AF541812

THE ĀʿĪN-I AKBARĪ

THE
Āᶜīn-i Akbarī

(The Complete English Translation)

Abū 'L-Faẓl ᶜAllāmī

Translated into English by
H. BLOCHMANN

Edited by
LIEUT.-COLONEL D.C. PHILLOTT

IN THREE VOLUMES
VOLUME ONE

MANOHAR
2026

First published 1868-94
Reprinted 2026

ISBN 978-93-91928-12-4 (Vol. 1)
ISBN 978-93-91928-36-0 (Set)

Published by
Ajay Kumar Jain *for*
Manohar Publishers & Distributors
4753/23 Ansari Road, Daryaganj
New Delhi 110 002

Printed and bound in India

THE

Āʿīn-i Akbarī

One

THE Āʿīn-i Akbarī

(A Gazetteer and Administrative Manual of Akbar's Empire and Past History of India)

by

Abū 'l-Faẓl ʿAllāmī

Vol. I

Translated into English by
H. BLOCHMANN

SECOND EDITION

Edited by
LIEUT.-COLONEL D.C. PHILLOTT

THE ASIATIC SOCIETY
1 PARK STREET ▪ KOLKATA-700 016

FOREWORD

The enormous importance of the Ain-i-Akbari of Abū 'L - Fazl as a historical document of the Mughal period of Indian history needs no elaboration. In his preface to the first edition of the English translation of the book, written in 1873, H. Blochmann had described it as 'by far the greatest work in the whole series of Mohammedan histories of India'. That assessment of the book as a source material has not changed much inspite of the significant progress in historical research of medieval India. Thorough editing of a work of this nature needs profound scholarship and years of painstaking dedicated research. This is borne out by the fact that it had taken more than half a century to bring out a new edition with only minor editorial additions and changes.

This is the first time that the Asiatic Society is bringing out the three volumes of Ain-i-Akbari in a single volume. We would have been happy if the book could be thoroughly re-edited in the light of the latest researches. That would have required much time besides versatile scholorship and dedicated single minded hard work and research. But the persistent demand from scholars for a handy volume of this great work has prompted the Society to publish the volume without waiting for an unknown period of time hoping for a new thoroughly revised edition. We hope the book will be welcomed by scholars as well as a wide circle of readers interested in one of the most fascinating periods of medieval India. ❑

22nd March, 1993

Chandan Roy Chaudhuri
General Secretary

THE

Ā'ĪN-I AKBARĪ

THE

Ā'ĪN-I AKBARĪ

BY

ABŪ 'L-FAZL 'ALLĀMĪ

TRANSLATED INTO ENGLISH BY

H. BLOCHMANN, M.A.

Calcutta, Madrasa

SECOND EDITION

EDITED BY

LIEUT.-COLONEL D. C. PHILLOTT, M.A., PH.D., F.A.S.B.

THE ASIATIC SOCIETY

1, PARK STREET

CALCUTTA - 700 016

PREFACE

SECOND EDITION OF BLOCHMANN'S TRANSLATION

OF THE

Ā'ĪN-I AKBARĪ

Some explanation is needed of the present edition. Blochmann's original translation has for some time been out of print. The Asiatic Society of Bengal has asked me to undertake the preparation of a reprint, and I lightly accepted the task, not realizing the amount of labour involved. Blochmann's translation and notes form a work of infinite detail and thorough scholarship; and though it has seldom been necessary to correct, it has often been necessary to investigate. This present edition is, however, in the main a mere reprint. This of itself is no small testimony to Blochmann's thoroughness. The transliteration, however, has been brought into line with a more modern system, and a few additional notes [in square brackets] have been added; those with a suffixed B. are Blochmann's own MS notes from a printed copy in my possession; I have not incorporated all of them, as many I was unable to decipher. Notes to which a P. is suffixed are my own.

D. C. P.

Felsted Bury,
Felsted, Essex.
1927.

PREFACE

(First Edition)

The Āʿīn-i Akbarī is the third volume of the Akbar-nāma, by Shaykh Abū 'l-Fazl, and is by far the greatest work in the whole series of Muhammadan histories of India. The first volume of this gigantic work contains the history of Tīmūr's family as far as it is of interest for the Indian reader, and the reigns of Bābar, the Sūr kings, and Humāyūn whilst the second volume is devoted to the detailed history of nearly forty-six years of the reign of the Great Emperor. The concluding volume, the Āʿīn-i-Akbarī, contains that information regarding Akbar's reign, which, though not strictly historical, is yet essential to a correct understanding of the times, and embodies, therefore, those facts for which, in modern times, we would turn to Administration Reports, Statistical compilations, or Gazetteers. It contains the *āʿīn* (i.e. mode of governing) of Akbar, and is, in fact, the Administration Report and Statistical Return of his government as it was about A.D. 1590. The contents, therefore, of the *Āʿīn* are naturally varied and detailed. The first of its five books treats of Akbar's household and court, and of the emperor himself, the soul of every department, who looks upon the performance of his duties as an act of divine worship, and who enters into the details of government in order to create a harmonious whole. Vouchsafed as king with a peculiar light from on high, his person is prominently put forward as the guide of the people in all matters temporal and spiritual; in whose character and temper the governed find that rest and peace which no constitution can give, and in whom, as the author of a new and advanced creed, the dust of intoleration is for ever allayed.

The second book treats of the servants of the throne, the military and civil services, and the attendants at court whose literary genius or musical skill receives a lustre from the encouragement of the emperor, and who in their turn reflect a brilliant light on the government.

The third book is entirely devoted to regulations for the judicial and executive departments, the establishment of a new and more practical era, the survey of the land, the tribal divisions, and the rent-roll of the great Finance minister whose name has become proverbial in India.

The fourth book treats of the social condition and literary activity, especially in philosophy and law, of the Hindus, who form the bulk of the population, and in whose political advancement the emperor saw the guarantee of the stability of his realm. There are also a few chapters on the foreign invaders of India, on distinguished travellers, and on Muhammadan saints and the sects to which they respectively belong.

The fifth book contains the moral sentences and epigrammatical sayings, observations, and rules of wisdom of the emperor, which Abū 'l-Faẓl has gathered as the disciple gathers the sayings of the master.

In the Āʿīn, therefore, we have a picture of Akbar's government in its several departments, and of its relations to the different ranks and mixed races of his subjects. Whilst in most Muhammadan histories we hear of the endless turmoil of war and dynastical changes, and are only reminded of the existence of a people when authors make a passing allusion to famines and similar calamities, we have in the Āʿīn the governed classes brought to the foreground: men live and move before us, and the great questions of the time, axioms then believed in, and principles then followed, phantoms then chased after, ideas then prevailing, and successes then obtained, are placed before our eyes in truthful, and therefore vivid, colours.

It is for this reason that the Āʿīn stands so unique among Muhammadan histories of India, and we need not wonder that long before curious eyes turned to other native sources of history and systematically examined their contents, the Ā'īn was laid under contribution. Le Père Tieffentaller, in 1776, published in his *Description Géographique de l'Indostan* long extracts from the rent-roll given in the Third Book; Chief Sarishtadár Grant used it largely for his Report on Indian Finances; and, as early as 1783, Francis Gladwin, a thorough Oriental scholar, dedicated to Warren Hastings his "*Ayeen Akberi*", of which in 1800 he issued a printed edition in London. In his translation, Gladwin has given the greater part of the First Book, more than one-half of the Second and Third Books, and about one-fourth of the Fourth Book; and although in modern times inaccuracies have been discovered in the portions translated by him—chiefly due, no doubt, to the fact that he translated from MSS. in every way a difficult undertaking—his translation has always occupied a deservedly high place, and it may confidently be asserted that no similar work has for the last seventy years been so extensively quoted as his. The magnitude of the task of translating the Ā'īn from uncollated MSS. will especially become apparent, when we remember that, even in the opinion of native writers, its style is "not intelligible to the generality of readers without great difficulty."

But it is not merely the varied information of the Ā'īn that renders the book so valuable, but also the trustworthiness of the author himself. Abū 'l-Fazl's high official position gave him access to any document he wished to consult, and his long career and training in various departments of the State, and his marvellous powers of expression, fitted him eminently for the composition of a work like the *Akbarnāmah* and the *Ā'īn*. His love of truth and his correctness of information are apparent on every page of the book, which he wished to leave to future ages as a memorial of the Great Emperor and as a guide for inquiring minds; and his wishes for the stability of the throne and the welfare of the people, his principles of toleration, his noble sentiments on the rights of man, the total absence of personal grievances and of expressions of ill-will towards encompassing enemies, show that the expanse of his large heart stretched to the clear offing of sterling wisdom. Abū 'l-Fazl has far too often been accused by European writers of flattery and even of wilful concealment of facts damaging to the reputation of his master. A study, though perhaps not a hasty perusal, of the *Akbarnāmah* will show that the charge is absolutely unfounded ; and if we compare his works with other historical productions of the East, we shall find that, while he praises, he does so infinitely less and with much more grace and dignity than any other Indian historian or poet. No native writer has ever accused him of flattery ; and if we bear in mind that all Eastern works on Ethics recommend unconditional assent to the opinion of the king, whether correct or absurd, as the duty of man, and that the whole poetry of the East is a rank mass of flattery at the side of which modern encomiums look like withered leaves—we may pardon Abū 'l-Fazl when he praises because he finds a true hero.

The issue of the several fasciculi of this translation has extended over a longer time than I at first expected. The simultaneous publication of my edition of the Persian Text, from which the translation is made, the geographical difficulties of the Third Book, the unsatisfactory state of the MSS., the notes added to the translation from various Muhammadan historians and works on the history of literature, have rendered the progress of the work unavoidably slow.

I am deeply indebted to the Council of the Philological Committee of the Asiatic Society of Bengal for placing at my disposal a full critical apparatus of the *Āʿīn*, and entrusting me with the edition of the text, for which the Indian Government had most liberally sanctioned the sum of five thousand Rupees. My grateful acknowledgments are also due to Dr. Thomas Oldham, Superintendent of the Geological Survey of India and late President of the Asiatic Society, for valuable advice and ever ready assistance in the execution of the work ; and to Col. H. Yule, C.B., and to H. Roberts, Esq., of the Doveton College, for useful hints and corrections.

I have thought it advisable to issue the first volume with a few additional notes, and two indexes, one of persons and things and the other of geographical names, without waiting for the completion of the whole work. I have thus had an opportunity of correcting some of the errors and inconsistencies in the spelling of names and supplying other deficiencies. That defects will still be found, notwithstanding my endeavours to remove them, none of my readers and critics can be more sensible than I myself am.

H. BLOCHMANN.

CALCUTTA MADRASAH.
23rd September, 1873.

CONTENTS

BOOK FIRST

[[1] *Āhū*, gazelle.—P.]

BOOK SECOND

[1 *Āhū*, gazelle.—P.]

NOTE

Lieut.-Col. Phillott, who most generously had undertaken to prepare a revised reprint of Blochmann's translation of the first volume of the Āʾīn-i-Akbarī, had progressed to the end of the text when illness precluded him from finishing his labours. What remained to be done was the revision of the index, the correction of the additional notes as already revised by him on the copy, and the entering of the modifications necessary in the proofs of pages xvii to xxxii, and xlix to lix of the preliminary matter, as also of pages 1 to 10 of the work itself.

For a long time lingering illness prevented the taking of immediate steps to terminate the volume, but in September, 1930, the regretted death of the learned Editor necessitated consideration of the problem of bringing the reprint to a close. The fact that the volume was being printed in England and that no details as to the method of the revision were at the disposal of the office of the Royal Asiatic Society of Bengal caused considerable delay, but ultimately arrangements were made to complete the work in the office of the Society.

Mr. D. K. Das was charged with the revision of the index, involving the changing of all page numbers, and the drawing up of a list of errata found in the body of the reprint during the course of his work. Mr. Das has performed his work with great care and has rendered valuable service in doing so. The new errata are to be found on page 690 of this volume. The plan adopted for the reprint has been explained by the Editor on page xi.

The circumstances explained above are responsible for the date of the Editor's Preface, as well as for the fact that the date of issue on the title page is given as 1927, whilst the actual publication was not possible till 1939.

The Council of the Society wishes to record its great indebtedness to the late Lieut.-Col. Phillott for his self-sacrificing labour on the present volume, and to pay its grateful homage to the memory of its late Member and Fellow, a devoted friend, a valued helper, and a distinguished scholar.

B. S. Guha,
General Secretary.

Royal Asiatic Society of Bengal,
1 Park Street, Calcutta.
12th July, 1939.

LIST OF PLATES

IN THE

FIRST VOLUME

OF THE

Ā'ĪN-I-AKBARĪ

Plates I to III. The Workmen of the Mint, p. 18.

1, 2. Preparation of acids.—3. Washing of ashes.—4, 9, 10, 12, melting and refining.—5. Weighing.—6, 8. Making of plates.

7. Work of the *ẓarrāb*, p. 22.—11. Engraving.—12. The *Sikkachī*, p. 22.

Plate IV. The Imperial Camp (p. 50).

a, *b*, *c*, *d*, *f*, *g*, roads and bāzārs. " The principal bāzār is laid out into " the form of a wide street, running through the whole extent of the army, now on the right, now on the left, of the Dīwān-i khāṣṣ."—*Bernier.*

1. The Imperial Harem (*shabistān-i iqbāl*). At the right hand side is the *Do-āshiyāna Manzil*; *vide* p. 56.
2. Open space with a canopy (*shāmyāna*).
3. Private Audience Hall (*Dīwān-i khāṣṣ*), p. 48.
4. The great camp light (*ākās-diya*), p. 52.

   " The *aquacy-die* resembles a lofty mast of a ship, but is very slender, and takes down in three pieces. It is fixed towards the king's quarters, near the tent called *Nagar-kane*, and during the night a lighted lantern is suspended from the top. This light is very useful, for it may be seen when every object is enveloped in impenetrable darkness. To this spot persons who lose their way resort, either to pass the night secure from all danger of robbers, or to resume their search after their own lodgings. The name ' Aquacy-die ' may be translated ' Light of Heaven ' the lantern when at a distance appearing like a star."—*Bernier.*
5. The *Naqqāra-khāna*, pp. 49, 50.

   AB, or distance from the Harem to the camp Light = 1,530 yards;
   AC = 360 yards; p. 49.
6. The house where the saddles were kept (*zīn-khāna*).
7. The Imperial stables (*iṣṭabal*).
8. Tents of the superintendents and overseers of the stables.
9. Tents of the clerk of the elephant stables.
10. The Imperial Office (*daftar*).
11. Tent for pālkīs and carts.
12. Artillery tent (*top-khāna*).
13. Tent where the hunting leopards were kept (*chīta-khāna*).
14. The Tents of Maryam Makānī (Akbar's mother), Gulbadan Begum (Humāyūn's sister, p. 49), and Prince Dānyāl; p. 49.
15. The tents of Sulṭān Salīm (Jahāngīr), to the right of the Imperial Harem.
16. The tents of Sulṭān Murād, to the left of the Imperial Harem; p. 50.
17. Store rooms and workshops (*buyūtāt*).
18. Tent for keeping basins (*āftābchī-khāna*).
19. Tent for the perfumes (*khushbū-khāna*).
20. Tent for storing mattress (*toshak-khāna*).

21. Tent for the tailors, etc.
22. Wardrobe (*kurkyarāq-khāna*), p. 93.
23. Tent for the lamps, candles, oil, etc. (*chirāgh-khāna*).
24. Tents for keeping fresh Ganges water (*ābdār-khāna*), p. 57.
25. Tent for making *sharbat* and other drinks.
26. Tent for storing *pān* leaves.
27. Tent for storing fruit (*mewa khāna*).
28. Tent for the Imperial plate (*rikāb-khāna*).
29. The Imperial kitchen (*maṭbakh*).
30. The Imperial bakery (*nānbā-khāna*).
31. Store room for spices (*hawej-khāna*).
32. The Imperial guard.
33. The Arsenal (*qur-khāna*).
34. Women's apartments.

35 to 41. Guard houses.

Round about the whole the nobles and Manṣabdārs with their contingents, pitched their tents.

" The king's private tents are surrounded by small *kanāts* (*qanāts*, standing screens), of the height of a man, some lined with Masulipatam chintz, worked over with flowers of a hundred different kinds, and others with figured satin, decorated with deep silken fringes."—*Bernier*. Bernier's description of the Imperial camp (second letter, dated Lāhor, 25th February, 1665), agrees with minute detail with the above.

Plate V. Candlesticks, p. 50.

1. Double candlestick (*dūshākha*).—2. Fancy candlestick with pigeons.—3. Single candlestick (*yakshākha*).
4. The *Ākās-diya*, or Camp-light; *vide* pl. iv, No. 4.

Plate VI. The Emperor Akbar Worships Fire, p. 50.

In front of Akbar twelve candles are placed, and the singer of sweet melodies sings to the praise of God, as mentioned on p. 51, l. 6 ff.

The faces of the emperor and the singer are left blank, in accordance with the Muhammadan dislike to paint likenesses of beings on, below, or above the earth. The emperor sits in the position called *dūzānū*.

Plate VII. Thrones, p. 52.

1, 2. Different kinds of thrones (*awrang*) with pillows (*masnad*) to lean against, the royal umbrella (*chatr*), and the footstool (*ṣandalī*).

Plate VIII. The Naqqāra Khāna, p. 52.

1. Cymbals (*sanj*).—2. The large drum (*kuwarga* or *damāma*).—3, 4, 5. The *Karanā*.—6. The *Surnā*.—7. The Hindī *Surnā*.—8. The *Nafīr*.—9. The *Singh*, or horn.—10. The *Naqqāras*.

Plate IX. The Ensigns or Royalty, p. 52.

1. The *Jhandā*, or Indian flag. " The Royal standard of the great Mogul is a *Couchant Lion* shadowing part of the body of a sun."—*Terry*.
2. The *Kawkaba*.
3. *Sāyabān* or *Āftābgīr*.
4. The *Tumantoq* (from the Turkish *toq*, or *togh*, a flag, and *tuman* or *tūmān*, a division of ten thousand).
5. The *Chatr*, or (red) royal umbrella.
6. A standard, or *ʿalam*.

7. The *Chatrtoq*. As Abū 'l-Faẓl says that this standard is *smaller* than the preceding, it is possible that the word should be pronounced ***chuturtoq***, from the Turkish *chutur*, or *chūtūr*, short. The flag is adorned with bunches of hair (*quṭās*) taken from the tails and the sides of the Tibetan Yak.

Plates X and XI. The Imperial Tents, p. 54.

Plate X.—The three tents on the top, commencing with the left, are (1) the *Shāmyāna*; (2) A *yakdart Kharyāh*, or tent of one door; (3) the *Dūdarī*, or tent of two doors; p. 57, 8. Rolled up over the door is the *chigh*; p. 236, Āʾīn 88.

Below these three tents, is the *Sarā-parda* and *Gulāl-bāṛ*, pp. 47, 57. At the foot of the plate is the *Nam-gīra* (*pr.* dew-catcher), with carpet and pillow (*masnad*); p. 48.

Plate XI.—On the top, the *bārgāh*, p. 55. Below it, on the left, is the *Do-āshiyāna Manzil*, or two-storied house; *vide* Pl. IV, No. 1. At the window of the upper story, the emperor showed himself; *vide* Index, darsan, and jharōka. To the right of this two-storied tent, is the *Chūbīn Rāwaṭī* (as the word ought to be spelt, from *chobīn*, wooden, and *rāwaṭī*, a square tent), p. 56. Below it, the common conical tent, tied to pegs stuck in the ground; hence it is called *zamīndōz*, with one tent pole (*yak-surugha*, from the Turkish *surugh*, or *surūgh*, a tent pole).

Below is a *Zamīndoz* with two poles (*dūsurugha*). At the bottom of the plate, to the left is the *Mandal*, p. 56; and to the right, the *ʿAjāʾibī*, p. 56.

Plate XII. Weapons, p. 116.

The numbers in brackets refer to the numbers on pp. 117 to 119.

1. The sword, *shamsher* (1).
2. The straight sword, *kheḍā* (2).
3, 3*a*. The *guptī ʿaṣā* (3).
4. The broad dagger, *jamdhar* (4).
5. The bent dagger, *khanjar* (5).
6. The *jam khāk*, or curved dagger (7).
7. The bent knife, *bāk* (8).
8. The *jhānbwa*, or hiltless dagger (9).
9. The *katāra*, a long and narrow dagger (10).
10. The *narsink moth* (*narsing moth* ?), a short and narrow dagger (11).
11. The bow, *kamān* (12).
12, 13. The small bow and arrow, *takhsh kamān* and *tīr* (13).
14*a*. Arrow.
14*b*. The *paikānkash*, or arrow-drawer (19).
15. The quiver, *tarkash* (16).
16. The lance, *neza* (20).
17. The Hindūstānī lance, *barchha* (21).
18. The *sāk*, or broad-headed lance (22).
19, 20. The *sainthī* (23) and *selara* (24).
21. The *shushbur*, or club. This I believe to be the correct name (instead of *shashpar*), from *shush*, lungs, and *bur*, tearing.
22. The axe, *tabar*.
23. The club, *gurz* (25). On p. 117, No. 29, the word *piyāzī* has been translated by "club", and this seems to be the correct meaning; but the plates in some MSS. call "piyāzī" a long knife, with straight back, ending in a point.
24. The pointed axe, *zāghnol*,[1] i.e. crow-bill (30).
25. The *chakar* (wheel) and *basola* (31).
26. The double axe, *tabar-zāghnōl* (32).

[[1] *Zāgh* a name largely applied to a chaugh, crow, jackdaw and magpie.—P.]

27. The *tarangāla* (33).
28. The knife, *kārd* (34).

PLATE XIII. WEAPONS (continued), p. 118.

29. The *guptī kārd*, or knife concealed in a stick (35).
30. The whip, *qamchī-kārd* (36).
31. The clasp knife, *chāqū* (37).
32. A bow, unstr g.
33. The bow for clay bullets, *kamṭha*, or *Kamān-i guroha* (38).
34. The tube, or pea-shooter, *tufak-i dahān*[1] (40).
35. The *pushtkhār* (41).
36. A lance called *girih-kushā*, i.e. a knot-unraveller (43).
37. The *khār-i māhī*, i.e. fish-spine (44).
38. The sling, *gobhan* (45).
39. The *gajbāg*, or *ānkus*, for guiding elephants (46).
40. The shield, *sipar* (47).
41. Another kind of shield, *dhāl* (48).
42. The plain cane shield, *pahrī*, or *pharī* (50).
43. The helmet, *dubalgha* (52).
44. The *ghūghuwa*, a mail coat for head and body, in one piece (55).
45. The helmet, with protection for the neck, *zirih kulāh* (54).
46. The mailed coat, *zirih* (57).
47. The mailed coat, with breast plate, *bagtar* (58).
48. An armour for chest and body, *jōshan* (59).
49. The breast and back-plates, *chār-āʾina* (60).

PLATE XIV. WEAPONS AND ARMOURS (continued), p. 118.

50. The coat with plates and helmet, *koṭhī* (61).
51. An armour of the kind called *ṣādiqī* (62).
52. A long coat worn over the armour, *angirkha* (63).
53. An iron mask, *chihrahzirih-i āhanī* (65).
54. A doublet worn over the armour, *chihilqad* (67).
55. The long glove, *dastwāna* (68).
56. The small one is the *moza-yi āhanī*, or iron stocking (71); and the large one the *rāk* (69).
57. The *kajem*, or *kejam*, a mailed covering for the back of the horse (72).
58, 59. The *artak-i kajēm*, the quilt over which the preceding is put (73).
60. The *qashqa*, or head protection for the horse (74).
61. The *Kanṭha sobhā* (70).
62. The rocket, *bān* (77).

PLATE XV. AKBAR'S MACHINE FOR CLEANING GUNS, p. 118; *vide* p. 122, Āʾīn 38, or the 1st Book.

PLATE XVI. HARNESS FOR HORSES, p. 144; Āʾīn 52, p. 143.

PLATE XVII. GAMES, p. 314.

The upper figure shows the board for *Chaupar*, p. 315, and the lower figure is the board for the Chandal Mandal game. Both boards were made of all sizes; some were made of inlaid stones on the ground in an open court yard, as in Fathpūr Sīkrī, and slave girls were used instead of pieces. The players at Chandal Mandal sat on the ground, round the circumference, one player at the end of each of the sixteen radii.

[[1] *Tufak-i dahan*, blowpipe.—P.]

BIOGRAPHY

OF

SHAYKH ABŪ 'L-FAẒL-I ʿALLĀMĪ

SHAYKH ABŪ 'L-FAẒL, Akbar's minister and friend, was born at Āgra on the 6th Muharram, 958,[1] during the reign of Islām Shāh.

The family to which he belonged traced its descent from Shaykh Mūsā, Abū 'l-Faẓl's fifth ancestor, who lived in the ninth century of the Hijra in Siwistān (Sindh), at a place called Rel (ریل). In " this pleasant village ", Shaykh Mūsā's children and grandchildren remained till the beginning of the tenth century, when Shaykh Khizr, the then head of the family, following the yearnings of a heart imbued with mystic lore, emigrated to Hindūstān. There he travelled about visiting those who, attracted by God, are known to the world for not knowing it ; and after passing a short time in Hijāz with the Arabian tribe, to which the family had originally belonged, he returned to India, and settled at Nāgor, north-west of Ajmīr, where he lived in the company of the pious, enjoying the friendship of Mīr Sayyid Yahyā of Bukhārā.

The title of Shaykh, which all the members of the family bore, was to keep up among them the remembrance of the home of the ancestors.

Not long afterwards, in 911, Shaykh Mubārak, Abū 'l-Faẓl's father, was born. Mubārak was not Shaykh Khizr's eldest child ; several children had been born before and had died, and Khizr rejoicing at the birth of another son, called him Mubārak, i.e. the blessed, in allusion, no doubt, to the hope which Islām holds out to the believers that children gone before bless those born after them, and pray to God for the continuance of their earthly life.

Shaykh Mubārak, at the early age of four, gave abundant proofs of intellectual strength, and fashioned his character and leanings in the company of one Shaykh ʿAṭan (عطن), who was of Turkish extraction and had come during the reign of Sikandar Lodī to Nāgor, where he lived in the service of Shaykh Sālār, and died, it is said, at the advanced age of one hundred and twenty years. Shaykh Khizr had now resolved to settle at Nāgor permanently, and with the view of bringing a few relations to his adopted home, he returned once more to Siwistān. His sudden death during the journey left the family at Nāgor in great

[1] 14th January, 1551.

distress; and a famine which broke out at the same time stretched numbers of the inhabitants on the barren sands of the surrounding desert, and of all the members of the family at Nāgor only Mubārak and his mother survived.

Mubārak grew up progressing in knowledge and laying the foundation of those encyclopedial attainments for which he afterwards became so famous. He soon felt the wish and the necessity to complete his education and visit the great teachers of other parts; but love to his mother kept him in his native town, where he continued his studies, guided by the teachings of the great saint Khwāja Aḥrār,[1] to which his attention had been directed. However, when his mother died, and when about the same time the Māldeo disturbances broke out, Mubārak carried out his wish, and went to Aḥmadābād in Gujarāt, either attracted by the fame of the town itself, or by that of the shrine of his countryman, Aḥmad of Khaṭṭū.[2] In Aḥmadābād he found a second father in the learned Shaykh Abū 'l-Faẓl, a khaṭīb, or preacher, from Kāzarūn, in Persia, and made the acquaintance of several men of reputation, as Shaykh ʿUmar of Tattah and Shaykh Yūsuf. After a stay of several years, he returned to Hindūstān, and settled, on the 6th Muḥarram, 950, on the left bank of the Jamunā, opposite Āgra, near the Chārbāgh Villa,[3] which Bābar had built, and in the neighbourhood of the saintly Mīr Rafīʿu 'd-Dīn Safawī of Injū (Shīrāz), among whose disciples Mubārak took a distinguished place. It was here that Mubārak's two eldest sons, Shaykh Abū 'l-Fayẓ[4] and, four years later, Shaykh Abu 'l-Faẓl, were born. Mubārak had now reached the age of fifty, and resolved to remain at Āgra, the capital of the empire; nor did the years of extraordinary drought which preceded the first year of Akbar's reign, and the dreadful plague, which in 963 broke out in Āgra and caused a great dispersion among the population, incline him to settle elsewhere.

The universality of learning which distinguished Mubārak attracted a large number of disciples, and displayed itself in the education he gave his sons; and the filial piety with which Abū 'l-Faẓl in numerous passages of his works speaks of his father, and the testimony of hostile writers as Badā,onī, leave no doubt that it was Mubārak's comprehensive-

---

[1] Died at Samarqand, 29th Rabīʿ I, 895, or 20th February, 1490.

[2] *Vide* p. 570, note. Aḥmad of Khaṭṭū is buried at Sarkhich near Aḥmadābād. He died in 849 (A.D. 1445).

[3] Later called Hasht Bihisht, or the Nūrafshān Gardens. It is now called the Rām Bāgh.

[4] Born A.H. 954, or A.D. 1547. *Vide* p. 548.

ness that laid in Abū 'l-Fayẓ and Abū 'l-Faẓl the foundation of those cosmopolitan and, to a certain extent, anti-Islamitic views, for which both brothers have been branded by Muhammadan writers as atheists, or as Hindūs, or as sun-worshippers, and as the chief causes of Akbar's apostacy from Islām.

A few years before A.H. 963, during the Afghān rule, Shaykh Mubārak had, to his worldly disadvantage, attached himself to a religious movement, which had first commenced about the year 900, and which continued under various phases during the whole of the tenth century. The movement was suggested by the approach of the first millennium of Islām. According to an often quoted prophecy, the latter days of Islām are to be marked by a general decadence in political power and in morals, which on reaching its climax is to be followed by the appearance of Imām Mahdī, "the Lord of the period,"[1] who will restore the sinking faith to its pristine freshness. Christ also is to appear; and after all men, through his instrumentality, have been led to Islām, the day of judgment will commence. Regarding this promised personage, the Rawẓatu 'l-A,imma, a Persian work on the lives of the twelve Imāms,[2] has the following passage—

Muslim, Abū Dā,ūd, Nisā,ī, Bayhaqī, and other collectors of the traditional sayings of the Prophet, state that the Prophet once said, "Muḥammad Mahdī shall be of my family, and of the descendants of Fāṭima (the Prophet's daughter and wife of ʿAlī)." And Aḥmad, Abū Dā,ūd, Tirmizī, and Ibn Mājah state that the Prophet at some other time said, "When of time one day shall be left, God shall raise up a man from among my descendants, who shall fill the world with justice, just as before him the world was full of oppression"; and again, "The world shall not come to an end till the King of the earth shall appear, who is a man of my family, and whose name is the same as mine." Further, Aḥmad and other collectors assert that the Prophet once said, "Muḥammad Mahdī belongs to my family, eight and nine years." Accordingly, people believe in the coming of Mahdī. But there is also a party in Islām who say that Imām Mahdī has already come into the world and exists at present; his patronymic is Abū 'l-Qāsim, and his epithets are "the elect, the stablisher, Mahdī, the expected, the Lord

---

[1] Ṣāḥib-i zamān. He is the 12th Imām. The first eleven succeeded the Prophet. 'Mahdī' (which in India is wrongly pronounced Mehndī, "myrtle") means "guided", Hādī means "a guide".

[2] By Sayyid ʿIzzat ʿAlī, son of Sayyid Pīr 'Alī of Rasūlpūr. Lithographed at Lakhnau A.H. 1271, 144 pp., royal 8vo.

of the age". In the opinion of this party, he was born at Surraman-raā (near Baghdād) on the 23rd Ramazān, 258, and in 265 he came to his Sardāba (prop. "a cool place", "a summer villa"), and disappeared whilst in his residence. In the book entitled *Shawāhid*, it is said that when he was born, he had on his right arm the words written, "Say, the truth has come and error has vanished, surely error is vanishing" (Qūrʿān, xvii, 83). It is also related that when he was born into the world, he came on his knees, pointed with his fingers to heaven, sneezed, and said, "Praise be to God, the Lord of the world." Some one also has left an account of a visit to Imām Ḥasan ʿAskarī (the eleventh Imām), whom he asked, "O son of the Prophet, who will be Khalīfa and Imām after thee?" ʿAskarī thereupon went into his room, and after some time came back with a child on his shoulders, that had a face like the full moon and might have been three years old, and said to the man, "If thou hadst not found favour in the eyes of God, He would not have shown you this child; his name is that of the Prophet, and so is his patronymic." The sect who believe Mahdī to be alive at present say that he rules over cities in the far west, and he is even said to have children. God alone knows the truth!

The alleged prophecies of the Founder regarding the advent of the Restorer of the Faith, assumed a peculiar importance when Islām entered on the century preceding the first millennium, and the learned everywhere agitated the question till at last the Mahdī movement assumed in India [1] a definite form through the teaching of Mīr Sayyid Muḥammad, son of Mīr Sayyid Khān of Jaunpūr. This man was a descendant of the Prophet, and bore his name; the fall of Jaunpūr was to him a sign that the latter days had come; extraordinary events which looked like miracles, marked his career; and a voice from heaven had whispered to him the words, "Anta Mahdī," "thou art Mahdī." Some people indeed say that Mīr Sayyid Muḥammad did not mean to declare that he was the promised Mahdī; but there is no doubt that he insisted on his mission as the Lord of the Age. He gained many adherents, chiefly

---

[1] Badā,onī, in his *'Najātu 'r-rashīd'*, gives a few particulars regarding the same movement in Badakhshān from where the idea seems to have spread over Persia and India. In Badakhshān, it was commenced by Sayyid Muḥammad Nūrbakhsh, a pupil of Abū Is-ḥāq Khatlānī, who gained numerous adherents and created such disturbances, that troops were sent against him. He was defeated and fled to ʿIrāq, in the mountainous districts of which country he is said to have gained thirty thousand followers. He had often to fight with the governors, but defied them all. Badā,onī has preserved a copy of the proclamation which Nūrbakhsh sent unto all the saints. One of his disciples was Shaykh Muḥammad Lāhijī, the commentator of the "Gulshan-i Rāz".

through his great oratorical powers, but pressed by enemies he went to Gujarāt, where he found an adherent in Sulṭān Maḥmūd I. From Gujarāt he proceeded, at the request of the king and to the joy of numerous enemies, on a pilgrimage to Makkah. From there also he seems to have been driven away. On his return, it was revealed to him that his teaching was vexatious, and he said to the disciples that accompanied him, "God has removed from my heart the burden of Mahdī. If I safely return, I shall recant all." But when he reached the town of Farāh in Balochistān, where his arrival had created a great sensation, he died (A.H. 911; A.D. 1505). His tomb became a place of general pilgrimage, although Shāh Ismāʿīl and Shāh Ṭahmāsp tried to destroy it. The movement, however, continued. Some of his followers adhered to their belief that he was Mahdī; and even the historian Badā,onī, who was strongly attached to the cause, speaks of him as of a great saint.

Other Mahdīs appeared in various parts of India. In 956 (A.D. 1549), a Mahdī of great pretensions arose in Biānah, S.W. of Āgra, in the person of Shay<u>kh</u> ʿAlā,ī. This man was a Bangālī Musalmān. His father had been looked upon in his country as a learned saint, and after visiting Makkah, he had settled in 935, with his younger brother Naṣr[u] 'llah, likewise a learned man, at Biānah, where they soon became respected and influential men. Shay<u>kh</u> ʿAlā,ī had shown from his youth the learning of the lawyer and the rigour of the saint; and on the death of his father, he gathered numerous pupils around himself. "But the love of power issues at last from the heads of the just," and on the day of the ʿId, he kicked an influential Shay<u>kh</u> from his *hauda*, and, supported by his brothers and elder relatives, he proclaimed that he alone was worthy of being the Shay<u>kh</u> of the town.

About the same time, one Miyān ʿAbd[u] 'llah, a Niyāzī Af<u>gh</u>ān and disciple of Mīr Sayyid Muḥammad of Jaunpūr, arrived from Makkah and settled at a retired spot near Biānah. Like his master, he was a man of oratorical powers and was given to street preaching; and in a short time he gained numerous followers among the woodcutters and water-carriers. Shay<u>kh</u> ʿAlā,ī also was overawed by the impressive addresses of Miyān ʿAbd[u]'llah; he gave up teaching and struggling for local influence, turned faqīr, told his wife either to follow him to the wilderness or to go, distributed his whole property, even his books, among the poor adherents of the Niyāzī, and joined the fraternity which they had formed. The brethren had established among themselves community of property divided the earnings obtained by begging, and gave up all work, because it was said in the Qurʾān, "Let not men be allured by trade or selling to give up meditating on God." Religious meetings, the object of which was to prepare people for the advent of the promised Mahdī, were daily held after the five prayers, which the brethren said together, and wherever they went they appeared armed to the teeth. They soon felt strong enough to interfere with municipal matters, and inspected the bāzārs and removed by force all articles forbidden in the law, defying the magistrates, if opposed to them, or assisting them, if of their opinion. Their ranks increased daily, and matters in Biānah had come to such a pass, that fathers separated themselves from their children and husbands from their wives. Shaykh ʿAlā,ī's former position and the thoroughness of his conversion had given him the rank of second leader; in fact, he soon outdid Miyān ʿAbdu'llāh in earnestness and successful conversions, and the later at last tried to rid himself of his rival by sending him with six or seven hundred armed men towards Makkah. ʿAla,ī marched with his band over Basāwar to Khawāṣpūr, converting and preaching on the way, but on account of some obstacles they all returned to Biānah.

Shaykh ʿAlā,ī's fame at last reached the ear of Islām Shāh, who summoned him to Āgra; and although the king was resolved to put him to death as a dangerous demagogue, and was even offended at the rude way in which ʿAlā,ī behaved in his presence, he was so charmed by an impromptu address which ʿAlā,ī delivered on the vanities of the world and the pharisaism of the learned, that he sent cooked provisions to ʿAlā,ī's men. To the amusement of the Afghān nobles and generals at court, ʿAlā,ī on another occasion defeated the learned on questions connected with the advent of Mahdī, and Islām Shāh was day after day informed that another of his nobles had gone to ʿAlā,ī's meetings and had joined the new sect.

It was at this time that Shaykh Mubārak also became a "disciple", and professed Mahdawī ideas. It is not clear whether he joined the sect from religious or from political motives, inasmuch as one of the objects of the brethren was to break up the party of the learned at Court, at whose head Makhdūmu'l-Mulk stood; but whatever may have been his reason, the result was, that Makhdūm became his inveterate enemy, deprived him of grants of land, made him flee for his life, and persecuted him for more than twenty years, till Mubārak's sons turned the tables on him and procured his banishment.[1]

---

[1] "'Makhdūmu'l-Mulk' was the title of ʿAbdu'llāh of Sulṭānpūr, regarding whom the reader may consult the index for references. The following biographical notice from the

The learned at Court, however, were not to be baffled by ʿAlā,ī's success, and Ma<u>kh</u>dūm's influence was so great, that he at last prevailed on the king to banish the Shay<u>kh</u>. ʿAlā,ī and his followers readily obeyed the command, and set out for the Dakhin. Whilst at Handiah on the Narbadā, the frontier of Islām Shāh's empire, they succeeded in converting Bahār Khān Aʿzam Humāyūn and half his army, and the king on hearing of this last success cancelled his orders and recalled Shay<u>kh</u> ʿAlā,ī.

About the same time (955) Islām Shāh left Āgra, in order to put down disturbances in the Panjāb caused by certain Niyāzī Af<u>gh</u>āns, and when he arrived in the neighbourhood of Biānah Ma<u>kh</u>dūm[u]'l-Mulk drew the king's attention to Miyān ʿAbd[u]'llāh Niyāzī, who after Shay<u>kh</u> ʿAlā,ī's departure for the Dakhin roamed about the hills of the Biānah district with three or four hundred armed men, and was known to possess great influence over men of his own clan, and consequently over the Niyāzī rebels in the Panjāb. Islām Shāh ordered the governor of Biānah, who had become a Mahdawī, to bring Miyān ʿAbd[u]'llāh to him. The governor advised his religious leader to conceal himself; but Miyān ʿAnd[u]'llāh boldly appeared before the king, and so displeased him by his neglect of etiquette, that Islām Shāh gave orders to beat him to death. The king watched on horseback for an hour the execution of the punishment, and only left when Miyān ʿAbd[u]'llāh lay apparently lifeless on the ground. But he was with much care brought back to life. He concealed himself for a long time, renounced all Mahdawī principles and got as late as 993 (A.D. 1585) from Akbar a freehold, because he,

---

<u>Kh</u>azīnat[u]'l- Aṣfiyā (Lāhor, pp. 443, 464) shows the opinion of good Sunnīs regarding Ma<u>kh</u>dūm.

"Mawlāna ʿAbd[u]'llāh Anṣārī of Sulṭānpūr belongs to the most distinguished learned men and saints of India. He was a Chishtī in his religious opinions. From the time of Sher Shāh till the reign of Akbar, he had the title of 'Ma<u>kh</u>dūm[u] 'l-Mulk' (*prop.* served by the empire). He was learned in the law and austere in practice. He zealously persecuted heretics. When Akbar commenced his religious innovations and converted people to his 'Divine Faith' and sun-worship, ordering them to substitute for the creed the words 'There is no God but Allah, and Akbar is the viceregent of God', Mawlānā ʿAbd[u] 'llāh opposed the emperor. Driven at last from Court, he retired to a mosque; but Akbar said that the mosque belonged to his realm, and he should go to another country. Ma<u>kh</u>dūm therefore went to Makkah. On his return to India, Akbar had him poisoned. He has written several works, as the كشف الغمة *Kashf[u] 'l-<u>gh</u>ummah*; the عفة الانبياء *ʿIffat[u] 'l-Anbiyā*, the منهاج الدين *Minhāj[u] 'd-dīn*, etc. He was poisoned in A.H. 1006.

"His son Ḥājī ʿAbd[u] 'l-Karīm went after the death of his father to Lāhor, where he became a religious guide. He died in 1045, and lies buried at Lāhor, near the Zīb[u] 'n-Nisā Villa, at Mawzaʿ Koṭ. His sons were Shay<u>kh</u> Yaḥyā, Ilāh Nūr, ʿAbd[u] 'l-Ḥaqq and Aʿlā Ḥuẓūr. Shay<u>kh</u> Yaḥyā, like his father, wrought miracles."

In this account the date is wrong; for Ma<u>kh</u>dūm[u] 'l-Mulk died in 990, and as Badā,onī, Ma<u>kh</u>dūm's supporter, says nothing of poison (Bad. II, 311) the statement of the <u>Kh</u>azīnat[u] 'l-Aṣfiyā may be rejected. Badā,onī also says that Ma<u>kh</u>dūm's sons were worthless men.

The titles of Ma<u>kh</u>dūm[u] 'l-Mulk's works are not correctly given either; vide p. 614.

too, had been one of Makhdūm^u'l-Mulk's victims. He died more than 90 years old, in 1000, at Sarhind.[1]

Islām Shāh, after quelling the Niyāzī disturbances, returned to Āgra, but almost immediately afterwards his presence was again required in the Panjāb, and it was there that Shaykh ʿAlā,ī joined the royal camp. When Islām Shāh saw the Shaykh he said to him in a low voice, "Whisper into my ear that you recant, and I will not trouble you." But Shaykh ʿAlā,i would not do so, and Islām Shāh, to keep up the appearance of authority ordered a menial to give him by way of punishment a few cuts with the whip in his presence. Shaykh ʿAlā,ī had then scarcely recovered from an attack of the plague, which for several years had been raging in India, and had a few badly healed wounds on his neck. Whilst he got the cuts, one of the wounds broke open, and ʿAlā,ī fainted and died. His body was now thrown under the feet of an elephant, and orders were given that no one should bury him, when all at once, to the terror of the whole camp and the king who believed that the last day had dawned, a most destructive cyclone broke forth. When the storm abated, ʿĀlā,ī's body was found literally buried among roses and other flowers, and an order was now forthcoming to have the corpse interred. This happened in 957 (A.D. 1550). People prophesied the quick end of Islām Shāh and the downfall of his house.[2]

Makhdūm^u'l-Mulk was never popular after that.

The features common to all Mahdawī movements, are (1) that the preachers of the latter days were men of education and of great oratorical powers, which gave them full sway over the multitudes; and (2) that the Mahdawīs assumed a hostile position to the learned men who held office at Court. Islām has no state clergy; but we find a counterpart to our hierarchical bodies in the ʿUlamās about Court, from whom the Ṣadrs of the provinces, the Mīr ʿAdls, Muftīs, and Qāẓīs were appointed. At Dihlī and Āgra, the body of the learned had always consisted of staunch Sunnīs, who believed it their duty to keep the kings straight.

---

[1] Badā,onī visited him in Sarhind, and it was from ʿAbd^u'llāh that he heard of Mīr Sayyid Muḥammad's repentance before death. Among other things, ʿAbd^u'llāh also told him that after the Mīr's death in Farāh, a well-known man of that town seized on lands belonging to Balochīs and proclaimed himself Christ; and he added that he had known no less than thirteen men of respectable parentage, who had likewise claimed to be Christ.

[2] The circumstances connected with ʿAlā,i's death resemble the end of Sīdī Mūlāh during the reign of Jalāl^u 'd-dīn Fīrūz Shāh.

The place in the Panjāb, where the scene took place, is called Ban. (Bad. I, 408).

The fact that Badā,onī spent his youth at Basāwar near Biānah, i.e. in the very centre of the Mahdawī movement, accounts perhaps for his adherence, throughout his life, to Mahdawī principles.

How great their influence was, may be seen from the fact that of all Muhammadan emperors only Akbar, and perhaps ʿAlāuʾd-Dīn Khiljī, succeeded in putting down this haughty set.

The death of Shaykh ʿAlā,ī was a great triumph for the Court ʿUlamās, and a vigorous persecution of all Mahdawī disciples was the immediate result. The persecutions lasted far into Akbar's reign. They abated only for a short time when the return of Humāyūn and the downfall of the Afghān power brought about a violent political crisis, during which the learned first thought of their own safety, well knowing that Humāyūn was strongly in favour of Shīʿism; but when Akbar was firmly established and the court at Āgra, after the fall of Bayrām Khān, who was a Shīʿa, again teemed with Hindūstānī Sunnīs, the persecutions commenced. The hatred of the court party against Shaykh Mubārak especially, rose to such a height that Shaykh ʿAbduʾn-Nabī and Makhdūmuʾl-Mulk represented to the emperor that inasmuch as Mubārak also belonged to the Mahdāwis and was, therefore, not only himself damned, but led also others into damnation, he deserved to be killed. They even obtained an order to bring him before the emperor. Mubārak wisely fled from Āgra, only leaving behind him some furniture for his enemies to reek their revenge on. Concealing himself for a time, he applied to Shaykh Salīm Chishtī of Fatḥpūr Sīkrī for intercession; but being advised by him to withdraw to Gujarāt, he implored the good offices of Akbar's foster-brother, the generous Khān-i Aʿẓam Mīrzā Koka, who succeeded in allaying all doubts in the mind of the emperor by dwelling on the poverty of the Shaykh and on the fact that, different from his covetous accusers, he had not cost the state anything by way of freeholds, and thus obtained at least security for him and his family. Mubārak some time afterwards applied indeed for a grant of land for his son ʿAbū ʾl-Fayẓ, who had already acquired literary fame, though he was only 20 years old, and waited personally with his son on Shaykh ʿAbdu ʾn-Nabī. But the latter, in his theological pride, turned them out of his office as men suspected of Mahdawī leanings and Shīʿa tendencies. Even in the 12th year of Akbar's reign, when Fayẓī's poems [1] had been noticed at Court—Akbar then lay before Chītor—and a summons had been sent to the young poet to present himself before his sovereign, the enemies at Āgra saw in the invitation a sign of approaching doom, and prevailed on the governor to secure the victim this time. The governor thereupon sent a detachment of Mughul soldiers to surround Mubārak's house. Fayẓī

[1] ʿAbdu ʾl-Fayẓ wrote under the nom-de-plume of Fayẓī.

was accidentally away from home, and the soldiers suspecting a conspiracy, subjected Mubārak to various sorts of ill-treatment; and when Fayẓī at last came, he was carried off by force to Chitor.[1] Nor did his fears for his father and his own life banish, till his favourable reception at court convinced him both of Akbar's good will and the blindness of his personal enemies.

Abū 'l-Faẓl had in the meantime grown up zealously studying under the care of his father. The persecutions which Shay<u>kh</u> Mubārak had to suffer for his Mahdawī leanings at the hands of the learned at Court, did not fail to make a lasting impression on his young mind. There is no doubt that it was in this school of misfortune that Abū 'l-Faẓl learned the lesson of toleration, the practice of which in later years formed the basis of Akbar's friendship for him; while, on the other hand, the same pressure of circumstances stimulated him to unusual exertions in studying, which subsequently enabled him during the religious discussions at Court to lead the opposition and overthrow by superior learning and broader sentiments the clique of the ʿUlamās, whom Akbar hated so much.

At the age of fifteen, he showed the mental precocity so often observed in Indian boys; he had read works on all branches of those sciences which go by the name of *ḥikamī* and *naqlī*, or *maʿqūl* and *manqūl*.[2] Following the footsteps of his father, he commenced to teach long before he had reached the age of twenty. An incident is related to show how extensive even at that time his reading was. A manuscript of the rare work of Iṣfahānī happened to fall into his hands. Unfortunately, however, one half of each page, vertically downwards from top to bottom, was rendered illegible, or was altogether destroyed, by fire. Abū'l-Faẓl determined to restore so rare a book, cut away the burnt portions, pasted new paper to each page, and then commenced to restore the missing halves of each line, in which attempt after repeated thoughtful perusals he succeeded. Some time afterwards, a complete copy of the same work turned up and on comparison, it was found that in many places there were indeed different words, and in a few passages new proofs even had been adduced; but on the whole the restored portion presented so many points of extraordinary coincidence that his friends were not a little astonished at the thoroughness with which Abū'l-Faẓl had worked himself into the style and mode of thinking of a difficult author.

---

[1] 20th Rabī' I, 975, or 24th September, 1567. The ode which Fayẓi presented will be found in the *Akbarnāma*.

[2] Page 609, note.

Abū'l-Faẓl was so completely taken up with study that he preferred the life of a recluse to the unstable patronage of the great, and to the bondage which attendance at court in those days rendered inevitable. But from the time Fayẓī had been asked by Akbar to attend the Court hopes of a brighter future dawned, and Abū'l-Faẓl, who had then completed his seventeenth year, saw in the encouragement held out by the emperor, in spite of Mubārak's numerous enemies at court, a guarantee that patient toil, on his part, too, would not remain without fruit. The skill with which Fayẓī in the meantime acquired and retained Akbar's friendship, prepared the way for Abū'l-Faẓl; and when the latter, in the very end of 981 (beginning of A.D. 1574) was presented to Akbar as Fayẓī's brother, the reception was so favourable that he gave up all thoughts of leading a life among manuscripts. "As fortune did not at first assist me," says Abū'l-Faẓl in the Akbarnāma, "I almost became selfish and conceited, and resolved to tread the path of proud retirement. The number of pupils that I had gathered around me, served but to increase my pedantry. In fact, the pride of learning had made my brain drunk with the idea of seclusion. Happily for myself, when I passed the nights in lonely spots with true seekers after truth, and enjoyed the society of such as are empty-handed, but rich in mind and heart, my eyes were opened and I saw the selfishness and covetousness of the so-called learned. The advice of my father with difficulty kept me back from outbreaks of folly; my mind had no rest, and my heart felt itself drawn to the sages of Mongolia, or to the hermits of Lebanon; I longed for interviews with the lamas of Tibet or with the pādrīs of Portugal, and I would gladly sit with the priests of the Pārsīs and the learned of the Zendavesta. I was sick of the learned of my own land. My brother and other relatives then advised me to attend the Court, hoping that I would find in the emperor a leader to the sublime world of thought. In vain did I at first resist their admonitions. Happy, indeed, am I now that I have found in my sovereign a guide to the world of action and a comforter in lonely retirement; in him meet my longing after faith and my desire to do my appointed work in the world; he is the orient where the light of form and ideal dawns; and it is he who has taught me that the work of the world, multifarious as it is, may yet harmonize with the spiritual unity of truth. I was thus presented at Court. As I had no worldly treasures to lay at the feet of his Majesty, I wrote a commentary to the *Āyat^u 'l-Kursī*,[1] and presented it when the emperor was at Āgra.

[1] Name of the 255th verse of the second chapter of the Qurʿān.

I was favourably received, and his Majesty graciously accepted my offering."

Akbar was at that time busily engaged with his preparations for the conquest of Bihār and Bengal. Fayẓī accompanied the expedition, but Abū'l-Faẓl naturally stayed in Āgra. But as Fayẓi wrote to his brother that Akbar had inquired after him, Abū'l-Faẓl attended Court immediately on the emperor's return to Faṭhpūr Sīkrī, where Akbar happened to notice him first in the Jāmiᶜ Mosque. Abū'l-Faẓl, as before, presented a commentary written by him on the opening of a chapter in the Qurᵉā entitled "Sūratᵘ 'l-Fatḥ", "the Chapter of Victory".[1]

The party of the learned and bigoted Sunnīs at Court, headed by Makhdūmᵘ 'l-Mulk and Shaykh ᶜAbdᵘ 'n-Nabī, had every cause to feel sorry at Fayẓī's and Abū'l-Faẓl's successes[2]; for it was now, after Akbar's return from Bihār, that the memorable Thursday evening discussions commenced, of which the historian Badā,onī has left us so vivid an account. Akbar at first was merely annoyed at the "Pharaoh-like pride" of the learned at court; stories of the endless squabbles of these pious casuits had reached his ear; religious persecutions and a few sentences of death passed by his Chief-Justice on Shīᶜas and "others heretics" affected him most deeply; and he now for the first time realized the idea that the scribes and the pharisees formed a power of their own in his kingdom, at the construction of which he had for twenty years been working. Impressed with a favourable idea of the value of his Hindū subjects, he had resolved when pensively sitting in the mornings on the solitary stone at Fathpūr Sīkrī, to rule with even hand men of all creeds in his dominions; but as the extreme views of the learned and the lawyers continually urged him to persecute instead of to heal, he instituted the discussions, because, believing himself to be in error, he thought it his duty as ruler to "inquire". It is not necessary to repeat here the course which these discussions took.[3] The unity that had existed among the learned disappeared in the very beginning; abuse took the place of argument, and the plainest rules of etiquette were, even in the presence of the emperor, forgotten. Akbar's doubts instead of being cleared up only increased; certain points of the Ḥanafī law, to which most Sunnīs cling, were found to be better established by the dicta of lawyers belong-

---

[1] The details of Abū 'l-Faẓl's introduction at Court given in Badā,onī differ slightly from Abū 'l-Faẓl's own account.

[2] Badā,onī ascribes to Makhdūmᵘ'l-Mulk an almost prophetic insight into Abū 'l-Faẓl's character; for the first time he saw Abū 'l-Faẓl, he said to his disciples, "What religious mischief is there of which that man is not capable?" Bad., III, 72.

[3] Vide pp. 179 ff.

ing to the other three sects; and the moral character of the Prophet was next scrutinized and was found wanting. Makhdūm[u] 'l-Mulk wrote a spiteful pamphlet against Shaykh ʿAbd[u] 'n-Nabī, the Ṣadr of the empire, and the latter retorted by calling Makhdūm a fool and cursing him. Abū'l-Faẓl, upon whom Akbar from the beginning had fixed as the leader of his party, fanned the quarrels, by skilfully shifting the disputes from one point to another, and at last persuaded the emperor that a subject ought to look upon the king not only as the temporal, but also as the only spiritual guide. The promulgation of this new doctrine was the making of Abū'l-Faẓl's fortune. Both he and Akbar held to it to the end of their lives. But the new idea was in opposition to Islām, the law of which stands above every king, rendering what we call a constitution impossible; and though headstrong kings as ʿAlāʾ[u] 'd-dīn Khiljī had before tried to raise the law of expediency (مصلحت وقت, *maṣlaḥat-i waqt*) above the law of the Qurʾān they never fairly succeeded in separating religion from law or in rendering the administration of the empire, independent of the Mullā. Hence when Abū'l-Faẓl four years later, in 986, brought up the question at the Thursday evening meetings, he raised a perfect storm; and while the disputations, bitter as they were, had hitherto dwelt on single points connected with the life of the Prophet, or with sectarian differences, they henceforth turned on the very principles of Islām. It was only now that the Sunnīs at Court saw how wide during the last four years the breach had become; that "the strong embankment of the clearest law and the most excellent faith had been broken through"; and that Akbar believed that there were sensible men in all religions, and abstemious thinkers and men endowed with miraculous power among all nations. Islām, therefore, possessed in his opinion no superiority over other forms of worship.[1] The learned party, seeing their official position endangered, now showed signs of readiness to yield, but it was too late. They even signed the remarkable document which Shaykh Mubārak in conjunction with his sons had drafted, a document which I believe stands unique in the whole Church History of Islām. Badā,onī has happily preserved a complete copy of it.[2] The emperor was certified to be a just ruler, and was as such assigned the rank of a "Mujtahid", i.e. an infallible authority in all matters relating to Islām. The "intellect of the just king" thus became the only source of legislation, and the whole body of the learned and the lawyers bound themselves to abide by Akbar's decrees in religious matters. Shaykh ʿAbd[u] 'n-Nabī and Makhdūm[u]'l-Mulk signed indeed the document against

[1] Pages 187, 189. [2] Vide p. 195.

their will, but sign they did ; whilst Shaykh Mubārak added to his signature the words that he had most willingly subscribed his name, and that for several years he had been anxiously looking forward to the realization of the progressive movement. " The document," says ˁAbū-'l-Fazl in the *Akbarnāma*, " brought about excellent results—(1) The Court became a gathering place of the sages and learned of all creeds ; the good doctrines of all religious systems were recognized, and their defects were not allowed to obscure their good features ; (2) perfect toleration (*ṣulḥ-i-kul* or " peace with all ") was established ; and (3) the perverse and evil-minded were covered with shame on seeing the disinterested motives of his Majesty, and thus stood in the pillory of disgrace." The copy of the draft which was handed to the emperor, was in Shaykh Mubārak's own handwriting, and was dated Rajab, 987 (September, 1579).

A few weeks afterwards, Shaykh ˁAbdᵘ 'n-Nabī and Makhdūmᵘ 'l-Mulk were sent to Makkah, and Shaykh Mubārak and his two sons triumphed over their enemies. How magnanimous Abū'l-Fazl was, may be seen from the manner in which he chronicles in the *Akbarnāma* the banishment of these men. Not a sentence, not a word, is added indicative of his personal grievances against either of them, though they had persecuted and all but killed his father and ruined his family ; the narrative proceeds as calm and statesmanlike as in every other part of his great work, and justifies the high praise which historians have bestowed upon his character that " neither abuse nor harsh words were ever found in his household ".

The disputations had now come to an end (A.D. 1579) and Fayẓī and Abū'l-Fazl had gained the lasting friendship of the emperor. Of the confidence which Akbar placed in Fayẓī, no better proof can be cited than his appointment, in the same year, as tutor to Prince Murād ; and as both brothers had entered the military, then the only, service and had received *manṣabs*, or commissions, their employment in various departments gave them repeated opportunities to gain fresh distinctions. Enjoying Akbar's personal friendship, both remained at court in Fatḥpūr Sīkrī, or accompanied the emperor on his expeditions. Two years later, Fayẓī was appointed Ṣadr of Āgra, Kālpī, and Kālinjar, in which capacity he had to inquire into the possibility of resuming free tenures (*sayurghāl*), which in consequence of fraudulent practices on the part of government officers and the rapaciousness of the holders themselves had so much increased as seriously to lessen the land revenue ; and Abū'l-Fazl in the very beginning of 1585,[1] was promoted to the *manṣab*

[1] *Akbarnāma*, iii, 463.

of Hazārī, or the post of a commander of one thousand horse, and was in the following year appointed Dīwān of the Province of Dihlī. Fayẕī's rank was much lower; he was only a commander of Four Hundred. But he did not care for further promotion. Devoted to the muse, he found in the appointment as Poet Laureate, with which Akbar honoured him in the end of 1588, that satisfaction which no political office, however high, would have given him. Though the emperor did not pay much attention to poetry, his appreciation of Fayẕī's genius was but just; for after Amīr Khusraw of Dihlī, Muhammadan India has seen no greater poet than Fayẕī.[1]

In the end of 1589, Abū'l-Fazl lost his mother, to whose memory he has devoted a page in the *Akbarnāma*. The emperor, in order to console him, paid him a visit, and said to him, " If the people of this world lived for ever and did not only once die, kind friends would not be required to direct their hearts to trust in God and resignation to His will; but no one lives long in the caravanserai of the world, and hence the afflicted do well to accept consolation." [2]

Religious matters had in the meantime rapidly advanced. Akbar had founded a new religion, the Dīn-i Ilāhī, or " the Divine Faith ", the chief feature of which, in accordance with Shaykh Mubārak's document mentioned above, consisted in belief in one God and in Akbar as His viceregent (*khalīfa*) on earth. The Islamitic prayers were abolished at court, and the worship of the " elect " was based on that of the Pārsīs and partly on the ceremonial of the Hindūs. The new era (*tārīkh-ilāhī*), which was introduced in all government records, as also the feasts observed by the emperor, were entirely Pārsī. The Muhammadan grandees at court showed but little resistance; they looked with more anxiety on the elevation of Hindū courtiers than on Akbar's religious innovations, which after all, affected but a few. But their feeling against Abū'l-Fazl was very marked, and they often advised the emperor to send him to the Dakhin hoping that some mismanagement in war or in administration would lessen his influence at court. Prince Salīm (Jahāngīr) also belonged to the dissatisfied, and his dislike to Abū'l-Fazl, as we shall see below, became gradually so deep-rooted, that he looked upon him as the chief obstacle to the execution of his wild plans. An unexpected visit to Abū'l-Fazl gave him an excellent opportunity to charge him with

---

[1] For his works, vide p. 161.

[2] اگر جهانیان طراز پایندگی داشتی و جزیکی راه نیستی نسپردی دوستان شناسا دل را از رضا و تسلیم گزیر نبود. هرگاه درین کاروان سرا هیچکس دیرنماند نکوهش ناشکیبائی را کجا اندازه توان گرفت ||

duplicity. On entering the house, he found forty writers busy in copying commentaries to the Qurʾān. Ordering them to follow him at once, he took them to the emperor, and showing him the copies he said, "What Abū'l-Faẓl teaches me is very different from what he practises in his house." The incident is said to have produced a temporary estrangement between Akbar and Abū'l-Faẓl. A similar, but less credible, story is told by the author of the *Zakhīratᵘ'l-Khawānīn*. He says that Abū'l-Faẓl repented of his apostacy from Islām, and used at night to visit *incognito* the houses of dervishes, and, giving them gold muhurs, requested them "to pray for the stability of Abū'l-Faẓl's faith", sighing at the same time and striking his knees and exclaiming, "What shall I do?" And just as writers on the history of literature have tried to save Fayẓī from apostacy and consequent damnation, by representing that before his death he had praised the Prophet, so have other authors succeeded in finding for Abū'l-Faẓl a place in Paradise; for it is related in several books that Shāh Abū 'l-Maʿalī Qādirī of Lāhor, a man of saintly renown,[1] once expressed his disapproval of Abū 'l-Faẓl's words and deeds. But at night, so runs the story, he saw in his dream that Abū' l-Faẓl came to a meeting held by the Prophet in Paradise; and when the Prophet saw him enter, he asked him to sit down, and said, "This man did for some time during his life evil deeds, but one of his books commences with the words, 'O God, reward the good for the sake of their righteousness, and help the wicked for the sake of thy love,' and these words have saved him." The last two stories flatter, in all probability, the consciences of pious Sunnīs; but the first, if true, detracts in no way from that consistency of opinion and uniform philosophic conviction which pervades Abū 'l-Faẓl's works; and though his heart found in pure deism and religious philosophy more comfort and more elements of harmony than in the casuistry of the Mullās, his mind from earlv youth had been so accustomed to hard literary work, that it was perfectly natural for him, even after his rejection of Islām to continue his studies of the Qurʾān, because the highest dialectical lore and the deepest philological research of Muhammadan literature have for centuries been concentrated on the explanation of the holy book.

To this period also belong the literary undertakings which were commenced under the auspices of the Emperor himself. Abū 'l-Faẓl, Fayẓī, and scholars as Badā,onī, Naqīb Khān, Shaykh Sulṭān, Ḥājī Ibrāhīm, Shaykh Munawwar and others, were engaged in historical and

[1] Born A.H. 960: died at Lāhor, 1024. *Khazīnatᵘ 'l-Aṣfiyā*, p. 139.

scientific compilations and in translations from the Sanskrit or Hindī into Persian.[1] Fayẓī took the Līlāwatī, a well-known book on mathematics, and Abū 'l-Faẓl translated the Kalīla Damna under the title of *ʿAyār Dānish* from Arabic into Persian. He also took a part in the translation of the *Mahābhārat*, and in the composition of the *Tārīkh-i Alfī*, the "History of the Millennium". The last-mentioned work, curious to say, has an intimate connexion with the Mahdawī movement, of which particulars have been given above. Although from the time of Shaykh ʿAlā,ī's death, the disciples of the millennium had to suffer persecution, and movement to all appearances had died out, the idea of a restorer of the millennium was revived during the discussions in Fatḥpūr Sīkrī and by the teachings of men of Sharīf-i Āmulī's stamp,[2] with this important modification, that Akbar himself was pointed to as the "Lord of the Age", through whom faded Islām was to come to an end. This new feature had Akbar's full approval, and exercised the greatest influence on the progress of his religious opinions. The *Tārīkh-i Alfī*, therefore, was to represent Islām as a thing of the past; it had existed a thousand (*alf*) years, and had done its work. The early history, to the vexation of the Sunnīs, was related from a Shīʿah point of view, and worse still, the chronology had been changed, inasmuch as the death of the Prophet had been made the starting point, not the *hijra*, or flight, of the Prophet from Makka to Madīna

Towards the middle of A.H. 1000 (beginning of A.D. 1592), Akbar promoted Abū 'l-Faẓl to the post of Dūhazārī, or commander of two thousand horse. Abū 'l-Faẓl now belonged to the great Amīrs (*umarā-yi kibār*) at court. As before, he remained in immediate attendance on the emperor. In the same year, Fayẓī was sent to the Dakhin as Akbar's ambassador to Burhānu 'l-Mulk, and to Rāja ʿAlī Khān of Khāndesh, who had sent his daughter to Prince Salīm. Fayẓī returned after an absence of more than sixteen months.

Shaykh Mubārak, who after the publication of his famous document had all but retired from the world, died in the following year at Lāhor (Sunday, 17th Ẕī Qaʿda, 1001, or 4th September, 1593). He had reached

---

[1] Vide pp. 110, 111.

[2] Page 502. We hear the last of the Mahdawī movement in 1628, at the accession of Shāhjahān. Akbar was dead and had not restored the Millennium; during Jahāngīr's reign, especially in the beginning, the court was indifferent to religion, and the king retained the ceremony of *sijda*, or prostration, which Muhammadans believe to be due to God alone. But Shāhjahān, on his accession, restored many Muhammadan rites that had fallen in abeyance at court; and as he was born in A.H. 1000, he was now pointed to as the real restorer. Since that time the movement has found no disciples.

the age of 90, and had occupied himself in the last years of his life with the compilation in four volumes of a gigantic commentary to the Qur*ān, to which he had given the title of *Manbaʕu Nafā,isu'l-ʕUyūn*. He completed it, in spite of failing eyesight, a short time before his death.

The historian Badā,onī speaks of him as follows :—

Shaykh Mubārak belonged to the most distinguished men of learning of the present age. In practical wisdom, piety, and trust in God, he stood high among the people of his time. In early life he practised rigorous asceticism ; in fact, he was so strict in his views regarding what is lawful and unlawful, that if any one, for example, came to a prayer meeting with a gold ring on his finger, or dressed in silk, or with red stockings on his feet, or red or yellow coloured clothes on him, he would order the offending articles to be removed. In legal decisions, he was so severe as to maintain that for every hurt exceeding a simple kick, death was the proper punishment. If he accidentally heard music while walking on the street, he ran away, but in course of time he became, from divine zeal, so enamoured of music, that he could not exist without listening to some voice or melody. In short, he passed through rather opposite modes of thought and ways of life. At the time of the Afghān rule, he frequented Shaykh ʕAlā,ī's fraternity ; in the beginning of His Majesty's reign, when the Naqshbandīs had the upper hand, he settled matters with that sect ; afterwards he was attached to the Hamadānī school, and lastly, when the Shīʕahs monopolized the court, he talked according to their fashion. " Men speak according to the measure of their understanding "—to change was his way, and the rest you know. But withal he was constantly engaged in teaching the religious sciences. Prosody also, the art of composing riddles, and other branches, he understood well ; and in mystic philosophy he was, unlike the learned of Hindūstān, a perfect master. He knew Shāṭibī[1] by heart, explained him properly, and also knew how to read the Qur*ān in the ten different modes. He did not go to the palaces of the kings, but he was a most agreeable companion and full of anecdote. Towards the end of his life, when his eyesight was impaired, he gave up reading and lived in seclusion. The commentary to the Qur*ān which he composed, resembles the *Tafsīr-i Kabīr* (the " Great Commentary "), and consists of four thick volumes, and is entitled *Mambaʕu ʕNafāisu 'l-ʕUyūn*. It is rather extraordinary that there is a passage in the preface in which he seems to point to himself

---

[1] A writer on " Tajwīd ", " the art of reading the Qur*ān correctly ".

as the renovator of the new century.[1] We know what this "renovating" means. About the time he finished his work he wisely committed the Fārizī Ode (in *t*) which consists of seven hundred verses, and the Ode Barda, the Ode by Kaʿb ibn Zubayr, and other Odes to memory, and recited them as daily homilies, till on the 17th Ẕī Qaʿda, 1001, he left this world at Lāhor for the judgment-seat of God.

I have known no man of more comprehensive learning; but alas! under the mantle of a dervish there was such a wicked love of worldly preferment, that he left no tittle of our religion in peace. When I was young, I studied at Āgra for several years in his company. He is indeed a man of merit; but he committed worldly and irreligious deeds, plunged into lust of possession and rank, was timeserving, practised deceit and falsehood, and went so far in twisting religious truth, that nothing of his former merit remains. "Say, either I am in the correct path or in clear error, or you" (Qurʾān, xxxiv, 23). Further, it is a common saying that the son brings the curse on the head of his father; hence people have gone beyond Yazīd and say, "Curse on Yazīd,[2] and on his father, too."

Two years after Shaykh Mubārak's death, Abū 'l-Fażl also lost his brother Fayżī, who died at the age of 50, after an illness of six months on the 10th Safar, 1004 (5th October, 1595). When in his last moments, Akbar visited him at midnight, and seeing that he could no longer speak, he gently raised his head and said to him, "Shaykh Jīo, I have brought Ḥakīm ʿAlī with me, will you not speak to me?" But getting no reply, the emperor in his grief threw his turban to the ground, and wept loud; and after trying to console Abū 'l-Fażl, he went away.[3] How deeply Abū l-Fażl loved his elder brother, is evident from the numerous passages in the *Akbarnāma* and the *Āʾīn* in which he speaks of him, and nothing is more touching than the lines with which he prefaces the selections in the *Āʾīn* made by him from his brother's poems. "The gems of thought in his poems will never be forgotten. Should leisure permit and my heart turn to worldly occupations, I would collect some

---

[1] Badā,onī says in his *Najātᵘ 'r-rashīd* that Jalālᵘ d-Dīn Suyūṭī, in his time the most universal scholar of all Arabia, pointed likewise to himself as the renovator of the tenth century.

[2] Ḥusayn, in whose remembrance the Muḥarram lamentations are chanted, was murdered by Yazid; hence the latter is generally called *Yazīd-i-malʿūn*, "Yazīd, the accursed". Badā,onī here calls Abū 'l-Fażl Yazīd. Poor Badā,onī had only the thousand bīghas which Akbar had given him rent-free, but his school fellow Yazīd Abū 'l-Fażl was a commander of two thousand and the friend of the emperor.

[3] Badā,onī, ii, 406.

of the excellent writings of this unrivalled author of the age, and gather, with the eye of a jealous critic, yet with the hand of a friend, some of his poems. But now it is brotherly love alone, which does not travel along the road of critical nicety, that commands me to write down some of his verses." Abū 'l-Faẓl, notwithstanding his onerous duties, kept his promise, and two years after the death of his brother, he collected the stray leaves of Fayẓī's *Markiz*[u] *'l-Adwār*, not to mention the numerous extracts which he has preserved in the *Akbarnāma*.

It was about the same time that Abū 'l-Faẓl was promoted to the post of a Commander of two thousand and five hundred horse. Under this rank he has entered his own name in the list of grandees in the *Ā*ʾ*īn-i Akbarī*, which work he completed in the same year when he collected his brother's literary remains (1596–7).

In the following year, the forty-third of Akbar's reign, Abū 'l-Faẓl went for the first time on active service. Sulṭān Murād had not managed matters well in the Dakhin, and Akbar now dispatched Abū 'l-Faẓl with orders to return with the Prince, whose excessive drinking caused the emperor much anxiety, provided the officers of the imperial camp made themselves responsible to guard the conquered territory. If the officers were disinclined to guarantee a faithful conduct of the war, he was to see the Prince off, and take command with Shāhrukh Mīrzā. The wars in the Dakhin, from their first commencement under Prince Murād and the Khān Khānān, are marked by a most astounding duplicity on the part of the imperial officers, and thousands of men and immense stores were sacrificed, especially during the reign of Jahāngīr, by treacherous and intriguing generals. In fact, the Khān Khānān himself was the most untrustworthy imperial officer. Abū 'l-Faẓl's successes, therefore, were chiefly due to the honesty and loyalty with which he conducted operations. When he arrived at Burhānpūr, he received an invitation from Bahādur Khān, king of Khāndesh, whose brother had married Abū 'l-Faẓl's sister. He consented to come on one condition, namely, that Bahādur Khān should vigorously assist him, and thus aid the cause of the emperor. Bahādur was not inclined to aid the imperialists in their wars with the Dakhin, but he sent Abū 'l-Faẓl rich presents, hoping that by this means he would escape the penalty of his refusal. Abū 'l-Faẓl, however, was not the man to be bribed. "I have made a vow," he said in returning the presents, "not to accept presents till four conditions are fulfilled—(1) friendship; (2) that I should not value the gift too high; (3) that I should not have been anxious to get a present; and (4) necessity to accept it. Now supposing that the first three are applicable to the present case, the favour of the emperor has extinguished every desire in me of accepting gifts from others."

Prince Murād had in the meantime retreated from Aḥmadnagar to Īlichpūr, and as the death of his infant son Mīrzā Rustam made him melancholy, he continued to drink, though dangerously ill with delirium tremens. When informed of Abū 'l-Fazl's mission, he returned at once towards Aḥmadnagar, in order to have a pretext for not going back to his father, and he had come to the banks of the Pūrnā,[1] twenty kos from Dawlatābād, when death overtook him. Abū 'l-Fazl arrived the same day, and found the camp in the utmost confusion. Each commander recommended immediate return; but Abū 'l-Fazl said that he was determined to march on; the enemy was near, the country was foreign ground, and this was no time for returning, but for fighting. Several of the commanders refused to march on, and returned; but Abū 'l-Fazl, nothing daunted, after a delay of a few days, moved forward, humoured the officers, and supplied in a short time all wants. Carefully garrisoning the country, he managed to occupy and guard the conquered districts with the exception of Nāsik, which lay too far to the west. But he sent detachments against several forts, and conquered Baiṭāla, Taltum, and Satondā. His headquarters were on the Godāwārī. He next entered into an agreement with Chānd Bībī, that, after punishing Abhang Khān Ḥabshī, who was at war with her, she should accept Janīr as fief and give up the fort of Aḥmadnagar.

Akbar had in the meantime gone to Ujjain. The Dakhin operations had also become more complicated by the refusal of Bahādur Khān to pay his respects to Prince Dānyāl, and war with Khāndesh had been determined on. Akbar resolved to march on Āsīr, Bahādur Khān's stronghold, and appointed Prince Dānyāl to take command at Aḥmadnagar. Dānyāl sent immediate instructions to Abū 'l-Fazl to cease all operations, as he wished to take Aḥmadnagar personally. When the Prince therefore left Burhānpūr, Abū 'l-Fazl at Akbar's request, left Mīrzā Shāhrukh, Mīr Murtazā, and Khwāja Abū 'l-Ḥasan in charge of his corps, and hastened to meet the emperor. On the 14th Ramazān, 1008 (beginning of the 44th year of Akbar's reign), he met Akbar at Khargō, near Bīlāgaṛh. The emperor received him with the following verse—

---

[1] The southern Pūrnā is meant. The northern Pūrnā flows into the Taptī in Khāndesh; whilst the southern Pūrnā, with the Dūdnā, flows into the Godāwarī. Prince Murād had gone from Īlichpūr to Narnāla, and from there to Shāhpūr, which he had built about eight miles south of Bālāpūr. It is now in ruins.

فرخنده شبے باید وخوش مهتابے تا با تو حکایت کنم از هربابے

Serene is the night and pleasant is the moonlight, I wish to talk to thee on many a subject.

and promoted him for his excellent management to a command of four thousand. The imperial army now marched on Āsīr and commenced the siege.[1] One day, Abū 'l-Faẓl inspected some of his trenches, when one of the besieged, who had deserted to Akbar's camp, offered to show him a way by which the Imperialists might get over the wall of the Mālai Fort, an important fortification below Āsīrgarh itself. Half way up the mountain, to the west and slightly to the north, were two renowned outworks, called the Mālai and Antar Mālai, which had to be conquered before Āsīr itself could be reached; and between the north-west and north, there was another bastion called Chūna Mālai. A portion of its wall was not finished. From east to south-west there were hills, and in the south was a high mountain called Korhia. A hill in the south-west, called Sāpan, was occupied by the Imperialists. Abū 'l-Faẓl determined on availing himself of the information given by the deserter, and selected a detachment to follow him. Giving orders to the officer commanding the trench to listen for the sound of the trumpets and bugles, when he was to hasten to his assistance with ladders, he went in the dark of night, whilst it was raining, with his selected men on Mount Sāpan, and sent a few of his men under Qarā Beg along the road that had been pointed out to him. They advanced, broke open a gate of Mālai Fort, and sounded the bugle. The besieged rose up to oppose them, and Abū 'l-Faẓl hastened to his men and joined them at break of day when the besieged withdrew in confusion to Āsīr. On the same

---

[1] "Akbar had no sooner crossed the Nerebada (Narbadā), when Radzia Bador-xa (Rāja Bahādur Shāh) who had possession of the fortress of Hasser (Āsīr) fortified the same against the king, and collected provisions from the neighbourhood. The king, thinking it dangerous to leave this fortress in his rear, considered how it might be captured. This fortress has three castles, of which the first is called *Cho-Tzanin*, the second *Commerghar*; and the third is placed on the very summit of the hill, so that it is a conspicuous object at the distance of six coss. The king with no delay surrounded it on all sides; and so energetically pressed the siege night and day, that at the end of six months it was on the point of being captured. Bador-xa however perceiving his danger, having obtained a pledge that his life and property should be safe, came as suppliant to the king and surrendered himself. . . . . Whilst the king was at this place, Abdul Fazel (Abū 'l-Faẓl) came to him, and so worked upon his mind, that he fully determined to set out for the war in the Deccan." From Professor Lethbridge's *Fragment of Indian History*, translated from De Laët's *India Vera*, and published in the *Calcutta Review* for 1873.

De Laët is wrong in a few minor details. I cannot identify the name Cho-Tzanin. "Commerghar" is the Persian "Kamargāh", "the middle of a mountain." The names of Fort Chūnah Mālai and of Mount Korhiah are doubtful, the MSS. having Khwāja Mālai and Korthah, Kortah, Koḍhiah, and similar variations.

Vide also, *Gazetteer*, Central Provinces, p. 8.

day, other detachments of the army occupied Chūna Mālai and Mount Korhia, and Bahādur Khān, unable to resist longer, sued for pardon (1009). Prince Dānyāl, who had in the meantime conquered Aḥmadnagar,[1] now joined his father at Āsīr.

About this time disturbances broke out in the Dakhin, caused by Rājū Mannā, and a party set up the son of ʿAlī Shāh as king. As the latter found numerous adherents, the Khān Khānān was ordered to march against him, and Abū 'l-Faẓl was sent to Nāsik; but a short time afterwards, he was told to join the Khān Khānān. Akbar returned, in the 46th year, to Āgra, leaving Prince Dānyāl in Burhānpūr. Abū 'l-Faẓl had no easy life in the Dakhin. The Khān Khānān stood idle at Aḥmadnagar, because he was disinclined to fight, and left the operations to Abū 'l-Faẓl, who looked upon him as a traitor. Abū 'l-Faẓl vigorously pushed on operations, ably assisted by his son ʿAbdu 'r-Raḥmān. After coming to terms with the son of ʿAlī Shāh, he attacked Rājū Mannā, recovered Jālnapūr and the surrounding district, and inflicted several defeats on him. Mannā found a temporary asylum in Dawlatābād, and in a subsequent engagement he was nearly captured.

As early as during the siege of Āsīr, Prince Salīm, who had been sent against the Rānā of Udaipūr, had rebelled against his father, and had moved to Ilāhābād, where he had assumed the title of king. Though on Akbar's return from Burhānpūr a reconciliation had been effected, the prince, in the forty-seventh year, showed again signs of rebellion, and as many of Akbar's best officers appeared to favour Salīm, the emperor recalled Abū 'l-Faẓl, the only trustworthy servant he had. As his presence at Court was urgently required, Akbar sent him orders to leave the troops of his contingent in the Dakhin. Putting his son ʿAbdu 'r-Raḥmān in charge of his corps, Abū 'l-Faẓl set out for Āgra, accompanied by a few men only. Salīm, who looked upon him with little concealed hatred, thought Abū 'l-Faẓl's journey unprotected, as he was, an excellent opportunity to get rid of him. He, therefore, persuaded Rāja Bir Singh, a Bundelā chief of Ūrcha (Ūḍchhā),[2] through whose territory Abū 'l-Faẓl was likely to pass, to lie in wait for him and kill him. Bir Singh, who was in disgrace at Court, eagerly seized the opportunity of pleasing the Prince, who no doubt would substantially reward him on his accession, and posted a large body of horse and foot near Narwar. When arrived at Ujjain, Abū 'l-Faẓl was warned of Salīm's

[1] Among the plunder taken at Aḥmadnagar was a splendid library. Fayẓī's library, having on his death lapsed to the state, had been incorporated with the Imperial Library.

[2] Vide p. 546.

intention, and his men tried to persuade him to go via Ghaṭī Chāndā; but Abū 'l-Fazl said that thieves and robbers had no power to stop him on his way to Court. He, therefore, continued his journey towards Narwar. On Friday, the 4th Rabīʿ I, 1011 (12th August, 1602), at a distance of about half a *kos* from Sarāy Bar, which lies six *kos* from Narwar, Bir Singh's men came in sight. The few men that Abū 'l-Faẓl had with him strongly advised him to avoid a fight, and an old servant, Gadā,ī Khān, Afghān, told him quickly to retreat to Antrī, which was three *kos* distant, as Rāy Rāyān and Sūraj Singh were stationed there with three thousand Imperial horse; he might first join them, and then punish Bir Singh. But Abū 'l-Faẓl thought it a disgrace to fly. He defended himself bravely; but in a short time he was surrounded and, pierced by the lance of a trooper, he fell dead to the ground. Bir Singh cut off Abū 'l-Faẓl's head, and sent it to Salīm in Ilāhābād, who, it is said, had it thrown " into an unworthy place ", where it lay for a long time.

The Dutch traveller De Laët gives the following account of Abū 'l-Faẓl's death :—[1]

Salīm returned to Halebassa (Ilāhbās, the old form of Ilāhābād), and began to coin gold and silver money in his own name, which he even sent to his father, to irritate him the more. The king, enraged at this, wrote an account of all that had happened to Abū 'l-Faẓl, who bade the king be of good courage, for he would come to him as quickly as possible; and added that his son should be brought bound to him, either by fair means or by foul. Accordingly, a little afterwards, having obtained leave of absence from Daniel Xa (Dānyāl Shāh), he took to the road with about two or three hundred horsemen, leaving orders for his baggage to follow him. Xa-Selim, to whom all these things were known, recalling how hostile Faẓl had always been towards him, and hence justly fearing that his father would be more exasperated than ever against him, judged it best to intercept him on his journey. So he begged Radzia Bertzingh Bondela, who lived in his province of Osseen (Ujjain), to lie in wait for Faẓl near Soor (Narwar ?) and Gualer (Gwāliyār) and to send his head to him, promising that he would be mindful of so great a benefit, and would give him the command of five thousand cavalry. The Radzia consented, and waited with a thousand cavalry and three thousand infantry about three or four coss from Gualer, having sent out scouts into the neighbouring

---

[1] From Professor E. Lethbridge's " Fragment of Indian History ", *Calcutta Review*, 1873.

The place near which Abū 'l-Faẓl was killed, is called in the MSS. سراي بر *Sarāi Bar*. De Laët's Soor appears to be a bad reading for Narwar.

villages, to give him early warning of the approach of Faẓl. Accordingly when the latter, ignorant of the ambuscade, had come as far as Collebaga (Kālābāgh), and was going towards Soor, Radzia Bertzingh and his followers fell upon him on all sides. Faẓl and his horsemen fought bravely, but being overpowered by numbers, they were gradually worn out. Faẓl himself, having received twelve wounds in the fight, was pointed out by a captive slave under a neighbouring tree, and was taken and beheaded. His head was sent to the prince, who was greatly pleased."

Prince Salīm, with that selfish nonchalance and utter indifference that distinguished him throughout life, openly confesses in his "Memoirs" that he brought about Abū 'l-Faẓl's murder, because he was his enemy, and with a naïveté exclusively his own, represents himself as a dutiful son who through the wickedness of others had been deprived of his father's love. He says :—

"On my accession, I promoted Rāja Bir Singh, a Bundelā Rājpūt, to a command of three thousand. He is one of my favourites, and he is certainly distinguished among his equals for his bravery, good character, and straightforwardness. My reason for promoting him was this. Towards the end of my father's reign, Shaykh Abū 'l-Faẓl, a Hindūstānī Shaykh by birth, who was well known for his learning and wisdom, and who had externally ornamented himself with the jewel of loyalty, though he sold himself at a high price to my father, had been called from the Dakhin. He was no friend of mine, and damaged openly and secretly my reputation. Now about that time, evil-minded and mischievous men had made my father very angry with me, and I knew that if Abū 'l-Faẓl were to come back to Court, I would have been deprived of every chance to effect a reconciliation. As he had to pass on his way through the territory of Bir Singh Bundelā, who at that time had rebelled against the emperor, I sent a message to the latter to say that, if he would waylay Abū 'l-Faẓl and kill him, I would richly reward him. Heaven favoured him, and when Abū 'l-Faẓl passed through his land, he stopped him on his way, dispersed after a short fight his men, and killed him, and sent his head to me at Ilāhābād. Although my father was at first much vexed, Abū 'l-Faẓl's death produced one good result: I could now without further annoyance go to my father, and his bad opinion of me gradually wore away."

At another place in his "Memoirs" when alluding to the murder, he says, as if an afterthought had occurred to him, that he ordered Bir Singh to kill Abū 'l-Faẓl because "he had been the enemy of the Prophet".

When the news of Abū 'l-Faẓl's death reached court, no one had the courage to break it to the emperor. According to an old custom observed by Tīmūr's descendants, the death of a prince was not in plain words mentioned to the reigning emperor, but the prince's vakīl presented himself before the throne with a blue handkerchief round his wrist; and as no one else would come forward to inform Akbar of the death of his friend, Abū 'l-Faẓl's vakīl presented himself with a blue handkerchief before the throne. Akbar bewailed Abū 'l-Faẓl's death more than that of his son; for several days he would see no one, and after inquiring into the circumstances he exclaimed, "If Salīm wished to be emperor, he might have killed me and spared Abū 'l-Faẓl," and then recited the following verse:

شیخ ما از شوق بیحد چون سوی ما آمده ز اشتیاق پای بوسی بی سر و پا آمده

My Shaykh in his zeal hastened to meet me,
He wished to kiss my feet, and gave up his life.

Akbar, in order to punish Bir Singh, sent a detachment under Patr Dās and Rāj Singh [1] to Ūṇḍchā. They defeated the Bundelā chief in several engagements, drove him from Bhānder and shut him up in Īrich. When the siege had progressed and a breach was made in the wall, Bir Singh escaped by one of Rāj Singh's trenches, and withdrew to the jungles closely pursued by Patr Dās. As it seemed hopeless to catch him, Akbar called Patr Dās to Court; but ordered the officers stationed about Ūṇḍchā to kill the rebel wherever he showed himself. In the beginning of the last year of Akbar's reign, Bir Singh was once surprised by Rāja Rāj Singh, who cut down a good number of his followers. Bir Singh himself was wounded and had a narrow escape. But the emperor's death, which not long afterwards took place, relieved Bir Singh of all fears. He boldly presented himself at Jahāngīr's Court, and received Ūṇḍchā and a command of three thousand horse as his reward.

"It has often been asserted," says the author of the *Maʿāsir*[u] *'l-Umarā*, that Abū 'l-Faẓl was an infidel. Some say he was a Hindū, or a fire-worshipper, or a free-thinker, and some go still further and call him an atheist; but others pass a juster sentence, and say that he was a pantheist, and that, like other Ṣūfīs, he claimed for himself a position above the law of the Prophet. There is no doubt that he was a man of lofty character,[2] and desired to live at peace with all men. He never

---

[1] Pages 523 and 509.
[2] I may remark here that Abū 'l-Faẓl never accepted a title.

said anything improper. Abuse, stoppages of wages, fines, absence on the part of his servants, did not exist in his household. If he appointed a man, whom he afterwards found to be useless, he did not remove him, but kept him on as long as he could; for he used to say that, if he dismissed him, people would accuse him of want of penetration in having appointed an unsuitable agent. On the day when the sun entered Aries, he inspected his whole household and took stock, keeping the inventory with himself, and burning last year's books. He also gave his whole wardrobe to his servants, with the exception of his trousers, which were burnt in his presence.

"He had an extraordinary appetite. It is said, that exclusive of water and fuel, he consumed daily twenty-two sers of food. His son ʿAbdu r-Raḥmān used to sit at table as *safarchī* [1] (head butler); the superintendent of the kitchen, who was a Muhammadan, was also in attendance and both watched to see whether Abū 'l-Fazl would eat twice of one and the same dish. If he did, the dish was sent up again the next day. If anything appeared tasteless, Abū 'l-Fazl gave it to his son to taste, and he to the superintendent, but no word was said about it. When Abū 'l-Fazl was in the Dakhīn, his table luxury exceeded all belief. In an immense tent (*chihilrāwaṭī*) one thousand rich dishes were daily served up and distributed among the Amīrs; and near it another large tent was pitched for all-comers to dine, whether rich or poor, and *khichrī* was cooked all day and was served out to any one that applied for it."

"As a writer, Abū 'l-Fazl stands unrivalled. His style is grand and is free from the technicalities and flimsy prettiness of other Munshīs [2]; and the force of his words, the structure of his sentences, the suitableness of his compounds, and the elegance of his periods, are such that it would be difficult for any one to imitate them."

It is almost useless to add to this encomium bestowed on Abū 'l-Fazl's style. ʿAbdu 'llāh, king of Bukhārā, said that he was more afraid of Abū 'l-Fazl's pen than of Akbar's arrow. Everywhere in India he is known as "the great Munshī". His letters are studied in all Madrasas, and though a beginner may find them difficult and perplexing, they are perfect models. But a great familiarity, not only with the Persian language, but also with Abū 'l-Fazl's style, is required to make the reading of any of his works a pleasure. His composition stands unique, and though everywhere studied, he cannot be, and has not been, imitated. The writers

[[1] *Sufra-chī.*—E.]
[2] This is also the opinion of the author of the *Haft Iqlīm*.

after him write in the style of the Pādishāhnāma, the ʿĀlamārā Sikandarī or in the still more turgid manner of the ʿĀlamgīrnāma, the Ruqʿāt Bedil, and other standard works on Inshā.

A praiseworthy feature of Abū 'l-Faẓl's works lies in the purity of their contents. Those who are acquainted with Eastern literature will know what this means. I have come across no passage where woman is lightly spoken of, or where immorality is passed over with indifference. Of his love of truth and the nobility of his sentiments [1] I have spoken in the Preface.

Abū 'l-Faẓl's influence on his age was immense. It may be that he and Fayẓī led Akbar's mind away from Islām and the Prophet—this charge is brought against them by every Muhammadan writer; but Abū 'l-Faẓl also led his sovereign to a true appreciation of his duties, and from the moment that he entered Court, the problem of successfully ruling over mixed races, which Islām in but few other countries had to solve, was carefully considered, and the policy of toleration was the result. If Akbar felt the necessity of this new law, Abū 'l-Faẓl enunciated it and fought for it with his pen, and if the Khān Khānāns gained the victories, the new policy reconciled the people to the foreign rule; and whilst Akbar's apostacy from Islām is all but forgotten, no emperor of the Mughul dynasty has come nearer to the ideal of a father of the people than he. The reversion, on the other hand, in later times to the policy of religious intoleration, whilst it has surrounded in the eyes of the Moslems the memory of Awrangzīb with the halo of sanctity and still inclines the pious to utter a *raḥim^{a}- 'llah-hū* (May God have mercy on him!) when his name is mentioned, was also the beginning of the breaking up of the empire.

Having elsewhere given numerous extracts from Badā,onī to show that Akbar's courtiers ascribed his apostacy from Islām to Fayẓī and Abū 'l-Faẓl, I need not quote other works, and will merely allude to a couplet by ʿUrfī [2] from one of his Odes in which he praises the Prophet—

یوسف نفس مرا ز آسیب اخوان دور دار کاین حسودان مروت سوز با این بے گناه
با قریت غول همزادند در راه سلوک با فساد گرگ انبازند در نزدیک چاه

O Prophet, protect the Joseph of my soul (i.e. my soul) from the harm of the brothers; for they are ungenerous and envious, and deceive me like evil sprites and lead me wolf-like to the well (of unbelief).

---

[1] Let the reader consult Gladwin's rendering of Abū 'l-Faẓl's introduction to the fourth book of the *Āʾīn*. Gladwin's *Āʾīn*, ii, pp. 285–91. The passage is anti-Islamitic.

[2] For ʿUrfī vide p. 639. The metre of the couplet is Long *Ramal*.

The commentators unanimously explain this passage as an allusion to the brothers Fayẓī and Abū 'l-Faẓl. I may also cite the Tārīkh of Abū 'l-Faẓl's death, which the Khān-i Aʿẓam Mīrzā Koka is said to have made :—

تیغ اعجاز نبی الله سر باغی برید

The wonderful sword of God's prophet cut off the head of the rebel.[1]

But Abū 'l-Faẓl appeared to him in a dream and said, "The date of my death lies in the words بندهٔ ابو الفضل, "The slave Abū 'l-Faẓl"— which likewise gives A.H. 1011.

Abū 'l-Faẓl's works are the following :—

(1) The *Akbarnāma* with the *Āʾīn-i Akbarī*, its third volume. The *Āʾīn-i Akbarī* was completed in the 42nd year of Akbar's reign ; only a slight addition to it was made in the 43rd year on account of the conquest of Barār (A.D. 1596–7). The contents of the *Akbarnāma* have been detailed in the Preface. The second volume contains an account of the first forty-six years of Akbar's reign.[2] There exists a continuation up to the end of Akbar's reign by ʿInāyatᵘ 'llah Muḥibb ʿAlī. Thus at least the continuator is called in two MSS. that I have seen. Elphinstone says that the name of the continuator is Muḥammad Salia, which seems to be a corruption of Muḥammad Ṣāliḥ.

(2) The *Maktūbāt-i ʿAllāmī*, also called *Inshā-yi Abū 'l-Faẓl*. This book contains letters written by Abū 'l-Faẓl to kings and chiefs. Among them are the interesting letters written to the Portuguese priests, and to ʿAbdᵘ 'llāh of Bukhārā, in reply to his question whether Akbar had renounced Islām. Besides, there are prefaces and reviews, a valuable essay on the progress of the art of writing, portions of which are given in the *Āīn*, etc. The collection was made after Abū 'l-Faẓl's death by ʿAbdᵘ 's-Ṣamad, son of Afẓal Muḥammad, who says that he was a son of Abū 'l-Faẓl's sister and also his son-in-law. The book, as above remarked, is frequently read in Madrasas, and there exist many lithographed editions. In all of them, the contents constitute three books ; but Amīr Haydar Ḥusaynī of Bilgrām says in the preface to his *Sawāniḥ-i Akbarī* [3] that he had a collection of four books, remarking at the same

---

[1] The word باغی *bāghī*, a rebel, has the numerical value of 1013 ; but the head (of the word, the letter ب) is cut off ; hence 1013 – 2 = 1011, the year of the Hijra in which Abū 'l-Faẓl was murdered. The metre of the hemistich is Long *Ramal*.

[2] The 46th year lasted from the 15th Ramaẓān, 1009, to 26th Ramaẓān, 1010, i.e. to about five months before Abū 'l-Faẓl's death.

[3] Regarding this valuable work, vide p. 331, note.

time that MSS. of the fourth are very rare. It looks, indeed, as if Amīr Haydar's copy was unique.

(3) The ˁ*Ayār Dānish*,[1] which is mentioned on p. 112.

Besides, I have seen in different books that Abū 'l-Faẓl also wrote a *Risālayi Munājāt*, or "Treatise of Prayers"; a *Jāmiˁu 'l-lughāt*, a lexicographical work; and a *Koshkol*. The last word means a "beggar's cup", or rather the small basket or bowl in which beggars in the East collect rice, dates, etc., given as alms, and hence the term is often applied to collections of anecdotes or short stories. But I have seen no copies of these works. It was also mentioned above that Abū 'l-Faẓl presented, on his introduction at Court, two commentaries, of which no MSS. seem to exist at present. Nor need I again refer to the part which he took in the translations from Sanskrit and the compilation of the *Tārīkh-i Alfī*.

The *Durarᵘ 'l-Manshūr*, a modern Tazkira by Muḥammad ˁAskarī Ḥusaynī of Bilgrām, selects the following inscription written by Abū 'l-Faẓl for a temple in Kashmīr[2] as a specimen both of Abū 'l-Faẓl's writing and of his religious belief. It is certainly very characteristic, and is easily recognized as Abū 'l-Faẓl's composition.

الهی بهر خانه که می نگرم جویاي تو اند و بهر زبان که من شفوم گویاي تو *سعر*

کفر و اسلام در رهت پویان وحده لا شریکَ له گویان

اگر مسجدست بیاد تو نعرهٔ قدوس میزنند و اگر کلیسیاست بشوق تو ناقوس می جنبانند *بیت*

ای تیوغمت رادل عشاق نشانه خلقی بتو مشغول وتو غایب از میانه

گه معتکف دیرم وگه ساکن مسجد یعنی که ترا میطلبم خانه بخانه

گه معتکف دیرم وگه ساکن مسجد یعنی که ترا می طلبم خانه بخانه

اگر خاصان ترا بکفر و اسلام کارے نیست این هردو را در پردهٔ اسلم تو بارے نه

کفر کافر را و دین دیندار را ذرهٔ وردی دل عطار را

---

[1] As the word is pronounced in India, instead of 'Iyār-i Dānish", "the test of wisdom." The author of the *Haft Iqlīm* seems to allude to this work; for he says that Abū 'l-Faẓl, when he saw him in A.H. 1000, was engaged in re-writing the *Nawādir-i Ḥikāyāt*.

[2] Abū 'l-Faẓl says in the fourth book of the *Āˁīn*—"The best people in Kashmīr are the Brahmans. Although they have not yet freed themselves from the fetters of blind belief and adherence to custom, they yet worship God without affectation. They do not sneer at people of other religions, utter no desires, and do not run after lucre. They plant fruit trees and thus contribute to the welfare of their fellow creatures. They abstain from meat, and live in celibacy. There are about two thousand of them in Kashmīr."

Akbar seems to have looked upon these Kashmīrī Rishis as model men.

این خانه بنیت ایتلاف قلوب مؤحدان هندوستان وخصوص معبود پرستان عرصهٔ کشمیر تعمیر یافته *

بفرمان خدیو تخت و افسر چراغ آفرینش شاه اکبر
نظام اعتدال هفت معدن کمال امتزاج چار عنصر

هر که نظر صدق نیند اخته این خانه را خراب سازد باید که نخست معبد خود را بیندازد چه اگر نظر بر دل است با همه ساختنی است واگر چشم بر آب و گل است همه برانداختنی *بیت*

خداوندا چو داد کار دادی مدار کار بر نیت نهادی
توئی بر بارگاه نیت آگاه به پیش شه داری نیت شاد

O God, in every temple I see people that seek Thee, and in every language I hear spoken people praise Thee!

Polytheism and Islām feel after Thee,
Each religion says, "Thou art one, without equal."

If it be a mosque, people murmur the holy prayer, and if it be a Christian Church, people ring the bell from love to Thee.

Sometimes I frequent the Christian cloister, and sometimes the mosque,
But it is Thou whom I search from temple to temple.

Thy elect have no dealings with either heresy or orthodoxy; for neither of them stands behind the screen of Thy truth.

Heresy to the heretic, and religion to the orthodox,
But the dust of the rose petal[1] belongs to the heart of the perfume-seller.

This temple was erected for the purpose of binding together the hearts of the Unitarians in Hindūstān, and especially those of His worshippers that live in the province of Kashmīr,

By order of the Lord of the throne and the crown, the lamp of creation, Shāh Akbar,
In whom the seven minerals find uniformity, in whom the four elements attain perfect mixture.[2]

He who from insincere motives destroys this temple, should first destroy his own place of worship; for if we follow the dictates of the heart, we must bear up with all men, but if we look to the external, we find everything proper to be destroyed.

---

[1] This line is Sūfistic. The longing of the heart after God is compared to the perfume which rises from the rose petals. The perfume-seller, i.e. the Unitarian, is truly religious, and is equally removed from heresy and orthodoxy.

[2] I.e. Akbar is the *insān-i kāmil*, or perfect man.

O God, Thou art just and judgest an action by the motive ;

Thou knowest whether a motive is sublime, and tellest the king what motives a king should have.

I have a few notes on Abū 'l-Fazl's family, which may form the conclusion of this biographical noticed. The *Aʿīn* gives the following list of Shaykh Mubārak's sons.

1. Shaykh Abū 'l-Fayz, better known under his poetical name of Fayzī. He was born in A.H. 954 (A.D. 1547) and seems to have died childless.

2. Shaykh Abū 'l-Fazl, born 14th January, 1551, murdered 12th August, 1602.

3. Shaykh Abū 'l-Barakāt, born 17th Shawwāl, 960 (1552). "Though he has not reached a high degree of learning, he knows much, is a practical man, and well versed in fencing. He is good-natured and fond of dervishes." He served under Abū 'l-Fazl in Khāndesh.

4. Shaykh Abū 'l-Khayr, born 22nd Jumāda I, 967. "He is a well-informed young man, of a regulated mind." He, too, must have entered the Imperial service ; for he is mentioned in the *Akbarnāma* as having been sent by the emperor to the Dakhin to fetch Prince Dānyāl.

5. Shaykh Abū 'l-Makārim, born 23rd Shawwāl, 976. He was wild at first, but guided by his father he learned a good deal. He also studied under Shāh Abū 'l-Fath Shīrāzī.

The above five sons were all by the same mother, who, as remarked above, died in 998.

6. Shaykh Abū Turāb, born 23rd Zil Hijjah, 988. "Though his mother is another one, he is admitted at Court, and is engaged in self-improvement."

Besides the above, Abū 'l-Fazl mentions two posthumous sons by *qummā*, or concubines, viz. Shaykh Abū 'l-Hāmid, born 3rd Rabī II, 1002, and Shaykh Abū Rāshid, born 1st Jumāda I, 1002. "They resemble their father."

Of Mubārak's daughters, I find four mentioned in the histories :—

1. One married to Khudāwand Khān Dakhinī ; vide p. 490. Badā,onī calls her husband a *Rafizī*, i.e. a Shīah, and says he died in Karī in Gujarāt.

2. One married to Husāmu 'd-Dīn ; vide p. 488.

3. One married to a son of Rāja ʿAlī Khān of Khandesh. Their son Safdar Khān[1] was made, in the 45th year of Akbar's reign, a commander of one thousand.

[1] The Lakhnau edition of the *Akbarnāma* (III, 830) calls him Sundar Khān.

4. Lāḍlī Begam, married to Islām Khān; vide p. 552, note 1. Mr. T.W. Beale of Agra, the learned author of the *Miftāḥ^{u}'-ttawārīkh*, informs me that Lāḍlī Begam died in 1017, or five years before the death of her husband. Her mausoleum, called the "Rawẓayi Lāḍlī Begam" is about two miles to the east of Akbar's mausoleum at Sikandra, near Āgra. The interior was built of marble, and the whole was surrounded by a wall of red Fatḥpūr sandstone. It was completed in 1004. In 1843, Mr. Beale saw in the Rawẓa several tombs without inscriptions, and a few years ago the place was sold by government to a wealthy Hindū. The new owner dug up the marble stones, sold them, and destroyed the tombs, so that of the old Rawẓa nothing exists nowadays but the surrounding wall. Mr. Beale thinks that the bodies of Shaykh Mubārak, Fayẓī, and Abū 'l-Faẓl were likewise buried there, because over the entrance the following inscription in Ṭughrā characters may still be seen:—

بسم الله الرحمن الرحيم و به ثقتى * هذه الروضة للعالم الربانى و العارف
الصمدانى جامع العلم شيخ مبارك الله قدس سره قد وقف ببنائه بحر العلوم
شيخ ابوالفضل سلم الله تعالى فى ظل دولة الملك العادل يطلبه المجد و
الاقبال و الكرم جلال الدنيا و الدين اكبر پادشاه غازى خلد الله تعالى ظلال
سلطنته باهتمام جضرت ابى البركات فى سنة اربع و الف اا

In the name of God the merciful, the clement, in whom I trust! This mausoleum was erected for the divine scholar, the sage of the eternal, the gatherer of knowledge, Shaykh Mubārakullah (may his secret be sanctified!), in filial piety by the ocean of sciences, Shaykh Abū 'l-Faẓl —may God Almighty preserve him!—in the shadow of the majesty of the just king, whom power, auspiciousness, and generosity follow, Jalāluddunyā waddīn Akbar, Pādishāh-i Ghāzī—may God Almighty perpetuate the foundations of his kingdom!—under the superintendence of Abū 'l-Barakat, in 1004 (A.D. 1595–96).

Thus it will appear that the Rawẓa was built in the year in which Fayzī died. Shaykh Mubārak, as mentioned above, died in A.D. 1593. It seems, however, as if Shaykh Mubārak and Fayẓī had been buried at a place opposite to Āgra, on the left bank of the Jamunā, where he first settled in 1551; for Abū 'l-Faẓl says in his description of Āgra in the *A'īn*[1]—"On the other side of the river is the Chār Bāgh Villa, built by Firdaws Makānī (the emperor Bābar). There the author was born, and

[1] My text edition, p. 441. Vide also p. 539; Keene's *Agra Guide*, p. 47, and regarding Lāḍlī Begum, p. 45. "Lāḍlī" means in Hindūstānī "a pet".

there are resting places of his father and his elder brother. Shaykh ʿAlāʾu 'd-Dīn Majzūb and Mīr Rafīʿu'd-dīn Safawī and other worthies are also buried there." We have no information regarding a removal of the bodies to the other side of the Jamunā, though Abū 'l-Fazl's inscription no doubt shows that such a removal was intended. It is a pity, however, that the Rawza was sold and destroyed.

Abū 'l-Fazl's son is the well-known

SHAYKH ʿABDU 'R-RAHMĀN AFZAL KHAN.

He was born on the 12th Shaʿbān, 979, and received from his grandfather the Sunnī name of ʿAbdu 'r-Rahmān. In the 35th year of Akbar's reign, when twenty years of age, Akbar married him to the daughter of Saʿādat Yār Koka's brother. By her ʿAbdu 'r-Rahmān had a son, to whom Akbar gave the name of Bishotan.[1]

When Abū 'l-Fazl was in command of the army in the Dakhin, ʿAbdu 'r-Rahmān was, what the Persians call, the *tīr-i-rū-yi tarkash-i-ū*, "the arrow at hand at the top of the quiver", ever ready to perform duties from which others shrank, and wisely and courageously settling matters of importance. He especially distinguished himself in Talingāna. When Malik ʿAmbar, in the 46th year, had caught ʿAlī Mardān Bahādur (p. 556) and had taken possession of the country, Abū 'l-Fazl dispatched ʿAbdu 'r-Rahmān and Sher Khwāja (p. 510) to oppose the enemy. They crossed the Godāwarī near Nānder, and defeated ʿAmbar at the Mānjarā.

Jahāngīr did not transfer to the son the hatred which he had felt for the father, made him a commander of two thousand horse, gave him the title of Afzal Khān, and appointed him, in the third year of his reign, governor of Bihār, *vice* Islām Khān (the husband of Abū 'l-Fazl's sister) who was sent to Bengal. ʿAbdu 'r-Rahmān also received Gorākhpūr as jāgīr. As governor of Bihār, he had his headquarters at Patna. Once during his absence from Patna, a dervish of the name of Qutbu 'd-dīn appeared in the district of Bhojpūr, which belonged to the then very troublesome Ujjainiya Rājās (p. 577, note), and gave out that he was Prince Khusra, whom his unsuccessful rebellion and imprisonment by Jahāngīr had made the favourite of the people. Collecting a large number of men, he marched on Patna, occupied the fort which Shaykh Banārasī and Ghiyās ʿAbdu 'r-Rahmān's officers, cowardly gave up, and plundered Afzal Khān's property and the Imperial treasury. ʿAbdu 'r-Rahmān returned from Gorākhpūr as soon as he heard of the

---

[1] Which name was borne by the brother of Isfandiyār, who is so often mentioned in Firdawsī's *Shāhnāma*.

rebellion. The pretender fortified Patna, and drew up his army at the Pun Pun River. ʿAbdᵘ 'r-Raḥmān charged at once, and after a short fight dispersed the enemy. Quṭb now retreated to the fort, followed by ʿAbdᵘ 'r-Raḥmān, who succeeded in capturing him. He executed the man at once, and sent his head to Court, together with the two cowardly officers. Jahāngīr, who was always minute in his punishments, had their heads shaved and women's veils put over the faces; they were then tied to donkeys, with their heads to the tails, and paraded through the towns (*tashhīr*) as a warning to others.

Not long after this affair, ʿAbdᵘ 'r-Raḥmān fell ill, and went to Court, where he was well received. He lingered for a time, and died of an abscess, in the 8th year of Jahāngīr's reign (A.H. 1022) or eleven years after his father's murder.

Bishotan, son of ʿAbdᵘ 'r-Raḥmān, son of Shaykh Abū 'l-Faẓl.

He was born on the 3rd Ẕī Qaʿda, 999. In the 14th year of Jahāngīr's reign, he was a commander of seven hundred, with three hundred horse. In the 10th year of Shāh Jahān's reign, he is mentioned as a commander of five hundred horse, which rank he held when he died in the 15th year of the same reign.

BOOK FIRST

THE IMPERIAL HOUSEHOLD

ABŪ 'L-FAẒL'S PREFACE

ALLĀH[u] AKBAR

O Lord, whose secrets are for ever veiled
And whose perfection knows not a beginning,
End and beginning, both are lost in Thee,
No trace of them is found, in Thy eternal realm.
My words are lame; my tongue, a stony tract;
Slow wings my foot, and wide is the expanse.
Confused are my thoughts; but this is Thy best praise,
In ecstasy alone I see Thee face to face!

It is proper for a man of true knowledge to praise God not only in words, but also in deeds, and to endeavour to obtain everlasting happiness, by putting the window of his heart opposite the slit of his pen, and describing some of the wondrous works of the Creator. Perhaps the lustre of royalty may shine upon him, and its light enable him to gather a few drops from the ocean, and a few atoms from the endless field of God's works. He will thus obtain everlasting felicity and render fertile the dreary expanse of words and deeds.

I, Abū 'l-Faẓl, son of Mubārak, return thanksgiving to God by singing the praises of royalty, and by stringing its kingly pearls upon the thread of description; but it is not my intention to make mankind, for the first time, acquainted with the glorious deeds and excellent virtues of that remarkable man,[1] who clothes our wonderful world in new colours, and is an ornament to God's noble creation. It would be absurd on my part to speak about that which is known; I should make myself the butt of the learned. It is only my personal knowledge of him, a priceless jewel, which I send to the market place of the world, and my heart feels proud of being engaged in such an undertaking. But it could not have been from self-laudation that I have taken upon myself to carry out so great a task—a work which even heavenly beings would find beset with difficulties; for such a motive would expose my inability and shortsightedness. My sole object in writing this work was, first, to impart to all that take an interest in this auspicious century, a knowledge of the wisdom, magnanimity, and energy of him who understands the minutest indications of all things, created and divine, striding as he does

[1] Akbar.

over the field of knowledge ; and, secondly to leave future generations a noble legacy. The payment of a debt of gratitude is an ornament of life and a provision for man's last journey. There may be some in this world of ambitious strife, where natures are so different, desires so numerous, equity so rare, and guidance so scarce, who, by making use of this source of wisdom, will escape from the perplexities of the endless chaos of knowledge and deeds. It is with this aim that I describe some of the regulations of the great King, thus leaving for far and near, a standard work of wisdom. In doing so, I have, of course, to speak of the exalted position of a king, and also to describe the condition of those who are assistants in this great office.

No dignity is higher in the eyes of God than royalty ; and those who are wise, drink from its auspicious fountain. A sufficient proof of this, for those who require one, is the fact that royalty is a remedy for the spirit of rebellion, and the reason why subjects obey. Even the meaning of the word Pādishāh shows this ; for *pād* signifies stability and possession, and *shāh* means origin, lord. A king is, therefore, the origin of stability and possession. If royalty did not exist, the storm of strife would never subside, nor selfish ambition disappear. Mankind, being under the burden of lawlessness and lust, would sink into the pit of destruction ; the world, this great market-place, would lose its prosperity, and the whole earth become a barren waste. But by the light of imperial justice, some follow with cheerfulness the road of obedience, whilst others abstain from violence through fear of punishment ; and out of necessity make choice of the path of rectitude. *Shāh* is also a name given to one who surpasses his fellows, as you may see from words like *shāh-suwār*, *shāh-rāh* ; it is also a term applied to a bridegroom—the world, as the bride, betrothes herself to the King, and becomes his worshipper.

Silly and shortsighted men cannot distinguish a *true* king from a *selfish* ruler. Nor is this remarkable, as both have in common a large treasury, a numerous army, clever servants, obedient subjects, an abundance of wise men, a multitude of skilful workmen, and a superfluity of means of enjoyment. But men of deeper insight remark a difference. In the case of the former, the things just now enumerated, are lasting ; but in that of the latter, of short duration. The former does not attach himself to these things, as his object is to remove oppression and provide for everything which is good. Security, health, chastity, justice, polite manners, faithfulness, truth, an increase of sincerity, etc., are the result. The latter is kept in bonds by the external forms of royal power, by vanity, the slavishness of men, and the desire of enjoyment; hence, everywhere there is insecurity, unsettledness, strife, oppression, faithlessness, robbery.

Royalty is a light emanating from God, and a ray from the sun, the illuminator of the universe,[1] the argument of the book of perfection, the receptacle of all virtues. Modern language calls this light *farr-i īzidī* (the divine light), and the tongue of antiquity called it *kiyān khura* (the sublime halo). It is communicated by God to kings without the intermediate assistance of any one, and men, in the presence of it, bend the forehead of praise towards the ground of submission. Again, many excellent qualities flow from the possession of this light. 1. *A paternal love towards the subjects.* Thousands find rest in the love of the King; and sectarian differences do not raise the dust of strife. In his wisdom, the King will understand the spirit of the age, and shape his plans accordingly. 2. *A large heart.* The sight of anything disagreeable does not unsettle him; nor is want of discrimination for him a source of disappointment. His courage steps in. His divine firmness gives him the power of requital, nor does the high position of an offender interfere with it. The wishes of great and small are attended to, and their claims meet with no delay at his hands. 3. *A daily increasing trust in God.* When he performs an action, he considers God as the real doer of it (and himself as the medium), so that a conflict of motives can produce no disturbance. 4. *Prayer and devotion.* The success of his plans will not lead him to neglect; nor will adversity cause him to forget God, and madly trust in man. He puts the reins of desire into the hands of reason; in the wide field of his desires he does not permit himself to be trodden down by restlessness, nor will he waste his precious time in seeking after that which is improper. He makes wrath, the tyrant, pay homage to wisdom, so that blind rage may not get the upper hand, and inconsiderateness overstep the proper limits. He sits on the eminence of propriety, so that those who have gone astray have a way left to return without exposing their bad deeds to the public gaze. When he sits in judgment, the petitioner seems to be the judge, and he himself, on account of his mildness, the suitor for justice. He does not permit petitioners to be delayed on the path of hope; he endeavours to promote the happiness of the creatures in obedience to the will of the Creator, and never seeks to please the people in contradiction to reason. He is for ever searching

---

[1] Akbar worshipped the sun as the visible representative of God, and the immediate source of life. Regarding his form of worship, *vide* below.

after those who speak the truth, and is not displeased with words that seem bitter, but are in reality sweet. He considers the nature of the words and the rank of the speaker. He is not content with not committing violence, but he must see that no injustice is done within his realm.

He is continually attentive to the health of the body politic, and applies remedies to the several diseases thereof. And in the same manner that the equilibrium of the animal constitution depends upon an equal mixture of the elements,[1] so also does the political constitution become well tempered by a proper division of ranks; and by means of the warmth of the ray of unanimity and concord, a multitude of people become fused into one body.

The people of the world may be divided into four classes.[2]—1. *Warriors*, who in the political body have the nature of fire. Their flames, directed by understanding, consume the straw and rubbish of rebellion and strife, but kindle also the lamp of rest in this world of disturbances. 2. *Artificers and merchants*, who hold the place of air. From their labours and travels, God's gifts become universal, and the breeze of contentment nourishes the rose-tree of life. 3. *The learned*, such as the philosopher, the physician, the arithmetician, the geometrician, the astronomer, who resemble water. From their pen and their wisdom, a river rises in the drought of the world, and the garden of the creation receives from their irrigating powers a peculiar freshness. 4. *Husbandmen* and *labourers*, who may be compared to earth. By their exertions, the staple of life is brought to perfection, and strength and happiness flow from their work.

It is therefore obligatory for a king to put each of these in its proper place, and by uniting personal ability with due respect for others, to cause the world to flourish.

And as the grand political body maintains its equilibrium by the above four ranks of men, so does royalty receive its final tint from a similar fourfold division.

1. *The nobles of the state*, who in reliance on their position lead everything to a happy issue. Illuminating the battle-field with the halo of devotedness, they make no account of their lives. These fortunate

---

[1] Thus, according to the medical theories of the middle ages.

[2] This passage resembles one in Firdausī's Shāhnāma, in the chapter entitled *dar dāstān-i Jamshīd*; *vide* also Vuller's *Persian Dictionary*, ii, 756, s. *kātūzī*. It is also found in the *Akhlāq i Muḥsinī*, chapter xv, *dar 'adl*, in the *Akhlāq-i Jalālī*, and the *Akhlāq-i Nāṣirī*, the oldest of the three Akhlāqs mentioned.

courtiers resemble fire, being ardent in devotion, and consuming in dealing with foes. At the head of this class is the *Vakīl*, who from his having attained by his wisdom the four degrees of perfection,[1] is the emperor's lieutenant in all matters connected with the realm and the household. He graces the Council by his wisdom, and settles with penetration the great affairs of the realm. Promotion and degradation, appointment and dismissal, depend on his insight. It requires therefore an experienced man who possesses wisdom, nobility of mind, affability, firmness, magnanimity, a man able to be at peace with any one, who is frank, single-minded towards relations and strangers, impartial to friends and enemies, who weighs his words, is skilful in business, well-bred, esteemed, known to be trustworthy, sharp and farsighted, acquainted with the ceremonies of the court, cognizant of the State secrets, prompt in transacting business, unaffected by the multiplicity of his duties. He should consider it his duty to promote the wishes of others, and base his actions on a due regard to the different ranks of men, treating even his inferiors with respect, from the desire of attaching to himself the hearts of all. He takes care not to commit improprieties in conversation, and guards himself from bad actions. Although the financial offices are not under his immediate superintendence, yet he received the returns from the heads of all financial offices, and wisely keeps abstracts of their returns.

The Mīr-māl,[2] the Keeper of the seal, the Mīr-ba<u>kh</u>shī,[3] the Bār-begī,[4] the Qurbegī,[5] the Mīr-tozak,[6] the Mīr-baḥrī,[7] the Mīr-barr,[8] the Mīr-Manzil,[9] the <u>Kh</u>wānsālār,[10] the Munshī,[11] the Qūsh-begī,[12] the A<u>kh</u>ta-begī,[13] belong to this class. Every one of them ought to be sufficiently acquainted with the work of the others.

---

[1] Akbar said that perfect devotedness consisted in the readiness of sacrificing four things—*jān* (life), *māl* (property), *dīn* (religion), *nāmūs* (personal honour). Those who looked upon Akbar as a guide in spiritual matters (*pīr*)—an honour which Akbar much coveted—promised to show this devotedness, and then belonged to the *dīn-i ilāhī*, or the Divine Faith, the articles of which Akbar had laid down, as may be seen below.

[2] Perhaps an officer in charge of the Emperor's private purse.

[3] Paymaster of the Court.

[4] An officer who presents people at Court, their petitions, etc. He is also called *Mīr ʿArẓ*.

[5] Bearer of the Imperial insignia.

[6] Master of Ceremonies.

[7] Harbour Master General and Admiral.

[8] Superintendent of the Imperial Forests.

[9] Quarter Master General of the Court. Akbar's court was frequently travelling.

[10] Superintendent of the Imperial Kitchen.

[11] Private Secretary.

[12] Superintendent of the aviaries (falcons, pigeons). [Head of the Mews.—P.]

[13] Superintendent of the Stud.

2. *The assistants of victory*, the collectors and those entrusted with income and expenditure, who in the administration resemble wind, at times a heart-rejoicing breeze, at other times a hot, pestilential blast. The head of this division is the *Vizier*, also called *Dīwān*. He is the lieutenant of the Emperor in financial matters, superintends the imperial treasuries, and checks all accounts. He is the banker of the cash of the revenue, the cultivator of the wilderness of the world. He must be a member of the *Divine Faith*, a skilful arithmetician, free from avarice, circumspect, warm-hearted, abstinent, active in business, pleasing in his style, clear in his writings, truthful, a man of integrity, condescending, zealous in his work. He is in reality a book-keeper. He explains all matters which appear too intricate for the *Mustawfī* [1]; and whatever is beyond his own ability he refers to the *Vakīl*. The Mustawfī, the Sāḥib-i Tawjī,[2] the Awārja Nawīs,[3] the Mīr-Sāmān,[4] the Nāẓir-i Buyūtāt,[5] the Dīwān-i Buyūtāt,[6] the Mushrif,[7] of the Treasury ; the Wāqiʿa Nawīs,[8] the ʿĀmil [9] of the domains, are under his orders, and act by the force of his wisdom.

Some princes consider the office of the Vizier as a part of that of the *Vakīl*, and are anxious to find in their realm a man who possesses the excellent qualities of these two pillars of the edifice of the State. But as they are not always able to find a person qualified for the office of a Vakīl, they make choice of a man who has some of his qualities, and appoint him as *Mushrif-i Dīwān*, which office is higher in rank than that of the Dīwān, but lower than that of the Vakīl.

3. *The companions of the king*, who are the ornaments of the court by the light of their wisdom, the ray of their sharpsightedness, their knowledge of the times, their intimate acquaintance with human nature, their frankness and polite address. Through the excellence of their religious faith and good will, thousands open in the market place of the world the stores of virtue. Wisely fettering ambition on the battle-field of the world, they extinguish the sparks of wrath by the rain of their

---

1 Deputy Dīwān.
2 The Accountant of the Army.
3 The Accountant of the daily expenditure at Court.
4 The officer in charge of the Court furniture, stores, etc.
5 Superintendent of the Imperial workshops
6 The Accountant of the Imperial workshops.
7 Clerk.
8 The Recorder.
9 Collector.

wisdom ; whence they resemble water in the affairs of the body political. When they are of a mild temperament, they remove the dust of affliction from the hearts of men, and bestow freshness upon the meadow of the nation ; but if they depart from moderation, they inundate the world with a deluge of calamity, so that numbers are driven by the flood of misfortunes into the current of utter extinction.

At the head of this class stands the philosopher, who with the assistance of his wisdom and example purifies the morals of the nation, and girds himself with the noble aim of putting the welfare of mankind upon a sound basis. The Ṣadr,[1] the Mīr-ʿAdl, the Qāẓī,[2] the physician, the astronomer, the poet, the soothsayer, belong to this class.

4. *The servants* who at court perform the duties about the king. They occupy in the system of the State the position of earth. As such, they lie on the high road of submission, and in dust before the majesty of the king. If free from chaff and dross, they are like an elixir for the body ; otherwise they are dust and dirt upon the face of success. The table servant, the armour bearer, the servants in charge of the *sharbat* and the water, the servant in charge of the mattresses and the wardrobe, belong to this class.

If the king be waited on by servants to whom good fortune has given excellent qualities, there arises sometimes a harmony, which is like a nosegay from the flower-bed of auspiciousness.

Just as the welfare of the whole world depends upon the successful working of the above-mentioned four classes, as settled by kings, so does the body politic depend upon the proper formation of the latter four divisions.

The sages of antiquity mention the following four persons as the chief supports of the State :—1. *An upright collector*, who protects the husbandman, watches over the subjects, develops the country, and improves the revenues. 2. *A conscientious commander* of the army, active and strict. 3. *A chief justice*, free from avarice and selfishness, who sits on the eminence of circumspection and insight, and obtains his ends by putting various questions, without exclusively relying on witnesses and oaths. 4. *An intelligencer*, who transmits the events of the time without addition or diminution, always keeping to the thread of truth and penetration.

---

[1] Also called *Ṣadr-i Jahān*, the Chief Justice and Administrator General of the empire.

[2] The Qāẓi hears the case ; the Mīr ʿAdl passes the sentence.

It is moreover incumbent on a just king to make himself acquainted with the characters of the following five kinds [1] of men of whom the world is composed, and act accordingly. 1. The most commendable person is *the sagacious man* who prudently does that which is proper and absolutely necessary. The fountain of his virtues does not only run along his channel, but renders verdant the fields of other men. Such a one is the fittest person for a king to consult in State affairs. After him comes, secondly, *the man of good intentions.* The river of his virtues does not flow over its bed, and does not therefore become an irrigating source for others. Although it may be proper to show him kindness and respect, yet he does not merit so high a degree of confidence. Inferior to him is, thirdly, *the simple man*, who does not wear the badge of excellence upon the sleeve of his action, yet keeps the hem of his garment free from the dust of wicked deeds. He does not deserve any distinction; but ought to be allowed to live at his ease. Worse than he is, fourthly, *the inconsiderate man*, who fills his house with furniture for his own mischief, without, however, doing harm to others. Him the king should keep in the hot place of disappointment, and bring him into the road of virtue by good advice and severe reprehension. The last of all is *the vicious man*, whose black deeds alarm others and throw, on account of their viciousness, a whole world into grief. If the remedies employed in the case of men of the preceding class, do not amend him, the king should consider him as a leper, and confine him separate from mankind; and provided this harsh treatment does not awaken him from his sleep of error, he should feel the torture of grief, and be banished from his dwelling; and if this remedy produce no effect either, he should be driven out of the kingdom to wander in the wilderness of disappointment; and if even this should not improve his vicious nature, he should be deprived of the instruments of his wickedness, and lose his sight, or his hand, or his foot. But the king ought not to go so far as to cut the thread of his existence; for inquiring sages consider the human form as an edifice made by God, and do not permit its destruction.

It is therefore necessary for just kings, to make themselves first acquainted with the rank and character of men, by the light of insight and penetration, and then to regulate business accordingly. And hence it is that the sages of ancient times have said that princes who wear the

---

[1] The following is a free paraphrase of a passage in the *Akhlāq-i Muḥsinī*, Chapter XXXII, entitled *dar siyāsat.*

jewel of wisdom do not appoint every low man to their service ; that they do not consider every one who has been appointed, to be deserving of daily admittance ; that those who are thus favoured, are not therefore deemed worthy to sit with them on the carpet of intercourse ; that those who are worthy of this station, are not necessarily admitted to the pavilion of familiar address that those who have this privilege, are not therefore allowed to sit in the august assembly ; that those upon whom this ray of good fortune falls, are not therefore let into their secrets ; and that those who enjoy the happiness of this station, are not therefore fit for admission into the Cabinet Council.

Praise be to God, the Giver of every good gift ! The exalted monarch of our time is so endowed with these laudable dispositions, that it is no exaggeration to call him their *exordium*. From the light of his wisdom, he discerns the worth of men, and kindles the lamp of their energy ; whilst ever clear to himself and without an effort, he adorns his wisdom with the beauty of practice. Who can measure, by the rules of speech, his power as a spiritual leader, and his works in the wide field of holiness[1] ; and even if it were possible to give a description of it, who would be able to hear and comprehend it ? The best thing I can do is to abstain from such an attempt, and to confine myself to the description of such of his wonderful doings as illustrate the worldly side of his nature, and his greatness as a king. I shall speak :—

First, of his regulations concerning *the household* ; *secondly,* of the regulations concerning *the army* ; *thirdly,* of the regulations concerning *the empire,* as these three contain the whole duty of a king. In doing so, I shall leave practical inquirers a present, which may seem difficult to understand, but which is easy ; or rather, which may seem easy, but is in reality difficult.

Experienced men who are acquainted with the art of governing, and versed in the history of the past, cannot comprehend how monarchs have hitherto governed, without these wise regulations and how the garden of royalty could have been fresh and verdant, without being irrigated by this fountain of wisdom.

This sublime volume then, is arranged under three heads ; it enables me, in some measure, to express my feelings of gratitude for favours received.

---

[1] Akbar as the spiritual leader of the members belonging to the Divine Faith wrought many miracles, of which some are related in the seventy-seventh *Āʾīn* of this book.

Remark by the Author.—As I had sometimes to use Hindī words, I have carefully described the consonants and vowels. Inquirers will therefore have no difficulty in reading; nor will any confusion arise from mistakes in copying. Letters like *alif, lām* and a few more, are sufficiently clear from their names. Some letters I have distinguished as *manqūṭa*, and letters similar in form, without such a limitation. Letters which are purely Persian, have been distinguished as such; thus the *p* in *padid*, the *che* in *chaman*, the *gāf* in *nigār*, the *zh* in *muzhda*. Sometimes I have added to the names of these letters, the phrase *having three points*. Letters peculiar to the Hindī language I have distinguished as *Hindī*. The letter *yā* as in *rūy*, I have called *taḥtūni*, and the *te*, as in *dast, fawqāni*. The *b* in *adab*, I have merely called *be*. Similarly, the letters *nūn, wāw, yā*, and *he*, when clearly sounded, have been merely described as *nūn, wāw*, etc. The nasal *nūn* I have called *nūn-i khafi*, or *nūn-i pinhān*. The final and silent *h*, as in *farkhunda*, I have called *maktūb*, i.e. written, but not pronounced. The *i* and *u*, when modified to *e* or *o* I have called *majhūl*. As consonants followed by an *alif* have the vowel *a*, it was not necessary to specify their vowels.

BOOK FIRST.

THE IMPERIAL HOUSEHOLD.

Āʿīn 1.

THE HOUSEHOLD.

He is a man of high understanding and noble aspirations who, without the help of others, recognizes a ray of the Divine power in the smallest things of the world; who shapes his inward and outward character accordingly, and shows due respect to himself and to others. He who does not possess these qualifications, ought not to engage in the struggle of the world, but observe a peaceable conduct. If the former be given to retirement, he will cultivate noble virtues; and if his position be a dependent one, he will put his whole heart in the management of his affairs, and lead a life free from distressing cares.

True greatness, in spiritual and in worldly matters, does not shrink from the minutiæ of business, but regards their performance as an act of Divine worship.[1]

If he cannot perform everything himself, he ought to select, guided by insight, and practical wisdom, one or two men of sagacity and understanding, of liberal views in religious matters, possessing diligence and a knowledge of the human heart, and be guided by their advice.

The wise esteem him not a king who confines his attention to great matters only, although some impartial judges excuse a king that does so, because avaricious sycophants who endeavour by cunning to obtain the position of the virtuous, often remind him of the difference of ranks, and succeed in lulling asleep such kings as are fond of external greatness, their only object being to make a trade of the revenues of the country, and to promote their own interests. But good princes make no difference between great and small matters; they take, with the assistance of God, the burden of this world and the responsibility of the world to come, on the shoulder of resolution, and are yet free and independent, as is the case with the king of our time. In his wisdom, he makes himself acquainted with the successful working of every department, which, although former monarchs

[1] A phrase which Akbar often used.

have thought it derogatory to their greatness, is yet the first step towards the establishment of a good government. For every branch he has made proper regulations, and he sees in the performance of his duty a means of obtaining God's favour.

The success of this vast undertaking depends upon two things : *first*, wisdom and insight, to call into existence suitable regulations ; *secondly*, a watchful eye, to see them carried out by men of integrity and diligence.

Although many servants of the household receive their salaries on the list of the army, there was paid for the household in the thirty-ninth year of the Divine era, the sum of 309,186,795 *dāms*.[1] The expenses of this account, as also the revenues, are daily increasing. There are more than one hundred offices and workshops each resembling a city, or rather a little kingdom ; and by the unremitting attention of his Majesty, they are all conducted with regularity, and are constantly increasing, their improvement being accompanied by additional care and supervision on the part of his Majesty.

Some of the regulations I shall transmit, as a present, to future enquirers, and thus kindle in others the lamp of wisdom and energy.

As regards those regulations which are of a general nature, and which from their subject matter belong to each of the three divisions of the work, I have put them among the regulations of the Household.

Āʿīn 2.

THE IMPERIAL TREASURIES.

Every man of sense and understanding knows that the best way of worshipping God, consists in allaying the distress of the times, and in improving the condition of man. This depends, however, on the advancement of agriculture, on the order kept in the king's household, on the readiness of the champions of the empire, and the discipline of the army. All this is again connected with the exercise of proper care on the part of the monarch, his love for the people, and with an intelligent management of the revenues and the public expenditure. It is only when cared for, that the inhabitants of the towns and those of the rural districts, are able to satisfy their wants, and to enjoy prosperity. Hence it is incumbent on just kings, to care for the former, and to protect the latter class of men. If some say that to collect wealth, and to ask for more

---

[1] Or, 7,729,669⅞ Rupees. One rupee (of Akbar) = 40 *dāms*. The Divine era, or *Tārīkh-i Ilāhī*, is Akbar's solar era, the commencement of which falls on the 19th February, 1556 ; hence the thirty-ninth year corresponds to A.D. 1595.

than is absolutely necessary, is looked upon as contemptible by people given to retirement and seclusion, whilst the opposite is the case with the inhabitants of the towns, who live in a dependent position, I would answer that it is after all only shortsighted men who make this assertion ; for in reality both classes of men try to obtain that which they think necessary. Poor, but abstemious people take a sufficient quantity of food and raiment, so as to keep up the strength necessary for the pursuit of their enquiries, and to protect them against the influence of the weather; whilst the other class think to have just sufficient, when they fill their treasuries, gather armies, and reflect on other means of increasing their power.

It was from such views, when lifting the veil and beginning to pay attention to these weighty concerns, that his Majesty entrusted his inmost secrets to the *K͟hwāja-sarā Iʿtimād K͟hān*,[1] a name which his Majesty had bestowed upon him as a fitting title. On account of the experience of the *K͟hwāja*, the reflections of his Majesty took a practical turn, widened by degrees, and shone at last forth in excellent regulations. An enquiry regarding the income of the different kinds of land was set on foot, and successfully concluded by the wisdom of upright and experienced men. With a comprehensiveness which knew no difference between friends and strangers, the lands which paid rents into the imperial exchequer were separated from the Jāgīr lands ; and zealous and upright men were put in charge of the revenues, each over one *karoṛ* of *dāms*. Incorruptible *bitakchīs* [2] were selected to assist them, and intelligent treasurers were appointed, one for each. And from kindness and care for the agricultural classes, it was commanded that the collectors should not insist upon the husbandman paying coin in full weight, but to give him a receipt for whatever species of money he might bring. This laudable regulation removed the rust of uncertainty from the minds of the collectors, and

---

[1] *Iʿtimād* means *trustworthiness*. *K͟hwāja-sarā* is the title of the chief eunuch. His real name was Phūl Malik. After serving *Salīm Shāh* (1545 to 1553), who bestowed upon him the title of *Muḥammad K͟hān*, he entered Akbar's service. Akbar, after the death of Shams^u 'd-Dīn Muḥammad Atgah K͟hān, his foster father, commenced to look into matters of finance, and finding the Revenue Department a den of thieves, he appointed Iʿtimād K͟hān, to remodel the finances, making him a commander of One Thousand (*vide* Abū 'l-Faẓl's list of Akbar's grandees, in part second, No. 119), and conferring upon him the title of *Iʿtimād K͟hān*. He appears to have performed his duties to Akbar's satisfaction. In 1565, he conveyed the daughter of Mīrān Mubārak, king of Khāndesh (1535 to 1566), to Akbar's harem, took afterwards a part in the conquest of Bengal, where he distinguished himself, and was, in 1576, appointed governor of Bhakkar. When in 1578 Akbar's presence was required in the Panjāb, Iʿtimād K͟hān desired to join him. In order to equip his contingent, he collected his rents and outstandings, as it appears, with much harshness. This led to a conspiracy against his life. In the same year he was murdered by a man named Maqṣūd ʿAlī. *Maʾāṣir^u 'l-Umarāʾ*.

[2] Writers.

relieved the subjects from a variety of oppressions, whilst the income became larger, and the state flourished. The fountain of the revenues having thus been purified, a zealous and honest man was selected for the general treasurership, and a *dārogha* and a clerk were appointed to assist him. Vigilance was established, and a standard laid down for this department.

Whenever a (provincial) treasurer had collected the sum of two lakhs of *dāms*, he had to send it to the Treasurer General at the Court, together with a memorandum specifying the quality of the sum.

A separate treasurer was appointed for the *peshkash* [1] receipts, another for receiving heirless property, another for *nazr* receipts,[2] and another for the moneys expended in weighing the royal person,[3] and for charitable donations. Proper regulations were also made for the disbursements ; and honest superintendents, *dāroghas* and clerks were appointed. The sums required for the annual expenditure, are paid at the General Treasury to each cashkeeper of the disbursements, and correct receipts granted for them. A proper system of accounts having thus been inaugurated, the empire began to flourish. In a short time the treasuries were full, the army was augmented, and refractory rebels led to the path of obedience.

In *Īrān* and *Tūrān*, where only one treasurer is appointed, the accounts are in a confused state : but here in India, the amount of the revenues is so great, and the business so multifarious that twelve treasurers are necessary for storing the money, nine for the different kinds of cash-payments, and three for precious stones, gold, and inlaid jewellery. The extent of the treasuries is too great to admit of my giving a proper description with other matters before me. From his knowledge of the work, and as a reward for labour, his Majesty very often expresses his satisfaction, or conveys reprimands ; hence everything is in a flourishing condition.

Separate treasurers were also appointed for each of the Imperial workshops the number of which is nearly one hundred. Daily, monthly, quarterly, and yearly accounts are kept of the receipts and disbursements, so that in this branch also the market-place of the world is in a flourishing condition.

Again by the order of his Majesty a person of known integrity keeps in the public audience hall, some gold and silver for the needy, who have their wants relieved without delay. Moreover, a *karoṛ* of *dāms* is kept in readiness within the palace, every thousand of which is kept in bags made of a coarse material. Such a bag is called in Hindī *sahsah*,[4]

---

[1] Tributes.

[2] Presents, vows, etc.

[3] *Vide* the eighteenth *Āʾīn* of the second book.

[[4] *Sahasra* S.—P.]

and many of them, when put up in a heap, *ganj*. Besides, his Majesty entrusts to one of the nobility a large sum of money, part of which is carried in a *purse*.[1] This is the reason, why such disbursements are called in the language of the country *kharj-i bahlah*.

All these benefits flow from the wonderful liberality of his Majesty, and from his unremitting care for the subjects of the empire. Would to God that he might live a thousand years!

Āʾīn 3.

THE TREASURY FOR PRECIOUS STONES.

If I were to speak about the quantity and quality of the stones it would take me an age. I shall therefore give a few particulars, "gathering an ear from every sheaf."

His Majesty appointed for this office an intelligent, trustworthy, clever treasurer, and as his assistants, an experienced clerk, a zealous *dārogha*, and also skilful jewellers. The foundation therefore of this important department rests upon those four pillars. They classified the jewels, and thus removed the rust of confusion.

Rubies.—1st class rubies, not less than 1000 muhrs in value; 2nd class from 999 to 500 muhrs; 3rd class, from 499 to 300; 4th class, from 299 to 200; 5th class, from 199 to 100; 6th class, from 99 to 60; 7th class, from 59 to 40; 8th class, from 39 to 30; 9th class, from 29 to 10; 10th class, from 9¾ to 5; 11th class, from 4¾ to 1 muhr; 12th class, from ¾ muhr to ¼ rupee. They made no account of rubies of less value.

Diamonds, emeralds, and the *red* and *blue yāqūts*, were classified as follows: 1st class, from 30 muhrs upwards; 2nd class, from 29¾ to 15 muhrs; 3rd class, from 14¾ to 12; 4th class, from 11¾ to 10; 5th class, from 9¾ to 7; 6th class, from 6¾ to 5; 7th class, from 4¾ to 3; 8th class, from 2¾ to 2; 9th class, from 1¾ to 1 muhr; 10th class, from 8¾ rupees to 5 rupees; 11th class, from 4¾ to 2 rupees; 12th class, from 1¾ to ¼ rupee.

The *Pearls* were divided into 16 classes, and strung by scores. The first string contained twenty pearls, each of a value of 30 muhrs and upwards; 2nd class pearls varied from 29¾ to 15 muhrs; 3rd class, from 14¾ to 12; 4th class, from 11¾ to 10; 5th class, from 9¾ to 7; 6th class, from 6¾ to 5; 7th class, from 4¾ to 3; 8th class, from 2¾ to 2; 9th class,

---

[1] A *purse* in Hindī is called *bahla*. [*Bahla*, P. a purse, a falconer's glove.—P.]

from 1¾ to 1 ; 10th class, less than a muhr, down to 5 rupees ; 11th class, less than 5, to 2 rupees ; 12th class, less than 2 rupees, to 1¼ rupees ; 13th class, less than 1¼ rupees, to 30 *dāms* ; 14th class, less than 30 *dāms*, to 20 *dāms* ; 15th class, less than 20 *dāms*, to 10 *dāms* ; 16th class, less than 10 *dāms*, to 5 *dāms*. The pearls are strung upon a number of strings indicating their class, so that those of the 16th class are strung upon 16 strings. At the end of each bundle of strings the imperial seal is affixed, to avoid losses arising from unsorting, whilst a description is attached to each pearl, to prevent disorder.

The following are the charges for boring pearls, independent of the daily and monthly wages of the workmen. For a pearl of the 1st class, ¼ rupee ; 2nd class, ⅛ ; 3rd class, $\frac{1}{10}$ rupee ; 4th class, 3 *dāms* ; 5th class, 1 *sūkī*[1] ; 6th class, 1 *dām* ; 7th class, ¾ *dām* ; 8th class, ½ *dām* ; 9th class, ¼ *dām* ; 10th class, ⅕ *dām* ; 11th class, ⅙ *dām* ; 12th class, $\frac{1}{7}$ *dām* ; 13th class, ⅛ *dām* ; 14th class, $\frac{1}{9}$ *dām* ; 15th class, $\frac{1}{10}$ *dām* ; 16th class, $\frac{1}{11}$ *dām*, and less.

The value of jewels is so well known that it is useless to say anything about it ; but those which are at present in the treasury of his Majesty may be detailed as follows :—

Rubies weighing 11 *tānks*,[2] 20 *surkhs*,[3] and diamonds of 5¼ *tānks*,[4] 4 *surkhs*, each one lākh of rupees ; emeralds weighing 17¾ *tānks*, 3 *surkhs*, 52,000 rupees ; *yāqūts* of 4 *tānks*, 7¾ *surkhs*, and pearls of 5 *tānks*, each 50,000 rupees.

Āʿīn 4.

THE IMPERIAL MINT.

As the successful working of the mint increases the treasure, and is the source of despatch for every department, I shall mention a few details.

The inhabitants of the towns and the country perform their transactions by means of money. Every man uses it according to the extent of his necessities ; the man whose heart is free from worldly desires

[[1] *Sūkī* s.m. and *sūkī* f. H., a four-anna bit.]

[[2] *Tāk* H. = 4 *māshā*.—P.]

[3] *Surkh* means *red* ; also, *a little seed with a black dot on it*, called in Hind. *ghungchī*, Abrus precatorius. The Persians called it *chashm-i khurūs*, cock's eye. The seeds are often used for children's bracelets. Abū 'l-Fazl means here the weight called in Hind. *ratī*, vulg. *rattī*. 8 *surkhs*, or 8 *ratīs* = 1 *māshā* ; 12 *māshās* = 1 *tōlā*, and 80 *tōlās* = 1 *ser*. A *tānk* is valued at 4 *māshās* ; but it must have weighed a little more, as in the tenth *Āʿīn*, Abū 'l-Fazl states that the weight of 1 *dām* was 5 *tānks*, or 1 *tōlā*, 8 *māshās*, 7 *surkhs* ; *i.e.*, 1 *tānk* = $\frac{167}{40}$ *māshās* = 4 *māshās*, 1 *surkhs*.

[4] Text 4½ *tānks*.

sustains by it his life, and the worldly man considers it the final stage of his objects—the wants of all are satisfied by it. The wise man looks upon it as the foundation, from which the fulfilment of his worldly and religious wishes flows. It is absolutely necessary for the continuance of the human race, as men obtain by money their food and clothing. You may indeed gain these two things by undergoing some labour, as sowing, rearing, reaping, cleaning, kneading, cooking, twisting, spinning, weaving, etc.; but these actions cannot well be performed without several helpers; for the strength of a single man is not sufficient, and to do so day after day would be difficult, if not impossible. Again, man requires a dwelling, for keeping his provisions. This he calls his *home*, whether it be a tent, or a cave. Man's existence, and the continuance of his life, depend on five things—a father, a mother, children, servants, food, the last of which is required by all. Moreover, money is required, as our furniture and utensils break; they last in no case very long. But money does last long, on account of the strength and compactness of its material, and even a little of it may produce much. It also enables men to travel. How difficult would it be to carry provisions for several days, let alone for several months or years!

By the help of God's goodness this excellent precious metal (gold) has come to the shore of existence, and filled the store of life without much labour on the part of man. By means of gold, man carries out noble plans, and even performs Divine worship in a proper manner. Gold has many valuable qualities: it possesses softness, a good taste, and smell. Its component parts are nearly equal[1] in weight; and the marks of the four elements are visible in its properties. Its colour reminds us of fire, its purity of air, its softness of water, its heaviness of earth: hence gold possesses many life-giving rays. Nor can any of the four elements injure it; for it does not burn in the fire; it remains unaffected by air; retains for ages its appearance although kept in water; and does not get altered when buried in the ground, whereby gold is distinguished from the other metals. It is for this reason that in old books on philosophy in which man's intellect is termed *the greater principle*, gold is called *the lesser principle*,[2] as the things required for human life depend upon it. Among its epithets I may mention "the guardian of justice"; "the universal adjuster"—and, indeed, the adjustment of things depends on gold,

---

[1] According to the chemists of the middle ages, gold consists of quicksilver and sulphur taken in equal proportions; the latter must, however, possess colouring properties. *Vide* the thirteenth *Āʾīn*.

[2] "Were it not for piety, I would bow down to gold and say, 'Hallowed be thy name!'"—*Harīrī*.

and the basis of justice rests upon it. To render it service, God has allowed silver and brass to come into use, thus creating additional means for the welfare of man. Hence just kings and energetic rulers have paid much attention to these metals, and erected mints, where their properties may be thoroughly studied. The success of this department lies in the appointment of intelligent, zealous, and upright workmen, and the edifice of the world is built upon their attention and carefulness.

Āʾīn 5.

THE WORKMEN OF THE MINT

1. The *Dārog͟ha.* He must be a circumspect and intelligent man, of broad principles, who takes the cumbrous burden of his colleagues upon the shoulder of despatch. He must keep every one to his work, and show zeal and integrity.

2. The *Ṣayrafī.*[1] The success of this important department depends upon his experience, as he determines the degrees of purity of the coins. On account of the prosperity of the present age, there are now numbers of skilful *ṣarrāfs* ;[1] and by the attention of his Majesty, gold and silver are refined to the highest degree of purity. The highest degree of purity is called in Persia *dahdahī*, but they do not know above 10 degrees of fineness ; whilst in India it it called *bārahbānī*, as they have twelve degrees. Formerly the old *hun*, which is a gold coin current in the Deccan, was thought to be pure, and reckoned at ten degrees ; but his Majesty has now fixed it at 8½ : and the round, small gold *dīnār* of ʿAlāʾ ʾd-Dīn,[2] which was considered to be 12 degrees, now turns out to be 10½.

Those who are experienced in this business have related wonderful stories of the purity of gold at the present time, and referred it to witchcraft and alchemy ; for they maintain, that gold ore does not come up to this fineness. But by the attention of his Majesty, it has come up to this degree ; hence the astonishment of people acquainted with this branch. It is, however, certain, that gold cannot be made finer, and of a higher degree. Honest describers and truthful travellers have indeed never mentioned this degree ; but, when gold is put into fusion, small particles separate from it, and mix with the ashes, which ignorant men look upon as useless dross, whilst the skilful recover the metal from it. Although malleable gold ore be calcined and reduced to ashes, yet by a

[1] The same as *Ṣayrāf* or *Ṣarrāf*; hence a *shroff*, a money lender.
[[2] طلاي دينار گرد خورد علائي—P.]

2
3
4

Pl. II

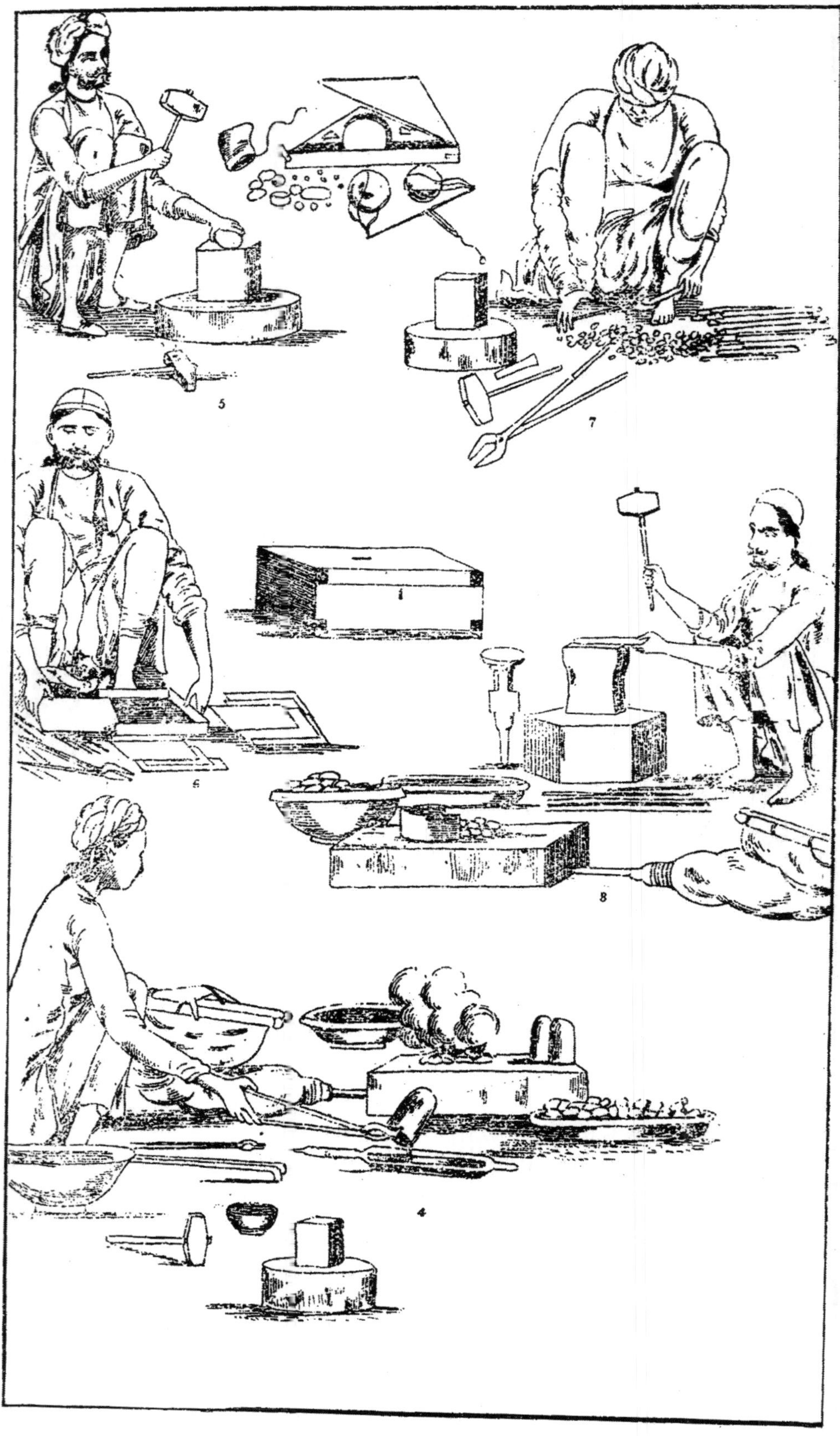

11
12
13
14

certain operation, it is brought back to its original state; but a part of it is lost. Through the wisdom of his Majesty, the real circumstances connected with this loss, were brought to light, and the fraudulent practices of the workmen thus put to the test.

Āʼīn 6.

BANWĀRĪ.[1]

An abbreviation for *bānwārī*. Although in this country clever ṣayrafīs are able from experience to tell the degree of fineness by the colour and the brightness of the metal, the following admirable rule has been introduced for the satisfaction of others.

To the ends of a few long needles, made of brass or such like metal, small pieces of gold are affixed, having their degree of fineness written on them. When the workmen wish to assay a new piece of gold, they first draw with it a few lines on a touchstone, and some other lines with the needles. By comparing both sets of lines, they discover the degree of fineness of the gold. It is, however, necessary that the lines be drawn in the same manner, and with the same force, so as to avoid deception.

To apply this rule, it is necessary to have gold of various degrees of fineness. This is obtained as follows. They melt together one *māsha* of pure silver with the same quantity of best copper; and let it get solid. This mixture they again melt with 6 *māshas* of pure gold of 10½ degrees of fineness. Of this composition one *māsha* [2] is taken, and divided into sixteen parts of half a *surkh* each. If now 7½ *surkhs* of pure gold (of 10½ degrees) are mixed with one of the sixteen parts of the composition, the touch of the new mixture will only be 10¼ *bān*.[3] Similarly, 7 *surkhs* pure gold and two parts of the composition melted together, will give gold of 10 *bān*; 6½ *s*. pure gold and three parts composition, 9¾ *bān*; 6 *s*. gold and four parts composition, 9½ *bān*; 5½ *s*. gold and five parts composition, 9¼ *bān*; 5*s*. gold and six parts composition, 9 *bān*; 4½ *s*. gold and seven parts composition, 8¾ *bān*; 4 *s*. gold and eight parts composition, 8½ *bān*; 3½ *s*. gold and nine parts composition, 8¼ *bān*; 3 *s*. gold and ten parts composition, 8 *bān*; 2½ *s*. gold and eleven parts composition, 7¾ *bān*; 2 *s*. gold and twelve parts composition, 7½ *bān*; 1½ *s*. gold and thirteen parts composition, 7¼ *bān*; 1 *s*. gold and fourteen parts composition, 7 *bān*; and

---

[1] This Hind. word, which is not given in the dictionaries, means the *testing of gold*.

[2] This *māsha* contains 6 parts gold, 1 part silver, and 1 part copper, *i.e.*, ¾ gold and ¼ alloy.

[3] The Hind. term *bān* means "temper, degree".

lastly, $\frac{1}{2}$ *s.* gold and fifteen parts composition, $6\frac{3}{4}$ *bān*. Or *generally*, every additional half *surkh* (or one part) of the composition diminishes the fineness of the gold by a quarter *bān*, the touch of the composition itself being $6\frac{1}{2}$ *bān*.

If it be required to have a degree less than $6\frac{1}{2}$ *bān*, they mix together $\frac{1}{2}$ *surkh* of the first mixture which consisted, as I said, of silver and copper, with $7\frac{1}{2}$ *surkhs* of the second composition (consisting of gold, copper, and silver), which, when melted together, gives gold of $6\frac{1}{4}$ *bān*; and if 1 *surkh* of the first mixture be melted together with 7 *surkhs* of the second composition, the result will be 6 *bān*; and if they require still baser compositions, they increase the mixtures by half *surkhs*. But in the *Banwārī*, they reckon to 6 *bāns* only, rejecting all baser compositions.

All this is performed by a man who understands the tests.

3. *The Amīn.* He must possess impartiality and integrity, so that friends and enemies can be sure of him. Should there be any differences, he assists the *dārogha* and the other workmen, maintains that which is right, and prevents quarrels.

4. The *Mushrif.* He writes down the daily expenditure in an upright and practical manner, and keeps a systematic day-book.

5. *The Merchant.* He buys up gold, silver, and copper, by which he gains a profit for himself, assists the department, and benefits the revenues of the State. Trade will flourish, when justice is everywhere to be had, and when rulers are not avaricious.

6. *The Treasurer.* He watches over the profits, and is upright in all his dealings.

The salaries of the first four and the sixth officers differ from each other, the lowest of them holding the rank of an *Aḥadī*.[1]

7. *The Weighman.* He weighs the coins. For weighing 100 *jalālī* gold-muhrs he gets $1\frac{3}{4}$ *dāms*; for weighing 1000 rupees, $6\frac{1}{2}\frac{9}{5}$ *dāms*; and for weighing 1000 copper *dāms*, $\frac{1}{2}\frac{1}{5}$ of a *dām*; and, after this rate, according to the quantity.

8. *The Melter of the Ore.* He makes small and large trenches in a tablet of clay, which he besmears with grease, and pours into them the melted gold and silver, to cast them into ingots. In the case of copper, instead of using grease, it is sufficient to sprinkle ashes. For the above-

---

[1] The *Aḥadīs* corresponds to our *warrant officers*. Most clerks of the Imperial offices, the painters of the court, the foremen in Akbar's workshops, etc., belonged to this corps. They were called *Aḥadīs*, or *single men*, because they stood under Akbar's immediate orders. The word *Aḥadī*, the *ḥ* of which is the Arabic ح, was spelt in official returns with the Persian ہ. So deep-rooted, says Badāonī, was Akbar's hatred for everything which was Arabic. [This word has come to mean in Urdu, lazy, indolent.—P.]

mentioned quantity of gold, he gets $2\frac{3}{5}$ *dāms*; for the same quantity of silver, 5 *dāms* and $13\frac{1}{4}$ *jetals*;[1] for the same quantity of copper, 4 *dāms* and $21\frac{1}{2}$ *jetals*.

9. *The Platemaker.* He makes the adulterated gold into plates of six or seven *māshas* each, six fingers in length and breadth; these he carries to the assay master, who measures them in a mould made of copper, and stamps such as are suitable, in order to prevent alterations and to show the work done. He receives as wages for the above-mentioned quantity of gold, $42\frac{1}{3}$ dāms.

Āʿīn 7.

THE MANNER OF REFINING GOLD.

When the above-mentioned plates have been stamped, the owner of the gold, for the weight of every 100 *jalālī* gold muhrs, must furnish[2] four sers of saltpetre, and four sers of brickdust of raw bricks. The plates, after having been washed in clean water, are stratified with the above mixture (of the saltpetre and brickdust), and put one above the other, the whole being covered with cowdung, which in Hindī is called *upla*. It is the dry dung of the *Wild*[3] *Cow*. Then they set fire to it, and let it gently burn, till the dung is reduced to ashes, when they leave it to cool; then, these ashes being removed from the sides, are preserved. They are called in Persian *k͟hāk-i k͟hāliṣ*, and in Hindī *salonī*. By a process, to be mentioned hereafter, they recover silver from it. The plates, and the ashes below them, are left as they are. This process of setting fire to the dung, and removing the ashes at the sides, is twice repeated. When three fires have been applied, they call the plates *sitāʿī*. They are then again washed in clean water, and stratified three times with the above mixture, the ashes of the sides being removed.

This operation must be repeated till six mixtures and eighteen fires have been applied, when the plates are again washed. Then the assay master breaks one of them; and if there comes out a soft and mild sound, it is a sign of its being sufficiently pure; but if the sound is harsh, the plates must undergo three more fires. Then from each of the plates one *māsha* is taken away, of which aggregate a plate is made. This is tried on the touchstone; if it is not sufficiently fine, the gold has again to pass through one or two fires. In most cases, however, the desired effect is obtained by three or four fires.

---

[1] Twenty-five *jetals* make one *dām*. *Vide* the 10th *Āʿīn*.

[[2] Use.—P.]

[[3] *Ṣaḥrāʿī*. This probably means *janglī*; *i.e.*, "not stalled or stall-fed."—P.]

The following method of assaying is also used. They take two *tolās* of pure gold, and two *tolās* of the gold which passed through the fire, and make twenty plates of each, of equal weight. They then spread the above mixture, apply the fire, wash them, and weigh them with an exact balance. If both kinds are found to be equal in weight, it is a proof of pureness.

10. *The Melter of the refined metal.* He melts the refined plates of gold, and casts them, as described above, into ingots. His fee for 100 gold *muhrs* is three *dāms*.

11. The *Ẕarrāb.* He cuts off the gold, silver and copper ingots, as exactly as he can, round pieces of the size of coined money. His fees are, for 100 gold *muhrs*, 21 *dāms*, 1¼ *jetals*; for the weight of 1000 rupees, 53 *dāms*, 8¾ *jetals*, if he cuts rupees; and 28 *dāms* in addition, if he cuts the same weight of silver into quarter rupees. For 1000 copper *dāms* his fee is 20 *dāms*; for the same weight of half and quarter *dāms*, 25 *dāms*; and for half-quarter *dāms*, which are called *damrīs*, 69 *dāms*.

In Īrān and Tūrān they cannot cut these pieces without a proper anvil; but Hindustani workmen cut them without such an instrument, so exactly, that there is not the difference of a single hair, which is remarkable enough.

12. *The Engraver.* He engraves the dies of the coins on steel, and such like metals. Coins are then stamped with these dies. At this day, Mawlā-nā ʿAlī Aḥmad of Delhi, who has not his equal in any country, cuts different kinds of letters in steel, in such a manner as to equal the copyslips of the most skilful caligraphers. He holds the rank of a *yūzbāshī*;[1] and two of his men serve in the mint. Both have a monthly salary of 600 *dāms*.

13. The *Sikkachī.* He places the round pieces of metal between two dies; and by the strength of the hammerer (*putk-chī*) both sides are stamped. His fees are for 100 gold *muhrs*, 1⅖ *dāms*; for 1000 rupees, 5 *dāms*, 9½ *jetals*; and for the weight of 1000 rupees of small silver pieces, 1 *dām*, 3 *jetals* in addition; for 1000 copper *dāms*, 3 *dāms*; for 2000 half-*dāms*, and 4000 quarter-*dāms*, 3 *dāms*, 18¾ *jetals*; and for 8000 half-quarter *dāms*, 10½ *dāms*. Out of these fees the *sikkachī* has to give one-sixth to the hammerer, for whom there is no separate allowance.

14. The *Sabbāk* makes the refined silver into round plates. For every 1000 rupees weight, he receives 54 *dāms*.

---

[1] This Turkish word signifies a *commander of one hundred men*, a captain. *Aḥadīs* of distinction were promoted to this military rank. The salary of a Yūzbāshī varied from five to seven hundred rupees *per mensem*; *vide* the third *Āʾīn* of the second book.

The discovery of an alloy in silver. Silver may be alloyed with lead, tin and copper. In Īrān and Tūrān, they also call the highest degree of fineness of silver *dahdahī* ; in Hindustān, the *ṣayrafīs* use for it the term *bīst biswa.* According to the quantity of the alloy, it descends in degree ; but it is not made less than five, and no one would care for silver baser than ten degrees. Practical men can discover from the colour of the compound, which of the alloys is prevailing, whilst by filing and boring it, the quality of the inside is ascertained. They also try it by beating it when hot, and then throwing it into water, when blackness denotes lead, redness copper, a white greyish colour tin, and whiteness a large proportion of silver.

THE METHOD OF REFINING SILVER.

They dig a hole, and having sprinkled into it a small quantity of wild [1] cow dung, they fill it with the ashes of *mughīlān* [2] wood ; then they moisten it, and work it up into the shape of a dish ; into this they put the adulterated silver, together with a proportionate quantity of lead. First, they put a fourth part of the lead on the top of the silver, and having surrounded the whole with coals, blow the fire with a pair of bellows, till the metals are melted, which operation is generally repeated four times. The proofs of the metal being pure are a lightning-like brightness, and its beginning to harden at the sides. As soon as it is hardened in the middle, they sprinkle it with water, when flames resembling in shape the horns of wild goats, issue from it. It then forms itself into a disc, and is perfectly refined. If this disc be melted again, half a *surkh* in every *tolā* will burn away, *i.e.*, 6 *māshas* and 2 *surkhs* in 100 *tolās.* The ashes of the disc, which are mixed with silver and lead, form a kind of litharge, called in Hindī *kharal*, and in Persian *kuhna* [3] ; the use of which will be hereafter explained. Before this refined silver is given over to the *Ẕarrāb*, 5 *māshas* and 5 *surkhs* are taken away for the Imperial exchequer out of every hundred *tolās* of it ; after which the assay master marks the mass with the usual stamp, that it may not be altered or exchanged.

In former times silver also was assayed by the *banwārī* system ; now it is calculated as follows :—if by refining 100 *tolās*, of *shāhī* silver, which is current in ʿIrāq and Khurāsān, and of the *lārī* and *miṣqālī*, which are

---

[1 See note 1, p. 21.—P.]

2 Called in Hind. *babūl*, a kind of acacia. Its bark is used in tanning. [The *kīkar* of the Panjab.—P.]

3 Some MSS. have *katah*.

current in Tūrān, there are lost three *tolās* and one *surkh* ; and of the same quantity of the European and Turkish *narjīl*, and the *maḥmūdī* and *muzaffarī* of Gujrāt and Mālwa, 13 *tolās* and 6½ *māshas* are lost, they become then of Imperial standard.

15. The *Qurṣ-kūb* having heated the refined silver, hammers it till it has lost all smell of the lead. His fee for the weight of 1000 rupees, is 4½ *dāms*.

16. The *Chāshnīgīr* examines the refined gold and silver, and fixes its purity as follows :—Having made two tolas of the refined gold into eight plates, he applies layers of the mixture as above described, and sets fire to it, keeping out, however, all draught ; he then washes the plates, and melts them. If they have not lost anything by this process, the gold is pure. The assay-master then tries it upon the touchstone, to satisfy himself and others. For assaying that quantity, he gets 1⅗ *dāms*. In the case of silver, he takes one tola with a like quantity of lead, which he puts together into a bone crucible, and keeps it on the fire till the lead is all burnt. Having then sprinkled the silver with water, he hammers it till it has lost all smell of the lead ; and having melted it in a new crucible, he weighs it ; and if it has lost in weight three[1] *birinj* (rice grains), it is sufficiently pure ; otherwise he melts it again, till it comes to that degree. For assaying that quantity, his fee is 3 *dāms*, 4½ *jetals*.

17. The *Niyāriya* collects the *khāk-i khāliṣ* and washes it, taking two sers at the time ; whatever gold there may be amongst it will settle, from its weight, to the bottom. The *khāk*, when thus washed, is called in Hindī *kukrah*,[2] and still contains some gold, for the recovery of which, directions shall hereafter be given. The above-mentioned adulterated sediment is rubbed together with quicksilver, at the rate of six *māshas* quicksilver per ser. The quicksilver from its predilective affinity, draws the gold to itself, and forms an amalgam which is kept over the fire in a retort, till the gold is separated from the quicksilver.

For extracting the gold from this quantity of *khāk*, the *Niyāriya* receives 20 *dāms*, 2 *jetals*.

The process of Kukrah.

They mix with the *kukrah* an equal quantity of *punhar*, and form a paste of *rasī* (aqua fortis), and cowdung. They then pound the first composition, and mixing it with the paste, work it up into balls of two sers weight, which they dry on a cloth.

---

[1] One MS. has *six*.

[[2] Word not traced.—P.]

Punhar is obtained as follows:—

They make a hole in the earth, and fill it with the ashes of *Babūl*-wood, at the rate of six fingers height of ashes for every maund of lead. The lead itself is put at the bottom of the hole, which has been smoothed; then they cover it with charcoals, and melt the lead. After that, having removed the coals, they place over it two plates of clay, fixed by means of thorns, and close up the bellows hole, but not the vent. This they keep covered with bricks, till the ashes have thoroughly soaked up the lead. The bricks they frequently remove to learn the state of the lead. For the above-mentioned quantity of lead, there are 4 *māshas* of silver mixed up with the ashes. These ashes they cool in water, when they are called *punhar*. Out of every *man* of lead two *sers* are burnt; but the mass is increased by four *sers* of ashes, so that the weight of the whole mass will be one *man* and two *sers*.

Rasī is a kind of acid made of *ashkhār*[1] and saltpetre.

Having thus explained what *punhar* and *rasī* are, I return to the description of the process of *Kukrah*. They make an oven-like vessel, narrow at both ends, and wide in the middle, one and a half yards in height, with a hole at the bottom. Then having filled the vessel with coals within four fingers of the top, they place it over a pit dug in the earth, and blow the fire with two bellows. After that, the aforementioned balls being broken into pieces, they throw them into the fire and melt them, when the gold, silver, copper and lead fall through the hole in the bottom of the vessel into the pit below. Whatever remains in the vessel, is softened and washed, and the lead separated from it. They likewise collect the ashes, from whence also by a certain process profit may be derived. The metal is then taken out of the pit, and melted according to the *punhar* system. The lead will mix with the ashes, from which thirty sers will be recovered, and ten sers will be burnt. The gold, silver and copper remain together in a mass, and this they call *bugrāwaṭī*, or according to some, *gubrāwatī*.

The process of Bugrāwaṭī.

They make a hole, and fill it with the ashes of *babūl*-wood, half a ser for every 100 tolas of *bugrāwaṭī*. These ashes they then make up in form of a dish, and mix them up with the *bugrāwaṭī*, adding one tola of copper, and twenty-five tolas of lead. They now fill the dish with coals, and cover it with bricks. When the whole has melted, they remove the coals and the

[1] The margins of some of the MSS. explain this word by the Hind. *sijjī*, impure carbonate of soda.

bricks, and make a fire of *babūl*-wood, till the lead and copper unite with the ashes, leaving the gold and silver together. These ashes are also called *kharal*, and the lead and copper can be recovered from them by a process, which will be hereafter explained.

Āʿīn 8.

THE METHOD OF SEPARATING THE SILVER FROM THE GOLD.

They melt this composition six times ; three times with copper, and three times with sulphur, called in Hind. *chhāchhiyā*. For every tola of the alloy, they take a *māsha* of copper, and two *māshas*, two *surkhs* of sulphur. First they melt it with copper, and then with sulphur. If the alloy be of 100 *tolas* weight, the 100 *māshas* of copper are employed as follows :—they first melt fifty *māshas* with it, and then twice again twenty-five *māshas*. The sulphur is used in similar proportions. After reducing the mixture of gold and silver to small bits, they mix with it fifty *māshas* of copper, and melt it in a crucible. They have near at hand a vessel full of cold water, on the surface of which is laid a broom-like bundle of hay. Upon it they pour the melted metal, and prevent it, by stirring it with a stick, from forming into a mass. Then having again melted these bits, after mixing them with the remaining copper in a crucible, they set it to cool in the shade ; and for every tola of this mixture two *māshas* and two *surkhs* of sulphur are used, *i.e.*, at the rate of one and one-half quarter *ser* ($1\frac{3}{8}$ ser) *per* 100 *tolas*. When it has been three times melted in this manner; there appears on the surface a whitish kind of ash, which is silver. This is taken off, and kept separate ; and its process shall hereafter be explained. When the mixture of gold and silver has thus been subjected to three fires for the copper, and three for the sulphur, the solid part left is the gold. In the language of the Panjāb, this gold is called *kail*, whilst about Dihlī, it is termed *pinjar*. If the mixture contains much gold, it generally turns out to be of $6\frac{1}{2}$ *bān*, but it is often only five, and even four.

In order to refine this gold, one of the following methods must be used : Either they mix fifty tolas of this with 400 tolas of purer gold, and refine it by the *Salonī* process ; or else they use the *Alonī* process. For the latter they make a mixture of two parts of wild-cow dung, and one part of saltpetre. Having then cast the aforesaid *pinjar* into ingots, they make it into plates, none of which ought to be lighter than $1\frac{1}{2}$ tolas, but a little broader than those which they make in the *salonī* process. Then having besmeared them with sesame-oil, they strew the above mixture over them, giving them for every strewing two gentle fires. This operation they repeat three or four times; and if they want the metal very pure, they repeat the process till it comes up to nine *bān*. The ashes are also collected, being a kind of *kharal*.

Āʾīn 9.

THE METHOD OF EXTRACTING THE SILVER FROM ASHES.

Whatever ashes and dross have been collected, both before and after the process of *alonī*, they mix with double the quantity of pure lead, put them into a crucible, and keep them for one watch over the fire. When the metal is cold, they refine it as described under the article *Sabbāk*, p. 22. The ashes of it are also *kharal*. The *salonī* process is also performed in other ways well known to those conversant with the business.

18. The *Panīwār* having melted the *kharal*, separates the silver from the copper. His fee for every tola of silver is 1½ *dāms*. As a return for the profit he makes, he pays monthly 300 *dāms* to the *dīwān*. Having reduced the *kharal* to small bits, he adds to every *man* of it 1½ sers of *tangār* (borax), and three sers of pounded natron,[1] and kneads them together. He then puts this mass, ser by ser, into the vessel above described, and melts it, when lead mixed with silver collects in the pit. This is afterwards refined by the process of the *sabbāk*, and the lead which separates from this, and mixes with the ashes, turns *punhar*.

19. The *Paikār* buys the *salonī* and *kharal* from the goldsmiths of the city, and carries them to the mint to be melted, and makes a profit on the gold and silver. For every *man* of *salonī*, he gives 17 *dāms*, and for the same quantity of *kharal* 14 *dāms*, to the exchequer.

20. The *Nichoʾī-wāla* brings old copper coins, which are mixed with silver, to be melted; and from 100 tolas of silver, 3½ rupees go to the *dīwān*; and when he wishes to coin the silver, he pays a fixed quantity for it as duty.

21. The *Khāk-shoy*. When the owners of the metals get their gold and silver in the various ways which have now been described, the *Khāk-shoy* sweeps the mint, takes the sweepings to his own house, washes them, and gains a profit. Some of the sweepers carry on a very flourishing trade. The state receives from this man a monthly gift of 12½ rupees.

And in like manner all the officers of the mint pay a monthly duty to the state, at the rate of three *dāms* for every 100 *dāms*.

[1 In the Persian *ashkhār-i kūfta*.—P.]

Āʿīn 10.

THE COINS OF THIS GLORIOUS EMPIRE.

As through the attention of his Majesty, gold and silver have been brought to the greatest degree of purity, in like manner the form of the coins has also been improved. The coins are now an ornament to the treasury, and much liked by the people. I shall give a few particulars.

A. *Gold Coins.*

1. The *sahansah* is a round coin weighing 101 *tolas*, 9 *māshas*, and 7 *surkhs*, in value equal to 100 *laʿl-i jalālī*-muhrs. On the field of one side is engraved the name of his Majesty, and on the five arches in the border, *Aṣ-sulṭānᵘ 'l-aʿẓamᵘ 'l-khāqānᵘ 'l-muʿaẓẓᵘ khalladᵃ Allāhᵘ mulkahᵘ wᵃ ṣulṭāna-hᵘ ẓarbᵘ dārⁱ 'l-khilāfatⁱ Āgra*, " the great sulṭan, the distinguished emperor, may God perpetuate his kingdom and his reign! Struck at the capital Āgra." On the field of the reverse is the *beautiful formula*,[1] and the following verse of the Qurʾān[2]: *Allāhᵘ yazraqᵘ man yashāʾᵘ bi-ghayrⁱ ḥisābⁱⁿ*, " God is bountiful unto whom He pleaseth, without measure "; and roundabout are the names of the first four Khalīfas. This is what was first cut by Maulānā Maqṣūd, the engraver; after which Mullā ʿAlī Aḥmad made with great skill the following additions. On one side *Afẓalᵘ dīnārⁱⁿ yanfuqu-hᵘ ar-rajulᵘ dīnārᵘⁿ yanfuquhᵘ ʿalą aṣḥābihⁱ fī sabīlⁱ 'llāh*, " the best coin which a man expends is a coin which he spends on his co-religionists in the path of God."

And on the other side he wrote,

Aṣ-ṣulṭānᵘ 'l- -ʿālī al-khalīfatᵘ al-mutaʿālī khalladᵃ allāhᵘ taʿālą mulkahᵘ wᵃ ṣulṭānahᵘ wᵃ abbadᵃ ʿadlahᵘ wᵃ iḥsānahᵘ, " the sublime *ṣulṭān*, the exalted *khalīfa*, may God the Almighty perpetuate his kingdom and his reign, and given eternity to his justice and bounty ! "

Afterwards all this was removed, and the following two *Rubāʿīs*[3] of the court-poet and philosopher *Shaykh Fayẓī* were engraved by him. On one side,

Khurshīd ki haft bahr azū gawhar yāft
Sang-i siyah az partav-i ān jawhar yāft
Kān az naẓar-i tarbiyat-i ū zar yāft
W'ān zar sharaf az sikka-yi Shāh Akbar yāft.

---

[1] Also called *Kalimah*, or the Confession of Faith, *lā ilāha ill-allāh, Muhammadun rasūl-ullāh.*

[2] Qur. Sur. II, 208. [[3] Quatrains.—P.]

"It is the Sun [1] from which the seven oceans get their pearls,
The black rocks get their jewels from his lustre.
The mines get their gold from his fostering glance,
And their gold is ennobled by Akbar's stamp."

and, *Allāh*[u] *akbar jall*[a] *jalāla-h*[u], "God is great, may His glory shine forth!" in the middle. And on the other side,

In sikka ki pīrāya-yi ummīd buvad
Bā naqsh-i davām u nām-i jāvīd buvad
Sīmā-yi saʿādat-ash hamīn bas ki bi-dahr
Yak zarra nazar-karda-yi khurshīd buvad.

"This coin, which is an ornament of hope,
Carries an everlasting stamp, and an immortal name.
As a sign of its auspiciousness, it is sufficient
That, once, for all ages the sun has cast a glimpse upon it."

and the date, according to the *Divine era*, in the middle.

2. There is another gold coin, of the same name and shape, weighing 91 tolas and 8 *māshas*, in value equal to 100 round muhrs, at 11 *māshas* each. It has the same impression as the preceding.

3. The *Rahas* is the half of each of the two preceding coins It is sometimes made square. On one side it has the same impression as the *sahansa*,[2] and on the other side the following *Rubāʿī* [3] by *Fayẓī*:—

Īn naqd-i ravān-i ganj-i shāhinshāhī
Bā kawkab-i iqbāl kunad hamrāhī
Khurshīd bi-parvar-ash az ān rū ki bi-dahr
Yābad sharaf az sikka-yi Akbarshāhī.

"This current coin of the Imperial treasure
Accompanies the star of good fortune.
O sun, foster it, because for all ages
It is ennobled by Akbar's stamp!"

4. The *Ātma* is the fourth part of the *sahansa*, round and square. Some have the same impression as the *sahansa* [4]; and some have on one side the following *Rubāʿī* by Fayẓī [5]:—

Īn sikka ki dast-i bakht rā zewar bād
Pīrāya-yi nuh sipihr u haft akhtar bād

---

[1] According to the Natural Philosophers of the Middle Ages, the influence of the sun calls the metals, the pearls, and precious stones into existence; *vide* the thirteenth Āʾīn. The allusion to the sun is explained by the note to page III.

[[2] In the Persian صدمهری.—P.]

[[3] Quatrains.—P.]

[[4] *Ṣad-muhrī* in the Persian text.—P.]

[[5] Maliku 'sh-Shuʿarāʾ in the Persian text.—P.]

Zarrīn naqdīst kār az-ū chūn zar bād
Dar dahr ravān bi-nām-i shāh akbar bād.

"This coin—May it adorn the hand of the fortunate,
And may it be an ornament of the nine heavens and the seven stars—
Is a gold coin,—May golden be its work!
Let it be current for all ages to the glory of Shāh Akbar."

And on the other side the preceding *Rubaʿī.*

5. The *Binsat,* of the same two forms as the *ātma,* in value equal to one-fifth of the first coin.

There are also gold coins of the same shape and impression, in value equal to one-eighth, one-tenth, one-twentieth, one twenty-fifth, of the *sahansa.*

6. The *Chugul,*[1] of a square form, is the fiftieth part of the *sahansa,* in value equal to two muhrs.[2]

7. The *round Laʿl-i Jalālī,*[3] in weight and value equal to two *round muhrs,* having on one side *Allāh^u akbar,* and on the other *Yā muʿīn^u,* "O helper."

8. The *Āftābī* is round, weighs 1 *tola,* 2 *māshas,* and 4¾ *surkhs,* in value equal to 12 rupees. On one side, "*Allāh^u akbar, jall^a jalālu-h^u,*" and on the other the date according to the Divine era, and the place where it is struck.

9. The *Ilāhī* is round, weighs 12 *māshas,* 1¾ *surkhs,* bears the same stamp as the *Āftābī,* and has a value of 10 rupees.

---

[1] Or *Jugul.* Abū 'l-Faẓl's spelling in the text is ambiguous.

[2] The MSS. differ. Most of them place the *Chugul* as the sixth coin *after* the *Binsat,* and read:—

"The *Chugul,* of a square form, weighing 3 *tolas,* 5¼ *surkhs*; its value is thirty rupees. Also, of a *round* form, weighing 2 *tolas,* 9 *māshas,* having a value of three *round muhrs,* of 11 *māshas* each (*i.e.,* 27 rupees). But the impression of both is the same. They are the *fiftieth* part of the *Sahansa.*"

The last sentence does not agree with the value and weight of the *Sahansa*; for the two *Chuguls,* as given by Abū 'l-Faẓl, would each be the hundred and third part of the two kinds of *Sahansa,* not the *fiftieth* part.

Mr. Thomas in his excellent edition of Prinsep's *Useful Tables,* pp. 5, 6, gives an *extract* from a MS. of the Āʾīn in his possession, which appears to agree with the above reading; but he only mentions the *square* form of the *Chugul,* weighing 3 *tolas,* 5¼ *surkhs,* worth 30 rupees; and then passes on to the *eighth* coin, the *Āftābī.*

Two other MSS.—among them Col. Hamilton's—read *after* the *Binsat* (*i.e.,* after the twenty-fifth line of p. 24 of my text edition)—

"6. The *Chahārgosha* (or *square*), weighing 3 *tolas,* 5¼ *surkhs,* worth 30 rupees.

"7. The *Gird* (or *round*); weighing 2 *tolas,* 9 *māshas,* in value equal to the 3 *round muhrs* of 11 *māshas* each.

"Both have the same impression.

"8. The *Chugul,* of a square form, the fiftieth part of a *Sahansa,* in value equal to two *Laʿl-i Jalālī muhrs.*"

This reading obviates all difficulties. But the real question is whether the *Chahārgosha,* the *Gird,* and the *Chugul* are *three* distinct coins.

[3] For *the round Laʿl-i Jalālī,* some MSS. only read, "*The Gird,*" *i.e.,* round, taking the words *Laʿl-i Jalālī* to the preceding. *Vide* the tenth coin.

10. The *square Laʕl-ī Jalālī* is of the same weight and value ; on one side " *Allāh*^{u} *akbar*," and on the other " *jall*^{a} *jalālu-h*^{u}."

11. The *ʕAdl-gutka* is round, weighs 11 *māshas*, and has a value of nine rupees. On one side " *Allāh*^{u} *akbar* ", and on the other, " *Yā muʕīn*^{u}."

12. The *Round muhr*, in weight and value equal to the *ʕAdl-guṭka*, but of a different[1] stamp.

13. *Miḥrābī*[2] is in weight, value, and stamp, the same as the *round muhr*.

14. The *Muʕīnī* is both square and round. In weight and value it is equal to the *Laʕl-i jalālī*, and the *round muhr*. It bears the stamp " *yā muʕīn*^{u}."

15. The *Chahārgosha*, in stamp and weight the same as the *Āftābī*.

16. The *Gird* is the half of the *Ilāhī*, and has the same stamp.

17. The *Dhan*[3] is half a *Laʕl-i Jalālī*.[4]

18. The *Salīmī* is the half of the *ʕAdl-guṭka*.

19. The *Rabī*[5] is a quarter of the *Āftābī*.

20. The *Man*, is a quarter of the *Ilāhī*, and *Jalālī*.

21. The *Half Salīmī* is a quarter of the *ʕAdl-guṭka*.

22. The *Panj* is the fifth part of the *Ilāhī*.

23. The *Panḍau* is the fifth part of the *Laʕl-i Jalālī* ; on one side is a lily,[6] and on the other a wild rose.

24. The *Ṣumnī*, or *Ashtsidd*, is one-eighth of the *Ilāhī* ; on one side " *Allāh*^{u} *akbar*," and on the other " *jall*^{a} *jalāla-h*^{u}."

25. The *Kalā* is the sixteenth part of the *Ilāhī*. It has on both sides a wild rose.

26. The *Ẕara* is the thirty-second part of an *Ilāhī* and has the same stamp as the *kalā*.

As regards gold coins, the custom followed in the imperial mint is to coin *Laʕl-i jalālīs*, *Dhans*, and *Mans*, each coin for the space of a month. The other gold coins are never stamped without special orders.

---

[1] It has the *Kalima*. (Sayyid Ahmad's edition of the *Aʕīn*.)

[2] The figure called *miḥrābī* is

[3] In Forbes's Dictionary, *dahan*.

[4] Several MSS. read—" *Half a quarter* Ilāhī and Laʕl-i Jalālī." Forbes gives six rupees (?).

[5] Several MSS. have *Rabī*. Perhaps we should write *Rabbī*.

[[6] *Lāla* in Persian text. This is the common red poppy in Afghānistān and the Panjāb ; and in Persia is also applied to the wild tulip.—P.]

B. *Silver Coins.*

1. The *Rūpiya* is round, and weighs eleven and one half *māshas.* It was first introduced in the time of *Sher Khān.* It was perfected during this reign, and received a new stamp, on one side "*Allāh*[u] *akbar, jall*[a] *jalālu-h*[u]," and on the other the date. Although the market price is sometimes more or less than forty *dāms,* yet this value is always set upon it in the payment of salaries.

2. The *Jalāla* is of a square form, which was introduced during the present reign. In value and stamp it is the same as No. 1.

3. The *Darb* is half a *Jalāla.*

4. The *Charn* is a quarter *Jalāla.*

5. The *Panḍau* is a fifth of the *Jalāla.*

6. The *Asht* is the eighth part of the *Jalāla.*

7. The *Dasā* is one-tenth of the *Jalāla.*

8. The *Kalā* is the sixteenth part of the *Jalāla.*

9. The *Sūkī* us one-twentieth of the *Jalāla.*

The same fractional parts are adopted for the [round] *Rūpiya,* which are, however, different in form.

C. *Copper Coins.*

1. The *Dām* weighs 5 *tāks,* i.e. 1 *tola,* 8 *māshas,* and 7 *surkhs* ; it is the fortieth part of the *rūpiya.* At first this coin was called *Paisa,* and also *Buhlolī* ; now it is known under this name (*dām*). On one side the place is given where it was struck, and on the other the date.

For the purpose of calculation, the *dām* is divided into twenty-five parts, each of which is called a *jetal.*[1] This imaginary division is only used by accountants.

2. The *Adhela* is half of a *dām.*

3. The *Pā*'*olā* is a quarter *dām.*

4. The *Damrī* is one-eighth of a *dām.*

In the beginning of this reign, gold was coined to the glory of his Majesty in many parts of the empire ; now gold coins are struck at four places only, viz. at the seat of the government, Bengal, Aḥmadābād (Gujrāt), and Kābul. Silver and copper are likewise coined in these four places, and besides in the following ten places : Ilāhabās, Āgra, Ujain, Sūrat, Dihlī, Patna, Kashmīr, Lāhor, Multān, Tānḍa. In twenty-eight towns copper coins only are struck, viz. Ajmīr, Avadh, Aṭak, Alwar, Badā'on, Banāras, Bhakkar, Bahīrah, Patan, Jaunpūr, Jālandhar, Hardwār, Hisār, Fīrūza, Kālpī, Gwāliyār, Gorakhpūr, Kalānūr,

---

[1] Often misspelt *chetal.* The text gives the correct spelling.

Lakhnau, Mandū, Nāgor, Sarhind, Siyālkot, Saronj, Sahāranpūr, Sārangpur, Sambal, Qanawj, Rantanbhūr.

Mercantile affairs in this country are mostly transacted in *round muhrs*, *rūyiyas*, and *dāms*.

Unprincipled men cause a great deal of mischief by rubbing down the coins, or by employing similar methods; and, in consequence of the damage done to the nation at large, his Majesty continually consults experienced men, and from his knowledge of the spirit of the age, issues new regulations in order to prevent such detrimental practices.

The currency underwent several changes. *First*, when (in the 27th year) the reins of the government were in the hands of Rāja Todarmal,[1] *four* kinds of muhrs were allowed to be current; *A*. There was a *Laʿl-i Jalālī*, which had the name of his Majesty stamped on it, and weighed 1 *tola*, 1¾ *surkhs*. It was quite pure, and had a value of 400 *dāms*. Again, there existed from the beginning of this glorious reign, a muhr with the imperial stamp, of which *three* degrees passed as current, viz.: *B*. This muhr, when perfectly pure and having the full weight of 11 *māshas*. Its value was 360 *dāms*. If from wear and tear it had lost in weight within three grains of rice it was still allowed to be of the same degree, and no difference was made. *C*. The same muhr, when it had lost in weight from four to six rice grains; its value was 355 *dāms*. *D*. The same muhr, when it had lost in weight from six to nine rice grains; its value was 350 *dāms*.

---

[1] Rāja Todarmal, a Khatrī by caste, was born at Lāhor. He appears to have entered Akbar's service during the 18th year of the emperor's reign, when he was employed to settle the affairs of Gujrāt. In the 19th year, we find him in Bengal in company with *Munʿim Khān*; and three years later again at Gujrāt. In the 27th year he was appointed *Dīwān* of the empire, when he remodelled the revenue system. After an unsuccessful attempt on his life made by a *Khatrī* in the 32nd year, he was sent against the Yūsufzāīs, to avenge the death of Bīr Bar. In the 34th year, old age and sickness obliged him to send in his resignation, which Akbar unwillingly accepted. Retiring to the banks of the Ganges, he died—or, *went to hell*, as Badāʾonī expresses himself in the case of Hindus—on the 11th day A.H. 998, or 10th November, 1589, the same year in which Rāja Bhagwān Dās died. Todarmal had reached the rank of a *Chahārhazārī*, or commander of Four Thousand, and was no less distinguished for his personal courage, than his financial abilities. His eldest son Dhārū, a commander of seven hundred, was killed in the war with T'hatha.

Abū 'l-Fazl did not like Todarmal personally, but praises him for his strict integrity and abilities; he charges him with vindictiveness of temper and bigotry. Awrangzeb said he had heard from his father that Akbar complained of the rāja's *independence*, *vanity*, and *bigoted adherence to Hinduism*. Abū 'l-Fazl openly complained of him to Akbar; but the emperor with his usual regard for faithful services, said that he could not drive away an old servant. In his adherence to Hinduism, Todarmal may be contrasted with Bīr Bar, who a short time before his death had become a member of the *Divine Faith*. Once when accompanying Akbar to the Panjāb, in the hurry of the departure, Todarmal's idols were lost; and as he transacted no business before his daily worship, he remained for several days without food and drink, and was at last with difficulty cheered up by the emperor.

Muhrs of less weight than this were considered as bullion.

Of *Rūpiyas*, three kinds were then current, viz.: *A*. one of a square form, of pure silver, and weighing 11½ *māshas*; it went under the name of *Jalāla*, and had a value of 40 *dāms*. *B*. The round, old *Akbarshāhī rūpiya*, which, when of full weight, or even at a *surkh* less, was valued at 39 *dāms*. *C*. The same rupees, when in weight two *surkhs* less, at 38 *dāms*.

Rupees of less weight than this were considered as bullion.

Secondly, on the 18th Mihr of the 29th year of the Divine era, ʿAẓudᵘ 'd-Daulah Amīr Fatḥᵘ 'llah [1] of Shīrāz coming at the head of affairs, a royal order was issued, that on the *muhrs*, as far as *three* grains; and on the *rūpiyas*, as far as *six* grains short weight, no account should be taken, but that they should be reckoned of full weight. If muhrs were still less, they should make a deduction for the deficiency, whatever their deficiency might be; but it was not ordered that only muhrs down to nine grains less should be regarded as muhrs. Again, according to the same regulation, the value of a muhr that was one *surkh* deficient was put down as 355 *dāms* and a fraction; and hence they valued the price of one *surkh* of *coined* gold at the low rate of *four dāms* and a fraction. According to Todarmal's regulation, a deduction of *five dāms* was made for a deficiency of one *surkh*; and if the muhr had lost something more than the three grains, for which he had made no account, even if it were only ½ *surkh*, full five

---

[1] Amīr Fatḥ 'llah of Shīrāz was the pupil of Khwāja Jamālᵘ 'd-Dīn Maḥmūd, Kamālᵘ d-Dīn of Shirwān, and Mīr Ghiyāṣᵘ 'd-Dīn Manṣūr of Shīrāz. He so excelled in all branches of natural philosophy, especially mechanics, that Abū 'l-Faẓl said of him, "If the books of antiquity should be lost, the Amīr will restore them." At the earnest solicitations of ʿAdl Shāh of Bījāpūr, he left Shīrāz for the Dekhan. In A.H. 991, after the death of ʿAdl Shāh, he was invited by Akbar, who raised him to the dignity of a *Ṣadr*, and bestowed upon him, three years later, the title of Amīnᵘ 'l-Mulk. He was appointed to assist Todarmal, and rendered good service in working up the old revenue books. His title, Amīnᵘ 'l-Mulk, to which Abū 'l-Faẓl alludes (*vide* p. 28, l. 9 of my text edition), was in the same year changed to ʿ*Aẓudᵘ 'd-Dawlah*, or *the arm of* [e]*mpire*. The Amīr went afterwards to Khāndesh. After his return in 997 to Akbar, who was then in Kashmīr, he was attacked with fever, of which he died. Thinking to understand the medical art, he refused the advice of the famous Ḥakīm ʿAlī, and tried to cure the fever by eating *harīsa* (*vide* the twenty-fourth Āʾīn), which caused his death.

Next to Abū '-Faẓl, Fayẓī, and Bīr Baṛ, the Amīr was perhaps most loved by Akbar. Several of his mechanical inventions, mentioned below, are ascribed by Abū 'l-Faẓl to Akbar himself (!). The Amīr was, however, on the best terms with Abū 'l-Faẓl, whose son he instructed. According to the author of the *Mirʾātᵘ 'l-ʿĀlam*, he was "a worldly man, often accompanying the emperor on hunting parties, with a rifle on his shoulder, and a powder-bag in his waistband, treading down science, and performing feats of strength which Rustam could not have performed."

It is stated by the author of the *Maʾāṣirᵘ 'l-Umarāʾ* that according to some, the Amīr was a *Sih-hazārī*, or Commander of three thousand; but I do not find his name among the lists of Akbar's grandees given in the *Tabaqāt-i Akbarī*, and the last Āʾīn of the second book of this work. Instead of *Amīr* Fatḥᵘ 'llāh, we also find, especially in Badāonī, *Shāh* Fatḥᵘ 'llāh. He lies buried on the *Takht-i Sulaymān*. Fayẓī's ode on his death is very fine.

dāms were subtracted ; and for a deficiency of 1½ *surkhs* he deducted ten *dāms*, even if the deficiency should not be quite 1½ *surkhs*. By the new law of ʿAẓudᵘ 'd-Dawlah, the value of a muhr was lessened by six *dāms* and a fraction, as its gold was worth 353 *dāms* and a fraction only.[1]

ʿAẓudᵘ 'd-Dawlah abolished also the regulation, according to which the value of a round *rūpiya* had been fixed at one *dām* less than the square one, notwithstanding its perfection in weight and purity, and fixed the value of the round *rūpiya*, when of full weight or not less than one *surkh*, at forty *dāms* ; and whilst formerly a deduction of two *dāms* was made for a deficiency of two *surkhs*, they now deduct for the same deficiency only one *dām* and a fraction.

Thirdly, when ʿAẓudᵘ 'd-Dawlah went to Khāndesh, the Rāja estimated the value of muhrs that had been expressed in Jalālā rupees, in round rupees ; and from his obstinate and wrangling disposition, fixed again the deficiencies on muhrs and rupees according to the old rates.

Fourthly, when Qulīj Khān[2] received the charge of the government he adopted the Rāja's manner of estimating the muhrs ; but he deducted ten *dāms* for a deficiency in the weight of a muhr, for which the Rāja had deducted five *dāms* ; and twenty *dāms* for the former deduction of ten *dāms* ; whilst he considered every muhr as bullion, if the deficiency was 1½ *surkhs*. Similarly, every *rūpiya*, the deficiency of which was one *surkh*, was considered as bullion.

---

[1] For ʿAẓudᵘ 'd-Dawlah having fixed the value of 1 *surkh* of coined gold at 4 *dāms* and a small fraction, the value of a muhr of full weight (11 *māshas* = 11 × 8 *surkhs*) was only 11 × 8 × (4 × a small fraction) *dāms*, *i.e.*, according to Abū 'l-Faẓl, 353 *dāms* and a fraction, instead of 360 *dāms*.

[2] *Qulīj Khān* is first mentioned during the 17th year of Akbar's reign, when he was made governor of the Fort of Sūrat, which Akbar after a siege of forty-seven days had conquered. In the 23rd year he was sent to Gujrāt ; and after the death of Shāh Manṣūr, he was, two years later, appointed as *Dīwān*. In the 28th year he accompanied the army during the conquest of Gujrāt. In the 34th year he received *Sambhal* as jāgīr. After the death of Todarmal, he was again appointed as *Dīwān*. This is the time to which Abū 'l-Faẓl refers. In 1002 he was made governor of Kābul, where he has not successful. After his removal, he accompanied, in 1005, his son-in-law Prince Dānyāl as *Atālīq*, or tutor, but he soon returned to Akbar. During the absence, in 1007, of the emperor in Khāndesh, he was governor of Āgra. Two years later he was promoted to the governorship of the Panjāb and Kābul. At the accession of Jahāngīr, he was sent to Gujrāt, but returned next year to the Panjāb, where he had to fight against the Rawshaniyyahs. He died, at an advanced age, in 1035, or A.D. 1625-26. Abū 'l-Faẓl, in the last *Āʾīn* of the second book, mentions him as *Chahārhazārī*, or Commander of Four Thousand, which high rank he must have held for some time, as *Niẓāmī-i Harawī*, in his *Ṭabaqāt-i Akbarī*, mentions him as such, and as *Dīwān*. When tutor to Prince Dānyāl, he was promoted to the command of Four Thousand Five Hundred. Qulīj Khān was a pious man, and a staunch Sunnī he was much respected for his learning. As a poet he is known under the name of *Ulfatī* ; some of his verses may be found in the concluding chapter of the *Mirʾātᵘ 'l-ʿĀlam*. The high rank which he held was less due to his talents as a statesman than to his family-connexion with the kings of Tūrān. Of his two sons, Mīrzā Ṣayfᵘ 'llāh and Mīrzā Ḥusayn Qulīj, the latter is best known. [*Vide* note 2 to No. 42 of *Āʾīn* 30.—B.]

Lastly, his Majesty, trusting to his advisers and being occupied by various important affairs, paid at first but little attention to this subject, till after having received some intimation of the unsatisfactory state of this matter, he issued another regulation, which saved the nation further losses, and was approved of by every one, far and near. On the 26th of Bahman, of the year 36, according to the Divine era (A.D. 1592), he adopted the second [i.e. ʿAẓudᵘ 'd-Dawlah] method, with one exception, namely, he did not approve of the provision that a muhr the deficiency of which did not exceed *three*, and a *rūpiya*, the deficiency of which did not exceed *six*, *surkhs*, should still be regarded as of full weight. And this regulation was the only effectual method for preventing the fraudulent practices of unprincipled men; for the former regulations contained no remedy in cases when the officers of the mint coined money of the above deficiency in weight, or when treasurers reduced full coins to the same deficiency. Besides, shameless thievish people made light grain weights, and used to reduce muhrs, deficient by three grains, to six grains deficiency, whilst they accepted muhrs six grains deficient as muhrs deficient by nine grains. This reduction of coins being continued, large quantities of gold were stolen, and the losses seemed never to end. By the command of his Majesty grain weights of *bābāghūrī* were made, which were to be used in weighing. On the same date other stringent regulations were issued, that the treasurers and revenue collectors should not demand from the tax-payers any particular species of coins, and that the exact deficiency in weight and purity, whatever it might be, should be taken according to the present rate and no more. This order of his Majesty disappointed the wicked, taught covetous men moderation, and freed the nation from the cruelty of oppressors.

Āʾīn 11.

THE *DIRHAM* AND THE *DĪNĀR*.

Having given some account of the currency of the empire, I shall add a few particulars regarding these two ancient coins, and remark on the value of ancient coinage.

The *Dirham*, or *Dirhām*, as the word is sometimes given, is a silver coin, the shape of which resembled that of a date-stone. During the *khilāfat* of *ʿUmar*,[1] it was changed to a circular form; and in the time of *Zubayr* it was impressed with the words *Allāhᵘ* (God), *barakat* (blessing). *Ḥajjāj*

[[1] *Fārūq*.—P.]

stamped upon it the chapter of the Qurʿān called *Ikhlāṣ* ; and others say that he imprinted it with his own name. Others assert, that ʿUmar was the first who stamped an impression on *dirhams* ; whilst, according to some, Greek, Khusravite, and Ḥimyarite *dirhams* were in circulation at the time of ʿAbd^u 'l-Malik, the son Marwān, by whose order Ḥajjāj, the son of Yūsuf, had struck *dirhams*. Some say that Ḥajjāj refined the base *dirhams*; and coined them with the words *Allāh^u aḥad* (God is one), and *Allāh^u aṣ-ṣamad* (God is eternal) ; and these *dirhams* were called *makrūha* (abominable), because God's holy name was thereby dishonoured, unless this term be a corruption of some other name. After Ḥajjāj, at the time of the reign of Yazīd bin ʿAbd^u 'l-Malik, ʿUmar bin Hubayrah coined in the kingdom of ʿIrāq better *dirhams* than Ḥajjāj had made ; and afterwards Khālid bin ʿAbd^u 'llāh Qasrī, when governor of ʿIrāq, made them still finer, but they were brought to the highest degree of purity by Yūsuf son of ʿUmar. Again, it has been said that Muṣʿab bin Zubayr was the first who struck *dirhams*. Various accounts are given of their weights ; some saying that they were of ten or nine, or six or five *miṣqāls* ; whilst others give the weights of twenty, twelve, and ten *qīrāts*, asserting at the same time that ʿUmar had taken a *dirham* of each kind, and formed a coin of fourteen *qīrāts*, being the third part of the aggregate sum. It is likewise said that at the time of ʿUmar there were current several kinds of *dirhams* : *first*, some of eight *dāngs*, which were called *baghlī*, after *Rās baghl*, who was an assay-master, and who struck *dirhams* by the command of ʿUmar ;[1] but others call them *baghallī*, from *baghal*, which is the name of a village ;[2] *secondly*, some of four *dāngs*, which were called *ṭabrī* ; *thirdly*, some of three *dāngs*, which were known as *maghribī* ; and *lastly*, some of one *dāng*, named *yamanī*, the half of which four kinds ʿUmar is said to have taken as a uniform average weight. Fāẓil of Khujand says that in former days *dirhams* had been of two kinds : *first*, full ones of eight and six *dāngs* (1 *dāng* of his = 2 *qīrāts* ; 1 *qīrāt* = 2 *ṭassūj* ; 1 *ṭassūj* = 2 *ḥabbah*) ; and *secondly*, deficient ones of four *dāngs* and a fraction. Some hold different opinions on this subject.

The *Dīnār* is a gold coin, weighing *one miṣqāl*, i.e. 1$\frac{3}{7}$ *dirhams*, as they put 1 *miṣqāl* = 6 *dāngs* ; 1 *dāng* = 4 *ṭassūj* ; 1 *ṭassūj* = 2 *ḥabbas* ; 1 *ḥabba* = 2 *javs* (barley grains) ; 1 *jav* = 6 *khardals* (mustard-grain) ; 1 *khardal* = 12 *fals* ; 1 *fals* = 6 *fatīls* ; 1 *fatīl* = 6 *naqīrs* ; 1 *naqīr* = 6 *qiṭmīrs* ; and 1 *qiṭmīr* = 12 *ẕaras*. One *miṣqāl*, by this calculation, would be equal to 96 barley grains. *Miṣqāl* is a weight, used in weighing gold ; and it is

[[1] عمر خطّاب in the Persian.—P.]

[2] According to some inferior MSS., the name of a kind of gold.

also the name of the coin.[1] From some ancient writings it appears that the Greek *misqāl* is out of use, and weighs two *qīrāts* less than this ; and that the Greek *dirham* differs likewise from others, being less in weight by $\frac{1}{6}$ or $\frac{1}{4}$ of a *misqāl.*

Āʿīn 12.

THE PROFIT OF THE DEALERS IN GOLD AND SILVER.

One round muhr of 11 *māshas* buys one tola of gold of 10 *bān* ; or one tola, 2 *surkhs* of 9¾ *bān* ; or 1 tola, 4 *s.* of 8½ *bān* ; or 1 tola 6 *s.* of 9¼ *bān* ; or 1 tola, 1 *māsha* of 9 *bān* ; and similarly, according to the same proportion, the decrease of one *bān* increases the quantity of gold which a muhr can buy by one *māsha.*

The merchant buys for 100 *Laʿl-i Jalālī* muhrs 130 *t.* 2 *m.* 0⅝ *s.* of *Hun* gold of 8¼ *bāns.* Of this quantity 22 *t.* 9 *m.* 7½ *s.* burn away in melting, and mix with the *khāk-i khalāṣ*, so that 107 *t.* 4 *m.* 1⅛ *s.* of pure gold remain, which are coined into 105 muhrs, leaving a remainder of nearly half a tola of gold, the value of which is 4 rupees. From the *khāk-i khalāṣ* are recovered 2 *t.* 11 *m.* 4 *s.* of gold, and 11 *t.* 11 *m.* 4½ *s.* of silver, the value of both of which is 35 rupees, 12½ *tangas,*[2] so that altogether the above-mentioned quantity of *Hun* gold yields 105 muhrs 39 Rs., and 25 *dāms.*

This sum is accounted for as follows. *First,* 2 *Rs.* 18 *d.* 12½ *j.*, due to the workmen according to the rates which have been explained above; *secondly,* 5 *Rs.* 8 *d.* 8 *j.* for ingredients ; which sum is made up of 1 *R.* 4 *d.* 1½ *j.* on account of articles used in refining the metal, viz. 26 *d.* 16½ *j.* dung [3] ; 4 *d.* 20 *j. salonī* ; 1 *d.* 10 *j.* water ; 11 *d.* 5 *j.* quicksilver, and 4 *Rs.* 4 *d.* 6¼ *j.* on account of the *khāk-i khalāṣ* (viz. 21 *d.* 7¼ *j.* charcoal, and 3 *Rs.* 22 *d.* 24 *j.* lead) ; *thirdly,* 6 *Rs.* 37½ *d.*, which the owners of the gold take from the merchant, as a consideration for lending him the gold ; this item goes to the *Dīwān* if the gold belongs to the exchequer ; *fourthly,* 100 *Laʿl-i Jalālī* muhrs, which the merchant gets in exchange for the gold which he brought ; *fifthly,* 12 *Rs.* 37 *d.* 3½ *j.* which the merchant takes as his profit ; *sixthly,* 5 muhrs 12 *Rs.* 3½ *d.*, which go to the exchequer.[4] According to this proportion, merchants make their profits.

Although gold is imported into Hindustan, it is to be found in abundance in the northern mountains of the country, as also in Tibet

---

[1] In text "a gold coin".—B.]

[2] One *tanga* = 2 *dāms* ; now-a-days one *tanga* = 2 *pais.*

[3] پاچک دشتي.—P.]

[4] There is a slight mistake of 1¼ *jetals*, as the several items added up give 105 *m.* 39 *Rs.* 24 *d.* 23¾ *j.*, but not 105 *m.* 39 *Rs.* 25 *d.*

Gold may also be obtained by the *Salonī*-process from the sands of the Ganges and Indus, and several other rivers, as most of the waters of this country are mixed with gold; however, the labour and expense greatly exceed the profit.

One Rupee buys 1 *t.* 0 *m.* 2 *s.* of pure silver; hence for 950 Rs. the merchant gets 969 *t.* 9 *m.* 4 *s.* of silver. Out of this quantity, 5 *t.* 0 *m.* 4¾ *s.* burn away in casting ingots. The remainder yields 1006 rupees, and a surplus of silver worth 27½ *dāms*. The several items are—*first*, 2 *Rs.* 22 *d.* 12 *j.*, as wages for the workmen (viz. The *Weighman* 5 *d.* 7¾ *j.*, the *Chāshnīgīr* 3 *d.* 4¼; the Melter 6 *d.* 12½ *j.*; the *Zarrāb* 2 *Rs.* 1 *d.* 0 *j.*; the *Sikkachī* 6 *d.* 12½ *j.*); *secondly*, 10 *d.* 15 *j.*, on account of requisites (viz. 10 *d.* charcoal, and 15 *j.* water); *thirdly*, 50 *Rs.* 13 *d.* 0 *j.*, payable to the *Dīwān*; *fourthly*, 950 Rs., which the merchant gets in exchange for the silver he brought; and *fifthly*, 3 *Rs.* 21 *d.* 10½ *j.*, being the profit of the merchant. If he refines the base silver at his own house, his profit will be much greater; but when he brings it to be coined, his profit cannot be so great.

Of the silver called *lārī* and *shāhī*, and the other above-mentioned baser coins, one rupee buys 1 *t.* 0 *m.* 4 *s.*, so that 950 rupees will buy 989 *t.* 7 *m.* In the *Sabbākī* process, 14 *t* 10 *m.* 1 *s.* burn away, being at the rate of 1½ *t.* per cent.; and in making the ingots, 4 *t.* 11 *m.* 3 *s.* are lost in the fire. The remainder yields 1012 rupees; and from the *khāk-i kharal* 3½ *Rs.* are recoverable. The several items are—*first*, 4 *Rs.* 27 *d.* 24¾ *j.* on account of the wages of the workmen (viz. the Weighman 5 *d.* 7¾ *j.*; the *Sabbāk* 2 *Rs.* 0 *d.* 19 *j.*; the *Qurskob* 4 *d.* 19 *j.*; the *Chāshnīgīr* 3 *d.* 4 *j.*; the Melter 6 *d.* 12½ *j.*; the *Zarrāb* 2 *Rs.* 1 *d.*; the *Sikkachī* 6 *d.* 12½ *j.*); *secondly*, 5 *Rs.* 24 *d.* 15 *j.* for necessaries (viz. 5 *Rs.* 14 *d.* lead; 10 *d.* charcoal, and 15 *j.* water); *thirdly*, 50 *Rs.* 24 *d.*, payable to the State; *fourthly*, 950 *Rs.* which the merchant receives for his silver; *fifthly*, 4 *Rs.* 29 *d.* his profit.[1] Sometimes the merchant gets the silver cheap, when his profit is much larger.

1044 *dāms* buy one *man* of copper, i.e. at the rate of 26 *d.* 2½ *j.* per *ser*. Out of this quantity, one *ser* is burnt away in melting; and as each *ser* yields 30 *dāms*, there are coined altogether 1170 *dāms*, from which the merchant takes his capital, and 18 *d.* 19½ *j.* as profit, 33 *d.* 10 *j.* go to the workmen; and 15 *d.* 8 *j.* for necessaries (viz. 13 *d.* 8 *j.* for charcoal; 1 *d.* for water; and 1 *d.* for clay); 58½ *d.* go to the state.

---

[1] These items added give *Rs.* 1015, 25 *d.* 14¾ *j.*, *i.e.*, a little more than the sum mentioned by Abū 'l-Faẓl (1015 *Rs.* 20 *d.*).

Ā'īn 13.

THE ORIGIN OF METALS.

The Creator by calling into existence the four elements, has raised up wonderful forms. *Fire* is absolutely warm, dry, light; *air* is relatively warm, moist, light; water is relatively cold, moist, heavy; earth is absolutely cold, dry, heavy. Heat is the cause of lightness, and cold of heaviness; moistness easily separates particles, whilst dryness prevents their separation. This wonderful arrangement calls four compounds into existence, *first*, the *āṣār-i ʿulavī*[1]; *secondly*, stones; *thirdly*, plants; *fourthly*, animals. From the heat of the sun, watery particles become lighter, mix with the air, and rise up. Such a mixture is called *bukhār* (gas). From the same cause, earthy particles mix with the air, and rise up. This mixture is called *dukhān* (vapour). Sometimes, however, airy particles mix with the earth. Several philosophers call both of the above mixtures *bukhār*, but distinguish the mixture of watery particles and air by the name of moist, or watery *bukhār*, whilst they call the mixture of earthy particles and air dry *bukhār*, or *dukhānī bukhār* (vapour-like gas). Both mixtures, they say, produce above the surface of the earth, clouds, wind, rain, snow, etc.; and, below the surface of our earth, earthquakes, springs, and minerals. They also look upon the *bukhār* as the body, and upon the *dukhān* as the soul of things. From a difference in their quality and quantity, various bodies are called into existence, as described in books on philosophy.

Minerals are of five kinds: *first*, those which do not melt on account of their dryness, as the *yāqūt*; *secondly*, those which do not melt, on account of their liquidity, as quicksilver; *thirdly*, those which can be melted, being at the same time neither malleable, nor inflammable, as blue stone; *fourthly*, those which can be melted, being, however, not malleable, but inflammable, as sulphur; *fifthly*, those which can be melted, and are malleable, but not inflammable, as gold. A body is said to melt when from the union of the inherent principles of dryness and moisture its particles are movable; and a body is called malleable when we can make it extend in such a manner as to yield a longer and wider surface without, however, either separating a part from it or adding a part to it.

When in a mixture of *bukhār* with *dukhān*, the former is greater in quantity, and when, after their mixture and complete union, the heat of the sun causes the whole to contract, quicksilver will be produced.

---

[1] Or *doings from on high*, as rain, snow, etc.

Since no part of it is destitute of *dukhān*, the dryness is perceptible; hence, on touching it, it does not affect the hand, but flees from it; and since its contraction was produced by heat, no warmth can dissolve it. Again, when in a mixture of *bukhār* and *dukhān*, both are nearly in equal proportion, a tenacious greasy moisture is produced. At the time of fermentation, airy particles enter, when cold causes the whole to contract. This mass is inflammable. If the *dukhān* and the greasiness are a little in excess, sulphur will be produced, in colour either red or yellow, or grey or white. If the proportion of the *dukhān* is large, and that of the grease less, arsenic will result, which is red and yellow. And if the quantity of the *bukhār* is greater, pure, black and yellow naphtha will arise, after the mixture gets solid. Since in all, cold was the cause of the contraction, they can be melted; and on account of the prevalence of greasiness and tenacious moistness, they are also inflammable, though, on account of the moistness, not malleable.

Although quicksilver and sulphur are the only component parts of "the seven bodies", there arise various forms from a difference in purity, or from peculiar circumstances of the mixture, or from a variety of the action of the component parts on each other. Thus *silver* will result, when neither of the two components mixes with earthy particles, when they are pure and become perfectly united, and when the sulphur is white, and less than the quicksilver. Or, when both are in equal proportions and the sulphur red, and capable of colouring, gold will originate. Again, under similar circumstances, if both contract after the mixture, but before a complete union has been effected, *khārchīnī* will be produced. This body is also called *Āhanchīnī*, and seems really to be raw gold; some say, it is a kind of copper. Again, if only the sulphur be impure, and the quicksilver the larger component, with an additional power of burning, copper will result. And if the mixture be not thorough, and the quicksilver larger, tin will be produced; some say that purity of the components is essential. If both compounds be of an inferior kind, closely mixed, and if the earthy particles of the quicksilver have a tendency of separating, and the power of burning be inherent in the sulphur, iron will result. And if under similar conditions the intermixture be not perfect, and the quicksilver quantitatively larger, lead will come into existence. These seven metals are called the *seven bodies*; and quicksilver has the name of *the mother of the bodies*, and sulphur, *the father of the bodies*. Quicksilver is also denominated *the spirit*, and arsenic and sulphur the *pivots of life*.

Jast (pewter),[1] which, according to the opinions of some, is *Rūḥ-i*

[[1] Or zinc ?—P.]

tūtiyā, and resembles lead, is nowhere mentioned in philosophical books, but there is a mine of it in Hindustan, in the territory of *Jālor*, which is a dependency of the Ṣūba of Ājmīr. Some practical mechanics[1] are of opinion that the metal called *riṣāṣ* is a silver in the state of leprosy, and quicksilver a silver in the state of apoplexy; that lead is gold apoplectic and burnt, and bronze crude gold; and that the chemist, like the doctor, can restore these diseased metals by the principles of similarity and opposition.

Practical men form of the above seven bodies, several compounds, used for ornaments, vessels, etc. Among them I may mention: 1. *Safīdrū*, which the people of Hindustan call *kā̃sī*. It is a mixture of 4 sers of copper to 1 ser of tin, melted together. 2. *Rūy*, 4 sers of copper to 1½ sers of lead. It is called in this country *bhangār*. 3. *Brass*, which the Hindūs call *pītal*, is made in three ways: *first*, 2½ sers copper to 1 ser *rūḥ-i tūtiyā*, which is malleable, when cold; *secondly*, 2 sers of copper to 1 ser of *rūḥ-i tūtiyā*, which is malleable, when heated; *thirdly*, 2 sers of copper to 1 ser of *rūḥ-i tūtiyā*, not worked with the hammer, but by casting. 4. *Sīm-i sūkhta*, composed of lead, silver, and bronze; it has a black lustre, and is used in painting. 5. *Haft-josh*, which, like the *Khārchīnī*, is nowhere to be found; it is said to consist of six metals. Some call it *ṭālīqūn*, whilst others give this name to common copper. 6. *Ashṭdhāt*, a compound of eight metals, viz. the six of the *haftjosh*, *rūḥ-i tūtiyā*, and *kā̃sī*. It is also made of seven compounds. 7. *Kaulpatr*, 2 sers of *safīdrū*, and 1 ser of copper. It is coloured, and looks well, and belongs to the inventions of his Majesty.[2]

Āʾīn 14.

ON SPECIFIC GRAVITY.

It has been said above that various compounds result from a mixture of *bukhār* and *dukhān*, which themselves consist of light and heavy elements. Besides, *bukhār* is *wet* or *dry*; and a complete union of the two sets in, sometimes before and after the mixture, and sometimes in either of these conditions. It is on this account that a compound whose fiery and airy particles are more numerous than its watery and earthy particles is lighter than a mineral in which there are more watery and earthy particles; and likewise, every mineral in which the *bukhār* predominates

---

[1] According to some MSS., the Hindūs.

[2] This phrase seems to mean that the invention was made at the time of Akbar.

over the *dukhān* is lighter than a mineral, in which the opposite is the case. Again, a mineral in which the complete union of the *bukhār* and *dukhān* has set in, is heavier than one which has not reached this degree, because the interstices between the particles, and the entering of air, make a body large and light. Bearing this in mind, we have a means of discovering the weight and lightness of every body. Some one,[1] now long ago dead, has expressed the weight of several bodies in verses (metre *Mujtaṣṣ*) :—

Z' rū-yi juṣṣa-yi haftād u yak diram sīmab,
Chil o shash ast, u z' arzīz siy u hasht shumār,
Ẕahab ṣad ast surb panjah u nuh, āhan chil,
Birinj o mis chihil o panj, nuqra panjah u chār.

"Quicksilver[2] is 71 ; Rūy is 46 ; Tin is 38 ; Gold 100 ; Lead 59 ; Iron 40 ; Brass and Copper 45 ; Silver 54." Others have expressed the numbers by mnemo-technical words in rhyme (metre *Ramal*) :—

Nuh filizz-i mustawiyy^u 'l ḥajm rā chūn bar-kashī,
Ikhtilāf-i wazn dārad har yak-ī bī ishtibāh.
Zar lakan, zībaq alam, usrub dahan, arzīz ḥal,
Fiẓẓa nad, āhan yak-ī, miss u shabuh mah, rūy māh.

"If you weigh equal volumes of the following *nine* metals, you will doubtlessly find their different weights as follows : gold *lakan*,[3] quicksilver *alam*, lead *dahan*, tin *ḥal*, silver *nad*, iron *yakī*, copper and brass *mah*, rūy *māh*." If of these nine metals, pieces be taken of equal dimensions, their weights will be different. Some sages ascribe this variety in weight to the difference in the qualitative constitution of the bodies, and trace to it their lightness or heaviness, their floating or sinking in water, and their weights as indicated by common and hydrostatic balances. Several deep-sighted philosophers compute the weight of bodies with a reference to water. They fill a suitable vessel with water, and throw into it 100 *misqāls* of each metal ; and from the quantities of water thrown out upon the introduction of the metals, are found the differences between them in volume and weight. The greater the quantity of the water which 100 *misqāls* of a body displace, the greater is its volume and the less its weight,

[1] *Abū Naṣr-i Farāhī*, of Farāh, a town in Sijistān. His real name is Muḥammad Badr^u 'd-Dīn. He has written a Vocabulary in rhyme, entitled *Niṣāb^u 's-Ṣibyān*, which for centuries has been read in nearly every Madrasa of Persia and India ; *vide Journal As. Soc. Bengal*, for 1868, p. 7.

[2] We fix the specific gravities as follows : *Gold* 19·26 ; *Mercury* 13·6 ; *Lead* 11·325 ; *Silver* 10·47 ; *Copper* 9 ; *Tin* 7·32 ; *Iron* 7·7, for which numbers water is unity. Abū 'l-Faẓl takes gold as standard ; and assuming, for his values, 19·26 as its specific gravity, we would get, *Mercury* 13·87 ; *Lead* 11·36 ; *Silver* 10·40 ; *Copper* 8·67 ; *Iron* 7·76 ; *Tin* 7·32 ; *Rūy* 8·86.

[3] The Arabic consonants of the mnemo-technical words *lakan*, *alam*, etc., represent numbers ; thus, $l + k + n = 30 + 20 + 50$; $a + l + m = 1 + 30 + 40$; etc.

and reversely. Thus 100 *m*. of silver displace $9\frac{3}{8}$ *m.* of water, and the same quantity of gold, $5\frac{1}{4}$ *m.* If the weight of the water displaced by a body be subtracted from its weight in air, its weight in water will be found. The scales of the air-balance are both suspended in air; those of the hydrostatic balance are both on the surface of the water. As the heavier body possesses the greater power for sinking, it will, in any case, move in the direction of the perpendicular; but, if either of the two scales be on the surface of the water, and the other in the air, the latter scale, although perhaps the lighter, will necessarily sink, as air, being a finer substance than water, does not offer so much resistance. A body will sink in water if the quantity of water displaced by it be less than the weight of the body, and a body will float if that quantity be greater; and if the water displaced be equal to the weight of the body, its upper side will coincide with the surface of the water. *Abū Rayḥān* [1] has drawn up a table which I shall insert here.

Quantity of water displaced by 100 *misqāls of*	*Misqāl.*	*Dāng.*	*Tassūj.*	*Apparent weight* (*weight in water*) *of* 100 *misqāls of*	*Misqāl.*	*Dāng.*	*Tassūj.*
Gold,[2]	5	1	2	Gold, ...	95	4	2
Quicksilver, ...	7	2	1	Quicksilver, ...	92	3	3
Lead, ...	8	5	3	Lead, ...	91	1	3
Silver, ...	9	4	1	Silver, ...	90	1	3
Rūy, ...	11	2	3	*Rūy*, ...	88	4	3
Copper, ...	11	3	3	Copper, ...	88	3	3
Brass, ...	11	4	3	Brass, ...	88	2	3
Iron, ...	12	5	2	Iron, ...	87	3	2
Tin, ...	13	4	3	Tin, ...	86	2	3
Yāqūt (light blue),	25	1	2	*Yāqūt* (light blue).	74	4	2
Yāqūt (red), ...	26	3	3	*Yāqūt* (red), ...	74	3	3
Ruby (*laʿl*), ...	27	5	2	Ruby (*laʿl*), ...	72	3	2
Zumurrud, ...	36	2	3	*Zumurrud*, ...	63	4	3
Pearl, ...	37	1	3	Pearl, ...	62	5	3
Lapis lazuli, ...	38	3	3	Lapis lazuli, ...	61	3	3
Cornelian, ...	38	3	3	Cornelian, ...	61	3	3
Amber, ...	39	3	3	Amber, ...	60	3	3
Bullūr, ...	40	3	3	*Bullūr*, ...	60	3	3

[1 ابو ريحان بيروني.—P.]

2 With the exception of *Quicksilver*, *Silver*, and *Yāqūt* (*light blue*), the numbers given in the MSS., and the above list, are slightly wrong, because the sum of the weights of the water displaced and the apparent weight, ought to give 100 *misqāls* (1 *m.* = 6 *d.*; 1 *d.* = 4 *t.*). But in most items there is an excess of *one dāng*.

The weight (in air) of the under-mentioned metals, the volume of 100 misqāls of gold being taken as the unit of volume.

	Misqāl.	*Dāng.*	*Tassūj.*
Gold, ...	100	0	0
Quicksilver, ...	71	1	1
Lead, ...	59	2	2
Silver, ...	54	3	3
Rūy, ...	46	2	3
Copper, ...	45	3	3
Brass, ...	45	3	5
Iron, ...	40	0	0
Tin, ...	38	2	2

The weight (in air) of the under-mentioned precious stones, the volume of 100 misqāls of the blue yāqūt being taken as the unit of volume.

	Misqāl.	*Dāng.*	*Tassūj.*
Yāqūt (light blue),	94	3	3
Yāqūt (red), ...	94	3	3
Ruby, ...	90	2	3
Zumurrud, ...	69	3	3
Pearls, ...	67	5	2
Lapis lazuli, ...	65	3	2
(?)Cornelian, ...	64	4	2
Amber, ...	64	3	1
Bullūr	63	3	3

Āʾīn 15.

THE IMPERIAL HAREM.

His Majesty is a great friend of good order and propriety in business. Through order, the world becomes a meadow of truth and reality; and that which is but external, receives through it a spiritual meaning. For this reason, the large number of women [1]—a vexatious question even for great statesmen—furnished his Majesty with an opportunity to display his wisdom, and to rise from the low level of worldly dependence to the eminence of perfect freedom. The imperial palace and household are therefore in the best order.

His Majesty forms matrimonial alliances with princes of Hindustan, and of other countries; and secures by these ties of harmony the peace of the world.

As the sovereign, by the light of his wisdom, has raised fit persons from the dust of obscurity, and appointed them to various offices, so does he also elevate faithful persons to the several ranks in the service of the seraglio. Short-sighted men think of impure gold, which will gradually turn into pure gold; [2] but the far-sighted know that his Majesty understands how to use elixirs [3] and chemical processes. Any kind of growth

---

[[1] پردگیان.—P.]

[2] So according to the opinion of the philosophers of the Middle Ages.

[3] Elixirs change *quickly* that which is worthless into pure gold.

will alter the constitution of a body; copper and iron will turn to gold, and tin and lead to silver; hence it is no matter of astonishment if an excellent being changes the worthless into men. "The saying of the wise is true that the eye of the exalted is the elixir for producing goodness." Such also are the results flowing from the love of order of his Majesty, from his wisdom, insight, regard to rank, his respect for others, his activity, his patience. Even when he is angry, he does not deviate from the right path; he looks at everything with kindly feelings, weighs rumours well, and is free from all prejudice; he considers it a great blessing to have the good wishes of the people, and does not allow the intoxicating pleasures of this world to overpower his calm judgment.

His Majesty has made a large enclosure with fine buildings inside, where he reposes. Though there are more than five thousand women, he has given to each a separate apartment. He has also divided them into sections, and keeps them attentive to their duties. Several chaste women have been appointed as *dāroghas,* and superintendents over each section, and one has been selected for the duties of writer. Thus, as in the imperial offices, everything is here also in proper order. The salaries are sufficiently liberal. Not counting the presents, which his Majesty most generously bestows, the women of the highest rank receive from 1610 to 1028 Rs. *per mensem.* Some of the servants have from 51 to 20, others from 40 to 2 Rs. Attached to the private audience hall of the palace is a clever and zealous writer, who superintends the expenditure of the Harem, and keeps an account of the cash and the stores. If a woman wants anything, within the limit of her salary, she applies to one of the *Taḥwīldārs* (cash-keepers) of the seraglio. The *Taḥwīldār* then sends a memorandum to the writer, who checks it, when the General Treasurer makes the payment in cash, as for claims of this nature no cheques are given.

The writer also makes out an estimate of the annual expenditure, writes out summarily a receipt, which is countersigned by the ministers of the state. It is then stamped with a peculiar imperial seal, which is only used in grants connected with the Harem, when the receipt becomes payable. The money itself is paid by the cash-keeper of the General Treasury to the General *Taḥwīldār,* who on the order of the writer of the Harem, hands it over to the several Sub-*Taḥwīldārs* for distribution among the servants of the seraglio. All moneys are reckoned in their salaries at the current rate.[1]

The inside of the Harem is guarded by sober and active women; the

---

[1] At 40 *dāms per rupee.*

most trustworthy of them are placed about the apartments of his Majesty. Outside the enclosure the eunuchs are placed; and at a proper distance, there is a guard of faithful *Rājpūts*, beyond whom are the porters of the gates. Besides, on all four sides, there are guards of Nobles, *Aḥadīs*, and other troops, according to their ranks.

Whenever *Begams*, or the wives of nobles, or other women of chaste character, desire to be presented, they first notify their wish to the servants of the seraglio, and wait for a reply. From thence they send their request to the officers of the palace, after which those who are eligible are permitted to enter the Harem. Some women of rank obtain permission to remain there for a whole month.

Notwithstanding the great number of faithful guards, his Majesty does not dispense with his own vigilance, but keeps the whole in proper order.

Āʿīn 16.

THE ENCAMPMENT ON JOURNEYS.[1]

It would be difficult to describe a large encampment; but I shall say something on the equipage used for hunting parties and short journeys.

1. The *Gulāl-bār* is a grand enclosure, the invention of his Majesty, the doors of which are made very strong, and secured with locks and keys. It is never less than one hundred yards square.[2] At its eastern end a pavilion of two entrances is erected, containing 54 divisions, 24 yards long and 14 broad; and in the middle there stands a large *chūbīn rā,oṭī*,[3] and round about it a *sarā-parda*.[3] Adjoining to the *chūbīn*, they built up a two-storied pavilion, in which his Majesty performs divine worship, and from the top of which, in the morning, he receives the compliments of the nobility. No one connected with the seraglio enters this building without special leave. Outside of it, twenty-four *chūbīn rā,oṭīs* are erected, 10 yards long and 6 yards wide, each separated by a canvas, where the favourite women reside. There are also other pavilions and tents for the servants, with *sāyabāns*[4] of gold embroidery, brocade, and velvet. Adjoining to this is a *sarā-parda* of carpet, 60 yards square, within which a few tents are erected, the place for the *Urdū-begīs*,[5] and other female

---

[[1] In text یورشها. *Yūrish*, properly means "attack, assault". *Yūrish-hā* seems to mean here "military expeditions.—P.]

[[2] صد گز در صد گز.—P.]

[3] Described in the twenty-first *Aʿīn*.

[4] Awnings.

[5] Armed women.

servants. Farther on up to the private audience hall, there is a fine open space, 150 yards long and 100 yards broad, called the *Mahtābī*; and on both sides of it, a screen is set up as before described, which is supported by poles 6 yards long, fixed in the ground at distances of two yards. The poles are one yard in the ground, and are ornamented with brass knobs on the top, and kept firm by two ropes, one passing inside and the other outside of the enclosure. The guards watch here, as has been described.

In the midst of the plain is a raised platform,[1] which is protected by an awning, or *Nam-gīra*, supported by four poles. This is the place where his Majesty sits in the evening, and none but those who are particularly favoured are here admitted. Adjoining to the *Gulāl-bār*, there is a circular enclosure, consisting of twelve divisions, each of thirty yards, the door of the enclosure opening into the *Mahtābī*; and in the midst of it is a *Chūbīn rā,oṭī*, ten yards long, and a tent containing forty divisions, over which twelve awnings are spread, each of twelve yards, and separated by canvases.[2] This place, in every division of which a convenient closet is constructed, is called *Ibachkī*,[3] which is the (*Chaghatā*ʼ*ī*) name used by his Majesty. Adjoining to this a *Sarā-parda* is being put up, 150 yards in length and breadth, containing sixteen divisions, of thirty-six square yards, the *Sarā-parda* being, as before, sustained by poles with knobs. In the midst of it, the state-hall is erected, by means of a thousand carpets; it contains seventy-two rooms, and has an opening fifteen yards wide. A tent-like covering, or *Qalandarī*, made of wax-cloth, or any other lighter material, is spread over it, which affords protection against the rain and the sun; and round about it, are fifty awnings, of twelve yards each. The pavilion, which serves as *Dīwān-i khāṣṣ* or private audience hall, has proper doors and locks. Here the nobles and the officers of the army, after having obtained leave through the *Bakhshīs*,[4] pass before the Emperor, the list of officers eligible for admission being changed on the first of every month. The place is decorated, both inside and outside with carpets of various colours, and resembles a beautiful flower-bed. Outside of it, to a distance of 350 yards, ropes are drawn, fastened to poles, which are set up at a distance of three yards from each other. Watchmen are stationed about them. This is the *Dīwān-i*ʼ*Āmm*, or public audience hall, round which, as above described,

---

[1] As may be still seen in the ruins of Fatḥpūr Sīkrī.

[[2] قنات "tent-wall".—P.]

[[3] In text *ibachkī-khānd.*—P.]

[4] Paymasters. The Commanding Officers were at the same time paymasters, as they collected the rents of the lands assigned to them for the payment of their contingents.

the various guards are placed. At the end of this place, at a distance of twelve *tanābs*[1] is the *Naqqāra Khāna*,[2] and in the midst of the area the *Ākās-diya*[3] is lighted up.

Some encampments, as just now described, are sent off, and one of them is put up by the *Farrāshes* on a piece of ground which the *Mīr Manzils*[4] have selected as an eligible spot, whilst the other camp furniture is sent in advance, to await the approach of his Majesty. Each encampment requires for its carriage 100 elephants, 500 camels, 400 carts, and 100 bearers. It is escorted by 500 troopers, *Manṣabdars*,[5] *Aḥadīs*. Besides, there are employed a thousand *Farrāshes*, natives of Īrān, Tūrān, and Hindustān, 500 pioneers, 100 water-carriers, 50 carpenters, tent-makers, and torch-bearers, 30 workers in leather, and 150 sweepers.

The monthly pay of the foot varies from 240 to 130 *dāms*.

Āʾīn 17.

THE ENCAMPMENT OF THE ARMY.

Although his Majesty but rarely collects his armies, a large number of troops accompany him in whatever direction an expedition may go; but a considerable number, in every province, are employed on various services, and are not allowed to follow him. On account of the crowding of camp-followers, and the number of the troops themselves, it would take a soldier days to find his tent; and how much worse would it be for a stranger? His Majesty has invented an admirable method of encamping his troops, which is a source of much comfort to them. On an open ground they pitch the imperial seraglio, the audience hall, and the *Naqāra-khāna*, all occupying a space the length of which is 1530 yards. To the right and left, and behind, is an open space of 360 yards, which no one but the guards is allowed to enter. Within it, at a distance of 100 yards to the left[6] and centre are the tents of Maryam Makān,[7] and Gulbadan Begum, and other chaste ladies, and the tents of Prince Dāniyāl; to the

[[1] طناب شصت گزی.—P.]

[2] A turret on the top of which the band plays. Regarding the *tanāb*, *vide* the tenth *Āʾīn* of the third book.

[3] A high pole to the top of which an immense lamp is fixed. *Vide* p. 50.

[4] Quartermasters.

[5] Grandees.

[[6] *Qol*, M. is said to be the *centre* of an army in battle array.—P.]

[7] *Maryam Makānī* (*i.e.*, dwelling with the Virgin Mary, who together with Āsiyah, the wife of Pharaoh, Khadīja, Muḥammad's first wife, and Fāṭimah, his daughter, are the four *perfect* women of Islām) is the title of Akbar's mother. Her name was *Ḥamīda Bānū Begum*; *vide* Badāonī, ed. Bibl. Ind. i, p. 437. Gulbadan Begum (*i.e.*, Lady Rose-body) appears to be the name of one of Akbar's favourite wives. [No, his aunt.—B.]

right, those of Prince Sulṭān Salīm, and to the left, those of Prince Shāh Murād. Behind their tents, at some distance, the offices and workshops are placed, and at a further distance of 30 yards behind them, at the four corners of the camp, the bāzārs. The nobles are encamped without on all sides, according to their rank.

The guards for Thursday, Friday, and Saturday encamp in the centre ; those for Sunday and Monday, on the right ; and those for Tuesday and Wednesday, on the left.

Āʾīn 18.

ON ILLUMINATIONS.

His Majesty maintains that it is a religious duty and divine praise to worship fire and light ; surly, ignorant men consider this forgetfulness of the Almighty, and fire-worship. But the deep-sighted know better. As the external form of the worship of "the select",[1] is based upon propriety, and as people think the neglect of some sort of worship abominable, there can be nothing improper in the veneration of that exalted element which is the source of man's existence, and of the duration of his life ; nor should base thoughts enter such a matter.

How beautifully has Shaykh Sharfᵘ 'd-Dīn [2] said : "What can be done with a man who is not satisfied with the lamp when the sun is down ? " Every flame is derived from that fountain of divine light (the sun), and bears the impression of its holy essence. If light and fire did not exist, we should be destitute of food and medicines ; the power of sight would be of no avail to the eyes. The fire of the sun is the torch of God's sovereignty.

At noon of the day, when the sun enters the 19th degree of Aries, the whole world being then surrounded by his light, they expose a round piece of a white and shining stone, called in Hindī *Sūrajkrānt*, to the rays of the sun. A piece of cotton is then held near it, which catches fire from the heat of the stone. This celestial fire is committed to the care of proper persons. The lamp-lighters, torch-bearers, and cooks of the household, use it for their offices ; and when the year has passed away in happiness, they renew the fire. The vessel in which this fire is preserved, is called *Agingir*, i.e. fire-pot.

---

[1] The members of the *Divine Faith*.

[2] This famous saint died in the beginning of the fifteenth century. Munair is a town in Bahār ; *vide Journal As. Soc. Bengal*, 1868, p. 7, l. 3, from below, and the biographies of Indian Saints in the fourth book. His works are to be found among the Persian MSS. of the Society's Library.

There is also a shining white stone, called *Chandrkrānt*, which, upon being exposed to the beams of the moon, drips water.

Every afternoon, one *gharī* [1] before sunset, his Majesty, if riding, alights, or, if sleeping, he is awakened. He then lays aside the splendour of royalty, and brings his external appearance in harmony with his heart. And when the sun sets, the attendants light twelve white candles,[2] on twelve candlesticks of gold and silver, and bring them before his Majesty, when a singer of sweet melodies, with a candle in his hand, sings a variety of delightful airs to the praise of God, beginning and concluding with a prayer for the continuance of this auspicious reign. His Majesty attaches the utmost importance to praise and prayer, and earnestly asks God for renewed light.

It is impossible to describe the beauty and various forms of the candle. sticks and shades, and to give an account of the offices of the workmen. Some of the candlesticks weigh ten *mans* and upwards, and are adorned with various designs; some single, others of two branches and more: they give light to the internal eye. His Majesty has invented a candlestick, one yard high. Five others are placed on the top of it, and each is adorned with the figure of an animal. White wax candles, three yards and upwards in length, are cast for it, so that a ladder is required to snuff it. Besides there are everywhere flambeaux,[3] both inside and outside, which increase the light very much. The first, second, and third nights of every lunar month, when there is moonlight but for a short time, eight wicks are used;[4] from the fourth to the tenth, they decrease one in number every night, so that on the tenth night, when the moon is very bright, one is sufficient; and they continue in this state till the fifteenth, and increase one wick every day from the sixteenth to the nineteenth. For the twentieth night the number is the same as on the nineteenth; on the twenty-first and twenty-second they increase one daily; the twenty-third is the same as the twenty-second; and from the twenty-fourth to the last, eight wicks are lighted up. They allow for every wick one ser of oil, and half a ser of cotton. In some places there are fat-burners, where grease is burnt instead of oil. The allowance varies according to the size of the wick.

In order to render the royal camp conspicuous to those who come from far, his Majesty has caused to be erected, in front of the Durbār, a pole upwards of forty yards high, which is supported by sixteen ropes;

[1] One *gharī* = 24 minutes.

[[2] كافوري شمعها, *i.e.*, wax candles.—P.]

[3] Oil-burners with several wicks are very common in India.

[4] For each flambeau.

and on the top of the pole is a large lantern, which they call *Ākās-diya*.[1] Its light, seen from great distances, guides the soldiers to the imperial camp, and helps them to find their tents. In former times, before the lamp was erected, the men had to suffer hardships from not being able to find the road.

In this department Manṣabdārs, Aḥadīs, and other troops are employed. The allowance of a foot soldier never exceeds 2400, and is never less than 80 *dāms*.

Aʾīn 19.

THE ENSIGNS OF ROYALTY.

The *Shamsa*[2] of the arch of royalty is a divine light, which God directly transfers to kings, without the assistance of men; and kings are fond of external splendour, because they consider it an image of the Divine glory. I shall mention some of the insignia used at present.

1. The *Awrang*, or throne, is made of several forms; some are inlaid with precious stones, and others are made of gold, silver, etc. 2. The *Chatr*, or umbrella, is adorned with the most precious jewels, of which there are never less than seven. 3. The *Sāya-bān* is of an oval form, a yard in length, and its handle, like that of the umbrella, is covered with brocade and ornamented with precious stones. One of the attendants holds it, to keep off the rays of the sun. It is also called *Āftābgīr*. 4. The *Kawkaba*,[3] of which several are hung up before the assembly hall.

These four insignia are used by kings only.

5. The *ʿAlam*, or standard. When the king rides out, not less than five of these are carried along with the *Qūr*,[4] wrapped up in scarlet cloth bags. On days of festivity, and in battle, they are unfurled. 6. The *Chatrtoq*, a kind of *ʿAlam*, but smaller than it, is adorned with the tails of Thibetan yaks. 7. The *Tumantoq* is like the *Chatrtoq*, but longer. Both insignia are flags of the highest dignity, and the latter is bestowed upon great nobles only. 8. The *Jhanḍā* is an Indian flag. The *Qūr* necessarily contains a flag of each kind; but on great occasions many are displayed.

Of musical instruments used in the *Naqārahkhāna*, I may mention, 1. *the Kuwarga*, commonly called *damāma*; there are eighteen pair of

---

[1] From *Ākās* sky, and *diya* lamp. The Ākāsdiya is also mentioned by *Bernier*.

[2] *Shamsa* is a picture of the sun affixed to the gates or walls of the palaces of kings. At night these pictures are illuminated.

[3] *Vide* the plates.

[4] The *Qūr* is a collection of flags, arms, and other insignia, which follow the king wherever he goes.

Pl. VII

1
2.
3.
4.
6
8
15

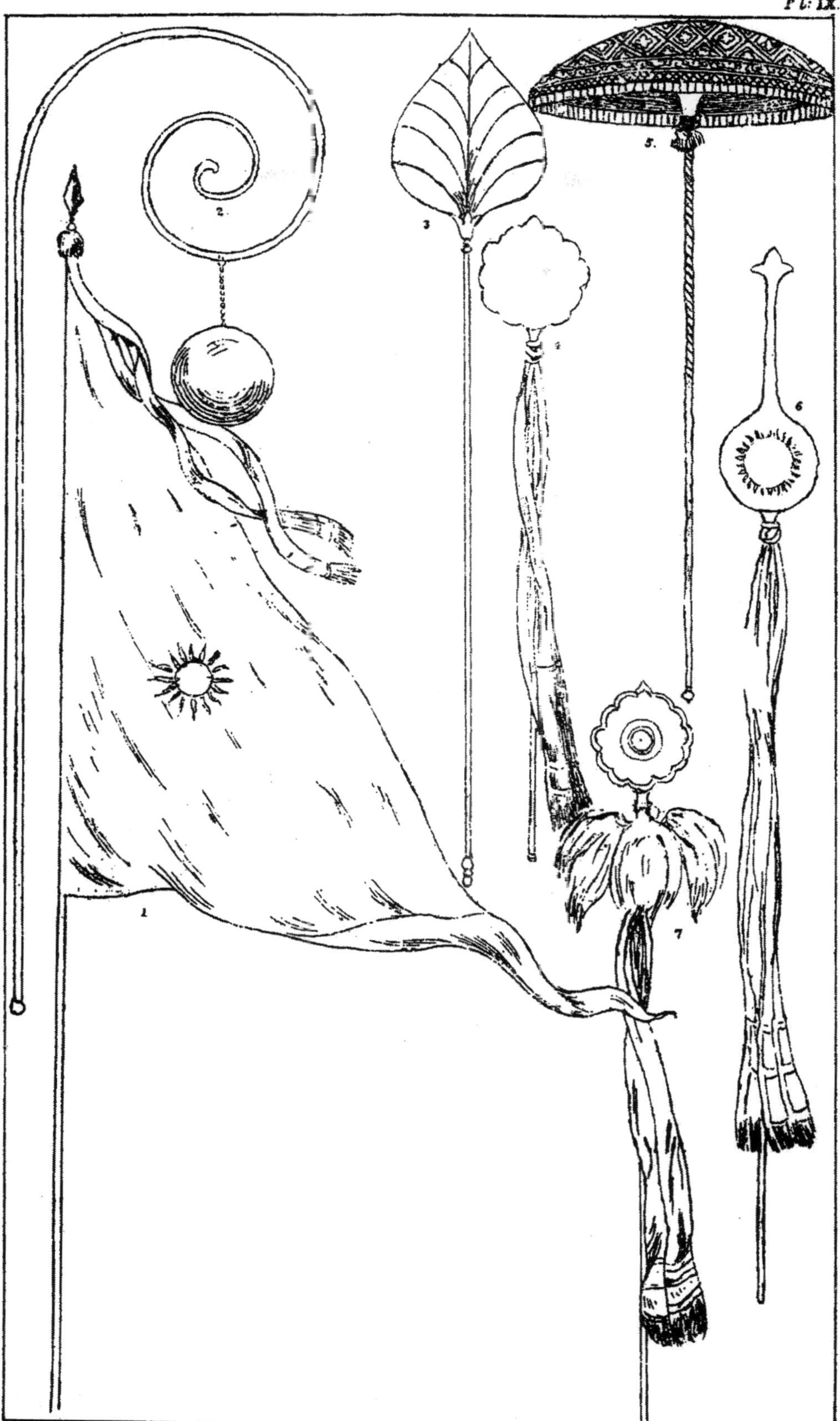
1
2
3
4
5.
6
7

them more or less ; and they give a deep sound. 2. *The naqāra*, twenty pair, more or less. 3. *The duhul,* of which four are used. 4. The *Karnā*[1] is made of gold, silver, brass, and other metals, and they never blow fewer than four. 5. *The surnā* of the Persian and Indian kinds ; they blow nine together. 6. The *nafīr,* of the Persian, European, and Indian kinds ; they blow some of each kind. 7. The *sing* is of brass and made in the form of a cow's horn ; they blow two together. 8. The *sanj*, or cymbal, of which three pair are used.

Formerly the band played four *gharīs* before the commencement of the night, and likewise four *gharīs* before daybreak ; now they play first at midnight, when the sun commences his ascent, and the second time at dawn. One *gharī* before sunrise, the musicians commence to blow the *surnā*, and wake up those that are asleep ; and one *gharī* after sunrise, they play a short prelude, when they beat the *kuwarga* a little, whereupon they blow the *karnā,* the *nafīr,* and the other instruments, without, however, making use of the *naqāra* ; after a little pause the *surnās* are blown again, the time of the music being indicated by the *nafīrs.* One hour later the *naqāras* commence, when all musicians raise "the auspicious strain."[2] After this they go through the following seven performances. 1. The *Mursalī,* which is the name of a tune played by the *mursil* ; and afterwards the *bardāsht,* which consists likewise of certain tunes, played by the whole band. This is followed by a pianissimo, and a crescendo passing over into a diminuendo ; 2. The playing of the four tunes, called *ikhlāṭī, ibtidā*ʿ*ī, shīrāzī, qalandarī nigar qaṭra,*[3] or *nukhūd qaṭra,* which occupies an hour. 3. The playing of the old[4] Khwārizmite tunes. Of these his Majesty has composed more than two hundred, which are the delight of young and old, especially the tunes *Jalālshāhī, Mahāmīr karkat* (?), and the *Nawrozī.* 4. The swelling play of the cymbals. 5. The playing of *Bā miyān dawr.* 6. The passing into the tunes *azfar*, also called *rāh-i bālā*, after which comes a pianissimo. 7. The Khwārizmite tunes, played by the *Mursil,* after which he passes into the *mursalī* ; he then pauses, and commences the blessings on his Majesty, when the whole band strikes up a pianissimo. Then follows the reading of beautiful sentences and poems. This also lasts for an hour. Afterwards the *surnā-*

[1] Or Karranā. [In text *karnā.*—P.]

[2] Probably blessings on his Majesty.

[3] Several of these names of melodies are unclear, and will in all probability remain so. Perhaps the words *shīrāzī qalandarī,* "a hermit of Shīrāz," belong to each other. *Nigar qaṭra* means, *behold the tear.* [*Qalandar* is a kind of *wandering* dervish of wild appearance.—P.]

[[4] In text "old and new."—P.]

players perform for another hour, when the whole comes to a proper conclusion.

His Majesty has such a knowledge of the science of music as trained musicians do not possess; and he is likewise an excellent hand in performing, especially on the *naqāra*.

Manṣabdārs, Aḥadīs, and other troops are employed in this department. The monthly pay of a foot-soldier does not exceed 340 and is not less than 74 *dāms*.

Āʿīn 20.

THE ROYAL SEALS.

Seals are used in the three [1] branches of the Government; in fact every man requires them in his transactions.[2] In the beginning of the present reign, Mawlānā Maqṣūd, the seal-engraver, cut in a circular form upon a surface of steel, in the *rīqāʿ* character, the name of his Majesty, and those of his illustrious ancestors up to Timūrlang; and afterwards he cut another similar seal, in the *nastaʿlīq* character, only with his Majesty's name. For judicial transactions a second kind of seal was made, *miḥrābī* in form,[3] which had the following verse round the name of his Majesty :—

Rāstī mūjib-i riẓā-yi khudāst kas nadīdam ki gum shud az rāh-ī rāst.

" Uprightness is the means of pleasing God; I never saw any one lost in the straight road."

Tamkīn made a new seal of the second kind; and afterwards Mawlānā ʿAlī Aḥmad of Dihlī improved both. The round small seal goes by the (*chaghatāʾī*) name of *Uzuk*, and is used for *farmān-i sabtīs*; [4] and the large one, into which he cut the names of the ancestors of his Majesty, was at first only used for letters to foreign kings, but nowadays for both. For other orders a square seal is used, engraved with the words *Allāhᵘ Akbar jallᵃ jalālahū*, whilst another of a peculiar stamp is used for all matters connected with the seraglio. For the seals attached to *farmāns*, another stamp is used of various forms.

Of seal-engravers I shall mention

1. *Mawlānā Maqṣūd of Hirāt,* one of the servants of Humāyūn, who writes well the *rīqāʿ* and *nastaʿlīq* characters. The astrolabe, globes, and

---

[1] Corresponding to the threefold division of the *Āʿīn-i Akbarī.*

[2] The word *muhr,* a seal, means also a *stamp,* and generally, the *signature of a man.* We *sign* documents, Orientals stamp their names to them. Sealing wax is rarely used on account of the climate; a tenacious black liquid, or the juice of the *Bhelā* nut is preferred. [The marking-nut tree commonly called *bhilāwā.*—P.]

[3] *Vide* note p. 30.

Vide the eleventh *Āʿīn* of the second book.

Pl. X

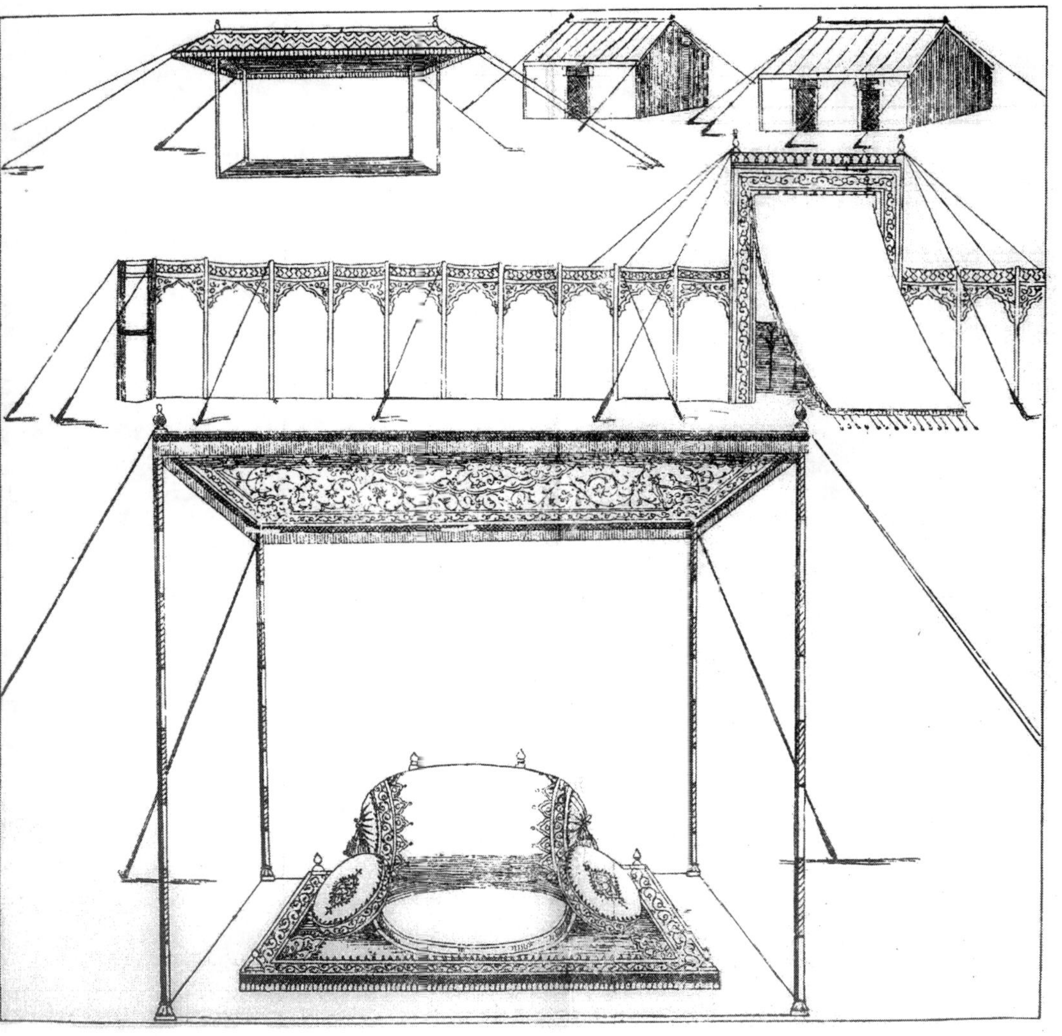

Pl. XI

various *mistars*[1] which he made, were much admired by people of experience. The patronage of his Majesty perfected his art.

2. *Tamkīn of Kābul.* He was educated in his native country, and brought his art to such a perfection as to excite the jealousy of the preceding engraver, whom he surpassed in the *nastaʿlīq.*

3. *Mīr Dost of Kābul.* He cuts both the *rīqāʿ* and *nastaʿlīq* characters in cornelian. He does not come up to the preceding artists. His *riqāʿ* is better than his *nastaʿlīq.* He also understands assaying.

4. *Mawlānā Ibrāhīm.* In the art of cutting cornelians he is the pupil of his brother Sharaf of Yazd. He surpasses the ancient engravers; and it is impossible to distinguish his *riqāʿ* and *nastaʿlīq* from the masterpieces of the best calligraphers. He engraved the words *laʿl jalālī,* or the glorious ruby, upon all imperial rubies of value.

5. *Mawlānā ʿAlī Aḥmad*[2] of Dihlī who, according to all calligraphers, stands unsurpassed as a steel-engraver, so much so that his engravings are used as copies. His *nastaʿlīq* is charming; but he writes also other characters as well. He learned the trade from his father Shaykh Ḥusayn, studied the manner of Mawlānā Maqṣūd, and eventually surpassed all.

Āʾīn 21.

THE FARRĀSH KHĀNA.

His Majesty considers this department[3] as an excellent dwelling-place, a shelter from heat and cold, a protector against the rain, as the ornament of royalty. He looks upon its efficiency as one of the insignia of a ruler, and therefore considers the care bestowed upon it as a part of Divine worship. The department has been much improved, both in the quality and the quantity of the stores, and also by the introduction of new fashions. I shall mention a few particulars as specimens for future enquirers.

1. The *Bārgāh,* when large, is able to contain more than ten thousand

[1] Copyists take a piece a pasteboard of the same size as the paper on which they write. Then they draw two parallel vertical lines, each about an inch from the two vertical sides of the pasteboard. Along these lines they make small holes at equal intervals, and draw a string from the first hole at the left hand to the first hole of the right of the pasteboard. Similarly, the two second holes are joined, and so on, care being taken that the horizontal strings are parallel. This contrivance is called *mistar,* from *saṭar,* a line. The copyist then puts the blank sheets on the top of the *mistar,* and presses on them with the hands, when the strings will leave marks on the paper sufficiently clear to prevent the writer from writing crookedly.

[2] *Niẓām* of Hirāt, in his Ṭabaqāt-i Akbarī, mentions him among the contemporaneous Persian poets, and gives a few of his verses.

[[3] کارخانه.—P.]

people. It takes a thousand *farrāshes*, a week to erect with the help of machines. There are generally two door poles, fastened with hinges. If plain (i.e. without brocade, velvet, or gold ornaments) a *bārgāh* costs 10,000 rupees and upwards, whilst the price of one full of ornaments is unlimited. The price of others may be estimated from the price of a plain one. 2. The *Chūbīn rāwaṭī* is raised on ten pillars. They go a little into the ground, and are of equal height, with the exception of two, which are a little higher, as the crossbeam rests upon them. The pillars have, above and below, a *dāsa*,[1] to keep them firm, and several rafters pass over the *dāsas* and the crossbeam, the whole being kept tightly together by clamps and bolts and nuts. The walls and the roof consist of mats. There is one door or two ; and at the height of the lower *dāsas* there is a raised platform. The inside is ornamented with brocade and velvet, and the outside with scarlet-sackcloth,[2] tied to the walls with silk tape. 3. The *Do-āshiyāna manzil*, or house of two storeys, is raised upon eighteen pillars, six yards in height, which support a wooden platform ; and into this, pillars of four cubits in length are fixed with bolt and nuts, forming an upper storey. The inside and outside are ornamented, as in the preceding. On the march it is used by his Majesty as a sleeping apartment, and also as a place of divine worship, where he prays to the Sun ; and hence the building resembles a man who strives after God without forgetting his worldly duties whose one eye is directed to the solitude of pure devotion, and the other eye to the motley *sarā* of the world. After the devotions are over, the women are allowed to enter to pay their compliments, and after them, outsiders. On journeys his Majesty inspects in this building the rations (of the elephants, camels, etc.), which is called *jharōka*,[3] or window. 4. The *Zamīndoz* is a tent made of various forms, sometimes with one, sometimes with two door poles ; screens are also hung up within it, so as to form divisions. 5. The *ʿAjāʾibī* consists of nine awnings on four pillars. Five of the awnings are square, and four tapering ; sometimes they make it so as to contain one division only, and four tapering ; sometimes they make it so as to contain one division only, supported by a single pole. 6. The *Mandal* is composed of five awnings joined together, and is supported by four poles. Four of the awnings are let down so as to form a private room ; sometimes all four are drawn up, or one side only is left open. 7. The *Aṭh-khamba* consists of seventeen awnings, sometimes

---

[1] A triangular piece of wood fixed into the angle formed by the vertical beam and the cross-beam, *a support*.

[2 *Saqirlāt*, perhaps a scarlet broad-cloth.—P.]

[3 *Jharokā*, a small window in an upper storey, especially one in a palace, to obtain a view.—P.]

separate, sometimes joined together; they are supported by eight poles. 8. The *Khargāh* is a folding tent made in various ways; some with one, others with two doors. 9. The *Shāmyāna*-awning is made of various sizes, but never more than of twelve yards square. 10. The *Qalandarī* has been described.[1] 11. The *Sarāparda* was made in former times of coarse canvas, but his Majesty has now caused it to be made of carpeting, and thereby improved its appearance and usefulness. 12. The *Gulābār* is a wooden screen, its parts being fastened together, like the walls of the *Khargāh*, with leather straps, so that it can be folded together when the camp breaks up. The *gulābār* is covered with red cloth, tied with tape.

Carpets.[2]

His Majesty has caused carpets to be made of wonderful varieties and charming textures; he has appointed experienced workmen, who have produced many masterpieces. The *gilīms* of Īrān and Tūrān are no more thought of, although merchants still import carpets from Goshkān,[3] Khūzistān, Kirmān, and Sabzwār. All kinds of carpet weavers have settled here, and drive a flourishing trade. These are found in every town, especially in Āgra, Fatḥpūr and Lāhor. In the imperial workshops single *gilīms* are made 20 *gaz* 7 *ṭassūjes* long, and 6 *gaz* 11½ *ṭassūjes* broad, at a cost of 1810 rupees, which those who are skilled in the business have valued at 2715 rupees.

Takya-namads, or woollen coverlets, are brought from Kābul and Persia,[4] but are also made in this country.

It would take up too much time to describe the *jājams*, *shaṭrinjīs*, *balūchīs*, and the fine mats which look as if woven of silk.

Āʾīn 22.

THE ĀBDĀR KHĀNA.

His Majesty calls this source of life "the water of immortality", and has committed the care of this department to proper persons. He does not drink much, but pays much attention to this matter. Both at home and

[1] *Vide* p. 48.

[[2] In text *gilīm*, which is a carpet without a pile.—P.]

[3] *Goshkān*, or *Joshaqān*, a town in ʿIrāq-i ʿAjamī, halfway between Kāshān and Iṣfahān. Khūzistān is the Persian province of which Shushtar, or Shustar, is the capital; the ancient *Susiana*. Kirmān is the capital of the Persian province Kirmān, which borders on Balūchistān. *Sabzwār* is one of the chief cities of the Persian province Khurāsān, between Mashhad (Meshed) and the Caspian Sea.

[[4] In text ولایت, *wilāyat*. Both countries are known by the name, as also England in modern times.—P.]

on travels he drinks Ganges water. Some trustworthy persons are stationed on the banks of that river, who dispatch the water in sealed jars. When the court was at the capital Āgra and in Fatḥpūr, the water came from the district of Sorūn,[1] but now[2] that his Majesty is in the Panjāb, the water is brought from Hardwār. For the cooking of the food, rain-water or water taken from the Jamna and the Chanāb is used, mixed with a little Ganges water. On journeys and hunting parties, his Majesty, from his predilection for good water, appoints experienced men as water-tasters.

Saltpetre, which in gunpowder produces the explosive heat, is used by his Majesty as a means for cooling water, and is thus a source of joy for great and small. Saltpetre is a saline earth. They fill with it a perforated vessel, and pour some water over it, and collecting what drops through, they boil it, clean it, and let it crystallize. One ser of water is then put into a goglet of pewter, or silver, or any other such metal, and the mouth closed. Then two and a half sers of saltpetre are thrown into a vessel, together with five sers of water, and in this mixture the goglet is stirred about for a quarter of an hour, when the water in the goglet will become cold. The price of saltpetre varies from ¾ to 4 *mans* per rupee.

Since the thirtieth year[3] of the *Divine Era,* when the imperial standards were erected in the Panjāb, snow and ice have come into use. Ice is brought by land and water, by post carriages or bearers, from the district of Panhān, in the northern mountains, about forty-five *kos* from Lāhor. The dealers derive a considerable profit, two to three sers of ice being sold per rupee. The greatest profit is derived when the ice is brought by water, next when by carriages, and least when by bearers. The inhabitants of the mountains bring it in loads, and sell it in piles containing from 25 to 30 sers, at the rate of 5 *dāms*. If they have to bring it very far, it costs 24 *d.* 17 *j.*; if the distance be an average one, 15 *d.*

Out of the ten boats employed for the transport of ice, one arrives daily at the capital, each being manned by four boatmen. The ice bundles contain from six to twelve sers, according to the temperature. A carriage brings two loads. There are fourteen stages, where the horses are changed, and besides, one elephant is used. Twelve pieces of ten to four sers arrive daily. By this kind of transport, a ser of ice costs in winter 3 *d.* 21 *j.*; during the rains 14 *d.* 20 *j.*; in the intermediate time 9 *d.* 21½ *j.*;

[1] The nearest station on the Ganges from Āgra.

[2] A.D. 1596. As in 1586 Fatḥpūr had ceased to be the capital, Akbar resided mostly in the Panjāb.

[3] A.D. 1586.

and in the average,[1] 5 *d.* 15½ *j.* If it is brought by bearers, twenty-eight men are required for the fourteen stages. They bring every day one load, containing four parcels. In the beginning of the year, the ice costs 5 *d.* 19½ *j.*; in the middle 16 *d.* 2⅛ *j.*; and in the end 19 *d.* 15⅝ *j.* per ser; in the average,[1] 8⅞ *d.*

All ranks use ice in summer; the nobles use it throughout the whole year.

Āʿīn 23.

THE IMPERIAL KITCHEN.

His Majesty even extends his attention to this department, and has given many wise regulations for it; nor can a reason be given why he should not do so, as the equilibrium of man's nature, the strength of the body, the capability of receiving external and internal blessings, and the acquisition of worldly and religious advantages, depend ultimately on proper care being shown for appropriate food. This knowledge distinguishes man from beasts, with whom, as far as mere eating is concerned, he stands upon the same level. If his Majesty did not possess so lofty a mind, so comprehensive an understanding, so universal a kindness, he would have chosen the path of solitude, and given up sleep and food altogether; and even now, when he has taken upon himself the temporal and spiritual leadership of the people, the question, "What dinner has been prepared to-day?" never passes over his tongue. In the course of twenty-four hours his Majesty eats but once, and leaves off before he is fully satisfied; neither is there any fixed time for this meal, but the servants have always things so far ready, that in the space of an hour, after the order has been given, a hundred dishes are served up. The food allowed to the women of the seraglio commences to be taken from the kitchen in the morning, and goes on till night.

Trustworthy and experienced people are appointed to this department; and all good servants attached to the court, are resolved to perform well whatever service they have undertaken. Their head is assisted by the Prime Minister himself. His Majesty has entrusted to the latter the affairs of the state. but especially this important department. Notwithstanding all this, his Majesty is not unmindful of the conduct of the servants. He appoints a zealous and sincere man as *Mīr Bakāwal*, or

---

[1] The text has *sarāsarī*, which may mean the *average*; but the price given by Abū'l-Fazl is not an average. The charges for ice at the time of Akbar may be compared to the prices of the present age. Here, in Calcutta, one ser of American ice costs two annas, or ⅛ rupee, i.e., $\frac{40}{8}$ = 5 *dāms* of Akbar.

Master of the Kitchen, upon whose insight the success of the department depends, and gives him several upright persons as assistants. There are also treasurers for the cash and the stores, several tasters, and a clever writer. Cooks from all countries prepare a great variety of dishes of all kinds of grains, greens, meats ; also oily, sweet, and spicy dishes. Every day such dishes are prepared as the nobles can scarcely command at their feasts, from which you may infer how exquisite the dishes are which are prepared for his Majesty.

In the beginning of the year the Sub-treasurers make out an annual estimate, and receive the amount ; the money bags and the door of the store-house being sealed with the seals of the *Mīr Bakāwal* and the writer ; and every month a correct statement of the daily expenditure is drawn up, the receipt for which is sealed by the same two officers, when it is entered under the head of the expenditure. At the beginning of every quarter,[1] the *Dīwān-i buyūtāt*[2] and the *Mīr Bakāwal*, collect whatever they think will be necessary ; e.g. *Sukhdās* rice from Bharāij,[3] *Dewzīra* rice from Gwāliār, *Jinjin* rice from Rājórī and Nīmlah, *ghī* from *Hiṣār Fīrūza* ; ducks,[4] water-fowls, and certain vegetables from Kashmīr. Patterns are always kept. The sheep, goats, berberies,[5] fowls, ducks,[6] etc., are fattened by the cooks ; fowls are never kept less than a month. The slaughter-house is without the city or the camp, in the neighbourhood of rivers and tanks, where the meat is washed, when it is sent to the kitchen in sacks sealed by the cooks. There it is again washed, and thrown into the pots. The water-carriers pour the water out of their leather bags into earthen vessels, the mouths of which are covered with pieces of cloth, and sealed up ; and the water is left to settle before it is used. A place is also told off as a kitchen garden, that there may be a continual supply of fresh greens. The *Mīr Bakāwal* and the writer determine the price of every eatable, which becomes a fixed rule ; and they sign the day-book, the estimates, the receipts for transfers, the list of wages of the servants, etc., and watch every transaction. Bad characters, idle talkers, unknown persons are never employed ; no one is entertained without a personal security, nor is personal acquaintance sufficient.

The victuals are served up in dishes of gold and silver, stone and earthenware ; some of the dishes being in charge of each of the *Sub-*

[[1] *Faṣl.*—P.]

[2] Superintendent of the stores, workshops, etc.

[[3] Bahrāich.—B.]

[[4] *Qāz* T. goose not duck.—P.]

[[5] Apparently the Barbary goat.—P.]

[[6] *Qāz* T. goose.—P.]

Bakāwals. During the time of cooking, and when the victuals are taken out, an awning is spread, and lookers-on kept away. The cooks tuck up their sleeves, and the hems of their garments, and hold their hands before their mouths and noses when the food is taken out; the cook and the *Bakāwal* taste it, after which it is tasted by the *Mīr Bakāwal*, and then put into the dishes. The gold and silver dishes are tied up in red cloths, and those of copper and china in white ones. The *Mīr Bakāwal* attaches his seal, and writes on it the names of the contents, whilst the clerk of the pantry writes out on a sheet of paper a list of all vessels and dishes, which he sends inside, with the seal of the *Mīr Bakāwal*, that none of the dishes may be changed. The dishes are carried by the *Bakāwals*, the cooks, and the other servants, and macebearers precede and follow, to prevent people from approaching them. The servants of the pantry send at the same time, in bags containing the seal of the *Bakāwal*, various kinds of bread, saucers of curds piled up, and small stands containing plates of pickles, fresh ginger, limes, and various greens. The servants of the palace again taste the food, spread the table cloth on the ground, and arrange the dishes; and when after some time his Majesty commences to dine, the table servants sit opposite him in attendance; first, the share of the derwishes is put apart, when his Majesty commences with milk or curds. After he has dined, he prostrates himself in prayer. The *Mīr Bakāwal* is always in attendance. The dishes are taken away according to the above list. Some victuals are also kept half ready, should they be called for.

The copper utensils are tinned twice a month; those of the princes, etc., once; whatever is broken is given to the braziers, who make new ones.

Āʼīn 24.

RECIPES FOR DISHES.

There are many dishes but the description is difficult. I shall give some particulars. Cooked victuals may be arranged under three heads, *first*, such in which no meat is used, called now-a-days *ṣūfiyāna*; *secondly*, such in which meat and rice, etc., are used; *thirdly*, meats with spices. I shall give ten recipes of each kind.

First, 1. *Zard birinj*: 10 *s*. of rice; 5 *s*. of sugarcandy; $3\frac{1}{2}$ *s*. of ghī; raisins, almonds, and pistachios, $\frac{1}{2}$ *s*. of each; $\frac{1}{4}$ *s*. of salt; $\frac{1}{8}$*s*. of fresh ginger; $1\frac{1}{2}$ *dāms* saffron, $2\frac{1}{2}$ *misqāls* of cinnamon. This will make four ordinary dishes. Some make this dish with fewer spices, and even without any: and instead of without meat and sweets, they prepare it also with meat and salt. 2. *Khushka*: 10 *s.* rice; ½ *s.* salt; but it is made in different ways. This will likewise give four dishes. One maund of *Dewzīra* paddy yields 25 *s.* of rice, of which 17 sers make a full pot; *jinjin* rice yields 22 sers. 3. *Khichṛī*: Rice, *mūng* dāl,[1] and ghī 5 *s.* of each; ⅓ *s.* salt; this gives seven dishes. 4. *Shīrbirinj*: 10 *s.* milk; 1 *s.* rice; 1 *s.* sugarcandy; 1 *d.* salt; this gives five full dishes. 5. *Thūlī*: 10 *s.* of wheat, ground, of which one-third will be lost; half of that quantity of ghī; 10 *misqāls* of pepper; 4 *m.* cinnamon; 3½ *m.* cloves and cardamums; ⅓ *s.* salt; some add milk and sweetmeats: this gives four dishes. 6. *Chikhī*: 10 *s.* of wheat-flour, made into a paste, and washed till it is reduced to 2 *s.* of fine paste. This is mixed with spices, and dressed with various kinds of meat. 1 *s.* ghī; 1 *s.* onions; saffron, cardmums, and cloves, ½ *d.* of each; cinnamon, round pepper, and coriander seed, 1 *d.* of each; fresh ginger, salt 3 *d.* of each: this gives two dishes; some add lime juice. 7. *Bādinjān*:[2] 10 *s.*; 1½ *s.* ghī: 3¾ *s.* onions; ¼ *s.* ginger and lime juice; pepper and coriander seed, 5 *m.* of each; cloves, cardamums, and assafœtida, each ½ *m.* This gives six dishes. 8. *Pahit*: For ten sers of dāl of vetches (or gram, or skinned lentils, etc.) take 2½ *s.* ghī; ½ *s.* of salt and fresh ginger; 2 *m.* cuminseed; 1½ *m.* assafœtida: this yields fifteen dishes. It is mostly eaten with *Khushka*. 9. *Sāg*: It is made of spinach, and other greens, and is one of the most pleasant dishes. 10 *s.* spinach, fennel, etc., 1½ *s.* ghī; 1 *s.* onions; ½ *s.* fresh ginger; 5½ *m.* of pepper; ½ *m.* of cardamums and cloves; this gives six dishes. 10. *Ḥalwā*: Flour, sugarcandy, ghī, 10 *s.* of each, which will give fifteen dishes; it is eaten in various ways.

There are also various kinds of sugared fruits, and drinks, which I cannot here describe.

Secondly, 1. *Qabūlī*: 10 *s.* rice; 7 *s.* meat; 3½ *s.* ghī; 1 *s.* gram skinned; 2 *s.* onions; ½ *s.* salt; ¼ *s.* fresh ginger; cinnamon, round pepper, cuminseed, of each 1 *d.*; cardamums and cloves, ½ *d.* of each; some add almonds and raisins: this gives five dishes. 2. *Duzdbiryān*. 10 *s.* rice, 3½ *s.* ghī; 10 *s.* meat; ½ *s.* salt: this gives five dishes. 3. *Qīma*[3] *Palāo*: Rice and meat as in the preceding; 4 *s.* ghī; 1 *s.* peeled gram; 2 *s.* onions; ½ s. salt; ¼ *s.* fresh ginger, and pepper; cuminseed, cardamums and cloves, 1 *d.* of each: this gives five dishes. 4. *Shulla*: 10 *s.* meat, 3½ *s.* rice; 2 *s.* ghī; 1 *s.* gram; 2 *s.* onions; ½ *s.* salt; ¼ *s.* fresh

[1 All *split* peas, pulse, lentils, vetches, etc., are called *dāl*.—P.]
[2 *Bādinjān* is the egg-plant or brinjāl.—P.]
[3 *Qīma* is pounded (or minced) meat.—P.]

ginger; 2 *d.* garlic, and round pepper, cinnamon, cardamums, cloves, 1 *d.* of each: this gives six dishes. 5. *Bughrā*: 10 *s.* meat; 3 *s.* flour; 1½ *s.* ghī; 1 *s.* gram; 1½ *s.* vinegar; 1 *s.* sugarcandy; onions, carrots, beets, turnips, spinach, fennel, ginger, ¼ *s.* of each; saffron, cloves, cardamums, cuminseed, 1 *d.* of each; 2 *d.* cinnamon; 8 *m.* round pepper: this gives twelve dishes. 6. *Qīma Shūrbā*: 10 *s.* meat; 1 *s.* rice; 1 *s.* ghī; ½ *s.* gram, and the rest as in the *Shulla*: this gives ten full dishes. 7. *Ḥarīsa*: 10 *s.* meat; 5 *s.* crushed wheat; 2 *s.* ghī; ½ *s.* salt; 2 *d.* cinnamon: this gives five dishes. 8. *Kashk*: 10 *s.* meat; 5 *s.* crushed wheat; 3 *s.* ghī; 1 *s.* gram; ¼ *s.* salt; 1½ *s.* onions; ½ *s.* ginger; 1 *d.* cinnamon; saffron, cloves, cardamums, cuminseed, 2 *m.* of each: this gives five dishes. 9. *Ḥalīm*: The meat, wheat, gram, spices, and saffron, as in the preceding; 1 *s.* ghī; turnips, carrots, spinach, fennel, ¼ *s.* of each: this gives ten dishes. 10. *Quṭāb*, which the people of Hind call *sanbūsa*: This is made in several ways. 10 *s.* meat; 4 *s.* fine flour; 2 *s.* ghī; 1 *s.* onions; ¼ *s.* fresh ginger; ½ *s.* salt; 2 *d.* pepper and coriander seed; cardamums, cuminseed, cloves, 1 *d.* of each; ¼ *s* of *summāq*. This can be cooked in twenty different ways, and gives four full dishes.

Thirdly, 1. *Biryān*. For a whole *Dashmandī* sheep, take 2 *s.* salt; 1 *s.* ghī; 2 *m.* saffron, cloves, pepper, cuminseed: it is made in various ways. 2. *Yakhnī* [1]: for 10 *s.* meat, take 1 *s.* onions, and ½ *s.* salt. 3. *Yulma*: A sheep is scalded in water till all the wool comes off; it is then prepared like *yakhnī*, or any other way; but a lamb, or a kid, is more preferable. 4. *Kabāb* is of various kinds. 10 *s.* meat; ½ *s.* ghī; salt, fresh ginger, onions, ¼ *s.* of each; cuminseed, coriander seed, pepper, cardamums, cloves, 1½ *d.* of each. 5. *Muṣamman*: They take all the bones out of a fowl through the neck, the fowl remaining whole; ½ *s.* minced meat; ½ *s.* ghī; 5 eggs; ¼ *s.* onions; 10 *m.* coriander; 10 *m.* fresh ginger; 5 *m.* salt; 3 *m.* round pepper; ½ *m.* saffron. It is prepared as the preceding. 6. *Dupiyāza*: 10 *s.* meat that is middling fat; 2 *s.* ghī; 2 *s.* onions; ¼ *s.* salt; ⅛ *s.* fresh pepper; cuminseed, coriander seed, cardamums, cloves, 1 *d.* of each; 2 *d.* pepper: this will give five dishes. 7. *Muṭanjana* [2] sheep: 10 *s.* meat that is middling fat; 2 *s.* ghī; ½ *s.* gram; ½ *s.* ginger; 1 *d.* cuminseed; round pepper, cloves, cardamums, coriander seed, 2 *d.* of each; this will give seven dishes full. It is also made of fowl and fish. 8. *Dampukht*: [3] 10 *s.* meat; 2 *s.* ghī; 1 *s.* onions; 11 *m.* fresh ginger; 10 *m.* pepper; 2 *d.* cloves; 2 *d.* cardamums. 9. *Qaliyy*:

[[1] *Yakhnī* is a gravy or broth.—P.]
[[2] Does this mean fried ?]
[[3] *Dam-pukht* means cooking slowly in a vessel with its lid closed by paste.—P.]

10 *s*. meat; 2 *s*. ghī; 1 *s*. onions; 2 *d*. pepper; cloves, cardamums, 1 *d*. each; ⅛ *s*. salt: this will give eight dishes. In preparing *qaliya*, the meat is minced and the gravy rather thick, in opposition to the *mutanjana*. Here in Hind they prepare it in various ways. 10. *Malghūba*: 10 *s*. meat; 10 *s*. curds; 1 *s*. ghī; 1 *s*. onions; ¼ *s*. ginger; 5 *d*. cloves: this will give ten dishes.

Āʾīn 25.

OF BREAD.

This belongs, properly speaking, to the preceding chapter. Bread is made in the pantry. There is a *large* kind,[1] baked in an oven, made of 10 *s*. flour; 5 *s*. milk; 1½ *s*. ghī; ¼ *s*. salt. They make also smaller ones. The *thin* kind is baked on an iron plate. One ser will give fifteen, or even more. There are various ways of making it; one kind is called *chapātī*, hich is sometimes made of *khushka*; it tastes very well when served ot. For the bread used at court, one *man* of wheat is made to yield ½ *m*. of fine flour; 2 *s*. coarsely pounded flour; and the rest bran; if this degree of fineness be not required, the proportions are altered.

Āʾīn 26.

THE DAYS OF ABSTINENCE. (*Sūfiyāna*.)[2]

His Majesty cares very little for meat, and often expresses himself to that effect. It is indeed from ignorance and cruelty that, although various kinds of food are obtainable, men are bent upon injuring living creatures, and lending a ready hand in killing and eating them; none seems to have an eye for the beauty inherent in the prevention of cruelty, but makes himself a tomb for animals. If his Majesty had not the burden of the world on his shoulders, he would at once totally abstain from meat; and now it is his intention to quit it by degrees, conforming, however, a little to the spirit of the age. His Majesty abstained from meat for some time on Fridays, and then on Sundays; now on the first day of every solar month, on Sundays, on solar and lunar eclipses, on days between two fasts, on the Mondays of the month of Rajab[3] on the feast-day of every

---

[[1] Probably a large flat cake.—P.]

[2] Living according to the manners of the Sūfīs.

[3] Akbar was born on the fifth of Rajab A.H. 949, a Sunday. This corresponds to the 15th October, 1542. The Mondays of the month of Rajab were observed as fasts, because the Sundays bad been included in the list of fast days. The members of the Divine *Faith* fasted likewise during the month of their birth.

solar month, during the whole month of *Farwardīn*,[1] and during the month in which his Majesty was born, viz. the month of *Ābān*. Again, when the number of fast days of the month of *Ābān* had become equal to the number of years his Majesty had lived, some days of the month of *Āzar* also were kept as fasts. At present the fast extends over the whole month. These fast days, however, from pious motives, are annually increased by at least five days. Should fasts fall together, they keep the longer one, and transfer the smaller by distributing its days over other months. Whenever long fasts are ended, the first dishes of meat come dressed from the apartments of Maryam Makānī, next from the other begums, the princes, and the principal nobility.

In this department nobles, *aḥadīs*, and other military, are employed. The pay of a foot soldier varies from 100 to 400 *dāms*.

Āʾīn 27.

STATISTICS OF THE PRICES OF CERTAIN ARTICLES.

The prices of course vary, as on marches, or during the rains, and for other reasons ; but I shall give here the average prices for the information of future enquirers.

A. The spring harvest.

Wheat, per *man*	12 *d.*	Safflower seed (carthamus), do.	8 *d.*
Kābul gram, do.	16 *d.*	Fenugreek, do.	10 *d.*
Black gram, do.	8 *d.*	Peas,[2] do.	6 *d.*
Lentils, do.	12 *d.*	Mustard seed, do.	12 *d.*
Barley, do.	8 *d.*	*Kewū*, do.	7 *d.*
Millet, do.	6 *d.*		
Linseed, per *man*	10 *d.*		

B. The autumnal harvest.

Mushkīn, paddy per *man*	110 *d.*	Jinjin rice, do.	80 *d.*
Sāda paddy, do.	100 *d.*	Dakah (?) rice, do.	50 *d.*
Sukhdās rice, do.	100 *d.*	Zirhī rice, do.	40 *d.*
Dūnaparsād rice, do.	90 *d.*	Sāṭhī rice, do.	20 *d.*
Sāmzīra rice, do.	90 *d.*	*Mūng* (black gram) do.	18 *d.*
Shakarchīnī rice, do.	90 *d.*	*Māsh* (a kind of vetch) per *man*	16 *d.*
Dewzīra rice, do.	90 *d.*		

[1] February–March ; [or March and April ?—P] ; *vide* the first *Āʾīn* of the third book ; *Ābān* corresponds to October–November.

[[2] *Mashang* or *mushang*, a pea ?—P.]

Moth (a kind of vetch), per *man* . . . 12 *d.*
White sesame, do. . . . 20 *d.*
Black sesame, do. . . . 19 *d.*
Lobiyā (a kind of bean), do. 12 *d.*
Juwārī (a kind of millet), do. . . . . . 10 *d.*
Lahdara, do . . . . 8 *d.*
Kōdram, do. . . . . 7 *d.*
Kūrī, do. . . . . 7 *d.*
Shamākh (Hind. *Sāwank*), do. . . . . . 6 *d.*
Gāl (Hind. *Kangnī*), do. . 8 *d.*
Millet (Hind. *chīna*), do. . 8 *d.*

Mūng dāl, per *man* . . 18 *d.*
Nukhūd dāl, do. . . 16½ *d.*
Dāl of Lentils, per *man* . 16 *d.*
Moth dāl, do. . . 12 *d.*

Wheat flour, per *man* . 22 *d.*
Do. coarse, do. . . 15 *d.*
Nukhūd flour, per *man* . 22 *d.*
Barley flour, do. . . 11 *d.*

C. Vegetables.

Fennel, per *man* . . 10 *d.*
Spinach, do. . . . 16 *d.*
Mint, do. . . . 40 *d.*
Onions, do. . . . 6 *d.*
Garlic, do. . . . 40 *d.*
Turnips, do. . . . 21 *d.*
Cabbage, per *ser* [1] . . 1 *d.*
Kankachhū, from Kashmīr, do . . . 4 *d.*
Dunwretū, . . . 2 *d.*
Shaqāqul (wild carrot [2]), do. 3 *d.*
Garlic flowers, per *ser* . 1 *d.*
Upalhāk, (from Kashmīr) do. . . . . . 1 *d.*
Jītū, do. . . . . 3 *d.*
Ginger (green), do. . 2½ *d.*
Po,ī, do. . . . . 1 *d.*
Kachnār buds, do. . . ½ *d.*
Chūkā (sorrel), do. . . ½ *d.*
Bathwa, do. . . . ¼ *d.*
Ratsakā, do. . . . 1 *d.*
Chaulā,ī, do. . . ¼ *d.*

D. Living animals and meats.

Dāshmandī sheep, per *head* 6½ *R.*
Afghān sheep, 1st kind, do. 2 *R.*
Do., 2nd kind, do. . . 1½ *R.*
Do., 3rd kind, do. . . 1¼ *R.*
Kashmīr sheep, do. . 1½ *R.*
Hindustānī sheep, do. . 1½ *R.*
Barbarī goat, 1st kind, do. 1 *R.*
Do., 2nd kind, do. . . ¾ *R.*
Mutton, per *man* . . 65 *d.*
Goat, do. . . . 54 *d.*
Geese, per *head* . . 20 *d.*
Duck, per *head* . . 1 *R.*
Tughdarī (bustard),[3] do. 20 *d.*
Kulang (crane),[4] do. . 20 *d.*
Jarz (a kind of bustard),[5] do. . . . . . 18 *d.*

[[1] *Turb* radish, not turnip.—P.]
[[2] Or wild parsnip ?—P.]
[[3] *Tughdarī* is the Hubara bustard.—P.]
[[4] *Kulang* is the Common Crane or "coolan".—P.]
[[5] For *charz*. In Baluchistan this is the name of the Hubara, but elsewhere of the Florican.—P.]

Durrāj (black partridge), per *head* . . . 3 *d.*
Kabg [1] (partridge), do. . 20 *d.*
Būdana,[2] do. . . 1 *d.*
Lāwah,[3] do. . . . 1 *d.*
Karwānak (stone curlew), do. . . . . . 20 *d.*
Fākhta (ringdove), do. . 4 *d.*

E. *Butter, Sugar, etc.*

Ghī, per *man* . . 105 *d.*
Oil, do. . . . 80 *d.*
Milk, do. . . . 25 *d.*
Curds, do. . . . 18 *d.*
Refined Sugar, per *ser* . 6 *d.*
White sugar candy, do. . 5½ *d.*
White sugar, per *man* . 128 *d.*
Brown sugar, do. . . 56 *d.*

F. *Spices.*

Saffron, per *ser* . . 400 *d.*
Cloves, do. . . . 60 *d.*
Cardamums, do. . . 52 *d.*
Round pepper, do. . 17 *d.*
Long pepper, do. . . 16 *d.*
Dry ginger, do. . . 4 *d.*
Fresh do., do. . . 2½ *d.*
Cuminseed, do. . . 2 *d.*
Aniseed, per *ser* . . 2 *d.*
Turmeric (Hind. *haldī*) do. . . . . . 10 *d.*
Coriander seed, do. . 3 *d.*
Siyāhdāna (Hind. *kalaunjī*), do. . . . . 1½ *d.*
Assafœtida, do. . . 2 *d.*
Sweet fennel, do. . . 1 *d.*
Cinnamon, do. . . 40 *d.*
Salt, per *man* . . 16 *d.*

G. *Pickles.*

Sour limes, per *ser* . . 6 *d.*
Lemon-juice, do. . . 5 *d.*
Wine vinegar . . 5 *d.*
Sugarcane vinegar, do. . 1 *d.*
Pickled *ashtarghār*, do. . 8 *d.*
Mangoes in oil, do. . 2 *d.*
Do. in vinegar, do. . 2 *d.*
Lemons in oil, do. . . 2 *d.*
Do. in vinegar, do. . 2 *d.*
Do. in salt, do. . . 1½ *d.*
Do. in lemon-juice, do. . 5 *d.*
Pickled ginger . . 2½ *d.*
Adarshākh, do. . . 2½ *d.*
Turnips in vinegar, do. . 1 *d.*
Pickled carrots, do. . ½ *d.*
Pickled bamboo, per *ser* 4 *d.*
Do. apples, do. . . 8 *d.*
Do. quinces, do. . . 9 *d.*
Do. garlic, do. . . 1 *d.*
Do. onions, do. . . ½ *d.*
Do. *bādinjān* (egg-plant), do. . . . . . 1 *d.*
Do. raisins and *munaqqa*,[4] do. . . . . . 8 *d.*
Do. *kachnār*, do. . . 2 *d.*
Do. peaches, do. . . 1 *d.*
Do. *sahajna* (horse-radish) . . . . 1 *d.*
Do. *karīl buds* (capparis), do. . . . . . ½ *d.*

[[1] *Kabk* the Chukor partridge.—P.]
[[2] The Common Quail.—P.]
[[3] The Rock Bush-quail.—P.]
[[4] *Kishmish* sultana raisins; *munaqqa* large black raisins.—P.]

Pickled *karīl berries*, per *ser*	½ *d.*	Do. cucumbers, do.	½ *d.*
Do. *sūran*, do.	1 *d.*	Do. *bādrang*,[1] (gourd) do.	½ *d.*
Do. mustard	¼ *d.*	Do. *kachālū*, do.	½ *d.*
Do. *torī* (a kind of cucumber)	½ *d.*	Do. radishes, do.	½ *d.*

Āʾīn 28.

THE FRUITERY.

His Majesty looks upon fruits as one of the greatest gifts of the Creator, and pays much attention to them. The horticulturists of Īrān and Tūrān have, therefore, settled here, and the cultivation of trees is in a flourishing state. Melons and grapes have become very plentiful and excellent; and water-melons, peaches, almonds, pistachios, pomegranates, etc., are everywhere to be found. Ever since the conquest of Kābul, Qandahār, and Kashmīr, loads of fruit are imported; throughout the whole year the stores of the dealers are full, and the bāzārs well supplied. Muskmelons come in season, in Hindūstān, in the month of *Farwardīn* (February–March),[2] and are plenty in *Urdībihish* (March–April).[3] They are delicious, tender, opening, sweet smelling, especially the kinds called *nāshpātī, bābāshaykhī, ʿalīsherī, alcha, barg-i nay, dūd-i chirāgh*, etc. They continue in season for two months longer. In the beginning of *Sharīwar* (August),[4] they come from Kashmīr, and before they are out of season plenty are brought from Kābul; during the month of *Āzar* (November),[5] they are imported by the caravans from Badakhshān, and continue to be had during *Day* (December).[6] When they are in season in Zābulistān, good ones also are obtainable in the Panjāb; and in Bhakkar and its vicinity they are plentiful in season, except during the forty cold days of winter. Various kinds of grapes are here to be had from *Khurdād* (May)[7] to *Amurdād* (July),[8] whilst the markets are stocked with Kashmīr grapes during *Shahrīwar*.[4] Eight sers of grapes sell in Kashmīr for one *dām*, and the cost of the transport is two rupees per *man*. The Kashmīris bring them on their backs in conical baskets, which look very curious.

[[1] *Bādrang*, not gourd. Perhaps a citron.—P.]
[[2] March–April.—P.]
[[3] April–May.—P.]
[[4] August–September.—P.]
[[5] November–December.—P.]
[[6] December–January.—P.]
[[7] May–June.—P.]
[[8] July–August.—P.]

From *Mihr* (September)[1] till *Urdībihist*[2] grapes come from Kābul, together with cherries,[3] which his Majesty calls *shāhālū*, seedless pomegranates, apples, pears, quinces, guavas, peaches, apricots, *girdālūs*, and *ālūchas*, etc., many of which fruits grow also in Hindūstān. From Samarqand even they bring melons, pears, and apples.

Whenever his Majesty wishes to take wine, opium, or *kūknār* (he calls the latter *sabras*), the servants in charge place before him stands of fruits; he eats a little, but most is distributed. The fruits are marked according to their degree of excellence: melons of the first quality are marked with a line drawn round the top; those of the second, with two lines; and so on.

In this department *Manṣabdārs*, *Aḥadīs*, and other soldiers are employed; the pay of a foot soldier varies from 140 to 100 *d.*

The following tables contain particulars regarding the names, seasons, taste, and prices of various fruits.

A. *Tūrānī Fruits.*

Arhang melons, 1st quality, at	2½ *R.*	Plums, do.	8 *d.*
Do., 2nd and 3rd do., at 1 to	2½ *R.*	*Khūbānī* (dried apricots), per *ser*	8 *d.*
Kābul melons, 1st do., at 1 to	1½ *R.*	Qandahar dry grapes, do.	7 *d.*
Do., 2nd do., at ¾ to	1 *R.*	Figs, per *ser*	7 *d.*
Do., 3rd do., at ½ to	¾ *R.*	*Munaqqa*, do.	6¾ *d.*
Samarqand apples, 7 to 15 for	1 *R.*	Jujubes, do.	3½ *d.*
Quinces, 10 to 30 for	1 *R.*	Almonds, without the shell, do.	28 *d.*
Pomegranates, per *man*, 6½ to	15 *R.*	Do., with do., do	11 *d.*
Guavas, 10 to 100 for	1 *R.*	Pistachios, do., do.	9 *d.*
Kābul and European apples, 5 to 10 for	1 *R.*	*Chilghūza*[4] nuts, per *ser*	8 *d.*
Kashmīr grapes, per *man*	108 *d.*	*Sinjid* (jujubes), do.	6½ *d.*
Dates, per *ser*	10 *d.*	Pistachios, without shell, do.	6 *d.*
Raisins (*kishmish*), do.	9 *d.*	*Jawz* (nuts), do.	4½ *d.*
Ābjosh (large raisins), do.	9 *d.*	Filberts, do.	3 *d.*
		Hazel[5] nuts, do.	2½ *d.*

[[1] September–October.—P.]

[2] The original has a word *kilās*, which is not to be found in our dictionaries. It may be *cerasus*. [Gīlās is the common name in Persia and in Kashmīr for the white sweet cherry.—P.]

[3] A town in Bada Khshān.

[[4] Edible seed of pinus Gerardiana.—P.]

[[5] *Girdgān* is properly the walnut.—P.]

B. The sweet fruits of Hindustan.

Mangoes, *per hundred*, up to	40 *d.*	*Tendū*, do.	2 *d.*
Pine-apples, one for	4 *d.*	*Ūsīrā*	*
Oranges,[1] two for	1 *d.*	Dates, per *ser*	4 *d.*
Sugarcanes, two for	1 *d.*	*Angūhal*	*
Jackfruits, two for	1 *d.*	*Delā*, do.	1 *d.*
Plantains, do.	1 *d.*	*Gūla*	*
Ber, per *ser*	2 *d.*	*Bholsarī*, per *ser*	4 *d.*
Pomegranates, per *man*, 80 to	100 *d.*	*Tarkul*, two for	1 *d.*
Guavas,[2] two for	1 *d.*	*Paniyāla*, per *ser*	2 *d.*
Figs, per *ser*	1 *d.*	*Lahsaura*, do.	1 *d.*
Mulberry, do.	2 *d.*	*Gumbhī*, do	4 *d.*
Custard-apples,[3] one for	1 *d.*	*Karahrī*	4 *d.*
Melons, per *man*	40 *d.*	*Tarrī*	*
Water-melons, one	2 to 10 *d.*	*Banga*, two for	1 *d.*
Khirnī, per *ser*	4 *d.*	*Gūlar*,[4] per *ser*	2 *d.*
Mahuwā, do.	1 *d.*	*Pīlū*, do.	2 *d.*
Dephal, do.	4 *d.*	*Barauta*	*
		Piyār, do.	4 *d.*

* The original does not mention the price.

Mulberries and *gūlars* are in season during *spring*; pine-apples, oranges, sugarcane, *bers*, *ūsīrās*, *bholsarīs*, *gumbhīs*, *déphals* during *winter*; jackfruits, *tarkuls*, figs, melons, *lahsauras*, *karahrīs*, *mahuwās*, *tendūs*, *pīlūs*, *barautas*, during *summer*; and mangoes, plantains, dates, *delās*, *gūlas*, pomegranates, guavas, water-melons, *paniyālas*, *bangas*, *khirnīs*, *piyārs*, during the rains.

C. Dried Fruits.

Coco-nuts, one for	4 *d.*	*Makhānā*, per *ser*	4 *d.*
Dry Dates, per *ser*	6 *d.*	*Sūpyārī*, do	8 *d.*
Walnuts, do.	8 *d.*	*Kaulgatta*, do.	2 *d.*
Chiraunchī, do.	4 *d.*		

Dates, walnuts, *chiraunchīs*, and *kaulgattas* are in seasons during *summer*, and coco-nuts, *makhānās*, and *supyārīs*, during *winter*.

[1 *Kāwla* ?]

[2 *Amrūd* guava, but in Persia and locally too in India, a pear.—P.]

[3 *Sadā-phal*. The custard-apple is *sītā-phal*.—P.] The original says that custard-apples are to be had throughout the whole year. This seems a mistake of the MSS. The remark suits the next fruit (melons).

[4 *Gūlar* wild fig.—P.]

D. Vegetables.

Palwal, per *ser* . .	2 *d.*	*Kachālū*, per *ser* . .	2 *d.*
Gourd,[1] one . . .	2½ *d.*	*Chachīndā*, do. . .	2 *d.*
Bādinjān, per *ser* . .	1½ *d.*	*Sūran*, do.	1 *d.*
Tura,ī, do. . . .	1½ *d.*	Carrots, do. . . .	1 *d.*
Kandūrī, do. . .	1½ *d.*	*Singhāra*, do.[2] . .	3 *d.*
Sēnb, do. . . .	1½ *d.*	*Sālak*, do. . . .	2 *d.*
Peṭh, do. . . .	1½ *d.*	*Pinḍālū*, do. . . .	2 *d.*
Karīla, do. . . .	1½ *d.*	*Siyātī*	*
Kakūra, do. . . .	1½ *d.*	*Kaserū*, do. . . .	3 *d.*

Sūrans and *siyātīs* are in season during *summer*; *palwals*, gourds, *tura,īs*, *kachālūs*, *chachīndās*, *kandūrīs*, *senbs*, *peṭhs*, *karīlas*, *kakūras*, and *singhāras* during the *rains*; and carrots, *sālaks*, *pinḍālūs*, and *kaserūs*, during *winter*. *Bādinjāns* are to be had throughout the year.

E. Sour Fruits.

Limes, *four* up to . .	1 *d.*	*Ghep*	*
Amalbet, do. . . .	1 *d.*	*Bijaurā*, one for . .	8 *d.*
Galgal, two up to . .	1 *d.*	*Āwlā*,[3] per *ser* . .	2 *d.*

Limes and *āwlas* are to be had in summer, the others during the rains.

F. Fruits somewhat acid.

Ambīlī, per *ser* . .	2 *d.*	*Kait*, four up to . .	1 *d.*
Badhal, one for . .	1 *d.*	*Kānkū*	*
Kamrak, four up to . .	1 *d.*	*Pākar*, per *ser* . .	½ *d.*
Nārangī,[4] two up to . .	1 *d.*	*Karnā*, one for . .	1 *d.*
Mountain grapes . .	*	*Labhīrā*	*
Jāman, per *ser* . .	1 *d.*	*Janbhīrī*, five up to .	1 *d.*
Phālsa, do . . .	1½ *d.*	*Garnal*	*
Karaundā, do. . .	1 *d.*		

* The original does not mention the price.

Kamraks and *nārangīs*,[4] are in season during *winter*; *ambīlīs*, *badhals*, mountain-grapes, *phālsas*, *labhīrās*, during *summer*; and *kaits*, *pākars*, *karnās*, *jāmans*, *karaundās*, *janbhīrīs*, during the *rains*.

The fruits of Hindustan are either sweet, or subacid, or sour; each kind is numerous. Some fruits also taste well when dry; others as above described are used when cooked. I shall give now a few details.

[[1] *Kadū* pumpkin.—P.]
[[2] The water-nut.—P.]
[[3] The emblic myrobalans.—P.]
[[4] The orange with *close* skin.—P.]

The Mangoe : The Persians call this fruit *Naghzak*, as appears from a verse of *Khusraw*.[1] This fruit is unrivalled in colour, smell, and taste ; and some of the gourmets of Tūrān and Īrān place it above muskmelons and grapes. In shape it resembles an apricot, or a quince, or a pear, or a melon, and weighs even one ser and upwards. There are green, yellow, red, variegated, sweet, and subacid mangoes. The tree looks well, especially when young ; it is larger than a walnut-tree, and its leaves resemble those of the willow, but are larger. The new leaves appear soon after the fall of the old ones in autumn, and look green and yellow, orange, peach-coloured, and bright red. The flower, which opens in spring, resembles that of the vine, has a good smell, and looks very curious.[2] About a month after the leaves have made their appearance, the fruit is sour, and is used for preserves and pickles. It improves the taste of *qalyas* (p. 64), as long as the stone has not become hard. If a fruit gets injured whilst on the tree, its good smell will increase. Such mangoes are called *koyilās*. The fruit is generally taken down when unripe, and kept in a particular manner. Mangoes ripened in this manner are much finer. They mostly commence to ripen during summer, and are fit to be eaten during the rains ; others commence in the rainy season, and are ripe in the beginning of winter ; the latter are called *Bhadiyya*. Some trees bloom and yield fruit the whole year ; but this is rare. Others commence to ripen, although they look unripe ; they must be quickly taken down, else the sweetness would produce worms. Mangoes are to be found everywhere in India, especially in Bengal, Gujrāt, Mālwah, Khāndesh, and the Dekhan. They are rarer in the Panjāb, where their cultivation has, however, increased, since his Majesty made Lāhor his capital. A young tree will bear fruit after four years. They put milk and treacle round about the tree, which makes the fruits sweeter. Some trees yield in one year a rich harvest, and less in the next one ; others yield for one year no fruit at all. When many mangoes are eaten, digestion is assisted by drinking milk with the kernels of the mangoe stones. The kernels of old stones are subacid, and taste well ; when two or three years old they are used as medicine. If a half-ripe mangoe, together with its stalk to a length of about two fingers, be taken from the tree, and the broken end of its stalk be closed with warm wax, and kept in butter, or honey, the fruit will retain its taste for two or three months, whilst the colour will remain even for a year.

---

[1] *Vide* the fourth note on p. 75 of my Persian text edition.

[[2] *Shigarf*, beautiful, fine.—P.]

Pine-apples [1] are also called *kaṭhal-i safarī*, or travelling jackfruits, because young plants, put into a vessel, may be taken on travels and will yield fruits. In colour and shape they resemble an oblong orange; and in taste and smell, a mangoe. The plant is about a yard long, and its leaves have the shape of a hand. The edges of the leaves are like a saw. The fruit forms at the end of the stalk and has a few leaves on its top. When the fruit is plucked, they cut out these leaves, separate them, and put them singly into the ground; they are the seedlings. Each plant bears only once, and one fruit only.

Oranges [2] have the colour of saffron, and the shape of quinces. They belong to the best fruits to be had in Hindūstān. The tree resembles the lime tree; its flower has a weak, but fine smell.

Sugarcane, which the Persians call *Nayshakar*, is of various kinds; one species is so tender and so full of juice, that a sparrow can make it flow out by pecking it; and it would break to pieces, if let fall. Sugarcane is either soft, or hard The latter is used for the preparation of brown sugarcandy, common sugar, white candy, and refined sugar, and thus becomes useful for all kinds of sweetmeats. It is cultivated as follows. They put some healthy sugarcane in a cool place, and sprinkle it daily with water. When the sun enters the sign of Aquarius, they cut off pieces, a cubit [3] and upwards in length, put them into soft ground, and cover them up with earth. The harder the sugarcane is, the deeper they put it. Constant irrigation is required. After seven or eight months it will come up.

Sugarcane is also used for the preparation of intoxicating liquor, but brown sugar is better for this purpose. There are various ways of preparing it. One way is as follows. They pound *Babūl* [4] bark mixing it at the rate of ten *sers* to one *man* of sugarcane, and put three times as much water over it. Then they take large jars, fill them with the mixture, and put them into the ground, surrounding them with dry horse-dung. From seven to ten days are required to produce fermentation. It is a sign of perfection, when it has a sweet, but a stringent taste. When the liquor is to be strong, they again put to the mixture some brown sugar, and sometimes even drugs and perfumes, as ambergris, camphor, etc. They also let meat dissolve in it. This beverage, when strained, may be used, but it is mostly employed for the preparation of arrack.

---

[1] Jahāngīr in his *Memoirs* (*Tuzuk-i Jahāngīrī*, ed. Sayyid Aḥmad, p. 3) states that the pine-apples at his time came from the harbour towns held by the Portuguese.

[[2] *Kāwtā*.—P.]

[[3] *Wajab*, a span.—P.]

[[4] A species of acaic, the *kīkar* of the Panjāb.—P.]

They have several methods of distilling it; *first*, they put the above liquor into brass vessels, in the interior of which a cup is put, so as not to shake, nor must the liquid flow into it. The vessels are then covered with inverted lids which are fastened with clay. After pouring cold water on the lids, they kindle the fire, changing the water as often as it gets warm. As soon as the vapour inside reaches the cold lid, it condenses, and falls as arrack into the cup. *Secondly*, they close the same vessel with an earthen pot, fastened in the same manner with clay, and fix to it two pipes, the free ends of which have each a jar attached to them, which stands in cold water. The vapour through the pipes will enter the jars and condense. *Thirdly*, they fill an earthen vessel with the above-mentioned liquor, and fasten to it a large spoon with a hollow handle. The end of the handle they attach to a pipe, which leads into a jar. The vessel is covered with a lid, which is kept full with cold water. The arrack, when condensed, flows through the spoon into the jar. Some distil the arrack twice, when it is called *Duătasha*, or twice burned. It is very strong. If you wet your hands with it, and hold them near the fire, the spirit will burn in flames of different colours without injuring the hands. It is remarkable that when a vessel containing arrack is set on fire you cannot put it out by any means; but if you cover the vessel, the fire gets extinguished at once.

The *Jackfruit* has the shape of a black-pudding,[1] looks greenish, and is sometimes a yard long, and half a yard broad. When small, it resembles a water-melon; its peel is full of thorns. It grows out of the branches, the trunk, and the roots. Those that grow below the ground are sweetest. On opening you see round clusters, so viscous, that the fingers stick together, when you take them out. The tree looks like a nut tree, but is somewhat bigger and has larger leaves. The flower, like the fruit, has a good smell. The fruits are also taken down when unripe. They then apply lime, etc., when the fruits will get ripe.

The *Plantain* tree looks straight like a spear; the leaves come out of the trunk thick and soft, and resemble an unsewn plaited [2] sleeve, but are much larger and wider. Out of the middle rises something looking like a spindle, of a lilac [3] colour; this is the bud. The fruit consists of a cluster of seventy to eighty plantains. In shape they resemble small cucumbers; the peel is easily removed. As plantains are very heavy, you cannot eat many. There are various kinds of plantains. The plant is every year

---

[1 *Kīpă* the gut of a sheep stuffed with mince and rice.—P.]
[2 أتو كنديده might mean ironed.—P.]
[3 *Sūsan* is the common purple flag-iris.—P.]

cut down, and a stump only is left of it: if this is not done, it will no longer bear fruit. The vulgar believe that the plantain tree yields camphor, but this is wrong; for the camphor tree, as shall be hereafter explained, is a different tree, although it has the same name. They also say that pearls originate in plantain trees—another statement upon which the light of truth does not shine.

The *Mahuwā* tree resembles the mangoe tree; its wood is used for building purposes. The fruit, which is also called *Gilaunda*, yields an intoxicating liquor.

The *Bholsīrī* tree is large and handsome,[1] the fruit has an orange colour, and resembles the jujube.

The *Tarkul* tree, and its fruit, resemble the coco-nut palm and its fruit. When the stalk of a new leaf comes out of a branch, they cut off its end and hang a vessel to it to receive the out-flowing juice. The vessel will fill twice or three times a day. The juice is called *tārī*; when fresh it is sweet; when it is allowed to stand for some time it turns subacid and is inebriating.

The *Paniyāla* fruit resembles the *Zardālū* [2] and its tree the lime tree; the leaves are like those of the willow. When unripe the fruit is green, and red when ripe.

The *Gumbhī* has a stem the branches of which are like creepers; its leaves and fruits, as those of the *kunār*, come from below the roots.

The *Tarrī* forms at the root; it grows mostly in the mountains, and weighs a *man*, more or less, when the creeper is a year old; and two, when two years old. It looks like a millstone. When older it grows larger according to the same proportion. Its leaves resemble those of the water melon.

The *Piyār* is like a small grape; brownish and sweet. The inside of the kernel is like butter, and is used in the preparation of food; it is called *Chiraunjī*. Its tree is about a yard high.

The *Coco-nut* is called by the Persians *Jawz-i Hindī*: the tree resembles the date tree, but is larger; its wood, however, looks better, and the leaves are larger. The tree bears fruit throughout the whole year; the fruits ripen in three months. They are also taken down, when unripe and green, and kept for some time. Their inside contains a cup full of milk-like juice, which tastes well, and is very often drunk in summer, mixed with sugar. When ripe, the fruit looks brown. The juice has now become solid, and

---

1 The text has here a few words the meaning of which I do not understand.
[2 *Zardā-lū* the acid apricot.—P.]

gets black when mixed with butter; it is sweet and greasy. When eaten with *pān*-leaves, it makes the tongue soft and fresh. The shell is used for spoons, cups, and *ghichaks* (a kind of violin). There are nuts having four, three, two, and one, holes or eyes; each kind is said to possess certain qualities, the last being considered the best. Another kind is used for the preparation of an antidote against poison. The nuts weigh sometimes twelve *sers* and upwards. The bark of the tree is used for ropes; the large ropes used on ships are made of it.

Dates are called in Hindi *Piṇḍ-khajūr*. The tree has a short stem, rising little above the ground, and produces from four to five hundred fruits.

The *Sūpyārī*, or betel nut, is called in Persian *fūfal*. The tree is graceful and slender, like the cypress. The wind often bends it, so that its crown touches the ground; but it rises up again. There are various kinds. The fruit when eaten raw tastes somewhat like an almond, but gets hard when ripe. It is eaten with betel leaves.

The *Singhāra* is a triangular fruit; its creeper grows in tanks, and the fruit is on the surface of the water. It is eaten raw or roasted.

The *Sālak* grows in tanks under the earth. They go into the water and dig it up.

The *Pindālū* is reared on lattice work, and grows about two yards high. Its leaf resembles the betel lead; they dig up the root.

The *Kaserū* grows in tanks. When the water gets low, they take it out of the ground and eat it, raw or boiled.

The *Siyālī* root is long and conical; the plant is a creeper, to whose root the fruit is attached.

The *Orange* [1] has the shape of an egg. One kind is called *kāghazī*.[1] Between the peel and the fruit is a thin white membrane. The fruit is juicy, and tastes well; one kind is to be had throughout the whole year.

The *Amalbet* is like a lime,[2] and very sour. If you put a steel needle into this fruit, the needle in a short time will dissolve; and a white shell when put into its juice will soon disappear.

The *Karnā* resembles an apple, and appears after the plant has reached the third year. At first the fruit is green, sour, and also somewhat bitter, but turns afterwards yellow and bitter; when ripe it is red and sweet. When it is kept long, it turns green again. The tree looks like an orange tree, but the leaves are somewhat broader, and the buds like fine arrows.[3]

[[1] *Nāranj*, orange ?—P.]

[[2] *Līmū*, lime. *Kāghazī* is applied to a small green lime with a skin as thin as paper.—P.]

[[3] *Paykān-i khākī* ?—P.]

The flower is white, and has four petals and yellow stamens. It has a fine smell, and is used for ambergris; but it is beyond my power to describe the process of the manufacture.

The Betel leaf is, properly speaking, a vegetable, but connoisseurs call it an excellent fruit. Mīr Khusraw of Dihlī, in one of his verses, says, "It is an excellent fruit like the flower of a garden, the finest fruit in Hindustān." The eating of the leaf renders the breath agreeable, and repasts odorous. It strengthens the gums, and makes the hungry satisfied, and the satisfied hungry. I shall describe some of the various kinds. 1. The leaf called *Bilahrī* is white and shining, and does not make the tongue harsh and hard. It tastes best of all kinds. After it has been taken away from the creeper it turns white, with some care, after a month, or even after twenty days when greater efforts are made. 2. The *Kāker* leaf is white with spots, and full, and has hard veins. When much of it is eaten, the tongue gets hard. 3. The *Jaiswār* leaf does not get white, and is profitably sold mixed with other kinds. 4. The *Kapūrī* leaf is yellowish, hard, and full of veins, but has a good taste and smell. 5. The *Kapūrkānt* leaf is yellowish-green, and pungent like pepper; it smells like camphor. You could not eat more than ten leaves. It is to be had at Banāras; but even there it does not thrive in every soil. 6. The *Bangla* leaf is broad, full, hard, plushy, hot, and pungent.

The cultivation is as follows. In the month of *Chait* (March–April), about New-Year's [1] time, they take a part of a creeper four or five fingers long with *Karhanj* leaves on it, and put it below the ground. From fifteen to twenty days after, according as leaves and knots form, a new creeper will appear from a knot, and as soon as another knot forms, a leaf will grow up. The creepers and new leaves form for seven months, when the plant ceases to grow. No creeper has more than thirty leaves. As the plant grows, they prop it with canes, and cover it, on the top and the sides, with wood and straw, so as to rear it up in the shade. The plant requires continually to be watered, except during the rains. Sometimes they put milk, sesame oil and its dregs, etc., about the plant. There are seven kinds of leaves, known under nine names: 1. The *Karhanj* leaf, which they separate for seedlings and call *Peṛī*. The new leaf is called *Gaḍauta*. 2. The *Nautī* leaf. 3. The *Bahutī* leaf. 4. The *Chhīw* leaf. 5. The *Adhinīḍā* leaf. 6. The *Agahniya* or *Lewār* leaf. 7. The *Karhanj* leaf itself. With the exception of the *Gaḍauta*, the leaves are taken away from the creeper when a month old. The last kind of leaf is eaten by some;

[[1] The 21st March is New Year's Day.—P.]

others keep it for seeding: they consider it very excellent, but connoisseurs prefer the *Peṛī*.

A bundle of 11,000 leaves was formerly called *Lahāsa*, which name is now given to a bundle of 14,000. Bundles of 200 are called *Ḍholī*; a *lahāsa* is made up of *ḍholīs*. In winter they turn and arrange the leaves after four or five days; in summer every day. From 5 to 25 leaves, and sometimes more, are placed above each other, and displayed in various ways. They also put some betel nut and *kath* [1] on one leaf, and some lime [2] paste on another, and roll them up; this is called a *bīṛā*. Some put camphor and musk into it, and tie both leaves with a silk thread. Others put single leaves on plates, and use them thus. They are also prepared as a dish.

Āʾīn 29.

ON FLAVOURS.

As I have mentioned various kinds of food, I shall also say something on flavours. *Heat* renders pungent that which is agreeable, bitter that which is greasy, and brackish that which has the proper flavour; *cold* makes the first acid, the second astringent, and the third tart. Astringency when affecting the tongue merely, is called in Arabic *qabẓ*; and *ʿufūṣat* when affecting the whole frame. A *moderate* temperature renders the first quality greasy, the second sweet, and the last tasteless. These are the fundamental flavours. Others count four, viz., the sweet, the bitter, the acid, the brackish. The flavours produced by combinations are endless; some have, however, names, e.g. *bashāʿat* is a bitter and tart flavour, and *zuʿūqa* a combination of the brackish and the bitter.

Āʾīn 30.

ON PERFUMES.

His Majesty is very fond of perfumes, and encourages this department from religious motives. The court-hall is continually scented with ambergris, aloewood, and compositions according to ancient recipes, or mixtures invented by his Majesty; and incense is daily burnt in gold and silver censers of various shapes; whilst sweet-smelling flowers are used

---

[1] An astringent vegetable extract eaten by the natives of India with the *pān* leaf. It looks brown, and stains the tongue and the gums red. [Catechu ?—P.]

[2] In Persian *chūna*; but in Anglo-Indice, *chunām*.

in large quantities. Oils are also extracted from flowers, and used for the skin and the hair. I shall give a few recipes.

1. *Santūk* is used for keeping the skin fresh: 1½ *tolās* Civet; 1 *t.* *Chūwa*[1]; 2 *māshas Chambelī* essence; 2 bottles of rose-water. 2. *Argaja* ¾ *s.* sandalwood; 2 *t.* *Iksīr* and *Mīd*; 3 *t.* *Chūwa*; 1 *t.* violet root, and *gehla* (the seed of a plant); ½ *m.* camphor; 11 bottles of rose-water. It is used in summer for keeping the skin cool. 3. *Gulkāma*: Pound together 1 *t.* best Ambergris; ½ *t.* *Lādan*; 2 *t.* best musk; 4 *t.* wood of aloes, and 8 *t.* *Iksīr-i ʿabīr*; and put it into a porcelain vessel, mix with it a *ser* of the juice of the flower called *Gul-i surkh*,[2] and expose it to the sun, till it dries up. Wet it in the evening with rose-water and with the extract of the flower called *Bahār*, and pound it again on *Samāq*[3] stone. Let it stand for ten days, mix it with the juice of the flower called *Bahār-i Nāranj*,[4] and let it dry. During the next twenty days, add occasionally some juice of the black *Rayḥān* (also called black *Nāzbū*).[5] A part of this mixture is added to the preceding. 4. *Rūḥ-afzā*, 5 *s.* Aloewood; 1¼ *s.* Sandalwood; 1¼ *s.* *Lādan*; *Iksīr*, *Lūbān*, *Dhūp* (a root brought from Kashmīr), 3½ *t.* of each; 20 *t.* violet root; 10 *t.* *Ushna*, called in Hind. *Chharīla*: Press till it gets tenacious like syrup. To be made into discs with four bottles of rose-water. It is burnt in censers, and smells very fine. 5. *Opatna* is a scented soap: 2¾ *s.* *Lādan*; 1½ *s.* 5 *d.* Aloewood; the same quantity of *Bahār-i Nāranj*,[4] and 1½ *s.* of its bark; 1 *s.* 10 *d.* Sandalwood; 1 *s.* 5 *d.* *Sumbulᵘ 't-ṭīb*, called in Hind *Chhaṛ*; the same quantity of *Ushna*; 38½ *t.* musk; 1 *s.* 4 *t.* *pācha* leaves; 36 *t.* apples; 11 *t.* *Suʿd*, called in Hind *Moṭh*; 5 *d.* violet root; 1 *t.* 2 *m.* *Dhūp*; 1½ *t.* *Ikankī* (a kind of grass); the same quantity of *Zurumbād*, called in Hind. *kachūr* (zerumbet); 1 *t.* 2 *m.* *Lūbān*; 106 bottles of rose-water; 5 bottles of extract of *Bahār*. Pound the whole, sift it, and boil slowly in rose-water. When it has become less moist let it dry. 6. *ʿAbīrmāya*,[6] 4 *d.* Aloewood; 2 *d.* Sandalwood; 1 *d.* violet root; 3 *d.* *Sumbulᵘ 't-ṭīb*; 3 *d.* *Duwālak*; 4 *t.* musk of *Khatā* (Cathay); 2½ *d.* *Lādan*; 7½ *d.* *Bahār-i Nāranj*. Pound and sift, boil over a slow fire in 10 bottles of rose-water, and put it into the shade to dry. 7. *Kisāta*, 24 *t.* Aloewood; 6½ *Lādan*, *Lūbān*, and Sandalwood; *Iksīr* and *Dhūp*, 2 *t.* of each; violet root and musk, 2 *t.*;

---

1 This and the following names of perfumes are explained further on in this chapter.

[2 *Gul-i surkh* in Persian is a pink fragrant rose that blooms in Spring.—P.]

[3 *Summāq* (vide *sumāq*) is the hardest kind of marble.—P.]

[4 Orange-flower bloom.—P.]

[5 Sweet basil.—P.]

6 *Vide* below the twelfth flower.

1 *t. Ushna*; mix with 50 *t.* refined sugar, and boil gently in two bottles of rose-water. It is made into discs. It smells very fine when burnt, and is exhilarating. 8. *Bukhūr*: 1 *s.* Aloewood and Sandalwood; ¼ *s. Lādan*; 2 *t.* musk; 5 *t. Iksīr*; mix with two *sers* of refined sugar and one bottle of rose-water over a slow fire. 9. *Fatīla*: 5 *s.* Aloewood; 72 *t.* Sandalwood; *Iksīr* and *Lādan*, 20 *t.* of each; 5 *t.* Violet root; 10 *t. Lūbān*; 3 *t.* refined sugar; mix with two bottles of rose-water, and make into tapers. 10. *Bārjāt*; 1 *s.* Aloewood; 5 *t. Lādan*; 2 *t.* musk; 2 *t.* Sandalwood; 1 *t. Lūbān*; ½ *t.* Camphor. Then distill it like *Chūwa* (*vide* below). 11. ʿ*Abīr-Iksīr*: ¾ *s.* Sandalwood; 26 *t. Iksīr*; 2 *t.* 8 *m.* musk. Pound it, and dry it in the shade. 12. *Ghasūl* (a liquid soap), 35 *t.* Sandalwood; 17 *t. Katūl* (?)[1]; 1 *t.* musk; 1 *t. Chūwa*; 2 *m.* Camphor; 2 *m. Mīd.* Mix with 2 bottles of rose-water.

A List of Perfumes[2] *and their Prices.*

ʿ*Ambar i ashhab*	1 to 3 Muhurs, per *tolā.*
Zabād (civet)	½ *R.* to 1 *M.*, *do.*
Musk	1 to 4½ *R.*, *do.*
Lignum aloes Hind. *Agar*	2 *R.* to 1 *M.*, per *ser.*
Chūwa (Distilled wood of Aloes)	⅛ *R.* to 1 *R.*, per *tolā.*
Gaura[3]	3 to 5 *R.*, *do.*
Bhīmsīnī Camphor	3 *R.* to 2 *M.*, *do.*
Mīd	1 to 3 *R.*, *do.*
Zaʿfarān.	12 to 22 *R.*, per *ser.*
Zaʿfarān-i Kamandī.	1 to 3 *M.*, *do.*
Zaʿfarān (from Kashmīr)	8 to 12 *R.*, *do.*
Sandalwood	32 to 55 *R.*, per *man.*
Nāfa-yi mushk	3 to 12 *M.*, per *ser.*
Kalanbak (Calembic)	10 to 40 *R.*, per *man.*
Silāras	3 to 5 *R.*, per *ser.*
ʿ*Ambar-i Lādan*	1½ to 4 *R.*, *do.*
Kāfūr-ī Chīna	1 to 2 *R.*, *do.*
ʿ*Araq-i Fitna*	1 to 3 *R.*, per *bottle.*
ʿ*Araq-i Bēd-i Mushk*	1 to 4 *R.*, *do.*
Rosewater	½ to 1 *R.*, *do.*
ʿ*Araq-i Bahār*	1 to 5 *R.*, *do.*
ʿ*Araq-i Chambelī*	⅛ to ¼ *R.*, *do.*
Violet-root	½ to 1 *R.*, per *ser.*

[1] According to some MSS. *Kanwal.*
[2] Most of the following names are explained below.
[3] In the text, p. 85, by mistake *Kaurah.* *Vide* my text edition, p. 94, l. 6.

Azfāru 'ṯ-ṯīb	1½ to 2 *R.*, per *ser.*
Barg-i Māj (brought from Gujrāt)	½ to 1 *R.*, *do.*
Sugandh Gūgalā	10 to 13 *R.*, *do.*
Lūbān (from Sargard ?)	⅓ to 3 *R.*, per *tolā.*
Lūbān (other kinds)	1 to 2 *R.*, per *ser.*
Alak, Hind. *Chhaṛ*	¼ to ½ *R.*, *do.*
Duwālak, Hind. *Chhaṛīla*	3 to 4 *d.*, *do.*
Gehla	*
Suʿd	*
Ikankī	*
Zurumbād	*

* The original does not mention the prices.

A List of fine smelling Flowers.

1. The *Sewtī.* Whitish; blooms the whole year, especially towards the end of the rains.
2. The *Bholsarī.* Whitish; in the rains.
3. The *Chambelī.* White, yellow, and blue. In the rains, and partly during winter.
4. *Rāy-bel.* White and pale yellow. In the end of the hot season, and the beginning of the rains.
5. The *Mongrā.* Yellow. In summer.
6. The *Champa.* Yellow. All the year; especially when the sun stands in Pisces and Aries.
7. *Ketkī.* The upper leaves are green, the inner ones yellowish-white. It blooms during the hot summer.
8. *Kūza.* White. During the hot season.
9. The *Pādal.* Brownish lilac. In spring.
10. The *Jūhī.* White and yellow, like jasmin. During the rains.
11. The *Niwāṛī.* Whitish. In spring.
12. The *Nargis.* White. In spring.
13. The *Kewara.* From Leo to Libra.
14. The *Chalta.*
15. The *Gulāl.* In spring.
16. The *Tasbīḥ Gulāl.* White. In winter.
17. The *Singārhār.* It has small white petals. In the hot season.
18. The *Violet.* Violet. In the hot season.
19. The *Karna.* White In spring.
20. The *Kapūr bél.*
21. The *Gul-i Zaʿfarān.* Lilac-colour. In autumn.

A List of Flowers notable for their beauty.

1. The *Gul-i Āftāb*. Yellow.

2. The *Gul-i Kāwal*. White and also bluish. In the rains.

3. The *Jaʿfarī*. A golden yellow, or orange coloured, or greenish. In spring.

4. The *Guḍhal*. Of different colours, red, yellow, orange, white. In the rains.

5. The *Ratan-manjanī*. Bright red. It is smaller than jasmin. All the year.

6. The *Kesū*. In the hot season.

7. The *Senbal*. Dark red. In spring.

8. The *Ratan-mālā*. Yellow. In spring.

9. The *Sonzard*. Yellow. In spring.

10. The *Gul-i Māltī*.

11. The *Karnphūl*. A golden red.

12. The *Karīl*. In spring.

13. The *Kaner*. Red and white.

14. The *Kadam*. Outside green; in the middle yellow threads; the inside leaves white. In spring.

15. The *Nāg-kesar*. In spring.

16. The *Surpan*. White, with red and yellow stripes in the middle. During the rains.

17. The *Sirī khanḍī*. Inside yellowish white, outside reddish. In spring.

18. The *Jait*. Inside yellow, outside a blackish red. In the rains.

19. The *Champala*. White, like orange blossoms. In spring.

20. The *Lāhī*. It blooms in Pisces.

21. The *Gul-i Karaunda*. White. It is smaller than the Chambēlī, and blooms during the rains.

22. The *Dhanantar* resembles the *Nīlūfar*. During the rains.

23. The *Gul-i Ḥinnā*.

24. The *Dupahriyā*. Bright red and white. All the year.

25. The *Bhūn Champā*. Peach coloured.

26. The *Sudarsan*. Yellow; it resembles the *Nīlūfar*, but is smaller.

27. The *Kanglā,ī*. There are two kinds, red and white.

28. The *Sirs*. Yellowish green. It is full of stamens. In spring.

29. The *San*. Yellow. During the rains.

On the Preparation of some Perfumes.

1. *ʿAmbar.* Some say that *ʿAmbar* grows at the bottom of the sea, and that it is the food brought up again after eating, by various animals living in the sea. Others say that fishes eat it and die from it, and that it is taken from their intestines. According to some, it is the dung of the sea-cow, called *sārā*; or the foam of the sea. Others again say, it trickles from the mountains of islands. Many look upon it as marine gum; others whose opinion I adopt, take it to be wax. It is said that on some mountains a great deal of honey is to be found, so much in fact that it runs into the sea; the wax rises to the surface, when the heat of the sun reduces it to a solid state. As the bees collect the honey from sweet smelling flowers, *ʿAmbar* is, naturally, scented. Bees are also occasionally found in it. *Abū Sīnā* thinks that there is a fountain at the bottom of the sea, from which *ʿAmbar* rills, when it is carried by waves to the shore. *ʿAmbar*, when fresh, is moist; the heat of the sun causes it to dry up. It is of various colours: the white is the best, and the black is the worst; the middling sort is pistachio-coloured and yellow. The best kind goes by the name of *ashhab*. It feels greasy, and consists of layers. If you break it, it looks yellowish white. The whiter, lighter, and more flexible it is the better. Next in quality is the pistachio-coloured *ʿAmbar*; and the inferior to it the yellow kind, called *Khashkhāshī*. The black kind is bad; it is inflammable. Greedy bāzār-dealers will mix it with wax, *Mandal*, and *Lādan*, etc.; but not every one has recourse to such practices. *Mandal* is a kind of *ʿAmbar* taken from the intestines of dead fishes; it does not smell much.

2. *Lādan* is also often called *ʿAmbar.* It is taken from a tree which grows in the confines of *Qibrus* (Cyprus) and *Qīsūs* (Chios) or *Qistūs*. It is a moisture that settles on the leaves of the tree. When goats in grazing pass near it, the hairs of their thighs and the horn of their hoofs stick to it, and the whole then dries up. Such *Lādan* as is mixed with goat's-hair is counted superior. It looks greenish, and has a good smell. But *Lādan* which is mixed with horn is looked upon as inferior. Sometimes people tie ropes round about the trees, and collect the *Lādan* which sticks to them. Afterwards they boil it in water, clean it, and make it into discs.

3. The *Camphor tree* is a large tree growing in the ghauts of Hindustan and in China. A hundred horsemen and upwards may rest in the shade of a single tree. Camphor is collected from the trunk and the branches. Some say that during summer a large number of snakes wind themselves round about the tree for the sake of its coolness; people then mark such trees by shooting an arrow into the trunks, and collect the camphor during

the winter. Others say that camphor trees are much frequented by leopards,[1] which like camphor so much that they seldom leave them. The camphor within the tree looks like small bits of salt ; that on the outside like resin. It often flows from the tree on the ground, and gets, after some time, solid. If there are earthquakes during the year or any other cosmical disturbances, camphor is found in large quantities.

Of the various kinds of camphor the best is called *Ribāḥī*, or *Qayṣūrī*.[2] Although different in name, they are the same ; for it is said that the first camphor was found by a king of the name of *Ribāḥ* near *Qayṣūr*, which is a place near the island of Ceylon. According to some books, it is white like snow ; and this is true, for I have broken it myself from the tree. Ibn Bayṭār, however, said that it was originally red and shining, and only got white by artificial crystallization. Whatever the case may be, there is certainly a kind of camphor which is white in its natural state. And of all kinds it is the best, the whitest, has the thinnest layers, and is the cleanest and largest. Inferior to it is the kind called *Qurqūy*, which is blackish and dirty. Still inferior is the light brown kind called *Kawkab*. The worst camphor is mixed with pieces of wood; it goes under the name of *Bālūs*. By artificial crystallization each kind will become clean and white. In some books, camphor in its natural state is called *Jūdāna or Bhīmsīnī*. If kept with a few barley grains, or peppercorns,[3] or *surkh dāna*, it will evaporate the less. The camphor which is made of *Zurumbād* by mixing it with other ingredients, is called *Chīnī* or *Mayyit*-camphor. White Zurumbād is finely pounded, and mixed with sour cream [4] of cow or buffalo ; on the fourth day they put fresh cream [4] to it, and beat it with the hand till foam appears, which they take away. With this they mix some camphor, put it into a box, and keep it for some time in the husks of grains. Or, they reduce some white stone to fine powder, mix it at the rate of ten dirhams of it with two dirhams of wax, and half a dirham of oil of Violet, or oil of *Surkh Gul*. The wax is first melted, and then mixed with the powder, so as to form a paste. They then put it between two stones, and make it thin and flat. When it gets cold, it looks like camphor, bits of which are mixed with it. Unprincipled men profit in this manner by the loss of others.

4. *Zabād* (civet) is also called *Shākh*. It is a moist substance secreted during the rutting season by an animal which resembles a cat, having, how-

[[1] *Yūz*, the cheeta or hunting-leopard.—P.]

[2] *Fanṣūrī* according to Marco Polo. *Fanṣūr* is a state in Sumatra.—B.

[3] Bāzār dealers give a few peppercorns along with every piece of camphor.

[[4] *Dogh* buttermilk, not cream.—P.]

ever, a larger face and mouth. The *zabād* which is brought from the harbour-town of Sumatra, from the territory of Āchīn, goes by the name of Sumatra zabād, and is by far the best. The moist substance itself is yellowish white. The animal has below its tail a bag, of the size of a small hazel nut, in which there are from five to six holes. The bag may be emptied every week or fortnight, and yields from half a *tolā* to eight *māshas*. Some civet cats become so tame as to keep still when the bag is being emptied; but in the case of most animals, they have to catch hold of the tail and draw it through the cage when they take out the *zabād* with a shell, or by pressing gently against the bag. The price of a civet cat varies from 300 to 500 Rs. The *zabād* of the male is better than that of the female, because in the latter the vulva is just above the bag. When removed, the *zabād* is washed, and becomes afterwards one of the finest perfumes. The perfume will remain a long time in the clothes, and even on the skin. There are several ways of washing it. If the quantity be small, they put in into a cup, or if greater, into a larger vessel, and wash it thirty times in cold water, and three times in warm water. The latter renders it thin and removes impurities. Then they wash it again in cold water till it gets solid, when they wash it three times in lime juice, which removes all unpleasant smell. After this, they wash it again three times in cold water, pass it through a piece of cloth, put it into a China cup, and wash it three times in rose-water. They then smear the *zabād* on the inside of the cup, keep it at night inverted in extract of *Chambelī*, or *Rāy-bel*, or *Surkh gul*, or *Gul-i Karna*, and expose it at daytime to the rays of the sun, covered with a piece of white cloth till all moisture goes away. It may then be used, mixed with a little rose-water.

5. *Gaura* looks greyish white, but does not smell so well as the preceding. It is a moisture secreted during the rutting season by an animal like the civet cat, but somewhat larger. It is also brought from the confines of Āchīn. The price of this animal varies from 100 to 200 Rs.

6. *Mīd* [1] resembles the preceding, but is inferior to it. They mix it with other substances; hence they sell it in larger quantities. The animal which yields *Mīd* is found in various countries, and sells for from five to six *dāms* only. Some say that *Mīd* is the dried bag of the civet cat, pounded and boiled in water; the greasy substance which rises to the surface is the *Mīd*.

7. ʿ*Ūd*, or wood of Aloes, called in Hind. *Agar*, is the root of a tree. They lop it off and bury it in the earth, when whatever is bad rots, and the

---

[1] ميد with the kasrah, a kind of perfume. *Kashf*^{u} *'l-lughāt*.

remainder is pure aloes. Some say that they do so with the whole tree. The statement occasionally found in some old books that the habitat of the tree is Central India, is an absurdity of fanciful writers. There are several kinds; the best is called *Mandalī*, and the second in quality, *Jabalī* or *Hindī*. The smell of the wood, especially that of the first kind, is a preventive against fleas; but some think both kinds equal in this respect. Of other good kinds I may mention the *Samandūrī*; the *Qumārī*, which is inferior to it; the *Qāqulī*, next in rank; the *Barrī*; the *Qiṭʿī*; and the Chinese, also called *Qismūrī*, which is wet and sweet. Still inferior are the *Jalālī*, the *Māyatāqī*, the *Lawāqī*, the *Riṭalī*.[1] But of all kinds, the *Mandalī* is the best. The *Samandūrī* is grey, fatty, thick, hard, juicy, without the slightest sign of whitishness, and burns long. The best of all is the black and heavy; in water it settles at the bottom, is not fibrous, and may be easily pounded. The wood which floats is looked upon as bad. Former kings transplanted the tree to Gujrāt, and nowadays it grows in Chānpānīr. It is generally brought from Āchīn and Dahnāsarī. Nothing is known of the *habitat* mentioned in old books. Aloewood is often used in compound perfumes; when eaten, it is exhilarating. It is generally employed in incense; the better qualities, in form of a powder, are often used for rubbing into the skin and clothes.

8. *Chūwa* is distilled wood of aloes; it is in general use. The preparation is as follows: They take fine clay, mix it with cotton or rice bran and beat it well. When properly intermixed, they take a small bottle large enough to put a finger in, smear it all over with the clay, and let it dry. After this, they put very small pieces of wood of aloes into it, so as nearly to fill the bottle. The wood must have been kept wet for a week before. Another vessel, with a hole in the middle, is now placed on a three-legged stand. Into this vessel, they pass the neck of the little bottle inverted, placing a cup full of water at the bottom of the vessel in such a manner that the mouth of the bottle reaches the surface of the water. On the top of the vessel they then put cow's dung, and light a gentle fire. Should flames break out they extinguish them with water. The wood of aloes will then secrete a moisture which trickles on the surface of the water where it remains. This is collected, and washed several times with water and rose water, to take off all smell of smoke. The oftener it is washed, and the older it gets, the better will be the scent. It looks black, although experienced people make it white. One *ser* of wood aloes will yield from two to fifteen *tolās* of Chūwa. Some avaricious dealers mix sandalwood or almonds with it, thereby to cheat people.

---

[1] The last three names are doubtful.

9. *Sandalwood* is called in Hind. *Chandan.* The tree grows in China. During the present reign, it has been successfully planted in India. There are three kinds, the white, the yellow, the red. Some take the red to be more refreshing than the white; others prefer the white. The latter is certainly more cooling than the red, and the red more so than the yellow. The best is that which is yellow and oily; it goes by the name of *Maqāṣarī.* Sandalwood is pounded and rubbed over the skin; but it is also used in other ways.

10. *Silāras* (storax) is called in Arabic *Mīʿah.* It is the gum of a tree that grows in Turkey. The kind which is clear is called *Mīʿah-yi sāyila* (liquid); the other kinds, *Mīʿah-yi yābisa* (dry). The best kind is that which spontaneously flows out of the trunk; it is yellowish.

11. *Kalanbak* (calembic) is the wood of a tree brought from Zīrbād (?)[1]: it is heavy and full of veins. Some believe it to be raw wood of aloes. When pounded it looks grey. They use it for compound perfumes; and they also make rosaries of it.

12. The *Malāgīr* is a tree resembling the former, only that the wood is lighter and not veined. When pounded it looks reddish white.

13. *Lubān* (frankincense) is the odorous gum of a tree which is found in Java. Some take it to be the same as *Mīʿah-yi yābisa.* When exposed to fire it evaporates like camphor. The *Lubān* which the Persians call *Kundur-i daryāʾī* (mastix) is a resin brought from Yaman; but it is not odorous.

14. *Aẓfāru 't-ṭīb*, or scented finger nails, are called in Hind *Nakh*, and in Persian *Nākhun-i boyā.* It is the house of an animal, consisting, like a shell, of two parts. It has a sweet smell, as the animal feeds on *sumbul*; it is found in the large rivers of Hindustan, Baṣrah, and Baḥrayan, the latter being considered the best. It is also found in the Red Sea, and many prefer it to the other kinds. It is heated in butter; some expose it to the fire, pound it, and mix it with other perfumes.

15. *Sugandh gūgalā* (bdellium) is a plant very common in Hindustan; it is used in perfumes.

As I have said something on perfumes, I shall make a few remarks on several beautiful flowers.

1. The *Sewtī* resembles the *Gul-i Surkh*, but is smaller. It has in

---

[1] **Zīrbād (Zīrābād), a town near the frontiers of Bengal. *Ghiyāṣu 'l-lughāt.***
[The Persian translation of the Malay *Bāwah angīn*, "below the wind, leeward," being the Malay name for the countries and islands to the East of Sumatra.—B.]

the middle golden stamens and from four to six petals. *Habitat*, Gujrāt and the Dakhin.

2. Of the *Chambelī* there are two kinds. The *Rāy Chambelī* has from five to six petals, outside red. The *Chambelī proper* is smaller, and has on the top a red stripe. Its stem is one and a half or two yards high, and trails over the ground. It has many long and broad branches. It flowers from the first year.

3. The *Rāybel* resembles the jasmin. There are various kinds ; single and double, etc. A quintuple is very common, so that each petal might be separated as a distinct flower. Its stem grows a yard high. The leaves of the tree resemble those of the lime tree ; but they are somewhat smaller and softer.

4. The *Mungrā* resembles the *Rāybel.* It is larger, but inferior in perfume. It has more than a hundred petals ; the plant grows to a large tree.

5. The *Champa* flower has a conical shape, of the size of a finger,[1] and consists of ten petals and more, lying in folds one above the other. It has several stamens. The tree looks graceful, and resembles in leaf and trunk the nut tree. It flowers after seven years.

6. The *Ketkī* has the form of spindle[2] of the size of a quarter of a yard, with twelve or more petals. Its smell is delicate and fragrant. It bears flowers in six or seven years.

7. The *Kewra* resembles the preceding, but is more than twice as big. The petals have thorns. As they grow on different places, they are not all equal. In the midst of the flower, there is a small branch with honey-coloured threads, not without smell. The flower smells even after it is withered. Hence people put it into clothes when the perfume remains for a long time. The stem of the tree is above four yards high; the leaves are like those of the maize, only longer, and triangular, with three thorns in each corner. It flowers from the fourth year. Every year they put new earth round about the roots. The plant is chiefly found in the Dakhin, Gujrāt, Mālwah, and Bihār.

8. The *Chalta* resembles a large tulip.[3] It consists of eighteen petals, six green ones above, six others, some red, some green, some greyish yellow, and six white. In the midst of the flower, as in the flower called *Hamesha Bahār*, there are nearly two hundred little yellow leaves, with a red globule in the centre. The flower will remain quite fresh for five or six

---

1 Orientals, as a rule, have very small hands and fingers.

[2 *Sanābarī-paykar*, a fir-cone ?—P.]

[3 *Lāla* is the name of the common red poppy, as well as of the tulip.—P.]

days after having been plucked. It smells like the violet. When withered, the flower is cooked and eaten. The tree resembles the pomegranate tree; and its leaves look like those of the lime tree. It blooms in seven years.

9. The *Tasbīḥ gulāl* has a fine smell. The petals have the form of a dagger. The stem of the plant is two yards high. It flowers after four years. They make rosaries of the flowers, which keep fresh for a week.

10. The *Bholsarī* is smaller than the jasmin; its petals are indented. When dry the flower smells better. The tree resembles the walnut tree, and flowers in the tenth year.

11. The *Singārhār* is shaped like a clove, and has an orange-coloured stalk. The stamens look like poppy seeds. The tree resembles the pomegranate tree, and the leaves are like the leaves of a peach tree. It flowers in five years.

12. The *Kūza* looks like a *Gul-i surkh*; but the plant and the leaves are larger. It has five or a hundred petals and golden coloured stamens in the middle. They make *ʿAbīrmāya* and an extract from it.

13. The *Pāḍal* has five or six long petals. It gives water an agreeable flavour and smell. It is on this account that people preserve the flowers, mixed with clay, for such times when the flower is out of season. The leaves and the stem are like those of a nut tree. It flowers in the twelfth year.

14. The *Jūhī* has small leaves. This creeper winds itself round about trees, and flowers in three years.

15. The *Niwārī* looks like a simple *Rāy-bel*, but has larger petals. The flowers are often so numerous as to conceal the leaves and branches of the plant. It flowers in the first year.

16. The *Kapūr bél* has five petals, and resembles the saffron flower. This flower was brought during the present reign from Europe.

17. The *Zaʿfarān* (saffron).[1] In the beginning of the month of *Urdībihisht*, the saffron seeds are put into the ground, which has been carefully prepared and rendered soft. After this, the field is irrigated with rain-water. The seed itself is a bulb resembling garlic. The flower appears in the middle of the month of Ābān; the plant is about a quarter of a yard long; but, according to the difference of the soil in which it stands, there are sometimes two-thirds of it above, and sometimes two-thirds below the ground. The flower stands on the top of the stalk, and consists of six petals and six stamens. Three of the six petals have a fresh lilac colour, and stand round about the remaining three petals. The stamens

[1] *Vide* a similar account of the saffron flower in the third book (Ṣūba Kābul).

are similarly placed, three of a yellow colour standing round about the other three, which are red. The latter yield the saffron. Yellow stamens are often cunningly intermixed. In former times saffron was collected by compulsory labour; they pressed men daily, and made them separate the saffron from the petals and the stamens, and gave them salt instead of wages, a man who cleaned two *pals* receiving two *pals* of salt. At the time of Ghāzī Khān,[1] the son of (Khājī) Chak, another custom became general; they gave the workmen eleven *tarks* of saffron flowers, of which one *tark* was given them as wages; and for the remaining ten they had to furnish two Akbarshāhī sers of clean, dry saffron, i.e., for two Akbarshāhī *mans* [2] of saffron flowers they had to give two sers of cleaned saffron. This custom, however, was abolished by his Majesty on his third visit to Kashmīr, to the great relief of the people.

When the bulb has been put into the ground, it will produce flowers for six years, provided the soil be annually softened. For the first two years, the flowers will grow sparingly; but in the third year the plant reaches its state of perfection. After six years the bulbs must be taken out; else they get rotten. They plant them again on some other place; and leave the old ground uncultivated for five years.

Saffron comes chiefly from the place Panpūr, which belongs to the district of Mararāj.[3] The fields there extend over nearly twelve *kós*. Another place of cultivation is in the Parganah of Paraspūr, near Indrakol, not far from Kamrāj, where the fields extend about a *kos*.

18. The *Aftābī* (sun-flower) is round, broad, and large, has a large number of petals, and turns continually to the sun. Its stem reaches a height of three yards.

19. The *Kanwal*. There are two kinds. One opens when the sublime Sun shines, turning wherever he goes, and closing at night. It resembles the *shaqāyiq*,[4] but its red is paler. Its petals which are never less than six in number, enclose yellow stamens, in the midst of which there is an excrescence of the form of a cone with the base upwards, which is the fruit, and contains the seeds. The other kind has four white petals, opens at night, and turns itself according to the moon, but does not close.

---

[1] He was the contemporary of Shér Khān; *vide* Abū 'l-Faẓl's list of Kashmīr Rulers in the third book. A good biography of *Ghāzī Khān* may be found in the beginning of the *Ma āṣir-i Raḥīmī*, Persian MS. No. 45 of the Asiatic Society of Bengal.

[2] One Kashmīrī *Tark*=8 *sers* (of Akbar)=4 Kashm. *mans*; 1 Kash. *man*= 4 Kash. *sers*; 1 Kash. *ser*=7½ *pals*.

[3] These places lie to the south of Srīnagar, the capital of Kashmīr; for *Marurāj* the text has مرراج. *Vide* Ṣūba Kābul, third book.

[[4] The *shaqāyiq* is probably the anemone.—P.]

20. The *Jaʿfarī* is a pretty, round flower, and grows larger than the *ṣadbarg*. One kind has five, another a hundred petals. The latter remains fresh for two months and upwards. The plant is of the size of a man, and the leaves resemble those of the willow, but are indented. It flowers in two months.

21. The *Guḍhal* resembles the *jūghāsū* tulip, and has a great number of petals. Its stem reaches a height of two yards and upwards ; the leaves look like mulberry leaves. It flowers in two years.

22. The *Ratanmanjanī* has four petals, and is smaller than the jasmin. The tree and the leaves resemble the *rāy-bel*. It flowers in two years.

23. The *Kesū* has five petals resembling a tiger's claw. In their midst is a yellow stamen of the shape of a tongue. The plant is very large, and is found on every meadow ; when it flowers, it is as if a beautiful fire surrounded the scenery.

24. The *Kaner* remains a long time in bloom. It looks well, but it is poisonous. Whoever puts it on his head is sure to fall in battle.[1] It has mostly five petals. The branches are full of the flowers ; the plant itself grows to a height of two yards. It flowers in the first year.

25. The *Kadam* resembles a *tumāgha* [2] (a royal cap). The leaves are like those of the walnut tree, which the whole tree resembles.

26. The *Nāg kesar*, like the *Gul-i surkh*, has five petals and is full of fine stamens. It resembles the walnut tree in the leaves and the stem; and flowers in seven years.

27. The *Surpan* resembles the sesame flower, and has yellow stamens in the middle. The stem resembles the *Ḥinnā* plant, and the leaves those of the willow.

28. The *Srīkandhī* is like the *Chambelī*, but smaller. It flowers in two years.

29. The *Ḥinna* has four petals, and resembles the flower called *Nāfarmān*. Different plants have often flowers of a different colour.

30. The *Dupahriyā* is round and small, and looks like the flower called *Hamesha-bahār*. It opens at noon. The stem is about two yards high.

31. The *Bhūn champā* resembles the *Nīlūfar*, and has five petals. The stem is about a span long. It grows on such places as are periodically under water. Occasionally a plant is found above the water.

32. The *Sudarsan* resembles the *Rāy-bel*, and has yellow threads inside. The stem looks like that of the *Sūsan* [3] flower.

[[1] باَویزه در اُفتد gets entangled in quarrels ?—P.]
[[2] *Tumāgha* locally survives in the sense of a hawk's hood.—P.]
[[3] *Sūsan* is properly the flag-iris.—P.]

33. *Senbal* has five petals, each ten fingers long, and three fingers broad.

34. The *Ratanmālā* is round and small. Its juice, boiled and mixed with vitriol and *muʿaṣfar*,[1] furnishes a fast dye for stuffs. Butter, sesame, oil, are also boiled together with the root of the plant, when the mixture becomes a purple dye.

35. The *Sūnzard* resembles the jasmin, but is a little larger, and has from five to six petals. The stem is like that of the *Chambelī*. It flowers in two years.

36. The *Māltī* is like the *Chamhelī*, but smaller. In the middle there are little stamens looking like poppyseed. It flowers in two years more or less.

37. The *Karīl* has three small petals. It flowers luxuriantly, and looks very well. The flower is also boiled and eaten; they also make pickles of it.

38. The *Jait* plant grows to a large tree; its leaves look like Tamarind leaves.

39. The *Chanpala* is like a nosegay. The leaves of the plant are like walnut leaves. It flowers in two years. The bark of the plant, when boiled in water, makes the water red. It grows chiefly in the hills; its wood burns bright like a candle.

40. The *Lāhī* has a stem one and a half yards high. The branches before the flowers appear are made into a dish, which is eaten with bread. When camels feed on this plant they get fat and unruly.

41. The *Karaunda* resembles the *Jūhī* flower.

42. The *Dhanantar* resembles the *Nīlūfar*, and looks very well. It is a creeper.

43. The *Siras* flower consists of silk-like threads, and resembles a *tumāgha*. It sends its fragrance to a great distance. It is the king of the trees, although the Hindus rather worship the *Pīpal* and *Baṛ*[2] trees. The tree grows very large; its wood is used in building. Within the stem the wood is black, and resists the stroke of the axe.

44. The *Kanglā,ī* has five petals, each four fingers long, and looks very beautiful. Each branch produces only one flower.

45. The *San* (hemp) looks like a nosegay. The leaves of the plant resemble those of the *Chinār*.[3] Of the bark of the plant strong ropes are made. One kind of this plant bears a flower like the cotton tree, and is called *Paṭ-san*. It makes a very soft rope.

[[1] *Muʿaṣfar* is perhaps bastard saffron —P.]
[[2] *Bar* the banyan tree.—P.]
[[3] *Chinār*, the plane tree.—P.]

It is really too difficult for me, ignorant as I am, to give a description of the flowers of this country: I have mentioned a few for those who wish to know something about them. There are also found many flowers of Īrān and Tūrān, as the *Gul-i surkh*, the *Nargis*, the violet, the *Yāsman-i kabūd*, the *Ṣūsan*,[1] the *Rayḥān*,[2] the *Raʿnā*, the *Zébā*, the *Shaqāyiq*,[3] the *Tāj-i khurūs*, the *Qalgha*, the *Nāfarmān*, the *Khaṭmī*,[4] etc. Garden and flower beds are everywhere to be found. Formerly people used to plant their gardens without any order, but since the time of the arrival in India of the emperor Bābar, a more methodical arrangement of the gardens has obtained; and travellers nowadays admire the beauty of the palaces and their murmuring fountains.

It would be impossible to give an account of those trees of the country whose flowers, fruits, buds, leaves, roots, etc., are used as food or medicine. If, according to the books of the Hindus, a man were to collect only one leaf from each tree, he would get eighteen *bārs* (or loads) (5 *surkhs* = 1 *māsha*; 16 *māshas* = 1 *karg*; 4 *kargs* = 1 *pal*; 100 *pals* = 1 *tulā*; 20 *tulās* = 1 *bār*); *i.e.*, according to the weights now in use, 96 *mans*. The same books also state that the duration of the life of a tree is not less than two *gharīs* (twice 24 minutes), and not more than ten thousand years. The height of the trees is said not to exceed a little above a thousand *jūjans*.[5] When a tree dies, its life is said to pass into one of the following ten things: fire, water, air, earth, plants, animals, animals of two senses, such as have three, or four, or five senses.

Āʾīn 31.

THE WARDROBE[6] AND THE STORES FOR MATTRESSES.

His Majesty pays much attention to various stuffs; hence Īrānī, European, and Mongolian articles of wear are in abundance. Skilful masters and workmen have settled in this country to teach people an improved system of manufacture. The imperial workshops, the towns of Lāhor, Āgra, Fatḥpūr, Aḥmadābād, Gujrāt, turn out many masterpieces of workmanship; and the figures and patterns, knots, and variety of

---

[[1] *Ṣūsan*, the iris.—P.]

[[2] *Rayḥān*, sweet basil.—P.]

[[3] *Shaqāyiq*, *vide* p. 85, note 1.—P.]

[[4] *Khaṭmī*, the hollyhock and the marsh mallow.—P.]

[5] Regarding this measure, *vide* the fourth book.

[6] The text has a word کرکیراق which occurs about three times in this work. I have also found it in Sayyid Aḥmad's edition of the Tuzuk i Jahāngīrī; but I cannot find it in any Persian or Chagatāi Dictionary. The meaning, *a wardrobe*, is however clear. [Also spelt کرک یراق.—B.]

fashions which now prevail, astonish experienced travellers. His Majesty himself acquired in a short time a theoretical and practical knowledge of the whole trade; and on account of the care bestowed upon them the intelligent workmen of this country soon improved. All kinds of hair-weaving and silk-spinning were brought to perfection; and the imperial workshops furnish all those stuffs which are made in other countries. A taste for fine material has since become general, and the drapery used at feasts surpasses every description.

All articles which have been bought, or woven to order, or received as tribute or presents, are carefully preserved; and according to the order in which they were preserved, they are again taken out for inspection, or given out to be cut and to be made up, or given away as presents. Articles which arrive at the same time, are arranged according to their prices. Experienced people inquire continually into the prices of articles used both formerly and at present, as a knowledge of the exact prices is conducive to the increase of the stock. Even the prices became generally lower. Thus a piece woven by the famous G͟hiyāṣ-i Naqshband may now be obtained for fifty muhrs, whilst it had formerly been sold for twice that sum; and most other articles have got cheaper at the rate of thirty to ten, or even forty to ten.[1] His Majesty also ordered that people of certain ranks should wear certain articles; and this was done in order to regulate the demand.

I shall not say much on this subject, though a few particulars regarding the articles worn by his Majesty may be of interest.

1. The *Takauchiya* is a coat without lining, of the Indian form. Formerly it had slits in the skirt, and was tied on the left side; his Majesty has ordered it to be made with a round skirt and to be tied on the right side.[2] It requires seven yards and seven *girihs*,[3] and five *girihs* for the binding. The price for making a plain one varies from one rupee to three rupees; but if the coat be adorned with ornamental stitching, from one to four and three quarters rupees. Besides a *miṣqāl* of silk is required.

2. The *peshwāz* (a coat open in front) is of the same form, but ties in front. It is sometimes made without strings.

---

[1] Or as we would say, the prices have become less by 66⅔, and even 75 per cent.

[2] The coats used nowadays both by Hindus and Muhammadans resemble in shape our dressing gowns (*Germ.* Schlafrock), but fitting tight where the lower ribs are. There the coat is tied; the Muhammadans make the tie on the *left*, and the Hindus on the *right* side. In the Eastern parts of Bengal, many Muhammadans adopt the old Hindu fashion of wearing a simple unsewn piece of muslin (*chādar*).

[3] It is not stated in *Aʿin* how many *girihs* the tailor's *gaz*, or yard, contains. It is probable that 16 *girihs* = 1 *gaz*, which is the usual division at present. For other yard measures, *vide* the 87th and 89th *Aʿīns* of this book. The Persian word *girih* is pronounced in India *girah*.

3. The *Dutāhī* (a coat with lining) requires six yards and four *girihs* for the outside, six yards lining, four *girihs* for the binding, nine *girihs* for the border. The price of making one varies from one to three rupees. One *misqal* of silk is required.

4. The *Shāh-ajīda* (or the royal stitch coat) is also called *Shast-khatt* (or sixty rows), as it has sixty ornamental stitches *per girih*. It has generally a double lining, and is sometimes wadded and quilted. The cost of making is two rupees *per* yard.

5. The *Sūzanī* requires a quarter of a *ser* of cotton and two *dāms* of silk. If sewed with *bakhya* [1] stitches, the price of making one is eight rupees; one with *ajīda* stitches costs four rupees.

6. The *Qalamī* requires $\frac{3}{8}$ *s.* cotton, and one *dām* silk. Cost of making, two rupees.

7. The *Qabā*, which is at present generally called *jāma-yi pumba-dār*, is a wadded coat. It requires 1 *s.* of cotton, and 2 *m.* silk. Price, one rupee to a quarter rupee.

8. The *Gadar* is a coat wider and longer than the *qabā*, and contains more wadding. In Hindustan it takes the place of a fur-coat. It requires seven *gaz* of stuff, six yards of lining, four *girihs* binding, nine for bordering, $2\frac{1}{2}$ *s.* cotton, 3 *m.* silk. Price, from one-half to one and one-half rupees.

9. The *Farjī* has no binding, and is open in front. Some put buttons to it. It is worn over the *jāma* (coat), and requires 5 *gaz* 12 *girih* stuff; 5 *gaz* 5 *girih* lining; 14 *girih* bordering; 1 *s.* cotton; 1 *m.* silk. Price, from a quarter to one rupee.

10. The *Fargul* resembles the *yāpanjī*,[2] but is more comfortable and becoming. It was brought from Europe,[3] but everyone nowadays wears it. They make it of various stuffs. It requires 9 *gaz* $6\frac{1}{2}$ *girih* stuff, the same quantity of lining, 6 *m.* silk, 1 *s.* cotton. It is made both single and double. Price from $\frac{1}{2}$ to 2 rupees.

---

[1] *Bakhya*, in Hind. *bakhiyā*, corresponds to what ladies call *backstitching*. *Ajīda* is the buttonhole stitch. These, at least, are the meanings which *bakhya* and *ajīda* now have. *Sūzanī*, a name which in the text is transferred to the coat, is a kind of embroidery, resembling our *satin-stitch*. It is used for working leaves and flowers, etc., on stuffs, the leaves lying pretty loosely on the cloth; hence we often find *sūzanī* work in rugs, small carpets, etc The rugs themselves are also called *sūzanī*. A term sometimes used in dictionaries as a synonym for *sūzanī* is *chikin*; but this is what we call *white embroidery*.

[2] A coat used in rainy weather. *Calcutta Chagatāi Dictionary*.

[3] The etymology of the word *fargul* is not known to me. The names of several articles of wear, nowadays current in India, are Portuguese; as *sāya*, a petticoat; *fīta*, a ribbon. Among other Portuguese words, now common in Hindustani, are *padrī*, clergyman; *girjā*, a church, Port. *igréja*; *kobī*, cabbage, Port. *cuóve*; *chābī*, a key, Port. *chāve*.

Abū 'l-Fazl's explanation (*vide* my text edition, p. 102, l. 16) corrects Vullers II, p. 663*a*.

11. The *Chakman*[1] is made of broadcloth, or woollen stuff, or wax cloth. His Majesty has it made of *Dārā*ʾ*ī* wax cloth, which is very light and pretty. The rain cannot go through it. It requires 6 *gaz.* stuff, 5 *girih* binding, and 2 *m.* silk. The price of making one of broadcloth is 2 *R.*; of wool, 1½ *R.*; of wax cloth, ½ *R.*

12. The *Shalwār* (drawers) is made of all kinds of stuff, single and double, and wadded. It requires 3 *gaz* 11 *girih* cloth, 6 *girih* for the hem through which the string runs, 3 *gaz* 5 *girih* lining, 1¼ *m.* silk, ½ *s.* cotton. Price, from ¼ to ½ rupee.

There are various kinds of each of these garments. It would take me too long to describe the *chīras, fawṭas,* and *dupaṭṭas*,[2] or the costly dresses worn at feasts or presented to the grandees of the present time. Every season, there are made one thousand complete suits for the imperial wardrobe, and one hundred and twenty, made up in twelve bundles, are always kept in readiness. From his indifference to everything that is worldly, His Majesty prefers and wears *woollen*[3] stuffs, especially shawls; and I must mention, as a most curious sign of auspiciousness, that his Majesty's clothes becomingly fit every one, whether he be tall or short, a fact which has hitherto puzzled many.

His Majesty has changed the names of several garments, and invented new and pleasing terms.[4] Instead of *jāma* (coat), he says *sarbgātī*, i.e. covering the whole body; for *izār* (drawers), he says *yār-pīrāhan* (the companion of the coat); for *nīmtana* (a jacket), *tanzeb*; for *fauṭa, patgat*; for *burqa*ʿ (a veil), *chitragupita*; for *kulāh* (a cap), *sīs sobhā*; for *mūy-bāf* (a hair ribbon), *kesghan*; for *paṭkā* (a cloth for the loins), *katzeb*; for *shāl* (shawl), *parmnarm*; for . . .,[5] *parmgarm*; for *kapārdhūr*, a Tibetan stuff, *kapūrnūr*; for *pāy-afzār* (shoes), *charndharn*; and similarly for other names.

---

[1] As this word is not given in any dictionary, the vowels are doubtful. So is Vuller's form *chaspán*.

[2] Stuffs of different shapes used for making turbans.

[3] In allusion to the practice of *Ṣūfīs*, who only wear garments made of wool (*ṣūf*). Abū 'l-Faẓl often tries to represent Akbar as a *Ṣūfī* of so high a degree as to be able to work miracles, and he states below that it was his intention to write a book on Akbar's miracles. The charge of fulsomeness in praise has often been brought against Abū 'l-Faẓl, though it would more appropriately lie against *Faiẓī*, who—like the poets of imperial Rome—represents the emperor as God, as may be seen in the poetical extracts of the second book. But the praises of the two brothers throw a peculiar light on Akbar's character, who received the most immoderate encomiums with self-complacency.

[4] The following passage is remarkable, as it shows Akbar's predilection for *Hindī* terms.

[5] The MSS. have an unintelligible word. The Banāras MS. has *pardak Firāng*, or European Pardak (?).

Á*īn 32.

ON SHAWLS, STUFFS, ETC.

His Majesty improved this department in *four* ways. The improvement is visible, *first*, in the *Ṭūs* shawls, which are made of the wool of an animal of that name; its natural colours are black, white, and red, but chiefly black. Sometimes the colour is a pure white. This kind of shawl is unrivalled for its lightness, warmth, and softness. People generally wear it without altering its natural colour; his Majesty has had it dyed. It is curious that it will not take a red dye. *Secondly*, in the *Safīd Alchas*,[1] also called *Ṭarḥdārs*, in their natural colours. The wool is either white or black. These stuffs may be had in three colours, white, black, or mixed. The first or white kind, was formerly dyed in three ways; his Majesty has given the order to dye it in various ways. *Thirdly*, in stuffs as *Zardozī*,[2] *Kalābatūn*, *Kashīda*, *Qalgha*ʾ*ī*, *Bāndhnūn*, *Chhīnṭ*, *Alcha*, *Purzdār*, to which his Majesty pays much attention. *Fourthly*, an improvement was made in the width of all stuffs; his Majesty had the pieces made large enough to yield the making of a full dress.

The garments stored in the Imperial wardrobe are arranged according to the days, months, and years, of their entries, and according to their colour, price, and weight. Such an arrangement is nowadays called *miṣl*, a set. The clerks fix accordingly the degree of every article of wear, which they write on a strip of cloth, and tack it to the end of the pieces. Whatever pieces of the same kind arrive for the imperial wardrobe on the *Urmuzd* day (first day) of the month of *Farwardīn*, provided they be of a good quality, have a higher rank assigned to them than pieces arriving on other days; and if pieces are equal in value, their precedence or otherwise, is determined by the character[3] of the day of their entry; and if pieces are equal as far as the character of the day is concerned, they put the lighter stuff higher in rank; and if pieces have the same weight, they arrange them according to their colour. The following is the order of colours: *ṭūs*, *safīdalcha*, ruby-coloured, golden, orange, brass-coloured, crimson, grass green, cotton-flower coloured, sandalwood-coloured, almond-coloured, purple, grape-coloured, *mauve* like the colour of some parrots, honey-coloured, brownish lilac, coloured like the *Ratanmanjanī*

[1] *Alcha*, or *Alācha*, any kind of corded (*mukhaṭṭaṭ*) stuff. *Ṭarḥdār* means *corded*.

[2] *Zardozī*, *Kalābatūn* (Forbes, *kalabattūn*), *Kashīda*, *Qalghaī*, are stuffs with gold and silk threads; *Bāndhnūn*, are stuffs dyed differently in different parts of the piece; *Chhīnt* is our *chintz*, which is derived from *Chhīnt*. *Purzdār* are all kinds of stuffs the outside of which is plush-like.

[3] Akbar, like the Parsees, believed in lucky and unlucky days. The arrangement of the stores of clothing must strike the reader as most unpractical. Similar arrangements, equally curious, will be found in the following *Á*ʾ*īns*. Perhaps they indicate a progress, as they show that some order at least was kept.

flower, coloured like the *Kāsnī* flower, apple-coloured, hay-coloured, pistachio, . . .,[1] *bhojpatra* coloured, pink, light blue, coloured like the *galghah* flower, water-coloured, oil-coloured, brown red, emerald, bluish like China-ware, violet, bright pink, mangoe coloured, musk-coloured, coloured like the *Fākhta.*[2]

In former times shawls were often brought from Kashmīr. People folded them up in four folds, and wore them for a very long time. Nowadays they are generally worn without folds, and merely thrown over the shoulder. His Majesty has commenced to wear them double, which looks very well.

His Majesty encourages, in every possible way, the manufacture of shawls in Kashmīr. In Lāhor also there are more than a thousand workshops. A kind of shawl, called *māyān,* is chiefly woven there ; it consists of silk and wool mixed. Both are used for *chīras* (turbans), *fotas* (loin bands), etc.

I subjoin the following tabular particulars.

A. Gold stuffs.

Brocaded velvet, from *Yazd,*[3] *per piece*	15 to 150 *M.*
Do. from Europe, do.	10 to 70 *M.*
Do. from *Gujrāt,* do.	10 to 50 *M.*
Do. from *Kāshān,* do..	10 to 40 *M.*
Do. from *Hirāt,* do.	*
Do. from *Lāhor,* do.	10 to 40 *M.*
Do. from *Barsah* (?), do.	3 to 70 *M.*
Mutabbaq, do.[4]	2 to 70 *M.*
Mīlak, do.	3 to 70 *M.*
Brocade, from Gujrāt, do.	4 to 60 *M.*
Tās [5]-Brocade, from do. do.	1 to 35 *M.*

[1] The text contains two doubtful words. The next word *bhojpatra* is the bark of a tree used for making *huqqa* tubes.

[[2] *Fākhta* is the Common Ring-dove of India, the *Turtur risoria* of Jerdon.—P.]

[3] *Yazd* is the principal city in the south of the Persian province of Khurāsān. *Kāshān* lies in *Irāq-i* ؏*Ajamī,* north of Iṣfahān. "The asses of Khāsān are wiser than the men of Iṣfahān," which latter town is for Persia what Bœotia is for Ancient Greece, or the Bretagne for France, of the kingdom of Fife for Scotland, or the town of Schilda for Germany, or Bihār for India—the home of fools. During the time of Moguls, the Sayyids of Bārhah enjoyed a similar notoriety.

[4] *Mutabbaq,* a kind of cloth, chiefly brought from *Khallukh,* and *Mīlak* from *Naushād* in Turkestān. *Ghiyās*[u] *l-lughat.*

[5] *Tās* means *generally* brocade ; *Dārāībāf* is a kind of brocaded silk ; *Muqayyash* is silk with stripes of silver—the *Ghiyās* says that *Muqayyash* comes from the Hind. *kesh,* hair to which the silver-stripes are compared, and that it is an Arabicized form of the *Hindī* word as *qaranful,* a clove, for the Hind. *karnphul* ; *itrīfal,* a kind of medicine for *trīphal,* as it consists of *three* fruits, etc. *Mushajjar* is a kind of silk with leaves and branches woven in it ; *Debā* is coloured silk ; *Khārā,* moirée antique ; *Khazz* is *filoselle*-silk. For *tafṣīla* (*vide* Freytag III, p. 353), we also find *tafsīla.*

Dārā'ī-bāf, from Gujrāt	2 to 50 *M*.
Muqayyash, do.	1 to 20 *M*.
Shirwānī Brocade, do.	6 to 17 *M*.
Mushajjar, from Europe, *per yard*	1 to 4 *M*.
Debā silk, do. do.	1 to 4 *M*.
Do., from *Yazd*, do.	1 to 1½ *M*.
Khārā, do.	5 *R*. to 2 *M*.
Satin, from Chinese Tartary	*
Nawār, from do.	*
Khazz silk	*
Tafṣīla (a stuff from Mecca)	from 15 to 20 *R*.
Kurtahwār, from Gujrāt	1 to 20 *M*.
Mindīl	1 to 14 *M*.
Chīra (for turbans)	½ to 8 *M*.
Dupaṭṭā, do.	9 to 8 *R*.
Foṭas (loin bands)	½ to 12 *M*.
Counterpanes	1 to 20 *M*.

* The Text does not give the prices.

B. Silks, etc., plain.

Velvet from Europe, *per yard*	1 to 4 *M*.
Do. from Kāshān, *per piece*	2 to 7 *M*.
Do. from Yazd, do.	2 to 4 *M*.
Do. from Mashhad, do.	2 to 4 *M*.
Do. from Hirāt, do.	1½ to 3 *M*.
Do. Khāfī, do.	2 to 4 *M*.
Do. from Lāhor, do.	2 to 4 *M*.
Do. from Gujrāt, *per yard*	1 to 2 *R*.
Qaṭīfa-yi i Pūrabī,[1] do.	1 to 1½ *R*.
Tāja-bāf, *per piece*	2 to 30 *M*.
Dārā'ī-bāf, do.	2 to 30 *M*.
Muṭabbaq, do.	1 to 30 *M*.
Shirwānī, do.	1½ to 10 *M*.
Mīlak, do.	1 to 7 *M*.
Kamkhāb, from Kābul and Persia, do.	1 to 5 *M*.
Tawār (?), do.	2 *R*. to 2 *M*.
Khūrī (?), do.	4 to 10 *R*.
Mushajjar, from Europe, *per yard*	2 *R*. to 1 *M*.
Do. from Yazd, *per piece*	1 to 2 *M*.

[1] A kind of velvet.

Satin, from Europe, *per yard*	2 *R.* to 1 *M.*
Satin, from Hirāt, *per piece*	5 *R.* to 2 *M.*
K͟hārā, *per yard*	1 *R.* to 6 *R.*
Sihrang,[1] *per piece*	1 to 3 *M.*
Quṭnī,[2] do.	$1\frac{1}{2}$ *R.* to 2 *M.*
Katān,[3] from Europe, *per yard*	$\frac{1}{2}$ to 1 *R.*
Tāfta,[4] do.	$\frac{1}{4}$ to 2 *R.*
Anbarī, do.	4 *d.* to $\frac{1}{2}$ *R.*
Dārāʻī, do.	$\frac{1}{5}$ *R.* to 2 *R.*
Sitīpūrī, *per piece*	6 *R.* to 2 *M.*
Qabāband, do.	6 *R.* to 2 *M.*
Ṭāt bandpūrī, do.	2 *R.* to $1\frac{1}{2}$ *M.*
Lāh, *per yard*	$\frac{1}{3}$ to $\frac{1}{7}$ *R.*
Miṣrī, *per piece*	$\frac{1}{2}$ to 1 *M.*
Sār, *per yard*	$\frac{1}{10}$ to $\frac{1}{5}$ *R.*
Ṭassar,[5] *per piece*	$\frac{1}{3}$ to 2 *R.*
Plain *Kurtawār* Satin, *per yard*	$\frac{1}{2}$ to 1 *R.*
Kapūrnūr, formerly called *Kapūrdhūr*, do.	$\frac{1}{8}$ to 1 *R.*
Alcha, do.	$\frac{1}{5}$ to 2 *R.*
Tafṣīla, *per piece*	7 to 12 *R.*

C. Cotton cloths.

K͟hāṣa, *per piece*	3 *R.* to 15 *M.*
Chautār, do.	2 *R.* to 9 *M.*
Malmal, do.	4 *R.*
Tansukh, do.	4 *R.* to 5 *M.*
Sirī Ṣāf, do.	2 *R.* to 5 *M.*
Gangājal, do.	4 *R.* to 5 *M.*
Bhīraun, do.	4 *R.* to 4 *M.*
Saḥan, do.	1 to 3 *M.*
Jhona, do.	1 *R.* to 1 *M.*
Aṭān, do.	$2\frac{1}{2}$ *R.* to 1 *M.*
Asāwalī, do.	1 to 5 *M.*
Bāfta, do.	$1\frac{1}{2}$ *R.* to 5 *M.*
Maḥmūdī, do.	$\frac{1}{2}$ to 3 *M.*

---

[1] Changing silk.

[2] A stuff made of silk and wool.

[3] Generally translated by *linen*. All dictionaries agree that it is exceedingly thin, so much so that it tears when the moon shines on it; it is *Muslin*.

[4] Properly, *woven*; hence *taffeta*.

[5] Nowadays chiefly made in Berhampore and Patna; *vulgo*, tessa.

Panchtoliya, per piece	1 to 3 *M.*
Jhola, do.	½ to 2½ *M.*
Sālū, per piece	3 *R.* to 2 *M.*
Doriva, per piece	6 *R.* to 2 *M.*
Bahādur Shāhī, do.	6 *R.* to 2 *M.*
Garba Sūtī, do.	1½ to 2 *M.*
Shela, from the Dakhin, do	½ to 2 *M.*
Mihrkul, do.	3 *R.* to 2 *M.*
Mindīl, do.	½ to 2 *M.*
Sarband, do.	½ to 2 *M.*
Dupaṭṭa, do.	1 *R.* to 1 *M.*
Katāncha, do.	1 *R.* to 1 *M.*
Foṭa, do.	½ to 6 *R.*
Goshpech, do.	1 to 2 *R.*
Chhīnt, per yard	2 *d.* to 1 *R.*
Gazīna, per piece	½ to 1½ *R.*
Silāhaṭī. per yard	2 to 4 *d.*

D. *Woollen stuffs.*

Scarlet Broadcloth, from Turkey, Europe,[1] and Portugal, *per yard*	2¼ *R.* to 4 *M.*
Do., from Nāgor and Lāhor *per piece*	2 *R.* to 1 *M.*
Ṣūf-i murabbaʿ, do.	4 to 15 *M.*
Ṣūf-i . . .,[2] do.	3 *R.* to 1⅛ *M.*
Parmnarm, do.	2 *R.* to 20 *M.*
Chīra-yi-Parmnarm, do.	2 *R.* to 25 *M.*
Foṭa, do.	½ to 3 *M.*
Jāmawār-i Parmnarm, do.	½ to 4 *M.*
Goshpech, do.	1½ *R.* to 1½ *M.*
Sarpech, do.	½ to 4 *M.*
Aghrī, do.	7 *R.* to 2½ *M.*

---

[1] The articles imported from Europe were chiefly broadcloth; musical instruments, as trumpets; pictures; curiosities (*vide* Badāonī II, p. 290, l. 2 from below; p. 338, l. 7) and, since 1600, tobacco. Of the names of cloths mentioned by Abū 'l-Faẓl several are no longer known, as native weavers cannot compete with the English Longcloth and the cheap European Muslins, Alpacas, Chintzes, and Mohairs, which are nowadays in common use with the natives all over the East. At the time of the Moguls, and before, the use of woollen stuffs and, for the poorer classes, blankets, was much more general than now. Even the light caps generally worn by Muhammadans in this country, called in Hind. *ṭopī*, and in Persian *takhfīfa* (*vide* Bahār-i ʿAjam) are mostly imported from England. I am not aware that the soldiers of the armies of the Moguls were uniformly dressed, though it appears that the commanders of the contingents at least looked to uniformity in the caps and turbans.

[2] The MSS. have an unintelligible word.

Parmgarm, per piece	3 *R.* to $2\frac{1}{2}$ *M.*
Katās, do.	$2\frac{1}{2}$ *R.* to 10 *M.*
Phūk, do.	$2\frac{1}{2}$ to 15 *R.*
Durman, do.	2 *R.* to 4 *M.*
Paṭū, do.	1 to 10 *R.*
Rewkār, do.	2 *R.* to 1 *M.*
Miṣrī, do.	5 to 50 *R.*
Burd-i Yamanī, do.	5 to 35 *R.*
Mānjī (?) *namad*, do.	2 *R.* to 1 *M.*
Kanpak (?) *namad*, do.	2 *R.* to 1 *M.*
Takyal namad, from Kābul and Persia	*
Do., country made, do.	$1\frac{1}{2}$ to 5 *R.*
Lo'ī, do.	14 *d.* to 4 *R.*
Blankets, do.	10 *d.* to 2 *R.*
Kashmīrian Caps, do.	2 *d.* to 1 *R.*

* The price is not given in the text.

Ā'īn 33.

ON THE NATURE OF COLOURS.

White and black are believed to be the origin of all colours. They are looked upon as extremes, and as the component parts of the other colours. Thus white when mixed in large proportions with an impure black, will yield *yellow* ; and white and black, in equal proportions, will give *red*. White mixed with a large quantity of black, will give a *bluish green*. Other colours may be formed by compounding these. Besides, it must be borne in mind that cold makes a juicy white body, and a dry body black ; and heat renders that which is fresh black, and white that which is dry. These two powers (heat and cold) produce, each in its place, a change in the colour of a body, because bodies are both *qābil*, i.e. capable of being acted upon, and *muqtaẓa*, i.e. subject to the influence of the heavenly bodies (chiefly the sun), the active origin of heat.

Ā'īn 34.

THE ARTS OF WRITING AND PAINTING.

What we call *form* leads us to recognize a body ; the body itself leads us to what we call *a notion, an idea*. Thus, on seeing the form of a letter, we recognize the letter, or a word, and this again will lead us to some idea. Similarly in the case of what people term *a picture*. But though it is true that painters, especially those of Europe, succeed in drawing figures expressive of the conceptions which the artist has of any of the mental states,[1] so much so, that people may mistake a picture for a reality: yet pictures are much inferior to the written letter, inasmuch as the letter may embody the wisdom of bygone ages, and become a means to intellectual progress.

I shall first say something about the art of writing, as it is the more important of the two arts. His Majesty pays much attention to both, and is an excellent judge of form and thought. And indeed, in the eyes of the friends of true beauty, a letter is the source from which the light confined within it beams forth; and, in the opinion of the far-sighted, it is the world-reflecting cup [2] in the abstract. The letter, a magical power, is spiritual geometry emanating from the pen of invention; a heavenly writ from the hand of fate; it contains the secret word, and is the tongue of the hand. The spoken word goes to the hearts of such as are present to hear it; the letter gives wisdom to those that are near and far. If it was not for the letter, the spoken word would soon die, and no keepsake would be left us of those that are gone by. Superficial observers see in the letter a sooty figure; but the deepsighted a lamp of wisdom. The written letter looks black, notwithstanding the thousand rays within it; or, it is a light with a mole on it that wards off the evil eye.[3] A letter is the portrait painter of wisdom; a rough sketch from the realm of ideas; a dark night ushering in day; a black cloud pregnant with knowledge; the wand for the treasures of insight; speaking, though dumb; stationary, and yet travelling; stretched on the sheet, and yet soaring upwards.

When a ray of God's knowledge falls on man's soul, it is carried by the mind to the realm of thought, which is the intermediate station between that which is conscious of individual existence (*mujarrad*) and that which is material (*māddī*). The result [4] is a concrete thing mixed with the absolute, or an absolute thing mixed with that which is concrete. This compound steps forward on man's tongue, and enters, with the assistance of the conveying air, into the windows of the ears of others. It then drops the

---

[1] *Khilqī* (from *khilqat*) referring to states of mind natural to us, as benevolence, wrath, etc. These, *Abū l'Fazl* says, a painter may succeed in representing; but the power of writing is greater.

[2] The fabulous cup of King Jamshed, which revealed the secrets of the seven heavens.

[3] Human beauty is imperfect unless accompanied by a mole. For the mole on the cheek of his sweetheart, Ḥāfiz would make a present of Samarqand and Būkhārā. Other poets rejoice to see at least one black spot on the beautiful face of the beloved who, without such an amulet, would be subject to the influence of the evil eye.

[4] The spoken word, the idea expressed by a sound.

burden of its concrete component, and returns, as a single ray, to its old place, the realm of thought. But the heavenly traveller occasionally gives his course a different direction by means of man's fingers, and having passed along the continent of the pen and crossed the ocean of the ink, alights on the pleasant expanse of the page, and returns through the eye of the reader to its wonted habitation.

As the letter is a representation of an articulate sound, I think it necessary to give some information regarding the latter.

The sound of a letter is a mode of existence depending on the nature of the air. By *qaraˁ* we mean the striking together of two hard substances; and by *qalaˁ*, the separation of the same. In both cases the intermediate air, like a wave, is set in motion; and thus the state is produced which we call *sound.* Some philosophers take sound to be the secondary effect, and define it as the air set in motion; but others look upon it as the primary effect, i.e. they define sound to be the very *qaraˁ*, or the *qalaˁ*, of any hard substances. Sound may be accompanied by modifying circumstances; it may be a piano, deep, nasal, or guttural, as when the throat is affected by a cold. Again, from the nature of the organ with which man utters a sound, and the manner in which the particles of the air are divided, another modifying circumstance may arise, as when two pianos, two deep, two nasal, or two guttural sounds separate from each other. Some, as Abū ˁAlī Sīnā, call this modifying element (*ˁāriz*) the sound of the letter; others define it as the original state of the sound thus modified (*maˁrūẓ*); but the far-sighted define an articulate sound as the union of the modifying element and the original state modified. This is evidently the correct view.

There are fifty-two articulate sounds in Hindī, so and so many[1] in Greek, and eighteen in Persian. In Arabic there are twenty-eight letters represented by eighteen signs, or by only fifteen when we count the joined letters, and if we take the *Hamzah* as one with the *alif*. The reason for writing an *alif* and a *lām* (لا) separately as the end of the single letters in the Arabic alphabet is merely to give an example of a *sākin* letter, which must necessarily be joined to another letter; and the reason why the letter *lām* is preferred[2] as an example is because the letter *lām* is the

---

[1] Abū 'l-Faẓl has forgotten to put in the number. He counts eighteen letters, or rather signs, in Persian, because ج, خ, and چ, have the same fundamental sign.

[2] Or rather, the *alif* was preferred to the *wāw* or *yā*, because these two letters may be either *sākin* or *mutaḥarrik*. But the custom has become established to call the *alif*, when mutaḥarrik, *hamzah*; and to call the *alif*, when *sākin*, merely *alif*. *ˁAbdulwāsī*, of *Hānsah*, in his excellent Persian Grammar, entitled *Risāla-yi ˁAbdul-wāsi*, which is read all over India, says that the *lām-alif* has the meaning of *not*,

middle letter of the word *alif*, and the letter *alif* the middle letter of the word *lām*.

The vowel-signs did not exist in ancient times, instead of which letters were dotted with a different kind of ink ; thus a red dot placed *over* a letter expressed that the letter was followed by an *a* ; a red dot in front of the letter signified a *u* ; and a red dot below a letter an *i*. It was Khalīl ibn-i Aḥmad,[1] the famous inventor of the Metrical Art of the Arabians, who fixed the forms of the vowel-signs as they are now in use.

The beauty of a letter and its proportions depend much on personal taste ; hence it is that nearly every people has a separate alphabet. Thus we find an Indian, Syriac, Greek, Hebrew, Coptic, *Maςqalī*, *Kūfī*, *Kashmīrī*, Abyssinian, *Rayḥānī*, Arabic, Persian, Himyaritic, Berbery, Andalusian, *Rūḥānī*, and several other ancient systems of writing. The invention of the Hebrew characters is traced in some poems to Ādam-i Hafthazārī ; [2] but some mention Idrīs [3] as the inventor. Others, however, say that Idrīs perfected the *Maςqalī* character. According to several statements, the Kūfic character was derived by the Khalīfah ςAlī from the *Maςqalī*.

The difference in the form of a letter in the several systems, lies in the proportion of straight and round strokes ; thus the Kūfic character consists of one-sixth curvature and five-sixths straight lines ; the *Maςqalī* has no curved lines at all ; hence the inscriptions which are found on ancient buildings are mostly in this character.

In writing we have to remember that black and white look well, as these colours best prevent ambiguities in reading.

In Īrān and Tūrān, India and Turkey, there are eight caligraphical

---

i.e., " do *not* read this compound *lām-alif*, but pass over it, when you say the Alphabet : look upon it as a mere example of a *sākin* letter."

The term *hamzah*, as used here in native schools, is carefully distinguished from the terms *Shakl-i Hamzah* and *Markiz-i Hamzah*. *Shakl-i Hamzah* is the small sign consisting of a semicircle, one extremity of which stands upon a straight line slightly slanting. *Markiz-i Hamzah* is either of the letters *alif*, *wāw*, or *yā*, but chiefly the latter, when accompanied by the *Shakl-i Hamzah*. *Hamzah* is a general term for either of the three letters *alif*, *wāw*, *yā*, when accompanied by the *Shakl-i Hamzah*. In European grammars, the chapter on the *Hamzah* is badly treated, because all explain the word *Hamzah* as the name of a *sign*.

Another peculiarity of European grammars is this, that in arranging the letters of the alphabet, the *wāw* is placed *after* the *he* ; here in the East, the *he* is invariably put before the *yā*.

[1] He is said to have been born A.H. 100, and died at Baṣrah, A.H. 175 or 190. He wrote several works on the science which he had established, as also several books on the rhyme, lexicographical compilations, etc.

[2] Ādam is called *Haft-hazārī*, because the number of inhabitants on earth at his death had reached the number *seven thousand*. A better explanation is given by Badāonī (II, p. 337, l. 10), who puts the creation of Ādam *seven thousand* years before his time. *Vide* the first *Āʾīn* of the Third Book.

[3] *Idrīs*, or Enoch.

systems [1] current, of which each one is liked by some people. Six of them were derived in A.H. 310 by *Ibn-i Muqlah* from the *Maʿqalī* and the Kūfic characters, viz., the *Ṣuls*, *Tauqīʿ*, *Muḥaqqaq*, *Naskh*, *Rayḥān*, *Riqāʿ*. Some add the *Ghubār*, and say that this seventh character had likewise been invented by him. The *Naskh* character is ascribed by many to *Yāqūt*, a slave of the Khalīfah Mustaʿṣam Billāh.[2] The *Ṣuls* and the *Naskh* consist each of one-third [3] curved lines, and two-thirds straight lines; the former (the *ṣuls*) is *jalī*,[4] whilst the latter (the *naskh*) is *khafī*. The *Taūqīʿ* and *Riqāʿ* consist of three-fourths curved lines and one-fourth straight lines; the former is *jalī*, the latter is *khafī*. The *Muḥaqqaq* and *Rayḥān* contain three-fourths straight lines; the former, as in the preceding, is *jalī*, and the *Rayḥān* is *khafī*.

Among famous copyists I must mention ʿAlī ibn-i Hilāl, better known under the name of *Ibn-i Bawwāb*; [5] he wrote well the six characters. Yāqūt brought them to perfection. Six of Yāqūt's pupils are noticeable; 1. Shaykh Aḥmad, so well known under the name of Shaykh-zāda-yi Suhrwardī; 2. Arghūn of Kābul; 3. Mawlānā Yūsuf Shāh of Mash,had; 4. Mawlānā Mubārik Shāh, styled *Zarrīn-qalam* (the golden pen; 5. Ḥaydar, called *Gandahnawīs* (i.e., the writer of the *jalī*); 6. Mīr Yaḥyā.

---

[1] It is remarkable that, in the whole chapter, there is not the slightest allusion to the art of printing. Nor do Abū 'l-Faẓl's letters, where nearly the whole of this *Āʾīn* is repeated, contain a reference to *printed* books. "The first book printed in India was the *Doctrina Christiana* of Giovanni Gonsalvez, a lay brother of the order of the Jesuits, who, as far as I know, first cast Tamulic characters in the year 1577. After this appeared, in 1578, a book entitled *Flos Sanctorum*, which was followed (?) by the Tamulic Dictionary of Father Antonio de Proenza, printed in 1679, at Ambalacate, on the coast of Malabar. From that Period the Danish Missionaries at Tranquebar have printed many works, a catalogue of which may be found in Alberti Fabricii *Salutaris lux Evangelii*." *Johnston's translation* of *Fra P. Da San Bartolomeo's Voyage to the East Indies*, p. 395. The Italian Original has the same years: 1577, 1578, 1679.

[2] He was the last caliph, and reigned from 1242 to 1258, when he was put to death by Hulāgū, grandson of Chingiz Khān. [*Billāh* is not in the text.—P.]

[3] Hence, the name *ṣuls*, or *one-third*.

[4] *Jalī* (i.e. clear) is a term used by copyists to express that letters are thick, and written with a pen full of ink. *Ghiās*.—*Khafī* (hidden) is the opposite.

[5] *Ibn Muqlah*, *Ibn Bawwāb*, and *Yāqūt* are the three oldest caligraphists mentioned in various histories. The following notes are chiefly extracted from Bakhātwar Khān's *Mīr-ātul ʿĀlam*:—

Ibn Muqlah, or according to his full name, Abū ʿAlī Muḥammad ibn-i ʿAlī ibn-i Ḥasan ibn-i Muqlah, was the vizier of the Khalīfahs Muqtadir billah, Alqāhir billah, and ArRāzī billah, who reigned from A.D. 907 to 940. The last, cut off Ibn-i Muqlah's right hand. He died in prison, A.H. 327, or A.D. 938–9.

Ibn-i Bawwāb, or Abū 'l-Ḥasan ʿAlī ibn i Hilāl, lived under the twenty-fifth Khalīfah, Alqādir billah (A.D. 992–1030), the contemporary of Maḥmūd of Ghaznī, and died A.H. 416, or A.D. 1025.

Yāqūt, or Shaykh Jamālᵘ 'd-Dīn, was born at Baghdād, and was the Librarian of Mustaʿṣam billah, the thirty-seventh and last Khalīfah, who imprisoned him some time on account of his Shīʿah tendencies. He survived the general slaughter (1258) of Halāgū Khān, and died, at the age of one hundred and twenty, A.H. 697, or A.D. 1297, during the reign of Ghāzān Khān Halāgū's great grandson.

The following caligraphists are likewise well-known: Ṣūfī Naṣr[u] 'llāh, also called Ṣadr-i ʿIrāqī; Arqūn; ʿAbd[u] 'llāh; Khwāja ʿAbd[u] 'llāh-i Ṣayrafī; Ḥājī Muḥammad; Mawlānā ʿAbd[u] 'llāh-i Āshpaz; Mawlānā Muḥī of Shīrāz; Muʿīn[u] 'd-Dīn-i Tanūrī; Shams[u] 'd-Dīn-i Khaṭāʾī; ʿAbd[u] 'r-Raḥīm-i Khalūlī (?); ʿAbd[u] 'l-Ḥayy; Mawlānā Jaʿfar[1] of Tabrīz; Mawlānā Shāh of Mash,had; Mawlānā Maʿrūf[2] of Baghdād; Mawlānā Shams[u] 'd-Dīn Bāyasanghur; Muʿīn[u] 'd-Dīn of Farāh; ʿAbd[u] 'l-Ḥaqq of Sabzwār; Maulānā Niʿmat[u] 'llāh-i Bawwāb; Khwājagī Mumin-i Marwārīd, the inventor of variegated papers and sands for strewing on the paper: Sulṭān Ibrāhīm, son of Mīrzā Shāhrukh; Mawlānā Muḥammad Ḥakīm Ḥāfiẓ Mawlānā Maḥmūd Siyā,ūsh; Mawlānā Jamāl[u] 'd-Dīn Ḥusayn; Mawlānā Pīr Muḥammad; Mawlānā Faẓl[u] 'l-Ḥaqq of Qazwīn.[3]

A *seventh* kind of writing is called *Taʿlīq*, which has been derived-from the *Riqāʿ* and the *Tawqīʿ*. It contains very few straight lines, and was brought to perfection by Khwāja Tāj-i Salmānī,[4] who also wrote well the other six characters. Some say that he was the inventor.

Of modern caligraphists I may mention: Mawlānā ʿAbd[u] 'l-Ḥayy, the Private Secretary[5] of Sulṭān Abū Saʿīd Mīrzā, who wrote *Taʿlīq* well; Mawlānā Darwīsh;[6] Amīr Manṣūr; Mawlānā Ibrāhīm of Astarābād; Khwāja Ikhtiyār;[7] Munshī Jamāl[u] 'd-Dīn; Muḥammad of Qazwīn; Mawlānā Idrīs; Khwāja Muḥammad Ḥusayn Munshī; and Ashraf Khān,[8]

---

[1] He lived in the beginning of the fifteenth century, at the time of Mīrzā Shāhrukh (1404-47).

[2] A contemporary and rival of the great poet Salmān of Sāwah (died 769). The name *Maʿrūf* appears to have been common in Baghdād since the times of the famous saint *Maʿrūf* of *Karkh* (a part of Baghdād).

[3] The *Maktūbāt* and the *Miʾāt* also mention Mullā Abā Bakr, and Shaykh Maḥmūd.

[4] According to the Maktūbāt and several MSS., *Sulaymānī*.

[5] In the original text, p. 114, l. 5, by mistake, Mawlānā ʿAbd[u] 'l-Ḥayy *and* the Munshī of Sulṭān Abū Saʿīd.

[6] Mawlānā Darwīsh Muḥammad was a friend of the famous Amīr ʿAlī Sher, the vizier of Sulṭān Ḥusayn Mīrzā, king of Khurāsān (A.D. 1470 to 1505), and the patron of the poet Jāmī. Mawlānā Darwīsh entered afterwards the service of Shāh Junayd-i Ṣafawī, king of Persia (A.D. 1499 to 1525). A biography of the Mawlānā may be found in the *Maʾāṣir-i Raḥīmī*, p. 751.

[7] Khwāja Ikhtiyār, the contemporary and successful rival of the preceding caligraphist. He was Private Secretary to Sulṭān Ḥusayn Mīrzā.

[8] This is the title of Muḥammad Aṣghar, a Sayyid from Mashhad—or according to the Tabaqāt-i Akbarī, from ʿArabshāhī. He served Humāyūn as Mīr Munshī, Mīr ʿArẓī, and Mīr Mālī. He accompanied Tardī Beg on his flight from Dihlī, was imprisoned by Bayrām, and had to go to Mecca. He rejoined Akbar in A.H. 968, when Bayrām had just fallen in disgrace, received in the following year the title of *Ashraf Khān*, and served under Munʿim Khān in Bengal. He died in the tenth year of Akbar's reign, A.H. 973. In Abū 'l-Faẓl's list of grandees, in the second book, Ashraf Khān is quoted as a commander of two thousand. Badā,onī mentions him among the contemporaneous poets. Abū 'l-Muẓaffar, Ashraf Khān's son, was, A.D. 1596, a commander of five hundred.

the Private Secretary of his Majesty, who improved the *Taˁlīq* very much.

The *eighth* character which I have to mention is the *Nastaˁlīq* ; it consists entirely of round lines. They say that Mīr ˁAlī of Tabrīz, a contemporary of Tīmūr, derived it from the *Naskh* and the *Taˁlīq*; but this can scarcely be correct because there exist books in the *Nastaˁlīq* character written before Tīmūr's time. Of Mīr ˁAlī's pupils, I may mention two:[1] Mawlānā Jaˁfar of Tabrīz, and Mawlānā Aẓhar; and of other caligraphists in *Taˁlīq*, Mawlānā Muḥammad of Awbah (near Hirāt), an excellent writer; Mawlānā Bārī of Hirāt; and Mawlānā Sulṭān ˁAlī[2] of Mash,had, who surpasses them all. He imitated the writing of Mawlānā Aẓhar, though he did not learn from him personally. Six of his pupils are well known : Sulṭān Muḥammad-i Khandān ;[3] Sulṭān Muḥammad Nūr ; Mawlānā ˁAlāˀu 'd-Dīn[4] of Hirāt; Mawlānā Zaynu 'd-Dīn (of Nīshāpūr); Mawlānā ˁAbdī of Nīshāpūr; Muḥammad Qāsim Shādī Shāh, each of whom possessed some distinguishing qualities.

Besides these, there are a great number of other good caligraphists, who are famous for their skill in *Nastaˁlīq*; as Mawlānā Sulṭān ˁAlī, of Qāyin ;[5] Mawlānā Sulṭān ˁAlī of Mashhad ;[6] Mawlānā Hijrānī ;[7] and after them the illustrious Mawlānā Mīr ˁAlī,[8] the pupil, as it appears, of Mawlānā Zaynu 'd-Dīn. He brought his art to perfection by imitating the writing of Sulṭān ˁAlī of Mash,had. The new method, which he established, is a proof of his genius; he has left many masterpieces. Some one asked him once what the difference was between his writing and that of the Mawlānā. He said, " I also have brought writing to perfection ; but yet, his method has a peculiar charm."

---

1 The *Mirˀāt* mentions a third immediate pupil of Mīr ˁAlī *Mawlānā Khwāja Muḥammad*, and relates that he put Mīr ˁAlī's name to his own writings, without giving offence to his master.

2 He also was a friend of Amīr ˁAlī Sher, and died A.H. 910, during the reign of Sulṭān Ḥusayn Mīrzā, mentioned in the fourth note.

3 He was called *Khandān*, as he was always *happy*. He was a friend of Amīr ˁAlī Sher, and died A.H. 915.

4 In the *Maktūbāt ˁAlāˀ 'd-Dīn Muḥammad* of Hirāt.

5 He was the instructor of Sulṭān Ḥusayn Mirzā's children, and died A.H. 914. *Qāyin* is a Persian town, S.E. of Khurāsān, near the frontier of Afghānistān. It is spelt *Ghayan* on our maps.

6 According to the *Maktūbāt*, Mawlānā Sulṭān ˁAlī *sher* of Mashhad, which is evidently the correct reading.

7 A poet and friend of Amīr ˁAlī Sher. He died A.H. 921.

8 Mawlānā Mīr ˁAlī, a Sayyid of Hirāt, died A.H. 924. As a poet he is often mentioned together with Mīr Aḥmad, son of Mīr Khusraw of Dihlī, and Bayrām Khān, Akbār's Khānkhānān, as a master of *Dakhl* poetry. *Dakhl*, or *entering*, is the *skilful* use which a poet makes of verses, or parts of verses, of another poet.

In conclusion, I may mention: Shāh Maḥmūd[1] of Nīshāpūr; Maḥmūd Is-ḥāq; Shamsᵘ 'd-Dīn of Kirmān; Mawlānā Jamshed, the riddle-writer; Sulṭān Ḥusayn of Khujand; Mawlānā ʿAyshī; Ghiyāsᵘ 'd-Dīn, the gilder; Mawlānā ʿAbdᵘ ṣ-Ṣamad; Mawlānā Malik; Mawlānā ʿAbdᵘ 'l-Karīm; Mawlānā ʿAbdᵘ 'r-Raḥīm of Khwārizm; Mawlānā Shaykh Muḥammad; Mawlānā Shāh Maḥmūd-i Zarrīnqalam (or gold pen); Mawlānā Muḥammad Ḥusayn[2] of Tabrīz; Mawlānā Ḥasan ʿAlī of Mash,had; Mīr Muʿizz of Kāshān; Mīrzā Ibrāhīm of Iṣfahān; and several others who have devoted their lives to the improvement of the art.

His Majesty shows much regard to the art, and takes a great interest in the different systems of writing; hence the large number of skilful caligraphists. *Nastaʿlīq* has especially received a new impetus. The artist who, in the shadow of the throne of his Majesty, has become a master of caligraphy, is Muḥammad Ḥusayn[3] of Kashmīr. He has been honoured with the title of *Zarrīnqalam*, the gold pen. He surpassed his master Mawlānā ʿAbdᵘ 'l-ʿAzīz; his *maddāt* and *dawāʾir*[4] show everywhere a proper proportion to each other, and art critics consider him equal to Mullā Mīr ʿAlī. Of other renowned caligraphists of the present age, I must mention Mawlānā Bāqir, the son of the illustrious Mullā Mīr ʿAlī; Muḥammad Amīn of Mash,had; Mīr Ḥusayn-i Kulankī; Mawlānā ʿAbdᵘ 'l-Ḥay; Mawlānā Dawrī;[5] Mawlānā ʿAbdᵘ 'r-Raḥīm; Mīr ʿAbdᵘ 'llah; Niẓāmī of Qazwīn; ʿAlī Chaman of Kashmīr; Nūrᵘ 'llah Qāsim Arsalān.

His Majesty's library is divided into several parts; some of the books are kept within, and some without, the Harem. Each part of the library

---

[1] According to the *Maktūbāt* and the *Mirʾāt*, Shāh *Muḥammad* of Nīshāpūr. Both mention another caligraphist, *Mīr Sayyid Aḥmad of Mashhad.*

[2] He was the teacher of the celebrated caligraphist ʿ*Imād*, whose biography will be found in the *Mirʾāt*. *Vide* also the preface of Dr. Sprenger's *Gulistān.*

[3] He died A.H. 1020, six years after Akbar's death.

[4] By *Maddāt* (extensions), caligraphists mean letters like ب, ف; by *dawāʾir* (curvatures), letters like ں, ح.

Draw four horizontal lines at equal intervals; call the spaces between them *a*, *b*, *c*, of which *a* is the highest. Every letter which fills the space *b* is called a *shūsha*; as ز, ـعـ, د, ذ. The diacritical points are immaterial. Every line above *b* is called a *markaz*; every line below *b*, i.e., in *c*, a *dāman*. Thus ك consists of a *shūsha* and a *markaz*; س of ع *shūsha* and a *dāman*. The knob of a ع, ف, or ق, is called *kalla*. Thus ف is a *Madda*, consisting of a *kalla*, and a *dāman*; so also ع, ج, ک. The ک consists of a *markaz* and a *dāman*.

In *Grammar* the word *markaz* means the same as *shūsha* in caligraphy; thus ؤ, ئ, consist of a *markaz*, and a *shakl-i hamza*.

By *iṣlāḥ*, caligraphists mean any additional ornamental strokes, or refilling a written letter with ink (Hind. *siyāhī bharnā*), or erasing (Hind. *chhīlnā*).

[5] His name is Sulṭān Bāyizīd; he was born at Hirāt. *Dawrī* is his poetical name. *Vide* Badāonī's list of poets (vol. iii of the Bibl. Indica). Akbar bestowed on him the title of *Kātibᵘ 'l-Mulk*, the writer of the empire. His pupil was Khwāja Muḥammad Ḥusayn, an Aḥadī (*vide* Badāonī, ii, p. 394, where for *Ibrāhīm*, in the Tārīkh, read *Barāhīm*).

is subdivided, according to the value of the books and the estimation in which the sciences are held of which the books treat. Prose books, poetical works, Hindī, Persian, Greek, Kashmīriān, Arabic,[1] are all separately placed. In this order they are also inspected. Experienced people bring them daily and read them before His Majesty, who hears every book from the beginning to the end. At whatever page the readers daily stop, His Majesty makes with his own pen a sign, according to the number of the pages; and rewards the readers with presents of cash, either in gold or silver, according to the number of leaves read out by them. Among books of renown, there are few that are not read in his Majesty's assembly hall; and there are no historical facts of the past ages, or curiosities of science, or interesting points of philosophy, with which His Majesty, a leader of impartial sages, is unacquainted. He does not get tired of hearing a book over again, but listens to the reading of it with more interest. The Akhlāq-i Nāṣirī, the Kīmiyā-yi Saʕādat, the Qābūsnāma, the works of Sharaf of Munayr (*vide* p. 50), the Gulistān, the Ḥadīqa of Ḥakīm Sanāʾī, the Masnawī of Maʕnawī, the Jām-i Jam, the Bustān, the Shāhnāma, the collected Masnawīs of Shaykh Niẓāmī, the works of Khusraw and Mawlānā Jāmī, the Dīwāns of Khāqānī, Anwarī, and several works on History, are continually read out to His Majesty. Philologists are constantly engaged in translating Hindī, Greek, Arabic, and Persian books, into other languages. Thus a part of the Zīchi-i Jadīd-i Mīrzāʾī (*vide* 3rd book, Āʾīn 1) was translated under the superintendence of Amīr Fatḥu 'llah of Shīrāz (*vide* p. 34), and also the Kishnjoshī, the Gangādhar, the Mohesh Mahānand, from Hindī (Sanscrit) into Persian, according to the interpretation of the author of this book. The Mahābhārat which belongs to the ancient books of Hindūstān has likewise been translated, from Hindī into Persian, under the superintendence of Naqīb Khān,[2] Mawlānā ʕAbdu 'l-Qādir of Badāon,[3] and Shaykh Sulṭān of

---

[1] Observe that the Arabic books are placed last. [But see p. 104, line 4.—B.]

[2] Regarding this renowned man, *vide* Abū 'l-Faẓl's list of Grandees, 2nd book, No. 161.

[3] Mullā ʕAbdu 'l-Qādir, poetically styled *Qādirī*, was born A.H. 947 [or 949] at Badāon, a town near Dihlī. He was thus two years older than Akbar. His father, whom he lost in 969, was called Shaykh Mulūk Shāh, and was a pupil of the Saint Bechū of Sambhal. ʕAbdu 'l-Qādir, or *Badāonī*, as we generally call him, studied various sciences under the most renowned and pious men of his age, most of whom he enumerates in the beginning of the third volume of his *Muntakhab*. He excelled in Music, History, and Astronomy, and was on account of his beautiful voice appointed Court *Imām* for Wednesdays. He had early been introduced to Akbar by Jalāl Khān Qūrchī (*vide* List of Grandees, 2nd book, No. 213). For forty years Badāonī lived in company with Shaykh Mubārak, and Fayẓī and Abū 'l-Faẓl, the Shaykh's sons; but there was no sincere friendship between them, as Badāonī looked upon them as heretics. At the command of Akbar, he translated the *Ramāyan* (*Badāonī*,

Thanesar.[1] The book contains nearly one hundred thousand verses: His Majesty calls this ancient history *Razmnāma*, the book of Wars. The same learned men translated also into Persian the Ramāyan, likewise a book of ancient Hindustan, which contains the life of Rām Chandra, but is full of interesting points of Philosophy. Ḥājī Ibrāhīm of Sarhind translated into Persian the *Atharban* [2] which, according to the Hindūs, is one of

II, pp. 336, 366), from the Sanscrit into Persian, receiving for twenty-four thousand *sloks* 150 Ashrafīs and 10,000 Tangahs; and parts of the Mahābhārat; extracts from the History of Rashīd; and the *Baḥru 'l-Asmār*, a work on the *Ḥadīs*. A copy of another of his works, entitled *Najātu 'r-Rashīd*, may be found among the Persian MSS. of the As. Soc. Bengal. His historical work, entitled *Muntakhatu 't-Tawārīkh*, is much prized as written by an enemy of Akbar, whose character, in its grandeur and its failings, is much more prominent than in the *Akbarnāma* or the *Ṭabaqāt-i Akbarī* or the *Maʿāṣir-i Raḥīmī*. It is especially of value for the religious views of the emperor, and contains interesting biographies of most famous men and poets of Akbar's time. The History ends with the beginning of A.H. 1004, or eleven years before Akbar's death, and we may conclude that Badāonī died soon after that year. The book was kept secret, and according to a statement in the *Mirʿatu 'l-ʿĀlam*, it was made public during the reign of Jahāngīr, who showed his displeasure by disbelieving the statement of Badāonī's children that they themselves had been unaware of the existence of the book. The Tuzuk-i Jahāngīrī unfortunately says nothing about this circumstance; but Badāonī's work was certainly not known in A.H. 1025, the tenth year of Jahāngīr's reign, in which the *Maʿāṣir-i Raḥīmī* was written, whose author complained of the want of a history beside the Ṭabaqāt, and the Akbarnāma.

In point of style, Badāonī is much inferior to Bakhtāwar Khān (*Mirʿatu 'l-ʿĀlam*) and Muḥammad Kāẓim (the *ʿĀlam-gīr Nāma*), but somewhat superior to his friend Mīrzā Niẓāmu 'd-Dīn Aḥmad of Hirāt, author of the *Ṭabaqāt*, and to ʿAbdu 'l-Ḥamīd of Lāhor, author of the *Pādishāhnāma*.

ʿAbdu 'l-Qādir of Badāon must not be confounded with Mawlānā Qādirī, another learned man contemporaneous with Akbar.

[1] *Vide* Badāonī II, p. 278; and for Ḥājī Ibrāhīm, iii, p. 139. [ii, p. 278.—B.]

[2] "In this year (A.H. 983, or A.D. 1575) a learned Brahmin, Shaykh Bhāwan, had come from the Dakhin and turned Muhammadan, when His Majesty gave me the order to translate the *Atharban*. Several of the religious precepts of this book resemble the laws of Islām. As in translating I found many difficult passages, which Shaykh Bhāwan could not interpret either, I reported the circumstance to His Majesty, who ordered Shaykh Fayẓī, and then Ḥājī Ibrāhīm, to translate it. The latter, though willing, did not write anything. Among the precepts of the *Atharban*, there is one which says that no man will be saved unless he read a certain passage. This passage contains many times the letter *l*, and resembles very much our *Lā illāha illā 'l-lāh*. Besides, I found that a Hindū, under certain conditions, may eat cow flesh; and another, that Hindūs *bury* their dead, but do not burn them. With such passages the Shaykh used to defeat other Brahmins in argument; and they had in fact led him to embrace Islām. Let us praise God for his conversion!" *Badāonī*, ii, p. 212.

The translation of the Mahābhārat was not quite a failure. "For two nights His Majesty himself translated some passages of the Mahābhārat, and told Naqīb Khān to write down the general meaning in Persian; the third night he associated me with Naqīb Khān; and, after three or four months, two of the eighteen chapters of these useless absurdities—enough to confound the eighteen worlds—were laid before His Majesty. But the emperor took exception to my translation, and called me a *Ḥarāmkhur* and a *turnip-eater*, as if that was my share of the book. Another part was subsequently finished by Naqīb Khān and Mullā Sherī, and another part by Sultān Ḥājī of Thanesar; then Shaykh Fayẓī was appointed, who wrote two chapters, prose and poetry; then the Ḥājī wrote two other parts, adding a *verbal* translation of the parts that had been left out. He thus got a hundred *juz* together, closely written, so exactly rendered, that even the accidental dirt of flies on the

the four divine books. The Līlawatī, which is one of the most excellent works written by Indian mathematicians on arithmetic, lost its Hindū veil, and received a Persian garb from the hand of my elder brother, Shaykh ʿAbd[u] 'l-Fayẓ-i Fayẓī.[1] At the command of His Majesty, Mukammal Khān of Gujrāt translated into Persian the Tājak, a well-known work on Astronomy. The Memoirs [2] of Bābar, the Conqueror of the world, which may be called a code of practical wisdom, have been translated from Turkish into Persian by Mīrzā ʿAbd[u]-'r-Raḥīm Khān, the present Khān Khānān (Commander-in-Chief). The History of Kashmīr, which extends over the last four thousand years, has been translated from Kashmīrian into Persian [3] by Mawlānā Shāh Muḥammad of Shāhābād. The *Muʿjam[u] 'l-Buldān,* an excellent work on towns and countries, has been translated from Arabic into Persian by several Arabic scholars, as Mullā Aḥmad of Thathah,[4] Qāsim Beg, Shaykh Munawwar, and others. The *Haribās*, a book containing the life of Krishna, was translated into Persian by Mawlānā Sherī (*vide* the poetical extracts of the second book). By order of His Majesty, the author of this volume composed a new version of the Kalīlah Damnah, and published it under the title of *ʿAyār Dānish*.[5] The original is a masterpiece of practical wisdom, but is full of rhetorical difficulties; and though Naṣr[u] 'llah-i Mustawfī and Mawlānā Ḥusayn-i Wāʿiẓ has translated it into Persian, their style abounds in rare metaphors and difficult words. The Hindī story of the love of Nal and Daman, which melts the hearts of feeling readers, has been metrically translated by my

original was not left out; but he was soon after driven from Court, and is now in Bhakkar. Other translators and interpreters, however, continue nowadays the fight between Panḍūs and the Kurūs. May God Almighty protect those that are not engaged in this work, and accept their repentance, and hear the prayer of pardon of every one who does not hide his disgust, and whose heart rests in Islām; for 'He allows men to return to Him in repentance!' This *Razmnāma* was illuminated, and repeatedly copied; the grandees were ordered to make copies, and ʿAbd[u] 'l-Faẓl wrote an introduction to it of about two *juz*, etc." *Badāonī*, ii, p. 302. A copy of this translation in two volumes, containing eighteen *fans* (فن) is among the MSS. of the As. Soc. of Bengal, No. 1329. One *juz* (جزو) = sixteen pages *quarto*, or two sheets.

[1] This work has been printed. Abū 'l-Faẓl's words *Hindū veil* are an allusion to Līlawatī's sex.

[2] *Vide* Tuzuk-i Jahāngīrī, p. 417. The Wāqiʿāt-i Tīmūr were translated into Persian, during the reign of Shāhjahān, by Mīr Abū Ṭālib-i Turbatī. *Pādshāhnāma* ii, p. 288, edit. Bibl. Indica. "Conqueror of the world," *getī sitānī*, is Bābar's title. Regarding the titles of the Mogul Emperors from Bābar to Bahādur Shāh, *vide* Journal As. Soc. Bengal for 1868, Part I, p. 39.

[3] "During this year (A.H. 999, or A.D. 1590–1), I received the order from His Majesty to re-write in an easy style, the History of Kashmīr, which Mullā Shāh Muhammad of Shāhābād, a very learned man, had translated into Persian. I finished this undertaking in two months, when my work was put into the Imperial Library, to be read out to His Majesty in its turn." *Badāonī*, ii, p. 374.

[4] Regarding the tragic end of this "heretic", *vide Badāonī*, ii, p. 364. Notices regarding the other two men will be found in the third volume of Badāonī.

[5] For *ʿIyār-i Dānish.* Such abbreviations are common in *titles.*

brother Shaykh Fayẓi-i Fayyāẓī, in the *masnawī* metre of the Layī Majnūn, and is now everywhere known under the title of *Nal Daman.*[1]

As His Majesty has become acquainted with the treasure of history, he ordered several well-informed writers to compose a work containing the events which have taken place in the seven zones for the last one thousand years. Naqīb Khān, and several others, commenced this history. A very large portion was subsequently added by Mullā Aḥmad of Thathah, and the whole concluded by Jaҁfar Beg-i Āṣaf Khān. The introduction is composed by me. The work has the title of *Tārīkh-i Alfī*,[2] the History of a thousand years.

The Art of Painting.

Drawing the likeness of anything is called *taṣwīr*. His Majesty, from his earliest youth, has shown a great predilection for this art, and gives it every encouragement, as he looks upon it as a means, both of study and amusement. Hence the art flourishes, and many painters have obtained great reputation. The works of all painters are weekly laid before His Majesty by the Dārōghas and the clerks; he then confers rewards according to excellence of workmanship, or increases the monthly salaries. Much progress was made in the commodities required by painters, and the correct prices of such articles were carefully ascertained. The mixture of colours has especially been improved. The pictures thus received a hitherto unknown finish. Most excellent painters are now to be found, and masterpieces, worthy of a *Bihzād*,[3] may be placed at the side of the wonderful works of the European painters who have attained world-wide fame. The minuteness in detail, the general finish, the boldness of execution, etc., now observed in pictures, are incomparable; even inanimate

---

[1] "Fayẓī's *Naldaman* (for *Nal o Daman* contains about 4,200 verses, and was composed, A.H. 1003, in the short space of five months). It was presented to Akbar with a few *ashrafīs* as *nazar*. It was put among the set of books read at Court, and Naqīb Khān was appointed to read it out to His Majesty. It is, indeed, a masnāwī, the like of which, for the last three hundred years, no poet of Hindustan, after Mīr Khusraw of Dihlī, has composed." *Badāonī*, ii, p. 296.

[2] In A.H. 1000, A.D. 1591-2, the belief appears to have been current among the Muhammadans that Islām and the world were approaching their end. Various men arose, pretending to be *Imām Mahdī*, who is to precede the reappearance of Christ on earth; and even Badāonī's belief got doubtful on this point. Akbar's disciples saw in the common rumour a happy omen for the propagation of the *Dīn-i Ilāhī*. The *Tārikh-i Alfī* was likewise to give prominence to this idea.

The copy of the *Tārīkh-i Alfī* in the Library of the As. Soc. of Bengal (No. 19) contains no preface, commences with the events subsequent to the death of the Prophet (8th June, 632), and ends abruptly with the reign of ҁUmar ibn-i ҁAbdu 'l-Malik (A.H. 99, or A.D. 717-18). The years are reckoned from the death of the Prophet, not from the Hijrah. For further particulars regarding this book, *vide* *Badāonī*, ii, p. 317.

[3] "*Bihzād* was a famous painter, who lived at the court of Shāh Ismaҁīl-i Ṣafawī of Persia." *Sirājullughāt.*

objects look as if they had life. More than a hundred painters have become famous masters of the art, whilst the number of those who approach perfection, or of those who are middling, is very large. This is especially true of the Hindus; [1] their pictures surpass our conception of things. Few, indeed, in the whole world are found equal to them.

Among the forerunners on the high road of art I may mention:

1. Mīr Sayyid ʿAlī of Tabrīz.[2] He learned the art from his father. From the time of his introduction at Court, the ray of royal favour has shone upon him. He has made himself famous in his art, and has met with much success.

2. Kh̲wāja ʿAbdᵘ 's-Ṣamad, styled *Shīrīnqalam*, or *sweet pen*. He comes from Shīrāz. Though he had learnt the art before he was made a grandee [3] of the Court, his perfection was mainly due to the wonderful effect of a look of His Majesty, which caused him to turn from that which is form to that which is spirit. From the instruction they received, the Kh̲wāja's pupils became masters.

3. Daswanth. He is the son of a palkee-bearer. He devoted his whole life to the art, and used, from love of his profession, to draw and paint figures even on walls. One day the eye of His Majesty fell on him; his talent was discovered, and he himself handed over to the Kh̲wāja. In a short time he surpassed all painters, and became the first master of the age. Unfortunately the light of his talents was dimmed by the shadow of madness; he committed suicide. He has left many masterpieces.

4. Basāwan. In back grounding, drawing of features, distribution of colours, portrait painting, and several other branches, he is most excellent, so much so that many critics prefer him to Daswanth.

The following painters have likewise attained fame: Kesū, Lāl, Mukund, Mushkīn, Farrukh̲ the Qalmāq (Calmuck), Mādhū,[4] Jagan, Mohesh, Khemkaran, Tārā, Sāwlā, Haribās, Rām. It would take me too long to describe the excellencies of each. My intention is "to pluck a flower from every meadow, an ear from every sheaf".

I have to notice that the observing of the figures of objects and the making of likenesses of them, which are often looked upon as an idle occupation, are, for a well regulated mind, a source of wisdom, and an

---

[1] Compare with Abū 'l-Faẓl's opinion, Elphinstone's ***History of India***, second edition, p. 174.

[2] Better known as a poet under the name of *Judā,ī*. *Vide* the poetical extracts of the second book. He illuminated the *Story of Amīr Hamzah*, mentioned on the next page.

[3] He was a *Chahārṣadī*. *Vide* the list of grandees in the second book, No. 266.

[4] Mentioned in the *Maʾaṣir-i Raḥīmī* (p. 753) as in the service of ʿAbdᵘ 'r-Raḥīm Kh̲ān Kh̲ānān, Akbar's commander-in-chief.

antidote against the poison of ignorance. Bigoted followers of the letter of the law are hostile to the art of painting; but their eyes now see the truth. One day at a private party of friends, His Majesty, who had conferred on several the pleasure of drawing near him, remarked: "There are many that hate painting; but such men I dislike. It appears to me as if a painter had quite peculiar means of recognizing God; for a painter in sketching anything that has life, and in devising its limbs, one after the other, must come to feel that he cannot bestow individuality upon his work, and is thus forced to think of God, the giver of life, and will thus increase in knowledge."

The number of masterpieces of painting increased with the encouragement given to the art. Persian books, both prose and poetry, were ornamented with pictures, and a very large number of paintings was thus collected. The *Story of Hamzah* was represented in twelve volumes, and clever painters made the most astonishing illustrations for no less than one thousand and four hundred passages of the story. The Chingiznāma, the Ẕafarnāma,[1] this book, the Razmnāma, the Ramāyan, the Nal Daman, the Kalīlah Damnah, the ʿAyār Dānish, etc., were all illustrated. His Majesty himself sat for his likeness, and also ordered to have the likenesses taken of all the grandees of the realm. An immense album was thus formed: those that have passed away have received a new life, and those who are still alive have immortality promised them.

In the same manner, as painters are encouraged, employment is held out to ornamental artists, gilders, line-drawers, and pagers.

Many *Manṣabdārs*, *Aḥadīs*, and other soldiers, hold appointments in this department. The pay of foot soldiers varies from 1,200 to 600 *dāms*.

Āʾīn 35.

THE ARSENAL.

The order of the household, the efficiency of the army, and the welfare of the country, are intimately connected with the state of this department; hence His Majesty gives it every attention, and looks scrutinizingly into its working order. He introduces all sorts of new methods, and studies their applicability to practical purposes. Thus a plated armour was brought before His Majesty, and set up as a target; but no bullet was so

---

[1] *A History of the House of Tīmūr*, by Sharafu 'd-Dīn of Yazd (died 1446). *Vide* Morley's *Catalogue of Historical MSS.*, p. 94.

powerful as to make an impression on it. A sufficient number of such armours has been made so as to supply whole armies. His Majesty also looks into the prices of such as are sold in the bāzārs.

All weapons for the use of His Majesty have names, and a proper rank is assigned to them. Thus there are thirty swords (*khāṣa* swords), one of which is daily sent to His Majesty's sleeping apartments. The old one is returned, and handed over to the servants outside the harem, who keep it till its turn comes again. Forty other swords are kept in readiness; they are called *kotal* swords. When the number of *khāṣa* swords (in consequence of presents, etc.) has decreased to twelve, they supply new ones from the *kotal* swords. There are also twelve *Yakbandī* (?),[1] the turn of every one of which recurs after one *week*. Of *Jāmdhars* and *Khapwas*, there are forty of each. Their turn recurs every week; and each has thirty *kotals*, from which deficiencies are supplied as before. Besides, eight knives, twenty spears and *barchhas*, are required monthly. Of eighty-six *Mash,hadī* bows, *Bhadāyan* bows, and twenty-four others, are returned monthly. . . .[2] In the same manner a rank is assigned to each.

Whenever His Majesty rides out, or at the time of the *Bār-i ʿĀm*, or Levee, the sons of the Amīrs, and other *Manṣabdārs* and *Aḥadīs*, carry the *Qur* in their hands and on their shoulders, i.e. every four of them carry four quivers, four bows, four swords, four shields; and besides, they take up lances, spears, axes, pointed axes, *piyāzī* war-clubs, sticks, bullet bows, pestles, and a footstool, all properly arranged. Several *qaṭār* [3] of camels and mules are loaded with weapons and kept in readiness; and on travels they use Bactrian camels, etc., for that purpose. At court receptions, the Amīrs and other people stand opposite the *Qur*, ready for any service; and on the march they follow behind it, with the exception of a few who are near His Majesty. Elephants in full trappings, camels, carriages, *naqqāras*, flags, the *kawkabas*, and other Imperial insignia, accompany the *Qur*, while eager macebearers superintend the march, assisted by the Mīrbakhshīs. In hunting expeditions several swift runners are in attendance, and a few others are in charge of harnesses.

In order to shorten the trouble of making references, I shall enumerate the weapons now in use in form of a table, and give pictures of some of them.

---

[1] I doubt the correctness of the translation. The word *yakbandī* is not in the dictionaries.

[2] The text has an unintelligible sentence.

[3] Five camels are called *qiṭār*, in Hind. *qaṭār*. A string of some length is tied to the tail of the front camel and is drawn through the nose holes of the next behind it, and so on. Young camels are put on the backs of their mothers.

Pl. XII

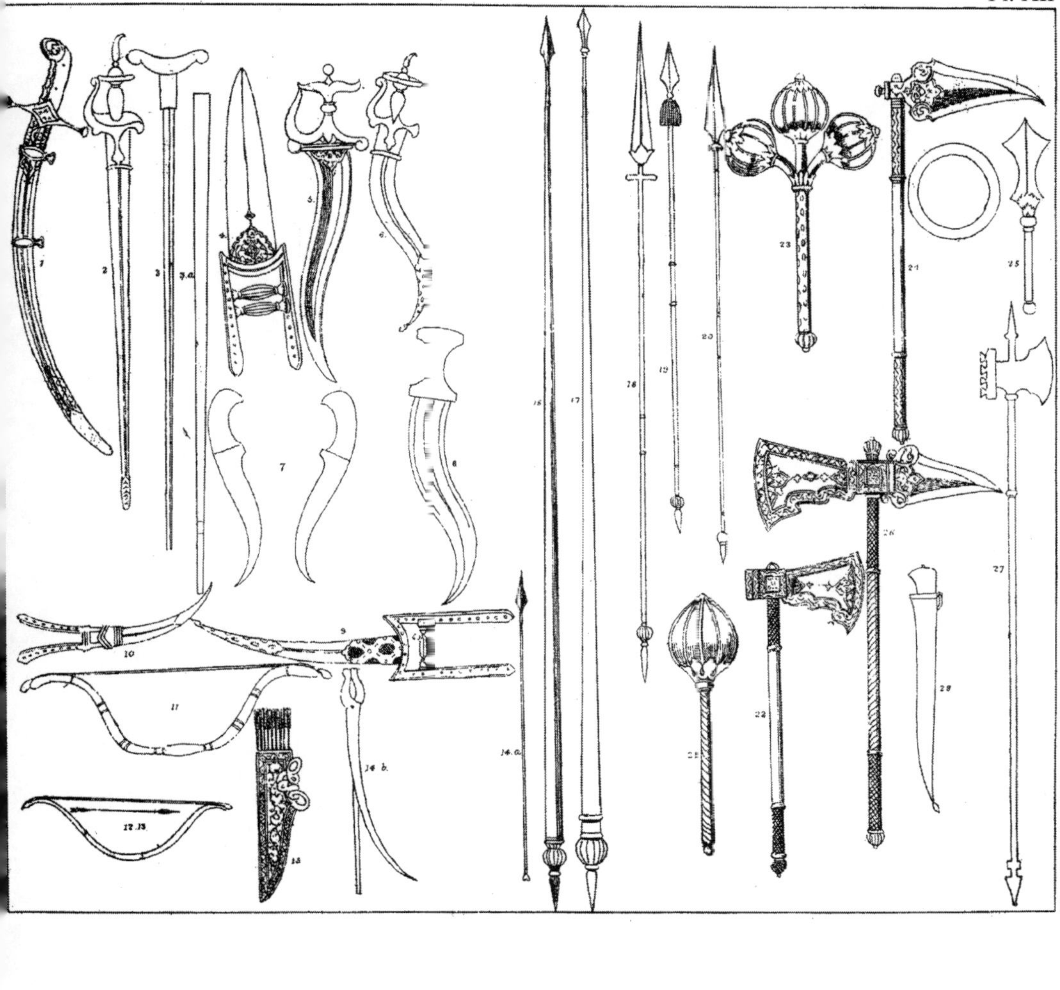

1.	Swords (slightly bent)	$\frac{1}{2}$ *R.* to 15 *Muhurs.*
2.	*Khāḍā* (straight swords)	1 to 10 *R.*
3.	*Guptī ʿaçā* (a sword in a walking stick)	2 to 20 *R.*
4.	*Jamdhar* (a broad dagger)	$\frac{1}{4}$ *R.* to $2\frac{1}{2}$ *M.*
5.	*Khanjar*	$\frac{1}{2}$ to 5 *R.*
6.	*Khapwa*	$\frac{1}{2}$ *R.* to $1\frac{1}{2}$ *M.*
7.	*Jam khāk*	$\frac{1}{2}$ *R.* to $1\frac{1}{2}$ *M.*
8.	*Bāk*	$\frac{1}{2}$ *R.* to 1 *M.*
9.	*Jhanbwa*	$\frac{1}{2}$ *R.* to 1 *M.*
10.	*Katāra*	$\frac{1}{2}$ *R.* to 1 *M.*
11.	*Narsink moth*	$\frac{1}{2}$ *R.* to 2 *M.*
12.	*Kamān* (bows)	$\frac{1}{4}$ *R.* to 3 *M.*
13.	*Takhsh kamān*	1 to 4 *R.*
14.	*Nāwak*	$\frac{1}{2}$ *R.* to 1 *M.*
15.	Arrows, *per bundle*	$\frac{1}{2}$ to 30 *R.*
16.	Quivers	$\frac{1}{4}$ *R.* to 2 *M.*
17.	*Ḍaḍī*	$\frac{1}{4}$ to 5 *R.*
18.	*Tīrbardār* (arrow drawers) [1]	$\frac{1}{2}$ to $2\frac{1}{2}$ *d.*
19.	*Paikānkash* (do.)	$\frac{1}{4}$ to 3 *R.*
20.	*Neza* (a lance)	$1\frac{3}{4}$ *R.* to 6 *M.*
21.	*Barchha*	$\frac{3}{4}$ *R.* to 2 *M.*
22.	*Sāk*	$\frac{1}{4}$ to $1\frac{1}{2}$ *R.*
23.	*Sainthī*	$\frac{1}{4}$ to 1 *R.*
24.	*Selara*	10 *d.* to $\frac{3}{4}$ *R.*
25.	*Gurz* (a war club)	$\frac{1}{4}$ to 5 *R.*
26.	*Shashpar* (do.)	$\frac{1}{2}$ *R.* to 3 *M.*
27.	*Kestan* (?) [2]	1 to 3 *R.*
28.	*Tabar* (a war axe)	$\frac{1}{4}$ *R.* to 2 *M.*
29.	*Piyāzī* (a club)	$\frac{1}{2}$ to 5 *R.*
30.	*Zāghnōl* (a pointed axe)	$\frac{1}{2}$ *R.* to 1 *M.*
31.	*Chakar-basola*	1 to 6 *R.*
32.	*Tabar zāghnol*	1 to 4 *R.*
33.	*Tarangāla*	$\frac{1}{4}$ to 2 *R.*
34.	*Kārd* (a knife)	2 *d.* to 1 *M.*
35.	*Guptī kārd*	3 *R.* to $1\frac{1}{2}$ *M.*
36.	*Qamchī kārd*	1 to $3\frac{1}{2}$ *R.*
37.	*Chāqū* (a clasp knife)	2 *d.* to $\frac{1}{4}$ *R.*

[1] If this spelling be correct, it is the same as the next (No. 19); but it may be *tīr-i pardār*, an arrow with a *feather* at the bottom of the shaft, a barbed arrow.

[2] This name is doubtful. The MSS. give all sorts of spellings. *Vide* my text edition, p. 121, l. 1. The dictionaries give no information.

38.	*Kamān-i guroha* (bullet bow)	2 *d.* to 1 *R.*
39.	*Kamtha*	5 *d.* to 3 *R.*
40.	*Tufak-i dahān* [1] (a tube; *Germ.* Blaserohr)	10 *d.* to ½ *R.*
41.	*Pushtkhār* [2]	2 *d.* to 2 *R.*
42.	*Shaṣtāwez* [3]	2 *d.* to 1 *R.*
43.	*Girihkushā*	1 *d.* to ¼ *R.*
44.	*Khār-i māhī*	1 to 5 *R.*
45.	*Gobham* (a sling)	1½ *d.* to ¼ *R*
46.	*Gajbāg*	1 to 5 *R.*
47.	*Sipar* (a shield)	1 to 50 *R.*
48.	*Dhāl*	½ *R.* to 4 *M.*
49.	*Khera*	1 *R.* to 4 *M.*
50.	*Pahrī*	1 *R.* to 1 *M.*
51.	*Udāna*	½ to 5 *R.*
52.	*Dubulgha*	½ *R.* to 3½ *M.*
53.	*Khōghī*	1 to 4 *R.*
54.	*Zirih kulāh*	1 to 5 *R.*
55.	*Ghūghuwa*	1 *R.* to 2 *M.*
56.	*Jaibāh* [4]	20 *R.* to 30 *M.*
57.	*Zirih*	1¾ *R.* to 100 *M.*
58.	*Bagtar* [5]	4 *R.* to 12 *M.*
59.	*Jōshan*	4 *R.* to 9 *M.*
60.	*Chār āʿina*	2 *R.* to 7 *M.*
61.	*Koṭhī*	5 *R.* to 8 *M.*
62.	*Ṣādiqī*	3 *R.* to 8 *M.*
63.	*Angirkha*	1½ *R.* to 5 *M.*
64.	*Bhanjū*	3 *R.* to 2 *M.*
65.	*Chihrahzirih-i āhanī*	1½ *R.* to 1 *M.*
66.	*Salhqabā*	5 *R.* to 8 *M.*
67.	*Chihilqad*	5 to 25 *R.*
68.	*Dastwāna*	1½ *R.* to 2 *M.*
69.	*Rāk* [6]	1 *R.* to 10 *M.*

[[1] A blow-pipe.—P.]

[2] *Vide Journal As. Society Bengal*, for 1868, p. 61.

[3] A weapon resembling the following. The word *Shaṣtāwez*, or more correctly *shastāwez*, means *a thing by which you can hook anything.* In Vullers' Persian Dicty., ii, p. 426b, read *bīz* for *panīr* (!).

[4] This word is used in a general sense, *an armour.* It is either *Turkish*, or a corruption of the Arab. *jubbah*. The form *jaibā* is occasionally met with; but *jabah*, as given by Vullers, i, p. 508a, is wrong, and against the metre of his quotation.

[[5] *Baktar* ?—P.]

[6] According to some MSS. *rāg*.

Pl. XIII

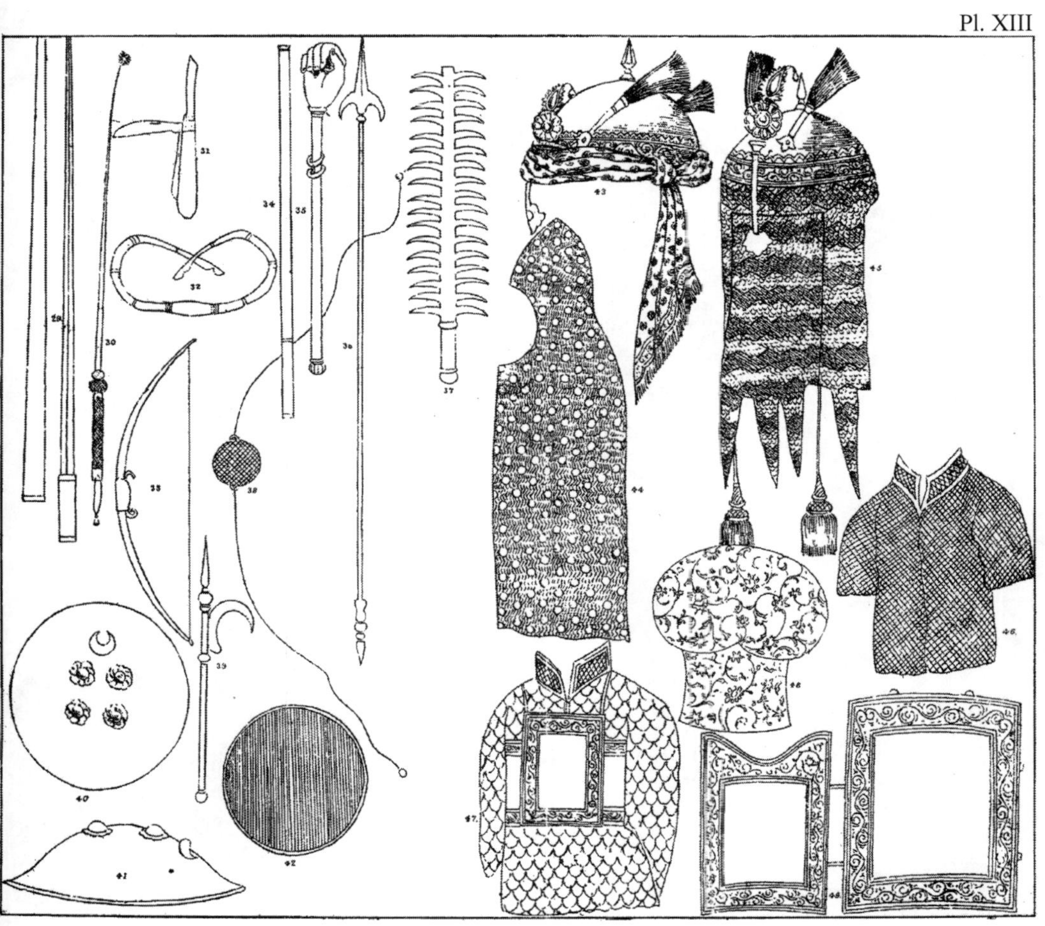

Pl. XIV

Pl: XV

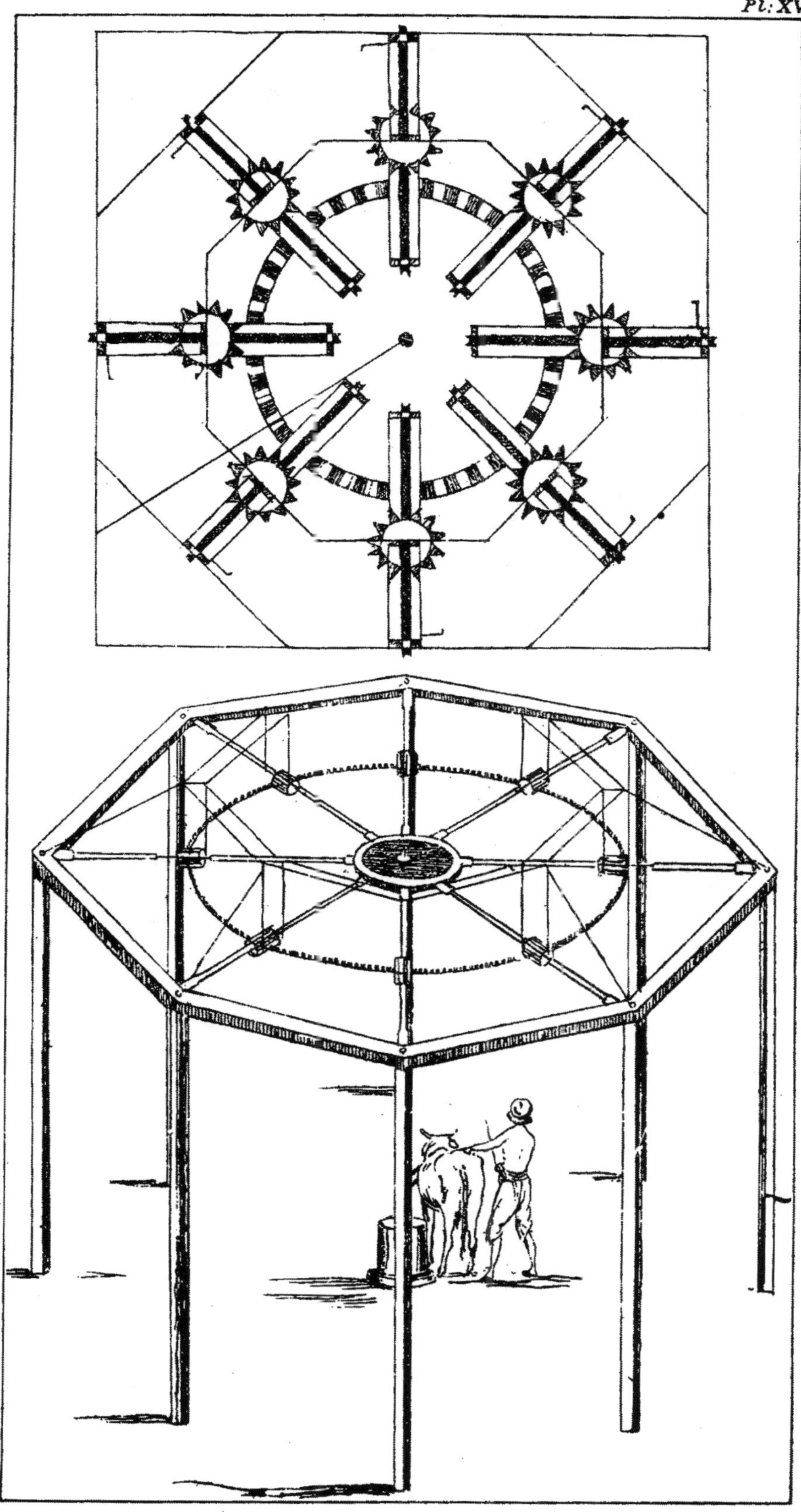

70. *Kaṉtha sobhā* [1] . . . . 1 to 10 *R.*
71. *Moza-yi āhanī* . . . . ½ to 10 *R.*
72. *Kajem* . . . . 50 to 300 *R.*
73. *Artak* (the quilt) *-i kajēm* . . . . . 4 *R.* to 7 *M.*
74. *Qashqa* . . . . 1 *R.* to 2½ *M.*
75. *Gardanī* [2] . . . . 1 *R.* to 1 *M.*
76. Matchlocks . . . . ½ *R.* to 1 *M.*
77. *Bān* (rockets) . . . . 2½ to 4 *R.*

Āʾīn 36.

ON GUNS.

Guns are wonderful locks for protecting the august edifice of the state ; and befitting keys for the door of conquest. With the exception of Turkey, there is perhaps no country which in its guns has more means of securing the government than this. There are nowadays guns made of such a size that the ball weighs 12 *mans* ; several elephants and a thousand cattle are required to transport one. His Majesty looks upon the care bestowed on the efficiency of this branch as one of the higher objects of a king, and therefore devotes to it much of his time. Dārog̲has and clever clerks are appointed to keep the whole in proper working order.

His Majesty has made several inventions which have astonished the whole world. He made a gun which, on marches, can easily be taken to pieces, and properly put together again when required. By another invention, His Majesty joins seventeen guns in such a manner as to be able to fire them simultaneously with one match. Again, he made another kind of gun, which can easily be carried by a single elephant ; such guns have the name *Gajnāls*. Guns which a single man may carry are called *Narnāls*.

The imperial guns are carefully distributed over the whole kingdom, and each Ṣūba has that kind which is fit for it. For the siege of fortresses and for naval engagements, His Majesty has separate guns made, which accompany his victorious armies on their marches. It is impossible to count every gun ; besides clever workmen make continually new ones, especially *Gujnāls* and *Narnāls*.

Amīrs and Aḥadīs are on staff employ in this branch. The pay of the foot varies from 100 to 400 *d.*

---

[1] The figure represents a long spear ; but the etymology, as also its position in the list of weapons, shows that it must be a part of the armour, *a neck-piece*.

[2] A round shield-like plate of iron attached to the *neck* of the horse and hanging down so as to protect the chest of the animal.

Āʾīn 37.

ON MATCHLOCKS, ETC.

These are in particular favour with His Majesty, who stands unrivalled in their manufacture, and as a marksman. Matchlocks are now made so strong that they do not burst, though let off when filled to the top. Formerly they could not fill them to more than a quarter. Besides, they made them with the hammer and the anvil by flattening pieces of iron, and joining the flattened edges of both sides. Some left them, from foresight, on one edge open ; but numerous accidents were the result, especially in the former kind. His Majesty has invented an excellent method of construction. They flatten iron, and twist it round obliquely in form of a roll, so that the folds get longer at every twist ; they then join the folds, not edge to edge, but so as to allow them to lie one over the other, and heat them gradually in the fire. They also take cylindrical pieces of iron, and pierce them when hot with an iron pin. Three or four of such pieces make one gun ; or, in the case of smaller ones, two. Guns are often made of a length of two yards ; those of a smaller kind are one and a quarter yards long, and go by the name of *Damānak*. The gunstocks are differently made. From the practical knowledge of His Majesty, guns are now made in such a manner that they can be fired off, without a match, by a slight movement of the cock. Bullets are also made so as to cut like a sword. Through the assistance of the inventive genius of His Majesty there are now many masters to be found among gunmakers, e.g., Ustād Kabīr and Ḥusayn.

Iron, when heated, loses about one-half of its volume.

When a barrel is completed lengthways, before the transverse bottom-piece is fixed to it, they engrave on it the quantity of its iron and the length, both being expressed in numerals. A barrel thus far finished, is called *Daul*. In this imperfect state they are sent to His Majesty, and delivered, in proper order, at the harem, to which place they are also brought for . . .[1] At the same time, the weight of the ball is fixed, and the order is given for the transverse section of the matchlock. For long guns the weight of a ball does not exceed twenty-five *tānks*, and for smaller ones fifteen. But balls of the former weight no one but His Majesty[2] would dare to fire. When the barrels are polished, they are again

---

[1] The text has an unintelligible word ; the *variantes lectiones* are marked on p. 125 of my text edition. Note (13). The Banāras MS. has ترقان. The word appears to be a foreign term.

[2] Akbar was remarkable for bodily strength. *Vide* Tusuk i Jahāngīrī, p. 16.

sent to the harem, and preserved in proper order. They are afterwards taken out, and closed, by the order of His Majesty, with a transverse bottom-piece. Having been put to an old stock, they are filled to one-third of the barrel with powder, and fired off. If no *tarāwish* [1] takes place, and the trial is satisfactory, they take the barrels again to His Majesty, who gives the order to finish the mouthpiece of the barrel. After this the gun is again placed on the stock, and subjected to a trial. If the ball issues in a crooked line, the barrel is heated, and straightened by means of a rod introduced into it, and, in the presence of His Majesty, handed over to a filer. He adorns the outside of the barrel in various ways, according to orders, when it is taken to the harem. The wood and the shape of the stock are then determined on. Several things are marked on every matchlock, viz., the weight of the raw and the manufactured iron, the former marks being now removed; the place where the iron is taken from; the workman; the place where the gun is made; the date; its number. Sometimes without reference to a proper order, one of the unfinished barrels is selected and completed at His Majesty's command. It is then entered in another place; the transverse bottom-piece is fixed; and the order is given to make the cock, the ramrod, the *pargaz,* [2] etc. As soon as all these things have been completed, a new trial is ordered; and when it succeeds, they send in the gun, and deliver it a third time at the harem. In this state the gun is called *sāda* (plain). Five bullets are sent along with it. His Majesty, after trying it in the manner above described, returns it with the fifth bullet. The order for the colour of the barrel and the stock is now given; one of the nine kinds of colour is selected for the stock. Guns also differ in the quality of inlaid gold and enamel; the colour of the barrel is uniform. A gun thus far completed is called *rangīn* (coloured). It is now, as before, handed over together with five bullets; His Majesty makes four trials, and returns it with the last ball. When ten of such guns are ready, His Majesty orders to inlay the mouth of the barrel and the butt end with gold. They are then again sent for trial into the harem, and whenever ten are quite complete they are handed over to the slaves.

---

[1] *Tarāwish* means a *trickling*; the particular meaning which it here has, is not clear and not given in the Dictionaries.

[2] *Pargaz,* or *Purgaz,* may mean the groove into which the ramrod is put, or the ramrod itself. The word is not in the dicts., and appears to be unknown at the present day.

Āʾīn 38.

THE MANNER OF CLEANING GUNS.

Formerly a strong man had to work a long time with iron instruments in order to clean matchlocks. His Majesty, from his practical knowledge, has invented a wheel, by the motion of which sixteen barrels may be cleaned in a very short time. The wheel is turned by a cow. Plate XV will best show what sort of a machine it is.

Āʾīn 39.

THE RANKS OF THE GUNS.

The Imperial arsenal contains *manufactured, purchased,* and *presented,* guns. Each of them is either *long,* or *short* ; and these are again subdivided into *sāda* (plain), *rangīn* (coloured), and *koftkār* (hammered) guns. His Majesty has selected out of several thousand guns, one hundred and five as *k͟hāṣa,* i.e. for his special use. *First,* twelve in honour of the twelve months ; each of them is brought back in its turn after eleven months. *Secondly,* thirty for every week ; after every seven days one goes out, and another is brought. *Thirdly,* thirty-two for the solar days ; one for every day. *Fourthly,* thirty-one *kotals.* Sometimes there are only twenty-eight. Whenever some of the former guns have been given away, *kotals* are brought, to supply their places. The order of precedence is as follows : the guns for the month ; the week ; days ; *kotals* ; plain ; coloured ; *koftkār,* not handed over to the slaves ; *koftkār,* handed over to the slaves ; long ones, selected from *peshkash* presents, or from such as were bought ; *damānaks,* selected from *peshkash,* or from bought ones ; such as have been chosen from selections of both. The one hundred and five *k͟hāṣa* guns are divided into seven parts ; every fifteen form a *kishk,* or guard, and are always kept ready by the slaves. On Sundays two are taken from the first ; four from the second ; five from the third ; four from the fourth This order is also followed on Mondays, Tuesdays, and Wednesdays. On Thursdays, two are again taken from the first, and four from the second ; four from the third ; five from the fourth. On Fridays, one is taken from the first ; five from the second ; four from the third ; five from the fourth. So also for Saturdays. In order to supply the places of such *k͟hāṣa* guns as have been given away, five other classes have been determined on : half kotals, fourteen ; quarter kotals, seven ; one-eighth kotals, four ; one-sixteenth kotals, two ; one-thirtysecond kotals, one. When *kotal* guns are given away, they bring half *kotals* ; similarly, the place of a gun, when given away, is taken by the next; and the place of the last is supplied by one selected from such as have been bought.

One hundred and one guns are continually kept in the harem. Their order is as follows. On the first day of every solar month eleven guns are handed over to the servants of the harem, one of each of the guns for the months, the weeks, the days, the *kotals*, the plain ones, the coloured ones, the *koftkār* not in charge of the slaves, the *koftār* in their charge, the selected long ones, the selected *Damānaks*, the chosen ones of the selected ones. On the second day only the guns of the months (i.e. ten) are handed over in the same order. For ten days an equal number is sent to the harem.

His Majesty practises often. When he has tried each gun, he commences from the beginning; and when each gun has been used four times it is sent away and replaced by a new one of each kind. If guns have been left unused at the beginning of a new month, they are placed last, and the guns for the current month are put first.

An order has also been given to the writers to write down the game killed by His Majesty with the particulars of the guns used. Thus it was found that with the gun which has the name of *Sangrām* one thousand and nineteen animals have been killed. This gun is the first of His Majesty's private guns, and is used during the *Farwardīn* month of the present era.

Ā'īn 40.

ON THE PAY OF THE MATCHLOCK BEARERS.

The pay of a *Mīrdaha*[1] is of four grades, 300 *dāms*, 280 *d.*, 270 *d.*, 260 *d.* The pay of the others is of five grades. Each grade is again subdivided into three classes. *First grade*, 250 *d.*, 240 *d.*, 230 *d.* *Second grade*, 220 *d.*, 210 *d.*, 200 *d.* *Third grade*, 190 *d.*, 180 *d.*, 170 *d.* *Fourth grade*, 160 *d.*, 150 *d.*, 140 *d.* *Fifth grade*, 130 *d.*, 120 *d.*, 110 *d.*

Ā'īn 41.

THE IMPERIAL ELEPHANT STABLES.

This wonderful animal is in bulk and strength like a mountain; and in courage and ferocity like a lion. It adds materially to the pomp of a king

[1] *A man placed over ten.* The rank of the *Mīrdaha* appears to have been the only *non-commissioned* rank in the Mogul armies. The lowest *commissioned* rank was that of a *Dahbāshī*, which word, though of the same *etymological* meaning, differs in usage, and signifies a man in *command* of ten. The rank of a *Dahbāshī* was the lowest *Manṣabdār* rank (*vide* the second book). *Mīrdaha* is also used in the sense *of a servant who looks after ten horses.*

and to the success of a conqueror ; and is of the greatest use for the army. Experienced men of Hindustan put the value of a good elephant equal to five hundred horses ; and they believe that, when guided by a few bold men armed with matchlocks, such an elephant alone is worth double that number. In vehemence on one side, and submissiveness to the reins on the other, the elephant is like an Arab, whilst in point of obedience and attentiveness to even the slightest signs, it resembles an intelligent human being. In restiveness when full-blooded, and in vindictiveness, it surpasses man. An elephant never hurts the female, though she be the cause of his captivity ; he never will fight with young elephants, nor does he think it proper to punish them. From a sense of gratitude, he does his keepers no harm, nor will he throw dust over his body when he is mounted, though he often does so at other times. Once an elephant, during the rutting-season was fighting with another. When he was in the height of excitement a small elephant came in his way ; he kindly lifted up the small one with his trunk, set him aside, and then renewed the combat. If a male elephant breaks loose during the rutting season in order to have his own way, few people have the courage to approach him ; and some bold and experienced man will have to get on a female elephant, and try to get near him and tie a rope round his foot. Female-elephants, when mourning the loss of a young one, will often abstain from food and drink ; they sometimes even die from grief.

The elephant can be taught various feats. He learns to remember such melodies as can only be remembered by people acquainted with music ; he will move his limbs to keep time and exhibit his skill in various ways. He will shoot off an arrow from a bow, discharge a matchlock, and will learn to pick up things that have been dropped and hand them over to the keeper. Sometimes they get grain to eat wrapped up in hay ; this they hide in the side of their mouth, and give it back to the keeper, when they are alone with him.

The teats of a female elephant, and the womb, resemble those of a woman. The tongue is round like that of a parrot. The testicles are not visible. Elephants frequently with their trunks take water out of their stomachs, and sprinkle themselves with it. Such water has no offensive smell. They also take out of their stomach grass on the second day, without its having undergone any change.

The price of an elephant varies from a lak [1] to one hundred rupees ;

---

[1] During the reigns of Akbar's successor, the price of a well-trained war elephant rose much higher. *Vide* Tuzuk-i Jahāngīrī, p. 198. At the time of Shāhjahān, the first white elephant was brought from Pégū, *Pādishāhnāma*, i, p. 267.

elephants worth five thousand, and ten thousand rupees, are pretty common.

There are four kinds of elephants. 1. *Bhaddar*. It is well proportioned, has an erect head, a broad chest, large ears, a long tail, and is bold, and can bear fatigue. They take out of his forehead an excrescence resembling a large pearl, which they call in Hindī *Gaj manik*.[1] Many properties are ascribed to it. 2. *Mand*. It is black, has yellow eyes, a uniformly sized belly, a long penis, and is wild and ungovernable. 3. *Mirg*. It has a whitish skin with black spots; the colour of its eyes is a mixture of red, yellow, black, and white. 4. *Mir*. It has a small head, and obeys readily. It gets frightened when it thunders.

From a mixture of these four kinds are formed others of different names and properties. The colour of the skin of elephants is threefold; white, black, grey. Again, according to the threefold division of the dispositions assigned by the Hindus to the mind, namely, *sat* benevolence, *raj* love of sensual enjoyment, and *tam* irascibility, which shall be further explained below,[2] elephants are divided into three classes. *First*, such in which *sat* predominates. They are well proportioned, good looking, eat moderately, are very submissive, do not care for intercourse with the female, and live to a very old age. *Secondly*, such in whose disposition *raj* prevails. They are savage-looking, and proud, bold, ungovernable, and voracious. *Lastly*, such as are full of *tam*. They are self-willed, destructive, and given to sleep and voraciousness.

The time of gestation of the female is generally eighteen [3] lunar months. For three months the *fluida germinalia* intermix in the womb of the female; when agitated the mass looks like quicksilver. Towards the fifth month the *fluida* settle and get gelatinous. In the seventh month, they get more solid, and draw to perfection towards the ninth month. In the eleventh, the outline of a body is visible; and in the twelfth, the veins, bones, hoofs, and hairs, make their appearance. In the thirteenth month the *genitalia* become distinguishable, and in the fifteenth, the

---

[1] This excrescence is also called *Gajmotī*, or *elephants'-pearl*. Forbes has also *Gajmanik*, and the *Dalīl-i Sāṭī*, گجوتي gaj wati (?).

[2] In the *fourth* book of this work.

[3] The time is differently given. The emperor Jahāngīr says in his Memoirs (p. 130) :—"During this month a female elephant in my stables gave birth before my own eyes. I had often expressed the wish to have the time of gestation of the female elephant correctly determined. It is now certain that a female birth takes place after sixteen, and a male birth after nineteen, months [the emperor means evidently *solar* months]; and the process is different from what it is with man, the fœtus being born with the feet foremost. After giving birth, the female at once covers the young one with earth and dust, and continually caresses it, whilst the young one sinks down every moment trying to reach the teats of the mother." *Vide* Lt. Johnstone's remarks on the same subject, in the *Proceedings of the Asiatic Society of Bengal* for May, 1868.

process of quickening commences. If the female, during gestation, gets stronger, the fœtus is sure to be a male; but if she gets weak it is the sign of a female. During the sixteenth month the formation becomes still more perfect, and the life of the fœtus becomes quite distinct. In the seventeenth month there is every chance[1] of a premature birth on account of the efforts made by the fœtus to move, till, in the eighteenth month, the young one is born.

According to others the sperm gets solid in the first month; the eyes, ears, the nose, mouth, and tongue are formed in the second; in the third month, the limbs made their appearance; in the fourth month, the fœtus grows and gets strong; in the fifth, it commences to quicken; in the sixth, it gets sense, which appears more marked during the seventh month; in the eighth, there is some chance of a miscarriage; during the ninth, tenth, and eleventh months the fœtus grows, and is born during the twelfth. It will be a male young one if the greater part of the sperm came from the male; and it will be a female young one if the reverse is the case. If the sperm of both the male and female is equal in quantity the young one will be a hermaphrodite. The male fœtus lies towards the right side; the female towards the left; a hermaphrodite in the middle.

Female elephants have often for twelve days a red discharge, after which gestation commences. During that period they look startled, sprinkle themselves with water and earth, keep ears and tail upwards, and go rarely away from the male. They will rub themselves against the male, bend their heads below his tusks, smell at his urine and dung, and cannot bear to see another female near him. Sometimes, however, a female shows aversion to intercourse with the male; and must be forced to copulate, when other female elephants, at hearing her noise, will come to her rescue.

In former times, people did not breed elephants, and thought it unlucky; by the command of His Majesty, they now breed a very superior class of elephants, which has removed the old prejudice in the minds of men. A female elephant has generally one young one, but sometimes two. For five years the young ones content themselves with the milk of the mother; after that period they commence to eat herbs. In this state they are called *bāl*. When ten years old they are named *pūt*; when twenty years old, *bikka*; when thirty years old, *kalba*. In fact the animal changes appearance every year, and then gets a new name. When sixty years old, the elephant is full grown. The skull then looks like two

---

[1] The words of the text are ambiguous. They may also mean: In the seventeenth month the effort of the fœtus to move causes the female to sink down.

halves of a ball, whilst the ears look like winnowing fans.[1] White eyes mixed with yellow, black, and red, are looked upon as a sign of excellence. The forehead must be flat without swellings or wrinkles. The trunk is the nose of the animal, and is so long as to touch the ground. With it, it takes up the food and puts it into the mouth ; similarly, it sucks up water with it, and then throws it into the stomach. It has eighteen teeth ; sixteen of them are inside the mouth, eight above and eight below, and two are the tusks outside. The latter are one and more yards long, round, shining, very strong, white, or sometimes reddish and straight, the end slightly bent upwards. Some elephants have four tusks. With a view to usefulness as also to ornament, they cut off the top of the tusks, which grow again. With some elephants they have to cut the tusks annually ; with others after two or three years ; but they do not like to cut them when an elephant is ten and eighty years old. An elephant is perfect when it is eight *dast* high, nine *dast* long, and ten *dast* round the belly, and along the back. Again, nine limbs, ought to touch the ground, namely, the fore feet, the hind feet, the trunk, the tusks, the penis, the tail. White spots on the forehead are considered lucky, whilst a thick neck is looked upon as a sign of beauty. Long hairs on and about the ears point to good origin.

Some elephants rut in winter, some in summer, some in the rains. They are then very fierce, they pull down houses, throw down stone walls, and will lift up with their trunks a horse and its rider. But elephants differ very much in the amount of fierceness and boldness.

When they are hot, a blackish discharge exudes from the soft parts between the ears and the temples, which has a most offensive smell ; it is sometimes whitish, mixed with red. They say that elephants have twelve holes in those soft parts, which likewise discharge the offensive fluid. The discharge is abundant in lively animals, but trickles drop by drop in slow ones. As soon as the discharge stops, the elephant gets fierce and looks grand ; in this state he gets the name of *Taftī* or *Sarharī*. When the above discharge exudes from a place a little higher than the soft parts between the ears and the temples, the elephant is called *Singāḍhāl* ; and when the fluid trickles from all three places, *Tal-jor*. When in heat, elephants get attached to particular living creatures, as men or horses ; but some elephants to any animal. So at least according to Hindu books.

---

[1] *G͟halla afshān*. This word, though common, is not in our dictionaries. It is a flat piece of wicker work, from one to two feet square. Three sides of the square are slightly bent upwards. They put grain on it, and seizing the instrument with both hands, they throw up the grain, till the husks, stones, and all other refuse collect near the side which is not bent upwards, when the refuse is removed with the hand. We use *sieves* for such purposes.

The *Bhaddar* ruts in Libra and Scorpio; the *Mand* in spring; the *Mirg* in Capricorn and Sagittarius; the *Mir* in any season. Elephant drivers have a drug which causes an artificial heat; but it often endangers the life of the beast. The noise of battle makes some superior elephants just as fierce as at the rutting season; even a sudden start may have such an effect. Thus His Majesty's elephant *Gajmukta*: he gets brisk as soon as he hears the sound of the Imperial drum, and gets the above-mentioned discharge. This peculiar heat generally makes its first appearance when elephants have reached the age of thirty; sometimes, however, earlier, at an age of twenty-five Sometimes the heat lasts for years, and some of the Imperial elephants have continued for five years in an uninterrupted alacrity. But it is mostly male elephants that get in heat. They then commence to throw up earth, and run after a female, or roll about in mud, and daub themselves all over with dirt. When in heat they are very irritable, and yawn a great deal, though they sleep but little. At last they even discontinue eating, and dislike the foot-chain: they try to get loose, and behave noisily.

The elephant, like man, lives to an age of one hundred and twenty years.

The Hindī language has several words for an elephant, as ***hastī***, ***gaj***, ***pīl***, ***hāthī***, etc. Under the hands of an experienced keeper it will much improve, so that its value in a short time may rise from one hundred to ten thousand rupees.

The Hindus believe that the eight points of the earth are each guarded by a heavenly being in the shape of an elephant; they have curious legends regarding them. Their names are as follows: 1. *Airāwata*, in the East; 2. *Pundarika*, south-east; 3. *Bāman*, south; 4. *Kumada*, south-west; 5. *Anjan*, west; 6. *Puhpadanta*, north-west; 7. *Sārbhabhūma*, north; 8. *Supratīka*, north-east. When occasions arise, people read incantations in their names, and address them in worship. They also think that every elephant in the world is the offspring of one of them. Thus, elephants of a white skin and white hairs are related to the first; elephants with a large head and long hairs, of a fierce and bold temper, and eyelids apart, belong to the second; such as are . . .[1] good-looking, black, and high in the back, are the offspring of the third; if tall, ungovernable, quick in understanding, short-haired, and with red and black eyes, they come from the fourth; if bright black, with one tusk longer than the other, with a white breast and belly, and long and thick fore-feet, from the

---

[1] The MSS. have an unintelligible word. Perhaps *khushsanj*, graceful, is the correct reading.

fifth; if fearful, with prominent veins, with a short hump and ears and a long trunk, from the sixth; if thin-bellied, red-eyed, and with a long trunk, from the seventh; and if of a combination of the preceding seven qualities, from the eighth.

The Hindus also make the following division into *eight* classes: 1. Elephants whose skin is not wrinkled, who are never sick, who are grand looking, do not run away from the battle-field, dislike meat, and prefer clean food at proper times, are said to be *Dew mizāj* (of a divine temper). 2. Such as possess all the good qualities of elephants, and are quick in learning, moving about the head, ears, trunk, forelegs, hind legs, and the tail, and do no one harm except they be ordered to do so, are *Gandharba mizāj* (angelic). 3. If irritable, of good appetite, fond of being in water, they are *Brahaman mizāj* (of a brahminical temper). 4. Such as are very strong, in good condition, fond of fighting, ungovernable, are said to have the temper of a *Khattrī*, or warrior. 5. Those which are of a low stature, and forgetful, self-willed in their own work, and neglectful in that of their master, fond of unclean food, and spiteful towards other elephants, are *Sūdra mizāj*. 6. Elephants which remain hot for a long time, and are fond of playing tricks, or are destructive, and lose the way, have the temper of a serpent. 7. Such as squint, and are slow to learn, or feign to be hot, have the temper of a *Pishācha* (spectre). 8. Those which are violent, swift, and do men harm, and are fond of running about at night, have the qualities of a *Rāchhas* (demon).

The Hindus have written many books in explanation of these various tempers, as also many treatises on the diseases of the elephants, their causes and proper remedies

Elephants are found in the Ṣūbah of Āgra, in the forests of Bayāwān and Narwar,[1] as far as Barār; in the Ṣūba of Ilāhābād (Allahabad), in the confines of Pannah, (Bhath) Ghoṛā, and Ratanpūr, Nandanpūr, Sirguja, and Bastar; in the Ṣūba of Mālwa, in Handiyah, Uchhod, Chanderī, Santwās, Bījāgaṛh, Rāisīn, Hoshangābād, Gaṛha, Haryāgaṛh; in the Ṣūba of Bihār, in the neighbourhood of Rahtās

[1] Narwar, where Abū 'l-Faẓl was subsequently murdered at the instigation of Prince Salīm (Jahāngīr), Long. 77° 58′, Lat. 25° 39′; *Ghoṛāghāt*, near Dinagepore, Long. 89° 17′, Lat. 25° 12′; *Ratanpūr* (Abū 'l-Faẓl evidently means the one south-east of Sargachh), Long. 82°, Lat. 22° 14′; *Sargachh*, Long. 83° 8′, Lat. 23° 8′; *Bustar*, Long. 81° 58′, Lat. 19° 13′. The towns from Handiya to Haryāgaḍh lie all between Long. 75° and 79°, and Lat. 21° and 24° (Gwāliār). For *Uchhod* (اچهود) the third book has *Ūnchhod* (اونچهود). The Fort of Rahtās, the scene of Sher Shāh's first exploit, lies Long. 84°, Lat. 24° 38′. The name *Pattah* (پته) is doubtful, each MS. having a different reading.

Wild elephants have nowadays disappeared in nearly all the places mentioned by Abū 'l-Faẓl.

and Jhārkhand; and in the Ṣūba of Bengal, in Orīsā, and Sātgāw. The elephants from Pannah are the best.

A herd of elephants is called in Hindī *sahn*. They vary in number; sometimes a herd amounts to a thousand elephants. Wild elephants are very cautious. In winter and summer, they select a proper place, and break down a whole forest near their sleeping place. For the sake of pleasure, or for food and drink, they often travel over great distances. On the journey one runs far in front of the others, like a sentinel; a young female is generally selected for this purpose. When they go to sleep they send out to the four sides of the sleeping place pickets of four female elephants, which relieve each other.

Elephants will lift up their young ones, for three or four days after their birth, with their trunks, and put them on their backs, or lay them over their tusks. They also prepare medicines for the females when they are sick or in labour pains and crowd round about them. When some of them get caught, the female elephants break through the nets, and pull down the elephant-drivers. And when a young elephant falls into a snare they hide themselves in an ambush, go at night to the place where the young one is, set it at liberty, and trample the hunters to death. Sometimes its mother slowly approaches alone, and frees it in some clever way. I have heard the following story from His Majesty: "Once a wild young one had fallen into a pit. As night had approached, we did not care to pull it out immediately, and left it; but when we came next morning near the place, we saw that some wild elephants had filled the pit with broken logs and grass, and thus pulled out the young one." Again, "Once a female elephant played us a trick. She feigned to be dead. We passed her, and went onwards; but when at night we returned, we saw no trace left of her."

There was once an elephant in the Imperial stables named *Ayāz*. For some reason it had got offended with the driver, and was for ever watching for an opportunity. Once at night, it found him asleep. It got hold of a long piece of wood, managed to pull off with it the man's turban, seized him by the hair, and tore him asunder.

Many examples are on record of the extraordinary cleverness of elephants; in some cases it is difficult to believe them.

Kings have always shown a great predilection for this animal, and done everything in their power to collect a large number. Elephant-keepers are much esteemed, and a proper rank is assigned to such as have a special knowledge of the animal. Wicked, low men see in an elephant a means of lawlessness; and unprincipled evildoers, with the help of this animal, carry on their nefarious trade. Hence kings of former times never succeeded in suppressing the rebellious, and were thus disappointed in their best intentions. But His Majesty, though overwhelmed with other important matters, has been able, through God's assistance and his numerous elephants, to check those low but haughty men; he teaches them to desire submission, and bestows upon them, by wise laws, the blessings of peace.

His Majesty divided the Imperial elephants into sections, which he put in charge of honest Dāroghas. Certain elephants were also declared *khāṣa*, i.e., appointed for the exclusive use of His Majesty.

Ā'īn 42.

THE CLASSIFICATION OF THE IMPERIAL ELEPHANTS.

His Majesty made a sevenfold division, based upon experience: 1. *Mast* (full blood); 2. *Shergīr* (tiger-seizing); 3. *Sāda* (plain); 4. *Manjhola* (middlemost); 5. *Karha*; 6. *Phandurkiya*; 7. *Mokal*. The first class comprises young elephants, possessed of the peculiar heat which renders the animal so strong. The second class contains likewise young ones which once or twice have given signs of perfection and exhibit an uninterrupted alacrity. The third class comprehends useful elephants, which are nearly as good as the preceding. The fourth class contains elephants of a somewhat inferior value. Those of the fifth class are younger than those of the fourth. The elephants of the sixth class are smaller than those of the fifth. The last class contains all young ones still unfit for use.

Each class is divided into three subdivisions, viz., *large sized, middle, young* ones; the last class contains ten kinds. A certain quantity of food has been fixed for each class.

Ā'īn 43.

THE FOOD ALLOWED TO THE ELEPHANTS.

Formerly the classification of the elephants was never attended to; hence in feeding them a large quantity of the stores was wasted. But when His Majesty, soon after lifting the veil,[1] commenced to care for the

---

[1] The same phrase as on p. 13, line 12. It refers to the year 1560, when Bayrām fell in disgrace, and Akbar assumed the reins of the government.

happiness of his subjects, this matter was properly inquired into, and wise regulations were issued for guidance. 1. *Mast elephants.* Large ones get daily 2 *mans* 24 *sers*; middle-sized, 2 *m.* 19 *s.*; small ones, 2 *m.* 14 *s.* 2. *Shergīrs.* Large ones, 2 *m.* 9 *s.*; middle-sized ones, 2 *m.* 4 *s.*; small ones, 1 *m.* 39 *s.* 3. *Sādas.* Large ones, 1 *m.* 34 *s.*; middle-sized ones, 1 *m.* 29 *s.*; small ones, 1 *m.* 24 *s.* 4. *Manjholas.* Large ones, 1 *m.* 22 *s.*; middle-sized ones, 1 *m.* 20 *s.*; small ones, 1 *m.* 18 *s.* 5. *Karhas.* Large ones, 1 *m.* 14 *s.*; middle-sized ones, 1 *m.* 9 *s.*; small ones, 1 *m.* 4 *s.* 6. *Phandurkiyas.* Large ones, 1 *m.*; middle-sized ones, 36 *s.*; small ones, 32 *s.* 7. *Mokals.* Large ones, 26 *s.*; middle-sized ones, 24 *s.*; third class, 22 *s.*; fourth class, 20 *s.*; fifth class, 18 *s.*; sixth class, 16 *s.*; seventh class, 14 *s.*; eighth class, 12 *s.*; ninth class, 10 *s.*; tenth class, 8 *s.*

Female elephants have been divided into four classes, viz., large ones, middle-sized ones, small ones, *mokals.* The first two classes are divided into three; the third, into four; the fourth, into nine subdivisions. 1. *Large ones:* Big, 1 *m.* 22 *s.*; middling, 1 *m.* 18 *s.*; small ones, 1 *m.* 14*s.* 2. *Middle-sized ones.* Big, 1 *m.* 10 *s.*; middling, 1 *m.* 6 *s.*; small, 1 *m.* 2 *s.* 3. *Small ones.* Big, 37 *s.*; middling, 32 *s.*; small, 27 *s.*; still smaller, 22 *s.* 4. *Mokals.* First class, 22 *s.*; second, 20 *s.*; third, 18 *s.*; fourth, 16 *s.*; fifth, 14 *s.*; sixth, 12 s.; seventh, 10 *s.*; eighth, 8 *s.*; ninth, 6 *s.*

Āʾīn 44.

THE SERVANTS OF THE ELEPHANT STABLES.

1. *Mast* elephants. There are five and a half [1] servants for each, viz., a *Mahāwat,* who sits on the neck of the animal and directs its movements. He must be acquainted with its good and bad properties, and thus contribute to its usefulness. He gets 200 *dāms* per month; but if the elephant be *khuṭahar,* i.e., wicked and addicted to pulling down the driver, he gets 220 *d.* *Secondly,* a *Bhoī,* who sits behind, upon the rump of the elephant, and assists in battle and in quickening the speed of the animal; but he often performs the duties of the *Mahāwat.* His monthly pay is 110 *d.* *Thirdly,* the *Meths,* of whom there are three and one-half, or only three in case of small elephants. A *meth* fetches fodder, and assists in caparisoning the elephant. *Meths* of all classes get on the march four *dāms* daily, and at other times three and a half.

2. For every *Shergīr,* there are five servants, viz., a *Mahāwat,* at 180 *d.*; a *Bhoī,* at 103 *d.*; and three *Meths* as before.

---

[1] i.e., either eleven servants for two elephants, or the last was a boy.

3. For every *Sāda*, there are four and a half servants, viz., a *Mahāwat*, at 160 *d.*, a *Bhoī* at 90 *d.* ; and two and a half *Meths*.

4. For every *Manjhola*, there are four servants ; viz., a *Mahāwat*, at 140 *d.* ; a *Bhoī*, at 80 *d* ; and two *Meths*.

5. For every *Karha*, there are three and a half servants ; viz., a *Mahāwat* at 120 *d.* ; a *Bhoī*, at 70 *d.* ; and one and a half *Meths*.

6. For every *Phandurkiya*, there are two servants ; viz., a *Mahāwat*, at 100 *d* ; and a *Meth*.

7. For every *Mokal*, there are likewise two servants ; viz., a *Mahāwat*, at 50 *d.* ; and a *Meth*.

Female Elephants. 1. Large ones have four servants, viz., a *Mahāwat*, at 100 *d.* ; a *Bhoī*, at 60 *d.* ; two *Meths*. 2. Middle-sized ones have three and a half servants ; viz., a *Mahāwat*, at 80 *d.* ; a *Bhoī*, at 50 *d.* ; and one and a half *Meths*. 3. Small ones have two ; viz., a *Mahāwat*, at 60 *d.* ; and a *Meth*. 4. *Mokals* have likewise two ; viz., a *Mahāwat*, at 60 *d.*, and a *Meth*.

The Fawjdār.

His Majesty has appointed a superintendent over every troop of ten, twenty, and thirty elephants. Such a troop is called a *ḥalqa* ; the superintendent is called *Fawjdār*. His business is to look after the condition and the training of the elephants ; he teaches them to be bold, and to stand firm at the sight of fire and at the noise of artillery ; and he is responsible for their behaviour in these respects. When a *Fawjdār* is raised to the dignity of a *Ṣadī* (a commander of one hundred) or higher, he has twenty-five elephants assigned to himself, the other *Fawjdārs*, as *Bīstīs* (commanders of twenty) and *Dahbāshīs* (commanders of ten) being under his orders. The same order is followed from the *Dahbāshīs* up to the *Hazārīs* (commanders of one thousand). The pay of officers above the *Ṣadī* is different. Some *Fawjdārs* have been raised to the dignity of grandees of the court. A *Ṣadī* marks two horses. A *Bīstī* of the first grade has 30 *rupees per mensem* ; second grade, 25 *R.* ; third grade, 20 *R.* A *Dahbāshī* of the first grade has twenty *R.* ; second grade, 16 *R.* ; third grade, 12 *R.* *Bīstīs* and *Dahbāshīs* mark one horse, and belong to the *Aḥadīs*. Such *Fawjdārs* as have thirty or twenty-five elephants assigned to themselves have to pay the wages of the *Mahāwat* and of one *Bhoī* of that elephant, which they select for their own use ; but such as have twenty or ten only pay for a *Mahāwat*.

The above arrangement regarding the servants was not thought sufficient by His Majesty, who has much experience in this matter. He therefore put several *ḥalqas* in charge of every grandee, and required him to look after them. The fodder also is now supplied by the government. A trustworthy clerk has, besides, been appointed, who is in charge of the correspondence of this branch ; he looks after the receipts and expenditure and sees that the orders of His Majesty are carried out. He also parades the elephants in the order described below (*Āʻīn* 78).

Āʻīn 45.

THE HARNESS OF ELEPHANTS.

1. The *Dharna* is a large chain, made of iron, gold, or silver. It is made of sixty oval links, each weighing three *sers* ; but the chain differs in length and thickness according to the strength of the elephant. One end of the chain is fixed in the ground, or fastened to a pillar ; the other end is tied to the left hind leg of the elephant. Formerly, they fastened this chain to the forefoot ; but as this is injurious for the chest of the elephant His Majesty ordered to discontinue the usage.

2. The *Āndū* is a chain, with which both forefeet are tied. As it annoys the elephant, His Majesty ordered it to be discontinued.

3. The *Beṛī* is a chain for fastening both hind feet.

4. The *Baland* is a fetter for the hind feet, an invention of His Majesty. It allows the elephant to walk, but prevents him from running.

5. The *Gaddh beṛī* resembles the *Āndū*, and is an additional chain for the hindlegs of unruly and swift elephants.

6. The *Loh langar* is a long chain, suitable for an elephant. One end is tied to the right fore foot, and the other end to a thick log, a yard in length. This the driver keeps near him, and drops it, when the elephant runs too swiftly, or gets so unruly as no longer to obey. The chain twists round his leg, and the log will annoy the animal to such extent that it necessarily stops. This useful invention, which has saved many lives, and protected huts and walls, is likewise due to His Majesty.

7. The *Char<u>kh</u>ī* is a piece of hollowed bamboo half a yard and two ṭassūjes long, and has a hole in the middle. It is covered with sinews and filled with gunpowder, an earthen partition dividing the powder into two halves. A fuzee wrapt in paper is put into each end. Fixed into the hole of the bamboo at right angles is a stick, which serves as a handle. Upon fire being put to both ends, it turns round and makes a frightful noise. When elephants fight with each other, or are otherwise unruly, a bold man on foot takes the burning bamboo into his hand, and holds it before the animals, when they will get quiet. Formerly, in order to separate two elephants that were fighting, they used to light a fire ; but people had

much trouble, as it seldom had the desired effect. His Majesty invented the present method, which was hailed by all.

8. *Andhiyārī*, i.e., darkness, a name which His Majesty changed into *Ujyālī*, i.e., light, is a piece of canvas above one and a half yards square. It is made of brocade, velvet, etc., and tied with two ends to the *Kilāwa* (*vide* next). When the elephant is unruly, it is let fall, so that he cannot see. This has been the saving of many. As it often gives way, especially when the elephant is very wild, His Majesty had three heavy bells attached to the ends of the canvas, to keep it better down. This completed the arrangement.

9. The *Kilāwa* [1] consists of a few twisted ropes, about one and a half yards long. They are laid at the side of each other, without, however, being interwoven among themselves, the whole being about eight fingers broad. A ring is drawn through both ends of the ropes, and fastened where the throat of the elephant is; the elephant driver rests his feet in it, and thus sits firmly. Sometimes it is made of silk or leather. Others fix small pointed iron-spikes to the *kalāwa*, which will prevent an unruly elephant from throwing down the driver by shaking its head.

10. The *Dulthī* is a rope, five yards long, as thick as a staff. This they tie over the *kalāwa* to strengthen it.

11. The *Kanār* is a small pointed spike, half a yard long. This they likewise attach to the *kalāwa*, and prick the elephant's ears with it in order to make the animal wild or to urge it on.

12. The *Ḍor* is a thick rope passing from the tail to the throat. When properly tied it is an ornament. They also catch hold of it, when the elephant makes an awkward movement. They also attach many other trappings to it.

13. The *Gadela* is a cushion put on the back of the elephant below the *dulthī*. It prevents galling, and is a source of comfort.

14. The *Gudauṭī* is a chain of brass. They attach it near the tail, which it prevents from getting injured by the *dulthī*. It is also ornamental.

15. The *Pichwa* is a belt made of ropes and is fastened over the buttocks of the elephant. It is a support for the *Bhoī*, and of much use to him in firing.

16. The *Chaurāsī* consists of a number of bells attached to a piece of

---

[1] This should be *Kalāwa*. Abū 'l-Faẓl spells the word wrong; *vide* my text edition, p. 136, l. 16. It looks as if Abū 'l-Faẓl had mistaken this *Persian* word for a *Hindī* term; else, why should he have any spelling at all. In Vullers' Persian Dictionary, ii, p. 862*b*, read *khait* for *khat*, and *ba tanīd* for his emendation (?) *tabyīn*.

broadcloth, which is tied on before and behind with a string passed through it. It looks ornamental and grand.

17. *Piṭkachh* is the name of two chains fastened over the elephant's sides. Attached to them, a bell hangs below the belly. It is of great beauty and grandeur.

18. Large chains. They attach six on both sides, and three to the *kalāwa*, the latter being added by His Majesty.

19. *Quṭās* (the tail of the Thibetan Yak). There are about sixty, more or less, attached to the tusk, the forehead, the throat, and the neck. They are either white, or black, or pied, and look very ornamental.

20. The *Ṭayyā* consists of five iron plates, each a span long, and four fingers broad, fastened to each other by rings. On both sides of the *Ṭayyā* there are two chains, each a yard long, one of which passes from above the ear, and the other from below it to the *kalāwa*, to which both are attached. Between them there is another chain, which is passed over the head and tied to the *kalāwa*; and below, crossways, there are four iron spikes ending in a curve, and adorned with knobs. The *Quṭās* are attached here. At their lower end there are three other chains similarly arranged. Besides, four other chains are attached to the knob; two of them, like the first, end in a knob, whilst the remaining two are tied to the tusks. To this knob again three chains are attached, two of which are tied round about the trunk, the middle one hanging down. *Quṭās* and daggers are attached to the former knobs, but the latter lies over the forehead. All this is partly for ornament, partly to frighten other animals.

21. The *Pākhar* is like an armour, and is made of steel; there are separate pieces for the head and the trunk.

22. The *Gaj-jhamp* is a covering put as an ornament above the *pākhar*. It looks grand. It is made of three folds of canvas, put together and sewn, broad ribbons being attached to the outside.

23. The *Megh dambar* is an awning to shade the elephant driver, an invention by His Majesty. It also looks ornamental.

24. The *Ranpiyal* is a fillet for the forehead made of brocade or similar stuffs, from the hem of which nice ribbons and *quṭās* hang down.

25. The *Gatelī* consists of four links joined together, with three above them, and two others over the latter. It is attached to the feet of the elephant. Its sound is very effective.

26. The *Pāy ranjan* consists of several bells similarly arranged.

27. The *Ānkus* is a small crook. His Majesty calls it *Gajbāga*.[1] It is used for guiding the elephant and stopping him.

---

[1] i.e., an elephant-rein. His Majesty had reason to change the name *Ānkus*, "which sounds offensive to a Persian ear." *Rashīdī*. Hence the Persians pronounce it *anguzh*.

28. The *Gaḍ* is a spear which has two prongs instead of an iron point. The *Bhoī* makes use of it, when the elephant is refractory.

29. The *Bangrī* is a collection of rings made of iron or brass. The rings are put on the tusks, and serve to strengthen as well as to ornament them.

30. The *Jagāwaṭ* resembles the *Gaḍ* (No. 28), and is a cubit long. The *Bhoī* uses it, to quicken the speed of the elephant.

31. The *Jhanḍā*, or flag, is hung round with *Quṭās*, like a *togh*.[1] It is fixed to the side of the elephant.

But it is impossible to describe all the ornamental trappings of elephants.

For each *Mast* and *Shergīr* and *Sāda*, seven pieces of cotton cloth are annually allowed, each at a price of 8½ *dāms*. Also, four coarse woollen pieces, called in Hindī *kambal*, at 10 *d*. each, and eight ox hides, each at 8 *d*. For *Manjhola* and *Karha* elephants, four of the first; three of the second; and seven of the third, are allowed. For *Phandurkiyas* and *Mokals*, and female elephants, three of the first; two of the second; four of the third. The saddlecloth is made of cloth, lining, and stuff for edging it round about; for sewing, half a *ser* of cotton thread is allowed. For every *man* of grain, the *ḥalqa-dār* is allowed ten *sers* of iron for chains, etc., at 2 *d*. per *ser*; and for every hide, one *ser* of sesame oil, at 60 *d*. per *man*. Also 5 *s*. coarse cotton thread for the *kalāwa* of the elephant on which the *Fawjdār* rides, at 8 *d*. per *ser*; but for other elephants, the men have to make one of leather, etc., at their own expense.

A sum of twelve *dāms* is annually subtracted from the servants; but they get the worn out articles.

Āʾīn 46.

THE ELEPHANTS FOR HIS MAJESTY'S USE (*KHĀṢA*).

There are one hundred and one elephants selected for the use of His Majesty. Their allowance of food is the same in quantity as that of the other elephants, but differs in quality. Most of them also get 5 *s*. of sugar, 4 *s*. of *ghī*, and half a *man* of rice mixed with chillies, cloves, etc.; and some have one and a half *man* [2] of milk in addition to their grain. In the sugar-cane season, each elephant gets daily, for two months, 300 sugar canes, more or less. His Majesty takes the place of the *Mahāwat*.

Each elephant requires three *bhoīs* in the rutting season, and two, when cool. Their monthly wages vary from 120 to 400 *d*., and are fixed by His

---

[1] *Togh* is the same as *tōq*. *Vide* Āʾīn 19, p. 52.

[2] Liquids are sold in India by the weight.

Majesty himself. For each elephant there are four *Meths.* In the *Ḥalqas*, female elephants are but rarely told off to accompany big male ones ; but for each *k͟hāṣa* elephant there are three, and sometimes even more, appointed. First class big female elephants have two and one-half *meths* ; second class do., two ; third class do., one and one-half ; for the other classes as in the *Ḥalqas*.

As each *Ḥalqa* is in charge of one of the grandees, so is every *k͟hāṣa* elephant put in charge of one of them. Likewise, for every ten *k͟hāṣa* elephants, a professional man is appointed, who is called *Dahā,īdār*. They draw, twelve, ten, and eight rupees *per mensem*. Besides, an active and honest superintendent is appointed for every ten elephants. He is called *Naqīb* (watcher) and has to submit a daily report, when elephants eat little, or get a shortened allowance, or in cases of sickness, or when anything unusual happens. He marks a horse, and holds the rank of an *Aḥadī*. His Majesty also weekly dispatches some of the servants near him, in the proportion of one for every ten elephants, who inspect them and send in a report.

Āʾīn 47.

THE MANNER OF RIDING *K͟HĀṢA*-ELEPHANTS.

His Majesty, the royal rider of the plain of auspiciousness, mounts on every kind of elephant, from the first to the last class, making them, notwithstanding their almost supernatural strength, obedient to his command. His Majesty will put his foot on the tusks, and mount them, even when they are in the rutting season, and astonishes experienced people.[1]

They also put comfortable turrets on the backs of swift-paced elephants, which serve as a travelling sleeping apartment. An elephant so caparisoned is always ready at the palace.

Whenever His Majesty mounts an elephant, a month's wages are given as a donation to the *bhoīs*. And when he has ridden ten elephants, the following donations are bestowed, *viz.*, the near servant who has weekly to report on the elephants, receives a present ; the former, 100 *R.* ; the *Dahā,ī*, 31 *R.* ; the *Naqīb*, 15 *R.* ; the *Mushrif* (writer), 7½ *R.* Besides, the regal rewards given to them at times when they display a particular zeal or attentiveness, go beyond the reach of speech.

Each elephant has his match appointed for fighting ; some are always

---

[1] Jahāngīr, in his Memoirs, gives several examples of Akbar's daring in this respect ; *vide* Tuzuk, p. 16.

ready at the palace, and engage when the order is given. When a fight is over, if the combatants were *khāṣa* elephants, the *bhoīs* receive 250 *dāms* as a present; but if other elephants, the *bhoīs* get 200 *d.*

The *Dahā,īdār* of *khāṣa* elephants receives one *dām* for every rupee paid as wages to the *bhoīs* and *meths*; the *Mushrif* is entitled to ½ *d.*, and the *Naqīb* to ¼ *d.* In the case of *ḥalqa* elephants, the *Ṣadīwāl*, the *Dahbāshī*, and the *Bīstī*, are entitled to 1 *d.* for every rupee; and the *Mushrif* and the *Naqīb* receive the allowance given for *khāṣa* elephants.

Āʾīn 48.

ON FINES.

In order to prevent laziness and to ensure attentiveness, His Majesty, as for all other departments, has fixed a list of fines. On the death of a male or a female *khāṣa* elephant the *Bhoīs* are fined three months' wages. If any part of the harness is lost, the *Bhoīs* and *Meths* are fined two-thirds of the value of the article; but in the case of a saddlecloth, the full price. When a female elephant dies from starvation, or through want of care, the *Bhoīs* have to pay the cost price of the animal.

If a driver mixes drugs with the food of an elephant to make the animal hot, and it dies in consequence thereof, he is liable to capital punishment, or to have a hand cut off, or to be sold as a slave. If it was a *khāṣa* elephant, the *Bhoīs* lose three months' pay and are further suspended for one year.

Two experienced men are monthly dispatched to inquire into the fatness or leanness of the *khāṣa* elephants. If elephants are found by them out of flesh to the extent of a quarter, according to the scale fixed by the *Pāgosht* Regulation (*vide* Āʾīn 83), the grandees in charge are fined, and the *bhoīs* are likewise liable to lose a month's wages. In the case of *ḥalqa* elephants, Aḥadīs are told off to examine them, and submit a report to His Majesty. If an elephant dies, the *Mahāwat* and the *Bhoī* are fined three months' wages. If part of an elephant's tusk is broken, and the injury reaches as far as the *kalī*—this is a place at the root of the tusks, which on being injured is apt to fester, when the tusks get hollow and become useless—a fine amounting to one-eighth of the price of the elephant is exacted, the *dārogha* paying two-thirds, and the *Fawjdār* one-third. Should the injury not reach as far as the *kalī*, the fine is only one-half of the former, but the proportions are the same. But, at present, a fine of one per cent has become usual; in the case of *khāṣa* elephants, however, such punishment is inflicted as His Majesty may please to direct.

Āʿīn 49.

THE IMPERIAL HORSE STABLES.

His Majesty is very fond of horses, because he believes them to be of great importance in the three branches of the government, and for expeditions of conquest, and because he sees in them a means of avoiding much inconvenience.

Merchants bring to court good horses from ʿIrāq-i ʿArab and ʿIrāq-i ʿAjam, from Turkey, Turkestan, Badakhshān, Shirwān, Qirghiz, Thibet, Kashmīr, and other countries. Droves after droves arrive from Tūrān and Īrān, and there are nowadays twelve thousand in the stables of His Majesty. And in like manner, as they are continually coming in, so there are others daily going out as presents, or for other purposes.

Skilful, experienced men have paid much attention to the breeding of this sensible animal, many of whose habits resemble those of man; and after a short time Hindustan ranked higher in this respect than Arabia, whilst many Indian horses cannot be distinguished from Arabs or from the *ʿIrāqī* breed. There are fine horses bred in every part of the country; but those of Cachh excel, being equal to Arabs. It is said that a long time ago an Arab ship was wrecked and driven to the shore of Cachh; and that it had seven choice horses, from which, according to the general belief, the breed of that country originated. In the Panjāb, horses are bred resembling ʿIrāqīs, especially between the Indus and the Bahat (Jhelum): they go by the name of *Sanūjī*; [1] so also in the district of Patī Haybatpūr,[2] Bajwāral, Tihāra, in the Ṣūbaof Āgra, Mewāt, and in the Ṣūba of Ājmīr, where the horses have the name of *pachwariya*. In the northern mountainous district of Hindustan, a kind of small but strong horse is bred, which are called *gūṭ*; and in the confine of Bengal, near Kūch [-Bahār], another kind of horses occurs, which rank between the *gūṭ* and Turkish horses, and are called *tānghan*,[3] they are strong and powerful.

His Majesty, from the light of his insight and wisdom, makes himself acquainted with the minutest details, and with the classification and the condition of every kind of article; he looks to the requirements of the times, and designs proper regulations. Hence he also pays much attention to everything that is connected with this animal, which is of so great an importance for the government and an almost supernatural means for the attainment of personal greatness.

---

[1] Several good MSS. read *Satūjī*.

[2] Haibatpūr, Lat. 29° 51′, Long. 76° 2′; Tihāra, Lat. 30° 57′, Long. 75° 25′.

[[3] *Ṭāghan*.—P.]

First, he has set apart a place for horse-dealers, where they may, without delay, find convenient quarters, and be secure from the hardships of the seasons. By this arrangement, the animals will not suffer[1] from that hardness and avariciousness so often observed in dealers of the present time; nor will they pass from the hands of well-intentioned merchants into those of others. But dealers who are known for their uprightness and humanity may keep their horses where they please, and bring them at an appointed time. *Secondly*, he appointed a circumspect man to the office of an *Amīn-i Kārwānsarā*, who from his superior knowledge and experience keeps the dealers from the path of disobedience and ties the mischievous tongues of such as are wicked and evasive. *Thirdly*, he has appointed a clever writer, who keeps a roll of horses that arrive and have been mustered, and who sees that the orders of His Majesty do not fall into abeyance. *Fourthly*, he has appointed trustworthy men acquainted with the prices of horses to examine the animals, and to fix their prices, in the order in which they are imported. His Majesty, from his goodness, generally gives half as much again above the price fixed by them, and does not keep them waiting for their money.[2]

Āʿīn 50.

THE RANKS OF THE HORSES.

There are two classes of horses: 1. *K͟hāṣa*; 2. Those that are not *k͟hāṣa*. The *k͟hāṣa* horses are the following—six stables, each containing forty choice horses of Arabia and Persia; the stables of the princes; the stables of Turkish courier horses; the stables of horses bred in the Imperial studs. They have each a name, but do not exceed the number thirty. His Majesty rides upon horses of the six stables.

The *second class* horses are of three kinds, viz., *sī-aspī*, *bīst-aspī*, *dah-aspī*, i.e., belonging to the stables of thirty, twenty, and ten. A horse

---

[1] Akbar abhorred cruelty towards domestic animals. Towards the end of his life, as shall be mentioned below, he even gave up hunting and animal fights.

[2] Abū 'l-Faẓl mentions this very often in the Āʿīn. Contractors generally received cheques on a local treasury; but they might be sent from there to another local treasury, unless they bribed the collector, or made over their cheques, for a *consideration*, to Mahājans (bankers). It was the same in Persia. "The clerks, whose habit it is to annoy people, gave him (Wazīr Mīrzā Ṣāliḥ, brother of the great Persian historian *Sikandar Beg*) in payment of his claims a lot of transfer receipts, and left him in the hands of the collectors (*muḥaṣṣil*), who, like the clerks, always pretend to be in a hurry: and although Mīrzā Raḥīm, a relation of his, tried to come to an understanding with them, in order to help Mīrzā Ṣāliḥ out of his wretched plight, they ruined him, in a short time, to such an extent that they had to provide in lieu a daily subsistence allowance. He died of a broken heart." *Ṭāhir Naṣrābādī's Taẕkira.*

whose value comes up to ten muhurs, is kept in a *Dah-muhrī* stable ; those worth from eleven to twenty muhurs, in a *Bīst-muhrī* stable, and so on.

Grandees and other *Manṣabdārs*, and *Senior Aḥadīs* are in charge of the stables. Hay and crushed grain are found by the government for all horses, except the horse which the *Yatāqdār* (guard) of every stable is allowed to ride, and which he maintains in grain[1] and grass at his own expense.

Āʾīn 51.

THE FODDER ALLOWED IN THE IMPERIAL STABLES.

A *k͟hāṣa* horse was formerly allowed eight *sers* fodder *per diem*, when the *ser* weighed twenty-eight *dāms*. Now that the *ser* is fixed at thirty *dāms* a *k͟hāṣa* horse gets seven and a half *sers*. In winter, they give boiled peas or vetch ; in summer, grain.[1] The daily allowance includes two *sers* of flour and one and a half *sers* of sugar. In winter, before the horse gets fresh grass, they give it half a *ser* of *ghī*. Two *dāms* are daily allowed for hay ; but hay is not given, when fresh grass [2] is available. About three *bīghās* of land will yield sufficient fodder for a horse. When, instead of sugar, the horses get molasses,[3] they stop the *ghī* ; and when the season of fresh grass [2] comes, they give no grain for the first three days, but allow afterwards six *sers* of grain and two *sers* of molasses *per diem*.[3] In other *ʿIrāqī* and *Turkī* stables, they give seven and a half *sers* of grain.[1] During the cool six months of the year, they give the grain [1] boiled, an allowance of one *dām* being given for boiling one *man* of it. The horses also get once a week a quarter *ser* of salt. When *ghī* and fresh grass [2] are given, each horse, provided its price be above thirty-one muhurs, gets also one *ser* of sugar ; whilst such as are worth from twenty-one to thirty muhurs, only get half a *ser*. Horses of less value get no sugar at all. Before green grass [2] is given, horses of a value from twenty-one to upwards of one hundred muhurs, get one *man* and ten *sers* of *ghī* ; such as are worth from eleven to twenty muhurs thirty *sers* ; but horses up to ten muhurs get neither *ghī*, brown sugar, nor green oats.[2] Salt is given at the *daily* rate one-fiftieth of a *dām*, though it is mostly given in a lump. *ʿIrāqī* and *Turkī* horses which belong to the court are daily allowed two *d.* for grass ; but such of them as are in the country only one and a half. In winter, each horse gets a *bīghā* of

---

[1 *Moṭh*, a small, hard, blue grain used, when well boiled, for fattening horses. *Dāna* "grain" colloquially amongst horse-dealers, etc., means "gram."—P.]

[2 *K͟havīd* is green wheat or barley (not oats) before the ear is well formed ; it is cut and used as fodder.—P.]

[3 *Qand-i siyāh* is probably *guṛ*.—P.]

Pl. XVI

fresh oats,[1] the price of which, at court, is 240 *d.*, and in the country 200 *d.* At the time of fresh oats,[1] each horse gets two *mans* of molasses,[2] the same quantity being subtracted from the allowance of grain.[3]

Experienced officers, attached to the Imperial offices, calculate the amount required, and make out an estimate, which in due course is paid. When a horse is sick, every necessary expense is paid on the certificate of the horse doctor.

Every stallion to a stud of mares receives the allowance of a *k͟hāṣa* horse. The *gūṭ* horses get five and a half *sers* of grain,[3] the usual quantity of salt, and grass at the rate of one and a half *d.* per diem, if at court, and at the rate of $1\frac{3}{25}$ *d.*, when in the country; but they do not get *ghī*, molasses, or green oats.[1] *Qisrāqs* [i.e., female horses] get, at court, four and a half *sers* of grain,[3] the usual allowance of salt, and one *d.* for grass; and in the country, the same, with the exception of the grass, for which only three fourths of a *dām* are allowed. Stud mares get two and three-fourths *sers* of grain,[3] but the allowance for grass, salt, and fuel, is not fixed.

A foal sucks its dam for three months; after which, for nine months, it is allowed the milk of two cows; then, for six months, two and three-fourths *sers* of grain [3] *per diem*; after which period, the allowance is every six months increased by a *ser*, till it completes the third year, when its food is determined by the above regulations.

Āʾīn 52.

ON HARNESS, ETC.

It would be difficult and tedious to describe the various ornaments, jewels, and trappings, used for the *k͟hāṣa* horses on which His Majesty rides.

For the whole outfit of a *k͟hāṣa* horse, the allowance is 277½ *d. per annum*; viz., an *artak*, or horse quilt, of wadded chintz, 47 *d.*; a *yālposh* (a covering for the mane), 32 *d.*; a woollen towel, 2 *d.*—these three articles are renewed every six months; in lieu of the old *artak*, half the cost price is deducted, and one-sixth for the old *yālposh*; a saddle-cloth, the outside of which is woven of hair, the lining being felt, 42 *d.*; halters for the

---

[[1] *K͟havīd* is green wheat or barley (not oats) before the ear is well formed; it is cut and used as fodder.—P.]

[[2] *Qand-i siyāh* is probably *gur*.—P.]

[[3] *Dāna* colloquially means, as here, gram.—P.]

nukhta [1] (headstall) and the hind feet,[2] 40 *d.*; a *pusht-tang* (girth), 8 *d.*; a *magas-rān* (a horse tail to drive away flies), 3 *d.*; a *nukhta* and *qayza* [3] (the bit), 14 *d.*; a curry-comb, 1½ *d.*; a grain bag, 6 *d.*; a basket, in which the horse gets its grain, 1[4] *d.* These articles are given *annually*, and fifteen *dāms*, ten *jetals*, subtracted in lieu of the old ones.

In the other stables, the allowance for horses whose value is not less than twenty-one muhurs, is 196½ *d. per annum*, the rate of the articles being the same. Twenty-five and a half *dāms* are subtracted in lieu of the old articles.

In stables of horses worth twenty to eleven muhurs, the annual allowance is 155¼ *d.*; viz., for the *artak*, 39¾ *d.*; the *yālposh*, 27¼ *d.*; a coarse saddle-cloth, 30 *d.*; the girth, 6 *d.*; the *nukhta* and *qayza*, 10 *d.*; and the *nukhta* ropes and feet-ropes, 32 *d.*; the *magas-rān*, 2 *d.*; a towel, 1½ *d.*; a curry-comb, 1¼ *d.*; a basket, 1 *d.*; a grain bag, 4½ *d.* Twenty *dāms* are subtracted for the old articles.

For horses worth up to ten muhurs, and *qisrāqs*, and *gūṭ*, the allowance is 117¼ *d.*; [5] viz., an *artak*, 37 *d.*; a *yālposh*, 24½ *d.*; a *jul*, 24 *d.*; a *nukhta band* and a *pāy-band*, 8 *d.*; a *nukhta* and *qayza*, 8 *d.*; a *pusht-tang*, 5 *d.*; a *magas-rān* and a towel, each 1½ *d.*; a curry-comb, 1¼ *d.*; a basket, 1 *d.*; a grain bag, 4½ *d.* The amount subtracted is the same as before.

1. The *Karāh* [6] is an iron vessel for boiling grain sufficient for ten horses. The price of a *karāh* is at the rate of one hundred and forty *dāms* per *man* of iron; but this includes the wages of the maker. 2. The *Missīn Saṯl*, or brass bucket, out of which horses drink. There is one for every ten *khāṣa* horses. The price of making one is 140 *d.* For other horses, as in the stables of thirty, etc., there is only one. 3. The *Kamand*, attached to iron pegs, is for fastening the horses. In stables of forty, there are three; in stables of thirty, two; in others, one. The weight of a halter is half a *man*; its cost price is 140 *d.*, and 16 *d.* the

---

[[1] *Nukhta* for *nuktā*.—P.]

[2] In consequence of the climate, horses are kept, in the East, much more outside than in the stables. When being cleaned or fed, each of the hindlegs is fastened by means of a rope to a peg in the ground. In the case of wicked horses, a rope is attached to each side of the head-stall, and fastened, like tent ropes, to pegs in the ground. Native grooms, in feeding horses, generally squat on the ground, pushing the grain in the basket towards the mouth of the horse. The word *nakhtah*, which, like hundreds of other words, is not given in our dictionaries, is generally pronounced *nuqta*. Similarly, *qaizah* is pronounced *qáizah*; *vide* Journal As. Soc. Bengal for 1868, I, p. 36 b.c.

[[3] In modern Urdu *qaza,ī* is a snaffle.—P.]

[4] The items added only give 116¼ *d.*

[5] Altogether 196½ *d.*, and 81 *d.* on account of the first three articles renewed after *six months*. The deduction in lieu of old articles refers, of course, to the wages of the grooms.

[[6] *Karwā* or *karu,ā*, H. ?—P.]

wages of the rope maker. 4. The *Āhanīn mekh*, or iron peg, of which there are two for every halter. Each peg weighs five *sers*, and costs 15 *d.* 5. The *Tabartukhmāq*, or hammer, weighs five *sers*, and is used for fixing the iron pegs. There is one in every stable.

All broken and old utensils of brass and iron, in the *khāṣa* stables, if repairable, are repaired at the expense of the Dāroghas; and when they are past mending, their present value is deducted, and the difference paid in cash. In other stables, a deduction of one-half of their value is made every third year.

6. *Naᶜl*, or horseshoes, are renewed twice a year. Formerly eight *dāms* were given for a whole set, but now ten. 7. *Kūndlān*. One is allowed for ten horses.[1] The price of it is 80¾ *R.*

Āᵉīn 53.

THE OFFICERS AND SERVANTS ATTACHED TO THE IMPERIAL STABLES.

1. The *Ātbegī* is in charge of all horses belonging to the government. He directs all officers charged with the management of the horses. This office is one of the highest of the State, and is only held by grandees of high rank: at present it is filled by the *Khān Khānān*[2] (Commander-in-Chief). 2. The *Dārogha*. There is one appointed for each stable. This post may be held by officers of the rank of commanders of five thousand down to Senior Aḥadīs. 3. The *Mushrif*, or accountant. He keeps the roll of the horses, manages all payments and fines, sees that His Majesty's orders are carried out, and prepares the estimate of the stores required for this department. He is chosen from among the grandees. 4. The *Dīda-war*, or inspector. His duty is occasionally to inspect the horses before they are mustered by His Majesty; he also determines the rank and the condition of the horses. His reports are taken down by the Mushrif. This office may be held by the Manṣabdārs or Aḥadīs. 5. The *Akhtachīs* look after the harness, and have the horses saddled. Most of them get their pay on the list of the Aḥadīs. 6. The *Chābuksuwār* rides the horses, and compares their speed with the road, which is likewise taken down by the Mushrif. He receives the pay of an Aḥadī. 7. The *Hāḍā*. This name is given to a class of Rājpūts, who teach horses the elementary

---

[1] This appears to be the same as the *Hind.* کندلا, which our meagre dictionaries describe as a "kind of tent".

[2] Or *Mīrzā Khān Khānān*, i.e., ᶜAbdᵘ-r-Raḥīm, son of Bayrām Khān; *vide* List of Grandees, 2nd book, No. 29.

steps. Some of them get their pay on the list of the Aḥadīs. 8. The *Mīrdaha* is an experienced groom placed over ten servants. He gets the pay of an Aḥadī; but in other *k͟hāṣa* stables, he only gets 170 *d.*; in the country-bred stables, 160 *d.*; in the other *si-aspī* stables, 140 *d.*; in the *bīst-aspī* stables, 100 *d.*; and in the *dah-aspī* stables, 30 *d.* Besides he has to look after two horses. 9. The *Bayṭar*, or horse-doctor, gets the pay of an Aḥadī. 10. The *Naqīb*, or watcher. Some active, intelligent men are retained for supervision. They report the condition of each stable to the *Dārog͟has* and the *Mushrif*, and it is their duty to have the cattle in readiness. The two head *Naqībs* are *Aḥadīs*, and they have thirty people under them, who receive from 100 to 120 *d.* 11. The *Sā,is*, or groom. There is one groom for every two horses. In the *chihil-aspī* stables, each groom gets 170 *d.*; in the stables of the eldest prince, 138 *d.*; in the stables of the other princes, and in the courier horse stables, 136 *d.*; in the country bred stables, 126 *d.*; in the other *si-aspī* stables, 106 *d.*; in the *bīst-aspī* stables, 103 *d.*; and in the *dah-aspī* stables, 100 *d.* 12. The *Jilawdār* (*vide* Āʾīn 60) and the *Payk* (a runner). Their monthly pay varies from 1,200 to 120 *d.*, according to their speed and manner of service. Some of them will run from fifty to one hundred *kroh* (*kos*) a day. 13. The *Naʿlband*, or farrier. Some of them are *Aḥadīs*, some foot soldiers. They receive 160 *d.* 14. The *Zīndār*, or saddle holder, has the same rank and pay as the preceding. In the *k͟hāṣa* stable of forty horses, one saddle is allowed for every two horses, in the following manner: for the first and twenty-first; for the second and twenty-second, and so on. If the first horse is sent out of the stable, the saddle remains at its place, and what was the second horse becomes first, and the second saddle falls to the third horse, and so on to the end. If a horse out of the middle leaves, its saddle is given to the preceding horse. 15. The *Ābkash*, or water-carrier. Three are allowed in the stables of forty; two in stables of thirty, and only one in other stables. The monthly pay is 100 *d.* 16. The *Farrāsh* (who dusts the furniture). There is one in every *k͟hāṣa* stable. His pay is 130 *d.* 17. A *Sipandsoz* [1] is only allowed in the stables of forty horses;

---

[1] The seeds of *sipand* (in Hind. *sarsõ*, a kind of mustard seed) are put on a heated plate of iron. Their smoke is an effectual preventive against the evil eye (*naẓar-i bad, chashm rasīdan*), which is even dangerous for Akbar's choice horses. The seeds burn away slowly, and emit a crackling sound. The man who burns them is called *Sipandsōz*. *Vide* the poetical extracts of the 2nd book, under *Shikebī*. Instead of *Sipand*, grooms sometimes keep a monkey over the entrance of the stable. The influence of the evil eye passes from the horses to the ugly monkey.

Another remedy consists in nailing old horseshoes to the gates of the stables. Hundreds of such shoes may still be seen on the gates in Fatḥpūr Sīkrī.

[*Sipand* P., or *ḥarmal* A., is wild rue not mustard.—P.]

his pay is 100 *d*. 18. The *Khākrūb*, or sweeper. Sweepers are called in Hindustan *Halālkhur*;[1] His Majesty brought this name *en vogue*. In stables of forty, there are two; in those of thirty and twenty, one. Their monthly pay is 65 *d*.

During a march, if the *dāroghas* are in receipt of a fixed allowance for coolies, they entertain some people to lead the horses. In the stables of thirty horses, fifteen are allowed. And in the same proportion does the government appoint coolies, when a *dārogha* has not received the extra allowance. Each cooly gets two *dāms per diem*.

Āʾīn 54.

THE BĀRGĪR.

His Majesty, from the regard which he pays to difference in rank, believes many fit for cavalry service, though he would not trust them with the keeping of a horse. For these he has told off separate stables, with particular *Dāroghas* and *Mushrifs*. When their services are required, they are furnished with a horse on a written order of the *Bitikchī* (writer); but they have not to trouble themselves about the keeping of the horse. A man so mounted is called a *Bārgīrsuwār*.

Āʾīn 55.

REGULATIONS FOR BRANDING HORSES.

In order to prevent fraudulent exchanges, and to remove the stamp of doubtful ownership, horses were for some time marked with the word نظر (*nazr*, sight), sometimes with the word داغ (*dāgh*, mark), and sometimes with the numeral ۷ (seven).[2] Every horse that was received by government had the mark burnt on the right cheek; and those that were returned, on the left side. Sometimes, in the case of ʿ*Irāqī* and *Mujannas*[3]

---

[1] Akbar was very fond of changing names which he thought offensive, or of giving new names to things which he liked; *vide* p. 46, l. 28; p. 55, l. 18; p. 65, l. 16; p. 90, l. 22; also Forbes' Dictionary under *rangtarā*. *Halālkhur*, i.e., one who eats that which the ceremonial law allows, is a euphemism for *harāmkhur*, one who eats forbidden things, as pork, etc. The word *halālkhur* is still in use among educated Muhammadans; but it is doubtful whether it was Akbar's invention. The word in common use for a sweeper is *mihtar*, a prince, which like the proud title of *khalīfa*, nowadays applied to cooks, tailors, etc., is an example of the irony of fate.

[2] *Vide* Āʾīns 7 and 8 of the second book. The branding of horses was revived in A.H. 981, A.D. 1573, when Shāhbāz had been appointed *Mīr Bakhshī*. He followed the regulations of ʿAlāʾ-ud-Dīn Khiljī and Sher Shāh; *vide* Badāonī, pp. 173, 190.

[3] *Mujannas*, i.e., put nearly equal (to an *Irāqī* horse); *vide* 2nd book, Āʾīn 2. [I think *mujannas* means half-bred.—P.]

horses, they branded the price in numerals on the right cheek; and in the case of Turkī and Arab horses, on the left. Nowadays the horses of every stable are distinguished by their price in numerals. Thus, a horse of ten muhurs is marked with the numeral ten; those of twenty muhurs have a twenty, and so on. When horses, at the time of the musters, are put into a higher or a lower grade, the old brand is removed.

Āʾīn 56.

REGULATIONS FOR KEEPING UP THE FULL COMPLEMENT OF HORSES.

Formerly, whenever there had been taken away either ten horses from the stables of forty, or from the stud-bred horses, or five from the courier horses, they were replaced in the following manner. The deficiency in the stables of forty was made up from horses chosen from the stables of the princes; the stud-bred horses were replaced by other stud-bred ones, and the courier horses from other stables. Again, if there were wanting fifteen horses in the stables of the eldest prince (Salīm), they were replaced by good horses of his brothers; and if twenty were wanting in the stables of the second prince (Murād), the deficiency was made up by horses taken from the stables of the youngest prince and from other stables; and if twenty-five were wanting in the stables of the youngest prince (Dānyāl), the deficiency was made up from other good stables.

But in the thirty-seventh year of the Divine Era (A.D. 1593), the order was given that, in future, one horse should annually be added to each stable. Thus, when, in the present year, the deficiency in the *khāṣa* stables had come up to eleven, they commenced to make up the complement, the deficiency of the other stables being made up at the time of the muster parades.

Āʾīn 57.

ON FINES.

When a *khāṣa* horse dies, the Dārogha has to pay one rupee, and the Mīrdaha ten *d.*, upon every muhur of the cost price; and the grooms lose one-fourth of their monthly wages. When a horse is stolen, or injured, His Majesty determines the fine, as it cannot be uniform in each case.

In the other stables they exacted from the Dārogha for a single horse that dies, one rupee upon every muhur; for two horses, two rupees upon every muhur ; and from the Mīrdaha and the grooms the above proportions. But now they take one rupee upon every muhur for one to three horses that die ; and two upon every muhur for four horses ; and three upon every muhur for five.

If the mouth of a horse gets injured, the Mīrdaha is fined ten *dāms* upon every muhur, which fine he recovers from the other grooms.

Āʼīn 58.

ON HORSES KEPT IN READINESS.

There are always kept in readiness two *k͟hāṣa* horses ; but of courier-horses,[1] three, and one of each stable from the seventy muhurs down to the ten muhur stables and the *gūts*. They are formed into four divisions, and each division is called a *miṣl*.

First *miṣl* : one from the *chihilaspī* stables ; one from the stable of the eldest prince ; one from those of the second prince ; one from the stable of *k͟hāṣa* courier horses. Second *miṣl* : one from the stable of the youngest prince ; one from the stud-bred ; one from the *chihilaspī* stables ; one courier horse. Third *miṣl*, one horse from the stables of the three princes ; one stud-bred. Fourth *miṣl*, one horse from each of the stables of horses of forty, thirty, twenty, and ten muhurs.

His Majesty rides very rarely on horses of the fourth *miṣl*. But when prince Shāh Murād joined his appointment,[2] His Majesty also rode the best horses of the stables of forty muhurs. The arrangement was then as follows. First *miṣl*, one horse from the stables of forty ; one horse from the stables of the eldest and the youngest prince, and a courier horse. Second *miṣl*, stud-bred horses from the stables of horses above seventy muhurs, *k͟hāṣa* horses of forty muhurs, and courier horses. Third *miṣl*, one horse from the stables of each of the two princes, the stud-bred, and the seventy-muhur horses. Fourth *miṣl*, horses from the stables of sixty, forty, and thirty muhurs.

Horses are also kept in readiness from the stables of twenty and ten muhurs and the *gūts*.

[[1] *Rāhwār*, ambling, a roadster.—P.]

[2] " Prince Murād in the beginning of the fortieth year (1596) of Akbar's reign, was put in command of the army of Gujrāt, and ordered to take Aḥmadnagar. But when, some time after, Akbar heard that Murād's army was in a wretched condition, chiefly through the carelessness and drunken habits of the prince, the emperor resolved to go himself (43rd year), and dispatched Abū 'l-Faẓl to bring the prince back to court. Abū 'l-Faẓl came just in time to see the prince die, who from the preceding year had been suffering from epileptic fits (*ṣarʻ*, delirium tremens ?) brought on by habitual drunkenness." *Mirʼāt.*

Āʾīn 59.

ON DONATIONS.

Whenever his Majesty mounts a horse belonging to one of the six *khāṣa* stables, he gives something, according to a fixed rule, with a view of increasing the zeal and desire for improvement among the servants. For some time it was a rule that, whenever he rode out on a *khāṣa* horse, a rupee should be given, viz., one *dām* to the Ātbegī, two to the Jilawdār; eighteen and one-half to the grooms, the rest being shared by the Mushrif, the Naqīb, the Akhtachī, and the Zīndār. In the case of horses belonging to the stables of the eldest prince, thirty *dāms* were given, each of the former recipients getting a quarter of a *dām* less. For horses belonging to stables of the second prince, twenty *dāms* were given, the donations decreasing by the same fraction; and for horses belonging to the stables of the youngest prince, as also for courier horses,[1] and stud-breds, ten *dāms*, according to the same manner of distribution.

Now, the following donations are given :—For a horse of a stable of forty, one rupee as before; for a horse belonging to a stable of the eldest prince, twenty *dāms*; for a horse belonging to the youngest prince, ten *dāms*; for courier horses, five; for stud-breds, four; for horses of the other stables, two.

Āʾīn 60.

REGULATIONS FOR THE JILAWĀNA.[2]

Whenever a horse is given away as a present, the price of the horse is calculated fifty *per cent.* higher, and the recipient has to pay ten *dāms* upon every muhur of the value of the horse. These ten *dāms per muhur* are divided as follows :—The Ātbegī gets five *dāms*; the Jilawbegī, two and a half; the Mushrif, one and a quarter; the Naqībs, nine *jetals*; the grooms, a quarter *dām*; the Taḥṣīldār, fifteen *jetals*; the remainder is equally divided among the Zīndār and Akhtachī.

In this country horses commonly live to the age of thirty years. Their price varies from 500 muhurs to 2 rupees.

[[1] *Rāhwār*, ambling; a roadster.—P.]

[2] *Jilaw* is the string attached to the bridle, by which a horse is led. A led horse is called *janība*. The adjective *jilawāna*, which is not in the dictionaries, means *referring to a led horse*. We have to write *jilawānah*, not *jilauāna*, according to the law of the Persian language, to break up a final diphthong in derivatives; as *na-īn*, *jawīn*, from *nai*, *jau*, not *nai-īn*, or *jau-īn*. The *jilaudār*, or *janībadar*, is the servant who leads the horse. The *jilaubegī* is the superintendent of horses selected for presents. The *taḥsīldār* collects the fee.

Āʿīn 61.

THE CAMEL STABLES.

From the time His Majesty paid regard to the affairs of the state, he has shown a great liking for this curiously shaped animal; and as it is of great use for the three branches of the government, and well known to the emperor for its patience under burdens, and for its contentment with little food, it has received every care at the hands of His Majesty. The quality of the country breed improved very much, and Indian camels soon surpassed those of Irān and Tūrān.

From a regard to the dignity of his court, and the diversion of others, His Majesty orders camel-fights, for which purpose several choice animals are always kept in readiness. The best of these *k͟hāṣa* camels, which is named *Shāhpasand* (approved of by the Shāh), is a country-bred twelve years old; it overcomes all its antagonists, and exhibits in the manner in which it stoops down and draws itself up every finesse of the art of wrestling.

Camels are numerous near Ājmīr, Jodhpūr, Nāgor, Bīkānīr, Jaisalmīr, Batindā, and Bhaṭnīr; the best are bred in the Ṣūba of Gujrāt, near Cachh. But in Sind is the greatest abundance; many inhabitants own ten thousand camels and upwards. The swiftest camels are those of Ājmīr; the best for burden are bred in Ṭhaṭha.

The success [1] of this department depends on the *Arwānas*, i.e., female camels. In every country they get hot in winter and couple. The male of two humps goes by the name of *Bug͟hur*. The young ones of camels are called *nar* (male) and *māya* (female), as the case may be; but His Majesty has given to the *nar* the name of *bug͟hdī*,[2] and to the female that of *jammāza*. The *bug͟hdī* is the better for carrying burdens and for fighting; the *jammāza* excels in swiftness. The Indian camel called *lok*, and its female, come close to them in swiftness, and even surpass them. The offspring of a *bug͟hur* and a *jammāza* goes by the name of *ghurd*; the female is called *māya ghurd*. If a *bug͟hdī*, or a *lok*, couples with a *jammāza*, the young one is called *bug͟hdī* or *lok* respectively. But if a *bug͟hdī* or a *lok* couples with an *arwāna*, the young male is named after its sire and the young female after its dam. The *lok* is considered superior to the *ghurd* and the *māya ghurd*.

---

[1] In the text *māya*, which also means *a female camel*—a very harmless pun. *Vide* Dr. Sprenger's Gulistān, preface, p. 6. Regarding the word *bug͟hur*, *vide* Journal Asiatic Society, Bengal, for 1868, p. 59.

[[2] Corruption of *buk͟htī*.—P.]

When camels are loaded and travel, they are generally formed into *qaṭārs* (strings), each *qaṭār* consisting of five camels The first camel of each *qaṭār* is called *peshang*[1]; the second, *peshdara*; the third, *miyāna qaṭār*; the fourth, *dumdast*; the last camel, *dumdār*.

Āʼīn 62.

THE FOOD OF CAMELS..

The following is the allowance of such *bughdīs* as are to carry burdens. At the age of two and a half, or three years, when they are taken from the herd of the stud dams, a *bughdī* gets 2 *s.* of grain; when three and a half to four years old, 5 *s.*; up to seven years, 9 *s.*; at eight years, 10 *s.* The same rule applies to *bughurs*. Similarly in the case of *jammāzas*, *ghurds*, *māyah ghurds*, and *loks*, up to four years of age; but from the fourth to the seventh year, they get 7 *s.*; and at the age of eight years, 7½ *s.*, at the rate of 28 *dāms* per *ser*. As the *ser* has now 30 *dāms*, a corresponding deduction is made in the allowance. When *bughdīs* are in heat, they eat less. Hence also concession is made, if they get lean, to the extent of 10 *s.*, according to the provisions of the *Pāgosht* rule (Āʼīn 83); and when the rutting season is over, the Dāroghas give out a corresponding extra allowance of grain to make up for the former deficiency. If they have made a definite entry into their day-book, and give out more food, they are held indemnified according to the *Pāgosht* rule; and similarly in all other cases, note is taken of the deductions according to that rule.

At Court, camels are found in grass by the government for eight months. Camels on duty inside the town are daily allowed grass at the rate of 2 *d.* per head; and those outside the town, 1½ *d.* During the four rainy months, and on the march, no allowance is given, the drivers taking the camels to meadows [2] to graze.

Āʼīn 63.

THE HARNESS OF CAMELS.

The following articles are allowed for *khāṣa* camels: an *Afsār* (head stall); a *Dum-afsār* (crupper); a *Mahār kāṭhī* (furniture resembling a horse-saddle, but rather longer—an invention of His Majesty); a *kūchī*

---

[1] So according to the best MSS. The word is evidently a vulgar corruption of *pesh-āhang*, the leader of a troop. *Peshdara* means "in front of the *belly*, or middle, of the *qaṭār*".

[[2] *Charā-gāh*, grazing-places.—P.]

(which serves as a saddle-cloth); a *Qaṭārchī*; a *Sarbchī*;[1] a *Tang* (a girth); a *Sartang* (a head-strap); a *Shebband* (a loin-strap); a *Jalājil* (a breast rope adorned with shells or bells); a *Gardanband* (a neck-strap); three *Chādars* (or coverings) made of broadcloth, or variegated canvas, or waxcloth. The value of the jewels, inlaid work, trimmings, and silk, used for adorning the above articles, goes beyond description.

Five *qaṭārs* of camels, properly caparisoned, are always kept ready for riding, together with two for carrying a *Miḥaffa*, which is a sort of wooden turret, very comfortable, with two poles, by which it is suspended, at the time of travelling, between two camels.

A camel's furniture is either coloured or plain. For every ten *qaṭārs* they allow three *qaṭārs* coloured articles.

For *Bughdīs*, the cost of the [coloured] furniture is 225¾ *d.*, viz., a head-stall studded with shells, 20½ *d.*; a brass ring, 1½ *d.*; an iron chain, 4½ *d.*; a *kallagī* (an ornament in shape of a rosette, generally made of peacock's feathers, with a stone in the centre), 5 *d.*; a *pushtpozī* (ornaments for the strap which passes along the back), 8 *d.*; a *dum-afsār* (a crupper), 1½ *d.*; for a *takaltū* (saddle-quilt) and a *sarbchī*, both of which require 5 *sers* of cotton, 20 *d.*; a *jul* (saddle-cloth),[2] 68 *d.*; a *jahāz-i gajkārī*,[3] which serves as a *mahārkāthī* (*vide* above), 40 *d.*; a *tang*, *shebband*, *gulūband* (throat-strap), 24 *d.*; a *ṭanāb* (long rope) for securing the burden—camel-drivers call this rope *ṭāqa ṭanāb*, or *kharwār*—38 *d.*; a *bālāposh*, or covering, 15 *d.*[4]

For *Jammāzas*, two additional articles are allowed, viz., a *gardanband*, 2 *d.*; and a *sīna-band* (chest-strap), 16 *d.*

The cost of a set of plain furniture for *Bughdīs* and *Jammāzas* amounts to 168½ *d.*, viz., an *afsār*, studded with shells, 10 *d.*; a *dum-afsār*, ½ *d.*; a *jahāz*, 16½ *d.*; a *jul*, 52½ *d.*; a *tang*, a *shebband*, and *gulūband*, 24 *d.*; a *ṭāqa ṭanāb*, 37½ *d.*; a *bālāposh*, 28 *d.*[5]

For *Loks*, the allowance for furniture is 143 *d.*, viz., an *afsār*, *jahāz*,

---

[1] The meaning is doubtful. The Arab. *sarb*, like *qiṭār*, signifies a troop of camels. From the following it appears that *sarbchī* is a sort of quilt.

[[2] A *jul* (=*jhūl* H.) is a heavy horse-covering of blanket and felt.—P.]

[3] *Gajkārī* appears to be the correct reading. The Arab. *jahāz* means *whatever is upon a camel*, especially *the saddle and its appurtenances*, generally made of coarse canvas steeped in lime (*gaj*). Hence *gajkārī*, white-washed.

[4] These items added up give 246 *d.*, not 225¾, as stated by Abū 'l-Faẓl. When discrepancies are slight, they will be found to result from a rejection of the fractional parts of the cost of articles. The difference of 20¼ *d.* in this case can only have resulted from an omission on the part of the author, because all MSS. agree in the several items. Perhaps some of the articles were not exchanged *triennially*, but had to last a longer time.

[5] These items added up give 159 *d.*, instead of Abū 'l-Faẓl's 168½ *d.*

kharwār, according to the former rates; a *jul*, 37½ *d.*; a *tang*, *shebband*, *gulūband*, 14½ *d.*; a *bālāposh*, 28 *d.*[1]

The coloured and plain furniture is renewed once in three years, but not so the iron bands and the woodwork. In consideration of the old coloured furniture of every *qaṭār*, sixteen *dāms*, and of plain furniture, fourteen *dāms*, are deducted by the Government. At the end of every three years they draw out an estimate, from which one-fourth is deducted; then, after taking away one-tenth of the remainder, an assignment is given for the rest.[2]

ʿ*Alafī* camels (used for foraging) have their furniture renewed annually, at the cost of 52½ *d.* for country-bred camels, and *loks*, viz. [for country bred camels] an *afsār*, 5 *d.*; a *jul*, 36½ *d.*; a *sardoz*, ½ *d.*; a *tang* and a *shebband*, 10¾ *d.*;[3] and [for *loks*], an *afsār*, a *tang*, and a *shebband*, as before; a *jul*, 45¾ *d.*; a *sardoz*, ¾ *d.*

From the annual estimate one-fourth is deducted, and an assignment is given for the remainder.

Shalīta ṭāts, or canvas sacks, for giving camels their grain, are allowed one for every *qaṭār*, at a price of 30¾ *d.* for *bughdīs* and *jammāzas*, and 24½ *d.* for *loks*.

Hitherto the cost of these articles had been uniformly computed and fixed by contract with the camel drivers. But when, in the forty-second year of the divine era [1598 A.D.], it was brought to the notice of His Majesty that these people were, to a certain extent, losers, this regulation was abolished, and the current market price allowed for all articles. The price is therefore no longer fixed.

On every New Year's day, the head camel-drivers receive permission for shearing the camels, anointing them with oil, injecting oil into the noses of the animals, and indenting for the furniture allowed to ʿ*alafī* camels.

Āʾīn 64.

REGULATIONS FOR OILING CAMELS, AND INJECTING OIL INTO THEIR NOSTRILS.

The scientific terms for these operations are *taṭliya* and *tajrīʿ*, though we might expect *taṭliya* and *tanshīq*, because *tanshīq* means *injecting into the nose*.

---

[1] The items added up give 144 *d.*, instead of Abū 'l-Faẓl's 143 *d.*

[2] Hence the Government paid, as a rule, $\frac{9}{10} \times \frac{3}{4} = \frac{27}{40}$ of the estimates presented.

[3] The addition gives 52¾ *d.*, instead of 52½. The following items, for *loks*, give added up 62¼.

For each *Bughdī* and *Jammāza* 3¾ *sers* of sesame oil are annually allowed, viz., three *sers* for anointing, and ¾ *ser* for injection into the nose. So also ¾ *s*. of brimstone and 6½ *s*. of butter-milk. For other kinds of camels the allowance is ⅝ *s*. of brimstone, 6½ *s*. of butter-milk, and ¾ *s*. of grease for injecting into the nose-holes.

Formerly these operations were repeated three times, but now only once, a year.

Āʾīn 65.

THE RANKS OF THE CAMELS, AND THEIR SERVANTS.

His Majesty has formed the camels into *qaṭārs*, and given each *qaṭār* in charge of a *sārbān*, or driver. Their wages are four-fold. The first class get 400 *d.*; the second, 340 *d.*; the third, 280 *d.*; the fourth, 220 *d.*, *per mensem*.

The *qaṭārs* are of three kinds—1. Every five *qaṭārs* are in charge of an experienced man, called *Bīstopanjī*, or commander of twenty-five. His salary is 720 *d*. He marks a *Yābū* horse, and has four drivers under him. 2. Double the preceding, or ten *qaṭārs*, are committed to the care of a *Panjāhī*, or commander of fifty. He is allowed a horse, draws 960 *d*., and has nine drivers under him. 3. Every hundred *qaṭārs* are in charge of a *Panjṣadī*, or commander of five hundred. Ten *qaṭārs* are under his personal superintendence. With the exception of one *qaṭār*, Government finds drivers for the others. The *Panjāhīs* and *Bīstopanjīs* are under his orders. Their salary varies; nowadays many *Yūzbāshīs*[1] are appointed to this post. One camel is told off for the *farrāshes*. A writer also has been appointed. His Majesty, from his practical knowledge, has placed each *Panṣadī* under a grandee of the court. Several active foot-soldiers have been selected to inquire from time to time into the condition of the camels, so that there may be no neglect. Besides, twice a year some people adorned with the jewel of insight inspect the camels as to their leanness or fatness at the beginning of the rains and at the time of the annual muster.

Should a camel get lost, the *Sārbān* is fined the full value; so also the *Panjāhī* and the *Panṣadī*. If a camel get lame or blind, he is fined the fourth part of the price.

Raibārī.

Raibārī is the name given to a class of Hindus who are acquainted with the habits of the camel. They teach the country-bred *lok* camel so to step

[1] Corresponding to our Captains of the Army, commanders of 100 soldiers.

as to pass over great distances in a short time. Although from the capital to the frontiers of the empire, in every direction, relay horses are stationed, and swift runners have been posted at the distance of every five *kos*, a few of these camel riders are kept at the palace in readiness. Each *Raibārī* is also put in charge of fifty stud *arwānas*, to which for the purpose of breeding, one *bughur* and two *loks* are attached. The latter (the males) get the usual allowance of grain, but nothing for grass. The fifty *arwānas* get no allowance for grain or grass. For every *bughur*, *bughdī*, and *jammāza* in the stud, the allowance for oiling and injecting into the nostrils is 4 *s.* of sesame oil, ¾ *s.* of brimstone, 6½ *s.* of butter-milk.[1] The first includes ¾ *s.* of oil for injection. *Loks, arwānas, ghurds*, and *māya ghurds*, get only 3⅝ *s.* of sesame oil—the deduction is made for injection—6½ *s.* of butter-milk,[1] and ⅝ *s.* of brimstone.

Botas and *Dumbālas*—these names are given to young camels; the former is used for light burdens; they are allowed 2½ *s.* of oil, inclusive of ½ *s.* for injection into the nostrils, ½ *s.* of brimstone, and 4½ *s.* of butter-milk.[1]

Full-grown stud-camels get weekly ½ *s.* of saltpetre and common salt; *botas* get ¼ *s.*

The wages of a herdsman is 200 *d. per mensem.* For grazing every fifty stud-camels, he is allowed five assistants, each of whom gets 2 *d. per diem.* A herdsman of two herds of fifty is obliged to present to His Majesty three *arwānas* every year; on failure, their price is deducted from his salary.

Formerly the state used to exact a fourth part of the wool sheared from every *bughdī* and *jammāza*, each camel being assessed to yield four *sers* of wool. This His Majesty has remitted, and in lieu thereof, has ordered the drivers to provide their camels with *dum-afsārs*, wooden pegs, etc.

The following are the prices of camels:—a *bughdī*, from 5 to 12 muhurs; a *jammāza*, from 3 to 10 *M.*; a *bughur*, from 3[2] to 7 *M.*;[3] a mongrel *lok*, from 8 to 9 *M.*; a country-bred, or a Balūchī *lok*, from 3 to 8 *M.*; an *arwāna*, from 2 to 4 *M.*

His Majesty has regulated the burdens to be carried by camels. A first class *bughdī*, not more than 10 *mans*; a second class do., 8 *m.*; superior *jammāzas*, *loks*, etc., 8 *m.*; a second class do., 6 *m.*

In this country, camels do not live above twenty-four years.

[[1] *Māst*, curds.—P.] [[2] In text "from 4 to 7".—P.]

[[3] The text has also here "a *māya bughur* from 3 to 5; a *ghurd* from 3 to 8; a *māya ghurd* and a *lok* from 3 to 7".—P.]

Āʾīn 66.

THE GĀW-KHĀNA OR COW [1]-STABLES.

Throughout the happy regions of Hindustan, the cow [1] is considered auspicious, and held in great veneration; for by means of this animal, tillage is carried on, the sustenance of life is rendered possible, and the table of the inhabitant is filled with milk, butter-milk,[2] and butter. It is capable of carrying burdens and drawing wheeled carriages, and thus becomes an excellent assistant for the three branches of the government.

Though every part of the empire produces cattle of various kinds, those of Gujrāt are the best. Sometimes a pair of them are sold at 100 muhurs. They will travel 80 kos [120 miles] in 24 hours, and surpass even swift horses. Nor do they dung whilst running. The usual price is 20 and 10 muhurs. Good cattle are also found in Bengal and the Dakhin. They kneel down at the time of being loaded. The cows give upwards of half a *man* of milk. In the province of Dihlī again, cows are not worth more than 10 Rupees. His Majesty once bought a pair of cows for two lacs of *dāms* [5,000 Rupees].

In the neighbourhood of Thibet and Kashmīr, the *Quṭās*, or Thibetan Yak, occurs, an animal of extraordinary appearance.

A cow will live to the age of twenty-five.

From his knowledge of the wonderful properties of the cow, His Majesty, who notices everything which is of value, pays much attention to the improvement of cattle. He divided them into classes, and committed each to the charge of a merciful keeper. One hundred choice cattle were selected as *khāṣa* and called *kotal*. They are kept in readiness for any service, and forty of them are taken unladen [1] on hunting expeditions, as shall be mentioned below (Book II, Āʾīn 27). Fifty-one others nearly as good are called half-*kotal*, and fifty-one more, quarter-*kotal*. Any deficiency in the first class is made up from the second, and that of the middle from the third. But these three form the cow [1]-stables for His Majesty's use.

Besides, sections of cattle have been formed, each varying in number from 50 to 100, and committed to the charge of honest keepers. The rank of each animal is fixed at the time of the public muster, when each gets its proper place among sections of equal rank. A similar proceeding is adopted for each section, when selected for drawing waggons and travelling carriages, or for fetching water (*vide* Āʾīn 22).

[[1] *Gāv*, ox. The bullock only is used for work.—P.] [[2] *Māst*, curds.—P.]

There is also a species of oxen, called *gainī*, small like *gūṭ* horses, but very beautiful.

Milch-cows and buffaloes have also been divided into sections, and handed over to intelligent servants.

Āʿīn 67.

THE DAILY ALLOWANCE OF FOOD.

Every head of the first *k͟hāṣa* class is allowed daily 6¼ *s.* of grain,[1] and 1½ *d.* of grass. The whole stable gets daily 1 *man* 19 *s.* of molasses,[2] which is distributed by the Dārog͟ha, who must be a man suitable for such a duty, and office. Cattle of the remaining *k͟hāṣa* classes get daily 6 *s.* of grain,[1] and grass as before, but no molasses [2] are given.

In other cow-stables the daily allowance is as follows. First kind, 6 *s.* of grain,[1] 1½ *d.* of grass at court, and otherwise only 1 *d.* The second kind get 5 *s.* of grain,[1] and grass as usual. The oxen used for travelling carriages get 6 *s.* of grain,[1] and grass as usual. First class *gainīs* get 3 *s.* of grain, and 1 *d.* of grass at court, otherwise only ¾ *d.* Second class do., 2½ *s.* of grain,[1] and ¾ *d.* of grass at court, otherwise only ½ *d.*

A male buffalo (called *arna*) gets 8 *s.* of wheat flour boiled, 2 *s.* of *ghī*, ½ *s.* of molasses,[2] 1½ *s.* of grain,[1] and 2 *d.* of grass. This animal, when young, fights astonishingly, and will tear a lion [3] to pieces. When this peculiar strength is gone, it reaches the second stage, and is used for carrying water. It then gets 8 *s.* of grain, and 2 *d.* for grass. Female buffaloes used for carrying water get 6 *s.* of grain, and 2 *d.* for grass. First class oxen for leopard-waggons [4] get 6¼ *s.* of grain; and other classes, 5 *s.* of grain, but the same quantity of grass. Oxen for heavy waggons got formerly 5 *s.* of grain, and 1½ *d.* for grass; but now they get a quarter *ser* less, and grass as before.

The milch-cows, and buffaloes, when at court, have grain given them in proportion to the quantity of milk they give. A herd of cows and buffaloes is called *ṭhāṭ*. A cow will give daily from 1 to 15 *s.* of milk; a buffalo from 2 to 30 *s.* The buffaloes of the Panjāb are the best in this respect. As soon as the quantity of milk given by each cow has been ascertained, there are demanded two *dāms* weight of *ghī* for every *ser* of milk.

[[1] *Dāna*=gram, see p. 142, note 1.—P.]
[[2] *Qand-i siyāh*, see p. 142, footnote 3.—P.]
[[3] *Sher* in India is the tiger, but *shīr* in Persia is the lion.—P.]
[4] Carriages for the transport of trained hunting leopards. *Vide* Book II, Āʿīn 27.

Ā'*īn* 68.

THE SERVANTS EMPLOYED IN THE COW[1]-STABLES.

In the *khāṣa* stables, one man is appointed to look after four head of cattle. Eighteen such keepers in the first stable get 5 *d. per diem*, and the remaining keepers, 4 *d.* In other stables, the salary of the keepers is the same, but each has to look after six cows.1 Of the carriage drivers, some get their salaries on the list of the Aḥadīs ; others get 360 *d.*, others 256 *d.* down to 112 *d.* *Bahals*, or carriages, are of two kinds :—1. *Chatrīdār* or covered carriages, having four or more poles (which support the *chatr*, or umbrella) ; 2. without a covering. Carriages suited for horses are called *ghur-bahal.*[2] For every ten waggons, 20 drivers and 1 carpenter are allowed. The head driver, or *Mīrdaha*, and the carpenter, get each 5 *d. per diem* ; the others 4 *d.* For some time 15 drivers had been appointed, and the carpenter was disallowed ; the drivers themselves undertook the repairs, and received on this account an annual allowance of 2,200 *dāms* [55 Rupees].

If a horn of an ox was broken, or the animal got blind, the Dārogha was fined one-fourth of the price, or even more, according to the extent of the injury.

Formerly the Dāroghas paid all expenses on account of repairs, and received for every day that the carriages were used, half a *dām* as *ūng* money—*ūng* is hemp smeared with ghī, and twisted round about the axle-tree which, like a pivot, fits into the central hole of the wheel, and thus prevents it from wearing away or getting broken. When afterwards the Dāroghaship was transferred to the drivers, they had to provide for this expense. At first, it was only customary for the carts to carry on marches a part of the baggage belonging to the different workshops ; but when the drivers performed the duties of the Dāroghas they had also to provide for the carriage of the fuel required at court and for the transport of building materials. But subsequently 200 waggons were set aside for the transport of building materials, whilst 600 others have to bring, in the space of ten months, 1,50,000 *mans* of fuel to the Imperial kitchen. And if officers of the government on any day use the Imperial waggons for other purposes, that day is to be separately accounted for, as also each service rendered to the court. The drivers are not subject to the *Pāgosht* regulation (*vide* Ā'īn 83). If, however, an ox dies, they have to buy another.

[[1] *Gāv*, ox ; *vide* p. 157, note 1.—P.] [[2] *Ghuṛ-bahal.*—P.]

But when it came to the ears of His Majesty that the above mode of contract was productive of much cruelty towards these serviceable, but mute animals, he abolished this system, and gave them again in charge of faithful servants. The allowance of grain for every cart-bullock was fixed at 4 *s.*, and $1\frac{1}{2}$ *d.* were given for grass. For other bullocks, the allowance is one-half of the preceding. But during the four rainy months no money is allowed for grass. There were also appointed for every eighteen carts twelve drivers, one of whom must understand carpenter's work. Now, if a bullock dies, government supplies another in his stead, and likewise pays for the *ūng*, and is at the expense of repairs.

The cattle that are worked are mustered once a year by experienced men who estimate their fatness or leanness; cattle that are unemployed are inspected every six months. Instead of the above mentioned transport of firewood, etc., the carters have now to perform any service which may be required by the government.

Āʾīn 69.

THE MULE STABLES.

The mule possesses the strength of a horse and the patience of an ass, and though it has not the intelligence of the former it has not the stupidity of the latter It never forgets the road which it has once travelled. Hence it is liked by His Majesty, whose practical wisdom extends to everything, and its breeding is encouraged. It is the best animal for carrying burdens and travelling over uneven ground, and it has a very soft step. People generally believe that the male ass couples with a mare, but the opposite connexion also is known to take place, as mentioned in the books of antiquity. The mule resembles its dam. His Majesty had a young ass coupled with a mare, and they produced a very fine mule.

In many countries just princes prefer travelling about on a mule; and people can therefore easily lay their grievances before them,[1] without inconveniencing the traveller.

Mules are only bred in Hindustan in Pakhalī,[2] and its neighbourhood. The simple inhabitants of the country used to look upon mules as asses, and thought it derogatory to ride upon them; but in consequence of the

---

[1] Which the subjects could not so easily do, if the princes, on their tours of administration of justice, were to ride on elephants, because the plaintiff would stand too far from the king.

[2] The Sarkār of Pakhalī lies between Aṭak (Attock) and Kashmīr, a little north of Rawul Pindee. *Vide* towards the end of Book III.

interest which His Majesty takes in this animal, so great a dislike is now nowhere to be found.

Mules are chiefly imported from ʿIrāq-i ʿArab and ʿIrāq-i ʿAjam. Very superior mules are often sold at Rs. 1,000 per head.

Like camels, they are formed into *qaṭārs* of five, and have the same names, except the second mule of each *qaṭār*, which is called *bardast*, [instead of *peshdara*, *vide* Āʾīn 61, end].

Mules reach the age of fifty.

Āʾīn 70.

THE DAILY ALLOWANCE OF FOOD FOR MULES.

Such mules as are not country-bred, get at court, 6 *s.* of grain, and 2 *d.* for grass; otherwise, only 1½ *d.* Country-bred mules get 4 *s.* of grain, and 1⅝ *d.* of grass, when at court; otherwise, 1 *d.* for grass. Each mule is allowed every week 3½ *jetals* for salt; but they give the salt in one lot.

Āʾīn 71.

THE FURNITURE OF MULES.

For imported mules, a head stall of leather, 20¼ *d.*; an iron chain weighing 2 *s.*, 10 *d.*; a *ranckī* (crupper) of leather, 4 *d.*; a *pālān* (pack-saddle), 102 *d.*; a *shāltang* (shawl strap), and a *palās-tang* (blanket strap), 36¼ *d.*; a *ṭāqa ṭanāb* (a rope for fastening the burden), 63 *d.*; a *qāṭir shalāq* (a short whip), 6 *d.*; a bell, one for every *qaṭār*, 10 *d.*; a horse-hair saddle, 40 *d.*; a *kalāwc* (*vide* Āʾīn 45, No. 9) of leather, 13 *d.*; a set of ropes, 9 *d.*; a saddle cloth, 4½ *d.*; a *sardoz* (a common head stall), 4 *d.*; a *khurjīn* (wallet), 15 *d.*; a fodder-bag, 4 *d.*; a *magas-rān* (to drive away flies) of leather, 1 *d.*; a curry-comb and a hair-glove (for washing), 4 *d.* Total 345¾ *d.*

For country-bred mules the allowance is 151¼ *d.*, viz., a head stall of leather, 4 *d.*; pack-saddle, 51 *d.* 18¾ *j.*; the two straps, 16½ *d.*; a *ṭāqa ṭanāb* and *sardoz*, 40 *d.*; a bell, 5 *d.*; a fodder-bag, 3 *d.*; a crupper, 3 *d.*; a saddle, 24 *d.*; a curry-comb and a hair-glove, 4 *d.*

The furniture is renewed every third year; but for all iron and wood work, half the price is deducted. The annual allowance for the repair of the furniture is 40 *d.*; but on the march, the time of renewal depends on the wear. Mules are shod every six months at a cost of 8 *d.* per head.

Each *qaṭār* is in charge of a keeper. Tūrānīs, Īrānīs, and Indians, are appointed to this office; the first two get from 400 to 1,920 *d.*; and the third class, from 240 to 256 *d. per mensem.* Such keepers as have monthly salaries of 10 R. [400 *d.*] and upwards, have to find the *peshang* [1] (first mule of their *qaṭār*) in grain and grass. Experienced people inspect the mules twice a year as to leanness or fatness. Once a year they are paraded before His Majesty.

If a mule gets blind or lame, the muleteer is fined one-fourth of the cost price ; ond one-half, if it is lost.

Asses also are employed for carrying burdens and fetching water. They get 3 *s.* of grain, and 1 *d.* for grass. The furniture for asses is the same as that for country-bred mules, but no saddle is given. The annual allowance for repairs is 23 *d.* The keepers do not get above 120 *d. per mensem.*

Ā'*īn* 72.

THE MANNER IN WHICH HIS MAJESTY SPENDS HIS TIME.

The success of the three branches of the government, and the fulfilment of the wishes of the subjects, whether great or small, depend upon the manner in which a king spends his time. The care with which His Majesty guards over his motives, and watches over his emotions, bears on its face the sign of the Infinite, and the stamp of immortality ; and though thousands of important matters occupy, at one and the same time, his attention, they do not stir up the rubbish of confusion in the temple of his mind, nor do they allow the dust of dismay to settle on the vigour of his mental powers, or the habitual earnestness with which His Majesty contemplates the charms of God's world. His anxiety to do the will of the Creator is ever increasing ; and thus his insight and wisdom are ever deepening. From his practical knowledge, and capacity for everything excellent, he can sound men of experience, though rarely casting a glance on his own ever extending excellence. He listens to great and small, expecting that a good thought, or the relation of a noble deed, may kindle in his mind a new lamp of wisdom, though ages have passed without his having found a really great man. Impartial statesmen, on seeing the sagacity of His Majesty, blotted out the book of their own wisdom, and commenced a new leaf. But with the magnanimity which distinguishes him, and with his wonted zeal, he continues his search for superior men, and finds a reward in the care with which he selects such as are fit for his society.

[[1] The *peshang* is selected for being a quick-stepper and for intelligence.—P.]

Although surrounded by every external pomp and display, and by every inducement to lead a life of luxury and ease, he does not allow his desires, or his wrath, to renounce allegiance to Wisdom, his sovereign—how much less would he permit them to lead him to a bad deed! Even the telling of stories, which ordinary people use as a means of lulling themselves into sleep, serves to keep His Majesty awake.

Ardently feeling after God, and searching for truth, His Majesty exercises upon himself both inward and outward austerities, though he occasionally joins public worship, in order to hush the slandering tongues of the bigots of the present age. But the great object of his life is the acquisition of that sound morality, the sublime loftiness of which captivates the hearts of thinking sages, and silences the taunts of zealots and sectarians.

Knowing the value of a lifetime, he never wastes his time, nor does he omit any necessary duty, so that in the light of his upright intentions, every action of his life may be considered as an adoration of God.

It is beyond my power to describe in adequate terms His Majesty's devotions. He passes every moment of his life in self-examination or in adoration of God. He especially does so at the time, when morning spreads her azure silk, and scatters abroad her young, golden beams; and at noon, when the light of the world-illuminating sun embraces the universe, and thus becomes a source of joy for all men; in the evening when that fountain of light withdraws from the eyes of mortal man, to the bewildering grief of all who are friends of light; and lastly at midnight, when that great cause of life turns again to ascend, and to bring the news of renewed cheerfulness to all who, in the melancholy of the night, are stricken with sorrow. All these grand mysteries are in honour of God, and in adoration of the Creator of the world; and if dark-minded, ignorant men cannot comprehend their signification, who is to be blamed, and whose loss is it? Indeed, every man acknowledges that we owe gratitude and reverence to our benefactors; and hence it is incumbent on us, though our strength may fail, to show gratitude for the blessings we receive from the sun, the light of all lights, and to enumerate the benefits which he bestows. This is essentially the duty of kings, upon whom, according to the opinion of the wise, this sovereign of the heavens sheds an immediate light.[1] And this is the very motive which actuates His Majesty to venerate fire and reverence lamps.

But why should I speak of the mysterious blessings of the sun, or of

[1] *Vide* Abū 'l-Faẓl's Preface, pp. iii and 49.

the transfer of his greater light to lamps? Should I not rather dwell on the perverseness of those weak-minded zealots, who, with much concern, talk of His Majesty's religion as of a deification of the Sun, and the introduction of fire-worship? But I shall dismiss them with a smile.

The compassionate heart of His Majesty finds no pleasure in cruelties, or in causing sorrow to others; he is ever sparing of the lives of his subjects, wishing to bestow happiness upon all.

His Majesty abstains much from flesh, so that whole months pass away without his touching any animal food, which, though prized by most, is nothing thought of by the sage. His august nature cares but little for the pleasures of the world. In the course of twenty-four hours he never makes more than one meal. He takes a delight in spending his time in performing whatever is necessary and proper. He takes a little repose in the evening, and again for a short time in the morning; but his sleep looks more like waking.

His Majesty is accustomed to spend the hours of the night profitably; to the private audience hall are then admitted eloquent philosophers and virtuous Ṣūfīs, who are seated according to their rank and entertain His Majesty with wise discourses. On such occasions His Majesty fathoms them, and tries them on the touch-stone of knowledge. Or the object of an ancient institution is disclosed, or new thoughts are hailed with delight. Here young men of talent learn to revere and adore His Majesty, and experience the happiness of having their wishes fulfilled, whilst old men of impartial judgment see themselves on the expanse of sorrow, finding that they have to pass through a new course of instruction.

There are also present in these assemblies, unprejudiced historians, who do not mutilate history by adding or suppressing facts, and relate the impressive events of ancient times. His Majesty often makes remarks wonderfully shrewd, or starts a fitting subject for conversation. On other occasions matters referring to the empire and the revenue are brought up, when His Majesty gives orders for whatever is to be done in each case.

About a watch before daybreak, musicians of all nations are introduced, who recreate the assembly with music and songs, and religious strains; and when four *gharīs* are left till morning His Majesty retires to his private apartments, brings his external appearance in harmony with the simplicity of his heart, and launches forth into the ocean of contemplation. In the meantime, at the close of night, soldiers, merchants, peasants, tradespeople, and other professions gather round the palace, patiently waiting to catch a glimpse of His Majesty. Soon after daybreak, they are allowed to make the *kornish* (*vide* Āʾīn 74). After this, His Majesty allows the attendants of the Harem to pay their compliments. During this time various matters of worldly and religious import are brought to the notice of His Majesty. As soon as they are settled, he returns to his private apartments and reposes a little.

The good habits of His Majesty are so numerous that I cannot adequately describe them. If I were to compile dictionaries on this subject they would not be exhaustive.

Āʿīn 73.

REGULATIONS FOR ADMISSION TO COURT.

Admittance to Court is a distinction conferred on the nation at large; it is a pledge that the three branches of the government are properly looked after, and enables subjects personally to apply for redress of their grievances. Admittance to the ruler of the land is for the success of his government what irrigation is for a flower-bed; it is the field, on which the hopes of the nation ripen into fruit.

His Majesty generally receives twice in the course of twenty-four hours, when people of all classes can satisfy their eyes and hearts with the light of his countenance. *First,* after performing his morning devotions, he is visible from outside the awning, to people of all ranks, whether they be given to worldly pursuits, or to a life of solitary contemplation, without any molestation from the mace-bearers. This mode of showing himself is called, in the language of the country, *darsan* (view); and it frequently happens that business is transacted at this time. The *second* time of his being visible is in the State Hall, whither he generally goes after the first watch of the day. But this assembly is sometimes announced towards the close of day, or at night. He also frequently appears at a window, which opens into the State Hall, for the transaction of business; or he dispenses there justice calmly and serenely, or examines into the dispensation of justice, or the merit of officers, without being influenced in his judgment by any predilections or anything impure and contrary to the will of God. Every officer of government then presents various reports, or explains his several wants, and is instructed by His Majesty how to proceed. From his knowledge of the character of the times, though in opposition to the practice of kings of past ages, His Majesty looks upon the smallest details as mirrors capable of reflecting a comprehensive outline; he does not reject that which superficial observers call unimportant and counting the happiness of his subjects as essential to his own, never suffers his equanimity to be disturbed.

Whenever His Majesty holds court they beat a large drum, the sounds of which are accompanied by Divine praise. In this manner, people of all classes receive notice. His Majesty's sons and grandchildren, the grandees of the Court, and all other men who have admittance, attend to make the *kornish*, and remain standing in their proper places. Learned men of renown and skilful mechanics pay their respects; the Dāroghas and Bitikchīs (writers) set forth their several wants; and the officers of justice give in their reports. His Majesty, with his usual insight, gives orders, and settles everything in a satisfactory manner. During the whole time, skilful gladiators and wrestlers from all countries hold themselves in readiness, and singers, male and female, are in waiting. Clever jugglers and funny tumblers also are anxious to exhibit their dexterity and agility.

His Majesty, on such occasions, addresses himself to many of those who have been presented, impressing all with the correctness of his intentions, the unbiasedness of his mind, the humility of his disposition, the magnanimity of his heart, the excellence of his nature, the cheerfulness of his countenance, and the frankness of his manners; his intelligence pervades the whole assembly, and multifarious matters are easily and satisfactorily settled by his truly divine power.

This vale of sorrows is changed to a place of rest: the army and the nation are content. May the empire flourish, and these blessings endure!

Āʾīn 74.

REGULATIONS REGARDING THE *KORNISH* AND THE *TASLĪM*.

Superficial observers, correctly enough, look upon a king as the origin of the peace and comfort of the subjects. But men of deeper insight are of opinion that even spiritual progress among a people would be impossible unless emanating from the king, in whom the light of God dwells; for near the throne, men wipe off the stain of conceit and build up the arch of true humility.[1]

With the view, then, of promoting this true humility, kings in their wisdom have made regulations for the manner in which people are to show their obedience. Some kings have adopted the bending down of the head. His Majesty has commanded the palm of the right hand to be placed upon the forehead and the head to be bent downwards. This

[1] Hence the presence of the king promotes humility, which is the foundation of all spiritual life. So especially in the case of Akbar, towards whom, as the head of the New Church, the subjects occupy the position of disciples. *Vide* Āʾīn 77 and the Note after it.

mode of salutation, in the language of the present age, is called *kornish*, and signifies that the saluter has placed his head (which is the seat of the senses and the mind) into the hand of humility, giving it to the royal assembly as a present, and has made himself in obedience ready for any service that may be required of him.

The salutation, called *taslīm*, consists in placing the back of the right hand on the ground, and then raising it gently till the person stands erect, when he puts the palm of his hand upon the crown of his head, which pleasing manner of saluting signifies that he is ready to give himself as an offering.

His Majesty relates as follows: " One day my royal father bestowed upon me one of his own caps, which I put on. Because the cap of the king was rather large, I had to hold it with my [right] hand, whilst bending my head downwards, and thus performed the manner of salutation (*kornish*) above described. The king was pleased with this new method and from his feeling of propriety ordered this to be the mode of the *kornish* and *taslīm*.

Upon taking leave, or presentation, or upon receiving a *manṣab*, a *jāgīr*, or a dress of honour, or an elephant, or a horse, the rule is to make three *taslīms*; but only one on all other occasions, when salaries are paid, or presents are made.

Such a degree of obedience is also shown by servants to their masters, and looked upon by them as a source of blessings. Hence for the disciples of His Majesty, it was necessary to add something, viz., prostration [1] (*sijda*); and they look upon a prostration before His Majesty as a prostration performed before God; for royalty is an emblem of the power of God, and a light-shedding ray from this Sun of the Absolute.

Viewed in this light, the prostration has become acceptable to many, and proved to them a source of blessings upon blessings.

But as some perverse and dark-minded men look upon prostration as blasphemous man-worship, His Majesty, from his practical wisdom, has

[1] The prostration, or *sijda*, is one of the positions at prayer, and is therefore looked upon by all Muhammadans as the exclusive right of God. When Akbar, as the head of his new faith, was treated by his flattering friends, perhaps against his calmer judgment, as the representative of God on earth, he had to allow prostration in the assemblies of the Elect. The people at large would never have submitted. The practice evidently pleased the emperor, because he looked with fondness upon every custom of the ancient Persian kings, at whose courts the *προσκυνεῖν* had been the usual salutation. It was *Niẓām* of Badakhshān who invented the prostration when the emperor was still at Fatḥpūr [before 1586]. The success of the innovation made Mullā Aʿlam of Kābul exclaim, " O that I had been the inventor of this little business! " *Bad.* III, p. 153. Regarding Niẓām, or Ghāzī Khān, *vide* Abū 'l-Fazl's list of Grandees, 2nd Book, No. 144. The *sijda* as an article of Akbar's Divine Religion, will be again referred to in the note to Āʾīn 77.

ordered it to be discontinued by the ignorant, and remitted it to all ranks, forbidding even his private attendants from using it in the *Darbār-i ʿĀm* (general court-days). However, in the private assembly, when any of those are in waiting, upon whom the star of good fortune shines, and they receive the order of seating themselves, they certainly perform the prostration of gratitude by bowing down their foreheads to the earth, and thus participate in the halo of good fortune.

In this manner, by forbidding the people at large to prostrate, but allowing the Elect to do so, His Majesty fulfils the wishes of both, and shows the world a fitting example of practical wisdom.

Āʾīn 75.

ON ETIQUETTE.

Just as spiritual leadership requires a regulated mind, capable of controlling covetousness and wrath, so does political leadership depend on an external order of things, on the regulation of the difference among men in rank, and the power of liberality. If a king possess a cultivated mind, his position as the spiritual leader of the nation will be in harmony with his temporal office; and the performance of each of his political duties will be equivalent to an adoration of God. Should anyone search for an example, I would point to the practice of His Majesty, which will be found to exhibit that happy harmony of motives, the contemplation of which rewards the searcher with an increase of personal knowledge, and leads him to worship this ideal of a king.[1]

When His Majesty seats himself on the throne, all that are present perform the *kornish*, and then remain standing at their places, according to their rank, with their arms crossed,[2] partaking, in the light of his imperial countenance, of the elixir of life, and enjoying everlasting happiness in standing ready for any service.

---

[1] The words of the text are ambiguous. They may also mean, *and leads him to praise me as the man who directed him towards this example.*

[2] The finger tips of the left hand touch the right elbow, and those of the right hand the left elbow; or, the fingers of each hand rest against the inner upper arm of the opposite side. The lower arms rest on the *kamarband.* When in this position, a servant is called *āmāda-yi khidmat*, or ready for service. Sometimes the right foot also is put over the left, the toes of the former merely touching the ground. The shoes are, of course, left outside at the *ṣaff-i niʿāl.* The emperor sits on the throne (*vide* Plate VII) with crossed legs, or *chahār-zānū*, a position of comfort which Orientals allow to persons of rank. This position, however, is called *firʿawnī nishast*, or Pharaoh's mode of sitting, if assumed by persons of no rank in the presence of strangers. Pharaoh—Orientals mean the Pharaoh of the time of Moses—is proverbial in the East for vainglory. The position suitable for society is the *duzānū* mode of sitting, i.e., the person first kneels down with his body straight; he then lets the body gently sink till he sits on his heels, the arms being kept extended and the hands resting on the knees.

The eldest prince places himself, when standing, at a distance of one to four yards from the throne, or when sitting, at a distance from two to eight. The second prince stands from one and one-half to six yards from the throne, and in sitting from three to twelve. So also the third; but sometimes he is admitted to a nearer position than the second prince, and at other times both stand together at the same distance. But His Majesty generally places the younger princes affectionately nearer.

Then come the Elect of the highest rank, who are worthy of the spiritual guidance of His Majesty, at a distance of three to fifteen yards, and in sitting from five to twenty. After this follow the senior grandees from three and a half yards, and then the other grandees, from ten or twelve and a half yards from the throne.

All others stand in the *Yasal*.[1] One or two attendants [2] stand nearer than all.

Āʾīn 76.

THE MUSTER OF MEN.

The business which His Majesty daily transacts is most multifarious; hence I shall only describe such affairs as continually recur.

A large number of men are introduced on such days, for which an *Anjuman-i Dād o Dihish*, or assembly of expenditure, has been announced. Their merits are inquired into, and the coin of knowledge passes current. Some take a burden from their hearts by expressing a wish to be enrolled among the members of the Divine Faith; others want medicines for their diseases.[3] Some pray His Majesty to remove a religious doubt; others again seek his advice for settling a worldly matter.[4] There is no end to such requests, and I must confine myself to the most necessary cases.

The salaries of a large number of men [5] from Tūrān and Īrān, Turkey and Europe, Hindustān and Kashmīr, are fixed by the proper officers in

---

[1] *Yasal* signifies the wing of an army, and here, the two wings into which the assembly is divided. The place before the throne remains free. One wing was generally occupied by the grandees of the Court and the chief functionaries; on the other wing stood the *Qur* (*vide* p. 116), the Mullās, and the ʿUlamā, etc.

[2] The servants who hold the *sāya-bān*, Āʾīn 19, or the fans.

[3] This is to be taken literally. The water on which Akbar breathed, was a universal remedy. *Vide* next Āʾīn.

[4] As settling a family-feud, recommending a matrimonial alliance, giving a new-born child a suitable name, etc.

[5] Abū 'l-Faẓl means men who were willing to serve in the several grades of the standing army. The standing army consisted of cavalry, artillery, and rifles. There was no regular infantry. Men who joined the standing army, in the beginning of Akbar's reign, brought their own horse and accoutrements with them; but as this was found to be the cause of much inefficiency (*vide* Second Book, Āʾīn 1) a horse was given to each recruit on joining, for which he was answerable.

a manner described below, and the men themselves are taken before His Majesty by the paymasters. Formerly it had been the custom for the men to come with a horse and accoutrements; but nowadays only men appointed to the post of an Aḥadī[1] bring a horse. The salary as proposed by the officers who bring them is then increased or decreased, though it is generally increased; for the market of His Majesty's liberality is never dull. The number of men brought before His Majesty depends on the number of men available. Every Monday all such horsemen are mustered as were left from the preceding week. With the view of increasing the army and the zeal of the officers, His Majesty gives to each who brings horsemen, a present of two *dāms* for each horseman.

Special *Bitikchīs*[2] [writers] introduce in the same manner such as are fit to be Aḥadīs. In their case, His Majesty always increases the stipulated salary. As it is customary for every Aḥadī to buy[3] his own horse, His Majesty has ordered to bring to every muster the horses of any Aḥadīs who may have lately died, which he hands over to the newly appointed Aḥadīs either as presents or charging the price to their monthly salaries.

On such occasions, Senior Grandees and other Amīrs introduce also any of their friends, for whom they may solicit appointments. His Majesty then fixes the salaries of such candidates according to circumstances; but appointments under fifty rupees *per mensem* are rarely ever solicited in this manner.

Appointments to the Imperial workshops also are made in such assemblies, and the salaries are fixed.

Āʾīn 77.

HIS MAJESTY[4] AS THE SPIRITUAL GUIDE OF THE PEOPLE.

God, the Giver of intellect and the Creator of matter, forms mankind as He pleases, and gives to some comprehensiveness, and to others narrowness of disposition. Hence the origin of two opposite tendencies

---

[1] As Aḥadīs drew a higher salary (II, Āʾīn 4) they could buy, and maintain, horses of a superior kind.

[2] Āʾīn 4 of the second book mentions only one officer appointed to recruit the ranks of Aḥadīs.

[3] So according to two MSS. My text edition, p. 158, l. 10, has *As it is* not *customary for Aḥadīs to buy a horse, etc.* Both readings give a sense, though I should prefer the omission of the negative word. According to Āʾīn 4 of the second book, an Aḥadī was supplied with a horse when his first horse had died. To such cases the negative phrase would refer. But it *was* customary for Aḥadīs to bring their own horse on joining; and this is the case which Abū 'l-Fazl evidently means; for in the whole Āʾīn he speaks of newcomers.

[4] A note will be found at the end of this Āʾīn.

among men, one class of whom turn to religious (*dīn*) and the other class to worldly thoughts (*dunyā*). Each of these two divisions selects different leaders,[1] and mutual repulsiveness grows to open rupture. It is then that men's blindness and silliness appear in their true light; it is then discovered how rarely mutual regard and charity are to be met with.

But have the religious and the worldly tendencies of men no common ground? Is there not everywhere the same enrapturing beauty [2] which beams forth from so many thousand hidden places? Broad indeed is the carpet [3] which God has spread, and beautiful the colours which He has given it.

> The Lover and the Beloved are in reality one; [4]
> Idle talkers speak of the Brahmin as distinct from his idol.
> There is but one lamp in this house, in the rays of which,
> Wherever I look a bright assembly meets me.

One man thinks that by keeping his passions in subjection he worships God; and another finds self-discipline in watching over the destinies of a nation. The religion of thousands of others consists in clinging to an idea; they are happy in their sloth and unfitness of judging for themselves. But when the time of reflection comes, and men shake off the prejudices of their education, the threads of the web of religious blindness [5] break, and the eye sees the glory of harmoniousness.

But the ray of such wisdom does not light up every house, nor could every heart bear such knowledge. Again, although some are enlightened, many would observe silence from fear of fanatics, who lust for blood, but look like men. And should anyone muster sufficient courage, and

---

[1] As prophets, the leaders of the Church; and kings, the leaders of the State.

[2] God. He may be worshipped by the meditative and by the active man. The former speculates on the essence of God, the latter rejoices in the beauty of the world, and does his duty as man. Both represent tendencies apparently antagonistic; but as both strive after God, there is a ground common to both. Hence mankind ought to learn that there is no real antagonism between *dīn* and *dunyā*. Let men rally round Akbar, who joins Ṣūfic depth to practical wisdom. By his example, he teaches men how to adore God in doing one's duties; his superhuman knowledge proves that the light of God dwells in him. The surest way of pleasing God is to obey the king. The reader will do well to compare Abū 'l-Faẓl's preface with this Āʾīn.

[3] The world.

[4] These Ṣūfic lines illustrate the idea that "the same enrapturing beauty" is everywhere. God is everywhere, in everything; hence everything is God. Thus God the Beloved, dwells in man, the lover, and both are one, Brahmin=man; the idol=God lamp=thought of God; house=man's heart. The thoughtful man sees everywhere "the bright assembly of God's works".

[5] The text has *taqlīd*, which means *to put a collar on one's own neck*, to follow another blindly, especially in religious matters. "All things which refer to prophetship and revealed religion they [Abū 'l-Faẓl, Ḥakīm, Abū 'l-Fatḥ, etc.] called *taqlīdiyāt*, i.e., things against reason, because they put the basis of religion upon reason, not testimony. Besides, there came [during A.H. 983, or A.D. 1575] a great number of Portuguese, from whom they likewise picked up doctrines justifiable by reasoning." *Badā,onī* II, p. 281.

openly proclaim his enlightened thoughts, pious simpletons would call him a mad man, and throw him aside as of no account, whilst ill-starred wretches would at once think of heresy and atheism, and go about with the intention of killing him.

Whenever, from lucky circumstances, the time arrives that a nation learns to understand how to worship truth, the people will naturally look to their king, on account of the high position which he occupies, and expect him to be their spiritual leader as well; for a king possesses, independent of men, the ray of Divine wisdom,[1] which banishes from his heart everything that is conflicting. A king will therefore sometimes observe the element of harmony in a multitude of things, or sometimes reversely, a multitude of things in that which is apparently one; for he sits on the throne of distinction, and is thus equally removed from joy or sorrow.

Now this is the case with the monarch of the present age, and this book is a witness of it.

Men versed in foretelling the future knew this when His Majesty was born,[2] and together with all others that were cognizant of the secret, they have since been waiting in joyful expectation. His Majesty, however, wisely surrounded himself for a time with a veil, as if he were an outsider, or a stranger to their hopes. But can man counteract the will of God? His Majesty, at first, took all such by surprise as were wedded to the prejudices of the age; but he could not help revealing his intentions; they grew to maturity in spite of him, and are now fully known. He now is the spiritual guide of the nation, and sees in the performance of this duty a means of pleasing God. He has now opened the gate that leads to the right path, and satisfies the thirst of all that wander about panting for truth.

But whether he checks men in their desire of becoming disciples, or admits them at other times, he guides them in each case to the realm of bliss. Many sincere inquirers, from the mere light of his wisdom, or his holy breath, obtain a degree of awakening which other spiritual doctors

---

[1] *Vide* Abū 'l-Faẓl's preface, p. iii, l. 19.

[2] This is an allusion to the wonderful event which happened at the birth of the emperor. Akbar spoke, "From Mirzā Shāh Muḥammad, called Ghaznīn Khān, son of Shāh Begkhān, who had the title of Dawrān Khān, and was an Arghūn by birth." The author heard him say at Lāhor, in A.H. 1053, "I asked Nawāb ʕAzīz Kokah, who has the title of Khān-i Aʕẓam [*vide* List of Grandees, second Book, Āʾīn 30], whether the late emperor, like the Messiah, had really spoken with his august mother. He replied, "His mother told me it was true." *Dabistān ul Maẓāhib*, Calcutta edition, p. 390. Bombay edition, p. 260. The words which Christ spoke in the cradle, are given in the Qurʾān, Sūr. 19, and in the spurious gospel of the *Infancy of Christ*, pp. 5, 111.

could not produce by repeated fasting and prayers for forty days. Numbers of those who have renounced the world, as *Sannāsīs*, *Jogīs*, *Seūrās*, *Qalandars*, *Ḥakīms*, and *Ṣūfīs*, and thousands of such as follow worldly pursuits as soldiers, tradespeople, mechanics, and husbandmen, have daily their eyes opened to insight, or have the light of their knowledge increased. Men of all nations, young and old, friends and strangers, the far and near, look upon offering a vow to His Majesty as the means of solving all their difficulties, and bend down in worship on obtaining their desire. Others again, from the distance of their homes, or to avoid the crowds gathering at Court, offer their vows in secret, and pass their lives in grateful praises. But when His Majesty leaves Court, in order to settle the affairs of a province, to conquer a kingdom, or to enjoy the pleasures of the chase, there is not a hamlet, a town, or a city that does not send forth crowds of men and women with vow-offerings in their hands, and prayers on their lips, touching the ground with their foreheads, praising the efficacy of their vows, or proclaiming the accounts of the spiritual assistance received. Other multitudes ask for lasting bliss, for an upright heart, for advice how best to act, for strength of the body, for enlightenment, for the birth of a son, the reunion of friends, a long life, increase of wealth, elevation in rank, and many other things. His Majesty, who knows what is really good, gives satisfactory answers to every one, and applies remedies to their religious perplexities. Not a day passes but people bring cups of water to him, beseeching him to breathe upon it. He who reads the letters of the divine orders in the book of fate, on seeing the tidings of hope, takes the water with his blessed hands, places it in the rays of the world-illuminating sun, and fulfils the desire of the suppliant. Many sick people [1] of broken hopes, whose diseases the most eminent physicians pronounced incurable, have been restored to health by this divine means.

A more remarkable case is the following. A simple-minded recluse had cut off his tongue, and throwing it towards the threshold of the palace, said, "If that certain blissful thought,[2] which I just now have, has been put into my heart by God, my tongue will get well; for the sincerity of my belief must lead to a happy issue." The day was not ended before he obtained his wish.

---

[1] "He [Akbar] showed himself every morning at a window, in front of which multitudes came and prostrated themselves; while women brought their sick infants for his benediction and offered presents on their recovery." From the account of the Goa Missionaries who came to Akbar in 1595, in *Murray's Discoveries in Asia*, II, p. 96.

[2] His thought was this. If Akbar is a prophet, he must, from his supernatural wisdom, find out in what condition I am lying here.

Those who are acquainted with the religious knowledge and the piety of His Majesty, will not attach any importance to some of his customs,[1] remarkable as they may appear at first; and those who know His Majesty's charity and love of justice, do not even see anything remarkable in them. In the magnanimity of his heart he never thinks of his perfection, though he is the ornament of the world. Hence he even keeps back many who declare themselves willing to become his disciples. He often says, "Why should I claim to guide men before I myself am guided?" But when a novice bears on his forehead the sign of earnestness of purpose, and he be daily enquiring more and more, His Majesty accepts him, and admits him on a Sunday, when the world-illuminating sun is in its highest splendour. Notwithstanding every strictness and reluctance shown by His Majesty in admitting novices, there are many thousands, men of all classes, who have cast over their shoulders the mantle of belief, and look upon their conversion to the New Faith as the means of obtaining every blessing.

At the above-mentioned time of everlasting auspiciousness, the novice with his turban in his hands, puts his head on the feet of His Majesty. This is symbolical,[2] and expresses that the novice, guided by good fortune and the assistance of his good star, has cast aside [3] conceit and selfishness, the root of so many evils, offers his heart in worship, and now comes to inquire as to the means of obtaining everlasting life. His Majesty, the chosen one of God, then stretches out the hand of favour, raises up the suppliant, and replaces the turban on his head, meaning by these symbolical actions that he has raised up a man of pure intentions, who from seeming existence has now entered into real life. His Majesty then gives the novice the *Shaṣt*,[4] upon which is engraved "The Great Name",[5] and His Majesty's symbolical motto, "*Allāh*ᵘ *Akbar*." This teaches the novice the truth that

---

[1] "He [Akbar] showed, besides, no partiality to the Muhammadans; and when in straits for money, would even plunder the mosques to equip his cavalry. Yet there remained in the breast of the monarch a stronghold of idolatry, on which they [the Portuguese missionaries] could never make any impression. Not only did he adore the sun, and make long prayers to it four times a day, he also held himself forth as an object of worship; and though exceedingly tolerant as to other modes of faith, never would admit of any encroachments on his own divinity." *Murray's Discoveries*, II, p. 95.

[2] The text has *zabān-i ḥāl*, and a little lower down, *zabān-i bezufānī*. *Zabān-i ḥāl*, or *symbolical* language is opposed to *zabān-i maqāl*, spoken words.

[3] Or rather, *from his head*, as the text has, because the casting aside of selfishness is symbolically expressed by taking off the turban. To wear a turban is a distinction.

[4] *Shaṣt* means *aim*; secondly, *anything round*, either a ring, or a thread, as the Brahminical thread. Here a ring seems to be meant. Or it may be the likeness of the Emperor which, according to Badāonī, the members wore on their turbans.

[5] The *Great Name* is a name of God. "Some say it is the word *Allah*; others say it is *Aṣ-Ṣamad*, the eternal; others *Al-Ḥayy*, the living; others *Al-Qayyūm*, the everlasting;

"The pure Shast and the pure sight never err."

Seeing the wonderful habits of His Majesty, his sincere attendants are guided, as circumstances require it; and from the wise counsels they receive they soon state their wishes openly. They learn to satisfy their thirst in the spring of divine favour, and gain for their wisdom and motives renewed light. Others, according to their capacities are taught wisdom in excellent advices.

But it is impossible, while speaking of other matters besides, to give a full account of the manner in which His Majesty teaches wisdom, heals dangerous diseases, and applies remedies for the severest sufferings. Should my occupations allow sufficient leisure, and should another term of life be granted me, it is my intention to lay before the world a separate volume on this subject.

Ordinances of the Divine Faith.

The members of the Divine Faith, on seeing each other, observe the following custom. One says, "*Allāh*[u] *Akbar*," and the other responds, "*Jall*[u] *Jallāluh*[u]."[1] The motive of His Majesty in laying down this mode of salutation, is to remind men to think of the origin of their existence, and to keep the Deity in fresh, lively, and grateful remembrance.

It is also ordered by His Majesty that, instead of the dinner usually given in remembrance of a man after his death, each member should prepare a dinner during his lifetime, and thus gather provisions for his last journey.

Each member is to give a party on the anniversary of his birthday,

---

others, *Ar-Raḥmān, ar-raḥīm*, the clement and merciful; others *Al-Muhaymin*, the protector." *Ghiyāṣ*. "Qāẓī Ḥamīd[u] 'd-Dīn of Nāgor says, the Great Name is the word *Hū*, or He (God), because it has a reference to God's nature, as it shows that He has no other at His side. Again, the word *hū* is a root, not a derivative. All epithets of God are contained in it." *Kashf*[u] *'l-Lughāt*.

[1] These formulæ remind us of Akbar's name, *Jallāl*[u] *'d-Dīn Muḥammad Akbar*. The words *Allāh*[u] *Akbar* are *ambiguous*; they may mean, *God is great*, or *Akbar is God*. There is no doubt that Abkar liked the phrase for its ambiguity; for it was used on coins, the Imperial seals, and the heading of books, farmāns, etc. His era was called the *Divine* era; his faith, the *Divine* faith; and the note at the end of this Āʾīn shows how Akbar, starting from the idea of the Divine right of kings, gradually came to look upon himself as the *Mujtahid* of the age, then as the prophet of God and God's Vice-regent on earth, and lastly as a Deity. "It was during these days [A.H. 983, or A.D. 1575–6] that His Majesty once asked how people would like it if he ordered the words *Allāh*[u] *Akbar* to be cut on the Imperial seal and the dies of his coins. Most said, people would like it very much. But Ḥājī Ibrāhīm objected, and said, the phrase had an ambiguous meaning, and the emperor might substitute the Qurʾan verse *La-ẕikr*[u] *'llāh*[i] *akbar*[u] (To think of God is the greatest thing), because it involved no ambiguity. But His Majesty got displeased, and said it was surely sufficient that no man who felt his weakness would claim Divinity; he merely looked to the sound of the words, and he had never thought that a thing could be carried to such an extreme." *Badāonī* p. 210.

and arrange a sumptuous feast. He is to bestow alms, and thus prepare provisions for the long journey.

His Majesty has also ordered that members should endeavour to abstain from eating flesh. They may allow others to eat flesh without touching it themselves; but during the month of their birth they are not even to approach meat. Nor shall members go near anything that they have themselves slain; nor eat of it. Neither shall they make use of the same vessels with butchers, fishers, and birdcatchers.

Members should not cohabit with pregnant, old, and barren women; nor with girls under the age of puberty.

Note by the Translator on the Religious Views of the Emperor Akbar.

In connexion with the preceding Āʿīn, it may be of interest for the general reader, and of some value for the future historian of Akbar's reign, to collect, in form of a note, the information which we possess regarding the religious views of the Emperor Akbar. The sources from which this information is derived, are, besides Abū 'l-Faẓl's Āʿīn, the *Muntakhab*ᵘ *'t-Tawārīkh* by ʿAbdᵘ l-Qādir ibn-i Mulūk Shāh of Badāon—regarding whom I would refer the reader to p. 110, and to a longer article in the *Journal of the Asiatic Society of Bengal* for 1869—and the *Dabistān*ᵘ *'l-Mazāhib*,[1] a work written about sixty years after Akbar's death by an unknown Muhammadan writer of strong Pārsī tendencies. Nor must we forget the valuable testimony of some of the Portuguese missionaries whom Akbar called from Goa, as Rodolpho Aquaviva, Antonio de Monserrato, Francisco Enriques, etc., of whom the first is mentioned by Abū 'l-Faẓl under the name of *Pādrī Radalf*.[2] There exist also two articles on Akbar's religious views, one by Captain Vans Kennedy, published in the second volume of the Transactions of the Bombay Literary Society, and another by the late Horace Hayman Wilson, which had originally appeared in the *Calcutta Quarterly Oriental Magazine*, vol. i, 1824, and has been reprinted in the second volume of Wilson's works, London, 1862. Besides, a few extracts from Badāonī, bearing on this subject, will be found in Sir H. Elliott's *Bibliographical Index to the Historians of Muhammadan India*, p. 243 ff. The proceedings of the Portuguese missionaries at Akbar's Court are described in Murray's

[1] Printed at Calcutta in 1809 with a short dictionary, and reprinted at Bombay A.H. 1272 [A.D. 1856]. This work has also been translated into English at the cost of the Oriental Translation Fund.

[2] Not *Padre Radīf*, پادري رديف, as in Elphinstone's history, but ردلف, the letter (*lām*) having been mistaken for a ي (*yā*).

Historical Account of Discoveries and Travels in Asia, Edinburgh, 1820, vol. ii.

I shall commence with extracts from Badāonī.[1] The translation is literal, which is of great importance in a difficult writer like Badāonī.

Abū 'l-Fazl's second introduction to Akbar. His pride.

[Badāonī, edited by Mawlawī Āghā Aḥmad ʿAlī, in the *Bibliotheca Indica*, vol. ii, p. 198.]

It was during these days [end of 982 A.H.] that Abū 'l-Faẓl, son of Shaykh Mubārak of Nāgor, came the second time to court. He is now styled *ʿAllāmī*. He is the man that set the world in flames. He lighted up the lamp of the *Ṣabāḥīs*, illustrating thereby the story of the man who, because he did not know what to do, took up a lamp in broad daylight, and representing himself as opposed to all sects, tied the girdle of infallibility round his waist according to the saying, "He who forms an opposition, gains power." He laid before the Emperor a commentary on the *Āyat^{u} 'l-kursī*,[2] which contained all subtleties of the Qurʿān; and though people said that it had been written by his father, Abū 'l-Faẓl was much praised. The numerical value of the letters in the words *Tafsīr-i Akbarī* (Akbar's commentary) gives the date of composition [983]. But the emperor praised it, chiefly because he expected to find in Abū 'l-Faẓl a man capable of teaching the Mullās a lesson, whose pride certainly resembles that of Pharaoh, though this expectation was opposed to the confidence which His Majesty had placed in me.

The reason of Abū 'l-Faẓl's opinionativeness and pretensions to infallibility was this. At the time when it was customary to get hold of, and kill such as tried to introduce innovations in religious matters (as had been the case with Mīr Ḥabshī and others), Shaykh ʿAbd^{u} 'n-Nabī and Makhdūm^{u} 'l-Mulk, and other learned men at court, unanimously

---

[1] As in the following extracts the years of the Hijrah are given, the reader may convert them according to this table :—

The year 980 A.H. commenced 14th May, 1572 [Old Style].

981—3rd May, 1573	993—24th December, 1584
982—23rd April, 1574	994—13th December, 1585
983—12th April, 1575	995—2nd December, 1586
984—31st March, 1576	996—22nd November, 1587
985—21st March, 1577	997—10th November, 1588
986—10th March, 1578	998—31st October, 1589
987—28th February, 1579	999—20th October, 1590
988—17th February, 1580	1000—9th October, 1591
989—5th February, 1581	1001—28th September, 1592
990—26th January, 1582	1002—17th September, 1593
991—15th January, 1583	1003—6th September, 1594
992—4th January, 1584	1004—27th August, 1595

[2] Qur., Sūr. II, 256.

represented to the emperor that Shaykh Mubārak also, in as far as he pretended to be *Mahdī*,[1] belonged to the class of innovators, and was not only himself damned, but led others into damnation. Having obtained a sort of permission to remove him, they dispatched police officers to bring him before the emperor. But when they found that the Shaykh, with his two sons, had concealed himself, they demolished the pulpit in his prayer-room. The Shaykh, at first, took refuge with Salīm-i Chishtī at Fatḥpūr, who then was in the height of his glory, and requested him to intercede for him. Shaykh Salīm, however, sent him money by some of his disciples, and told him it would be better for him to go away to Gujrāt. Seeing that Salīm took no interest in him, Shaykh Mubārak applied to Mīrzā ʕAzīz Koka [Akbar's foster-brother], who took occasion to praise to the emperor the Shaykh's learning and voluntary poverty, and the superior talents of his two sons, adding that Mubārak was a most trustworthy man, that he had never received lands as a present, and that he [ʕAzīz] could really not see why the Shaykh was so much persecuted. The emperor at last gave up all thoughts of killing the Shaykh. In a short time matters took a more favourable turn; and Abū 'l-Faẓl when once in favour with the emperor (officious as he was, and time-serving, openly faithless, continually studying His Majesty's whims, a flatterer beyond all bounds) took every opportunity of reviling in the most shameful way that sect whose labours and motives have been so little appreciated,[2] and became the cause not only of the extirpation of these experienced people, but also of the ruin of all servants of God, especially of Shaykhs, pious men, of the helpless, and the orphans, whose livings and grants he cut down..

He used to say, openly and implicitly :—

> O Lord, send down a proof [3] for the people of the world !
> Send these Nimrods [4] a gnat as big as an elephant !
> These Pharaoh-like fellows have lifted up their heads ;
> Send them a Moses with a staff, and a Nile !

---

[1] *Vide* p. 113, note 2.

[2] Badāonī belonged to the believers in the approach of the Millennium. A few years later, Akbar used Mahdawī rumours for his own purposes ; *vide* below. The extract shows that there existed before 982, heretical innovators, whom the emperor allowed to be persecuted. Matters soon took a different turn.

[3] That is, a man capable of teaching the ʕUlamās a lesson. Abū 'l-Faẓl means himself.

[4] Nimrod, or Namrūd, and Pharaoh, are proverbial in the East for their pride. Nimrod was killed by a gnat which had crept through the nose to his brain. He could only relieve his pains by striking the crown of his head ; but at last he died from the effects of his own blows.

And when in consequence of his harsh proceedings, miseries and misfortunes broke in upon the ʿUlamās (who had persecuted him and his father), he applied the following *Rubāʿī* to them :—

I have set fire to my barn with my own hands,
As I am the incendiary, how can I complain of my enemy ?
No one is my enemy but myself,
Woe is me ! I have torn my garment with my own hands.

And when during disputations people quoted against him the edict of any *Mujtahid*,[1] he used to say, " Oh don't bring me the arguments of this sweetmeat-seller and that cobbler, or that tanner ! " He thought himself capable of giving the lie to all Shaykhs and ʿUlamās.

Commencement of the Disputations. [Badāonī II, p. 200.]

" During the year 983 A.H., many places of worship were built at the command of His Majesty. The cause was this. For many years previous to 983 the emperor had gained in succession remarkable and decisive victories. The empire had grown in extent from day to day ; everything turned out well, and no opponent was left in the whole world. His Majesty had thus leisure to come into nearer contact with ascetics and the disciples of the Muʿīniyyah sect, and passed much of his time in discussing the word of God (Qurʾān), and the word of the prophet (the *Ḥadīs*, or Tradition). Questions of Ṣūfism, scientific discussions, inquiries into philosophy and law, were the order of the day. His Majesty passed whole nights in thoughts of God ; he continually occupied himself with pronouncing the names *Yā Hū* and *Yā Hādī*, which had been mentioned to him,[2] and his heart was full of reverence for Him who is the true Giver. From a feeling of thankfulness for his past successes, he would sit many a morning alone in prayer and melancholy, on a large flat stone of an old building which lay near the palace in a lonely spot, with his head bent over his chest, and gathering the bliss of early hours."

In his religious habits the emperor was confirmed by a story which he had heard of Sulaymān,[3] ruler of Bengal, who, in company with 150

---

[1] A man of infallible authority in his explanations of the Muhammadan law. There are few Mujtahids. Among the oldest there were several who plied a trade at the same time. The preceding *Rubāʿī* is translated by Sir H. Elliot in the *Muhammadan Historians of India*, p. 244.

[2] By some ascetic. *Yā Hū* means O He (God), and *Yā Hādī*, O Guide. The frequent repetition of such names is a means of knowledge. Some faqīrs repeat them several thousand times during a night.

[3] The edition of Badāonī calls him كراراني *Kararānī.* He is sometimes called *Karānī*, sometimes *Karzānī.* He reigned in Bengal from 971 to 980, or A.D. 1563 to 1573.

Shaykhs and ʿUlamās, held every morning a devotional meeting, after which he used to transact state business; as also by the news that Mīrzā Sulaymān, a prince of Ṣūfī tendencies, and a *Ṣāḥib-i ḥāl* [1] was coming to him from Badakhshān.

Among the religious buildings was a meeting place near a tank called *Anūptalāo*, where Akbar, accompanied by a few courtiers, met the ʿUlamās and lawyers of the realm. The pride of the ʿUlamās, and the heretical (Shīʿitic) subjects discussed in this building, caused Mullā Sherī, a poet of Akbar's reign, to compose a poem in which the place was called a temple of Pharaoh and a building of Shaddād (*vide* Qur., Sūr. 89). The result to which the discussions led will be seen from the following extract.

[Bad. II, p. 202.]

"For these discussions, which were held every Thursday [2] night, His Majesty invited the Sayyids, Shaykhs, ʿUlamās, and grandees, by turn. But as the guests generally commenced to quarrel about their places, and the order of precedence, His Majesty ordered that the grandees should sit on the east side; the Sayyids on the west side; the ʿUlamās to the south; and the Shaykhs to the north. The emperor then used to go from one side to the other and make his inquiries . . . when all at once, one night, 'the vein of the neck of the ʿUlamās of the age swelled up,' and a horrid noise and confusion ensued. His Majesty got very angry at their rude behaviour, and said to me [Badāonī], 'In future report any of the ʿUlamās that cannot behave and that talks nonsense, and I shall make him leave the hall.' I gently said to Āsaf Khān, 'If I were to carry out this order, most of the ʿUlamās would have to leave,' when His Majesty suddenly asked what I had said. On hearing my answer, he was highly pleased, and mentioned my remark to those sitting near him."

Soon after, another row occurred in the presence of the Emperor.

[Bad. II, p. 210.]

"Some people mentioned that Ḥājī Ibrāhīm of Sarhind had given a decree, by which he made it legal to wear red and yellow clothes,[3] quoting at the same time a Tradition as his proof. On hearing this, the Chief Justice, in the meeting hall, called him an accursed wretch, abused him, and lifted up his stick in order to strike him, when the Ḥājī by some subterfuges managed to get rid of him."

---

[1] *Ḥāl* is the state of ecstasy and close union with God into which Ṣūfīs bring themselves by silent thought, or by pronouncing the name of God.

[2] The text has *shāb-i Jumʿa*, the night of Friday; but as Muhammadans commence the day at sunset, it is our *Thursday* night.

[3] As women may use.

Akbar was now fairly disgusted with the ʿUlamās and lawyers; he never pardoned pride and conceit in a man, and of all kinds of conceit, the conceit of learning was most hateful to him. From now he resolved to vex the principal ʿUlamās; and no sooner had his courtiers discovered this, than they brought all sorts of charges against them.

[Bad. II, p. 203.]

"His Majesty therefore ordered Mawlānā ʿAbdu 'llāh of Sulṭānpūr, who had received the title of *Makhdūmu 'l-Mulk,* to come to a meeting, as he wished to annoy him, and appointed Ḥājī Ibrāhīm Shaykh Abū 'l-Faẓl (who had lately come to court, and is at present the infallible authority in all religious matters, and also for the New Religion of His Majesty, and the guide of men to truth, and their leader in general), and several other newcomers, to oppose him. During the discussion, His Majesty took every occasion to interrupt the Mawlānā when he explained anything. When the quibbling and wrangling had reached the highest point, some courtiers, according to an order previously given by His Majesty, commenced to tell rather queer stories of the Mawlānā, to whose position one might apply the verse of the Qurʿān (Sūr. XVI, 72), 'And some one of you shall have his life prolonged to a miserable age, etc.' Among other stories, Khān Jahān said that he had heard that Makhdūmu 'l-Mulk [1] had given a *fatwą* that the ordinance of pilgrimage was no longer binding, but even hurtful. When people had asked him the reason of his extraordinary *fatwą*, he had said, that the two roads to Makkah, through Persia and over Gujrāt, were impracticable, because people, in going by land (Persia) had to suffer injuries at the hand of the *Qizilbāshes* (i.e., the Shīʿah inhabitants of Persia), and in going by sea, they had to put up with indignities from the Portuguese, whose ship-tickets had pictures of Mary and Jesus stamped on them. To make use, therefore, of the latter alternative would mean to countenance idolatry; hence both roads were closed up.

"Khān Jahān also related that the Mawlānā had invented a clever trick by which he escaped paying the legal alms upon the wealth which he amassed every year. Towards the end of each year, he used to make over all his stores to his wife, but he took them back before the year had actually run out.[2].

[1] This extract as given by Sir H. Elliott on p. 244, conveys a wrong impression. Akbar did not prohibit pilgrimages before A.H. 990.

[2] Alms are due on every surplus of stock or stores which a Sunnī possesses at the end of a year, provided that surplus have been in his possession for a whole year. If the wife, therefore, had the surplus for a part of the year, and the husband took it afterwards back, he escaped the paying of alms.

" Other tricks also, in comparison with which the tricks of the children of Moses are nothing, and rumours of his meanness and shabbiness, his open cheating and worldliness, and his cruelties said to have been practised on the Shaykhs and the poor of the whole country, but especially on the Aimadārs and other deserving people of the Panjāb—all came up, one story after the other. His motives, ' which shall be revealed on the day of resurrection ' (Qur. LXXXVI, 9), were disclosed ; all sorts of stories, calculated to ruin his character and to vilify him, were got up, till it was resolved to force him to go to Makkah.

" But when people asked him whether pilgrimage was a duty for a man in his circumstances, he said *No* ; [1] for Shaykh ʿAbdᵘ 'n-Nabī had risen to power, whilst the star of the Mawlānā was fast sinking."

But a heavier blow was to fall on the ʿUlamās. [Bad. II, p. 207.]

" At one of the above-mentioned meetings, His Majesty asked how many *freeborn* women a man was legally allowed to marry (by *nikāḥ*). The lawyers answered that four was the limit fixed by the prophet. The emperor thereupon remarked that from the time he had come of age, he had not restricted himself to that number, and in justice to his wives, of whom he had a large number, both freeborn and slaves, he now wanted to know what remedy the law provided for his case. Most expressed their opinions, when the emperor remarked that Shaykh ʿAbdᵘ 'n-Nabī had once told him that one of the Mujtahids had had as many as nine wives. Some of the ʿUlamās present replied that the Mujtahid alluded to was Ibn Abī Layā ; and that some had even allowed eighteen from a too literal translation of the Qurʿān verse (Qur., Sūr. IV, 3), ' Marry whatever women ye like, two and two,[2] and three and three, and four and four,' but this was improper. His Majesty then sent a message to Shaykh ʿAbdᵘ 'n-Nabī, who replied that he had merely wished to point out to Akbar that a difference of opinion existed on this point among lawyers, but that he had not given a *fatwa* in order to legalize irregular marriage proceedings. This annoyed His Majesty very much. ' The Shaykh,' he said, ' told me at that time a very different thing from what he now tells me.' He never forgot this.

" After much discussion on this point the ʿUlamās, having collected

---

[1] I.e., he meant to say he was poor, and thus refuted the charges brought against him.

[2] Thus they got 2+2, 3+3, 4+4=18. But the passage is usually translated, " Marry whatever women ye like, two, or three, or four." The Mujtahid, who took nine unto himself, translated " two+three+four "=9. The question of the emperor was most ticklish, because, if the lawyers adhered to the number four, which they could not well avoid, the *ḥarāmzādagī* of Akbar's *freeborn* princesses was acknowledged.

every tradition on the subject, decreed, *first*, that by *mutˁah* [not by *nikāḥ*] a man might marry any number of wives he pleased; and, *secondly*, that *mutˁah* marriages were allowed by Imām Mālik. The Shīˁahs, as was well known, loved children born in *mutˁah* wedlock more than those born by *nikāḥ* wives, contrary to the Sunnīs and the Ahl-i Jamāˁat.

"On the latter point also the discussion got rather lively, and I would refer the reader to my work entitled *Najāt*[u] *'r-rashīd* [*vide* note 2, p. 104], in which the subject is briefly discussed. But to make things worse, Naqīb Khān fetched a copy of the *Muwaṭṭa* of Imām Mālik, and pointed to a Tradition in the book, which the Imām had cited as a proof against the legality of *mutˁah* marriages.

"Another night, Qāẓī Yaˁqūb, Shaykh Abū 'l-Faẓl, Ḥājī Ibrāhīm, and a few others were invited to meet His Majesty in the house near the *Anūptalā,o* tank. Shaykh Abū 'l-Faẓl had been selected as the opponent, and laid before the emperor several traditions regarding *mutˁah* marriages, which his father (Shaykh Mubārak) had collected, and the discussion commenced. His Majesty then asked me, what my opinion was on this subject. I said, 'The conclusion which must be drawn from so many contradictory traditions and sectarians customs, is this:—Imām Mālik and the Shīˁahs are unanimous in looking upon *mutˁah* marriages as legal; Imām Shāfiˁī and the Great Imām (Ḥanīfah) look upon *mutˁah* marriages as illegal. But, should at any time a Qāẓī of the Mālikī sect decide that *mutˁah* is legal, it is legal, according to the common belief, even for Shāfiˁī's and Ḥanafīs. Every other opinion on this subject is idle talk.' This pleased His Majesty very much."

The unfortunate Shaykh Yaˁqūb, however, went on talking about the extent of the authority of a Qāẓī. He tried to shift the ground; but when he saw that he was discomfited, he said, "Very well, I have nothing else to say—just as His Majesty pleases."

"The Emperor then said, 'I herewith appoint the Mālikī Qāẓī Ḥasan ˁArab as the Qāẓī before whom I lay this case concerning my wives, and you, Yaˁqūb, are from to-day suspended.' This was immediately obeyed, and Qāẓī Ḥasan on the spot gave a decree which made *mutˁah* marriages legal.

"The veteran lawyers, as Makhdūm[u] 'l-Mulk, Qāẓī Yaˁqūb, and others, made very long faces at these proceedings.

"This was the commencement of 'their sere and yellow leaf'.

"The result was that, a few days later, Mawlānā Jalāl[u] 'd-Dīn of Multān, a profound and learned man, whose grant had been transferred, was ordered from Āgra (to Fatḥpūr Sīkrī) and appointed Qāẓī of the realm. Qāẓī Yaʿqūb was sent to Gaur as District Qāẓī.

" From this day henceforth, ' the road of opposition and difference in opinion ' lay open, and remained so till His Majesty was appointed Mujtahid of the empire." [Here follows the extract regarding the formula *Allāhᵘ Akbar*, given on p. 175, note 1.]

[Badāonī II, p. 211.]

" During this year [983], there arrived Ḥakīm Abū 'l-Fatḥ, Hakīm Humāyūn (who subsequently changed his name to Humāyūn Qulī, and lastly to Ḥakīm Humām), and Nūrᵘ 'd-Dīn, who as poet is known under the name of *Qarārī*. They were brothers, and came from Gīlān, near the Caspian Sea. The eldest brother, whose manners and address were exceedingly winning, obtained in a short time great ascendency over the Emperor ; he flattered him openly, adapted himself to every change in the religious ideas of His Majesty, or even went in advance of them, and thus became in a short time a most intimate friend of Akbar.

" Soon after there came from Persia, Mullā Muḥammad of Yazd, who got the nickname of Yazīdī, and attaching himself to the emperor, commenced openly to revile the *Ṣaḥābah* (persons who knew Muhammad, except the twelve Imāms), told queer stories about them, and tried hard to make the emperor a Shīʿah. But he was soon left behind by Bīr Baṛ—that bastard !--and by Shay*kh* Abū 'l-Faẓl and Ḥakīm Abū 'l-Fatḥ, who successfully turned the emperor from the Islām, and led him to reject inspiration, prophetship, the miracles of the prophet and of the saints, and even the whole law, so that I could no longer bear their company.

" At the same time, His Majesty ordered Qāẓī Jalālᵘ 'd-Dīn and several ʿUlamās to write a commentary on the Qurʾān ; but this led to great rows among them.

" Deb Chand Rāja Manjhola—that fool—once set the whole court in laughter by saying that Allah after all had great respect for cows, else the cow would not have been mentioned in the first chapter (*Sūratᵘ 'l-baqarah*) of the Qurʾān.

" His Majesty had also the early history of the Islām read out to him, and soon commenced to think less of the *Ṣaḥābah*. Soon after, the observance of the five prayers and the fasts, and the belief in everything connected with the prophet, were put down as *taqlīdī*, or religious blindness, and man's reason was acknowledged to be the basis of all religion. Portuguese priests also came frequently ; and His Majesty inquired into the articles of their belief which are based upon reason."

[Badāonī II, p. 245.]

" In the beginning of the next year [984], when His Majesty was at Dīpālpūr in Mālwah, Sharīf of Āmul arrived. This apostate had run from country to country, like a dog that has burnt its foot, and turning from one sect to the other, he went on wrangling till he became a perfect heretic. For some time he had studied Ṣūfic nonsense in the school of Mawlānā Muḥammad Zāhid of Balkh, nephew of the great Shaykh Ḥusayn of Khwārazm, and had lived with derwishes. But as he had little of a derwish in himself, he talked slander, and was so full of conceit that they hunted him away. The Mawlānā also wrote a poem against him, in which the following verse occurs :—

" There was a heretic, Sharīf by name,
Who talked very big, though of doubtful fame.

" In his wanderings he had come to the Dakhin, where he made himself so notorious, that the king of the Dakhin wanted to kill him. But he was only put on a donkey, and shown about in the city. Hindustān, however, is a nice large place, where anything is allowed, and no one cares for another, and people go on as they may. He therefore made for Mālwah, and settled at a place five *kos* distant from the Imperial camp. Every frivolous and absurd word he spoke was full of venom, and became the general talk. Many fools, especially Persian heretics (whom the Islām casts out as people cast out hairs which they find in dough—such heretics are called *Nuqṭawīs* and are destined to be the foremost worshippers of Antichrist) gathered round him, and spread, at his order, the rumour that he was the restorer of the Millennium. The sensation was immense. As soon as His Majesty heard of him, he invited him one night to a private audience in a long prayer room, which had been made of cloth, and in which the emperor with his suite used to say the five daily prayers. Ridiculous in his exterior, ugly in shape, with his neck stooping forward, he performed his obeisance, and stood still with his arms crossed, and you could scarcely see how his blue eye (which colour[1] is a sign of hostility to our prophet) shed lies, falsehood, and hypocrisy. There he stood for a long time, and when he got the order to sit down, he prostrated himself in worship, and sat down *duzānū* (*vide* p. 168, note 2), like an Indian camel. He talked privately to His Majesty ; no one dared to draw near them, but I sometimes heard from a distance the word *ʿilm* (knowledge), because he spoke pretty loud. He called his silly views ' the truth of truths ', or ' the groundwork of things '.

---

[1] *Chashm-i azraq*. Europeans have blue eyes. The expression is as old as Ḥarīrī and the Crusades.

"A fellow ignorant of things external and internal,
From silliness indulging idle talk.
He is immersed in heresies infernal,
And prattles—God forbid!—of truth eternal.

"The whole talk of the man was a mere repetition of the ideas of Maḥmūd of Basakhwān (a village in Gīlān), who lived at the time of Tīmūr. Maḥmūd who had written thirteen treatises of dirty filth, full of such hypocrisy as no religion or sect would suffer, and containing nothing but *tūtāl*, which name he had given to the 'science of expressed and implied language'. The chief work of this miserable wretch is entitled *Baḥr o Kūza* (the Ocean and the Jug), and contains such loathsome nonsense, that on listening to it one's ear vomits. How the devil would have laughed in his face, if he had heard it, and how he would have jumped for joy! And this Sharīf—the dirty thief—had also written a collection of nonsense, which he styled *Tarashshuḥ-i Ẓuhūr*, in which he blindly follows Mīr ʿAbdᵘ 'l-Awwal. This book is written in loose, deceptive aphorisms, each commencing with the words *mīfarmūdand* (the master said), a queer thing to look at, and a mass of ridiculous, silly nonsense. But notwithstanding his ignorance, according to the proverb, 'Worthies will meet,' he has exerted such an influence on the spirit of the age, and on the people, that he is now [in 1004], a commander of One Thousand and His Majesty's apostle for Bengal, possessing the four degrees of faith, and calling, as the Lieutenant of the emperor, the faithful to these degrees."

The discussions on Thursday evenings were continued for the next year. In 986, they became violent, in as far as the elementary principles of the Islām were chosen as subject, whilst formerly the disputations had turned on single points. The ʿUlamās, even in the presence of the emperor, often lost their temper, and called each other *Kāfirs*, or *accursed.*

[Bad. II, p. 255.]

"Makhdūm also wrote a pamphlet against Shaykh ʿAbdᵘ 'n-Nabī, in which he accused him of the murder of Khizr Khān of Shīrwān, who was suspected to have reviled the prophet, and of Mīr Ḥabshī, whom he had ordered to be killed for heresy. But he also said in the pamphlet that it was wrong to say prayers with ʿAbdᵘ 'n-Nabī, because he had been undutiful towards his father, and was, besides, afflicted with piles. Upon this, Shaykh ʿAbdᵘ 'n-Nabī called Makhdūm a fool, and cursed him. The ʿUlamās now broke up into two parties, like the Sibṭīs and Qibṭīs, gathering either round the Shaykh, or round Makhdūmᵘ l-Mulk; and the heretic innovators used this opportunity, to mislead the emperor by their wicked opinions and aspersions, and turned truth into falsehood, and represented lies as truth.

"*His Majesty till now* [986] *had shown every sincerity, and was diligently searching for truth. But his education had been much neglected; and surrounded as he was by men of low and heretic principles, he had been forced to doubt the truth of the Islām. Falling from one perplexity into the other, he lost sight of his real object, the search of truth; and when the strong embankment of our clear law and our excellent faith had once been broken through, His Majesty grew colder and colder, till after the short space of five or six years not a trace of Muhammadan feeling was left in his heart. Matters then became very different.*"

[Bad. II, p. 239.]

"In 984 the news arrived that Shāh Ṭahmāsp of Persia had died, and Shāh Ismāʿīl II had succeeded him. The Tārīkh of his accession is given in the first letters of the three words دولت, فتح, and ظفر [د+ف+ظ =984]. Shāh Ismāʿīl gave the order that any one who wished to go to Makkah could have his travelling expenses paid from the royal exchequer. Thus thousands of people partook of the spiritual blessing of pilgrimage, whilst here you dare not now [1004] mention that word, and you would expose yourself to capital punishment if you were to ask leave from court for this purpose."

[Bad. II, p. 241.]

"In 985, the news arrived that Shāh Ismāʿīl, son of Shāh Ṭahmāsp had been murdered, with the consent of the grandees, by his sister *Parī Jān Khānum*. Mīr Ḥaydar, the riddle writer, found the Tārīkh of his accession in the words *Shahinshāh-i rūi zamīn* [984] 'a king of the face of the earth'. and the Tārīkh of his death in *Shahinshāh-i zer-i zamīn* [985] 'a king below the face of the earth'.[1] At that time also there appeared in Persia the great comet which had been visible in India (p. 240), and the consternation was awful, especially as at the same time the Turks conquered Tabrīz, Shīrwān, and Māzandarān. Sulṭān Muḥammad Khudābanda, son of Shāh Ṭahmāsp, but by another mother, succeeded; and with him ended the time of reviling and cursing the *Ṣaḥābah*.

"*But the heretical ideas had certainly entered Hindūstān from Persia.*"

---

[1] As Ṭahmāsp in his short Memoirs (Pers. Ms. 782, As. Soc. Bengal) gives the word ظل *ẓil* [930] as the Tārīkh of his accession, we have:—

Ṭahmāsp from 930 to 984; Ismāʿīl II, 984 to 985.

Prinsep's Tables (IInd edition, p. 308) give:—Ṭahmāsp, 932 to 983; Ismāʿīl II, from 983 to 985.

BADĀ,ONĪ'S SUMMARY OF THE REASONS WHICH LED AKBAR TO RENOUNCE THE ISLĀM.

[Bad. II, p. 256.]

The following are the principal reasons which led His Majesty from the right path. I shall not give all, but only some, according to the proverb, "That which is small, guides that which is great, and a sign of fear in a man points him out as the culprit."

The principal reason is the large number of learned men of all denominations and sects that came from various countries to court, and received personal interviews. Night and day people did nothing but inquire and investigate; profound points of science, the subtleties of revelation, the curiosities of history, the wonders of nature, of which large volumes could only give a summary abstract, were ever spoken of. His Majesty collected the opinions of every one, especially of such as were not Muhammadans, retaining whatever he approved of, and rejecting everything which was against his disposition and ran counter to his wishes. From his earliest childhood to his manhood, and from his manhood to old age, His Majesty has passed through the most various phases, and through all sorts of religious practices and sectarian beliefs, and has collected everything which people can find in books, with a talent of selection peculiar to him, and a spirit of inquiry opposed to every [Islāmitic] principle. Thus a faith based on some elementary principles traced itself on the mirror of his heart, and as the result of all the influences which were brought to bear on His Majesty, they grew, gradually as the outline of a stone, the conviction in his heart that there were sensible men in all religions, and abstemious thinkers and men endowed with miraculous powers, among all nations. If some true knowledge was thus everywhere to be found, why should truth be confined to one religion, or to a creed like the Islām, which was comparatively new, and scarcely a thousand years old; why should one sect assert what another denies, and why should one claim a preference without having superiority conferred on itself.

Moreover, Sumanīs [1] and Brahmins managed to get frequent private interviews with His Majesty. As they surpass other learned men in their treatises on morals, and on physical and religious sciences, and reach a high degree in their knowledge of the future, in spiritual power and human perfection, they brought proofs based on reason and testimony,

---

[1] Explained in Arab. dictionaries as a sect in Sind who believe in the transmigration of souls (*tanāsukh*). Akbar, as will be seen from the following, was convinced of the transmigration of souls, and therefore rejected the doctrine of resurrection.

for the truth of their own and the fallacies of other religions, and inculcated their doctrines so firmly and so skilfully represented things as quite self-evident which require consideration, that no man, by expressing his doubts, could now raise a doubt in His Majesty, even if mountains were to crumble to dust, or the heavens were to tear asunder.

Hence His Majesty cast aside the Islāmitic revelations regarding resurrection, the day of judgment, and the details connected with it, as also all ordinances based on the tradition of our prophet. He listened to every abuse which the courtiers heaped on our glorious and pure faith, which can be so easily followed; and eagerly seizing such opportunities, he showed in words and gestures, his satisfaction at the treatment which his original religion received at their hands.

How wise was the advice which the guardian gave a lovely being,

"Do not smile at every face, as the rose does at every zephyr."[1]

When it was too late to profit by the lesson,

She could but frown, and hang down the head.

For some time His Majesty called a Brahmin, whose name was Purukhotam, author of a commentary on the . . .,[2] whom he asked to invent particular Sanscrit names for all things in existence. At other times, a Brahmin of the name of Debī was pulled up the wall of the castle,[3] sitting on a *chārpāe*, till he arrived near a balcony where the emperor used to sleep. Whilst thus suspended, he instructed His Majesty in the secrets and legends of Hinduism, in the manner of worshipping idols, the fire, the sun, and stars, and of revering the chief gods of these unbelievers, as Brahma, Mahādev, Bishn, Kishn, Rām, and Mahāmāī, who are supposed to have been men but very likely never existed, though some, in their idle belief, look upon them as gods, and others as angels. His Majesty, on hearing further how much the people of the country prized their institutions, commenced to look upon them with affection. The doctrine of the transmigration of souls especially took a deep root in his heart, and he approved of the saying—"There is no religion in which the doctrine of transmigration has not taken firm root." Insincere flatterers composed treatises in order to fix the evidence for this doctrine; and as His Majesty relished inquiries into the sects of these infidels (who cannot be counted, so numerous they are, and who have no end of

---

[1] Just as Akbar liked the zephyr of inquiry into other religious systems. But zephyrs are also destructive; they scatter the petals of the rose.

[2] The text has a few unintelligible words.

[3] Perhaps in order not to get polluted, or because the balcony belonged to the Harem.

revealed books, but nevertheless, do not belong to the *Ahl-i Kitāb*, Jews, Christians, and Muhammadans), not a day passed but a new fruit of this loathsome tree ripened into existence.

Sometimes again, it was *Shaykh Tāj^u 'd-Dīn* of Dihlī, who had to attend the emperor. This Shaykh is the son of Shaykh Zakariyā of Ajodhan. The principal ˁUlamās of the age call him *Tāj^u 'l-ˁĀrifīn*, or crown of the Ṣūfīs. He had learned under Shaykh Zamān of Pānīpat, author of a commentary on the Liwāˁiḥ, and of other very excellent works, was in Ṣūfism and pantheism second only to Shaykh Ibn ˁArabī, and had written a comprehensive commentary on the *Nuzhat^u 'l-Arwāḥ*. Like the preceding, he was drawn up the wall of the castle. His Majesty listened whole nights to his Ṣūfic trifles. As the Shaykh was not over strict [1] in acting according to our religious law, he spoke a great deal of the pantheistic presence, which idle Ṣūfīs will talk about, and which generally leads them to denial of the law and open heresy. He also introduced polemic matters, as the ultimate salvation by faith of Pharaoh —God's curse be upon him!—which is mentioned in the *Fuṣūṣ^u 'l-Ḥikam*,[2] or the excellence of hope over fear,[3] and many other things to which men incline from weakness of disposition, unmindful of cogent reasons, or distinct religious commands, to the contrary. The Shaykh is therefore one of the principal culprits who weakened His Majesty's faith in the orders of our religion. He also said that infidels would, of course, be kept for ever in hell, but it was not likely, nor could it be proved, that the punishment in hell was eternal. His explanations of some verses of the Qurˀān or of the Tradition of our prophet, were often far-fetched. Besides, he mentioned that the phrase *Insān-i Kāmil* (perfect man) referred to the ruler of the age, from which he inferred that the nature of a king was holy. In this way, he said many agreeable things to the emperor, rarely expressing the proper meaning, but rather the opposite of what he knew to be correct. Even the *sijdah* (prostration), which people mildly call *zamīnbos* (kissing the ground), he allowed to be due to the Insān-i Kāmil; he looked upon the respect due to the king as a religious command, and called the face of the king *Kaˁba-yi Murādāt*, the sanctum of desires,

---

[1] As long as a Ṣūfī conforms to the Qurˀān he is *sharˁī*; but when he feels that he has drawn nearer to God, and does no longer require the ordinances of the *profanum vulgus*, he is *āzād*, free, and becomes a heretic.

[2] Pharaoh claimed divinity, and is therefore *malˁūn*, accursed by God. But according to some books, and among them the *Fuṣūṣ*, Pharaoh repented in the moment of death, and acknowledged Moses to be a true prophet.

[3] The Islām says, *Al-īmān bayn^a 'l-khawf^i wa 'r-rijāˁ*, "Faith stands *between* fear and hope." Hence it is sin to fear God's wrath more than to hope for God's mercy; and so reversely.

and *Qibla-yi ḥājāt*, the cynosure of necessities. Such blasphemies[1] other people supported by quoting stories of no credit, and by referring to the practice followed by disciples of some heads of Indian sects. And after this, when . . .[2]

Other great philosophical writers of the age also expressed opinions, for which there is no authority. Thus Shay<u>kh</u> Yaʿqūb of Kashmīr, a well-known writer, and at present the greatest authority in religious matters, mentioned some opinions held by ʿAynᵘ 'l-Quẓāt of Hamadān, that our prophet Muḥammad was a personification of the divine name of *Al-hādī* (the guide), and the devil was the personification of God's name of *Al-muẓill* (the tempter),[3] that both names, thus personified, had appeared in this world, and that both personifications were therefore necessary.

Mullā Muḥammad of Yazd, too, was drawn up the wall of the castle, and uttered unworthy, loathsome abuse against the first three <u>Kh</u>alīfahs, called the whole Ṣaḥābah, their followers and next followers, and the saints of past ages, infidels and adulterers, slandered the Sunnīs and the *Ahl-i Jamāʿat*,[4] and represented every sect, except the Shīʿah, as damned and leading men into damnation.

The differences among the ʿUlamās, of whom one called lawful what the other called unlawful, furnished His Majesty with another reason for apostacy. The emperor also believed that the ʿUlamās of his time were superior in dignity and rank to Imām-i <u>Gh</u>azzālī and Imām-i Rāẓī,[5] and knowing from experience the flimsiness of his ʿUlamās, he judged those great men of the past by his contemporaries, and threw them aside.

Learned monks also came from Europe, who go by the name of *Pādre*.[6] They have an infallible head, called *Pāpā*. He can change any religious ordinances as he may think advisable, and kings have to submit to his authority. These monks brought the gospel, and mentioned to the emperor their proofs for the Trinity. His Majesty firmly believed in the truth of the Christian religion, and wishing to spread the doctrines of

---

[1] As the *zamīnbos*, or the use of holy names as *Kaʿbah* (the temple of Makkah) or *Qiblah* (Makkah, in as far as people turn to it their face when praying).

[2] The text has an unintelligible sentence.

[3] According to the Islām, God leads (*hādī*) men to salvation, but also to sin and damnation. God created also wickedness.

[4] *Ahl-i jamāʿat* is a term which is often joined with the word *Sunnīs*. All religious ordinances are either based upon the Qurʾān, or upon the Tradition; or upon the opinion (*qiyāṣ*) of famous *Ṣaḥābīs*; or lastly, upon *ijmāʿ* agreement, or the custom generally followed during the first century of the *Hijrah*. Hence *Ahl-i jamāʿat* comprises all such as believe *ijmāʿ* binding.

[5] Two famous authorities in religious matters. The most popular books of *Imām <u>Gh</u>azzālī* are the *Iḥyāᵘ 'l-ʿutlūm* and the *Kīmiyā-yi saʿādat* which, according to p. 103, was one of the few books which Akbar liked.

[6] The text has پادری.

Jesus, ordered Prince Murād [1] to take a few lessons in Christianity by way of auspiciousness, and charged Abū 'l-Fazl to translate the Gospel. Instead of the usual *Bism*[i] *'llāh*[i] *'r-raḥmān*[i] *'r-raḥīm*[i], [2] the following lines were used—

Ay nām-i tu Jesus o Kiristū

(O thou those names are Jesus and Christ)

which means, " O thou whose name is gracious and blessed " ; and Shaykh Fayzī added another half, in order to complete the verse

Subḥāna-k[a] *lā siwā-k*[a] *Yā hū.*

(We praise Thee, there is no one besides Thee, O God !)

These accursed monks applied the description of cursed Satan, and of his qualities, to Muḥammad, the best of all prophets—God's blessings rest on him and his whole house !—a thing which even devils would not do.

Bīr Baṛ also impressed upon the emperor that the sun was the primary origin of everything. The ripening of the grain in the fields, of fruits and vegetables, the illumination of the universe, and the lives of men, depended upon the Sun. Hence it was but proper to worship and reverence this luminary ; and people in praying should face towards the place where he rises, instead of turning to the quarter where he sets. For similar reasons, said Bīr Baṛ, should men pay regard to fire and water, stones, trees, and other forms of existence, even to cows and their dung, to the mark on the forehead and the Brahminical thread.

Philosophers and learned men who had been at Court, but were in disgrace, made themselves busy in bringing proofs. They said the sun was " the greatest light ", the source of benefit for the whole world, the nourisher of kings, and the origin of royal power.

This was also the cause why the Nawrūz-i Jalālī [3] was observed, on which day, since His Majesty's accession, a great feast was given. His Majesty also adopted different suits of clothes of seven different colours,

---

[1] Prince Murād was then about eight years old. Jahāngīr (Salīm) was born on Wednesday, the 17 *Rabī*ʿ[u] *'l-awwal* 977. Three months after him, his sister *Shāhzāda Khānum* was born ; and after her in the year 978 on 3rd Muḥarram (Bad. II, 132) *Shāh Murād*, who got the nickname of *Pahāṛī*, as he was born in the hills of Fathpūr Sīkrī. Dānyāl was born in Ajmīr during the night between Tuesday and Wednesday, the 10th, the Jumāda 'l-awwal 979.

[2] The formula " *Bism*[i] *'llāh*[i], etc." is said by every schoolboy before he commences to read from his text book.

The words *Ay nām-i tu Jesus o Kiristo* are taken from the Dabistān ; the edition of Badā,onī has *Ay nāmī wai zhazho Kiristo*, which, though correct in metre (*vide* my " Prosody of the Persians ", p. 33, No. 32), is improbable. The formula as given in the Dabistān has a common Masnawī metre (*vide* my " Prosody ", p. 33, No. 31), and spells *Jesus* ژزو *dezuz*. The verse as given by H. Wilson (Works II, p. 387) has no metre.

[3] *Vide* the *Tārīkh-i Mulkī*, in the beginning of Book III.

each of which was worn on a particular day of the week in honour of the seven colours of the seven planets.

The emperor also learned from some Hindus, formulæ to reduce the influence of the sun to his subjection, and commenced to read them mornings and evenings as a religious exercise. He also believed that it was wrong to kill cows, which the Hindus worship; he looked upon cow-dung as pure, interdicted the use of beef, and killed beautiful men (?) instead of cows. The doctors confirmed the emperor in his opinion, and told him it was written in their books that beef was productive of all sorts of diseases and was very indigestible.

Fire-worshippers also had come from Nausārī in Gujrāt, and proved to His Majesty the truth of Zoroaster's doctrines. They called fire-worship "the great worship", and impressed the emperor so favourably that he learned from them the religious terms and rites of the old Pārsīs, and ordered Abū 'l-Faẓl to make arrangements that sacred fire should be kept burning at court by day and by night, according to the custom of the ancient Persian kings, in whose fire-temples it had been continually burning; for fire was one of the manifestations of God, and "a ray of His rays".

His Majesty, from his youth, had also been accustomed to celebrate the *Hom* (a kind of fire-worship) from his affection towards the Hindu princesses of his Harem.

From the New Year's day of the twenty-fifth year of his reign [988], His Majesty openly worshipped the sun and the fire by prostrations; and the courtiers were ordered to rise when the candles and lamps were lighted in the palace. On the festival of the eighth day of Virgo, he put on the mark on the forehead, like a Hindu, and appeared in the Audience Hall, when several Brahmins tied, by way of auspiciousness, a string with jewels on it round his hands, whilst the grandees countenanced these proceedings by bringing, according to their circumstances, pearls and jewels as presents. The custom of Rākhī (or tying pieces of clothes round the wrists as amulets) became quite common.

When orders in opposition to the Islām were quoted by people of other religions, they were looked upon by His Majesty as convincing, whilst Hinduism is in reality a religion in which every order is nonsense. The originator of our belief, the Arabian Saints, all were said to be adulterers and highway robbers, and all the Muhammadans were declared worthy of reproof, till at length His Majesty belonged to those of whom the Qur'ān says (Sūr 61, 8): "They seek to extinguish God's light with their mouths: But God will perfect his light though the infidels be averse thereto." In fact, matters went so far that proofs were no longer required when anything connected with the Islām was to be abolished.

Akbar publicly assumes the spiritual leadership of the nation.

[Bad. II, p. 268.]

"In this year [987], His Majesty was anxious to unite in his person the powers of the State and those of the Church; for he could not bear to be subordinate to any one. As he had heard that the prophet, his lawful successors, and some of the most powerful kings, as Amīr Tīmūr Ṣāḥib-qirān, and Mīrzā Ulugh Beg-i Gurgān, and several others, had themselves read the *Khuṭba* (the Friday prayer), he resolved to do the same, apparently in order to imitate their example, but in reality to appear in public as the Mujtahid of the age. Accordingly, on Friday, the first *Jumāda 'l-awwal* 987, in the Jāmiʿ Masjid of Fatḥpūr, which he had built near the palace, His Majesty commenced to read the Khuṭba. But all at once he stammered and trembled, and though assisted by others, he could scarcely read three verses of a poem, which Shaykh Fayẓī had composed, came quickly down from the pulpit, and handed over the duties of the Imām (leader of the prayer) to Ḥāfiẓ Muḥammad Amīn, the Court *Khaṭīb*. These are the verses:—

The Lord has given me the empire,
And a wise heart, and a strong arm,
He has guided me in righteousness and justice,
And has removed from my thoughts everything but justice.
His praise surpasses man's understanding,
Great is His power, Allāh[u] Akbar!"

[p. 269.]

"As it was quite customary in those days to speak ill of the doctrine and orders of the Qurʾān, and as Hindu wretches and Hinduizing Muhammadans openly reviled our prophet, irreligious writers left out in the prefaces to their books the customary praise of the prophet, and after saying something to the praise of God, wrote eulogies of the emperor instead.[1] It was impossible even to mention the name of the prophet, because these liars (as Abū 'l-Faẓl, Fayẓī, etc.) did not like it. This wicked innovation gave general offence, and sowed the seed of evil throughout the country;[2] but notwithstanding this, a lot of low and mean fellows

---

[1] As Abū l'Faẓl has done in the Āʾīn. "But Fayẓī added the usual praise of the prophet (*naʿt*) to his *Nal Daman*, a short time before his death, at the pressing request of some friends." *Badāonī.*

[2] Because books were sure to be copied; hence many would see the innovation and imitate it. As the formula "*Bismi 'llāh*, etc.", had been changed to *Allāh[u] Akbar*, we also find *Allāh[u] Akbar* in the heading of books, as in the Āʾīn.

put piously on their necks the collar of the Divine Faith, and called themselves disciples, either from fear or hope of promotion, though they thought it impossible to say our creed."

[pp. 270 to 272.]

" In the same year [987] a document made its appearance, which bore the signatures and seals of Makhdūm[u] 'l-Mulk, of Shaykh ʿAbd[u] 'n-Nabī, ṣadr[u] ṣ-ṣudūr, of Qāẓī Jalāl[i] 'd-Dīn of Multān, Qāẓiy[u] 'l-quẓāt of Ṣadr Jahān, the muftī of the empire, of Shaykh Mubārak, the deepest writer of the age, and of Ghāzī Khān of Badakhshān, who stood unrivalled in the various sciences. The objects of the document was to settle the superiority of the *Imām-iʿādil* (just leader) over the *Mujtahid*, which was proved by a reference to an ill-supported authority. The whole matter is a question, regarding which people differ in opinion ; but the document was to do away with the possibility of disagreeing about laws, whether political or religious, and was to bind the lawyers in spite of themselves. But before the instrument was signed, a long discussion took place as to the meaning of *ijtihād*, and as to whom the term *Mujtahid* was applicable, and whether it really was the duty of a just *Imām* who, from his acquaintance with politics, holds a higher rank than the *Mujtahid*, to decide, according to the requirements of the times, and the wants of the age, all such legal questions on which there existed a difference of opinion. At last, however, all signed the document, some willingly, others against their convictions.

I shall copy the document *verbatim*.

The Document.

" ' Whereas Hindūstān has now become the centre of security and peace— and the land of justice and beneficence, a large number of people, especially learned men and lawyers, have immigrated and chosen this country for their home. Now we, the principal ʿUlamās, who are not only well versed in the several departments of the law and in the principles of jurisprudence, and well-acquainted with the edicts which rest on reason or testimony, but are also known for our piety and honest intentions, have duly considered the deep meaning, *first*, of the verse of the Qurʾān (Sūr. IV, 62), " *Obey God, and obey the prophet, and those who have authority among you*," and *secondly*, of the genuine tradition, " *Surely, the man who is dearest to God on the day of judgment, is the Imām-i ʿĀdil : whosoever obeys the Amīr, obeys Me ; and Whosoever rebels against him, rebels against Me*," and *thirdly*, of several other proofs based on reasoning or testimony ; and we have agreed that the rank of a *Sulṭān-i ʿādil* (a just ruler) is higher in the eyes of God than the rank of a *Mujthahid.* Further we declare that the king of Islām, Amīr of the Faithful, shadow of God in the world, ʿ*Abd 'l-Fatḥ Jalāl*ᵘ *'d-Dīn Muḥammad Akbar Pādishāh-i ghāzī*, whose kingdom God perpetuate, is a most just, a most wise, and a most God-fearing king. Should therefore, in future, a religious question come up, regarding which the opinions of the *Mujtahids* are at variance, and His Majesty, in his penetrating understanding and clear wisdom, be inclined to adopt, for the benefit of the nation and as a political expedient, any of the conflicting opinions which exist on that point, and issue a decree to that effect, we do hereby agree that such a decree shall be binding on us and on the whole nation.

" ' Further, we declare that, should His Majesty think fit to issue a new order, we and the nation shall likewise be bound by it, provided always that such an order be not only in accordance with some verse of the Qurʾān, but also of real benefit for the nation ; and further, that any opposition on the part of the subjects to such an order as passed by His Majesty, shall involve damnation in the world to come, and loss of religion and property in this life.

" ' This document has been written with honest intentions, for the glory of God, and the propagation of the Islām, and is signed by us, the principal ʿUlamās and lawyers in the month of Rajab of the year 987 of the Hijrah.'

" The draft of this document when presented to the emperor, was in the handwriting of Shaykh Mubārak. The others had signed it against their will, but the Shaykh had added at the bottom that he had most willingly signed his name ; for this was a matter which, for several years, he had been anxiously looking forward to.

" No sooner had His Majesty obtained this legal instrument, than the road of deciding any religious question was open ; the superiority of intellect of the Imām was established, and opposition was rendered impossible. All orders regarding things which our law allows or disallows, were abolished, and the superiority of intellect of the Imām became law.

" But the state of Shaykh Abū 'l-Faẓl resembled that of the poet *Ḥayratī* of Samarqand,[1] who after having been annoyed by the cool and sober people of Mā-wara 'n-nahr (Turkistān), joined the old foxes of Shīʿitic Persia, and chose ' the roadless road '. You might apply the proverb to him— ' He prefers hell to shame on earth.'

[1] The birthplace of the poet *Ḥayratī* is not exactly known, though he belongs to Turkistān. It is said that he was a great wine-bibber, and travelled about in search of places where wine-drinking was connived at. At last he settled at Kāshān, and became a Shīʿa. He was murdered there by a robber in 961.

" On the 16th Rajab of this year, His Majesty made a pilgrimage to Ajmīr. It is now fourteen years that His Majesty has not returned to that place. On the 5th Shaʿbān, at the distance of five *kos* from the town, the emperor alighted, and went on foot to the tomb of the saint (Muʿīnᵘ 'd-Dīn). But sensible people smiled, and said, it was strange that His Majesty should have such a faith in the Khwāja of Ajmīr, whilst he rejected the foundation of everything, our prophet, from whose ' skirt ' hundreds of thousands of saints of the highest degree had sprung."

[p. 273.]

" After Makhdūmᵘ 'l-Mulk and Shaykh ʿAbdᵘ 'n-Nabī had left for Makkah (987), the emperor examined people about the creation of the Qur'ān, elicited their belief or otherwise, in revelation, and raised doubts in them regarding all things connected with the prophet and the imāms. He distinctly denied the existence of *Jinns*, of angels, and of all other beings of the invisible world, as well as the miracles of the prophet and the saints ; he rejected the successive testimony of the witnesses of our faith, the proofs for the truths of the Qur'ān as far as they agree with man's reason, the existence of the soul after the dissolution of the body, and future rewards and punishments in as far as they differed from metempsychosis.

Some copies of the Qur'ān, and a few old graves
Are left as witnesses for these blind men.
The graves, unfortunately, are all silent,
And no one searches for truth in the Qur'ān.
An ʿ*Īd* has come again, and bright days will come—like the face of the bride.
And the cupbearer will again put wine into the jar—red like blood.
The reins of prayer and the muzzle of fasting—once more
Will fall from these asses—alas, alas ! [1]

" His Majesty had now determined publicly to use the formula, ' There is no God, but God, and Akbar is God's representative.' But as this led to commotions, he thought better of it, and restricted the use of the formula to a few people in the Harem. People expressed the date of this event by the words *fitnahā-yi ummat*, the ruin of the Church (987). The emperor tried hard to convert Quṭbᵘ 'd-Dīn Muḥammad Khān and Shāhbāz Khān (*vide* List of grandees, 2nd book, Nos. 28 and 80), and several others. But they staunchly objected. Quṭbᵘ 'd-Dīn said, ' What would the kings of the West, as the Sulṭān of Constantinople, say, if he

[1] Badā,onī bewails the blindness of Akbar, Abū 'l-Fazl, etc., who threw away the means of grace of the Islām (prayers, fasts).

heard all this. Our faith is the same, whether a man hold high or broad views.' His Majesty then asked him, if he was in India on a secret mission from Constantinople, as he showed so much opposition; or if he wished to keep a small place warm for himself, should he once go away from India, and be a respectable man there; he might go at once. Shāhbāz got excited, and took a part in the conversation; and when Bīr Baṛ—that hellish dog—made a sneering remark at our religion, Shāhbāz abused him roundly, and said, 'You cursed infidel, do you talk in this manner? It would not take me long to settle you.' It got quite uncomfortable when His Majesty said to Shāhbāz in particular, and to the others in general, 'Would that a shoeful of excrements were thrown into your faces.'"

[p. 276.]

"'In this year the *Tamghā* (inland tolls) and the *Jazya* (tax on infidels), which brought in several krors of *dāms*, were abolished, and edicts to this effect were sent over the whole empire.'

"In the same year a rebellion broke out at Jaunpūr, headed by Muḥammad Maʕṣūm of Kābul, Muḥammad Maʕṣūm Khān, Muʕizzᵘ 'l-Mulk, ʕArab Bahādur, and other grandees. They objected to Akbar's innovations in religious matters, in as far as these innovations led to a withdrawal of grants of rent-free land. The rebels had consulted Mullā Muḥammad of Yazd (*vide* above, pp. 184, 191), who was Qāẓiyᵘ 'l-quẓāt at Jaunpūr; and on obtaining his opinion that, under the circumstances, rebellion against the king of the land was lawful, they seized some tracts of land, and collected a large army. The course which this rebellion took is known from general histories; *vide* Elphinstone, p. 511. Mullā Muḥammad of Yazd and Muʕizzᵘ 'l-Mulk, in the beginning of the rebellion, were called by the emperor to Āgra, and drowned, on the road, at the command of the emperor, in the Jamnā.

"In the same year the principal ʕUlamās, as Makhdūᵘ 'l-Mulk, Shaykh Munawwar, Mullā ʕAbdᵘ 'sh-Shukūr, etc., were sent as exiles to distant provinces."

[p. 278.]

"Ḥājī Ibrāhīm of Sarhind (*vide* above, p. 111) brought to court an old, worm-eaten MS. in queer characters, which, as he pretended, was written by Shaykh Ibn ʕArabī. In this book, it was said that the *Ṣāḥib-i Zamān*[1] was to have many wives, and that he would shave his beard. Some of the characteristics mentioned in the book as belonging to him

[1] *Ṣāḥib-i Zamān*, or "Man of the Period", is a title frequently given to Imām Mahdi.

were found to agree with the usages of His Majesty. He also brought a fabricated tradition that the son of a *Ṣaḥābī* (one who knew Muḥammad) had once come before the prophet with his beard cut off, when the prophet had said that the inhabitants of Paradise looked like that young man. But as the Ḥājī during discussions, behaved imprudently towards Abū 'l-Faẓl, Ḥakīm Abū 'l-Fatḥ and Shāh Fatḥᵘ 'llāh, he was sent to Rantanbhūr, where he died in 994.

"Farmāns were also sent to the leading Shaykhs and ʿUlamās of the various districts to come to Court, as His Majesty wished personally to inquire into their grants (*vide* 2nd book, *Āʾīn* 19) and their manner of living. When they came, the emperor examined them singly, giving them private interviews, and assigned to them some lands, as he thought fit. But when he got hold of those who had disciples, or held spiritual soirées, or practised similar tricks, he confined them in forts, or exiled them to Bengal or Bhakkar. This practice become quite common . . . . The poor Shaykhs, who were, moreover, left to the mercies of Hindu Financial Secretaries, forgot in exile their spiritual soirées, and had no other place where to live, except mouseholes."

[p. 288.]

"In this year [988] low and mean fellows, who pretended to be learned, but were in reality fools, collected evidences that His Majesty was the *Ṣāḥib-i Zamān*, who would remove all differences of opinion among the seventy-two sects of the Islām. Sharīf of Āmul brought proofs from the writings of Maḥmūd of Basakhwān (*vide* above, p. 186), who had said that, in 990, a man would rise up who would do away with all that was wrong . . .[1] And Khwāja Mawlānā of Shīrāz, the heretic of Jafrdān, came with a pamphlet by some of the Sharīfs of Makkah, in which a tradition was quoted that the earth would exist for 7,000 years, and as that time was now over, the promised appearance of Imām Mahdī would immediately take place. The Mawlānā also brought a pamphlet written by himself on the subject. The Shiʿahs mentioned similar nonsense connected with ʿAlī, and some quoted the following *Rubāʿī*, which is said to have been composed by Nāṣir-i Khusraw,[2] or, according to some, by another poet :—

In 989, according to the decree of fate,
The stars from all sides shall meet together.
In the year of Leo, the month of Leo, and on the day of Leo,
The Lion of God will stand forth from behind the veil.

[1] The text here does not give a clear meaning.

[2] A Persian poet of the fifth century of the *Hijrah.* As he was a free-thinker and Shīʿah, his poems were much read at the time of Akbar. The *Farhang-i Jahāngīrī* is full of verses from the works of this ancient poet.

" All this made His Majesty the more inclined to claim the dignity of a prophet, perhaps I should say, the dignity of something else." [1]

[p. 291.]

" At one of the meetings, the emperor asked those who were present to mention each the name of a man who could be considered the wisest man of the age; but they should not mention kings, as they formed an exception. Each then mentioned that man in whom he had confidence. Thus Ḥakīm Humām (*vide* above, p. 184) mentioned himself, and Shaykh Abū 'l-Fazl his own father.

" During this time, the four degrees of faith in His Majesty were defined. The four degrees consisted in readiness to sacrifice to the Emperor property, life, honour, and religion. Whoever had sacrificed these four things possessed four degrees; and whoever had sacrificed one of these four possessed one degree.

" All the courtiers now put their names down as faithful disciples of the throne."

[p. 299.]

" At this time (end of 989), His Majesty sent Shaykh Jamāl Bakhtyār to bring Shaykh Quṭbᵘ 'd-Dīn of Jalesar who, though a wicked man, pretended to be ' attracted by God '. When Quṭbᵘ 'd-Dīn came, the emperor brought him to a conference with some Christian priests, and rationalists, and some other great authorities of the age. After a discussion the Shaykh exclaimed, ' Let us make a great fire, and in the presence of His Majesty I shall pass through it. And if any one else gets safely through, he proves by it the truth of his religion.' The fire was made. the Shaykh pulled one of the Christian priests by the coat, and said to him, ' Come on, in the name of God ! ' But none of the priests had the courage to go.

" Soon after the Shaykh was sent into exile to Bhakkar, together with other faqīrs, as His Majesty was jealous of his triumph.

" A large number of Shaykhs and Faqīrs were also sent to other places, mostly to Qandahār, where they were exchanged for horses. About the same time, the emperor captured a sect consisting of Shaykhs and disciples, and known under the name of *Ilāhīs*. They professed all sorts of nonsense, and practised deceits. His Majesty asked them whether they repented of their vanities. They replied, ' Repentance is our Maid.' And so they had invented similar names for the laws and religious commands of the Islām, and for the fast. At the command of His Majesty,

---

[1] God.

they were sent to Bhakkar and Qandahār, and were given to merchants in exchange for Turkish colts."

[p. 301.]

"His Majesty was now [990] convinced that the Millenium of the Islāmitic dispensation was drawing near. No obstacle, therefore, remained to promulgating the designs which he had planned in secret. The Shaykhs and ʿUlamās who, on account of their obstinacy and pride, had to be entirely discarded, were gone, and His Majesty was free to disprove the orders and principles of the Islām, and to ruin the faith of the nation by making new and absurd regulations. The first order which was passed was that the coinage should show the era of the Millenium,[1] and that a history of the one thousand years should be written, but commencing from the death of the Prophet. Other extraordinary innovations were devised as political expedients, and such orders were given that one's senses got quite perplexed. Thus the *sijda*, or prostration, was ordered to be performed as being proper for kings; but instead of *sijda*, the word *zamīnbos* was used. Wine also was allowed, if used for strengthening the body, as recommended by doctors; but no mischief or impropriety was to result from the use of it, and strict punishments were laid down for drunkenness, or gatherings and uproars. For the sake of keeping everything within proper limits, His Majesty established a wine-shop near the palace, and put the wife of the porter in charge of it, as she belonged to the caste of wine-sellers. The price of wine was fixed by regulations, and any sick persons could obtain wine on sending his own name and the names of his father and grandfather to the clerk of the shop. Of course, people sent in fictitious names, and got supplies of wine; for who could strictly inquire into such a matter? It was in fact nothing else but licensing a shop for drunkards. Some people even said that pork formed a component part of this wine! Notwithstanding all restrictions, much mischief was done, and though a large number of people were daily punished there was no sufficient check.

"Similarly, according to the proverb,[2] 'Upset, but don't spill,' the prostitutes of the realm (who had collected at the capital, and could scarcely be counted, so large was their number), had a separate quarter of the town assigned to them, which was called *Shaiṭānpūra*, or Devilsville.

[[1] The coin showed the word الف .—B.]

[2] *Kaj dār o marīz,* which is impossible. Akbar's order was well meant; but according to Badā,onī, his Act of Segregation was unpractical. The passage is remarkable, as it shows the open profligacy among the Grandees, which annoyed Akbar very much. For another instance, *vide* Bad. II, p. 20.

A Dārogha and a clerk also were appointed for it, who registered the names of such as went to prostitutes, or wanted to take some of them to their houses. People might indulge in such connexions, provided the toll collectors knew of it. But without permission, no one was allowed to take dancing girls to his house. If any well-known courtiers wanted to have a virgin, they should first apply to His Majesty and get his permission. In the same way, boys prostituted themselves, and drunkenness and ignorance soon led to bloodshed. Though in some cases capital punishment was inflicted, certain privileged courtiers walked about proudly and insolently doing what they liked.

"His Majesty himself called some of the principal prostitutes and asked them who had deprived them of their virginity. After hearing their replies, some of the principal and most renowned grandees were punished or censured, or confined for a long time in fortresses. Among them His Majesty came across one whose name was Rāja Bīr Baṛ, a member of the Divine Faith, who had gone beyond the four degrees and acquired the four cardinal virtues.[1] At that time he happened to live in his jāgīr in the Pargana of Karah; and when he heard of the affair, he applied for permission to turn Jogī; but His Majesty ordered him to come to Court, assuring him that he need not be afraid.

'Beef was interdicted, and to touch beef was considered defiling. The reason of this was that, from his youth, His Majesty had been in company with Hindu libertines, and had thus learnt to look upon a cow—which in their opinion is one of the reasons why the world still exists—as something holy. Besides, the Emperor was subject to the influence of the numerous Hindu princesses of the Harem, who had gained so great an ascendancy over him as to make him forswear beef, garlic, onions, and the wearing of a beard,[2] which things His Majesty still avoids. He had also introduced, though modified by his peculiar views, Hindu customs and heresies into the court assemblies, and introduces them still, in order to please and win the Hindus and their castes; he abstained from everything which they think repugnant to their nature, and looked upon shaving the beard as the highest sign of friendship and affection for him. Hence this custom has become very general. Pandering pimps also expressed the opinion that the beard takes its nourishment from the testicles; for no eunuch had a beard; and one could not exactly see of what merit or

[1] *Fazāʾil-i arbaʕa*, or the four virtues, viz., *ḥikmat* wisdom; *shujāʕat* courage; *ʕiffat* chastity; *ʕadālat* justice. Books on *Akhlāq* divide each into several kinds. Compare the above with the cardinal virtues of the ancient justice, prudence, temperance, and fortitude.

[2] "The last three things are inconvenient in kissing."

importance it was to cultivate a beard. Moreover, former ascetics had looked upon carelessness in letting the beard grow as one way of mortifying one's flesh, because such carelessness exposed them to the reproach of the world; and as, at present, the silly lawyers of the Islām looked upon cutting down the beard as reproachful, it was clear that shaving was now a way of mortifying the flesh, and therefore praiseworthy, but not letting the beard grow. (But if any one considers this argument calmly, he will soon detect the fallacy.) Lying, cheating Muftīs also quoted an unknown tradition, in which it was stated that 'some Qāẓīs' of Persia had shaved their beards. But the words *ka-mā yafˁalū baˁẓᵘ-'l-quẓātⁱ* (as *some Qāẓīs* have done), which occur in this tradition, are based upon a corrupt reading, and should be *ka-mā yafˁalū baˁẓᵘ 'l-ˁuṣāt* (as some *wicked men* have done) . . .

"The ringing of bells as in use with the Christians, and the showing of the figure of the cross, and [1] . . . and other childish playthings of theirs, were daily in practice. The words *Kufr shāyiˁ shud*, or 'heresy became common', express the *Tārīkh* (985). Ten or twelve years after the commencement of these doings, matters had gone so far that wretches like Mīrzā Jānī, chief of Tattah, and other apostates, wrote their confessions on paper as follows:—'I, such a one, son of such a one, have willingly and cheerfully renounced and rejected the Islām in all its phases, whether low or high, as I have witnessed it in my ancestors, and have joined the Divine Faith of Shāh Akbar, and declare myself willing to sacrifice to him my property and life, my honour and religion.' And these papers—there could be no more effective letters of damnation—were handed over to the Mujtahid (Abū 'l-Fazl) of the new Creed, and were considered a source of confidence or promotion. The Heavens might have parted asunder, and earth might have opened her abyss, and the mountains have crumbled to dust!

"In opposition to the Islām, pigs and dogs were no longer looked upon as unclean. A large number of these animals was kept in the Harem, and in the vaults of the castle, and to inspect them daily was considered a religious exercise. The Hindus, who believe in incarnations, said that the boar belonged to the ten forms which God Almighty had once assumed.

"'God is indeed Almighty—but not what they say.'

"The saying of some wise men that a dog had ten virtues, and that a man, if he possesses one of them, was a saint, was also quoted as a proof. Certain courtiers and friends of His Majesty, who were known for their

---

[1] The text has *o balbalān* (?) [كنابلان *cunabula* B.] *kih khushgāh-i īshānast*, which I do not understand.

excellence in every department, and proverbial as court poets,[1] used to put dogs on a tablecloth and feed them, whilst other heretical poets, Persians and Hindustānīs, followed this example, even taking the tongues of dogs into their own mouths, and then boasting of it.

"Tell the Mīr that thou hast, within thy skin, a dog and a carcass.[2]

"A dog runs about in front of the house ; don't make him a messmate.

"The ceremonial ablution after emission of *semen* [3] was no longer considered binding, and people quoted as proof that the essence of man was the *sperma genitale*, which was the origin of good and bad men. It was absurd that voiding urine and excrements should not require ceremonial ablutions, whilst the emission of so tender a fluid should necessitate ablution ; it would be far better, if people would first bathe, and then have connexion.

"Further, it was absurd to prepare a feast in honour of a dead person ; for the corpse was mere matter, and could derive no pleasure from the feast. People should therefore make a grand feast on their birthdays.[4] Such feasts were called *Āsh-i ḥayāt*, food of life.[5]

"The flesh of a wild boar and the tiger was also permitted, because the courage which these two animals possess would be transferred to any one who fed on such meat.

"It was also forbidden to marry one's cousins or near relations, because such marriages are destructive of mutual love. Boys were not to marry before the age of 16, nor girls before 14, because the offspring of early marriages was weakly. The wearing of ornaments and silk dresses at the time of prayer was made obligatory.[6] . . .

"The prayers of the Islām, the fast, nay even the pilgrimage, were henceforth forbidden. Some bastards, as the son of Mullā Mubārak, a worthy disciple of Shaykh Abū 'l-Faẓl wrote treatises, in order to revile and ridicule our religious practices, of course with proofs. His Majesty liked such productions, and promoted the authors.

"The era of the Hijrah was now abolished, and a new era was introduced, of which the first year was the year of the emperor's accession (963). The months had the same names as at the time of the old Persian kings, and as given in the *Niṣāb*ᵘ *'ṣ-ṣibiyān*.[7] Fourteen festivals also were

---

1 Fayẓī.

2 I.e., that you are a dog.

3 According to the law, bathing is required after *jimāʕ* and *iḥtilām*.

4 For the poor.

5 Provisions for the life to come.

6 The Muhammadan law enjoins Muslims to go to the Mosques simply dressed. Silk is forbidden. Muhammadans disapprove of our "Sunday dresses" and pewage.

7 *Vide* p. 43, note 1.

introduced, corresponding to the feasts of the Zoroastrians; but the feasts of the Musalmāns, and their glory were trodden down, the Friday prayer alone being retained, because some old, decrepit, silly people [1] used to go to it. The new era was called *Tārīkh-i Ilāhī*, or 'Divine Era'. On copper coins and gold muhrs, the era of the Millennium [2] was used, as indicating that the end of the religion of Muḥammad, which was to last one thousand years, was drawing near. Reading and learning Arabic was looked upon as a crime; and Muhammadan law, the exegesis of the Qur'ān, and the Tradition, as also those who studied them, were considered bad and deserving of disapproval. Astronomy, philosophy, medicine, mathematics, poetry, history, and novels, were cultivated and thought necessary. Even the letters which are peculiar to the Arabic language, as the ث, ع, ح, ص, ض, and ظ, were avoided. Thus for عبدالله ʕAbdᵘ 'llah, people wrote ابدالله Abdullah; and for احدی Aḥadī, اهدی Ahadī, etc. All this pleased His Majesty. Two verses from the Shāhnāma, which Firdawsī gives as part of a story, were frequently quoted at court—

From eating the flesh of camels and lizards
The Arabs have made such progress,
That they now wish to get hold of the kingdom of Persia.
Fie upon Fate! Fie upon Fate!

"Similarly other verses were eagerly seized, if they conveyed a calumny, as the verses from the . . .,[3] in which the falling out of the teeth of our prophet is alluded to.

"In the same manner, every doctrine and command of the Islām, whether special or general, as the prophetship, the harmony of the Islām with reason, the doctrines of *Ru'yat*, *Taklīf*, and *Takwīn*,[4] the details of the day of resurrection and judgment—all were doubted and ridiculed.

---

[1] The text has an unintelligible sentence.

[2] That is, the word *alf* (one thousand) was put on the coins. From this passage it would appear that coins with *alf* on it (*vide* Marsden, p. 599) were struck about 991.

[3] The word in the text is *Sagarāk* (?). In an engagement Muḥammad lost two of his teeth.

[4] *Rūyat*, or *dīdār-i Ilāhī dar jannat*, the actual seeing of God in Paradise, is a doctrine in high favour with the Sunnīs. The Shiʕahs say there will be no actual seeing.

Taklīf. A man is called *mukallaf bi-sh-sharʕ*, bound by the law, *first*, if he belong to the *Islām*; *secondly*, if he have ʕ*aql* or a sound mind; *thirdly*, if he have reached *bulūgh*, i.e., if he be of age.

Takwīn means existence between two non-existences (ʕ*adamayn*). Thus a present event stands between a past and a future non-existence. This, the Islām says, is the case with the world, which will come to an end. But Akbar denied it, as he did not believe in a day of judgment.

And if anyone did object to this mode of arguing, his answer was not accepted. But it is well known how little chance a man has who cites proofs against one who will reject them, especially when his opponent has the power of life and death in his hands; for equality in condition is a *sine quâ non* in arguing.

A man who will not listen if you bring the Qur*ān and the Tradition,
Can only be replied to by not replying to him.

"Many a family was ruined by these discussions. But perhaps 'discussions' is not the correct name; we should call them meetings for arrogance and defamation. People who sold their religion were busy to collect all kinds of exploded errors, and brought them to His Majesty, as if they were so many presents. Thus Laṯīf Khwāja, who came from a noble family in Turkistān, made a frivolous remark on a passage in Tirmizī's *Shamā*il*,[1] and asked how in all the world the neck of the Prophet could be compared to the neck of an *idol*. Other remarks were passed on the straying camel.[2] Some again expressed their astonishment, that the Prophet, in the beginning of his career, plundered the carvans of Quraysh; that he had fourteen wives; that any married woman was no longer to belong to her husband if the Prophet thought her agreeable, etc. . . . At night, when there were social assemblies, His Majesty told forty courtiers to sit down as 'The Forty',[3] and every one might say or ask what he liked. If then any one brought up a question connected with law or religion, they said, 'You had better ask the Mullās about that, as we only settle things which appeal to man's reason.' But it is impossible for me to relate the blasphemous remarks which they made about the *Ṣaḥābah*, when historical books happened to be read out, especially such as contained the reigns of the first three Khalīfahs, and the quarrel about Fadak, the war of Ṣiffīn,[4] etc.—would that I were

[1] The book of the famous *Muḥaddis* (Collector of Traditions) Tirmizī, which contains all Traditions regarding the figure and looks of the prophet. The word *idol* is expressive of great beauty; but the courtiers laughed at the phrase as unsuited to Muḥammad, who had abolished idols.

[2] This refers to the charge of adultery brought against ςĀyisha Muhammad's favourite wife. The whole story will be found in Sale's Qur*ān, Sur. 24, p. 288.

[3] The *Chihil tanān*, or 40 *Abdāls*. After the death of Muḥammad, the last of the long series of prophets, the earth complained to God, that henceforth she would no longer be honoured by prophets walking on her surface. God promised her that there should always be on earth *forty* (according to some, *seventy-two*) holy men, Abdāls, for whose sake He would let the earth remain. The chief of the Forty is called *Ghaws*.

[4] *Fadak* is a village not far from Makkah, which Fāṯimah claimed as her own; but Abū Bakr would not let her have it. *Siffīn* is a place near the Euphrates, where a battle took place between ςAlī and Muςāwiyah.

Both affairs form, even now-a-days, subjects of quarrel between Sunnīs and Shīςahs. Hence the author of the Dabistān has also made use of them in his Dialogues. The reader will find more particulars in the notes to the English translation of the Dabistān.

deaf! The Shīʿahs, of course, gained the day, and the Sunnīs were defeated; the good were in fear, and the wicked were secure. Every day a new order was given, and a new aspersion or a new doubt came up; and His Majesty saw in the discomfiture of one party a proof for his own infallibility, entirely forgetful of the proverb, 'Who slanders others, slanders himself.' . . . The ignorant vulgar had nothing on their tongues but '*Allāhᵘ Akbar*', and they looked upon repeating this phrase, which created so much commotion, as a daily religious exercise. Mullā Sherī, at this time, composed a *qiṭʿa* of ten verses, in which the following occur:

It is madness to believe with the fool that love towards our prophet
Will ever vanish from the earth.
I smile, if I think that the following verse, in all its silliness,
Will be repeated at the feast of the rich, and as a prayer by the poor:

'This year the emperor has claimed prophetship,
Next year, if God will, he will be god.'

"At the new year's day feasts, His Majesty forced many of the ʿUlamās and the pious, nay even the Qāẓīs and the Muftī of the realm, to drink wine. . . . And afterwards the Mujtahids of the Divine Faith, especially Fayẓī, called out, 'Here is a bumper to the confusion of the lawyers!' On the last day of this feast, when the sun enters the nineteenth degree of Aries (a day called *Sharafᵘ'sh-sharaf*, and considered particularly holy by His Majesty), the grandees were promoted, or received new jāgīrs, or horses, or dresses of honour, according to the rules of hospitality, or in proportion of the tribute they had brought.'

"In this year Gulbadan Begum [Akbar's aunt] and Salīma Sulṭān Begum returned from a pilgrimage to Makkah. Soon after Shāh Abū Turāb also, and Iʿtimād Khān of Gujrāt, returned from the pilgrimage, and brought an immense stone with them, which had to be transported on an elephant. The stone contained, according to Abū Turāb, an impression of the foot of the Prophet. Akbar—though it is difficult to guess the motive—went four *kos* to meet it, and the grandees were ordered to carry the stone themselves by turns, and thus it was brought to town."

[p. 312.]

"In this year, Shaykh Mubārak of Nāgor said in the presence of the emperor to Bīr Bar, 'Just as there are interpolations in your holy books, so there are many in ours (Qurʾān); hence it is impossible to trust either.'

"Some shameless and ill-starred wretches also asked His Majesty, why at the approaching close of the Millenium, he did not make use of the sword, 'the most convincing proof,' as Shāh Ismāʿīl of Persia had done. But His Majesty, at last, was convinced that confidence in him as a leader was a matter of time and good counsel, and did not require the sword. And indeed, if His Majesty, in setting up his claims, and making his innovations, had spent a little money, he would have easily got most of the courtiers, and much more the vulgar, into his devilish nets.

"The following Rubāʿī of Nāṣir-i Khusraw was often quoted at court—

I see in 992 two conjunctions,
I see the sign of Mahdī and that of Antichrist:
Either politics must change or religion.
I clearly see the hidden secret.

"At a council meeting for renovating the religion of the empire, Rāja Bhagawān said, 'I would willingly believe that Hindūs and Musalmāns have each a bad religion; but only tell us where the new sect is, and what opinion they hold, so that I may believe.' His Majesty reflected a little, and ceased to urge the Rāja. But the alteration of the orders of our glorious faith was continued. The *Tārīkh* was found in the words *Iḥdās-i bidʿat*, the innovation of heresy (990).

"During those days also the public prayers and the *azān*, which was chanted five times a day for assembly to prayer in the state hall, were abolished. Names like *Aḥnad, Muḥammad, Muṣṭafa*, etc., became offensive to His Majesty, who thereby wished to please the infidels outside, and the princesses inside the Harem, till, after some time, those courtiers who had such names, changed them; and names as *Yār Muḥammad, Muḥammad Khān*, were altered to *Raḥmat*. To call such ill-starred wretches by the name of our blessed prophet would indeed be wrong, and there was not only room for improvement by altering their names, but it was even necessary to change them, according to the proverb, 'It is wrong to put fine jewels on the neck of a pig.'

"And this destructive fire all broke out in Āgra, burnt down great and small families, and did not even spare their family tombs—May God forsake these wretches!"

[p. 315.]

"In *Rabīʿᵘ 's-ṣānī* 990, Mīr Fatḥᵘ 'llāh came from the Dakhin (*vide* above, p. 34). . . . As he had been an immediate pupil of Mīr Ghiyāṣᵘ 'd-Dīn Manṣūr of Shīrāz, who had not been overstrict in religious matters, His Majesty thought that Fatḥᵘ 'llāh would only be too glad to enter into his religious scheme. But Fatḥᵘ 'llāh was such a staunch Shīʿah, and at the same time such a worldly office-hunter, and such a worshipper of mammon and of the nobility that he would not give up a jot of the tittles of bigoted Shīʿsm. Even in the state hall he said, with the greatest composure, his Shīʿah prayers—a thing which no one else would have dared to do. His Majesty, therefore, put him among the class of the bigots; but he connived at his practices, because he thought it desirable to encourage a man of such attainments and practical knowledge. Once the emperor in Fatḥᵘ 'llāh's presence,[1] said to Bīr Baṛ, 'I really wonder how any one in his senses can believe that a man, whose body has a certain weight, could, in the space of a moment, leave his bed, go up to heaven, there have 90,000 conversations with God, and yet on his return find his bed still warm?' So also was the splitting of the moon ridiculed. 'Why,' said His Majesty, lifting up one foot, 'it is really impossible for me to lift up the other foot! What silly stories men will believe.' And that wretch (Bīr Baṛ) and some other wretches—whose names be forgotten—said, 'Yea, we believe! Yea, we trust!' This great foot-experiment was repeated over and over again. But Fatḥᵘ 'llāh—His Majesty had been every moment looking at him, because he wanted him to say something, for he was a new-comer—looked straight before himself, and did not utter a syllable, though he was all ear."

Here Badā,onī mentions the translations from Sanscrit into Persian, which have been alluded to above, p. 110. It is not quite certain whether the translations were made from Sanscrit or from Hindī translations, or from both. Badā,onī clearly states that for some translations, as at the Atharban, Hindus were used as interpreters. For other works as the Mahābhārat, there may have been Hindī translations or extracts, because Akbar himself (*vide* p. 111, note 2) translated passages to Naqīb K͟hān. Abū 'l-Faẓl also states that he was assisted by Paṇḍits when writing the fourth book of the *Āʾīn*. Compare Sir H. Elliott's *Index to the Historians of India*, p. 259.

[p. 321.]

"In these days (991) new orders were given. The killing of animals on certain days was forbidden, as on Sundays, because this day is sacred to the Sun; during the first eighteen days of the month of Farwardīn; the whole month of Ābān (the month in which His Majesty was born); and on several other days, to please the Hindus. This order was extended over the whole realm, and capital punishment was inflicted on every one

[1] As Fatḥᵘ 'llāh was a good mechanic, Akbar thought that by referring to the weight of a man, and the following experiment with his foot, he would induce Fatḥᵘ 'llāh to make a remark on the Prophet's ascension (*miʿrāj*).

who acted against the command. Many a family was ruined. During the time of these fasts, His Majesty abstained altogether from meat, as a religious penance, gradually extending the several fasts during a year over six months and even more, with the view of eventually discontinuing the use of meat altogether.

"A second order was given that the Sun should be worshipped four times a day, in the morning and evening, and at noon and midnight. His Majesty had also one thousand and one Sanscrit names of the Sun collected, and read them daily, devoutly turning towards the sun; he then used to get hold of both ears, and turning himself quickly round about, used to strike the lower ends of the ears with his fists. He also adopted several other practices connected with sun-worship. He used to wear the Hindu mark on his forehead, and ordered the band to play at midnight and at break of day. Mosques and prayer-rooms were changed into store rooms, or given to Hindu Chaukīdārs. For the word *jamāʿat* (public prayer), His Majesty used the term *jimāʿ* (copulation), and for *hayya* [1] *ala*, he said *yalalā talalā*.

"The cemetery within the town was ordered to be sequestered."

[p. 324.]

"In the same year (991) His Majesty built outside the town two places for feeding poor Hindus and Muhammadans, one of them being called *Khayr-pūra* and the other *Dharmpūra*. Some of Abū'l-Fazl's people were put in charge of them. They spent His Majesty's money in feeding the poor. As an immense number of *Jogīs* also flocked to this establishment, a third place was built, which got the name of *Jogīpūra*. His Majesty also called some of the Jogīs, and gave them at night private interviews, inquiring into abstruse truths; their articles of faith; their occupations; the influence of pensiveness; their several practices and usages; the power of being absent from the body; or into alchemy, physiognomy, and the power of omnipresence of the soul. His Majesty even learned alchemy, and showed in public some of the gold made by him. Once a year also during a night called *Sīvrāt*, a great meeting was held of all Jogīs of the empire, when the emperor ate and drank with the principal Jogīs, who promised him that he should live three and four times as long as ordinary men. His Majesty fully believed it, and connecting their promises with other inferences he had drawn, he got quite convinced of it. Fawning court doctors, wisely enough, found proofs

---

[1] *Hayya ʿala*, for "*hayya ʿala 's-salāh*" [the *waqf* form of *salāt*], "Come quick to the prayer," is a phrase which occurs in the *Azān*. *Yalalā talalā* is a phrase used by drunkards in the height of mirth.

for the longevity of the emperor, and said that the cycle of the moon, during which the lives of men are short, was drawing to its close, and that the cycle of Saturn [1] was at hand, with which a new cycle of ages, and consequently the original longevity of mankind would again commence. Thus they said, it was mentioned in some holy books that men used to live up to the age of one thousand years, whilst in Sanscrit books the ages of some men were put down as ten thousand years ; and in Thibet there were even now a class of *Lāmās*, or Mongolian devotees, and recluses, and hermits, that live two hundred years, and more. For this reason, His Majesty, in imitation of the usages of these Lāmās, limited the time he spent in the harem, curtailed his food and drink, but especially abstained from meat. He also shaved the hair of the crown of his head, and let the hairs at the sides grow, because he believed that the soul of perfect beings, at the time of death, passes out by the crown (which is the tenth opening [2] of the human body) under a noise resembling thunder, which the dying man may look upon as a proof of his happiness and salvation from sin, and as a sign that his soul, by metempsychosis, will pass into the body of some grand and mighty king.

" His Majesty gave his religious system the name of *Tawḥīd-i Ilāhī*, or ' Divine Monotheism '.

" He also called, according to the manner of the Jogīs, a number of special disciples *Chelās* (slaves). A lot of vile, swindling, wicked birds, who were not admitted to the palace, stood every morning opposite to the window, near which His Majesty used to pray to the sun, and declared they had made vows not to rinse their mouths, nor to eat and drink, before they had seen the blessed countenance of the emperor ; and every evening there was a regular court assembly of needy Hindus and Muhammadans, all sorts of people, men and women, healthy and sick, a queer gathering, and a most terrible crowd. No sooner had His Majesty finished saying the 1,001 names of the ' Greater Luminary ', and stepped out into the balcony, than the whole crowd prostrated themselves. Cheating, thieving Brahmins collected another set of 1,001

---

[1] *Zuḥal*, in Persian *Kaywān*, Saturn. This planet is looked upon as the fountain of wisdom. Niẓāmī says *sawād-i safīna ba-kaywān süpurd*, " He (Muḥammad) gave Saturn the power of writing." *Anwār Suhaylī*, in praise of some physician, *Zuḥal shāgird-i ū dar nuqṭa-dānī*, " Saturn in wisdom is his pupil." Hence the famous astronomer Abū'l-Qāsim has the *laqab* (title) of *Ghulām-i Zuḥal*. Besides, there are several cycles of years, over which each of the seven planets reigns. The first cycle was that of Saturn, during which the ages of men were long. The last cycle is that of the moon, during which people do not attain a very old age. It existed already at the time of Ḥāfiẓ, who says, *In chi shorīst ki dar dawr-i qamar mībīnīm.* " What misfortune is this which we witness in the cycle of the moon ? "

[2] *Vide* my text edition, fourth book, p. 8, l. 9.

names of 'His Majesty the Sun', and told the emperor that he was an incarnation, like Rām Kishn and other infidel kings; and though Lord of the world, he had assumed his shape, in order to play with the people of our planet. In order to flatter him, they also brought Sanscrit verses, said to have been taken from the sayings of ancient sages, in which it was predicted that a great conqueror would rise up in India, who would honour Brahmins and cows, and govern the earth with justice. They also wrote this nonsense on old looking paper, and showed it to the emperor, who believed every word of it.

"In this year also, in the state hall of Fatḥpur, the ten cubit square of the Ḥanafīs and the *Qullatayn* [1] of the Shāfiʕīs and Shīʕahs were compared. The fluid quantum of the Ḥanafīs was greater than that of the others.

"His Majesty once ordered that the Sunnīs should stand separately from the Shīʕahs, when the Hindustānīs, without exception, went to the Sunnī side, and the Persians to the Shīʕah side."

[p. 336.]

"During this year [992], Mullā Ilāhdād of Amrohah and Mullā Sherī attended at Court, in order to flatter the emperor; for they had been appointed to *ṣadrships* in the Duāb of the Panjāb. Mullā Sherī presented to His Majesty a poem made by him, entitled *Hazār Shuāʕ* or 'The Thousand Rays', which contained 1,000 *qiṭaʕs* in praise of the Sun. His Majesty was much pleased."

At the feast of the emperor's accession in 992, numerous conversions took place. [Bad. II, p. 338.]

"They were admitted as disciples in sets of twelve, one set at a time, and declared their willingness to adopt the new principles, and to follow the new religion. Instead of the usual tree,[2] His Majesty gave his likeness, upon which the disciples looked as a symbol of faith and the advancement of virtue and prosperity. They used to wrap it up in cloth studded with jewels, and wore it on the top of their turbans. The phrase '*Allāh*[u] *Akbar*' was ordered to be used as the heading in all writings. Playing with dice, and taking interest, were allowed, and so in fact was everything else admitted which is forbidden in the Islām. A play-house was even

---

[1] *Qullatayn*, two large jars containing 1,200 *raṭl-i ʕrāqī* (ʕirāqī pounds) of water. According to the Shīʕahs and the Shāfiʕī sect, water does not become *najis*, or soiled, from its being used, provided the quantity of water weigh not less than 1,200 *raṭl*, or the cube of 3½ spans. Hanīfah fixed (10 ذراع),[2] just deep enough that the hand, in passing over it, do not touch the bottom. The experiment which Akbar made had for its object to throw blame on the Ḥanafī Sunnīs.

[2] Heads of sects give their pupils trees, not of genealogy, but of discipleship as, Aḥmad, disciple of ʕAlī, disciple of Muʕīn, disciple of Bayazīd, etc., ending with their own name and the name of that disciple to whom the tree (*shajara*) is given.

built at Court, and money from the exchequer was lent to the players on interest (*vide* Second book, *Āʾīn* 15). Interest and *shatal* (money given at the end of the play to the bystanders) were looked upon as very satisfactory things.

" Girls before the age of fourteen, and boys before sixteen, were not to marry, and the story of the marriage night of the Prophet with *Ṣiddīqa*[1] was totally disapproved of. But why should I mention other blasphemies ?—May the attention which any one pays to them run away like quicksilver—really I do not know what human ears cannot bear to hear !

" The sins which all prophets are known to have committed, were cited as a reason why people should not believe the words of the prophets. So especially in the case of David[2] and the story of Uriah. And if any one dared to differ from the belief of these men, he was looked upon as fit to be killed, or as an apostate and everlastingly damned, or he was called a lawyer and enemy of the emperor. But according to the proverb, ' What people sow, that they shall reap,' they themselves became notorious in the whole world as the greatest heretics by their damnable innovations, and ' the infallible ' authority got the nickname of *Abū-jahl*.[3] Yes, ' If the king is bad, the Vizier is worse.' Looking after worldly matters was placed before religious concerns ; but of all things, these innovations were the most important, and everything else was accessory.

" In order to direct another blow at the honour of our religion, His Majesty ordered that the stalls of the fancy bāzārs, which are held on New Year's day, should, for a stated time, be given up for the enjoyment of the Begums and the women of the Harem, and also for any other married ladies. On such occasions, His Majesty spent much money ; and the important affairs of harem people, marriage-contracts, and betrothals of boys and girls, were arranged at such meetings.

" The real object of those who became disciples was to get into office ;

---

[1] *Ṣiddīqa* is the title of ʿ*Āyisha*, the daughter of Abū Bakr. " She was six years old, when she was engaged to Muḥammad, who was then fifty years old. The actual marriage took place when she was nine years old. ' I sat,' she relates, ' with other girls in a swing, when my mother called me. I went to her, not knowing what she wanted. She took my hand and led me to the door of the house. I now guessed what she wished to do with me ; my heart throbbed, but I soon got again composed. I washed my face and my head, and was taken inside, where several women were assembled, who congratulated me, and dressed me up. When they had done, they handed me over to the Prophet.' As she was so young, she took her toys to the house of the Prophet. The Prophet loved her so much, that even in the mosque, at the time of the service, he put his head under her veil and caressed her, and played with her hair (Thaʿlabī Tafsīr 2, 180) ; and he told the faithful that she would be his wife in Paradise." From Sprenger's Life of Muhammad, III, p. 62.

[2] David counts as a prophet. The book revealed to him is the *zabūr*, or the Psalms.

[3] Properly *father of ignorance*. Badāʾonī means Abū 'l-Faẓl, which name signifies *father of wisdom*. Besides, Abū 'l-Faẓl had the title (*takhallus*) ʿ*Allāmī*, the most learned.

and though His Majesty did everything to get this out of their heads, he acted very differently in the case of Hindus, of whom he could not get enough; for the Hindus, of course, are indispensable; to them belongs half the army and half the land. Neither the Hindūstānīs nor the Moghuls can point to such grand lords as the Hindus have among themselves. But if others than Hindus came, and wished to become disciples at any sacrifice, His Majesty reproved or punished them. For their honour and zeal he did not care, nor did he notice whether they fell in with his views or not."

[p. 340.]

"In this year Sulṭān Khẉāja died. He also belonged to the elect disciples of His Majesty. After burying him, they laid down a new rule. They put a grate over his grave in such a manner that the light of the rising sun, which cleanses from all sins, could shine on the face of the corpse. People said, they had seen fiery tongues resting over his mouth, but God knows best."

During the month of *Ṣafar* (the second month of the year) 994, Akbar's troops were defeated by the Yūsuf-zā,īs. Badā,onī says (p. 350):

"Nearly 8,000 men, perhaps even more, were killed. Bīr Baṛ also, who had fled from fear of his life, was slain, and entered the row of the dogs in hell, and thus got something for the abominable deeds he had done during his lifetime. During the last night attack, many grandees and persons of renown were killed, as Ḥasan Khān,[1] and Khẉāja ʿArab, paymaster (colonel) of Khān Jahān and Mullā Sherī, the poet, and many others whose names I cannot specify. The words *az Khẉāja ʿArab ḥayf*[2] express the Tārīkh of the defeat, by one less. Ḥakīm Abū 'l-Faẓl and Zayn Khān on the 5th Rabīʿu l-awwal, reached with their defeated troops the fort of Āṭak. . . . But His Majesty cared for the death of no grandee more than for that of Bīr Baṛ. He said, 'Alas! they could not even get his body out of the pass, that it might have been burned'; but at last, he consoled himself with the thought that Bīr Baṛ was now free and independent of all earthly fetters, and as the rays of the sun were sufficient for him, there was no necessity that he should be cleansed by fire."

New orders were given in the beginning of 995. [Page 356.]

"No one was to marry more than one wife, except in cases of barrenness; but in all other cases the rule was, 'One God, and one wife.' Women,

---

[1] *Vide* List of grandees, Text edition of the Āʿīn, p. 227, No. 220, where for *Husayn* read *Ḥasan*. In the MSS. of the Āʿīn he is called بتني or بثني. My MS. of the Ṭabaqāt reads بثنى افغان *Patanī Afghān*, and calls him a *Hazārī*. The edition of Badā,onī has wrong بنى. His biography is not given in the *Maʿāṣiru 'l-umarā*.

[2] The letters give 993; hence one more=994.

on reaching the limit of their period of fertility, when their courses stop, should no longer wish for the husband. If widows liked to re-marry, they might do so, though this was [1] against the ideas of the Hindus. A Hindu girl, whose husband had died before the marriage was consummated, should not be burnt. If, however, the Hindus thought this a hardship, they should not be prevented (from burning the girl); but then a Hindu widow should take the girl . . . [2]

"Again, if disciples meet each other, one should say '*Allāh*ᵘ *Akbar*', and the other should respond '*Jall*ᵃ *Jallālu-h*ᵘ'. These formulas were to take the place of our *salām*, and the answer to the *salām*. The beginning of counting Hindu months should be the 28th day, and not the 16th, because the latter was the invention and innovation of Bikramājīt. The Hindu feasts, likewise, were to take place in accordance with this rule. But the order was not obeyed, though farmāns to that effect, as early as 990, had been sent to Gujrāt and Bengal.

"Common people should no longer learn Arabic, because such people were generally the cause of much mischief. Cases between Hindus should be decided by learned Brahmins, and not by Musalmān Qāẓīs. If it were necessary to have recourse to oaths they should put heated irons into the hands of the accused, who was guilty if his hands were burnt, but innocent if not; or they should put the hands of the accused into hot, liquid butter; or the accused should jump into water, and if he came to the surface before an arrow had returned to the ground, which had been shot off when the man jumped into the water, he was guilty.

"People should be buried with their heads towards the east and their feet towards the west.[3] His Majesty even commenced to sleep in this position."

[p. 363.]

"In the same year the prohibition of the study of Arabic was extended to all. People should learn astronomy, mathematics, medicine, and philosophy. The *Tārīkh* of this order is *Fasād-i fazl* (995) . . .

"On the 10th day of Muḥarram 996, His Majesty had invited the Khān Khānān, and Mān Singh (who had just been appointed governor of Bahār, Ḥājīpūr and Patna); and whilst they were drinking, His Majesty commenced to talk about the Divine Faith, in order to test Mān Singh. He said without reserve, 'If Your Majesty mean by the

[1] The text has *was not against the ideas of the Hindus* (?).

[2] The text of the whole passage is doubtful. The readings of the three MSS. which Mawlawī Āghā Aḥmad ʿAlī had in editing Badā,onī, give no sense.

[3] This was an insult, because the Muhammadans in India face the west during prayer. *Vide* Journal Asiatic Society, Bengal, for 1868, p. 56.

term of membership, willingness to sacrifice one's life, I have given pretty clear proofs, and Your Majesty might dispense with examining me; but if the term has another meaning, and refers to religion, surely I am a Hindu. And if I am to become a Muhammadan, Your Majesty ought to say so—but besides Hinduism and Islām, I know of no other religion.' The emperor then gave up urging him.

"During the month of *Ṣafar* 996, Mīrzā Fūlād Beg Barlās managed to get one night Mullā Aḥmad of Thathah, on some pretext, out of his house, and stabbed at him, because the Mullā openly reviled [as Shīʿahs do] the companions of the prophet. The *Tārīkh* of this event is expressed by the words *Zihe khanjar-i Fūlād*, 'Hail, steel of Fūlād,' or by *Khūk-i saqarī*, 'hellish hog!' And really, when this dog of the age was in his agony, I saw that his face looked just like the head of a pig,[1] and others too witnessed it—O God! we take refuge with Thee against the evil which may befall us! His Majesty had Mīrzā Fūlād tied to the foot of an elephant and dragged through the streets of Lāhor; for when Ḥakīm Abū-Fatḥ, at the request of the emperor, had asked the Mīrzā, whether he had stabbed at the Mullā from religious hatred, he had said, 'If religious hatred had been my motive, it would have been better to kill a greater one[2] than the Mullā.' The Ḥakīm reported these words to His Majesty, who said, 'This fellow is a scoundrel; he must not be allowed to remain alive,' and ordered his execution, though the people of the harem asked the emperor to spare him for his general bravery and courage. The Mullā outlived the Mīrzā three or four days. The Shīʿahs, at the time of washing his corpse, say that, in conformity with their religion, they put a long nail into the *anus*, and plunged him several times into the river.[3] After his burial, Shaykh Fayẓī and Shaykh Abū'l-Faẓl put guards over his grave; but notwithstanding all precaution, during the year His Majesty went to Kashmīr, the people of Lāhor one night took the hideous corpse of the Mullā from the grave, and burned it."

[pp. 375, 376, 380.]

"In 999, the flesh of oxen, buffaloes, goats, horses, and camels, was forbidden. If a Hindu woman wished to be burnt with her husband, they should not prevent her; but she should not be forced. Circumcision was

---

[1] Sunnīs assert that this transfiguration into an animal (*maskh*) happens very often to Shīʿahs, because they revile the *Ṣaḥābah*. Fayẓī, according to Badā,onī, looked and barked like a dog, when dying. Another thing which the Sunnīs all over India quote as a great proof of the correctness of their *mazhab*, is that no Shīʿah can ever become a *ḥāfiẓ*, i.e., no Shīʿah can commit the Qorān to memory.

[2] Either Akbar or Abū 'l-Faẓl.

[3] This was done to clean the intestines of *faeces*, which were thrown into the river from which the Sunnīs got their water.

forbidden before the age of twelve, and was then to be left to the will of the boys. If any one was seen eating together with a butcher, he was to lose his hand, or if he belonged to the butcher's relations, the fingers which he used in eating.

" In 1000, the custom of shaving off the beard was introduced."

" In 1002, special orders were given to the *kotwāls* to carry out Akbar's commands. They will be found in the Third book of the *Āʿīn*, *Āʿīn* 5. The following are new :—

" If any of the *darsanīyya* [1] disciples died, whether man or woman, they should hang some uncooked grains and a burnt brick round the neck of the corpse, and throw it into the river, and then they should take out the corpse, and burn it at a place where no water was. But this order is based upon a fundamental rule, which His Majesty indicated, but which I cannot here mention.

" If a woman was older than her husband by twelve years, he should not lie with her, and if a young girl was found running about town, whether veiled or not, or if a woman was bad, or quarrelled with her husband, she should be sent to the quarter of the prostitutes, to do there what she liked."

[p. 391.]

" At the time of famines and distress, parents were allowed to sell their children, but they might again buy them, if they acquired means to pay their price. Hindus who, when young, had from pressure become Musalmāns, were allowed to go back to the faith of their fathers. No man should be interfered with on account of his religion, and every one should be allowed to change his religion, if he liked. If a Hindu woman fall in love with a Muhammadan, and change her religion, she should be taken from him by force, and be given back to her family. People should not be molested if they wished to build churches and prayer rooms, or idol temples, or fire temples."

[p. 398.]

" In this year Aʿẓam Khān returned from Makkah, where he had suffered much harm at the hands of the Sharīfs,[2] and throwing away the blessing which he had derived from the pilgrimage, joined, immediately on his return, the Divine Faith, performing the *sijda* and following all other rules of discipleship ; he cut off his beard, and was very forward at social meetings and in conversation. He learnt the rules of the new faith

---

[1] From *darsan*, for which *vide* p. 165.

[2] This is the title of the rulers of Makkah.

from the Reverend Master Abū 'l-Faẓl, and got Ghāzīpūr and Ḥājīpūr as *jāgīr*."

[p. 404.]

"During the Muḥarram of 1004, Ṣadr Jahān, muftī of the empire, who had been promoted to a commandership of One Thousand, joined the Divine Faith, as also his two over-ambitious sons; and having taken the *Shaṣt* [1] of the new religion, he ran into the net like a fish, and got his *Hazārīship*. He even asked His Majesty what he was to do with his beard, when he was told to let it be. On the same day, Mullā Taqī of Shushtar [2] joined, who looks upon himself as the learned of all learned, and is just now engaged in rendering the Shāhnāma into prose, according to the wishes of the emperor, using the phrase *jall^a ʿaẓmatu-h^u w^a ʿazz^a shānu-h^u*,[3] wherever the word *Sun* occurs. Among others that joined were Shaykhzāda Gosāla Khān of Banāras; Mullā Shāh Muḥammad of Shāhābād [4]; and Ṣūfī Aḥmad, who claimed to belong to the progeny of the famous Muḥammad Ghawṣ. They all accepted the four degrees of faith, and received appointments as Commanders from One Hundred to Five Hundred, gave up their beards agreeably to the rules, and thus looked like the youths in Paradise. The words *mū-tarāsh-i chand*, or 'several shavers', express the *tārīkh* of this event (1004). The new candidates behaved like Hindus that turn Muhammadan,[5] or like those who are dressed in red clothes, and look in their joy towards their relations, who say to them 'My dear little man, these rags will be old to-morrow, but the Islām will still remain on your neck'. This Aḥmad, 'the little Ṣūfī,' is the same who claimed to be the pupil, or rather the perfect successor, of Shaykh Aḥmad of Egypt. He said that at the express desire of that religious leader of the age, he had come to India and the Shaykh had frequently told him to assist the Sulṭān of India, should he commit an error, and lead him back from everlasting damnation. But the opposite was the case."

So far, Badā,onī. We have, therefore, the following list of members of the Divine Faith. With the exception of Bīr Bar, they are all Muḥammadans; but to judge from Badā,onī's remarks, the number of those that took the *Shaṣt* must have been much larger.

1. Abū 'l-Faẓl.
2. Fayẓī, his brother, Akbar's court-poet.

---

[1] *Shaṣt*, which has been explained on p. 174, also means *a fish hook*.
[2] *Vide* List of Grandees, Second Book, No. 352.
[3] Because Muhammadans use such phrases after the name of God.
[4] *Vide* p. 112, note 3.
[5] That is, over-zealous.

3. Shaykh Mubārak, of Nāgor, their father.
4. Ja'far Beg Āṣaf Khān, of Qazwīn, a historian and poet.
5. Qāsim-i Kāhī, a poet.
6. 'Abdᵘ 's-Ṣamad, Akbar's court-painter ; also a poet.
7. A'ẓam Khān Koka, after his return from Makkah.
8. Mullā Shāh Muḥammad of Shāhābād, a historian.
9. Ṣūfī Aḥmad.
10 to 12. Ṣadr Jahān, the crown-lawyer, and his two sons.
13. Mīr Sharīf of Āmul, Akbar's apostle for Bengal.
14. Sulṭān Khwāja, a ṣadr.
15. Mīrzā Jānī, chief of Thathah.
16. Taqī of Shustar, a poet and commander of two hundred.
17. Shaykhzāda Gosāla of Banāras.
18. Bīr Bar.

Nos. 4 to 6 are taken from the *Ā'īn* ; the others are mentioned in the above extracts from Badāonī. The literary element is well represented in the list.

The above extracts from Badāonī possess a peculiar value, because they show the rise and progress of Akbar's views, from the first doubt of the correctness of the Islām to its total rejection, and the gradual establishment of a new Faith combining the principal features of Hinduism and the Fireworship of the Pārsīs. This value does not attach to the scattered remarks in the *Ā'īn*, nor to the longer article in the Dabistān.

As the author of the latter work has used Badāonī, it will only be necessary to collect the few remarks which are new.

The following two miracles are connected with Akbar's birth.

[*Dabistān*, p. 390.[1]]

" Khwāja Mas'ūd, son of Khwāja Maḥmūd, son of Khwāja *Murshidᵘ 'l-Ḥaqq*, who was a gifted *Ṣāḥib-i ḥāl*,[2] said to the writer of this book, " My father related, he had heard from great saints, that the Lord of the faith and the world 'reveals himself'. I did not know, whether that august personage had appeared, or would appear, till, at last, one night I saw that event, and when I awoke, I suddenly arrived at that place, where the blessed [2] Lord was born, namely on a Sunday of the month of Rajab of the year 949, the lord Jalālᵘ 'd-Dīn Akbar, the august son of Humāyūn Pādishāh and Ḥamīda Bānū Begum."

The second miracle has been related above, on p. 172, note 2. These two miracles make up the first of the four chapters, into which the author

---

[1] *Vide* also *Shea and Troyer's* English translation of the Dabistān, III, p. 49.
[2] *Vide* p. 171, note 2.

of the Dabistān has divided his article on the "Divine Faith". The second chapter contains religious dialogues, and extracts from Badā,onī, which are rather conjecturally rendered in Shea's Translation. The third chapter contains remarks on the worship of the sun and stars, chiefly with reference to the sun-worship of the Tātārs.[1] The last chapter contains extracts from the third and fifth books of the *Ā'īn*.

p. 410. "His Majesty also sent money to Īrān, to bring to India a wise Zoroastrian of the name of Ardsher."[2]

p. 412. Abū 'l-Fazl wrote, *as a counterpart to his commentary on the Āyatu 'l-kursī* (p. 177), a preface to the translation of the Mahābhārat (*vide* p. 111) of two *juz*.

p. 413. "When Sultān Khwāja,[3] who belonged to the members of the Divine Faith, was near his death, *he said that he hoped His Majesty would not have him buried like a mad man.* He was therefore buried in a grave *with a peculiar lamp,* and a grate was laid over it, so that the greater luminary, whose light cleanses from all sins, might shine upon him. . . .

"Should a Hindu woman fall in love with a Muhammadan, and be converted to the Islām, she would be taken away by force and handed over to her family; *but so should also a Musalmān woman, who had fallen in love with a Hindu, be prevented from joining Hinduism.*"[4]

p. 414. "I heard from Mullā Tarson of Badakhshān, who was a Ḥanafī by sect, that once during the year 1058 he had gone on a pilgrimage to Sikandrah, the burial place of Akbar. 'One of my companions,' he said, 'declined to enter the pure mausoleum, and even abused the Representative of God [Akbar]. My other companions said, 'If Akbar possesses hidden knowledge, that man will certainly come to grief.' Soon after a piece of a broken stone fell down, and crushed his toe."

p. 431. "In Multān, I saw *Shāh Salāmu 'llah,* who has renounced the world, and is a *muwaḥḥid* (Unitarian). He is very rigid in discipline and avoids the society of men. He said, he had often been in company with Jalālu 'd-Dīn Akbar, and had heard him frequently say, 'Had I

---

[1] The author of the Dabistān gives much prominence to the idea that the power and success of the Tātārs was in some way mysteriously connected with their sun and star worship, and that their conversion to the Islām was looked upon as the beginning of their decline. It looks as if the writer wished to connect this idea with Akbar's successes and sun worship.

[2] Regarding this Ardsher, *vide* Journal Asiatic Society, Bengal, for 1868, p. 14. Akbar's fire temple was in the Harem.

[3] *Vide* above, p. 214.

[4] The words in italics are not in Badā,onī. The object of the order was evidently to prevent a woman from doing what she liked; for, according to the Muhammadans, women are looked upon as *nāqiṣu 'l-ʕaql*.

formerly possessed the knowledge which I now have, I would never have chosen a wife for myself; for upon old women I look as mothers, on women of my age as sisters, and on girls as daughters.' A friend of mine said, he had heard Nawāb ˁAbdᵘ 'l-Ḥasan called Lashkar Khān of Mash,had, report the same as having been said by Akbar.

"Salāmᵘ 'llāh also said that God's Representative (Akbar) had often wept and said, 'O that my body were larger than all bodies together, so that the people of the world could feed on it without hurting other living animals.'

"A sign of the sagacity of this king is this, that he employed in his service people of all classes,[1] Jews, Persians, Tūrānīs, etc., because one class of people, if employed to the exclusion of others, would cause rebellions, as in the case of the Uzbaks and Qizilbāshes (Persians), who used to dethrone their kings. Hence Shāh ˁAbbās, son of Sulṭān Khudā-banda-yi Ṣafawī, imitated the practice of Akbar, and favoured the Gurjīs (Georgians). Akbar paid likewise no regard to hereditary power, or genealogy and fame, but favoured those whom he thought to excel in knowledge and manners."

The passages in the Āˀīn which refer to Akbar's religious views are the following:—p. III; 11; 50; 51; 56; 59; 60; 61, ll. 20 to 24; Āˀīn 26, p. 64; p. 96, notes 3 and 4, the Sanscrit names being very likely those which were alluded to by Badā,onī, *vide* above p. 189, l. 19; p. 103, note 3; p. 110, note 1; 111–113; p. 115, l. 4, because the "making of likenesses" is as much forbidden by the Islām as it was interdicted by the Mosaic law; Āˀīn 72, p. 162; 168; Āˀīn 77, p. 162; Āˀīn 81, p. 226. In the Second Book, Āˀīns 18, 19, 22–5; in the Third Book, end of Āˀīn 1 (Tārīkh Ilāhī); Āˀīns 2, 5, 9, 10; and lastly, the greater part of the Fifth Book.

It will be observed that the remarks on Akbar's religious views do not extend beyond the year 1596, when the greater part of the Āˀīn had been completed. Badā,onī's history ends with A.H. 1004, or A.D. 1595; but his remarks on Akbar's religion become more and more sparing towards the end, and as subsequent historians, even Jahāngīr "Memoirs", are almost entirely silent on the religious ideas of the emperor, we have no means of following them up after 1596. Akbar, in all probability, continued worshipping the sun, and retained all other peculiarities of his monotheistic Pārsī-Hinduism, dying as he had lived. The story related in that edition of Jahāngīr's Memoirs, which has been translated by Major Price, that Akbar died as a good Musalmān, and

[1] *Vide* the notes of Āˀīn 30 of the Second Book.

"repented" on his death-bed, is most untrustworthy, as every other particular of that narrative.[1]

With Akbar's death,[2] the Divine Faith died out. Akbar, solely relying on his influence and example, had established no priesthood, and had appointed no proper person for propagating his faith. If we except the influence which his spirit of toleration exerted, the masses had remained passive. Most of the members, mentioned on p. 219, had died before Akbar; such as were still alive, as Sharīf of Āmul took again to sophistry, and tried to create sensations under Jahāngīr.[3] As Jahāngīr did not trouble himself about any religion, Akbar's spirit of toleration soon changed to indifference, and gradually died out, when a reaction in favour of bigotry set in under Awrangzeb. But people still talked of the Divine

---

[1] The story of Akbar's "conversion" is also repeated in Elphinstone's History, second edition, p. 531. The Mullā whom Akbar, according to Price's Memoirs, is said to have called is Ṣadr Jahān, who, as remarked above on p. 219 was a member of the Divine Faith. This in itself is improbable. Besides, the Tuzuk-i Jahāngīrī, as published by Sayyid Aḥmad, says nothing about it. Nor does the Iqbālnāma, a poor production (though written in beautiful Irānī Persian), or Khāfī Khān, allude to the conversion which, if it had taken place, would certainly have been mentioned. Khāfī Khān especially would have mentioned it, because he says of Badā,onī, that he said and wrote about the religious views of the Emperor things which he should not have related (*vide Khāfī Khān*, I, p. 196). The silence of the author of the Dabistān is still more convincing, whilst the story of Mullā Tarson, and the abuse uttered by his companion against Akbar (p. 220), are proofs that Akbar did not "repent". To this we have to add that Jahāngīr, in his Memoirs, adopts a respectful phraseology when mentioning the sun, which he calls *Ḥaẓrat Nayyir-i Aʕẓam*; he also continued the *sijda*, though offensive to pious Muhammadans, and Akbar's Solar Era, though it involved a loss to the revenue because for every 33 lunar years, the state only received taxes for 32 solar years; he allowed some Hindu customs at Court, as the *Rākhī* (*vide* above p. 193), and passed an order not to force Hindus to join the Islām (*Tuzuk*, p. 100).

[2] Akbar died on the *Shab-i Chahārshambih*, 12*th Jumāda 'l-ukhrā* 1014 A.H., which, according to note 3 of p. 180, is our Tuesday night [not Wednesday, as in Price, and all European Historians], the 15th October, 1605, old style. Hence Akbar would have died in the night which followed the day on which he celebrated his sixty-third birthday if we adopt our mode of reckoning; *vide* p. 64, note 1.

There is some confusion in the histories regarding the exact day of Akbar's death.

The *Pādishāhnāma* (vol. I, p. 66) says that Akbar died at the age of sixty-three (solar) years and one day, in the night of the *Chahārshambih* (the night between Tuesday and Wednesday) of the 12th *Jumāda 'l-ukhrā*, corresponding to the 2nd *Abān* of Akbar's Era. The *Mirʕāt* and *Khāfī Khān* (I, p. 235) give the same; the latter adds that Akbar died at midnight.

Pādishāhnāma (p. 69) and Khāfī Khān (p. 246) fix the *julūs* or accession, of Jahāngīr for Thursday, the 20th *Jumāda 'l-ukhrā*, or the 10th Ābān, i.e. 8 days after Akbar's death.

Muḥammad Hādī, in his preface to the *Tuzuk-i Jahāngīrī*, says that Akbar died on the *Shab-i Chahārshambih*, 13*th Jumada 'l-ukhrā*; and Sayyid Aḥmad's edition of the Tuzuk refers the *Julūs* to Thursday, the *eighth Jumada 'l-ukhrā*; but the word هشتم is often confounded in MSS. with بیستم.

Again the *Mirʕāt*, and Sharīf-i Īrānī in his *Iqbālnāma*, mention the *Julūs* as having taken place on Thursday, the *eleventh Jumada 'l-ukhrā*. Lastly, the prefaces of the *Farhang-i Jahāngīrī* refer the *julūs* to the third Thursday [the twentieth day] of *Jumāda 'l-awwal* [a mistake for *al-ukhrā*], corresponding to the *roz-i khur*, or the *eleventh* of Ābān.

[3] *Vide* Tuzuk, p. 22.

Faith in 1643 or 1648, when the author of the Dabistān collected his notes on Akbar's religion.[1]

Āʾīn 78.

THE MUSTER OF ELEPHANTS.

The beginning of the musters is made with this animal. The *Khāṣa* elephants with their furniture and ornaments are the first which are daily brought before His Majesty, namely, ten on the first day of every solar month. After this, the *Ḥalqa* elephants are mustered, according to their number. On Tuesdays from ten to twenty are mustered. The Bitikchī, during the muster, must be ready to answer any questions as to the name of each animal (there are more than five thousand elephants, each having a different name. His Majesty knows to which section most of the elephants belong—ten elephants form a section of ten (*dahā,ī*), and are in charge of an experienced officer); as to how each elephant came into the possession of His Majesty; the price; the quantity of food; the age of the animal; where it was born; the period of heat, and the duration of that state each time; the date when an elephant was made *khāṣa*; its promotion in the *ḥalqas*; the time when the tusks are cut; how many times His Majesty has mounted it; how many times it was brought for riding out; the time of the last muster; the condition of the keepers; the name of the Amīr in charge. For all other elephants eight things are to be reported, *viz.*, the change of its name (?); the repetition of it; its price; how it came into the possession of His Majesty; whether it is fit for riding, or for carrying burdens; its rank; whether it has plain furniture or not; which rank the Fawjdār has assigned to it. The rule is, that every Fawjdār divides his elephants into four classes, separating those that are best from those that are worst, whether they are to remain with him or whether he has to give some to other Fawjdārs.

Each day five *taḥwīlī* (transferable) elephants are inspected by an

---

[1] Only one of Akbar's innovations, the *Sijda* was *formally* abolished by Shāhjahān. "During the reigns of ʿ*Arsh-āshyānī* [Akbar], and *Jannat-makānī* [Jahāngīr], it was customary for courtiers on meeting their Majesties, or on receiving a present, to prostrate themselves, placing the forehead on the ground. . . . This custom had also obtained in antiquity, but had been abolished by the Islām. . . . When His Majesty [Shāhjahān] mounted the throne, he directed his imperial care to *the reintroduction of the customs of the Islām, the strict observance of which had died away*, and turned his august zeal to re-building the edifice of the law of the Prophet, *which had all but decayed.* Hence on the very day of his accession, His Majesty ordered that putting the forehead on the ground should be restricted to God. Mahābat Khān, the Commander-in-Chief, objected at first, etc. His Majesty would not even allow the *Zamīnbos*, or kissing the ground, and subsequently introduced a fourth *Taslīm* [Akbar had fixed three, *vide* p. 166, l. 5]." *Pādishāhnāma*, I, p. 110.

experienced man. The following custom is observed: When new elephants arrive for the government, they are handed over in fifties or hundreds to experienced officers, who fix their ranks. Such elephants are called *Taḥwīlī* elephants. When His Majesty inspects them, their rank is finally settled, and the elephants are transferred to the proper sections. Every Sunday one elephant is brought before His Majesty, to be given away as a present to some deserving servant. Several *ḥalqas* are set apart for this purpose. The rank of the *k͟hāṣa* elephants formerly depended on the number of times they had been inspected by His Majesty; but now their precedence is fixed by the number of times His Majesty has mounted them. In the *ḥalqas*, the precedence of elephants is determined by the price. When all elephants have been mustered, the *k͟hāṣa* elephants are again examined, ten every day. Then come the elephants of the princes, who mostly march them past themselves. After them come the *ḥalqas*. As they are arranged in sections according to the price, some elephants have, at every muster, their value either enhanced or lowered, and are then put among their equals. For this reason, many Fawjdārs are anxious to complete their sets, and place themselves for this purpose in a row at the time of the musters. His Majesty then gives the elephants to whomsoever he likes. If the number of the elephants of any Fawjdār is found correct, some more are put in his charge; for such officers are thought of first. Fawjdārs, whose elephants are found to be lean, are preferred, in making up the complements, to such as bring less than their original number. Each Fawjdār receives some, provided he musters all his elephants. The Mushrif (accountant) receives orders where to keep the elephants.

The elephants of the grandees also, though not belonging to the fixed establishment, are almost daily brought before His Majesty, who settles their rank, and orders them to be branded with a peculiar mark. Elephants of dealers also are brought before His Majesty, who fixes their rank and value.

Āʾīn 79.

THE MUSTER OF HORSES.

They begin with the stables of forty; then come the stables of the princes; then the *k͟hāṣa* courier horses; then the country-bred, and all other stables. When the ten-muhr horses have been inspected, they bring the *Gūṭs*, *Qisrāqs*, the horses on which the hunting leopards ride, and the *Bārgīr* horses (*vide* p. 146, l. 25; p. 143, l. 10 from below, and Āʾīn 54, p. 147). The place of the horses at the musters, is determined by their value, and in the case of horses of the same value, the precedence is determined by the time of service. Before the musters, the horses are inspected by clever officers, who again fix their value, and divide them into three classes. When the rank of a horse has been put higher or lower, it is placed among his proper class-fellows. Those horses which belong to the third class, form separate stables, and are given away as presents. If horses have their value raised, they are given over to such keepers as bring to the musters either the full complement of their horses, or at least a complement not more deficient than by two. Incomplete stables are daily filled up during the musters; or if not filled up, they are put in charge of separate keepers. Twenty horses are daily mustered. On Sundays, horses are the first that are mustered. Double the usual number are then inspected. Several horses are also kept in waiting at Court, viz., one from each of the sixty to the forty-muhr stables, and one more from each of the thirty to the ten-muhr stables. They are given away as presents or as parts of salaries. The precedence at musters of bāzār-horses is fixed according to the price. According to the number of horses available, from twenty to a hundred are daily mustered. Before the musters, experienced officers fix the prices, which are generally enhanced at the time of the parades. Horses above thirty muhrs, have their value fixed in the presence of His Majesty. A cash-keeper attached to the State-hall is entrusted with money, so that horse-dealers have not to wait long for payment of their claims. When horses have been bought they are marked with a peculiar brand, so that there may be no fraudulent exchange.

From foresight, and on account of the large profits of the horse-dealers, His Majesty enforces a tax of three rupees for every ʿ*Irāqī*, *Mujannas* (*vide* p. 147, note 3), and Arab, imported from Kābul and Persia; two and a half rupees for every Turkish and Arabian horse imported from Qandahār; and two from Kābul horses, and Indian Arab bred.

Āʾīn 80.

THE MUSTER OF CAMELS.

The beginning is made with country-bred camels, of which five *qaṭārs* are daily inspected. Those *panṣadīs* (officers in charge of five hundred camels) come first who are oldest. The Head Dārogha has the permission to parade before His Majesty a *qaṭār* of excellent Bughdīs and Jammāzas. Then come the Bughdīs, and after them the Jammāzas, the Ghurds, the Loks, and all other camels. The commencement of the muster takes place on Fridays, on which day double the usual number marches past. The precedence of camels is determined by their value.

Āʿīn 81.

THE MUSTER OF CATTLE.

Cattle are mustered according to their value, ten yokes daily. The muster commences on Wednesdays, on which day double the usual number is inspected.

On the day of the *Dīwālī*—an old festival of this country, on which the Hindus pray to the cow, as they look upon reverence shown to cows as worship—several cows are adorned and brought before His Majesty. People are very fond of this custom.

Āʿīn 82.

THE MUSTER OF MULES.

The muster of this beast of burden commence on Thursdays, when six *qaṭārs* are inspected in order of their value. Mules are mustered once a year.

Formerly all musters took place as above described. But now horses are inspected on Sundays; camels, cows, and mules, on Mondays; the soldiers, on Tuesdays; on Wednesdays, His Majesty transacts matters of finance; on Thursdays, all judicial matters are settled; Fridays His Majesty spends in the Harem; on Saturdays the elephants are mustered.

Āʿīn 83.

THE *PĀGOSHT* REGULATION.[1]

His Majesty has taught men something new and practical, and has made an excellent rule, which protects the animal, guards the stores,

[1] The object of this curious regulation was to determine the amount of the fines which Akbar could justly inflict on the officers in charge of the animals belonging to the Court, if the condition of the animals did not correspond to his expectations. The daily extra quanta of food supplied to the animals, had been fixed by minute rules (Āʿīns 43, 51, 62, 67, 70), and the several Dāroghas (store-keepers) entered into their *roznāmchas*, or day-books, the quantum daily given to each animal. These day-books were produced at the musters, and special officers measured the fatness of each animal, and compared it with the food it had been receiving since the last muster, as shown in the day-book. Akbar determined a maximum fatness (A), which corresponded to a maximum quantity of daily food. (*a*) Similarly, he determined a fatness (B), resulting from a daily quantity of food (*b*), though Abū 'l-Faẓl does not specify how this was done. The quantities A, B, etc.,

teaches equity, reveals the excellent and stimulates the lazy man. Experienced people saw their wisdom increased, and such as inquired into this secret obtained their desires.

His Majesty first determined the quantity of daily food for each domestic animal, and secondly determined the results, which different quanta of food produce in the strength of an animal. In his practical wisdom and from his desire of teaching people, His Majesty classifies the dishonest practices of men. This is done by the *Pāgosht* regulation. From time to time an experienced man is sent to the stables of these dumb creatures. He inspects them, and measures their fatness and leanness. At the time of the musters also the degrees of fatness or leanness are first examined into, and reports are made accordingly. His Majesty then inspects the animals himself, and decreases or increases the degrees of their fatness or leanness as reported, fixing at the same time the fine for leanness. If, for some reason, the allowance of grain or grass of an animal had been lessened, proper account is taken of such a decrease. The leanness of an elephant has been divided into thirteen classes. . . .[1]

For all other animals beside the elephant, six degrees have been laid down, viz., the second, third, fifth, seventh, ninth, and tenth [degrees of the thirteen for the elephant]. And as it is the custom of the Fawjdārs, to mark, at the time of the musters of the *ḥalqas*, one *ḥalqa* which is the best in their opinion, and to put separate that which is the worst, the officers who inquire into the leanness and fatness, deduct fifty per cent. from the degree of the former, and count one half for the latter *ḥalqa*. If the Fawjdār works in concert with the Dārogha, and both sign the entries in the day-book, the Fawjādr is responsible for one-fourth, and the Dārogha for the remaining part of the food. The leanness of old elephants is fixed by the condition of the whole *ḥalqa*. In the horse stables the grooms, water-carriers, and sweepers are fined one-fourth of the wages. In the case of camels, the Dārogha is fined the amount

---

were then divided into several fractions or degrees, as $\frac{8A}{8}$, $\frac{7A}{8}$, $\frac{6A}{8}$ etc. Thus in the case of elephants the maximum fatness (A) was divided into 13 degrees.

Pā-gosht means *a quarter of flesh*, and evidently expresses that the food *a* only produced $\frac{3}{4}$A, instead of $\frac{4}{4}$A. The name was then transferred to the regulation.

We do not know how the mustering officers applied Akbar's rule, whether by measuring the circumference of an animal or by weighing it. The rule may appear fanciful and unpractical; but it shows how determined Akbar was to fathom the dishonesty of his Dāroghas. Hence the carefulness which he showed in assessing fines (Āʿīns 48, 57), in ordering frequent musters of animals and men, in reviving the regulations of branding animals as given by ʿAlāʿu 'd-Dīn Khiljī and Sher Shāh, in fixing the perquisites, in paying cash for all supplies, in allowing veterinary surgeons certain powers, etc.

[1] The text (p. 163, l. 19) enumerates several fractions, or degrees of leanness, but they give no sense. The confusion of the MSS. is due to the want of interpunctuation.

of the grain, and the driver for the share of the grass. In the case of oxen used for carriages, the Dārogha is fined for the part of the grass and the grain ; but the driver is not liable. In case of heavy carriages, half the fine is remitted.

Āʾīn 84.

ON ANIMAL FIGHTS. REGULATIONS FOR BETTING.

His Majesty is desirous of establishing harmony among people of different classes. He wishes to arrange feasts of friendship and union, so that everything may be done with propriety and order. But as all men do not possess a mind capable of selecting that which is true, and as every ear is not fit to listen to wisdom, His Majesty holds social meetings for amusement, to which he invites a large number of people. Through the careful arrangements of His Majesty, the court has been changed from a field of ambitious strife to a temple of a higher world, and the egotism and conceit of men have been directed to the worship of God. Even superficial, worldly people thus learn zeal and attachment, and are induced by these gatherings to inquire after the road of salvation.[1]

Deer [2]-fights.

The manner of fighting of this animal is very interesting, and its method of stooping down and rising up again is a source of great amusement. Hence His Majesty pays much attention to this animal, and has succeeded in training this stubborn and timid creature. One hundred and one deer are *khāṣa* ; each has a name, and some peculiar qualities. A keeper is placed over every ten. There are three kinds of fighting deer, *first,* those which fight with such as are born in captivity and with wild ones ; *secondly,* such as fight best with tame ones ; and *thirdly,* such as fiercely attack wild deer. The fights are conducted in three different ways. *First,* according to number, the first fighting with the second, the third with the fourth, and so on, for the whole. At the second go, the first fights with the third, the second with the fourth, and so on. If a deer runs away, it is placed last ; and if it is known to have run away three times, it ceases to be *khāṣa.* Betting on these fights is allowed ; the stake does not exceed 5 *dāms.* *Secondly,* with those belonging to the princes. Five *khāṣa* pair fight with each other, and afterwards, two *khāṣa* pair from His Majesty's hunting-ground ; then five other *khāṣa* pair. At the

---

[1] To join Akbar's Divine Faith.

[[2] The text has *āhū* which is the Persian name of the *chikārā* (H.), the "ravine-deer" of Anglo-Indian sportsmen.—P.]

same time two pair from the deer park of His Majesty's hunting-ground fight, and afterwards five khāṣa deer engage with five deer of the eldest prince. Then fourteen khāṣa pair engage with each other, and fight afterwards with the deer of the prince, till the fight with the deer of the prince is finished. Upon this, the deer of princes fight with each other, and then khāṣa deer. The betting on such fights must not exceed one muhr. *Thirdly*, with the deer of other people.

His Majesty selects forty-two from his nearer friends, and appoints every two of them as opponents, forming thus one and twenty sets. The first winners receive each thirty deer, and all others get one less, so that the last get each eleven. To every set a *Mal*,[1] a water-buffalo, a cow, a *quchqār* (fighting ram), a goat, and a cock, are given. Fights between cows[2] and goats are rarely mentioned to have been held in ancient times. Before the fighting commences, two khāṣa deer are brought in trimmed up, and are set against two deer belonging to people of various sets. First, with a deer belonging to a powerful grandee, and then the fight takes place before His Majesty. If a general assembly is announced, the fight may also take place, if the deer belongs to a commander of One Thousand. The betting on khāṣa deer is eight muhrs, and on deer belonging to one of a set, five muhrs, if it be an *Aṭkal*; and four, if an *Anīn*. As deer have not equal strength and impetuosity of attack, the rule among deer-keepers is, once to select each of their deer in turn and take it to the arena. Such deer are called *Anīn*. Another then estimates its strength, and brings a deer as opponent. The latter is called *Aṭkal*. In case of *Mals*, the betting is five muhrs; for water buffaloes and cocks, four; for cows[2] and fighting rams, and goats, two. A commander of One Thousand is allowed to bet six muhrs on a khāṣa deer; and with one of his own rank,[3] $3\frac{3}{4}$ muhrs, if the bet is on an *Aṭkal*; and three on an *Anīn*; and so also in the same proportion on *Mals*, water-buffaloes, and cocks; but on cows,[4] fighting rams, and goats, two. A commander of Nine Hundred may bet on a khāṣa deer 50 rupees; and with one of his own rank, $30\frac{1}{4}$ *R.* on an *Aṭkal*, and 25 *R.* on an *Anīn*; on a *Mal* $3\frac{1}{8}$ muhrs; on a water-buffalo and a cock $3\frac{1}{4}$ *M.*; and on all other animals, $1\frac{1}{2}$ *M.* A commander of Eight Hundred is allowed to bet 48 *R.* on a khāṣa deer; with one of his own rank, 30 *R.* on an *Aṭkal*; and 24 *R.* on an *Anīn*;

---

[1] *Mal*, according to Āʾīn 6 of the second book, is the name for a Gujrāt wrestler.

[[2] In text *gāv*, which in Persian is applied to the bull, cow, and bullock. It is improbable that *cows* were used for fighting.—P.]

[3] Or perhaps with his opponent in the set (*miṣl*).

[[4] See note 2 on previous page.]

on a *Mal* 3⅓ *M.*; on a water buffalo and cock, 2½ *M.*, and on other animals as before. A commander of Seven Hundred is allowed to bet 44 *R.* on a *k͟hāṣa* deer; with one of his own rank on an *Aṭkal* 27½ *R.*; on an *Anīn* 22 *R.*; on a *Mal* 3 *M.*; on other animals as before. A commander of Six Hundred may bet 40 *R.* on a *k͟hāṣa* deer; with one of his own rank, 25 *R.* on an *Aṭkal*; 20 *R.* on an *Anīn*; on other animals as before. A commander of Five Hundred may bet 4 *M.* [36 *R.*] on a *k͟hāṣa* deer; with one of his own rank 2½ *M.* on an *Aṭkal*, and 2 *M.* on an *Anīn*; on other animals, as the preceding. A commander of Four Hundred may bet 34 *R.* on a *k͟hāṣa* deer; with one of his own rank 21½ *R.* on an *Aṭkal*; 17 *R.* on an *Anīn*; on a *Mal* 2¾ *M.*; on a water-buffalo and cock, 2 *M.*; on a cow, a fighting ram, and goat, 1 *M.* A commander of Three Hundred may bet 30 *R.* on a *k͟hāṣa* deer; with one of his own rank, 18¾ *R.* on an *Aṭkal*; 15 *R.* on an *Anīn*; 2½ *M.* on a *Mal*; on other animals as the preceding. A commander of Two Hundred may bet 24 *R.* on a *k͟hāṣa* deer; with one of his own rank 15 *R.* on an *Aṭkal*, 12 *R.* on an *Anīn*, and on other animals as before. A commander of One Hundred may bet 2 *M.* on a *k͟hāṣa* deer; with one of his own rank 1½ *M.* on an *Aṭkal*; 1 *M.* on an *Anīn*; and on other animals as before. A commander of Eighty may bet 16 *R.* on a *k͟hāṣa* deer; with one of his own rank 10 *R.* on an *Aṭkal*; 8 *R.* on an *Anīn*; 17 *R.* on a *Mal*; 1½ *M.* on a water-buffalo and a cock; on other animals as before. A commander of Forty may bet 12 *R.* on a *k͟hāṣa* deer; with one of his own rank 7½ *R.* on an *Aṭkal*; 6 *R.* on a *Anīn*; on other animals as before. A commander of Twenty may bet 10 *R.* on a *k͟hāṣa* deer; 6½ *R.* with one of his own rank on an *Aṭkal*; 5 *R.* on an *Anīn*; on other animals as before. A commander of Ten may bet 8 *R.* on a *k͟hāṣa* deer, and 5 *R.* on an *Aṭkal*, with one of his own rank; 4 *R.* on an *Anīn*; on other animals as before. People who hold no *manṣabs*, bet 4 *R.* on a *k͟hāṣa* deer; with one of their own rank, 2½ *R.* on an *Aṭkal*; 2 *R.* on an *Anīn*; 15 *R.* on a *Mal*; on other animals as before.

But if the opponent hold a less rank, the amount of the bet is determined according to the amount which the opponent is allowed to bet on an *Anīn*. When the last pair comes, the betting is everywhere on the deer. A fourth part of what people take from each other in *Mal* fights, is given to the victorious wrestler. The presents which His Majesty makes on such occasions have no limits.

The rule is that every one of such as keep animals brings on the fourteenth night of the moon one deer to the fight. The Bitikchī of this department appoints half the number of deer as *Anīns*, and the other half as *Atkals*. He then writes the names of the *Aṭkals* on paper slips, folds them up, and takes them to His Majesty, who takes up one. The animal chosen has to fight with an *Anīn*. As such nights are clear, fights are generally announced for that time.

Besides, there are two other classes of deer, *kotal* and *half kotal*. The number of each is fixed. As often the number of *khāṣa* deer decreases, the deficiency is made up from the *kotal* deer; and the deficiency in the number of *kotals* is made up from *half kotals*. One pair of *kotals* also is brought to the fight, so that they may be tried. Hunters supply continually wild deer, and bring them to His Majesty, who fixes the price. A fat superior deer costs 2 *M.*; a thin superior one, 1 *M.* to 15 *R.*; a fat middling one, 12 *R.*; Do. lean, 8 *R.*; a third class fat one, 7 *R.*; Do. thin, 5 *R.*; a fourth class fat one, 4 *R.*; Do. lean, 2 to 2½ *R.*

Deer are kept and fed as follows; *Khāṣa* deer selected for fighting before His Majesty, get 2 *s.* grain, ½ *s.* boiled flour, ⅓ *s.* butter, and 1 *d.* for grass. Such as are kept on His Majesty's hunting-grounds, *kotals*, and fighting deer of the sets, get 1¾ *s.* of grain, and flour and butter as before. The grass is supplied by each amateur himself. All *khāṣa*, home-bred, *kotal* deer, and those of His Majesty's hunting-ground, have each one keeper. The fighting deer of the sets have one keeper for every two; the single last one has a keeper for itself. Nothing is given for grass. Deer which are given to people to have them fattened get 1¾ *s.* grain, and ½ *d.* for grass. They have one keeper for every four; but one for every two, if they are fit to become *khāṣa*. Some deer are also sent to other towns; they get 1½ *s.* grain, and have each one keeper. If deer are newly caught, they get no regular food for seven days, after which they get ½ *s.* of grain for a fortnight. They then get 1 *s.* and when one month is over, 1½ *s.*

In the deer park, Manṣabdārs, Aḥadīs, and other soldiers are on staff employ. The pay of foot-soldiers varies from 80 to 400 *d.*

His Majesty has 12,000 deer; they are divided into different classes, and proper regulations are made for each of them. There is also a stud for deer, in which new results are obtained. A large female gets 1½ *s.* grain, and ½ *d.* for grass. A new-born deer drinks the milk of the dam for two months, which is reckoned as equivalent to ¼ *s.* of grain. Afterwards, every second month, the allowance is increased by a quarter *ser* of grain, so that after a period of two years, it gets the same as its dam. For grass, ¼ *d.* is given from the seventh to the tenth month. Young males also get weaned after two months, when they get ⅜ *s.* of grain, which is increased by that quantity every second month, so that, after two years, they get 2¼ *s.* From the fifth to the eighth month, they get ½ *d.* for grass, after which period they get ½ *d.* for grass.

I have given a short description of animal fights as announced for general assemblies. His Majesty announces them also for day time; but as often a more important act of worship is to be performed, he announces them for the night. Or else His Majesty thinks of God, and seeks for wisdom in self-examination; he cares neither for cold nor heat; he spends the time which others idle away in sleep, for the welfare of the people, and prefers labour to comfort.

Ā‘īn 85.

ON BUILDINGS.

Regulations for house-building in general are necessary; they are required for the comfort of the army, and are a source of splendour for the government. People that are attached to the world will collect in towns, without which there would be no progress. Hence His Majesty plans splendid edifices, and dresses the work of his mind and heart in the garment of stone and clay. Thus mighty fortresses have been raised, which protect the timid, frighten the rebellious, and please the obedient. Delightful villas, and imposing towers have also been built. They afford excellent protection against cold and rain, provide for the comforts of the princesses of the Harem, and are conducive to that dignity which is so necessary for worldly power.

Everywhere also *Sarā,is* have been built, which are the comfort of travellers and the asylum of poor strangers. Many tanks and wells are being dug for the benefit of men and the improvement of the soil. Schools and places of worship are being founded, and the triumphal arch of knowledge is newly adorned.

His Majesty has inquired into every detail connected with this department, which is so difficult to be managed and requires such large sums. He has passed new regulations, kindled the lamp of honesty, and put a stock of practical knowledge into the hands of simple and inexperienced men.

Ā‘īn 86.

THE PRICES OF BUILDING MATERIAL, ETC.

Many people are desirous of building houses; but honesty and conscientiousness are rare, especially among traders. His Majesty has carefully inquired into their profits and losses, and has fixed the prices of articles in such a manner, that both parties are satisfied.

Red sandstone costs 3 *d. per man*. It is obtainable in the hills of Fatḥpūr Sīkrī, His Majesty's residence, and may be broken from the rocks at any length or breadth. Clever workmen chisel it so skilfully, as no turner could do with wood; and their works vie with the picture book of *Mānī* [the great painter of the Sassanides]. Pieces of red sandstone (*sang-i gulūla*), broken from the rocks in any shape, are sold by the *pharī*, which means a heap of such stones, without admixture of earth, 3 *gaz* long, 2½ *g.* broad, and 1 *g.* high. Such a heap contains 172 *mans*, and has a value of 250 *d.*, i e. at the rate of 1 *d.* 11¼ *j. per man.*

Bricks[1] are of three kinds; burnt, half burnt, unburnt. Though the first kind are generally made very heavy, they weigh in the average three *sers*, and cost 30 *d. per* thousand. The second class cost 24 *d.*, and the third 10 *d. per* thousand.

Wood. Eight kinds of wood are in general use. 1. *Sīsaū*,[2] unrivalled for its beauty and durability. A block 1 *Ilāhī gaz* long, and 8 *Ṭassūj* broad and high, costs 15 *d.* 6 *j.* But if the height be only 5 or 6 *Ṭ.*, 11 *d.* 10¾ *j.* Other sizes according to the same proportion. 2. *Nāzhū*, called in Hindī *Jīḍh.*[3] A beam, 10 *Ṭ.* broad and high, costs *per gaz* 5 *d.* 13¾ *j.*; and a half size beam, from 7 to 9 *Ṭ.* broad and high, costs *per gaz* 5 *d.* 3¾ *j.* 3. *Dasang* (?), called in Hindī *Karī*[4]; a beam 3 *Ṭ.* broad, and 4 *gaz* long, costs 5 *d.* 17½ *j.* 4. *Ber*,[5] 1 *Ṭ.* broad and high, 4 *gaz* long, 5 *d.* 17¾ *j.*; so also *Tūt*, or Mulberry. 5. *Mug͟hīlān* (Babūl), of the same cubic contents as No. 4, 5 *d.* 2 *j.* 6. *Sirs*, size as before, 10 *d.* 4 *j.* 7. *Dayāl*, same size, first quality 8 *d.* 22¼ *j.*; second quality, 8 *d.* 6½ *j.* 8. *Bakāyin*, same size, 5 *d.* 2 *j.*

Gaj-i shīrīn, or sweet limestone. There is a quarry near Bahīrah. When a merchant brings it, it costs 1 *R. per three mans*; but if any one sends his own carriers, only 1 *d.* *Qalʿī-yi sangīn*, *per man* 5 *d.* 5 *j.* *Ṣadafī* 5 *d.* *Chūna*, or quicklime, 2 *d. per man*; it is mostly boiled out of *kangur*, a kind of solid earth resembling stone in hardness.

Iron cramps, if tinned 13 for 18 *d.*; plain ones, for 6 *d.*

Iron door-knockers, from Persia and Tūrān, tinned; large ones, 8 *d. per pair*; small ones, 4 *d.* Indian do., tinned, 5½ *d.*; plain ones, 4 *d.* 12 *j.*

Gul-mek͟h (large nails with broad heads), 12 *d. per ser.* *Dīnārīn* nails,

---

[[1] *K͟hisht* in text. In modern Persian this word means a sun-dried brick as opposed to *ājur*, a kiln-burnt brick.—P]

[[2] In Platt's *sīsō*.—P.]

[3] This word is spelt *Chīḍh* in Āʾīn 90, No. 59.

[[4] *Karī*.—P.]

[5] "The *Ber* was in great request in Akbar's time as a building timber, but is now little used, except for kingposts and tiebeams, as the direct cohesion of its fibres is equal to that of Salwood." *Balfour's Timber Trees of India.*

5 *d. per ser*. *Goga*, or small nails, tinned, first quality 7 *d*. for one hundred; second quality, 5 *d*.; smallest, 4 *d*.

Screws and nuts, chiefly used for doors and boxes. Tinned, 12 *d*. *per ser*; plain, 4 *d*.

Rings, tinned, 6 *d*. *per ser*; plain, 4 *d*.

Khaprel, or tiles. They are one hand long and ten fingers broad, are burnt, and are used for the roofs of houses, as a protection against heat and cold. Plain ones, 86 *d*. *per* thousand; enamelled, 30 *d*. for ten.

Qulba, or spouts, to lead off water. Three for 2 *d*.

Bās, or bamboo. It is used for spears. First quality, 15 *d*. for twenty pieces; second quality, 12 *d*. for do.; third quality, 10 *d*. for do. The price of some kinds of bamboo is much higher. Thus a peculiar kind is sold at 8 *Ashrafīs* [muhrs] *per* piece. They are used for making thrones.[1] Bamboo, at a rupee *per* piece, is common. *Patal*, is made of the reed which is used for *qalams* (pens). It is used for covering ceilings. First quality, cleaned, 1½ *d*. *per* square *gaz*; second quality, 1 *d*. Sometimes they sell *patal* at 2 *d*. for pieces 2 *gaz* long, and 1½ *g*. broad. *Sirkī* is made of very fine *qalam* reeds, looks well, and is very smooth; it is sold at the rate of 1½ *d*. *per* pair, 1½ *g*. long, and 16 *girihs* broad. The ceilings and walls of houses are adorned with it.

K͟has[2] is the sweet-smelling root of a kind of grass which grows along the banks of rivers. During summer, they make screens of it, which are placed before the door and sprinkled with water. This renders the air cool and perfumed. Price 1½ *R*. *per man*.

Kāh-i chappar[3] (reeds for thatching) is sold in bundles, which are called in Hindī *pūla*, *per ser* from 100 to 10 *d*.

Bhus, or wheat straw, used for mixing with mortar, 3 *d*. *per man*.

Kāh-i ḍābh, straw, etc., which is put on roofs, 4 *d*. for a load of 2 *mans*.

Mūnj, the bark of *qalam* reeds, used for making ropes to fasten the thatching, 20 *d*. *per man*.

San[4] is a plant. Peasants mix it with quicklime. People also make ropes of it for well-buckets, etc., 3 *d*. *per man*.

Gum, of an inferior quantity, is mixed with quicklime, 70 *d*. *per man*.

Sirīsh-i kāhī, or reed glue, is mixed with sweet limestone, 4 *d*. *per ser*.

Luk is the flower-bunch of the reed which is used for matting. People burn it and use it as a candle. It is also mixed with quicklime and *qalʿī*. Price, 1 *R*. *per man*.

[[1] سکاسن ?—P.]
[[2] Or Hindi *khas-khas*.—P.]
[[3] For *chhappar*, H.—P.]
[[4] *San*, H., hemp, flax ?—P.]

Sīmgil (silver clay) is a white and greasy clay, 1 *d. per man.* It is used for white-washing houses. It keeps a house cool and looks well. *Gil-i surkh,* or red clay, called in Hindī, *gerū.*[1] 40 *d. per man.* There is a quarry of it in the hills of Gwāli,ār.

Glass is used for windows; price, 1 *R.* for 1¼ *s.* or one pane for 4 *d.*

Āʾīn 87.

ON THE WAGE OF LABOURERS.

Gilkārs (workers in lime), first class workmen, 7 *d.*; second class, 6 *d.*; third class, 5 *d.*

Sang-tarāsh (stone-masons). The tracer gets 6 *e.* for each *gaz*; one who does plain work, 5 *d.* A labourer employed in quarries gets for every *man* he breaks, 22 *j.*

Carpenters, first class, 7 *d.*; second do., 6 *d.*; third do., 4 *d.*; fourth do., 3 *d.*; fifth do., 2 *d.* For plain job-work, a first class carpenter gets 1 *d.* 17 *j.* for one *gaz*; second class do., 1 *d.* 6 *j.*; third class do., 21 *j.*

Pinjara-sāz (lattice worker and wicker worker). *First,* when the pieces are joined (fastened with strings), and the interstices be dodecagonal, 24 *d.* for every square *gaz* when the interstices form twelve circles, 22 *d.*; when hexagonal, 18 *d.*; when *jaʿfarī* [or rhombus-like, one diagonal being vertical, the other horizontal], 16 *d.*; when *shatranjī* [or square fields, as on a chess board], 12 *d.* for every square *gaz.*

Secondly, when the work is *ghayr-waṣlī* (the sticks not being fastened with strings, but skilfully and tightly interwoven), for first class work, 48 *d.* per square *gaz*; for second class do., 40 *d.*

Arra-kash (one who saws beams). For job-work, *per square gaz* 2½ *d.*, if *sīsaū* wood; if *nāzhū* wood, 2 *d.* A labourer employed for the day, 2 *d.* There are three men for every saw, one above, two below.

Bīldārs (bricklayers),[2] first class, daily 3½ *d.*; second class do., 3 *d.* If employed by the job, for building fortress walls with battlements, 4 *d.* per *gaz*; for laying foundations, 2½ *d.*; for all other walls, 2 *d.* For digging ditches, ½ *d. per gaz.*

The *gaz* of a labourer contains 32 *tassūj.*

Chāh-kan, or well-diggers, first class workmen, 2 *d. per gaz*; second class do., 1½ *d.*; third class, 1½ *d.*

[[1] *Gerū,* H. Armenian bole.—P.]
[[2] *Bel-dār* a digger, a pioneer.—P.]

Ghoṭa-khur, or divers. They clean wells. In the cold season, 4 *d. per diem*; in the hot season, 3 *d.* By the job, 2 *R.* for cleaning a depth of 1 *gaz.*

Khisht[1]*-tarāsh*, or tile makers, for 100 moulds, smoothened, 8 *d.*

Surkhī-kob (pounders of old bricks), 1½ *d.* for a heap of 8 *mans.*

Glass-cutters, 100 *d. per gaz.*

Bamboo-cutters, 2 *d. per diem.*

Chappar-band,[2] or thatchers, 3 *d. per diem*; if done by the job, 24 *d.* for 100 *gaz.*

Patal-band (*vide* p. 234), 1 *d.* for 4 *gaz.*

Lakhīra. They varnish reeds, etc., with lac. Wages, 2 *d. per diem.*

Ābkash, or water-carriers. First class, 3 *d. per diem*; second class do., 2 *d.* Such water-carriers as are used for furnishing house-builders with water for mortar and quicklime, get 2 *d. per diem.*

Āʾīn 88.

ON ESTIMATES OF HOUSE BUILDING.

Stonebuildings. For 12 *gaz*, one *pharī* (*vide* above *Āʾīn* 86) is required; also 75 *mans* of *chūna*; but if the walls be covered with red stone, 30 *mans* of *chūna* are required *per gaz.*

Brickbuildings. For every *gaz*, there are required 250 bricks of three *ser* each, 8 *mans chūna*, and 2 *m.* 27 *s.* pounded brick (*surkhī*).

Claybuildings. 300 bricks are required for the same; each brick-mould contains 1 *s.* of earth and ½ *s.* of water.

Astarkārī work. For every *gaz*, 1 *man chūna*, 10 *s. qalʿī*, 14 *s. surkhī*, and ¼ *s. san* (*vide* p. 234) are required.

Ṣandalakārī work. For every *gaz*, 7 *s.* of *qalʿī*, and 3 *s. surkhī* are required.

Safīdkārī work. 10 *s.* of *qalʿī* are required *per gaz.*

Gajkārī work (white-washing). For walls and ceilings, 10 *s. per gaz*; for pantries, 6 *s.*; chimneys, 10 *s.*

Windows require 24 *s.* of lime, 2½ *s.* of glass, 4 *s.* of *sirīsh-i kāhī* (putty).

Plaster for walls, for 14 *gaz* 1 *m.* of straw, and 20 *m.* earth; for roofs and floors, do. for 10 *gaz.* For ceilings, and the inside of walls, do. for 15 *gaz.*

Lac (varnish work) used for *chighs*[3] [sliced bamboo sticks, placed

---

[[1] See note 1 to Āʾīn 86.—P.]
[[2] Chhappar-band.—P.]
[[3] *Chiq* T., f.—P.]

horizontally, and joined by strings, with narrow interstices between the sticks. They are painted, and are used as screens]. If red, 4 *s*. of lac, and 1 *s*. of vermilion ; if yellow, 4 *s*. of lac, 1 *s*. of *zarnīkh* (auripigment). If green, ¼ *s*. of indigo is mixed with the lac, and *zarnīkh* is added ; if black, 4 *s*. of lac and 8 *s*. of indigo.

Āʼīn 89.

RULES FOR ESTIMATING THE LOSS IN WOOD CHIPS.[1]

One *gaz*=24 *tassūj*
1 *tassūj*=24 *tiswānsa*
1 *tiswānsa*=24 *khām*
1 *khām*=24 *zarra*.

Whatever quantity of wood be used, the chippings (?) are reckoned at one-eighth (?). In *Sīsaū* wood, *per tassūj*, 26¼ *sers* 15 *tānks* ; ***Babūl*** **wood,** 23½ *s*. 5 *d*. ; *Sirs* wood, 21½ *s*. 15 *tānks* ; *Nāzhū* wood, 20 *s*. ; ***Ber*** **wood,** 18½ *s*. ; *Dayāl* wood, 17 *s*. 20 *tānks*.

Āʼīn 90.

THE WEIGHT OF DIFFERENT KINDS OF WOOD.

His Majesty, from his practical knowledge, has for several reasons experimented on the weight of different kinds of wood, and has thus adorned the market place of the world. One cubic *gaz* of dry wood of every kind has been weighed, and their differences have thus been established. *Khanjak* wood has been found to be the heaviest, and ***Safīdār*** the lightest wood. I shall mention 72 kinds of wood.

The weight of one cubic *gaz* of

		Mans.	Sers.	Tanks.
1.	Khanjak . . . . is	27	14	—
2.	Amblī (*Tamarindus indica*)	24	8¾	25
3.	Zaytūn (*Gyrocarpus asiaticus* [2] ?) . .	21	24	—
4.	Balūṭ (Oak)			
5.	Kher (*Acacia catechu*)	21	16	—
6.	Khirnī (*Mimusops*)			
7.	Parsiddh	20	14	17
8.	Ābnūs (Ebony)	20	9	20

[1] I am not sure whether this Āʼīn has been correctly translated.

[2] So according to Watson's Index. But Voigt, in his *Hortus Bengalensis*, says the wood of *Zaytūn*, or *Gyrocarpus*, is very light, and is used for boats. Abū 'l-Faẓl puts *Zaytūn* among the heaviest woods.

		Mans.	Sers.	Tanks.
9.	Sain (*Acacia suma*)	19	32	10
10.	Baqam (*Caesalpina sappan*)	19	22½	10
11.	Kharhar	19	11¼	5
12.	Mahwā (*Bassia latifolia*)	18	32½	2
13.	Chandanī }	18	20½	10
14.	Phulāhī }			
15.	Red Sandal, in Hindī *Rakt Chandan* (*Pterocarpus santalinus*)	18	4½	10
16.	Chamrī	18	2	7½
17.	Chamar Mamrī	17	16¼	—
18.	ʿUnnāb (*Zizyphus sativus*)	17	5	4
19.	Sisaū Patang (*vide* No. 40)	17	1¾	7
20.	Sāndan	17	1	28
21.	Shamshād (*Buxus sempervirens*)	16	18	25
22.	Dhau (*Grislea tomentosa*)	16	1	10
23.	Āṃla, *Hind* Āṇwlah, (*Emblica officinalis*)	16	1½	1
24.	Karīl (*Sterculia fetida*)	16	1	10
25.	Ṣandal	15	17	20
26.	Sāl (*Shorea robusta*)	15	4¾	7
27.	Banaus. His Majesty calls this tree *Shāh Ālū*; but in Kābul and Persian it is called *Ālū Bālū* [1] (Cherry)	14	36½	10
28.	Kailās [2] (Cherry-tree)	14	35½	—
29.	Nīṃb (*Azadirakhta indica*)	14	32¼	31
30.	Dārhard (*Berberis aristata*)	14	32¼	19
31.	Main }	14	22¾	—
32.	Babūl (*Acacia arabica*) }			
33.	Sāgaun	14	10	20
34.	Bijaysār }	13	34	—
35.	Pīlū }			
36.	Mulberry	13	28½	15
37.	Dhāman	13	25	20
38.	Bān Barās	13	10	29
39.	Sirs (*Acacia odoratissima*)	12	38	21
40.	Sīsaū (*Dalbergia sissoo*; *vide* No. 19)	12	34¼	5
41.	Finduq	12	26	4

[1. *Alū-bālū* is a sour dark cherry.—P.]
[2 *Gīlās* in Persia and Kasmīr is a sweet cherry.—P.]

No.	Tree	Mans.	Sers.	Tanks.
42.	Chhaukar	12	17½	22
43.	Duddhī			
44.	Haldī	12	13½	32
45.	Kaim (*Nauclea parviflora*)	12	12½	30
46.	Jāman (*Jambosa*)	12	8	20
47.	Farās			
48.	Bar (*Ficus indica*)	12	3¼	5
49.	Khandū	11	29	—
50.	Chanār [1]			
51.	Chārmaghz (Walnut-tree)	11	9¼	17
52.	Champā (*Michelia champaca*)			
53.	Ber (*Zizyphus jujuba*)	11	4	—
54.	Āmb (Mango, *Mangifera indica*)	11	2	20
55.	Pāparī (Ulmus)			
56.	Diyār (*Cedrus deodar*)	10	20	—
57.	Bed (Willow)			
58.	Kunbhīr (*Gunbhīr* (?) *gmelina arborea*)	10	19½	22
59.	Chīḍh (*Pinus longifolia*)			
60.	Pīpal. The Brahmins worship this tree (*Ficus religiosa*)	10	10¼	21
61.	Kaṭhal (Jacktree, *Artocarpus integrifolia*)	10	7½	34
62.	Gurdaiṇ			
63.	Ruherā (*Terminalia belerica*)	10	7	30
64.	Palās (*Butea frondosa*)	9	34	—
65.	Surkh Bed	8	25	20
66.	Āk (*Calotropis gigantea*)	8	19¼	25
67.	Senbal (*Cotton-tree*)	8	13	34
68.	Bakāyin (*Melea composita*)	8	9	30
69.	Lahsorā (*Cordia mixa*)	8	9	20
70.	Padmākh (*Cerasus caproniana*)			
71.	Aṇd	7	7	31
72.	Safīdār	6	7	22½

In the above weights the *ser* has been taken at 28 *dāms*.

[1 *Chanār*, the Plane.—P.]

END OF THE FIRST BOOK.

BOOK SECOND.

THE ARMY.

Áʼín 1.

THE DIVISIONS OF THE ARMY.

His Majesty guides the Imperial Army by his excellent advice and counsel, and checks in various ways attempts at insubordination. He has divided the army, on account of the multitude of the men, into several classes, and has thereby secured the peace of the country.

With some tribes, His Majesty is content, if they submit; he does not exact much service from them, and thus leads many wild races towards civilization.

The Zamīndārs of the country furnish more than four million, four hundred thousand men, as shall be detailed below (Third Book).

Some troopers are compelled by His Majesty to mark their horses with the Imperial brand. They are subject to divisions into ranks, and to musters.

Some soldiers are placed under the care and guidance of *one* commander. They are called *Aḥadīs,* because they are fit for a harmonious *unity*. His Majesty believes some capable of commanding, and appoints them as commanders.

A large number are worthy but poor; they receive the means of keeping a horse, and have lands assigned to themselves, without being obliged to mark their horses with the Imperial brand. Tūrānīs and Persians get 25 *Rupees*; and Hindūstānīs, 20 *R.* If employed to collect the revenue, they get 15 *R.* Such troopers are called *Barāwardī.*

Some commanders, who find it troublesome to furnish men, get a number of such soldiers as accept the Imperial brand. Such troops are called *Dakhilīs*.

In the contingent of a commander (*manṣabdār*) of Ten Thousand, other *manṣabdārs* as high as *Hazārīs* (commanders of One Thousand) serve; in the contingent of a commander of Eight Thousand, Manṣabdārs up to *Hashtṣadīs* (commanders of Eight Hundred) serve; in the contingent of a commander of Seven Thousand, Manṣabdārs up to Haftṣadīs (commanders of Seven Hundred) serve; in the contingent of a commander of Five Thousand, other Manṣabdārs as high as *Panṣadīs* (commanders of Five Hundred) serve ; and in the contingent of a *Panṣadī*, Manṣabdārs as high as *Ṣadīs* (commanders of One Hundred) serve. Manṣabdārs of lower ranks do not serve in the contingents of high Manṣabdārs.

Some commanders also receive auxiliaries. Such reserves are called *Kumakīs*.

At the present time, those troopers are preferred whose horses are marked with the Imperial brand. This class of soldiers is superior to others. His Majesty's chief object is to prevent the soldiers from borrowing horses (for the time of musters) or exchanging them for worse ones, and to make them take care of the Imperial horses ; for he knows that avarice makes men so short-sighted that they look upon a loss as a gain. In the beginning of the present reign, when His Majesty was still " behind the veil ", many of his servants were given to dishonest practices, lived without check, and indulged, from want of honour, in the comforts of married life.[1] Low, avaricious men sold their horses, and were content to serve as foot-soldiers, or brought instead of a superior horse, a *tātū*[2] that looked more like an ass. They were magniloquent in their dishonesty and greediness of pay, and even expressed dissatisfaction, or rebelled. Hence His Majesty had to introduce the Descriptive Roll System, and to make the issue of pay dependent upon the inspection of these rolls (*vide* below Āʾīn 7). This stopped, in a short time, much lawlessness, and regenerated the whole military system. But at that time the regulations regarding the Imperial brand were not issued, as His Majesty had adopted the advice of some inexperienced men, who look upon branding an animal as an act of cruelty ; hence avaricious men (who cannot distinguish that which is good from that which is bad, having neither respect for themselves, nor their master, and who think to promote a cause by ruining it, thus acting against their own interest) adopted other vicious practices, which led to a considerable want of efficiency in the army. Horse borrowing was then the order of the day. His Majesty, therefore, made the branding of the horses compulsory, in addition to the Descriptive Roll System. Easy-minded idlers thus passed through a school of discipline and became worthy men, whilst importunate, low men were taught honourableness and manliness. The unfeeling and avaricious learned the luxury of magnanimity. The army resembled a newly irrigated garden. Even for the Treasury the new regulations proved

[1 In text نوکر گسسته مهار زیستي.—P.]
[2 For *taṭṭū* H. pony.—P.]

beneficial. Such are the results which wisdom and practical knowledge can produce! Branding a horse may indeed inflict pain; but when viewed from a higher point, it is the cause of much satisfaction to the thinking man.

Āʾīn 2.

ON THE ANIMALS OF THE ARMY.

In the 18th year of his reign, His Majesty introduced the branding system [*vide* p. 147, note 2]. The ranks of the men were also laid down in the best manner, and the classification of the animals belonging to the army was attended to. The requirements for each were noted down, and excellent regulations were issued. The maximum and minimum prices were inquired into by His Majesty, and average prices were fixed. A proper check by accounts was enforced, and regulations on this subject were laid down. The Bak͟hshīs were also freed from the heavy responsibility of bringing new men, and everything went on smoothly.

1. *Horses.* They have been divided into seven classes. The rate of their daily food has also been fixed. These seven classes are *Arabs, Persian horses, Mujannas, Turkī horses, Yābūs, Tāzīs,* and *Jangla horses.*

The *first* class are either Arab bred, or resemble them in gracefulness and prowess. They cost 720 *dāms per mensem*; and get daily 6 *s.* of grain (the price of which, in the estimates for each animal, is put down at 12 *d. per man*), 2½ *d.* of *ghī*, 2 *d.* for sugar, and 3 *d.* for grass. Also, for a *jul, artak, yālposh,* girth [1] (His Majesty does not call it *tang*, but a *farāk͟hī*),[1] *gaddī nak͟htaband*,[2] *qayza* (which the vulgar pronounces *qāyiza*), *magassān*, curry-comb, *hatthī* (a bag made of horse hair for washing the horse), towel, *pāy-band*, nails, etc. [*vide* p. 144], 70 *d. per mensem*, which outlay is called *k͟harj-i yarāq-i asp* (outlay for the harness of the horse). Besides, 60 *d.* for the saddle, and an *apchī* (?) every second month; 7 *d. per mensem* for shoes; and 63 *d.* for a groom, who gets double this allowance if he takes charge of two horses. Total, 479 *d.* But as His Majesty cares for the comfort of the army and inquires into the satisfactory condition of the soldiers, he increased, in the very beginning, this allowance of 479 *d.* by 81 *d.*; and when the value of the Rupee was increased from 35 to 40 *dāms*, His Majesty granted a second additional allowance of 80 *d.* This coin [the Rupee] is always counted at 40 *d.* in salaries. Afterwards a third additional allowance of 2 *R.* (80 *d.*) was ordered to be given for

---

[[1] *Tang* is girth, but *farāk͟hī* is a body-roller, not a girth.—P.]
[[2] *Nak͟hta-band* for *naktā-band* headstall ?—P.]

each class of horses, except *Janglas*, which horses are nowadays entirely left out in the accounts.

The *second* class are horses bred in Persia,[1] or such as resemble Persian [2] horses in shape and bearing. Monthly allowance, 680 *d.* Of this, 458 *d.* are necessary expenses, being 21 *d.* less than the former, viz., 10 *d.* for the *yarāq*, 10 *d.* for saddle and bridle, and 1 *d.* for shoes. The first increase which was given amounted to 67 *d.*; the second to 75 *d.*; the third to 80 *d.* Total 680 *d.*

The *third* class, or *Mujannas* horses, resemble Persian horses [*vide* p. 147, note 3], and are mostly Turkī, or Persian geldings.[3] Monthly cost 560 *d.* Of this, 358 *d.* are for necessaries. The allowance for these horses is 100 *d.* less than the preceding, viz., 30 *d.* less for sugar; 30 *d.* less for saddle, bridle, etc.; 15 *d.* less in *ghī*; 3 *d.* less for the groom; 2 *d.* less for shoeing. First increase sanctioned by His Majesty, 72 *d.*; second, 50 *d.*; third, 80 *d.*

The *fourth* class are horses imported from Tūrān; though strong and well-formed, they do not come up to the preceding. Monthly allowance, 480 *d.* Of this, 298 *d.* are for necessaries. The allowance is 60 *d.* less than for *Mujannas* horses, viz., 30 *d.* less for sugar, 30 *d.* less for grass; 10 *d.* less for the *yarāq*; 4 *d.* less for the saddle, bridle, etc.; 2 *d.* less for shoeing; 2 *d.* less for *ghī*. But the daily allowance of grain was increased by 2 *sers* (which amounts to 18 *d.* *per mensem*), as the sugar had been left out. First increase, 52 *d.*; second, 50 *d.*; third, 80 *d.*

The *fifth* class (*yābū* horses) are bred in this country, but fall short in strength and size. Their performances also are mostly bad. They are the offspring of Turkī horses with an inferior breed. Monthly cost 400 *d.* Of this, 239 *d.* are for necessaries. The allowance is 59 *d.* less than the preceding; viz., 28 *d.* for *ghī*; 15 *d.* less for the groom; 10 *d.* less for the *yarāq*; and 6 *d.* less for the saddle, bridle, etc. First increase, 41 *d.*; second increase, 40 *d.*; third, 80 *d.*

The last two classes also are mostly Indian breed. The best kind is called *Tāzī*; the middling, *Janglas*; the inferior ones, *Tātū*.[4]

Good mares are reckoned as *Tāzīs*; if not, they are counted as *Janglas*.

1. *Tāzī*. Monthly cost, 320 *d.*, of which 188 *d.* are for necessaries. The allowance is 51 *d.* less than for the *Yābū*, viz., 18 *d.* less for grain, as they only get 6 *sers per diem*; 15 *d.* less for grass; 10 *d.* less for *ghī* and sugar; 8 *d.* less for *yarāq*. First increase, 22 *d.*; second, 30 *d.*; third, 80 *d.*

[[1] ʿIrāq-i ʿAjam.—P.] [[2] "ʿ*Irāqī horses*."—P.]

[[3] *Ikdish* does not mean gelding but "of mixed breed".—P.]

[[4] For *ṭaṭṭū*, H.—P.]

2. *Jangla.* Monthly cost, 240 *d.*, of which 145½ *d.* are for necessaries. The allowance is 42½ *d.* less than for *Tāzīs*. The daily allowance of grain has been fixed at 5 *sers*. Hence there are 15 *d.* less for grass; 9 *d.* less for grain; 6 *d.* less for *ghī* and molasses; [1] 4½ *d.* less for the *yarāq*; 2 *d.* less for shoeing. First increase, 29½ *d.*; second, 25 *d.*; third, 40 *d.*

Formerly mules were reckoned as *Tāzī* horses; but nowadays, as *Jangla*.

For *Tātūs* [2] the monthly expenditure is 160 *d.*; but this animal is now altogether thrown out.

Note by the Translator. We may arrange Abū 'l-Faẓl's items in a tabular form. From several remarks in Badā,onī, we may conclude that the horses of the Imperial army were mostly fourth and sixth class horses. The exportation of horses from Hindūstān was strictly prohibited by Akbar, who made the kotwāls responsible for it; *vide Bad.* II, p. 390, l. 5 from below. Many recruits on joining the contingent of a *Manṣabdār*, brought horses with them, for which the *Manṣabdār* received from the treasury an allowance according to the following table:—

	I	II.	III.	IV.	V.	VI.	VII.	VIII.
	Arabs.	Persian Horses.	Mujannas Horses.	Turkī Horses.	Yābūs.	Tāzīs.	Janglahs.	Tātūs.
Gram	54 *d.*	54 *d.*	54 *d.*	72 *d.*	72 *d.*	54 *d.*	45 *d.*	
Ghī	75 *d.*	75 *d.*	60 *d.*	} 58	} 30 *d.*	10 *d.*	4 *d.*	
Sugar	60 *d.*	60 *d.*	30 *d.*			10 *d.*	4 *d.*	
Grass	90 *d.*	90 *d.*	90 *d.*	60 *d.*	60 *d.*	45 *d.*	30 *d.*	Not specified.
Yarāq	70 *d.*	60 *d.*	40 *d.*	30 *d.*	20 *d.*	12 *d.*	7½ *d.*	
Saddle, &c	60 *d.*	50 *d.*	20 *d.*	16 *d.*	10 *d.*	10 *d.*	10 *d.*	
Shoes	7 *d.*	6 *d.*	4 *d.*	2 *d.*	2 *d.*	2 *d.*	—	
Groom	63 *d.*	63 *d.*	60 *d.*	60 *d.*	45 *d.*	45 *d.*	45 *d.*	
Original Allowance	479 *d.*	458 *d.*	358 *d.*	298 *d.*	239 *d.*	188 *d.*	145½ *d.*	
1st Increase	81 *d.*	67 *d.*	72 *d.*	52 *d.*	41 *d.*	22 *d.*	29½ *d.*	Not specified.
2nd Ditto	80 *d.*	75 *d.*	30 *d.*	50 *d.*	40 *d.*	30 *d.*	25 *d.*	
3rd Ditto	80 *d.*	80 *d.*	80 *d.*	80 *d.*	80 *d.*	80 *d.*	40 *d.*	
Total monthly cost in *dāms*	720 *d.*	680 *d.*	560 *d.*	480 *d.*	400 *d.*	320 *d.*	240 *d.*	160 *d.*

The allowance of sugar, or molasses, according to Abū 'l-Faẓl ceases from Class IV; but as he goes on mentioning it in the inferior classes, I have made brackets. *Ghī* and molasses were generally given together; *vide* p. 142.

[[1] *Qand-i siyāh* is probably *gur*, H.—P.]
[[2] See footnote 4, p. 244.—P.]

3. *Elephants*. The branded elephants of the army are divided into *seven* classes : *Mast, Shergīr, Sāda, Manjhola, Karha, Phanḍurkiya*, and *Mokal*, elephants ; but there are no subdivisions, as in His Majesty's elephant stables [*vide* p. 131, l. 27].

The monthly allowance for *Mast* elephants is 1,320 *dāms* [33 Rupees]. Daily allowance of grain, 2½ *māns*. No elephant has more than three servants, a *Mahāwat*, a *Bho,ī*, and a *Meṭh*, of whom the first gets 120 *d*., and the two last 90 *d*. An increase of 120 *d*. was given. From the beginning, elephants were branded ; but now certain differences are made.

Shergīr elephants. Monthly cost, 1,100 *d*., which is 220 *d*. less than the former. Grain, 2 *m*. *per diem*, which makes 180 *d*. less *per mensem* ; also 15 *d*. less for the *Mahāwat* and the *Bho,ī*. His Majesty increased the allowance by 110 *d*.

Sāda elephants. Monthly cost, 800 *d*., which is 300 *d*. less than the preceding. Grain 1½ *m*. *per diem*, which gives 180 *d*. less *per month*. Besides 30 *d*. less for the *Meṭh*, and 15 *d*. less for the *Mahāwat* and the *Bho,ī*. An increase of 50 *d*. was sanctioned.

Manjhola elephants. Monthly cost, 600 *d*. Grain 1 *m*. The decrease is the same as in the preceding ; but an additional allowance of 90 *d*. was sanctioned.

Karha elephants. Monthly cost, 420 *d*. ; grain, 30 *s*. Hence there is a decrease of 30 *d*. on this account ; and of 15 *d*. for the *Mahāwat*. No *Bho,ī* is allowed. The additional grant is 60 *d*.

Phanḍurkiya elephants. Monthly cost, 300 *d*. Grain, 15 *s*. *per diem*, which gives a decrease of 135 *d*. *per mensem*. Only one servant is allowed. at 60 *d*. *per month*. An additional grant of 105 *d*. was sanctioned.

Mokal elephants were formerly not counted. Now they are considered worthy of entering the classes. Monthly allowance, 280 *d*.

In all payments on account of elephants, *dāms* are taken, not rupees, so that there is no possibility of fluctuation.

4. *Camels*. Monthly cost, 240 *d*. Grain, 6 *s*. ; grass, 1 *d*. ; furniture, 20 *d*. ; the driver, 60 *d*. An addition of 58 *d*. was sanctioned ; and when the value of the Rupee was fixed at 40 *dāms*, 20 *d*. more were allowed.

5. *Oxen*. Monthly allowance, 120 *d*. Grain, 4 *s*. ; grass, 1 *d*. ; furniture, 6 *d*. Additional grant, 38 *d*. At the time when the value of the rupee was raised, 10 *d*. more were given.

6. *Oxen for the waggons*. For each waggon, the monthly expenditure is 600 *d*., viz. 480 *d*. for four oxen ; 120 *d*. for grease, repairs, and additional comforts.

Elephants and waggons are only allowed to Mansabdārs, and to those who bring good horses and camels, and middling oxen to be branded.

Āʾīn 3.

THE MANṢABDĀRS.[1]

Wise inquirers follow out the same principles, and the people of the present age do not differ in opinion from those of ancient times. They all agree that if that which is numerous be not pervaded by a principle of harmony, the dust of disturbances will not settle down, and the troubles of lawlessness will not cease to rise. It is so with the elements; as long as the uniting principle is absent, they are dead, and incapable of exhibiting the wonders of the kingdoms of nature. Even animals form unions among themselves, and avoid wilful violence; hence they live comfortably and watch over their advantages and disadvantages. But men, from the wickedness of their passions, stand much more in need of a just leader round whom they may rally; in fact, their social existence depends upon their being ruled by a monarch; for the extraordinary wickedness of men, and their inclination to that which is evil, teach their passions and lusts new ways of perversity, and even cause them to look upon committing bloodshed and doing harm as a religious command.[2] To disperse this cloud of ignorance, God chooses one, whom he guides with perfect help and daily increasing favour. That man will quell the strife among men by his experience, intrepidity, and magnanimity, and thus infuse into them new vigour.

But as the strength of one man is scarcely adequate to such an arduous

---

[1] The Arabians say *manṣib* in Persia and India, the word is pronounced *manṣab*. It means a post, an office, hence *manṣabdār*, an officer; but the word is generally restricted to high officials.

[2] "When the Collector of the Dīwān asks them (the Hindus) to pay the tax, they should pay it with all humility and submission. And if the Collector wishes to spit into their mouths, they should open their mouths without the slightest fear of contamination (*taqazzuz*), so that the Collector may do so. In this state [with their mouths open] they should stand before the Collector. The object of such humiliations and spitting into their mouths is to prove the obedience of infidel subjects under protection, and to promote the glory of Islām, the true religion, and to show contempt to false religions: God himself orders us to despise them; for He says (Sur. 9. 29), 'Out of hand, whilst they are reduced low.' To treat the Hindus contemptuously is a religious duty, because they are the greatest enemies of Muṣṭafa (Muḥammad), because Muṣṭafa, regarding the killing and plundering of Hindus, and making slaves of them, has ordered, 'They must either accept the Islām, or be killed, or be made slaves, and their property must be plundered'; and with the exception of the Imām-i Aʿẓam (Abū Ḥanīfah), to whose sect we all belong, there is no other authority for taking the *Jizya* from Hindus; but all other lawyers say, 'Either death or the Islām.'" *Tārīkh-i Fīrūz Shāhī*, p. 290. Akbar often reproached the Muhammadans for converting with the sword. This, he said, was inhuman. And yet, he allowed the suttee.

undertaking, he selects, guided by the light of his knowledge, some excellent men to help him, appointing at the same time servants for them. For this cause did His Majesty establish the ranks of the Manṣabdārs, from the *Dahbāshī* (Commander of Ten) to the *Dah Hazārī* (Commander of Ten Thousand), limiting, however, all commands above Five Thousand to his august sons.

The deep-sighted saw a sign, and inquirers got a hint from above when they found the value of the letters of God's holy name ; [1] they read in it glad tidings for the present illustrious reign, and considered it a most auspicious omen. The number of Manṣabs is sixty-six, the same as the value of the letters in the name of *Allāh*, which is an announcement of eternal bliss.

In selecting his officers, His Majesty is assisted by his knowledge of the spirit of the age, a knowledge which sheds a peculiar light on the jewel of his wisdom. His Majesty sees through some men at the first glance,[2] and confers upon them high rank. Sometimes he increases the manṣab of a servant, but decreases his contingent. He also fixes the number of the beasts of burden. The monthly grants made to the Manṣabdārs vary according to the condition of their contingents. An officer whose contingent comes up to his manṣab, is put into the first class of his rank ; if his contingent is one half and upwards of the fixed number, he is put into the second class ; the third class contains those contingents which are still less, as is shown in the table below.

Yūzbāshīs (Commanders of One Hundred) are of eleven classes. The *first* class contains such as furnish one hundred troopers. Their monthly salary is 700 Rupees. The *eleventh* class contains such as have no troops of their own, in accordance with the statement made above, that *Dākhilī* troops are nowadays preferred. This class gets 500 Rupees. The nine intermediate classes have monthly allowances decreasing from 700 Rupees by 20 Rupees for every ten troopers which they furnish less.

In the live stock accounts of the *Du-bīstīs*, the fixed number of *Turkī* and *Jangla* horses, and of elephants, is not enforced. For Commanders of Thirty and Twenty, four horses are reckoned generally *Mujannas*, rarely

---

[1] *Jalālah.* This curious word is, according to *Bahār-i ϛAjām*, an abbreviation of the phrase *Jall^a jalālu-h^u*, "May His glory shine forth." It is then used in the sense of *God* ; thus the dual *jalālatayn*, saying *Allah* ! *Allah* ! ; and *khatm-i jalāla* saying the word *Allah* 125,000 times. Similarly here ; the 66 *manṣabs* correspond to the value of the letters of *Jalālah*, i.e. الله =1+30+30+5=66. Abū 'l-Faẓl makes much of the coincidence, for Akbar's name was *Jalāl^u 'd-Dīn*, and Akbar was a divinity. Perhaps I should not say *coincidence*, because of the sixty-six *manṣabs* only one half existed.

[2] Abū 'l-Faẓl often praises Akbar as a good physiognomist. Badā,onī says Akbar learnt the art from the Jogīs.

Yābūs ; and *Dahbāshīs* are excused the *Turkī* horse, though their salaries remain as before.

NOTE BY THE TRANSLATOR ON THE MANṢABS.

The sixty-six Manṣabs, detailed by Abū 'l-Faẓl in the following table, appear to be the result of a minute classification rather than a representation of the Manṣabs which actually existed at the time of Akbar. The table may represent Akbar's plan ; but the list of grandees, as given by Abū 'l-Faẓl himself in the 30th Āʾīn of this Book, only mentions *thirty-three*—the three commands of the three Princes from 10,000 to 7,000 ; and thirty commands of the Manṣabdārs, namely commands of 5,000, 4,500, 4,000, 3,500, 3,000, 2,500, 2,000, 1,500, 1,250, 1,000, 900 ?, 800, 700, 600, 500, 400, 350, 300 ?, 250, 200, 150, 120, 100, 80, 60, 50, 40, 30, 20, 10. Of the last thirty commands, two are somewhat doubtful (the commands of 900 and 300), as not given in all MSS. of the Āʾīn, though the List of Grandees of Shāh Jahān's time (*Pādishāhnāma,* II, p. 717) mentions a command of 900. It does not specify a command of 300, because no Manṣabs under 500 are enumerated in that list.

Abū 'l-Faẓl specifies below the names of all of Akbar's Commanders up to the Manṣabdārs of 500 ; he then gives the names of the Commanders of 500 to 200, who were living, when he made the list. Of the Commands below 200, he merely gives the numbers of those that were alive, viz. :— of Commanders of

150	53
120	1
100 (*Yūzbāshīs*) . .	250
80	91
60	204
50	16
40	260
30	39
20	250
10	224

in all, 1,388 commanders from 150 to 10. The number of the higher Manṣabdārs from 5,000 to 200 is 412, of which about 150 may have been dead, when Abū 'l-Faẓl made his list.

As Abū 'l-Faẓl's List (Āʾīn 30), according to the testimony of Niẓām-i Harawī is a complete list,[1] it is certain that of the 66 Manṣabs of the

[1] Niẓām says, in the introduction to his List of the principal grandees of Akbar's Court, that it was unnecessary for him to specify all, because *tafṣīl-i asāmī-yi har yak rā afāẓilpanāh Shaykh Abū 'l-Faẓl dar kitāb-i Akbarnāma marqūm-i qalam-i badāʾiʿ raqam gardānīda.*

following table, only 33 existed in reality. The first eighteen of these 33 are commands down to 500, which corresponds to the List of Shāhjahān's grandees in the *Pādishāhnāma*, which likewise gives 18 commands to 500.

The commands as detailed in the *Pādishāhnāma* are :—Four commands of the princes (Dārā Shikoh, 20,000 ; Shāh Shujāʿ, 15,000 ; Awrangzeb, 15,000 ; Murād Bakhsh, 12,000) and commands of 9,000, 7,000, 6,000, 5,000, 4,000, 3,000, 2,500, 2,000, 1,500, 1,000, 900, 800, 700, 600, 500.

From the fact that Abū 'l-Faẓl only gives names up to commanders of 200, and the *Pādishāhnāma* up to 500, we may conclude that, at Akbar's time, Manṣabs under 200, and at Shāhjahān's time, Manṣabs under 500, did not entitle the holder to the title of *Amīr*. To judge from *Niẓām's Ṭabaqāt* and the *Maʾāṣir-i Raḥīmī*, Manṣabdārs from the Hazārī (Commander of 1,000) were, at Akbar's time, styled *umarāʾ-i kibār*, or *umarā-i ʿiẓām*, great Amīrs ; and I am not quite sure whether the title of Amīr is not restricted to Manṣabdārs from the *Hazārīs* upwards. Niẓām does restrict his phrases *ba-martaba-yi imārat rasīd*, or *dar jarga* (or *silk*, or *zumra*)*-yi umarā muntaẓim gasht*, to commanders from Hazārīs.

The title *Amīr*ᵘ *'l-umarā* (the Amīr of the Amīrs, principal Amīr), which from its meaning would seem to be applicable to one at the time, seems to have been held by several simultaneously. Niẓām gives his title to Adham Khān, Khizr Khwāja Khān, Mīr Muḥammad Khān Atkah, Muẓaffar Khān, Quṭbᵘ 'd-Dīn Muḥammad Khān, and to the three commanders-in-chief, Bayrām Khān, Munʿim Khān, and Mīrzā ʿAbdᵘ 'r-Raḥīm, the three latter being styled *Khān Khānān*,[1] or *Khān Khānān o Sipahsālār*.

In the *Pādishāhnāma*, however, the title of *Amīr*ᵘ *'l-Umarā* is restricted to the first living grandee (ʿAlī Mardān Khān).

It is noticeable that Niẓām only mentions commanders of 5,000, 4,000, 3,000, 2,500, 2,000, 1,500, and 1,000—for lower Manṣabs he does not specify names. Abū 'l-Faẓl gives three intermediate Manṣabs of 4,500, 3,500, and 1,250 ; but as he only gives five names for these three ranks we may conclude that these Manṣabs were unusual. This agrees also with the salaries of the commanders ; for if we leave out the commands of 4,500, 3,500, and 1,250, we have, according to Āʾīn 30, *twelve* steps from 5,000 to 500, and the monthly salary of a commander of 500 (Rs. 2,500) is the *twelfth* part of the salary of a commander of 5,000 (Rs. 30,000). The *Pādishāhnāma* gives *fourteen* steps between the

[1] For *Khān-i Khānān*, the Khān of the Khāns. In such titles the Persian *Iẓāfat* is left out.

commanders of 7,000 and 500, and fixes the salary of a commander of 7,000 at one *kror* of *dāms per annum*, or 250,000 Rs., stating at the same time that the salaries decrease in proportion. The Persian Dictionary, entitled *Ghiyās*ᵘ *'l-lughāt* states that the salary of a commander of 5,000 is one *kror*, or 250,000 *Rs* , and that the salary of a *Panṣadī*, or commander of 500, is 20,000 Rs. *per annum*, the 12½th part of the former.

It would thus appear that the salaries of the Manṣabdārs, as given by Abū 'l-Faẓl in the following table, are somewhat *higher* than those given in the *Pādishāhnāma* and the *Ghiyāṣ*, whatever may have been the source of the latter.

The salaries appear to be unusually high ; but they would be considerably reduced, if each Manṣabdār had to keep up the establishment of horses, elephants, camels, carts, etc., which Abū 'l-Faẓl specifies for each rank. Taking the preceding Āʾīn and the table in the note as a guide, the establishment of horses, etc., mentioned in the following table, would amount, for a commander of

5,000 (monthly salary 30,000 *R.*) to 10,637 *R.*
1,000 („ „ 8,200 *R.*) to 3,015½ *R.*
100 („ „ 700 *R.*) to 313 *R.*

The three classes which Abū 'l-Faẓl mentions for each Manṣab differ very slightly, and cannot refer to p. 249, l. 23.

A commander of 5,000 was not necessarily at the head of a contingent of 5,000 men. In fact, the numbers rarely even approach the number expressed by the title of a Manṣabdār. Thus Niẓām says of Todar Mall and Quṭbᵘ 'd-Dīn Muḥammad Khān, as if it was something worth mentioning, that the former had 4,000 cavalry, and the latter 5,000 *nawkars*, or servants, i.e., soldiers, though Todar Mall was a commander of 4,000 (Niẓām says 5,000), and Quṭbᵘ 'd-Dīn a commander of 5,000. Of ʿAbdul majīd Āṣaf Khān, a commander of 3,000 (*vide* Āʾīn 30, No. 49), Niẓām says, " he reached a point when he had 20,000." In the *Pādishāhnāma*, where more details are given regarding the number of men under each commander, we find that of the 115 commanders of 500 under Shāhjahān, only six had contingents of 500, whilst the last had only 50 troopers. This also explains the use of the word ذات *ẕāt* after the titles of Manṣabdārs ; as *panj hazārī-yi ẕāt sihhazār suwār*, " a commander of 5,000, personally (*ẕāt*, or by rank), and in actual command of 3,000 cavalry." Sometimes we meet with another phrase, the meaning of which will be explained below, as *Shāyista Khān panjhazārī, panj hazār suwār-i duaspa sihaspa*, " Shāyista Khān, a commander of 5,000, contingent 5,000 cavalry, *with two horses, with three horses*." A trooper is called *duaspa,* if he has two horses, and *sihaspa,* if three, in order to change horses during *elghārs* or forced marches. But keeping *duashpa sihaspa* troopers was a distinction, as in the *Pādishāhnāma* only the senior Manṣabdars of some ranks are so designated, viz., 8 (out of 20) Panjhazārīs; 1 Chahārhazārī; 2 Sihhazārī; 2 Duhazārī; 2 Hazār o panṣadī; 1 Hazārī; and 1 Haftṣadī.

The higher Manṣabdārs were mostly governors of Ṣūbas. The governors were at first called *sipahsālārs*; towards the end of Akbar's reign we find them called *Ḥākims,* and afterwards *Ṣāhib Ṣūbah,* or *Ṣūba-dārs,* and still later merely *Ṣūbas.* The other Manṣabdārs held *Jāgīrs,* which after the times of Akbar were frequently changed. The Manṣabdārs are also called *taʕīnatiyān* (appointed), whilst the troops of their contingents are called *tābīnāt* (followers);[1] hence *tābīnbāshī,* the Manṣabdār himself, or his *Bakhshī* (pay-master, colonel).

The contingents of the Manṣabdārs, which formed the greater part of the army, were mustered at stated times, and paid from the general or the local treasuries; *vide* Āʾīns 6, 7, 8. Akbar had much trouble with these musters, as fraudulent practices were quite common. The reform of the army dates from the time when Shāhbāz Khān (*vide* pp. 148, 197) was appointed *Mīr Bakhshī.* The following passage from Badā,onī (II, p. 190) is interesting:—

"The whole country, with the exception of the *Khāliṣa* lands (domains), was held by the Amīrs as *jāgīr*; and as they were wicked and rebellious, and spent large sums on their stores and workshops, and amassed wealth, they had no leisure to look after the troops or take an interest in the people. In cases of emergency, they came themselves with some of their slaves and Moghul attendants to the scene of the war; but really useful soldiers there were none. Shāhbāz Khān,[2] the Mīr Bakhshī, introduced the custom and rule of the *dāgh o maḥallī,* which had been the rule of ʕAlaᵘ 'd-Dīn Khiljī,[3] and afterwards the law under Sher Shāh. It was settled that every Amīr should commence as a commander of twenty (*bīstī*), and be ready with his followers to mount guard and . . .,[4] as had

---

[1] تعیناتیان, pl. of تعینی, from تعین *taʕīn,* the Indian pronunciation of تعیین *taʕyīn,* to appoint *tābīn,* تابین, *to follow*; then as an adj. *one who follows.* This corrects the erroneous meanings of *tābīn* on p. 62 of the *Journal A. S. of Bengal* for 1868.

[2] The passage in the printed edition is frightfully unintelligible. For *kih* read *Kanbū*; for *baū daḥanīda,* we have perhaps to read *yād dahānīda,* having brought to the memory of (Akbar); for *tābtān,* read *tābīnān*; for *panāh Khudā,* read *panāh ba-Khudā*; for *ān hām,* read *ān hamah.*

[3] The *Tārīkh-i Fīrūz Shāhī* says but little regarding it. The words *dāgh o maḥallī* occur very often together.

[4] *Ojār o maljār* (?). For *jār,* a Turkish word, *vide* Vullers.

been ordered ; and when, according to the rule, he had brought the horses of his twenty troopers to be branded, he was then to be made a *Ṣadī*, or commander of 100 or more. They were likewise to keep elephants, horses, and camels, in proportion to their Manṣabs, according to the same rule. When they had brought to the musters their new contingent complete they were to be promoted according to their merits and circumstances to the post of *Hazārī*, *Duhazārī*, and even *Panjhazārī*, which is the highest Manṣab ; but if they did not do well at the musters, they were to be put down. But notwithstanding this new regulation, the condition of the soldiers got worse, because the Amīrs did what they liked ; for they put most of their own servants and mounted attendants into soldiers' clothes (*libās-i sipāhī*), brought them to the musters, and performed everything according to their duties. But when they got their *jagīrs*, they gave leave to their mounted attendants, and when a new emergency arose, they mustered as many 'borrowed' soldiers as were required, and sent them away again, when they had served their purpose. Hence while the income and expenditure of the Manṣabdār remained *in statu quo*, 'dust fell into the platter of the helpless soldier,' so much so, that he was no longer fit for anything. But from all sides there came a lot of low tradespeople, weavers, and cotton-cleaners (*naddāf*), carpenters, and greengrocers, Hindu and Musalmān, and brought borrowed horses, got them branded, and were appointed to a Manṣab, or were made *Krorīs* (*vide* p. 13, l. 7 from below), or Aḥadīs, or Dākhilīs to some one (*vide* p. 231) ; and when a few days afterwards no trace was to be found of the imaginary horse and the visionary saddle, they had to perform their duties on foot. Many times it happened at the musters, before the emperor himself in the *Dīwān-khāna-yi khāṣṣ*, that they were weighed in their clothes, with their hands and feet tied, when they were found to weigh from 2½ to 3 *man*, more or less (?) and after inquiry, it was found that all were hired, and that their very clothes and saddles were borrowed articles. His Majesty then used to say, 'With my eyes thus open, I must give these men pay, that they may have something to live on.' After some time had passed away, His Majesty divided the Aḥadīs into *du-aspa*, *yakaspa* (having one horse), and *nīmaspa* (having half a share in a horse), in which latter case two troopers kept one horse together, and shared the stipulated salary, which amounted to six rupees.[1]

Weigh well these facts, but put no question !

These were things of daily occurrence . . . ;[2] but notwithstanding

---

[1] So according to one MS. The passage is not quite clear.
[2] Here follows a sentence which I do not know how to translate.

all this, His Majesty's good luck overcame all enemies, so that large numbers of soldiers were not so very necessary, and the Amīrs had no longer to suffer from the inconvenient reluctance of their servants."

Hence the repeated musters which Akbar held, both of men and of animals, carts, etc. ; the minuteness of some of the regulations recorded in the Āʾīn; and the heavy fines imposed on neglectful servants (pp. 226–7, note). The carefulness with which Akbar entered into details (*kas̤rat*), in order to understand the whole (*waḥdat*)—an unusual thing for rulers of former times—is the secret of his success.[1]

We have not sufficient data to form an exact estimate of the strength of Akbar's army. We may, however, quote a statement in the *Pādishāhnāma* regarding the strength of Shāhjahān's army ; *vide Pādishāhn.* II, p. 715.

" The paid army of the present reign consists of 200,000 cavalry, according to the rule of branding the fourth part, as has been mentioned above. This is exclusive of the soldiers that are allowed to the Fawjdārs, Krorīs, and tax-collectors, for the administration of the Parganas. These 200,000 cavalry are made up as follows :—

8,000 Manṣabdārs.

7,000 mounted *Aḥadī* and mounted *Barqandāz*.

185,000 cavalry, consisting of the contingents (*tābīnān*) of the princes, the chief grandees, and the other Manṣabdārs.

" Besides these 200,000 cavalry, there are 40,000 foot, musketeers, artillery, and rocket-bearers. Of these 40,000, 10,000 accompany the emperor, and the remaining 30,000 [2] are in the ṣūbas and the forts."

The " Rule of branding the fourth part " is described among the events of the year 1056 as follows (II, p. 506) :—

" The following law was made during the present reign (Shāhjahān). If a Manṣabdār holds a jāgīr in the same ṣūba, in which he holds his manṣab, he has to muster *one-third* of the force indicated by his rank.[3] Accordingly a *Si Hazārī-yi ẕāt sih-hazār suwār* (a commander of 3,000, personal rank ; contingent 3,000 cavalry) has to muster (bring to the brand) 1,000 cavalry. But if he holds an appointment in another ṣūba, he has only to muster *a fourth* part. Accordingly, a *Chahārhazārī chahār-hazār suwār* (a commander of 4,000 ; contingent, 4,000) has only to muster 1,000 cavalry.

---

[1] *Vide* p. 11, note.

[2] The edition of the *Pādishāhnāma* has wrongly 3,000.

[3] Literally, *he has to bring his followers* (*troopers*) *to the brand* (*dāgh*) *according to the third part.*

"At the time the Imperial army was ordered to take Balkh and Samarqand [1055], His Majesty, on account of the distance of those countries, gave the order that as long as the expedition should last, each Manṣabdār should only muster one-fifth. Accordingly a *Panjhazārī panjhazār suwār* (a commander of 5,000; contingent, 5,000) mustered only 1,000; viz., 300 *sihaspa* troopers, 600 *du-aspa* troopers, 100 *yak-aspa* troopers [i.e., 1,000 men with 2,200 horses], provided the income (*ḥāṣil*) of his jāgīr was fixed at 12 months; or 250 *sihaspa* troopers, 500 *du-aspa* troopers, and 250 *yak-aspa* troopers [i.e., 1,000 men with 2,000 horses], provided the income of his jāgīr was fixed at 11 months; or 800 *du-aspa* troopers, and 200 *yak-aspa* troopers [i.e., 1,000 men and 1,800 horses], if the income of his jāgīr was fixed at 10 months; or 600 *du-aspa* troopers and 400 *yak-aspa*, if at 9 months; or 450 *du-aspa* and 550 *yak-aspa* troopers, if at 8 months; or 250 *du-aspa* and 750 *yak-aspa* troopers, if at 7 months; or 100 *du-aspa* and 900 *yak-aspa* troopers, if at 6 months; or 1,000 *yak-aspa*, if at 5 months.

"But if the troopers to a manṣab had all been fixed as *si-aspa du-aspa* [in other words, if the commander was not a *Panj hazārī, panj hazār suwār*, but a *Panj hazārī panj hazār suwār-i du-aspa si-aspa*] he musters, as his proportion of *duaspa* and *sihaspa* troopers, double the number which he would have to muster, if his manṣab had been as in the preceding. Accordingly, a *Panj hazārī panj hazār tamām du-aspa si-aspa* (a commander of 5,000; contingent, only *du-aspa* and *si-aspa*) would muster 600 troopers with three horses, 1,200 troopers with two horses, and 200 troopers with one horse each [i.e., 2,000 men with 4,400 horses], provided the income of his jāgīr be fixed at 12 months and so on."

From this important passage, it is clear that one-fourth of that number of troopers, which is indicated by the title of a Manṣabdār, was the average strength of the contingents at the time of Shāhjahān. Thus if a commander of 1,000 troopers had the title of *Hazārī hazār suwār*, the strength of his contingent was $\frac{1000}{4}$ = 250 men with 650 horses, viz., 75 *si-aspa*, 150 *du-aspa*, and 25 *yak-aspa*; and if his title was *Hazārī hazār suwār-i du-aspa si-aspa*, the strength of his contingent was 500 men with 1,300 horses, viz., 150 *si-aspa*, 300 *du-aspa*, and 50 *yak-aspa*, if the income of his jāgīr was drawn by him for every month of the year. The above passage also indicates that the proportions of *si-aspa*, and *du-aspa*, and *yak-aspa* troopers was for all manṣabs as 300 : 600 : 100, or as 3 : 6 : 1.

As the author of the *Pādishāhnāma* does not mention the restriction as to the number of months for which the Manṣabdārs drew the income, we may assume that the difference in strength of the contingents mentioned after the name of each grandee depended on the value of their jāgīrs.

From an incidental remark (*Pādishāhnāma*, I, p. 113), we see that the pay of a commander of *sihaspa du-aspa* troopers was double the pay allowed to a commander of *yak-aspas*. This agrees with the fact that the former had double the number of men and horses of the latter.

The strength also of Awrangzeb's army, on a statement by Bernier, was conjectured to have been 200,000 cavalry, *vide* Elphinstone's *History*, second edition, p. 546, last line.

Akbar's army must have been smaller. It is impossible to compute the strength of the contingents, which was continually fluctuating, and depended rather on emergencies. We can, however, guess at the strength of Akbar's *standing* army. At the end of Āʾīn 30, Abū 'l-Faẓl states that there were alive at the time he wrote the Āʾīn

250 Commanders of 100 (Yūzbāshīs)
204 ,, ,, 60 ,,
260 ,, ,, 40 ,,
250 ,, ,, 20 ,,
224 ,, ,, 10 ,,

As these numbers are very uniform, the regular army could not have been larger than 250 × 100, or 25,000 men (troopers, musketeers, and artillery). The Imperial stables contained 12,000 horses (*vide* p. 132, l. 6 from below) which were under the immediate charge of Mīrzā ʿAbdᵘ 'r-Raḥīm Khān Khānān, Akbar's Commander-in-Chief. Hence there may have been about 12,000 standing cavalry. The rest were matchlock-bearers and artillery. In Āʾīn 6, Abū 'l-Faẓl states that there were 12,000 matchlock-bearers. The number of Aḥadīs, of which Shāhjahān had 7,000, cannot have been very large. Many of them were on staff employ in the various offices, store-houses, Imperial workshops; others were employed as adjutants and carriers of important orders. They were, at Akbar's time, gentlemen rather than common soldiers, as they had to buy their own horse on joining. Badā,onī mentions an Aḥadī of the name of Khwāja Ibrāhīm Ḥusayn as one of his friends (II, p. 394). The number of Manṣabdārs, which under Shāhjahān amounted to 8,000, was also much less. Of the 415 Manṣabdārs whose names are given in Āʾīn 30, about 150 were dead when Abū 'l-Faẓl wrote it,[1] so that there would be about

[1] The list of grandees in Āʾīn 30 is quoted in Niẓām's Ṭabaqāt which do not go beyond A.H. 1002, as the author died in October, 1594; but it may be still older, as Niẓām assigns to several Manṣabdārs a higher rank than the one mentioned by Abū 'l-Faẓl. In fact, the list refers to a time prior to the year 993, when the three princes (*Bad.* II, p. 342) were appointed Commanders of 12,000, 9,000, and 7,000 respectively, whilst in Abū 'l-Faẓl's List, Prince Salīm (Jahāngīr) is still put down as a Commander of 10,000, Murād as Commander of 8,000, and Dānyāl as of 7,000.

Table showing the Establishments and Salaries of the Manṣabdārs.[1]

Number.	Commanders of	Horses.						Elephants.					Beasts of Burden and Carts.			Monthly Salaries.		
		ʿIraqi.	Mujannas.	Turkī.	Yābū.	Tāzī.	Jangla.	Shergīr.	Sāda.	Manjhola.	Karha.	Phandurkiya.	Qaṭārs of Camels.	Qaṭārs of Mules.	Carts.	Classes. 1st Rs.	2nd Rs.	3rd Rs.
1	10,000	68	68	136	136	136	136	40	60	40	40	20	160	40	320	60,000	—	—
2	8,000	54	54	108	108	108	108	35	50	36	34	15	130	34	260	50,000	—	—
3	7,000	49	49	98	98	98	98	30	42	29	27	12	110	27	220	45,000	—	—
4	5,000	34	34	68	68	68	68	20	30	20	20	10	80	20	160	30,000	29,000	28,000
5	4,900	33	33	67	67	67	67	20	30	19	19	10	77	19	157	27,600	27,400	27,300
6	4,800	32	32	66	66	65	65	20	29	19	19	9	77	$19\frac{2}{5}$	152	27,600	27,400	27,300
7	4,700	31	31	65	65	63	63	19	29	19	18	9	75	$19\frac{1}{5}$	151	26,800	26,600	26,500
8	4,600	31	31	63	63	62	62	18	28	19	18	9	74	$18\frac{4}{5}$	148	26,400	26,200	26,100
9	4,500	31	30	61	61	61	61	18	28	19	17	8	$72\frac{3}{5}$	$18\frac{3}{5}$	145	26,000	25,800	25,700
10	4,400	30	29	60	60	59	59	18	28	19	16	7	71	$18\frac{1}{5}$	142	25,200	25,000	24,800
11	4,300	29	28	59	59	58	58	17	27	19	16	7	$69\frac{3}{5}$	18	139	24,400	24,200	24,000
12	4,200	28	27	58	58	57	56	16	26	19	16	7	68	$17\frac{3}{5}$	136	23,600	23,400	23,200
13	4,100	27	27	56	56	56	55	16	26	18	16	6	68	$17\frac{2}{5}$	133	22,800	22,400	22,400
14	4,000	27	27	54	54	54	54	16	25	18	15	6	65	17	130	22,000	21,800	21,600
15	3,900	26	26	53	53	52	52	16	24	18	15	6	$63\frac{3}{5}$	$16\frac{4}{5}$	127	21,400	21,200	21,100
16	3,800	26	26	51	51	51	51	16	23	18	15	6	62	$16\frac{2}{5}$	124	20,800	20,600	20,500
17	3,700	25	25	50	50	50	49	16	23	17	15	6	$60\frac{3}{5}$	$16\frac{1}{5}$	121	20,200	20,000	19,900
18	3,600	25	25	49	48	48	47	16	23	17	14	6	59	$15\frac{4}{5}$	118	19,600	19,400	19,300
19	3,500	24	24	47	47	47	46	16	23	17	14	5	$57\frac{3}{5}$	$15\frac{3}{5}$	115	19,000	18,800	18,700
20	3,400	23	23	46	46	46	44	16	22	17	14	5	56	$15\frac{1}{5}$	112	18,300	18,014	18,300
21	3,300	22	22	45	45	44	43	15	22	17	14	5	$54\frac{3}{5}$	15	109	18,200	18,000	17,900
22	3,200	21	21	44	44	42	42	15	21	17	14	5	53	$14\frac{3}{5}$	106	17,800	17,600	17,500
23	3,100	20	20	43	43	41	40	15	20	17	14	5	$51\frac{3}{5}$	$14\frac{2}{5}$	103	17,400	17,200	17,100
24	3,000	20	20	40	40	40	40	15	20	16	14	5	50	14	100	17,000	16,800	16,700
25	2,900	19	19	39	39	39	39	15	19	16	13	4	48	$13\frac{1}{5}$	96	16,400	16,200	16,100
26	2,800	18	18	38	38	38	38	15	18	14	12	3	46	$12\frac{2}{5}$	92	15,800	15,600	15,500
27	2,700	17	17	37	37	37	37	14	17	13	11	3	44	$11\frac{3}{5}$	88	15,200	15,000	14,900
28	2,600	17	17	36	36	35	35	13	15	12	11	3	42	$10\frac{4}{5}$	84	14,600	14,400	14,300
29	2,500	17	17	34	34	35	34	12	14	12	10	2	40	10	80	14,000	13,800	13,700
30	2,400	17	17	33	33	33	33	12	13	11	10	2	38	$9\frac{2}{5}$	76	13,600	13,400	13,300
31	2,300	16	16	33	33	32	32	12	12	10	10	2	36	$8\frac{4}{5}$	72	13,200	13,000	12,900
32	2,200	16	16	32	32	31	31	11	12	9	10	2	34	$8\frac{1}{5}$	68	12,800	12,600	12,500
33	2,100	15	15	31	31	31	31	10	12	9	9	2	32	$7\frac{3}{5}$	64	12,400	12,200	12,100
34	2,000	15	15	30	30	30	30	10	12	9	7	2	30	7	60	12,000	11,900	11,800
35	1,900	14	14	29	29	29	30	10	12	9	7	2	$28\frac{4}{5}$	$6\frac{3}{5}$	58	11,950	11,350	11,450
36	1,800	14	13	28	28	28	29	10	11	9	7	2	$27\frac{3}{5}$	$6\frac{1}{5}$	56	11,400	11,650	11,300
37	1,700	14	13	27	27	27	27	9	11	9	7	2	$26\frac{2}{5}$	$5\frac{4}{5}$	54	11,220	11,000	10,800
38	1,600	13	13	26	26	25	25	9	10	9	7	2	$25\frac{1}{5}$	$5\frac{2}{5}$	52	10,600	10,400	10,200
39	1,500	12	12	24	24	24	24	8	10	8	7	2	24	5	50	10,000	9,800	9,700
40	1,400	12	12	24	24	23	23	8	10	8	7	2	$23\frac{2}{5}$	$4\frac{4}{5}$	49	9,600	9,400	9,300
41	1,300	12	12	23	23	23	22	8	10	7	7	2	23	$4\frac{3}{5}$	48	9,200	9,100	9,050
42	1,200	11	11	22	22	22	22	7	9	7	7	2	22	$4\frac{3}{5}$	46	9,000	8,900	8,800
43	1,100	11	11	22	22	21	21	7	9	7	7	2	22	$4\frac{2}{5}$	44	8,700	8,500	8,400
44	1,000	10	10	21	21	21	21	7	8	7	7	2	21	$4\frac{1}{5}$	42	8,200	8,100	8,000
45	900	10	10	20	20	20	20	7	8	6	7	2	20	4	40	7,700	7,400	7,100
46	800	10	14	17	17	9	3	7	8	5	5	2	17	$3\frac{2}{5}$	34	5,000	4,700	4,400
47	700	6	13	9	13	14	7	5	6	4	4	1	$15\frac{2}{5}$	3	27	4,400	4,000	3,800
48	600	5	7	11	9	4	4	4	3	5	2	1	13	$2\frac{2}{5}$	21	3,500	3,200	3,000
49	600	4	7	8	8	4	3	4	2	4	2	1	14	2	15	2,800	2,750	2,700

[1] For differences in reading I must refer the reader to my Text edition, p. 185.

Number.	Commanders of	Horses.						Elephants.					Beasts of Burden and Carts.			Monthly Salaries.		
																Classes.		
		ʿIrāqī.	Mujannas.	Turkī.	Yābū.	Tāzī.	Jangla.	Shergir.	Sāda.	Manjhola.	Karha.	Phandurkiya.	Qaṭārs of Camels.	Qaṭārs of Mules.	Carts.	1st Rs.	2nd Rs.	3rd Rs.
50	500	4	6	8	8	4	—	3	4	2	2	1	10	2	15	2,500	2,300	2,100
51	400	3	4	5	6	2	—	2	2	2	2	1	5	—	12	2,000	1,751	1,500
52	350	3	4	4	4	2	—	1	1	2	3	1	4⅖	—	11	1,450	1,305	1,350
53	300	3	3	3	4	2	—	1	1	2	2	1	4	—	10	1,400	1,250	1,200
54	250	3	3	3	4	1	—	1	1	2	2	—	3⅖	—	8	1,150	1,100	1,000
55	200	2	3	3	3	1	—	1	2	1	2	—	3	—	7	975	950	900
56	150	2	3	3	3	—	—	1	1	1	—	—	2	—	6	875	850	800
57	125	2	2	2	3	2	—	—	1	1	2	—	2⅕	—	5	780	760	750
58	120	2	2	2	3	2	—	—	1	1	2	—	2⅕	—	5	745	740	730
59	100	2	2	2	2	2	—	—	1	1	1	—	2	—	5	700	600	500
60	80	2	1	2	2	1	1	—	—	1	2	—	2	—	3	410	380	350
61	60	1	1	2	2	1	1	—	—	1	1	—	1⅖	—	2	301	285	270
62	50	1	1	2	2	1	1	—	—	1	1	—	1⅖	—	2	250	240	230
63	40	1	2	1	1	1	—	—	1	—	—	—	1⅖	—	1	223	200	185
64	30	—	1	1	2	1	1	—	—	—	1	—	1⅕	—	1	185	165	155
65	20	—	1	1	1	2	—	—	—	—	1	—	1⅕	—	1	135	125	115
66	10	—	—	2	2	—	—	—	—	—	—	—	—	—	—	100	82½	75

250 higher Manṣabdārs, to which we have to add 1,388 lower Manṣabdārs, from the Commanders of 150 downwards ; hence altogether about 1,600 Manṣabdārs.

But Akbar's Manṣabdārs, on the whole, had larger contingents, especially more horses, than the Manṣabdārs of the following reigns, during which the brevet ranks (*ẕat*) were multiplied.

In the beginning of Akbar's reign, Manṣabdārs had even to furnish men with four horses (*chahār-aspa*). A *Dahbāshī*, or Commander of ten, had to furnish 10 men with 25 horses ; but in later times (*vide* Āʼīn 5) the *Chahār-aspas* were discontinued, and a *Dahbāshī* furnished 10 men with 18 horses. As the other ranks had to furnish horses in proportion, one of Akbar's Hazārīs would have had to bring 1,800 horses, whilst a Hazārī at the time of Shāhjahān only furnished 650.

Of non-commissioned officers a *Mīrdaha* is mentioned ; *vide* note 1, p. 116. The pay of a Mīrdaha of matchlock-bearers varied from 7½ to 6½ *R. per mensem.* Common matchlock-bearers received from 6¼ to 2¾ *R.* As they were standing (household) troops, Abū 'l-Faẓl has put them into the first book of this work (Āʼīns 36 to 40) ; and, generally, the reader will have to bear in mind that the second book, relating to the army, treats chiefly of the contingents of the Manṣabdārs.

Badā,onī, in the above extract, p. 253, speaks of a *libās-i sipāhī*, or soldier's uniform (armour ?).

The distinctions conferred by the emperor on the Manṣabdārs consisted in certain flags (*vide* p. 52, l. 6, from below), and the *gharyāl* or gong (*vide* in the beginning of the fourth book, *Āʾīn-i Gharyāl*).

Āʾīn 4.

THE AḤADĪS.

There are many brave and worthy persons whom His Majesty does not appoint to a Manṣab, but whom he frees from being under the orders of any one. Such persons belong to the immediate servants of His Majesty, and are dignified by their independence. They go through the school of learning their duties, and have their knowledge tested. As it is the aim of His Majesty to confer a spiritual meaning on that which is external, he calls such persons *Aḥadīs* (from *aḥad*, one). They are thus reminded of the *unity* of God.

A new regulation regarding rank was given.

For the sake of the convenience of the Aḥadīs, a separate Dīwān and a paymaster were appointed, and one of the great Amīrs is their chief. A fit person has also been selected to introduce to His Majesty such as are candidates for Aḥadīships. Without partiality or accepting bribes, he takes daily several before His Majesty, who examines them. When they have been approved of, they pass through the *Yād-dāsht*, the *Taʿlīqa*, the descriptive roll, and accounts [*vide* Āʾīn 10]. The paymaster then takes security and introduces the candidate a second time to His Majesty, who generally increases his pay from an eighth to three-fourths, or even to more than six-sevenths.[1] Many Aḥadīs have indeed more than 500 Rupees *per mensem*.[2] He then gets the number *nine* as his brand [*vide* Āʾīn 7]. In the beginning, when their rank was first established, some Aḥadīs mustered eight horses; but now the limit is five. On his *sar-khaṭ* [*vide* Āʾīn 11] each receives a *farmāncha* (rank and pay certificate), on which year after year the treasurer makes payments.

Aḥadīs are mustered every four months, when on a certificate signed by the Dīwān and the Bakhshī, which is called nowadays *Taṣḥīḥa*,[3] the

---

[1] Or, as we would say, by 75 or even 85⅐ *per cent*. *Vide* note 4, p. 88.

[2] This agrees with a statement which I have seen in some historian of Akbar's reign that a senior *Aḥadī* was promoted to a *Yūzbāshīship* as the next step. *Vide* p. 20, note 1.

[3] The *Taṣḥīḥa* corresponds, therefore, to a "life certificate". Arabic Infinitives II take in modern Persian a final ة; thus *taʿlīqa* [*vide* below, Āʾīn 10], *takhfīfa* [*vide* p. 101, note 1], etc.

clerk of the treasury writes out a receipt, to be countersigned by the principal grandees. This the treasurer keeps, and pays the claim. Before the period (of four months) is over, he gets one month's salary in advance. In the course of the year, he receives cash for ten months, after deducting from it one-twentieth of the sum, the total stoppage being made on account of his horses and other expenses. On joining the service, an Aḥadī generally finds his own horse; but afterwards he gets it from the Government; and if the certificate of the inspectors, which is called *Saqaṯnāma*,[1] explains the reason why the horse is not forthcoming he is held indemnified for his dead horse, but does not receive the money for keeping a horse until he gets a new one. But if he has no *Saqaṯnāma* to show, he is not allowed anything from the time of the last muster. Those who are in want of horses are continually taken before His Majesty, who gives away many horses as presents or as part of the pay, one-half being reckoned as *irmās* money,[2] and the other half being deducted in four instalments at the subsequent four musters; or if the Aḥadī be in debt, in eight instalments.

Āʿīn 5.

OTHER KINDS OF TROOPERS.

As I have said something about the Manṣabdārs and the Aḥadīs, I shall give a few details regarding the third class of troopers.

The horse-dealer fixes the quality of the horses, which are carefully inspected by the Ba<u>kh</u>shīs. The description of the man is then taken down in writing. If a trooper has more than one horse they add to his establishment a camel or an ox, for which he gets half the allowance usually given to troopers of a superior class; or if this be not given he gets an addition of two-fifths.

A *Yak-aspa* trooper is paid according to the following rates. If his horse be an ʿIrāqī, he gets 30 *R. per mensem*; if *mujannas*, 25 *R.*; if *Turkī*, 20 *R.*; if a *Yābū*, 18 *R*.; if a *Tāzī*, 15 *R.*; if a *Jangla*, 12 *R.*

The revenue collectors of domain lands got formerly 25 *R.*, but now only 15 *R.*

Troopers of this kind mustered formerly up to four horses, but now the order is not to exceed three.

---

[1] From *saqaṯa*, he fell.

[2] Or *armās* money. The word ارماس may be Inf. IV, or plural of *rams*, a grave. Badā,oni evidently reads *irmās*, because in II, p. 202, he explains *irmās* by *zawāl-i dushman* the burying or destruction of the foes, 'which word the grandees used instead of *ṯalab-i ajnās*, requesting stores, etc.' Hence *irmās*, a request made for military supplies or for salary.

Every *Dah-bāshī* had to muster 2 *chahār-aspa*, 3 *si-aspa*, 3 *du-aspa*, and 2 *yak-aspa* troopers [i.e., 10 troopers with 25 horses], and the other Manṣabdārs in the same proportion. But now a Dah-bāshī's contingent consists of 3 *si-aspa*, 4 *du-aspa*, and 3 *yak-aspa* troopers [i.e., 10 troopers with 18 horses].

Āʾīn 6.

THE INFANTRY.

As I have said something about the Cavalry, I shall make a few remarks on foot soldiers. They are of various kinds, and perform remarkable duties. His Majesty has made suitable regulations for their several ranks, and guides great and small in the most satisfactory manner.

The writer of these . . .[1] is the *Awāra-navīs*. Inasmuch as they are of importance, they are counted as belonging to the infantry. There are several classes of them. The first class gets 500 *dāms* ; the second, 400 *d.* ; the third, 300 *d.* ; the fourth, 240 *d.*

The *Bandūq-chīs*, or Matchlock-bearers.

There are 12,000 Imperial Matchlock-bearers. Attached to this service is an experienced *Bitikchī*, an honest treasurer, and an active *Dārogha*. A few *Bandūq-chīs* are selected for these offices ; the others hold the following ranks Some are distinguished by their experience and zeal, and are therefore appointed over a certain number of others, so that uniformity may pervade the whole, and the duties be performed with propriety and understanding. The pay of these [non-commissioned] officers is of four grades, *first*, 300 *d.* ; *second*, 280 *d.* ; *third*, 270 *d.* ; *fourth*, 260 *d.*

Common *Bandūq-chīs* are divided into *five* classes, and each class into three subdivisions. *First class*, 250, 240, and 230 *d.* *Second class*, 220, 210, 200 *d.* *Third class*, 190, 180, and 170 *d.* *Fourth class*, 160, 150, and 140 *d.* *Fifth class*, 130, 120, and 110 *d.*

The *Darbāns*, or Porters.

A thousand of these active men are employed to guard the palace. The pay of the *Mīrdahas* is five fold, 200, 160, 140, 130, and 120 *d.* Common *Darbāns* have from 100 to 120 *d.*

The *Khidmatiyyas*.

The *Khidmatiyyas* also belong to the infantry. They guard the environs of the palace, and see that certain orders are carried out. *Panjāhīs*

[1] The text has a word which does not suit.

to *Bīstīs* have 200 *d.*; and a *Dah-bāshī* gets 180 and 140 *d.* The others get 120, 110, and 100 *d.*

The caste to which they belong was notorious for highway robbery and theft; former rulers were not able to keep them in check. The effective orders of His Majesty have led them to honesty; they are now famous for their trustworthiness. They were formerly called *Māwīs*. Their chief has received the title of *Khidmat Rā,ī*. Being near the person of His Majesty, he lives in affluence. His men are called *Khidmatiyyas*.[1]

The *Mewṛas*.[2]

They are natives of Mewāṭ, and are famous as runners. They bring from great distances with zeal anything that may be required. They are excellent spies, and will perform the most intricate duties. There are likewise one thousand of them, ready to carry out orders. Their wages are the same as the preceding.

The *Shamsherbāz*, or Gladiators.

There are several kinds of them, each performing astonishing feats. In fighting they show much swiftness and agility, and join courage to skill in stooping down and rising up again. Some of them use shields in fighting, others use cudgels. The latter are called *Lakrāit*. Others again use no means of defence, and fight with one hand only; these are called *yak-hāth*. The former class come chiefly from the Eastern districts, and use a somewhat smaller shield, which they call *chirwa*. Those who come from the southern districts make their shields large enough to conceal a horseman. This kind of shield they call *tilwa*.

Another class goes by the name of *Pharāits*. They use a shield not quite so large as to conceal a man, but a *gaz* broad.

Some again are called *Banāits*. They use a long sword, the handle of which is more than a *gaz* long, and seizing it with both hands, they perform extraordinary feats of skill.

The class which goes by the name of *Bankūlīs* are likewise famous. They use a peculiar sword which, though bent towards the point, is straight near the handle. But they do not make use of a shield. The skill which they exhibit passes all description. Others make various kinds of daggers and knives, and perform with them the most extraordinary feats. Each class of these men has a different name; they also

---

[1] They are called in the Tuzuk-i Jahāngīrī *Piyādahā-yi Khidmatiyya*. The name of their chief under Jahāngīr was *Rai Mān*. He once picked up the young Shāh Shujāʿ who had fallen from an upper window to the ground. *Tuzuk-i Jahāngīrī*, p. 303.

[2] "Among the innovations made by Akbar are the *Ḍāk-Mewṛas*, of whom some were stationed at every place." *Khāfī Khān*, I, p. 243. Hence the *Mewṛas* were chiefly postmen.

differ in their performances. But it is really impossible to give a mere description of them; nor would mere listening to my descriptions be sufficient.

There are more than a hundred thousand of them. At Court one thousand of them are always in readiness. Their *Ṣadī* (commander of one hundred) holds the rank of an Aḥadī, and even a higher one. Their salaries vary from 80 to 600 *d*.

The *Pahluwāns*, or Wrestlers.

There are many Persian and Tūrānī wrestlers and boxers at Court, as also stone-throwers, athletes of Hindūstān, clever *Mals* from Gujrāt, and many other kinds of fighting men. Their pay varies from 70 to 450 *d*. Every day two well-matched men fight with each other. Many presents are made to them on such occasions. The following belong to the best wrestlers of the age—Mīrzā K͟hān of Gīlān; Muḥammad Qulī of Tabrīz, to whom His Majesty has given the name of *Sher-ḥamla*, or Lion-attacker; Ṣādiq of Buk͟hārā; ʿAlī of Tabrīz; Murād of Turkistān; Muḥammad ʿAlī of Tūrān; Fūlād of Tabrīz; Qāsim of Tabrīz; Mīrzā Kuhna-suwār of Tabrīz; Shāh Qulī of Kurdistān; Hilāl of Abyssinia; Sadhū Dayāl; ʿAlī; Srī Rām; Kanhyā; Mangol; Ganesh; Ānbā; Nānkā; Balbhadr; Bajrnāth.

The *Chelas*, or Slaves.[1]

His Majesty, from religious motives, dislikes the name *banda*, or slave; for he believes that mastership belongs to no one but God. He therefore calls this class of men *Chelas*, which Hindī term signifies a *faithful disciple*.[2] Through His Majesty's kindness, many of them have chosen the road to happiness.[3]

Various meanings attach to the term *slave*.[4] *First*, that which people in general mean by a slave. Some men obtain power over such as do not belong to their sect, and sell and buy them. The wise look upon this as abominable. *Secondly* he is called a slave who leaves the path of selfishness and chooses the road of spiritual obedience.[5] *Thirdly*, one's

[1 *Chela*, H., disciple, etc.—P.]

2 The word *Chela* is the same as the Arab. *murīd*, a disciple who places implicit belief in his *murshid* or *pīr*, the head of the sect. "And many of His Majesty's special disciples, in 991, called themselves *chelas* in imitation of the use of this term among Jogīs."—*Badā,onī* II, p. 325.

The author of the pretty Tazkira, entitled *Kalimātu 'sh-Shuʿarā*, which contains biographies of the poets of the eleventh century, was called *Chela*. His real name is Mīrzā Muḥammad Afẓal; as a poet he is known as *Sark͟hush*.

3 By joining the Divine Faith.

[4 *Chela*?—P.]

5 Inasmuch as such a man blindly follows his *pīr*.

child. *Fourthly,* one who kills a man in order to inherit his property. *Fifthly,* a robber who repents and attaches himself to the man whom he had robbed. *Sixthly,* a murderer whose guilt has been atoned by payment of money, in which case the murderer becomes the slave of the man who releases him. *Seventhly,* he who cheerfully and freely prefers to live as a slave.

The pay of Chelas varies from 1 *R.* to 1 *d. per diem.* His Majesty has divided them into several sections, and has handed them over to active and experienced people who give them instruction in several things. Thus they acquire knowledge, elevate their position, and learn to perform their duties with propriety.

His Majesty, who encourages everything which is excellent and knows the value of talent, honours people of various classes with appointments in the ranks of the army ; and raises them from the position of a common soldier to the dignity of a grandee.

The *Kuhārs,* or *Pālkī* bearers.

They form a class of foot-servants peculiar to India. They carry heavy loads on their shoulders, and travel through mountains and valleys. With their *pālkīs, singhāsans, chaudols,* and *ḍūlīs,* they walk so evenly that the man inside is not inconvenienced by any jolting. There are many in this country ; but the best came from the Dakhin and Bengal. At Court, several thousand of them are kept. The pay of a head bearer varies from 192 to 384 *d.* Common bearers get from 120 to 160 *d.*

Dākhilī troops.

A fixed number of these troops are handed over to the Manṣabdārs ; but they are paid by the State. His Majesty has ordered to designate these infantry soldiers in the descriptive rolls as *nīma suwārān,* or half troopers.

The fourth part of Dākhilī troops are matchlock-bearers ; the others carry bows.

Carpenters, workers in iron, water-carriers, pioneers, belong to this class.

A non-commissioned officer of the matchlock-bearers receives 160 *d.* or 4 *R.* ; common matchlock-bearers get 140 *d.* The Mīrdahas of the archers get from 120 to 180 *d.* ; common archers from 100 to 120 *d.*

I could say much more on this subject, but I must content myself with having described the principal classes. I have also given some details in speaking of the several workshops and offices of the Household.

Āʾīn 7.

REGULATIONS REGARDING THE BRANDING OF ANIMALS.

When His Majesty had fixed the ranks of the army, and inquired into the quality of the horses, he ordered that upright *Bitikchīs* should make out descriptive rolls of the soldiers and write down their peculiar marks. Their ages, the names of their fathers, dwelling-places, and race, were to be registered. A Dārogha also was appointed, whose duty it is to see that the men are not unnecessarily detained. They were to perform their duties without taking bribes or asking for remunerations.

Every one who wishes to join the army is taken before His Majesty, in whose presence his rank is fixed, after which the clerks make out the *Taʿlīqa* [*vide* Āʾīn 10].

Dākhilī troops are admitted on the signature of the Manṣabdārs.

His Majesty has also appointed five experienced officers who have to look after the condition of the men, their horses, and the stipulated amount of pay. His Majesty has the men assembled in an open place, and receives the several descriptive rolls, when the men with their horses are handed over to the above five officers. The amount of their pay is then entered at the bottom of the descriptive rolls, and is countersigned by those officers, which serves as a proof, and prevents fraudulent alterations. Each roll is then handed over to the inspecting Dārogha. He takes them in the manner described above [*vide* Āʾīn 4] to His Majesty, who orders the pay to be increased or decreased. His Majesty discerns the value of a man by the lineaments of his forehead, and can therefore increase or decrease his pay. He also distinguishes a tradesman by the look of his face from a soldier, so much so that experienced people are astonished, and refer His Majesty's power of discernment to 'hidden knowledge'. When the roll is thus certified, it is also signed by the *Wāqiʿa Nawīs* (Āʾīn 10), the *Mīr ʿArz*, and the officer commanding the guards. On the strength of this certificate, the Dārogha of the *dāgh* (brand) marks the horses.

When the brand was first introduced, it was made in the shape of the head of the letter *sīn* (i.e. like this, ٣], and was put on the right side of the neck of the horse. For some time, it was made in shape of two *alifs* intersecting at right angles, the heads of the *alif* being made heavy as in this figure ✢, and put on the right thigh. For some time again, it was made like a bow with the string taken off. At last, numerals were introduced, which plan best frustrates fraudulent practices. They make iron numerals, by which all indistinctness is avoided. These new signs are likewise put on the right thigh. Formerly, each horse on being mustered for the first time, was marked with a 1 ; the second time with a 2, and so on ; but now His Majesty has ordered that separate numerals should be used for the horses of the princes, the Manṣabdārs, the governors of the provinces, and all other dignitaries attached to the Court.

The carefulness with which the system of marking horses was attended to resulted at once in truthful reports regarding dead horses ; for when a soldier, after the introduction of the system of repeated marks (*vide* next Āʾīn), brought a horse which had been exchanged, he would demand his pay from the time he had last received his pay, whilst the Bakhshī commenced to count from the day be brought his (exchanged) horse. But since the present mark was introduced, the rule was made that each horse with which, instead of with his old one, a trooper came to the muster, should be described, and should get the same mark as the dead one ; the Bakhshīs, at the subsequent musters held for repeating the marks, were to inspect it and go by the brand. Horses answering the description in the rolls were even hired and substituted for the old ones ; but as the mark was not forthcoming, the deception was detected, and the soldiers thus learnt to be honest.

Āʾīn 8.

ON THE REPETITION OF THE MARK.

The servants (Manṣabdārs) of His Majesty have their horses every year newly marked, and thus maintain the efficiency of the army, as by their endeavours unprincipled people learn to choose the path of honesty. If a Manṣabdār delays bringing his men to the muster, one-tenth of his jāgīr (*aqṭāʿ*) [1] is withheld. Formerly, when the mark was repeated, they put the number on the muster of the horse, marking, for example, a horse with a 2 when it was mustered the second time, and so on ; but now, as each class of soldiers had a particular mark, the mark is merely repeated at the subsequent musters. In the case of Aḥadīs, the former custom was retained. Some Bitikchīs, and near servants of His Majesty, who have no leisure to look after jāgīrs, receive their monthly salaries in cash, and

[1] Properly *iqṭāʿ*, Inf. IV, of *qaṭʿā* ; but in India the word is mostly pronounced as *aqṭā*. The king is therefore called *muqtīʿ*, one who confers lands on the nobles ; abstr. n. *muqṭīʿī*, the giving of lands to nobles, of which the Moghul historians accuse Sher Shāh. *Vide* end of Āʾīn 10, third book, *Muqṭaʿ*, past part., one on whom lands have been conferred ; so often in the *Tārīkh-i Fīrūz Shāhī*. From the times of Akbar the words *aqṭāʿ*, and *jāgīr* are used as synonyms ; before his time we only find *aqṭāʿ* used ; but *jājīr* occurs, or *jāygīr*, in its etymological sense. In later Historians the word *aqṭāʿ* is but rarely met with.

muster their horses every eighteen months. Grandees whose jāgīrs are very remote, do not bring their horses to muster before twelve years have elapsed ; but when six years have elapsed since the last muster, one-tenth of their income is retrenched. And if a Manṣabdār has been promoted to a higher Manṣab, and three years have elapsed since he last presented his horses at muster, he receives a personal (ذات) increase of salary, but draws the allowance for the increased number of his men after the first muster. His old and his new men then get their assignments. If at the renewal of the mark at subsequent musters, any soldier brings a superior horse in exchange for his old one, he is taken before His Majesty, who inspects and accepts it.

Āʾīn 9.

RULES ABOUT MOUNTING GUARD.

Mounting guard is called in Hindī *chaukī*. There are three kinds of guards. The four divisions of the army have been divided into seven parts, each of which is appointed for one day, under the superintendence of a trustworthy Manṣabdār. Another, fully acquainted with all ceremonies at Court, is appointed as *Mīr ʿArẓ*. All orders of His Majesty are made known through these two officers (the *Mīr ʿArz,* and the commander of the Palace). They are day and night in attendance about the palace, ready for any orders His Majesty may issue. In the evening, the Imperial *Qur* (*vide* p. 116) is taken to the State hall. The mounting guards stand on the right ; the ranks of the guards to be relieved are drawn up on the other side. His Majesty generally inspects the guards himself, and takes notice of the presence or absence of the soldiers. Both ranks salute His Majesty. If His Majesty be prevented by more important affairs from attending, one of the princes is ordered to inspect the guards. From predilection and a desire to teach soldiers their duties, as also from a regard to general efficiency, His Majesty pays much attention to the guards. If any one is absent without having a proper excuse, or from laziness, he is fined one week's pay, or receives a suitable reprimand.

The Imperial army has been divided into twelve parts, each of which mounts guard for the space of one month. This gives all troops, whether near or far, an opportunity to come to Court, and to partake of the liberality of His Majesty. But those who are stationed at the frontiers, or told off for any important duty, merely send in reports of their exact condition, and continue to perform His Majesty's special orders. On the first of every solar month, the guards are drawn up to salute His Majesty, as is usual on weekly parades, and are then distinguished by royal marks of favour.

The Imperial army has also been divided into twelve other divisions, each of which is selected in turn, to come to Court for one year and do duty near the person of His Majesty.

Āʾīn 10.

REGULATIONS REGARDING THE WĀQIʿA-NAWĪS.[1]

Keeping records is an excellent thing for a government; it is even necessary for every rank of society. Though a trace of this office may have existed in ancient times, its higher objects were but recognized in the present reign. His Majesty has appointed fourteen zealous, experienced, and impartial clerks, two of whom do daily duty in rotation, so that the turn of each comes after a fortnight.[2] Some other suitable men are selected as supernumeraries, each of whom is appointed for one day; and if any of the fourteen be detained by an important business, this additional person acts for him. Hence they are called *kotal* (supernumeraries).

Their duty is to write down the orders and the doings of His Majesty and whatever the heads of the departments report; what His Majesty eats and drinks; when he sleeps, and when he rises; the etiquette in the State hall; the time His Majesty spends in the Harem; when he goes to the general and private assemblies; the nature of hunting-parties; the slaying of animals;[3] when he marches, and when he halts; the acts of His Majesty as the spiritual guide of the nation; vows made to him; his remarks (*vide* Fifth Book); what books he has read out to him; what alms he bestows; what presents he makes; the daily and monthly exercises[4] which he imposes on himself; appointments to manṣabs; contingents of troops; salaries; jāgīrs; *Irmās* money (*vide* above, p. 260, note 2); *sayūrghāls* (rent-free land); the increase or decrease of

---

[1] From *wāqiʿa* an event and *nawīs* a writer. Instead of *wāqiʿa-nawīs* we also find *majlis-nawīs*.

There was a *wāqiʿa-nawīs*, or recorder, in each Ṣūba. From several places in the *Tuzuk-i Jahāngīrī*, we see that the Bakhshīs of the Ṣūbas often held the posts of *Wāqiʿa-nawīs* at the same time. *Vide* Tuzuk, p. 121, l. 2; p. 137, l. 1; p. 171, l. 5.

[2] Hence the arrangement must have been as follows—first day, first and second writers; second day, second and third writers; third day, third and fourth writers, and so on.

[3] Akbar wished to restrict the slaying of animals. *Vide* above, p. 200, l. 9.

[4] Especially fasts.

taxes; contracts; sales, money transfers; *peshkash* (tribute receipts); dispatch; the issue of orders; the papers which are signed by His Majesty; the arrival of reports; the minutes thereon; the arrivals of courtiers; their departures; the fixing[1] of periods; the inspection of the guards; battles, victories, and peace; obituaries of well-known persons; animal-fights and the bettings on them; the dying of horses; capital punishments; pardons granted by His Majesty; the proceedings of the general assemblies; marriages, births; *chawgān* games (*vide* Āʾīn 29); *chaupar nard*, chess, card games, etc.; extraordinary phenomena; the harvests of the year; the reports on events.

After the diary has been corrected by one of His Majesty's servants, it is laid before the emperor, and approved by him. The clerk then makes a copy of each report, signs it, and hands it over to those who require it as a voucher, when it is also signed by the *Parwānchī*, by the *Mīr ʿArẓ*, and by that person who laid it before His Majesty. The report in this state is called *yād-dāsht*, or memorandum.

Besides, there are several copyists who write a good hand and a lucid style. They receive *yād-dāsht* when completed, keep it with themselves, and make a proper abridgement of it. After signing it, they return this instead of the *yād-dāsht*, when the abridgement is signed and sealed by the *Wāqiʿa-nāwīs*, and the *Risāla-dār*,[2] the *Mīr ʿArẓ*, and the *Dārogha*. The abridgement, thus completed, is called *Taʿlīqa*, and the writer is called *Taʿlīqa-nawīs*.

The *Taʿlīqa* is then signed, as stated above, and sealed by the ministers of state.

His Majesty's object is, that every duty be properly performed; that there be no undue increase, or decrease in any department; that dishonest people be removed, and trustworthy people be held in esteem; and that active servants may work without fear, and negligent and forgetful men be held in check.

Āʾīn 11.

ON SANADS.

Every money matter will be satisfactorily settled, when the parties express their minds clearly, then take a pen and write down the

[1] *Taʿīn-i mudlat*, the fixing of periodical inspections; opp. *be-taʿīnī āmadan* to come at times not appointed beforehand, unexpectedly.

[2] The text has *risāla*, which stands for *risāla-dār*, as, in later times, *Ṣūba* for *Ṣūba-dār*.

For *Mīr ʿArẓ* we find in the early historians *ʿāriẓ*.

statement in legible handwriting. Every written statement of accounts is called a *sanad*. All classes of men adopt such a practice.

The *sanad* is the voucher which relieves the treasurer of all responsibility, and on which people receive payment of their claims. Honest experienced officers, upon whose forehead the stamp of correctness shines, write the agreement upon loose pages and leaves, so that the transaction cannot be forgotten. These loose sheets into which all *sanads* are entered are called the *Daftar*.

His Majesty has made himself acquainted with this department and brought it into proper working order. He has appointed clever, honest, incorruptible, experienced writers, and entrusts the *daftar* to impartial officers, who are under his immediate control.

The *Daftar* of the empire is divided into three parts :—

1. The *Abwāb*ᵘ *'l-māl* or entries referring to the revenue of the country. This part of the *Daftar* explains the revenue of the empire, details any increase or decrease, and specifies every other source of income (as presents, etc.).

2. The *Arbāb*ᵘ *'t-taḥāwīl.*[2] This part explains the manner in which the sums for the Household have been expended ; it contains the debits and credits entered on account of the cashkeepers employed at Court ; and lastly, contains the accounts of daily expenditure, etc., for things bought or sold.

3. The *Tawjīh.*[3] This part contains all entries referring to the pay of the army, and shows the manner in which the pay is given out.

Some *sanads* are merely sealed with the imperial seal. Other *sanads* are first signed and sealed by the ministers of State, and are afterwards laid before His Majesty for signature. Many *sanads*, however, are only signed and sealed by the grandees of the Court. This will be explained in the following.

The *Farmān-i ṣabtī.*

Farmān-i ṣabtīs are issued for three purposes :—

1. For appointments to a Manṣab ; to the Vakīlship ; to the post of *Sipāh-sālār* (governor of a province and Commander-in-Chief) ; to the

[1] English writers of the last century often refer to this system of keeping all documents in loose sheets, instead of bound books. The sheets were kept together by a string drawn through them. This custom, I am informed, is still in use in Persia ; and suits Eastern countries, the hot and damp climate of which soon destroys the binding of books. The word *daftar* is the Greek διφθέρα, a tanned hide, parchment, *ṣaḥib-i daftar*, Minister of Finance, the same as *Dīwān* and *Vazīr*. *Daftarī* means in India a man kept in every office for mending pens, ruling paper and forms, etc.

[2] *The men who get transfer receipts on the Treasury.* This part of the *Daftar* contained all Household accounts, as specified above. Though all MSS. read *Arbāb*, it is probable that *abwāb* is the more usual expression.

[3] Or, *the giving of wajh* (pay) *to the army* ; hence *tawjīh*, military accounts. For *tawjīh*, some MSS. read *tawjīhah*.

tutorship of the princes; to the rank of *Amīr*ᵘ *'l-umarā* (*vide* p. 250); to a *Nāḥiyatī*, or districtship; to the post of *Vazīr*, or Finance Minister; to the *Bakhshīship* (Paymaster and Adjutant-General); to the post of a *ṣadr*, or a judge.

2. For appointments to *jāgīrs*, without military service;[1] for taking charge of a newly conquered territory; sometimes . . .[2]

3. For conferring *Sayū-ghāls* (*vide* Āʾīn 19); for grants on account of daily subsistence allowance; and for grants for beneficent purposes.

When the *Taʿlīqa* has been made out, the *Dīwān-i Jāgīr* (who keeps the Jāgīr accounts) pays the stipulated grant. If the jāgīr is given for military services, with the order of bringing horses to the muster, the grant is once more sent to the *Bakhshīs* for inspection, when the following words are written either on the back or the corner of the paper—*khāṣa, o mardum barāward numāyand; kārgarān-i īn shughl chihra-nawīsī kunand* (this is special; the estimate for the salary may be made out. The proper officers are to prepare the descriptive rolls). When the horses are then branded at the time of the muster, the *Bakhshī general* takes the *Taʿlīqa*, keeps it, and hands instead of it a writing specifying the amount of the monthly salary, duly signed and sealed.

This paper, which the *Bakhshī* grants instead of the *Taʿlīqa*, is called *Sarkhaṭ*.

The *Sarkhaṭs* are entered in the *daftars* of all *Sub-Bakhshīs*, and are distinguished by particular marks. The Dīwān then keeps the *Sarkhaṭ* with himself, prepares an account of the annual and monthly salary due on it, and reports the matter to His Majesty. If His Majesty gives the order to confer a jāgīr on the person specified in the *Sarkhaṭ*, the following words are entered on the top of the report: *Taʿlīqa-yi tan qalamī numāyand* (they are to write out a *Taʿlīqa-yi tan* (certificate of salary)). This order suffices for the clerks; they keep the order, and make out a draft to that effect. The draft is then inspected by the Dīwān, who verifies it by writing on it the words *ṣabt numāyand* (ordered to be entered). The mark of the daftar, and the seal of the Dīwān, the Bakhshī, and the Accountant the Dīwān, are put on the draft in order, when the Imperial grant is

---

[1] *Jāgīrs*, to which no military service attaches, appear to be called ***bedāgh o maḥallī***, i.e., the holder had nothing to do with the army and the musters, at which the Manṣabdārs drew the salaries of their contingents, nor with the collection of the taxes of the several *Maḥalls* or Parganas. Thus *Fatḥ*ᵘ *'llah* of Shīrāz (*vide* p. 209) received Basāwar as his jāgīr, *bedāgh o maḥallī*. *Badāʾonī*, p. 315. Badāʾonī also had a jāgīr of 1,000 Bīghas at which he often grumbles, calling himself by way of joke *Hazārī*, or Commander of One Thousand.

[2] The text has *jāe* (sometimes ?) *ba ʿunwān-i mulk* (*milk* ?) *dādan*—which I do not understand.

written on the outside. The draft thus completed is sent for signature to the Dīwān.

The *Ṣāḥib-i Tawjīh*, or military accountant, keeps the former *Taʿlīqa* with himself, writes its details on the *Farmān*, and seals and signs it. It is then inspected by the *Mustaufī*, and is signed and sealed by him. Afterwards the *Nāẓir* and the *Bakhshīs* do so likewise, when it is sealed by the Dīwān, his accountant, and the *Vakīl* of the State.

If His Majesty's order specifies a cash payment, the *farmān* is made out in the same manner, but is generally called *barāt* (cheque). A statement of accounts of the transaction is appended at the bottom of it. After the *Nāẓir*, the *Dīwān-i Buyūtāt* signs it, and when it has passed through the hands of the Bakhshīs and the Dīwān, it is sealed and signed by the *Khān Sāmān*. The receipts and expenditure of the Imperial workshops, the deposits and payments of salaries to the workmen (of whom some draw their pay on [military] descriptive rolls, and others according to the services performed by them, as the men engaged in the Imperial elephant and horse stables, and in the waggon department) are all made by *barāts*. The accountant of each workshop (or stable) writes out annually two *barāts*, one for the six months from *Farwardīn* (February–March) to *Shahrīwar*, and the other from *Mihr* (September) to *Isfandiyārmuz*. He writes down the allowances on account of grain, grass, etc., both in shape of cash and stores, and the salaries of the workmen, and signs the statement. The *Dīwān-i Buyūtāt* inspects them, passes the order for payment, inquires into the increase or decrease, if any, and writes on the margin *az taḥwīl-i falānī barāt nawīsand*, 'Let a *barāt* be made out showing the amount to be deposited with such and such a *Mushrif*.' The Mushrif of the workshop or stable then takes it, writes out an order and the receipt, and seals and signs it. In all cash payments, one-fourth is deducted, as another *sanad* is given for this amount. The *Dīwān-i Buyūtāt* then gives the order to have it entered. The Mushrif does so, signs and seals the *barāt* and the receipt. It then passes through the hands of the military accountant, the Nāẓir, the Dīwān-i Buyūtāt, the Dīwān-i Kul, the Khān Sāmān, the Mushrif of the Dīwān, and the Vakīl, who sign and seal it. In every case the estimate is sent along with it, so that there may be no mistake. When it has been laid before His Majesty, the Mushrif writes out the receipt, which is then in the same manner entered into the several *daftars*. The mode of payment also is detailed on the back of it, viz., one-fourth is to be paid in gold (*ashrafīs*), one-half in silver (*rūpīs*), and one part in copper (*dāms*), according to the fixed values of the coins.

The *Farmāns* in favour of Manṣabdārs are made out in the same manner; they are, however, never sent to the officers of the workshops and stables.

In case of *Sayūrghāls* (*vide* Āʾīn 19), the farmāns, after having been signed by the Mustawfī, are entered in the *daftars* of the *Dīwān-i Saʿādat* (*vide* Āʾīn 19); they are then signed and sealed by the *Ṣadr*, and the *Dīwān-i Kul*.

Farmāns are sometimes written in *Ṭughrā* character; but the two first lines are not made short. Such a Farmān is called a *Parwāncha*.

Parwānchas are made out for the stipulated salaries of the Begums and the princes; for the stipends of people under the care of the *Dīwān-i Saʿādat* (*vide* Āʾīn 19); the salaries of the Aḥadīs, Chelas, and of some officers in the workshops; and for the allowances on account of the food of *Bārgīr* horses (*vide* p. 147, Āʾīn 54). The treasurer does not annually demand a new *sanad*, but pays the allowances on the mere receipt, signed and sealed by the ministers of the State. The Mushrif (accountant) writes out the receipt which is signed by the recipient, and is then sent to the Dīwān for orders. It is then signed by the Mushrif, the Mustawfī, the Nāẕir-i buyūtāt, the Dīwān-i kul, the Khān-Sāmān, the Mushrif of the Dīwān. In the *Parwānchas* given to Aḥadīs, the signature, seal, and orders of the *Aḥadībāshī*, or Commander of the Aḥadīs, are required after those of the Mustawfī, the Dīwān, and the Bakhshīs, because His Majesty from motives of kindness, and from a desire to avoid delay, has ordered that these *Parwānchas* need not be laid before him.

Nor does His Majesty sign *sarkhaṭs*, sale and purchase receipts, price-lists, *ʿarẓ-nāmchas* (statements of sums forwarded to Court by the collectors of the Imperial domains), *qarār-nāmas* (which specify the revenue collections of the collectors on account of the ryots), and the *muqāsā* (statements of account which *Tahwīldārs* take from the Mustawfī, showing that the sums which they had received as deposits, have been correctly expended).

Āʾīn 12.

THE ORDER OF THE SEALS.

Farmāns, Parwānchas, and Barāts, are made into several folds, beginning from the bottom. On the first fold which is less broad, at a place towards the edge where the paper is cut off, the Vakīl puts his seal; opposite to it, but a little lower, the Mushrif of the Dīwān puts his seal, in such a manner that half of it goes to the second fold. Then, in like manner, but a little lower, comes the seal of the Ṣadr. But when Shaykh

ʿAbdᵘ 'n-Nabī and Sulṭān Khwāja were Ṣadrs (*vide* note to Āʾīn 19), they used to put their seals opposite to that of the Vakīl. In the middle of that fold is the place where that person puts his seal who comes nearest in rank to the Vakīl, as Atka Khān did at the time of Munʿim Khān, and Adham Khān. The Mīr Māl, the Khān Sāmān, the Parwānchī, etc., seal on the second fold, but in such a manner that a smaller part of their seals goes to the first fold. The seals of the Dīwān, and the Bakhshī do not go beyond the edge of the second fold, whilst the Dīwān-i juz, the Bakhshī-yi juz, and the Dīwān-i buyūtāt put their seals on the third fold. The Mustawfī puts his seal on the fourth, and the Ṣāḥib-i Tawjīh on the fifth fold. The seal of His Majesty is put above the *Tughrā* lines on the top of the Farmān, where the princes also put their seals in *Taʿlīqas*.

Āʾīn 13.

THE FARMĀN-I BAYĀẒĪ.

Some matters connected with the Government do not admit of delay, or must not to be known to every one. Such an order receives only the Imperial seal, and is called a *Farmān-i bayāẓī*.[1] The farmān is folded up, and two edges are made to meet, when a knot of paper is put over them, which is sealed up in such manner that the contents cannot be seen. The sealing wax is made of the gum [2] of the Kunār, the Baṛ, the Pīpal, and other trees. Like wax, it gets warm when exposed to fire, but gets afterwards cool and hard. When thus sealed, the farmān is put into a golden cover; for His Majesty looks upon the use of external signs of grandeur as an act of divine worship. Such farmāns are carried by Manṣabdārs, Aḥadīs, or common foot-soldiers, to the parties concerned.

When an officer receives such an order he proceeds a proper distance to meet it, performs various acts of obeisance, puts it on the crown of his head, makes the *sijda*, and rewards the messenger according to the favour conferred upon himself, or according to his circumstances. According to His Majesty's wishes, the bags in which reports are sent, are secured in the same manner as a *Farmān-i bayāẓī*, so that no alterations are possible. In consequence of this, much trouble is avoided, and dishonest practices are put a stop to.

---

[1] That is, a *blank* farmān.

[[2] *Lāk*. The author probably means "sap". It is from the exudations from slits made overnight in the bark of the *baṛ* and the *pīpal* tree that the best bird-lime is made.—P.]

Āʿīn 14.

ON THE MANNER IN WHICH SALARIES ARE PAID.

When any one has the good fortune of joining the army, he receives, on bringing his horses to the muster, a proper *sanad* without delay and without costs. All accounts of salaries are made out in *dāms* ; but at the time of making out the estimate he receives one half in rupees, reckoned at thirty-eight *dāms* [1] each. Half of the remainder is paid in muhurs at nine rupees each, and the last quarter is given in *dāms* for stores. When the value of the rupee was raised to forty *dāms*, the soldiers, through His Majesty's kindness, received *dāms* at the same rate. Every year one month's pay is subtracted on account of the horse, the value of which is raised fifty per cent. above prime cost, and for accoutrements ; but, as much care is shown in buying horses, this increase is not productive of any loss for the soldier. Besides, Aḥadīs are continually employed for affairs of importance, and are permitted to carry the orders of His Majesty ; and whatever is given to them as an acknowledgment for their services by the recipients of the orders, is allowed to be kept by the Aḥadīs as a present if they bear a good character ; but if not, a part of it is reckoned as monthly pay.

With the view of teaching zeal and removing the stamp of laziness, His Majesty fines soldiers for absence from guard ; an Aḥadī loses fifteen days' pay, and other soldiers one week's.

The Commander of every contingent (*Tābīnbāshī*) is allowed to keep for himself the twentieth part of the pay of his men, which reimburses him for various expenses.

Āʿīn 15.

MUSĀʿADAT, OR LOANS TO OFFICERS.

Higher Officers, who receive lands or monthly salaries may occasionally come into difficulties when it would be against the rules of the government for them to ask for a present. For this reason His Majesty appointed a treasurer and a separate *Mīr ʿArẓ*, and those who wish to borrow money may now do so without prejudice to their honour, or annoyance of delay. For the first year, nothing is charged ; in the second, the loan is increased by a sixteenth part of it ; in the third year, by one-eighth ; in the fourth year, by one-fourth ; from the fifth to the seventh, by one-half ; from the eighth to the tenth year, by three-fourths ; from the tenth year and longer, double the original loan is charged, after which there is no further increase.

---

[1] The MSS. have forty-eight.

His Majesty's only object [1] is to teach propriety in transactions; else mutual esteem will never increase among men from the nature of their mercantile affairs.

This regulation brought unprincipled usurers to the proper path, and thus prevented much impropriety.

Ā'īn 16

ON DONATIONS.

His Majesty, from his knowledge of man's nature, gives donations in various ways. It looks as if he lends, but in his heart, he makes a present; or he calls the donation a loan, but never asks it back. The far and near, the rich and poor, share His Majesty's liberality. He gives away elephants, horses, and other valuable articles. The Bakhshīs read out daily the names of the guards and other soldiers, mentioning such first as have never received anything. His Majesty gives them horses. When a soldier has received a horse, he is not recommended to His Majesty for the space of a year for any other donation.

Ā'īn 17.

ON ALMS.

His Majesty bestows upon the needy money and necessaries, winning the hearts of all in public or private. Many enjoy daily, monthly, or yearly allowances, which they receive without being kept waiting. It is impossible for me to detail the sums which some people receive in consequence of representations having been made of their circumstances by such as stand near the throne; and it would take up too much time to describe the presents made daily to beggars, or the eating houses which have been established for the poor.[2]

There is a treasurer always waiting [3] at Court; and every beggar whom His Majesty sees is sure to find relief.

Ā'īn 18.

THE CEREMONY OF WEIGHING HIS MAJESTY.

From reasons of auspiciousness, and as an opportunity of bestowing presents upon the poor, His Majesty is weighed twice a year. Various articles are put into the scales.

---

[1] It is needless to remind the reader that charging interest on loans is against the Muhammadan law. But Akbar was a Hindu in such matters.

[2] *Vide* p. 210, l. 19.

[3] *Vide* p. 15, l. 1.

On the first day of the month of Ābān [15th October], which is the solar anniversary of the emperor, His Majesty is weighed twelve times against the following articles: gold, quicksilver, silk, perfumes, copper, *rūḥ-i tūtiyā*, drugs, *ghī*, iron, rice-milk, seven kinds of grain, salt; the order of these articles being determined by their costliness. According to the number of years His Majesty has lived, there is given away an equal number of sheep, goats, fowls, to people that breed these animals. A great number of small animals are also set at liberty.

His Majesty is weighed a second time on the 5th of Rajab,[1] against eight articles, viz., silver, tin, cloth, lead, fruits, mustard oil, and vegetables. On both occasions the festival of *Sālgirih* (birthday) is celebrated, when donations, or grants of pardon, are bestowed upon people of all ranks.

The Imperial princes, sons, and grandsons of His Majesty are weighed once in every solar year. They are for the first time weighed when two years old, but only against one thing. Every year, however, a new additional thing is put on the scales. When grown up, they are generally weighed against seven or eight things, but not against more than twelve. Animals are set free as usual.

A separate treasurer and an accountant are appointed for this purpose, so that the expenditure may be made with every propriety.[2]

---

1. The lunar birthday of the emperor. As this was the *Muhammadan* birthday, the articles were, of course, fewer and less valuable.

2. According to the *Tuzuk-i Jahāngīrī* (p. 163) and *Pādishāhnāma* (I, p. 243), the weighing of the Royal person was introduced by Akbar. It is an old Hindu custom. At first the weighing took place once a year, on the birthday of the Emperor; but with the introduction of Akbar's Divine (solar) Era, we find in the history of every year the record of a *wazn-i shamsī*, or *solar* weighing, and a *wazn-i qamarī*, or *lunar* weighing. There was of course, a *jashn*, or feast, on such occasions, and courtiers on the same day were promoted to higher Manṣabs, or presented their *peshkash*. The feast was of special importance for the Harem. It appears (*vide* Pādishāhnāma, p. 243) that the articles against which the royal person was weighed were sent from the Harem, or by the mother of the reigning emperor. Jahāngīr, according to several remarks in the *Tuzuk* (pp. 69, 70, 276, etc.), was even weighed in the palace of his august mother, to whom the *Tuzuk* gives the title of *Maryam Zamānī*, the Mary of the age, as Akbar's mother had been styled *Maryam Makānī* (*vide* p. 49, note 7). The solar *wazn* was even retained by Aurangzeb; *vide* ʿĀlamgīrnāma, p. 229.

The birthday of the emperor was of importance for the Harem, as there the string was kept, which numbered as many knots as the emperor numbered years; hence also *sālgirih* (or *sālgirah*, as the word is pronounced all over India) "the year's knot", or birthday.

Tying knots, or bits of string, or ribbon, to the tombs of saints is considered by barren women as a means of obtaining a son, and the tomb of *Salīm-i Chishtī* in Fathpūr Sīkrī, in whose house Jahāngīr was born, is even nowadays visited by Hindu and Musalman women, who tie bits of strong to the marble trellis surrounding the tomb. Similar vows are even placed on Akbar's tomb in Sikandra, near Āgra.

Akbar's regulation, as given in the above Āʾīn, appears to have been continued under Jahāngīr. Shāhjahān made some alterations, in asfar as he was weighed on each feast first against gold and silver, and then against other articles. The articles themselves were given away to the courtiers, or to pious men and beggars, as a means of keeping the royal

Āʿīn 19.

ON SUYŪRGHĀLS.[1]

His Majesty, in his care for the nation, confers benefits on people of various classes ; and in the higher wisdom which God has conferred upon him, he considers doing so an act of divine worship.

His Majesty, from his desire to promote rank distinctions, confers lands and subsistence allowances on the following four classes of men, *first*, on inquirers after wisdom who have withdrawn from all worldly occupation, and make no difference between night and daytime in searching after true knowledge ; *secondly*, on such as toil and practise self-denial, and while engaged in the struggle with the selfish passions of human nature, have renounced the society of men ; *thirdly*, on such as are weak and poor, and have no strength for inquiry ; *fourthly*, on honourable men of gentle birth who from want of knowledge are unable to provide for themselves by taking up a trade.

Subsistence allowances, paid in cash, are called *Waẓīfa* ; lands conferred are called *Milk*, or *Madad-i maʿāsh*. In this way krors are given away, and yet the grants are daily increasing in number.

As the circumstances of men have to be inquired into before grants are made, and their petitions must be considered in fairness, an experienced man of correct intentions is employed for this office. He ought to be at peace with every party, and must be kind towards the people at large in word and action. Such an officer is called *Ṣadr*. The *Qāẓī* and the *Mīr ʿAdl* are under his orders. He is assisted in his important duties by a clerk, who has to look after the financial business, and is now-adays styled *Dīwān-i Saʿādat*.

His Majesty, in his mercy, orders his servants to introduce to him such

---

person from all bodily and mental harm. The gold and the silver against which Jahāngīr was once weighed amounted to Rs. 33,000 ; but according to the *Tuzuk*, the money was distributed among the women of the Harem. On another occasion (*Tuzuk*, p. 163), Jahāngīr was found to weigh 6,514 *tolas*. Taking the *tola* as 186 grains (Prinsep's useful Tables, by E. Thomas, p. 111), Jahāngīr at the age of forty-seven would have weighed 210¼ lbs. Troy.

Akbar, in accordance with his Hindu tendencies, used to give the money to Brahmins. " On the fifth of Rajab 973, which is the day on which the Emperor was born, the feast of weighing His Majesty was held at Niẓāmābād, a town belonging to the Sirkār of Jaunpūr, for according to established custom the emperor is weighed twice a year, on his solar and lunar birthdays, against gold, silver, etc., which is given as a present to the Brahmins of India, and others. Poets used, and still use, such opportunities for presenting nice poems," *Badā,onī*, ii, p. 84.

Occasionally, courtiers were weighed for important personal services. Thus Jahāngīr had once his Court doctor *Rūḥᵘ 'llāh* weighed in silver (*Tuzuk*, p. 283), the sum being given him as a fee in addition to three villages, which were bestowed upon him as *jāgīr*.

[1] *Vide* the note at the end of this Āʿīn.

as are worthy of grants, and a large number receive the assistance they desire.

When His Majesty commenced to inquire into this department, it was discovered that the former *Ṣadrs* had been guilty of bribery and dishonest practices. He therefore appointed, at the recommendation of near friends, Shaykh ʿAbdᵘ 'n-Nabī to this important office. The lands which were then held by Afghāns and Chaudrīs were taken away, and became domain lands (*khalṣā*),[1] whilst all others that held grants were referred to the Shaykh who inquired into, and certified, their grants. After some time it was reported that those who held grants had not the lands in one and the same place, whereby the weak whose grounds lay near *khāliṣa* lands or near the jāgīrs of Manṣabdārs, were exposed to vexations, and were encroached upon by unprincipled men. His Majesty then ordered that they should get lands on one spot, which they might choose. This order proved beneficial for both parties. The officers of the government, on receiving this order, told off certain villages for this purpose; those who were weak were protected, and the encroachments of the unprincipled were put a stop to.

But when Time, according to his custom, commenced to tear the veil of secrets, rumours also regarding this *Ṣadr* [ʿAbdᵘ 'n-Nabī] came to the ears of His Majesty. An order was therefore given that all those who held more than five hundred *bīghas* should lay their *farmāns* personally before His Majesty, and in default, should lose their lands. As, however, the practices of these grant-holders did not come up to the wise counsels of His Majesty, the order was passed that the excess of all lands above one hundred *bīghas*, if left unspecified in the *farmāns*, should be reduced to two-fifths of it, three-fifths of the excess being annexed to the domain lands. Irānī and Tūrānī women alone were excepted from this rule.

As it was reported that impudent, avaricious people used to leave their old grounds and take possession of new places, it was ordered that every one who should leave his place, should lose one-fourth of his lands and receive a new grant.

Again, when His Majesty discovered that the Qāẓīs were in the habit of taking bribes from the grant-holders, he resolved, with the view of obtaining God's favour, to place no further reliance on these men [the Qāẓīs], who wear a turban as a sign of respectability, but are bad at heart, and who wear long sleeves, but fall short in sense. He examined into the whole matter, and dismissed all Qāẓīs, except those who had been appointed during the *Ṣadrship* of Sulṭān Khwāja. The Īrānī and Tūrānī

[1] This is the Indian pronunciation for the Arabic and Persian *khāliṣa*.

women also were convicted of fraud, and the order was passed that every excess of land above one hundred *bīghas* held by them should be inquired into, whether it was correctly held or not.

During the *Ṣadrship* of ʿAzīzᵘ 'd-Dawla [Mīr Fatḥᵘ 'llāh of Shīrāz] the following order was given :—If any one held a Suyūrg̲h̲āl together with a partner, and the farmān contained no reference to the share possessed by each partner, the *Ṣadr* should, in the event of one of the partners dying, proceed without further inquiry to a division, the share of the deceased partner lapsing to the Crown, and remaining domain land till the heirs should personally apply to His Majesty. The new *Ṣadr* was at the same time prevented from granting, without previous reference to His Majesty, more than fifteen bīghas.

On account of the general peace and security in the empire, the grant-holders commenced to lay out their lands in gardens, and thereby derived so much profit, that it tempted the greediness of the Government officers, who had certain notions of how much was sufficient for Suyūrg̲h̲āl-holders, to demand revenue taxes ; but this displeased His Majesty, who commanded that such profits should not be interfered with.

Again, when it was found out that holders of one hundred bīghas and even less were guilty of bribery, the order was given that Mīr Ṣadr Jahān should bring these people before His Majesty ; and afterwards it was determined that the Ṣadr with the concurrence of the writer of this work should either increase or decrease the grants. The rule now followed is this, that all Suyūrg̲h̲āl land should consist of one-half of tilled land, and of one-half of land capable of cultivation ; if the latter half be not so (i.e., if the whole be tilled land), one fourth of the whole should be taken away and a new grant be issued for the remainder.

The revenue derived from each bīgha varies in the several districts, but is never less than one rupee.

His Majesty, with the view of teaching wisdom and promoting true piety, pays much attention to this department, and appoints disinterested men as *Ṣadrs* of districts and *Ṣadr* of the realm.

Note by the Translator on the Ṣadrs of Akbar's reign.

In this Āʾīn—one of the most interesting in the whole work—the Chag̲h̲atāʾī word *suyūrg̲h̲āl* is translated by the Arabic *madadᵘ l-maʿāsh*, in Persian *madad-i maʿāsh*, for which we often find in MSS. *madad o maʿāsh*. The latter term signifies " assistance of livelihood ", and, like its equivalent *milk*, or property, it denotes *lands given for benevolent purposes*, as specified by Abū 'l-Faẓl. Such lands were hereditary, and differ for this reason from *jāgīr* or *tuyūl* lands, which were conferred for a specified time on Manṣabdārs in lieu of salaries.

This Ā*īn proves that Akbar considerably interfered with *suyūrghāl* lands, arbitrarily resuming whatever lands he liked, and increasing the domain, or *khāliṣa*,[1] lands to the ruin of many a Muhammadan (Afghān) family. He also completely broke the power of the *Ṣadr*, whose dignity, especially before the Moghul dynasty, had been very great. It was the *Ṣadr*, or as he was generally styled, *Ṣadr-i Jahān*, whose edict legalized the *julūs*, or accession, of a new king. During the reign of Akbar also, he ranked as the fourth officer of the empire (*vide* end of Ā*īn 30). Their power was immense. They were the highest law-officers, and had the powers which Administrators-General have among us; they were in charge of all lands devoted to ecclesiastical and benevolent purposes, and possessed an almost unlimited authority of conferring such lands independently of the king. They were also the highest ecclesiastical law-officers, and might exercise the powers of High Inquisitors. Thus ˁAbdᵘ 'n-Nabī, during his *Ṣadrship*, ordered two men to be killed for heresy (*vide* p. 186, l. 7, from below).

In the times before the Moghuls, the terms *idrārāt*, *waẓāif*, *milk*, *inˁām-i dehhā*, *inˁām-i zamīnhā*, etc., occur for the word *suyūrghāl* (or *siyūrgāl*, or *sughurghāl*, as some dictionaries spell it).

Among the former kings, ˁAlāˁᵘ 'd-Dīn-i Khiljī is notorious for the disregard with which he cancelled the grants of former rulers. He resumed the greater part of the *madad-i maˁāsh* tenures, and made them domain lands. He also lowered the dignity of the *Ṣadr* by appointing his keybearer to this high office (*Tārīkh-i Fīrūzshāhī*, p. 353). Quṭbᵘ 'd-Dīn Mubārakshāh, however, during the four years and four months of his reign, reinstated many whom ˁAlāᵘ 'd-Dīn had deprived (*T. F.*, p. 382). Fīrūz Shāh is still more praised for his liberality in conferring lands (*T. F.*, p. 558).

That Sher Shāh has often been accused by Moghul Historians for his bounty in conferring lands, has been mentioned above (p. 266, note); and this may have been one of the reasons why Akbar showed such an unexpected severity towards the grant-holders of his time.

Each *Ṣūbā* had a *Ṣadr-i juz*, or provincial *Ṣadr*, who was under the orders of the Chief *Ṣadr* (*Ṣadr-i Jahān*, or *Ṣadr-i kul*, or *Ṣadr-i Ṣudūr*).

As in every other department, bribery was extensively carried on in the offices of the *Ṣadrs*. The land specified in the *farmān* of a holder

---

[1] Regarding the turning out of *Atamghā* and *Madad-i maˁāsh* holders, *vide* Elliot's Glossary, under *Altamghā*, p. 13.

rarely corresponded in extent to the land which he actually held ; or the language of the *farmān* was ambiguously worded to enable the holder to take possession of as much as he could and keep it, as long as he bribed the *Qāẓīs* and provincial *Ṣadrs*. Hence Akbar had every reason, after repeated inquiries, to cancel grants conferred by former rulers. The religious views of the emperor (*vide* p. 176) and the hatred which he showed to the ʿUlamā, most of whom held lands, furnished him with a personal, and therefore stronger, reason to resume their grants, and drive them away to *Bhakkar* in Sind, or to Bengal, the climate of which in those days was as notorious as, in later days, that of Gombroon. After the fall of ʿAbdᵘ 'n-Nabī—a man whom Akbar used once to honour by holding the slippers before his feet—Sulṭān K͟hwāja, *a member of the Divine Faith* (*vide* p. 214), was appointed as *Ṣadr* ; and the *Ṣadrs* after him were so limited in conferring lands independently of Akbar, and had so few grants to look after, as to tempt Badā,onī to indulge in sarcastical remarks. The following were Akbar's *Ṣadrs* :—

1. Shayk͟h Gadāʾī, a Shīʿah, appointed at the recommendation of Bayrām K͟hān, till 968.
2. K͟hwāja Muḥammad Ṣāliḥ, till 971.
3. Shayk͟h ʿAbdᵘ 'n-Nabī, till 986.
4. Sulṭān K͟hwāja, till his death in 993.
5. Amīr Fatḥᵘ 'llāh of Shīrāz, till 997.
6. Ṣadr Jahān, whose name coincides with the title of his office.

Abū 'l-Faẓl also mentions a *Ṣadr* Mawlānā ʿAbdᵘ 'l-Bāqī ; but I do not know when he held office.

I extract a few short passages from Badā,onī.

Page 29. Shayk͟h Gadāʾī cancelled the *Madad-i maʿāsh* lands, and took away the legacies[1] of the *K͟hānzādas* (Afg͟hāns) and gave a Suyūrg͟hāl to any one that would bear up with humiliating treatment, but not otherwise. Nevertheless, in comparison with the present time, when obstacles are raised to the possession of every *jarīb* of ground, nay, even less, you may call the Shayk͟h an ʿĀlambak͟hsh (one who gives away a world).

Page 52. After Shayk͟h Gadāʾī, K͟hājagī Muḥammad Ṣāliḥ was, in 968, appointed *Ṣadr* ; but he did not possess such extensive powers in conferring lands as *madad-i maʿāsh*, because he was dependent on the Dīwāns.

Page 71. In 972, or perhaps more correctly in 971, Shayk͟h ʿAbdᵘ 'n-Nabī was made *Ṣadr*. In giving away lands, he was to consult Muẓaffar K͟hān, at that time Vazīr and Vakīl. But soon after, the Shayk͟h acquired

[1] *Awqāf*. The text of Badā,onī has wrongly *auqāt*. For *bār* read *bārah*.

such absolute powers that he conferred on deserving people whole worlds of subsistence allowances, lands, and pensions, so much so that if you place the grants of all former kings of Hindūstān in one scale, and those of the Shaykh into the other, his scale would weigh more. But several years later the scale went up, as it had been under former kings, and matters took an adverse turn.

Page 204. In 983, His Majesty gave the order that the *Ayimas* of the whole empire should not be let off by the *krorīs* of each Pergana, unless they brought the *farmāns* in which their grants, subsistence allowances and pensions were described, to the *Ṣadr* for inspection and verification. For this reason, a large number of worthy people, from the eastern districts up to Bhakkar on the Indus, came to Court. If any of them had a powerful protector in one of the grandees or near friends of His Majesty, he could manage to have his affair settled; but those who were destitute of such recommendations had to bribe Sayyid ˁAbdᵘ 'r-Rasūl, the Shaykh's head man, or make presents to his farrāshes, darbāns (porters), syces (grooms), and mihtars (sweepers), "in order to get their blanket out of the mire." Unless, however, they had either strong recommendations, or had recourse to bribery, they were utterly ruined. Many of the *Ayimas*, without obtaining their object, died from the heat caused by the crowding of the multitudes. Though a report of this came to the ears of His Majesty, no one dared to take these unfortunate people before the emperor. And when the Shaykh, in all his pride and haughtiness, sat upon his *masnad* (cushion), and influential grandees introduced to him, in his office, scientific or pious men, the Shaykh received them in his filthy way, paid respect to no one,[1] and after much asking, begging, and exaggerating he allowed, for example, a teacher of the *Hidāya* (a book on law) and other college books 100 Bīghas, more or less; and though such a man might have been for a long time in possession of more extensive lands, the Shaykh took them away. But to men of no renown, to low fellows, even to Hindus, he gave primitive lands as marks [2] of personal favour. Hence science and scientific men fell in estimation. . . . At no time had a *Ṣadr* for so long a time exercised more tyrannical powers.

The fate of ˁAbdᵘ 'n-Nabī has been related above. Akbar gave him money for the poor of Makkah, and sent him on a pilgrimage. When he came back, he was called to account for the money, was put in prison, and murdered "by some scoundrel" in 992.

---

[1] Badā,onī says that even in the State hall when before the time of prayer he washed his hands and feet, he took care to spirt water on the grandees standing near him.

[2] For *batafẓīl* in the text (p. 205) one MS. of Badāonī reads *zamīn-i ibtidāˁī ba-tafaẓẓul az khūd mīdād.*

The next *Ṣadr* was Sulṭān Khwāja. Matters relating to suyūrghāls now took a very different course. Akbar had rejected the Islām, and the new *ṣadr*, who had just returned from Makkah,[1] become a member of the Divine Faith. The systematic persecution of the learned and the lawyers had commenced, and His Majesty inquired personally into all grants (*vide* p. 199, second para.). The lands were now steadily withdrawn, and according to Badā,onī, who had managed to get 1,000 bīghas, at first to the great disgust of ʿAbdu 'n-Nabī, many a Muhammadan family was impoverished or utterly ruined.

In 993, Fatḥu 'llāh of Shīrāz (*vide* p. 34) was appointed *Ṣadr*. As the *Suyūrghāl* duties, and with them the dignity of the *Ṣadr*, had dwindled down to nothing, Fatḥu 'llāh, though *Ṣadr*, could be spared for missions to the Dakhin, *Bad.*, p. 343.

" His Shīrāzī servant *Kamāl* officiated for him during his absence, and looked after these lacklands of Ayima-dārs,[2] who had a few spots here and there ; for the dignity of the *Ṣadr* had approached its *kamāl* (perfection). Fatḥu 'llāh had not even the power of conferring five bīghas ; in fact he was an imaginary *Ṣadr*, as all lands had been withdrawn. And yet, the lands which had been withdrawn became the dwelling-places of wild animals, and thus belonged neither to the *Ayima-dārs*, nor to farmers. However, of all these oppressions, there is at least a record left in the books of the *Ṣadr*, though of the office of the *Ṣadr* the name only is left.

Page 368. Fatḥu 'llāh [the *Ṣadr* himself] laid before His Majesty a bag containing the sum of Rs. 1,000, which his collector by means of oppression or under the pretext that an Ayima-dār was not forthcoming or dead, had squeezed out of the widows and unfortunate orphans of the Pargana of Basāwar [which was his jāgīr] and said " My collectors have this much collected from the *Ayima-dārs* as a *kifāyat* (i.e., because the collectors thought the Suyūrghāl holders had more than *sufficient* to live upon)" But the emperor allowed him to keep the sum for himself.

The next *Ṣadr*, Ṣadr Jahān, was a member of the Divine Faith. Though appointed *Ṣadr* immediately after the death of Fatḥu 'llāh, Badā,onī continues calling him *Muftī-yi mamālik-i maḥrūsa*, the Muftī of

---

[1] The same happened afterwards to Mīrzā ʿAzīz Koka. In fact, several examples are on record that devout pilgrims returned so disappointed and " fleeced " from Makkah as to assume a hostile position to the Islām. There is a proverb current in the East, *Ash-shayṭān fī 'l-ḥaramayn*, " The Devil dwells in Makkah and Madīnah."

[2] *Maqtūʿu 'l-arāẓī* a pun reminding of *muqtaʿ* (past part. IV), one on whom lands have been conferred, and *muqṭiʿ* (part act. IV), one who confers lands. Observe that Badā,onī uses the word *ayima* not only in the plural sense of *ayima-dārs*, but as an equivalent of *those who hold a Suyūrghāl.*

Regarding the punishments which grasping Ṣadrs were subject to, *vide* Elliot's Index, p. 253, note, of which, however, the first para. ought to be expunged as unhistorical.

the empire, which had been his title before. Perhaps it was no longer necessary to have a separate officer for the *Ṣadr*ship. Ṣadr Jahān continued to serve under Jahāngīr.

A great portion of the Suyūrghāl lands is specified by Abū 'l-Faẓl in the geographical tables of the Third Book.

Āʾīn 20.

ON THE CARRIAGES, ETC., INVENTED BY HIS MAJESTY.

His Majesty has invented an extraordinary carriage, which has proved a source of much comfort for various people. When this carriage is used for travelling, or for carrying loads, it may be employed for grinding corn.[1]

His Majesty also invented a large cart, which is drawn by one elephant. It is made sufficiently large so as to hold several bath-rooms, and thus serves as a travelling bath. It is also easily drawn by cattle.

Camels and horses also are used for pulling carriages, and thus contribute to the comfort of mankind. Finely built carriages are called *bahals*;[2] if used on even ground several may sit together and travel on.

Water wheels and carts have also been so constructed that water may be fetched from far, low places. Two oxen may pull four such wheels at the same time, or one ox two.

Another machine exists which conveys water from a well, and moves at the same time a millstone.

Āʾīn 21.

THE TEN SER TAX (*DAHSERĪ*).

His Majesty takes from each *bīgha* of tilled land ten sers of grain as a royalty. Store-houses have been constructed in every district. They supply the animals belonging to the State with food, which is never bought in the bāzārs. These stores prove at the same time of great use for the people; for poor cultivators may receive grain for sowing purposes, or people may buy cheap grain at the time of famines. But the stores are only used to supply necessities. They are also used for benevolent purposes; for His Majesty has established in his empire many houses[3]

---

[1] This was, according to Niẓām's Ṭabaqāt, an invention of Fatḥᵘ 'llāh of Shīrāz (*vide* p. 38, note). Niẓām says, "He constructed a millstone which was placed on a cart. It turned itself and ground corn. He also invented a looking-glass which, whether seen near or at a distance, showed all sorts of curious figures. Also a wheel, which cleaned at once twelve barrels." The last mentioned wheel also is ascribed by Abūʿl-Faẓl to Akbar; *vide* Book I, Āʾīn 38, p. 122

[2] Regarding English carriages (*rath-i angrezī*) brought to India under Jahāngīr, *vide* Tuzuk, pp. 167, 168.

[3] *Vide* pp. 210 and 211.

for the poor, where indigent people may get something to eat. He also appoints everywhere experienced people to look after these store-houses, and selects for this purpose active Dārogahs and clever writers, who watch the receipts and charges.

Āʼīn 22.

ON FEASTS.

His Majesty inquires into the excellent customs of past ages, and without looking to the men of the past in particular, he takes up that which is proper, though he have to pay a high price for it. He bestows his fostering care upon men of various classes, and seeks for occasions to make presents. Thus, when His Majesty was informed of the feasts of the Jamsheds, and the festivals of the Pārsī priests, he adopted them, and used them as opportunities of conferring benefits. The following are the most important feasts. 1. *The New Year's Day feast.*[1] It commences on the day when the Sun in his splendour moves to Aries, and lasts till the nineteenth day of the month (Farwardīn). Two days of this period are considered great festivals, when much money and numerous other things are given away as presents ; the first day of the month of Farwardīn, and the nineteenth, which is the time of the *Sharaf.* Again, His Majesty followed the custom of the ancient Pārsīs, who held banquets on those days the names of which coincided with the name of a month.[2] The following are the days which have the same name as a month : 19th *Farwardīn* ; 3rd *Urdībihisht* ; 6th *Khūrdād* ; 13th *Tīr* ; 7th *Amurdād* ; 4th *Shahrīwar* ; 16th *Mihr* ; 10th *Ābān* ; 9th *Āzar* ; 8th, 15th, 23rd *Day* ; 2nd, *Bahman* ; 5th *Isfandārmuz.* Feasts are actually and ideally held on each of these days. People in their happiness raise the strain of inward joy. In the beginning of each *pahr* the *naqqāras* (*vide* p. 51, l. 1) are beaten, when the singers and musicians fall in. On the first of the above feasts coloured lamps are used for three nights ; on the second for one night, and the joy is general.

I have given a few particulars in the first book (Āʼīn 18).

Āʼīn 23.

THE *KHUSHROZ* OR DAY OF FANCY BĀZĀRS.

On the third feast-day of every month, His Majesty holds a large assembly for the purpose of inquiring into the many wonderful things

[1] Badā,onī generally calls this day *Nawrūz-i Jalālī* ; *vide* p. 192, note 3.

[2] Thus *Ābān* was the name of the eighth month (October-November) ; but the tenth day also of every month had the same name.

found in this world. The merchants of the age are eager to attend, and lay out articles from all countries. The people of His Majesty's Harem come, and the women of other men also are invited, and buying and selling is quite general. His Majesty uses such days to select any articles which he wishes to buy, or to fix the price of things, and thus add to his knowledge. The secrets of the empire, the character of the people, the good and bad qualities of each office and workshop, will then appear. His Majesty gives to such days the name of *Khushrūz*, or the joyful day, as they are a source of much enjoyment.

After the fancy bāzārs for women, bāzārs for the men are held. Merchants of all countries then sell their wares. His Majesty watches the transactions, and such as are admitted to Court indulge in the pleasure of buying. Bāzār people, on such occasions, may lay their grievances before His Majesty, without being prevented by the mace-bearers, and may use the opportunity of laying out their stores, in order to explain their circumstances. For those who are good, the dawn of success rises, whilst wicked bāzār people are called to account.

His Majesty has appointed for this purpose a separate treasurer and an accountant, so that the sellers may get paid without delay. The profit made by tradesmen on such occasions is very great.[1]

Āʾīn 24.

REGULATIONS REGARDING MARRIAGES.

Every care bestowed upon this wonderful tie between men is a means of preserving the stability of the human race, and ensuring the progress of the world; it is a preventive against the outbreak of evil passions, and leads to the establishment of homes. Hence His Majesty, inasmuch as he is benign, watches over great and small, and imbues men with his notions of the spiritual union and the equality of essence which he sees in marriage. He abhors marriages which take place between man and woman before the age of puberty. They bring forth no fruit, and His Majesty thinks them even hurtful; for afterwards, when such a couple ripens into manhood, they dislike having connexion, and their home is desolate.

Here in India, where a man cannot see the woman to whom he is betrothed, there are peculiar obstacles; but His Majesty maintains that the consent of the bride and bridegroom, and the permission of the parents, are absolutely necessary in marriage contracts.

[1] Regarding these fancy bāzārs, *vide* above Badā,onī's remarks on p. 213, l. 4.

Marriage between near relations His Majesty thinks highly improper. He says, " The fact that, in ancient times (?) even, a girl was not given to her twin brother[1] ought to silence those who are fond of historical proofs. Marriage between first cousins, however, does not strike the bigoted followers of Muḥammad's religion as wrong; for the beginning of a religion resembles, in this regard, the beginning of the creation of mankind.

His Majesty disapproves of high dowries; for as they are rarely ever paid, they are mere sham; but he admits that the fixing of high dowries is a preventive against rash divorces. Nor does His Majesty approve of every one marrying more than one wife; for this ruins a man's health, and disturbs the peace of the home. He censures old women that take young husbands, and says that doing so is against all modesty.

He has also appointed two sober and sensible men, one of whom inquires into the circumstances of the bridegroom, and the other into those of the bride. These two officers have the title of *Tūʾī-begī*, or masters of marriages. In many cases, the duties are performed by one and the same officer. His Majesty also takes a tax from both parties, to enable them to show their gratitude. The payment of this tax is looked upon as auspicious. Manṣabdārs commanding from five to one thousand, pay 10 *Muhrs*; do. from one thousand to five hundred, 4 *M.*; do. to Commanders of one hundred, 2 *M.*; do. to Commanders of forty, 1 *M.*; do. to Commanders of ten, 4 *R.* The latter fee is also paid by rich people. The middle classes pay 1 *R.*, and common people 1 *dām*.[2] In demanding this tax, the officers have to pay regard to the circumstances of the father of the bride.

Āʾīn 25.

REGULATIONS REGARDING EDUCATION.

In every country, but especially in Hindūstān, boys are kept for years at school, where they learn the consonants and vowels. A great portion of the life of the students is wasted by making them read many books. His Majesty orders that every school boy should first learn to write the letters of the Alphabet, and also learn to trace their several forms.[3] He ought to learn the shape and name of each letter, which may

---

[[1] و برزبان قدسي چنان رود آنکه در باستان دختربتوام ندادی.—P.]

[2] "The sons and daughters of common people were not allowed to marry, unless they came to the office of the kotwāl, and were stared at by the kotwāl's men, who had to take down their respective ages; and you may imagine what advantages and fine opportunities the officers thus had, especially the people of the kotwāl, and the *khānū-yi kalāl* (?), and their other low assistants outside." *Bad.* II, p. 391. *Vide* also Third Book, Āʾīn 5.

[3] Boys in the East generally learn to write by running their pens over the characters of the copyslips (*qiṭʿas*).

be done in two days, when the boy should proceed to write the joined letters. They may be practised for a week, after which the boy should learn some prose and poetry by heart, and then commit to memory some verses to the praise of God, or moral sentences, each written separately. Care is to be taken that he learns to understand everything himself; but the teacher may assist him a little. He then ought for some time to be daily practised in writing a hemistich or a verse, and will soon acquire a current hand. The teacher ought especially to look after five things: knowledge of the letters; meanings of words; the hemistich; the verse; the former lesson. If this method of teaching be adopted, a boy will learn in a month, or even in a day, what it took others years to understand, so much so that people will get quite astonished. Every boy ought to read books on morals, arithmetic, the notation peculiar to arithmetic, agrculture, mensuration, geometry, astronomy, physiognomy, household matters, the rules of government, medicine, logic, the *ṭabīʿī*, *riyāẓī*, and *ilāhī*, sciences,[1] and history; all of which may be gradually acquired.

In studying Sanscrit, students ought to learn the Bayākaran, Nīyā,ī, Bedanta, and Pātanjal. No one should be allowed to neglect those things which the present time requires.

These regulations shed a new light on schools, and cast a bright lustre over Madrasas.

Āʾīn 26.

THE ADMIRALTY.

This department is of great use for the successful operations of the army, and for the benefit of the country in general; it furnishes means of obtaining things of value, provides for agriculture, and His Majesty's household. His Majesty, in fostering this source of power, keeps four objects in view, and looks upon promoting the efficiency of this department as an act of divine worship.

First.—The fitting out of strong boats, capable of carrying elephants. Some are made in such a manner as to be of use in sieges and for the conquest of strong forts. Experienced officers look upon ships as if they were houses and dromedaries, and use them as excellent means of conquest. So especially in Turkey, Zanzibar, and Europe. In every part of His

[1] This is the three-fold division of sciences. *Ilāhī*, or *divine*, sciences comprise everything connected with theology and the means of acquiring a knowledge of God. *Riyāẓī* sciences treat of quantity, and comprise mathematics, astronomy, music, mechanics. *Ṭabī-ʿī* sciences comprehend physical sciences.

Some dictionaries call the last class of sciences *ṭabaʿʾī*, instead of *ṭabīʿī*.

Majesty's empire ships are numerous; but in Bengal, Kashmīr, and Thathah (Sind) they are the pivot of all commerce. His Majesty had the sterns of the boats made in shape of wonderful animals, and thus combines terror with amusement. Turrets and pleasing kiosks, markets, and beautiful flower-beds, have likewise been constructed on the rivers. Along the coasts of the ocean, in the west, east, and south of India, large ships are built, which are suitable for voyages. The harbours have been put into excellent condition, and the experience of seamen has much improved. Large ships are also built at Ilāhābās and Lāhor, and are then sent to the coast. In Kashmīr, a model of a ship was made which was much admired.

Secondly.—To appoint experienced seamen, acquainted with the tides, the depths of the ocean, the time when the several winds blow, and their advantages and disadvantages. They must be familiar with shallows and banks. Besides, a seaman must be hale and strong, a good swimmer, kind hearted, hard working, capable of bearing fatigue, patient; in fact, he must possess all good qualities. Men of such character can only be found after much trouble. The best seamen come from Malībār (Malabar).

Boatmen also bring men and their things from one side of the river to the other.

The number of sailors in a ship varies according to the size of the vessel. In large ships there are twelve classes. 1. The *Nā<u>kh</u>udā*, or owner of the ship. This word is evidently a short form of *Nāv<u>kh</u>udā*. He fixes the course of the ship. 2. The *Muᶜallim*, or Captain. He must be acquainted with the depths and the shallow places of the ocean, and must know astronomy. It is he who guides the ship to her destination, and prevents her from falling into dangers. 3. The *Tamḍīl*,[1] or chief of the *<u>kh</u>alāṣīs*, or sailors. Sailors, in seamen's language, are called *<u>kh</u>alāṣīs* or *<u>kh</u>ārwas*. 4. The *Nā<u>kh</u>udā-<u>kh</u>ashab*. He supplies the passengers with firewood and straw, and assists in shipping and unlading the cargo. 5. The *Sarhang*, or mate, superintends the docking and landing of the ship, and often acts for the *Muᶜallim*. 6. The *Bhanḍārī* has the charge of the stores. 7. The *Karrānī*[2] is a writer who keeps the accounts of the ship, and serves out water to the passengers. 8. The *Sukkāngīr*,[3] or helmsman. He steers the ship according to the orders of the *Muᶜallim*. Some ships carry several helmsmen, but never more than twenty. 9. The *Panjarī* looks out from

---

[[1] *Tanḍail* or *tanḍel*, H.—P.]

[2] This word is nowadays pronounced *Kirānī*, and is applied to any clerk. The word is often used contemptuously.

[[3] There is a modern Anglo-Indian word used in Calcutta, 'sea-cunny,' derived from *sukkānī*.—P.]

the top of the mast, and gives notice when he sees land or a ship, or a coming storm, etc. 10. The *Gūmtī* belongs to the class of *khalāṣīs*. He throws out the water which has leaked through the ship. 11. The *Top-andāz*, or gunner, is required in naval fights; the number depends on the size of the ship. 12. The *Khārwa* or common sailors. They set and furl the sails. Some of them perform the duty of divers, and stop leaks, or set free the anchor when it sticks fast. The amount of their wages varies, and depends on the voyage, or *kūsh*, as seamen call it. In the harbour of *Sātgāw* (*Hūglī*) a *Nākhudā* gets 400 *R.*; besides he is allowed four *malīkh*, or cabins, which he fills with wares for his own profit. Every ship is divided into several divisions, for the accommodation of passengers and the stowage of goods, each of the divisions being called a *malīkh*. The *Muʿallim* gets 200 *R.* and two *malīkhs*; the *Tanḍīl*, 120 *R.*; the *Karrānī*, 50 *R.* and one *malīkh*; the *Nākhudā khashab*, 30 *R.*; the *Sarhang*, 25 *R.*; the *Sukkāngīr*, *Panjarī*, and *Bhanḍārī*, each 15 *R.*; each *Khārwa* or common sailor, 40 *R.*, and his daily food in addition; the *Degandāz*, or gunner, 12 *R.*

In *Kambhāyat* (Cambay), a *Nākhudā* gets 800 *R.*, and the other men in the same proportion.

In *Lāharī*, a nākhudā gets 300 *R.*, and the rest in proportion.

In *Āchīn* he gets half as much again as in southern harbours; in Portugal, two and a half as much again; and in Malacca,[1] twice as much again. In Pegu, and Dahnāsarī, he gets half as much again as in Cambay. All these rates vary according to the place and the length of the voyage. But it would take me too long to give more details.

Boatmen on rivers have wages varying from 100 to 500 *d. per mensem*.

Thirdly, an experienced man has been appointed to look after the rivers. He must be an imposing and fearless man, must have a loud voice, must be capable of bearing fatigue, active, zealous, kind, fond of travelling, a good swimmer. As he possesses experience, he settles every difficulty which arises regarding fords, and takes care that such places are not overcrowded, or too narrow, or very uneven, or full of mud. He regulates the number of passengers which a ferry may carry; he must not allow travellers to be delayed, and sees that poor people are passed over *gratis*. He ought not to allow people to swim across, or wares to be deposited anywhere else but at fording places. He should also prevent people from crossing at night, unless in cases of necessity.

Fourthly, the remission of duties. His Majesty, in his mercy, has remitted many tolls, though the income derived from them equalled the

[[1] Malāgha.—P.]

revenue of a whole country. He only wishes that boatmen should get their wages. The state takes certain taxes in harbour places; but they never exceed two and a half *per cent.*, which is so little compared with the taxes formerly levied, that merchants lock upon harbour taxes as totally remitted.

The following sums are levied as river tolls. For every boat, 1 *R. per kos* at the rate of 1,000 *mans*, provided the boat and the men belong to one and the same owner. But if the boat belongs to another man and everything in the boat to the man who has hired it, the tax is 1 *R.* for every $2\frac{1}{2}$ *kos*. At ferry places, an elephant has to pay 10 *d.* for crossing; a laden cart, 4 *d.*; do. empty, 2 *d.*; a laden camel, 1 *d.*; empty camels, horses, cattle with their things, $\frac{1}{2}$ *d.*; do. empty, $\frac{1}{4}$ *d.* Other beasts of burden pay $\frac{1}{16}$ *d.*, which includes the toll due by the river. Twenty people pay 1 *d.* for crossing; but they are often taken *gratis*.

The rule is that one-half or one-third of the tolls thus collected go to the State (the other half goes to the boatmen).

Merchants are therefore well treated, and the articles of foreign countries are imported in large quantities.

Āʾīn 27.

ON HUNTING.

Superficial, worldly observers see in killing an animal a sort of pleasure, and in their ignorance stride about, as if senseless, on the field of their passions. But deep inquirers see in hunting a means of acquisition of knowledge, and the temple of their worship derives from it a peculiar lustre. This is the case with His Majesty. He always makes hunting a means of increasing his knowledge, and besides, uses hunting parties as occasions to inquire, without having first given notice of his coming, into the condition of the people and the army. He travels *incognito*, and examines into matters referring to taxation, or to *Sayūrg̲h̲āl* lands, or to affairs connected with the household. He lifts up such as are cppressed. and punishes the oppressors. On account of these higher reasons His Majesty indulges in the chase, and shows himself quite enamoured of it. Short-sighted and shallow observers think that His Majesty has no other object in view but hunting; but the wise and experienced know that he pursues higher aims.

When His Majesty starts on a hunting party, active *Qarāwals* [men employed by the *Mīr Shikār*,[1] or Master of Hunting] surround the hunting

[[1] *Mīr shikār* in India is now applied to *any* assistant falconer, bird-catcher, etc. etc.—P.]

ground, the *Qur* (p. 116), remaining at a distance of about five *kos* from it. Near the *Qur* the grandees and other people await the arrival of His Majesty. The men who look after the things sit down and watch. About a yard behind them the *Mīr Tūzak* stands ready for service, and about a *kos* and one-half behind them stand some of the *Khidmatiyya* (p. 252) and other servants of His Majesty. The *Khidmatiyya* are told off to watch at that place. At about the same distance there stands a vigilant officer with some of His Majesty's servants. He advances very slowly and guards the private hunting ground. Behind them an experienced officer is stationed to superintend the whole. Several near servants of His Majesty have admission to this place; but generally only such are allowed to come as are required to render services at the chase.

When a certain distance has been passed over, His Majesty selects a few to accompany him, and then moves on; and after having gone over another distance, he generally goes alone, or accompanied by one or two. When the hour of rest comes, both parties which had been left behind again join His Majesty

As I have stated the views of His Majesty regarding the chase, and have written down some remarks on the arrangements which are made during hunting parties, I shall give a few particulars as to the several modes of chasing, and the wonderful contrivances which people have recourse to.

1. *Tiger Hunting.*

They make a large cage, and having fastened it (on the ground) with strong iron ties, they put it in places frequented by tigers. The door is left open; but it is arranged in such a manner that the slightest shaking will cause it to close. Within the cage they put a goat, which is protected by a screen so constructed that the tiger can see the goat, but not get hold of it. Hunger will lead the tiger to the cage. As soon as he enters, he is caught.

Another method.—They put a poisoned arrow on a bow, painted green, in such a manner that a slight movement will cause the arrow to go off. The bow is hung upon a tree, and when the tiger passes, and shakes it a little, the arrow will hit the animal and kill it.

Another method.—They tie a sheep to a place in a road frequented by tigers, putting round about the sheep on the ground small blades of grass covered with glue.[1] The tiger comes rushing forward and gets his claws full of the glue. The more he tries to get rid of it, the more will the glue

[1 *Shilim*, probably bird-lime made from the exudations from slits made in the bark of the *bar* (banyan) or the *pīpal* tree.—P.]

stick to his feet, and when he is quite senseless and exhausted, the hunters come from the ambush and kill him. Or they take him alive, and tame him.

His Majesty, from his straightforwardness, dislikes having recourse to such tricks, and prefers with bows or matchlocks openly to attack this brute, which destroys so many lives.

Another method.—An intrepid experienced hunter gets on the back of a male buffalo and makes it attack the tiger. The buffalo will quickly catch the tiger on its horns, and toss it violently upwards, so that it dies. It is impossible to describe the excitement of this manner of hunting the tiger. One does not know what to admire more, the courage of the rider, or his skill in standing firm on the slippery back of the buffalo.

One day, notice was given that a man-eating tiger had made its appearance in the district of Bārī. His Majesty got on the elephant *Nāhir Khān*, and went into the jungle. The brute was stirred up; and striking its claws into the forehead of the huge animal, it pulled its head close down to the ground, when the tiger was killed by the men. This occurrence astonished the most intrepid and experienced hunters.

On another occasion, His Majesty hunted near Ṭoḍa. The tiger had stretched one of the party to the ground. His Majesty aimed at the brute, killed it, and thus saved the life of the man.

Once during a *qamargha*[1] chase, a large tiger was stirred up. The animal attacked His Majesty, when he shot it in time through the head and killed it.

Once a tiger struck his claws into a man. All who witnessed it despaired of his life. His Majesty shot the tiger through the body and released the unfortunate man.

A remarkable scene took place in the forest of Mathurā. Shujāʿat Khān (*vide* Āʾīn 30, No. 51), who had advanced very far, got suddenly timid. His Majesty remained standing where he was, and looked furiously at the tiger. The brute cowered[2] down before that divine glance, and turned right about trembling all over. In a short time it was killed.

The feats of His Majesty are too numerous to be imagined; much less can a Hindustānī, as I am, describe them in a dignified style.

He slays lions,[3] but would not hurt an ant.
He girds himself for the fray; but the lion[3] drops his claws from fear.[4]

---

[1] *Qamargha* is a chase for which drivers are employed. [The game is apparently enclosed in a living ring.—P.]

[2] This is one of Akbar's miracles.

[[3] *Sher*, tiger.—P.]

[4] These two verses are taken from Fayẓī's *Nal Daman*; *vide* p. 113, note 1.

2. *Elephant-catching.*

There are several modes of hunting elephants.

1. *Kheda.*[1] The hunters are both on horseback and on foot. They go during summer to the grazing places of this wonderful animal, and commence to beat drums and blow pipes, the noise of which makes the elephants quite frightened. They commence to rush about, till from their heaviness and exertions no strength is left in them. They are then sure to run under a tree for shade, when some experienced hunters throw a rope made of hemp or bark round their feet or necks, and thus tie them to the trees. They are afterwards led off in company with some trained elephants, and gradually get tame. One-fourth of the value of an elephant thus caught is given to the hunters as wages.

2. *Chor kheda.* They take a tame female elephant to the grazing place of wild elephants, the driver stretching himself on the back of the elephant, without moving or giving any other sign of his presence. The elephants then commence to fight, when the driver manages to secure one by throwing a rope round the foot.

3. *Gād.*[2] A deep pit is constructed in a place frequented by elephants, which is covered up with grass. As soon as the elephants come near it the hunters from their ambush commence to make a great noise. The elephants get confused, and losing their habitual cautiousness, they fall rapidly and noisily into the hole. They are then starved and kept without water, when they soon get tame.

4. *Bār.* They dig a ditch round the resting-place of elephants, leaving only one road open, before which they put up a door, which is fastened with ropes. The door is left open, but closes when the rope is cut. The hunters then put both inside and outside the door such food as elephants like. The elephants eat it up greedily; their voraciousness makes them forget all cautiousness, and without fear they enter at the door. A fearless hunter, who has been lying concealed, then cuts the rope, and the door closes. The elephants start up, and in their fury try to break the door. They are all in commotion. The hunters then kindle fires and make much noise. The elephants run about till they get tired, and no strength is left in them. Tame females are then brought to the place, by whose means the wild elephants are caught. They soon get tame.

From times of old people have enjoyed elephant hunts by any of the above modes; His Majesty has invented a new manner, which

---

[1] Hence our elephant *kheddas.*

[[2] For *gāḍ* or *gāṛā* f., a pit ?—P.]

admits of remarkable *finesse*. In fact, all excellent modes of hunting are inventions of His Majesty. A wild herd of elephants is surrounded on three sides by drivers, one side alone being left open. At it several female elephants are stationed. From all sides, male elephants will approach to cover the females. The latter then go gradually into an enclosure, whither the males follow. They are now caught as shown above.[1]

3. *Leopard*[2] *Hunting.*

Leopards, when wild, select three places. In one part of the country they hunt; in another part they rest and sleep; and in a third district they play and amuse themselves. They mostly sleep on the top of a hill. The shade of a tree is sufficient for the leopard. He rubs himself against the trunk. Round about the tree they deposit their excrements, which are called in Hindī *ākhar*.

Formerly, hunters used to make deep holes and cover them with grass. These pits were called *odī*. The leopards on coming near them, fell down to the bottom; but they often broke their feet or legs, or managed by jumping to get out again. Nor could you catch more than one in each pit. His Majesty therefore invented a new method, which has astonished the most experienced hunters. He made a pit only two or three *gaz* deep, and constructed a peculiar trapdoor, which closes when the leopard falls into the hole. The animal is thus never hurt. Sometimes more than one go into the trap. On one occasion no less than seven leopards were caught. At the time of their heat, which takes place in winter, a female leopard had been walking about on the field, and six male leopards were after her. Accidentally she fell into a pit, and her male companions, unwilling to let her off, dropped in one after the other—a nice scene, indeed.

His Majesty also catches leopards by tiring them out, which is very interesting to look at.

---

[1] "A large number of people had surrounded the whole jungle, outside of which, on a small empty space, a throne made of wood had been put on a tree, as a seat for the emperor [Jahāngīr], and on the neighbouring trees beams had been put, upon which the courtiers were to sit and enjoy the sight. About two hundred male elephants, with strong nooses, and many females were in readiness. Upon each elephant there sat two men of the *Jhariyyah* caste, who chiefly occupy themselves in this part of India [Gujrāt] with elephant hunting. The plan was to drive the wild elephants from all parts of the jungle near the place where the emperor sat, so that he might enjoy the sight of this exciting scene. When the drivers closed up from all sides of the jungle, their ring unfortunately broke on account of the density and impenetrability of the wood, and the arrangements of the drivers partially failed. The wild elephants ran about as if mad; but twelve male and female elephants were caught before the eyes of the emperor." *Iqbālnāma*, p. 113.

[[2] *Yūz*, the *chītā* or hunting leopard.—P.]

Another method is to fasten nooses to the foot of the above mentioned tree. When the animal comes to scratch itself, it gets entangled.

His Majesty generally hunts leopards thirty or forty *kos* from Āgra, especially in the districts of Bārī, Sīmāwalī, Alāpūr, Sunnām, Bhaṭinḍa, Bhaṭnīr, Paṭan in the Panjāb, Fatḥpūr Jhinjhanū, Nāgor, Mīrath, Jodhpūr, Jaisalmīr, Amrsarnāyin; but several other more remote spots have been selected as hunting grounds. His Majesty used often to go to the first mentioned places, take out the leopards that had fallen into a pit, and hand them over to the keepers. He would often travel over great distances, and was perhaps just on the point of resting a little; but before he had done so, good news were brought from some hunting ground, when he hastened away on a fleet courser.

In former times people managed to train a newly caught leopard for the chase in the space of three months, or if they exerted themselves, in two months. From the attention which His Majesty pays to this animal, leopards are now trained in an excellent manner in the short space of eighteen days. Old and active keepers were surprised at such results, and extolled the charm of His Majesty's knowledge. From good motives, and from a desire to add splendour to his court, His Majesty used to take it upon himself to keep and train leopards, astonishing the most experienced by his success.

A rather remarkable case is the following. Once a leopard had been caught, and without previous training, on a mere hint by His Majesty, it brought in the prey like trained leopards. Those who were present had their eyes opened to truth, and experienced the blessing of prostrating themselves in belief on His Majesty.[1]

Attracted by the wonderful influence of the loving heart of His Majesty, a leopard once followed the imperial suite without collar or chain, and like a sensible human being, obeyed every command, and at every leopard chase enjoyed it very much to have its skill brought to the test.

There are two hundred keepers in charge of the *k͟hāṣa* leopards. A proper system of training has been laid down.

Āʾīn 28.

THE FOOD ALLOWED TO LEOPARDS. THE WAGES OF THE KEEPERS.

First class leopards get 5 *s.* of meat every day; second class, $4\frac{1}{2}$ *s.* third class, 4 *s.*; fourth class, $3\frac{3}{4}$ *s.*; fifth class, $3\frac{1}{2}$ *s.*; sixth class, $3\frac{1}{4}$ *s.*;

---

[1] Two more miracles of Akbar's.

seventh class, 3 *s.* ; eighth class, $2\frac{3}{4}$ *s.* The meat is given in a lump ; and as on Sundays no animals are killed,[1] double the daily portion is given on Saturdays.

Formerly every six months, but now annually, four *sers* of butter and one-tenth of a *ser* of brimstone are given as ointment, which prevents itch. Four men also were appointed to train and look after each leopard ; but now there are three men told off for such leopards as sit on horses when taken to the hunting ground, and only two for such as sit on carts and on doolies. The wages of the keepers vary from 30 *R.* to 5 *R. per mensem* ; but they have at the same time to look after the cattle which draw the leopard carts. The servants who look after the cattle are divided into seniors and juniors, each class being subdivided into five divisions. The seniors get 300 *d.*, 260 *d.*, 220 *d.* 200 *d.*, and 180 *d.*, which is the lowest allowance ; the juniors get 160 *d.*, 140 *d.*, 120 *d.*, 110 *d.*, and 100 *d.* For the sake of show, the leopards get brocaded saddle cloths,[2] chains studded with jewels, and coarse blankets, and *Gushkānī* [3] carpets to sit on. Grandees of the court also are appointed to superintend the keepers of each leopard ; they are to take care that the animals are nicely dressed, and that new ones are added to the establishment. Each leopard has a name which indicates some of his qualities. Every ten leopards form a *Miṣl* or *Ṭaraf* (set) ; they are also divided according to their rank as follows. One thousand [4] leopards are kept in His Majesty's park, and an interesting encampment they form. The three first sets are *khāṣa* ; they are kept at Court together with two other sets. For their conveyance two litters (*miḥaffa*) are hung over the back of an elephant, one litter on each side. On each litter one leopard sits, looking out for a prey. Litters are also put on camels, horses, and mules. Carts even are made for the leopards, and are drawn by horses or cattle ; or they are made to sit on horses ; and sometimes they are carried by men in doolies. The best leopard which His Majesty has goes by the name of *Samand-mānik* ; he is carried on a *chau-ḍol*, and proceeds with much pomp. His servants,

---

[1] According to the order mentioned on p. 209, 2nd para.

[[2] *Jul*, a covering for any animal.—P.]

[3] In my text edition, p. 208, l. 8, گشکانی. This should perhaps be گشکانی or گوشکانی *goskhānī*, Goshkān (in Arabic *Joshqān*), being a town in Irān, famous for its carpets.

[4] " Among the curious events which happened during the present [Jahāngīr's] reign I must mention that a leopard in captivity covered a female leopard, which gave birth to three cubs. The late emperor [Akbar] during his youth, was passionately fond of leopards and hunting with leopards. He had about 9,000 leopards collected during his reign, and tried much to pair them, so as to get cubs, but in vain. He even allowed some leopards to run about in the gardens without collars, letting them walk about and hunt after their fashion ; but they would not pair. During this year a male leopard broke its collar, and covered a female, which after a space of two months and a half gave birth to three cubs. They went on well, and grew big." *Iqbālnāma*, p. 70.

fully equipped, run at his side; the *naqqāra* (a large drum) is beaten in front, and sometimes he is carried by two men on horseback, the two ends of the pole of the *chau-ḍol* resting on the necks of their horses. Formerly two horses were kept for every leopard; but now three horses are given to two leopards. Others have a dooly, or a cart drawn by four oxen. Many travel along on one and the same dooly. A tame, trained leopard has the dooly carried by three men, others by two.

Skill exhibited by hunting leopards.

Leopards will go against the wind, and thus they get scent of a prey, or come to hear its voice. They then plan an attack, and give the hunters notice where the prey is.[1] The hunters keep the animal near themselves, and proceed to catch the prey. This is done in three ways.

1. *Ūparghaṭī.* The hunters let off the leopard to the right from the place where the deer[2] was seen. The leopard swiftly seizes it with his claws. 2. *Righnī.* The leopard lies concealed, and is shown the deer[2] from a distance. The collar is then taken off, when the leopard, with perfect skill, will dash off, jumping from ambush to ambush till he catches the deer.[2] 3. *Muhārī.* The leopard is put in an ambush, having the wind towards himself. The cart is then taken away to the opposite direction. This perplexes the deer,[2] when the leopard will suddenly make his way near it and catch it.

It is impossible to describe the wonderful feats of this animal; language fails to express his skill and cunning. Thus he will raise up the dust with his forefeet and hind legs, in order to conceal himself; or he will lie down so flat, that you cannot distinguish him from the surface of the ground.

Formerly a leopard would not kill more than three deer[2] at one and the same chase; but now he will hunt as many as twelve.

His Majesty has also invented a method called *chatrmanḍal.* The hunters lie in ambush near a place frequented by deer,[2] and commence the chase from this place as if it was a *qamargha* hunt (in which drivers are used). The leopards are then let off in all directions, and many deer[2] are thus caught.

The men employed to train and keep the imperial leopards receive presents on all occasions when the animals exhibit skill, as an encouragement to further exertions. A special present has been fixed for each animal, but I cannot specify this.

Once, from the kindness shown by His Majesty, a deer[2] made friendship

---

[[1] The translation of this passage is doubtful.—P.]
[[2] *Āhū*, gazelle.—P.]

with a leopard. They lived together and enjoyed each other's company. The most remarkable thing was this, that the leopard when let off against other deer,[1] would pounce upon them as any other leopard.

In former times leopards were never allowed to remain loose towards the close of the day; for people were afraid of their stubbornness and anxiety to run away. But now, in consequence of the practical rules made by His Majesty, they are let loose in the evenings and yet remain obedient. Formerly, leopards were also kept blindfolded,[2] except at the time of the chase; for the leopards used to get brisk and run about as if mad. But nowadays they are kept without covers for their heads. The grandees of the court are allowed to bet on forty *kh̲āṣa* leopards; whoever wins takes the amount of his bet from the others. If a leopard is first in bringing twenty deer, his *Ḍoriya* [3] gets five rupees from his equals. The grandee in charge of the *kh̲āṣa* leopards, Sayyid Aḥmad of Bārha,[4] gets one muhr from each bet, by which he makes a good deal of money. As often as a grandee lays before His Majesty twenty pair of deer horns,[5] he takes an *Ashrafī* from each of his equals. So also do the *Ṭarafdārs* and *Qarāwals* [6] bet; in fact every one shows his zeal in trying to get as many deer[1] as possible. The skins of the deer [1] are often given to poor people as part of money presents.

It is remarkable that His Majesty can at once tell by seeing a hide to what hunting ground the deer [1] belonged.

His Majesty, in fulfilment of a vow made by him before the birth of the eldest prince, never hunts on Fridays.[7]

[[1] *Āhū*, gazelle.—P.]

[[2] *i.e.* hooded.—P.]

[3] The man who holds the chain to which the leopard is fastened.

[4] He was a *Duhazārī*; *vide* Āʾīn 30, No. 91.

[5] Akbar required the horns of deer.

"In this year (981), His Majesty built several edifices and castles on the road from Āgra to Ajmīr. The reason was this. He thought it incumbent upon him once a year to make a pilgrimage to the tomb (*dargāh*) of Muʿīn-i Chishtī at Ajmīr; he therefore had houses built at every stage on the road to that town. He also erected at every *kos* a tower (*manāra*), and had a well made near it. The towers were studded with several hundred thousand horns of deer which His Majesty had killed during his lifetime. The words *mīl-i shāk̲h̲* contain the *Tārīk̲h̲* (981). I wished His Majesty had made gardens and *sarāīs* for travellers instead." *Badā,onī*, ii, p. 173. *Vide* also Elliot's Index, p. 243, note.

[6] *Ṭarafdārs*, the men in charge of a *ṭaraf*, which word Abū'l-Faẓl above used in the same sense as *miṣl*, or set. *Ṭarafdār* means also a Zamīndār. A *Qarāwal* is a driver.

[7] "It was at this time [1027 A.H. or A.D. 1618] that Shāhzāda Shujā, son of Shāhjahān, fell ill, and as I am so much attached to him, and the doctors could not cure him of the insensibility in which he had lain for several days, I humbly prayed to God, and asked Him a favour. During the prayer, it occurred to me that I had already made a contract with my God and had promised Him to give up hunting after reaching the age of fifty, not to touch after that an arrow or a gun, and never again to slay an animal with my own hands; and I thought that if I should carry into effect my former vow from the present time, which would prevent so many animals from being killed, God might grant my

The Siyāh-gosh.[1]

His Majesty is very fond of using this plucky little animal for hunting purposes. In former times it would attack a hare or a fox; but now it kills black deer.[2] It eats daily 1 *s.* of meat. Each has a separate keeper, who gets 100 *d. per mensem.*

Dogs.

His Majesty likes this animal very much for his excellent qualities, and imports dogs from all countries. Excellent dogs come from Kābul, especially from the Hazāra district [north of Rawūl Pindī]. They even ornament dogs, and give them names.[3] Dogs will attack every kind of animals, and more remarkable still, they will attack a tiger. Several also will join and hunt down the enemy. *Khāṣa* dogs get daily 2 *s.* of meat; others get 1¼ *s.* There is one keeper for every two *Tāzī* [4] (hunting) dogs; their wages are 100 *d. per mensem.*[5]

Hunting Deer [6] *with Deer.*

This timid animal also may be tamed and trained. They put a net [7] over his horns, and let it off against wild deer,[6] which from fear will fight with them. During the struggle, the horn, or the foot, or the ears of the wild deer will get entangled in the net; the hunters who have been lying in ambush, will then run up to it, and catch it. The deer thus caught

---

prayer for the prince's recovery, I then made this contract with God, and promised, in all singleness of intention and true belief, never again to harm an animal with my own hand. Through God's mercy, the sufferings of the prince were entirely allayed. When I was in the womb of my mother, it happened one day that I did not quicken as usual. The servants of the Harem grew alarmed, and reported the fact to my august father [Akbar]. In those days my father was continually hunting with leopards. That day happened to be Friday. My father then, with a view to making God inclined to preserve me, made a vow never again, to the end of his life, to hunt on Fridays. I have followed the practice of my father, and have never hunted with leopards on a Friday." *Tuzuk-i Jahāngīrī*, p. 249.

Jahāngīr's self-denial was not great; for when the prince was sick, Jahāngīr was fifty years of age!

[1] Or *black ear*, the Persian translation of the Turkish *qara-qolaq*, whence our *Felis caracal.*

[The Red Lynx of India, Persia, and Arabia. It is trained to take, besides the quarry mentioned, partridges, pigeons, cats, and Egyptian vultures, etc.—P.]

[[2] *Āhū-yi siyāh*, a wrong term.—P.]

[3] This would not strike us as something worth mentioning. But as dogs are considered unclean animals by Muhammadans, they are not looked upon as domestic. Nowadays we hear occasionally names, as *kallū, bachhū*; or English names as *fenī* (Fanny), *buldāg* (bull dog), etc.

European bloodhounds were early imported by the Portuguese. Jahāngīr once said to Roe, " I only desire you to help me to a horse of the greatest size, and a male and female of mastiffes, and the tall Irish greyhounds, and such other dogges as hunt in your land." Regarding European dogs in India, *vide* also *Tuzuk*, p. 138, l. 3, from below.

[[4] *Tāzī* is the Arab greyhound.—P.]

[[5] For a note on hunting Dogs and Cheetas *vide Jl. and Pro. As. Soc. Beng.*, 1907.—P.]

[[6] *Āhū*, gazelle.—P.]

[[7] *Dām*, probably a noose of thick gut.—P.]

passes through a course of instruction, and gets tame. If the net[1] should break, or the deer get tired during the struggle, it will return to the keeper, who either puts a new net[1] on it, or sends out a fresh deer.[2]

Sulṭān Fīrūz-i Khiljī used to indulge in this sport; but His Majesty reduced this manner of hunting to a proper system.

Sometimes it happens that a wild deer will carry on the struggle from morning till evening, defeating as many as four tamed deer; but at last it will succumb to the fifth. Deer are nowadays rendered so perfectly obedient as to hunt at night; of their own accord they will return to their keepers, should the net break, or the wild deer run away; on hearing the call, they will discontinue a fight, come back, and then again engage, if ordered to do so.

In former times deer were never let loose at night time; for people were afraid, lest they should run away. Hence they attached a heavy ball to one of their feet, when the deer were let loose.

Many stories are related of the sagacity and faithfulness of trained deer.

Only lately a deer created much sensation. It had run away from Ilāhābād, and after bravely crossing rivers and plains, returned to the Panjāb, its home, and rejoined its former keeper.

In former times, two persons at most enjoyed together the pleasures of deer hunting. They would even, from fear of the timidity of the deer, alter the style of their dress, and lie concealed among shrubs. Nor would they employ other than wild deer; they caught them somehow, and taught them to hunt. His Majesty has introduced a new way, according to which more than two hundred may at the same time go deer hunting. They drive slowly about forty cattle towards a place where deer are; the hunters are thus concealed, and when arrived enjoy the chase.

There are nowadays also deer-studs; the deer born in captivity are employed as hunting-deer.

The keepers will also bend forward and allow the trained deer to jump on them from behind. Wild deer, on seeing this, will think that they are in the act of copulation, and come near to fight. This way of hunting is disapproved of by His Majesty, who uses female deer as a means of making wild deer fight.

Once a deer caught a leopard, whose foot had got entangled in the net.[1] Both were brought together from Gujrāt, as mentioned above (?).

Ghanṭāhera is the name given to the following mode of hunting. The

---

[[1] *Dām*, probably a noose of thick gut.—P.] [[2] *Āhū*, gazelle.—P.]

hunter takes a shield, or a basket, the concave[1] side being turned from him. He then lights a lamp, which being put in the concavity of the shield, will conceal him, and commences to ring bells. Other hunters lie at the same time in wait. The light of the lamp, and the sound of the bells, will attract the animals towards the place, when they are shot by the hunters in ambush. The sound of musical instruments will so enchant deer that they are easily caught; or sometimes hunters will charm them with a song, and when the deer approach will rise up and cruelly slay them. From a long time His Majesty has disapproved of these two methods.

Thāngī. The hunter manages to get opposite a wild deer; and bareheaded, from a distance, he commences to throw himself into odd attitudes. The deer then mistakes him for a mad man, and from curiosity will approach him. At this moment the hunters come from the ambush and kill it.

Baukāra. The hunters lie in ambush, against the scent, at a good distance from each other. Some others drive the deer towards them, each of the drivers swinging a white sheet above his head. The deer naturally will take fright, and run towards the hunters in ambush, who kill them.

Ḍaḍāwan. Two good shots, dressed in green, place themselves as before, and have the deer driven towards themselves. This manner of hunting yields much amusement, as the deer get quite perplexed.

Ajāra. The hunters tie green twigs round their bodies from head to foot, and similarly conceal their bows and arrows. They then move boldly to a place where deer generally pass, and enjoy the chase. Or they make ropes of deer skin, and attach them to trees, or let them hang down from poles all round about the place where wild deer sleep. They then lay down some nooses at a place situate against the wind. When the hunters show themselves from the side, the deer are compelled to run towards the spot where the nooses lie, and thus get caught. Sometimes the hunter will take his place behind a tree, and imitate the voice of deer. As soon as deer approach him, he kills them. Or, they tie a female deer to a place in a plain, or they let a trained deer go to the pasture place of wild deer. The latter will soon come near it, and get entangled with their feet.

Ṭhāngī. The hunter . . .[2] walks about bareheaded as if mad; his clothes are stained all over with *pān* juice, and the man himself acts as if he were wounded. Wild animals and others will soon gather round him, waiting for his death; but their greediness and desire lead them to destruction.

[[1] *Wāzhgūn.* The concave side towards him ?—P.]

[2] The text has *dar khāna-yi zīn,* in the hollow of a saddle (?).

Buffalo Hunts.

At a place where buffaloes sleep, a rope is laid in the ground; but the end forming a loop is left outside. Another long rope is attached to it. To this they tie a female buffalo that wants the male. A courageous active man lies in ambush. As soon as a wild male buffalo comes to the spot, and covers the female, the hunter makes use of the opportunity, and fastens the foot of the male; but it frequently happens that the man loses courage, and has to pay for the attempt with his life.

Another mode of catching them is to go near the ponds which they frequent. They put snares round the ponds; and sitting on tame buffaloes the hunters go into the water with spears in their hands. Some buffaloes are then killed with spears, others are caught in the snares. A similar method may be adopted when buffaloes are attacked in their jungle pastures.

On Hunting with Hawks.

His Majesty is very fond of these remarkable animals, and often uses them for hunting purposes. Though he trains the *bāz*,[1] *shāhīn*,[2] *shunqār*,[3] and *burkat*[4] falcons, and makes them perform wonderful deeds, His Majesty prefers the *bāsha*,[5] to which class of hawks he gives various names.

As I am compelled to hurry on, and must restrict myself to summary accounts, it is impossible to say much about this matter, or about the skill of the several birds, especially as I know little about it, being by nature averse to destroying life. I shall, however, give a few details, and lead inquirers to the retired spot of knowledge.

In the middle of spring the birds are inspected; after this they are allowed to moult, and are sent into the country. As soon as the time of moulting is over, they are again inspected. The commencement is made with the <u>kh</u>āṣa falcons (*bāz*) which are inspected in the order in which they have been bought. The precedence of *jurras*[1] is determined by the number of game killed by them. Then come the *bāshas*,[5] the *shāhīns*,[2] the *khelas*,[6] the *chappak*[7] *bāshas*, the *baḥrīs*, the young *baḥrīs*,[8] the *shikaras*,[7]

[[1] *Bāz*, the female goshawk, the *jurra* being the male.—P.]

[[2] *Shāhīn*, fem., the male being the *shāhīncha*, is in India the Shahin Falcon, but in Persia the Peregrine is included in this term. *Vide Journ. As. Soc. Beng.*, 1907.—P.]

[[3] The *Shunqār* was a Jer falcon, of which an occasional specimen found its way to India. It is doubtful whether it ever lived in India long enough to be trained. *Vide* Note in *Journ.* and *Proc. As. Soc. Beng.*, vol. iii, No. 2, 1907.—P.]

[[4] *Barkat, bargud*, etc., was the Golden Eagle.—P.]

[[5] *Bāsha* is the female of the Common English Sparrow-hawk, the male being called *bāshīn*.—P.]

[[6] *Khela*, word not traceable; evidently the Hindi name of some hawk.—P.]

[[7] *Chappak* is the Hindi name of the *male* of the Shikara or Indian Sparrow-hawk. The dictionaries make the former term masculine, and the latter feminine, but Akbar being a falconer knew better.—P.]

[[8] *Baḥrī* is the female peregrine, and *baḥrī bachcha* the tiercel or male, which is a *third* smaller; *bachcha* does not mean "young".—P.]

the *chappak shikaras*, the *turmatīs*,[1] the *rekīs*,[2] the *besras*,[3] the *dhotīs*, the *charghs*, the *charghela*,[4] the *lagars*, and the *jhagars*,[5] (which His Majesty calls the *chappak*[6] kind of the *lagar*). The *Molchīns*[7] also are inspected—the *molchīn* is an animal resembling the sparrow, of yellowish plumage, like the *shāhīn*; it will kill a *kulang*[8] crane. People say that, whilst flying, it will break the wing[9] of the *kulang*, and others maintain that it pierces its eyes; but this cannot be proved. *Odhpapars*[10] also are brought from Kashmīr. This bird has a bluish (*sabz*) colour and is smaller than a parrot; its beak is red, straight, and long;[11] its tail is rather elongated. It brings down small birds, and returns to the hand of the keeper.

Many other birds can be trained for the chase, though I cannot specify all. Thus the crow, the sparrow, the *bodna*,[12] and the *sārū*[13] will learn to attack.

His Majesty, from motives of generosity and from a wish to add splendour to his Court, is fond of hunting with falcons, though superficial observers think that merely hunting is his object.

In this department many Manṣandārs, Aḥadīs, and other soldiers are employed. The footmen are mostly Kashmīrīs or Hindūstānīs. Their pay is as follows. *First class* of the former first grade, 7½ *R.*; second, 7 *R.*; third, 6¾ *R.* *Second class*, first grade, 6½ *R.*; second, 6¼ *R.*; third, 5¾ *R.* *Third class*, first grade, 5½ *R.*; second, 5 *R.*; third, 4½ *R.* *First class* of the latter (Hindūstānī), first grade, 5 *R.*; second, 4¾ *R.*; third, 4½ *R.* *Second class*, first grade, 4¼ *R.*; second, 4 *R.*; third, 3¾ *R.* *Third class*, first grade, 3½ *R.*; second, 3¼ *R.*; third, 3 *R.*

Allowance of Food.

In Kashmīr and in the aviaries[14] of Indian amateurs, the birds are generally fed once a day; but at Court they are fed twice. A *bāz* falcon

---

[[1] *Turmatī* or vulg. *turumtī*, is the Red-headed Merlin.—P.]

[[2] *Regī*, the common English Merlin.—P.]

[[3] The Besra Sparrow-hawk male and female, sexes transposed in the dictionaries.—P.]

[[4] *Chargh* or *charkh* is the female, and *charghela* the male of F. Sakar of Jerdon.—P.]

[[5] *Lagar* is the female, and *jhagar* the male of F. Jugger.—P.]

[6] See n. 7, p. 304.

[[7] *Molchīn*, obviously the Falconet. Apparently it was occasionally trained to alight on a crane's head, the startled quarry being then gathered by hand.—P.]

[[8] *Kulang*, the common Crane (in the Panjab *kūnj*), the coolan of Anglo-Indian sportsmen.—P.]

[[9] *Kulang rā az pā andāzad*, "brings down a crane."—P.]

[10] The name of this bird is doubtful. It is not to be found among the names of *Kashmīrī* birds given in the *Iqbālnāma*, p. 159.

[[11] Probably the Green Jay, *Sissa Sinensis*, No. 673, of Jordan, vol. ii.—P.]

[[12] *Bodna* for *būdana*, the common Quail, which is used for fighting.—P.]

[[13] *Sārū*, the common Maina.—P.]

[[14] *Qūsh-khāna*, mews for hawks.—P.]

gets a quantity of meat weighing 7 *dāms*; the *jurra*, 6 *d.*; the *baḥrī*, *lāchīn*,[1] and *k͟hela*, 5 *d.*; the *bāsha*, 3 *d.*; the *chappak bāsha*, *shikara*, *chappak shikara*, *besra*, *dhotī*, etc., 2 *d.* Towards the close of every day, they are fed on sparrows, of which the *bāz*, *jurra*, and *baḥrī*, get each seven; the *lāchīn*, five; the *bāsha*, three; others, two. *Charg͟hs* and *lagaṛs* get at the same time meat. *Shunqārs*, *shāhbāzes*; *burkats*, get one *ser*. On the hunting grounds they feed them on the game they take.

Prices of Falcons.

From eagerness to purchase, and from inexperience, people pay high sums for falcons. His Majesty allows dealers every reasonable profit; but from motives of equity, he has limited the prices. The dealers are to get their gain, but buyers ought not to be cheated. In purchasing falcons people should see to which of the following three classes birds belong. First, *k͟hāna-kurīz* birds; they have moulted whilst in charge of experienced trainers, and have got new feathers. Second, *chūz* birds; they have not yet moulted. Third, *Tarīnāk* birds; they have moulted before they were captured. *First class*, a superior *bāz* costs 12 *muhrs*; second grade do., 9 *M.*; third do., 6 *M.* *Second class*, first, 10 *M.*; second, 7 *M.*; third, 4 *M.* A *third class bāz* is somewhat cheaper than second class ones.

Jurras. First class, 8, 5, 2, 1 *M.* Second class, 6, 4, 1½, 1 *M.*, 5 *R.*

Bāshas. First class, 3, 2, 1 *M.*, 4 *R.* Second class, 2, 1 *M.*, 5 *R.*

Shāhīns of both kinds, 3, 2, 1 *M.*

Baḥrīs, 2, 1½, 1 *M.* Young *Baḥrīs*[2] a little less.

Khelas, 1½, 1, ½ *M.*

Charg͟hs, 2½ *R.*, 2, 1½ *R.*

Chappak bāshas, 1 *R.*; ½, ¼ *R.*

Shikaras, 1½ *R.*, 1, ½ *R.*

Besras, 2 *R.*, 1½, 1 *R.*

Chappak shikarahs, *lagaṛs*, *jhagaṛs*, *turmatīs*, *rekīs*, 1 *R.*, ½, ¼ *R.* Their prices are not classified.

His Majesty rewards the *Mīr Shikārs* (superintendents[3] of the chase) according to their ranks, with suitable presents. There are also fixed donations for each game brought in, varying from 1 *M.* to 1 *d.* If the falcons bring down the game alive or dead, attention is paid to the skill which it exhibited and to the size of the quarry. The man who keeps the falcon gets one-half of the allowance. If His Majesty hunts himself, fifty

---

[[1] *Lāchīn* is the Turki-name of the Shāhīn.—P.]

[[2] *Baḥrī bachcha*, peregrine tiercel.—P.]

[[3] *Mīr shikār* is a term applied to any bird-catcher, assistant falconer, etc.—P.]

per cent. of the donation is stopped. If birds are received by the Imperial aviary[1] as *peshkash* (tribute), the *Qushbegī* (Superintendent of the Aviary)[1] gets for every *bāz* 1½ *R.*, and the accountant ½ *R.* For *jurras*, the Qushbegī gets 1 *R.*; the accountant, ¼ *R.*; for *bāshas*, the former receives ¼ *R.*; the latter, ⅛ *R.*; for every *lāchīn*, *chargh*, *charghela*, *khela*, *bahrī-bachcha*, the former gets ⅛ *R.*, the latter 1/10 *R.*; for every *chhappak*, *bāsha*, *dhotī*, etc., the former receives 1/10, the other 1/20 *R.* (*sūkī*).

The minimum number of *bāz* and *shāhīn* falcons, kept at Court, is forty; of *jurras*, thirty; of *bāshas*, one hundred; of *bahrīs*, *charghs*, twenty; of *lagars*, and *shikaras*, ten.

Waterfowl.

Hunting waterfowl affords much amusement. A rather curious way of catching them is the following. They make an artificial bird of the skin of a waterfowl with the wings, the beak, and the tail on it. Two holes are made in the skin for looking through. The body is hollow. The hunter puts his head into it, and stands in the water up to his neck. He then gets carefully near the birds, and pulls them one after the other below the water. But sometimes they are cunning and fly away.

In Kashmīr they teach *bāz* falcons to seize the birds whilst swimming about, and to return with them to the boat of the hunter. Or the hawk will keep a waterfowl down, and sit on it [till the man in the boat comes].

Another method is to let water buffaloes go into the water, between which the hunter conceals himself, and thus catches the birds.

Durrāj[2] catching. There are various methods. Some get a young one and train it till it obeys every call. It will fight with other birds. They put it into a cage, and place hair-nets[3] round about it. At the signal of the fowler, the bird commences to sing,[4] when wild ones come near it either from friendship or a desire to fight, and get entangled in the snares.

Bodnas.[5] The hunter makes a claypot with a narrow neck and, at night time, blows into it, which produces a noise like an owl's cry. The *bodnas*, frightened by the noise, come together. Another man then lights a bundle of straw, and swings it about, so that the eyes of the birds get dazzled. The fowlers thereupon seize the birds, and put them into cages.

Lagars. They resemble *charghs*; in body they are as large *jurras*. They hang nets[3] (about the body of a trained *lagar*) and put birds'

[[1] Mews.—P.]

[[2] The *durrāj* is the francolin or black partridge. Abū 'l-Fazl was evidently not a sportsman and probably meant the red-legged partridge, the *chukor* of India and the *kubk* of Persia.—P.]

[[3] Hair nooses.—P.] [[4] *I.e.* utter its challenging call.—P.]

[[5] *Būdina* in Persia is the Common Quail.—P.]

feathers into its claws. It is then allowed to fly up. The birds think that it has got hold of prey, and when they get entangled in the nets,[1] they commence to fight, and fall to the ground.

Ghaughā,ī. They fasten together on a cross-stick an owl and a *ghaughā,ī,*[2] and hang hair nets [1] round about them. The owl will soon get restless ; the birds think that the owl wishes to fight, and commence to cry out. Other *ghaughā,īs* and owls will come to their assistance ; and get entangled in the nets.[1]

Frogs.

Frogs also may be trained to catch sparrows. This looks very funny.

His Majesty, from curiosity, likes to see spiders fight [3] and amuses himself in watching the attempts of the flies to escape, their jumps, and combats with their enemy.

I am in the power of love ; and if I have thousands of wishes, it is
no crime ;
And if my passionate heart has an (unlawful) desire, it is no crime.

And in truth, His Majesty's fondness for leopards is an example of the power of love,[4] and an instance of his wonderful insight.

It would take me too long to give more details. It is impossible to enumerate all particulars ; hence it is better to go to another subject.

Āʾīn 29.

ON AMUSEMENTS.

His Majesty devises means of amusement, and makes his pleasures a means of testing the character of men.

There are several kinds of amusements, of which I shall give a few details.

[[1] *Dām*, a noose. The nooses are attached to the claws. A hawk so prepared is called in the Panjab, a *bārak (urānā).* For Plate and description, vide *Journ. As. Soc. Beng.*, vol. iii, 1907.—P.]

[[2] *Ghaughā,ī* is probably the Large Grey Babbler or *sāt bhā,ī*, 436 of Jerdon.—P.]

[[3] *Ba-shikār-i ʿankabūt dil nihad* means "catch their prey".—P.]

[4] The Historian may thank Abū 'l-Faẓl for having preserved this little trait of Akbar's character. In several places of the Āʾīn, Abū 'l-Faẓl tries hard to ascribe to His Majesty higher motives in order to bring the emperor's passion for hunting in harmony with his character as the spiritual guide of the nation. But as "higher motives" were insufficient to explain the fancy which Akbar took in frog and spider fights, Abū 'l-Faẓl has to recognize the fact that peculiar leanings will lead even a sensible man to oddities and to actions opposed to the general tenor of his character.

The game of Chaugān (hockey).[1]

Superficial observers look upon this game as a mere amusement; and consider it mere play; but men of more exalted views see in it a means of learning promptitude and decision. It tests the value of a man, and strengthens bonds of friendship. Strong men learn in playing this game the art of riding; and the animals learn to perform feats of agility and to obey the reins. Hence His Majesty is very fond of this game. Externally, the game adds to the splendour of the Court; but viewed from a higher point, it reveals concealed talents.

When His Majesty goes to the *maydān* (open field) in order to play this game, he selects an opponent and some active and clever players, who are only filled with one thought, namely, to show their skill against the opponent of His Majesty. From motives of kindness, His Majesty never orders any one to be a player; but chooses the pairs by the cast of the die. There are not more than ten players; but many more keep themselves in readiness. When one *gharī* (20 minutes) has passed, two players take rest, and two others supply their place.

The game itself is played in two ways. The first way is to get hold of the ball with the crooked end of the *chaugān* stick, and to move it slowly from the middle to the *ḥāl*.[2] This manner is called in Hindī *rol*. The other way consists in taking deliberate aim, and forcibly hitting the ball with the *chaugān* stick out of the middle; the player then gallops after it, quicker than the others, and throws the ball back. This mode is called *bela*, and may be performed in various ways. The player may either strike the ball with the stick in his right hand, and send it to the right forwards or backwards; or he may do so with his left hand; or he may send the ball in front of the horse to the right or to the left. The ball may be thrown in the same direction from behind the feet of the horse or from below its body; or the rider may spit [3] it when the ball is in front of the horse; or he may lift himself upon the back leather [3] of the horse, and propel the ball from between the feet of the animal.

His Majesty is unrivalled for the skill which he shows in the various

---

[1] There is scarcely a Muhammadan Historian that does not allude to this game. Bābar says it is played all over Thibet. In the East of India the people of Munnipore (Assam) are looked upon as clever hockey players. *Vide* Vigni's Travels in Cashmir, ii, p. 289.

Sayyid ʿAbdu 'llah Khān, son of Mīr Khwānda, was Akbar's *chaugānbegī*, or Superintendent of the game of *chaugān*; *vide* Bad. II, p. 368. In the beginning of Akbar's reign, after 970, Gharīwalī, which lies a *farsang* from Āgra, was the favourite spot for *chaugān* playing. Bad. II, p. 70. [*Chaugān*, polo.—P.]

[2] The pillars which mark the end of the playground.

[[3] Meaning not clear.—P.]

ways of hitting the ball; he often manages to strike the ball while in the air, and astonishes all. When a ball is driven to the *ḥāl*, they beat the *naqqāra*, so that all that are far and near may hear it. In order to increase the excitement, betting is allowed. The players win from each other, and he who brought the ball to the *ḥāl* wins most. If a ball be caught in the air, and passes, or is made to pass, beyond the limit (*mīl*), the game is looked upon as *burd* (drawn). At such times the players will engage in a regular fight about the ball, and perform admirable feats of skill.

His Majesty also plays at *chaugān* in dark nights, which caused much astonishment even among clever players. The balls which are used at night, are set on fire.[1] For this purpose, *palās* wood is used, which is very light, and burns for a long time. For the sake of adding splendour to the games, which is necessary in worldly matters, His Majesty has knobs of gold and silver fixed to the tops of the *chaugān* sticks. If one of them breaks, any player that gets hold of the pieces may keep them.

It is impossible to describe the excellency of this game. Ignorant as I am, I can say but little about it.

ʿIshqbāzī (pigeon-flying).

His Majesty calls pigeon-flying *ʿishqbāzī* (love-play). This occupation affords the ordinary run of people a dull kind of amusement; but His Majesty, in his wisdom, makes it a study. He even uses the occupation as a way of reducing unsettled, worldly-minded men to obedience, and avails himself of it as a means productive of harmony and friendship. The amusement which His Majesty derives from the tumbling and flying of the pigeons reminds one of the ecstasy and transport of enthusiastic dervishes; he praises God for the wonders of creation. It is therefore from higher motives that he pays so much attention to this amusement.

The pigeons of the present age have reached a high state of perfection. Presents of pigeons are sent by the kings of Īrān and Tūrān; but merchants also bring very excellent ones in large numbers.

When His Majesty was very young, he was fond of this amusement; but afterwards, when he grew older and wiser, he discontinued pigeon-flying altogether. But since then, on mature consideration, he has again taken it up.

A well-trained pigeon of bluish colour, formerly belonging to the K͟hān-i

[1] "In the beginning of 974 (July, 1566), the emperor returned (from Jaunpur) to Āgra, and passed his time in amusements. He went to *Nagarchīn*, a new town which he had built near Āgra, and enjoyed the *chaugān* game, dog-hunting, and pigeon-flying. He also invented a fire ball with which he could play at *chaugān* during dark nights." Bad. II, p. 48.

The town of *Nagarchīn* was subsequently deserted.

Aʿẓam Kokaltāsh (ʿAzīz, Akbar's foster-brother), fell into His Majesty's hands. From the care which was bestowed upon it by His Majesty, it has since become the chief of the imperial pigeons, and is known under the name of *Mohana*. From it descended several excellent pigeons as *Ashkī* (the weeper), *Parīzād* (the fairy), *Almās* (the diamond), and *Shāh ʿūdī* (Aloe Royal). Among their progeny again there are the choicest pigeons in the whole world, which have brought the trained pigeons of ʿUmar Shaykh Mīrzā (father of Bābar), Sulṭān Ḥusayn Mīrzā (*vide* p. 107, note 6) into oblivion. Such improvement, in fact, has been made in the art of training, as to astonish the amateurs of Īrān and Tūrān, who had to learn the art from the beginning.

In former times pigeons of all kinds were allowed to couple; but His Majesty thinks equality in gracefulness and performance a necessary condition in coupling, and has thus bred choice pigeons. The custom is to keep a male and a female pigeon, if not acquainted with each other, for five or six days together, when they become so familiar that, even after a long separation, they will again recognize each other. The hen generally lays her eggs from eight to twelve days after coupling, or more if she be small or sickly. Pigeons couple in *Mihrmāh* (September–October), and separate in *Farwardīn* (February–March). A hen lays two eggs, but sometimes only one. The cock will sit upon the eggs by daytime, and the hen during the night, and thus they keep them warm and soft. In winter they hatch for twenty-one days; but if the air be warm, they only take seventeen or eighteen. For about six days, the pigeons feed their young ones with *falah*, which means grain reduced to pap in the crops of the old ones. Afterwards they feed them from the grain in their crops, which they bring up before it is fully digested. This they continue for about a month, and as soon as they see that the young ones can pick up their own grain, the old ones will go away. Eggs, or even young ones, are sometimes given to other pigeons to take care of. Home bred young ones are trained. Some are kept in a *tor* (?) till they get stronger, and get acquainted with the place. As soon as these two things have been attained, the pigeons only get one-third or one-fourth of their daily allowance of food. When they have got a little accustomed to hunger, they are gradually allowed to take flights. They take daily about forty *hawās* (air), i.e., forty flights. At this period the trainers pay no regard to what is called *charkh* and *bāzī* (*vide* below). Of feathers, they count ten, and if eight of them have fallen out, the keepers no longer allow the pigeons to fly, but keep them at rest (*khwābānīdan*). After two months, the pigeons get new feathers, and become very strong. They are then again let off. This is the best time for showing their skill. As soon as the pigeons learn to perform the *bāzī* and the *charkh*, they are sent to His Majesty for inspection, and are kept for four months in readiness, to exhibit their skill. *Charkh* is a lusty movement ending with the pigeon throwing itself over in a full circle. If this circular turn be not completely carried out, the movement is called *kitf* (shoulder), and is held in no esteem. *Bāzī* is the same as *muʿallaq zadan* (lying on the back with the feet upwards, and quickly turning round, in Hind. *kaḷā*). Some thought that the two wings (*kitf*) meet, which appears to the observer as if it were a *muʿallaq*; but His Majesty had one wing of a pigeon blackened, when the erroneousness of that opinion became evident. Some pigeons get confused during the *bāzī* and *charkh*, and come stupefied to the ground. This is called *gulūla*, and is disliked. Sometimes pigeons hurt themselves and fall down; but often they get all right again when they come near the ground; and taking courage and collecting their strength they fly up again. A pigeon of the *khāṣa* pigeon cots will perform fifteen *charkhs* and seventy *bāzīs*, a feat which will certainly astonish the spectators. In former times, they let eleven or twenty-one pigeons fly at a time; but nowadays they let off as many as one hundred and one. From the attention which His Majesty has bestowed upon pigeons, they are now so carefully trained as to be let fly at night, even to great heights.

At the time of departure and the breaking of the camp, the pigeons will follow, the cots being carried by bearers (*kahār*). Sometimes they will alight and take rest for a while, and then rise again.

It would be difficult to count the pigeons at Court; but there are more than twenty thousand. Five hundred of them are *khāṣa*. They have a great reputation, and remarkable stories are told of their skill.

Pigeon trainers of former times, in order to determine the value of a pigeon, used to twist the foot,[1] or looked to the slit of the eyes, or the openings on the top of the bill; but they failed to discover more signs of the value of a breed. His Majesty has discovered many more; and the fixing the value of a pigeon, in former times a matter of great difficulty, has now become very easy. *First.* His Majesty subdivided the three marks of former trainers as follows: the two eyes, and their upper and lower signs;[2] the eight claws; the two sides of the beak, above and below. The mutual comparison of these signs has led to many additional means of fixing the value of a pigeon. *Secondly.* His Majesty looks to the variety and the colour of the annular protuberances on the feet of pigeons. A book

---

[[1] *Ba-tāflan-i pā.* Can this mean the angle made by the feet?—P.]

[[2] *Du chashm bālā u pāʿīn.*—P.]

has been made in which the systematic order of these signs has been laid down. According to them, His Majesty distinguishes ten classes, for each of which separate aviaries have been constructed. The price of pigeons in the first house has not been limited. Many a poor man anxious to make his way has found in the training of superior pigeons a means of getting rich. A pair of second class pigeons has a value of 3 *R.*; third class, 2½ *R.*; fourth class, 2 *R.*; fifth class, 1½ *R.*; sixth class, 1 *R.*; seventh class, ¾ *R.*; eighth class, ½ *R.*; ninth and tenth classes, ⅜ *R.*

When inspections are held, the stock of *Mohana* first pass in review; then the young ones of *Ashkī*. Though the latter belong to the former, they are now separately counted. Then come the four *zirihī* pigeons; they are the stock of a pigeon which belonged to Hājī ʿAlī, of Samarqand, which coupled with an *ʿUdī* hen, of which I do not know the owner; their stock has become famous. The precedence of all other pigeons is determined by their age or the time they were bought.

The Colours of Khāṣa Pigeons.

Magasī (flea-bitten); *zirihī* (steelblue); *amīrī* (?); *zamīrī* (a colour between *zirihī* and *amīrī*; His Majesty invented this name); *chīnī* (porcelain blue); *noftī* (grey like naptha); *shafaqī* (violet); *ʿūdī* (aloe-wood coloured); *surmaī* (dark grey, like powder of antimony); *kishmishī*[1] (dark brown, like currants[1]); *ḥalwāʾī* (light-brown, like *ḥalwā* sweetmeat); *ṣandalī* (light-brown, like sandalwood); *jigarī* (brown); *nabātī* (greyish white); *dūghī* (bluish-white, like sour milk); *wushkī* (of the same colour as the gum called *wushk*); *jīlānī* (*chīlānī* ?); *kūraʾī* (brown, like a new earthen pot ?); *nīlūfarī* (bluish-white); *azraq* (a colour between yellow and brown; His Majesty applies this name in this sense); *ātashī* (black brown); *shaftālū* (peach coloured); *gul-i gaz* coloured (?), yellow; *kāghazī* (yellowish, like native paper); *zāgh* (grey like a crow); *agrī* (a colour between white and brown); *muḥarraqī* (a dirty black); *khiẓrī* (a colour between greenish and *ʿūdī*); *ābī* (water coloured);[2] *surmag* (a name invented by His Majesty to express a colour between *surma,ī* and *magasī*).

Pigeons of these colours have often different names, as *gulsar* (whose head resembles a flower); *dumghāza* (stumptail); *yakrang* (of one colour); *ḥalqūm-safīd* (white throat); *parsafīd* (white wing); *kalla* (big head); *ghazghazh* (wild chick); *māgh*[3] (name of an aquatic bird); *bābarī* (?); *ālpar* (red wing ?); *kalta par* (short wing); *māhdum*[4] (moontail);

[1 *Kishmish*, Sultana raisins.—P.]

[2 *Ābī*, blue.—P.]

[3 *Māgh*, a cormorant ?—P.]

[4 *Māhdum*, with white on the tail.—P.]

ṯawqdār (ring-bearer) ; *marwārīd-sar* (pearl head) ; *mashʿala-dum* (torch-tail) ; etc.

Some trainers of the present age gave pigeons such names as indicate their colours. His Majesty rather calls them according to their qualities, as *bughur* (?), *qarapilk* (with black eyelids) ; *abyārī* ; *palangnīgārī* ; *rekhta pilk*.

There are also many pigeons which do not perform *charkhs* and *bāzīs*, but are distinguished by their colours, or by peculiar tricks. Thus the *Kokah* [1] pigeon, the voice of which sounds like the call to prayer. 2. The *Bagha*, which utters a peculiar voice in the morning to wake up people. 3. The *Luqqan*,[2] which struts about proudly, wagging its head, neck, and tail. 4. The *Loṭan*.[3] They turn it about, and let it off on the ground, when it will go through all the motions which a half-killed fowl goes through. Some pigeons will do so when the keeper strikes his hand against the ground, and others will show the same restlessness when on leaving the cage their beak is made to touch the ground. 5. The *Khernī*. The cock shows a remarkable attachment to the hen. Though he fly up so high as to be no longer visible, if the hen be exposed in a cage, he will get restless and drop down instantly to join her. This is very remarkable. Some of them come down with both wings spread, others close one ; some close both ; or they change alternately the wing which they close in flying. 6. The *Raṭh* pigeon is chiefly used for carrying letters, though any other kind may be trained to bring letters even from great distances. 7. The *Nishāwarī* pigeon will fly up, and follow its cage to whatever place it be taken. It will fly out of sight, and stay away for a day or two, when it comes down and remains in its cage. 8. The *parpā* (having feet covered with feathers) will inhale air (?) and act as if it sighed.

Some pigeons are merely kept for the beauty of their plumage, the colours of which receive peculiar names. Thus some are called *shīrāzī*, *shūstarī*, *kāshānī*, *jogiya*, *reza-dahan*, *magasī*, and *qumrī*.[4] Wild pigeons are called *gola*. If some of them are caught, they will be joined by a thousand others ; they soon get domesticated. They return daily to the fields, and get on their return salt water to drink. This makes them vomit the grain which they had eaten on the fields. The grain is collected and given as food to other pigeons.

People say that pigeons will but rarely live above thirty years.

[[1] Can this be for *kokla*, a species of green pigeon which has a call like the human voice, *vide* Jerdon No. 778.—P.]

[[2] *Laqā*, *laqa*, etc., the fantail pigeon.—P.]

[[3] *Loṭan*, the ground-tumbler.—P.]

[[4] *Qumrī*, a white dove.—P.]

17

18

Four *sers* of grain will be sufficient for one hundred of such pigeons as are made to fly ; but for other pigeons five *sers* are required ; or seven and a half if they pair. But flying pigeons get millet, not mixed with other grain ; the others get a mixture of the seven kinds of grain, viz., rice, *dāl* [1]*-i nukhūd* (gram), *mūng dāl* [1] (millet), *karar, lahdara, juwār* (*vide* p. 66). Though most servants of His Majesty keep pigeons and show much skill in training them, there are a few that have risen to eminence, as *Qulʿ Alī* of Bukhārā, Mastī of Samarqand, Mullāzāda, Pūr-i Mullā Aḥmad Chand, Muqbil Khān Chela, Khwāja Ṣandal Chela, Mūmin of Harāt, ʿAbdu 'l-Laṭīf of Bukhārā, Ḥājī Qāsim of Balkh, Ḥabīb of Shahrsabz, Sikandar Chela, Māltū, Maqṣūd of Samarqand, Khwāja Phūl, Chela Hīrānand.

The servants attached to the pigeon houses draw their pay on the list of the army. The pay of a foot soldier varies from 2 *R.* to 48 *R. per mensem.*

The game of Chaupar.

From times of old, the people of Hindūstān have been fond of this game. It is played with sixteen pieces of the same shape ; but every four of them must have the same colour. The pieces all move in the same direction. The players use three dice. Four of the six sides of each dice are greater than the remaining two, the four long sides being marked with one, two, five, and six dots respectively. The players draw two sets of two parallel lines, of which one set bisects the other at right angles. These parallel lines are of equal length. The small square which is formed by the intersection of the two sets in the centre of the figure is left as it is ; but the four rectangles adjoining the sides of the square are each divided into twenty-four equal spaces in three rows, each of eight equal spaces, as shown in Pl. XVII, Fig. 17. The game is generally played by four players, of whom two play against the other two. Each player has four pieces, of which he puts two in the sixth and seventh spaces of the middle row of the parallellogram before him, and the other two in the seventh and eighth spaces of the right row. The left row remains empty. Each player moves his pieces, according to his throw, in the outer row, always keeping to the right, till he arrives at the outer left row of the parallelogram, from which he started ; and from there he moves to the middle row. When arrived at the latter place, he is *pukhta* (ripe), and from here, he must throw for each of his pieces the exact number which will carry them to the empty square in the centre of the figure. He is now *rasīda*, or arrived.

When a player is *pukhta* or *rasīda*, he may commence to play from

[[1] Pulse of *mūng*.—P.]

the beginning, which leads to amusing combinations. As long as a player keeps two of his pieces together, the adversary cannot throw them out. If a player throws a double six, he can move two pieces over twelve spaces, provided the two pieces stand together on one field; but he is allowed to move them only six fields onwards should he prefer doing so. A similar rule holds for double fives, etc. A throw consisting of a six, a five, and a one, is called *k͟hām* (raw); and in this case, two pieces, provided they are togdther on the same field, may each be moved six fields forwards, and every single piece twelve fields. If a player throws three sixes, and three of his four pieces happen to stand on one field, he may move each of them over twelve fields. A similar rule holds, if a player throw three twos, or three ones. There are many other rules for particular cases. If a player has brought his four pieces into the central square, he throws, when his turn comes, for his companion, to get him out too. Formerly the custom was that when a piece had come to the last row, and . . . [1] His Majesty thinks it proper to do so from the very eighth field. If the throws of two players are the same as the throw of the preceding players, His Majesty counts them as *qāyim*, or standing. Formerly he did not allow such equal throws. If the four pieces of an opponent are *puk͟hta*, and he yet lose his bet, the other players are entitled to double the amount of the bet. Should any of the players leave the game for some reason he may appoint anyone to play for him; but he will have to be responsible for the betting of his substitute. Of all winnings, the substitute is entitled to two *per cent*; if a player loses a bet, his substitute has to pay one *per cent*. If a player drops one of his pieces, or any of the players be late or inattentive, he is fined one rupee. But a fine of a muhur is exacted if any one prompts the other, or moves his pieces over too many fields, or tries to get two throws.

Formerly many grandees took part in this game; there were often as many as two hundred players, and no one was allowed to go home before he had finished sixteen games, which in some cases lasted three months. If any of them lost his patience and got restless, he had to drink a cup of wine.

Superficially considered, all this is mere play; but His Majesty has higher aims; he weighs the talents of a man, and teaches kindness.

The game of Chandal Mandal.

This game was invented by His Majesty. The figure, or board, which is required, consists of sixteen parallelograms, arranged in a circular form

[1] The MSS. have *az khānayi hashtum pāyān shavad, hangām-i k͟hān shudan āmāda gardad*, which words are not clear to me.

round a centre. Each parallelogram is divided into twenty-four fields, every eight of which form a row ; *vide* Pl. XVII, Fig. 18. The number of pieces is sixty-four, and four dice are used, of which the four longer sides are marked with one, two, ten, and twelve points respectively. The number of players is sixteen. Each gets four pieces, which are placed in the middle. As in Chaupar, the pieces are moved to the right, and pass through the whole circle. The player who is out first, is entitled to receive the stipulated amount from the other fifteen players ; the second that is out, from fourteen players, and so on. The first player, therefore, wins most, and the last loses most ; the other players both lose and win. His Majesty plays this game in several ways ; one way in which the pieces are moved as if the fields were squares of a chess board, is very often played. I shall give a few particulars and directions how to play the different kinds of this game.

First kind, no piece can throw out another piece, but moves on by itself. *Second* way, single pieces may be thrown out. Each player whose piece has thus been thrown out, commences again from his starting point. *Third* way, at each throw two pieces are moved at a time, either with or without the permission of throwing out pieces. *Fourth* way, the preceding rule is applied to three or four pieces at a time. *Fifth* way, the dice are thrown four times, and four pieces are moved at each throw. These different ways may, moreover, be varied by some players playing to the right, others to the left, or all in the same direction. *Sixth* way, a player is out when he comes to the place from which the player opposite to him commenced to play, moving from the middle row of his opponent into the empty space in the centre of the board. Or the game ends when each player arrives at the place from which his left hand neighbour commenced to play. *Seventh* way, each player puts his pieces before himself, and has three throws. At the first throw, he moves two of his pieces ; at the second, one of his own pieces and one belonging to his right hand neighbour ; at the third throw, he moves any piece of his own, and allows his left hand neighbour to move one of his pieces. In this way of playing, no player throws out the pieces of his neighbours ; and when the game is in full swing, he allows each piece which happens to come into the row in which he is, to move according to his own throw, as a sort of compliment to a guest. *Eighth* way, two pieces when together may throw out another set of two pieces ; but single pieces do not throw out each other. *Ninth* way, four pieces together may throw out three together ; three together, sets of two ; and two together, single ones ; but single pieces do not throw out each other. *Tenth* way, each player moves his pieces according to the number of points which he throws, but at the same time, the player who sits opposite to him moves his pieces according to the number of points on the reverse side of the dice, whilst the two players to the right and left of the player who threw the dice, move their pieces according to the number of points to the right and left sides of the dice. *Eleventh* way, the players use five dice and four pieces. Each player, in his turn, throws the five dice, and moves his pieces according to the sum of the two highest points of his throw. The next highest point is taken by his *vis-à-vis*, and the two lowest points by his right and left hand neighbours. *Twelfth* way, the players have each five dice and five pieces. At every throw, he gives the points of one die to his right hand neighbour, and uses the others for himself. Sometimes the thrower mentions beforehand the names of four players to whom he wishes to give the points of four dice, he himself taking the points of the fifth die. And when a player requires only a few points, to get *pukhta*, he must give the remaining points to those near whom the dice fall.

The game may also be played by fifteen or less players, the figure being lessened accordingly. So also may the number of the dice be increased or decreased.

Cards.

This is a well-known game. His Majesty has made some alterations in the cards. Ancient sages took the number twelve as the basis, and made the suit to consist of twelve cards ; but they forgot that the twelve kings should be of twelve different kinds. His Majesty plays with the following suits of cards. 1*st*, *Ashwapatī*, the lord of horses. The highest card represents a king on horseback, resembling the king of Dihlī, with the umbrella (*chatr*), the standard (*ʿalam*), and other imperial ensigns. The second highest card of the same suit represents a *vazīr* on horseback ; and after this card come ten others of the same suit with pictures of horses, from one to ten. 2*nd*, *Gajpati*, the king whose power lies in the number of his elephants, as the ruler of Oṛīsah. The other eleven cards represent, as before, the vazīr, and elephants from ten to one. 3*rd*, *Narpati*, a king whose power lies in his infantry, as is the case with the rulers of Bījāpūr. The card represents a king sitting on his throne in imperial splendour ; the vazīr sits on a footstool (*ṣandalī*), and the ten cards completing this suit have foot soldiers, from one to ten. 4*th*, *Gaḍhpati*. The card shows a man sitting on a throne over a fort ; the vazīr sits on a *ṣandalī* over a fort ; and the remaining ten cards have forts from one to ten, as before. 5*th*, *Dhanpati*, the lord of treasures. The first card of this suit shows a man, sitting on a throne, and gold and silver heaps ; the vazīr sits upon a *ṣandalī*, as if he took account of the Treasury, and the remaining cards show jars full of gold and silver, from one to ten. *6th, Dalpati*, the hero of battle. The first card of this suit shows a king in armour, sitting on his throne and surrounded by warriors on coats of mail. The vazīr sits on a *ṣandalī* and wears a *jayba* (breast armour) ; the ten other cards show individuals clad in armour. *7th, Nawāpati*, the lord of the fleet. The card shows a man sitting on a throne in a ship ; the vazīr sits, as usual, on a *ṣandalī*, and the other ten cards have boats from one to ten. *8th, Tīpati*, a queen sitting on the throne, surrounded by her maids. The second card shows a woman as *vazīr* on a *ṣandalī*, and the other ten cards have pictures of women, from one to ten. *9th, Surapati*, the king of the divinities (*deota*) also called *Indar*, on a throne. The vazīr sits on a *ṣandalī*, and the ten other cards have pictures of divinities from one to ten. *10th, Asrpati*, the lord of genii (*deo*). The card represents Sulaymān, son of Dāʾūd, on the throne. The vazīr sits on a *ṣandali*, and the other ten cards have genii. *11th, Banpatī*, the king of wild beasts. The card represents a tiger (*sher*) with some other animals. The vazīr is drawn in the shape of a leopard (*palang*) and the other ten cards are pictures of wild beasts, as usual from one to ten. *12th, Āhipatī*, the king of snakes. The first card shows a serpent mounted on a dragon, whilst the vazīr is a serpent riding on another serpent of the same kind. The remaining ten cards show serpents, from one to ten.

The first six of these twelve suits are called *bīshbar* (powerful), and the six last, *kambar* (weak).

His Majesty has also made some suitable alterations in the cards. Thus the *Dhanpati*, or lord of treasures, is represented as a man distributing money. The vazīr sits on a *ṣandalī*, and inspects the Treasury ; but the ten other cards of this suit are representations of the ten classes of workmen employed in the Treasury, viz., the jeweller, the melter, the piece-cutter (*muṭallas-sāz*), the weighman, the coiner, the *muhr* counter, the *bitikchī* (writer) of *dhan* pieces (*vide* p. 31, No. 17), the *bitīkchī* of *man* pieces (*vide* p. 31, No. 20), the dealer, the *qurṣgar* (*vide* p. 24, No. 15). His Majesty had also the king of assignments painted on the cards, who inspects *farmāns*, grants, and the leaves of the *daftar* (*vide* p. 270) ; the vazīr sits on a *ṣandalī* with the *daftar* before him ; the other cards show officers employed in the Financial Department, as the paper maker, the *misṭar* maker (*vide* p. 55, note 1), the clerk who makes the entries in the *daftar*, the illuminator (*muṣawwir*), the *naqqāsh* (who ornaments the pages), the *jadwal-kash* (who draws blue and gold lines on the pages), the *farmān* writer, the *mujallid* (bookbinder), the *rangrez* [1] (who stains the paper with different colours). The *Pādishāh-i qimāsh* also, or king of manufacturers, is painted in great state, looking at different things, as Thibetan yaks, silk, silken stuffs. The vazīr sits near him on a *ṣandalī*, inquiring into former proceedings. The other ten cards represent beasts of burden. Again, the *Pādishāh-i Chang*, or lord of the lyre, is painted sitting on a throne, and listening to music; the vazīr sits before him, inquiring into the circumstances of the performers, of whom pictures are given on the remaining cards. Next, the *Pādishāh-i zar i safīd*, or king of silver, who is painted distributing rupees and other silver coins; the vazīr sits on a *ṣandalī*, and makes inquiries regarding donations. On the other cards, the workmen of the silver mint are depicted, as before those of the gold mint. Then comes the *Pādishāh-i Shamsher*, or king of the sword, who is painted trying the steel of a sword. The vazīr sits upon a *ṣandalī*, and inspects the arsenal; the other cards contain pictures of armourers, polishers, etc. After him comes the *Pādishāh-i Tāj*,[2] or king of the diadem. He confers royal insignia, and the *ṣandalī* upon which the vazīr sits, is the last of the insignia. The ten other cards contain pictures of workmen, as tailors, quilters, etc. Lastly, the *Pādishāh-i Ghulāmān*, or king of the slaves, sits on an elephant, and the vazīr on a cart. The other cards are representations of servants, some of whom sit, some lie on the ground in worship, some are drunk, others sober, etc.

Besides these ordinary games of cards, His Majesty also plays chess, four-handed and two-handed. His chief object is to test the value of men, and to establish harmony and good fellow-feeling at Court.

Āʾīn 30.

THE GRANDEES OF THE EMPIRE.[3]

At first I intended, in speaking of the Grandees of the Court, to record the deeds which raised them to their exalted positions, to describe their

[1] This is the Hindūstānī corruption of the Persian *rang-raz*. [*Rang-rīz* is the common word in modern Persian.—P.]

[2] *Tāj* is often translated by a *crown*; but *tāj* is a *cap* worn by oriental kings instead of the crown of occidental kings. Hence the word *diadem* does not express the meaning of *tāj* either. [It apparently is also used of a *crown* as well as the cap worn by dervishes.—P.]

[3] From the fact that Abū 'l-Faẓl mentions in his list of Grandees Prince Khusraw, (*vide* No. 4) who was born in 995, but not Prince Parwīz, who was born in 997, we might conclude that the table was compiled prior to 997. But from my note to p. 256, it would appear that the beginning of the list refers to a time prior to 993, and Abū 'l-Faẓl may have afterward added Khusraw's name, though it is difficult to say why he did not add the names of Parwīz and Shāhjahān, both of whom were born before the Āʾīn was completed.

Again, Mīrzā Shāhrukh (No. 7) and Mīrzā Muẓaffar Ḥusayn (No. 8) are mentioned as

qualities, and to say something of their experience. But I am unwilling to bestow mere praise; in fact, it does not become the encomiast of His Majesty to praise others, and I should act against my sense of truthfulness, were I but to mention that which is praiseworthy, and to pass in silence over that which cannot be approved of. I shall therefore merely record, in form of a table, their names and the titles which have been conferred upon them.

I. Commanders of Ten Thousand.

1. **Shāhzāda** Sulṭān Salīm, eldest son of His Majesty.

II. Commanders of Eight Thousand.

2. **Shāhzāda** Sulṭān Murād, second son of His Majesty.

III. Commanders of Seven Thousand.

3. **Shāhzāda** Sulṭān Dānyāl, third son of His Majesty.

Akbar had *five* sons :—

1. Ḥasan }
2. Ḥusayn } twins, born 3rd Rabī' I, 972. They only lived one month.
3. Sulṭān Salīm **[Jāhangīr]**.
4. Sulṭān Murād.
5. Sulṭān Dānyāl.

Of daughters, I find three mentioned—(*a*) Shāhzāda Khānum, born three months after Salīm, in 977. (*b*) Shukr^u 'n-Nisā Begum, who in 1001 was married to Mīrzā Shāhrukh (No. 7, below, p. 326); and (*c*) Ārām Bānū Begum; both born after Sulṭān Dānyāl. Regarding the death of the last Begum, *vide* Tuzuk, p. 386.

Of Akbar's wives the following are mentioned [1]:—1. Sulṭān Ruqayyah Begum (a daughter of Mīrzā Hindāl), who died 84 years old, 7th Jumāda I, 1035 (*Tuzuk*, p. 401). She was Akbar's first wife (*zan-i kalān*), but had no child by him. She tended Shāhjahān. Nūr Jahān (Jahāngīr's wife), also stayed with her after the murder of Sher Afkan. 2. Sulṭān Salīma Begum. She was a daughter of Gulrukh (?) Begum [2] (a daughter of Bābar)

Commanders of Five Thousand, though they were appointed in 1001 and 1003 respectively, i.e., a short time before the Ā'īn was completed.

The biographical notices which I have given after the names of the more illustrious grandees are chiefly taken from a MS. copy of the *Mu'āsir^u 'l- Umarā'* (No. 77 of the MSS. of the As. Soc. Bengal), the *Tuzuk-i Jahāngīrī*, the *Ṭabaqāt-i Akbarī*, *Badā,onī*, and the *Akbarnāma*. For the convenience of the student of Indian History, I have added a genealogical table of the House of Tīmūr, and would refer the reader to a more detailed article on the Chronology of Tīmūr and his Descendants published by me in the *Proceedings of the Asiatic Society of Bengal* for August, 1869.

[1] *Vide* Additional notes.

[2] Regarding her, *vide Jour. As. Soc. Bengal* for 1869, p. 136, note.

and Mīrzā Nur^u 'd-Dīn Muḥammad. Humāyūn had destined her for Bayrām Khān, who married her in the beginning of Akbar's reign. After the death of Bayrām, Akbar, in 968, married her. She died 10th Zī Qaʿda, 1021. As a poetess, she is known under the name *Makhfī* (concealed), and must not be confounded with *Zeb^u 'n-Nisā*[1] (a daughter of Awrangzeb's) who has the same poetical name. 3. The daughter of Rāja Bihārī Mal and sister of Rāja Bhagawān Dās. Akbar married her in 968, at Sābhar. 4. The beautiful wife of Abd^u l-Wāṣī, married in 970 (*vide* Bad. II, 61). 5. Bībī Dawlat Shād, mother of (*b*) and (*c*); *vide* Tuzuk, p. 16. 6. A daughter of ʿAbd^u 'llah Khān Mughul (964). 7. A daughter of Mīrān Mubarak Shāh of Khandes; *vide* p. 13, note 1.

Sulṭān Salīm. Title as Emperor, Jahāngīr. Title after death, *Jannatmakānī*. Born at Fatḥpūr Sīkrī, on Wednesday, 17th Rabī' I, 997, or 18th Shahrīwar of the 14th year of Akbar's Era. He was called *Salīm* because he was born in the house of Shaykh Salīm-i Chishtī. Akbar used to call him *Shaykhū Bābā* (*vide* Tuzuk, p. 1). For his wives and children, *vide* below, No. 4. Jahāngīr died on the 28th Ṣafar 1037 (28th October, 1627) near Rājor on the Kashmīr frontier. *Vide* my article on Jahāngīr in the *Calcutta Review* for October, 1869.

Sulṭān Murād, Akbar's fourth son, was born on Thursday, 3rd Muḥarram, 978, and died of *delirium tremens* in 1006, at Jalnāpūr in Barār (Tuzuk, p. 15; Akbarnāma II, p. 443; Khāfī Khān, p. 212). He was nicknamed *Pahāṛī* (Bad. II, 378). He was *sabzrang* (of a livid[2] complexion), thin, and tall (*Tuzuk*). A daughter of his was married to Prince Parwīz, Jahāngīr's son (*Tuzuk*, p. 38).

Sulṭān Dānyāl was born at Ajmīr, on the 10th Jumāda I, 979, and died of *delirium tremens*, A.H. 1013. Khāfī Khān, I, p. 232, says the news of his death reached Akbar in the beginning of 1014. He was called Dānyāl in remembrance of Shaykh Dānyāl, a follower of Muʿīn-i Chishtī, to whose tomb at Ajmīr Akbar, in the beginning of his reign, often made pilgrimages. Dānyāl married, in the beginning of 1002, the daughter of Qulij Khān (No. 42), and towards the end of 1006, Jānān Begum, a daughter of Mīrzā ʿAbd^u 'r-Raḥīm Khān Khānān (Khāfī Khān, p. 213), and was betrothed to a daughter of Ibrāhīm ʿĀdlishāh of Bījlāpūr; but he died before the marriage was consummated. He had three sons:—1. Ṭahmūras, who was married to Sulṭān Bahār Begum, a daughter of Jahāngīr. 2. Bāyasanghar (بايسنغر). 3. Hoshang, who was married to Hoshmand

[1] Her charming Dīwān was lithographed at Lucknow, A.H. 1284. She was the eldest daughter of Awrangzeb, and was born in A.H. 1048.

[[2] Sallow ?—P.]

Bānū Begum, a daughter of Khusraw. Besides, he had four daughters, whose names are not mentioned. One of them, Bulāqī Begum, was married to Mīrzā Wālī (Tuz., p. 272). Ṭahmūras and Hoshang were killed by Āṣaf Khān after the death of Jahāngīr (*vide Proceedings Asiatic Society of Bengal*, for August, 1869). Nothing appears to be known regarding the fate of Bāyasanghar. *Vide Calcutta Review* for October, 1869.

Dānyāl is represented as well built, good looking, fond of horses and elephants, and clever in composing Hindūstānī poems.

IV. Commanders of Five Thousand.

4. **Sulṭan Khusraw,** eldest son of Prince Salīm [Jahāngīr].

Jahāngīr's wives (*Tuzuk*, p. 84, and Preface, p. 6). A daughter of Rāja Bhagwān Dās, married in 993, gave birth, in 994, to Sulṭān[u] 'n-Niṣā Begum [*Khāfī Khān*, Sulṭān Begum], and in 995 to Prince Khusraw. She poisoned herself with opium in a fit of madness apparently brought on by the behaviour of Khusraw and her younger brother Madhū Singh, in 1011 (Khāfī Khān, p. 227). 2. A daughter of Rāy Rāy Singh, son of Rāy Kalyan Mal of Bīkānīr, married 19th Rajab 994, Bad. II, p. 353. She is not mentioned in the *Tuzuk* among Jahāngīr's wives. 3. A daughter of Oday Singh [Moth Rāja], son of Rāja Māldeo, married in 994. The *Tuzuk* (p. 5) calls her Jagat Gosāyinī. She is the mother of Shāhjahān, and died in 1028 (*Tuzuk*, p. 268). 4. A daughter of Khwāja Ḥasan, the uncle of Zayn Khān Koka. She is the mother of Prince Parwīz. She died 15th Tīr, 1007. 5. A daughter of Rāja Keshū Dās Rāṭhor. She is the mother of Bahār Bānū Begum (born 23rd Shahrīwar 998). 6 and 7. The mothers of Jahāndār and Shahryār. 8. A daughter of ʿAlī Rāy, ruler of little Thibet (*Bad.*, II, 376), married in 999. 9. A daughter of Jagat Singh, eldest son of Rāja Mān Singh (*Tuzuk*, p. 68). 10. Mihr[u] 'n-Nisā Khānum, the widow of Sher Afkan. On her marriage with Jahāngīr she received the title of Nūr Maḥall, and was later called Nūr Jahan (*Tuz.*, p. 156). Jahāngīr does not appear to have had children by Nūr Jahān.

Jahāngīr's children. 1. Sulṭān Khusraw. 2. Sulṭān Parwīz. 3. Sulṭān Khurram (Shāhjahān). 4. Sulṭān Jahāndār. 5. Sulṭān Shahryār. Two daughters are mentioned :—(*a*) Sulṭān[u] 'n-Niṣa Begum ; (*b*) Sulṭān Bahār Bānū Begum. There were " several children " after Parwīz ; but the *Tuzuk* (p. 8) does not give their names. They appear to have died soon after their birth.

Sulṭān Khusraw was born on the 24th Amurdād 995 (*Tuzuk*, Preface) ; but Khāfī Khān says 997. He was married to a daughter of Aẓam Khān

Koka. His sons—1. Baland Akhtar, who died when young, *Tuzuk*, p. 73. 2. Dāwar Bakhsh (also called *Bulāqī*),[1] whose daughter, Hoshmand Bānū Begum, was married to Hoshang, son of Dānyāl. 3. Garshasp.

Khusraw died on the 18th Isfandiyārmuz, 1031. He lies buried in the Khusraw Gardens in Allahabad. Dāwar Bakhsh was proclaimed Emperor by Āṣaf Khān after the death of Jahāngīr; but at an order of Shāhjahān, he was killed, together with his brother Garshasp, by Āṣaf Khān.

Sulṭān Parwīz, born 19th Ābān, 997. He was married to a daughter of Mīrzā Rustam-i Ṣafawī (No. 9) and had a son who died when young (*Tuz.*, p. 282). A daughter of Parwīz was married to Dārā Shikoh. Parwīz died of *delirium tremens* in 1036.

Sulṭān Khurram (Shāhjahān) was born at Lāhor on the 30th Rabīʿ I, 1000 A.H. Regarding his family, *vide Proceedings As. Soc. Bengal* for August, 1869, p. 219. He was Akbar's favourite.

Sulṭān Jahāndār had no children. He and *Sulṭān Shahryār* were born about the same time, a few months before Akbar's death (*Tuz.*, Preface, p. 17). Shahryār was married, in the 16th year of Jahāngīr, to Mihr^{u}'n-Nisā, the daughter of Nūr Jahān by Sher Afkan, and had a daughter by her, Arzānī Begum (*Tuzuk*, p. 370). The *Iqbāl-nāma* (p. 306) calls her الاردلي بيگم. From his want of abilities, he got the nickname *Nāshudanī* (fit for nothing). Khusraw, Parwīz, and Jahāndār died before their father.

Shahryār, at the instigation of Nūr Jahān, proclaimed himself Emperor of Lāhor a few days after the death of Jahāngīr. He was killed either at the order of Dāwar Bakhsh or of Āṣaf Khān; *vide Proceedings As. Soc. Bengal* for August, 1869, p. 218.

5. **Mīrzā Sulaymān**, son of Khān Mīrzā, son of Sulṭān Maḥmūd, son of Abū Saʿīd.

6. **Mīrzā Ibrāhīm**, son of Mīrzā Sulaymān (No. 5).

Mīrzā Sulaymān was born in 920, and died at Lāhor in 997. He is generally called *Wālī-yi Badakhshān*. As grandson of Abū Saʿīd Mīrzā, he is the sixth descendant from Tīmūr. Ābū Saʿid killed Sulṭān Muḥammad of Badakhshān, the last of a series of kings who traced their descent to Alexander the Great, and took possession of Badakhshān, which after his death fell to his son, Sulṭān Maḥmūd, who had three sons, Bāyasanghar Mīrzā, ʿAlī Mīrzā,[2] Khān Mīrzā. When Maḥmūd died, Amīr Khusraw

---

[1] The MSS. spell this name بلاقي and بولاقي.

[2] The *Maʿāṣir^{u} 'l-Umarā* calls the second son, Mīrzā Masʿūd.

Khān, one of his nobles blinded Bāyasanghar, killed the second prince, and ruled as usurper. He submitted to Bābar in 910. When Bābar took Qandahār, in 912, from Shāh Beg Arghūn, he sent Khān Mīrzā as governor to Badakhshān. Mīrzā Sulaymān is the son of this Khān Mīrzā.[1]

After the death of Khān Mīrzā, Badakhshān was governed for Bābar by Prince Humāyūn, Sulṭān Uways (Mīrzā Sulaymān's father-in-law), Prince Hindāl, and lastly, by Mīrzā Sulaymān, who held Badakhshān till 17 Jumāda II, 948, when he had to surrender himself and his son, Mīrzā Ibrāhīm, to Prince Kāmrān. They were released by Humāyūn in 952, and took again possession of Badakhshān. When Humāyūn had taken Kābul, he made war upon and defeated Mīrzā Sulāymān who once in possession of his country, had refused to submit; but when the return of Kāmrān from Sind obliged Humāyūn to go to Kābul, he reinstated the Mīrzā, who held Badakhshān till 983. Bent on making conquests, he invaded in 967 Balkh, but had to return. His son, Mīrzā Ibrāhīm, was killed in battle.[2]

In the eighth year when Mīrzā Muḥammad Ḥakīm's (Akbar's brother) mother had been killed by Shāh Abū 'l-Maʿānī Mīrzā S. went to Kābul, and had Abū 'l-Maʿalī hanged; he then married his own daughter to M. M. Ḥakīm, and appointed Umed ʿAlī, a Badakhshān noble, M. M. Ḥakīm's Vakīl (970). But M. M. Ḥakīm did not go on well with Mīrzā Sulaymān, who returned next year to Kābul with hostile intentions; but M. M. Hakīm fled and asked Akbar for assistance, so that Mīrzā S., though he had taken Jalālābād, had to return to Badakhshān. He returned to Kābul in 973, when Akbar's troops had left that country, but retreated on being promised tribute.

Mīrzā Sulaymān's wife was Khurram Begum, of the Qibchāk tribe. She was clever and had her husband so much in her power, that he did nothing without her advice. Her enemy was Muḥtaram Khānum, the widow of Prince Kāmrān. M. Sulaymān wanted to marry her; but Khurram Begum got her married, against her will, to Mīrzā Ibrāhīm, by whom she had a son, Mīrzā Shāhrukh (No. 7). When Mīrzā Ibrāhīm fell in the war with Balkh, Khurram Begum wanted to send the Khānum to her father, Shāh Muḥammad of Kāshghar; but she refused to go. As soon as Shāhrukh had grown up, his mother and some Badakhshī nobles excited him to rebel against his grandfather M. Sulaymān. This he did,

---

[1] The *Maʾāṣir* says Khān Mīrzā died in 917; but this is impossible, as Mīrzā Sulaymān was born in 920, the *Tārīkh* of his birth being the word يخشي.

[2] Hence he never was a grandee of Akbar's Court, and has been put on the list according to the rules of etiquette.

alternately rebelling and again making peace. Khurram Begum then died. Shāhrukh took away those parts of Badakhshān which his father had held, and found so many adhreents, that M. Sulaymān, pretending to go on a pilgrimage to Makkah, left Badakhshān for Kābul, and crossing the Nīlāb went to India (983). Khān Jahān, governor of the Panjāb, received orders to invade Badakhshān, but was suddenly ordered to go to Bengal, as Munʿīm Khān had died and Mīrzā Sulaymān did not care for the governorship of Bengal, which Akbar had given him.

M. Sulaymān then went to Ismāʿīl II of Persia. When the death of that monarch deprived him of the assistance which he had just received, he went to Muzaffar Ḥusayn Mīrzā (No. 8) at Qandahār, and then to M. M. Ḥakīm at Kābul. Not succeeding in raising disturbances in Kābul, he made for the frontier of Badakhshān, and luckily finding some adherents, he managed to get from his grandson the territory between *Tāqān* and the Hindū Kush. Soon after Muḥtaram Khānum died. Being again pressed by Shāhrukh, M. Sulaymān applied for help to 'Abd[u] 'llah Khān Uzbak, king of Tūrān, who had long wished to annex Badakhshān. He invaded and took the country in 992; Shāhrukh fled to Hundūstān, and M. Sulaymān to Kābul. As he could not recover Badakhshān, and being rendered destitute by the death of M. M. Ḥakīm, he followed the example of his grandson, and repaired to the court of Akbar, who made him a Commander of six thousand.

A few years later he died, at Lāhor, at the age of seventy-seven.

7. **Mīrzā Shāhurkh**, son of Mīrzā Ibrāhīm.

Vide Nos. 5 and 6. Akbar, in 1001, gave him his daughter Shukr[u] n'-Nisā Begum, and made him governor of Mālwa, and he distinguished himself in the conquest of the Dakhin. Towards the end of Akbar's reign, he was made a Commander of seven thousand, and was continued in his *Manṣab* by Jahāngīr.

He died at Ujain in 1016. His wife, *Kābulī Begum*, was a daughter of Mīrzā Muḥammad Ḥakīm. She wanted to take his body to Madīnah, but was robbed by the Badawīs; and after handing over the body to some "scoundrels" she went to Baṣra, and then to Shīrāz. In 1022, Shāh ʿAbbās married her to Mīrzā Ṣulṭān ʿAlī, his uncle, whom he had blinded; but the Begum did not like her new husband.

Shāhrukh's Children.—1. Ḥasan and Ḥusayn, twins. Ḥasan fled with Khusraw and was imprisoned by Jahāngīr. 2. Badīʿ[u] 'z-Zamān (or Mīrzā Fatḥpūrī), "a bundle of wicked bones," murdered by his brothers in Patan (Gujrāt). 3. *Mīrzā Shujāʿ* rose to honours under Shāhjahān, who called him Najābat Khān. 4. Mīrzā Muḥammad Zamān. He held a town in Badakhshān, and fell against the Uzbaks. 5. Mīrzā Sulṭān, a favourite of Jahāngīr. He had many wives, and Jahāngīr would have given him his own daughter in marriage if he had not perjured himself in trying to conceal the number of his wives. He fell into disgrace, and was appointed governor of Ghāzīpūr, where he died. 6. Mīrzā Mughul, who did not distinguish himself either. The *Tuzuk* (p. 65) says that after the death of Shāhrukh, Jahāngīr took charge of four of his sons and three of his daughters, "whom Akbar had not known." "Shāhrukh, though twenty years in India, could not speak a word of Hindī."

8. Mīrzā Muẓaffar Ḥusayn, son of Bahrām Mīrzā, son of Shāh Ismā'īl-i Ṣafawī.

In 965, Shāh Ṭahmāsp of Persia (930 to 984) conquered Qandahār, which was given, together with Dāwar and Garmsīr as far as the river Hīrmand, to Sulṭān Ḥusayn Mīrzā,[1] his nephew. Sulṭān Ḥusayn M. died in 984, when Shāh Isma'īl II (984 to 985) was king of Persia, and left five children, Muḥammad Ḥusayn Mīrzā, Muẓaffar Ḥusayn Mīrzā, Rustam Mīrzā, Abū Sa'īd Mīrzā, and Sanjar Mīrzā. The first was killed by Shāh Isma'īl Īrān. The other four in Qandahār had also been doomed; but the arrival of the news of the sudden death of the Shāh saved their lives. The new Shāh Khudābanda, gave Qandahār to Muẓaffar Ḥusayn Mīrzā, and Dāwar as far as the Hīrmand to Rustam Mīrzā, who was accompanied by his two younger brothers, their Vakīl being Hamza Beg 'Abdu 'llah, or Kor Hamza, an old servant of their father. The arbitrary behaviour of the Vakīl caused Muẓaffar Ḥusayn Mīrzā to take up arms against him, and after some alternate fighting and peace-making, Muẓaffar had the Vakīl murdered. This led to fights between Muẓaffar and Mīrzā Rustam who, however, returned to Dāwar.

Not long after the invasion of Khurāsān by the Uzbaks under Dīn Muḥammad Sulṭān and Bāqī Sulṭān (a sister's son of 'Abdu 'llah Khān of Tūrān) took place, and the Qandahār territory being continually exposed to incursions, the country was unsettled. Most of the Qizilbāsh grandees fell in the everlasting fights, and the Shāh of Persia promised assistance, but rendered none; Mīrzā Rustam who had gone to Hindūstān, was appointed by Akbar Governor of Lāhor, and kept Qandahār in anxiety; and Muẓaffar hesitatingly resolved to hand over Qandahār to Akbar, though 'Abdu 'llah Khān of Tūrān advised him not to join the Chaghatā'ī kings (the Mughuls of India). At that time Qarā Beg (an old servant of Muẓaffar's father, who had fled to India, and was appointed *Farrāshbegī*

[[1] Son of Bahrām Mīrzā *vide* 95.—P.]

by Akbar) returned to Qandahār, and prevailed upon Muẓaffar's mother and eldest son to bring about the annexation of Qandahār to India.

Akbar sent Shāh Beg K͟hān Arg͟hūn, Governor of Bangash, to take prompt possession of Qandahār, and though, as in all his undertakings, Muẓaffar wavered at the last moment and had recourse to trickery, he was obliged by the firm and prudent behaviour of Beg K͟hān in 1003, to go to Akbar. He received the title of *Farzand* (son), was made a Commander of five thousand, and received Sambhal as Jāgīr, " which is worth more than all Qandahār."

But the ryots of his jāgīr preferred complaints against his grasping collectors, and Muẓaffar, annoyed at this, applied to go to Makkah. No sooner had Akbar granted this request than Muẓaffar repented. He was reinstated, but as new complaints were preferred, Akbar took away the jāgīr, and paid him a salary in cash (1005). Muẓaffar then went to Makkah, but returned after reaching the first stage, which displeased Akbar so much, that he refused to have anything to do with him.

Muẓaffar found everything in India bad, and sometimes resolved to go to Persia, and sometimes to Makkah. From grief and disappointment, and a bodily hurt, he died in 1008.

His daughter, called *Qandahār Maḥall,* was in 1018 married to Shāhjahān, and gave birth, in 1020, to Nawāb Parhez Bānū Begum.

Three sons of his remained in India, Bahrām Mīrzā, Ḥaydar Mīrzā (who rose to dignity under Shāhjahān, and died in 1041), and Ismāʿīl Mīrzā. The *Maʾāṣir* mentions two other sons, Alqās Mīrzā and Ṭahmās Mīrzā.

Muẓaffar's younger brothers, Mīrzā Abū Saʿīd, and Mīrzā Sanjar, died in 1005. They held commands of Three hundred and fifty. (*Vide* Nos. 271 and 272.)

9. **Mīrzā Rustam.**—He is the younger, but more talented brother of the preceding. As the revenue of Dāwar was insufficient for him and his two younger brothers, he made war on Malik Maḥmūd, ruler of Sīstān. Muẓaffar Ḥusayn assisted him at first, but having married Malik Maḥmūd's daughter, he turned against Rustam. This caused a rupture between the brothers. Assisted by Lalla (guardian) Hamza Beg, M. Rustam invaded Qandahār, but without result. During the invasion of the Uzbaks into K͟hurāsān, he conquered the town of Farāh, and bravely held his own. Some time after, he again attacked Malik Maḥmūd. The latter wished to settle matters amicably. During an interview, Rustam seized him and killed him, when Jalālᵘ 'd-Dīn, Maḥmūd's son, took up arms. Rustam was defeated, and hearing that

his brother Muẓaffar had occupied Dāwar, he quickly took the town of Qalāt. Being once absent on a hunting expedition, he nearly lost the town, and though he took revenge on the conspirators who had also killed his mother, he felt himself so insecure, that he resolved to join Akbar. Accompanied by his brother, Sanjar Mīrzā, and his four sons Murād, Shāhrukh, Ḥasan, and Ibrāhīm, he went in 1001 to India. Akbar made him a *Panjhazārī*, and gave him Multān as jāgīr, " which is more than Qandahār." His inferiors being too oppressive, Akbar, in 1003, wished to give him Chitor, but recalled him from Sarhind, gave him Pathān as *tuyūl*, and sent him, together with Āṣaf Khān against Rāja Bāsū. But as they did not get on well together, Akbar called M. Rustam to court, appointing Jagat Singh, son of Rāja Mān Singh, in his stead. In 1006, M. Rustam got Rāysīn as jāgīr. He then served under Prince Dānyāl in the Dakhin. In 1021, Jahāngīr appointed him Governor of That'hah, but recalled him as he ill-treated the Arghūns. After the marriage of his daughter with Prince Parwīz, Jahāngīr made him *Shashhazārī*, and appointed him Governor of Allāhābād. He held the fort against ʿAbd[u] 'llah Khān, whom Shāhjahān, after taking possession of Bengal and Bihār, had sent against Allāhābād, and forced ʿAbd[u] 'llah to retire to Jhosī. In the 21st year, he was appointed Governor of Bihār, but was pensioned off as too old by Shāhjahān at 120,000 Rs. *per annum*, and retired to Āgra. In the sixth year, M. Rustam married his daughter to Prince Dārā Shikoh. He died, in 1051, at Āgra, 72 years old.

As a poet he is known under the *takhalluṣ* of *Fidāʾī*. He was a man of the world and understood the spirit of the age. All his sons held subsequently posts of distinction.

His first son *Murād* got from Jahāngīr the title of *Iltifāt Khān*. He was married to a daughter of ʿAbd[u] r-Raḥīm Khān Khānān. Murād's son, Mīrzā Mukarram Khān, also distinguished himself; he died in 1080.

His third son *Mīrzā Ḥasan-i Ṣafawī*, a *Hazār o panṣadī* under Jahāngīr, was Governor of *Kūch* died 1059. Ḥasan's son, *Mīrzā Ṣafshikan*, was Fawjdār of Jessore in Bengal, retired, and died in 1073. *Ṣafshikan's* son, *Sayf[u] 'd-Dīn-i Ṣafawī*, accepted the title of Khān under Awrangzeb.

10. **Bayrām Khān**, the fifth in descent from Mīr ʿAlī Shukr Beg Bahārlū.

Bahārlū is the name of a principal clan of the Qarāqūilū Turks. During the time of their ascendency under Qarā Yūsuf, and his sons Qarā Sikandar and Mīrzā Jahān Shāh, rulers of ʿIrāq-i ʿArab and Āzarbāyjān, ʿAlī Shukr Beg held Daynūr, Hamadān, and Kurdistān, " which tracts are still called the territory of ʿAlī Shukr." His son Pīr ʿAlī Beg stayed some time with Sulṭān Maḥmūd Mīrzā, and attacked afterwards the Governor of Shirāz, but was defeated. He was killed by some of the Amīrs of Sulṭān Ḥusayn Mīrzā. Pīr ʿAlī Beg's son, in the reign of Shāh Ismāʿīl-i Ṣafawī, left ʿIrāq, settled in Badakhshān, and entered the service of Amīr Khusraw Shāh (*vide* p. 324, last line) at Qunduz. He then joined, with his son Sayf ʿAlī Beg, Bābar's army, as Amīr Khusraw had been deposed. Sayf ʿAlī Beg is Bayrām's father.

Bayrām Khān was born at Badakhshān. After the death of his father he went to Balkh to study. When sixteen years old, he entered Humāyūn's army, fought in the battle of Qanawj (10th Muḥarram, 947), and fled to the Rāja of Lakhnor (Sambhal). Sher Shāh met Bayrām in Mālwa, and tried to win him over. But Bayrām fled from Barhāmpūr with Abū 'l-Qāsim, governor of Gwāliyār, to Gujrāt. They were surprised, on the road, by an ambassador of Sher Shāh who had just returned from Gujrāt. Abū 'l-Qāsim, a man of imposing stature, being mistaken for Bayrām, the latter stepped forward and said in a manly voice, "I am Bayrām." "No," said Abū 'l-Qāsim, "he is my attendant, and brave and faithful as he is, he wishes to sacrifice himself for me. So let him off." Abū 'l-Qāsim was then killed, and Bayrām escaped to Sulṭan Maḥmūd of Gujrāt. Under the pretext of sailing for Makkah, Bayrām embarked at Sūrat for Sindh. He joined Humāyūn on the 7th Muḥarram, 950, when the Emperor, after passing through the territory of Rāja Māldeo, was pressed by the Arghūns at Jon. On the march to Persia, he proved the most faithful attendant. The King of Persia also liked him, and made him a Khān. On Humāyūn's return, Bayrām was sent on a mission to Prince Kāmrān. When Humāyūn marched to Kābul, he took Qandahār by force and treachery from the Qizilbāshes, and making Bayrām governor of the district, he informed the Shāh that he had done so as Bayrām was "a faithful servant of both". Subsequently rumours regarding Bayrām's duplicity reached Humāyūn; but when in 961, the Emperor returned to Qandahār, the rumours turned out false.

The conquest of India may justly be ascribed to Bayrām. He gained the battle of Māchhīwāra, and received Sambhal as jāgīr. In 963, he was appointed *atālīq* (guardian) of Prince Akbar, with whom he went to the Panjāb against Sikandar Khān. On Akbar's accession (2nd Rabīʿ II, 963) at Kalānūr, he was appointed *Wakīl* and *Khān Khānān*, and received the title of *Khān Bābā*. On the second of Shawwāl, 964, shortly after the surrender of Mānkoṭ, when Akbar returned to Lāhor, an imperial elephant ran against Bayrām's tent, and Bayrām blamed Atgah Khān

(No. 15), who never had been his friend, for this accident. The Atgah, after arrival at Lāhor, went with his whole family to Bayrām, and attested his innocence by an oath upon the Qurʿān.[1] In 965, Bayrām married Salīma Sulṭān Begum (p. 321, note), and soon after the estrangement commenced between Akbar and him. Badāonī (II, p. 36) attributes the fall of Bayrām to the ill-treatment of Pīr Muḥammad (No. 20) and the influence of Adham Khān and his mother Māhum Anagah (Akbar's nurse), Ṣiddiq Muḥammad Khān, Shāhābu 'd-Dīn Aḥmad, etc., who effectually complained of the wretchedness of their jāgīrs, and the emptiness of the Treasury, whilst Bayrām Khān's friends lived in affluence. The *Ṭabaqāt-i Akbarī* says that no less than twenty-five of Bayrām's friends reached the dignity of Panjhazārīs—rather a proof of Bayrām's gift of selecting proper men. Bayrām's fall is known from the Histories. "Akbar's trick resembles exactly that which Sulṭān Abū Saʿīd-i Mughul adopted towards his minister Amīr Chaubān." (Bad.)

On hearing the news that Akbar had assumed the reigns of the government, Bayrām left Āgra, and sent his friends who had advised him to go to Akbar, to Court. He himself went under the pretext of going to Makkah to Mewāt and Nāgor, from where he returned his *insignia*, which reached Akbar at Jhujhar; for Akbar was on his way to the Panjāb, which Bayrām, as it was said, wished to invade. The *insignia* were conferred on Pīr Muḥammad Khān, Bayrām's old *protégé*; and he was ordered to see him embark for Makkah. Bayrām felt much irritated at this; and finding the road to Gujrāt occupied by Rāja Māldeo, his enemy, he proceeded to Bīkānīr to his friend Kalyān Mal

---

[1] So *Bad.* II, 19. The story in Elphinstone (fifth edition), p. 497, does not agree with the sources. The Akbarnama says, Bayrām was on board a ship on the Jamna, when one of Akbar's elephants ran into the water and nearly upset the boat. Abū 'l-Faẓl, moreover, refers it to a later period than 964. The author of the *Sawāniḥ-i Akbarī* has a fine critical note on Abū 'l-Faẓl's account. I would remark here that as long as we have no translation of *all* the sources for a history of Akbar's reign, European historians should make the *Sawāniḥ-i Akbarī* the basis of their labours. This work is a modern compilation dedicated to William Kirkpatrick, and was compiled by Amīr Ḥaydar of Belgrām from the Akbarnāma, the Ṭabaqāt Bad,āonī, Firishta, *the Akbarnāma by Shaykh Ilāhdād of Sarhind* (poetically called *Fayẓī*; *vide* Journal As. Soc. Bengal for 1868, p. 10) and *Abū 'l-Faẓl's letters*, of which the compiler had *four* books. The sources in *italics* have never been used by preceding historians. This work is perhaps the only critical historical work written by a native, and confirms an opinion which I have elsewhere expressed, that those portions of Indian History for which we have several sources, are full of the most astounding discrepancies as to details.

Belgrām was a great seat of Muhammadan learning from the times of Akbar to the present century. For the *literati* of the town *vide* the Tazkira by Ghulām ʿAlī Āzād, entitled *Sarw-i Āzād*.

The author of the *Sawāniḥ-i Akbarī* states that Abū 'l-Faẓl does not show much friendliness to Bayrām, whilst Erskine (Elphinstone, p. 495, note) represents Abū 'l-Faẓl as " Bayrām's warm panegyrist ".

(No. 93). But unable to restrain himself any longer, he entrusted his property, his family, and his young son ʿAbḍu ʾr-Raḥīm (No. 29) to Sher Muḥammad Dīwāna, his adopted son and jāgīr holder of Tabarhinda, and broke out in open rebellion. At Dīpālpūr, on his way to the Panjāb, he heard that Dīwāna had squandered the property left in his charge, had insulted his family, and had sent Muẓaffar ʿAlī (whom Bayrām had dispatched to Dīwāna to settle matters) to Court a prisoner. Mortified at this, Bayrām resolved to take Jālindhar. Akbar now moved against him; but before he reached him, he heard that Bayrām had been defeated[1] by Atgah K͟hān (No. 15). Bayrām fled to Fort Tilwāra on the banks of the Biyāh, followed by Akbar. Fighting ensued. In the very beginning, Sulṭān Ḥusayn Jalāir was killed; and when his head was brought to Bayrām,[2] he was so sorry that he sent to Akbar and asked forgiveness. This was granted, and Bayrām, accompanied by the principal grandees, went to Akbar's tent, and was pardoned. After staying for two days longer with Munʿim K͟hān, he received a sum of money, and was sent to Makkah. The whole camp made a collection (*chandog͟h*). Hājī Muḥammad of Sīstān (No. 55) accompanied Bayrām over Nāgor to Patan (Nahrwāla) in Gujrāt, where he was hospitably received by Mūsa K͟hān Fūlādī, the governor. On Friday, 14th Jumāda I, 968, while alighting from a boat after a trip on the Sahansa Lang Tank, Bayrām was stabbed by a Lohānī Afg͟hān of the name of Mubārak, whose father had been killed in the battle of Māchhīwara. "With an *Allāhu Akbar* on his lips, he died." The motive of Mubārak K͟hān is said to have merely been revenge. Another reason is mentioned. The Kashmīrī wife of Salīm Shāh with her daughter had attached herself to Bayrām's suite, in order to go to Ḥijāz, and it had been settled that Bayrām's son should be betrothed to her, which annoyed the Afg͟hāns. Some beggars lifted up Bayrām's body, and took it to the tomb of Shayk͟h Ḥusāmu ʾd-Dīn. Seventeen years later the body was interred in holy ground at Mash,had.

Akbar took charge of ʿAbdu ʾr-Raḥīm, Bayrām's son (*vide* No. 29), and married soon after Salīma Sulṭān Begum, Bayrām's widow.

For بیرام *Bayrām*, we often find the spelling بیرم *Bayram*. Firishta generally calls him Bayrām K͟hān Turkmān. Bayrām was a Shīʿah, and a poet of no mean pretensions (*vide* Badāonī III, p. 190).

---

[1] Near کرناجور (or کوناچور) in the Parganah دکهدار [Bad.; دکدار *Maʿāṣir*; دکدهار *Sawāniḥ*] near Jālindhar. For کوناجور, Bad. (II. 40) has کنورپهلور. Firishta says (Lucknow edit., p. 249) the fight took place outside of Māchhīwāra.

[2] The *Maʿāṣir* mentions this fact without giving the source.

11. **Munʿim Khān**, son of Bayrām[1] Beg.

Nothing appears to be known of the circumstances of his father. Munʿim Khān was a grandee of Humāyūn's Court, as was also his brother Fazīl Beg. When Humāyūn, on his flight to Persia, was hard pressed by Mīrzā Shāh Ḥusayn of Thathah, one grandee after another went quietly away. M. and Fazīl Beg also were on the point of doing so, when Humāyūn made them prisoners, as he had done from motives of prudence and policy with several other nobles. M. did not, however, accompany Humāyūn to Persia. He rejoined him immediately on his return, and rose at once to high dignity. He rejected the governership of Qandahār, which was given to Bayrām Khān. In 961, he was appointed *atālīq* of Prince Akbar; and when Humāyūn invaded India, M. was left as governor of Kābul in charge of Mīrzā Muḥammad Ḥakīm, Akbar's brother, then about a year old. In Kābul M. remained till Bayrām fell into disgrace. He joined Akbar, in Ẕī Ḥijja, 967, at Lūdhiyāna, where Akbar encamped on his expedition against Bayrām. M. was then appointed *Khān Khānān* and *Vakīl*.

In the seventh year of Akbar's reign, when Adham Khān (No. 19) killed Atgah Khān (No. 15), Munʿim who had been the instigator, fled twice from Court, but was caught the second time in Saror (Sirkār of Qanawj) by the collector of the district, and was brought in by Sayyid Maḥmūd Khān of Bārha (No. 75). Akbar restored M. to his former honours.

Munʿim Khān's son, Ghanī Khān, whom his father had left in charge of Kābul, caused disturbances from want of tact. Māh Jūjak Begum, Prince M. Muḥammad Ḥakīm's mother, advised by Fazīl Beg and his son Abu 'l-Fatḥ, who hated Ghanī Khān, closed the doors of Kābul when Ghanī Khān was once temporarily absent at Fālīz. Ghanī Khān, not finding adherents to oppose her, went to India. Māh Jūjak Begum then appointed Fazīl Beg as Vakīl and Abu 'l-Fatḥ as *Nāʾib*; but being dissatisfied with them, she killed them both, at the advice of Shāh Walī, one of her nobles. On account of these disturbances, Akbar, in the eighth year, sent M. to Kābul. Thinking he could rely on the Kābulīs, M. left before his contingent was quite ready. He was attacked near Jalālābād by Māh Jūjak Begum (who in the meantime had killed Shāh Walī and had taken up, apparently criminally, with Ḥaydar Qāsim Koh-bar, whom she had made *Vakīl*) and defeated. M. fled to the Ghakhars, and ashamed and hesitating he joined Akbar, who appointed him Commander of the Fort of Āgra.

[1] Some MSS. read *Mīram*; but *Bayrām* is the preferable reading.

In the 12th year, after the defeat and death of Khān Zamān (No. 13), M. was appointed to his jāgīrs in Jaunpūr (Bad. II, 101), and then concluded peace with Sulaymān Kararānī of Bengal, who promised to read the Khuṭba and strike coins in Akbar's name.

In 982, Akbar, at M.'s request, went with a flotilla from Āgra to Bihār, and took Ḥājīpūr and Paṭna from Dā'ūd, Sulaymān's son. M. was then appointed Governor of Bihār, and was ordered to follow Dā'ūd into Bengal. M. moved to Ṭānḍa (opposite Gaur, on the right side of the Ganges) to settle political matters, and left the pursuit to Muḥammad Qulī Khān Barlās (No. 31). But as the latter soon after died, M., at the advice of Ṭoḍar Mal, left Ṭānḍa, and followed up Dā'ūd, who after his defeat at تکروه submitted at Katak. In Ṣafar 983, M. returned, and though his army had terribly suffered from epidemics on the march through Southern Bengal, he quartered them against the advice of his friends at Gaur, where M. soon after died of fever.

The great bridge of Jaunpūr was built by Mun'im Khān in 981. Its *tārīkh* is صراط المستقیم. M.'s son Ghanī Khān went to 'Ādilshāh of Bījāpūr, where he died.

12. **Tardī Beg Khān**, of Turkistān.

A noble of Humāyūn's Court. After the conquest of Gujrāt, he was made Governor of Champānīr (Pāwangarh). On Mīrza 'Askarī's defeat by Sulṭān Bahādur, Tardī Beg also succumbed to him, and retreated to Humāyūn. During the emperor's flight from India, Tardī Beg distinguished himself as one of the most faithless[1] companions. When passing through the territory of Rāja Māldeo, he even refused Humāyūn a horse, and at Amarkoṭ, he declined to assist the emperor with a portion of the wealth he had collected while at court. Hence Rāy Parsād advised H. to imprison some of his nobles and take away part of their property by force. H., however, returned afterwards most of it. In Qandahār, Tardī Beg left the emperor and joined Mīrzā 'Askarī. But Mīrzā 'Askarī put most of them on the rack, and forced also Tardī Beg to give him a large sum as ransom.

On Humāyūn's return from 'Irāq, Tardī Beg asked pardon for his former faithlessness, was restored to favour, and was sent, in 955, after the death of Mīrzā Ulugh Beg, son of Mīrzā Sulṭān, to Dāwar. During the conquest of India, T. distinguished himself and received Mewāt as

---

[1] Elphinstone, p. 452, note, says Tardī Beg was one of the most *faithful* followers of Humāyūn, a statement which is contradicted by all native historians.

jāgīr. In 963, when Humāyūn died (7th Rabīʿ I), T. read the *khuṭba* in Akbar's name, and sent the crown-insignia with M. Abū 'l-Qāsim, son of Prince Kāmrān, to Akbar in the Panjāb. Akbar made T. a Commander of Five Thousand, and appointed him governor of Dihlī. T. drove away Ḥājī Khān, an officer of Sher Shāh, from Narnaul. On Hemū's approach, after some unsuccessful fighting, T. too rashly evacuated Dihlī, and joined Akbar at Sarhind. Bayrām Khān, who did not like T. from envy and sectarian motives, accused him, and obtaining from Akbar "a sort of permission" (Bad. II, 14) had him murdered (end of 963). Akbar was displeased. Bayrām's hasty act was one of the chief causes of the distrust with which the Chaghatāʾī nobles looked upon him. Tardī Beg was a Sunnī.

13. Khān Zamān-i Shaybānī.

His father Ḥaydar Sulṭān Uzbak-i Shaybānī had been made an Amīr in the Jām war with the Qizilbāshes. When Humāyūn returned from Persia, Ḥaydar joined him, together with his two sons ʿAlī Qulī Khān [Khān Zamān] and Bahādur Khān (No. 22), and distinguished himself in the conquest of Qandahār. On the march to Kābul, an epidemic broke out in Humāyūn's camp, during which Ḥaydar Sulṭān died.

ʿAlī Qulī Khān distinguished himself in Kābul and in the conquest of Hindūstān, was made Amīr and sent to the Du,āb and Sambhal, where he defeated the Afghāns. At the time of Akbar's accession, ʿAlī Qulī Khān fought with Shādī Khān, an Afghān noble; but when he heard that Hemū had gone to Dihlī, he thought fighting with this new enemy more important; but before ʿAlī Qulī arrived at Dihlī, Tardī Beg (No. 12) had been defeated, and A. returned from Meerut to Akbar at Sarhind. ʿAlī Qulī was sent in advance with 10,000 troopers, met Hemū near Pānīpat and defeated him. Though Akbar and Bayrām were near, they took no part in this battle. ʿAlī Qulī received the title of *Khān Zamān*. Next to Bayrām, the restoration of the Mughul Dynasty may be justly ascribed to him. Khān Zamān then got Sambhal again as jāgīr, cleared the whole north of India up to Lakhnau of the Afghāns, and acquired an immense fortune by plunder. In 964, he held Jaunpūr as *Qāʾim maqām* for Sikandar, after the latter had surrendered Mānkeṭ. In the third year of Akbar's reign, Khān Zamān became the talk of the whole country in consequence of a love scandal with Shāham Beg, a page of Humāyūn, and as he refused to send the boy back to Court, Akbar took away some of Khān Zamān's *tuyūl's*, which led him to rebel. Bayrām from generosity did not interfere; but when Pīr Muḥammad, Khān Zamān's enemy, had been appointed Vakīl, he took away, in the 4th year, the whole of his *maḥalls*, and had him appointed commander against the Afg͟hāns who threatened the Jaunpūr District. Pīr Muḥammad had also Burj ʿAlī thrown from the walls of Fīrūzābād, whom K͟hān Zamān had sent to him to settle matters. K͟hān Zamān now thought it was high time to send away Shāham Beg, went to Jaunpūr, and drove away the Afg͟hāns. Upon the fall of Bayrām, they appeared again under Sher Shāh, son of ʿĀdlī,[1] with a large army and 500 elephants. K͟hān Zamān, however, defeated them in the streets of Jaunpūr, and carried off immense plunder and numerous elephants, which he retained for himself.

In Ẕī Qaʿda of the 6th year, Akbar moved personally against him; but at Kaṛah (on the Ganges) K͟hān Zamān and his brother Bahādur submitted and delivered the booty and the elephants. They were pardoned and sent again to Jaunpūr. Soon after, he defeated the Afg͟hāns, who had attacked him in a fortified position near the Son.

In the 10th year, K͟hān Zamān rebelled again in concert with the Uzbaks, and attacked the Tuyūldārs of the province. As soon as an imperial army marched against him, he went to G͟hāzīpūr, and Akbar on arrival at Jaunpūr sent Munʿim K͟hān against him. Being a friend of K͟hān Zamān, he induced him to submit, which he did. But a body of imperial troops under Muʿizzᵘ 'l-Mulk and Rāja Ṭodaṛ Mal, having been defeated by Bahādur and Iskandar Uzbak (No. 48), the rebellion continued, though repeated attempts were made to bring about a conciliation. Having at last sworn to be faithful, K͟hān Zamān was left in possession of his jāgīrs, and Akbar returned to Āgra. But when the emperor, on the 3rd Jumāda I, 974, marched against M. Muḥammad Ḥakīm, K͟hān Zamān rebelled again, read the *K͟huṭba* at Jaunpūr in M. Muḥammad Ḥakīm's name, and marched against Shergaṛh (Qanawj). Akbar was now resolved no longer to pardon; he left the Panjāb, 12th Ramaẓān 974, and Āgra on the 26th Shawwāl. At Sakīṭ, east of Āgra, Akbar heard that K͟hān Zamān had fled from Shergaṛh to Mānikpūr where Bahādur was, and from there marching along the Ganges, had bridged the river near the frontier of Singror (Nawābganj, between Mānikpūr and Allāhābād). Akbar sent a detachment of 6,000 troopers under Muḥammad Qulī K͟hān Barlās and Ṭodaṛ Mal to Audh to oppose Iskandar K͟hān Uzbak, and marched over Rāy Barelī to Mānikpūr, crossed the Ganges with about 100 men, and slept at night near the banks of the river, at a short distance from K͟hān Zamān's camp, who must have gone from Nawābganj back again on the right side of the river to Kaṛah. Next morning, 1st Ẕī

[[1] *Mubāriz K͟hān ʿĀdlī.*—B.]

Ḥijja, 974, Akbar with some reinforcements attacked Khān Zamān. Bahādur was captured, and brought to Akbar, and he had scarcely been dispatched, when Khān Zamān's head was brought in. He had been half killed by an elephant whose driver was called Somnāt, when a soldier cut off his head; for Akbar had promised a muhr for every Mughul's head. But another soldier snatched away the head and took it to Akbar. The fight took place *dar ʿarṣa-yi Sakrāwal* (in Badā,onī, *Mungarwāl*), "which place has since been called *Fatḥpūr*." The Trig. S. maps show a small village Faṭhpūr about 10 or 12 miles south-east of Kaṛah, not far from the river.

On the same day, though the heat was terrible, Akbar started for and reached Allāhābād.

Khān Zamān as a poet styled himself Sulṭān (*vide Proceedings Asiatic Society*, September, 1868). *Zamāniyā* (now a station on the E. I. Railway) was founded by him. Though an Uzbak, Khān Zamān, from his long residence in Persia was a staunch Shīʿah. Khān Zamān must not be confounded with No. 124.

14. **ʿAbdu 'llah Khān Uzbak.**

A noble of Humāyūn's Court. After the defeat of Hemū, he received the title of Shujāʿat Khān, got Kālpī as *tuyūl*, and served under Adham Khān (No. 19) in Gujrāt. When Bāz Bahādur, after the death of Pīr Muḥammad, had taken possession of Mālwa, ʿAbdu 'llah was made a *Panjhazārī*, and was sent to Mālwa with almost unlimited authority. He re-conquered the province, and "reigned in Mandū like a king". Akbar found it necessary to move against him. ʿAbdu 'llah, after some unsuccessful fighting, fled to Gujrāt, pursued by Qāsim Khān of Nīshāpūr (No. 40). Leaving his wives in the hands of his enemies, he fled with his young son to Changīz Khān, an officer of Sulṭān Maḥmūd of Gujrāt. Ḥakīm ʿAynu 'l-Mulk was dispatched to Changīz with the request to deliver up ʿAbdu 'llah, or to dismiss him. Changīz Khān did the latter. ʿAbdu 'llah again appeared in Mālwa, and was hotly pursued by Shahābu 'd-Dīn Aḥmad Khān (No 26), who nearly captured him. With great difficulties he eluded his pursuers, and managed to reach Jaunpūr, where he died a natural death during the rebellion of Khān Zamān (No. 13).

15. **Shamsu 'd-Dīn Muḥammad Atga Khān.**

Son of Mīr Yār Muḥammad of Ghaznī, a simple farmer. Shamsu 'd-Dīn, when about twenty years old, once dreamed that he held the moon under his arm, which dream was justified by the unparalleled luck which he owed to a little deed of kindness. Shamsu 'd-Dīn entered

Prince Kāmrān's service as a common soldier, and was present in the fatal battle of Qanawj (10th Muḥarram, 947). Humāyūn, after the defeat, crossed the river "on an elephant", and dismounted on the other side, where a soldier who had escaped death in the current, stretched out his hand to assist the emperor to jump on the high bank. This soldier was Shams^{u} 'd-Dīn. Humāyūn attached him to his service, and subsequently appointed his wife wet nurse (*angā*) to Prince Akbar at Amarkoṭ, conferring upon her the title of *Jī Jī Anaga*. Shams^{u} 'd-Dīn remained with the young prince whilst Humāyūn was in Persia, and received after the emperor's restoration the title of *Atga* (foster father) *Khān*. Humāyūn sent him to Ḥiṣār, which Sirkār had been set aside for Prince Akbar's maintenance.

After Akbar's accession, Atga Khān was dispatched to Kābul to bring to India the Empress mother and the other Begums. Soon after, on the march from Mankoṭ to Lāhor, the elephant affair took place, which has been related under *Bayrām Khān*, p. 331. He held Khushāb in the Panjāb as jāgīr, and received, after Bayrām's fall, the *insignia* of that chief. He was also appointed Governor of the Panjāb. He defeated Bayrām Khān near Jālindhar, before Akbar could come up, for which victory Akbar honoured him with the title of Aʿẓam Khān. In the sixth year, he came from Lāhor to the Court, and acted as Vakīl either in supersession of Munʿim Khān or by "usurpation", at which Akbar connived. Munʿim Khān and Shahāb Khān (No. 26) felt much annoyed at this, and instigated Adham (*vide* No. 19) to kill Atga Khān,[1] 12th Ramaẓān, 969.

For Atga Khān's brothers *vide* Nos. 16, 28, 63, and for his sons, Nos. 18 and 21. The family is often called in Histories *Atga Khāyl*[2] "the foster father battalion."

16. **Khān-i Kalān Mīr Muḥammad**, elder brother of Atga Khān.

He served under Kāmrān and Humāyūn, and rose to high dignity during the reign of Akbar. Whilst Governor of the Panjāb, where most of the *Atgas* (*Atga Khayl*) had jāgīrs, he distinguished himself in the war with the Ghakkars, the extirpation of Sulṭān Ādam, and in keeping down Kamāl Khān. In the ninth year he assisted Mīrzā Muḥammad Ḥakīm against Mīrzā Sulaymān (No. 5), restored him to the throne of Kābul, settled the country, and sent back the imperial troops under

---

[1] He stabbed at the *Atga*, and ordered one of his own servants, an Uzbak, of the name of Khusham Beg, to kill him. *Badā,onī* (p. 52) and Elphinstone (p. 502, l. 1) say that Adham himself killed Atga.

[[2] *Khayl*, troop, tribe, etc.—P.]

his brother Quṭbᵘ 'd-Dīn (No. 28), though Akbar had appointed the latter *Atālīq* of the Prince. But Khān-i Kalān did not get on well with M. M. Ḥakīm, especially when the Prince had given his sister Fakhrᵘ 'n-Nisā Begum (a daughter of Humāyūn by Jūjak Begum, and widow of Mīr Shāh ʿAbdᵘ 'l-Maʿālī) to Khwāja Ḥasan Naqshbandī in marriage. To avoid quarrels, Khān-i Kalān left Kābul one night and returned to Lāhor.

In the 13th year (976) the *Atga Khayl* was removed from the Panjāb, and ordered to repair to Āgra. Khān-i Kalān received Sambhal as jāgīr, whilst Ḥusayn Qulī Khān (No. 24) was appointed to the Panjāb. In 981, he was sent by Akbar in advance, for the reconquest of Gujrāt (*Bad.* II, 165). On the march, near Sarohī (Ajmīr), he was wounded by a Rājpūt, apparently without cause; but he recovered. After the conquest, he was made governor of Patan (Nahrwāla). He died at Patan in 983.

He was a poet and wrote under the *takhalluṣ* of "Ghaznawī", in allusion to his birthplace. Badā,onī (III, 287) praises him for his learning.

His eldest son, Fāẓil Khān (No. 156), was a *Hazārī*, and was killed when Mīrzā ʿAzīz Koka (No. 21) was shut up in Aḥmadnagar. His second son, Farrukh Khān (No. 232) was a *Panṣadī*. Nothing else is known of him.

17. **Mīrzā Sharafᵘ 'd-Dīn Ḥusayn,** son of Khwāja Muʿīn.

He was a man of noble descent. His father, Khāwja Muʿīn, was the son of Khāwand Maḥmūd, second son of Khwāja Kalān (known as Khwājagān Khwāja), eldest son of the renowned saint Khwāja Nāṣirᵘ 'd-Dīn ʿUbaydᵘ 'llah Aḥrār. Hence Mīrzā Sharafᵘ 'd-Dīn Ḥusayn is generally called *Aḥrārī.*

His grandfather, Khāwand Maḥmūd, went to India, was honorably received by Humāyūn, and died at Kābul.

His father, Khwāja Muʿīn, was a rich, but avaricious man; he held the tract of land called "Rūdkhāna-yi Nasheb", and served under ʿAbdᵘ 'llāh Khān, ruler of Kāshghar. He was married to Kījak Begum, daughter of Mīr ʿAlāʿᵘ 'l-Mulk of Tirmiz, who is a daughter of Fakhr Jahān Begum, daughter of Sulṭān Abū Saʿid Mīrzā. "Hence the blood of Tīmūr also flowed in the veins of Mīrzā Sharafᵘ 'd-Dīn Ḥusayn." As the son did not get on well with his father, he went to Akbar. Through the powerful influence of Māhum, Akbar's nurse, and Adham Khān, her son (No. 19), Mīrzā Sharaf was appointed *Panjhazārī*. In the 5th year, Akbar gave him his sister Bakhshī Bānū Begum in marriage, and made him governor of Ajmīr and Nāgor. In 969, when Akbar went to Ajmīr, Mīrzā Sharaf joined the emperor, and distinguished himself in the siege of Mairtha, which was defended by Jagmal and Devīdās, the latter of whom was killed in an engagement subsequent to their retreat from the fort.

In 970, Mīrzā Sharaf's father came to Āgra, and was received with great honours by Akbar. In the same year, Mīrzā Sharaf, from motives of suspicion, fled from Āgra over the frontier, pursued by Ḥusayn Qulī Khān (No. 24), and other grandees. His father, ashamed of his son's behaviour, left for Ḥijāz, but died at Cambay. The ship on which was his body, foundered. Mīrzā Sharaf stayed for some time with Changīz Khān, a Gujrāt noble, and then joined the rebellion of the Mīrzās. When Gujrāt was conquered, he fled to the Dakhin, and passing through Baglāna, was captured by the Zamīndār of the place, who after the conquest of Sūrat handed him over to Akbar. To frighten him, Akbar ordered him to be put under the feet of a tame elephant, and after having kept him for some time imprisoned, he sent him to Muẓaffar Khān, Governor of Bengal (No. 37), who was to give him a jāgīr, should be find that the Mīrzā showed signs of repentance ; but if not, to send him to Makkah. Muẓaffar was waiting for the proper season to have him sent off, when Mīr Maʿṣūm-i Kābulī rebelled in Bihār. Joined by Bābā Khān Qāqshāl, the rebels besieged Muẓaffar Khān in Ṭānḍa and overpowered him. Mīrzā Sharaf fled to them, after having taken possession of the hidden treasures of Muẓaffar. But subsequently he became Maʿṣūm's enemy. Each was waiting for an opportunity to kill the other. Maʿṣūm at last bribed a boy of the name of Maḥmūd, whom Mīrzā Sharaf liked, and had his enemy poisoned. Mīrzā Sharaf's death took place in 988. He is wrongly called *Siefuddeen* in Stewart's History of Bengal (p. 108).

18. **Yūsuf Muḥammad Khān**, eldest son of Atga Khān (No. 15).

He was Akbar's foster brother (*koka* or *kūkaltāsh*). When twelve years old, he distinguished himself in the fight with Bayrām (p. 332, l. 9), and was made Khān. When his father had been killed by Adham Khān (No. 19) Akbar took care of him and his younger brother ʿAzīz Koka (No. 21). He distinguished himself during the several rebellions of Khān Zamān (No. 13).

He died from excessive drinking in 973. *Bad.* II, p. 84.

19. **Adham Khān**,[1] son of Māhum Anga.

The name of his father is unknown ; he is evidently a royal bastard.

---

[1] Generally called in European histories Ādam Khān ; but his name is ادهم, not آدم.

His mother Māhum was one of Akbar's nurses (*angā*),[1] and attended on Akbar " from the cradle till after his accession ". She appears to have had unbounded influence in the Harem and over Akbar himself, and Munʿim Khān (No. 11), who after Bayrām's fall had been appointed *Vakīl*, was subject to her counsel. She also played a considerable part in bringing about Bayrām's fall; *Bad.* II, p. 36.

Adham Khān was a *Panjhazārī*, and distinguished himself in the siege of Mānkot.[2] Bayrām Khān, in the third year, gave him Hatkānth,[3] South-East of Āgra, as jāgīr, to check the rebels of the Bhadauriya clan, who even during the preceding reigns had given much trouble. Though he accused Bayrām of partiality in bestowing bad jāgīrs upon such as he did not like, Adham did his best to keep down the Bhadauriyas. After Bayrām's fall, he was sent, in 968, together with Pīr Muḥammad Khān to Mālwah, defeated Bāz Bahādur near Sārangpūr, and took possession of Bahādur's treasures and dancing girls. His sudden fortune made him refractory; he did not send the booty to Āgra, and Akbar thought it necessary to pay him an unexpected visit, when Māhum Anga found means to bring her son to his senses. Akbar left after four days. On his departure, Adham prevailed on his mother to send back two beautiful dancing girls; but when Akbar heard of it, Adham turned them away. They were captured, and killed by Māhum's orders. Akbar knew the whole, but said nothing about it. On his return to Āgra, however, he recalled Adham, and appointed Pīr Muḥammad governor of Mālwah.

At Court, Adham met again Atga Khān, whom both he and Munʿim Khān envied and hated. On the 12th Ramaẓān 969, when Munʿim Khān, Atga Khān, and several other grandees had a nightly meeting in the state hall at Āgra, Adham Khān with some followers, suddenly

---

[1] This is the pronunciation given in the Calcutta Chaghatāī Dictionary. Misled by the printed editions of Badā,onī, Firishta, Khāfī Khān, etc., I put on p. 223 of my text edition of the Āʿīn, *Māhum Atgah*, as if it was the name of a man. *Vide* Khāfī Khān I, p. 132, l. 6 from below.

[2] The *Maʿāṣir* gives a short history of this fort, partly taken from the Akbarnāma.

[3] Hatkānth was held by Rājpūts of the Bhadauriya clan. *Vide* Beames's edition of Elliot's Glossary, II, p. 86, and I, 27, where the word لہاور is doubtful, though it is certainly not *Lahore*; for the old spelling " Luhāwar " for " Lāhor " had ceased when the author of the *Makhzan-i Afghānī* wrote. Besides, a place in Gwāliār is meant, not far from the Sindh river. For لہاور the two editions of Badā,onī have لہایر; Dorn has بہاير Behair; Briggs has *Yehar*; the Lucknow edition of Firishta has يہار. There is a town and Pargana of the name of لہاور in Sirkār Rantanbhūr.

The passage in the Akbarnāma regarding Adham Khān quoted by Elliot may be found among the events of the third year.

Another nest of robbers was the eight villages, called Āthgah, near Sakīt, in the Sirkār of Qanawj.

entered. All rose to greet him, when Adham struck Atga with his dagger, and told one of his companions (*vide* p. 338) to kill him. He then went with the dagger in his hand towards the sleeping apartments of Akbar, who had been awakened by the noise in the state hall. Looking out from a window, he saw what had happened, rushed forward sword in hand, and met Adham on a high archway (*aywān*) near the harem. "Why have you killed my foster father, you son of a bitch?" (*bachcha-yi lāda*), cried Akbar. "Stop a moment, Majesty," replied Adham, seizing Akbar's arms, "first inquire." Akbar drew away his hands and struck Adham a blow in the face, which sent him "spinning" to the ground. "Why are you standing here gaping?" said Akbar to one of his attendants of the name of Farḥat Khān; "bind this man." This was done, and at Akbar's orders Adham Khān was twice thrown down from the dais (*ṣuffa*) of the *Aywān* to the ground, with his head foremost. The corpses of Adham and Atga were then sent to Dihlī.

Māhum Anga heard of the matter, and thinking that her son had been merely imprisoned, she repaired, though sick, from Dihlī to Āgra. On seeing her, Akbar said, "He has killed my foster father, and I have taken his life." "Your Majesty has done well," replied Māhum, turning pale, and left the hall. Forty days after, she died from grief, and was buried with her son in Dihlī in a tomb which Akbar had built for them. For Adham's brother, *vide* No. 60.

20. **Pīr Muḥammad Khān** of Shīrwān.[1]

Nothing is known of his father. Pīr Muḥammad was a Mullā, and attached himself to Bayrām in Qandahār. Through Bayrām's influence he was raised to the dignity of Amīr on Akbar's accession. He distinguished himself in the war with Hemū, and received subsequently the title of Nāṣir^{u} 'l-Mulk. His pride offended the Chaghatā'ī nobles, and, at last, Bayrām himself to whom he once refused admittance when he called on him at a time he was sick.

Bayrām subsequently ordered him to retire, sent him, at the instigation of Shaykh Gadā'ī (*vide* p. 282) to the Fort of Biyāna, and then forced him to go on a pilgrimage. Whilst on his way to Gujrāt, Pīr Muḥammad received letters from Adham Khān (No. 19) asking him to delay. He stayed for a short time at Rantanbhūr; but being pursued by Bayrām's men, he continued his journey to Gujrāt. This harsh treatment annoyed Akbar, and accelerated Bayrām's fall. Whilst in Gujrāt, P. M. heard of

---

[1] In my text edition, p. 223, No. 20, *dele* بسر. Shīrwān is also the birth-place of Khāqānī. The spelling *Sharwān* given in the Mu'jam does not appear to be usual.

Bayrām's disgrace, and returned at once to Akbar who made him a Khān. In 968, he was appointed with Adham Khān to conquer Mālwah, of which he was made sole governor after Adham's recall. In 969, he defeated Bāz Bahādur who had invaded the country, drove him away, and took Bījāgarh from Iʿtimād Khān, Bāz Bahādur's general. He then made a raid into Khandes, which was governed by Mīrān Muḥammad Shāh, sacked the capital Burhānpūr, slaughtered most unmercifully the inhabitants, and carried off immense booty, when he was attacked by Bāz Bahādur and defeated. Arriving at night on his flight at the bank of the Narbaddah, he insisted on crossing it, and perished in the river.

21. **Khān-i Aʿẓam Mīrzā ʿAzīz Koka,** son of Atga Khān (No. 15).

His mother was Jī Jī Anaga (*vide* p. 338). He grew up with Akbar, who remained attached to him to the end of his life. Though often offended by his boldness Akbar would but rarely punish him; he used to say, "Between me and ʿAzīz is a river of milk which I cannot cross."

On the removal of the *Atga Khāyl* (p. 338) from the Panjāb, he retained Dīpālpūr, where he was visited by Akbar in the 16th year (978) on his pilgrimage to the tomb of Shaykh Farīd-i Shakkarganj at Ajhodhan (Pāk Patan, or Patan-i Panjāb).

In the 17th year, after the conquest of Aḥmadābād, Mīrzā ʿAzīz was appointed governor of Gujrāt as far as the Mahindra river, whilst Akbar went to conquer Sūrat. Muḥammad Ḥusayn Mīrzā and Shāh Mīrzā, joined by Sher Khān Fūlādī, thereupon beseiged Patan; but they were at last defeated by Mīrzā ʿAzīz and Qulbu 'd-Dīn. ʿAzīz then returned to Aḥmadābād. When Akbar, on the 2nd Ṣafar 981, returned to Fatḥpūr Sīkrī, Ikhtiyāru 'l-Mulk, a Gujrātī noble, occupied Īdar, and then moved against ʿAzīz in Aḥmadābād. Muḥammad Ḥusayn Mīrzā also came from the Dakhin, and after attacking Kambhāyit (Cambay), they besieged Aḥmadābād. ʿAzīz held himself bravely. The siege was raised by Akbar, who surprised the rebels[1] near Patan. During the fight Muḥammad Ḥusayn Mīrzā and Ikhtiyāru 'l-Mulk were killed. The victory was chiefly gained by Akbar himself, who with 100 chosen men fell upon the enemy from an ambush. ʿAzīz had subsequently to fight with the sons of Ikhriyāru l-Mulk.

In the 20th year Akbar introduced the *Dāgh* (Āʾīn 7), which proved a source of great dissatisfaction among the Amīrs. Mīrzā ʿAzīz especially

---

[1] Akbar left Āgra on the 6th Rabīʿ I, and attacked the Mīrzās on the ninth day after his departure. The distance between Āgra and Patan being 400 *kos*, Akbar's forced march has often been admired. Briggs, II, p. 241. [This differs from the Akbar-nāma.—B.]

showed himself so disobedient that Akbar was compelled to deprive him temporarily of his rank.

Though restored to his honours in the 23rd year, M. ʿAzīz remained unemployed till the 25th year (988), when disturbances had broken out in Bengal and Bihār (*vide* Muẓaffar K͟hān, No. 37). ʿAzīz was promoted to a command of Five Thousand, got the title of Aʿẓam K͟hān, and was dispatched with a large army to quell the rebellion. His time was fully occupied in establishing order in Bihār. Towards the end of the 26th year, he rejoined the emperor, who had returned from Kābul to Fatḥpūr Sīkrī. During ʿAzīz's absence from Bihār, the Bengal rebels had occupied Ḥājīpūr, opposite Patna; and ʿAzīz, in the 27th year, was again sent to Bihār, with orders to move into Bengal. After collecting the Tuyūldārs of Ilāhābād, Audh, and Bihār, he occupied Gaṛhī, the "key" of Bengal. After several minor fights with the rebels under Maʿṣūm-i Kābulī, and Majnūn K͟hān Qāqshāl, ʿAzīz succeeded in gaining over the latter, which forced Maʿṣūm to withdraw. The imperial troops then commenced to operate against Qutlū, a Lohānī Afg͟hān, who during these disturbances had occupied Oṛīsā and a portion of Bengal. ʿAzīz, however, took this ill, and handing over the command to Shāhbāz K͟hān-i Kambū, returned to his lands in Bihār. Soon after, he joined Akbar at Ilāhābād, and was transferred to Gaṛha and Rāisīn. (993).

In the 31st year (994), M. ʿAzīz was appointed to the Dakhin; but as the operations were frustrated through the envy of Shahābᵘ 'd-Dīn Aḥmad (No. 26) and other grandees, ʿAzīz withdrew, plundered Ilichpūr in Barār, and then retreated to Gujrāt, where the K͟hān K͟hānān was (Briggs, II, 257).

In the 32nd year, Prince Murād married a daughter of M. ʿAzīz. Towards the end of the 34th year, ʿAzīz was appointed Governor of Gujrāt in succession to the K͟hān K͟hānān. In the 36th year, he moved against Sulṭān Muẓaffar, and defeated him in the following year. He then reduced Jām and other zamindārs of Kachh to obedience, and conquered Somnāt and sixteen other harbour towns (37th year). Jūnāgaṛh also, the capital of the ruler of Sorath, submitted to him (5th Ẕī Qaʿda 999), and Miyān K͟hān and Tāj K͟hān, sons of Dawlat K͟hān ibn-i Amīn K͟hān-i G͟horī, joined the Mug͟huls. ʿAzīz gave both of them jāgīrs. He had now leisure to hunt down Sulṭān Muẓaffar, who had taken refuge with a Zamīndār of Dwārkā. In a fight the latter lost his life, and Muẓaffar fled to Kachh, followed by ʿAzīz. There also the Zamīndārs submitted, and soon after delivered Sulṭān Muẓaffar into his hands. No sooner had he been brought to the Mīrzā than he asked for permission to step aside to perform a call of nature, and cut his throat with a razor.

In the 39th year Akbar recalled M. ʿAzīz, as he had not been at Court for several years; but the Mīrzā dreading the religious innovations at Court,[1] marched against Diu under the pretext of conquering it. He made, however, peace with the "Farangī" and embarked for Ḥijāz at Balāwal, a harbour town near Somnāt, accompanied by his six younger sons (Khurram, Anwar, ʿAbdᵘ 'llah, ʿAbdᵘ 'l-Laṭīf, Murtaẓā, ʿAbdᵘ 'l-Ghafūr), six daughters, and about one hundred attendants. Akbar felt sorry for his sudden departure, and with his usual magnanimity, promoted the two eldest sons of the Mīrzā (M. Shamsī and M. Shādmān).

M. ʿAzīz spent a great deal of money in Makkah; in fact he was so "fleeced", that his attachment to Islām was much cooled down; and being assured of Akbar's good wishes for his welfare, he embarked for India, landed again at Balāwal, and joined Akbar in the beginning of 1003. He now became a member of the "Divine Faith" (*vide* p. 217, l. 33), was appointed Governor of Bihār, was made *Vakīl* in 1004, and received Multān as Jāgīr.

In the 45th year (1008) he accompanied Akbar to Āsīr. His mother died about the same time, and Akbar himself assisted in carrying the coffin. Through the mediation of the Mīrzā, Bahādur Khan, ruler of Khandes, ceded Āsīr to Akbar towards the end of the same year. Soon after, Prince Khusraw married one of ʿĀzīz's daughters.

At Akbar's death, Mān Singh and M. ʿAzīz were anxious to proclaim Khusraw successor; but the attempt failed, as Shaykh Farīd-i Bukhārī and others had proclaimed Jahāngīr before Akbar had closed his eyes. Mān Singh left the Fort of Āgra with Khusraw, in order to go to Bengal. ʿAzīz wished to accompany him, sent his whole family to the Rāja, and superintended the burial of the deceased monarch. He countenanced Khusraw's rebellion, and escaped capital punishment through the intercession of several courtiers, and of Salīma Sulṭān Begum and other princesses of Akbar's harem. Not long after, Khwāja Abū 'l-Ḥasan laid before Jahāngīr a letter written some years ago by ʿAzīz to Rāja ʿAlī Khān of Khandes, in which ʿAzīz had ridiculed Akbar in very strong language. Jahāngīr gave ʿAzīz the letter and asked him to read it before

---

[1] M. ʿAzīz ridiculed Akbar's tendencies to Hinduism and the orders of the "Divine Faith". He used to call Fayẓī and Abū 'l-Faẓl, ʿUsmān and ʿ*Alī*. His disparaging remarks led to his disgrace on the accession of Jahāngīr, as related below.

the whole Court, which he did without the slightest hesitation, thus incurring the blame of all the courtiers present. Jahāngīr deprived him of his honours and lands, and imprisoned him.

In the 3rd year of Jahāngīr's reign (1017), M. ʿAzīz was restored to his rank, and appointed (nominally) to the command of Gujrāt, his eldest son, Jahāngīr Qulī Khān, being his *nāʾib*. In the 5th year, when matters did not go on well in the Dakhin, he was sent there with 10,000 men. In the 8th year (1022), Jahāngīr went to Ajmīr, and appointed, at the request of ʿAzīz, Shāhjahān to the command of the Dakhin forces, whilst he was to remain as adviser. But Shāhjahān did not like M. ʿAzīz on account of his partiality for Khusraw, and Mahābat Khān was dispatched from Court to accompany ʿAzīz from Udaipūr to Āgra. In the 9th year, ʿAzīz was again imprisoned, and put under the charge of Āṣaf Khān in the Fort of Gwāliyār (*Tuzuk*, p. 127). He was set free a year later, and soon after restored to his rank. In the 18th year, he was appointed *Atālīq* to Prince Dāwar Bakhsh, who had been made Governor of Gujrāt. M. ʿAzīz died in the 19th year (1033) at Aḥmadābād.

ʿAzīz was remarkable for ease of address, intelligence, and his knowledge of history. He also wrote poems. Historians quote the following aphorism from his "pithy" sayings. "A man should marry four wives—a Persian woman to have somebody to talk to; a Khurāsānī woman, for his housework; a Hindu woman, for nursing his children; and a woman from Māwarānnahr, to have some one to whip as a warning for the other three." *Vide* Ibqālnāma, p. 230.

Koka means "foster brother", and is the same as the Turkish *Kūkaldāsh* or *Kūkaltāsh.*

Mīrzā ʿAzīz's sons. 1. *Mīrzā Shamsī* (No. 163). He has been mentioned above. During the reign of Jahāngīr he rose to importance, and received the title of Jahāngīr Qulī Khān.

2. *Mīrzā Shādmān* (No. 233). He received the title of Shād Khān. *Tuzuk*, p. 99.

3. *Mīrzā Khurrum* (No. 177). He was made by Akbar governor of Jūnāgaṛh in Gujrāt, received the title of Kāmil Khān under Jahāngīr, and accompanied Prince Khurram (Shāhjahān) to the Dakhin.

4. *Mīrzā ʿAbdᵘ 'llah* (No. 257) received under Jahāngīr the title of Sardār Khān. He accompanied his father to Fort Gwāliyār.

5. *Mīrzā Anwar* (No. 206) was married to a daughter of Zayn Khān Koka (No. 34).

All of them were promoted to commanderships of Five and Two Thousands. ʿAzīz's other sons have been mentioned above.

A sister of M. ʿAzīz, Māh Bānū, was married to ʿAbd[u] 'r-Raḥīm Khān Khānān. (No. 29).

22. **Bahādur Khān-i Shaybānī,** (younger) brother of Khān Zamān. (No. 13).

His real name is Muḥammad Saʿīd. Humāyūn on his return from Persia put him in charge of the District of Dāwar. He then planned a rebellion and made preparations to take Qandahār, which was commanded by Shāh Muḥammad Khān of Qalāt (No. 95). The latter, however, fortified the town and applied to the king of Persia for help, as he could not expect Humāyūn to send him assistance. A party of Qizilbāshes attacked Bahādur, who escaped.

In the 2nd year, when Akbar besieged Mānkoṭ, Bahādur, at the request of Bayrām Khān, was pardoned, and received Multān as jāgīr. In the 3rd year, he assisted in the conquest of Mālwa. After Bayrām's fall, through the influence of Māhum Anga (*vide* p. 340), he was made *Vakīl*, and was soon after appointed to Iṭāwa (Sirkār of Āgra).

Subsequently he took an active part in the several rebellions of his elder brother (*vide* p. 336). After his capture, Shāhbāz Khān i-Kambū (No. 80) killed him at Akbar's order.

Like his brother he was a man of letters (Bad. III, 239).

23. **Rāja Bihārī Mal,** son of Prithirāj Kachhwāha.

In some historical MSS. he is called *Bihārā Mal*. There were two kinds of Kachhwāha, Rājāwat and Shaykhāwat, to the former of which Bihārī Mal belonged. Their ancient family seat was Amber in the Ṣūba of Ajmīr. Though not so extensive as Marwāṛ, the revenues of Amber were larger.

Bihārī Mal was the first Rājpūt that joined Akbar's Court. The flight [1] of Humāyūn from India had been the cause of several disturbances. Ḥājī Khān, a servant of Sher Khān, had attacked Nārnaul, the jāgīr of Majnūn Khān Qāqshāl (No. 50), who happened to be a friend of the Rāja's. Through his intercession both came to an amicable settlement; and Majnūn Khān, after the defeat of Hemū (963), brought Bihārī Mal's services to the notice of the emperor. The Rāja was invited to come to court, where he was presented before the end of the first year of Akbar's reign. At the interview Akbar was seated on a wild (*mast*)[2] elephant,

---

[1] The "flight" of Humāyūn from India was a delicate subject for Mughul historians. Abū 'l-Faẓl generally uses euphemisms, as *ān wāqiʿa-yi nāguzīr*, "that unavoidable event," or *riḥlat* (departure); or *āmadan-i Sher Khān*, the coming of Sher Khān (*not* Sher Shāh), etc.

[[2] *Mast*, in rut; furious.—P.]

and as the animal got restive and ran about, the people made way; only Bihārī Mal's Rājpūt attendants, to the surprise of Akbar, stood firm.

In the 6th year of his reign (969), Akbar made a pilgrimage to the tomb of Muʿīn-i Chishtī at Ajmīr, and at Kalālī, Chaghtā Khān reported to the Emperor, that the Rāja had fortified himself in the passes, as Sharafu 'd-Dīn Ḥusayn (No. 17), Governor of Mālwa, had made war upon him, chiefly at the instigation of Sojā, son of Pūran Mal, elder brother of the Rāja. Sharafu 'd-Dīn had also got hold of Jagnāth (No. 69), son of the Rāja, Rāj Singh (No. 174), son of Askaran, and Kangār, son of Jagmal (No. 134), his chief object being to get possession of Amber itself. At Deosa, 40 miles east of Jaipūr, Jaima, son of Rūpsī (No. 118), Bihārī Mal's brother, who was the chief of the country, joined Akbar, and brought afterwards, at the request of the emperor, his father Rūpsī. At Sangānīr, at last, Bihārī Mal with his whole family, attended, and was most honorably received. His request to enter Akbar's service and to strengthen the ties of friendship by a matrimonial alliance, was granted. On his return from Ajmīr, Akbar received the Rāja's daughter at Sambhar, and was joined, at Ratan, by the Rāja himself, and his son Bhagawant Dās, and his grandson Kūwar Mān Singh. They accompanied Akbar to Āgra, where Bihārī Mal was made a Commander of Five Thousand. Soon after Bihārī Mal returned to Amber. He died at Āgra (Ṭabaqāt).

Amber is said to have been founded A.D. 967 by Dholā Rāy, son of Sorā, of whom Bihārī Mal was the 18th descendant.[1]

The Akbernāma mentions the names of four brothers of Bihārī Mal. 1. Pūran Mal; 2. Rūpsī (No. 118); 3. Askaran (*vide* No. 174); 4. Jagmal (No. 134). Bihārī Mal is said to have been younger than Pūran Mal, but older than the other three.

Three sons of Bihārī Mal were in Akbar's service—1. Bhagwān Dās (No. 27); 2. Jagannāth (No. 69); and 3. Salhadī (No. 267).

24. **Khān Jahān Ḥusayn Qulī Khān,**[2] son of Walī Beg Ẕū 'l-Qadr.

He is the son of Bayrām Khān's sister. His father Walī Beg Ẕū 'l-Qadr was much attached to Bayrām, and was captured in the fight in the Pargana of دکدار (Jālindhar, *vide* p. 332, l. 5), but died immediately afterwards from the wounds received in battle. Akbar looked upon him as the chief instigator of Bayrām's rebellion, and ordered his head to

---

[1] The present Mahārāja of Jaipūr is the 34th descendant; *vide* Selections Government of India, No, LXV, 1868. Amber was deserted in 1728, when Jai Singh II founded the modern Jaipūr.

[2] Ḥusayn Qulī Beg. *Maʾāṣir.*

be cut off, which was sent all over Hindūstān. When it was brought to Iṭāwa, Bahādur Khān (No. 22) killed the foot soldiers (*tawāchīs*) that carried it. Khān Jahān had brought Bayrām's *insignia* from Mewāt to Akbar, and as he was a near relation of the rebel, he was detained and left under charge of Āṣaf Khān ʿAbdu 'l-Majīd, Commander of Dihlī. When Bayrām had been pardoned, Khān Jahān was released. He attached himself henceforth to Akbar.

In the 8th year (end of 971) he was made a Khān and received orders to follow up Sharafu 'd-Dīn Ḥusayn (No. 17). Ajmīr and Nāgor were given him as *tuyūl*. He took the Fort of Jodhpūr from Chandar Sen, son of Rāy Māldeo, and distinguished himself in the pursuit of Udai Singh during the siege of Chītor.

In the 13th year (976) he was transferred to the Panjāb, whither he went after assisting in the conquest of Rantanbhūr.

In the 17th year he was ordered to take Nagarkoṭ, which had belonged to Rāja Jai Chand. Badā,onī says (II, p. 161) that the war was merely undertaken to provide Bīr Baṛ with a jāgīr. Akbar had Jai Chand imprisoned, and Budī[1] Chand, his son, thinking that his father was dead, rebelled. Khān Jahān, on his way, conquered Fort Kotla, reached Nagarkoṭ in the beginning of Rajab 980, and took the famous Bhawan temple outside of the Fort. The siege was progressing and the town reduced to extremities, when it was reported that Ibrāhīm Ḥusayn Mīrzā and Masʿūd Mīrzā had invaded the Panjāb. Khān Jahān therefore accepted a payment of five *mans* of gold and some valuables, and raised the siege. He is also said to have erected a *Masjid* in front of Jai Chand's palace in the Fort, and to have read the *Khuṭba* in Akbar's name (Friday, middle of Shawwāl 980).

Accompanied by Ismāʿīl Qulī Khān and Mīrzā Yūsuf Khān-i Riẓawī (No. 35), Khān Jahān marched against the Mīrzās, surprised them in the Pargana of Talamba, 40 *kos* from Multān, and defeated them. Ibrāhīm Ḥusayn Mīrzā escaped to Multān, but Masʿūd Ḥusayn and several other Mīrzās of note were taken prisoners.

In the 18th year (981) when Akbar returned to Āgra after the conquest of Gujrāt, he invited his Amīrs to meet him, and Khān Jahān also came with his prisoners, whom he had put into cow skins with horns on, with their eyelids sewn together. Akbar had their eyes immediately opened, and even pardoned some of the prisoners. The victorious

---

[1 General Cunningham tells me that the correct name is Bidhi (Sansk. Vriddhi), not Budī, *vide* Index.—B.]

general received the title of Khān Jahān, "a title in reputation next to that of Khān Khānān." About the same time Sulaymān, ruler of Badakhshān (p. 326) had come to India, driven away by his grandson Shāhrukh (No. 7), and Khān Jahān was ordered to assist him in recovering his kingdom. But as in 983 Munʿim Khān Khānān died, and Bengal was unsettled, Khān Jahān was recalled from the Panjāb, before he had moved into Badakhshān, and was appointed to Bengal, Rāja Ṭoḍar Mal being second in command. At Bhāgalpūr, Khān Jahān was met by the Amīrs of Bengal, and as most of them were Chaghtāʾī nobles, he had, as Qizilbāsh, to contend with the same difficulties as Bayrām Khān had had. He repulsed the Afghāns who had come up as far as Gaṛhī and Ṭānḍa; but he met with more decided opposition at Āg Maḥal, where Dāʾūd Khān had fortified himself. The Imperialists suffered much from the constant sallies of the Afghāns. Khān Jahān complained of the wilful neglect of his Amīrs, and when Akbar heard of the death of Khwāja ʿAbdu 'llah Naqshbandī, who had been purposely left unsupported in a skirmish, he ordered Muẓaffar Khān, Governor of Bihār (No. 37) to collect his Jāgīrdārs and join Khān Jahān (984). The fights near Āg Maḥal were now resumed with new vigour. During a skirmish a cannon ball wounded Junayd-i Kararānī, Dāʾūd's uncle,[1] which led to a general battle (15th Rabīʿ II, 984). The right wing of the Afghāns, commanded by Kālā Pahāṛ, gave way when the soldiers saw their leader wounded, and the centre under Dāʾūd was defeated by Khān Jahān. Dāʾūd himself was captured and brought to Khān Jahān, who sent his head to Akbar.

After this great victory, Khān Jahān dispatched Ṭoḍar Mal to Court, and moved to Sātgāw̃ (Hūglī) where Dāʾūd's family lived. Here he defeated the remnant of Dāʾūd's adherents under Jamshed and Mittī, and reannexed Sātgāw̃, which since the days of old had been called *Bulghākkhāna*,[2] to the Mughul empire. Dāʾūd's mother came to Khān Jahān as a suppliant.

Soon after Malkū Sā,ī,[3] Rāja of Kūch Bihār sent tribute and 54 elephants, which Khān Jahān dispatched to Court.

With the defeat and death of Dāʾūd, Bengal was by no means conquered. New troubles broke out in Bhāṭī,[4] where the Afghāns had

---

[1] The Ed: Bibl. Indica of *Badā,onī* (II, 238) has by mistake 'uncle'. Badā,onī says that the battle took place near Colgong (Khalgāw̃).

[2] This nickname of Sātgāw̃ is evidently old. Even the word *bulghāk* (rebellion), which may be found on almost every page of the *Tārīkh-i Fīrūz Shāhī*, is scarcely ever met with in historical works from the 10th century. It is now quite obsolete.

[[3] Bāl Gosā,ī.—B.]

[4] For *Bhāṭī*, *vide* below under No. 32.

collected under Karīm Dād, Ibrāhīm, and the rich Zamīndār ʿĪsā (عیسیٰ). With great difficulties Khān Jahān occupied that district, assisted by a party of Afghāns who had joined him together with Dāʾūd's mother at Go,ās; and returned to Ṣihhatpūr, a town which he had founded near Ṭanḍa. Soon after, he felt ill, and died after a sickness of six weeks in the same year (19th Shawwāl, 986).

Abū 'l-Fazl remarks that his death was opportune, inasmuch as the immense plunder collected by Khān Jahān in Bengal, had led him to the verge of rebellion.

Khān Jāhān's son, Rizā Qulī (No. 274) is mentioned below among the Commanders of Three Hundred and Fifty. In the 47th year he was made a Commander of Five Hundred with a contingent of 300 troopers. Another son, Raḥīm Qulī, was a Commander of Two Hundred and Fifty (No. 333). For Khān Jahān's brother, *vide* No. 46.

25. **Saʿīd Khan**, son of Yaʿqūb Beg, son of Ibrāhīm Jābūq.

He is also called Saʿīd Khān-i Chaghtāʾī. His family had long been serving under the Tīmūrides. His grandfather Ibrāhīm Beg was an Amīr of Humāyūn's, and distinguished himself in the Bengal wars. His son, Yūsuf Beg, was attacked near Jaunpūr by Jalāl Khān (i.e., Salīm Shāh), and killed. His other son also, Yaʿqūb, Saʿīd's father, distinguished himself under Humāyūn. According to the *Ṭabaqāt*, he was the son of the brother of Jahāngīr Qulī Beg, governor of Bengal under Humāyūn.

Saʿīd rose to the highest honours under Akbar. He was for some time Governor of Multān, and was appointed, in the 22nd year, *atālīq* of Prince Dānyāl. Some time after, he was made Ṣūbahdār of the Panjāb, in supercession to Shāh Qulī Muḥrim (No. 45), of whom the inhabitants of the Panjāb had successfully complained. Saʿīd again was succeeded in the governorship by Rāja Bhagwān Dās (No. 27), and received Sambhal as *tuyūl*. In the 28th year, he was called to Court, was made a Commander of Three Thousand, and was sent to Ḥājīpūr (Patna) as successor to Mīrzā ʿAzīz Koka (No. 21). In the 32nd year, when Vazīr Khān (No. 41) had died in Bengal, Saʿīd was made Governor of Bengal, which office he held till the 40th year. He was also promoted to the rank of *Panjhazārī*. In the 40th year, Mān Singh (No. 30) being appointed to Bengal, he returned to Court, and was, in the following year, again made Governor of Bihār. In the 48th year (1001), when Mīrzā Ghāzī rebelled in Thatha after the death of his father, Mīrzā Jānī Beg (No. 47), Saʿīd was appointed to Multān and Bhakkar, and brought about the submission of the rebel.

After the accession of Jahāngīr, he was offered the Governorship of the Panjāb on the condition that he should prevent his eunuchs from committing oppressions, which he promised to do. (*Tuzuk*, p. 6, l. 2.) He died, however, before joining his post, and was buried " in the garden of Sarhind ".

His affairs during his lifetime were transacted by a Hindū of the name of Chetr Bhoj. Saʿīd had a passion for eunuchs, of whom he had 1,200.[1] One of these Khwājasarās, Hilāl, joined afterwards Jahāngīr's service; he built Hilālābād, six *kos* N.W. from Āgra, near Rankaṭṭa,[2] regarding which the *Maʾāṣir* tells an amusing incident. Another eunuch, Ikhtiyār Khān, was his Vakīl, and another, Iʿtibār Khān, the Fawjdār of his jāgīr. For Saʿīd's brother, *vide* No. 70.

26. **Shihāb Khān**, a Sayyid of Nīshāpūr.

His full name is Shihābu 'd-Dīn Aḥmad Khān. He was a relation and friend of Māhum Anga (p. 341), and was instrumental in bringing about Bayrām's fall. From the beginning of Akbar's reign, he was Commander of Dihlī. When Akbar, at the request of Māhum, turned from Sikandarābād to Dihlī to see his sick mother, Shihāb Khān told him that his journey, undertaken as it was without the knowledge of Bayrām Khān, might prove disastrous to such grandees as were not Bayrām's friends; and the Chaghtāʾī nobles took this opportunity of reiterating their complaints, which led to Bayrām's disgrace.

As remarked on p. 337, Shihāb served in Mālwah against ʿAbdu 'llah-Khan.

In the 12th year (975) he was appointed Governor of Mālwah, and was ordered to drive the Mīrzās from that province. In the 13th year, he was put in charge of the Imperial domain lands, as Muẓaffar Khān (No. 37) had too much to do with financial matters.

In the 21st year, he was promoted to a command of Five Thousand, and was again appointed to Mālwah; but he was transferred, in the following year, to Gujrāt, as Vazīr Khān (No. 41) had given no satisfaction. He was, in the 28th year, succeeded by Iʿtimād Khān (No. 119), and intended to go to Court; but no sooner had he left Aḥmadābād than he was deserted by his servants, who in a body joined Sulṭān Muẓaffar. The events of the Gujrāt rebellion are known from the histories. When Mīrzā Khān Khānān (No. 29) arrived, Shihāb was attached to Qulij

[1] If not acquired in Bengal, this predilection could not have been better satisfied elsewhere. The eunuchs of Bengal and Silhaṭ were renowned; for interesting passages *vide* below, Third Book, Ṣūba of Bengal, and *Tuzuk-i Jahāngīrī*, pp. 72, 328.

[2] Sikandra (or Bihishtābād), where Akbar's tomb is, lies halfway between Āgra and Rankaṭṭā.

Khān (Mālwah Corps). He distinguished himself in the conquest of Bahrōch (992), and received that district as *tuyūl*. In the 34th year (997), he was again made Governor of Mālwa, in succession to M. ʿAzīz Koka (No. 21).

Shihāb died in Mālwah (Ujain, *Ṭabaqāt*) in 999. His wife, Bābā Āghā, was related to Akbar's mother ; she died in 1005.

During the time Shihāb was Governor of Dihlī, he repaired the canal which Fīrūz Shāh had cut from the Parganah of Khizrābād to Safīdūn ; and called it *Nahr-i Shihāb*. This canal was again repaired, at the order of Shāhjahān, by the renowned Makramat Khān, and called فيض نهر, *Fayẓ Nahr*, (20th year of Shāhjahān). During the reign of Awrangzeb it was again obstructed, but has now again been repaired and enlarged by the English. (*Āṣār^u 's-ṣanādīd.*)

27. **Rāja Bhagwān Dās**, son of Rāja Bihārī Mal.

In the histories we find the spellings *Bhagwant, Bhagwānt, and Bhagwān*. He joined Akbar's service with his father (No. 23). In 980, in the fight with Ibrāhīm Ḥusayn Mīrzā near Sarnāl (*Briggs*, Sartāl), he saved Akbar's life. He also distinguished himself against the Rānā of Īdar, whose son, Amr Singh, he brought to Court. When, in the 23rd year, the Kachwāhas had their tuyūls transferred to the Panjāb, Rāja Bh. D. was appointed Governor of the province. In the 29th year, Bh.'s daughter was married to Prince Salīm, of which marriage Prince Khusraw was the offspring. In the 30th year, Bh. D. was made a commander of Five Thousand and Governor of Zābulistān, as Mān Singh was sent against the Yūsufza,īs. But Akbar, for some reason, detained him. In Khayrābād, Bh. D. had a fit of madness, and wounded himself with a dagger ; but he recovered soon after in the hands of the Court Doctors. In the 32nd year, the jāgīrs of the Rāja and his family were transferred to Bihār, Mān Singh taking the command of the province.

Rāja Bh. D. died in the beginning of 998 at Lāhor, a short time after Rāja Ṭoḍar Mal (No. 39). People say that on returning from Ṭoḍar Mal's funeral, he had an attack of stranguary, of which he died. He had the title of *Amīr^u 'l-ʿUmarā*.

The Jāmi ʿMasjid of Lāhor was built by him.

Regarding his sons, *vide* Nos. 30, 104, 336.

28. **Quṭb^u 'd-Dīn Khān**, youngest brother of Atga Khān (15).

As he belonged to the *Atga Khayl* (*vide* p. 338), his *tuyūl* was in the Panjāb. He founded several mosques, etc., at Lāhor.

In the 9th year (972), Akbar sent him to Kābul. During his stay there, he built a villa at Ghaznīn, his birth-place. On the transfer of the

" Atga Khayl " from the Panjāb, Q. was appointed to Mālwa. After the conquest of Gujrāt, he received as jāgīr the Sirkār of Bahrōch (Broach), " which lies south of Aḥmadābād, and has a fort on the bank of the Narbuddā near its mouth." Subsequently he returned to Court, and was made a Commander of Five Thousand.

In the 24th year (12th Rajab, 987), he was appointed *atālīq* to Prince Salīm, received a *dāgū*,[1] and the title of *Beglar Begī*. Akbar also honoured him by placing at a feast Prince Salīm on his shoulders. Afterwards Q. was again appointed to Bahrōch " as far as Nazrbār ". In the 28th year (991), Muẓaffar of Gujrāt tried to make himself independent. Q. did not act in concert with other officers, and in consequence of his delay and timidity he was attacked and defeated by Muẓaffar near Baroda. Q.'s servants even joined Muẓaffar, whilst he himself retreated to the Fort of Baroda. After a short time he capitulated and surrendered to Muẓaffar, who had promised not to harm him or his family. But at the advice of a Zamīndār, Muẓaffar went to Bahrōch, occupied the fort in which Q.'s family lived, and confiscated his immense property (10 *krors* of rupees), as also 14 lacs of imperial money. Immediately after, Muẓaffar had Q. murdered.

His son, Nawrang Khān, served under Mīrzā Khān Khānan (No. 29) in Gujrāt (992), received a jāgīr in Mālwa and subsequently in Gujrāt. He died in 999.

The MSS. of the *Ṭabaqāt*, which I consulted, contain the remark that Nawrang Khān was a Commander of Four Thousand, and was, in 1001, governor of Jūnāgaṛh.

His second son, Gūjar Khān, was a *Haftṣadī* (No. 193), and served chiefly under M. Aʿzam Khān Koka (No. 21). He also had a *tuyūl* in Gujrāt.

29. **Khān Khānān Mīrzā ʿAbdᵘ 'r-Raḥīm**, son of Bayrām Khān.

His mother was a daughter of Jamāl Khān of Mewāt.[2] In 961, when Humāyūn returned to India, he enjoined his nobles to enter into matrimonial alliances with the Zamīndārs of the country, and after marrying the eldest daughter of Jamāl Khān, he asked Bayrām Khān to marry the younger one.

M. ʿAbdᵘ 'r-Raḥīm was born at Lāhor, 14th Ṣafar 964. When Bayrām Khān was murdered at Patan in Gujrāt (p. 332), his camp was plundered

---

[1] A kind of warm mantle—a great distinction under the Tīmūrides.

[2] He was the nephew of Ḥasan Khān of Mewāt (*Bad.* I, p. 361). In the fourth Book of the Āʾīn, ʿAbū'l-Faẓl says that the Khānzādas of Mewāt were chiefly converted Janūha Rājpūts.

by some Afghāns; but Muḥammad Amīn Dīwāna and Bābā Zambūr managed to remove the child and his mother from the scene of plunder and bring them to Aḥmadābād, fighting on the road with the Afghān robbers. From Aḥmadābād, M. ʿAbdᵘ 'r-Raḥīm was taken to Akbar (969), who, notwithstanding the insinuations of malicious courtiers, took charge of him. He gave him the title of *Mīrzā Khān*, and married him subsequently to Mah Bānū, sister of M. ʿAzīz Koka (No. 21).

In 981, M. ʿAbdᵘ 'r-Raḥīm accompanied Akbar on his forced march to Patan (p. 343). In 984 M. ʿA. was appointed to Gujrāt, Vazīr Khān having the management of the province. In the 25th year, he was made *Mīr ʿArẓ*, and three years later, *atālīq* to Prince Salīm. Soon after, he was sent against Sulṭān Muẓaffar of Gujrāt. Muẓaffar, during the first Gujrātī war, had fallen into the hands of Akbar's officers. He was committed to the charge of Munʿim Khān (No. 11), and after his death, to the care of Shāh Manṣūr the Dīwān (No. 122). But Muẓaffar managed, in the 23rd year, to escape, and took refuge with the Kāthīs of Jūnāgaṛh, little noticed or cared for by Akbar's officers. But when Iʿtimād Khān was sent to Gujrāt to relieve Shihābᵘ d-Dīn (No. 26), the servants of the latter joined Muẓaffar, and the Gujrāt rebellion commenced. Muẓaffar took Aḥmadābād, and recruited, with the treasures that fell into his hands (*vide* Quṭbᵘ 'd-Dīn, No. 28), an army of 40,000 troopers. Mīrzā ʿAbdᵘ 'r-Raḥīm had only 10,000 troopers to oppose him, and though his officers advised him to wait for the arrival of Qulij Khān and the Mālwa contingent, Dawlat Khān Lodī (No. 309), M. ʿA.'s *Mīr Shamsher*, reminded him not to spoil his laurels and claims to the Khān Khānānship. M. ʿA. then attacked Muẓaffar, and defeated him in the remarkable battle of Sarkich, three *kos* from Aḥmadābād. On the arrival of the Mālwa contingent, M. ʿA. defeated Muẓaffar a second time near Nādot. Muẓaffar concealed himself in Rajpīpla.

For these two victories Akbar made M. ʿA. a Commander of Five Thousand, and gave him the coveted title of Khān Khānān. For this reason historians generally call him Mīrzā Khān Khānan.

When Gujrāt was finally conquered, M. Khān Khānān gave his whole property to his soldiers, even his inkstand, which was given to a soldier who came last and said he had not received anything. The internal affairs of Gujrāt being settled, Qulij Khān was left in the province, and M. ʿA. rejoined the Court.

In the 34th year he presented to Akbar a copy of his Persian translation of Bābar's Chaghtā,ī Memoirs (*Wāqiʿāt-i Bābarī*).[1]

---

[1] *Vide* p. 105, last line.

Towards the end of the same year, he was appointed *Vakīl* and received Jaunpūr as *tuyūl*; but in 999 his jāgīr was transferred to Multān, and he received orders to take Thatha (Sind). Passing by the Fort of Sahwān,[1] he took the Fort of Lakhī, "which was considered the key of the country, just as Gaḍhī is in Bengal and Bārahmūla in Kashmīr." After a great deal of fighting Mīrzā Jānī Beg (No. 47), ruler of Thatha, made peace, which M. ʿA., being hard pressed for provisions, willingly accepted. Sahwān was to be handed over to Akbar, M. Jānī Beg was to visit the emperor after the rains, and Mīrzā Īrich, M. ʿA.'s eldest son, was to marry Jānī Beg's daughter. But as M. Jānī Beg, after the rains, delayed to carry out the stipulations, M. ʿA. moved to Thatha and prepared himself to take it by assault, when M. Jānī Beg submitted and accompanied M. ʿA. to Court.[2] Thus Sindh was annexed.

When Sulṭān Murād assembled at Bahrōch (Broach) his troops for the conquest of the Dakhin, Akbar dispatched M. ʿA. to his assistance, giving him Bhīlsā as jāgīr. After delaying there for some time, M. ʿA. went to Ujain, which annoyed the Prince, though M. ʿA. wrote him that Rāja ʿAlī Khān,[3] of Khāndes was on the point of joining the Imperialists, and that he would come with him. When M. ʿA. at last joined headquarters at Fort Chāndor, 30 *kos* from Aḥmadnagar, he was slighted by the Prince; and, in consequence of it, he hesitated to take an active part in the operations, leaving the command of his detachment chiefly in the hands of M. Shāhrukh (No. 7). Only on one occasion after Murād's departure from Aḥmadnagar, he took a prominent part in the war. Muʿtamidᵘ 'd-Dawla Suhayl Khān (Briggs II, 274; III, 308) threatened Prince Murād, who had been persuaded by his officers not to engage with him. M. ʿA., Rāja ʿAlī Khān, and M. Shāhrukh, therefore, took it upon themselves to fight the enemy. Moving in Jumāda II, 1005, from Shāhpūr, M. ʿA. met Suhayl near the town of Ashtī, 12 *kos* from Pathrī. The fight was unusually severe. Rāja ʿAlī Khān with five or six of his principal officers and five hundred troopers were killed (Briggs IV, 324). The night put an end to the engagement; but each party, believing itself victorious, remained under arms. When next morning, M. ʿA.'s troopers went to the river [near Sūpā, *Firishta*] to get water, they were attacked by 25,000 of the enemy's horse. Dawlat Khān, who commanded

---

[1] Also called Siwastān, on the right bank of the Indus. Lakhī (Lukkee) lies a little south of Sahwān.

[2] The conquest of Sindh forms the subject of a Maṣnawī by Mullā Shikebī, whom Abū'l-Faẓl mentions below among the poets of Akbar's age.

[3] Khāfī Khān calls him *Rājī* ʿAlī Khān.

M. ʿA.'s avantguard, said to him, "It is dying a useless death to fall fighting with but 600 troopers against such odds." "Do you forget Dihlī ?", asked M. ʿA. "If we keep up," replied Dáwlat Khān, "against such odds, we have discovered a hundred Dihlīs ; and if we die, matters rest with God." Qāsim of Bārha [1] and several other Sayyids were near ; and on hearing M. ʿA.'s resolution to fight, he said, " Well, let us fight as Hindūstānīs, nothing is left but death ; but ask the Khān Khānān what he means to do." Dawlat Khān returned, and said to M. ʿA. " Their numbers are immense, and victory rests with heaven ; point out a place where we can find you, should we be defeated." " Under the corpses," said M. ʿA. Thereupon they charged the flank of the enemy and routed them. After this signal victory, M. ʿA. distributed 75 lacs of rupees among his soldiers. At the request of the Prince, M. ʿA. was soon after recalled (1006).

In the same year Mah Bānū, M. ʿA.'s wife, died.

In the 44th year Prince Dānyāl was appointed to the Dakhin, and M. ʿA. was ordered to join the Prince, and besiege Aḥmadnagar. The town, as is known from the histories, was taken after a siege of 4 months and 4 days.[2] M. ʿA. then joined the Court, bringing with him Bahādur ibn-i Ibrāhīm, who had been set up as Niẓām Shāh. Dānyāl was appointed governor of the newly conquered territory, which was called by Akbar *Dāndes*,[3] and married to Jānā Begum, M. ʿA.'s daughter. The Khān Khānān was also ordered to repair to Aḥmadnagar, to keep down a party that had made the son of Shāh ʿAlī, uncle of Murtaẓā, Niẓām Shāh.

After the death of Akbar, matters in the Dakhin did not improve. In the 3rd year of Jahāngīr (1017), M. ʿA. promised to bring the war to a close in two years if he received a sufficient number of troops. Shāhzāda Parwīz, under the *Atālīq*-ship of Āṣaf Khān, Mān Singh, Khān Jahān Lodī, and others, were appointed to assist M. ʿA. He took the Prince in the rains from Burhānpūr to Bālāghāt ; but in consequence of the usual duplicity and rancour displayed by the Amīrs, the imperial army suffered from want of provisions and loss of cattle, and M. ʿA. was compelled to conclude a treaty dishonourable for Jahāngīr, who appointed

---

[1] The Sayyids of Bārha considered it their privilege to fight in the *Harāwal* or van. *Vide No.* 75.

[2] Abū'l-Faẓl and the Lucknow edition of Firishta call the eunuch who murdered Chānd Bībī جیته خان or جیته. Briggs has Hamid Khān. For *Nihang Khān*, which Briggs gives, all copies of the Akbarnāma and the Maʿāṣir have *Abhang Khān*. The Lucknow Ed. of Firishta has *Ahang Khān*. The differences, moreover, between Abū 'l-Faẓl and Firishta in details are very remarkable.

[3] A combination of the words *Dānyāl* and *Khāndes*.

K͟hān Jahān Lodī as his successor, and sent Mahābat K͟hān, subsequently M. ʿA.'s enemy, to bring the unsuccessful commander to Court.

In the 5th year, M. ʿA. received Kālpī and Qanawj as *tuyūl*, with orders to crush the rebels in those districts (*vide* p. 341, note). Some time afterwards, M. ʿA. was again sent to the Dakhin, as matters there had not improved ; but he did not gain any advantage either.

In the 11th year (1025) Jahāngīr, at last, dispatched Prince K͟hurram, to whom he had given the title of Shāh.[1] Jahāngīr himself fixed his residence at Māndū in Mālwa, in order to be nearer the scene of war, while Shāh K͟hurram selected Burhānpūr as Head Quarters. Here the Prince also married the daughter of Shāhnawāz K͟hān, M. ʿA.'s son. ʿĀdil Shāh and Quṭb^{u} 'l-Mulk sent tribute and submitted, and Jahāngīr bestowed upon ʿĀdil Shāh the title of *Farzand* (son) ; and ʿAmbar Malik handed over the keys of Aḥmadnagar and other Forts, together with the Parganas of Bālāghāt, which he had conquered. Shāh K͟hurram then appointed M. ʿA. Ṣūbahdār of K͟hāndes, Barār, and Aḥmadnagar, whilst Shāhnawāz K͟hān was appointed to Bālāghāt. Leaving 30,000 horse and 7,000 artillery in the Dakhin, Shāh K͟hurram joined his father at Māndū, where new honours awaited him.[2]

In the 15th year, Malik ʿAmbar "broke" the treaty, and fell upon the Thānadārs of the Mug͟huls. Dārāb K͟hān, M. ʿA.'s second son, retreated from Bālāg͟hāt to Bālāpūr ; and driven from there, he went to Burhānpūr, where he and his father were besieged. On Shāhjahān's approach, the besiegers dispersed.

In the 17th year (1031) Shāh ʿAbbās of Persia attacked Qandahār, and Shāhjahān and ʿAbd^{u} 'r-Raḥīm were called to Court to take command against the Persians ; but before they joined, Prince Parwīz, through Nūr Jahān's influence, had been appointed heir-apparent, and Mahābat K͟hān had been raised to the dignity of *K͟hān K͟hānān*. Shāhjahān rebelled, returned with M. ʿA. to Māndū, and then moved to Burhānpūr. On the march thither, Shāhjahān intercepted a letter which M. ʿA. had secretly

---

[1] "Since the time of Tīmūr no Prince had received this title." *Maʿāṣir*. *Shāh K͟hurram* received subsequently the title of *Shāhjahān*, which he retained as king, in conjunction with the titles of *Ṣāḥib Qirān-i Ṣānī* and *Aʿlā Ḥaẓrat* (اعلیٰ حضرت). The last title had also been used by Sulaymān-i Kararāni, King of Bengal. Awrangzeb, in imitation of it, adopted the title of *Aʿlā K͟hāqān*.

[2] He received the title of *Shāhjahān* and was made a *Sīhāzārī*, or Commander of Thirty Thousand, personal (brevet) rank, and a contingent of 20,000 (*az aṣl wa iẓāfa*, i.e., his former contingent *plus* an increase in troops). He was also allowed a *Ṣandalī* (*vide* p. 318), likewise a custom that had not been observed since the age of Tīmūr. Jahāngīr even came down from the *Jharoka* (the window in the State hall, familiar to all that have seen the halls of the palaces of Agra and Fatḥpūr Sīkrī), and placed a dish full of jewels and gold on Shāhjahān's head, distributing the whole (as *niṣār*) among the Amīrs.

written to Mahābat Khān, whereupon he imprisoned him and his son Dārāb Khān, and sent him to Fort Āsīr, but released them soon after on *parole*. Parwīz and Mahābat Khān had, in the meantime, arrived at the Narbadda to capture Shāhjahān. Bayrām Beg, an officer of Shāhjahān's, had for this reason removed all boats to the left side of the river, and successfully prevented the imperials from crossing. At M. ʿA.'s advice, Shāhjahān proposed, at this time, an armistice. He made M. ʿA. swear upon the Qurʾān not to betray him, and sent him as ambassador to Parwīz. Mahābat Khān, knowing that the fords would not now be so carefully watched as before, effected a crossing, and M. ʿA., forgetful of his oath, joined Prince Parwīz, and did not return to Shāhjahān, who now fled from Burhānpūr, marching through Talingāna to Orīsa and Bengal. Mahābat and M. ʿA. followed him up a short distance beyond the Taptī. M. ʿA. wrote to Rāja Bhīm, a principal courtier of the Dawlatshāhī party, to tell Shāhjahān, that he (M. ʿA.) would do everything in his power to detain the imperial army, if the prince would allow his sons to join him. Rāja Bhīm replied that the prince had still from five to six thousand followers, and that he would kill M. ʿA.'s sons should it come to a fight. Shāhjahān then moved into Bengal and Bihār, of which he made Dārāb Khān, who had evidently attached himself to the prince, Governor. Mahābat Khān had in the meantime returned to Ilāhābād to oppose Shāhjahān, and had placed M. ʿA., who looked upon him with distrust, under surveillance.

In the 21st year, Jahāngīr ordered Mahābat Khān to send M. ʿA. to court, where he was reinstated in his titles and honours. He afterwards retired to his jāgīr at Lāhor, when Mahābat Khān followed him and sent him back to Dihlī. Soon after the failure of his scheme of retaining possession of Jahāngīr's person, and the return of the monarch from Kābul, Mahābat Khān had to fly. Nūr Jahān now appointed M. ʿA. to follow up Mahābat, and contributed herself twelve lacs of rupees to the expedition. But before the necessary preparations had been completed, M. ʿA. fell ill at Lāhor, and on his arrival at Dihlī, he died at the age of seventy-two, in the end of Jahāngīr's 21st year (1036). The words *Khān Sipahsālār kū* (where is the Khān Commander?) are the *tārīkh* of his death.

M. ʿA.'s great deeds are the conquests of Gujrāt and Sind and the defeat of Suhayl Khān of Bījāpūr. During Jahāngīr's reign, he did nothing remarkable; nor was he treated with the respect which he had enjoyed during the lifetime of Akbar, though he was allowed to retain his rank. For nearly thirty years he had been serving in the Dakhin.

Every grandee, and even the princes, accused him of secret friendship with the rulers of the Dakhin, and ʿAbd 'l-Faẓl, on one occasion, gave his *fatwa* that M. ʿA. was a rebel. Under Jahāngīr, he was the open friend of Malik ʿAmbar; and Muḥammad Maʿṣūm, one of his servants, once informed the emperor that he would find Malik ʿAmbar's correspondence in the possession of ʿAbdᵘ 'r-Raḥīm of Lakhnau (No. 197), who was much attached to M. ʿA. Mahābat Khān was appointed to inquire into this; but ʿAbdᵘ 'r-Raḥīm of Lakhnau would not betray his friend. People said, M. ʿA.'s *motto* was, "people should hurt their enemies under the mask of friendship," and all seem to have been inclined to blame him for maliciousness and faithlessness. He used to get daily reports from his newswriters whom he had posted at various stations. He read their reports at night, and tore them up. But he was also proverbial for his liberality and love of letters. The *Mā'āsir-i Raḥīmī*[1] is a splendid testimony of his generosity; it shows that he was the Mœcenas of Akbar's age. People, by a happy comparison, called him Mīr ʿAlī Sher (*vide* p. 107, note 6). M. ʿA. wrote Persian, Turkish, Arabic, and Hindī with great fluency. As poet he wrote under the name of *Raḥīm*.

Though his father had been a Shīʿah, M. ʿA. was a Sunnī; but people said he was a Shīʿah, but practised *taqiyya*.[2]

M. ʿA.'s most faithful servant was Miyān Fahīm. People said, he was the son of a slave girl; but he appears to have been a Rājpūt. He grew up with M. ʿA.'s sons, and was as pious as he was courageous. He fell with his son Fīrūz Khān and 40 attendants in a fight with Mahābat Khān, who had imprisoned his master. M. ʿA. built him a tomb in Dihlī, which is now called *Nīla Burj*, near Humāyūn's tomb. (*Āsārᵘ 'ṣ-ṣanādīd.*)

M. ʿA. outlived his four sons.

1. *Mīrzā Īrich* (or *Īrij*), *Shahnawāz Khān Bahādur* (No. 255). When young he used to be called *Khān Khānān-i jawān*. He distinguished himself by his courage. In the 40th year of Akbar he was made a Commander of 400. In the 47th year, after a fight[3] with Malik ʿAmbar who got wounded, he received the title of *Bahādur*. During the reign of Jahāngīr he was called Shahnawāz Khān (*vide* Tuzuk, p. 95), and was made a Commander of Five Thousand. He died in 1028, from excessive drinking. (*Vide* Tuzuk, p. 270.)

---

[1] Called *Ma'āsir-i Raḥīmī* in allusion to his name M. ʿAbdᵘ-'r-Raḥīm. *Vide* Elliot's Index (1st edition), p 377.

[2] Wherever Shīʿahs are in the minority, they practise, if necessary, *taqiyya* (تقیہ, fear, caution), i.e., they do as if they were Sunnīs. A Shīʿha may even vilify his own sect, if his personal safety requires it.

[[3] Near Nānder.—B.]

Two of his sons are mentioned in the *Pādishāhnāma*. 1. Mīrzā Khān. He was Fawjdār of Kāngrah, and retired "foolishly" from public life in Rabīʿ II, 1046. But he was re-employed and was a Commander of Three Thousand in 1055 (*Pādishāhnāma* II, pp. 483, 723). 2. Lashkar-shikan Khān. He got in 1047 a present of 4,000 R., and received an appointment in Bengal.

Historians call Shahnawāz Khān generally *Shahnawāz Khān-i Jahāngīrī*, to distinguish him from Shahnawāz Khān-i Ṣafawī, a grandee of Shāhjahān.

2. *Mīrzā Dārāb Dārāb-Khān*. He has been mentioned above (p. 337). When Shāhjahān made him Governor of Bengal, he retained his wife, a son and a daughter, and a son of Shahnawāz Khān as hostages (*yarghamāl*). When the prince after the fight near the Tons (Benares) had again to go to the Dakhin, he wrote to Dārāb Khān to move to Gaḍhī (N.W. entrance of Bengal) and join him. Dārāb wrote him that he could not come, being besieged by the zamīndārs of the place. He fell at last into the hands of Parwīz and Mahābat Khān, and as Jahāngīr had "no objections", Mahābat executed him (1035), wrapped his head in a table cloth, and sent it to his father M. ʿA. as a present of a "melon". A short time before ʿAbduʿ 'llah Khān had killed Dārāb's son and a son of Shahnawāz Khān.

3. *Mīrzā Raḥmān Dād*. His mother belonged to the Sandahas of Amarkoṭ. Though very dissolute, he was the most liked by his father. He died, at Bālāpūr, about the same time as his eldest brother. *Vide* Tuzuk, p. 315. No one dared to inform his father of the event, till people sent at last the famous saint Ḥaẓrat ʿIsā of Sindh to M. ʿA. on a visit of condolence.

4. *Mīrzā Amru 'llah*. He grew up without education, and died when young.

30. **Rāja Mān Singh**, son of Bhagwān Dās.

He was born at Amber, and is the son of Rāja Bhagwān Dās (No. 27). European historians say that he was the adopted son of Rāja Bh. D., but Muhammadan historians do not allude to this circumstance, perhaps because Hindūs make absolutely no difference between a real and an adopted son. He is also known under the title of *Mīrzā Rāja*, and Akbar bestowed upon him the title of *Farzand* (son).

He joined Akbar with Bihārī Mal (p. 329). In 984 he was appointed against Rānā Kīkā, and gained, in 985,[1] the great battle near Goganda.[2]

[[1] Corrected in No. 109.—B.]
[2] The best account of this battle is to be found in Badā,onī, who was an eye-witness. *Bad.* II, 230 to 237. The whole is left out in Briggs.

Rāja Rāmsāh of Gwāliyār was killed with his sons, whilst the Rānā himself in the *melée* was wounded by Mān Singh. Akbar, however, felt annoyed, because M. S. did not follow up his victory, and so recalled him.

When Bhagwān Dās was appointed governor of the Panjāb, M. S. commanded the districts along the Indus. In the year 993, Prince M. Muḥammad Ḥakīm died, and M. S. was sent to Kābul to keep the country in order. He rejoined Akbar near the Indus with M. Muḥammad Ḥakīm's sons (M. Afrāsyāb and M. Kayqubād); but was soon after sent back to Kābul, where he chastised the Raushānīs who, like other Afg͟hān tribes, were given to predatory incursions. After the death of Rāja Bīr Baṛ, in the war with the Yūsufzāʿīs, M. S. was appointed to the command of the army in Kābul, in supercession of Zayn K͟hān Koka (No. 34) and Ḥakīm Abū 'l-Fatḥ. He was also put in charge of Zābulistān, as Bhagwān Dās had a fit of madness (p. 358). In the 32nd year, M. S. was recalled in consequence of loud complaints of the people against the Rājpūts and M. S.'s indifference to the Kābulīs, and was appointed Governor of Bihār, to which province the *tuyūls* of the Kachhwāhas had been transferred.

After the death of Bhagwān Dās in 998, M. S., who hitherto had the title of *Kũwar*, received from Akbar the title of Rāja and a Command of Five Thousand. In Bihār he punished several refractory Zamindārs, as Pūrān Mal and Rāja Sangrām, and received their tribute.

The principal events in Mān Singh's life from 997 to 1015 are given in Stewart's History of Bengal (pp. 114 to 121).[1] In the 35th year, M. S. invaded Oṛīsa by way of Jhārkand (Chuttiā Nāgpūr). The result of this expedition was the cession of Pūrī. In the 37th year, when the Afg͟hāns under K͟hwāja Sulaymān and K͟hwāja ʿUṣmān attacked Pūrī, M. S. again invaded Oṛīsa, and re-annexed, in 1000, that province to the Dihlī empire. In the 39th year, M. S. continued his conquests in Bhāṭī (the eastern portions of the Sundarban), and built, in the following year, Akbarnagar, or Rājmaḥall, at a place which Sher Shāh, before him, had selected as a convenient spot, as also Salīmnagar, the Fort of Sherpūr Murcha (Mymensing). The whole of Eastern Bengal on the right side of the Brahmaputra was likewise annexed. In the 41st year, M. S. married the sister of Lachmī Narāʿin, Rāja of Kūch Bihār, who had

---

[1] The name of "Sayyid" K͟hān (سید خان) which occurs several times in Stewart, *l.c.*, should be corrected to Saʿīd Khān (سعید خان), the same grandee whose biography was given above (p. 351). Such as take an interest in the History of Bengal and Oṛīsa should make use of the Akbarnāma, which contains many new facts and details not given in Stewart.

declared himself a vassal of the Mughul empire. In the same year, M. S. fell dangerously ill at Ghorāghāt, when the Afghāns attacked him. They were soon after driven back by Himmat Singh, one of M. S.'s sons,[1] into the Sundarban. In the 42nd year, M. S. had to send a detachment under Ḥijāz Khān into Kūch Bihār for the protection of Lachmī Narāʿin. In the 44th year M. S., at Akbar's request, joined the Dakhin war. Thinking that the Afghāns, in consequence of the death of their leader, the rich ʿĪṣa of Ghorāghāt, would remain quiet, M. S. appointed his son Jagat Singh (No. 160) his deputy, and joined Prince Salīm at Ajmīr. Jagat Singh died after a short time, and was succeeded by Mahā Singh, a grandson of M. S. The Afghāns under ʿUṣman used this opportunity, defeated, in the 45th year, the imperials near Bhadrak in Oṛīsa, and occupied a great portion of Bengal. M. S. then hastened back over Rahtās, and defeated the Afghāns near Sherpūr ʿAṭāī, a town of the Sirkār of Sharīfābād, which extended from Bardwān to Fatḥ Singh, S. of Murshibābād. After this victory, which obliged ʿUṣmān to retreat to Oṛīsa, M. S. paid a visit to the emperor, who promoted him to a (full) command of Seven Thousand. Hitherto Five Thousand had been the limit of promotion. It is noticeable that Akbar in raising M. S. to a command of Seven Thousand, placed a Hindū above every Muhammadan officer, though, soon after, M. Shāhrukh (*vide* p. 326) and M. ʿAzīz Koka (No. 21), were raised to the same dignity.

M. S. remained in Bengal till 1013, when the sickness of the emperor induced him to resign his appointment in order to be in the capital. The part which he played at the time of Akbar's death is known from the histories. Jahāngīr thought it prudent to overlook the conspiracy which the Rāja had made, and sent him to Bengal. But soon after (1015), he was recalled and ordered to quell disturbances in Rohtās (Bihār), after which he joined the Emperor. In the 3rd year of Jahāngīr's reign, he was permitted to go to his home, where he raised levies, in order to serve with M. ʿAbdᵘ 'r-Raḥīm (No. 29) in the Dakhin war.

M. S. died a natural death in the 9th year of J.'s reign, whilst in the Dakhin. Sixty of his fifteen hundred wives burned themselves on the funeral pile. At the time of his death, only one of his numerous sons was alive, Bhā,o Singh, regarding whose succession to the title, *vide* Tuzuk-i Jahāngīrī, p. 130

The ground on which the Tāj at Āgra stands, belonged to Mān Singh.

---

[1] He died in 1005.

31. **Muḥammad Qulī Khān Barlās**, a descendant of the Barmaqs (?).[1]

He served under Humāyūn, and held Multān as *jāgīr*. In the beginning of Akbar's reign, he conveyed, together with Shams^{u} 'd-Dīn Atga (No. 15) the princesses from Kābul to India. His *tuyūl* was subsequently transferred to Nāgor. For a short time he was also Governor of Mālwa.

In the 12th year, he was sent against Iskandar Khān Uzbak (*vide* No. 48) in Audh. After the death of Khān Zamān, Iskandar fled to Bengal, and Audh was given to Muḥammad Qulī Khān as *jāgīr*.

He subsequently served under Munʿim Khān in Bihār and Bengal. In the 19th year when Dāʾūd had withdrawn to Sātgāw (Hūglī) Munʿim Khān dispatched M. Q. Kh. to follow up the Afghāns, whilst he remained with Rāja Ṭoḍar Mal in Ṭānḍa to settle financial matters. When M. Q. Khān arrived at Sātgāw Dāʾūd withdrew to Oṛīsa, to which country neither M. Q. Khān nor his officers had much inclination to go. From Sātgāw M. Q. Khān invaded the district of Jesar (Jessore), where Ṣarmadī, a friend of Dāʾūd's, had rebelled; but the imperialists met with no success, and returned to Sātgāw. Munʿim Khān at last ordered Ṭoḍar Mal to join M. G. Khān, and subsequently both moved into Oṛīsa. Soon after passing the frontier M. Q. Khān died at Mednīpūr (Midnapore), Ramaẓān, 982. He seems to have died a natural death, though some accused one of his eunuchs of foul play.

His son, *Mīrzā Farīdūn Barlās* (No. 227). He served under M. ʿAbd^{u} 'r-Raḥīm (No. 29) in Sind, and accompanied, in 1001, Jānī Beg (No. 47) to Court. He was a Commander of Five Hundred. Under Jahāngīr, he was rapidly promoted, and held, in the 8th year, a command of Two Thousand, when he served under Prince Khurram against Rānā Amr Singh. He died during the expedition.

His son Mihr ʿAlī Barlās was made by Jahāngīr a Commander of One Thousand.

32. **Tarson Khān**, sister's son of Shāh Muḥammad Sayf^{u} 'l-Mulk.

In Histories he is called Tarson Muḥammad Khān. Sayf^{u} 'l-Mulk had been an independent ruler in Gharjistān (a part of Khurāsān); but he had to submit to Ṭahmasp (A.H. 940).

---

[1] So in the MSS.; but the name *Baṛmaq* is very doubtful. Being a "Barlās", he belonged to that Chaghtā,ī tribe which traced its descent to برد مجي or ايرد مجي—the MSS. have various forms for this name—who is the 8th ancestor of Tīmūr. If برد مجي be the correct form, the substitution of برمق, a renowned name in Muhammadan history, would not appear altogether impossible. The MSS. of the *Maʾāṣir* have *Barantaq* برنتق. In the beginning of the Akbarnāma, Abū 'l-Faẓl says that this 8th ancestor of Tīmūr was the first that held the title of *barlās*, which means the same as شجاع *shujāʿ*, brave. Another Barlās had been mentioned above on p. 216. An Amīr Chākū Barlās served with distinction under Tīmūr.

Tarson Khān was in the service of Bayrām Khān (No. 10), and joined Akbar when Bayrām fell into disgrace. Akbar sent him, together with Ḥājī Muḥammad Sīstānī (No. 55), to see Bayrām on his way to Makkah, as far as Nāgor, then the frontier of the empire. T. Kh. was subsequently promoted to the post of a Commander of Five Thousand, and was for some time Governor of Bhakkar (*vide* No. 107), and then of Patan in Gujrāt. In the 21st year he served in Rājpūtānā, *vide* No. 44. In the 23rd year he was made Fawjdār of Jaunpūr, at the same time that Mullā Muḥammad Yazdī (*vide* p. 198) was appointed Qāẓiyu 'l-Quẓāt and Ṣadr of the Sirkār. When the Jaunpūr Rebellion broke out, T. Kh. with other faithful Amīrs moved to Bihār against Bahādur Khān and ʕArab Khān, who were joined by Maʕṣūm Khān Farankhūdī (No. 157). In the 27th year he served under M. ʕAzīz Koka in Bihār. When the Qāqshāls (No. 50) left Maʕṣūm Khān and joined the Imperialists, M. ʕAzīz sent T. Kh. to Ghorāghāt, where most of the Qāqshāls had jāgīrs. T. Kh. stayed at Tājpūr (Dinagepore), settling matters, when Maʕṣūm Khān came with a large army from Bhāṭī (بهاتی),[1] and plundered Western Bengal, approaching even the environs of Ṭānda ; he also sent a detachment against T. Kh., who was besieged in the fort of Tājpūr. The siege was raised by a corps sent by Shāhbāz Khān-i Kambū (No. 80) from Patna, and T. Kh. was thus enabled to join Shāhbāz and drive away the rebels from Upper Bengal. Maʕṣūm fled again to Bhāṭī, and Shāhbāz and T. Kh. planned an expedition against ʕĪṣā, who had afforded Maʕṣūm shelter. They crossed the Ganges at Khizrpūr, which stands on the frontier of Bhāṭī, took Sunnārgāw, plundered Baktarāpūr (?), where ʕĪṣā used to live, and nearly caught Maʕṣūm. At this juncture, ʕĪṣā returned from an expedition to Kūch Bihār, and attacked the Imperialists near Bhowāl (N. of Dacca). The Imperialists had entrenched themselves

---

[1] Abū 'l-Faẓl gives this spelling in the Akbarnāma, and says it means *lowland* (from the Hindūstanī بهاتی *down the river*), and extends nearly 400 *kos* from east to west, and 300 *kos* from N.S., from Thibet to the ocean. It would thus include the Sundarban and the tracts along the Megna. Grant, in the Vth Report, p. 260, note, defines *Bhāṭī* as comprising the Sunderban and all the neighbouring low lands, even Hijlī, overflowed by the tide.

ʕĪṣā's father, according to Abū 'l-Faẓl, was a Rājpūt of the Bais clan, if I read correctly my MSS. He came in contact with Salīm Khān and Tāj Khān of Bengal, was killed ; and his two sons, ʕĪṣā and Ismāʕīl, were sold as slaves. They were subsequently traced by Quṭbu 'd-Dīn Khān, ʕĪṣā's uncle, to Tūrān, and brought back. ʕĪṣā soon became the chief of Bhāṭī, and had twelve great zamīndārs dependent on him. Hence he is generally called by Abū 'l-Faẓl *Marzbān-i Bhāṭī*, ruler of *Bhāṭī*. He gave the Imperialists no end of trouble. He must not be confounded with ʕĪṣa, the Vakīl of Qutlū Khān of Orīsā, who ceded Pūrī to Mān Singh.

near the Brahmaputra, and the fighting was continued for a long time both by land and on the river. At one time T. Kh. with a small detachment came too near a position held by the enemy, and was attacked by Maʿṣūm Khān and wounded. Immediately afterwards he was caught and killed by Maʿṣūm (992). For a relation of his, *vide* No. 400.

33. **Qiyā Khān Gung.**

Qiyā is a Turkish word and means *zeb*, ornament. *Gung*, if it is the Persian word, means "dumb". He served under Humāyūn, and held Kol Jalālī. On the approach of Hemū, he joined Tardī Beg (No. 12) in Dihlī, and retreated with him. After Hemū's defeat, Qiyā was sent to Āgra, and was raised to the dignity of a Commander of Five Thousand. Several parganas in Gwāliār having been given to him as *tuyūl*, Qiyā Khān, in the 2nd year of Akbar's reign, besieged Gwāliyār, which was held by Bhīl Khān, a general of Salīm Shāh, during whose reign Gwāliyār had been the capital of the empire. Bhīl Khān, thinking it impossible to hold the Fort for a long time, wished [1] to hand it over for a consideration to Rāja Rāmsāh, whose ancestors had held Gwāliār, when Qiyā Khān arrived, and after defeating the Rāja, prepared himself to besiege Bhīl Khān. When Akbar, in 966, came to Āgra, he sent a detachment to assist Qiyā, and Bhīl Khān submitted.

He was a friend of Bayrām, but was the first that left him and joined Akbar.

A few years later, Qiyā Khān joined Khān Zamān's rebellion, but repented and was pardoned, at the request of Munʿim Khān.

After the first conquest of Bengal, Q. Kh. was sent to Oṛīsa, to settle matters. He remained in Oṛīsa and Bengal during the Bengal rebellion, and when, in the 25th year, the Imperialists withdrew from that country, Qutlū Khān seized upon Oṛīsa, and besieged Qiyā Khān in some fort. Deserted by his soldiers, Q. Kh. was killed (989).[2]

---

[1] So the *Maʾāṣir*. The *Sawāniḥ* says that Rāja Rāmsāh with a large force of Rājpūts, had come to besiege Gwāliyār. Firishta instead of Bhīl Khān (Akbarnāma, Sawāniḥ, Badā,onī) has Suhayl Khān (?), and Iqbāl Khān (?) for *Qiyā Khān*, *vide* Briggs, II, p. 194. The change from بهیل to سهیل is not remarkable; but the alteration of قیا to اقبال is more violent, as we have an additional *alif* and *lām*.

How untrustworthy our printed editions are may be seen from Khāfī Khān's List of Commanders of Five Thousand under Akbar (*Ed. Bibl. Indica* I, p. 237), where the native editors have given three wrong names among twelve, viz.:—

P. 237, last line, for *Amīn Khān Kokā*, read *Zayn Khān Koka* (No. 34).

P. 238, l. 1, for *Shujāʿ Khān*, read *Shujāʿat Khān* (No. 14).

P. 238, l. 2, for *Rasūl Khān*, read *Tarson Khān* (No. 32).

Moreover Khāfī Khān's list is most incomplete, and does not coincide, although he says so, with the number of Panjhazārīs given in the *Ṭabaqāt*.

[2] Several copies of the *Ṭabaqāt* which I have consulted, say that Qiyā Khān died in 984 (?).

Tardī Khān (No. 101), his son, was a Commander of Fifteen Hundred. He accompanied Prince Dānyāl to the Dakhin, but fell later in disgrace. In the 49th year he was restored and promoted to a command of Two Thousand Five Hundred, and got a present of 5 lacs of Rupees.

V. *Commanders of Four Thousand Five Hundred.*

34. **Zayn Khān,**[1] son of Khwāja Maqṣūd of Harāt.

His father, Khwāja Maqṣūd ʿAlī, was a servant of Akbar's mother. The name of his mother was Pīcha Jān Anaga; she was one of Akbar's nurses. On Humāyūn's flight to Persia, Maqṣūd was always near the howdah of Akbar's mother, and remained attached to her in all her misfortunes. His brother was Khwāja Ḥasan (Zayn Khān's uncle), whose daughter married Prince Salīm. She is the mother of Prince Parwīz.

In 993, Mīrzā Muḥammad Ḥakīm, Akbar's brother, had died, and Akbar crossed the Indus for Zābulistān. Zayn Khān was at that time a Commander of Two Thousand and Five Hundred, and was sent against the Yūsufzā,īs. This tribe, says ʿAbu 'l-Faẓl, had formerly been in Qarābāgh and Qandahār, and had invaded Kābul, where a great number of them were killed by M. Ulugh Beg. The remainder settled at Lamghānāt, and subsequently at Ishtaghar. For the last one hundred years they had held the territory of Bajor,[2] and were notorious robbers. In Bajor, there was also a tribe of the name of Sulṭānī, who traced their descent to a daughter of Sulṭān Sikandar. The Yūsufzāʾīs deprived them treacherously of their district; a few of the Sulṭānīdes, however, remained in Bājor from attachment to their old country.

On a former occasion, when Akbar had moved against M. Muḥammad Ḥakīm, the chiefs of the Yūsufzāʾīs submitted, and one of them, Kālū, went with Akbar to Āgra and was hospitably treated. He fled, however, but was caught by Shamsᵘ 'd-Dīn Khāfī (No. 159) near Aṭak, and was sent back; and although Akbar continued to treat him kindly, he fled again and stirred up his countrymen.

Zayn Khān moved into the District of Bajor[2] (north of Pashāwar), and punished the Yūsufzāʾīs. Several chiefs asked for pardon. After this he erected a fort in Jakdara, in the middle of the country, and defeated the enemies in twenty-three fights. He had at last to ask

---

[1] As he was Akbar's foster-brother; he is generally called in histories, Zayn Khān Koka.

[[2] Or Bijūr (?).—P.]

for reinforcements, and Akbar sent to him Rāja Bīr Baṛ and Ḥakīm Abū 'l-Fatḥ with some troops. Zayn Khān asked them to attack the Afghāns whilst he would occupy the conquered districts, or he would attack the enemies and they should hold the district. But Bīr Baṛ and Ḥakīm Abū 'l-Fatḥ, who were no friends of Zayn Khān, proposed that they should attack the Yūsufzāʿīs together and then go back. Z. Kh. said it would not do to return without better results from a country which had cost so many sacrifices; else, the best thing they could do, was to return the same way they had come. But to this they would not listen, and returned by another road (over کراکر). Z. Kh. paid no attention to their insubordination and joined them, chiefly because he was afraid they would denounce him at Court. As soon as the Afghāns saw the Imperialists returning, they attacked them in every narrow valley. On passing the Girewa[1] Balandrī (گریوه بلندری), Z. Kh. who commanded the rear (*chandāwal*), was so severely attacked that he had to face them. Arrows and stones were showered from all sides on the Imperialists, the soldiers got bewildered, and the horses ran into the train of elephants. Many lives were lost. Z. Kh., unable to prevent a rout, rushed among the Afghāns seeking death, when Jānish Bahādur (No. 235) got hold of the reins of his horse, and led him by force out of the *melée*. In the greatest disorder the Imperialists reached the next station, when the mere rumour of an approach of the Afghāns dispersed the soldiers. In the darkness of night most of them lost their way, and several detachments entered the valleys occupied by the Afghāns. Their enemies being engaged in plundering, they were at first safe; but next day were all cut off. This was the occasion when Bīr Baṛ with 500 officers fell (*vide* p. 214).

In the 31st year (994), Z. Kh. operated successfully against the Mahmands and Ghorīs near Pashāwar, who under their chief Jalālᵘ 'd-Dīn Rawshānī had committed numerous predations. In the next year, Z. Kh. was made governor of Zābulistān *vice* Mān Singh, and moved, in the 33rd year, against the Yūsufzāʿīs. After eight months' fighting they submitted, but Z. Kh. insisted on occupying their territory. He followed the same policy as before, and erected a large Fort on the banks of the river Pajkora[2] (پجکوره, where their district commences. During the festival of the ʿĪd-i Qurbānī (Baqr ʿĪd, in Ẕī Ḥijjah), he surprised the Afghāns and took possession of the whole district, erecting a fort wherever

[1] *Girewa* means *a hill*.
[2] Or Panjkora.

he thought necessary, and leaving in each a sufficient number of soldiers [1] (*Vide* No. 46.)

In the 35th year he was sent to punish several rebellious zamīndārs in the Himālayas. Most of them, as Rāja Budī (Badhī) Chand of Nagarkoṭ (*vide* p. 349), Rāy Pertāb of Mānkoṭ, Rāja Parisrām of Mount Jamū, Rāja Bāsū of Mau, Rāy Baldhadr of Lakhinpūr, etc., submitted and accompanied Z. Kh. to Court, though they had an army of 10,000 horse and a lac of foot soldiers.

After having been made, in the 36th year, a Commander of Four Thousand, Z. Kh. was allowed an ʿ*alam* and a *naqqāra* (*vide* p. 52), and was appointed, in the following year, governor of the districts beyond the Indus up to the Hindūkush, when new opportunities offered for punishing the mountaineers.

In the 41st year he was made a Commander of Five Thousand and governor of Kābul, *vice* Qulij Khān. In the same year, Prince Salīm fell in love with Z. Kh.'s daughter, and married her soon after, though Akbar was displeased (*vide* p. 288, l. 1, from below). With the death of Jalāl Khān Rawshānī the disturbances in Zābulistān came to an end, and Z. Kh. was ordered to Lāhor, from where Akbar, on his return from Burhānpūr, called him to Āgra.

Z. Kh. died in 1010, partly from excessive drinking. He played on several instruments, and composed poems. As Saʿīd Khān (No. 25) for his eunuchs, and Qulij Khān (No. 42) for his horses, so was Z. Kh. famous for his elephants.

A son of his, Shukr[u] 'Ullah (No. 373), *vide* below, was a Commander of Two Hundred. The *Maʿāṣir* mentions another son, Mughul Khān, who served under Jahāngīr and Shāhjahān (*vide* Pādishāhn. II, p. 641) and died 19th Ramaẓān, 1067. He commanded for some time Fort Odgīr in the Dakhin, where the author of the *Maʿāṣir* later found an inscription referring to his appointment. For a second daughter, *vide* p. 346.

For Zayn Khān's brother, *vide* No. 38.

35. **Mīrzā Yūsuf Khān**, son of Mīr Aḥmad-i Raẓawī.

He was a real Sayyid of Mashhad, and was much liked by Akbar. In the 30th year he was a Commander of Two Thousand and Five Hundred.

---

[1] Such forts were called *Thānas*, now the common word for a police station. "*Thāna* means a corps of cavalry, matchlockmen, and archers, stationed within an enclosure. Their duty is to guard the roads, to hold the places surrounding the *Thāna*, and to dispatch provisions (*rasad*) to the next *Thāna*." *Pādishāhnāma*, I, p. 167.

How old the use of the word *Thāna* is, may be seen from the fact that it occurs frequently on Tribenī and Sātgāw inscriptions of the eighth and ninth centuries of the Hijrah.

When Shāhbāz Khān left Bihār for Bengal, M. Yūsuf Khān was sent from Audh to keep Bihār. In the 32nd year (995), when Qāsim Khān (No. 59) resigned, M. Y. was sent to Kashmīr as ruler. He was much liked by the people of that country, conciliated Shams Chak, the claimant to the throne, and sent him to Court. In the 34th year (997), Akbar visited Kashmīr, and issued several orders regarding the taxation of the country. In the districts of Mararāj and Kamrāj, i.e., the upper and lower districts on both sides of the Bahat river, he fixed the taxes at one-fourth.

In Kashmīr every piece of ground is called *patta*, though a *patta* originally is equal to 1 Bīgha, 1 Biswa (*Ilāhī*) of Akbar. Two and a half *pattas* and a little more are equal to 1 *Kashmīrī* Bīgha. Three kinds of grain pay taxes in Kashmīr, and each village is assessed at some *kharwārs* of *shālī*. A *kharwār* is equal to 3 *mans*, 8 *sers* of Akbar. The principal weight used in Kashmīr is the *tark*, which is equal to 8 *sers* of Akbar (*vide* p. 90, note 2). At the time of the *Rabīʿ* crop, they take 2 *tarks* from each *patta* of wheat and vetches (*māsh*). The country having been recently annexed, was assessed very lightly, at 22 lacs *kharwārs*, which was 2 lacs more than before, the *kharwār* being reckoned at 16 *dāms*. For this sum, Akbar handed over Kashmīr to M. Y. Kh.

In the 36th year, one of M. Y. Kh.'s Mutaṣaddīs (revenue clerks) fled to Court, and stated that the revenue should be 50 *per cent* (*dah-pānzdah*) higher, and the *kharwār* should be valued at 29 *dāms*. M. Y. Kh. informed Akbar that so high an assessment was an impossibility; but Akbar sent Qāẓī Nurᵘ 'llah and Qāẓī ʿĀlī to Kashmīr to report on the revenue. As M. Y. Khān's people assumed a threatening attitude, Nūrᵘ 'llah returned, and Akbar sent Ḥasan Beg Shaykh ʿUmarī (No. 167) to Kashmīr. On his arrival, some of M. Y. Kh.'s people made a conspiracy, and stirred up the malcontents of the country, who collected under Yādgār, the son of M. Y. Kh.'s uncle. The disturbances became so serious that Qāẓī ʿĀlī and Ḥasan Beg returned to Hindūstān; but the rebels blockaded the roads and killed Qāẓī ʿĀlī. Ḥasan Beg escaped, not without wounds. Yādgār then read the *khuṭba* in his name, and had dies prepared for striking coins. Several bad omens foreshadowed his speedy ruin. Without having any knowledge of this rebellion, Akbar revisited Kashmīr; but when he was informed of the state of the country, he put M. Y. Kh. under the charge of Abū 'l-Faẓl. Yādgār in vain tried to oppose Akbar at the frontier passes, and fled from Srīnagar to Hīrāpūr, where some of M. Y. Kh.'s men spread at night the rumour that Akbar had suddenly arrived. In the confusion which ensued, Yādgār fled outside of the camp, accompanied by a servant of the name of Yūsuf. His camp was plundered and M. Y. Kh.'s men got hold of Yūsuf, who had returned to get a horse for his master. They tortured him, till he confessed where Yādgār was. Soon after, they caught him and cut off his head.

As M. Y. Kh. refused to remain in charge of Kashmīr under the increased revenue, the country was made *khāliṣa*, and Shamsu 'd-Dīn Khāfī (No. 159) was appointed Governor with 3,000 troops. Some time after, at Prince Salīm's request, M. Y. Kh. was re-instated.

In the 38th year, M. Y. Kh. was appointed Dārogha of the Topkhāna, and received Jaunpūr as *tuyūl*, *vice* Qulij Khān (1002); but in the 41st year his *jāgīr* was transferred to Gujrāt, to enable him to serve in the Dakhin. In the following year, when Ṣādiq of Harāt (No. 43) died, M. Y. Kh. was appointed *atālīq* to Prince Murād, whom he joined in Bālāpūr (Barār). After the death of Prince Murād (p. 322), M. Y. Kh. distinguished himself, together with Abū 'l-Faẓl, in the Dakhin wars, and later, under Prince Dānyāl, in the conquest of Aḥmadābād, on which occasion M. Y. Kh. is said to have been more energetic than other grandees.

After joining Akbar's Court at Burhānpūr, in the 46th year, M. Y. Kh. went again to Prince Dānyāl, who, in 1010, sent him to assist Abū 'l-Faẓl and the Khān-Khānān at Bālāghāt. But soon after, he died of an abscess at Jalnāpūr,[1] in Jumāda II, of the same year. His body was taken to Mash,had.

M. Y. Kh. generally stayed at Sulṭānpūr, which he looked upon as his Indian home. His contingent consisted exclusively of Rohīlas, whose wages he paid monthly.

His sons. 1. *Mīrzā Lashkarī Ṣafshikan Khān* (No. 375). He was under Akbar Thānadār of Bīr (East of Aḥmadnagar), and got from Jahāngīr the title of Ṣafdar Khān, and a *tuyūl* in Bihār. In the 5th year (of Jahāngīr), he was promoted to the post of a Commander of 1,500, with 700 horse, and was made in the following year Ṣūbadār of Kashmīr. In the 8th year, he was removed from his office. In the 21st year, when Mahābat Khān had fled, he was sent towards Dihlī to intercept Mahābat's treasures which were known to have arrived from Bengal. This he did. In the beginning of Shāh Jahān's reign, he was made a Commander of 2,500, and 2,000 horse, received the title of Ṣafshikan Khān, and was

---

[1] My copy of the *Ṭabaqāt* as also another MS. which I have seen, contains the following entry—"*At the time he was appointed to operate against Rājū, he died at Jannatābad in the Dak'hin, which is generally called Jalnāpūr.*" It is difficult to say how these words have found their way into some MS. of the *Ṭabaqāt*, which was finished in A.H. 1001, or nine years before M. Y. Khān's death.

again sent to Bīr, where he remained for a long time. He withdrew at last from public life, got a pension of Rs. 12,000 *per annum*, and lived at Lāhor. He died in 1055.

He was frank to a fault. Once he invited the Manṣabdārs of Kābul, and feasted them on pork; and when called to Court, to answer for his conduct, he gave Jahāngīr a lesson by saying that not only pork, but also wine was forbidden in the law. For this answer he fell into disgrace.

2. *Mīrzā ʿIvaẓ* (عوض). He was a good prose writer, and wrote a history of the world, entitled *Chaman*.

3. *Mīrzā Aflāṭūn*. "He lived with his brother." He was subsequently made Mutawallī of Sikandra (Akbar's tomb), where he died.

A relation of M. Y. Kh., Mīr ʿAbdᵘ 'llah, was under Shāhjahān a Commander of 1,500 and 600 horse. He was for some time Governor of Fort Dharūr, E. of Bīr, mentioned above. He died in the 8th year of Shāhjahān.

VI. *Commanders of Four Thousand.*

36. **Mahdī Qāsim Khān.**

The *Ṭabaqāt* mentions him among the Commanders of Five Thousand. He served under M. ʿAskarī, Bābar's third son, whose foster brother he was. His brother was Ghaẓanfar Koka [1] (غضنفر). Humāyūn, after the conquest of Gujrāt, had appointed ʿAskarī to Aḥmadābād. One night, when half drunk, M. ʿAskarī said, "I am king and the shadow of God"; when Ghaẓanfar gently replied, "Thou art drunk, and hast lost thy senses," at which all who were present laughed. ʿAskarī got enraged, and imprisoned Ghaẓanfar; but he escaped, went to Sulṭān Bahādur, king of Gujrāt, who had retreated to Fort Diu, and betrayed the plans of ʿAskarī. Bahādur thereupon collected an army, marched to Aḥmadābād and drove the Prince away (*vide* No. 12).

Mahdī Qāsim Khān joined Humāyūn on his return from Persia, and was made in the beginning of Akbar's reign, a Commander of Four Thousand. In the 10th year, ʿAbdᵘ 'l-Majīd Āṣaf Khān (No. 49) had been ordered to pursue Khān Zamān (No. 13); but entertaining doubts regarding his own safety, he fled to Gaṛha (Jabalpūr). M. Q. Kh. was, therefore, sent to Gaṛha, after Akbar had, in 973, returned from Jaunpūr to Āgra, and was ordered to capture ʿAbdᵘ 'l-Majīd. When M. Q. Kh. arrived

---

[1] *Ghaẓanfar* means *a lion*. *Badāonī* (II. p. 125, l. 8) calls him *Ghazanfar Beg*. The Ed. Bibl. Indica Edition has, by mistake, *Ghanazfar*.

at Garha, ˁAbdᵘ 'l-Majīd fled to Khān Zamān; but the wretched state of the country displeased M. Q. Kh. so much, that without asking Akbar's permission, he left Garha and went to Makkah. From there he returned over Persia and Qandahār, and arrived, towards the end of the 13th year, at Rantanbhūr (which Akbar besieged), and asked to be forgiven, sending at the same time a fine batch of Persian horses as a present. Akbar pardoned him, restored him to his old rank, and gave him Lakhnau as *tuyūl*.

"Nothing else is known of him" (*Maˁāṣir*). He had been dead for some time in 1001, when the *Ṭabaqāt* was completed. Ḥusayn Khān Tukriya (No. 53) was the son of his sister and his son-in-law.

He had a villa at Lāhor, which was called *Bāgh-i Mahdī Qāsim Khān*, *vide* Badāonī II, 90, 292, and Calcutta Review for October, 1869 (Jahāngir's Death).

37. **Muẓaffar Khān-i Turbatī.**

Turbat is the name of a tribe (*ulūs*) in Khurāsān. His full name is Khwāja Muẓaffar ˁAlī Khān-i Turbatī. He was Bayrām's Dīwān. Bayrām delegated him from Dīpālpūr to Sher Muḥammad Dīwāna (p. 332), who sent him in chains to Akbar. Though several courtiers advised the Emperor to kill Muẓaffar, he pardoned him, and made him ˁ*Āmil* (Collector) of the Pargana of Parsaror. Subsequently Akbar made him *Dīvān-i Buyūtāt* (Collector of the Imperial Stores, etc.), and at last Dīvān of the Empire, with the title of Muẓaffar Khān (971). Rāja Ṭoḍar Mal was then under him. According to Badā,onī, the two quarrelled incessantly, though people said that the Rāja was a better financier than Muẓaffar, whose accession to office was honoured by the short *tārikh* ظالم, *ẓā,im* (=971), or "Tyrant".

In the 11th year he abolished the *Jamˁ-i Raqmī*. This is the name of the assessment of the Dihlī empire, which had existed since the time of Bayrām; but the rent roll showed an assessment very different from the actual state of things; "for, on account of the number of men (*kaṣrat-i mardum*, i.e. Jāgīr-holders) and the unsettled state (*qalb-i wilāyat*) of the country, the revenue was increased in name (*ba-nām afzūda*) for the sake of mere show (*barā-yi mazīd-i iˁtibār*)." This *Jamˁ-i Raqmī* was now abolished (*vide* Third Book, *Āˁīn-i Dahsāla*), and Muẓaffar prepared a rent roll according to his experience and the returns of *Qānūngos*. The new rent roll was called *Jamˁ-i Ḥāṣil-i Ḥāl*, or the roll of the present actual income (*vide* p. 352). As the *Dāgh* law (pp. 265, 266, and p. 252) did not then exist, Muẓaffar Khān fixed the number of soldiers which the contingents of the *Amīrs* and the *Mulāzims* (friends of the king) should contain, and the soldiers were divided into three classes.[1]

In the 12th year it was reported that Muẓaffar loved a boy of the name of Quṭb. Akbar had the boy forcibly removed, whereupon Muẓaffar assumed the garb of a Faqīr, and went into the forest. Akbar was thus obliged to recall him, and restored the beloved.

In the 17th year a mania for *Chaupar* (p. 315) had seized Akbar's Court. Muẓaffar lost not only his gold muhurs, but also his temper, and annoyed the Emperor so much that he was told to go to Makkah. But he was recalled, and joined the Court at Sūrat, which Akbar then besieged. In the 18th year (981), after having been for some time in Sārangpūr in Mālwa, he was appointed *Vakīl* of the Empire, with the title of *Jumlat^u 'l-Mulk*. But he did several things which Akbar did not approve of, and when the Emperor returned from Patna, from where he had dispatched a corps to take Rahtās in South Bihār, he ordered Muẓaffar to join the expedition, without allowing him first to pay his respects (*vide* Briggs II, 249). Like his companion, Khwāja Shams^u 'd-Dīn Khāfī (No. 159), M. distinguished himself in the campaign, punished the rebels on several occasions, and took Ḥājīpūr, of which the Afghāns had again taken possession. For these services, M. was appointed, in the 20th year, Governor of Bihār, from Chausā to Gaṛhī. Soon after the taking of Ḥājīpūr, M. was nearly caught by a party of Afghāns, who saw him reconnoitering the banks of the Ghandak.

In the 22nd year, M. returned to Court, where Shāh Manṣūr (No. 122) and Rāja Ṭoḍaṛ Mal continued, under his superintendence, their financial reforms.

On the death of Khān Jahān (No. 24) in 986, he was made Governor of Bengal.

In the 25th year (988), Shāh Manṣūr subjected the Amīrs of Bihar and Bengal to strict inquiries, and called on them to refund sums which they had spent without permission. When he insisted on his

---

[1] The *Ma'āṣir* says, he allowed the *first* class 48,000 *dāms*, the second 32,000 *d.*, and the third 24,000 *d. per annum*. These numbers appear to be very large, when compared with p. 241. But what was the value of a *dām* in those days ? In the 40th year of Akbar's reign, the following pay regulation was introduced :—

Mughul, Afghān, or Hindī		
Sih-aspas .	1,000 *d.*	*per mensem.*
Du-aspas .	800 *d.*	,,
Yak-aspas .	600 *d.*	,,
1st Class Rājputs	800 *d.*	,,
2nd ditto ditto	600 *d.*	,,

(Akbarnāma). But at that time 40 *dāms* were equal to 1 Akbarshāhī Rupee, which differed very little from our rupee.

demands, Maʿṣūm-i Kābulī and several other grandees that held jāgīrs in Bihār, rebelled. Muẓaffar imitated Shāh Manṣūr's policy in Bengal, and when he commenced vigorously to collect outstandings, Bābā Khān Qāqshāl and other Jāgīrdārs of Bengal rebelled likewise. M. defeated them on several occasions, but would not listen to proposals of peace. At last the Bihār rebels joined those of Bengal, and mustered a sufficient force to take the field against Muẓaffar. Notwithstanding this, the rebels would have gladly come to terms and gone to Orīsā, had not Muẓaffar betrayed his weakness by moving to the Fort of Ṭānḍa, which, according to Badā,onī, consisted of nothing but four old walls. The rebels thus emboldened demanded full pardon, permission to go to Makkah, and restoration of one-third of their property. At this juncture, Sharafᵘ 'd-Dīn Ḥusayn (No. 17) escaped from Muẓaffar's custody, joined the rebels, and informed them of M.'s miserable condition. They moved, therefore, against Ṭānḍa, took it, captured M., and killed him (Rabīʿ I, 988).[1]

The Jāmiʿ Masjid in Āgra was built by Muẓaffar. I am told the Masjid is now in ruins, which still go by the name of *Nawāb Muẓaffar Khān kī Masjid* or *Kālī Masjid.* The *Maʾāṣir* says it stood in the *Kaṭra Miyān Raqīq*, but this name does not appear to be now-a-days in use. The Masjid now called the Jāmiʿ Masjid of Āgra was built, in 1058, by Jahān Ārā Begum, Shāhjahān's daughter, at a cost of five lacs of Rupees.

According to the *Mirʾatᵘ 'l-ʿĀlam*, his youngest daughter was married to Shāh Fatḥᵘ 'llah of Shīrāz.

38. **Sayf Khan Koka**, elder brother of Zayn Khān Koka (No. 34).

His mother had only daughters, and when she was pregnant with Sayf Khān, her husband threatened to divorce her, should it again turn out to be a daughter. She complained of this to Akbar's mother, and Akbar, though then a child, told her husband that he would incur his displeasure if he should do so ; "besides," said he, "it shall be this time a fine boy." The mother looked upon Prince Akbar's words as a prophecy from heaven, and in course of time Sayf Khān was born.

Akbar was very fond of Sayf Khān, and made him, though quite young, a Commander of Four Thousand. He distinguished himself by his bravery, especially in the 17th year, at the taking of Sūrat, where he was wounded by a bullet. In the beginning of the next year (981), he accompanied Akbar on his forced march from Āgra to Aḥmadābād (p. 343), and was killed bravely fighting with Muḥammad Ḥusayn Mīrzā.

---

[1] According to Bādā,onī (II, p. 282), Muẓaffar capitulated, left the fort, and was then captured and slain.

How Akbar appreciated his services may be seen from the fact, that having heard that Sayf Khān was heavily involved, he paid, on his return to Āgra, every debt due by him.

His two sons, Sher Afkan (355), and Amān^{u} 'llah (356) are mentioned below as Commanders of Two Hundred and Fifty.

39. **Rāja Ṭoḍar Mal**, a Khatrī.

He was born at Lāhor. The *Ma'āṣir^{u} 'l-Umarā* does not record his services before the 18th year of Akbar's reign ; but T. M. appears to have entered Akbar's service at a very early period. In 971, he was employed under Muẓaffar (*Bad.* II, 65), and in 972, he served under Akbar against Khān Zamān (*vide* No. 61). He held the first important post in the 18th year, when after the conquest of Gujrāt he was left there to assess that province. In the 19th year, after the conquest of Patna, he got an ʿ*alam* and a *naqqāra* (Āʾīn 19), and was ordered to accompany Munʿim Khān to Bengal. He was the soul of the expedition. In the battle with Dāʾūd Khān-i Kararānī, when Khān ʿĀlam (*vide* No. 58) had been killed, and Munʿim Khān's horse had run away, the Rāja held his ground bravely, and "not only was there no defeat, but an actual victory". "What harm," said Ṭoḍar Mal, "if Khān ʿĀlam is dead ; what fear, if the Khān Khānān has run away, the empire is ours !" After settling several financial matters in Bengal and Orīsā, Ṭoḍar Mal went to Court, and was employed in revenue matters. When Khān Jahān (No. 24) went to Bengal, Ṭoḍar Mal was ordered to accompany him. He distinguished himself, as before, in the defeat and capture of Dāʾūd. In the 21st year, he took the spoils of Bengal to Court, among them 300 to 400 elephants. In the following year, he was again sent to Gujrāt, *vice* Vazīr Khān (No. 41), who had given no satisfaction. Whilst arranging at Aḥmadābād matters with Vazīr Khān, Muẓaffar Ḥusayn, at the instigation of Mihr ʿAlī Kolābī, rebelled. Vazīr Khān proposed to retreat to the Fort, but Ṭoḍar Mal was ready to fight, and defeated Muẓaffar in the 22nd year, near Dholqah, which lies 12 *kos* from Aḥmadābād. Vazīr Khān would have been lost in this battle, if Ṭoḍar Mal had not come to his assistance. Muẓaffar, after his defeat, fled to Jūnāgaṛh.

In the same year Ṭoḍar Mal was appointed *Vazīr*. When Akbar left Ajmīr for the Panjāb, the house idols of the Rāja were lost, as mentioned on p. 33, note.

When the news of Muẓaffar's death (No. 37) and the occupation of the whole of Bengal and Bihār by the rebels reached Akbar, he sent Ṭoḍar Mal, Ṣādīq Khān, Tarson Khān, etc., from Faṭhpūr Sīkrī to Bihār. Muḥibb ʿAlī (No. 107), Governor of Rahtās and Muḥammad Maʿṣūm

Khān-i Farankhūdī (No. 157) were appointed *kumakīs*, or auxiliaries. The latter joined the Rāja with 3,000 well-equipped horse, evidently bent on rebellion. Ṭodar Mal managed to keep him quiet; but he reported the matter to Court. The Bengal rebels, under Maʿṣūm-i Kābulī, the Qāqshāls, and Mīrzā Sharafu 'd-Dīn Ḥusayn, with 30,000 horse, 500 elephants, and many ships and artillery, had collected near Mungīr, and Ṭodar Mal, from fear of treachery among his auxiliaries, shut himself up in the Fort of Mungīr, instead of risking a general engagement. During the siege, two of his officers, Humāyūn Farmilī and Tarkhān Dīwāna, joined the rebels. Though suffering from want of provisions, Ṭodar Mal held himself bravely, especially as he received timely remittances from Court. After the siege had lasted for some time, Bābā Khān Qāqshāl died, and Jabārī, son of Majnūn Khān Qāqshāl desired to leave. The rebel army dispersed; Maʿṣūm-i Kābulī went to South Bihār, and ʿArab Bahādur wished to surprise Patna, and take possession of the Imperial treasury, which Pahāṛ Khān (perhaps No. 407) had safely lodged in the Fort of that town. After sending Maʿṣūm-i Farankhūdī to Patna, to assist Pahāṛ Khān, Ṭodar Mal, and Ṣādīq Khān followed Maʿṣūm-i Kābulī to Bihār. Maʿṣūm made a fruitless attempt to defeat Ṣādīq Khān in a sudden night attack, but was obliged to retreat, finding a ready asylum with ʿĪṣā Khān, Zamīndār of Oṛīsā. Ṭodar Mal was thus enabled to report to Akbar that South Bihār, as far as Gaṛhī, was re-annexed to the Dihlī empire.

In the 27th year (990) Ṭodar Mal was made Dīvān, or rather *Vakīl*. During this year he introduced his financial reforms which have made him so famous. The third book of the Āʾīn contains his new rent-roll, or *Aṣl-i Jamʿ-i Ṭūmār*, which superseded Muẓaffar's assessment (p. 373). His regulations regarding the coinage have been alluded to above, and others may be found in the Akbarnāma.

The most important reform introduced by Ṭodar Mal is the change in the language and the character used for the revenue accounts. Formerly they had been kept in Hindī by Hindū *Muharrirs*. Ṭodar Mal ordered that all government accounts should henceforth be written in Persian. He thus forced his co-religionists to learn the court language of their rulers—a circumstance which may well compare to the introduction of the English language in the courts of India. The study of Persian therefore became necessary for its pecuniary advantages.

Ṭodar Mal's order, and Akbar's generous policy of allowing Hindūs to compete for the highest honours—we saw on p. 363 that Mān Singh [1] was the first Commander of Seven Thousand—explain two facts, *first*, that before

[[1] Or Mahā Singh ?—P.]

the end of the 18th century the Hindūs had almost become the Persian teachers of the Muhammadans ; *secondly*, that a new dialect could arise in upper India, the *Urdū*, which without the Hindūs as receiving medium, never could have been called into existence. Whether we attach more influence to Ṭodar Mal's order or to Akbar's policy, which once initiated, his successors, willing or not, had to follow, one fact should be borne in mind that before the times of Akbar, the Hindūs, as a rule, did not study Persian, and stood therefore politically below their Muhammadan rulers.

In the 29th year, Akbar honoured him by paying him a visit. In the 32nd year, a Khatrī, from private hatred, wounded Ṭ. M. on a march at night time. The man was at once cut down.

When Bīr Baṛ (No. 85) had been killed in the war with the Yūsufzāʾīs, Ṭ. M. was ordered to accompany Mān Singh, who had been appointed commander-in-chief. In the 34th year, when Akbar went to Kashmīr, Ṭ. M. was left in charge of Lāhor. Soon after, he applied for leave to go to the banks of the Ganges, as he was old and wished to die. Akbar let him go ; but he recalled him from Hardwār, and told him that looking after his duties was more virtuous than sitting on the banks of the Ganges. Ṭ. M. unwillingly returned, but died soon after, on the 11th day of the year 998 (*vide* No. 27, p. 353).

Though often accused of headstrongness and bigotry by contemporaneous historians, Ṭodar Mal's fame, as general and financier, has outlived the deeds of most of Akbar's grandees ; together with Abū 'l-Faẓl and Mān Singh, he is best known to the people of India at the present day.

His son Dhārū (No. 190) was a Commander of Seven Hundred, and was killed during the Sindh expedition, while serving under Khān Khānān (p. 335). People say that he used to shoe his horses with golden shoes.

The name *Ṭoḍaṛ Mal* is often spelt in MSS. with the Hindī *Ṭ*, *ḍ*, and *ṛ*, which explains the spelling " Torel Mall ", which we find in old histories. Under Shāhjahān also there lived a distinguished courtier of the name " Ṭoḍaṛ Mal ".

The *Tafrīḥᵘ 'l-ʿImārat*[1] says Ṭodar Mal's father died when Ṭ. M. was quite young, and that the widow was in great distress. Ṭ. M., at an early

---

[1] This is the title of a Persian MS. preserved in the Library of the Asiatic Society of Bengal. It was composed by Sīl Chand, of the Government College of Āgra, and treats of the antiquities of that town. The book gives many valuable and interesting particulars. In the preface an English gentleman is praised, whose Christian names are James Stephen, but the surname is not legible. The name clearly ends in *gton*, and may be Babington or some other similar name. The style is bombastic, and there is no proper arrangement.

age, showed much clearness and common sense, and received an appointment as writer, from which humble position he rose to the greatest honours.

40. **Muḥammed Qāsim Khān**, of Nīshāpūr.

The *Maᶜāṣir* calls him Qāsim Muḥammad Khān, and has put his name under the letter *Q*; but Abū 'l-Faẓl, Badā,onī, and the *Ṭabaqāt* give his name in the above order.

He was a rich landowner of Nīshāpūr, and fled after the invasion of the Uzbaks to India, where he served under Bayrām Khān. He distinguished himself in the war with Sikandar Sūr, and served as *Harāwal*, or leader of the van, under Khān Zamān (No. 13) in the battle with Hemū. Immediately after, but still in the first year of Akbar's reign, he was sent against Ḥājī Khān, who had defeated Rānā Udai Sing of Maiwār, and taken possession of Nāgor and Ajmīr. Ḥājī Khān was an old servant of Sher Khān, and was distinguished for his wisdom and bravery. On the appearance of the Imperialists, however, Ḥājī Khān's army dispersed, and he himself withdrew to Gujrāt. M. Q. Kh. thus took possession of Nāgor and Ajmīr, which for a long time remained the south-western frontier of Akbar's empire.

In the 5th year, he left Bayrām's party, and joined the Chaghtā,i nobles. He commanded the left wing of Shamsᵘ 'd-Dīn Atga's corps in the fight in which Bayrām was defeated (p. 332). After the victory, he received Multān as jāgīr.

He was next sent to Sārangpūr in Mālwa, where, in the 9th year, he was visited by Akbar on his sudden hunting expedition to that province, the object of which was to get hold of ᶜAbdᵘ 'llah Khān Uzbak (No. 14). M. Q. Kh. assisted in the pursuit.

According to the *Ṭabaqāt*, M. Q. Kh. died soon after at Sārangpūr.

41. **Vazīr Khān**, brother of ᶜAbdᵘ 'l-Majīd-i Āṣaf Khān (I), of Harāt (No. 49).

When Vazīr Khān escaped with his brother (*vide* below, No. 49) from Bahādur Khān (No. 21), he fled to Kaṛa, and obtained subsequently, through the mediation of Muẓaffar Khān (No. 37), free pardon for himself and Āṣaf Khān.

In the 21st year, when ᶜAzīz Koka (p. 344) had incurred Akbar's displeasure, V. Kh. was sent to Gujrāt to govern in ᶜAzīz's name, and when that chief had been called to Court, he was appointed governor (*sipahsālār*) of the province. But he did not distinguish himself, and Akbar, in the 22nd year, sent Ṭoḍar Mal (No. 39) to Gujrāt, to take the administration out of V. Kh.'s hands. It happened that about the same time, Mihr ʿAlī Gulābī, a friend of M. Ibrāhīm Ḥusayn, rebelled and set up as king Muẓaffar Ḥusayn Ibrāhīm's young son, whom he had brought from the Dakhin. As mentioned above, the rebellion was crushed through Ṭoḍar Mal's bravery. When the Rāja left, Mihr ʿAlī appeared again, and V. Kh., most of whose soldiers had joined the rebel, shut himself up in the fort of Aḥmadābād. In one of the assaults, Mihr ʿAlī was killed by a bullet, and Muẓaffar Ḥusayn Mīrzā, from timidity, raised the siege. Notwithstanding this success, matters in Gujrāt did not improve, and oppressions became so numerous, that Akbar deposed V. Kh. and called him to Court.

In the 25th year, Akbar appointed him *vazīr* in the place of Shāh Manṣūr of Shīrāz (No. 122), and soon after governor of Audh.

In the 27th year, when M. ʿAzīz (No. 21) had been sent to Bihār, V. Kh. was ordered to join him with his contingent, and as after the flight of Maʿṣūm Khān sickness obliged ʿAzīz to return to Bihār, he left V. Kh. in charge of the province, till a new Ṣūbadār should be appointed. V. Kh. made use of the opportunity, and moved against Qutlū Khān, ruler of Orīsā, whom he defeated (*vide* p. 383). Qutlū, in the following (29th) year, sent tribute, and was left in possession of Orīsā. V. Kh. returned to Ṭānḍa, and applied himself, with the assistance of Ṣādiq Khān (No. 43) and Shāhbāz Khān-i Kambū (No. 80) to financial matters.

In the 31st year, Akbar ordered that each ṣūba should, in future, be ruled by two Amīrs, and Vazīr Khān was appointed Ṣūbadār of Bengal, with Muḥibb ʿAlī Khān (No. 107) as assistant. In the following year, 995, V. Kh. died.

Shāhbāz Khān, who was Bakhshī of Bengal, allowed Mīrzā Muḥammad Ṣāliḥ, V. Kh.'s son, to take command of his father's contingent. But M. M. Ṣāliḥ showed much inclination to rebel, and Akbar sent Mīr Murād (282, or 380) to bring him and his contingent to Court. On the route, at Fatḥpūr Hanswah, he behaved so rebelliously, that Mīr Murād imprisoned him with the assistance of the jāgīrdārs of the district, and took him fettered to Akbar. He was kept imprisoned for some time.

42. **Qulij Khān.**

He is called *Andajānī*, from Andajān, a province of *Farghāna*, south of the Sayḥūn. His ancestors had been for many years serving under the Tīmūrides. His grandfather was a noble at Sulṭān Ḥusayn Mīrzā Bāyqrā's court.

The principal facts of his life have been mentioned on p. 35, note 2. In mentioning his appointment to Sūrat, the "iron fort", which Akbar, in the 17th year, conquered in one month and seventeen days, Abū 'l-Faẓl says that the Fort had been built in 947 (A.D. 1540–41), by Ṣafar Āg͟hā, *alias* K͟hudāwand K͟hān, a Turkish slave of Sulṭān Maḥmūd of Gujrāt. The *tarīk͟h* of its construction is characteristic (metre *long Ramal*).

سد بود برسینه وجان فرنگی این بنای

"May this structure prove a barrier for the chest and the life of the Firingī." [1]

Qulij K͟hān died at the age of eighty, on the 10th Ramaẓān 1022 (end of A.D. 1613),[2] at Peshāwar. He was at his death a Commander of Six Thousand, Five Thousand horse.

The *Maʿāṣir* and Badā,onī (III. p. 188) say that he belonged to the tribe of جاني قرباني *Jānī Qurbānī* (?) ; but for the latter word the MSS. have different readings, as *Qurbānī Farbānī*, *Faryānī*, etc.

The *Maʿāṣir* copies from the *Zak͟hīratᵘ lk͟hawānīn* the following story which is said to have taken place in A.H. 1000, when Jaunpūr was Q.'s jāgīr. "Q. was building a house, when the working men in digging came to a cupolalike-structure. Q. and several other respectable men were called, and they remained on the spot till the newly discovered building was fully dug out. It had a door with an immense lock attached to it weighing one *man*. When forced open, an old man made his appearance, who asked the bystanders in Sanscrit, whether Rām Chandr's *avatār* (incarnation) had taken place; whether he had got back his Sītā; whether Krishnā's *avatār* had taken place at Mathurā; and, lastly, whether Muḥammad had appeared in Arabia. On receiving affirmative answers to these questions, the old man further wished to know, whether the Ganges still flowed. This also being affirmed, he expressed a wish to be taken out. Q. then put up seven tents, joined to each other, in each of which the sage remained for a day. On the 8th day he came out, and said prayers according to the way of Muhammadans. In sleep and

---

[1] The numbers added give 947. The last *yā*, though somewhat irregular, cannot be left out.

[2] So according to the *Tuzuk-i Jahāngīrī* (ed. Sayyid Ahmad, p. 123, l. 1).

Misled by bad MSS., I mentioned on p. 35, note, the year 1035 as the year of his death. The *Mirʾātu 'l-ʿAlam* and the *Maʿāṣir* give as *tārīk͟h* of his death the Arabic words, *Almawtᵘ-jasrᵘⁿ yuṣilᵘ al-ḥabība ila al-ḥābībⁱ*; "Death is the bridge which joins the beloved to the Beloved;" but the letters added give 1023, not 1022, as in the *Tuzuk*.

For *Ḥusayn* in the last line of the note on p. 35, which is given in inferior MSS., better copies have *Chīn Qulij*, which is to be substituted for it.

His *tak͟hallus* "Ulfatī" has been mentioned above. The *Ṭabaquāt* says that another poet of the same *tak͟hallus* was in the service of Zayn K͟hān Koka (No. 34), and Badā,onī (III, 188, 189) mentions two other poets of the same *tak͟hallus*.

Qulij, properly *qülüj*, means in Turkish *a sword*, and "Qulij K͟hān" is the same as *Shamsher K͟hān*. The word is variously spelled in MSS., sometimes with long vowels and a final *ch*.

eating he differed from other men ; he spoke to no one, and died after six months."

Qulij Khān's sons. 1. Mīrzā Sayf[u] 'llah (No. 292). 2. Mīrzā Chīn Qulij (No. 293), regarding whom *vide* below.

43. **Ṣādiq Khān**, son of Bāqir of Harāt.

Other historians call him Ṣādiq Muḥammad Khān.[1] His father, Muḥammad Bāqir, had been *vazīr* to Qarā Khān Turkmān, ruler of Khurāsān. Qarā had rebelled against Shāh Ṭadmāsp, and fled to India. Ṣādiq entered Bayrām's service as *Rikābdār* (spur-holder),[2] and got soon after a *manṣab*, and was made, after Bayrām's death, an Amīr. *Badā,onī* (II, 220) alludes to his services under Humāyūn in Qandahār, and the *Ṭabaqāt* says that he had been since his youth in Akbar's service.

After the conquest of Patna, Akbar returned by boat to Jaunpūr. On the road, in crossing the river at Chausā, a valuable elephant perished through Ṣ.'s carelessness. Akbar confiscated his jāgīr, excluded him from Court, and told him to go to Bhath (Bhath Ghorā, or Banda-Rewa), to get another elephant. After passing over "the heights and the low places" of fortune, Ṣādiq, in the 20th year, returned to Court with 100 elephants, and was restored to favour. He was made governor of *Garha, vice* Rāi Sarjan (No. 96). In the 22nd year (985), Ṣ., with several other grandees, was ordered to punish Rāja Madhukar, should he not submit peacefully. Passing the confines of Narwar, Ṣ. saw that kindness would not do ; he therefore took the fort of Karharā (کرهرا), and cutting down the jungle, advanced to the river Dasthārā, close to which Ūndchha lay, Madhukar's residence. A fight ensued. Madhukar was wounded and fled with his son Rām Sāh. Another son of his, Horal Deo (*Ma'āṣir*, Horal Rāo), and about 200 Rājpūts were killed. Ṣ. remained encamped in the Rāja's territory. Driven to extremities, Madhukar sent Rām Chand (No. 248), a relation of his, to Akbar at Bahīra, and asked and obtained pardon. On the 3rd Ramaẓān, 986, Ṣādiq with the penitent Rāja arrived at Court.

Soon after Ṣ.'s *aqṭā*ʿ were transferred to the Eastern Districts of the empire, so that he might take part in the suppression of the revolt in Bengal. In the 27th year, during the temporary absence of ʿAzīz Koka

---

[1] Akbar disliked the names *Muḥammad* and *Aḥmad* ; hence we find that Abū' l-Faẓl leaves them out in this list. Similar omissions occurred above, as Munʿim Khān (No. 11), Mīrzā ʿAzīz (No. 21), for Muḥammad Munʿim and M. Muhammad ʿAzīz ; or, Shihāb Khān (No. 26), for Shihāb[u]'d-Dīn Aḥmad Khān. More examples will be found below.

[[2] *Rikābdar* "stirrup-holder, one that runs at the stirrup of a great man, retinue." The pointed corner of the plate that forms the foot-rest of the Indian stirrup is used as a spur.—P.]

(No. 21), Ṣādiq and Muḥibb ʿAlī Khān (No. 107), defeated Khabīṭa,[1] one of Maʿṣum's officers, on the Ghanḍak near Ḥājīpūr, and sent his head to Akbar. In the beginning of the 28th year, he paid his respects at Court, but was immediately ordered to rejoin Mīrzā Koka, who had again left for Bihār.

In the beginning of the 29th year, he was ordered to move to Vazīr Khān (No. 41), who at a place six *kos* from Bardwān was treating with Qutlū.[2] Through Ṣ.'s skill, a sort of peace was concluded, which confirmed Qutlū in the possession of Orīsā. Ṣ. then returned to his *tuyūl* at Patna.

When Shāhbāz Khān (No. 80) returned from his expedition to Bhāṭī, the *tuyūldārs* of Bengal and Bihār were ordered to move to him. Ṣ., however, was no friend of Shāhbāz. The mutual dislike rose to the highest pitch, when once Ṣ.'s elephant ran against Shāhbāz, who believed the accident premeditated: and Akbar sent Khwāja Sulaymān (No. 327) to Bengal to settle their differences. One was to remain in Bengal, the other to go to Bihār; but Ṣ., in the 30th year, left Bengal without permission, and went to Court, where he was not admitted. But when Shāhbāz went from Bihār to Bengal, Ṣ. went again to Court, and was appointed governor of Multān.

When the Rawshānīs in the District of Mount Terāh (تیراه), "which lies west of Pashāwar, and is 32 *kos* long, and 12 *kos* broad," commenced disturbances, Ṣ., in the 33rd year, was ordered to bring them to obedience, which he did with much tact and firmness. After the return of Zayn Khān (No. 34) from Bijor, Ṣ. was sent there, to subjugate the Yūsafzā,īs.

In the 36th year, Prince Murād was sent from Mālwa to Gūjrāt, and as Ismāʿīl Qulī Khān (No. 46) had not given satisfaction as *Vakīl*, Ṣ. was appointed *atālīq* to the Prince,[3] whom in the 40th year he accompanied to the Dakhin. Shāhbāz Khān, being one of the auxiliaries, the old enmity broke out again. After the siege of Aḥmadnagar had been raised, Ṣ. distinguished himself in protecting the frontiers of Barār.

In the beginning of the 41st year he was made a Commander of Five Thousand. In the same year he defeated Sarāwar Khān, and made much

[1] Khabīṭa (خبیطه) was a Mughul, and had risen by bravery under Maʿṣum-i Kābulī from a humble position to the post of a Commander. In *Badā,oni* (Ed. Bibl. Indica, p. 310), he is called Khabīṣa Bahādur (خبیثه) and *Khasta* (خسته) in my MS. of the *Ṭabaqāt*, where, moreover, the event, according to the erroneous chronology of that history, is put in the 28th year.

[2] The spelling *Qutlū* is perhaps preferable to *Qatlū* if this name is a shortened form of Qutlugh.

[3] From several passages in the *Akbarnāma* it is clear that *atālīq* (*pr.* a tutor) means the same as *Vakīl* or *Vazir*. The imperial princes kept up Courts of their own, and appointed their *Vazīrs*, their *Dīvāns*, *Bākhshīs*, etc. The appointment of the *Vakīl*, however, appears to have rested with the emperor.

booty. He was then made governor of Shāhpūr, which town Prince Murād had founded six *kos* from Bālāpūr.

Ṣādiq died at Shāhpūr in the beginning of 1005. At Dholpūr, which "lies 20 *kos* from Agra, near the left bank on the Chambal river," Ṣ. had erected splendid buildings and a mausoleum. He had also done much for the cultivation of the surrounding country.

He was one of the best officers Akbar had.

His sons. 1. Zāhid Khān (No. 286), a Commander of Three Hundred and Fifty. In the 47th year, he was made a *Khān*, and, on the accession of Jahāngīr, a Commander of Two Thousand.

2. Dost Muḥammad (No. 287). 3. Yār Muḥammad (No. 288). "Neither of them was alive at the time of Shāhjahān." *Maʿāṣir.*

44. **Rāy Rāysingh,** son of Rāy Kalyān Mal (No. 93).

Rāy Singh belonged to the Rāṭhors of Bīkānīr, and is the fourth descendant from Rāy Māldeo. His father, Kalyān Mal, was a friend of Bayrām (p. 316), and paid, in the 15th year, his respects to Akbar at Ajmīr, when he together with his son entered the emperor's service. He also sent his brother's daughter to Akbar's harem. Kalyān Mal was in the 40th year a Commander of Two Thousand.

Rāy Singh, in the 17th year, when Akbar made preparations to crush the rebellion in Gujrāt, occupied Jodhpūr, the old seat of Māl Deo, in order to prevent the rebels from invading the Dihlī territory; but Ibrāhīm, after his defeat at Sarnāl, invaded Akbar's territory, and besieged Nāgor, which at that time was the *tuyūl* of Khān-i Kalān (No. 16), and was defended by his son, Farrukh Khān (p. 339). R. came to his relief, and the Mīrzā had not only to raise the siege, but was pursued and defeated by R. In the following year also, R. distinguished himself in the engagement with Muḥammad Ḥusayn Mīrzā (p. 343).

In the 19th year, R. and Shāh Qulī Maḥram (No. 45) were ordered to punish Chandr Sen, son of Rāja Māl Deo; but as they were unable to take Siwāna, Chandr Sen's stronghold, notwithstanding the auxiliaries which Akbar had sent them at R.'s request, R., in the 21st year, was called to Court, and Shāhbāz Khān (No. 80) took the command. Before the end of the same year, however, R. and Tarson Muḥammad Khān (No. 32) were sent against the refractory zamīndārs of Jālor and Sarohī; but as they applied to Akbar for pardon, R. and Sayyid Hāshim of Bārha (No. 143) garrisoned Nādot to watch the Rānā of Udaipūr, and bring the rebels of those districts to obedience. As at this time Saltān Deoda, the zamīndār of Sarohī, from distrust again assumed a hostile attitude, R. marched against Sarohī and besieged it. During the siege,

R. called his family to his camp; but Saltān Deoda fell upon the caravan, killed several relations of R., and then withdrew to Abūgaṛh.[1] R. in the meantime took Sarohī, and hastened to Abūgaṛh, which Saltān surrendered. R. left a garrison there, and took Saltān to Court.

In the 26th year, when Mīrzā Muḥammad Ḥakīm, Akbar's brother, threatened to invade the Panjāb, R. together with several other grandees was sent in advance. They were soon followed by Prince Murād. When the imperial army, in the end of the same year, returned to Āgra, R. and several others were sent as *tuyūldārs* to the Panjāb. In the 28th year he served in Bengal.

In the 30th year R. and Ismāʿīl Qulī Khān (*vide* No. 46) led successfully an expedition against the Balūchīs. In the following year (19th Rajab, 994), R.'s daughter was married to Prince Salīm. In the 35th year he went for some time to Bīkānīr, and served, in the end of the 36th year, in Sindh under M. ʿAbdu r-Raḥīm (No. 29).

In the 38th year Akbar paid R. a visit of condolence. The son of Rāja Rāmchand Baghela of Bāndhū died suddenly on his way to Bāndhū, to which he had only lately, after the death of his father, been appointed. The young Rāja had married a daughter of R. Akbar interceded for their young children, and prevented R.'s daughter from burning herself. Soon after, R. stayed away from Court for some reason, during which time one of his servants complained of him to Akbar. The emperor called the man to Court; but R. concealed him, and gave out he had run away. Akbar was annoyed, and excluded R. for some time from the darbārs; but after some time he restored him and sent him as governor to Sūrat, with the order to assist in the Dakhin wars. R., however, delayed in Bīkānīr, and when he had at last left, delayed on the road to Sūrat. Akbar advised him to be obedient; but seeing that he would not go, called him to Court, but without allowing him to attend the darbārs. After some time he was pardoned.

In the 45th year, R. was ordered to accompany Abū 'l-Faẓl to Nāsik; but as his son Dalpat[2] (No. 252) had caused disturbances in Bīkānīr

---

[1] "Abūgaṛh is a fort near Sarohī, and not far from the frontier between Gujrāt and Ajmīr." Abū 'l-Faẓl says in the Akbarnāma (events of the 21st year) that the old name of Abūgaṛh was *Arbudā Achal, Arbudā* being the name of a spirit, who, disguised as a female, shows wanderers the way, and *achal* meaning *mountain*. The fort on the top of this high mountain was difficult of access; it could, moreover, hold out for a long time, as there were several springs and fields within it. My copies of the *Sawāniḥ* and the *Akbarnāma* have *Sulṭān Deora* (سلطان ديوره) for Saltān Deoda (سلطان ديوده) of the *Maʿāṣir*.

[2] For *Dalpat*, the *Tuzuk-i Jahāngīrī* (pp. 36, 106, and 126) has wrongly *Dalīp*.

The *Tuzuk* and the *second* volume of the *Pādishāhnāma* (Edit. Bibl. Indica, p. 635) have *Sūraj* Singh, for Sūr Singh. But the *Maʿāṣir* and the *first* volume of the *Pādishāhnāma* have *Sūr* Singh (pp. 297, 302, at the end of the first *decade*.)

(*vide* p. 386), R. got leave to go home. In the following year, he went again to Court. In the 48th year he served under Prince Salīm against the Rānā of Udaipūr.

At the death of the emperor, R. was a Commander of Four Thousand. Jahāngīr, on his accession, made him a Commander of Five Thousand. When the emperor set out for the Panjāb to pursue Khusraw, R. was put in charge of the travelling harem; but on the road he left without order and went to Bīkānīr. In the second year, when Jahāngīr returned from Kābul, R., at the advice of Sharīf Khān, presented himself before the emperor with a *fūṭa* round his neck, to show his willingness to suffer punishment for his crimes, and was again pardoned. He died in 1021.

His sons. 1. *Dalpat* (No. 252). He was a Commander of Five Hundred. In the 36th year, he served in the Sindh war, but was looked upon as a coward. In the 45th year, when Akbar was in the Dakhin, Muẓaffar Ḥusayn Mīrẓā, in consequence of his differences with Khwājagī Fath[u] 'llah had fled; and Dalpat, under the pretext of following him up, had gone to Bīkānīr and created disturbances. In the 46th year, his father brought him to his senses. D. asked to be pardoned, and was ordered again to come to Court.

In the third year of Jahāngīr's reign (1017), he appears to have offended the emperor; but at the request of Khān Jahān Lodī he was pardoned. After the death of his father, D. came from the Dakhin to Court, was appointed successor, and got the title of *Rāy*, although his younger brother (by another mother), Sūr Singh, claimed the right of succession, which Rāy Singh had promised him from affection to his mother. Sūr Singh, however, disgusted Jahāngīr by the bold way in which he preferred his claim.

D. was then ordered to join M. Rustam-i Ṣafawī (No. 8), the governor of Sindh. In the 8th year, it was reported to Jahāngīr that Sūr Singh had attacked and defeated his brother, who in consequence had created disturbances in Ḥiṣār. Hāshim, the Fawjdār of the Sarkār, caught him and sent him fettered to court, where he was executed as a warning to others.

For Dalpat's son, Mahes Dās, and grandson, Ratan, *vide* Pādishāhnāma, pp. 635, 723; 684, 729.

2. *Sūr Singh.* After the death of his brother he rose to favour. In Histories he is generally called *Rāo* Sūr Singh, a title which he received from Shāhjahān. He died in 1040. He had two sons, Karan and Satr Sāl, the former of whom inherited the title of *Rāo* (*vide* Pādishāhnāma II, p. 727).

VII. Commanders of Three Thousand Five Hundred.

45. **Shāh Qulī Maḥram-i** Bahārlū.

He was in Bayrām's service, and distinguished himself in the war with Hemū. It was Shāh Qulī that attacked Hemū's elephant, though he did not know who his opponent was. The driver, however, made him a sign, and he led the elephant with Hemū, whose eye had been pierced by an arrow, from the battle-field, and brought the wounded commander to Akbar.[1] Soon after, before the end of the first year, Sh. Q. served with Muḥammad Qāsim Khān (No. 40) against Ḥājī Khān in Nāgor and Ajmīr.

In the third year, it was brought to Akbar's notice, that Sh. Q. was passionately attached to a dancing boy of the name of Qabūl Khān; and as the emperor had the boy forcibly removed,[2] Sh. Q. dressed as a Jogī, and went into the forests. Bayrām traced him with much trouble, and brought him back to court, where the boy was restored to him.

Like Bābā Zambūr, he remained faithful to Bayrām to the last, and was pardoned together with his master in Tilwāra (p. 332).

After Bayrām's death, he was rapidly promoted and made an Amīr. In the 20th year, when Khān Jahān (No. 24) was sent from the Panjāb to Bengal, Sh. Q. was appointed Governor of the Panjāb, rising higher and higher in Akbar's favour.

It is said that the Emperor, from goodwill towards him, admitted him to his female apartments. After the first time he had been allowed to enter the Harem, he went home, and had his testicles removed (*majbūb*). From the circumstances, he was everywhere called *Maḥram*,[3] i.e., one who is admitted to the Harem and knows its secrets.

In the 34th year, Akbar, after his return from Zābulistān, crossed the Bahat (Jhelum) near Rasūlpūr, and encamped at Hailān. During his stay there, he mounted a female elephant, and was immediately attacked by a *mast* male elephant. Akbar was thrown down and sustained severe contusions. A rumour of his death spread over the whole country; in some provinces even disturbances broke out. The Rājpūts of Shaykhāwat, especially, plundered the districts from Mewāt to Rewārī; and in the

[1] " Before the end of the first year, Pīr Muḥammad was dispatched against Ḥājī Khān in Alwar, and as he withdrew, the imperialists took possession of the Sarkār of Alwar as far as Deolī Sājārī [or *Sāchārī*], the birth-place of Hemū, and performed many brave deeds. They also caught Hemū's father alive, and brought him to Pīr Muḥammad, who asked him to embrace Islām. As he would not, he was killed by him. After gathering his spoils, Pīr M. returned to Akbar." *Sawāniḥ from the Akbarnāma.*

[2] For similar examples, *vide* p. 335, which also happened in the third year, and No. 37, p. 374.

[3] Or *Muḥrim.*

35th year, Akbar had to send Sh. Q. against them. He soon restored order.

In the 41st year, he was made a commander of Four Thousand, and soon after of Five Thousand. The *Ṭabaqāt* says that in 1001 he had been a commander of Three Thousand for thirty years.

He died at Āgra in 1010. At Nārnaul, where he chiefly lived, he erected splendid buildings, and dug large tanks. When he felt death approaching, he gave the soldiers of his contingent two years' pay in advance, and left, besides, many legacies. As he had no heirs, his remaining property lapsed to the state (*Tuzuk*, p. 22).

46. **Ismāʿīl Qulī K͟hān**, brother of K͟hān Jahān (No. 24).

He must not be confounded with No. 72. He was caught in the battle near Jālindhar (p. 317). He joined Akbar's service with his brother, under whom he mostly served. When his brother had died in Bengal, he came with the immense property he had left behind him to Court, and was favourably received. In the 30th year, he was sent against the Balūchīs (*vide* No. 44). On his arrival in Balūchistān the people soon submitted, and their chiefs, G͟hāzī K͟hān Wajhiya and Ibrāhīm K͟hān, repaired to Court, and were allowed to retain the country. In the 31st year, when Bhagwān Dās (No. 27), on account of his madness, had not been allowed to go to Zābulistān, I. Q. was sent there instead. But he committed certain improprieties and fell into disgrace, and was ordered to go from Bhakkar to Makkah. He begged hard to be forgiven; but he was not allowed to see the Emperor, and was sent against the Yūsufzāʾīs.

At that time epidemics were raging in Bijor, and the chiefs of the Yūsufzāʾīs came forward and submitted to I. Q., whilst Zayn K͟hān (No. 34), governor of Zābulistān pressed hard upon Jalāla Rawshānī, who had left Terāh and entered Bijor. Zayn K͟hān therefore entered the district, determined to use the opportunity to wipe off the disgrace of his former defeat. The arrival of Ṣādiq K͟hān (No. 43), however, who had been sent from Court, to occupy the district, and capture Jalāla, annoyed I. Q. still more, as he thought that that duty might have been left to him as Ṭhānadār of the district. I. Q. forgot himself so far as to allow Jalāla to escape. He then went to Court, where he was severely reprimanded for his conduct.

In the 33rd year, he was made Governor of Gujrāt. In the 36th year, when Prince Murād had been made Governor of Mālwa, I. Q. was appointed his *atālīq* or Vakīl; but he gave no satisfaction, and was called to Court, Ṣādiq K͟hān having been appointed in his stead.

In the 39th year, he was sent to Kālpī, to look after his jāgīr. In the 42nd year (1005), he was made a Commander of Four Thousand.

He was given to luxury, and spent large sums on carpets, vessels, dress, etc. He kept 1,200 women, and was so jealous of them, that whenever he went to Court, he put his seal over the strings attached to their night drawers. The women resented this and other annoyances, made a conspiracy, and poisoned him.

Three sons of his are mentioned below—1. Ibrāhīm Qulī (No. 322), a commander of Three Hundred: 2. Salīm Qulī (No. 357), and 3, K͟halīl Qulī (No. 358), both commanders of Two Hundred. They do not appear to have distinguished themselves.

VII. Commanders of Three Thousand.

47. **Mīrzā Jānī Beg**, ruler of Thatha.

He belonged to the *Arg͟hūn* clan, and therefore traced his descent to Chingīz Khān. Abū'l-Faẓl in the Akbarnāma gives his tree as follows:—

Chingīz K͟hān
|
Tūlī K͟hān.
|
Hulāgū K͟hān (the brother of Mangū Qāān)
|
Abāg͟h (or, Abāg͟hā) K͟hān, [*d.* 663
|
Arghūn K͟hān, *d.* 690.
|
Four generations intervening
|
Atkū Tīmūr
|
Shankal Beg Tarkhān
|
Several generations not known.
|
ʿAbd^{u} 'l-K͟hāliq Tark͟hān
|
Mīrzā ʿAbd^{u} 'l-ʿAlī Tark͟hān
|

Of his ancestors Atkū Tīmūr had been killed in the war with Tuqtamish K͟hān, and the Emperor Tīmūr took care of Shankal Beg, and made him a *Tark͟hān* (*vide* the note at the end of this biography).

Mīrzā ʿAbd^{u}'l ʿAlī, fourth ancestor of M. Jānī Beg, had risen to high dignities under Sulṭān Maḥmūd, son of M. Abū Saʿīd, and received the government of Buk͟hārā. He was treacherously killed, together with his five eldest sons, by Shaybānī K͟hān Uzbak; only his sixth son, M. Muḥammad ʿIsā escaped. The Arg͟hūn clan in Buk͟hārā, being thus left without a head, emigrated to K͟hurāsān, where they attached themselves to Mīr Ẕū 'l-Nūn Beg Arg͟hūn, who was the Amīr^{u} 'l-Umarā and Sipahsālar of Sulṭan Husain Myrzā. He also was *atālīq* and father-in-law to Prince Badīʿ^{u} 'z-Zamān Mīrzā, and held Qandahār as jāgīr. When the prince's career ended, his two sons, Badīʿu 'z-Zamān and Muẓaffar Mīrzā, proclaimed themselves kings of Khurāsān. Anarchy prevailed ; and matters grew worse, when Shaybān Khān invaded the country. Zu 'l-Nūn Beg fell in battle against him.

M. Muḥammad ʿI'ṣā [Tarkhān, *d.* 975.
|
M. Muḥammad Bāqī [Tarkhān, *d.* 993.
|
Mīrzā Pāyanda Muḥammad Tarkhān.
|
Mīrzā Jānī Beg Tarkhān.
|
Mīrzā Ghāzī Beg Tarkhān.

Shujāʿ Beg, better known as Shāh Beg, Zū 'l-Nūn's son, held Qandahār during the absence of his father, and succeeded him in the government. He was bent on conquest. In 890, he took Fort Sewe from Jām Niẓāmu 'd-Dīn (generally called in Histories *Jām Nandā*), king of Sindh. He continued to interfere, as related by Abū 'l-Faẓl below in the Third Book, (Ṣūba of Sindh), and managed, at last, in 929, to conquer the country, thus compensating himself for the loss of Qandahār, which had been occupied by Bābar. A short time before his death, which took place in 930,[1] he invaded Multān, then in the hands of the *Langāhs*.

Shāh Beg Arghūn was succeeded by his son Mīrzā Shāh Ḥusayn Arghūn, who took Multān from Sulṭān Ḥusayn Langāh (*vide* Third Book, Ṣūba of Multān). M. Shāh Ḥusayn Arghūn was afflicted with a peculiar fever, which only left him when he was on the river Indus. He therefore used to travel down the Indus for six months of the year, and upwards for the remaining portion. On one occasion, he went towards Bhakkar, when some of the nobles deserted him, and elected Mīrzā Muḥammad ʿIsa, third ancestor of M. Jānī Beg, as their chief. M. Shāh Ḥusayn, assisted by his foster brother, Sulṭān Maḥamūd, Governor of Bhakhar, opposed him; but he had at last to come to terms, and ceded a large part of Sindh to M. ʿIsa. On Shāh Ḥusayn's death, in 963, the whole country fell to ʿIsa.

In this manner the older branch of the Arghūns came to the throne of Thatha.

ʿIsa died in 975, and was succeeded by his son M. Muḥammad Bāqī, who successfully crushed the revolt of his younger brother, M. Jān Bābā. M. Bāqī, in 993, committed suicide during an attack of insanity ; and as his son, M. Pāyanda Muḥammad, was also subject to fits of madness, the government passed into the hands of M. Jānī Beg, the son of M. Pāyanda.

---

[1] Shāh Begwas a learned man, like his renowned opponent Bābar. He wrote a Commentary to the well-known Arabic grammar *Kāfiya* (شرح کافیه), and commentaries to the *Maṭāliʿ* (شرح مطالع) and the ʿAqāʾid-i Nasafī (شرح عقاید نسفي).

Akbar had often felt annoyed that, notwithstanding his frequent stays in the Panjāb, M. Jānī Beg had shown no anxiety to pay him a visit. In the 35th year therefore (999), when the Khān Khānān was ordered to invade Qandahār, he was told to send some one to M. J. B., and draw his attention to this neglect; if no heed was paid, he was to invade Sindh on his return. Multān and Bhakkar being the *tuyūl* of the Khān Khānān, he did not move into Qandahār by way of Ghaznīn and Bangash, but chose a round-about way through his jāgīr. In the meantime the conquest of Thatha had been determined upon at Court, and the Khān Khānān set out at once for Sindh (*vide* p. 356, and Brigg's *Firishta*). After bravely defending the country, M. J. B. had at last to yield. In the 38th year (1001), accompanied by the Khān Khānān, he paid his respects to Akbar at Lāhor, was made a Commander of Three Thousand, and received the Ṣūba of Multān as *tuyūl*, Sindh itself being assigned to M. Shāhrukh (No. 7). But before this arrangement was carried out, a report reached Akbar that the Arghūn clan, about 10,000 men, women, and children, moved up the river, to follow M. J. B. to his new *tuyūl*, and that great distress had thereby been caused both among the emigrants and those who were left behind. Akbar felt that under such circumstances policy should yield to mercy, and M. J. B. was appointed to Sindh. Lāharī Bandar, however, became *khāliṣa*, and the Sarkār of Siwistān which had formerly paid *pīshkash*, was parcelled out among several grandees.

In the 42nd year, M. J. B. was promoted to a command of Three Thousand and Five Hundred. He was much liked by Akbar for his character, religious views (*vide* p. 218–9), pleasing manners, and practical wisdom. It is perhaps for this reason that Abū 'l-Faẓl has placed him first among the Commanders of Three Thousand, though names much more renowned follow. From his youth, M. J. B. had been fond of wine, but had not indulged in excesses; his habitual drinking, however, undermined his health, and brought on delirium (*sarsām*), of which he died, in 1008, at Burhānpūr in the Dakhin, after the conquest of Āsīr.

A short time before his death, he offended Akbar by declaring that had he had an Āsīr, he would have held it for a hundred years.

M. J. B. was fond of poetry; he was himself a poet and wrote under the *takhalluṣ* of *Halīmī*.[1]

---

[1] Here follows in the *Maʿāṣiru 'l-Umarā*, a description of Sindh taken from the Third Book of the Āʾīn, concluding with the following remark:—

"At present (when the author of the *Maʿāṣir* wrote), the whole of Sindh is under Khudā Yār Khān Latī (لتی). From a long time he had farmed (*ijāra kard*) the Ṣūba of Thathah, and the Sarkars of Siwistān and Bhakkar. Subsequently when the district on the other side of the Indus were ceded to Nādir Shāh, Khudā Yār Khān administered them for Nādir Shāh."

Mīrzā Ghāzī Beg, son of M. Jānī Beg. At the death of his father, he was only 17 years old; and though not at Court, Akbar conferred Sindh on him. He was opposed by Mīrzā ʕĪsạ Tarkhān, son of Mīrzā Jān Bābā (brother of M. Muḥammad Bāqī, grandfather of M. Jānu Beg); but Khusraw Khān Chirgis, an old servant of the Arghūns and *Vakīl* to his father, espoused his cause, and M. ʕĪsạ Tarkhān fled from Sindh. The army which M. Ghāzī Beg and Khusraw Khān had at their disposal, seems to have made them inclined to rebel against Akbar; but the Emperor sent promptly Saʕīd Khān (No. 25) and his son Saʕdu 'llāh[1] to Bhakkar, and M. Ghāzī Beg came to Court, and was confirmed in the government of Sindh.

After the accession of Jahāngīr, M. Ghāzī Beg received Multān in addition to Sindh, was made a Commander of Seven Thousand, and was sent to relieve Qandahār (*Tuzuk*, pp. 33, 72, 109), which had been besieged by Ḥusayn Khān Shāmlū, the Persian Governor of Harāt. He also received the title of *Farzand* (son). Shāh ʕAbbās of Persia often tried to win him over, and sent him several *khiʕlats*.

He died suddenly at the age of twenty-five in 1018,[2] the word *Ghāzī* being the *Tārīkh* of his death. Suspicion attaches to Luṭfu 'llah, his *Vakīl* and son of Khusraw Khān Chirgis, who appears to have been treated unkindly. M. Ghāzī does not appear to have had children.

Like his father, he was a poet. He wrote under the *takhalluṣ* of *Vaqārī*, which he had bought of a Qandahār poet. He played nearly every instrument. Poets like Ṭālibī of Āmul, Mullā Murshid-i Yazdjirdī, Mīr Niʕmatu 'llāh Vacili, Mullā Asad Qiṣṣa-khwān, and especially Fughfūrī of Gīlān enjoyed his liberality. The last left him, because his verses were too often used for *dakhl* (*vide* p. 108, note 8). In his private life, M. Ghāzī was dissolute. Not only was he given to wine, but he required every night a virgin; girls from all places were brought to him, and the

---

[1] Saʕdu 'llāh has been omitted to be mentioned on p. 351. He received the title of *Nawāzish Khān* in 1020; *vide Tuzuk*, pp. 34, 96.

[2] So the *Maʕāṣir*. The *Tuzuk* (p. 109), perhaps more correctly, places the death of M. Ghāzī in the 7th year of Jahāngīr's reign, 1021.

After M. Ghāzī Beg's death, Sindh was taken away from the Tarkhāns, and M. Rustam was appointed Governor (*vide* p. 314).

Khusraw Chirgis tried to set up some ʕAbdu 'l-ʕAlī Tarkhan, whose pedigree is not known; but Jahāngīr bestowed his favours on Mīrzā ʕĪsạ Tarkhān, son of M. Jān Bābā (uncle of M. Jānī Beg). He rose to the highest honours under Shāhjahān, and died more than a hundred years old, in 1062, at Sāmbhar. He had *four* sons—1. Mīrzā ʕInāyatu, who died in the 21st year of Shāhjahān; 2. Mīrzā Muḥammad Ṣālih, who played some part during Awrangzeb's war with Dārā Shikoh; 3. Fatḥu 'llāh, 4. M. ʕĀqil. Mīrzā Bihrūz, M. Muḥammad Ṣaliḥ's son, is mentioned as a Commander of Five Hundred under Shāhjahān.

women of the town of Thatha are said to have been so debauched, that every bad woman, even long after his death, claimed relationship with the Mīrzā.

Note on the meaning of the title of "Tarkhān".

Abū 'l-Fazl, in the Akbarnāma (38th year) has a valuable note regarding the meaning and the history of this ancient title. The title was hereditary, and but rarely given. Chingīz Khān conferred it on Qishliq and Bātā for having given him correct information regarding the enemy. The title in this case, as in all others, implied that the holder was excused certain feudal services, chiefly attendance at Court *taklīf-i bār*).[1] Chingīz Khān, moreover, did not take away from the two nobles the royal share of the plunder. Under Tīmūr, a Tarkhān had free access to every place of the palace, and could not be stopped by the macebearers; nor was he or his children liable to be punished for any crime, provided the number of his or their crimes did not exceed the number *nine*.[2]

Some say, a Tarkhān had *seven* distinctions and privileges—1. a *tabl*; 2, a *tūmāntogh*; 3, a *naqqāra*; 4, he can confer on two of his men a *qushūn togh*, or *chatr togh*;[3] 5, his *Qur* (p. 116) was carried (*qūr-i ū nīz bardārand*). Among the Mughuls no one but the king was allowed to use a quiver. 6. He could enclose (*qurq*) a forest as his private hunting ground, and if any one entered the enclosure, he forfeited his personal liberty. 7. He was looked upon as the head of the clan to which he belonged. In the state hall the Amīrs sat behind him to his right and left arranged in form of a bow (*kamānwār*).

When Tughluq Tīmūr conferred this title upon an Amīr,[4] he put all financial matters (*dād o sitad*) as far as a Hazārī (?) in his charge; nor were his descendants, to the ninth generation, liable to be called to account; but should their crimes exceed the number nine, they were to be called to account. When a Tarkhān had to answer for blood shed by him (*pādāsh-i khūn*), he was placed on a silver-white horse two years old, and a white cloth was put below the feet of the animal. His statement was made by a chief of the Barlās clan (*vide* p. 364 note), and the

[[1] *Taklīf* duty.—P.]

[2] *Nine* was looked upon as an important number by the Mughuls. Thus kings received *nine* presents, or the present consisted of *nine* pieces of the same article. Hence also the Chaghtāʿī *tuquz* (or *tūqūz* or *tuqūz*), nine came to mean *a present*, in which sense it occurs in the *Pādishāhnāma* and the *ʿAlamgīr-nama*, especially in reference to presents of stuffs, as *haft tuquz pārcha*, "a present of seven pieces of cloth."

[3] *Vide* p. 52.

[4] The MSS. call him لولاخی or یولاجی, with every variety of diacritical points.

sentence was communicated to him by a chief of the Arkīwat (ارکیوت) clan. His neck vein was then opened, the two chiefs remaining at his side, and watching over him till he was dead. The king was then led forth from the palace, and sat down to mourn over him.

Khizr Khwāja in making Mīr Khudādād a *Tarkhān*, added three new privileges. 1. At the time of wedding feasts (*tūī*), when all grandees have to walk on foot, and only the *yasāwal* (chief mace-bearer) of the king on horseback to keep back the crowds, the *Tarkhān* also proceeds on horseback. 2. When during the feast the cup is handed to the king from the right side, another cup is at the same time handed to the Tarkhān from the left. 3. The Tarkhān's seal is put on all orders; but the seal of the king is put to the beginning of the last line and below his.

Abū 'l-Faẓl, in concluding these remarks, says that these distinctions are extraordinary enough; he believes it possible that a king may grant a virtuous man immunity for nine crimes; but he thinks it absurd to extend the immunity to nine generations.

48. **Iskandar Khān**, a descendant of the Uzbak Kings.

He distinguished himself under Humāyūn, who on his return to India made him a *Khān*. After the restoration, he was made Governor of Āgra. On Hemū's approach, he left Āgra, and joined Tardī Beg at Dihlī. Both opposed Hemū, Iskandar commanding the left wing (*jūranghār*). His wing defeated the right wing (*burunghār*) and the van (*harāwal*) of Hemū, and hotly pursued them, killing many fugitives. The battle was almost decided in favour of the Imperialists, when Hemū with his whole force broke upon Tardī Beg, and put him to flight. The victorious Iskandar was thus obliged to return. He afterwards joined Akbar at Sarhind, fought under Khān Zamān (No. 13) against Hemū, and received after the battle for his bravery, the title of *Khān ʿĀlam*.

As Khizr Khwāja Khān,[1] the Governor of the Panjāb, had retreated

---

[1] Khizr had descended from the kings of Mūghulistān; but according to the *Tabaqāt* from the kings of *Kāshghar*. He was a grandee of Humāyūn, left him on his flight to Persia, and was with M. ʿAskarī in Qandahār, when Humāyūn on his return besieged that town. Before the town surrendered, Khizr Khwāja threw himself down from the wall, managed to reach Humāyūn's tent, and implored forgiveness. He was restored to favour, was made *Amīr*ᵘ *'l-Umarā*, and married Gulbadan Begam, H.'s sister. When Akbar marched against Hemū. Khizr Khān was made Governor of the Pānjāb and ordered to operate against Sikandar. Sūr, who during Humāyūn's lifetime had retreated to the Sawāliks. Leaving Ḥājī Khān Sīstānī in Lāhor, Khizr Khān moved against Sikandar, whom he met near a place called in the MSS. جمیاری. Kh. selected two thousand horsemen to reconnoitre; but Sikandar was on the alert, fell upon the detachment, and defeated the Imperialists. Kh. without further fighting retreated to Lāhor. Sikandar used the respite, and collected a large army, till Akbar himself had to move against him. Finding Akbar's army too strong, Sikandar shut himself up in Mānkot. After a siege of six months, Sikandar bribed Shams[u] 'd-Dīn Atgah (No. 15) and Pīr Muḥammad (No. 20) who prevailed

before Sikandar Khān Sūr, and fortified himself in Lāhor, leaving the country to the Afghāns, Akbar appointed Iskandar to move to Siyālkoṭ and assist Khizr Khwāja.

Afterwards he received Audh as *tuyūl.* "From want of occupation," he rebelled in the tenth year. Akbar ordered Ashraf Khān (No. 74) to bring him to Court but Isk. joined Khān Zamān (No. 13). Together with Bahādur Khān (No. 22), he occupied Khāyrābād (Audh), and attacked Mīr Muʿizzu 'l-Mulk (No. 61). Bahādur ultimately defeated the Imperialists; but Isk. had in the first fight been defeated and fled to the north of Audh.

When in the 12th year Khān Zamān and Bahādur again rebelled, Isk. in concert with them occupied Audh. He was attacked by Muḥammad Qulī Khān Barlās (No. 31), and besieged in Avadh. When Isk. heard that Khān Zamān and Bahādar had been defeated and killed, he made proposals of peace, and managed during the negotiation to escape by boat with his family to Gorākhpūr, which then belonged to Sulaymān, king of Bengal. He appears to have attached himself to the Bengal Court, and accompanied, in 975, Bāyazīd, Sulaymān's son, over Jhārkand to Oṛīsā. After Sulaymān's return from the conquest of Oṛīsā,[1] Isk.'s presence in Bengal was looked upon as dangerous, as Sulaymān wished at all hazards to be at peace with Akbar, and the Afghāns waited for a favourable opportunity to kill Iskandar. He escaped in time, and applied to Munʿim Khān, who promised to speak for him. At his request, Isk. was pardoned. He received the Sarkār of Lakʿhnau as *tuyūl*, and died there in the following year (980).

49. **Āṣaf Khān ʿAbdu 'l-Majīd** (of Hirāt), a descendant of Shaykh Abū Bakr-i Tāybādī.

His brother Vazīr Khān has been mentioned above (No. 41). Shaykh Zaynu 'd-Dīn Abū Bakr-i Tāybādī[2] was a saint (*ṣāḥib kamāl*) at the time of Tīmūr. When Tīmūr, in 782, set out for the conquest of Hirāt, which was in the hands of Malik Ghiyāsu 'd-Dīn, he sent, on his arrival at

---

upon Akbar to pardon him. Sikandar sent his son ʿAbdu 'r-Raḥmān with some elephants as *pīshkash,* and was allowed by Akbar to occupy Bihār as *tuyūl* (*vide* p. 335). Mānkot surrendered on the 27th Ramaẓān 964. Sikandar died two years later.

It is difficult to say why Abu l-Faẓl had not entered Khizr Khān in the List of Grandees. His name is given in the *Ṭabaqāt*. Similarly Khwāja Muʿaẓẓim and Mīr Shāh ʿAbdu 'l-Maʿālī are left out. For Kh.'s son, *vide* No. 153.

[1] On Sulaymān's return from Oṛīsā, he appointed Khān Jahān Lodhī, his Amīr-ul-Umarā, Governor of Oṛīsā. Qutlū Khān, who subsequently made himself king of Oṛīsā, was then Governor of Pūrī (Jagganath) Bad. II, 174.

[2] He died A.H. 791. His biography is given in Jāmī's *Nafhatu 'l-Uns.* Taybād belongs to Jām-i Khurāsān.

Tāybād, a messenger to the Shaykh, to ask him why he had not paid his respects to the conqueror of the world. "What have I," replied the Shaykh, "to do with Tīmūr?" Tīmūr, struck with this answer, went himself to the Shaykh, and upbraided him for not having advised Malik Ghiyās. "I have indeed done so," said the Shaykh, "but he would not listen, and God has now appointed you over him. However, I now advise you, too, to be just, and if you likewise do not listen, God will appoint another over you." Tīmūr afterwards said that he had seen many dervishes; every one of them had said something from selfish motives, but not so Shaykh Abū Bakr, who had said nothing with reference to himself.

Khwāja ʿAbdu 'l-Majīd was a Grandee of Humāyūn, whom he served as Dīwān. On Akbar's accession, he also performed military duties. When the Emperor moved to the Panjāb, to crush Bayrām's rebellion, ʿAbdu 'l-Majīd received the title of *Āṣaf Khān*, regarding which *vide* the note after this biographical notice. Subsequently Āṣaf was appointed Governor of Dihlī, received a flag and a drum, and was made a Commander of Three Thousand. When Fattū, a servant of ʿAdlī, made overtures to surrender Fort Chanāḍh (Chunar), Ā., in concert with Shaykh Muḥammad Ghawṣ, took possession of it, and was appointed Governor of Kaṛa-Mānikpūr on the Ganges. About the same time, Ghāzī Khān Tannūrī, an Afghān noble who had for a time been in Akbar's services, fled to Bhath Ghorā, and stirred up the Zamīndārs against Akbar. Ā., in the 7th year, sent a message to Rāja Rām Chand, the ruler of Bhath, to pay tribute to Akbar, and surrender the enemies. But the Rāja prepared for resistance. Ā. marched against the Rāja, defeated him, and executed Ghāzī Khān. The Rāja, after his defeat, shut himself up in Bāndhū,[1] but obtained Abbar's pardon by timely submission, chiefly through the influence of several Rāja's at Court. Ā. then left the Rāja in peace; but the spoils which he had collected and the strong contingent which he had at his disposal (*vide* p. 251, l. 29), made him desirous of further warfare and he planned the famous expedition against Gaḍha-Katangah,[2]

[1] Abū 'l-Faẓl in the events of the 42nd year of the Akbarnāma, says that ʿAlāʾu 'd-Dīn-i- Khiljī besieged Bāndhū in vain.

[2] Gaḍha (Gurh, Gurhah, Gurrah) lies close to Jabalpūr in Central India. Katangah is the name of two small places, one due south of Jubalpūr below lat. 22, as on the map in Journal A. S. B., Decr. 1837, pl. lvii; another apparently larger place of the same name lies N.W. of, and nearer to, Jabalpūr and Gaḍha, about lat. 23° 30′, as on the map of Central India in Sir J. Malcolm's Malwa; but both are called on the maps *Katangī*. In Muḥammadan Histories, the country is generally called Gaḍha-Katangah. Abū 'l-Faẓl says, it had an extent of 150 *kos* by 80 *kos*, and there were in ancient times 80,000 flourishing cities. The inhabitants, she says, are all Gonds, who are looked upon by Hindūs as very low.

The Rājas of Gaḍha-Katangah are generally called the Gaḍha-Mandlā Rājas. Mandlā lies S.E. of Jabalpūr, on the right side of the Narbaddah.

or Gondwānah, south of Bhath, which was then governed by Durgāwatī,[1] the heroine of Central India. Her heroic defence and suicide, and the death of her son, Bīr Sāh, at the conquest of Chaurāgaḍh (about 70 miles west of Jabalpūr) are well-known. The immense spoils which Ā. carried off, led him temporarily into rebellion, and of the 1,000 elephants which he had captured, he only sent 200 to Court. But when Khān Zamān (No. 13), in the 10th year, rebelled and besieged Majnūn Qāqshāl (No. 50) in Mānikpūr, Ā. came with 5,000 troopers to his relief, presented himself before Akbar, who had marched against Khān Zamān, and handed over the remainder of the Gaḍha spoils. He thereby regained Akbar's confidence and was appointed to follow up the rebels. At this juncture the imperial Mutaṣaddīs, whom Ā. before had handsomely bribed, reported, from envy, his former unwillingness to hand over the spoils, and exaggerated his wealth. Hypocritical friends mentioned this to Ā.; and afraid of his personal safety, he fled to Gaḍha (Ṣafar, 973).

Akbar looked upon his flight as very suspicious, and appointed Mahdī Qāsim Khān (No. 36) to Gaḍhā. Ā. then left Central India " with a sorrowful heart ", and joined, together with his brother (No. 41), Khān Zamān at Jaunpūr. But he soon saw that Khān Zamān only wanted his wealth and watched for a favourable moment to kill him. Ā. therefore made use of the first opportunity to escape. Khān Zamān had sent his brother Bahādur (No. 22) against the Afghāns, and Ā. was to accompany him. Vazīr Khān, whom Khān Zamān had detained, managed likewise to escape, and was on the road to Mānikpūr, which Ā. had appointed as place of rendezvous. No sooner had Ā. escaped than Bahādūr followed him up, defeated his men, and took Ā. prisoner. Bahādur's men immediately dispersed in search of plunder, when suddenly Vazīr Khān fell over Bahādur. Bahādur made some one a sign to kill Ā., who sat fettered on an elephant, and Ā. had just received a wound in his hand and nose, when Vazīr in time saved his life, and carried him away. Both reached, in 973, Karah, and asked Muẓaffar Khān (No. 37) to intercede for them with the emperor. When Muẓaffar, in 974, was called by the emperor to the Panjāb, he took Vazīr with him, and obtained full pardon for the two brothers. Ā. was ordered to join Majnūn Qāqshāl at Kaṛa-Mānikpūr. His bravery in the last struggle with Khān Zamān induced Akbar, in 975, to give him Piyāg as *tuyūl*, *vice* Ḥājī Muḥammad Sīstānī (No. 55), to enable him to recruit a contingent for the expedition against

[1] Capt. Sleeman in his " History of the Gurha Mandala Rājas ", Journal A.S. Bengal, vol. vi, p. 627, spells her name *Durghoutee*. He calls her son *Bīr Narāin*. *Vide* also *Badā,onī*, ii, 66.

Rānā Udai Singh. Ā. was sent in advance (*manqalā*). In the middle of Rabīʿ I, 975, Akbar left Āgra for Chītor. The Rānā had commissioned Jay Mal, who had formerly been in Mīrtha, to defend the fort, whilst he himself had withdrawn to the mountains. During the siege, which lasted four months and seven days, Ā. distinguished himself, and when, on the 25th Shaʿbān 975, the fort fell Ā. was made Governor of Chītor.

Neither the *Ma*ʾ*āṣir*, nor the *Tabaqāt*, mentions the year of his death. He must have been dead in 981, because the title of Āṣaf Khān was bestowed upon another noble.[1]

Note on the Title of "Āṣaf Khān".

Āṣaf was the name of the Vazīr of Sulaymān (Solomon), who like his master is proverbial in the East for his wisdom. During the reign of Akbar three grandees received this title. Badā,onī, to avoid confusion, numbers them Āṣaf Khān I, II, and III. They are :—

ʿAbdu 'l-Majīd, Āṣaf Khān I, *d.* before 981 (No. 49).

Khwāja Mīrzā Ghiyāṣu 'd-Dīn ʿAlī Āṣaf Khān II, *d.* 989 (No. 126).

Mīrzā Jaʿfar Beg Āṣaf Khān III (No. 98).

The three Āṣafs were Dīwāns or Mīr Bakhshīs. The third was nephew to the second, as the following tree will show :—

Āghā Mullā Dawātdār.

1. Ghiyāṣu 'd-Dīn ʿAli, Beg. *Āṣaf Khān II.*
   - Mīrzā Nūru 'd-Dīn.
   - A daughter
     - Mumtāz Mahall, (Shāhjahān's wife).
2. Mīrzā Badīʿu-z-Zamān
   - Mīrzā Jaʿfar Beg, *Āṣaf Khān III.*
3. Mīrzā Ahmad

Jahāngīr conferred the title of "Āṣaf Khān" (IV) on Abū 'l-Ḥasan, elder brother of Nūr Jahān, and father of Mumtāz Mahall (or Tāj Bībī, Shāhjahān's wife), whose mother was a daughter of Āṣaf Khān II. During the reign of Shāhjahān when titles containing the word *Dawla*[2] were

[1] Stewart (History of Bengal, p. 120) says, ʿAbdu 'l-Majīd Āṣaf Khān officiated in 1013 for Mān Singh in Bengal. This is as impossible as his statement on p. 112, that Farīdu 'd-Dīn Bukhārī [No. 99] is the author of the History of the Emperor Jahāngīr.

[2] They had been in use among the Khalīfas and the Ghaznawīs. Thus *Yamīnu 'd-Dawla* which title Shāhjahān bestowed on Abū 'l-Ḥasan Āṣaf Khān IV, had also been the title of Mahmūd of Ghaznī when prince. The kings of the Dakhin occasionally conferred titles

revived, *Āṣaf Khān* was changed to *Āṣafᵘ 'd-Dawla*, and this title was conferred on Āṣafᵘ 'd-Dawla Jumlatᵘ 'l-Mulk Asadjang (Shāhjahān-Awrang-zeb), a relation of Āṣaf Khān IV. Under Aḥmad Shāh, lastly, we find Āsafᵘ 'd-Dawla Amīrᵘ 'l-Mamālik, whose name like that of his father, Niẕāmᵘ 'l-Mulk Aṣaf Jāh, occurs so often in later Indian History.

50. **Majnūn Khān-i Qāqshāl.**[1]

He was a grandee of Humāyūn, and held Nārnaul as *jāgīr*. When Humāyūn fled to Persia, Ḥājī Khān besieged Nārnaul, but allowed Majnūn Khān to march away unmolested, chiefly at the request of Rāja Bihārī Mal, who, at that time, was with Ḥājī Khān (*vide* p. 347).

On Akbar's accession, he was made Jāgīrdār of Mānikpūr, then the east frontier of the Empire. He remained there till after the death of Khān Zamān (No. 13), bravely defending Akbar's cause. In the 14th year, he besieged Kālinjar. This fort was in the hands of Rāja Rām Chand, ruler of Bhath, who during the Afghan troubles had bought it for a heavy sum, from Bijlī Khān, the adopted son of Pahār Khān. When, during the siege, the Rāja heard of the fall of Chītor and Rantanbhūr, he surrendered Kālinjar to M. (29th Ṣafar, 997). Akbar appointed M. Commander of the Fort, in addition to his other duties.

In the 17th year (980), he accompanied Munʿim Khān (No. 11) on his expedition to Gorakhpūr. At the same time the Gujrātī war had commenced, and as Bābā Khān Qāqshāl[2] had words with Shāhbāz Khān (No. 80), the Mīr Tozak, regarding certain arrangements, he was reproved by Akbar. But the rumour spread in Munʿim's army that Bābā Khān Jabārī (Majnūn's son), Mīrzā Muḥammad, and other Qāqshāls, had killed Shāhbāz Khān, and joined the rebellion of the Mīrzās in Gujrāt; and that Akbar had therefore ordered Munʿim to imprison Majnūn. In consequence of these false rumours, M. and others of his clan withdrew from Munʿim, who in vain tried to convince them of the absurdity of the rumours; but

---

with *Dawla*. This is very likely the reason why Akbar conferred the title of Āzādᵘ 'd-Dawla on Mīr Fatḥᵘ 'llah of Shīrāz, who had come from the Dakhin.

The title *Malik*, so common among the Pathāns, was never conferred by the Mughūl (Chaghtāi) Kings of Delhi.

Titles with *Jang*, as *Fīrūzjang*, *Nuṣratjang*, etc., came into fashion with Jahāngīr.

[1] Name of a Turkish clan. Like the Uzbaks, they were disliked by Akbar, and rebelled. Majnūn Khān was certainly the best of them.

[2] *Bābā Khān Qāqshāl* also was a grandee of Akbar, but Abū 'l-Faẓl has left him out in this list. Like Majnūn he distinguished himself in the war with Khān Zamān and the Mīrzās. During Munʿim's expedition to Bengal, the Qāqshāls received extensive jāgirs in Ghorāghāt. Bābā Khān was looked upon as the head of the clan after Majnūn's death. He rebelled with Maʿṣūm Khān-i Kābulī, partly in consequence of Mūzaffar Khān's (No. 37) exactions, and assumed the title of Khān Khānān. He died in the same year in which Muẕaffar died, of cancer in the face (*Khūra*), which he said he had brought on himself by his faithlessness.

[*Khura* chancre ?—P.]

when M. soon after heard that Bābā Khān and Jabārī had been rewarded by Akbar for their brave behaviour in the Gujrāti war, he was ashamed of his hastiness, and rejoined Munʿim who, in the meantime, had taken Gorākhpūr.

M. accompanied Munʿim on his Bengal expedition. When, in 982, Dā,ūd, retired to Oṛīsā, and Kālā Pahār,[1] Sulaymān Manklī and Bābū Manklī had gone to Ghorāghāt, Munʿim sent M. against them. M. conquered the greater part of Northern Bengal, and carried off immense spoils. On the death of Sulaymān Manklī, the acknowledged ruler of Ghorāghāt, a great number of the principal Afghān nobles were caught, and M. with the view of securing peace, married the daughter of Sulaymān Manklī to his son Jabārī. He also parcelled out the whole country among his clan. But Bābū Manklī and Kālā Pahāṛ had taken refuge in Kūch Bihār, and when Munʿim was in Kaṭak, they were joined by the sons of Jalālᵘ 'd-Dīn Sūr, and fell upon the Qāqshāls. The latter, without fighting, cowardly returned to Ṭānḍa, and waited for Munʿim, who, on his return from Oṛīsā, sent them with reinforcements to Ghorāghāt. The Qāqshāls re-occupied the district. Majnūn died soon after at Ghorāghāt.

The *Ṭabaqāt* says that he was a Commander of Five Thousand, and had a contingent of 5,000 troopers.

His son Jabārī,[2] distinguished himself by his zeal and devotion. The enforcing of the *Dāgh* law led him and his clan into rebellion. Jabārī then assumed the title of *Khān Jahān*. When the Qāshāls left Maʿṣūm (p. 344), Jabārī went to Court. Akbar imprisoned him, but pardoned him in the 39th year.

51. **Shujāʿat Khān, Muqīm-i ʿArab.**

He is the son of Tardī Beg's sister (No. 12). Hūmāyūn made Muqīm-a *Khān*. On the emperor's flight to Persia, he joined Mīrzā ʿAskarī. When Humāyūn took Qandahār on his return, Muqīm, like most old nobles,

---

[1] The renowned conqueror of the temple of Jagannath at Pūrī in S. Oṛīsā. *Vide* below Third Book, Ṣūbas of Bengal and Oṛīsā. A minute description of his conquest is given in the *Makhzan-i Afghānī* and by Stirling in his Account of Orissa, Asiatic Researches, vol. xv. But Stirling's account, taken as it is from the Pūrī Vynsavali (a chronicle kept for the last six hundred years in the temple of Pūrī) differs considerably from the Akbarnāma. Kālā Pahār was killed by a gun-shot in one of the fights between Maʿṣūm and Qutlū of Oṛīsā, and ʿAzīz Koka (*vide* p. 344) which, in 990, took place between Khalgāw (Colgong) and Gadhī (near Rajmahall).

Bābū Manklī subsequently entered Akbar's service (*vide* No. 202). European historians generally spell his name Bābū *Mangalī*, as if it came from the Hindī *mangal*, Tuesday. This may be correct; for common people in India do still use such names. But *manklī* is perhaps preferable. Two of Tīmūr's ancestors had the same name. The Turkish *manklī* means خالدار, *khāldār*, spotted.

[2] The best MSS. of the Akbarnāma, Badā,onī, and the Maʾāsir have جباري. Stewart (p. 109) calls him *Jebbaburdy* (?).

presented himself before the emperor with a sword hanging from his neck, and was for a short time confined. After his release, he remained with Munʿim Khān (No. 11) in Kābul, and followed him to India, when Akbar called Munʿim to take Bayrām's place.

In the 9th year, Muqīm distinguished himself in the pursuit of ʿAbdᵘ 'llāh Khān Uzbak (No. 14), "the king of Mandū," and received the title of *Shujāʿat Khān*, which Akbar had taken away from the rebellious ʿAbdᵘ 'llāh.

In the beginning of the 15th year, Akbar honoured him by being his guest for a day.

In the 18th year, he accompanied the Emperor on his forced march to Aḥmadābād (p. 343). Once he slandered Munʿim, and Akbar sent him to the Khān Khānān to do with him what he liked; but Munʿim generously forgave him, and had him restored.

In the 22nd year, he was made a Commander of Three Thousand, and Governor and Commander-in-Chief of Mālwah.

In 988, when troubles in Bihār and Bengal had broken out, Shujāʿat Khān, at Akbar's order, left Sārangpūr for Fatḥpūr (*Badā,onī* II, 284). At the first stage, ʿIwaẓ Beg Barlās who complained of arrears of pay and harsh treatment of the men, created a tumult, made a man of the name Ḥājī Shihāb Khān leader, fell upon Shujāʿat's tent, and killed his son Qawīm Khān.[1] Shujāʿat himself was mortally wounded. Some of his adherents, at last, managed to put the dying Sh. on an elephant, and led him off to Sārangpūr. Though Sh. had expired before they reached the town, they did not spread the news of his death, and thus kept the greater part of the soldiers together, and joined Akbar in Sārangpūr.

Akbar punished the rebels severely. According to p. 294, Akbar once saved Shujāʿat's life in the jungles.

From Badā onī (II, 284), we learn that Qawīm Khān was a young man, renowned for his musical talents.

Muqīm Khān (No. 386) is Shujāʿat Khān's second son. He was promoted under Akbar to a Commandership of seven hundred.

Qāʾim Khān was the son of Muqīm Khān. Qāʾim's son, Abdᵘ 'r-Rāḥīm, was under Jahāngīr a Commander of seven hundred and 400 horse, got the title of Tarbiyat Khān, and was made in the 5th year, Fawjdār of Alwar. Qāʾim's daughter, *Ṣāliḥa Bānū*, was received (3rd year) by Jahāngīr in his harem, and went by the title of *Pādishāh Maḥall*. She adopted *Miyān Joh*, son of the above, Abdᵘ 'r-Raḥīm. Miyān Joh was

---

[1] So the Maʾāṣir and the Akbarnāma. Badā,onī (ii, 284) has *Qāʾim Khān*; but this is perhaps a mistake of the native editors of the Bibl. Indica.

killed by Mahābat Khān when near the Bahat (Jhelam) he had taken possession of Jahāngīr's person.

No. 52. **Shāh Budāgh Khān,** a descendant of Uymāqs[1] of Miyāṅkāl, Samarqand.

The Turkish *Budāgh* means " a branch of a tree ". He distinguished himself under Humāyūn and was made by Akbar a Commander of Three Thousand.

In the 10th year he accompanied Mīr Muʿizzᵘ 'l-Mulk (No. 61) against Bahādur (No. 22). Though the imperialists were defeated, B. Kh. fought bravely, and was captured. His son ʿAbdᵘ 'l-Maṭlab (No. 83) ran away. In the 12th year, B. Kh. went with Shihābᵘ 'd-Dīn Aḥmad (No. 26) against Mīrzās in Mālwah, received Sārangpūr as *tuyūl,* fought under ʿAzīz Koka (No. 21) in the battle of Patan (18th Ramaẓān 980), and was for a long time Governor of Mandū, where he died. The *Ṭabaqāt* says, he had the title of *Amīrᵘ 'l-Umarā.* He was alive in 984, when he met Akbar at Mohinī.

Inside Fort Mandū, to the south, close to the walls, he had erected a building, to which he gave the name of *Nīlkānth,* regarding the inscriptions on which the *Maʾāṣir* gives a few interesting particulars.

53. **Ḥusayn Khān** (Ṭukṛiya), sister's son of Mahdī Qāsim Khān (No. 36.)

" He is the Bayard and the Don Quixote of Akbar's reign." In his *jihāds* he was *sans peur,* and his private life *sans reproche* ; he surpassed all grandees by his faithfulness and attachment to his masters, but his contingent was never in order ; he was always poor, though his servants, in consequence of his liberality, lived in affluence. He slept on the ground, because his Prophet had enjoyed no greater luxuries ; and his motto in fight was " death or victory " ; and when people asked him why he did not invert the order and say " victory or death ", he would reply, " O ! I so long to be with the saints that have gone before."

He was the patron of the historian Badā,onī,[2] who served Ḥusayn as almoner to his estate (Shamsābād and Patyālī).

---

[1] There were two tribes of the Qarā Turks called أیماق or أویماق *üymāq.* They were renowned in India as horsemen. Hence ایماق as the word is generally spelt by Mughul Historians, means *a kind of superior cavalry* ; *vide* Tuzuk, p. 147, l. 17. How this Turkish word lost its original meaning in India, may be seen from p. 57, l. 1 of the second volume of my Aʾīn text, where Abū 'l-Faẓl applies the word to Rājpūt cavalry of the Rāṭhor clan. The word is pronounced *aimāq* in India.

The meaning of *Miyān Kāl* is still unclear to me. To judge from Abū 'l-Faẓl's phrase it must be the name of the head or founder of a clan. The adjective *Miyān Kālā* occurs frequently. Two Miyān Kālīs may be found below among the list of learned men (Qāẓī ʿAbdᵘ 's-Samīʿ) and the poets (Qāsim-i Kāhī).

[2] *Vide* my Essay on Badā,onī and his Works in J.A.S. Bengal, for 1869, p. 120.

Ḥusayn Khān was not only sister's son, but also son-in-law to Mahdī Qāsim Khān (No. 36). He was in Bayrām's service. In the second year, after the conquest of Mānkoṭ, Akbar made him Governor of Lāhor, where he remained four months and four days. When Akbar in Ṣafar 965, marched to Dihlī, he appointed Ḥ. Kh. Governor of the Panjāb. During his incumbency, he showed himself a zealous Sunnī. As the Christians did with the Jews, he ordered the Hindūs as unbelievers to wear a patch (Hind. *ṭukrā*) near the shoulders, and thus got the nickname of *Ṭukriya* "Patcher".

Like Shāh Qulī Khān Maḥram (No. 45), he stuck to Bayrām to the last, and did not meet Akbar at Jhūjhar; but after Bayrām had been pardoned, he entered Akbar's service. When Mahdī Qāsim Khān, from dislike to Gaḍha, went by way of the Dakhin to Makkah, Ḥ. Kh. accompanied him a short distance on the road. On his return, he reached Satwās in Mālwah, when the rebellion of the Mīrzās broke out, and in concert with Muqarrib Khān, the *tuyūldār* of that place, he tried to fortify himself in Satwās. But Maqarrib lost heart and fled; and Ḥ. Kh. was forced to leave the Fort, and asked Ibrāhīm Ḥusayn Mīrzā for an interview. Though urged to join the Mīrzā, Ḥ. Kh. remained faithful to Akbar.

In the 12th year, when Akbar moved against Khān Zamān, Ḥ. Kh. was to take a command, but his contingent was not ready. In the 13th year his jāgīr was transferred from Lakhnau, where he and Badā,onī had been for about a year, to Kānto Gola.[1] His exacting behaviour towards Hindūs and his religious expeditions against their temples annoyed Akbar very much. In the 19th year, when the Emperor went to Bihār, Ḥ. Kh. was again absent; and when Akbar returned after the conquest of Ḥājīpūr, he confiscated Ḥ.'s jāgīr; but on satisfying himself of his harmlessness, he pardoned him, restored his jāgīr, and told him to get his contingent ready. His *mania*, however, again overpowered him. He made an expedition against Basantpūr in Kamā,on, which was proverbially rich, and got wounded by a bullet in the shoulder. Akbar was almost convinced that he had gone into rebellion, and sent Ṣādiq Khān (No. 43) to him to bring him by force to Court. Ḥ. Kh. therefore left Gaṛh Muktesar, with the view of going to Munʿim Khān, through whose influence he hoped to obtain pardon. But he was caught at Bārha, and was taken to Faṭhpūr Sīkrī, where in the same year (983) he died of his wounds.

[1] Elliot (Index, p. 235, First Edition) has by mistake *Lakhnor* (on the Rāmganga) instead of *Lakhnau* (in Audh), and he calls Ḥusayn Khān a *Kashmīrī*. This must be an oversight.

The Ṭabaqāt says, he was a Commander of Two Thousand; but according to the Akbarnāma, he had since the 12th year been a Commander of Three Thousand.

His son, Yūsuf Khān, was a grandee of Jahāngīr. He served in the Dakhin in the corps of ʿAzīz Kokā (No. 21), who, in the 5th year, had been sent with 10,000 men to reinforce Prince Parwīz, the Khān Khānān, and Mān Singh, because on account of the duplicity of the Khān Khānān (*Tuzuk* p. 88) the imperialists were in the greatest distress (*vide* pp. 344 and 357). Yūsuf's son, ʿIzzat Khān, served under Shāhjahān, (*Pādīshāhn.* II, 121).

54. **Murād Khān,** son of Amīr Khān Mughul Beg.

His full name is Muḥammad Murād Khān. In the 9th year he served under Āṣaf Khān (No. 48) in Gaḍha Katanga. In the 12th year, he got a jāgīr in Mālwa, and fought under Shihābu 'd-Dīn Aḥmad against the Mīrzās. After the Mīrzās had returned to Gujrāt, M. got Ujjain as *tuyūl.*

In the 13th year, the Mīrzās invaded Mālwa from Khandesh, and Murād Khān, together with Mīr ʿAzīzu 'llah, the Dīwān of Mālwah, having received the news two days before the arrival of the enemies, shut themselves up in Ujjain, determined to hold it for Akbar. The Emperor sent Qulij Khān (No. 42) to their relief, when the Mīrzās retreated to Mandū. Followed up by Qulij and Murād they retreated at last across the Narbaddah.

In the 17th year, the Mīrzās broke out in Gujrāt, and the jāgīrdārs of Mālwah assembled under the command of M. ʿAzīz Koka (No. 21). Murād held a command in the left wing, and took part, though not very actively, in the confused battle near Patan (Ramaẓān, 980).

In 982, he was attached to Munʿim's expedition to Bengal. He conquered for Akbar the district of Fatḥābād, Sarkār Boglā (S.E. Bengal), and was made Governor of Jalesar (Jellasore) in Oṛīsā, after Dāʾūd had made peace with Munʿim.

When in 983, after Munʿim's death, Dāʾūd fell upon Naẓar Bahādur, Akbar's Governor of Bhadrak (Oṛīsā), and treacherously killed him, Murād wisely retreated to Ṭāṇḍa.[1]

Subsequently M. was again appointed to Fatḥābād, where he was when the Bengal rebellion broke out. Murād at Fatḥābād Qiyā Khān in

[1] As Munʿim left T'hānahdārs in Bhadrak and Jalesar, Dāʾūd must have been restricted to Kaṭak proper. Munʿim's invasion of Oṛīsā was certainly one of the most daring exploits performed during Akbar's reign.

Having mentioned Kaṭak, I may here state that the name "Aṭak" (Attock, in the Panjāb) was chosen by Akbar who built the town, because *it rhymes with Kaṭak.* The two frontier towns of his empire were to have similar names. *Akbarnāma.*

Orīsā, Mirzā Najāt at Sātgāw, were almost the only officers of Akbar's Bengal corps that did not take part in the great military revolt of 988. Qiyā was killed by Qutlū (p. 366), and Murād died at Fatḥābād immediately after the first outbreak of the revolt in 988, "before the veil of his loyalty was rent".

After his death, Mukand, the principal Zamīndār of Fatḥābād, invited Murād's sons to a feast, and treacherously murdered them.

Vide No. 369.

55. **Hājī Muḥammed Khān** of Sīstān.

He was in the service of Bayrām, who was much attached to him. In 961, when Bayrām held Qandahār, rumours of treason reached Humāyūn. The Emperor went from ʿKābul to Qandahār, and personally investigated the matter, but finding Bayrām innocent, he went back, taking Ḥājī Muḥammad with him, who during the investigation had been constantly referred to as inclined to rebellion.[1]

After the conquest of Hindūstān, Ḥ. M. at Bayrām's request, was made a Khān, and was rapidly promoted.

In the 1st year of Akbar's reign, Ḥ. M. was ordered to accompany Khizr Khwāja'n (p. 394, note 1) on his expedition against Sikandar Sūr. Tardī Beg's (No. 12) defeat by Hemū had a bad effect on the Emperor's cause; and Mullā ʿAbdᵘ'llāh Makhdūmᵘ'l- Mulk who, though in Akbar's service, was said to be devoted to the interests of the Afghān's, represented to Sikandar that he should use this favourable opportunity and leave the Sawāliks. As related above Khizr Khwāja moved against Sikandar, leaving Ḥ. M. in charge at Lāhor. Being convinced of Makhdūm's treason, Ḥ. M. tortured him, and forced him to give up sums of money which he had concealed.

In 966, Bayrām fell out with Pīr Muḥammad (No. 20), and deprived him of his office and emoluments which were given to Ḥ. M. When Bayrām fell into disgrace, he sent Ḥ. M. with several other Amīrs to Dihlī with expressions of his humility and desire to be pardoned. But Ḥ. M. soon saw that all was lost. He did not receive permission to go back to Bayrām. After Bayrām had been pardoned (p. 318) Ḥ. M. and Muḥammad Tarsō Khān (No. 32) accompanied him on his way to Ḥijāz as far as Nāgor, then the frontier of the Empire. Once, on the road, Bayrām charged Ḥ. M. with faithlessness, when the latter gently reminded him that he had at least never drawn his sword against his master.

---

[1] Ḥājī Muḥammad is the same to whom Erskine's remark refers quoted by Elphinstone (Fifth Edition), p. 470 note.

Ḥ. M. was present in almost every campaign, and was promoted to the post of *Sih-hazārī*. In the 12th year, when Akbar set out for the conquest of Chītor, he sent Ḥ. M. and Shibāb[u] 'd-Dīn Aḥmad (No. 26) from Gāgrūn against the sons of Sulṭān Muḥammad Mīrzā, who had fled from Sambhal and raised a revolt in Mālwah. Ḥ. M. then received the Sarkār of Mandū as *jāgīr*.

In the 20th year, Ḥ. M. accompanied Munʿim Khān on his expedition to Bengal and Oṛīsā, and got wounded in the battle of Takaroī (20th Ẕī Qaʿda, 982). He then accompanied the Khān Khānān to Gaur, where soon after Munʿim's death he, too, died of malaria (983).

Note on the Battle of Takaroī, or Mughulmārī, in Oṛīsā.

This battle is one of the most important battles fought by Akbar's generals. It crushed the Afghāns, and decided the possession of Bengal and Upper Oṛīsā. The MSS. of the *Akbarnāma* and the *Maʾāṣir* have تكروهي *Takarohī*, and تكروئي *Takaroī*. My copy of the Sawāniḥ has the former spelling. A few copies of the *Akbarnāma* have نكروهي *Nakrohī*. In *Badā,onī* and the *Ṭabaqāt* the battle of Takaroī is called the battle of بجهوره (*vide* p. 334) which may be *Bajhorah*, *Bachhorah*, *Bajhorh*, or *Bachhorh*. Stewart's account of Munʿim's Oṛīsā expedition (5th Section), differs in many particulars from the *Akbarnāma* and the Ṭabaqāt. He places the battle in the environs of Kaṭak, which is impossible, and his "Bukhtore" is a blunder for بچتوا *ba-chittū,ā*, "in Chittuā," the final *alif* having assumed the shape of a ر *re*, and the چ that of خ. The Lucknow lithograph of the *Akbarnāma*, which challenges in corruptness the worst possible Indian MS., has *ba-chitor*, "in Chitor."

The *Akbarnāma*, unfortunately, gives but few geographical details. Todar Mal moved from Bardwān over Madāran[1] into the Pargana of Chittuā (چتوه), where he was subsequently joined by Munʿim. Dāʾūd had taken up a strong position at هرپور, Harpūr or Harīpūr, "which lies intermediate (*barzakhe*) between Bengal and Oṛīsā." The same phrase (*barzakhe*), in other passages of the *Akbarnāma*, is applied to Chittuā itself. Dāʾūd's object was to prevent the Imperialists from entering Oṛīsā into which led but few other roads; "but Ilyās Khān Langāh

[1] Madāran lies in Jahānābād, a Pargana of the Hūglī district, between Bardwān and Mednīpūr (Midnapore). Regarding the importance and history of this town, *vide* my "Places of Historical Interest in the Hūglī District", in the April Proceedings of the As. Soc. of Bengal for 1870.

showed the victorious army an easier road," and Munʿim entered the country, and thus turned Dāʾūd's position. The battle then takes place (20th Ẕī Qaʿda, 982, or A.D., 3rd March, 1575). After the battle Ṭoḍar Mal leads the pursuit and reaches with his corps the town of Bhadrak. Not long after, he writes to Munʿim to come and join him, as Dāʾūd had collected his troops near Kaṭak, and the whole army moves to Kaṭak, where a peace was concluded, which confirmed Dāʾūd in the possession of Kaṭak.

Now from the facts that the battle took place soon after the Imperialists had left Chittuā, which lies a little E.E.N. of Midnīpūr (Midnapore), and that after the victory Rāja Ṭoḍar Mal, in a pursuit of several days, pushed as far as Bhadrak, I was led to conclude that the battle must have taken place near Jalesar (Jellasore), and probably north of it, as Abū 'l-Faẓl would have mentioned the occupation of so large a town. On consulting the large Trigonometrical Map of Oṛīsā lately published, I found on the road from Midnipūr to Jalesar the village of Mogulmaree [1] (Mughulmārī, i.e., Mughul's Fight) and about seven miles southwards, half way between Mughulmārī and Jalesar, and two miles from the left bank of the Soobanreeka river, the village of Tookaroe.

According to the map the latitude of Mughulmārī is 22°, and that of Tookaroe, 21° 53 nearly.

There can be no doubt that this Tookaroe is the تکروئی, *Takaroī*, of the *Akbarnāma*.

The battle extended over a large ground. Badā,onī (II, p. 195, l. 3) speaks of *three, four kos*, *i.e.* about six miles, and thus the distance of Takaroī from Mughulmārī is accounted for.

I can give no satisfactory explanation of the name بجهوره, by which the battle is called in the Ṭabaqāt and Badā,onī (II, 194, l. 2). It looks as if the name contained the word *chaur* which occurs so often in the names of Parganas in the Jalesar and Balesar districts.

In Badā,onī (Edit. Bibl. Indica, p. 196) and the *Ṭabaqāt*, it is said that Ṭoḍar Mal in his pursuit reached کل کل گهاتی *Kalkalghāṭī* (?), not Bhadrak.

List of Officers who died in 983, after their return from Oṛīsā, at Gaur, of malaria.

1. Munʿim Khān, Khān Khānān, (18th Rājab). *Vide* p. 334.
2. Ḥājī Khān Sīstānī (No. 55).
3. Ḥaydar Khān (No. 66).

[1] Another "Mughulmārī" lies in the Bardwān district between Bardwān and Jahānābād (Hūglī district) on the old high road from Bardwān over Madāran to Midnīpūr.

4. Mīrzā Qulī Khān, his brother.
5. Ashraf Khān (No. 74).
6. Muʿīnu 'd-Dīn Aḥmad (No. 128).
7. Laʿl Khān (No. 209).
8. Ḥājī Yūsuf Khān (No. 224).
9. Shāh Ṭāhir (No. 236).
10. Hāshim Khān.
11. Muḥsin Khān.
12. Qunduz Khān.
13. Abū'l-Ḥusayn.
14. Shāh Khalīl.

56. **Afẓal Khān**, Khwāja Sulṭān ʿAlī[1] -yi Turbatī.

Regarding *Turbatī vide* No. 37. He was *Mushrif* (accountant) of Humāyūn's Treasury, and was, in 956, promoted to the post of *Mushrif-i Buyūtāt* (store accountant). In 957, when Mīrzā Kāmrān took Kābul, he imprisoned A. Kh., and forced him to pay large sums of money. On Humāyūn's return to India, A. Kh. was made *Mīr Bakhshī*, and got an *ʿalam*. He was together with Tardī Beg (No. 12) in Dihlī, when Humāyūn died. In the battle with Hemū, he held a command in the centre (*qol*), and his detachment gave way during Hemū's charge. A. Kh., together with Pīr Muḥammad (No. 20) and Ashraf Khān (No. 74), fled from the battlefield, partly from hatred towards Tardī Beg—the old hatred of Khurāsānīs towards Uzbaks—and retreated to Akbar and Bayrām. As related above, Tardī Beg was executed by Bayrām for this retreat, and A. Kh. and Ashraf Khān were convicted of malice and imprisoned. But both escaped and went to Makkah. They returned in the 5th year, when Bayrām had lost his power, and were favourably received at Court. A. Kh. was made a Commander of three-thousand.

"Nothing else is known of him." *Maʿāṣir*.

57. **Shāhbeg Khān**, son of Irbāhīm Beg Ḥarīk (?).[2]

He is sometimes called *Beg Khān* (p. 327). He was an *Arghūn*; hence his full name is *Shāh Beg Khān Arghūn*. Under Jahāngīr he got the title of *Khān Dawrān*.

He was in the service of Mīrzā Muḥammad Ḥakīm of Kābul, Akbar's brother, and was Governor of Peshāwar. When after the Prince's death, Mān Singh, in 993, crossed the Nīlāb (p. 362) for Kābul, Shāh Beg took M. M. Ḥakīm's two sons, Kay Qubād and Afrāsiyāb, to Akbar, and received a *manṣab*. Sh. B. distinguished himself in the war with the Yūsufzāʾīs, and got *Khushāb* as *jāgīr*. He then served under the Khān Khānān in Sindh, and was for his bravery promoted to a command of 2,500. In the 39th year Akbar sent him to Qandahār (p. 327), which,

---

[1] The word ʿAlī has been omitted in my text edition on p. 224.

[2] So the Maʿāṣir. My MSS. of the Āʾīn have حرک, which may be *Ḥarīk*, *Ḥarmak*, *Ḥarbak*, etc. Some MSS. read clearly *Ḥarmak*.

Muẓaffar Ḥusayn had ceded. During the time of his Governorship Sh. B. succeeded in keeping down the notorious Kākar کاکر tribe. In the 42nd year, he was made a Commander of 3,500. In the 47th year, Ghaznīn was placed in his charge (*vide* No. 63).

Immediately after the accession of Jahāngīr, Ḥusayn Khān Shāmlū, the Persian Governor at Hirāt, thinking Akbar's death would lead to disturbances, made war upon Sh. B. and besieged Qandahār, which he hoped to starve out. To vex him, Sh. B. gave every night feasts on the top of the castle before the very eyes of the enemies (*Tuzuk*, p. 33). One day Ḥusayn Khān sent an ambassador into the Fort, and Sh. B., though provisions had got low, had every available store of grain spread out in the streets, in order to deceive the enemies. Not long after, Ḥusayn Shāh received a reprimand from Shāh ʿAbbās for having besieged Qandahār " without orders ", and Ḥusayn Khān, without having effected anything, had to raise the siege.

When Jahāngīr in 1016 (18th Ṣafar) visited Kābul,[1] Sh. B. paid his respects, was made a Commander of 5,000, and received the title of *Khān Dawrān*. He was also made Governor of Kābul (in addition to Qandahār), and was ordered to prepare a financial settlement for the whole of Afghānistān. After having held this office till the end of 1027 he complained of the fatigues incident to a residence in Kābul, horse-travelling and the drizzly state of the atmosphere of the country,[2] paid in the beginning of 1028 his respects at Court (*Tuz.*, p. 257), and was appointed Governor of Thatha.[3] He resigned, however, in the same year (*Tuz.*, p. 275) and got the revenue of the Pargana of Khushāb assigned as pension (75,000 Rs.).

Before he went to Thatha, he called on Āṣaf to take leave and Āṣaf recommended to him the brothers of Mullā Muḥammad of Thatha, who had been a friend of Āṣaf. Shāhbeg had heard before that the Mullā's brothers, in consequence of Āṣaf's support, had never cared for the Governors of the province ; hence he said to Āṣaf, " Certainly, I will take an interest in their welfare, if they are sensible (*sarḥisāb*) ; but if not, I shall flay them." Āṣaf got much annoyed at this, opposed him in everything, and indirectly forced him to resign.

---

[1] According to the *Tuzuk* p. 53), Sh. B. then held the Pargana of Shor as *jāgīr*, regarding which *vide* Elliot's Index, first edition, p. 198.

[2] The text has *qaṭra*, which is mentioned as a peculiarity of Kābul. I do not know whether I have correctly translated the term.

[3] Sayyid Aḥmad in his edition of the *Tuzuk* (p. 266) makes him governor of *Patna*—a confusion of پتنه and تته.

Sh. B. was a frank Turk. When Akbar appointed him Governor of Qandahār, he conferred upon him an ʿ*alam* and a *naqqāra* (p. 52); but on receiving the *insignia*, he said to Farīd (No. 99), "What is all this trash for? Would that His Majesty gave me an order regarding my *manṣab*, and a *jāgīr*, to enable me to get better troopers for his service.' On his return, in 1028, from Kābul, he paraded before Jahāngīr his contingent of 1,000 picked Mughul troopers, whose appearance and horses created much sensation.

He was much given to wine drinking. He drank, in fact, wine, *cannabis*, opium, and *kūknār*, mixed together, and called his beverage of four ingredients *Chār Bughrā* (p. 63, l. 2), which gave rise to his nickname *Chār Bughrā Khur*.

His sons. 1. *Mīrzā Shāh Muḥammad Ghaznīn Khān*, a well educated man. Jahāngīr, in 1028, made him a Commander of One Thousand, six-hundred horse.

2. *Yaʿqūb Beg*, son-in-law to Mīrzā Jaʿfar Āṣaf Khān (III), (No. 98), a Commander of Seven Hundred, 350 horse. The *Maʾāṣir* says, he was a fatalist (*azalparast*), and died obscure.

3. *Asad Beg* (*Tuz.*, p. 275), a Commander of Three Hundred, 50 horse. The *Maʾāṣir* does not mention him.

The *Tuzuk*, p. 34, mentions a Qāsim Beg Khān, a relation of Sh. B. This is perhaps the same as No. 350.

Shāhbeg Khān Arghān must not be confounded with No 148.

58. **Khān ʿAlam Chalma Beg,**[1] son of Hamdam who was Mīrzā Kāmrān's foster brother.

Chalma Beg was Humāyūn's *safarchī*, or table attendant. Mīrzā Kāmrān had, in 960, been blinded, and at the Indus asked for permission to go to Makkah. Before he left, Humāyūn, accompanied by some of his courtiers, paid him a visit, when the unfortunate prince, after greeting his brother, quoted the verse—

کلاه گوشهٔ درویش برفلک ساید که سایه همچو تو شاهی فکند برسر او

"The fold of the poor man's turban touches the heaven, when a king like thee casts his shadow upon his head."

And immediately afterwards he said the following verse *extempore* :—

بر جانم از تو هرچه رسد جاي منت است گر ناوک جفاست وگر خنجر ستم

[1] For *Chalma*, the MSS. of the Āʾīn have, at this place, *Ḥalīm*. In No. 100, the same name occurs. The *Maʾāṣir* and good MSS. of the *Akbarnāma* have *Chalmah*. Turkish dictionaries give *chalmah* (چلمه) in the meaning of *wild goat's dung* and *chālma* (چالمه) in that of *dastār*, a turban.

In the Edit. Bibl. Indica of Badāonī, Khān ʿĀlam is wrongly called خاناعلم, instead of خان عالم.

"Whatever I receive at thy hands is kindness, be it the arrow of oppression or the dagger of cruelty."

Humāyūn felt uncomfortable and tried to console him. He gave next day orders that any of Kāmrān's old friends might accompany him free to Makkah; but as no one came forward, he turned to Chalmah Beg, and said, "Will you go with him, or stay with me?" Chalmah Beg, though he knew that Humāyūn was much attached to him, replied that he thought he should accompany the Prince in the "gloomy days of need and the darkness of his solitude". The Emperor approved of his resolution, and made liberal provisions for Kāmrān and his companion.

After Kāmrān's death, Chalma Beg returned to India, and was favourably received by Akbar, who made him a Commander of 3,000, bestowing upon him the title of *K͟hān ʿĀlam*. He served under the emperor against the Mīrzās in Gujrāt, and was present in the fight at Sarnāl (p. 353, No. 27).

In the 19th year, when Akbar moved against Dāʾūd in Patna, K͟hān ʿĀlam commanded a corps, and passing up the river in boats towards the mouth of the Ghandak, effected a landing, though continually exposed to the volleys of the enemies. Akbar praised him much for his daring. In the same year he was attached to Munʿim's corps. In the battle of Takaroī (p. 406), he commanded the *harāwal* (van). He charged the Afg͟hāns, and allowing his corps to advance too far, he was soon hard pressed and gave way, when Munʿim sent him an angry order to fall back. But before his corps could be brought again into order, Gūjar K͟hān, Dāʾūd's best general, attacked the Imperialists with his line of elephants, which he had rendered fierce looking by means of black Yak tails (*quṭas*) and skins of wild beasts attached to them. The horses of the Imperialists got frightened, nothing could make them stand, and their ranks were utterly broken. K͟h. ʿĀ's' horse got a sword cut, and reared, throwing him on the ground. He sprang up, and mounted it again, but was immediately thrown over by an elephant, and killed by the Afg͟hāns who rushed from all sides upon him (20th Ẕī Qaʿda, 982).

It is said that before the battle he had presentiment of his death, and begged of his friends, not to forget to tell the Emperor that he had willingly sacrificed his life.

K͟h. ʿĀ. was a poet and wrote under the *Tak͟halluṣ* of *Hamdamī* (in allusion to the name of his father).

A brother of his, Muẓaffar, is mentioned below (No. 301) among the Commanders of Three Hundred, where for اعظم, in my Text edition, p. 229, read عالم.

59. **Qāsim Khān**, Mīr Baḥr Chamanārāī (?) Khurāsān.[1]

He is the son of Mīrzā Dost's sister, who was an old servant of the Tīmūrides. When Mīrzā Kāmrān was, in 954, besieged in Kābul, Humāyūn had occupied Mount Aqābīn, which lies opposite the Fort of Kābul. Whilst the siege was going on, Qāsim Khān and his younger brother, Khwājagī Muḥammad Ḥusayn (No. 241) threw themselves down from a turret between the Āhanīn Darwāza and the Qāsim Barlās bastion, and went over to Humāyūn, who received them with distinction.

Soon after Akbar's accession, Q. Kh. was made a Commander of Three Thousand. He superintended the building of the Fort of Āgra, which he completed "after eight years at a cost of 7 *krors of tankas*, or 35 lacs of rupees. The Fort stands on the banks of the Jamna river, E. of the town of Āgra, on the place of the old Fort, which had much decayed. The breadth of the walls is 30 yards, and the height from the foundation to the pinnacles 60 *gaz*. It is built of red sandstone, the stones being well joined together and fastened to each other by iron rings which pass through them. The foundation everywhere reaches water ".[2]

In the 23rd year, Q. was made Commander of Āgra. In the beginning of Shaʿbān 995 (32nd year), he was ordered to conquer Kashmīr, "a country which from its inaccessibility had never tempted the former kings of Dihlī." Though six or seven roads lead into Kashmīr, the passes are all so narrow that a few old men might repel a large army. The then ruler of Kashmīr was Yaʿqūb Khān, son of Yūsuf Khān Chak. He had fortified a pass;[3] but as his rule was disliked, a portion of his men went over to Q., whilst others raised a revolt in Srīnagar. Thinking it more important to crush the revolt, Yaʿqūb left his fortified position, and allowed Q. to enter the country. No longer able to oppose the Imperialists, he withdrew to the mountains, and trusted to an active guerilla warfare;

---

[1] I am doubtful regarding the true meaning of the odd title *chaman-ārāyi Khurāsān*, "Ruler of Khurāsān." The Maʿāṣir, not knowing what to do with it, has left it out. *Mīr Baḥr* means "admiral". If *chamanārāī Kh.* be a genitive, the words mean, "Admiral of the ruler of Khūrāsān," which from his biography does not appear to be correct. His brother (No. 241) is styled *Mīr Bar*, an officer whose duties seem to have been confined to looking after arrangements during trips, hunting expeditions, etc.

[2] The old Fort of Āgra was called *Badalgaṛh* (Bad. I, 429). It suffered much during the earthquake of 911 (3rd Ṣafar), and was nearly destroyed during an explosion which happened in 962.

The Fort *Bādalgaḍh* بادلگڈہ, not بدلگڈہ, which Elliot (Index, First Edit., p. 229) identifies with the Fort of Āgra, cannot be the old Fort of Āgra, because Badā,onī (I, 327) clearly says that it was a lofty structure at the foot of the Fort of Gwāli,ār, not "one of the Forts dependent on Gwāli,ār".

For Udantgīr, on the same page in Elliot, read *Ūtgar* (اوتنگر). It was a Fort in the Sarkār of Mandlā,ir, on the left side of the Chambal. Our maps have *Ootgir* or *Deogurh*.

[3] Called in the MSS. کتل کتریل. The word *kutal*, means "a mountain" or "a mountain-pass". [Bad. II. 353, کتل کتریل—B.]

but disappointed even in this hope, he submitted and became "a servant of Akbar". The Kashmīrīs, however, are famous for love of mischief and viciousness, and not a day passed without disturbances breaking out in some part of the country. Q., tired of the incessant petty annoyances, resigned his appointment (*vide* No. 35). In the 34th year he was made Governor of Kābul. At that time a young man from Andajān (Farghāna) gave out that he was a son of Shāhrukh.[1] He met with some success in Badakhshān but was defeated by the Tūrān Shāh. The pretender then made friendship with the Zābulī Hazāras, and when Q., on one occasion, had repaired to Court, he entered Akbar's territory giving out that he was going to pay his respects to the Emperor. But Hāshim Beg, Q.'s son, who officiated during the absence of his father, sent a detachment after the pretender, who now threw himself on the Hazāras. But Hāshim Beg followed him, and took him a prisoner to Kābul. Q., on his return from India, let him off and even allowed him to enter his service. The pretender, in the meantime, rearranged his old men, and when he had five hundred together, he waited for an opportunity to fall on Q. At this juncture, Akbar ordered the pretender to repair to Court. Accompanied by his ruffians, he entered at noon Q.'s sleeping apartments, when only a few females were present, and murdered his benefactor (1002). Hāshim Beg soon arrived, and fired upon the pretender and his men. In the *melée*, the murderer was killed.

For Qāsim's brother, *vide* No. 241, and for his son, No. 226.

60. **Bāqī Khān** (elder), brother of Adham Khān (No. 19).

His mother is the same Māhum Anaga, mentioned on p. 340. "From Badā,onī (II, 340) we learn that Bāqī Khān died in the 30th year as Governor of Gadha-Katanga." This is all the *Maʾāṣir* says of him.

His full name is Muḥammad Bāqī Khān Koka. From Badā,onī II, 81, we see that Bāqī Khān took part in the war against Iskandar Khān and Bahādur Khān (972–3), and fought under Muʿizzu'l-Mulk (No. 61)

---

[1] In 1016 another false son of Mīrzā Shāhrukh (p. 326) created disturbances and asked Jahāngīr for assistance against the Tūrānīs.

The fate of Mīrzā Shāhrukh's second son, Mīrzā Ḥusayn, is involved in obscurity, "He ran away from Burhānpūr, went to sea and to Persia, from where he went to Badakhshān. People say that he is still alive (1016); but no one knows whether this new pretender is Shāhrukh's son or not. Shāhrukh left Badakhshān about twenty-five years ago, and since then the Badakhshīs have set up several false Mīrzās, in order to shake off the yoke of the Uzbaks. This pretender collected a large number of Uymāqs (p. 402, note 1) and Badakhshī Mountaineers, who go by the name of *Gharjas* [غرجه, whence *Gharjistān*], and took from the Uzbaks a part of the country. But the enemies pressed upon him, caught him, and cut off his head, which was carried on a spear all over Badakhshān. Several false Mīrzās have since been killed; but I really think their race will continue as long as a trace of Badakhshīs remain on earth." *Tuzuk i-Jahāngīrī*, p. 57.

in the battle of Khayrābād, in which Budāgh Khān (No. 52) was captured. The battle was lost, chiefly because Bāqī Khān, Mahdī Qāsim Khān (No. 36), and Ḥusayn Khān Tukriya (No. 53) had personal grievances —their Uzbak hatred—against Muʕizzᵘ 'l-Mulk and Rāja Toḍar Mal.

61. **Mīr Muʕizzᵘ l'-Mulk-i** Mūsawī of Mashhad.

He belongs to the Mūsawī Sayyids of Mashhad the Holy, who trace their descent to ʕAlī Mūsā Raẓā, the 8th Imām of the Shīʕahs. A branch of these Sayyids by a different mother is called *Raẓawī*.

In the 10th year, Akbar moved to Jaunpūr to punish Khān Zamān (No. 13), who had dispatched his brother Bahādur and Iskandar Khān Uzbak (No. 48) to the district of *Sarwār*.[1] Against them Akbar sent a strong detachment (*vide* No. 60) under Muʕizzᵘ 'l-Mulk. Bahādur, on the approach of the Imperialists, had recourse to negotiations, and asked for pardon, stating that he was willing to give up all elephants. M. M., however, desired war, and though he granted Bahādur an interview, he told him that his crimes could only be cleansed with blood. But he reported the matter to Akbar, who sent Lashkar Khān (No. 90) and Rāja Toḍar Mal to him, to tell him that he might make peace with Bahādur, if he was satified with his good intentions. But here also the rancour of the Khurāsānīs towards the Uzbaks decided matters, and Toḍar Mal only confirmed M. M. in his resolution.[2] Although a few days later the news arrived that Akbar had pardoned Khān Zamān, because he sent his mother and his uncle Ibrāhīm Khān (No. 64) to Court as guarantees of his loyalty, M. M. attacked Bahādur near Khayrābād. Muḥammad Yār, son of Iskandar Khān's brother, who commanded the van of the rebels, fell in the first attack, and Iskandar who stood behind him, was carried along and fled from the field. The Imperialists, thinking that the battle was decided, commenced to plunder, when suddenly Bahādur, who had been lying in wait, fell upon M. M.'s left wing and put it to flight. Not only was Budāgh Khān (No. 52) taken prisoner but many soldiers went over to Bahādur. Flushed with victory, he attacked the

---

[1] Most MSS. have سروار. The Edit. Bibl. Indica of Badā,onī, p. 78, has سردار *Sardār*; but again سروار, on p. 83. There is no doubt that the district got its name from the *Sarw* River (آب‌سروار آب‌سرو, آب‌سرو).

[2] Badā,onī says Toḍar Mal's arrival was "*naphta* on Muʕizzᵘ 'l-Mulk's fire". Throughout his work, Badā,onī shows himself an admirer of Khān Zamān and his brother Bahādur. With Muʕizzᵘ 'l-Mulk a Shīʕāh of the Shīʕahs, he has no patience. "Muʕizzᵘ'l-Mulk's ideas," he says, were "I and nobody else"; he behaved as proudly as Firʕaūn and Shaddād; for pride is the inheritance of all Sayyids of Mashhad. Hence people say: "*Ahl-i Mashhad ba-juz Imām-i shumā, Laʕnatᵘ llāhⁱ bar tamām-i shumā,*" "O people of Mashkad, with the exception of your Imām [Mūsā Raẓā], may God's curse rest upon all of you. And also, "The surface of the earth rejoices in its inhabitants; how fortunate would it be, if a certain Mashhad vanished from the surface of the earth."

centre, where the grandees either fled or would not fight from malice (*vide* No. 60). Toḍar Mal's firmness was of no avail, and the day was lost

After the conquest of Bihār, M. M. got the Pargana of Āra (Arrah) as *jāgīr*. In the 24th year the nobles of Bihār under Maʿṣūm-i Kābulī, *tuyūldār* of Patna, rebelled. They won over M. M., and his younger brother Mīr ʿAlī Akbar (No. 62); but both soon left the rebels, and M. M. went to Jaunpūr recruiting, evidently meditating revolt independently of the others. In the 25th year, Akbar ordered Asad Khān Turkmān, *jāgīrdār* of Mānikpūr, to hasten to Jaunpūr and convey M. M. with all his suspicious adherents to Court. Asad Khān succeeded in catching M. M., and sent him by boat to the Emperor. Near Itāwah, however, the boat "foundered", and M. M. lost his life.

62. **Mīr ʿAlī Akbar** (younger), brother of the preceding.

He generally served with his brother, and held the same rank. In the 22nd year he presented Akbar, according to the *Ṭabaqāt* with a *Mawlūdnāma*, or History of the birth of the Emperor. It was in the handwriting of Qāẓī Ghiyāṣ[u] 'd-Din-i Jāmī, a man of learning, who had served under Humāyūn, and contained an account of the vision which Humāyūn had in the night Akbar was born. The Emperor saw in his dream the new born babe, and was told to call his name Jalāl[u] 'd-Dīn Muḥammad Akbar. This Mawlūdnāma Akbar prized very much, and rewarded Mīr ʿAlī Akbar with a pargana [1] as *inʿām*.

When his brother was sent to Bihār, M. ʿA. A. was ordered to accompany him. He established himself at Zamāniya, which "lies 6 *kos* from Ghāzīpūr (*vide* p. 336), and rebelled like his brother in Jaunpūr. After the death of his brother, Akbar ordered M. ʿAzīz (No. 21), who had been appointed to Bihār, to send M. ʿA. A. fettered to Court. Notwithstanding his protests that he was innocent, he was taken to the Emperor, who imprisoned him for life.

63. **Sharīf Khān**, brother of Atga Khān (No. 15).

He was born at Ghaznīn. After Bayrām's fall, he held a *tuyūl* in the Panjāb, and generally served with his elder brother Mīr Muḥammad Khān (No. 16).

On the transfer of the *Atga Khayl* from the Panjāb, Sh. was appointed to the Sarkār of Qannawj. In the 21st year, when Akbar was at Mohinī, he sent Sh., together with Qāẓī Khān-i Badakhshī (No. 144), Mujāhid Khān, Subḥān Qulī Turk, against the Rānā. He afterwards distinguished

---

[1] Called in the *Maʾāṣir* ندیه (though it cannot be Nuddea in Bengal); in my copy of the *Sawāniḥ* مدینه; but Nadīnah in Sambhal appears to be meant.

himself in the conquest of Kōbhalmīr. In the 25th year, he was made *atālīq* to Prince Murād, and was in the same year sent to Mālwah as Governor, Shujāʿat K͟hān (No. 51) having been killed. His son Bāz Bahādur (No. 188) was ordered to join his father from Gujrāt. In the 28th year, he served against Muẓaffar, and distinguished himself in the siege of Bahrōch, which was held for Muẓaffar by Chirkis-i Rūmī and Naṣīrā, brother of Muẓaffar's wife. The former having been killed, Naṣīrā escaped in the 7th month of the siege, through the trench held by Sharīf, and the Fort was taken. In the 30th year, he was sent with Shihābᵘ 'd-Dīn (No. 26) to the Dak͟hin, to assist Mīrzā ʿAzīz (No. 21).

In the 35th year he went from Mālwah to Court, and was made in the 39th year Governor of G͟haznīn, an appointment which he had long desired. There he remained till the 47th year, when Shāh Beg (No. 57) was sent there.

"Nothing else is known of him." *Maʾāṣir.*

His son, Bāz Bahādur (No. 188), held a *jāgīr* in Gujrāt, and was transferred to Mālwah as related above. He served in the siege of Āsīr, and in the Aḥmadnagar war. In the 46th year, he was caught by the Talingahs, but was released, when Abū 'l-Faẓl made peace, and the prisoners were exchanged.

IX.—Commanders of Two Thousand and Five Hundred.

64. **Ibrāhīm K͟hān-i Shaybānī** (uncle of K͟hān Zamān, No. 13).

He served under Humāyūn. After the conquest of Hindūstān, Humāyūn sent him with Shāh Abū 'l-Maʿālī to Lāhor, to oppose Sikandar Sūr, should he leave the Sawāliks. After the fall of Mānkoṭ, he received the Pargana of Sarharpūr,[1] near Jaunpūr, as *jāgīr*, and remained with K͟hān Zamān. During K͟hān Zamān's first rebellion, Ibrāhīm K͟hān and K͟hān Zamān's mother repaired at Munʿim K͟hān's request to Court as hostages of his loyalty. Ibrāhīm appearing, as was customary, with a shroud and a sword round his neck, which were only taken off when the Emperor's pardon had been obtained.

In the 12th year, however, K͟hān Zamān again rebelled, and Ibrāhīm went with Iskandar (No. 48) to Audh. When the latter had gone to Bengal, Ibrāhīm, at Munʿim's request, was pardoned, and remained with the K͟hān K͟hānān.

---

[1] It is difficult to reconcile this statement with Badāonī II, 23, where Sarharpūr, which "lies 18 *kos* from Jaunpūr", is mentioned as the *jāgīr* of Abdᵘ 'r-Raḥmān, Sikandar Sūr's son, who got it after the surrender of Mānkoṭ.

In the *Tabaqāt*, Ibr. is called a Commander of Four Thousand.

His son, Ismaʿīl Khān, held from Khān Zamān the town of Sandelah in Audh. In the 3rd year, Akbar gave this town to Sulṭān Ḥusayn Khān Jalā,ir. Ismāʿīl opposed him with troops which he had got from Khān Zamān; but he was defeated and killed.

65. **Khwāja Jalālᵘ 'd-Dīn Maḥmūd Bujūq**, of Khurāsān.

The MSS. of the Āʾīn have *Muḥammad*, instead of *Maḥmūd*, which other histories have, and have besides a word after *Muḥammad* which reads like الحق and بحق. This should be no doubt بجق *bujuq*, the *scriptio defectiva* of the Turkish بجوق *bujūq*, "having the nose cut," as given in the copy of the *Maʾāṣir*.

Jalālᵘ 'd-Dīn was in the service of M. ʿAskarī. He had sent him from Qandahār to Garmsīr, to collect taxes, when Humāyūn passed through the district on his way to Persia. The Emperor called him, and Jalāl presented him with whatever he had with him of cash and property, for which service Humāyūn conferred on him the title of *Mīr Sāmān*, which in the circumstances was an empty distinction. On Humāyūn's return from Persia, Jalāl joined the Emperor, and was ordered, in 959, to accompany the young Akbar to Ghaznīn, the *tuyūl* of the Prince. His devotion to his master rendered him so confident of the Emperor's protection that he treated the grandees rudely, and incessantly annoyed them by satirical remarks. In fact, he had not a single friend.

Akbar on his accession made him a Commander of Two Thousand Five Hundred, and appointed him to Ghaznīn. His enemies used the opportunity and stirred up Munʿim Khān, who owed Jalāl an old grudge. Jalāl soon found his post in Ghaznīn so disagreeable that he determined to look for employment elsewhere. He had scarcely left Ghaznīn, when Munʿim called him to account. Though he had promised to spare his life, Munʿim imprisoned him, and had a short time after his eyes pierced. Jalāl's sight, however, had not been entirely destroyed, and he meditated a flight to India. Before he reached the frontier, Munʿim's men caught him and his son, Jalālᵘ 'd-Dīn Masʿūd.[1] Both were imprisoned and shortly afterwards murdered by Munʿim.

This double murder is the foulest blot on Munʿim's character, and takes us the more by surprise, as on all other occasions he showed himself generous and forbearing towards his enemies.

---

[1] He must not be confounded with the Jalālᵘ 'd-Dīn Masʿūd mentioned in *Tuzuk*, p. 67, who "ate opium like cheese out of the hands of his mother".

66. **Ḥaydar Muḥammad Khān**, Akhta Begī.

He was an old servant of Ḥumāyūn, and accompanied him to Persia. He gave the Emperor his horse, when, in the defeat near Balkh, Ḥumāyūn's horse had been shot. On the march against Kāmrān, who had left Kābul for Afghānistān, the imperialists came to the River Surkhāb, Ḥaydar, with several other faithful Amīrs, leading the van. They reached the river Siyāh-āb, which flows near the Surkhāb, before the army could come up. Kāmrān suddenly attacked them by night; but Ḥaydar bravely held his ground. He accompanied the Emperor to Qandahār and to India, and was appointed to Bayānah (*Bad.* I, 463), which was held by Ghāzī Khān Sūr, father of Ibrāhīm Khān. After the siege had lasted some time, Ḥaydar allowed Ghāzi to capitulate; but soon after, he killed Ghāzī. Humāyūn was annoyed at this breach of faith, and said he would not let Ḥaydar do so again.

After Akbar's accession, Ḥ. was with Tardī Beg (No. 12) in Dihlī, and fought under Khān Zamān (No. 13) against Hemū. After the victory, he went for some reason to Kābul. At Munʿim's request he assisted Ghanī Khān (*vide* p. 333) in Kābul. But they could not agree, and Ḥ. was called to India. He accompanied Munʿim in the 8th year, on his expedition to Kābul and continued to serve under him in India.

In the 17th year, Ḥ. served with Khān-i Kalān (No. 16) in Gujrāt. In the 19th year, he was, together with his brother Mīrzā Qulī, attached to the Bengal Army, under Munʿim. Both died of fever, in 983, at Gaur (*vide* p. 407).

A son of Ḥ. is mentioned below (No. 326).

Mīrzā Qulī, or *Mīrzā Qulī Khān*, Ḥaydar's brother, distinguished himself under Ḥumāyūn during the expedition to Badakhshān. When Kāmrān, under the mask of friendship, suddenly attacked Humāyūn, M. Q. was wounded and thrown off his horse. His son, *Dost Muḥammad*, saved him in time.

According to the *Ṭabaqāt*, M. Q. belonged to the principal grandees (*umarā-i kibār*), a phrase which is never applied to grandees below the rank of Commanders of One Thousand. His name occurs also often in the *Akbarnāma*. It is, therefore, difficult to say why his name and that of his son have been left out by Abū 'l-Faẓl in this list.

67. **Iʿtimād Khān**, of Gujrāt.

He must not be confounded with No. 119.

Iʿtimād Khān was originally a Hindū servant of Sulṭān Maḥmūd, king of Gujrāt. He was "trusted" (*iʿtimād*) by his master, who had allowed him to enter the harem, and had put him in charge of the women.

It is said that, from gratitude, he used to eat camphor, and thus rendered himself impotent. He rose in the king's favour, and was at last made an Amīr. In 961, after a reign of 18 years, the king was foully murdered by a slave of the name of Burhān, who besides killed twelve nobles. Iˁtimād next morning collected a few faithful men, and killed Burhān. Sulṭān Maḥmūd having died without issue, Iˁt. raised Raẓiyᵘ 'l-Mulk, under the title of Aḥmad Shāh, to the throne. Raẓī was a son of Sulṭān Aḥmad, the founder of Aḥmadābād; but as he was very young, the affairs of the state were entirely in Iˁt.'s hands. Five years later, the young king left Aḥmadābād, and fled to Sayyid Mubārak of Bukhārā [1] a principal courtier; but Iˁt. followed him up, defeated him, and drove him away. Sulṭān Aḥmad then thought it better to return to Iˁt., who now again reigned as before. On several occasions did the king try to get rid of his powerful minister; and Iˁt. at last felt so insecure that he resolved to kill the king, which he soon afterwards did. Iˁt. now raised a child of the name of Nathū (نتهو) [2] to the throne, "who did not belong to the line of kings"; but on introducing him to the grandees, Iˁt. swore upon the Qur'ān that Nathū was a son of Sulṭān Maḥmūd; his mother when pregnant had been handed over to him by Sulṭān Maḥmūd, to make her miscarry; but the child had been five months old, and he had not carried out the order. The Amīrs had to believe the story, and Nathū was raised to the throne under the title of Sulṭān Muẓaffar.

This is the origin of Sulṭān Muẓaffar, who subsequently caused Akbar's generals so much trouble (*vide* pp. 344, 354, 355).

Iˁt. was thus again at the head of the government; but the Amīrs parcelled out the country among themselves, so that each was almost independent. The consequence was that incessant feuds broke out among them. Iˁt. himself was involved in a war with Chingiz Khān, son of Iˁtimādᵘ 'l-Mulk, a Turkish slave. Chingiz maintained that Sulṭān Muẓaffar, if genuine, should be the head of the state; and as he was strengthened by the rebellious Mīrzās, to whom he had afforded protection against Akbar, Iˁt saw no chance of opposing him, left the Sulṭān, and went to Dūngarpūr. Two nobles, Alif Khān and Jhujhār Khān took Sulṭān Muẓaffar to him, went to Chingiz in Aḥmadābād and killed him (Chingiz) soon after. The Mīrzās, seeing how distracted the country was, took possession of Bahrōch and Sūrat. The general confusion only increased, when Sulṭān Muẓaffar fled one day to Sher Khān Fūlādī and

---

[1] Regarding this distinguished Gujrātī noble, *vide* the biography of his grandson, S. Ḥāmid (No. 78).

[2] Some MSS. read *Nahtū*.

his party, and Iʿt. retaliated by informing Sher Khān that Nathū was no prince at all. But Sher Khān's party attributed this to Iʿt.'s malice, and besieged him in Aḥmadābād. Iʿt. then fled to the Mīrzās and soon after to Akbar, whose attention he drew to the wretched state of Gujrāt.

When Akbar, in the 17th year, marched to Patan, Sher Khān's party had broken up. The Mīrzās still held Bahrōch ; and Sulṭān Muẓaffar, who had left Sher Khān, fell into the hands of Akbar's officers (*vide* No. 361). Iʿtimād and other Gujrātī nobles had in the meantime proclaimed Akbar's accession from the pulpits of the mosques and struck coins in his name. They now waited on the Emperor. Baroda, Champānīr, and Sūrat were given to Iʿt. as *tuyūl* ; the other Amīrs were confirmed, and all charged themselves with the duty of driving away the Mīrzās. But they delayed and did nothing ; some of them, as Iʿtimād^{u} 'l-Mulk, even fled, and others who were attached to Akbar, took Iʿt. and several grandees to the Emperor, apparently charging them with treason. Iʿt. fell into disgrace, and was handed over to Shāhbāz Khān (No. 80) as prisoner.

In the 20th year, Iʿt. was released, and charged with the superintendence of the Imperial jewels and gold vessels. In the 22nd year, he was permitted to join the party who under Mīr Abū Turāb (*vide* p. 207) went to Makkah. On his return he received Patan as *jāgīr*.

In the 28th year, on the removal of Shihāb^{u} 'd-Dīn Aḥmad (No. 26), he was put in charge of Gūjrāt, and went there accompanied by several distinguished nobles, though Akbar had been warned ; for people remembered Iʿt.'s former inability to allay the factions in Gujrāt. No sooner had Shihāb handed over duties than his servants rebelled. Iʿt. did nothing, alleging that Shihāb was responsible for his men ; but as Sulṭān Muẓaffar had been successful in Kāthīwār, Iʿt. left Aḥmadābāb, and went to Shihāb, who on his way to Court had reached Karī, 20 *kos* from Aḥmadābād. Muẓaffar used the opportunity and took Aḥmadābād, Shihāb's men joining his standard.

Shihāb and Iʿt. then shut themselves up in Patan, and had agreed to withdraw from Gujrāt, when they received some auxiliaries, chiefly a party of Gujrātīs who had left Muẓaffar, to try their luck with the Imperialists. Iʿt. paid them well, and sent them under the command of his son Sher Khān, against Sher Khān Fūlādī, who was repulsed. In the meantime, M. ʿAbd^{u} 'r-Raḥīm (No. 29) arrived. Leaving Iʿt. at Patan, he marched with Shihāb against Muẓaffar.

Iʿtimād died at Patan in 995. The *Ṭabaqāt* puts him among the Commanders of Four Thousand.

In Abū 'l-Faẓl's opinion, Gujrātīs are made up of cowardice, deceit, several good qualities, and meanness; and Iʿtimād was the very type of a Gujrātī.

68. **Pāyanda Khān**, Mughul, son of Ḥājī Muḥammad Khān Kokī's brother.

Ḥājī Muḥammad and Shāh Muḥammad, his brother, had been killed by Humāyūn for treason on his return from Persia. Ḥājī Muḥammad was a man of great daring, and his value, when he was faithful, was often acknowledged by the Emperor.

Pāyanda, in the 5th year of Akbar's reign came with Munʿim from Kābul, and was ordered to accompany Adham Khān (No. 19) to Mālwa. In the 19th year, he accompanied Munʿim to Bengal. In the 22nd year, he served under Bhagwān Dās against Rānā Partāb. In the Gujrāt war, he commanded M. ʿAbd[u] 'r-Raḥīm's (No. 29) *harāwal*.

In the 32nd year, he received Ghorāghāt as jāgīr, whither he went.

This is all the *Maʾāṣir* says regarding Pāyanda.

His full name was Muḥammad Pāyanda. He had a son Walī Beg who is mentioned below (No. 359).

From the *Tuzuk*, p. 144, we see that Pāyanda died in 1024 A.H., Jahāngīr, in 1017, had pensioned him off, as he was too old. *Tuz.*, p. 68.

69. **Jagannāth**, son of Rāja Bihārī Mal (No. 23).

He was a hostage in the hands of Sharaf[u] 'd-Dīn Ḥusayn (No. 17; *vide* p. 339). After some time he regained his freedom and was well received by Akbar. He generally served with Mān Singh. In the 21st year, when Rānā Partāb of Maiwār opposed the Imperialists, Jagannāt'h during an engagement when other officers had given way, held his ground, and killed with his own hands the renowned champion Rām Dās, son of Jay Mal. In the 23rd year, he received a jāgīr in the Panjāb, and was, in the 25th year, attached to the van of the army which was to prevent Mīrzā Muḥammad Ḥakīm from invading the Panjāb. In the 29th year, he again served against the Rānā. Later he accompanied Mīrzā Yūsuf Khān (No. 35) to Kashmīr. In the 34th year, he served under Prince Murād in Kābul, and accompanied him, in the 36th year, to Mālwa, of which the Prince had been appointed Governor. In the 43rd year, after several years' service in the Dakhin, he left Murād without orders, and was for some time excluded from Court. On Akbar's return from the Dakhin, J. met the emperor at Rantanbhūr, his jāgīr, and was then again sent to the Dakhin.

In the 1st year of Jahāngīr, he served under Prince Parwīz against the Rānā, and was in charge of the whole army when the emperor, about the time Khusraw had been captured, called Parwīz to Court (*Tuzuk*, p. 33). In the same year, J. suppressed disturbances which Dalpat (p. 386) had raised at Nāgor.

In the 4th year, he was made a Commander of Five Thousand, with 3,000 horse.

Rām Chand,[1] his son. He was under Jahāngīr a Commander of Two Thousand, 1,500 horse.

Rāja Manrūp, a son of Rām Chand. He accompanied Prince Shāhjahān on his rebellion, and got on his accession a Command of Three Thousand, with 2,000 horse. He died in the 4th year of Shāhjahān. He had a son *Gopāl Singh.*

70. **Makhṣūṣ Khan** (younger), brother of Saʿīd Khān (No. 25).

He served under his brother in Multān. In the 23rd year, he served under Shāhbāz Khān (No. 80) against Gajpatī, and three years later he accompanied Prince Murād to Kābul, where he also served under Akbar, who had gone thither and pardoned his brother, M. Muḥammad Ḥakīm.

Subsequently, Makhṣūṣ served under Prince Salīm. In the 49th year, he was a Commander of Three Thousand.

He was alive in the beginning of Jahāngīr's reign. The author of the *Maʾāṣir* has not recorded the date of his death.

He had a son Maqṣūd who did not get on well with his father, for which reason Jahāngīr would not give him a *manṣab.*

71. **The author of the Āʾīn, Abū 'l-Faẓl,** son of Shaykh Mubārak of Nāgor.

Abū 'l-Faẓl's biography will be found elsewhere.

X. Commanders of Two Thousand.

72. **Ismaʿīl Khān Dulday.**

Dulday, or Dūlday, is the name of a subdivision of the Barlās clan (*vide* p. 364, note).

The *Maʾāṣir* calls him Ismāʿīl Qulī *Beg* Dūlday. A similar difference was observed in the name of Ḥusayn Qulī Khān (No. 24), and we may conclude that *Beg*, at least in India, was considered a lower title than *Khān*, just as *Beglar Begī* was considered inferior to *Khān Khānān.*

Ismāʿīl Qulī was a grandee of Bābar and Humāyūn, distinguished in the field and in council. When Humāyūn besieged Qandahār, and the grandees one after the other left M. ʿAskarī, Ism. also joined the Emperor, and was appointed, after the conquest of Qandahār, Governor of Dāwar.

---

[1] The *Tuzuk*, p. 74, calls him Karm Chand. *Vide* also *Pādishāhnāma*, I, *b*. 318.

When Kābul was besieged, Ism. and Khizr Khwāja (*vide* p. 394, note) attacked Sher ʿAlī, an officer of Mīrzā Kāmrān, who at the prince's order had followed up and plundered the Persian caravan (*qāfila-yiwilāyat*) on its way to Chārīkān;[1] but as the roads were occupied by the Imperialists, Sher ʿAlī could not reach Kābul, and marched towards Ghaznīn, when he was overtaken and defeated. Ism. and Khizr spoiled the plunderer, and went again to Humāyūn. A short time after, Ism. and several other grandees left the emperor, because they resented the elevation of Qarācha Khān, and followed Mīrzā Kāmrān to Badakhshān. Humāyūn followed them up and caught them together with Kāmrān, Ism. among them. Ism. was, however, pardoned at Munʿim's request.

Ism. accompanied the emperor on his march to India, and was sent, after the capture of Dihlī together with Shāh Abū 'l-Maʿālī to Lāhor.

"Nothing else is known of him." *Maʾāṣir.*

73. **Mīr Babus** (?), the Īghur (Uighur?).

The Īghurs are a well known Chaghtā,ī tribe. The correct name of this grandee is a matter of doubt, as every MS. has a different *lectio*; *vide* my Text edition, p. 224, note 6. The *Maʿāṣir* has left out the name of this grandee; nor do I find it in the List of the Ṭabaqāt.

74. **Ashraf Khān Mīr Munshī,** Muḥammad Aṣghar. of Sabzwār (?).

He was a Ḥusaynī Sayyid of Mashhad (*Maʿāṣir*, Mirʾātᵘ 'l-ʿĀlam). The author of the *Ṭabaqāt* says, he belonged to the ʿ*Arabshāhī* Sayyids; "but people rarely make such fine distinctions." Abū 'l-Faẓl says, he was of Sabzwār; but in the opinion of the *Maʿāṣir*, this is an error of the copyists.

Ashraf Khān was a clever writer, exact in his style, and a renowned calligrapher, perhaps the first of his age in writing the *Taʿlīq* and *Nastaʿlīq* character (pp. 107–8). He also understood *jafar*, or witchcraft.[2]

Ashraf was in Humāyūn's service, and had received from him the post and title of Mīr Munshī. After the conquest of Hindūstān, he was made Mīr ʿ*Arẓ* and *Mīr Mal.* At Akbar's accession, he was in Dihlī, and took part in the battle with Hemū (p. 394, No. 48). He was imprisoned by Bayrām, but escaped and went to Makkah. He returned in 968, when Akbar was at Māchhīwāra on his way to the Siwāliks where Bayrām

[1] So the *Maʾāṣir.* Our maps have *Charikar* (lat. 35°, long. 69), which lies north of Kābul, and has always been the centre of a large caravan trade. Istālif (استالف, or استاليف) lies half-way between Kābul and Charikar. [Dowson, v., 225, has Chārīkārān.—B.]

[[2] *Jafr* divination, etc.—P.]

was. He was well received and got a *manṣab*. In the 6th year, when the emperor returned from Malwa, he bestowed upon him the title of *Ashraf Khān*.

In the 19th year, he went with Munʿim to Bengal, was present in the battle of Takaroī, and died in the twentieth year (983) [1] at Gaur (*vide* p. 407).

Ashraf was a poet of no mean pretensions.

His son, Mīr Abū 'l-Muẓaffar (No. 240) held a Command of 500. In the 38th year, he was Governor of Awadh.

Ashraf's grandsons, Ḥusaynī and Burhānī held inferior commands under Shāhjahān.

75. **Sayyid Maḥmūd of Bārha** (Kūndlīwāl).

"Sayyid Maḥmūd was the first of the Bārha Sayyids that held office under the Tīmūrides." He was with Sikandar Sūr (*Badā,onī* II, 18) in Mānkot, but seeing that the cause of the Afghāns was hopeless, he left Sikandar and went over to Akbar. He was a friend of Bayrām, and served in the first year under ʿAlī Qulī Khān Zamān (No. 13) against Hemū. In the second year, he took part in the expedition against Ḥājī Khān in Ajmīr (*vide* Nos. 40, 45). In the 3rd year, he conquered with Shāh Qulī Maḥram (No. 45) Fort Jaitāran,[2] and served in the same year under Adham Koka against the Bhadauriyahs of Hatkānth (*vide* p. 341, l. 8).

After Bayrām's fall, Sayyid Maḥmūd got a jāgīr near Dihlī. In the 7th year, he brought Munʿim Khān to Court (*vide* p. 333). In the 17th year, he served under the Khān-i Kalān (No. 16) and the emperor in Gujrāt, was present in the battle of Sarnāl, and followed up Mīrzā Ibrāhīm Ḥusayn. On every occasion he fought with much bravery. Towards the end of the 18th year, he was sent with other Sayyids of Bārha, and Sayyid Muḥammad of Amroha (No. 140) against Rāja Madhukar, who had invaded the territory between Sironj and Gwāliyār. S. Maḥmud drove him away, and died soon after, in the very end of 981.

Sayyid Maḥmūd was a man of rustic habits, and great personal courage and generosity. Akbar's court admired his valour and chuckled at his boorishness and unadorned language; but he stood in high favour with the emperor. Once on his return from the war with Madhukar he gave in the State hall a verbal account of his expedition, in which his

---

[1] The *Mirʾāt* says in the tenth year (973), as stated on p. 101, note 6. This is clearly a mistake of the author of the *Mirʾāt*.

[2] The best MSS. have جیتارن. The name is doubtful. Akbar passed it on one of his marches from Ajmīr over Pālī to Jālor.

"I" occurred oftener than was deemed proper by the assembled Amīrs. "You have gained the victory," interrupted Āṣaf Khān, in order to give him a gentle hint, "because His Majesty's good fortune (*iqbāl-i pādishāhī*) accompanied you." Mistaking the word "Iqbāl" for the name of a courtier, "Why do you tell an untruth?" replied Maḥmūd, "Iqbāl-i Pādishāhī did not accompany me: I was there, and my brothers; *we* licked them with our sabres." The emperor smiled, and bestowed upon him praise and more substantial favours.

But more malicious were the remarks of the Amīrs regarding his claim to be a Sayyid of pure blood. Jahāngīr (*Tuzuk*, p. 366) also says that people doubt the claim of the Bārha family to be Sayyids. Once Maḥmūd was asked how many generations backwards the Sayyids of Bārha traced their descent. Accidentally, a fire was burning on the ground near the spot where Maḥmūd stood. Jumping into it, he exclaimed, "If I am a Sayyid, the fire will not hurt me; if I am no Sayyid, I shall get burnt." He stood for nearly an hour in the fire, and only left it at the earnest request of the bystanders. "His velvet-slippers showed, indeed, no trace of being singed."

For Sayyid Maḥmūd's brother and sons, *vide* Nos. 91, 105, and 143.

Note on the Sayyids of Bārha (Sādāt-i Bārha).

In MSS. we find the spelling بارهه *bārha*, and بارہ *barāh*. The lexicographist Bahār-i ʿAjam (Tek Chand) in his grammatical treatise, entitled *Jawāhir*ᵘ *'l-Ḥurūf*, says that the names of Indian towns ending in ہ form adjectives in وي, as تته, *Tatta* or تهتهه *Thatha*, forms an adjective تتوي *tatawī*: but of بارهه no adjective is formed, and you say *sādat-i bārha* instead of *sādāt-i bārhawī*

The name *Bārha* has been differently explained. Whether the derivation from the Hindī numeral *bārah*, 12, be correct or not, there is no doubt that the etymology was believed to be correct in the times of Akbar and Jahāngīr; for both the *Ṭabaqāt* and the *Tuzuk* derive the name from 12 villages in the Du,āb (Muẓaffarnagar District), which the Sayyids held.

Like the Sayyids of Bilgrām, the Bārha family trace their origin to one Sayyid Abū 'l-Farah of Wāsiṭ [1]; but their *nasabnāma*, or genealogical tree, was sneered at, and even Jahāngīr, in the above-quoted passage from the *Tuzuk*, says that the personal courage of the Sayyids of Bārha—but

---

[1] "From him are descended the most renowned Musalmān families in Northern India, the Bārha and Belgrām Sayyids, and in Khyrābād, Futtehpore Huswā, and many other places, branches of the same stem are found." C. A. Elliot, *The Chronicles of Onao*, Allahabad, 1862, p. 93.

nothing else—was the best proof that they were Sayyids. But they clung so firmly to this distinction, that some of them even placed the title of Sayyid before the titles which they received from the Mughul emperors, as Sayyid Khān Jahān (Sayyid Abū 'l-Muẓaffar) and several others.

But if their claim to be Sayyids was not firmly established, their bravery and valour had become a by-word. Their place in battle was the van (*harāwal*); they claimed to be the leaders of the onset, and every emperor from the times of Akbar gladly availed himself of the prestige of their name. They delighted in looking upon themselves as Hindūstānīs (*vide* p. 336). Their military fame completely threw to the background the renown of the Sayyids of Amrohah, of Mānikpūr, the Khānzādas of Mewāt, and even families of royal blood as the Ṣafawīs.

The Sayyids of Bārha are divided into four branches, whose names are 1. *Tihanpūrī*; 2. *Chatbanūrī* or *Chātrauṛī* [1]; 3. *Kūndlīwāl*; 4. *Jagnerī*. The chief town of the first branch was Jānsaṭh; of the second, Sambalhaṛa; of the third, Majhaṛa; of the fourth Biḍaulī on the Jamna. Of these four lines Muhammadan Historians, perhaps accidentally, only mention two, viz., the *Kūndlīwāl* (كوندلي وال) to which Sayyid Maḥmūd (No. 75) belonged; and the *Tihanpūrī* (تهنپوري), of which Sayyid Khān Jahān was a member.

The Histories of India do not appear to make mention of the Sayyids of Bārha before the times of Akbar; but they must have held posts of some importance under the Sūrs, because the arrival of Sayyid Maḥmūd in Akbar's camp (p. 424) is recorded by all historians as an event of importance. He and other Sayyids, were moreover, at once appointed to high *manṣabs*. The family boasts also traditionally of services rendered to Humāyūn; but this is at variance with Abū 'l-Faẓl's statement that Sayyid Maḥmūd was the first that served under a Timuride.

The political importance of the Sayyids declined from the reign of Muḥammad, Shāh (1131 to 1161) who deposed the brothers Sayyid ʿAbdᵘ 'llah Khān and Sayyid Ḥusayn ʿAli Khān, in whom the family reached the greatest height of their power. What a difference between the rustic and loyal Sayyid Maḥmūd and Akbar, and the above two

---

[1] *Vide* Sir H. Elliot's Glossary (Beames' Edition) I, p. 11 and p. 297. On p. 12 of the Glossary read *Sayyid Maḥmūd* twice for *Sayyid Muḥammad*; *Sayyid ʿAlī Aṣghar* for *Sayyid ʿAlī Aṣaf Dilīr Khān* for *Debī Khān*. Instead of *Chatbanūrī* (or *Chātrauṛī*), which Mr. R. J. Leeds, C.S., gives in his valuable Report on the Castes and Races of the Muẓaffarnagar District (Glossary, p. 297 ff.), Sir H. Elliot has *Chantraudī*.

brothers, who made four Timurides emperors, dethroned and killed two and blinded and imprisoned three.[1]

The Sayyids of Bārha are even nowadays numerous and "form the characteristic element in the population of the Muẕaffarnagar district" (Leeds' Report).

Abū 'l-Faẕl mentions nine Sayyids in this List of grandees, *viz.* :—

1. Sayyid Maḥmūd (No. 75).
2. Sayyid Aḥmad, his brother (No. 91).
3. Sayyid Qāsim (No. 105). } sons of 1.
4. Sayyid Hāshim (No. 143). } sons of 1.
5. Sayyid Rājū (No. 165).
6. Sayyid Jamālᵘ 'd-Dīn (No. 217), son of 2.
7. Sayyid Chajhū (No. 221).
8. Sayyid Bāyazid (No. 295).
9. Sayyid Lāḍ (No. 409).

The Akbarnāma mentions several other Sayyids without indicating to what family they belong. Thus S. Jamālᵘ 'd-Dīn, a *grandson* of S. Maḥmūd (*vide* under 91) ; S. Sālim ; S. Fāth Khān (Bad. II, 180) ; etc.

The following trees are compiled from the *Tuzuk*, *Pādishāhnāma*, and *Maʾāṣir*.

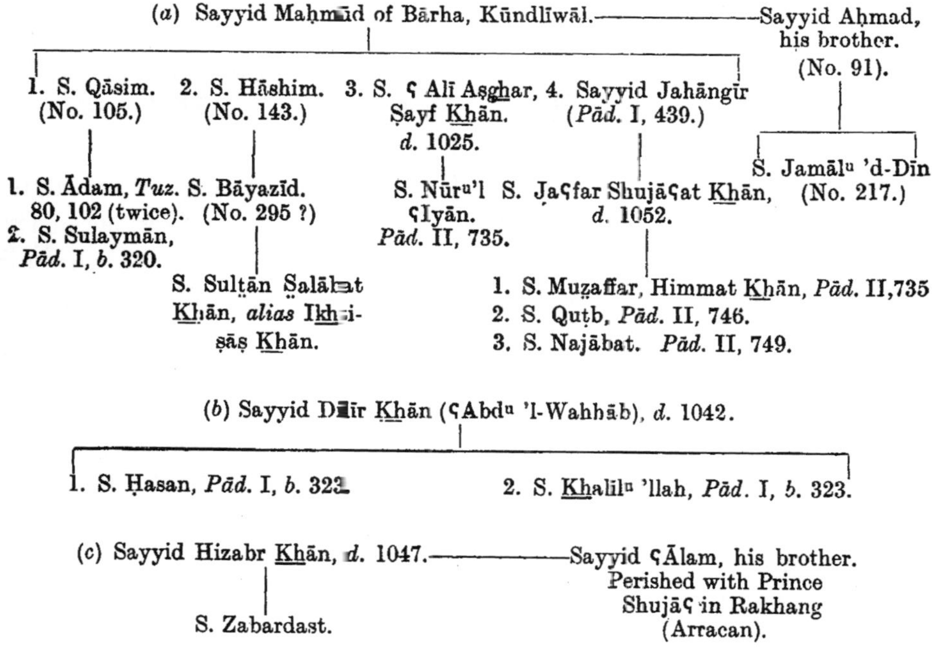

[1] They made Farrukh Siyar, Rafīʿᵘ 'd-Darajāt, Rafīʿᵘ 'd-Dawla and Muḥammad Shāh emperors ; they dethroned and killed Jahāndār Shāh and Farrukh Siyar, whom they had moreover blinded ; and they blinded and imprisoned Princes Aʿazzᵘ 'd-Dīn, ʿAlī Tabār, and Humāyūn Bakht.

(*d*) Sayyid Khān Jahān-i Shāhjahānī, Tihanpūrī —— A brother.
(*alias* S. ʕAbdᵘ 'l-Muẓaffar Khān), *d.* 1055.

1. S. Manṣūr. 2. Sher Zamān, *title*, S. Muẓaffar Khān. 3. S. Munawwar, Lashkar Khān. — S. Wajīhᵘ 'd-Dīn Khān.

(A brother:) 1. S. ʕAlī. *Pād.* II, 748. 2. S. Fīrūz, Ikhtiṣāṣ Khān, *d.* 1077.

The *Pādishāhnāma* (I, b., 312, 319; II, p. 733, 734, 735, 741, 752) mentions also S. Mākhan, *d.* 9th year of Shāhjahān; S. Sīkhan; S. ʕAbdᵘ 'llāh; S. Muḥammad, son of S. Afẓal; S. Khādim; S. Sālār; S. Shihāb.

(*e*) Sayyid Qāsim, Shahāmat Khān [Chātraurī] —— a brother
(was alive in the 24th year of Awrangzīb).
(a brother:) 1. S. Nuṣrat Yār Khān (under Muḥammad Shāh).

(*f*) Sayyid Ḥusayn Khān, *d.* 1120.

1. S. Abū Saʕīd Khān. 2. Ghayrat Khān. 3. Ḥasan Khān.

(*g*) Sayyid ʕAbdᵘ 'llah Khān [Tihanpūrī].
alias Sayyid Miyān (under Shāh ʕĀlam I.)

1. S. Ḥasan ʕAlī Khān; *title* Quṭbᵘ 'l-Mulk S. ʕAbdᵘ 'llah Khān. 2. Amīrᵘ 'l-Mamālik S. Ḥusayn ʕAlī Khān. (killed by Muḥammad Shāh).
3. Ṣayfᵘ 'd-Dīn Ḥusayn ʕAlī Khān. 4. S. Najmᵘ 'd-Dīn ʕAlī Khān

For the following notes, I am indebted to R. J. Leeds, Esq., C.S., Mirzapore, who kindly sent me two Urdū MSS. containing a short family history of the *Sādāt-i Bārha*, composed in 1864 and 1869 by one of the Sayyids themselves. As Mr. Leeds has submitted together with his Report " a detailed account in English of the history of the Sayyids," the following extracts from the Urdū MSS. will suffice.

The date of the arrival in India of the above-mentioned Abū 'l-Farah from Wāsiṭ is doubtful. The two MSS. mention the time of Iltitmish (Altamsh), and trace the emigration to troubles arising from Hulāgū's invasion of Baghdād and the overthrow of the empire of the Khalīfas; while the sons of Abū 'l-Farah are said to have been in the service of Shihābᵘ 'd-Dīn Ghorī—two palpable anachronisms.

Abū 'l-Farah is said to have arrived in India with his twelve sons, of whom four remained in India on his return to his country. These four brothers are the ancestors of the four branches of the Sayyids. Their names are:—

1. Sayyid Dāʾūd, who settled in the *mawẓaʕ* of *Tihanpūr*.
2. Sayyid Abū 'l-Faẓl, who settled in the *qaṣba* of *Chhatbanūrā* (چهت بنورا).

3. Sayyid Abū 'l-Faẓāʿil, who settled in the *mawẓaʿ* of *Kūndlī*.

4. Sayyid Najm[u] 'd-Dīn Ḥusayn, who settled in the *mawẓaʿ* of *Jhujar*.

These four places are said to lie near Patiyālā in the Panjāb, and have given rise to the names of the four branches. Instead of *Chhatbanūrī*, the name of the second branch, the MSS. have also *Chhātrauḍī*, چهاترودي or چهاتروزي, and *Jagnerī* (جگنيري) instead of *Jhujarī* (جهجري), although no explanation is given of these alterations.

From Patiyālā the four brothers went to the Du,āb between the Ganges and Jamna, from where a branch was established at Bilgrām in Audh.

The etymology of *bārha* is stated to be uncertain. Some derive it from *bāhir*, outside, because the Sayyids encamped *outside* the imperial camp; some from *bārah imām*, the twelve Imāms of the Shīʿahs, as the Sayyids were Shīʿahs; some derive it from twelve (*bārah*) villages which the family held, just as the district of Balandshahr, Taḥṣīl Anūpshahr, is said to contain a *bārha* of Paṭhāns, i.e. 12 villages belonging to a Paṭhān family; and others, lastly, make it to be a corruption of the Arabic *abrār*,[1] pious.

The descendants of S. Dāʿūd settled at *Dhāsrī*; and form the *Tihanpūrī* branch, those of S. Abū 'l-Faẓl at Sambalhaṛa, and form the Chhatbanūrī or Chhātrauṛī branch; those of S. Abū 'l-Faẓāʿil went to Majhaṛa, and are the Kūndlīwāls; and those of S. Najm[u] 'd-Dīn occupied Biḍaulī, and form the Jhujarī, or Jagnerī branch.

A. The Tihanpūrīs.

The eighth descendant of S. Dāʿūd was S. Khān Qīr (?) (خان قير)[2] He had four sons:—

1. *Sayyid ʿUmar Shahīd*, who settled in Jānsaṭh, a village then inhabited by Jāts and Brahmins. To his descendants belong the renowned brothers mentioned on p. 428 (*g*).

The occurrence of the name *ʿUmar* shows that he, at any rate, was no Shīʿah.

2. *Sayyid Chaman*, who settled at Chatora (چتوره), in the Pargana of Jolī-Jānsaṭh. To his descendants belongs S. Jalāl, who during the reign

---

[[1] Plural.—P.]

[2] The word قير occurs also in the lists of Paṭhān nobles in the *Tārīkh-i Fīrūzshāhī*. The title of قيربک *qīrbak*, which is mentioned in the same work, appears to be the same as the later قوربيک or قوربيگي, *qurbegī*, the officer in charge of the *qūr* (p. 116). But the name *Khān Qīr* is perhaps wrong; the MS. calls him خوان فير, or خوان قير, *Khwān Fīr* or *Khwān Qīr* (?).

of Shāhjahān[1] is said to have founded Kharwa Jalālpūr in the ʿIlāqa of Sirdhana, district Mīrath. His son S. Shams left the imperial service; hence the family declined. He had two sons, Asad ʿAlī and ʿAlī Aṣghar, whose descendants still exist in Chatora and Jalālpūr respectively. They are very poor, and sold in 1843–44 the bricks of the ruined family dwelling, in Chatora for Rs. 10,000 to the Government for the construction of works of irrigation. The buildings in Chatora are ascribed to S. Muḥammad Ṣalāḥ Khān, who served in Audh, and died childless.

3. *Sayyid Hunā* (هنا). He settled at Bihārī, Muẓaffarnagar. He had six sons :—

I. Sayyid Quṯb, whose descendants occupy the village of Bilāspūr in the Muẓaffarnagar District. From this branch come the Ratheri Sayyids.

II. S. Sulṯān, whose descendants hold Sirdhāolī.[2]

III. S. Yūsuf, whose posterity is to be found in Bihārī and Vhalna (one MS. reads *Dubalna*).

IV and *V. S. Jān* and *S. Mān*, had no offspring.

*VI. S. Naṣīr*ᵘ *'d-Dīn*. To his descendants belongs S. Khān Jahān-i Shāhjahānī, p. 428 (*d*). On him the Sayyids appear to look as the second founder of their family. His first son, *S. Manṣūr*, built Manṣūrpūr and his descendants hold nowadays Manṣūrpūr and Khataulī; his second son *Muẓaffar Khān* [Sher Zamān] built Muẓaffarnagar, where his descendants still exist, though poor or involved.

4. *Sayyid Aḥmad*. He settled at کڑال in Jolī-Jānsaṭh, where his descendants still are. The MSS. mention Tātār Khān, and Dīwān Yār, Muḥammad Khān as having distinguished themselves in the reign of Awrangzīb.

B. The Chhatbanūrī, or Chhātrauṛī, Clan.

One of the descendants of S. Abū 'l-Faẓl is called S. Ḥasan Fakhr[u] 'd-Dīn who is said to have lived in the reign of Akbar at Sambalhaṛa, the rājas of which place were on friendly terms with the family. His son, S. Nadhah, is said to have had four sons :—

I. Sayyid ʿAlī.

II. Sayyid Aḥmad, a descendant of whom, S. Rawshan ʿAlī Khān, served under Muḥammad Shāh.

---

[1] The *Pādishāhnāma*, though very minute, does not mention S. Jalāl and S. Shams. A S. *Jalāl* is mentioned *Tuz.*, p. 30. He died of his wounds received in the fight at Bhaironwāl (*vide* No. 99).

[[2] Sandhā,olī ?—P.]

III. *S. Taj*[u] *'d-Dīn*, whose son, S. ʿUmar settled at Kakraulī.

IV. *S. Sālār* (perhaps the same on p. 428*d*, last line of) who had two sons S. Ḥaydar Khān, and S. Muḥammad Khān. The descendants of the former settled at Mīrānpūr, which was founded by Nawab S. Shahāmat Khān, evidently the same as on p. 428. S. Muḥammad Khān settled at Khatora ("a village so called, because it was at first inhabited by Kā,iths"). Among his descendants are S. Nuṣrat Yār Khān (p. 428) and Rukn[u] 'd-Dawla.

C. *The Kūndlīwāls.*

S. Abū 'l-Faẓāil settled at Majhaṛa,[1] which is said to have been so called because the site was formerly a jungle of *mūnj*[1] grass. The MSS. say that many Sayyids of the branch are *mafqūd*[u] *khabar*, i.e. it is not known what became of them. The Kūndlīwāls which now exist, are said to be most uneducated and live as common labourers, the condition of Majhaṛa[1] being altogether deplorable.

The Kūndlīwāls are now scattered over Majhaṛa,[1] Hāshimpūr, Tisang,[2] Tandera, etc.

D. *The Jagnerīs.*

The son of S. Najm[u] 'd-Dīn, S. Qamar[u] 'd-Dīn, settled at Biḍaulī. A descendant of his, S. Fakhr[u] 'd-Dīn, left Biḍaulī and settled at پلري in Jolī-Jānsaṭh, and had also zamīndārīs in Chandaurī Chandaura, Tulsīpūr, and Kharī. Nowadays many of this branch are in Biḍaulī, ʿIlāqa Pānīpat, and Dihlī.

* * *

The chief places where the Sayyids of Bārha still exist are Mīrānpūr, Khataulī, Muẓaffarnagar, Jolī, Tis-ha, Bakheṛa, Majhaṛa, Chataura, Sambalhaṛa, Tisang, Bilāspūr, Morna, Sandhā,olī, Kailā,odha, Jānsaṭh.

[[1] On maps Munjherah.—B.]

[2] As this place is said to have been founded by Hizabr Khān [p. 427 (c.)] it would seem as if this Sayyid also was a Kūndlīwāl. His brother, S. ʿĀlam perished with Prince Shujāʿ in Arracan; and it is noticeable that of the 22 companions of the unfortunate prince, *ten* were Bārha Sayyids, the remaining twelve being Mughuls.

The value of the above-mentioned two Urdū MSS. lies in their geographical details and traditional information. A more exhaustive History of the Sādāt-i Bārha, based upon the Muhammadan Historians of India—now so accessible—and completed from inscriptions and sanads and other documents still in the possession of the clan, would be a most welcome contribution to Indian History, and none are better suited for such a task than the Sayyids themselves.

There is no doubt that the Sayyids owe their renown and success under the Timurides to the Kūndlīwāls, who are the very opposite of *Mafqūd*[u] *'l-khabar*.

After the overthrow of the Tihanpūrī brothers (p. 428, (*g*)), many emigrated. Sayyids of Bārha exist also in Lakhnau, Barelī, Āwla, in Audh; also in Nagīna, Maiman, and Chāndpūr in the Bijnor district. A branch of the Jolī Sayyids is said to exist in Pūrnia (Bengal), and the descendants of the saint ʿAbdu 'llāh Kirmānī of Bīrbhūm claim likewise to be related to the Bārha Sayyids.

During the reign of Awrangzīb, the Sayyids are said to have professed Sunnī tendencies.

The political overthrow of the Sādāt-i Bārha under Muḥammad Shāh (*vide* Elphinstone, Vth edition, p. 693) was followed by the disastrous fight at Bhainsī (بهینسی), which lies on the Khataulī road, where the Sayyids were defeated by the Imperialists, and robbed of the jewels and gold vessels which their ancestors, during their palmy days, had collected.

76. **ʿAbdu 'llāh Khān** Mughul.

I cannot find the name of this grandee in the *Maʿāṣir* or the *Ṭabaqāt*. He has been mentioned above, p. 322, l. 10. Akbar's marriage with his daughter displeased Bayrām, because ʿAbdu 'llāh's sister was married to Kāmrān, of whose party Bayrām believed him to be. When Bayrām, during his rebellion (p. 332) marched from Dīpālpūr to Jālindhar, he passed over Tihāra, where Abdu 'llāh defeated a party of his friends under Walī Beg (No. 24).

ʿAbdu 'llāh Khān *Mughul* must not be confounded with ʿAbdu 'llāh Khān *Uzbak* (No. 14).

77. **Shaykh Muḥammad**-i Bukhārī.

He was a distinguished Hindūstānī Sayyid, and maternal uncle (*tughāi* (?)) to Shaykh Farīd-i Bukhārī (No. 99). Akbar liked him for his wisdom and faithfulness. Fattū Khāṣa Khayl Afghān handed over the Fort of Chanāṛ to Akbar, through the mediation of Shaykh Muḥammad.

In the 14th year, Akbar gave him a *tuyūl* in Ajmīr, and ordered him to take charge of Shaykh Muʿīn-i Chishtī's tomb, as the *khādims* were generally at feud about the emoluments and distribution of vows presented by pilgrims. Nor had the efficacy of their prayers been proved, though they claimed to possess sufficient influence with God to promise offspring to the barren and childless.

In the 17th year, Shaykh M. was attached to the corps under Mīrzā ʿAzīz (No. 21), whom Akbar had put in charge of Aḥmadābād. After the Emperor's victory at Sarnāl, Ibrāhīm Mīrzā joined Ḥusayn Mīrzā, Shāh Mīrzā, and ʿĀqil Mīrzā, at Patan (Gujrāt); but having quarrelled with them, he left them, and invaded the District of Āgra. The other three Mīrzās remained in Patan and entered into a league with the Fūlādī party (*vide* No. 67). Mīrzā ʿAzīz had been reinforced by the Mālwa contingent under Quṭbᵘ 'd-Dīn (No. 28), Shāh Budāgh (No. 52), and Maṭlab Khān (No. 83). His army was further increased by the contingent of Shaykh M., whom Akbar had ordered to move from Dholqa to Sūrat. Mīrzā ʿAzīz Koka left Sayyid Ḥāmid (No. 78) in Aḥmadābād, and moved against the Mīrzās in Patan. The Mīrzās and Sher Khān Fūlādī, however, wished to delay the fight, as their reinforcements had not arrived, and Sher Khān sent proposals of peace through Shaykh M. to M. ʿAzīz. Shāh Budāgh advised M. ʿAzīz not to listen to them, as the enemies only wished to gain time, and ʿAzīz drew up his army. He himself, Shāh Budāgh, Muʿīnᵘ 'd-Dīn-i Farankhūdī (No. 128), Maʿṣūm Khān and his son, and Maṭlab Khān (No. 83) stood in the centre (*qol*); Quṭbᵘ 'd-Dīn (No. 28), and Jamālᵘ'd-Din Injū (No. 164), on the right wing; Shaykh Muḥammad, Murād Khān (No. 54), Shāh Muḥammad (No. 95), Shāh Fakhrᵘ 'd-Dīn (No. 88), Muẓaffar Mughul, Pāyanda (No. 68), Ḥājī Khān Afghān, and the son of Khawā Khān, on the left wing; Dastam Khān (No. 79), Nawrang Khān (*vide* p. 354), Muḥammad Qulī Toqbāī (No. 129), and Mihr ʿAlī Sildoz (No. 130), led the van (*harāwal*); Bāz Bahādur (No. 188) occupied the *Altimash* (between the van and the commander); and Mīrzā Muqīm and Chirgis Khān formed the reserve behind the centre. The centre of the enemies was held by Sher Khān Fūlādī and Junayd-i Kararānī; the right wing by the three Mīrzās; the left wing by Muḥammad Khān (Sher Khān's eldest son) and Sādāt Khān; and their van was led by Badr Khān, younger son of Sher Khān. The battle then commenced in the neighbourhood of Patan, 18th Ramaẓān, 980 (22nd January, 1573). The left wing of the Imperialists was defeated by the Mīrzās. Murād Khān (No. 54) preferred to look on. Shāh Muḥammad (No. 95) was wounded, and carried off by his men to Aḥmadābād. Shaykh Muḥammad himself was killed with several of his relations, as the son of Sayyid Bahāʾᵘ 'd-Dīn, and Sayyid Jaʿfar, brother of Shaykh Farīd (No. 99). The Mīrzās also fell upon Shāh Fakhrᵘ 'd-Dīn and repulsed him. Quṭbᵘ 'd-Dīn even was hard pressed, when M. ʿAzīz by a timely attack with his centre put the enemies to flight. As usual, the soldiers of the enemies had too early commenced to plunder.

Sher Khān fled to Jūnāgaḍh, and the Mīrzās to the Dakhin.

78. **Sayyid Ḥāmid**-i Bukhārī.

Sayyid Ḥāmid was the son of S. Mīrān, son of S. Mubārik. Sayyid Mubārak was a Gujrātī Courtier (*vide* p. 419, note) who, it is said, arrived from Bukhārā with but a horse. One day he was attacked by a *mast* elephant, when he discharged an arrow that entered the forehead of the animal so deep, that only the notch of the arrow was visible. From this event, the people of Gujrāt swore by S. Mubārak's arrow. He gradually rose to higher dignities. When Iᶜtimād Khān (No. 67) raised Nathū to the throne, under the title of Muẓaffar Shāh, S. Mubārak got several Maḥalls of the Patan, Dholqa, and Dandoqa (W. of the Peninsula) Districts. After his death, Dholqa and Dandoqa were given to his son Sayyid Mīrān, and after him to his grandson Sayyid Ḥāmid.

When Akbar, on his invasion of Gujrāt, arrived on 1st Rajab, 980, at Patan, Sayyid Ḥāmid went over to him, and was favourably received. During the war of Mīrzā ᶜAzīz Koka with the Mīrzās (*vide* No. 77), S. Ḥ. was put in charge of Aḥmadābād. In the 18th year, Dholqa and Dandoqa were again given him as *tuyūl*. Subsequently, he served under Quṭbᵘ 'd-Dīn in Kambhā,it.

In the 22nd year he was appointed to Multān, and served in the end of the same year with M. Yūsuf Khān-i Raẓawī (No. 35), against the Balūchīs. In the 25th year, when M. Muḥammad Ḥakīm invaded Lāhor, S. Ḥ. with the other *tuyūldārs* of the Panjāb assembled and joined the army of Prince Murād, S. Ḥ. commanding the left wing. He also served under Akbar in Kābul. On the Emperor's return he was permitted to go from Sirhind to his *jāgīr*.

In the 30th year he served under Mān Singh in Kābul. On his arrival at Peshāwar, his jāgīr, S. Ḥ. sent most of his men to Hindūstān, and lived securely in Bigrām (on our Maps, *Beghram*), leaving his affairs in the hands of a man of the name of Mūsa. This man oppressed the Maḥmand and Gharbah (?) Khayl tribes, "who have ten thousand homes near Peshāwar." The oppressed Afghāns, instead of complaining to Akbar, chose Jalāla-yi Tarīkī as leader, and attacked S. Ḥ. He first resolved to shut himself up in Bigrām; but having received an erroneous report regarding the strength of the enemies, he left the town, and was defeated and killed (31st year). The *Maᶜāṣir* says he was killed in 993. In this fight forty of his relations and clients also perished. The Afghāns then besieged the Fort, which was held by Kamāl, son of S. Ḥ. He held it till he was relieved.

S. Kamāl, during Akbar's reign, was promoted to a command of Seven Hundred, and, on the accession of Jahāngīr, to a Hazārīship. He was made Governor of Dilhī, *vice* Shaykh ᶜAbdᵘ 'l-Wahhāb, also a Bukhārī Sayyid (*Tuz.* p. 35, l. 8 from below). Kamāl served under Farīd-i Bukhārī (No. 99) in the expedition against Prince Khusraw, and commanded the left wing in the fight near Bhairōwāl, rendering timely assistance to the Sayyids of Bārha who, as was customary, led the van.

Sayyid Yaʿqūb, son of S. Kamāl, was a Commander of Fifteen Hundred, 1,000 horse, and died in the third year of Shāhjahān's reign. The *Maʾāṣir* says, in the 2nd year.

The two lists of Shāhjahān's grandees given in the *Pādishāhnāma* (I, b., 322; II, 740) mention another son of Sayyid Ḥāmid, of the name of Sayyid Bāqir, who held a Command of Five Hundred, 400 horse.

79. **Dastam Khān**, son of Rustam-i Turkistānī.

The correct name of this grandee is *Dastam* دستم, a very unusual name though most MSS. of the Āʾīn and many of the Akbarnāma give رستم, *Rustam*. The *Maʾāṣir* correctly places his name under the letter *D*.

His father's name was Rustam. His mother—her name is not clearly written in the MSS. of the *Maʾāṣir* and *Akbarnāma*, which I have seen, either *Najība* or *Bakhya*—was a friend of Māhum Anaga (*vide* No. 19) and had free access to the Harem. Dastam appears to have been a play-fellow of Prince Akbar.

Dastam Khān in the 9th year, served under Muʿizzᵘ 'l-Mulk (No. 61) against ʿAbdᵘ 'llāh Khān Uzbak (No. 14). In the 17th year he served under Mīrzā ʿAzīz Koka in the battle of Patan (*vide* No. 77), distinguished himself in the war with Muḥammad Ḥusayn Mīrzā, and got a flag. In the 22nd year he was appointed to the Ṣūba of Ajmīr, and got Rantanbhūr as *tuyūl*. His administration was praiseworthy; he kept down the rebellious, and protected the oppressed.

In the 25th year Uchlā, son of Balbhadr, and Mohan, Sūr Dās, Tilūksī, sons of Rāja Bihārī Mal's brother, came without permission from the Panjāb to Lūnī (?), their native town, and caused disturbances. Dastam, from a wish not to be too hard on Kachhwāhas, advised them to return to obedience; but his leniency only rendered the rebels more audacious. Akbar then ordered D. to have recourse to threats, and if this was not sufficient, to proceed against them. D. had at last to do so; but he did it hastily, without collecting a sufficient number of troops. In the fight,[1] the three nephews of the Rāja were killed. Dastam received a

[1] The geographical details given in the Akbarnāma are unsatisfactory.

Abū 'l-Faẓl mentions the *Qaṣba* (small town) of Lūnī (لونی) as the birth-place of the Kachhwāha rebels; the fight, he says, took place in a village (*mawzaʿ*) of the name of تهوری *Thorī*, and Dastam died at *Sherpūr*, which is also called a *Qaṣba*. But the Akbarnāma leaves the reader to find out where these three places are. The *Ṭabaqāt*, in its list of grandees, fortunately says that Dastam Khān was killed in the neighbourhood of Rantanbhūr. The only places near Rantanbhūr which resemble the above three are Bounlee, Tohra, and Shergaṛh, as given on the Trig. Map of the Jodhpūr Territory for 1850. The road from Shergaṛh (about 4 miles S.E. of Rantanbhūr) to Bounlee is bisected

wound from Uchlā, who had attacked him from an ambush. Wounded as he was, he attacked Uchlā, and killed him. Immediately afterwards he fainted and fell from his horse. His men put him again on horseback—a usual expedient, in order not to dishearten the soldiers. The rebels were totally defeated and their estates plundered (988).

Dastam died of his wounds, two days later, at Sherpūr. Akbar said that even D.'s mother could not feel the loss of her son as much as he did, because D., with the exception of three years, had never been away from him.

The *Maʿāṣir* says he was a Commander of Three Thousand. Rantanbhūr was then given to Mīrzā ʿAbdurrahīm (No. 29) as jāgīr.

A son of Dastam is mentioned below (No. 362).

80. **Shāhbāz Khān-i** Kambū.

Regarding the tribe called *Kambū, vide* Beames' Edition of Sir H. Elliot's Glossary, I, 304. The Persian hemistich quoted (Metre *Hazaj*) :—

[اگر قحط الرجال فتد بسه کس کم انس گیري]
یکے افغان دوم کنبو سیوم بدذات کمشیري

" The Afghāns are the first, the Kambūs the second, and the Kashmīrīs the third, set of scoundrels "

must be very modern ; for during the reigns of Akbar and Jahāngīr, it was certainly a distinction to belong to this tribe, as will be seen just now.

The sixth ancestor of Shāhbāz was Ḥājī Ismāʿīl, a disciple of the renowned saint Bahāʿu d-Dīn Zakariyā of Multān. Once a beggar asked the saint to give him an *ashrafī*, or gold muhr, for the name of every prophet he would mention ; but as Bahāʿu 'd-Dīn could not pay the money, Ḥājī Ismāʿīl took the beggar to his house, and gave him an Ashrafī for each of the ten or twenty names he mentioned. Another time, Ḥājī Ismaʿīl acknowledged to the saint that his power of understanding was defective, whereupon the saint prayed for him, and from that time the Kambūs are proverbial in Hindūstān for sagacity and quickness of apprehension.

Shāhbāz at first devoted himself to a life of abstinence and austerity, as his ancestors had done ; but the excellent way in which he performed

---

by the Banas River. Rantanbhūr lies in the angle formed by the confluence of the Chambal and the Banas, and Bounlee lies about 30 miles N.W. of it. There are two villages of the names of *Tohra*, one about 3 miles S.W. of Bounlee, and the other S. of it, on the right bank of the Banas. *Bounlee*, or Baūlī, would be بونلي, or بولي, which will be found below as the head of a Pargana in Sarkār Rantanbhūr, and the change of بولي to بونلي is very simple. The greatest difference lies in Sherpūr and *Shergarh*.

The Akbarnāma says the fight took place on the 10th Ābān of the 25th year

the duties of *kotwāl*, drew Akbar's attention to him, and he was made an Amīr and appointed *Mīr Tozak* (quarter master).

In the 16th year, when Lashkar Khān (No. 90) fell into disgrace, Sh. was appointed Mīr Bakhshī. In the 21st year he was sent against the rebels in Jodhpūr, especially against Kallah, son of Rāy Rām, and grandson of Rāy Māldeo, and was ordered to take Fort Siwāna. Shāhbāz first took Fort Daigūr (?),[1] where a large number of Rāṭhor rebels were killed; after this he took Dūnāra, from where he passed on to Siwānah, which on his arrival capitulated (984).

In the same year, Shāhbāz was sent against Rāja Gajpatī.[2] This Rāja was the greatest Zamīndār in Bihār, and had rendered good services during Munʿim's expedition to Bengal. But when Dāʾūd, king of Oṛīsā, invaded Bengal after Munʿim's death at Gaur in 983, Gajpatī rebelled and plundered several towns in Bihār. Farḥat Khān (No. 145) *tuyūldār* of Āra, his son Farhang Khān, and Qarāṭāq Khān, opposed the Rāja, but perished in the fight. When Shāhbāz approached, Gajpatī fled; but Sh. followed him up, and gave him no rest, and conquered at last Jagdespūr, where the whole family of the Rāja was captured. Sh. then conquered Shergaḍh, which was held by Srī Rām, Gajpatī's son. About the same time, Sh. took possession of Rahtās. Its Afghān commander, Sayyid Muḥammad, who commanded the Fort on the part of Junayd-i Kararānī, had been hard pressed by Muẓaffar (No. 37); he therefore fled to Shāhbāz, asked for protection, and handed over the Fort. Sh. then repaired to court, where he received every distinction due to his eminent services.

In the 23rd year (986) Sh. marched against the proud Rānā Partāb, and besieged the renowned Fort of Kōbhalmīr (called on our maps Komalnair, on the frontier between Udaipūr and Jodhpūr, lat. 25° 10′). The Rānā, unable to defend it, escaped in the disguise of a *Sannāsī* when the fort was taken. Goganda and Udaipūr submitted likewise. Sh. erected no less than 50 thānas in the hills and 35 in the plains, from Udaipūr to Pūr Manḍal. He also prevailed upon the rebellious Daudā, son of Rāy Surjan Hāḍā (No. 96), to submit, and took him to Court. After this, Sh. was sent to Ajmīr, where disturbances frequently occurred.

---

[1] The MSS. have دیگور, which I cannot find on the maps. There are many places of a similar name, S.W. of Jodhpūr, near which it must lie. *Dūnūra* (most MSS. have دوتاره) lies on the right bank of the Lūnī, S.W. of Jodhpūr. Here Shāhbāz crossed (*ʿubūr*) and went to *Siwānah*, which lies N.W. S. of Dūnāra, about 10 miles from the left bank of the Lūnī.

[2] So according to the best MSS. Stewart calls him *Gujety*, the Lakhnau Akbarnāma (III, 140) *Kajī*, and the Edit. Bibl. Indica. of Badā,onī, *Kachītī*, (p. 179, 284, 285) and *Kajītī* (p. 237), which forms are also found in the Lakhnau edition of the Akbarnāma.

When the military revolt of Bengal broke out, Sh. was ordered to go to Bihār; but he did not agree with M. ʿAzīz Koka—for Sh. could not bear to be second or third—and carried on the war independently of him, defeated ʿArab Bahādur, and marched to Jagdespūr. At that time the report reached him that Maʿṣūm Khān Farankhūdī (No. 157) had rebelled. and ʿArab Bahādur and Niyābat Khān had joined him. Sh. therefore marched to Audh, and met the enemies near Sulṭānpūr Bilkarī, 25 *kos* from Awadh (Fayẓābād). Maʿṣūm, by a timely centre-attack, put Sh. to flight, and followed him up, Sh. fighting all the way to Jaunpūr, a distance of 30 *kos*. Accidentally a rumour spread in the army of the enemy that Maʿṣūm had been killed, which caused some disorder. At this moment, Sh.'s right wing attacked the enemy, Maʿṣūm got wounded, and withdrew to Awadh (Fayẓābād). Sh. now pursued him, and seven miles from that town, after a hard fight, totally routed him. Maʿṣūm could not hold himself in Awadh, and his army dispersed.

After this, Sh. again went to court, where he was received by the emperor on his return from Kābul. At court, Sh. generally gave offence by his pride; and when once, at a parade, the Bakhshīs had placed the young Mīrzā Khān (No. 29) above him, he gave vent openly to his anger, was arrested, and put under the charge of Rāy Sāl Darbārī (No. 106).

But an officer of Sh.'s usefulness could ill be spared, and when M. ʿAzīz in the 28th year applied for transfer from Bihār, Sh. with other Amīrs was sent there. He followed up Maʿṣūm Khān Kābulī to Ghorāghāt, and defeated him. He then followed him to Bhāṭī (p. 365), plundered Baktarāpūr, the residence of ʿIsạ, took Sunnārgā̃w, and encamped on the Brahmaputra. 'Isạ afforded Maʿṣūm means and shelter; but being hard pressed by the imperialists, he made proposals of peace: an Imperial officer was to reside as Sunnārgā̃w; Maʿṣūm was to go to Makkah; and Sh. was to withdraw. This was accepted, and Sh. crossed the river expecting the terms would be carried out. But the enemy did nothing; and when Sh. prepared to return, his officers showed the greatest insubordination, so that he had to retreat to Ṭānḍa, all advantage being thus lost. He reported matters to Court, and the *tuyūldārs* of Bihār were ordered to join him. Sh. then took the field and followed up Maʿṣūm. In the 30th year, he and Ṣādiq Khān (*vide* No. 43) quarrelled. Subsequently, Sh. marched again to Bhāṭī, and even sent a detachment "to Kokra (کوکره), which lies between Oṛīsā and the Dakhin". Mādhū Singh, the Zamīndār of the district, was plundered, and had to pay tribute. In the 32nd year, when Sāʿīd (No. 25) was made Governor of Bengal, and the disturbances had mostly been suppressed, Sh. returned to Court. In the 34th year, he was made *Kotwāl* of the army. He was then sent against the Afghāns of Sawād; but he left his duties without orders, and was again imprisoned.

After two years he was released, was made *atālīq* to M. Shāhrukh, who had been appointed to Mālwa, and was on his way to Prince Murād in the Dakhin. During the siege of Aḥmadnagar, the inhabitants of Shahr-i Naw, "which is called *Burhānābād,*" asked the Imperialists for protection; but as they were mostly Shīʿas, Sh., in his bigotry, fell upon them, plundered their houses, especially the quarter called *Langar-i-Duwāzda Imām*, the very name of which must have stunk in Sh.'s nostrils. The inhabitants "seeing that they could not rely on the word of the Mughuls" emigrated. The Prince was irritated; and when Ṣādīq Khān (No. 43) was appointed his *atālīq*, Sh. left without permission for Mālwa. Akbar gave his jāgīr to Shāhrukh, and transferred Shāhbāz.

In the 43rd year Sh. was sent to Ajmīr as Commander of the *manqalā* of Prince Salīm (Jahāngīr), whom Akbar had asked to go from Ilāhābād against the Rānā. But Sh. was now about seventy years old, and as he had been in the habit of eating quicksilver, he commenced to suffer from pain in his hands and wrists. He got well again, but had in Ajmīr another attack; he rallied again, but died suddenly in the 44th year (1008). Salīm took quickly possession of Sh.'s treasures, went back to Ilāhābād without having done anything, and continued in his rebellious attitude towards his father.

Shāhbāz had expressed a dying wish to be buried in Ajmīr within the hallowed enclosure of Muʿīn-i Chishtī. But the custodians of the sacred shrine refused to comply, and Sh. was buried outside. At night, however, the saint appeared in the dreams of the custodians, and told them that Shāhbāz was his favourite, whereupon the hero was buried inside, north of the dome.

Shāhbāz was proverbial for his rigid piety and his enormous wealth. His opposition to Akbar's "Divine Faith" had been mentioned above (p. 197). He would neither remove his beard to please the emperor, nor put the word *murīd* (disciple) on his signet. His Sunnī zeal, no doubt, retarded his promotion as much as his arrogance; for other less deserving officers held higher commands. He observed with great strictness the five daily prayers, and was never seen without a rosary in his hand. One day the emperor took a walk along the tank at Fatḥpūr and seized Shāhbāz's hand to accompany him. It was near the time of the ʿaṣr, or afternoon prayer, and Sh. was restless and often looked up to the sun, not to miss the proper time. Ḥakīm Abū 'l-Fatḥ (No. 112) saw it from a distance, and said to Ḥakīm ʿAlī who stood near him, "I shall indeed call Shāhbāz a pious man, if he insists on saying the prayer alone, as he is with the emperor"; (for the prayer had been abolished by Akbar at Court). When the time of prayer had come, Sh. mentioned it to the emperor. "Oh," replied Akbar, "you can pray another time, and make amends for this omission." But Sh. drew away his hand from the grasp of the emperor, spread his *dupaṭṭa* shawl on the ground, and said not only his prayer but also his *vird* (voluntary daily religious exercise), Akbar his head slapping all the while, and saying, "Get up!" Abū 'l-Faẓl stepped up and interceded for Shāhbāz, whose persistency he admired.

Abū 'l-Fatḥ says that Shāhbāz was an excellent and faithful servant; but he blames him for his bigotry. In liberality, he says, he had no equal, and people whispered that he found the *Pāras* stone (*vide* Book III, Ṣūba of Mālwa). His military contingent was always complete and in good order; during his fights near the Brahmaputr he had 9,000 horse. Every Thursday evening he distributed 100 *Ashrafīs* to the memory of the renowned *Ghawṣ*[u] *'ṣ-ṣiqlayn* (?) (ʿAbd[u] 'l-Qādu-i Jīlānī). To the Kambūs he gave so much, that no Kambū in India was in bad circumstances.

During the time he was Mīr Bakhshī he introduced the *Dāgh* law, the most important military reform of Akbar's reign (*vide* pp. 252, 265, 266).

Shāhbāz's brother, Karam[u] 'llāh, was likewise pious. He died in 1002 at Saronj (*Maʾāṣir*). The *Maʾāṣir* mentions a son of Shāhbāz, Ilhām[u] 'llāh. He was *Wāqiʿa-nawīs* (p. 268) of the Sarkār of Baglāna, where he died.

The *Tuzuk* (p. 248) mentions another son of his, Ranbāz Khān, who during the reign of Shāhjahān was a Commander of Eight Hundred, 400 horse. He was, in the 13th year, *Bakhshī* and *Wāqiʿa-nawīs* of the corps which was sent to Bangash. He held the same rank in the 20th year of Shāhjahān's reign.[1]

81. **Darwīsh Muḥammad** Uzbak.

The *Maʾāṣir* says nothing about this grandee; the MSS. of the *Ṭabaqāt* merely say that he was dead in 1001.

---

[1] Ranbāz Khān is wrongly called *Niyāz Khān* in the Ed. Bibl. Indica of the Pādishāh, I. b., p. 314; but in II, p. 740, of the same work, *Ranbāz Khān* as in the *Tuzuk*.

Sayyid Aḥmad's edition of the *Tuzuk*, p. 159, says that Ranbāz's name was *Khūb*[u] *'llāh*; but this is a most extraordinary name, and therefore likely to be wrong. It should, perhaps, be *Ḥabīb*[u] *'llāh*.

In the list of Akbar's grandees in the *Ṭabaqāt*, Niẓām says, "At present (in 1001) Shāhbāz is Mīr Bakhshī of Mālwa."

From the *Akbarnāma* (Lucknow edition, II, p. 137) we see that he was a friend of Bayrām. He was sent by Bayrām together with Muẓaffar ʿAlī (No. 37, and p. 332, l. 6) to Sher Muḥammad Dīwāna, who dispatched both fettered to Court.

His name occurs again in the *Akbarnāma* (Lucknow edition, II, p. 250 —where for *Darwīsh Uzbak Khwāja*, read *Darwīsh Uzbak o Muẓaffar Khwāja*). From the fact that Abū 'l-Faẓl has given his name in this list, it is evident that Akbar pardoned him on Bayrām's submission.

82. **Shaykh Ibrāhīm**, son of Shaykh Mūsa, elder brother of Shaykh Salīm of Fatḥpūr Sīkrī.

His father, Shaykh Mūsa, lived a retired life in Sīkrī. As Akbar had at first no children, he asked the Sīkrī Shaykhs to pray for him, which they did; and as at that time one of Akbar's wives became pregnant (with Salīm), Akbar looked upon the Shaykhs with particular favour. To this lucky circumstance, the Sīkrī family owes its elevation.

Shaykh Ibrāhīm lived at first at Court, chiefly in the service of the princes. In the 22nd year he was made Thānahdār of Lāḍlā,ī, and suppressed the disturbances. In the 23rd year he was made Governor of Fatḥpūr Sīkrī. In the 28th year he served with distinction under M. ʿAzīz Koka (No. 21) in Bihār and Bengal, and was with Vazīr Khān (No. 41) in his expedition against Qutlū of Orīsā. When Akbar, in the 30th year, went to Kābul, he was made Governor of Āgra, which post he seems to have held till his death in 999 (36th year).

According to the *Tabaqāt*, he was not only the brother but also the son-in-law of Shaykh Salīm-i Sīkrīwāl.

83. **ʿAbdu 'l-Maṭlab Khān**, son of Shāh Budāgh Khān (No. 52).

The *Maʾāṣir* makes him a Commander of Two Thousand Five Hundred.

ʿAbdu 'l-Maṭlab accompanied Sharafu 'd-Dīn Ḥusayn (No. 17) on his expedition to Mīrtha. In the 10th year he served together with his father under Muʿizzu 'l-Mulk (No. 61) against Iskandar and Bahādur Khān, and fled from the battlefield of Khayrābād. In the 12th year he served under Muḥammad Qulī Khān Barlās (No. 31) against Iskandar Khān in Audh. He then retired to his *tuyūl* in Mālwa.

In the 17th year he belonged to the auxiliaries of M. ʿAzīz Koka and was present in the battle of Patan (p. 433). In the 23rd year, when Quṭbu 'd-Dīn's men (No. 28) brought Muẓaffar Ḥusayn Mīrzā from the Dakhin to Court, ʿAbdu 'l-Maṭlab attached himself as convoy and saw the Mīrzā safely to Court. In the 25th year he accompanied Ismāʿīl Qulī Khān (No. 46) on his expedition against Niyābat Khān ʿArab. In the following year he received a reprimand for having murdered Fatḥ Dawlat, son of ʿAlī Dost. He was, however, subsequently pardoned, and was put in command of the left wing of the army which was sent to Kābul. In the 27th year, Akbar honoured him by being his guest in Kālpī, his jāgīr.

In the 30th year he accompanied M. ʿAzīz Koka to the Dakhin, and was sent, two years later, against Jalāla Tārīkī, the Afghān rebel. One day, Jalāla fell upon the van of the Imperialists, which was commanded by Beg Nūrīn Khān (No. 212), Salīm Khān (No. 132), and Sheroya Khān (No. 168). They were in time, and, assisted by Muḥammad Qulī Beg, routed Jalāla, who escaped to the mountains. ʿAbdu 'l-Maṭlab "had not the good fortune of even mounting his horse to take part in the fight". He seems to have taken this to heart; for when the victorious army returned to Bangash, he had an attack of madness and was sent to Court. He died soon after.

His son, Sherzād, was under Jahāngīr, a Commander of Three Hundred, 200 horse.

84. **Iʿtibār Khān**, the Eunuch.

His name, like that of many other Eunuchs, was ʿAmbar. He was one of Bābar's Eunuchs. When Humāyūn left Qandahār for ʿIrāq, he despatched Iʿtibār and others to conduct Maryam Makānī (Akbar's mother) to his camp. In 952 he left Kābul and joined the emperor, who attached him to Prince Akbar's suite.

In the 2nd year of Akbar's reign he accompanied Akbar's mother and the other Begams from Kābul to India. Akbar appointed him Governor of Dihlī, where he died.

He must not be confounded with No. 86.

85. **Rāja Bīr Bal** [Bīr Baṛ], the Brahman.

He was a Brahman of the name of Mahesh Dās (*Maʾāṣir*; the *Ed. Bibl. Indica of Badā,onī*, II, p. 161, calls him *Brahman Dās*) and was a *Bhāt*, or minstrel, a class of men whom the Persians call *bādfarosh*, "dealers in encomiums." He was very poor, but clear-headed, and remarkable for his power of apprehension. According to Badā,onī, he came soon after Akbar's accession from Kālpī to Court, where his *bonmots* in a short time made him a general favourite. His Hindī verses also were much liked, and Akbar conferred on him the title of *Kab Rāy*, or (Hindu) Poet Laureate,[1] and had him constantly near himself.

---

[1] Just as *Jotik Rāy* the (Hindū) Court Astrologer. The (Persian) Poet Laureate [Fayẓī] had the title of *Maliku 'sh-Shuʿarā*, or "King of Poets".

In the 18th year Rāja Jai Chand of Nagarkoṭ, who was at Court happened to displease the emperor, and was imprisoned. Nargakoṭ was given to Kab Rāy as jāgīr. He also received the title of Rāja Bīr Baṛ. But Jai Chand's son, Budh Chand (or Budhī Ch., or Badī Ch.—the MSS. differ) shut himself up in Nagarkoṭ, and Ḥusayn Qulī Khān (No. 24) was ordered to conquer it. The invasion of Ibrāhīm Ḥusayn Mīrzā, as related above, forced Ḥusayn Qulī to raise the siege, and Bīr Baṛ, in all probability, did not get his jāgīr. He accompanied Akbar on his forced march to Patan and Aḥmadābād, 24th Rabīʿ II, 981. (*Vide* note to No. 101.)

He was often employed in missions. Thus in the 21st year he was sent with Rāy Lon Karan to Dūngarpūr, the Ṛāy of which town was anxious to send his daughter to Akbar's Harem. In the 28th year, again, B. B. and Zayn Koka (No. 34) conducted Rāja Rām Chand (No. 89) to Court.

Bīr Baṛ spent his time chiefly at Court. In the 34th year Zayn Khān Koka marched against the Yūsufzā,īs in Bijūr and Sawād; and as he had to ask for reinforcements, Bīr Baṛ was sent there together with Ḥakīm Abū 'l-Fatḥ (No. 112). It is said that Akbar determined by lot whether Abū 'l-Faẓl or Bīr Baṛ should go, and the lot fell on the latter, much against Akbar's wish.

The result of this campaign has been related above (pp. 214, 367). Bīr Baṛ and nearly 8,000 Imperialists were killed during the retreat—the severest defeat which Akbar's army ever suffered.[1]

How Akbar felt Bīr Baṛ's loss has been mentioned on p. 214. There is also a letter on this subject in Abū 'l-Faẓl's *Maktūbāt*.

The following passages from Badā,onī (*Ed. Bibl. Ind.*, pp. 357, 358) are of interest—" Among the silly lies—they border on absurdities—which during this year (995) were spread over the country, was the rumour that Bīr Baṛ, the accursed, was still alive, though in reality he had then for some time been burning in the seventh hell. The Hindūs by whom His Majesty is surrounded, saw how sad and sorry he was for Bīr Baṛ's loss, and invented the story that Bīr Baṛ had been seen in the hills of Nagarkoṭ, walking about with Jogīs and Sannāsīs. His Majesty believed the rumour, thinking that Bīr Baṛ was ashamed to come to Court on account of the defeat which he had suffered at the hands of the Yūsufzā,īs; and it was, besides, quite probable that he should have been seen with Jogīs,

---

[1] A similar catastrophe befell Awrangzīb, when several thousand soldiers of the army commanded by Amīn Khān were killed in the Khaibar Pass, on the 3rd Muḥarram, 1083, or 21st April, 1672. *Maʾāṣir-i ʿĀlamgīrī*, p. 117. *Vide Journal A. S. Bengal* for 1862, p. 261.

inasmuch as he had never cared for the world. An Aḥadī was therefore sent to Nagarkoṭ to inquire into the truth of the rumour, when it was proved that the whole story was an absurdity."

"Soon after, His Majesty received a report that Bīr Baṛ had been seen at Kālinjar (which was the jāgīr of this dog), and the collector of the district stated that a barber had recognized him by certain marks on his body, which the man had distinctly seen, when one day Bīr Baṛ had engaged him to rub his body with oil; from that time, however, Bīr Baṛ had concealed himself. His Majesty then ordered the barber to come to Court; and the Hindū Krorī (collector) got hold of some poor innocent traveller, charged him with murder, and kept him in concealment, giving out that he was Bīr Baṛ. The Krorī could, of course, send no barber to Court; he therefore killed the poor traveller, to avoid detection, and reported that it was Bīr Baṛ in reality, but he had since died. His Majesty actually went through a second mourning; but he ordered the Krorī and several others to come to Court. They were for some time tortured as a punishment for not having informed His Majesty before, and the Krorī had, moreover, to pay a heavy fine."

Bīr Baṛ was as much renowned for his liberality, as for his musical skill and poetical talent. His short verses, bon-mots, and jokes, are still in the mouths of the people of Hindūstān.

The hatred which Badā,onī Shāhbāz Khān (No. 80) and other pious Muslims showed towards Bīr Baṛ (*vide* pp. 192, 198, 202, 209, 214) arose from the belief that Bīr Baṛ had influenced Akbar to abjure Islām.

Bīr Baṛ's eldest son, *Lāla*, is mentioned below among the commanders of Two Hundred (No. 387). He was a spendthrift; and as he got no promotion, and his property was squandered away, he resigned court life, and turned *faqīr*, in order to live free and independent (end of 46th year).

86. **Ikhlāṣ Khān** Iʿtibār, the Eunuch.

The *Maʾāṣir* does not give his name. The list of Akbar's grandees in the *Ṭabaqāt* has the short remark that Ikhlāṣ Khān was a Eunuch, and held the rank of a Commander of *One Thousand*.

87. **Bahār Khān** (Muḥammad) Aṣghar, a servant of Humāyūn.

The name of this grandee is somewhat doubtful, as some MSS. read *Bahādur Khān*. The *Maʾāṣir* does not give his name. The list of the *Ṭabaqāt* mentions a "Bahār Khān, a Khāṣa Khayl Afghān, who held a command of Two Thousand". Bahār Khān Khāṣa Khayl is also mentioned in several places in the *Akbarnāma*. He is therefore most probably the same as given by Abū 'l-Faẓl in this list. Perhaps we have to read *Pahāṛ Khān*, instead of *Bahār Khān* ; *vide* No. 407. The notice in the *Ṭabaqāt* implies that he was dead in 1001.

88. **Shāh Fakhr^u 'd-Dīn**, son of Mīr Qāsim, a Mūsawī Sayyid of Mashhad.

Shāh Fakhr^u 'd-Dīn came, in 961, with Humāyūn to India. In the 9th year of Akbar's reign he served in the army which was sent against ʿAbd^u 'llāh Khān Uzbak (No. 14). In the 16th year he was in the *manqalā*, or advance corps, commanded by Khān-i Kalān (No. 16). When Akbar arrived at Patan, he sent Sh. F. and Ḥakīm ʿAyn^u 'l-Mulk to Mīr Abū Turāb and Iʿtimād Khān (No. 67). On the road he fell in with the former, and went to Iʿtimād whom he likewise induced to pay his respects to Akbar. He was among the auxiliaries of M. ʿAzīz Koka (No. 21) and was present in the battle of Patan (p. 433). He was also among the grandees who accompanied Akbar on his forced march to Gujrāt (p. 343, note, where according to the *Akbarnāma* we have to read *24th Rabīʿ* II, for *4th Rabīʿ* I). After this, he was made Governor of Ujjain, and received the title of *Naqābat Khān*.[1] In the end of the 24th year, he was made Governor of Patan (Gujrāt), *vice* Tarsō Muḥammad Khān (No. 32), where he soon after, probably in the beginning of 987, died (986, *Ṭabaqāt*).

89. **Rāja Rām Chand Baghela.**

A few MSS. read *Bhagela*, which form Tod says is the correct one. *Baghela*, however, is the usual spelling.

Rām Chand was Rāja of Bhath (or *Bhattah*, as the *Maʾāṣir* spells it). Among the three great Rājas of Hindūstān whom Bābar mentions in his Memoirs, the Rājas of Bhath are the third.

Rām Chand was the patron of the renowned musician and singer Tānsīn, regarding whom *vide* the List of Musicians at the end of this book. His fame had reached Akbar ; and in the 7th year, the Emperor sent Jalāl^u 'd-Dīn Qūrchī (No. 213) to Bhath, to induce Tānsīn to come to Āgra. Rām Chand feeling himself powerless to refuse Akbar's request, sent his favourite, with his musical instruments and many presents to Āgra, and the first time that Tānsīn performed at Court, the Emperor made him a present of two lākhs of rupees. Tānsīn remained with Akbar. Most of his compositions are written in Akbar's name, and his melodies are even nowadays everywhere repeated by the people of Hindūstān.

When Āṣaf Khān (I) led his expedition to Gaḍha (p. 396)[2] he came in

---

[1] The Lucknow Edition of the *Akbarnāma* (III, p. 222) calls him *Naqīb-Khān* (?).

[2] On p. 396, *Rām Chand* is by mistake called *Rām Chandr*.

contact with Rām Chand; but by timely submission the Rāja became "a servant" of Akbar. In the 14th year Yām Chand lost Fort Kālinjar, as related on p. 399. He sent his son, Bīr Bhadr, to Court, but from distrust would not pay his respects personally. In the 28th year, therefore, when Akbar was at Shāhābād, he ordered a corps to march to Bhath; but Bīr Bhadr, through the influence of several courtiers, prevailed upon the Emperor to send a grandee to his father and convey him to Court. Rāja Bīr Baṛ and Zayn Koka were selected for this office, and Rām Chand came at last to Court, where he was well received.

R. Ch. died in the 37th year, and Bīr Bhadr succeeded to the title of Rāja. But on his way from Court to Bhath he fell from his palanquin, and died soon after, in the 38th year (1001; *vide* p. 385). His sudden death led to disturbances in Bāndhū, of which Bikramājīt, a young relation of Rām Chand, had taken possession. Akbar therefore sent Rāja Patrdās (No. 196) with troops to Bāndhū, and the Mug͟huls, according to custom, erected throughout the district military stations (*thānas*). At the request of the inhabitants, Akbar sent Ismāʿīl Qulī K͟hān (No. 46) to Bāndhū, to convey Bikramājīt to Court (41st year), their intention being to prevent Bāndhū from being conquered. But Akbar would not yield; he dismissed Bikramājīt, and after a siege of eight months and several days, Bāndhū was conquered (42nd year).

In the 47th year Durjodhan, a grandson of Rām Chand, was made Rāja of Bāndhū. In the 21st year of Jahāngīr's reign Amr Singh, another grandson of Rām Chand, acknowledged himself a vassal of Dihlī. In the 8th year of Shāhjahān when ʿAbdu 'llāh K͟hān Bahādur marched against the refractory zamīndār of Ratanpūr, Amr Singh brought about a peaceful submission. Amr Singh was succeeded by his son Anūp Singh. In the 24th year, when Rāja Pahāṛ Singh Bundela, Jāgīrdār of Chaurāgaḍh, attacked Anūp, because he had afforded shelter to Dairām, a zamīndār of Chaurāgaḍh, Anūp Singh, with his whole family, withdrew from Rewā (which after the destruction of Bāndhū had been the family seat) to the hills. In the 30th year, however, Sayyid Ṣalābat K͟hān, Governor of Ilāhābād (*vide* p. 427), conducted him to Court, where Anūp turned Muḥammadan. He was made a Commander of Three Thousand, 2,000 horse, and was appointed to Bāndhū and the surrounding districts.

90. **Lashkar K͟hān**, Muḥammad Ḥusayn of K͟hurāsān.

He was *Mīr Bak͟hshī* and *Mīr ʿArẓ*. In the 11th year Muẓaffar K͟hān (No. 37) had him deposed. In the 16th year he came one day drunk to the Darbār, and challenged the courtiers to fight him. Akbar punished him by tying him to the tail of a horse, and then put him into prison.

He was subsequently released, and attached to Mun˓im's Bengal corps. In the battle of Takaroī (p. 406) he was severely wounded. Though his wounds commenced to heal, he did not take sufficient care of his health, and died, a few days after the battle, in Oṛīsā.

He is mentioned as having had a contingent of 2,000 troopers (*Ma˓āṣir*, 1,000).

The *Ma˓āṣir* has a long note in justification of the extraordinary punishment which Akbar inflicted on him.

The title of *Lashkar Khān* was conferred by Jahāngīr on Abū 'l-Ḥasan Mashhadī, and by Shāhjahān on Jān Niṣār Khān Yādgār Beg.

91. **Sayyid Aḥmad of Bārha.**

He is the younger brother of Sayyid Maḥmūd (p. 427). In the 17th year he served in the *manqāla*, which, under the command of Khān-i Kalān (No. 16), was sent to Gujrāt. After the conquest of Aḥmadābād, he was ordered with other Amīrs to pursue the sons of Sher Khān Fūlādī (p. 432), who had removed their families and property from Patanto Īdar. A portion of their property fell into the hands of Imperialists. When Akbar afterwards encamped at Patan, he gave the town to Mīrzā Abd^u 'r-Raḥīm (No. 29), but appointed S. A. as Governor. In the same year, Muḥammad Ḥusayn Mīrzā, Shāh Mīrzā, and Sher Khān Fūlādī, besieged Patan; but they dispersed on the approach of M. ˓Azīz.

In the 20th year S. A. and his nephews S. Qāsim and S. Hāshim quelled the disturbances in which Jalāl^u d'-Dīn Qūrchī (No. 213) had lost his life. In 984 he served under Shahbāz Khān (No. 80) in the expedition to Siwānah. According to the *Ṭabaqāt*, which calls him a Commander of Three Thousand, he died in 985.

Abū 'l-Faẓl mentioned Sayyid Aḥmad above on p. 300, l. 11 from below.

Sayyid Aḥmad's son, *S. Jamāl^u 'd-Dīn* was killed by the untimely explosion of a mine during the siege of Chītor (p. 398).

This S. Jamāl^u 'd-Dīn must not be confounded with the notorious S. Jamāl^u 'd-Dīn who was executed in 993 (*Badā,onī* II, 345). He was a grandson of S. Maḥmūd (No. 75) S. Qāsim being called his uncle.

92. **Kākar ˓Alī Khān-i** Chishtī.

He came with Humāyūn to Hindūstān. In the 11th year (973) he was sent together with Shāh Qulī Nāranjī (No. 231) to Gaḍha-Katanga, because Mahdī Qāsim Khān (No. 36) had gone without leave to Makkah. Kākar served also under Mu˓izz^u 'l-Mulk (No. 61) and was present in the battle of Khayrābād. He took part in the bloody fight at Sarnāl (middle of Sha˓bān, 980; *vide* p. 353). He was then attached to Mun˓im's corps, and served in the siege of Patna, during which he and his son were killed (end of 981; *Maʿāṣir*, 980).

93. **Rāy Kalyān Mal**, Zamīndār of Bīkānīr.

He is the father of Rāy Singh (No. 44), and has been mentioned above, p. 384.

94. **Ṭāhir Khān**, Mīr Farāghat, son of Mīr Khurd, who was *atālīq* to Prince Hindāl.

His name is not given in the *Maʾāṣir*. The *Ṭabaqāt* merely says that he was a grandee of Humāyūn, and reached, during the reign of Akbar, the rank of a Commander of Two Thousand. According to the same work, he had a son *Bāqī Khān*, who likewise served under Akbar.

From the *Akbarnāma* (Lucknow Edition, II, p. 274) we see that he was one of Akbar's companions. Together with Dastam Khān (No. 79) Qutluq Qadam Khān (No. 123), Peshraw Khān (No. 280), Ḥakīm[u]'l-Mulk, Muqbil Khān, and Shimāl Khān (No. 154), he assisted in the capture of the wild and mad Khwāja Muʿazzam, brother of Akbar's mother.

95. **Shāh Muḥammad Khān** of Qalāt.

As Qalāt belongs to Qandahār, he is often called Shāh Muḥammad Khān-i Qandahārī. The *Maʾāṣir* says that the name of the town of Qalāt is generally spelt with a ق, *Q*; but that the Hazāras pronounce *Kalāt*, with a *K*.

Shāh Muḥammad Khān was a friend of Bayrām, and was with him in Qandahār, which Humāyūn had given Bayrām as *jāgīr*. Bayrām, however, left it entirely in S. M.'s hands. Bahādur Khān (No. 22) was then governor of Dāwar, and had bribed several grandees to hand over Qandahār to him; but S. M. discovered the plot and killed the conspirators. Bahādur then marched against Qandahār. S. M. knew that he could expect no assistance from Humāyūn, and wrote to Shāh Ṭahmāsp of Persia that it was Humāyūn's intention to cede Qandahār; he should therefore send troops, defeat Bahādur, and take possession of the town. Ṭahmāsp sent 3,000 Turkmān troopers furnished by the *jāgīrdārs* of Sīstān, Farāh, and Garmsīr. Their leader, ʿAlī Yār, surprised Bahādur and defeated him so completely, that Bahādur could not even keep Dāwar. He therefore fled to India. S. M. had thus got rid of one danger; he treated the Persian Commander with all submissiveness, but would not hand over the town. Shāh Ṭahmāsp then ordered his nephew, Sulṭān Ḥusayn Mīrzā, son of Bahrām Mīrzā (*vide* No. 8), Walī Khalīfa Shāmlū, and others, to besiege Qandahār. The siege had lasted for some time, when Sulṭān Ḥusayn Mīrzā felt disgusted and withdrew.

Ṭahmāsp felt annoyed, and sent again Sulṭān Ḥusayn Mīrzā with ʿAlī Sulṭān, Governor of Shīrāz, to Qandahār, with positive orders to take the town. ʿAlī Sulṭān was shot during the siege, and Sulṭān Ḥusayn Mīrzā remained encamped before the town without doing anything. At this juncture, Akbar, who in the meantime had succeeded to the throne, ordered S. M. to hand over Qandahār to the Persians, according to Humāyūn's promise, and come to India.

This account of the cession of Qandahār, observes the author of the *Maʾāṣir*, differs from Munshī Sikandar's version of his great work entitled *ʿĀlamārā-yi Sikandarī*. According to that history, Ṭahmāsp, at the very first request of Shāh Muḥammad sent Sulṭān Ḥusayn Mīrzā with Walī Khalīfa and other nobles to Qandahār. They defeated Bahādur; but as S. M. would not hand over Qandahār, Ṭahmāsp sent ʿAlī Sulṭān with a stronger army, and appointed Sulṭān Ḥusayn Mīrzā governor of Dāwar and Qandahār. Shāh Muḥammad held out for six months; but as he got no assistance from India, he capitulated, and withdrew to Hindūstān.

Be this as it may, S. M. arrived in the end of the third year of Akbar's reign in India, was made a Khān, and gradually rose to the rank of a Commander of Two Thousand. In the beginning of the 6th year (968) he led the van in the battle near Sārangpūr, in which Bāz Bahādur lost Mālwa, and served, in the 9th year, in the war against ʿAbdu 'llah Khān Uzbak (No. 14). In the 12th year he was made governor of Kotha. In the 17th year he was among the auxiliaries of Mīrzā ʿAzīz Koka, and was wounded in the battle of Patan (p. 432).

Regarding ʿĀdil Khān, S. M.'s son, *vide* below, No. 125.

96. **Rāy Surjan Hāḍā.**

He is often merely called Rāy Hāḍā. The Hāḍās are a branch of the Chauhāns. The Sarkār of Rantanbhūr is called after them *Hāḍautī*.

Rāy Surjan was at first in the service of the Rānā, and defied the Mughuls, because he thought himself safe in Rantanbhūr. Akbar, after the conquest of Chītor (p. 398), besieged in the end of the 13th year, Rantanbhūr, and R. S., despairing of holding out longer—the siege having lasted about a month—sent his sons Daudā and Bhoj (No. 175) to Akbar's camp to sue for peace. The Emperor received them well, and gave each a dress of honour. When they were taken behind the tent enclosure to put on the garments, one of their men, suspecting foul play, rushed sword in hand towards the audience tent, and killed several people, among them Shaykh Bahāu'' Dīn Majzūb of Badā,on, but was cut down by one of Muẓaffar Khān's men. As R. S.'s sons were entirely innocent, the accident did not change Akbar's goodwill towards them;

and he sent them back to their father. At R. S.'s request, Ḥusayn Qulī Khān (No. 24) was then sent to the Fort and escorted R. S. to the Emperor. Rantanbhūr was annexed (Shawwāl, 976, or beginning of the 14th year).

R. S. was made Governor of Gaḍha-Katanga, from where, in the 20th year, he was transferred to Fort Chanāḍh (Chunār).

Soon after, Daudā fled and created disturbances in Būndī. Zayn Khān Koka (No. 34), R. S. and his second son Bhoj were therefore sent to Būndī, which was conquered in the beginning of 985. After the conquest, R. S. was made a commander of Two Thousand. Daudā who had escaped, submitted, in the 23rd year, to Shāhbāz Khān (p. 436). Not long after, Daudā fled again. He died in the 30th year.

R. S. served in the 25th year, after Muẓaffar's (No. 37) death in Bihār. The *Maʿāṣir* does not mention the year of his death. From the *Ṭabaqāt*, it is clear, that he had been dead for some time in 1001.

For R. S.'s son, Rāy Bhoj, *vide* below, No. 175.

97. **Shāham Khān** Jalā,ir.

Jalā,ir is the name of a Chaghtā,ī tribe.

Shāham's father was Bābā Beg, who had been under Humāyūn, governor of Jaunpūr. Bābā Beg also took part in the battle of Chausā, in which Humāyūn was defeated by Sher Shāh. The Emperor fled to Āgra, and ordered Bābā Beg and other grandees to bring up the camp and the Begams. In attempting to rescue the ladies of the Harem, Bābā Beg was killed by an Afghān near the imperial tent.

Shāham Khān was made an Amīr by Akbar.

In the beginning of the 4th year (966) he served together with the two Jalā,irs, mentioned below, Ḥājī Muḥammad Khān-i Sīstānī (No. 55), Chalma Beg (58), Kamāl Khān, Ghakkar, and Qiyā Khān Gung (No. 33), under Khān Zamān (No. 13) in the Jaunpūr District against the Afghāns. The war continued till the sixth year, in which Sher Shāh, son of ʿAdlī, Mubāriz Khān, after Bayrām's death, made a final attempt to overthrow the Mughuls. In the 10th year Sh. Kh. served against Khān Zamān.

In the 19th year he served under Munʿim in the Bengal and Oṛīsā wars, was present in the battle of Takaroī and pursued with Toḍar Mal the Afghāns to Bhadrak (p. 406). After Munʿim's death at Gaur (p. 407), the grandees put Sh. Kh. in command of the army till the Emperor should send a new commander. In the 21st year he took part in the battle near Āg Maḥall (p. 350). In the 24th year he was *jāgīrdār* of Ḥājīpūr (opposite Patna). After Muẓaffar's death (No. 37) in 988, before Toḍar Mal had arrived, he defeated and killed Saʿīd-i Badakhshī, one of the Bengal rebels. Subsequently, he pursued ʿArab Bahādūr, whom Shāhbāz Khān

(p. 438) had defeated. In the 26th year Sh. Kh. was stationed at Narhan. In this year, Maʿṣūm Khān-i Farankhūdī (No. 157) had been driven by the imperialists from Bahrā,ich over Kalyānpūr to Muḥammadābād, which he plundered, and prepared to attack Jaunpūr. Sh. Kh. from Narhan, Pahāṛ Khān (No. 407) from Ghāzīpūr and Qāsim from Jaldpūr, united their contingents and pursued Maʿṣūm so effectually that he applied to M. ʿAzīz Koka to intercede for him with the Emperor. In the 32nd year he was made Governor of Gaḍha, and soon after, of Dihlī. In the end of the same year he accompanied Sulṭān Murād, who conducted M. Sulaymān (No. 5) to Court. In the beginning of the 33rd year he assisted Ṣādiq Khān (No. 43) in his expedition against Jalāla Tārīkī in Terāh.

In the 43rd year, after a stay of fourteen years in the Panjāb, Akbar made Dihlī his residence. It was proved that Sh. had been oppressive, and he was therefore reprimanded. Two years later, he served in the Āsīr war, and died during the siege of that fort, Ẕī Ḥijjah, 1009.

The *Ṭabaqāt* says that Shāham Khān was in 1001 a Commander of Two Thousand.

The *Akbarnāma* mentions two other Jalā,ir Grandees :—

1. *Sulṭān Ḥusayn Khān Jalā,ir.* He was mentioned above, p. 417, l. 3.

2. *Muḥammad Khān Jalā,ir.* The *Ṭabaqāt* says of him, " he is an old Amīr, and is at present (1001) mad." He served under Khān Zamān in the war with Hemū. In the beginning of the 4th year all three Jalā,irs served under Khān Zamān against the Afghāns in the Jaunpūr District.

98. **Āsaf Khān (III)**, [Mīrzā Qiwāmᵘ d'-Dīn] Jaʿfar Beg, son of Badīʿᵘ 'z-Zamān of Qazwīn.

His father Mīrzā Badīʿᵘ 'z-Zamān was the son of Āghā Mullā Dawātdār of Qazwīn (*vide* p. 398). M. Badī, during the reign of Shāh Ṭahmāsp, had been *vazīr* of Kāshān, and Jaʿfar had also been introduced at the Persian Court.

In the 22nd year of Akbar's reign (985), Jaʿfar Beg came to India, and was presented to Akbar by his uncle M. Ghiyāsᵘ 'd-Dīn ʿAlī Āṣaf Khān II (No. 126), on his return from the Īdar expedition. The new *Dāgh* law having then been introduced, Akbar made Jaʿfar a Commander of Twenty (*Bistī*) and attached him to the *Dākhilīs* (p. 252) of his uncle. According to *Badā,onī* (III, 216) people attributed this *minimum* of royal favour to the malice of Jaʿfar's uncle. The post was so low that Jaʿfar threw it up in disgust and went to Bengal, to which province Muẓaffar Khān (No. 37) had just been appointed governor. He was with him when the Bengal military revolt broke out, and fell together with Shams[u] 'd-Dīn-i Khāfī (No. 159) into the hands of the rebels. Jaˁfar and Shams found means to escape, the former chiefly through his winning manners. On arriving at Fatḥpūr, Jaˁfar met with a better reception than before, was in a short time made a Commander of Two Thousand, and got the title of *Āṣaf Khān*. He was also appointed Mīr Bakhshī, *vice* Qāẓī ˁAlī. In his first expedition, against the Rānā of Udaipūr, Āṣaf was successful.

In the 32nd year he was appointed Thānadār of Sawād (Swat), *vice* Ismāˁīl Qulī Khān, who had been reprimanded (p. 388, where for *Waijūr* read *Bijūr*). In the 37th year Jalāla Rawshānī fled to ˁAbd[u] 'llah Khān Uzbak, king of Tūrān; but finding no support, he returned to Terāh, and stirred up the Āfrīdī and Ūrakzā,ī Afghāns. Āṣaf was sent against him, and with the assistance of Zayn Khān Koka, defeated Jalāla. The family of the rebel fell into the hands of the imperialists; his women were given to Waḥdat ˁAlī, who was said to be Jalāla's brother, while the other members of his family were taken to Court.

In the 39th year Āṣaf was sent to Kashmīr, M. Yūsuf Khān (No. 35) having been recalled. He re-distributed the lands of the Jāgīr holders, of whom Aḥmad Beg Kābulī (No. 191), Muḥammad Qulī Afshār, and Ḥasan ˁArab were the most important. The cultivation of *Zaˁfarān* (saffron, *vide* p. 89) and hunting were declared monopolies, and the revenue was fixed according to the assessment of Qāẓī ˁAlī, *i.e.* at one lākh of *kharwārs*, at 24 *dāms* each (*vide* p. 370). Āṣaf stayed only three days in Kashmīr, and returned to Lāhor. In the 42nd year, when Kashmīr had become all but desolated through the oppressions of the Jāgīr holders, Āṣaf was made Governor of the province. In the 44th year (beginning of 1008) he was appointed *Dīwān-i kull vice* Patr Dās (No. 196).

In 1013 Prince Salīm (Jahāngīr) rebelled against Akbar; but a reconciliation was effected by Akbar's mother, and Salīm was placed for twelve days under surveillance. After this, he received Gujrāt as *tuyūl*, and gave up the Ṣūbas of Ilāhābād and Bihār, of which during his rebellion he had taken possession. Bihār was given to Āṣaf, who, moreover, was appointed to a Command of Three Thousand.

On Jahāngīr's accession, Āṣaf was called to Court, and appointed *atālīq* to Prince Parwīz, who had taken the command against the Rānā. The expedition was, however, interrupted by the rebellion of Prince Khusraw. In the 2nd year, 1015, Jahāngīr, after suppressing Khusraw's revolt, left Lāhor for Kābul, and as Sharīf Khān Amīr[u] 'l-Umarā remained dangerously ill in India, Āṣaf was made Vakīl and Commander of Five Thousand. He also received a pen-box studded with jewels.[1] But he never trusted Jahāngīr, as the Emperor himself found out after Āṣaf's death (*Tuzuk*, p. 109).

From the time of Akbar's death, the kings [2] of the Dakhin had been restless, and Malik ʿAmbar had seized upon several places in the Bālāghāt District. The Khān Khānān (No. 29), with his usual duplicity, had done nothing to recover the loss, and Jahāngīr sent Prince Parwīz to the Dakhin, with Āṣaf Khān as *atālīq*, and the most renowned grandees of the Court, as Rāja Mān Singh (No. 30), Khān Jahān Lodī, Khān-i Aʿẓam (No. 21), ʿAbdᵘ 'llah Khān, "each in himself sufficient for the conquest of a country." But incessant drinking on the part of the Prince, and the jealousy and consequent insubordination of the Amīrs, spoiled everything, and the Mughuls suffered a check and lost their prestige. Not long after, in 1021, Āṣaf died at Burhāmpūr. The *Tārīkh* of his death is :—

صد حیف ز آصف‌خان. A hundred times alas ! for Āṣaf Khān.

The *Tuzuk* (p. 108) says that he died at the age of sixty-three.

Āṣaf Khan is represented as a man of the greatest genius. He was an able financier, and a good accountant. A glance is said to have been sufficient for him to know the contents of a page. He was a great horticulturist, planting and lopping off branches with his own hands in his gardens ; and he often transacted business with a garden spade in his hand. In religious matters, he was a free-thinker, and one of Akbar's disciples (p. 218–9). He was one of the best poets of Akbar's age, an age most fruitful in great poets. His Masnawī, entitled *Nūrnāma* ranks after Niẓam's *Shīrīn Khusraw*. *Vide* below among the poets of Akbar's reign.

Āṣaf kept a great number of women, and had a large family.

His sons. 1. *Mīrzā Zaynᵘ 'l-ʿĀbidīn.* He was a Commander of Fifteen Hundred, 500 horse, and died in the second year of Shāhjahān's reign. He had a son *Mīrzā Jaʿfar*, who like his grandfather was a poet, writing under the same *takhalluṣ* (Jaʿfar). He, Zāhid Khān Koka, and M. Shāfī (*Pādishāhnāma* ; Sāqī, *Maʾāṣir*) son of Sayf Khān, were such intimate friends, that Shāhjahān dubbed them *sih yār*, "the three friends." He

---

[1] It was customary under the Mughul Government to confer a pen-box or a golden inkstand, or both, as *insignia* on Dīwāns. When such officers were deposed, they generally returned the presents.

[2] Mughul historians do not like to call the rulers of the Dakhin *kings*. The word which they generally use, is *dunyādār*, which is a meaningless title. I have not found this title used in histories written before the *Akbarnāma*.

later resigned the service, and lived in Āgra on the pension which Shāhjahān granted and Awrangzīb increased. He died in 1094.

2. *Suhrāb Khān.* He was under Shāhjahān a Commander of Fifteen Hundred, 1,200 horse, and died in the 13th year of Shāhjahān.

3. *Mīrzā ˁAlī Aṣghar.* He was a hasty youth, and could not bridle his tongue. In the Parenda expedition, he created dissensions between Shāh Shujāˁ and Mahābat Khān. He served in the war against Jujhār Bandela, and perished at the explosion of a tower in Fort Dhamūnī, as related in the *Pādishāhnāma.* He had just been married to the daughter of Muˁtamid Khān Bakhshī (author of the *Iqbālnāma-yi Jahāngīrī*); but as no cohabitation had taken place, Shāhjahān married her to Khān Dawrān. He was a Commander of Five Hundred, 100 horse.

4. *Mīrzā ˁAskarī.* He was in the 20th year of Shāhjahān a Commander of Five Hundred, 100 horse.

The lists of grandees in the *Pādishāhnāma* mention two relations of Āṣaf—1. *Muḥammad Ṣāliḥ,* son of Mīrzā Shāhī, brother or nephew of Āṣaf. He was a Commander of One Thousand, 800 horse, and died in the second year of Shāhjahān's reign. 2. *Muqīm,* a Commander of Five Hundred, 100 horse.

XI. Commanders of One Thousand and Five Hundred.

99. **Shaykh Farīd-i Bukhārī.**

The *Iqbālnāma,* according to the *Maˁāṣir,* says he belonged to the *Mūsawī* Sayyids; but this is extraordinary, because the Bukhārī Sayyid's trace their descent to Sayyid Jalāl-i Bukhārī, seventh descendant of Imām ˁAlī Naqī Alhādī.

The fourth ancestor of Shaykh Farīd was Shaykh ˁAbdᵘ 'l-Ghaffār of Dihlī, who when dying desired his family to give up depending on Suyūrghāl tenures, but rather to enter the military service of the kings. This they seem to have done.

Shaykh Farīd was born at Dihlī (*Tuzuk,* p. 68). He entered Akbar's service early. In the 28th year, when M. ˁAzīz (No. 21) resigned from ill-health the command of the Bihār army, S. F. accompanied Vazīr Khān (No. 41) to the neighbourhood of Bardwān, where Qutlū of Oṛīsā had collected his Afghāns. Qutlū having made proposals of peace, S. F. was ordered to meet him. In doing so he nearly perished through Qutlū's treachery (*vide* Stewart's Bengal). In the 30th year, he was made a Commander of 700, and gradually rose, till the 40th year, to a command of 1,500. He was also appointed Mīr Bakhshī, and had also for some time the *Daftar-i Tan* in his charge, i.e., he had to settle all matters relating to the grants of Jāgīr holders.

His elevation under Jahāngīr was due to the decided support he gave Jahāngīr, immediately before his accession, and to the victory he obtained over Prince Khusraw at Bhairōwāl. When Prince Salīm occupied Ilāhābād during his rebellion against his father, appointing his servants to *manṣabs* and giving them *jāgīrs*, Akbar favoured Prince Khusraw so openly, that every one looked upon him as successor. Soon after, a sort of reconcilation was effected, and Salīm's men were sent to Gujrāt. When Akbar lay on the death-bed, he ordered Salīm to stay outside the Fort of Āgra; and M. ʿAzīz Koka (No. 21) and Rāja Mān Singh, who from family considerations favoured Khusraw's succession, placed their own men at the gates of the fort, and asked Shaykh Farīd to take command. But S. F. did not care for their arrangements and went over to Prince Salīm outside, and declared him emperor, before Akbar had closed his eyes. On the actual accession, S. F. was made a commander of 5,000, received the title of *Ṣāḥib^u 's-sayf w^a 'l qalam*,[1] and was appointed *Mīr Bakhshī*.

A short time after, on the 8th Ẕī Ḥijjah, 1014, Prince Khusraw suddenly left Āgra, and went plundering and recruiting to Lāhor. S. F., with other Bukhārī and many Bārha Sayyids, was sent after him, whilst Jahāngīr himself followed soon after, accompanied by Sharīf Khān Amīr^u 'l-Umarā^e and Mahābat Khān, who were hostile to S. F., and took every possible opportunity of slandering him. Sulṭān Khusraw had gone to Lāhor and besieged the town, when he heard of S. F.'s arrival with 12,000 horse at the *Āb-ī Sulṭānpūr*. He raised the siege, and arrived at the Bi,āh, which S. F. had just crossed. Khusraw was immediately attacked. The fight was unusually severe. The Bārha and Bukhārī Sayyids had to bear the brunt of the fight, the former in the van under the command of Sayf Khān, son of Sayyid Maḥmūd Khān Kundlīwāl (p. 427) and Sayyid Jalāl. There were about 50 or 60 of the Bārha Sayyids opposed to 1,500 Badakhshī troopers, and had not S. Kamāl (*vide* No. 78) come in time to their rescue, charging the enemy with loud cries of *Pādishāh salāmat* the Bārha Sayyids would have been cut down to a man. Sayyid Sayf Khān got seventeen wounds, and S. Jalāl died a few days after the battle. About four hundred of Khusraw's troopers were killed, and the rest dispersed. Khusraw's jewel-box fell

---

[1] **This title we also find in old inscriptions, e.g. in those of Tribenī and Sātgāw, Hūglī District. It means *Lord of the sword and the pen.***

into the hands of the Imperialists. The fight took place in the neighbourhood of Bhairõwāl.[1] In the evening Jahāngīr arrived, embraced S. F., and stayed the night in his tent. The District was made into a Pargana of the name of Fatḥābād, and was given S. F. as a present. He received, besides, the title of *Murtaẓā Khān*, and was appointed governor of the Ṣūba of Gujrāt.

In the 2nd year, S. F. presented Jahāngīr with an immense ruby made into a ring, which weighed 1 *misqāl*, 15 *surkhs*, and was valued at 25,000 Rs. As the relations of the Shaykh oppressed the people in Gujrāt, he was recalled from Aḥmadābād (*Tuzuk*, p. 73). In the 5th year he was made governor of the Panjāb. In 1021 he made preparations to invade Kāngra. He died at Pathān in 1025, and was buried at Dihlī (*Tuz.* p. 159). At the time of his death, he was a Commander of Six Thousand, 5,000 horse.

Sayyid Aḥmad, in his work on the antiquities of Dihlī, entitled *Āṣār*ᵘ *'ṣ-Ṣanādīd*, No. 77, says that the name of S. F.'s father was Sayyid Aḥmad-i Bukhārī. Of Farīd's tomb, he says, nothing is left but an arcade (*dālān*). But he wrongly places the death of the Shaykh *in the 9th year, or* 1033 A.H., instead of *in the eleventh year*, or 1025 A.D. Sayyid Aḥmad also mentions a *Sārā,ī*, built by Shaykh Farīd in Dihlī, which has since been repaired by the English Government, and is now used as a jail (جیل خانه, *jel khāna*).

According to the *Tuzuk*, p. 65, Salīmgaḍh (Dihlī) belonged to S. Farīd. It had been built by Salīm Khān the Afghān during his reign in the midst (*dar miyān*) of the Jamna. Akbar had given it to Farīd.[2]

When Shaykh Farīd died, only 1,000 Ashrafīs were found in his house, which very likely gave rise to the *Tārīkh* of his death :—

---

[1] Bhairõwāl, on our maps *Bhyrowal*, lies on the road from Jālindhar to Amritsir, on the right bank of the Bi,āh. After the defeat Khusraw fled northwards with the view of reaching Rohtās beyond the right bank of the Jhelum. He had therefore to cross the Rāwī, the Chanāb, and the Jhelam. On coming to the Chanāb, at a place called *Shāhpūr* (a very common name in the Panjāb), he could not get boats. He therefore went to Sodhara, which is also mentioned as a place for crossing in the *Ṭabaqāt-i Nāṣirī*—on our maps *Sodra*, N.E. of Vazīrābād—and induced some boatmen to take him over. But they left him in the lurch, landed him on an island in the middle of the Chanāb, and swam back. This came to the ears of the Chaudī of Sodhara, and a report was sent to ʿAbdᵘ 'l-Qāsim Namakīn (No. 199), one of Jahāngīr's officers stationed at Gujrāt (at some distance from the right bank of the Chanāb, opposite to Vazīrābād). He came, took Khusraw from the island, and kept him confined in Gujrāt. The news of the capture reached Jahāngīr at Lāhor on the last Muḥarram 1015, i.e. 52 days after Khusraw's flight from Āgra. On the 3rd Ṣafar, Khusraw Ḥasan Beg-i Badakhshī (No. 167), and ʿAbdᵘ 'r-Raḥīm Khar, were brought to Jahāngīr in the Bāgh-i Mīrzā Kāmrān.

[2] The family must have had large possessions in Dihlī; for when Akbar, in the 22nd year, visited Dihlī, he stayed in Sh. Farīd's mansion, and Abū 'l-Faẓl (*Akbarnāma*, III, p. 196) speaks of his extensive possessions along the Jamna.

دادِ خرد[1] برد *dād, khurd burd* (1025 A.H.).
"He gave,[1] and left (carried off) little."

Shaykh Farīd was indeed a man of the greatest liberality. He always gave with his own hands. Once a beggar came to him seven times on one day, and received money; and when he returned the eighth time, Farīd gave him again money, but told him not to tell others; else they might take the money from him. He gave widows a great deal, and his jāgīr lands were given as free land tenures to the children of his servants or soldiers who had been killed. When in Gujrāt, he had a list made of all Bukhārī Sayyids in the province,[2] and paid for every marriage feast and outfit; he even gave pregnant women of his clan money for the same purpose for the benefit of their yet unborn children. He never assisted singers, musicians, or flatterers.

He built many *sarā,īs*. The one in Dihlī has been mentioned above. In Aḥmadābād, a *maḥalla* was adorned by him and received as a memorial of him the name of Bukhārā. In the same town he built the Masjid and Tomb of Shāh Wajīh[u] 'd-Dīn (*died* 988; *Badā,onī*, III, 43). He also built *Farīdābād* near Dihlī, the greater part of the old pargana of Tilpaṭ being included in the pargana of Farīdābād (Elliot's Glossary, Beame's Edition, II, p. 123). In Lāhor also, a Maḥalla was built by him, a large bath, and a *chauk*, or bāzār. The Government officers under him received annually three *khilʿats*; to his footmen he gave annually a blanket, and his sweepers got shoes. He never made alterations in his gifts.

His contingent consisted of 3,000 picked troopers. Neither in the reign of Akbar, nor that of Jahāngīr did he build a palace for himself. He always lived as if on the march. He paid his contingent personally, little caring for the noise and tumult incident to such offices. One of his best soldiers, an Afghān of the name of Sher Khān, had taken leave in Gujrāt, and rejoined after an absence of six years, when Sh. Farīd was in Kalānūr on his march to Kāngra. The Shaykh ordered Dwārkā Dās, his Bakhshī, to pay the man his wages, and the Bakhshī wrote out the Descriptive Roll, and gave the man one day's pay. But Farīd got angry, and said, "He is an old servant, and though he comes rather late, my affairs have not fared ill on account of his absence; give him his whole pay." The man got 7,000 Rs., his whole pay for six years.

[[1] *Khurd*, eat, enjoyed.—P.]

[2] In Dihlī, Aḥmadābād, and many other places in Gujrāt do we find Bukhārī Sayyids. *Vide* Nos. 77, 78.

"Night and day," exclaims the author of the *Maʿāṣir*, "change as before, and the stars walk and the heavens turn as of old, but India has no longer such men. Perhaps they have left for some other country!"

Shaykh Farīd had no son. His daughter also died childless. He had adopted two young men, Muḥammad Saʿīd and Mīr Khān. They lived in great pomp, and did not care for the emperor. Though often warned, they would noisily pass the palace in pleasure boats to the annoyance of the emperor, their boats being lighted up with torches and coloured lamps. One night they did so again, and Mahābat Khān, whom Jahāngīr had given a hint, sent one of his men and killed Mīr Khān. S. F. demanded of the emperor Mahābat's blood; but Mahābat got together several "respectable" witnesses who maintained before the emperor that Mīr Khān had been killed by Muḥammad Saʿīd, and Shaykh F. had to remain quiet.

Muḥammad Saʿīd was alive in the 20th year of Shāhjahān, and was a Commander of Seven Hundred, 300 horse (*Pādishāhn*, II, 743).

Sayyid Jaʿfar, S. F.'s brother, was also in Akbar's service. He was killed in the battle of Patan (p. 433).

The *Pādishāhnāma* (I, b., 316, 313; II, 739) also mentions *Sayyid Badr*, son of Shaykh Farīd's sister, a Commander of 700, 500 horse; and *Sayyid Bhakar*, son of Sh. F.'s brother, a Commander of Five Hundred, 300 horse.

100. **Samānjī Khān**, son of Chalma Beg.

For *Samānjī* we often find in MSS. *Samājī*. The Turkish *samān* means *hay*, so that *Samānjī* or *Samānchī* would mean *one who looks after the hay*.

The name of this grandee is neither given in the *Maʿāṣir*, nor the *Ṭabaqāt*. Nor have I come across his name in the *Akbarnāma*. It remains, therefore, doubtful whether he is the son of No. 58.

Another Samānjī Khān will be found below, No. 147.

101. **Tardī Khān**, son of Qiyā Khān Gung (No. 33).

He has been mentioned above, on p. 367. The *Ṭabaqāt* says that, in 1001, he was governor of Patan (Gujrāt).[1]

---

[1] Tardī Khān is also mentioned in Sayyid Aḥmad's edition of the *Tuzuk*, p. 19, l. 15. But this is a mistake. It should be *Tar Khān*, not *Tardī Khān*. The word *toqnāī*, *l.c.*, also is a mistake, and should be *Toqbāī*. Pages 18, 19, of the *Tuzuk* treat of Akbar's forced march to Patan in Gujrāt (*vide* p. 343, note, and p. 445). The *Maʿāṣir* (MS. 77 of the Library As. Soc. Bengal, p. 163, *b.*) mentions the 4th Rabīʿ I, as the day when Akbar left Āgra; but from the Akbarnāma (Lucknow Edition, III, 18 ff.) it is clear that Akbar left Āgra on the 24th Rabīʿ II, 981, and engaged the enemies on the 9th day after his

102. **Mihtar Khān**, Anīs[u] 'd-Dīn, a servant of Humāyūn.

The word *mihtar*, prop. a prince, occurs very often in the names of Humāyūn's servants. Thus in the *Akbarnāma* (Lucknow Edition, Vol. I, p. 269—a very interesting page, which gives the names of the grandees, etc., who accompanied the emperor to Persia).

Mihtar Khān was the title of Anīs[u] 'd-Dīn. He was Humāyūn's treasurer on his flight to Persia, and returned with the emperor.

In the 14th year, when Rantanbhūr had been conquered (*vide* No. 96), the fort was put in his charge. In the beginning of the 21st year (beginning of 984) he accompanied Mān Singh on his expedition against Rānā Partāb of Maiwār, and distinguished himself as leader of the *Chandāwul* (rear). In the 25th year he held a *jāgīr* in Audh, and distinguished himself in the final pursuit of Maʕṣūm Khān Farankhūdī (No. 157).

Anīs was gradually promoted. He was at the time of Akbar's death a Commander of Three Thousand. According to the *Ṭabaqāt*, he was in 1001 a Commander of 2,500.

He died in the 3rd year of Jahāngīr's reign, 1017, eighty-four years old. If I read the MSS. of the *Maʕāṣir* correctly, he was a Kātī, and looked upon his tribe with much favour. He was a man of great simplicity. It is said that he paid his contingent monthly.

Mūnīs Khān, his son, was during the reign of Jahāngīr a Commander of Five Hundred, 130 horse. *Abū Ṭālib*, son of Mūnis Khān, was employed as treasurer (*Khizānchī*) of the Ṣūba of Bengal.

103. **Rāy Durgā** Sīsodia.

Rāy Durgā is generally called in the *Akbarnāma*, Rāy Durgā Chandrāwaṭ, (چندراوت). The home of the family was the Pargana of Rāmpūr, also called Islāmpūr, near Chītor.

In the 26th year of Akbar's reign Rāy Durgā accompanied Prince Murād on his expedition against Mīrzā Muḥammad Ḥakīm of Kābul. In the 28th year he was attached to Mīrzā Khān's (No. 29) corps, and distinguished himself in the Gujrāt war. In the 30th year he was with M. ʕAzīz Koka (No. 21) in the Dakhin. In the 36th year he followed Prince Murād to Mālwa, and later to the Dakhin.

In the 45th year Akbar sent him after Muẓaffar Ḥusayn Mīrzā. He then accompanied Abū 'l-Faẓl to Nāsik, and went afterwards home on

---

departure, i.e. on the 5th Jumāda I, 981. Hence the date 5th Jumāda I, 980, which Sayyid Aḥmad gives, *Tuzuk*, p. 8, l. 16, should be corrected to 5th Jumāda I, 981.

The comparison of the several sources for a history of Akbar's reign, and the correction of the MSS. is a truly herculean labour, which the want of critical acumen on the part of the editors of our printed historical editions has very much increased. *Vide* No. 104.

leave. He returned, but after six weeks went again home, apparently without permission.

He died towards the end of the 2nd year of Jahāngīr's reign.

According to the *Tuzuk* (p. 63) he had served Akbar for upwards of forty years. Jahāngīr says, he had at first been in the service of Rānā Ūdai Singh, and reached, during the reign of Akbar, the dignity of Commander of Four Thousand. He is said to have been a good tactician.

The *Ṭabaqāt* says that he was in 1001 a Commander of Fifteen Hundred.

The *Maʾāṣir* continues the history of his descendants, from which the following tree has been taken.

Genealogy of the Rā,os of Rāmpūr (Islāmpūr), Chītor.

1. Rāy Durgā Sīsodiya (Chandrāwaṭ)
   |
2. Rā,o Chandā (Jahāngīr)
   |
   (a) A son ———— (b) Rūp Mukund
   |
3. Rā,o Daudā (Shāhjahān)
   |
4. Rā,o Hattī Singh (Do.)[1] [died childless]

5. (a) Rā,o Rūp Singh [died childless] ———— 6. (b) Rā,o Amr Singh (Awrangzīb)
   |
7. Rā,o Muhkam Singh
   |
8. Rā,o Gopāl Singh
   |
9. Rā,o Ratan Singh

Rā,o Ratan Singh turned Muhammadan, and got the title of *Muslim Khān* (Awrangzīb-Jahāndār Shāh).

104. **Mādhū Singh,** son of Rāja Bhagwān Dās (No. 27).

He was present in the fight at Sarnāl (p. 353). In the beginning of the 21st year (Muḥarram, 984) he served under Mān Singh against Rānā Kīkā, and distinguished himself in the battle of Goganda (21st Rabīʿ I, 984).[2] In the 30th year he accompanied Mīrzā Shāhrukh (No. 7)

[1] There is some confusion in the MSS. and printed editions regarding his name. Thus in the *Pādishāhnāma*, Ed. Bibl. Indica, I, b. 305, he is called *Mathī Singh*; but *Hattī Singh* in the same work, Vol. II, p. 730, and *Hathī*, on p. 374.

[2] It was said above, p. 361, note 2, that the battle of Goganda was fought in 985. This is the statement of the *Ṭabaqāt*, which the *Maʾāṣir* follows in its biographical note of Rāja Mān Singh. But from the *Akbarnāma* and the History of Badā,onī, who was present in the battle, and brought Akbar Mān Singh's report, it is clear that Mān Singh set out on the 2nd Muḥarram, 984, and that the battle took place on the 21st Rabī I, of the same year.

It has been remarked above (p. 383, note 1) that the chronology of the *Ṭabaqāt* is erroneous. Badā,onī ascribes the errors to the omission of the intercalary days, and a confusion of solar and lunar years. Historians should bear this in mind. The *Akbarnāma* is the only source for a history of Akbar's reign, and the *Sawāniḥ* should be the guide of Historians.

on his expedition to Kashmīr. In the 31st year, after the death of Sayyid Ḥāmid (No. 78), he took the contingent of Rāja Bhagwān from Thāna Langar, where he was stationed, to ʿAlī Masjid, where Mān Singh was.

In the 48th year he was made a Commander of Three Thousand, 2,000 horse. According to the *Ṭabaqāt*, he had been, in 1001, a Commander of 2,000.

His son, *Chatr Sāl*, or *Satr Sāl*, was at the end of Jahāngīr's reign a Commander of Fifteen Hundred, 1,000 horse. He was killed together with his two sons, Bhīm Singh and Anand Singh, in the Dakhin, in the 3rd year of Shāhjahān's reign. His third son, *Ugar* Sen, was a Commander of Eight Hundred, 400 horse (*vide* Pādishāhn, I, p. 294; I, b., pp. 305, 314).

105. **Sayyid Qāsim**, and 143. **Sayyid Hāshim**, sons of Sayyid Maḥmūd Khān of Bārha, Kūndlīwāl (No. 75).

In the 17th year S. Qāsim served under Khān ʿĀlam (No. 58) in the pursuit of Muḥammad Ḥusayn Mīrzā, who after his defeat by M. ʿAzīz Koka (No. 21) had withdrawn to the Dakhin.

S. Hāshim served, in the 21st year, with Rāy Rāy Singh (No. 44) against Sulṭān De,ora, ruler of Sarohī, and distinguished himself in the conquest of that place.

In the 22nd year both brothers served under Shāhbāz Khān (No. 80) against the Rānā. In the 25th year, when Chandr. Sen., son of Māldeo, raised disturbances, both brothers, who had *jāgīrs* in Ajmīr, were ordered to march against him. Both again distinguished themselves in the 28th year, and served in the *harāwal* of Mīrzā Khān (No. 29) in the Gujrāt war.

S. Hāshim was killed in the battle of Sarkich, near Aḥmadābād. S. Qāsim was wounded. He was subsequently appointed Thānadār of Patan. When Mīrzā Khān went to Court, leaving Qulij Khān as Governor of Aḥmadābād, Qāsim was again appointed to a command and operated successfully against Muẓaffar, Jām (zamīndār of Little Kachh), and Khangār (zamīndār of Great Kachh).

On the transfer of Mīrzā Khān, Khān-i Aʿẓam (No. 21) was appointed Governor of Gujrāt. Qāsim continued to serve in Gujrāt, and distinguished himself especially in the 37th year. Later, he commanded the left wing of Sulṭān Murād's Dakhin corps.

Qāsim died in the 44th year (1007). He was at his death a Commander of 1,500.

Regarding their sons, *vide* p. 427.

XII. Commanders of Twelve Hundred and Fifty.

106. **Rāy Sāl Darbārī**, Shaykhāwat.

He is also called Rāja Rāy Sāl Darbārī, and is the son of Rājā Sojā, son of Rāy Rāy Mal Shaykhāwat, in whose service Ḥasan Khān Sūr (father of Sher Shāh) was for some time.

As remarked above (No. 23), the Kachhwāhas are divided into Rājāwats and Shaykhāwats. To the latter branch belong Rāja Lō Karan, Rāy Sāl, etc.; the former contains Mān Singh's posterity (the present rulers of Jaipūr).

The term *Shaikhāwat*, or *Shekhāwat*, as it is generally pronounced, is explained as follows. One of the ancestors of this branch had no sons. A Muḥammadan Shaykh, however, had pity on him, and prayed for him till he got a son. From motives of gratitude, the boy was called *Shaykh*.[1] Hence his descendants are called the Shaykhāwat Branch.

Rāy Sāl was employed at Court, as his title of *Darbārī* indicates. He was in charge of the Harem. During the reign of Jahāngīr, he was promoted, and served in the Dakhin. He died there at an advanced age. He had twenty-one sons, each of whom had a numerous posterity.

Whilst Rāy Sāl was in the Dakhin, Mādhū Singh and other grandchildren of his, collected a lot of ruffians, and occupied Rāy Sāl's paternal possessions.[2] But Mathurā Dās, a Bengalī, who was Rāy Sāl's Munshī and Vakīl, recovered a portion of his master's lands.

After Rāy Sāl's death, his sons and grandsons lived, according to the custom of the Zamīndārs of the age, in feud with their neighbours and with each other. Rāja Girdhar, Rāy Sāl's son, is almost the only one that distinguished himself at Court.

From the *Akbarnāma* we see that Rāy Sāl entered early Akbar's service; for he was present in the battle of Khayārbād (p. 414) in the fight at Sarnāl (*vide* 27), and accompanied the Emperor on his forced march to Patan and Aḥmadābād (p. 458, note).

The *Pādishāhnāma* (I, b., p. 314) mentions another son of Rāy Sāl's, Bhoj Rāj, who was a Commander of Eight Hundred, 400 horse.

The *Ṭabaqāt* says that Rāy Sāl, was in 1001 a Commander of Two Thousand. Abū 'l-Faẓl calls him in this list a Commander of 1250. This *manṣab* is unusual, and Rāy Sāl stands alone in this class. It does not

---

[1] He is the same as the *Shaykhjī* of Jaipūr genealogies. Shaykhjī is said to have been a grandson of Udaikaran, twelfth descendant of Dholā Rāy (p. 348).

[2] Called in the *Maʾāsir* کهندار, Khandār or Ghandār, "near Amber." Tod mentions a Khandhar near Amber. *Vide* Geogr. Index, Khandār.

occur in the lists of Grandees in the *Pādishāhnāma*. From other histories also it is clear that the next higher Manṣab after the *Hazārī* was the *Hazār o pānṣadī*, or Commander of Fifteen Hundred.

XIII. Commanders of One Thousand.

107. **Muḥibb ʿAlī Khān**, son of Mīr Khalīfa.

This grandee must not be confounded with *Muḥibb ʿAlī Khān Rahṭāsī* (p. 466).

Muḥibb ʿAlī Khān is the son of Mīr Niẓāmᵘ 'd-Dīn ʿAlī Khalīfa, the "pillar of Bābar's government". He had no faith in Humāyūn, and was opposed to his accession. He therefore favoured Mahdī Khwāja, Bābar's son-in-law. Mahdī, a short time before Bābar's death, assumed a royal deportment. One day, Mīr Khalīfa happened to be in Mahdī's tent; and when he left, Mahdī, thinking himself alone, put his hand to his beard, and exclaimed, "Thou shalt by and by follow me." He had scarcely uttered these words, when he observed Muqīm-i Harawī[1] in the corner of the tent. Muqīm reported these words to Mīr Khalīfa, and upbraided him for giving Mahdī his support. Mīr Khalīfa thereupon changed his mind, forbade people to visit Mahdī, and raised, on Bābar's death, Humāyūn to the throne.

His son Muḥibb ʿAlī Khān distinguished himself under Bābar and Humāyūn. His wife was Nāhīd Begam, daughter of Qāsim Koka. Qāsim had sacrificed himself for Bābar. Bābar had fallen into the hands of ʿAbdᵘ 'llāh Khān Uzbak, when Qāsim stepped forward and said that *he* was Bābar. He was cut to pieces, and Bābar escaped. In 975, Nāhīd Begam went to Thatha, to see her mother, Ḥājī Begam (daughter of Mīrzā Muqīm, son of Mīrzī Ẕū 'l-Nūn). After Qāsim Koka's death, Ḥājī Begam married Mīrzā Ḥasan, and after him, Mīrzā ʿĪsa Tarkhān, king of Sindh (p. 390). Before Nāhīd Begam reached Thatha Mīrzā ʿĪsa died. His successor, Mīrzā Bāqī, ill-treated Ḥājī Begam and her daughter. Ḥājī Begam therefore collected a few desperate men and watched for an opportunity to get hold of M. Bāqī's person. The plot was, however, discovered, and Ḥājī Begam was put into prison. Nāhīd Begam escaped and went to Bhakkar, where she was well received by Sulṭān Maḥmūd, ruler of the District. He persuaded her to ask Akbar to send her husband Muḥibb ʿAlī to Bhakkar; and he would give him an army, if he liked to attack Thatha. Nāhīd Begam did so on coming to Court, and Akbar,

[1] Father of the Historian Niẓāmᵘ 'd-Dīn Aḥmad, author of the *Ṭabaqāt-i Akbarī*. Muqīm was then *Dīwān-i Buyūtāt*.

in the 16th year (978), called for Muḥibb, who had then retired from court-life, and ordered him to proceed to Bhakkar.

Muḥibb set out, accompanied by *Mujāhid Khān*, a son of his daughter. Saʿīd Khān (No. 25), Governor of Multān, had also received orders to assist Muḥibb; but at Sulṭān Maḥmūd's request, Muḥibb came alone, accompanied by only a few hundred troopers. When he arrived at Bhakkar, Sulṭān Maḥmūd said that he had changed his mind: he might go and attack Thatha without his assistance; but he should do so from Jaisalmīr, and not from Bhakkar. Muḥibb, though he had only 200 troopers, resolved to punish Sulṭān Maḥmūd for his treachery, and prepared himself to attack Bhakkar. Maḥmūd had 10,000 horse assembled near Fort Māthīla (ماتهيله). Muḥibb attacked them, dispersed them, and took soon after the fort itself. He then fitted out a larger corps, and moved to Bhakkar, where he again defeated Maḥmūd. The consequence of this victory was that Mubārak Khān, Sulṭān Maḥmūd's *vazīr*, left his master and went with 1,500 horse over to Muḥibb. But as Mubārak's son, Beg Oghlū, was accused of having had criminal intercourse with a concubine of Sulṭān Maḥmūd, Muḥibb wished to kill Beg Oghlū. Mubārak, who had not expected this, now tried to get out of Muḥibb's power. Muḥibb therefore killed Mubārak, and used the money which fell into his hands to complete his preparations for the siege of Bhakkar.

The siege had lasted three years, when famine and disease drove the inhabitants to despair. The swelling which is peculiar to the district decimated the people; and the bark of the *Sirs* tree (p. 238), the best remedy for it, could only be had for gold. Sulṭān Maḥmūd at last sent a message to Akbar, and offered the fort as a present to Prince Salīm, if Muḥibb were recalled, and another grandee sent in his stead, who was to take him (Maḥmūd) to Court; for he said, he could not trust Muḥibb. Akbar accepted the proposal, and sent Mīr Gesū, Bakāwal-begī, to Bhakkar.[1] Before Mīr Gesū arrived, Sulṭān Maḥmūd had died. New complications arose on his arrival. Mujāhid Khān just besieged Fort Ganjāba,[2] and his mother Sāmiʿa Begam (Muḥibb's daughter), who felt offended at Akbar's proceedings, dispatched a few ships against Mīr Gesū, and nearly captured him. In the meantime Muqīm-i Harawī also arrived and dissuaded Muḥibb from hostilities against Mīr Gesū.

---

[1] The conquest of Bhakkar is minutely related in the *Tārīkh-i Maʿṣūmī* (*vide* No. 329), from which Prof. Dowson in his edition of Elliot's History of India (I, p. 240 ff.) has given extracts. But Abū 'l-Faẓl's account contains a few interesting particulars and differences. For Dowson's Mīr Kisū, we have to read *Mīr Gesū*. His biography is given in the *Maʾāṣir*.

[2] Generally called *Ganjāwa*.

The latter now entered Bhakkar (981) and the inhabitants handed the keys over to him.

But neither Muḥibb nor Mujāhid felt inclined to leave for the Court, though their stay was fraught with danger. Muḥibb therefore entered into an agreement with Mīr Gesū, according to which Mujāhid should be allowed to go to Thatha, and that he himself with his whole family should be accommodated in Loharī. The arrangement had been partially carried out, when Mīr Gesū dispatched a flotilla after Mujāhid. Muḥibb upon this withdrew to Māthīla. Sāmiʿa Begam fortified the environs, and when attacked by Gesū's men, she successfully repulsed them for one day and one night. Next day, Mujāhid arrived by forced marches, defeated the enemy,[1] and occupied the land east of the river.

In the meantime, Akbar had sent Muḥammad Tarsō Khān (No. 32) as governor to Bhakkar, and Muḥibb thought it now wise to go to Court.

In the 21st year, Muḥibb received an appointment at Court, as a sort of *Mīr ʿArẓ*. As he gave the emperor satisfaction, Akbar, in the 23rd year, allowed him to choose one of four appointments, the office of *Mīr ʿArẓ*, the guard of the Harem, the governorship of a distant province, or the governorship of Dihlī. Muḥibb chose the last, and entered at once upon his office.

He died as Governor of Dihlī in 989.

Muḥibb is placed in the *Ṭabaqāt* among the Commanders of Four Thousand.

Regarding the town of Bhakkar, Abū 'l-Faẓl says that it is called in old books *Manṣūra*. Six rivers united pass by it in several branches; two branches lie to the south, one to the north. The town at the latter branch is called Bhakkar. On the second branch another town lies, called Loharī, and near it is the Indus.

Mīrzā Shāh Ḥusayn Arghūn, king of Thatha, had Bhakkar fortified, and appointed as Commander his foster-brother, Sulṭān Maḥmūd. After Shāh Ḥusayn's death, Sulṭān Maḥmūd declared himself independent at Bhakkar, and Mīrzā ʿĪsā Tarkhān (p. 390) at Thatha. Both were often at war with each other. Sulṭān Maḥmūd is said to have been a cruel man.

As Bhakkar was conquered and annexed before Thatha, it was attached to the Ṣūba of Multān.

---

[1] If Prof. Dowson's MSS. agree with his version (I, p. 241), the *Tārīkh-i Maʿṣūmī* would contradict the *Akbarnāma*. Mujāhid Khān is again mentioned, *l.c.*, p. 282.

[Muḥibb ʿAlī Khān Rahtāsī.]

Like Muḥibb ʿAlī Khān, son of Mīr Khalīfa, Muḥibb ʿAlī Khān Rahtāsī is put in the *Ṭabaqāt* among the Commanders of Four Thousand. It is impossible to say why Abū 'l-Faẓl had not mentioned him in this list. His name, however, occurs frequently in the *Akbarnāma* and other histories. As he was a long time Governor of Rahtās in S. Bihār, he is generally called *Rahtāsī*. This renowned Fort had passed, in 945, into the hands of Sher Shāh. During his reign, as also that of Salīm Shāh, Fatḥ Khān Baṭnī commanded the Fort. Subsequently it came into the hands of Sulaymān and Junayd-i Karrarānī. The latter appointed Sayyid Muḥammad commander. As related above (p. 437), he handed it over to Shāhbāz Khān (No. 80), at the time of the war with Gajpatī and his son Srī Rām (984).

In the same year, Akbar appointed Muḥibb ʿAlī Khān governor of Rahtās, and Shāhbāz Khān made over the Fort to him.

Muḥibb rendered excellent services during the Bengal Military Revolt. His son also, Ḥabīb ʿAlī Khān (*vide* No. 133), distinguished himself by his bravery, but was killed in a fight with one Yūsuf Miṭṭī, who had collected a band of Afghāns and ravaged S. Bihār. His death affected his father so much that he became temporarily insane.

In the 31st year, two officers having been appointed to each Ṣūba, Muḥibb was ordered to join Vazīr Khān (No. 41), Governor of Bengal. In the 33rd year Bihār was given to the Kachhwāhas as *jāgīr*, and Akbar called Muḥibb to Court, intending to make him governor of Multān. But as the emperor was just about to leave for Kashmīr (997), Muḥibb accompanied him.

Soon after entering Kashmīr, Muḥibb fell ill, and died, on the emperor's return, near the *Koh-i Sulaymān*. Akbar went to his sick-bed and saw him the moment he died.

In the *Akbarnāma* (III, p. 245) a place *Muḥibb ʿAlīpūr* [1] is mentioned which Muḥibb founded near Rahtās.

108. **Sulṭān Khwāja,** ʿAbdᵘ 'l-ʿAẓīm, son of Khwāja Khāwand Dost.

He is also called Sulṭān Khwāja *Naqshbandī*.[2] His father Khāwand Dost was a pupil of Khwāja ʿAbdᵘ 'sh-Shahīd, fifth son of Khwāja

[1] Not given on the maps.

[2] *Naqshband* was the epithet of the renowned saint Khwāja Bahāᵘ 'd-Dīn of Bukhārā, born 728, died 3rd Rabīʿ I, 791. He was called *naqshband*, because according to his own words, he and his parents used to weave *kamkhābs* adorned with figures (*naqsh*).

ʿAbdᵘ 'llāh (generally called Khwājagān Khwāja; *vide* No. 17), son of the renowned saint Khwāja Aāṣirᵘ 'd-Dīn Aḥrār (born 806, died 29th Rabiʿ I, 895).

When ʿAbdᵘ 'sh-Shahīd came from Samarqand to India, he was well received by Akbar, and got as present the Pargana Chamārī. He remained there some time, but returned in 982 to Samarqand, where he died two years later.

Sulṭān Khwāja, though neither learned in the sciences nor in *taṣawwuf* (mysticism), had yet much of the saintly philosopher in him. He possessed in a high degree the confidence and the friendship of the emperor. In 984 he was made *Mīr Ḥajj*, and as such commanded a numerous party of courtiers during the pilgrimage to Makkah. Never before had so influential a party left for Arabia: Sulṭān Khwāja was to distribute six *lākhs* of rupees and 12,000 *khilʿats* to the people of Makkah.

On his return in 986 (23rd year) he was made a Commander of One Thousand, and appointed *Ṣadr* of the realm (p. 284). He held that office till his death, which took place in the 29th year (992). He was buried outside the Fort of Fatḥpūr, to the north.

His daughter, in the beginning of the 30th year, was married to Prince Dānyāl.

His son, Mīr Khwāja, was in the 46th year a Commander of 500.

According to Badā,onī and Abū 'l-Faẓl, Sulṭān Khwāja belonged to the elect of the "Divine Faith" (*vide* p. 214).

109. **Khwāja ʿAbdᵘ 'llāh**, son of Khwāja ʿAbdᵘ 'l-Laṭīf.

His name is not given in the *Maʿāṣir* and the *Ṭabaqāt*. The *Akbarnāma* mentions a Khwāja ʿAbdᵘ 'llah who served in the war against Abdᵘ 'llāh Khān Uzbak (No. 14), in Mālwah (971–2), during the last rebellion of Khān Zamān (No. 13), and in the fight at Sarnāl (middle of Shaʿbān, 980; *vide* No. 27). He also accompanied the emperor on his forced march to Patan and Aḥmadābād. *Vide* the Lucknow Edition of the *Akbarnāma*, II, 285, 287, 367; III, 24.

110. **Khwāja Jahān**, Amīnā of Hirāt.

His full name is Khwāja Amīnᵘ 'd-Dīn Maḥmūd of Hirāt. The form Amīnā is modern Īrānī, which likes to add a long *ā* to names.

Amīn was an excellent accountant and a distinguished calligrapher. He accompanied Humāyūn on his flight to Persia. On the return of the emperor, he was made Bakhshī of Prince Akbar.

On Akbar's accession, Amīn was made a Commander of One Thousand, and received the title of *Khwāja Jahān*. He was generally employed in financial work, and kept the great seal. In the 11th year he was accused by Muzaffar Khān (No. 37) of want of loyalty shown in the rebellion of Khān Zamān. Amīn was reprimanded, the great seal was taken from him, and he was dismissed to Makkah.

On his return, he was pardoned. In the 19th year (981–2) Akbar besieged Ḥājīpūr; but Amīn had been compelled by sickness to remain behind at Jaunpūr. When the emperor returned from Ḥājīpūr over Jaunpūr to Āgra, Amīn followed him. On the march, he was once charged by a *mast* elephant; his foot got entangled in a tent rope, and he fell to the ground. The accident had an injurious effect on Amīn, convalescent as he was. He died near Lakhnau in the beginning of Shaʿbān, 982.

According to the chronology of the *Ṭabaqāt*, his death took place in 983.

A son of Amīn's brother is mentioned. His name was Mīrzā Beg. He was a poet and wrote under the *takhalluṣ* of *Shahrī*. He withdrew from Court, and died in 989.

Jahāngīr also conferred the title of Khwāja Jahān on the officer (Dost Muḥammad of Kābul) who had served him as Bakhshī while Prince.

111. **Tātār Khān**, of Khurāsān.

His name is Khwāja Ṭāhīr Muḥammad. In the 8th year he accompanied Shāh Budāgh Khān (No. 52) and Rūmī Khān (No. 146), and pursued Mīr Shāh Abū 'l-Maʿālī, who withdrew from Ḥiṣār Fīrūza to Kābul.

He was then made governor of Dihlī, where he died in 986.

The *Ṭabaqāt* says he was for some time *Vazīr*, and died in 985.

Regarding his enmity with Mullā Nūr[u] 'd-Dīn Tarkhān, *vide* Badā,onī, III, 199.

112. **Ḥakīm Abū 'l-Fatḥ**, son of Mullā ʿAbd[u] r-Razzāq of Gīlān.

His name is Masīḥ[u] 'd-Dīn Abū 'l-Fatḥ. Mawlānā ʿAbd[u] 'r-Razzāq, his father, was a learned and talented man, and held for a long time the post of *Ṣādr* of Gīlān. When Gīlān, in 974, came into the possession of Ṭahmāsp, Aḥmad Khān, ruler of the country was imprisoned, and ʿAbd[u] 'r-Razzāq was tortured to death. Ḥakīm Abū 'l-Fatḥ, with his distinguished brothers, Ḥakīm Humām (No. 205) and Ḥakīm Nūr[u] 'd-Dīn,[1] left the country, and arrived, in the 20th year, in India (p. 184). They went to Court and were well received. Abū 'l-Fatḥ, in the 24th year, was made *Ṣadr* and *Amīn* of Bengal. At the outbreak of the military

[1] He is mentioned below among the poets of Akbar's reign. His *takhalluṣ* is "Qarārī". Their fourth brother, Hakīm Luṭf[u] 'llāh, came later from Īrān to India, and received through Abū'l-Fatḥ's influence a Command of Two Hundred (No. 354). He did not live long.

revolt, he was captured with several other officers (*vide* Nos. 98 and 159); but he escaped from prison, and went again to Court. He rose higher and higher in Akbar's favour, and possessed an immense influence in state matters and on the emperor himself. Though only a Commander of One Thousand, he is said to have had the power of a *Vakīl.*

As related above (p. 367), he accompanied Bīr Baṛ on the expedition against the Yūsufzā,īs in Sawād and Bijor. On his return, he was reprimanded; for the emperor, correctly enough, ascribed the disastrous issue of the campaign to Abū 'l-Fatḥ's insubordinate conduct towards Zayn Koka (No. 34).

In the 34th year (997) he went with the emperor to Kashmīr and from there to Zābulistān. On the march he fell sick, and died. According to Akbar's order, Khwāja Shams[u] d'-Dīn (No. 159) took his body to Ḥasan Abdāl, and buried him in a vault which the Khwāja had made for himself (*Tuzuk*, p. 48). On his return, the emperor said a prayer at Abū 'l-Fatḥ's tomb.

The great poet ʿUrfī of Shīrāz (*vide* below, among the poets) is Abū 'l-Fatḥ's encomiast. Fayẓī also has composed a fine *marṣiya*, or elegy, on his death.

Abū 'l-Faẓl and Badā,onī speak of the vast attainments of Abū 'l-Fatḥ. A rare copy of his *Munshiyāt* [1] is preserved in the Library of the As. Soc. Bengal (No. 780). He had a profound contempt for old Persian poets: thus he called Anwarī diminutively *Anwariyak*; and of Khaqānī he said, he would give him a box on the ears if he were to come to him to rouse him from his sleepiness, and would send him to Abū 'l-Faẓl, who would give him another box, and both would then show him how to correct his verses (Badā,onī, III, 167).

Badā,onī mentions Abū 'l-Fatḥ's influence as one of the chief reasons why Akbar abjured Islām (p. 184).

Abū 'l-Fatḥ had a son, Fatḥ[u] 'llāh. He was killed by Jahāngīr, as he was an accomplice of Khusraw (*Tuzuk*, p. 58).

A grandson of Abū 'l-Fatḥ is mentioned in the *Pādishāhnāma* (II, p. 739). His name is Fatḥ Ziyā; he was a Commander of Nine Hundred, 150 horse.

113. **Shaykh Jamāl**, son of Muḥammad Bakhtyār.

His full name is Shaykh Jamāl Bakhtyār, son of Shaykh Muḥammad Bakhtyār. The Bakhtyār clan had possessions in Jalesar, near Dihlī.

Shaykh Jamāl's sister held the post of superintendent in Akbar's

---

[1] His *Munshiyāt* contain interesting letters addressed by Abū 'l-Fatḥ to his brother Ḥakīm Humām, the Khān Khānān (No. 29), Khwāja Shams (No. 159) and others.

harem, and procured for her brother a command of One Thousand. Jamāl's elevation excited much envy. One day, after taking some water, he felt suddenly ill. Rūp also, one of Akbar's servants, who had drunk of the same water, fell immediately ill. Akbar had antidotes applied, and both recovered.

In the 25th year he accompanied Ismāˁīl Qulī Khān (No. 46) on his expedition against the rebel Niyābat Khān. Niyābat Khān was the son of Mīr Hāshim of Nīshāpūr; his name was ˁArab. Before his rebellion he held Jhosī and Arail (Jalālābās) as jāgīr. In the fight which took place near "Kantit, a dependency of Panna,"[1] Shaykh Jamāl was nearly killed, Niyābat Khān having pulled him from his horse.

In the 26th year he marched with Prince Murād against Mīrzā Muḥammad Ḥakīm of Kābul.

Shaykh Jamāl drank a great deal of wine. One day he brought such a smell of wine to the audience hall that Akbar felt offended, and excluded him from Court. Jamāl therefore squandered and destroyed the things he had with him, and assumed the garb of a *jogī*. This annoyed the emperor more, and Jamāl was put into prison. Soon after, he was pardoned; but he continued his old vice, and brought *delirium tremens* on himself. In the 30th year, when Akbar set out for Zābulistān, Shaykh Jamāl had to remain sick in Lūdhiyāna. He died there in the same year (993).

Jamāl has been mentioned above on p. 200.

114. **Jaˁfar Khān**, son of Qazāq Khān.

He is generally called in the histories *Jaˁfar Khān Taklū*, Taklū being the name of a Qizilbāsh tribe.

His grandfather, Muḥammad Khān Sharafᵘ 'd-Dīn Oghlū Taklū was at the time of Humāyūn's flight governor of Hirāt and *lalla*[2] to Sulṭān Muḥammad Mīrzā, eldest son of Shāh Ṭahmāsp-i Ṣafawī. At the Shāh's order, he entertained Humāyūn in the most hospitable manner. When he died he was succeeded in office by his son Qazāq Khān. But Qazāq showed so little loyalty, that Ṭahmāsp, in 972, sent

---

[1] The Bibl. Indica edition of *Badā,onī* (II, 289) says, the fight took place at *Gasht* (گشت), *a dependency of Patna* (پتنه), but this is a mistake of the editors. Sir H. Elliot (Beames' Glossary II, 166) has drawn attention to the frequent mistakes which MSS. make in the name of *Panna* (پنه), to which Kantit belonged. There is no doubt, that above, on p. 130, l. 2, and p. 129, note, we have likewise to read *Panna*, which was famous for its wild elephants.

[2] The word *lalla* is not in our dictionaries, though it occurs frequently in Persian Historians, as the *Memoirs of Ṭahmāsp*, the *ˁĀlamārā*, etc. I have never seen it used by Indian Historians. From the passages where it occurs, it is plain that it has the same meaning as *atālīq*, which so often occurs in Indian Histories, *vide* p. 383, note 3. [*Lala* a tutor.—P.]

Ma^cṣūm Beg-i Ṣafawī against him. Qazāq fell ill, and when the Persians came to Hirāt, he died. Maʿṣūm seized all his property.

Jaʿfar thinking himself no longer safe in Persia, emigrated to India, and was well received by Akbar. He distinguished himself in the war with K͟hān Zamān, and was made a *K͟hān* and a Commander of One Thousand. From *Badā,onī* (II, p. 161), we see that he had a *jāgīr* in the Panjāb, and served under Ḥusayn Qulī K͟hān (No. 24) in the expedition to Nagarkoṭ.

According to the *Ṭabaqāt*, Jaʿfar's father did not die a natural death, but was killed by the Persians.

Jaʿfar had been dead for some time in 1001.

115. **Shāh Fanā'ī,** son of Mīr Najafī.

His name is not given in the *Ma'āṣir* and the *Ṭabaqāt*. From the *Akbarnāma* (Lucknow Edition, II, 170, 172) we see that he served in the conquest of Mālwa and took part in the battle near Sārangpūr (beginning of the 6th year; *vide* No. 120).

The poet *Fanā'ī* who is mentioned in *Badā,onī* (III, 296), the *Ṭabaqāt*, and the *Mir'ātᵘ 'l ʿĀlam*, appears to be the same. He travelled a good deal, was in Makkah, and distinguished himself by personal courage in war. Akbar conferred on him the title of *K͟hān*. He was a Chag͟htā'ī Turk of noble descent. Once he said, in Akbar's presence, that no one surpassed him in the three *C*'s—chess, combat, composition, when the emperor replied that he had forgotten a fourth, viz. conceit. For some reason, he was imprisoned, and when set at liberty it was found that he had become mad. He ran into the wilderness, and was no more heard of.

116. **Asadᵘ 'llāh K͟hān,** of Tabrīz.

His name is not given in the *Ma'āṣir* and the *Ṭabaqāt*. An Asadᵘ 'llāh K͟hān is mentioned in the *Akbarnāma* (end of the 12th year). He served under K͟hān Zamān (No. 13) and commanded the town of *Zamāniyā* (p. 337, l. 14). After K͟hān Zamān's death, he wished to make over the town to Sulaymān, king of Bengal. But Munʿim (No. 11) sent a man to him to convince him of his foolishness, and quickly took possession of the town, so that the Afg͟hāns under their leader, K͟hān K͟hānān Lodī, had to withdraw. This incident, however, brought the Afg͟hān's into contact with Munʿim; and as they found him a tractable man, a meeting was arranged, which took place in the neighbourhood of Patna. This meeting was of importance, inasmuch as K͟hān K͟hānān Lodī, on the part of Sulaymān, promised to read the *K͟huṭba*, and to strike coins in

Akbar's name. Bengal therefore enjoyed peace till the death of Sulaymān in 980.[1]

The *Akbarnāma* mentions another officer of a similar name, *Asad*ᵘ *'llāh Turkmān*. He was mentioned above under 61.

117. **Saʿādat ʿAlī Kh̲ān**, of Badak̲h̲shān.

From the *Akbarnāma* (III, 295) we see that he was killed in 988 in a fight with the rebel ʿArab Bahādur. Shāhbāz Kh̲ān had sent Saʿādat to a Fort [2] near Rahtās, where he was surprised by ʿArab, defeated and slain. It is said that ʿArab drank some of his blood.

118. **Rūpsī Bairāgī**, brother of Rāja Bihārī Mal (No. 23).

The *Maʾāṣir* says that Rūpsī was *the son* of Rāja Bihārī Mal's brother. He was introduced at Court in the 6th year.

According to the *Ṭabaqāt*, he was a commander of Fifteen Hundred.

Jaymal, Rūpsī's son, was the first that paid his respects to Akbar (under 23). He served some time under Sharafᵘ 'd-Dīn (No. 17), jāgīrdār of Ajmīr, and was Thānadār of Mīrtha. When Sharaf rebelled, Jaymal went to Court. In the 17th year he served in the *manqalā* of Kh̲ān Kalān (*vide* No. 129) and accompanied the emperor on the forced march to Patan and Aḥmadābād (p. 458, note). In the 21st year he served in the expedition against Daudā, son of Rāy Surjan (No. 96), and the conquest of Būndī (Muḥarram, 985). Subsequently, he was sent by Akbar on a mission to the grandees of Bengal; but on reaching Chausā, he suddenly died.

Jaymal's wife, a daughter of Moth Rāja (No. 121), refused to mount the funeral pile; but Ūdai Singh, Jaymal's son, wished to force her to become a *Satī*. Akbar heard of it, and resolved to save her. He arrived just in time. Jagnāth (No. 69) and Rāy Sāl (No. 106) got hold of Ūdai Singh, and took him to Akbar, who imprisoned him.

The story of the heavy armour which Jaymal wore in the fight with Muḥammad Ḥusayn Mīrzā, after Akbar's forced march to Patan and Aḥmadābād, is known from Elphinstone's History (Fifth Edition, p. 509, note). Rūpsī was offended, because the emperor ordered Karan (a grandson of Māldeo) to put on Jaymal's armour, and angrily demanded it back. Akbar then put off his own armour. Bhagwān Dās, however, thought it necessary to ask the emperor to pardon Rūpsī's rudeness.

---

[1] According to the *Akbarnāma, Badā,onī*, and the *Ṭabaqāt*, Sulayman died in 980. In Prinsep's Tables, Stewart's Bengal, etc., 981 is mentioned as the year of his death. The *Riyāẓ*ᵘ *'s-Salāṭīn*, upon which Stewart's work is based, has also 981; but as this Hitory is quite modern and compiled from the *Akbarnāma* and the *Ṭabaqāt*, 981 may be looked upon as a mistake. *Vide note* 3, p. 179.

[2] The MSS. call the Fort کیست, کسیت, کبست, etc. It is said to be a dependency (*az muẓāfāt*) of Rohtās.

119. **Iˁtimād <u>Kh</u>ān**, <u>Kh</u>wājasarā.

He has been mentioned above, p. 13, note. His appointment to Bhakkar was made in 984, when Sayyid Muḥammad Mīr ˁAdl (*vide* No. 140) had died.

Maqṣūd ˁAlī, who killed Iˁtimād, is said to have been blind in one eye. When he explained to Iˁtimād his miserable condition, his master insulted him by saying that someone should put urine into his blind eye. Maqṣūd stabbed him on the spot. According to another account, Iˁtimād was murdered by Maqṣūd, whilst getting up from bed.

Iˁtimād built *Iˁtimādpūr*, 6 *kos* from Āgra. He had there a villa and a large tank. He also lies buried there.[1]

120. **Bāz Bahādur**, son of Shajāwal <u>Kh</u>ān [Sūr].

Abū 'l-Faẓl says below (Third Book, Ṣūba of Mālwa) that his real name was *Bāyazīd.*

Bāz Bahādūr's father was Shujāˁat <u>Kh</u>ān Sūr, who is generally called in histories *Shajāwal*, or *Sajāwal*, *<u>Kh</u>ān*. The large town Shajāwalpūr, or Sajāwalpūr, in Mālwa bears his name;[2] its original name, *Shujāˁatpūr*, which Abū 'l-Faẓl gives below under Sarkār Sārangpūr, Mālwa, appears to be no longer in use.

When Sher Shāh took Mālwa from Mallū (Qādir <u>Kh</u>ān), Shujāˁat <u>Kh</u>ān was in Sher Shāh's service, and was made by him governor of the conquered province. In Salīm's reign, he returned to Court; but feeling dissatisfied with the king, he returned to Mālwa. Salīm dispatched a corps after him, and Shujāˁat fled to the Rāja of Dūngarpūr. Some time after, he surrendered to Salīm, and remained with him, Mālwa being divided among the courtiers. Under ˁAdlī, he was again appointed to Mālwa. After a short time, he prepared himself to assume the royal purple, but died (962).

Bāz Bahādur succeeded him. He defeated several opponents, and declared himself, in 963, king of Mālwa. His expedition to Gaḍhā was not successful, Rānī Dūrgāwatī (p. 397) having repulsed him. He now gave himself up to a life of ease and luxury: his singers and dancing women were soon famous throughout Hindūstān, especially the beautiful *Rūpmatī*, who is even nowadays remembered.

---

[1] The trigonometrical maps have a village of the name of *Iˁtimādpūr Mandra* about 9 miles E. of Āgra, in the Pargana of Fatḥābād, near Samūgar, where Awrangzīb defeated Dārā Shikoh.

[2] A few MSS. have *Shujāˁ <u>Kh</u>ān* for *Shujāˁat <u>Kh</u>ān*, just as one MS. read *Shujāˁpūr* for *Shujāˁatpūr*. Elphinstone also has *Shujāˁ* (p. 501, note 1). The word "Shujāˁat" should be spelled "Sh*a*jāˁat", whilst شجاع is pronounced *Shujā*; but the former also is pronounced with a *u* over all India.

In the very beginning of the 6th year of Akbar's reign Adham Koka (No. 19) was ordered to conquer Mālwa. Pīr Muḥammad Khān (No. 20) ʿAbdu '-llah Khān Uzbak (No. 14), Qiyā Khān Gung (No. 33), Shāh Muḥammad Khān of Qandahār (No. 95) and his son ʿĀdil Khān (No. 125), Ṣādiq Khān (No. 43), Ḥabīb ʿAlī Khān (No. 133), Ḥaydar Muḥammad Khān (No. 66), Muḥammad Qulī Toqbāʾī (No. 129), Qiyā Khān (No. 184), Mīrak Bahādur (No. 208), Samānjī Khān (No. 147), Pāyanda Muḥammad Mughul (No. 68), Mihr ʿAlī Sildoz (No. 130), Shāh Fanāʾī (No. 115), and other grandees accompanied Adham. They met Bāz Bahādur three *kos* from Sārangpūr and defeated him (middle of 968).[1] Bāz Bahādur fled to the jungles on the Khāndesh frontier. He collected a new army, but was defeated by Pīr Muḥammad, who had succeeded Adham. He then fled to Mīrān Shāh of Khāndesh, who assisted him with troops. Pīr Muḥammad in the meantime conquered Bījāgaḍh, threw himself suddenly upon Burhānpūr, sacked the town, and allowed an indiscriminate slaughter of the inhabitants. B. B. marched against him, and defeated him. As related above, Pīr Muḥammad fled, and was drowned in the Narbadā. The imperialists thereupon got discouraged, and the jāgīrdārs left for Āgra, so that Bāz Bahādur without opposition re-occupied Mālwa.

In the 7th year Akbar sent ʿAbdu '-llah Khān Uzbak to Mālwa. Before he arrived, B. B. fled without attempting resistance, and withdrew to the hills. He lived for some time with Bharjī, Zamīndār of Baglāna, and tried to obtain assistance from Chingiz Khān and Sher Khān of Gujrāt, and lastly even from the Niẓāmu 'l-Mulk. Meeting nowhere with support, B. B. went to Rānā Udai Singh. He then appears to have thrown himself on Akbar's generosity; for in the 15th year Akbar ordered Ḥasan Khān Khizānchi[2] to conduct Bāz Bahādur to Court. He now entered the emperor's service, and was made on his arrival a commander of One Thousand. Some time later, he was promoted to a *manṣab* of Two Thousand. He had been dead for some time in 1001.

Bāz Bahādur and his Rūpmatī lie buried together. Their tomb stands in the middle of a tank in Ujjain. *Vide* No. 188.

121. **Ūdai Singh, Moth Rāja,** son of Rāy Māldeo.

The *Ṭabaqāt* says that he was in 1001 a Commander of Fifteen Hundred and ruler of Jodhpūr.

---

[1] The 6th year of Akbar's reign commences on the 24th Jumāda II, 968, and the battle of Sārangpūr took place in the very beginning of the 6th year.

[2] This officer was often employed on missions. In the beginning of Akbar's reign, he was sent to Mukund Deo, the last Gajpatī of Oṛisā.

In 981 he was at Kambhā,it, which he left on the approach of Muḥammad Ḥusayn Mīrzā, and withdrew to Aḥmadābād to M. ʿAzīz Koka (No. 21).

Akbar, in 994, married Ūdai Singh's daughter to Jahāngīr. On p. 8 of the *Tuzuk*, Jahāngīr says that her name was *Jagat Gosā'inī*. She was the mother of Prince Khurram (Shāhjahān); *vide* p. 323, l. 18.

Mīrzā Hādī in his preface to Jahāngīr's Memoirs (the Tuzuk-i Jahāngīrī) has the following remark (p. 6): "Rāja Udai Sing is the son of Rāja Māldeo, who was so powerful that he kept up an army of 80,000 horse. Although Rānā Sānkā, who fought with Firdaws-makānī (Bābar) possessed much power, Māldeo was superior to him in the number of soldiers and the extent of territory; hence he was always victorious."

From the *Akbarnāma* (Lucknow Edition, III, p. 183) we see that Moth Rāja accompanied in the 22nd year Ṣādiq Khān (No. 43), Rāja Askaran, and Ulugh Khān Ḥabshī (No. 135) on the expedition against Madhukar (26th Rabīʿ I, 985). In the 28th year he served in the Gujrāt war with Muẓaffar (*Akbarnāma*, III, 422).

Another daughter of Moth Rāja was married to Jaymal, son of Rūpsī (No. 118).

122. **Khwāja Shāh Manṣūr**, of Shīrāz.

Manṣūr was at first *mushrif* (accountant) of the *Khushbū-Khāna* (Perfume Department). Differences which he had with Muẓaffar Khān (No. 37) induced Sh. Manṣūr to go to Jaunpūr, where Khān Zamān made him his *Dīwān*. Subsequently he served Munʿim Khān Khānān in the same capacity. After Munʿim's death he worked for a short time with Toḍar Mal in financial matters. In the 21st year (983), he was appointed by the emperor *Vazīr*. He worked up all arrears, and applied himself to reform the means of collecting the land revenue. The custom then was to depend on experienced assessors for the annual rate of the tax; but this method was now found inconvenient, because the empire had become greater; for at different places the assessment differed, and people and soldiers suffered losses. For this reason, the Khwāja in the 24th year, prepared a new rent roll, based upon the preceding *Dahsāla* roll, and upon the prices current in the 24th year. The empire itself, which did not then include Oṛīsā, Thathah, Kashmīr, and the Dakhin, was divided into 12 parts, called *Ṣūbas*; and to each ṣūba a *sipahsālār* (Military Governor), a *Dīwān*, a *Bakhshī* (Military Paymaster and Secretary), a *Mīr ʿAdl*, a *Ṣadr*, a *Kotwāl*, a *Mīr Baḥr*, and a *Wāqiʿa Nawīs* (p. 268) were to be appointed. The strictness which the Khwāja displayed towards jāgīr-holders led to serious results. In the 25th year he lowered the value of the jāgīrs of the grandees in Bengal by one-fourth of their former value, and those in Bihār by one-fifth. As Bengal and South Bihār were then not completely subjugated, and the Afghāns still mustered large forces in Eastern and Southern Bengal, in Orīsā, and along the Western frontier of Bengal, Manṣūr's rigour was impolitic; for Akbar's officers looked upon the old jāgīr emoluments as very moderate rewards for their readiness to fight the Afghāns. Akbar some time before, in consideration of the troubled state of both provinces, and the notorious climate of Bengal, had doubled the allowances of Bengal officers and increased by 50 *per cent* the emoluments of those in Bihār. This Manṣūr cut down: he allowed Bengal officers an increase of 50, and Bihār officers an increase of only 20 *per cent*. He then wrote to Muẓaffar to enforce the new arrangements. But the dissatisfaction was also increased by the innovations of the emperor in religious matters, and his interference with Suyurghāl tenures brought matters to a crisis. The jāgīr-holders in Jaunpūr, Bihār, and Bengal rebelled. That religious excitement was one of the causes of this military revolt, which soon after was confined to Bengal, is best seen from the fact that not a single Hindū was on the side of the rebels.[1] Toḍar Mal tried to prevent the outbreak by reporting Manṣūr and charging him with unnecessary harshness shown especially towards Maʿṣūm Khān-i Farankhūdī (No. 157) and Muḥammad Tarsō (No. 32). Akbar deposed Manṣūr and appointed temporarily Shāh Qulī Maḥram (No. 45); but having satisfied himself of the justice of Manṣūr's demands, he reinstated him in his office, to the great anxiety of the courtiers.

In the same year, Mīrzā Muḥammad Ḥakīm, at Maʿṣūm Khān-i Kābulī's instigation, threatened to invade the Panjāb, and Akbar prepared to leave for the north. Manṣūr's enemies charged him with want of loyalty, and showed Akbar letters in the handwriting of Mīrzā M. Ḥakīm's Munshī, addressed to Manṣūr. Accidentally Malik Ṣānī Ḥakīm's Dīwān, who had the title of *Vazīr Khān*, left his master, and paid his

---

[1] The chief rebel was Maʿṣūm Khān-i Kābulī, who has been frequently mentioned above (pp. 198, 365, 377, 438, etc.). He was a *Turbatī* Sayyid (*vide* p. 373, No. 37). His uncle, Mīrzā ʿAzīz, had been Vazīr under Humāyūn, and Maʿṣūm himself was the foster-brother (*koka*) of Mīrzā Muḥammad Ḥakīm, Akbar's brother. Having been involved in quarrels with Khwāja Ḥasan Naqshbandī (p. 339) who had married the widow of Mīr Shāh Abu 'l-Maʿālī, Maʿṣūm, in the 20th year, went to Akbar and was made a commander of Five Hundred. He distinguished himself in the war with the Afghāns, and was wounded in a fight with Kālā Pahāṛ. For his bravery he was made a commander of One Thousand. In the 24th year, he received Orīsā as *tuyūl*, when Manṣūr and Muẓaffar's strictness drove him into rebellion. Historians often call him *Maʿṣūm Khān-i ʿĀṣī*, "Maʿṣūm Khān, the rebel". His fights with Muzaffar and Shāhbāz have been mentioned above. He was at last driven to *Bhāṭī* (p. 365, note), where he died in the 44th year (1007).

His son *Shujāʿ-i Kābulī* was under Jahāngīr Thānadār of Ghaznīn, and a commander of Fifteen Hundred under Shāhjahān, who bestowed upon him the title of *Asad Khān*. He died in the 12th year of Shāhjahān's reign. His son, *Qubād*, was a commander of Five Hundred.

The editors of the *Pādishāhnāma*, Ed. Bibl. Indica, have entered Shujā's name twice, I, *b*. 304, and p. 308. As he was a Commander of Fifteen Hundred, the second entry is wrong. [Regarding his death *vide* Akbarn. III, 810.—B.]

respects to Akbar at Sonpat. As he put up with Manṣūr, new suspicions got afloat. Several words which Manṣūr was said to have uttered, were construed into treason, and letters which he was said to have written to M. M. Ḥakīm were sent to Akbar. Another letter from Sharaf Beg, his collector, was likewise handed to the emperor, in which it was said that Farīdūn Khān (maternal uncle to M. M. Ḥakīm) had presented the Beg to the Mīrzā. Akbar, though still doubtful, at the urgent solicitations of the grandees, gave orders to arrest Manṣūr; he should remain in arrest till any of the grandees should stand bail for him; but as none dared to come forward, they ordered the Khidmat Rāy (p. 262) to hang Manṣūr on a tree near Sarā Koṭ Khachwa (beginning of 989).[1]

This foul murder gave the nobles the greatest satisfaction. But when Akbar came to Kābul (10th Rajab 989) he examined into Manṣūr's treasonable correspondence. It was then found, to the sorrow of Akbar, that every letter which had been shown to him had been a forgery, and that Manṣūr was not guilty of even one of the malicious charges preferred against him.

It is said, though at the time it was perhaps not proved, that Karamᵘ 'llah, brother of Shāhbāz Khān-i Kambū (p. 440, l. 23), had written the letters, chiefly at the instigation of Rāja Toḍar Mal.

Manṣūr had been Vazīr for four years.

123. **Qutlugh Qadam Khān**, Ākhta-begī.[2]

The Turkish word *qutlugh* means *mubārak*, and *qadam-i mubārak*, is the name given to stones bearing the impression of the foot of the Prophet. The *Tabaqāt* calls him *Qutlū*, instead of *Qutlugh*, which confirms the conjecture in note 2, p. 383.

Qutlugh Qadam Khān was at first in the service of Mīrzā Kāmrān, and then went over to Humāyūn.

In the 9th year of Akbar's reign, he assisted in the capture of Khwāja Muʿaẓẓam, and served in the same year in Mālwa against ʿAbdᵘ 'llah Khān Uzbak (No. 14). In the battle of Khayrābād, he held a command in the van.

---

[1] So the *Akbarnāma* سراي كوت كچهوه. Koṭ Khachwa is a village on the road from Karnāl to Ludhiyāna, Lat. 30° 17′; Long. 76° 53′. In the Ed. Bibl. India of Badā,onī (II, pp. 293, 294) the place is called كجه كوت *kajh koṭ*, probably by mistake. Sharaf Beg, moreover, is called *Musharraf Beg*, and a few lines lower, again *Sharaf Beg*. Badā,onī says nothing of Toḍar Mal's intrigues. Manṣūr was hanged in the very beginning of 989, i.e. the end of the 25th year. The 26th year of Akbar's reign commences on the 5th Ṣafar 989 (the Lucknow Edition III, 325, has wrongly 990); and the 27th year commences 15th Ṣafar 990, which in the Bibl. Indica Edit. of Badā,onī (II, p. 300, l. 2 from below) is wrongly called the 28th year.

[2] *Ākhta* means "a gelding", and *ākhta-begī*, the officer in charge of the geldings (*vide* No. 66). This title is not to be confounded with the much higher title *Ātbegī*, from the Turkish *āt*, a horse; *vide* p. 145, Āʾīn 53.

In the 19th year, he was attached to Munʿim's Bengal corps, and was present in the battle of Takaroī (p. 406). He was no longer alive in 1001.

His son, Asad (?) Khān, served under Prince Murād in the Dakhin, and was killed by a cannon ball before Dawlatābād.

124. **ʿAlī Qulī Khān**, Indarābī.

Indarāb is a town of Southern Qunduz. A straight line drawn from Kābul northwards to Tālīkhān passes nearly through it.

ʿAlī Qulī had risen under Humāyūn. When the Emperor left Kābul for Qandahār to inquire into the rumours regarding Bayrām's rebellion, he appointed ʿAlī Qulī governor of Kābul. Later, he went with Humāyūn to India.

In the first year of Akbar's reign, he served under ʿAlī Qulī Khān Zamān (No. 13) in the war with Hemū, and accompanied afterwards Khizr Khwāja (p. 394, note 1) on his unsuccessful expedition against Sikandar Sūr.

In the fifth year, he served under Atga Khān (No. 15), and commanded the van in the fight in which Bayrām was defeated.

The *Ṭabaqāt* says that he was commander of Two Thousand, and was dead in 1001.

125. **ʿĀdil Khān**, son of Shāh Muḥammad-i Qalātī (No. 95).

He served under Adham Khān (No. 19) in Mālwa, and took a part in the pursuit of ʿAbdᵘ 'l-Khān Uzbak. Later, he assisted Muḥammad Qulī Khān Barlās (No. 31) on his expedition against Iskandar Uzbak, and was present at the siege of Chītor (p. 397). In the beginning of the 13th year (Ramaẓān, 975), Akbar was on a tiger-hunt between Ajmīr and Alwar. ʿĀdil, who was at that time *muʿtāb, i.e.*, under reprimand and not allowed to attend the Darbārs, had followed the party. A tiger suddenly made its appearance, and was on the point of attacking the Emperor, when ʿĀdil rushed forward and engaged the tiger, putting his left hand into its mouth, and stabbing, with the dagger in his right, at the animal's face. The tiger got hold of both hands of his opponent, when others came up and killed the brute with swords. In the struggle ʿĀdil received accidentally a sword cut.

He died of his wounds after suffering for four months. In relating his end, Abū 'l-Faẓl says that the wrath of heaven overtook him. He had been in love (*taʿalluq-i khāṭir*) with the wife of his father's Dīwān; but he was not successful in his advances. His father remonstrated with him, and ʿĀdil in his anger struck at him with a sword.

Qiyām Khān, brother of ʿĀdil Khān. Jahāngīr made him a Khān. He served the Emperor as *Qarāwalbegī* (officer in charge of the drivers).

126. **Khwāja Ghiyāsu 'd-Dīn** [ʕAlī Khān, Āṣaf Khān II] of Qazwīn. He is not to be confounded with Mīr Ghiyāsu 'd-Dīn ʕAlī Khān (No. 161). For his genealogy, *vide* p. 398. The family traced its descent to the renowned saint Shaykh Ghiyāsu 'd-Dīn Suhrawardī,[1] a descendant of Abū Bakr, the Khalīfa

Khwāja Ghiyāṣ was a man of learning. On his arrival from Persia in India, he was made a *Bakhshī* by Akbar. In 981, he distinguished himself in the Gujrātī war and received the title of *Āṣaf Khān*. He was also made Bakhshī of Gujrāt, and served as such under M. ʕAzīz Koka (No. 21). In the 21st year, he was ordered to go with several other Amīr's to Īdar, "to clear this dependency of Gujrāt of the rubbish of rebellion." The expedition was directed against Zamīndār Narāʿin Dās Rāṭhor. In the fight which ensued, the van of the Imperialists gave way, and Muqīm-i Naqshbandī, the leader, was killed. The day was almost lost, when Āṣaf, with the troops of the wings, pressed forward and routed the enemies.

In the 23rd year, Akbar sent him to Mālwa and Gujrāt, to arrange with Shihāb Khān (No. 26) regarding the introduction of the *Dāgh* (pp. 252, 265).

He died in Gujrāt in 989.

Mīrzā Nūru 'd-Dīn, his son. After the capture of Khusraw (p. 455) Jahāngīr made Āṣaf Khān III (No. 98), Nūru 'd-Dīn's uncle, responsible for his safety. Nūru 'd-Dīn, who was an adherent of the Prince, found thus means to visit Khusraw and told him that at the first opportunity he would let him escape. But soon after, Khusraw was placed under the charge of Iʕtibār Khān, one of Jahāngīr's eunuchs, and Nūru 'd-Dīn had to alter his plans. He bribed a Hindū, who had access to Khusraw, and sent the Prince a list of the names of such grandees as favoured his cause. In four or six months, the number had increased to about 400, and arrangements were made to murder Jahāngīr on the road. But it happened that one of the conspirators got offended, and revealed the plot to Khwāja Waisī, Dīwān of Prince Khurram, who at once reported matters to his august father. Nūru 'd-Dīn and Muḥammad Sharīf, son of Iʕtimadu 'd-Dawla, and several others were impaled. The paper containing the list of names was also brought up; but Jahāngīr, at the request of Khān Jahān Lodī, threw it into the fire without having read it; "else many others would have been killed."

---

[1] Author of the *ʕAwārifu 'l-Maʕārif*. He died at Baghdād in 632. His uncle ʕAbdu 'l-Najīb (died 563) was also a famous saint. Wüstenfeld's Jacut, III, p. 203. *Nafhātu 'l-Uns*, pp. 478, 544. *Safinatu 'l-Aṣfiyā* (Lahore Edition), pp. 681, 683.

127. **Farrukh Ḥusayn Khān**, son of Qāsim Ḥusayn Khān. His father was an Uzbak of Khwārazm ; his mother was a sister of Sulṭān Ḥusayn Mīrzā.

The *Maʾāṣir* and the *Ṭabaqāt* say nothing about him. A brother of his is mentioned in the *Akbarnāma* (II, p. 335).

128. **Muʿīnᵘ 'd-Dīn [Aḥmad] Khān-i** Farankhūdī.[1]

Muʿīn joined Humāyūn's army when the Emperor left Kābul for Hindūstān. In the 6th year of Akbar's reign, he was made Governor of Āgra during the absence of the Emperor in the Eastern provinces. In the 7th year, when ʿAbdᵘ 'llah Khān Uzbak was ordered to re-conquer Mālwa, Muʿīn was made a Khān. After the conquest, he divided the province into *khāliṣa* and jāgīr lands, and performed this delicate office to Akbar's satisfaction. In the 18th year, Muʿīn was attached to Munʿim's Bihār corps. He then accompanied the Khān Khānān to Bengal, was present in the battle of Takaroī, and died of fever at Gaur (*vide* p. 407).

The *Ṭabaqāt* merely says of him that he had been for some time *Mīr Sāmān*.

For his son, *vide* No. 157.

Badā,onī (III, p. 157) mentions a Jāmiʿ Masjid built by Muʿīn at Āgra.

129. **Muḥammad Qulī Toqbā.**

Toqbāʾī is the name of a Chaghtāʾī clan.

Muḥammad Qulī served under Adham Khān (No. 19) in the conquest of Mālwa (end of the 5th and beginning of the 6th year), and in the pursuit of Mīrzā Sharafᵘ 'd-Dīn (No. 17) in the 8th year. In the 17th year (980) he served in the *manqalā* of the Khān-i Kalān (No. 16).[2] In the 20th

[1] Many MSS. have *Faranjūdī*. The *Muʿjam* mentions a place فرنکد, *Farankad*, which is said to be near Samarqand.

[2] Akbar left Fatḥpūr Sīkrī for Gujrāt, in the 20th Ṣafar 980 (17th year), passed over Sangānīr (8 miles south of Jaipūr), and arrived on the 15th Rabīʿ I, at Ajmīr. On the 2nd Rabīʿ II, 980, he ordered the Khān-i Kalān (No. 16) to march in advance (*manqalā*), and left Ajmīr on the 22nd Rabīʿ II. Shortly before his arrival at Nāgor on the 9th Jumāda I, Akbar heard that Prince Dānyāl had been born at Ajmīr on the 2nd Jumāda I, 980. He reached Patan on the 1st Rajab, 980, and Aḥmadābād on the 14th of the same month. In the middle of Shaʿbān, 980, the fight at Sarnāl took place with Ibrāhīm Ḥusayn Mīrzā. On the 25th Shaʿbān, Akbar reached Baroda, and arrived at Sūrat on the 7th Ramaẓān, 980. On the 18th Ramaẓān, 980, Mīrzā ʿAzīz defeated Muḥammad Ḥusayn Mīrzā and the Fūlādīs at Patan. Sūrat surrendered on the 23rd Shawwāl.

There are serious discrepancies in the MSS. regarding the day and year of Prince Dānyāl's birth. The *Tuzuk* (Sayyid Aḥmad's edition, p. 15) has the 10th Jumāda I, 979, which has been given above on p. 309. *Badā,onī* (II, p. 139) has the 2nd Jumāda I, 980. The *Akbarnāma* has the 2nd Jumāda I, and relates the event as having taken place in 980. The MSS. of the *Sawāniḥ* also place the event in 980, but say that Dānyāl was born on the 2nd Jumāda I, 979.

On the 6th Ẕī Qaʿda, 980, the 18th year of Akbar's reign commences. After the ʿĪd-i Qurbān (10th Ẕī Ḥijjah, 980) Akbar returned over Patan and Jālor to Āgra, which he reached on the 2nd Ṣafar, 981. After this, Muḥammad Ḥusayn Mīrzā invaded Gujrāt, and took Bahronch and Kambhā,it, but was defeated by Qulij Khān and S. Ḥāmid (No. 78).

year, he was attached to Munʿim's corps, and was present in the battle of Takaroī, and the pursuit of the Afghāns to Bhadrak (p. 375).

130. **Mihr ʿAlī Khān Sildoz.**

Sildoz is the name of a Chaghtā,ī clan. According to the *Ṭabaqāt*, he was at first in Bayrām's service. In the end of 966, Akbar sent him to Fort Chanāḍh (Chunār) which Jamāl Khān, the Afghān Commander, wished to hand over to the Imperialists for a consideration (*vide* Badā,onī II, 32). Akbar offered him five parganas near Jaunpūr, but Jamāl did not deem the offer sufficiently advantageous, and delayed Mihr ʿAlī with vain promises. Mihr ʿAlī at last left suddenly for Āgra.

On his journey to Chanāḍh, he had been accompanied by the Historian Badā,onī, then a young man, to whom he had given lodging in his house at Āgra. On his return from the Fort, Badā,onī nearly lost his life during a sudden storm whilst on the river. Badā,onī calls him Mihr ʿAlī *Beg*, and says that he was later made a Khān and Governor of Chītor.

He served under Adham Khān (No. 10) in Mālwa, and in the Gujrāt wars of 980 and 981. In the 22nd year, Akbar was on a hunting tour near Ḥiṣar, and honoured him by being his guest. In the following year, he attended Sakīna Bānū Begum, whom Akbar sent to Kābul to advise his brother, Mīrzā Muḥammad Ḥakīm. In the 25th year, he served under Toḍar Mal against the rebel ʿArab.

The *Ṭabaqāt* makes him a Commander of Fifteen Hundred, and says that he was dead in 1001.

131. **Khwāja Ibrāhīm-i Badakhshī.**

He is not mentioned in the *Ma,āṣir* and the *Ṭabaqāt*. From the *Akbarnāma* (II, p. 207) we see that he was Jāgīrdār of Sakīt (in the Mainpūrī District). Near this town there were eight villages inhabited by robbers. In consequence of numerous complaints, Akbar resolved to surprise the dacoits. A great number were killed, and about one thousand of them were burnt in dwellings in which they had fortified themselves. Akbar exposed himself to great dangers ; no less than seven

---

Ikhtiyāru 'l-Mulk also appeared and marched upon Aḥmadābād. Muḥammad Ḥusayn Mīrzā joined him. Both besieged Aḥmadābād. Akbar now resolved again to go to Gujrāt. This is the famous nine days' march (24th Rabīʿ II, 981, to 4th Jumāda I, 981); *vide* p. 458, note. Muḥammad Ḥusayn Mīrzā was captured and killed, apparently without the order of the Emperor. Ikhtiyār was also killed. Akbar then returns, and arrives, *after an absence of forty-three days*, at Fatḥpūr Sīkrī, 8th Jumāda II, 981.

It has been above remarked (p. 406, l. 24) that the Lucknow Edition of the *Akbarnāma* is not a trustworthy edition. An extraordinary error occurs in the events of the 17th year. The editors have divided the work into *three*, instead of *two* parts—the Ā,īn-i Akbarī, is the third part—and have ended their second volume with the birth of Dānyāl (2nd Jumāda I, 980). Their third volume opens with the beginning of the 18th year (6th Zī Qa,da, 980). Hence they have omitted the important events which took place between those two days, *viz.*, the conquest of Gujrāt and the first defeat of the Mīrzās.

arrows struck in his shield, and his elephant fell with one foot in a grain pit, which threw the officer who was seated behind him with much force upon him. The fight chiefly took place in a village called in the MSS. بروزنکه or بروزنکه.[1]

The *Tabaqāt* mentions a Sulṭān Ibrāhīm of Awba (near Hirāt) among Akbar's grandees. His name is not given in the Āʾīn. He was the maternal uncle of Niẓāmᵘ 'd-Dīn Aḥmad, author of the *Tabaqāt*. He conquered Kamā,on and the Dāman-i Koh.

132. **Salīm Khān Kākar.**[2]

Several MSS. of the Āʿīn call him *Salīm Khān Kākar ʿAlī*. The *Akbarnāma* calls him *Salīm Khān Kākar*, or merely Salīm Khān, or *Salīm Khān Sirmūr*. The *Tabaqāt* has *Salīm Khān Sirmūr Afghān*.

He served in the beginning of the 6th year in the conquest of Mālwa, and later under Muʿizzᵘ 'l-Mulk (No. 61) in Audh, and was present in the battle of Khayrābād. In 980, he took a part in the fight of Sarnāl. He then served in Bengal, and was jāgīrdar of Tājpūr. In the 28th year, he accompanied Shāhbāz Khān (No. 80) to Bhāṭī. As there were no garrisons left in Upper Bengal, Vazīr Khān having gone to the frontier of Orīsā, Jabārī (*vide* p. 400, note 2) made an inroad from Kūch Bihār into Ghorāghāt, and took Tājpūr from Salīm's men, and Pūrni,a from the relations of Tarsō Khān (No. 32). Jabārī moved as far as Ṭānḍa. The Kotwāl, Ḥasan ʿAlī, was sick, and Shaykh Allah Bakhsh Ṣadr fled in precipitate haste. Fortunately, Shaykh Farīd arrived, and Jabārī withdrew to Tājpūr. In the 32nd year, Salīm served under Maṭlab Khān (No. 83) against the Tārikīs, and shortly after, in the 33rd year, under Ṣadīq Khān against the same Afghān rebels.

He was no longer alive in 1001.

133. **Ḥabīb ʿAlī Khān.**

He is not to be confounded with the Ḥabīb ʿAlī Khān mentioned on p. 466.

Ḥabīb was at first in the service of Bayrām Khān. In the third year when Akbar had marched to Āgra, he ordered Ḥabīb to assist Qiyā Khān (No. 33) in the conquest. Towards the end of the fourth year, Akbar sent him against Rantanbhūr. This fort had formerly been in the possession of the Afghāns, and Salīm Shāh had appointed Jhujhār Khān governor. On Akbar's accession, Jh. saw that he would not be able to hold it against the Imperialists, and handed it over to Rāy Surjan (No. 96), who was then in the service of Rāna Ūdai Singh. But Ḥabīb had to raise the siege.

[1 Parōkh, nineteen *kos* south of Siyālkoṭ.—B.]
[2 Should be *Ormaṛ*.—B.]

Abū 'l-Faẓl attributes this want of success partly to fate, partly to the confusion which Bayrām's fall produced.

In the 6th year (968) he served under Adham (No. 19), in Mālwa. According to the *Ṭabaqāt*, he died in 970.

134. **Jagmāl,** younger brother of Rāja Bihārī Mal (No. 23).

He must not be confounded with No. 218. Jagmāl was mentioned on p. 348. In the 8th year, he was made governor of Mīrtha. In the 18th year, when Akbar marched to Patan and Aḥmadābād, he was put in command of the great camp.

His son Kangār. He generally lived with his uncle Rāja Bihārī Mal at Court. When Ibrāhīm Ḥusayn Mīrzā threatened to invade the Āgra District, he was ordered by the Rāja to go to Dihlī. In the 18th year, he joined Akbar at Patan. In the 21st year, he accompanied Mān Singh's expedition against Rānā Partāb. Later, he served in Bengal, chiefly under Shahbāz Khān (No. 80). When Shahbāz returned unsuccessfully from Bhātī (p. 438) Kangār, Sayyid ʿAbdᵘ 'llah Khān (No. 189), Rāja Gopāl Mīrzāda ʿAlī (No. 152) met a detachment of rebels, and mistook them for their own men. Though surprised, the Imperialists held their ground and killed Nawrūz Beg Qāqshāl, the leader. They then joined Shāhbāz, and arrived after a march of eight days at Sherpūr Mūrcha.

According to the *Ṭabaqāt*, Kangār was in 1001 a Commander of Two Thousand. The phraseology of some MSS. implies that he was no longer alive in 1001.

135. **Ulugh Khān Ḥabshī,** formerly a slave of Sulṭān Maḥmūd of Gujrāt.

Ulugh Khān is Turkish for the Persian *Khān-i Kalān* (the great Khān).

He rose to dignity under Maḥmūd of Gujrāt. The word *Ḥabshī*, for which MSS. often have *Badakhshī*, implies that he was of Abyssinian extraction, or a eunuch. In the 17th year, when Akbar entered for the first time Aḥmadābād, he was one of the first Gujrātī nobles that joined the Imperialists.

In the 22nd year, he served with distinction under Ṣādiq (No. 43) against Rāja Madhukar Bundela, Zamīndār of Ūndcha. In the 24th year, he followed Ṣādiq who had been ordered to assist Rāja Toḍar Mal on his expedition against the rebel ʿArab (Niyābat Khān) in Bihār. He commanded the left wing in the fight in which Khabīta (p. 383, note 1) was killed.

He died in Bengal.

136. **Maqṣūd ʿAlī Kor.**

The *Ṭabaqāt* says that Maqṣūd was at first in Bayrām Khān's service. He had been dead for a long time in 1001.

From the *Akbarnāma* (II, 96) we see that he served under Qiyā Khān (No. 33) in the conquest of Gwāliyār.

137. **Qabūl Khān.**

From the *Akbarnāma* (II, p. 450, last event of the 15th year of Akbar's reign) we see that Qabūl Khān had conquered the District of Bhimbar on the Kashmīr frontier. One of the Zamīndārs of the District, named Jalāl, made his submission, and obtained by flattery a great power over Qabūl, who is said to have been a good-hearted Turk. Jalāl not only managed on various pretexts to send away Qabūl's troops, but also his son Yādgār Ḥusayn (No. 338), to Nawshahra. The Zamīndārs of the latter place opposed Yādgār, and wounded him in a fight. Exhausted and wounded as he was, Yādgār managed to escape and took refuge with a friendly Zamīndār. About the same time Jalāl collected his men and fell over Qabūl, and after a short struggle killed him (5th Ramaẓān, 978).

Akbar ordered Khān Jahān to invade the District. The lands of the rebellious Zamīndārs were devastated and summary revenge was taken on the ringleaders.

Yādgār Ḥusayn recovered from his wounds. He is mentioned below among the commanders of Two Thousand.

The *Akbarnāma* mentions another Qabūl Khān among the officers who served in the Afghān war in Bengal under Munʿim Khān Khānān. He was present in the battle of Takaro,ī and pursued the Afghāns under Todar Mal to Bhadrak (p. 406).

Neither of the two Qabūl Khāns is mentioned in the *Ṭabaqāt* and the *Maʾāṣir*.

Commanders of Nine Hundred.[1]

138. **Kūchak ʿAlī Khān-i Kolābī.**

Kolāb is the name of a town and a district in Badakhshān, long. 70°, lat. 30°. The District of Kolāb lies north of Badakhshān Proper, from which it is separated by the ʿĀmū (Oxus); but it was looked upon as part of the kingdom of Badakhshān. Hence Kūchak ʿAlī is often called in the *Akbarnāma* Kūchak ʿAlī Khān-i Badakhshī.

[1] Not all MSS. of the Āʾīn have these words; they count the officers from No. 138 to 175 amongst the Hazārīs. But the best MSS. have this *manṣab*. In the lists of grandees in the *Pādishāhnāma* also the *manṣab* of Nine Hundred occurs.

He served under Mun'im Khān Zamān, and was present at the reconciliation of Baksar (Buxar) in the 10th year.

He also served under Mun'im Khān in Bengal, and held a command in the battle of Takaro,ī (p. 406).

His sons are mentioned below, No. 148 and No. 380.

139. **Sabdal Khān,** Sumbul, a slave of Humāyūn.

140. **Sayyid Muhammad,** Mīr 'Adl, a Sayyid of Amroha.

Amroha, formerly a much more important town than now, belongs to the Sarkār of Sambal. Its Sayyids belonged to old families of great repute throughout India. Mīr Sayyid Muhammad had studied the Hadīs and law under the best teachers of the age. The father of the Historian Badā,onī was his friend. Akbar made Sayyid Muhammad, *Mīr 'Adl.* When the learned were banished from Court (*ikhrāj-i 'ulamā*) he was made governor of Bhakkar.[1] He died there two years later in 984 (*vide* Nos. 119 and 251).

From the *Akbarnāma*, we see that S. Muhammad with other Amroha Sayyids served, in the 18th year, under S. Mahmūd of Bārha in the expedition against Rāja Madhukar.

He advised the Historian Badā,onī to enter the military service of the emperor, instead of trusting to learning and to precarious *Madad-i ma'āsh* tenures, an advice resembling that of 'Abd[u] 'l-Ghaffār (*vide* No. 99, p. 454). S. Muhammad's sons were certainly all in the army; *vide* Nos. 251, 297, 363.

141. **Razawī Khān,** Mīrzā Mīrak, a Razawī Sayyid of Mashhad.

He was a companion of Khān Zamān (No. 13). In the 10th year, he went to the camp of the Imperialists to obtain pardon for his master. When in the 12th year Khān Zamān again rebelled, Mīrzā Mīrak was placed under the charge of Khān Bāqī Khān (No. 60), but fled from his custody (at Dihlī, *Badā,onī* II, 100). After Khān Zamān's death, he was captured, and Akbar ordered him daily to be thrown before a *mast* elephant; but the driver was ordered to spare him as he was a man of illustrious descent. This was done for five days, when at the intercession of the courtiers he was set at liberty. Shortly afterwards he received a mansab, and the title of *Razawī Khān.* In the 19th year, he was made Dīwān of Jaunpūr, and in the 24th year, Bakhshī of Bengal in addition to his former duties.

At the outbreak of the Bengal Military Revolt (25th year), he was with Muzaffar Khān (No. 37). His harsh behaviour towards the dissatisfied grandees is mentioned in the histories as one of the causes of

[1] In 983, the 20th year (*Akbarnāma* III, 138). *Badā,onī* (III, p. 75) has 984.

the revolt. When the rebels had seceded (9th Ẕī Ḥijjah, 987) and gone from Ṭānḍa to Gaur, Muẓaffar sent Raẓawī Khān, Rāy Patr Dās (No. 196) and Mīr Aḥmad Munshī to them to try to bring them back to obedience. Things took indeed a good turn, and everything might have ended peacefully when some of Rāy Patr Dās's Rājpūts said that the opportunity should not be thrown away to kill the whole lot. Rāy Patr Dās mentioned this to Raẓawī Khān, and through him, it appears, the rebels heard of it. They took up arms and caught Rāy Patr Dās. Raẓawī Khān and Mīr Aḥmad Munshī surrendered themselves.

The *Maʿāṣir* says that nothing else is known of Raẓawī Khān. The *Ṭabaqāt* says that he was a Commander of Two Thousand, and was dead in 1001.

Mīrzā Mīrak is not to be confounded with *Mīrak Khān*, "an old grandee, who died in 975" (*Ṭabaqāt*); or with *Mīrak Bahādur* (208).

Shāhjahān conferred the title of *Raẓawī Khān* on Sayyid ʿAlī, son of Ṣadrᵘ ṣ'-Ṣudūr Mīrān S. Jalāl of Bukhārā.

142. **Mīrzā Najāt Khān,** brother of Sayyid Barka, and

149. **Mīrzā Ḥusayn Khān,** his brother.

Both brothers, according to the *Ṭabaqāt*, were dead in 1001. Their names are often wrongly given in MSS., which call them *Najābat*, instead of *Najāt*, and *Ḥasan* instead of *Ḥusayn*.

From the *Akbarnāma* (I, 411) we see that both brothers accompanied Humāyūn on his march to India.

Mīrzā Najāt served, in the 10th year, against Khān Zamān (No. 13). In the end of the 21st year, he was attached to the corps which under Shihāb Khān (No. 26) moved to Khandesh, the king of which, Rāja ʿAlī Khān, had shown signs of disaffection. Later, he served in Bengal. When the Military Revolt broke out, Bābā Khān Qāqshāl (*vide*, p. 399, note 2), Jabārī (p. 400), Vazīr Jamīl (No. 200), Saʿīd-i Toqbāʾī, and other grandees, marched on the 9th Ẕī Ḥijja, 987, from Ṭānḍa to Gaur across the Ganges. Mīr Najāt was doubtful to which party to attach himself; and when Muẓaffar sent his grandees [Mīr Jamālᵘ 'd-Dīn Ḥusayn Injū (No. 164), Raẓawī Khān (No. 141), Tīmūr Khān (No. 215), Rāy Patr Dās (No. 196), Mīr Adham, Ḥusayn Beg, Ḥakīm Abū 'l-Fatḥ (No. 112), Khwāja Shamsᵘ 'd-Dīn (No. 159), Jaʿfar Beg (No. 98), Muḥammad Qulī Turkmān (No. 203), Qāsim Khān-i Sīstānī, ʿIwaẓ Bahādur, Zulf ʿAlī Yazdī, Sayyid Abū Is-ḥāq-i Ṣafawī (No. 384), Muẓaffar Beg, etc.] to the banks of the Ganges, where the rebels had drawn up their army, Mīr Najāt stayed with Vazīr Jamīl, although Muẓaffar, who was Najāt's father-in-law, fully expected him to join. He must have soon after left the rebels and gone to Southern Bengal; for in the end of the 25th year he was at Sātgāw (Hūglī). Abū 'l-Faẓl mentions him together with Murād Khān at Fatḥābād (No. 34), and Qiyā Khān in Orīsā (No. 33), as one of the few that represented Imperialism in Bengal (*Akbarn.* III, 291). But these three were too powerless to check the rebels. Murād died, and Qiyā was soon after killed by the Afghāns under Qutlū, who looked upon the revolt as his opportunity. Mīr Najāt also was attacked by Qutlū and defeated near Salīmābād (Sulaymānābād), S. of Bardwān. He fled to the Portuguese governor of Hūglī.[1] Bābā Khān Qāqshāl sent one of his officers to get hold of Najāt; but the officer hearing of Qutlū's victory, attacked the Afghāns near Mangalkoṭ, N.E. of Bardwān. Qutlū, however, was again victorious.

143. **Sayyid Hāshim** son of Sayyid Maḥmūd of Bārha. *Vide* No. 105, p. 461.

144. **Ghāzī Khān-i Badakhshī.**

In MSS., *Ghāzī* is often altered to *Qāẓī*, and *Badakhshī* to *Bakhshī*, and as Ghāzī Khān's first title was *Qāẓī Khān*, his name is often confounded with No. 223. Other *Ghāzī Khāns* have been mentioned above, on pp. 396, 418.

Ghāzī Khān's name was Qāẓī Niẓām. He had studied law and Ḥadīs, under Mullā ʿIṣāmu 'd-Dīn Ibrāhīm, and was looked upon as one of the most learned of the age. He was also the *murīd* of Shaykh Ḥusayn of Khwārazm, a renowned Ṣūfī. His acquirements procured him access to the court of Sulaymān, king of Badakhshān (No. 5), who conferred upon him the title of *Qāẓī Khān*. At the death of Humāyūn, Sulaymān, wishing to profit by the distracted state of the country, moved to Kābul and besieged Munʿim (No. 11). After the siege had lasted for some time, Sulaymān sent Qāẓī to Munʿim to prevail on him to surrender. But Munʿim detained him for several days, and treated him "to the most sumptuous fare, such as Badakhshīs cannot enjoy even in peaceful times". The good dinners made such an impression on Qāẓī Khān that he advised Sulaymān to raise the siege, as there was no lack of provisions in the fort. Sulaymān thereupon returned to Badakhshān.

Subsequently Qāẓī Khān left his master, and went to India. At Khānpūr he was introduced to the emperor on his return from Jaunpūr (*Akbarn.*, III, 85). He received several presents, and was appointed *Parwānchī* writer (p. 273). Akbar soon discovered in him a man of great insight, and made him a Commander of One Thousand. He also bestowed upon

[1] The MSS. of the *Akbarnāma* call him *Bartab Bār Firingī*, or *Partāb Firingī*.

him the title of *Ghāzī Khān*, after he had distinguished himself in several expeditions.

In the 21st year, Ghāzī Khān commanded the left wing of Mān Singh's corps in the war with the Rānā. Though his wing gave way, he returned with the troops and joined the van, and fought bravely. He then received Awadh as *tuyūl*, and distinguished himself in Bihār against the rebellious grandees.

He died at Awadh in the 29th year (992) at the age of seventy, about the same time that Sulṭān Khwāja died (No. 108).

Ghāzī Khān is the author of several works (*vide* Badā,onī III, 153).

The *sijda*, or prostration, which formed so important a part in the ceremonies of the Court, was his invention (*vide* p. 167, note).

His son *Ḥusāmᵘ 'd-Dīn*. Akbar made him a Commander of One Thousand, and sent him with the Khān Khānān (No. 29) to the Dakhin. Suddenly a change came over Ḥusām, and though a young man, he expressed to the commander his wish to resign the service and live as a faqīr at the tomb of Niẓāmᵘ 'd-Dīn Awliyā in Dihlī. The Khān Khānān persuaded him in vain to give up this mad idea; but Ḥusām next day laid aside his clothes, smeared his body with clay and mud, and wandered about in the streets and bazars. Akbar permitted his resignation. Ḥusām lived for thirty years as an ascetic in Dihlī. Khwāja Bāqī Billah (born at Kābul and buried at Dihlī) conferred on him power of "guiding travellers on the road of piety". He died in 1034. His wife was Abū 'l-Faẓl's sister. She gave at the request of her husband her ornaments to Darwīshes, and fixed an annual sum of 12,000 Rupees as allowance for the cell of her husband. *Vide* Tuzuk, p. 80.

145. **Farḥat Khān**, Mihtar Sakā,ī, a slave of Humāyūn.

The MSS. have *Sakāʿī* and *Sakāhī*. Farḥat Khān is first mentioned in the war between Humāyūn and Mīrzā Kāmrān, when many grandees joined the latter. In a fight, Beg Bābā of Kolāb lifted up his sword to strike Humāyūn from behind. He missed and was at once attacked by Farḥat, and put to flight. When Humāyūn left Lāhor on his march to Sarhind, where Sikandar Khān was, Farḥat was appointed *Shiqdār* of Lāhor.[1] Subsequently, Mīr Shāh Abū 'l-Maʿālī was appointed Governor of Lāhor. He sent away Farḥat, and appointed his own men instead. Farḥat therefore joined Prince Akbar on his arrival in the Panjāb.

---

[1] *Akbarnāma* I, 416. At the same time, Mīr Bābūs (No. 73) was appointed *Fawjdār* of the Panjāb, Mīrzā Shāh Sulṭān was made Amīn, and Mihtar Jawhar, treasurer.

Humāyūn was on the 29th Muḥarram, 962, at Bigrām, crossed the Indus on the 5th Safar, when Bayrām arrived from Kābul, was at Lāhor on the 2nd Rabīʿ II, and at Sarhind, on the 7th Rajab.

After Akbar's accession, Farhat was made *Tuyūldār* of Korra. He distinguished himself in the war with Muḥammad Ḥusayn Mīrzā near Aḥmadābād. When the Mīrzā was brought in a prisoner, Farhat refused him a drink of water which he had asked for ; but Akbar gave him some of his own water, and remonstrated with Farhat for his cruelty. In the 19th year, he served in Bihār and was made *jāgīrdār* of Āra. In the 21st year (984), Gajpatī (p. 437) devastated the district. Farhang Khān, Farhat's son, marched against him, but was repulsed and slain. Farhat then moved against the enemy to avenge the death of his son, but met with the same fate (*vide* No. 80).

146. **Rūmī Khān**, Ustād Jalabī (?), of Rūm.

He is not mentioned in the *Tabaqāt* and the *Maʿāṣir*, and but rarely in the *Akbarnāma*. In the 20th year, he and Bāqī Khān (No. 60) and ʿAbdᵘ'r-Raḥmān Beg (No. 186) accompanied a party of Begams from Court on their road to Makkah. The party consisted of Gulbadan Begam, Salīma Sulṭān Begam, Ḥājī Begam, Gulʿazār Begam, Sulṭān Begam (wife of Mīrzā ʿAskarī), Umm Kulsūm Begam (granddaughter of Gulbadan Begam), Gujnār Āghā (one of Bābar's wives), Bībī Ṣafiya, Bībī Sarw-i Sahī and Shāham. Āghā (wives of Humāyūn), and Salīma Khānum (daughter of Khizr Khwāja). They left in Rajab, 983.

Rūmī Khān has also been mentioned above (No. 111).

147. **Samānjī Khān Qurghūjī** (*vide* No. 100).

He was a grandee of Humāyūn. During the reign of Akbar, he reached the dignity of a Commander of Fifteen Hundred. The *Tabaqāt* says he was, in 1001, a Commander of 2,000. In the same work he is called a *Mughul*.

In the beginning of the 6th year (middle of 968) he served in Mālwa under Adham Khān (No. 19) and was present in the battle of Sārangpūr. In the 9th year, he accompanied Muḥammad Qāsim Khān-i Nīshāpūrī (No. 40) and pursued ʿAbdᵘ 'llah Khān Uzbak (No. 14). In the 13th year, he was ordered, together with Ashraf Khān Mīr Munshī (No. 74), to go to Rantanbhūr and suppress the disturbances created by Mīrzā Muḥammad Ḥusayn in Mālwa. Later, he held a *jāgīr* in Āra.[1] He joined at first the rebellious grandees, but convincing himself of their selfishness, he went back to the Imperial camp.

In the 39th year, he was allowed to come to Court, and died a few years later. His sons received employments in the army.

From the *Akbarnāma* (III, 156) we see that he also served in the

---

[1] **The *Maʿāṣir* has *Awadh*. At the outbreak of the Bengal Military Revolt, he was Jāgīrdār of the Āra District (*Akbarn.* III, 244).**

21st year under Khān Jahān (No. 24) and was present in the battle of Āg Maḥall. In the 30th year, he was in Mālwa and was ordered to join the Dakhin corps. Two years later, he served under Shihāb Khān (No. 26) against Rāja Madhukar.

148. **Shāhbeg Khān**, son of Kūchak ʿAlī Khān of Badakhshān (Nos. 138 and 380).

His name is not given in the *Maʿāṣi* and the *Ṭabaqāt*. Amīr Beg, a Pānṣadī under Shāhjahān, appears to be his son.

149. **Mīrza Ḥusayn Khān**, brother of Mīrzā Najāt Khān (*vide* No. 142).

150. **Ḥakīm Zanbīl**, brother of Mīrzā Muḥammad Ṭabīb of Sabzwār.

Zanbīl means " a basket ". In the list of the physicians of the Court, lower down, he is called Ḥakīm Zanbīl Beg. Badā,onī says, he was a *muqarrib*, or personal attendant on the emperor.[1]

151. **Khudāwand Khān-i Dakhinī.**

Khudāwand Khān was a Niẓāmshāhī Grandee. As his father was born at Mash,had, Kh. is often called *Mash,hadī*. He was of course a Shīʿah.

He was a man of imposing stature, and well known for his personal courage. When Khwāja Mīrak of Iṣfahān, who had the title of Chingiz Khān, was the Vakīl of Murtaẓā Niẓām Shāh, Kh. rose to dignity. He held several districts in Barār as jāgīr. The Masjid of Rohankhera [2] was built by him.

In 993, when Mīr Murtaẓā of Sabzwār (No. 162) commanded the army of Barār, and was no longer able to withstand Ṣalābat Khān Chirgis in the Dakhin, Kh. accompanied M. Murtaẓā to Hindūstān. Both were well received by Akbar, and Kh. was made a Commander of One Thousand. He received Paṭan in Gujrāt as *tuyūl*.

He was married to Abū 'l-Faẓl's sister, and died at Karī in the end of the 34th year, before the middle of 998 (*Badā,onī* II, 372, where in the *Tārīkh* of his death the word *Dakhinī* must be written without an *h*).

Once Abū 'l-Faẓl had invited several grandees, Khudāwand among them. The dishes placed before Kh. contained fowls and game and different kinds of vegetables, whilst the other guests had roast meat. He remarked it, took offence, and went away. Although Akbar assured him that Abū 'l-Faẓl had treated him to fowls and game according to a Hindūstānī custom, Kh. disliked Abū 'l-Faẓl, and never went again to his house. " Hence Dakhinīs are notorious in Hindūstān for stupidity."

---

[1] The Edit. Bibl. Indica of Badā,onī (III, 164) calls him wrongly *Ḥakīm Zīnal Shīrāzī*. Zīnal is the reading of bad MSS., and *Sabzwārī* is often altered to *Shīrāzī*. Other bad MSS. have *Ranbal*.

[2] Rohankhera lies in West Barār, in the district of Buldāna. In Abū 'l-Faẓl's list of parganas in Sarkār Talingāna, there is one called *Qiryāt-i Khudāwand Khān*.

The *Ṭabaqāt* puts Kh. among the Commanders of Fifteen Hundred, and says that he died in 995. The *Maʿāṣir* has 997.

152. **Mīrzāda ʿAlī Khān,** son of Muḥtaram Beg.[1]

He served in the 9th year in Mālwa during the expedition against ʿAbdu 'llah Khān Uzbak (No. 14). In the 17th year, he served in the Gujrāt war under the Khān-i Kalān (No. 16). Two years later, he commanded an expedition against Qāsim Khān Kāsū, who with a corps of Afghāns ravaged the frontiers of Bihār. In the 23rd year, he accompanied Shāhbāz Khān in the war with Rānā Partāb.[2] He then served in Bihār under Khān-i Aʿzam (25th year) and in Bengal under Shāhbāz Khān (*vide* No. 134, p. 483). In the 30th year (993) he was present in the fight with Qutlū near Mangalkoṭ (Bardwān). In the 31st year, he was ordered to join Qāsim Khān (No. 59), who was on his way to Kashmīr. Not long after, in 995 (32nd year) he was killed in a fight with the Kashmīrīs who defeated an Imperial detachment under Sayyid ʿAbdu 'llah Khān (No. 189).

Badā,onī (III, p. 326) says he was a poet. He places his death in 996.

153. **Saʿādat Mīrzā,** son of Khizr Khwāja Khān (p. 394, note).

154. **Shimāl Khān Chela.**

Chela means " a slave ". The *Ṭabaqāt* says he was a Qurchī, or armour-bearer of the emperor, and a genial companion. He was made a *Hazārī*. and was no longer alive in 1001.

In the 9th year, he assisted in the capture of Khwāja Muʿaẓẓam, In the 20th year, he served in the war against Chandr Sen, during which Jalāl Khān (No. 213) had lost his life, and afterwards under Sayyid Aḥmad (No. 91) and Shāhbāz (No. 80) in the expedition to Siwāna.

155. **Shāh Ghāzī Khān,** a Sayyid from Tabrīz.

The *Ṭabaqāt* calls him a Turkmān, and says, he was dead in 1001. He served in the 19th year with Mīrzāda ʿAlī Khān (No. 152) against Qāsim Khān Kāsū.

He may be the Shāh Ghāzī Khān mentioned below under No. 161.

156. **Fāẓil Khān,** son of Khān-i Kalān (No. 16).

He was mentioned above, on p. 339.

157. **Maʿṣūm Khān,** son of Muʿīnu 'd-Dīn Aḥmad Faraṇkhūdī (No. 128).

He is not to be confounded with Maʿṣūm Khān-i Kābulī (p. 476, note).

---

[1] He is also called *Mīrzād* ʿAlī Khān. My text edition has wrongly *Mīrzā ʿAlī Khān*. For *Muḥtaram* many MSS. read wrongly *Maḥram*.
His father, Muḥtaram Beg, was a grandee of Humāyūn's Court.

[2] Generally called in the Histories *Rānā Kīkā*.

Ma$^{\varsigma}$ṣūm was made a *Hazārī* on the death of his father, and received Ghāzīpūr as *tuyūl.* He joined Toḍar Mal in Bihār, though anxious to go over to the rebels (pp. 376–7). Not long afterwards, Mīrzā Muḥammad Ḥakīm, Akbar's brother, threatened to invade the Panjāb, and as the emperor had resolved to move personally against him, Ma$^{\varsigma}$ṣūm thought it opportune to rebel. He seized Jaunpūr and drove away Tarsõ Khān's men (No. 32). As Akbar kad known him from a child, he was inclined to pardon him, provided he left Jaunpūr, and accepted Awadh as *tuyūl.* This M. did ; but he continued to recruit, and when Shāh Qulī Maḥram and Rāja Bīr Baṛ had failed to bring him to his senses, Shāhbāz Khān, on hearing of his conduct, determined to punish him. The events of the expedition have been related on p. 437.

After his defeat near Awadh, M. threw himself into the town ; but as several rebel chiefs had left him, he absconded, without even taking his family with him. He applied to two Zamīndārs for assistance ; but the first robbed him of his valuables, and the latter waylaid him, and had it not been for a bribe, M. would not have escaped. About this time one of his friends of the name of Maqṣūd joined him and supplied him with funds. M. collected men and surprised and plundered the town of Bahrā,ich. Vazīr Khān (No. 41) and others moved from Ḥājīpūr against him ; but M. escaped them. After plundering the town of Muḥammadābād, he resolved to surprise Jaunpūr, when the tuyūldārs of the district marched against him. Being hard pressed, he applied to M. $^{\varsigma}$Azīz Koka (No. 21) to intercede for him. Akbar again pardoned him, and gave him the Pargana Mihsī, Sarkār Champāran, as *tuyūl.* But M. continued in a rebellious attitude, and when M. $^{\varsigma}$Azīz prepared to punish him, he applied for leave to go to Court. He arrived, in the 27th year, in Āgra, and was again pardoned, chiefly at the request of Akbar's mother.

Soon after, on going home one night from the Darbār, he was killed on the road. An inquiry was ordered to be held, but without result, and people believed that Akbar had connived at the murder. Compare with this the fate of Nos. 61 and 62, two other Bihār rebels.

158. **Tolak Khān Qūchīn.**

Tolak commenced to serve Bābar. He joined Humāyūn on his return from Persia. When the emperor had seized on Kābul, and M. Kārām came near the town under the mask of friendship, many of Humāyūn's grandees went over to him, and the emperor was obliged to retreat northwards to Ẓaḥāk (ضحاک) and Bāmiyān, where he hoped to find faithful officers. He sent, however, Tolak and several others to Kābul, to bring him correct information, but Tolak alone returned. For his faithfulness he was made Qurbegī.

Tolak accompanied Humāyūn to India. After the emperor's death, he belonged to those who supported the young Akbar, and was instrumental in the capture at a dinner party of Mīr Shāh Abū 'l-Maʿālī. Afterwards, T. went to Kābul, where he remained for a long time. In the 7th year of Akbar's reign, he was suddenly imprisoned by the young and hasty Ghanī Khān, son of Munʿim Khān (No. 11), who was in charge of Kābul. Tolak managed to escape, and went to Bābā Khātūn, his jāgīr, collecting men to take revenge on Ghānī. A favourable opportunity presented itself when Ghanī one day had left Kābul for a place called Khwāja Sayyārān (خواجه سیاران), to waylay a caravan from Balkh. He was just feasting with his companions, when Tolak Khān fell upon them. Ghanī, who was drunk, was caught, and Tolak marched to Khwāja Awāsh (خواجه اواش), a place two *kos* distant from Kābul. But he was opposed by Fazīl Beg (Munʿim's brother) and his son Abū 'l-Fatḥ (called wrongly *ʿAbdᵘ 'l-Fatḥ*, on p. 318), and thought it advisable to let Ghanī go. Ghanī immediately collected men and pursued Tolak, who now prepared himself to go to Hindūstān. Ghanī overtook him near the Āb-i Ghorband and killed Bābā Qūchīn, and several other relations and friends of Tolak. Tolak himself and his son Isfandiyār managed to cut their way through the enemies, and arrived safely in India. Akbar gave Tolak a jāgīr in Mālwa, where he remained for a long time.

In the 28th year, T. served under Khān Khānān (No. 29) in Mālwa and Gujrāt, and defeated Sayyid Dawlat in Kambhā,it. He distinguished himself in the fights with Muzaffar, and served under Qulij Khān (No. 42) in the conquest of Bahrōch. In the 30th year, he was attached to the corps which under M. ʿAzīz Koka was to be sent to the Dakhin. Having indulged in slander during the disagreement between M. ʿAzīz Koka and Shihābᵘ 'd-Dīn, he was imprisoned. After his release he was sent to Bengal, where in the 37th year he served under Mān Singh against the Afghāns.

He died in the beginning of the 41st year (1004).

159. Khwāja Shamsᵘ 'd-Dīn Khawafī.

Khawāfī means "coming from Khawāf", which is a district and town in Khurāsān. Our maps have "Khāff" or "Khāf", due west of Hirāt, between Lat. 60° and 61°. According to the *Muʿjamᵘ 'l-Buldān*, "Khawāf is a large town belonging [at the time the author wrote] to the revenue district of Nīshāpūr. Near it lies on one side Būshanj which belongs to the districts of Hirāt, and on the other Zūzan. Khawāf contains one hundred villages and three towns (Sanjān, Sīrāwand, and Kharjard)." Amīn Rāẓī in his excellent *Haft Iqlīm* says that the district of Khawāf is famous for the kings, ministers, and learned men it has produced. The dynasty called, Āl-i Muẓaffar, of whom seven kings ruled for 59 years over Fārs and Shīrāz,[1] were Khawāfīs. The author of the *Zakhīrat*ᵘ *'l Khawānīn* says that the people of Khawāf were known to be bigoted Sunnīs. When Shāh ʿAbbās-i Ṣafawī, in the beginning of his reign, came to Khawāf, he forced the inhabitants to abuse, as is customary with Shīʿas, the companions of the Prophet (*sabb-i ṣaḥāba*); but as the people refused to do so, he had seventy of the principal men thrown down from a Masjid. Although then no one was converted, the Khwāfīs are now as staunch Shīʿas as they were formerly bigoted Sunnīs.

Khwāja Shams[u] 'd-Dīn was the son of Khwāja ʿAlāʿ[u] 'd-Dīn, who was a man much respected in Khawāf. Shams accompanied Muẓaffar Khān (No. 37), his countryman, to Bihār and Bengal. At the outbreak of the Military Revolt, he was caught by the rebels, and Maʿṣūm-i Kābulī had him tortured with a view of getting money out of him. Shams was half dead, when at the request of ʿArab Bahādur he was let off and placed under ʿArab's charge, who lay under obligations to him. But Shams eluded his vigilance, and fled to Singrām, Rāja of Kharakpūr (Bihār).[2] As the roads were all held by the rebels, Shams could not

---

[1] They succumbed to Tīmūr. The Histories disagree regarding the length of their reign, some give 57 years, from A.H. 741 to 798.

Amīn Rāẓī mentions also several learned men and vazīrs besides those mentioned in the *Muʿjam*, and relates some anecdotes illustrating the proverbial sagacity and quick-wittedness of the inhabitants of Khawāf.

The number of Khawāfīs in the service of the Mughul emperors was considerable. One is mentioned below, No. 347. The Maʾāṣir has notes on the following :—Mīrzā ʿIzzat (under Jahāngīr); Mīrzā Aḥmad, and Muʿtamid Khān Muḥammad Ṣalīh (under Shāhjahān); Sayyid Amīr Khān Shaykh Mīr, Khwāja Mīr Khawāfī Ṣalābat Khān, ʿInāyat Khān, and Muṣṭafā Khān (under Awrangzīb). The lists of grandees in the *Pādishāhnāma* mention several other Khawafīs. In later times we have the name of ʿAbd[u] 'r-Razzāq Ṣamṣām[u] 'd-Dawla Awrangābādī, who was murdered in 1171. His ancestor, Mīr Kamāl[u] 'd-Dīn Khawāfī, has served under Akbar.

For *Khawāfī* some MSS. have *Khāfī*. The Historian Muḥammad Hāshim Khāfī Khān has also been supposed to be a Khawāfī, though it must be observed that geographical titles are rare. There are a few, as *Rūmī Khān, Ghaznīn Khān, Habshī Khān*. The authors of the *Pādishāhnāma* and the *Maʾāṣir* never use the form *Khāfī*.

[2] Singrām later fought with Shāhbāz Khān (No. 80), and ceded Fort Mahdā. Though he never went to Court, he remained in submission to the Imperial governors of Bihār and Bengal. In the first year of Jahāngīr's reign, Jahāngīr Qulī Khān Lāla Beg, governor of Bihār, sent a corps against Singrām, who was killed in a fight. His son turned Muḥammadan, and received the name " Rāja Roz-afzūn ", was confirmed in his zamīndārīs, and reached, under Jahāngīr, the dignity of a Commander of Fifteen Hundred. Under Shāhjahān, he served with Mahābat Khān in Balkh, against Jhujār Singh Bundela, in the siege of Parenda, and was at his death in 1044 a Commander of Two Thousand. His son, Rāja Bihrūz served in Qandahār, in the war between Awrangzīb and Shāh Shujāʿ, and distinguished himself in the second conquest of Palāmau (4th year of Awrangzīb). Rāja Bihrūz died in the 8th year of Awrangzīb's reign. *Vide* Proceedings, Asiatic Society Bengal, for December, 1870.

make his way to the Imperial army. He collected men, attacked the rebels, and carried off some of their cattle ; and when some time after dissensions broke out among the mutineers, he found means to escape. Akbar received him with every distinction, and appointed him, in the same year (26th) to superintend the building of Fort Aṭak (built 990–1) on the Indus, near which the Imperial camp then was.[1]

After this, Shams was for some time Dīwān of Kābul. In the 39th year, when Qulij Khān (No. 42) after the death of Qāsim Khān (No. 59) was made Ṣūbadār of Kābul, Shams was made Dīwān of the empire (*Dīwān-i kull*), *vice* Qulij.[2] When Akbar in the 43rd year, after a residence of fourteen years in the Panjāb, moved to Āgra to proceed to the Dakhin, the Begams with Prince Khurram (Shāhjahān) were left in Lāhor, and Shams was put in charge of the Panjāb, in which office he continued, after Akbar's mother had returned, in the 44th year, with the Begams to Āgra.

Shams died at Lāhor in the 45th year (1008). The family vault which he had built near Bābā Ḥasan Abdāl having been used for other purposes (p. 469) he was buried in Lāhor in that quarter of the town which he had built, and which to his honour was called *Khawāfīpūra*.

He is said to have been a man of simple manners, honest and faithful, and practical in transacting business.

Like Shaykh Farīd-i Bukhārī (No. 99), whom he in many respects resembles, he died childless.

His brother, Khwāja Mūmin Khawāfī, was made, on his death, Dīwān of the Panjāb. Mūmin's son, ʿAbdu 'l-Khāliq was a favourite of Āṣaf Khān IV (p. 398). He was killed by Mahābat Khān, when Āṣaf had been removed by Mahābat from Fort Aṭak and imprisoned.

160. **Jagat Singh,** eldest of Rāja Mān Singh (No. 30).

Kūwar Jagat Singh served in the 42nd year under Mīrzā Jaʿfar Āṣaf Khān (No. 98) against Rāja Bāsū, zamīndār of Mau and Paṭhān (Nūrpūr, N.E. Panjāb). In the 44th year (1008) when Akbar moved to Mālwa, and Prince Salīm (Jahāngīr) was ordered to move against Rānā Amr Singh,

---

[1] The author of the *Maʾāṣir* repeats Abū 'l-Faẓl's etymology of the name "Aṭak", which was given on p. 404, note. He also says that some derive it from the Hindī, *aṭak*, prevention, a bar, "because Hindūs will not go beyond the Indus." But there is no instance on record that Hindūs ever did object to cross the Indus. Bhagwān Dās, Mān Singh, and others were governors of Kābul and Zābulistān, and had their Rājpūts there ; and during the reign of Shāhjahān, the Rājpūts distinguished themselves in the conquest of Balkh and the siege of Qandahār. [Fort *Aṭak* built in 990-91.—B.]

Abū 'l-Faẓl's etymology is also doubtful ; for in the *Akbarnāma* (II, 302) he mentions the name "Aṭak" long before the building of the Fort (III, 335).

[2] The twelve Dīwāns, who in 1003 had been appointed to the 12 Ṣūbas, were under his orders. *Dīwān-i kull* is the same as *Vazīr-i kull* or *Vazīr-i muṭlaq*, or merely *Vazīr*.

Mān Singh was called from Bengal, and Jagat Singh was ordered to go to Bengal, as *nā*ʾ*ib* of his father. While still at Āgra, he died from excessive drinking. Regarding J. S.'s daughter, *vide* p. 323 and No. 175.

Mahā Singh, Jagat's younger son, was appointed in his stead. His youth and inexperience inclined the Afghāns under ʿUsmān and Shujāwal Khān to attack him. They defeated him and Partāb Singh, son of Rāja Bhagwān Dās (No. 336), near Bhadrak in Oṛīsā (45th year). Mān Singh hastened to Bengal, and after defeating in 1009 the Afghāns near Sherpūr ʿAtā,ī, between Shi,ūṛī (Sooree) in Bīrbhūm and Murshidābād, recovered Lower Bengal and Oṛīsā.

Mahā Singh died soon after, like his father, from excessive drinking.

161. **Naqīb Khān**, son of Mīr ʿAbdu ’l-Laṭīf of Qazwīn.

Naqīb Khān is the title of Mīr Ghiyāṣu ’d-Dīn ʿAlī. His family belongs to the Sayfī Sayyids of Qazwīn, who were known in Īrān for their Sunnī tendencies. His grandfather Mīr Yaḥyā was "a well-known theologian and philosopher, who had acquired such extraordinary proficiency in the knowledge of history, that he was acquainted with the date of every event which had occurred from the establishment of the Muḥammadan religion to his own time."

"In the opening of his career, Mīr Yaḥyā was patronized by Shāh Ṭahmāsp-i Ṣafawī, who called him Yaḥyā Maʿṣūm,[1] and was treated by the king with such distinction, that his enemies, envious of his good fortune, endeavoured to poison his patron's mind against him, by representing that he and his son, Mīr ʿAbdu ’l-Laṭīf, were the leading men among the Sunnīs of Qazwīn. They at last prevailed so far as to induce the king, when he was on the borders of Āzarbāyjān, to order Mīr Yaḥyā and his son, together with their families, to be imprisoned at Iṣfahān. At that time, his second son, ʿAlāʿu ’d-Dawla was in Āzarbāyjān, and sent off a special messenger to convey his intelligence to his father. Mīr Yaḥyā, being too old and infirm to flee, accompanied the king's messenger to Iṣfahān, and died there, after one year and nine months, in A.H. 962, at the age of 77 years."[2]

"Mīr ʿAbdu ’l-Laṭīf, however, immediately on receipt of his brother's

---

[1] *I.e.* exempt, probably from losing life and property for his attachment to Sunnism.

[2] Mīr Yaḥyā is the author of an historical compendium called *Lubbu ’d-tawārīkh*, composed in 1541. *Vide* Elliot's Bibl. Index to the Historians of India, p. 129. His second son ʿAlaʿu ’d-Dawla wrote under the poetical name of *Kāmī*, and is the author of the *Nafāʾisu ’l-Maʾāṣir*, a "*tazkira*", or work on literature. Badā,onī (III, 97) says he composed a Qaṣīda in which, according to the manner of Shīʿahs, he abused the companions of the Prophet and the Sunnīs, and among the latter his father and elder brother (ʿAbdu ’l-Laṭīf), whom he used to call *Ḥaẓrat-i Āqā*, as he had been his teacher. But the verse in which he cursed his relations is ambiguously worded.

Some fix the date of Mīr Yaḥyā's death two years earlier.

communication, fled to Gīlān,[1] and afterwards at the invitation of the emperor Humāyūn went to Hindūstān, and arrived at Court with his family just after Akbar had ascended the throne. By him he was received with great kindness and consideration, and appointed in the second year of his reign as his preceptor. At that time Akbar knew not how to read and write, but shortly afterwards he was able to repeat some odes of Ḥāfiẓ. The Mīr was a man of great eloquence and of excellent disposition, and so moderate in his religious sentiments,[2] that each party used to revile him for his indifference."

"When Bayrām Khān had incurred the displeasure of the emperor and had left Āgra and proceeded to Alwar with the intention, as it was supposed, of exciting a rebellion in the Panjāb, the emperor sent the Mīr to him, to dissuade him from such an open breach of fidelity to his sovereign." *Elliot, Index, l.c.*

Mīr ʿAbdu 'l-Laṭīf died at Sīkrī on the 5th Rajab, 981,[3] and was buried at Ajmīr near the Dargāh of Mīr Sayyid Ḥusayn Khing-Suwār.

ʿAbdu 'l-Laṭīf had several sons. The following are mentioned: 1. Naqīb Khān; 2. Qamar Khān; 3. Mīr Muḥammad Sharīf. The last was killed in 984 at Fatḥpūr by a fall from his horse, while playing hockey with the emperor (Bad. II, 230). For Qamar Khān, *vide* No. 243.

Naqīb Khān arrived with his father in India, when Akbar after his accession was still in the Panjāb (*Akbarn.* II, 23) and soon became a personal friend of the emperor (II, 281). In the 10th year, he conveyed Akbar's pardon to Khān Zamān, for whom Munʿim Khān had interceded (II, 281). In the 18th year N. accompanied the emperor on the forced march to Patan and Aḥmadābād (p. 481, note), and in the following year to Patan. In the end of the 21st year, he took part in the expedition to Īdar (III, 165) and was sent in the following year to Mālwa or Gujrāt, after the appointment of Shihāb to the latter province. After the outbreak of the Military Revolt in Bengal, N. with his brother Qamar Khān served under Toḍar Mal and Ṣādiq Khān in Bihār against Maʿṣūm-i Kābulī (III, 273). In the 26th year, he received the title of *Naqīb Khān*.[4] Though

---

[1] The MSS. of the *Maʾāṣir* have جبال کیلانات ; so also Badā,onī, *l.c.*

[2] He was the first that taught Akbar the principle of *ṣulḥ-i kull*, "peace with all," the Persian term which Abū 'l-Faẓl so often uses to describe Akbar's policy of toleration. Abū 'l-Faẓl (*Akbarn.* II, 23) says that ʿAbdu 'l-Laṭīf was accused in Persia of being a Sunnī and in Hindūstān of being a Shīʿah.

[3] Elliot has by mistake 971. The *Tārīkh* of his death in the *Maʾāṣir* and *Badā,onī* (III, p. 99) is *fakhr-i āl-i Yā-Sīn*, "the pride of the descendants of Yāsīn (the Prophet)" = 981, if the long *alif* in *āl* be not counted 2, but 1.

[4] Kewal Rām, according to Elliot, says in the *Tazkirātu 'l-Umarāʾ* that the title was conferred on Naqīb Khān in the 25th year for his gallant conduct in repelling a night attack made by Maʿṣūm Khān-i Kābulī on the Imperialists under Toḍar Mal and Ṣādiq Khān. This night attack is related in the *Akbarnāma* (III, 293). The fight took place in the 25th year, near Gayā; but Abū 'l-Faẓl says nothing of Naqīb's "gallant conduct"; he does not even mention his name.

during the reign of Akbar, he did not rise above the rank of a *Hazārī*, he possessed great influence at Court. He was Akbar's reader, and superintended the translations from Sanscrit into Persian, mentioned on p. 110. Several portions of the *Tārīkh-i Alfī* also (p. 113) are written by him.

Naqīb had an uncle of the name of Qāẓī ʿĪṣā, who had come from Irān to Akbar's Court, where he died in 980. His son was Shāh Ghāzī Khān (*vide* No. 155). Akbar married the latter to Sakīna Bānū Begam, sister of Mīrzā Muḥammad Ḥakīm (Akbar's half-brother); and as Naqīb Khān, in the 38th year, reported that Qāẓī ʿĪṣā had expressed a dying wish to present his daughter to Akbar, the emperor married her. Thus two of Naqīb's cousins married into the imperial family.

On the accession of Jahāngīr, N. was made a Commander of 1,500 (*Tuzuk*, p. 12). He died in the 9th year of J.'s reign (beginning of 1023) at Ajmīr, and was buried at the side of his wife within the enclosure of Muʿīn-i Chishtī's tomb (*Tuzuk*, p. 129). His wife was a daughter of Mīr Maḥmūd, *Munshiyᵘ 'l-Mamālik*, who had been for twenty-five years in Akbar's service (Badā,onī III, 321).

Naqīb's son, ʿAbdᵘ'l-Laṭīf, was distinguished for his acquirements. He was married to a daughter of M. Yūsuf Khān (No. 35) and died insane.

Naqīb Khān, like his grandfather, excelled in history. It is said that he knew the seven volumes of the *Rawżatᵘ 'ṣ-ṣafā* by heart. Jahāngīr, in his Memoirs, praises him for his remarkable memory, and Badā,onī, who was Naqīb's schoolfellow and friend, says that no man in Arabia or Persia was as proficient in history as Naqīb. Once on being asked how many pigeons there were in a particular flock then flying, he responded instantly, without making a mistake of even one.

162 **Mīr Murtaẓā Khān**, a Sabzwārī Sayyid.

Mīr Murtaẓā Khān was at first in the service of ʿĀdil Shāh of Bījāpūr. Murtaẓā Niẓām Shāh called him to Aḥmadnagar, and made him Military Governor of Barār, and later Amīrᵘ 'l-Umarā. He successfully invaded, at Niẓam Shāh's order, ʿĀdil Shāh's dominions. But Niẓām Shāh suffered from insanity, and the government was left in the hands of his Vakīl, Shāh Qulī Ṣalābat Khān; and as he reigned absolutely, several of the nobles, especially the *tuyūldārs* of Barar, were dissatisfied. Ṣalābat Khān being bent on ruining them, Mīr Murtaẓā Khudāwand Khān (No. 151), Jamshed Khān-i Shīrāzī and others, marched in 992 to Aḥmadnagar. Ṣalābat Khān and Shāhzāda Mīrān Ḥusayn surprised them and routed them. Mīr Murtaẓā lost all his property, and unable to resist Ṣalābat Khān, he went with Khudāwand Khān to Akbar, who made him a Commander of One Thousand.

M. M. distinguished himself under Shāh Murād in the Dakhin invasion. When the Prince left Aḥmadnagar, Ṣādiq Khān (No. 43) remained in Mahkar (South Barār), and M. M. in Ilichpūr, to guard the conquered districts. During his stay there, he managed to take possession of Fort Gāwīl, near Īlichpūr (43rd year, 1007), persuading the commanders Wajīhᵘ 'd-Dīn and Biswās Rā,o, to enter Akbar's service. Later, M. M. distinguished himself in the conquest of Aḥmadnagar under Prince Dānyāl, and received a higher *Manṣab*, as also a flag and a *naqqāra*.

Mīr Murtaẓā is not to be confounded with the learned Mīr Murtaẓā Sharīf-i Shīrāzī (Badā,onī III, 320), or the Mīr Murtaẓā mentioned by Badā,onī III, 279.

163. **Shamsī**, son of Khān-i Aʿẓam Mīrzā Koka (No. 21).

He was mentioned above on pp. 345 and 346. At the end of Akbar's reign, Shamsī [1] was a Commander of Two Thousand.

In the third year of Jahāngīr's reign, he received the title of Jahāngīr Qulī Khān, vacant by the death of Jahāngīr Qulī Khān Lāla Beg, Governor of Bihār, and was sent to Gujrāt as *nā'ib* of his father. Mīrzā ʿAzīz had been nominally appointed Governor of that Ṣūba; but as he had given the emperor offence, he was detained at Court. Subsequently Shamsī was made a Commander of Three Thousand, and Governor of Jaunpūr. Whilst there, Prince Shāhjahān had taken possession of Bengal, and prepared himself to march on Patna, sending ʿAbdᵘ 'llāh Khān Fīrūz-Jang and Rāja Bhīm in advance towards Ilāhābād. On their arrival at Chausā, Shamsī left Jaunpūr, and joined Mīrzā Rustam (No. 9), Governor of the Ṣūba of Ilāhābād.

On Shāhjahān's accession, Shamsī was deposed, but allowed to retain his Manṣab. A short time after, he was appointed to Sūrat [2] and Jūnāgaḍh, *vice* Beglar Khān. He died there in the 5th year of Shāhjahān's reign (1041).

Shamsī's son, Bahrām, was made by Shāhjahān a Commander of 1,000, 500 horse (*Pādishāhn.* I, b., 309) and appointed to succeed his father. Whilst in Gujrāt, he built a place called after him *Bahrāmpūra*. He died in the 18th year of Shāhjahān's reign (*Pādishāhn.* II, p. 733).

164. **Mīr Jamālᵘ 'd-Dīn Ḥusayn**, an Injū Sayyid.

From a remark in the *Waṣṣāf* it appears that a part of Shīrāz was called *Injū*; *vide Journal Asiatic Society Bengal*, 1868, p. 67 to p. 69.

Mīr Jamālᵘ 'd-Dīn Injū belongs to the Sayyids of Shīrāz, who trace their descent to Qāsimarrasī (?) ibn-i Ḥasan ibn-i Ibrāhīm Ṭabāṭibā'ī Ḥusaynī. Mīr Shāh Maḥmūd and Mīr Shāh Abū Turāb, two later members

[1] *Shamsī* is an abbreviation for *Shamsᵘ 'd-Dīn*.

[[2] Sorath.—B.]

of this renowned family, were appointed during the reign of Shāh Ṭahmāsp-i Ṣafawī, at the request of the Chief Justice of Persia, Mīr Shams^u 'd-Dīn Asad^u 'llāh of Shushtar, the first as Shaykh^u 'l-Islām of Persia, and the second as Qāẓiy^u 'l-Quẓāt. Mīr Jamāl^u 'd-Dīn is one of their cousins.

Mīr Jamāl^u 'd-Dīn went to the Dakhin, the kings of which had frequently intermarried with the Injūs. He afterwards entered Akbar's service, took part in the Gujrāt wars, and was present in the battle of Patan (p. 432). Later he was sent to Bengal. At the outbreak of the Military Revolt, he was with Muẓaffar (*Akbarnāma* III, p. 255). In the 30th year (993) he was made a Commander of Six Hundred, and accompanied, shortly after, Aʿẓam Khān (No. 21) on his expedition to Gadha and Rāʾīsīn (*Akbarn.* III, 472). In the 36th year, he had a jāgīr in Mālwa, and served under Aʿẓam Khān in the Dakhin. His promotion to the rank of a Hazārī took place in the 40th year. When in the 45th year the fort of Āsīr had been conquered, ʿĀdil Shāh, king of Bījāpūr wished to enter into a matrimonial alliance with Akbar, and offered his daughter to Prince Dānyāl. To settle matters, Akbar dispatched the Mīr in 1009 (*Akbarn.* III, 846) to the Dakhin. But the marriage only took place in 1013, near Patan. After this, accompanied by the Historian Firishta, he went to Āgra, in order to lay before the emperor " such presents and tribute, as had never before come from the Dakhin ".

At the end of Akbar's reign, Mīr J. was a Commander of Three Thousand. Having been a favourite of Prince Salīm, he was promoted after the Prince's accession to the post of a Chahar-Hazārī, and received a *naqqāra* and a flag. When Khusraw rebelled, the Mīr received the order to effect an understanding by offering Khusraw the kingdom of Kābul with the same conditions under which M. Muḥammad Ḥakīm, Akbar's brother, had held that province. But the Prince did not consent; and when he was subsequently made a prisoner (p. 455) and brought before his father, Ḥasan Beg (No. 167), Khusraw's principal agent told Jahāngīr that all Amīrs of the Court were implicated in the rebellion; Jamāl^u 'd-Dīn had only a short time ago asked him (Ḥasan Beg) to promise him an appointment as *Panjhazārī*. The Mīr got pale and confused, when Mīrzā ʿAzīz Koka (No. 21) asked the emperor not to listen to such absurdities; Ḥasan Beg knew very well that he would have to suffer death and therefore tried to involve others; he himself (ʿAzīz) was the chief conspirator, and ready as such to undergo any punishment. Jahāngīr consoled the Mīr, and appointed him afterwards Governor of Bihār. In the 11th year, Mīr Jamāl received the title of *ʿAṣad^u 'd-Dawla.*

On this occasion, he presented to the emperor a dagger, inlaid with precious stones, the making of which he had himself superintended when at Bījāpūr. At the top of the handle, he had a yellow *yāqūt* fixed, perfectly pure, of the shape of half an egg, and had it surrounded by other *yāqūts* and emeralds. The value was estimated at 50,000 Rupees.

In 1621, Jahāngīr pensioned him off, because he was too old, allowing him four thousand rupees *per mensem*. The highest rank that he had reached was that of a brevet Panjhazārī with an actual command of Three Thousand and Five Hundred. In 1623, at the eighteenth anniversary of Jahāngīr's accession, he presented the emperor a copy of the great Persian Dictionary, entitled *Farhang-i Jahāngīrī*, of which he was the compiler. The first edition of it had made its appearance in 1017.[1]

After having lived for some time in Bahrāich, Mīr Jamāl returned to Āgra, where he died.

Mīr Jamālu 'd-Dīn had two sons. 1. *Mīr Amīnu 'd-Dīn.* He served with his father, and married a daughter of ʿAbdu 'r-Raḥīm Khān Khānān (No. 29). He died when young.

2. *Mīr Ḥusamu 'd-Dīn.* He married the sister of Aḥmad Beg Khān, brother's son of Ibrāhīm Khān Fatḥ-Jang (Nūr Jahān's brother). Jahāngīr made him Governor of Āsīr, which fort he handed over to Prince Shāhjahān during his rebellion. On Shāhjahān's accession, he was made a Commander of 4,000, with 3,000 horse, received a present of 50,000 Rupees, and the title of *Murtaẓā Khān.* He was also made Governor of Thathah, where he died in the second year (1039).

Mīr Ḥusām's sons—1. *Ṣamṣāmu 'd-Dawla.* He was made Dīwān of Shāh Shujāʿ in the 21st year. In the 28th year, he was appointed Governor of Oṛīsā with a command of 1,500, and 500 horse. He died in the end of the same year. 2. *Nūru 'llāh.* He is mentioned in the *Pādishāhnāma* (I, b., p. 312) as a Commander of Nine Hundred, 300 horse.

165. **Sayyid Rājū,** of Bārha.

Historians do not say to which of the four divisions (*vide* p. 427) the Bārha clan Rājū belongs.

He served in the 21st year, under Mān Singh, and in the 28th year, under Jagannāth (No. 69), against the Rānā. While serving under the latter, Rājū commanded the Imperial garrison of Mandalgaṛh, and successfully conducted an expedition against a detachment of the Rānā's troops. In the 30th year Jagannāth and Rājū attacked the Rānā in his residence; but he escaped.

[1] Regarding the *Farhang-i Jahāngīrī*, *vide Journal Asiatic Society Bengal,* 1868, pp. 12 to 15, and 65 to 69.

Later, Rājū served under Prince Murād, Governor of Mālwa, whom, in the 36th year, he accompanied in the war with Rāja Madhukar; but as the Prince was ordered by Akbar to return to Mālwa, Rājū had to lead the expedition. In the 40th year, he served in the siege of Aḥmadnagar. Once the enemies surprised the Imperialists, and did much damage to their cattle. Rājū attacked them, but was killed in the fight, together with several of his relations (A.H. 1003).

166. **Mīr Sharīf-i Āmuli.**

His antecedents and arrival in India have been mentioned above on p. 185. In the 30th year (993) Prince Mīrzā Muḥammad Ḥakīm of Kābul died, and the country was annexed to India. Mīr Sharīf was appointed Amīn and Ṣadr of the new province. In the following year, he served under Mān Singh in Kābul. In the 36th year,[1] he was appointed in the same capacity, though with more extensive powers, to Bihār and Bengal. In the 43rd year, he received Ajmīr as *aqṭāʿ*, and the Pargana of Mohān near Lakhnau, as *tuyūl*. During the siege of Āsīr, he joined the Imperial camp with his contingent, and was well received by the emperor.

He is said to have risen to the rank of a Commander of Three Thousand. He was buried at Mohān. On his death, neither books nor official papers were found; his list of soldiers contained the names of his friends and clients, who had to refund him six months' wages *per annum*.

Jahāngīr in his memoirs (*Tuzuk*, p. 22) praises him very much.

The *Ṭabaqāt* says, "Mīr Sharīf belongs to the heretics of the age. He is well acquainted with ṣūfism and is at present (1001) in Bihār."

Note on the *Nuqṭawiyya* Sect (نقطویه).

It was mentioned above (p. 186) that Mīr Sharīf spread in India doctrines which resembled those of Maḥmūd of Basakhwān.[2] The curious sect which Maḥmūd founded, goes by the name of *Maḥmūdiyya*, or *Wāḥidiyya*, or *Nuqṭawiyya*, or *Umanā*.[3] Maḥmud called himself *Shakhṣ-i wāḥid*, or "the individual", and professed to be the Imām Mahdī, whose appearance

[1] The Lucknow edition of the *Akbarnāma* (III, p. 629) says he was made at the same time a Commander of Four Thousand. This must be a mistake, because Mīr Sharīf was at Jahāngīr's accession a Commander of 2,500 (*Tuzuk*, p. 22).

[2] Badā,onī (Ed. Bibl. Indica) has *Basakhwān*; the MSS. of the Maʾāṣir, *Basākhwān* (with a long penultima) and in other places *Basākhān* without a *w*; the Calcutta edition of the Dabistān (p. 374) and Shea and Troyer's Translation have *Masajwān*—a shifting of the diacritical points.

[3] The name *nuqṭawī* was evidently used by Badā,onī, though the MSS. from which the Bibl. Indica edition was printed, have *Nabaṭī*, which was given on p. 185. For *Umanā*, Shea's translation of the Dabistān has *Imanā*; but امنا (*umanā*) is, no doubt, the plural of امین *amīn*.

on earth ushers in the end of the world. According to the Calcutta edition of the Dabistān and Shea's Translation, he lived about A.H. 600; but the MSS. of the *Maʿāṣir* have A.H. 800, which also agrees with Badā,oni's statement that Maḥmūd lived at the time of Tīmūr. The sect found numerous adherents in Īrān, but was extinguished by Shāh ʿAbbās-i Māẓī,[1] who killed them or drove them into exile.

Maḥmūd had forced into his service a passage from the Qurʾān (Sur. XVII, 81), *ʿasā an yabʿaṣa-ka rabbu-ka maqāman makmūdan*, "peradventure thy Lord will raise thee to an honorable (*maḥmūd*) station." He maintained that the human body (*jasad*) had since its creation been advancing in purity, and that on its reaching a higher degree of perfection "Maḥmūd" would arise, as indicated in the passage from the Qurʾān, and with his appearance the dispensation of Muḥammad would come to an end. He taught the transmigration of souls, and said that the beginning of everything was the *nuqṭa-yi khāk*, or earth-atom, from which the vegetables, and from these the animals, arose. The term *nuqṭa-yi khāk* has given rise to their name *Nuqṭawīs*. For other of Maḥmūd's tenets, *vide* Shea's translation of the Dabistān, vol. III, pp. 12 to 26.

Some of Maḥmūd's doctrines must have been of interest to Akbar, whose leanings towards the "man of the millennium", transmigration of souls, etc., have been mentioned above, and Mīr Sharīf-i Āmulī could not have done better than propounding the same doctrine at Court, and pointing out to Akbar as the restorer of the millennium.

The author of the ʿAlam Ārāʾ-yi Sikandarī, as the *Maʿāṣir* says, mentions Mīr Sharīf-i Āmulī under the following circumstances. In 1002, the 7th year of Shāh ʿAbbās-i Māẓī's reign, the astrologers of the age predicted, in consequence of certain very inauspicious conjunctions, the death of a great king, and as this prediction was universally referred to Shāh ʿAbbās Jalālu 'd-Dīn Muḥammad of Tabrīz, who was looked upon as the greatest astronomer of the period, it was proposed that Shāh ʿAbbās should lay aside royalty for the two or three days the dreaded conjunction was expected to last, and that a criminal who had been sentenced to death should sit on the throne. This extraordinary expedient was everywhere approved of; the criminals threw lots, and Yūsuf the quiver-maker, who belonged to the heretical followers of Darwīsh Khusraw of Qazwīn, was raised to the throne. He reigned for three days, and was then killed. Soon after, Darwīsh Khusraw was hanged. His ancestors had been well-diggers, but he was a dervish, and though he had been wise enough

[1] *Māẓī* (ماضی), *i.e.*, who passed away, is the epithet which Historians give to Shāh ʿAbbās I of Persia, the contemporary of Akbar and Jahāngīr.

never to speak of his *Nuqṯawiyya* belief, he was known as one of the sect, and was accordingly killed. So also Mīr Sayyid Aḥmad of Kāshān, whom ʕAbbās killed with his own sword. Among his papers treatises were found on the *Nuqṯa* doctrine, and also a letter addressed to him by Abū 'l-Fazl in Akbar's name. *Mīr Sharīf-i Āmulī, a good poet and the head of the sect, heard of these persecutions, and fled from Astrābād to Hindūstān.*

Regarding the last sentence, the author of the *Maʕāṣir* remarks that it involves an anachronism, for Mīr Sharīf was in India in 984, when Akbar was at Dīpālpūr in Mālwa; and besides, Sharīf-i Āmulī was mentioned in no Tazkira as a poet.

167. **Hasan Beg Khān-i Badakhshī Shaykh ʕUmarī.**[1]

Ḥasan Beg was a good soldier. In the 34th year, Akbar after his stay in Kashmīr, marched to Zābulistān, and passed through the district of Pakhalī, " which is 35 *kos* long and 25 broad, and lies west of Kashmīr. In Pakhalī, Sulṭān Ḥusayn Khān-i Pakhalīwāl (No. 301) paid his respects. This Zamīndār belonged to the descendants of the Qārlughs (قارلوغ), whom Tīmūr on his return from India to Tūrān had left in Pakhalī as garrison. After following Akbar's Court for a few days, Sulṭān Ḥusayn Khān withdrew without leave, and the emperor ordered Ḥasan Beg to occupy Pakhalī (*Akbarnāma* III, 591, 598). He speedily subdued the district. In the 35th year, during Ḥasan Beg's temporary absence at Court, Sulṭān Ḥusayn Khān again rebelled, assumed the title of Sulṭān Nāṣirᵘ 'd-Dīn, and drove away Ḥasan Beg's men. But soon after, he had again to submit to Ḥasan Beg. In the 46th year, Ḥasan was made a Commander of Two Thousand and Five Hundred for his services in Bangash, and was put, towards the end of Akbar's reign, in charge of Kābul, receiving Fort Rohtās[2] (in the Panjab) as jāgīr.

In the beginning of Jahāngīr's reign, he was called from Kābul to Court. On his way, at Mathurā (Muttra), Ḥasan Beg met Prince Khusraw, who had fled from Āgra on Sunday, the 8th Zī Ḥijjah, 1014.[3] From

---

[1] *Badakhshī* is the adjective formed from *Badakshān*, as *Kāshī* from *Kāshān*. The words *Shaykh ʕUmarī* are to be taken as an adjective formed like *Akbarshāhī*, *Jahāngīrī*, etc., which we find after the names of several grandees. Thus *Shaykh ʕUmarī* would mean " belonging to the servants of Shaykh ʕUmar ", and this explanation is rendered more probable by the statement of historians that Ḥasan Beg belonged to the *Bābariyān* or " nobles of Bābar's Court ".

Ḥasan Beg is often wrongly called *Ḥusayn Beg*. Thus in the *Tuzuk*, p. 25 ff.; *Pādishāhn* I, p. 306; *Akbarn.* III, 598.

[2] Generally spelt روهتاس. The fort in Bihār is spelt without *wāw*, رهتاس, though both are identical.

[3] So the *Tuzuk*. The *Maʕāṣir* has the 20th, instead of the 8th. MSS. continually confound هشتم and بیستم. But Jahāngīr on his pursuit reached Hoḍal on the 10th Zī Ḥijjah and the *Tuzuk* is correct.

distrust as to the motives of the emperor, which led to his recall from Kābul, or " from the innate wickedness of Badakhshīs ", he joined the Prince with his three hundred Badakhshī troopers, received the title of Khān Bābā, and got the management of all affairs. Another officer who attached himself to Khusraw, was ʿAbdu 'r-Raḥīm, Dīwān of Lāhor. After the defeat near Bhairōwāl on the Bi,āh,[1] the Afghāns who were with the prince, advised him to retreat to the Eastern provinces of the Empire ; but Ḥasan Beg proposed to march to Kābul, which, he said, had always been the starting-place of the conquerors of India ; he had, moreover, four lacs of rupees in Rohtās, which were at the Prince's service. Ḥasan Beg's counsel was ultimately adopted. But before he could reach Rohtās, Khusraw was captured on the Chanāb. On the 3rd Ṣafar 1015, the Prince, Ḥasan Beg, and ʿAbdu 'r-Raḥīm, were taken before Jahāngīr in the Bāgh-i Mīrzā Kāmrān, a villa near Lāhor, Khusraw himself, according to Chingiz's law (*batorah i Chingīzī* (?)), with his hands tied and fetters on his feet. Ḥasan Beg after making a useless attempt to incriminate others (p. 500), was put into a cow-hide and ʿAbdu 'r-Raḥīm into a donkey's skin, and in this state they were tied to donkeys, and carried through the bazars. " As cow-hides get dry sooner than donkey-skins," Ḥasan died after a few hours from suffocation : but ʿAbdu 'r-Raḥīm was after 24 hours still alive, and received, at the request of several courtiers, free pardon.[2] The other accomplices and the troopers of Khusraw were impaled ; their corpses were arranged in a double row along the road which leads from the Bāgh-i Mīrzā Kāmrān to the Fort of Lāhor, and Khusraw, seated on a sorry elephant, was led along that way. People had been posted at short intervals, and pointing to the corpses, kept calling out to Khusraw, " Behold, your friends, your servants, do homage to you."

Ḥasan Beg was mentioned above on p. 370. His son *Isfandiyār Khān*, was under Shāhjahān, a commander of 1,500. He served in Bengal, and died in the 16th year of Shāhjahān's reign (*Pādishāhn.* I, 476 ; I, b. 304). The ʿĀrif Beg-i Shaykh ʿUmarī mentioned in the *Pādishāhn.* (I, b. 319) appears to be a relation of his.

168. **Sheroya Khān**, son of Sher Afkan Khān.

Sher Afkan Khān was the son of Qūch Beg. Qūch Beg served under Humāyūn, and was killed in the successful attempt made by several

---

[1] *Vide* p. 456 note. There is another Bhairōwāl between Wazīrābād and Siyālkoṭ, south of the Chanāb.

[2] In Zū 'l-Ḥijjah, 1018, he got an appointment as a Yūzbāshī, or commander of 100 and was sent to Kashmīr (*Tuzuk*, p. 79). In the *Tuzuk*, he is called *ʿAbdu 'r-Raḥīm Khar*, Abdu 'r-Raḥīm " the Ass ".

grandees to save Maryam Makānī, Akbar's mother, after the fatal battle of Chausā (*vide* No. 96, p. 450). When Humāyūn fled to Persia, Sher Afkan remained with Mīrzā Kāmrām in Kābul; but he joined the emperor on his return from Īrān, and was made governor of Qalāt. Later he received Ẓaḥāk-Bāmiyān as jāgīr, but went again over to Kāmrān. Humāyūn's, soon after, captured and killed him.

Sheroya Khān served at first under Munʿim (No. 11) in Bengal and Oṛīsā. In the 26th year he was appointed to accompany Prince Murād to Kābul. In the 28th year, he served under ʿAbdu 'r-Raḥīm (No. 29) in Gujrāt, and was present in the battle of Sarkich (*Akbarnāma* III, 408, 422). In the 30th year, he served under Maṭlab Khān (No. 83) against Jalāla Tārīkī (p. 442). In the 39th year, he was made a Khān, and was appointed to Ajmīr. According to the *Ṭabaqāt* he was a Hazārī in 1001.

169. **Naẓar Be Uzbak.**

The *Akbarnāma* (III, p. 500) says, "On the same day [1] Naẓar Be, and his sons, Qanbar Be, Shādī Be (No. 367), and Bāqī Be (No. 368), were presented at Court, and were favourably received by the emperor."

Shādī Be distinguished himself in the expedition under Maṭlab Khān (No. 83) against the Tārīkīs. He may be the Shādī Khān Shādī Beg, mentioned in the *Pādishāhnāma* (I, b. 308) as a commander of One Thousand. *Be* is the abbreviation of *Beg*. Naẓar Be is not to be confounded with Naẓar (?) Beg (No. 247).

170. **Jalāl Khān**, son of Muḥammad Khān, son of Sulṭān Ādam, the Gakkhar.

171. **Mubārak Khān**, son of Kamāl Khān, the Gakkhar.

The Gakkhars are a tribe inhabiting, according to the *Maʾāṣir*, the hilly districts between the Bahat and the Indus.[2] At the time of Zaynu 'l-ʿĀbidīn, king of Kashmīr, a Ghaznīn noble of the name of Malik Kid (كد or كيد), who was a relation of the then ruler of Kābul, took away

[1] When the news was brought to Akbar that Mān Singh, soon after the defeat of the Imperialists, and the death of Bīr Baṛ in the Khaybar Pass, had defeated the Tārīkīs at ʿAlī Masjid (end of the 30th year, or beginning of Rabīʿ I, 994).

[2] Mr. J. G. Delmerick informs me that the Gakkhars inhabited the hilly parts of the Rawul Pinḍī and Jhelam districts from Khānpūr on the borders of the Hazāra district along the lower range of hills skirting the Taḥṣīls of Rāwul Pinḍī, Kuhūta, and Gūjar Khān, as far as Domeli in the Jehlam district. Their ancient strongholds were Pharwāla, Sulṭānpūr, and Dāngalī. They declare that they are descended from the Kaianian kings of Īrān. Their ancestor Kid invaded Tibet, where he and his descendants reigned for ten generations. His tenth descendant Kab conquered Kashmīr, and took possession of half of it. The Gakkhars then reigned for 16 generations after Kab in Kashmīr. The 16th descendant, Zayn Shāh, fled to Afghānistān, where he died. His son, Gakkhar Shāh, came to the Panjāb with Maḥmūd of Ghaznī, and was made lord of the Sind Sāgar Du,āb. Malik Bīr is said to have been the grandfather of Tatār, whose father was Malik Pīlū. *Vide* Mr. Delmerick's History of the Gakkhars, *Journal A.S.B.*, 1871. *Vide* p. 621.

these districts from the Kashmīrīs, and gradually extended his power over the region between the Nīlāb (Indus) and the Sawāliks and the frontier of modern Kashmīr.[1] Malik Kid was succeeded by his son Malik Kalān, and Malik Kalān by Malik Bīr. After Bīr, the head of the tribe was Sulṭān Tatār, who rendered Bābar valuable service, especially in the war with Rānā Sānkā. Sulṭān Tatār had two sons, Sulṭān Sārang and Sulṭān Ādam. Sārang fought a great deal with Sher Shāh and Salīm Shāh, capturing and selling a large number of Afghāns. The Fort Rohtās was commenced by Sher Shāh with the special object of keeping the Gakkhars in check. Sher Shāh in the end captured Sulṭān Sārang and killed him, and confined his son Kamāl Khān in Gwāliyār, without, however, subjugating the tribe. Sulṭān Ādam was now looked upon as the head of the clan. He continued to oppose the Afghāns. Once Salīm Shāh gave the order to blow up a portion of the Gwāliyār Fort, where the state prisoners were kept. Kamāl Khān, who was still confined, had a miraculous escape and was in consequence pardoned. Kamāl went to his kinsfolk; but as Sulṭān Ādam had usurped all power, he lived obscurely, with his brother Saʿīd Khān, avoiding conflict with his uncle. Immediately after Akbar's accession, however, Kamāl paid his respects to the emperor at Jālindhar, was well received, and distinguished himself in the war with Hemū and during the siege of Mānkoṭ. In the 3rd year he was sent against the Myāna Afghāns, who had revolted near Saronj (Mālwa) and was made on his return jāgīrdār of Karah and Fathpūr Huswah. In the 6th year, he served under Khān Zamān (No. 13) against the Afghāns under the son of Mubāriz Khān ʿAdlī (p. 326). In the 8th year (970), he was called to Court, and as Akbar wished to reward him, Kamāl Khān begged the emperor to put him in possession of the Gakkhar district, which was still in the hands of his usurping uncle. Akbar ordered the Khān-i Kalān (No. 16) and other Panjābī grandees to divide the district into two parts, and to give one of them to Kamāl Khān; if Sulṭān Ādam was not satisfied with the other, they should occupy the country and punish Sulṭān Ādam. The latter alternative was rendered necessary by the resistance of Sulṭān Ādam. The Panjāb,

[1] The *Maʿāsir* says, he subjected the tribes called بهوكيال جترنيه ' ايوان ' جانوهه ' كهتر (*vide* p. 487) 'جهيه, باريه and ميكرال. Mr. Delmerick says, the Khatars inhabit the western parts of the Rāwul Piṇḍī district. The second tribe is that of the *Janjū,as* who inhabit the Salt Range. The third, *Awān* (اوان) are found in the southern parts of the Rāwul Pindī and the Jhelam districts; their tract is called *Awānkārī* to this day. The fourth, he says, may be the *Jodras* (جودره), a great clan about Piṇḍī Gheb. The fifth, he believes, is intended for the *Khokarān* (كهوكران), a tribe of some importance in Piṇḍ Dādan Khān. The sixth and the eighth are the *Chibh* (چهبه) and Mangarāl (منگرال), large tribes in Jammū. The seventh he supposes to be a mistake for پهاريه *pahāṛiya* or hill tribes, which were the Dhūnds (دهوند) and Satīs (ستي). *Vide* Additional Notes at end to p. 507.

army, therefore, and Kamāl Khān entered the Gakkhar district, and defeated and captured Ādam after a severe engagement near the "Qaṣba of Hīlā".[1] Sulṭān Ādam and his son Lashkarī were handed over to Kamāl Khān, who was put in possession of the district. Kamāl Khān killed Lashkarī, and put Sulṭān Ādam into prison, where he soon after died. (*Akbarnāma*, II, 240 ff.)

It is stated in the *Ṭabaqāt* that Kamāl Khān was a Commander of Five Thousand, distinguished for courage and bravery, and died in 972.[2]

Mubārak Khān and Jalāl Khān served in the 30th year under Mīrzā Shāhrukh, Bhagwān Dās, and Shāh Qulī Māḥram, in Kashmīr (*Akbarnāma*, III, 485). The *Ṭabaqāt* calls both, as also Saʿīd Khān, Commanders of Fifteen Hundred. A daughter of Saʿīd Khān was married to Prince Salīm; *vide* No. 225, note.

172. **Tāsh Beg Khān Mughul**, [Tāj Khān].

Tāsh Beg served at first under Mīrzā Muḥammad Ḥakīm, king of Kābul, and entered, after the death of his master, Akbar's service. He received a jāgīr in the Panjāb. According to the *Akbarnāma* (III, 489), he went with Bīr Baṛ (No. 85) to Sawād and Bijor, and distinguished himself under ʿAbdᵘ 'l-Maṭlab (No. 83) against the Tārīkīs (III, 541).

In the 40th year, he operated against the ʿĪsā Khayl Afghāns, though with little success. Two years later, he served under Āṣaf Khān (No 98) in the conquest of Mau, and received the title of *Tāj Khān*. When Rāja Bāsū again rebelled (47th year), Khwāja Sulaymān, Bakhshī of the Panjāb, was ordered to march against him with the contingents of Qulij Khān (No. 42), Ḥusayn Beg-i Shaykh ʿUmarī (No. 167), Aḥmad Beg-i Kābulī (No. 191), and Tāj Khān. Without waiting for the others, T. Kh. moved to Paṭhān. Whilst pitching his tents, Jamīl Beg, T. Kh.'s son, received news of Bāsū's approach. He hastily attacked him, and was killed with fifty men of his father's contingent.

Jahāngīr, on his accession, promoted him to a command of 3,000. In the second year of his reign, he officiated as governor of Kābul till the arrival of Shāh Beg Khān (No. 57). He was afterwards appointed governor of Thathah, where he died in the ninth year (1023).

---

[1] Not Hailā (هيلان), south of Chiliānwālā between the Jhelam and the Chanāb; but Hīlā, or Hīl, which, Mr. Delmerick says, is a ferry on the Jhelam near Dāngalī, Sulṭān Ādam's stronghold.

[2] So in my MSS. of the *Ṭabaqāt*. The author of the *Maʾāṣir* found 970 in his MS., which would be the same year in which Kamāl Khān was restored to his paternal inheritance; hence he adds a والله اعلم. He was certainly alive in the middle of 972. (*Akbarnāma*, I, p. 302.)

173. **Shaykh ʿAbd^u 'llāh**, son of Shaykh Muḥammad Ghawṣ [of Gwāliyār].

Shaykh ʿAbd^u 'llāh at first lived a retired and saintly life, but entered subsequently the Emperor's service. He distinguished himself, and is said to have risen to the dignity of a Commander of Three Thousand. He died when young.

His brother *Ẓiyāʾ^u 'llāh* lived as a Faqīr, and studied during the lifetime of his father under the renowned saint Wajīh^u 'd-Dīn in Gujrāt, who himself was a pupil of Muḥammad Ghawṣ.

Biographies of Muḥammad Ghawṣ (died 970 at Āgra, buried in Gwāliyār) will be found in the *Maʿāṣir*, *Badā,onī* (III, p. 4), and the *Khazīnat^u 'l-Aṣfiyāʾ* (p. 969). He was disliked by Bayrām Khān, Shaykh Gadā,ī, and Shaykh Mubārak, Abū 'l-Faẓl's father. *Vide* also *Maʾāṣir-i ʿĀlamgīrī*, p. 166.

174. **Rāja Rājsingh**, son of Rāja Askaran, the Kachhwāha.

Rāja Askaran is a brother of Rāja Bihārī Mal (No. 23). He served in the 22nd year with Ṣādiq Khān (No. 43) against Rāja Madhukar of Ūḍcha,[1] and in the 25th year under Toḍar Māl in Bihār. In the 30th year, he was made a Commander of One Thousand, and served in the same year under ʿAzīz Koka (No. 21) in the Dakhin. In the 31st year, when Akbar appointed two officers to each ṣūba, Askaran and Shaykh Ibrāhīm (No. 82) were appointed to Āgra. In the 33rd year, he served a second time against Rāja Madhukar under Shihāb Khān (No. 26), and died soon after.

Abū 'l-Faẓl has not given his name in this list of grandees. The *Ṭabaqāt* says he was a Commander of Three Thousand.

Rāj Sing, his son, received the title of Rāja after the death of his father. He served for a long time in the Dakhin, was called in the 44th year to Court, and was appointed commandant of Gwāliyār. In the 45th year, he joined the Imperial army, which under Akbar besieged Fort Āsīr. In the 47th year, he pursued, together with Rāy Rāyān Patr Dās (No. 196) the notorious Bir Singh Deo Bundela, who at Jahāngīr's instigation had murdered Abū 'l-Faẓl. For his distinguished services in the operations against the Bundela clan, he was promoted, and held, in the 50th year the rank of a Commander of 4,000, 3,000 horse. In the 3rd year, of Jahāngīr's reign, he served in the Dakhin, where he died in 1024 (10th year).

---

[1] *Ūḍcha* is generally spelt on our maps *Oorcha*. It lies near Jhānsī on the left bank of the Betwa. The name of the river "Dasthārā" mentioned on p. 382, is differently spelled in the MSS. In one place the *Maʾāṣir* has *Satdahārā*.

Rām Dās, his son, was a Commander of 1,000, 400 horse. He received, in the 12th year, the title of Rāja, and was made, in the same year, a Commander of 1,500, 700 horse.

One of his grandsons, Prasuttam Singh, turned Muḥammadan in the 6th year of Shāhjahan's reign, and received the name of *ʿIbādatmand*.[1]

175. **Rāy Bhoj**, son of Rāy Surjan Hāḍā (No. 96).

When Būndī, in the 22nd year, was taken from Daudā, elder brother of Rāy Bhoj, the latter was put in possession of it. Bhoj served under Mān Singh against the Afghāns of Oṛīsā, and under Shaykh Abū 'l-Faẓl in the Dakhin (*Akbarn.*, III, 851, 855).

His daughter was married to Jagat Singh (No. 160).

In the first year of his reign, Jahāngīr wished to marry Jagat Singh's daughter. Rāy Bhoj, her grandfather, refused to give his consent, and Jahāngīr resolved to punish him on his return from Kābul. But Rāy Bhoj, in the end of 1016, committed suicide. The marriage, however, took place on the 4th Rabīʿ I, 1017, (*Tuzuk*, pp. 68, 69).

It is said that Rāthoṛ and Kachhwāha princesses entered the imperial Harem; but no Hāḍā princess was ever married to a Timuride.

XIV. Commanders of Eight Hundred.

176. **Sher Khwāja.**

He belonged to the Sayyids of Itāwa (سادات اتانی). His mother was a *Naqshbandī* (p. 466, note 2). Sher Kh.'s name was "Pādishāh Khwāja", but Akbar called him on account of his bravery and courage *Sher Khwāja*.

In the 30th year, Sh. Kh. served under Saʿīd Khān Chaghtā'ī (No. 25) against the Yūsufzā,īs, and afterwards under Sulṭān Murād in the Dakhin. In the 40th year, the Prince sent with him a corps to Paṭan, where he distinguished himself against Ikhlāṣ Khān. He continued to serve in the Dakhin under Abū 'l-Faẓl. In the engagement near Bīr he was wounded. He entered the town victoriously but was besieged. From want of provisions, his men had to subsist on horse-flesh. As in consequence of the swelling of the Gangā (Godāvarī) he did not expect assistance from the north, he resolved to try a last sortie and perish, when Abū 'l-Faẓl arrived and raised the siege. Abū 'l-Faẓl proposed to leave his own son ʿAbd^u 'r-Raḥmān at Bīr; but Sh. Kh. refused to quit his post. In the 46th year, he received a drum and a flag.

---

[1] Regarding the Kachhwāhas, see my article in the *Calcutta Review*, for April, 1871, entitled "A Chapter from Muḥammadan History".

Sh. Kh. remained in favour during the reign of Jahāngīr. He was with the emperor when Mahābat Khān near the Bahat had taken possession of Jahāngīr's person. After Jahāngīr's death, he served with Āṣaf Khān against Shahryār in Lāhor.

. In the 1st year of Shāhjahan's reign, he was made a Commander of 4,000, with 1,000 horse, and received the title of *Khwāja Bāqī Khān.* He was also appointed governor of Thathah, *vice* Mīrzā ʿĪsā Tarkhān (p. 392). He died on his way to his province in 1037. *Pādishāhn.*, I, 181, 200.

His son *Khwāja Hāshim* was made a commander of 500 (*Pādishāhnāma,* I, b. 327). Another son, *Asad^{u} 'llah,* is mentioned as a Commander of 900, 300 horse, (*Pādishāhn.*, II, 738).

177. **Mīrzā Khurram,** son of Khān-i Aʿẓam Mīrzā ʿAzīz Koka (No. 21).

He has been mentioned above, p. 346.

XV. Commanders of Seven Hundred.

178. **Quraysh Sulṭān,** son of Abd^{u} 'r-Rashīd Khān, king of Kāshghar.

182. **Sulṭān ʿAbd^{u} 'llāh,** brother (by another mother) of Quraysh Sulṭān

310. **Shāh Muḥammad,** son of Quraysh Sulṭān.

Quraysh Sulṭān is a descendant of Chingiz Khān.[1] His genealogical tree is given in the *Akbarnāma* (III, 584) and the *Tārīkh-i Rashīdī* as on following page.

After the death of ʿAbd^{u} 'r-Rashīd Khān (16), ʿAbd^{u} 'l-Karīm Khān, elder brother of Quraysh Sulṭān, succeeded to the throne of Kāshghar. He treated his relations well, partly in fulfilment of his father's wish, partly from natural benevolence. But Khudābanda, son of Quraysh Sulṭān, quarrelled with Muḥammad Khān, his uncle, and Khudābanda occupied the town of Tarfān. ʿAbd^{u} 'llāh, doubting the loyalty of his relations, ordered Quraysh Sulṭān to go to Makkah. Q. went first with his family to Badakhshān and Balkh, and lastly, with the permission of ʿAbd^{u} 'llāh Khān of Tūrān, to Hindūstān. He met Akbar, in the 34th year, at Shihāb^{u} 'd-Dīn-pūr, when the emperor was just returning from Kashmīr, was well received, and appointed to a command of Seven Hundred.

Quraysh died in the 37th year (1000), at Ḥājīpūr.

179. **Qarā Bahādur,** son of Mīrzā Maḥmūd, who is the paternal uncle of Mīrzā Ḥaydar [Gurgānī].

---

[1] Chingiz Khān in the histories is often called *Qāʾān-i Buzurg.*

1. Chingiz Khān.
2. Chaghtāʾi Khān.
3. Mawātkān (second son of Chaghtāʾī Khān).
4. بيسون توا (the MSS. give various readings).
5. Yarāq [1] Khān (called after his conversion Sultān Ghiyasu 'd-Dīn).
6. Dawā Khān.[2]
7. Alsīnūqā, or Alsānūqā, Khān.
8. Tughluq Tīmūr Khān.
9. Khizr Khwāja Khān [3] (father-in-law of Tīmūr).
10. (a) Muhammad Khān . . . (b) Shamς Jahān Khān . . . (c) Naqsh Jahān Khān.
11. (a) Sher Muhammad Khān. (b) Sher ςAlī Ughlān.
12. Uwais Khān, son of Sher ςAlī Ughlān.
13. Yūnas Khān, father of Bābar's mother.
14. Sultān Ahmad Khān, known as *Alāncha Khān.*
15. Sultān Abū Saςid Khān.
16. ςAbdu 'r-Rashīd Khān.
17. (1) ςAbdu 'l-Karīm Khān. (2) Quraysh Sultān (No. 168). (3) Sultān ςAbdu 'llah (No. 178).
    - (1) Shāh Muhammad (No. 310).
    - (2) Khudābanda.

Like the preceding, Qarā Bahādur belonged to the royal family of Kāshghar. Mīrzā Haydar's father, Muhammad Husayn, was the son of Bābar's maternal aunt.

Mirzā Haydar,[4] during his stay in Kāshghar, had accompanied the

---

[[1] Burāq, Vamςbery, p. 153.—B].

[2] Dawā invaded India during the reign of ςAlāʾu 'd-Dīn; *vide Journal As. Soc. Bengal* for 1869, p. 194, and 1870, p. 44.

[3] His daughter is called Tukul Khānum تكل خانم. It is said that Tīmūr after the marriage received the title of Gurgān گرگان, the Mughul term for the Persian *dāmād,* a son-in-law. Hence Timurides are often called *Gurgānīs.*

[4] Mīrzā Haydar was a historian and poet. He wrote in 951 the *Tārīkh-i ςAbdu 'r-Rashīdī,* in honour of *ςAbdu 'r-Rashīd,* king of Kāshghar. The villa known as *Bāgh-i Safā* was erected by him. *Akbarnāma,* III, 585.

The MS. of the Tārīkh-i Rashīdī in the Library of the Asiatic Society (Persian MSS., No. 155, three parts, 19 lines per page) is a fair, though modern copy, and was brought by Capt. H. Strachey from Yārkand.

The Tārīkh commences with the reign of Tughluq Tīmūr, who was converted to Islām by Mawlānā Arshadu 'd-Dīn, and goes down to the reign of ςAbdu 'r-Rashīd. The second *daftar* contains the Memoirs of Mīrzā Haydar. The style is elegant.

son of Sulṭān Abū Saʿīd on several expeditions to Kashmīr, and had thus acquired some knowledge of the people and the state of that province. He subsequently went over Badakhshān to India, and arrived at Lāhor, where Mīrzā Kāmrān made him his *nāʾib* during his absence on an expedition to Qandahār, which the Shāh of Persia had taken from Khwāja Kalān Beg. M. Ḥaydar afterwards accompanied Kāmrān to Āgra, and tried on several occasions to persuade Humāyūn to take possession of Kashmīr. When the emperor after his second defeat by Sher Shāh retreated to Lāhor, he gave M. Ḥaydar a small corps and sent him to Kashmīr. The country being in a distracted state, M. H. took possession of it without bloodshed, and ruled as absolute king for ten years. But afterwards he ordered the *khuṭba* to be read, and coins to be struck, in Humāyūn's name. He was killed in 958 by some treacherous Kashmīrīs.

The father of Qarā Bahādur was Mīrzā Maḥmūd ; hence Q. B. was M. Ḥaydar's cousin. As he had been with M. Ḥ. in Kashmīr, Akbar, in the 6th year, ordered him to re-conquer the province, and gave him a large corps. But Q. B. delayed his march, and when he arrived in the hot season at Rājor, he found the passes fortified. Soon afterwards, he was attacked and defeated by Ghāzī Khān, who had usurped the throne of Kashmīr. Q. B. discomfited returned to Akbar.

In the 9th year, he accompanied the emperor to Mālwa, and was appointed, on Akbar's return, governor of Mandū. He died soon after.

For a relation of Qarā Bahādur, *vide* No. 183.

180. **Muẓaffar Ḥusayn Mīrzā**, son of Ibrāhīm Ḥusayn Mīrzā [son of Muḥammad Sulṭān Mīrzā].

Muẓaffar Ḥusayn Mīrzā is a Timuride. His tree is as follows :—

ʿUmar Shaykh Mīrzā (second son of Tīmūr).
|
Mīrzā Bāyqrā.
|
Mīrzā Manṣūr.
|
M. Bāyqrā.[1]
|
Wais Mīrzā.
|
Muḥammad Sulṭān Mīrzā.

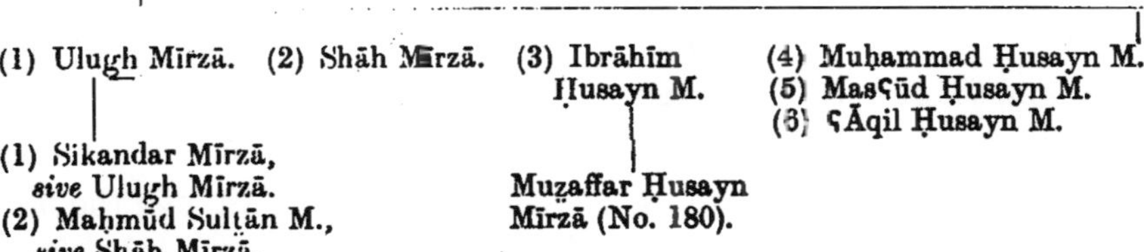

[1 His brother is Abū 'l-Ghāzī Sulṭān Ḥasayn Mīrzā.—B.]

The mother of Muḥammad Sulṭān Mīrzā was the daughter of the renowned Sulṭān Ḥusayn Mīrzā, king of Khurāsān, at whose Court Muḥammad Sulṭān Mīrzā held a place of distinction. After Sulṭān Ḥusayn's death, Muḥammad Sulṭān Mīrzā went to Bābar, who treated him with every distinction. Humāyūn also favoured him, though on several occasions he rebelled, and extended his kindness to his sons, Ulugh Mīrzā and Shāh Mīrzā, who had given him repeatedly cause of dissatisfaction. Ulugh Mīrzā was killed in the expedition against the Hazāras, and Shāh Muḥammad died, soon after, a natural death.

Ulugh Mīrzā had two sons, Sikandar Mīrzā and Maḥmūd Sulṭān Mīrzā ; but Humāyūn changed their names, and gave Sikandar the name of Ulugh Mīrzā, and Maḥmūd Sulṭān Mīrzā that of Shāh Mīrzā.

As Muḥammad Sulṭān Mīrzā was old, Akbar excused him from attending at Court (*taklīf-i bār*), and gave him the pargana of Aʿẓampūr in Sambhal as.a pension. He also bestowed several other places upon his grandsons Ulugh and Shāh Mīrzā. At Aʿẓampūr in his old age, Muḥammad Sulṭān M. had four other sons born to him—1. Ibrāhīm Ḥusayn Mīrzā, 2. Muḥammad Ḥusayn Mīrzā, 3. Masʿūd Ḥusayn Mīrzā, and 4. ʿĀqil Ḥusayn Mīrzā.

In the 11th year of Akbra's reign, Mīrzā Muḥammad Ḥakīm, king of Kābul, invaded India and besieged Lāhor ; and when Akbar marched against him, Ulugh M. and Shāh M. rebelled. They were joined in their revolt by their (younger) uncles Ibrāhīm Ḥusayn M. and Muḥammad Ḥusayn M. The rebellious Mīrzās went plundering from Sambhal, to Khān Zamān (No. 13) at Jaunpūr ; but as they could not agree with him, they marched on Dihlī, and from there invaded Mālwa, the governor of which, Muḥammad Qulī Khān Barlās (No. 31), was with the emperor. The consequence of their revolt was, that Akbar imprisoned the old Muḥammad Sulṭān Mīrzā. He died a short time after in his prison at Bi,ānā. In the 12th year, when Akbar had defeated and killed Khān Zamān, and conquered Chītor, he made Shihāb Khān (No. 26) governor of Mālwa, and ordered him to punish the Mīrzās.

About this time Ulugh M. died. The other Mīrzās unable to withstand Shihāb Khān fled to Chingiz Khān (p. 419), who then ruled over a portion of Gujrāt. Chingiz Khān was at war with Iʿtimād Khān (No. 67) of Aḥmadābād ; and as the Mīrzās had rendered him good service, he gave them Bahṛōch as jāgīr. But their behaviour in that town was so cruel that Chingiz Khān had to send a corps against them. Though the Mīrzās defeated his troops they withdrew to Khāndesh, and re-entered Mālwa. They were vigorously attacked by Ashraf Khān (No. 74), Ṣādīq Khān

No. 43), and others, who besieged Rantanbhūr (13th year), and were pursued to the Narbadā, where many soldiers of the Mīrzās perished in crossing. In the meantime Chingiz Khān had been murdered by Jhujhār Khān and as Gujrāt was in a state of disorder, the Mīrzās with little fighting, occupied Champānīr, Bahrōch, and Sūrat.

In the 17th year, Akbar entered Gujrāt and occupied Aḥmadabad. Dissensions having broken out among the Mīrzās, Ibrāhīm Ḥusayn M. left Bahrōch, and arrived at a place 8 miles from Akbar's camp. Most of Akbar's Amīrs had the day before been sent away towards Sūrat in search of Muḥammad Ḥusayn M. Hearing of Ibrāhīm Ḥusayn's arrival, the emperor dispatched Shāhbāz Khān (No. 80) after the Amīrs whilst he himself marched to the Mahindrī River, where it flows past the town of Sarnāl. Akbar had about 40 men with him, few of whom had armour ; but when the Amīrs returned, the number rose to about 200. The signal of attack was given and after a hard fight, Ibrāhīm Ḥusayn M. was defeated. He fled towards Āgra, whilst his wife, Gulrukh Begam, a daughter of Mīrzā Kāmrān, on hearing of his defeat, fled with Muẓaffar Ḥusayn Mīrzā from Sūrat to the Dakhin.

Akbar now resolved to invest Sūrat, and left M. ʿAzīz Koka (No. 21) with a garrison in Aḥmadābād, ordering at the same time Quṭbᵘ 'd-Dīn (No. 28) to join ʿAzīz with the Mālwa contingent. Muḥammad Ḥusayn M. and Shāh M. thereupon united their troops with those of Sher Khān Fūlādī, a Gujrātī noble, and besieged Paṭan. ʿAzīz marched against them, and defeated them (p. 432). Muḥammad Ḥusayn M. then withdrew to the Dakhin.

Ibrāhīm Ḥusayn M. and his younger brother Masʿūd Ḥusayn M. having met with resistance at Nāgor (p. 384), invaded the Panjāb. The governor, Ḥusayn Qulī Khān (No. 24) at that time besieged Nagarkoṭ, and hearing of the inroad of the Mīrzās, made peace with the Rāja, attacked the rebels, defeated them, and captured Masʿūd. Ibrāhīm Ḥusayn fled towards Multān, and was soon afterwards wounded, and captured by some Balūchīs. He then fell into the hands of Saʿīd Khān (No. 25) and died of his wounds.

After Akbar's return to Āgra, Muḥammad Ḥusayn Mīrzā left the Dakhin, invaded Gujrāt, and took possession of several towns. He was defeated at Kambhā,it by Nawrang Khān (p. 354) and joined the party of Ikhtiyārᵘ 'l-Mulk and the sons of Sher Khān Fūlādī. They then marched against Aḥmadābad and besieged M. ʿAzīz Koka. To relieve him Akbar hastened by forced marches from Āgra to Paṭan, and arrived, on the 5th Jumāḍa I, 981 (p. 458), with about 1,000 horse, at a place 3 *kos* from Aḥmadābād. Leaving Ikhtiyār to continue the siege, Muḥammad Ḥusayn opposed the emperor, but was defeated and wounded. In his flight his horse fell over a bramble, when two troopers captured him, and led him to Akbar. Each of the two men claimed the customary reward, and when Bīr Baṛ, at Akbar's request, asked Muḥammad Ḥusayn which of the two had taken him prisoner, he said, " The salt of the emperor has caught me ; for those two could not have done it." Ikhtiyār, on hearing of the defeat and capture of Muḥammad Ḥusayn, raised the siege, and fled with his 5,000 troopers. Akbar at once pursued him. Ikhtiyār got detached from his men, and in jumping over a shrub fell with his horse to the ground, when Suhrāb Turkmān who was after him, cut off his head, and took it to the emperor. Muḥammad Ḥusayn also had, in the meantime, been executed by Ray Singh (No. 44), whom Akbar had put over him.

Shāh Mīrzā had fled in the beginning of the battle.

In the 22nd year, Muẓaffar Ḥusayn Mīrzā, whom his mother had taken to the Dakhin, entered Gujrāt and created disturbances. He was defeated by Rāja Toḍar Mal and Vazīr Khān (p. 379) and fled to Jūnāgaḍh. When the Rāja had gone, Muẓaffar besieged Vazīr in Aḥmadābād. During the siege he managed to attach Vazīr's men to his cause, and was on the point of entering the town, when a cannon ball killed Mihr ʿAlī Kolābī, who had led the young Muẓaffar into rebellion. This so affected Muẓaffar that he raised the siege, though on the point of victory, and withdrew to Nazrbār. Soon after, he was captured by Rāja ʿAlī of Khāndesh, and handed over to Akbar. He was kept for some time in prison ; but as he showed himself loyal, Akbar, in the 36th year, released him, and married him to his eldest daughter, the Sulṭān Khānum. He also gave him the Sarkār of Qanawj as *tuyūl*. Muẓaffar, however, was addicted to the pleasures of wine, and when complaints were brought to Akbar, he cancelled the *tuyūl*, and again imprisoned him. But he soon after set him at liberty. In the 45th year (1008), when Akbar besieged Āsīr, he sent Muẓaffar to besiege Fort Lalang. But he quarrelled with Khwāja Fatḥu 'llāh, and one day, he decamped for Gujrāt. His companions deserted him ; and dressing himself in the garb of a faqīr, he wandered about between Sūrat and Baglāna, when he was caught by Khwāja Waisī and taken before the Emperor. After having been imprisoned for some time, he was let off in the 46th year. He died, not long after, a natural death.

His sister, Nūru 'n-Nisā, was married to Prince Salīm (*vide* No. 225, note). Gulrukh Begam, Muẓaffar's mother, was still alive in 1023, when she was visited on her sick-bed by Jahāngīr at Ajmīr.

181. **Qundūq Khān**, brother of the well-known Bayrām Oghlān.

The *Akbarnāma* (I, 411) mentions a Qundūq Sulṭān, who accompanied Humāyūn on his march to India.

For *Qundūq*, some MSS. read *Qundūz*. A grandee of this name served in Bengal under Munᶜim, and died at Gaur (p. 407).

182. **Sulṭān ᶜAbdᵘ 'llāh**, brother (by another mother) of Quraysh Sulṭān (No. 178).

183. **Mīrzā ᶜAbdᵘ 'r-Raḥmān**, son of Mīrzā Ḥaydar's brother (*vide* No. 179).

184. **Qiyā Khān**, son of Ṣāḥib Khān.

In the *Ṭabaqāt* and the *Akbarnāma* he is generally called قیا صاحب حسن, which may mean 'Qiyā, the beautiful", or "Qiyā, son of Ṣāḥib Ḥasan". Proper nouns ending in a long vowel rarely take the Izāfat.[1] It looks as if the reading صاحب خان of the Āᵉīn MSS. was a mistake. The words صاحب حسن are intended to distinguish him from Qiyā Gung (No. 33).

Qiyā served under Shamsᵘ 'd-Dīn Atga against Bayrām (p. 332). He was also present in the battle of Sārangpūr (*vide* No. 120).

185. **Darbār Khān**, ᶜInāyat [ullah], son of Takaltū Khān, the Reader.

Darbār's father was Shāh Ṭahmāsp's reader. ᶜInāyat, on his arrival in India, was appointed to the same post by Akbar, and received the title of Darbār Khān. He served in the 9th year (end of 971) in Mālwa, and in the 12th year, in the last war with Khān Zamān. He accompanied the emperor to Rantanbhūr, and when Akbar, in the 14th year, after the conquest of the fort made a pilgrimage to the tomb of Muᶜīn-i Chishtī in Ajmīr, Darbār Khān took sick leave, and died on his arrival at Āgra.

According to his dying wish—to the disgust of the author of the *Maᵉāṣir*—he was buried in the mausoleum of one of Akbar's dogs, which he had built. The dog had shown great attachment to its imperial master.

186. **ᶜAbdᵘ 'r-Raḥmān**, son of Muᶜayyid Dūlday.

The name *Dūlday* had been explained above on p. 388. ᶜAbdᵘ 'r-Raḥmān's great-grandfather, Mīr Shāh Malik, had served under Tīmūr. ᶜAbdᵘ 'r-Raḥmān was killed in a fight with the Bihār rebel Dalpat. *Vide* under his son Barkhurdār, No. 328, and under No. 146. Another son is mentioned below, No. 349.

---

[1] Thus you say هلاگو ملعون, for هلاگوی ملعون; the accursed Hulāgū.

187. **Qāsim ʿAlī Khān.**

When Akbar, in the 10th year, moved against Khān Zamān (No. 13), Qāsim ʿAlī Khān held Ghāzīpūr. In the 17th year, he served in the siege of Sūrat, and in the following year, with Khān ʿĀlam (No 58) in the conquest of Patna under Munʿim. For some reason he returned to Court, and took Shujāʿat Khān (No. 51) a prisoner to Munʿim, whom he had slandered. In the 22nd year, he served under Ṣādiq (No. 43) against Madhukar Bundela, and in the 25th year, under ʿAzīz Koka (No. 21) in Bihār. In the 26th year, he was employed to settle the affairs of Ḥājī Begam, daughter of the brother of Humāyūn's mother (*taghāʾī zāda-yi wālida-yi Jannat-āstānī*), who after her return from Makkah (see under 146) had been put in charge of Humāyūn's tomb in Dihlī, where she died. In the 31st year, when Akbar appointed two officers for each Ṣūba, Q. A. and Fatḥ Khān Tughluq were sent to Audh. He returned, in the 35th year, from Khayrābād to Court, and soon after received Kālpī as jāgīr. "Nothing also is known of him."[1] *Maʾāṣir.* For his brother, *vide* No. 390.

188. **Bāz Bahādur,** son of Sharīf Khān (No. 63).

Vide above, p. 415.

189. **Sayyid ʿAbdᵘ 'llāh,** son of Mīr Khwānanda.

Some MSS. have "Khwānd" instead of "Khwānanda." Sayyid ʿAbdᵘ 'llāh had been brought up at Court. In the 9th year, he served in the pursuit of ʿAbdᵘ 'llāh Khān Uzbak. In the 17th year, he was with the Khān-i Kalān (No. 16) in the first Gujrāt war. Later, he served under Munʿim in Bengal, and was with Khān ʿĀlam (No. 58) in the battle of Takaroī (p. 406). In 984, he brought the news of Dāʾūd's defeat and death at Āgmaḥal (p. 350) to Akbar. During the Bengal military revolt, he served under Mīrzā ʿAzīz (No. 21) and under Shāhbāz Khān (No. 80), chiefly against Maʿṣūm-i Farankhūdī (No. 157). In the 31st year, Akbar sent him to Qāsim Khān (No. 59) in Kashmīr. In the 34th year (997), he was one night surprised by a body of Kashmīrīs, and killed with nearly three hundred Imperialists.

190. **Dhārū,** son of Rāja Toḍar Mal (No. 39).

Vide above, p. 378.

191. **Ahmad Beg-i Kābulī.**

Aḥmad Beg traces his origin to Mīr Ghiyāṣᵘ 'd'Dīn Tarkhān, a Chaghtāʾī noble who served under Tīmūr. Like Shāh Beg (No. 57), Tāj Khān

---

[1] Sayyid Aḥmad's edition of the *Tuzuk* mentions a Qāsim ʿAlī on p. 58, l. 2 from below; but according to the *Maʾāṣir*, we have there to read *Qāsim Beg* for *Qāsim ʿAlī*.

(No. 172), Abū 'l-Qāsim (No. 199), Maˁṣūm Khān (p. 476, note 1), and Takhta Beg (No. 195), A. B. entered, after M. Muḥammad Ḥakīm's death, Akbar's service. He was made a commander of 700, and received, in 1003, on the removal of Yūsuf Khān-i Raẓawī (No. 35), a jāgīr in Kashmīr. He married the sister of Jaˁfar Beg Āṣaf Khān. (No. 98).

During the reign of Jahāngīr he rose to the post of a commander of 3,000, and received the title of *Khān*, and also a flag. He was for some time governor of Kashmīr. On his removal, he went to Court, and died.

From the *Tuzuk* we see that Aḥmad Beg in the first year of Jahāngīr was made a commander of 2,000, and held Peshāwar as jāgīr. In the second year he was ordered to punish the Afghān tribes in Bangash, and was for his services there promoted, in the 5th year, to a command of 2,500. In the 9th year, in consequence of complaints made by Qulij Khān (No. 42), he was called to Court, and confined to Fort Rantanbhūr (*Tuzuk*, p. 136). In the following year, he was released (*l.c.*, p. 146) and sent to Kashmīr (*l.c.*, p. 149).

Aḥmad Beg's sons, especially his second eldest, were all distinguished soldiers. They are :—

1. *Muḥammad Masˁūd* [1] (eldest son). He was killed in the war with the Tārīkīs. His son, Ardsher, was a commander of 1,000, six hundred horse, and died in the 18th year of Shāhj.'s reign.

2. *Saˁīd Khān Bahādur Ẓafar-jang* (second son). He rose during the reign of Shāhjahān to the high dignity of a commander of 7,000, and distinguished himself in every war. He was governor of Kābul, the Panjāb, and Bihār. He died on the 2nd Ṣafar, 1062. Of his twenty-two sons, the two eldest, Khānazād Khān and Luṭfᵘ 'llāh, were killed in the Balkh war, where Saˁīd also was severely wounded. Two other sons, ˁAbdᵘ 'llāh and Fatḥᵘ 'llāh, rose to high commands.

3. *Mukhliṣᵘ 'llāh Khān Iftikhār Khān*. He rose under Shāhjahān to a command of 2,000, one thousand horse, and was Fawjdār of Jammū (*Pādishāhn.*, I, p. 258), and died in the 4th year of Shāhj.'s reign.

4. *Abū 'l-Baqā*. He was the younger brother (by the same mother) of Saˁīd, under whom he served. He was thānadār of Lower Bangash. In the 15th year, after the Qandahār expedition, he got the title of *Iftikhār Khān*, at the same time that his elder brother received that of *Ẓafar-jang*, and was made a commander of 1,500, one thousand horse.

192. **Ḥakīm ˁAlī, of Gīlān.**

ˁAlī came poor and destitute from Persia to India, but was fortunate

[[1] Mentioned Tuzuk, p. 307.—B.]

enough to become in course of time a personal attendant (*mulāzim*) and friend of Akbar. Once the emperor tried him by giving him several bottles of urine of sick and healthy people, and even of animals. To his satisfaction, ʿAlī correctly distinguished the different kinds. In 988, he was sent as ambassador to ʿAlī ʿĀdil Shāh of Bījāpūr, and was well received; but before he could be sent back with presents for his master, ʿĀdil Shāh suddenly died.[1]

In the 39th year, Ḥakīm ʿAlī constructed the wonderful reservoir (*ḥawẓ*), which is so often mentioned by Mughul historians. A staircase went to the bottom of the reservoir, from where a passage led to an adjoining small room, six *gaz* square, and capable of holding ten or twelve people. By some contrivance, the water of the reservoir was prevented from flowing into the chamber. When Akbar dived to the bottom of the reservoir and passed into the room, he found it lighted up and furnished with cushions, sleeping apparel, and a few books. Breakfast was also provided.

In the 40th year, ʿAlī was a commander of 700, and had the title of *Jālīnūsᵘ 'z-Zamānī*, "the Galenus of the age." His astringent mixtures enjoyed a great reputation at Court.

He treated Akbar immediately before his death. It is said that the Emperor died of dysentery or acute diarrhœa, which no remedies could stop. ʿAlī had at last recourse to a most powerful astringent, and when the dysentery was stopped, costive fever and strangury ensued. He therefore administered purgatives, which brought back the diarrhœa, of which Akbar died. The first attack was caused, it is said, by worry and excitement on account of the behaviour of Prince Khusraw at an elephant fight. Salīm (Jahāngīr) had an elephant of the name of *Girānbār*, who was a match for every elephant of Akbar's stables, but whose strength was supposed to be equal to that of *Ābrūp*, one of Khusraw's elephants. Akbar therefore wished to see them fight for the championship, which was done. According to custom, a third elephant, *Rantahman*, was selected as *ṭabāncha*, i.e., he was to assist either of the two combatants when too severely handled by the other. At the fight, Akbar and Prince Khurram (Shāhjahān) sat at a window, whilst Salīm and Khusraw were on horseback in the arena. Girānbār completely worsted Ābrūp, and as he mauled

---

[1] ʿĀdil Shāh was murdered in 988 by a young handsome eunuch, whom he attempted to use for an immoral purpose. The king was known as much for his justice and goodwill towards his subjects as for his mania for boys and unnatural crimes. He obtained with some exertion two young and handsome eunuchs from Malik Barīd of Bedar, and was stabbed by the elder of the two at the first attempt of satisfying his inordinate desires. Mawlānā Raẓā of Mashhad, poetically styled Raẓāī, found the *tarīkh* of his death in the words *Shāh-i jāhān shud shahīd* (988), "The king of the world became a martyr."

him too severely, the *tabāncha* elephant was sent off to Ābrūp's assistance. But Jahāngīr's men, anxious to have no interference, pelted Rantahman with stones, and wounded the animal and the driver. This annoyed Akbar, and he sent Khurram to Salīm to tell him not to break the rules, as in fact all elephants would once be his. Salīm said that the pelting of stones had never had his sanction, and Khurram, satisfied with the explanation, tried to separate the elephants by means of fireworks, but in vain. Unfortunately Rantahman also got worsted by Girānbār, and the two injured elephants ran away, and threw themselves into the Jamna. This annoyed Akbar more; but his excitement was intensified, when at that moment Khursaw came up, and abused in unmeasured terms his father in the presence of the emperor. Akbar withdrew, and sent next morning for ʿAlī, to whom he said that the vexation caused by Khursaw's bad behaviour had made him ill.

In the end of 1017, Jajāngīr also visited ʿAlī's reservoir, and made him a commander of 2,000. He did not long enjoy his promotion, and died on the 5th Muḥarram, 1018. Jahāngīr says of him (*Tuzuk*, p. 74) that he excelled in Arabic, and composed a commentary to the *Qānūn*. "But his subtlety was greater than his knowledge, his looks better than his walk of life, his behaviour better than his heart; for in reality he was a bad and unprincipled man." Once Jahāngīr hinted that ʿAlī had killed Akbar. On the other side it is said that he spent annually 6,000 Rupees on medicines for the poor[1]

He had a son, known as *Ḥakīm ʿAbdᵘ 'l-Wahhāb*. He held a *manṣab*. In the 15th year of Jahāngīr's reign, he claimed from certain Sayyids in Lāhor the sum of 80,000 Rs., which, he said, his father had lent them. He supported his claim by a certificate with the seal of a Qāẓī on it, and the statements of two witnesses. The Sayyids, who denied all knowledge, seeing that the case went against them, appealed to the Emperor. Jahāngīr ordered Āṣaf Khān (No. 98) to investigate the case. ʿAbdᵘ 'l-Wahhāb got afraid, and tried to evade the investigation by proposing to the Sayyids a compromise. This looked suspicious, and Āṣaf by cross-questioning found that the claim was entirely false. He therefore reported ʿAbdᵘ 'l-Wahhāb, and the Emperor deprived him of his manṣab and jāgīr. He seems to have been afterwards restored to favour, for in the *Pādishāh-nāma* (I, 6, 328) he is mentioned as a commander of 500, fifty horse.

---

[1] *Badā,onī* (III, 166) says that ʿAlī was the son of the sister of Ḥakīmᵘ 'l-Mulk of Gīlān, and learned medicine and science under Shāh Fatḥᵘ 'llāh of Shīrāz. He was a rabid Shīʿah, and a bad doctor who often killed his patients. Thus he killed Fatḥᵘ 'llāh by prescribing *harīsa* (*vide* p. 3[illegible], note). [*Harīsa* is said to be some concoction of meat and wheat.—P.]

193. **Gūjar Khān**, son of Quṭbu 'd-Dīn Khān Atga (No. 28).

He was mentioned above under No. 28.

194. **Ṣadr Jahān Muftī.**

Mīrān Ṣadr Jahān was born in Pihānī, a village near Qanawj.[1] Through the influence of Shaykh ʿAbdu 'n-Nabī he was made *Muftī*. When ʿAbdu 'llāh Khān Uzbak, king of Tūrān, wrote to Akbar regarding his apostacy from Islām, Mīrān Ṣadr and Ḥakīm (No. 205) were selected as ambassadors. The answer which they took to ʿAbdu 'llāh contained a few Arabic verses which ʿAbdu 'llāh could construe into a denial of the alleged apostacy—

قيل ان الاله ذو ولد   قيل. ان الرسول قد كهنا

ما نجا الله والرسول معا   من لسان الوري فكيف انا

"Of God people have said that He had a son; of the Prophet some have said that he was a sorcerer. Neither God nor the Prophet has escaped the slander of men—Then how should I ?"

Mīrān returned in the 34th year, and was made *Ṣadr* (*vide* p. 284). In the 35th year, at the feast of Ābānmāh, the Court witnessed a curious spectacle. The Ṣadr and ʿAbdu 'l-Ḥay (No. 230), the Chief Justice of the empire, took part in a drinking feast, and Akbar was so amused at seeing his ecclesiastical and judicial dignitaries over their cups, that he quoted the well-known verse from Hāfiz :—

در دور پادشاه خطابخش جرم پوش حافظ قرابه کش شد و مفتي پياله‌نوش

Up to the 40th year, he had risen to the dignity of a commander of 700 ; but later, he was made an Amīr, and got a manṣab of 2,000 (*vide* p. 217–18).

During the reign of Jahāngīr, who was very fond of him, he was promoted to a command of 4,000, and received Qanawj as *tuyūl*. As Ṣadr under Jahāngīr he is said to have given away more lands in five years than under Akbar in fifty. He died in 1020, at the age, it is believed, of 120 years. His faculties remained unimpaired to the last.

His position to Akbar's "Divine Faith" has been explained above (p. 217–18). There is no doubt that he temporized, and few people got more for it than he. He also composed poems, though in the end of his life, like Badā,onī, he repented and gave up poetry as being against the spirit of the Muhammadan law.

He had two sons :—

1. *Mīr Badr-i ʿĀlam.* He lived a retired life.
2. *Sayyid Niẓām Khān.* His mother was a Brāhman woman, of

---

[1] So Badā,onī. The *Maʾāṣir* says, Pihānī lies near Lakhnau.

whom his father had been so enamoured that he married her; hence Niẓām was his favourite son. He was early introduced at Court, and, at the death of his father, was made a commander of 2,500, two thousand horse. In the first year of Shāhjahān's reign, he was promoted to a command of 3,000, and received, on the death of Murtaẓā Khān Injū (p. 501) the title of *Murtaẓā Khān*. He served a long time in the Dakhin. His *tuyūl* was the Pargana of Dalamau, where he on several occasions successfully quelled disturbances. He was also Fawjdār of Lakhnau. In the 24th year of Shāhj.'s reign he was pensioned off, and received 20 lacs of dāms *per annum* out of the revenue of Pihānī, which was one kror. He enjoyed his pension for a long time.

His sons died before him. On his death, his grandsons, ˁAbdᵘ 'l-Muqtadir and ˁAbdᵘ 'llāh were appointed to manṣabs, and received as *tuyūl* the remaining portion of the revenue of Pihānī. ˁAbdᵘ 'l-Muqtadir rose to a command of 1,000, six hundred horse, and was Fawjdār of Khayrābād.

195. **Takhta Beg-i** Kābulī [Sardār Khān].

He was at first in the service of M. Muḥammad Ḥakīm, and distinguished himself in the wars with India; but on the death of his master (30th year) he joined Akbar's service. He served under Mān Singh and Zayn Koka against the Yūsufzāīs. As Thānahdār of Peshāwar he punished on several occasions the Tārīkīs. In the 49th year, he was made a *Khān*.

After Jahāngīr's accession, he was made a commander of 2,000, and received the title of *Sardār Khān*. He was sent with Mīrzā Ghāzī Tarkhān (p. 392), to relieve Shāh Beg Khān (No. 57) in Qandahār. As Shāh Beg was appointed governor of Kābul, Takhta was made governor of Qandahār, where, in 1016, he died.

He had a villa near Peshāwar, called the *Bāgh-i Sardār Khān*. His two sons, Ḥayāt Khān and Hidāyatᵘ 'llāh got low manṣabs.

196. **Ray Patr Dās** [Rāja Bikramājīt], a Khatrī.

Patr Dās was in the beginning of Akbar's reign accountant (*mushrif*) of the elephant stables, and had the title of *Rāy Rāyān*. He distinguished himself, in the 12th year, during the siege of Chītor. In the 24th year, he and Mīr Adham were made joint dīwāns of Bengal. At the outbreak of the Bengal military revolt, he was imprisoned by the rebels (p. 485), but got off and served for some time in Bengal. In the 30th year, he was made dīwān of Bihār. In the 38th year, he was ordered to occupy Bāndhū (p. 446), the capital of which after a siege of 8 months and 25 days surrendered (42nd year). In the 43rd year, he was made dīwān of Kābul, but was in the following year again sent to Bāndhū. In the 46th year, he was made a commander of 3,000. When Abū 'l-Faẓl, in the 47th year, had been murdered by Bīr Singh, Akbar ordered Patr Dās to hunt down the rebel, and bring his head to Court. Patr defeated Bīr Singh in several engagements, and blockaded him in Īrich. When the siege had progressed, and a breach was made in the wall, Bīr Singh eṣcaped and withdrew to the jungles with Patr close at his heels. Akbar, at last, in the 48th year, called P. to Court, made him in the next year a commander of 5,000, and gave him the title of Rāja Bikramājīt.

After Jahāngīr's accession, he was made *Mīr Ātash,* and was ordered to recruit and keep in readiness 50,000 artillery (*topchī*) with a train of 3,000 gun-carts, the revenue of fifteen parganas being set aside for the maintenance of the corps (*Tuzuk*, p. 10).

When the sons of Muẓaffar of Gujrāt created disturbances, and Yatīm Bahādur had been killed, Patr was sent to Aḥmadābād with powers to appoint the officers of the rebels who submitted up to commands of Yūzbāshīs, or to recommend them, if they had held higher commands, for appointments to the Emperor.

" The year of his death is not known." *Maᶜāṣir.*

The Rāy Mohan Dās mentioned occasionally in the *Akbarnāma* and the *Tuzuk* (p. 50) appears to be his son.

197. **Shaykh ᶜAbdᵘ 'r-Raḥīm,** of Lakhnau.

He belongs to the Shaykhzādas of Lakhnau, and was in the 40th year a commander of 700. He was a great friend of Jamāl Bakhtyār (No. 113), from whom he learned wine-drinking. In fact he drank so hard that he frequently got insane. In the 30th year, when Akbar was in the Panjāb, ᶜAbdᵘ 'r-Raḥīm wounded himself in a fit whilst at Siyālkoṭ in Ḥakīm Abū 'l-Fatḥ's dwelling. Akbar looked after the wound himself.

His wife was a Brāhman woman of the name of Kishnā. After the death of her husband, she spent his money in laying out gardens and villas. In one of them her husband was buried, and she entertained every one who passed by the tomb, from a *panjhazārī* to a common soldier, according to his position in life.

ᶜAbdᵘ 'r-Raḥīm was mentioned above on p. 359–60.

198. **Mednī Rāy Chauhān.**

From the *Akbarnāma* we see that he served, in the 28th and 32nd years, in Gujrāt. Niẓāmᵘ 'd-Dīn Aḥmad, who was with him in Gujrāt, says in the *Ṭabqāt*—" Mednī Rāy is distinguished for his bravery and liberality, and is now (i.e., in 1001) a commander of 1,000."

199. **Mīr Abū 'l-Qāsim Namakīn** [Qāsim Khān].

The MSS. have almost invariably *Tamkīn* (تمکین) instead of *Namakīn*. He is not to be confounded with Nos. 240 and 250.

Mīr Abū 'l-Qāsim was a Sayyid of Hirāt. He was at first in the service of Mīrzā Muḥammad Ḥakīm, Akbar's brother and king of Kābul. But he left Kābul, and on entering Akbar's service, he received Bhīra and Khushāb in the Punjāb as jāgīr. As his lands lay within the *Namaksār*,[1] or salt range, he once presented Akbar, evidently in allusion to his faithful intentions (*namak-ḥalālī*), with a plate and a cup made of salt (*namakīn*), from which circumstance he received the nickname of *Namakīn*.

Abū 'l-Qāsim served in the war with Dā'ūd of Bengal. In the 26th year, he was in Kābul, and accompanied, in the 30th year, Ismāʿīl Qulī Khān (No. 46) on his expedition against the Balūchīs. In the 32nd year, the Afghān chiefs of Sawād and Bajor, and Terāh waited with their families on Akbar, who made Abū 'l-Qāsim Krorī and Fawjdār of those districts, and ordered him to take the families of the chiefs back to Afghānistān. The chiefs themselves were retained at Court. Renewed fights, in the 33rd year, gave him frequent occasions of distinguishing himself.

Up to the 40th year, he rose to a command of 700. In the 43rd year, he was appointed to Bhakkar. He built the great mosque in Sukkhar, opposite to Bhakkar. The inhabitants accused him of oppressions, and he was deposed. A party of the oppressed arrived with him at Court, and lodged a new complaint against him with ʿAbdu 'l-Ḥay (No. 230), the Qāẓī of the imperial camp (*urdū*). But Abū 'l-Qāsim, though summoned, did not appear before the judge, and when the matter was reported to Akbar, he was sentenced to be tied to the foot of an elephant, and paraded through the bazars. To avoid the disgrace, he came to an immediate settlement with the complainants, chiefly through the mediation of Shaykh Maʿrūf, Ṣadr of Bhakkar, and prevailed on them to return the very day to their homes The next day he went to the Emperor, and complained of the Qāẓī, stating that there were no complainants, and ʿAbdu 'l-Ḥay tried in vain to produce the oppressed parties. This case led to the order that Qāẓīs should in future prepare descriptive rolls of complainants, and present them to the Emperor.

---

[1] The *namaksār*, or salt-range, says the *Ma'āṣir*, is a district 20 *kos* long, and belongs to the Sind Sāgar Du,āb, between the Bahat and the Indus. People break off pieces from the salt rocks, and carry them to the banks of the river, where the price is divided between the miners and the carriers, the former taking ¾ and the latter ¼ of the amount realized. Merchants buy the salt at a price varying from half a dām to two dāms (one rupee = 40 dāms) per *man*, and export it. The Government takes 1 Rupee for every 17 *mans*. The salt is also often made into ornaments.

Abū 'l-Qāsim was, soon after, made a Khān, got a higher manṣab, and received Gujrāt in the Panjāb as *tuyūl*. In the first year of Jahāngīr's reign, he was made a commander of 1,500. The part which he played in the capture of Prince Khusraw has been mentioned above (p. 456, note 1, where *Tamkīn* is to be altered to *Namakīn*). For his services he was again appointed to Bkakkar with the rank of a commander of 3,000. He now resolved to make Bhakkar his home. Most of his illustrious descendants were born there. On a hill near the town, southwards towards Loharī, near the branch of the river called *Kahārmātrī* (کہار,ماتری), he built a mausoleum, to which he gave the name of *Ṣuffa-yi Ṣafā* (the dais of purity). He and several of his descendants were buried in it.

He is said to have been a most voracious man. He could eat—historians do not specify the time—1,000 mangoes, 1,000 sweet apples, and 2 melons, each weighing a *man*. The *Maʿāṣir* says, he had 22 sons, and the *Tuzuk* (p. 13) says he had 30 sons and more than 15 daughters.

The following tree is compiled from several notes in the *Maʿāṣir*:—

Mīr Abū 'l-Qāsim Namakīn (settled at Bhakkar in 1015).

- 1. Mīr Abū 'l-Baqā. Amīr Khān. (died 1057 A.H.)
  - 1. M. ʿAbd^{u} 'r-Razzāq.
  - 2. Ziyāʾ^{u} 'd-Dīn Yūsuf. Khān.
    - A son.
      - M. Abū 'l-Wafā. (end of Awrangzīb's reign).
  - 3. Mīr ʿAbd^{u} 'l-Karīm Sindhī Amīr Khān. (under Awrangzīb to Farrukh Siyar).
    - Abū 'l-Khayr Khān. (under Farrukh Siyar).
  - A daughter, married in 1066 to Prince Murād Bakhsh.
- 2. Mirzā Kashmīrī.
- 3. M. Ḥusām^{u} 'd-Dīn.
- 4 M. Zāid^{u} 'llāh.

Mīr Abū 'l-Baqā Amīr Khān rose under Jahāngīr to a command of 2,500, fifteen hundred horse. Through the influence of Yamīn^{u} 'd-Dawla he was made governor of Multān, and in the 2nd year of Shāhjahān, he was made a commander of 3,000, two thousand horse, and appointed to Thathah, *vice* Murtaẓā-yi Injū deceased (p. 501). In the 9th year, he was made Tuyūldār of Bīr in the Dakhin, and was sent, in the 14th year, to Sīwistān *vice* Qarāq Khān. In the following year he was again appointed to Thathah, where, in 1057 (20th year), he died. He was buried in the mausoleum built by his father. Under Jahāngīr he was generally called Mīr Khān. Shāhjahān gave him the title of Amīr Khān.

One of his daughters was married in 1066, after his death, to Prince Murād Bakhsh, who had no children by his first wife, a daughter of

Shāhnawāz Khān-i Ṣafawī.[1] Amīr Khān had a large family. His eldest son, Mīr ʿAbdᵘ r'Razzāq, was a commander of 900, and died in the 26th year of Shāhjahān's reign. His second son, Ẓiyāʾᵘ 'd-Dīn Yūsuf, was made a Khān, and held under Shāhjahān a manṣab of 1,000, six hundred horse. Ẓiyāʾ's grandson, Abū 'l-Wafā, was in the end of Awrangzīb's reign in charge of his majesty's prayer room (*dārogha-yi jā-namāz*). Amīr Khān's youngest son, Mīr ʿAbdᵘ 'l-Karīm, was a personal friend of Awrangzīb. He received in succession the titles of Multafit Khān, Khānazād Khān (45th year of Awrangzīb), Mīr Khānazād Khān, and Amīr Khān (48th year), and held a command of 3,000. After Awrangzīb's death, he was with Muḥammad Aʿẓam Shāh ; but as he had no contingent, he was left with the baggage (*bungāh*) at Gwāliyār. After the death of Muḥammad Aʿẓam in the battle of Sarāy Jājū,[2] Bahādur Shāh made him a commander of 3,500. He was generally at Court, and continued so under Farrukh Siyar. After Farrukh's death, the Bārha brothers made Amīr Khān *ṣadr* of the empire. He died shortly after. His son, Abū 'l-Khayr, was made a Khān by Farrukh Siyar ; the other sons held no manṣabs, but lived on their zamīndārīs.

2. *Mīrzā Kashmīrī* was involved in the rebellion of Prince Khusraw. As the associates were to be punished in an unusual way (*siyāsat-i ghayr-mukarrar, Tuzuk*, p. 32) Jahāngīr ordered his *penis* to be cut off.

3. *Mīrzā Husānᵘ 'd-Dīn.* He held a manṣab, but died young.

4. *Mīrzā Zāʾidᵘ 'llāh.* He was in the service of Khān Jahān Lodī.

200. **Wazīr Beg Jamīl.**[3]

Wazīr Jamīl, as he is often called, served in the 9th year of Akbar's reign against ʿAbdᵘ 'llāh Khān Uzbak, and in the war with Khān Zamān (No. 13). In the final battle, when Bahādur Khān (No. 22) was thrown off his horse, W. J., instead of taking him prisoner, accepted a bribe from him, and let him off. But Naẓar Bahādur, a man in the service of Majnūn Khān (No. 50) saw it, and took Bahādur prisoner. Afterwards, he received a jāgīr in the Eastern Districts, and took part in the expeditions to Bengal and Orīsā under Munʿim Khān. At the outbreak of the Bengal military revolt, he joined the Qāqshāls ; but when they separated from Maʿṣūm-i

---

[1] Shahnawāz Khān-i Ṣafawī is the title of Mīrzā Badīʿᵘ 'z-Zamān, *alias* Mīrzā Dakhinī, son of Mīrzā Rustam (No. 9). One of his daughters, Dilras Bānū Begum, was married, in the end of 1046, to Awrangzīb. Another was married, in 1052, to Prince Murād Bakhsh. Elphinstone (*History of India*, 5th edition, p. 607) calls Shahnawāz Khān by mistake the brother of Shāyista Khān ; but Shāyista is the son of Yamīnᵘ 'd-Dawla Āṣaf Khān, elder brother of Nūr Jahān.

[2] Sarāy Jājū, near Dholpūr. The battle was fought on the 18th Rabīʿ I, 1119, and Muḥammad Aʿẓam was killed with his two sons, Bedar Bakht and Wālā-jāh.

[3] Jamīl is a common name among Turks. It is scarcely ever used in Hindūstān.

Kābulī (p. 476, note) and tendered their submission, W. J. also was pardoned. In the 29th year, he came to Court, and served in the following year under Jagnāth (No. 69) against the Rānā. He seems to have lived a long time. Jahāngīr, on his accession, made him a commander of 3,000 (*Tuzuk*, p. 8.).

He is not to be confounded with the Jamīl Beg mentioned under No. 172.

201. **Ṭāhir,** [son of] Sayf^{u} 'l-Mulūk.

The *Ṭabaqāt* says that Ṭāhir was the son of Shāh Muḥammad Sayf^{u} 'l-Mulūk.[1] His father was governor of G͟harjistān in K͟hurāsān, and was killed by Shāh Ṭahmāsp of Persia. Ṭāhir went to India, was made an Amīr at Akbar's Court, and served in Bengal, where he was when the author of the Ṭabaqāt wrote (1001).

He is also mentioned in Dowson's Edition of *Elliot's Historians*, I, pp. 241, 242.

202. **Bābū Manklī.**

Regarding the name "Manklī", *vide* p. 400, note 1. The *Ṭabaqāt* says that Bābū Manklī was an Afg͟hān, and a commander of 1,000.

He was at first in Dāᶜūd's service, and occupied Ghorāghāt at the time when Munᶜim K͟hān had invaded Oṛīsā (p. 400). Soon after, he entered Akbar's service, but continued to be employed in Bengal. In the 30th year, he suppressed disturbances at Ghorāghāt (*Akbarn.* III, 470), and took part, in the 35th year, in the operations against Qutlū K͟hān. Two years later he accompanied Mān Singh's expedition to Oṛīsā.

He may have lived under Jahāngīr; for the Manklī K͟hān mentioned in the *Tuzuk* (pp. 70, 138) can only refer to him. The *Tuzuk* (p. 12) mentions a son of his, Ḥātim. Another son, Maḥmūd, appears to have been a commander of 500, three hundred horse, under Shāhjahān (*Pādishāhn.*, I, b., p. 323) though the text edition of the *Bibl. Indica* calls him *son of Yābū Maikalī* (يابو ميكلي, for بابو منكلي).

XVI. Commanders of Six Hundred.

203. **Muḥammad Qulī K͟hān Turkmān** [*Afshār*, p. 452].

He served at first in Bengal. At the outbreak of the military revolt, he took the side of the rebels, but left them, and was pardoned by Akbar. In the 30th year, he marched with Mān Singh to Kābul, where he greatly distinguished himself. In the 39th year, when Qulij K͟hān (No. 42) was

[[1] *Vide* No. 401.—B.]

appointed to Kābul, Muḥammad Qulī Khān, his brother Hamza Beg (perhaps No. 277), and others, were sent to Kashmīr, *vice* Yūsuf Khān (No. 35, and p. 452). In the 45th year, a party of Kasmīrīs tried to set up Ambā Chak[1] as king; but they were defeated by ʿAlī Qulī, son of M. Q. Kh. In the 47th year, M. Q. Kh. was made a commander of 1,500, six hundred horse; and Hamza Beg, one of 700, three hundred and fifty horse. New disturbances broke out when in the following year ʿAlī Rāy, king of Little Tibet, invaded the frontier districts of Kashmīr. He retreated on M. Q. Kh.'s arrival, and was vigorously pursued, when the imperialists were enforced by Sayfu 'llāh (No. 262) from Lāhor. In the 49th year, Ambā again appeared, but was driven, with some difficulty, from his mountains.

In the 2nd year of Jahāngīr's reign, M. Q. Kh. was removed from Kashmīr. Hamza Beg was, in the 49th year of Akbar's reign, a commander of 1,000.

204. **Bakhtyār Beg Gurd-i Shāh Manṣūr.**

The *Iẓāfat* most likely means that he was the son of Shāh Manṣūr, in which case the word *gurd* (athlete) would be Bakhtyār's epithet. Two MSS. have the word *pisar* (son) instead of *gurd*.

The *Ṭabaqāt* says: "Bakhtyār Beg Turkmān is an Amīr, and governs at present (1001) Sīwistān." In the 32nd year, he served against the Tārīkīs.

205. **Ḥakīm Ḥumām,**[2] son of Mīr ʿAbdu 'r-Razzāq of Gīlān.

Regarding his family connection, *vide* No. 112, p. 468. Ḥumām's real name is Humāyūn. When he came to Akbar's Court, he discreetly called himself Humāyūn Qulī, or "slave of Humāyūn"; but soon afterwards Akbar gave him the name of Ḥumām. He held the office of Bakāwal Beg (p. 59), and though only a commander of 600, he was a personal friend of Akbar, and possessed great influence at Court. In the 31st year he was sent with Ṣadr Jahān (No. 194) to Tūrān as ambassador. Akbar often said that he did not enjoy his meals on account of Ḥumām's absence. He returned to India about a month after his brother's death. He died in the 40th year, on the 6th Rabīʿ I, 1004. *Badā,onī* (II, p. 406) says, the day after Ḥumām's death, Kamālā (p. 264) also died, and their property was at once put under seal and escheated to the government, so that they were destitute of a decent shroud.

---

[1] The MSS. have انبا. The *Tuzuk* mentions "a Kashmīrī of royal blood", of the name of انبه. He was killed by Sher Afkan (*vide* No. 394) at Bardwān, on the 3rd Ṣafar, 1016.
[2] Humām, not Hammām, is the Indian pronunciation.

Ḥumām had two sons :—

1. *Ḥakim Ḥāẕiq* (حاذق). He was born at Fatḥpūr Sīkrī, and was a young man when his father died. At Shāhjahān's accession, he was made a commander of 1,500, six hundred horse, and was sent, in the 1st year, to Tūrān as ambassador. He rose to a command of 3,000. Later, for some reason, his manṣab was cancelled, and he lived at Āgra on a pension of 20,000 rupees *per annum*, which in the 18th year was doubled. He died in the 31st year (1068).[1] He was a poet of some distinction, and wrote under the name of *Ḥāẕiq*. His vanity is said to have been very great. A copy of his dīwān was kept on a golden stool in his reception room, and visitors, when it was brought in or taken away, were expected to rise and make salāms ; else he got offended.

2. *Ḥakīm Khushʿḥāl*. He grew up with Prince Khurram. Shāhjahān, on his accession, made him a commander of 1,000. He was for some time Bakhshī of the Dakhin.

206. **Mīrzā Anwar**, son of Khān-i Aʿẓam Mīrzā Koka (No. 21).

He was mentioned above on page 346.

XVII. Commanders of Five Hundred.

207. **Baltū Khān** of Turkistān.

He was a grandee of Humāyūn, and served in the Kābul war, and in the battles which led to H.'s restoration.

208. **Mīrak Bahādur Arghūn.**

The *Ṭabaqāt* says he reached a command of 2,000, and died.[2] From the *Akbarnāma* (II, 170, 248) we see that he served in the conquest of Mālwa (*vide* No. 120) and in the pursuit of Sharafᵘ 'd-Dīn Ḥusayn (No. 17).

209. **Laʿl Khān Kolābī.**

He is also called Laʿl Khān *Badakhshī* (*vide* p. 484), and served under Humāyūn in the war of the restoration (*Akbarn.* I, 411). He distinguished himself in the defeat of Hemū. Later, he served under Munʿim in Bengal and Oṛīsā, and died of fever at Gaur (p. 407).

210. **Shaykh Aḥmad,** son of Shaykh Salīm.

He is the second (*miyānī*) son of Shaykh Salīm of Fatḥpūr Sīkrī. He served at Court with Shaykh Ibrāhīm (No. 82), and died in the 22nd year (985).[3]

---

[1] The *Maʾāṣir* says that the author of the *Mir-ʾātᵘ 'l-ʿĀlam* mentions 1080 as the year of his death ; but my MS. of the *Mirʾ-āt* (Chapter on the poets of the period from Humāyūn to Awrangzīb) mentions no year.

[[2] Died in 975. He was blown up before Chitor ; *Sawāniḥ*, p. 201.—B.]

[[3] *Sawāniḥ*, p. 370.—B.]

211. **Iskandar Beg-i Badakhshī.**

He is mentioned in the *Akbarnāma* (II, 251) as having served in the pursuit of Abūl 'l-Maʿālī (end of the 8th year).

212. **Beg Nūrīn Khān Qūchīn.**

He served under Muʿizzᵘ 'l-Mulk (No. 61) in the battle of Khayrābād. In the 32nd and 33rd years, he served under ʿAbdᵘ 'l-Maṭlab (No. 83) and Ṣadīq Khān (No. 43) against the Tārīkīs.

The *Ṭabaqāt* says he was a commander of 1,000, and was dead in 1001.

213. **Jalāl Khān Qūrchi.**

Akbar was much attached to him. In the 7th year, he was sent to Rām Chand Bhagela (No. 89) with the request to allow Tānsīn to go to Court. In the 11th year, it came to the Emperor's ears that J. was passionately attached to a beautiful boy. Akbar had the boy removed; but J. managed to get him again, and fled with him from Court. M. Yūsuf Raẓawī pursued and captured them. After some time, J. was restored to favour. Later, he took a part in the expedition to Siwāna and distinguished himself, in the 20th year, in the war with Rāja Chandr Sen of Mārwār. During the expedition a Rājpūt introduced himself to him who pretended to be Devī Dās, who had been killed at Mīrtha, evidently with a view of obtaining through him an introduction to Court. The stranger also reported that Chandr Sen had taken refuge with Kallā, son of Rām Rāy, and brother's son to Ch. S., and a detachment of imperialists was sent to Kallā's palace. Kallā now wished to take revenge on the stranger for spreading false reports, and induced Shimāl Khān (No. 154) to help him. Shimāl therefore invited the stranger; but though surrounded by Sh.'s men, the pretender managed to escape. He collected a few men and entered one night a tent which he supposed to belong to Shimāl. But it happened to be that of Jalāl, who was cut down by the murderers (end of 983; *Akbarn.*, III, 140).

It was Jalāl who introduced the historian Badā,onī at Court.

214. **Parmānand**, the Khatrī.

He is mentioned in Dowson's edition of *Elliot's Historians*, I, p. 244.

215. **Tīmūr Khān Yakka.**

He served under Munʿim (No. 11) in Kābul, and, in the 10th year, against Khān Zamān (*Akbarn.*, II, 236, 326).

The Tīmūr-i Badakhshī mentioned several times in the *Akbarnāma* (III, 165, 174) appears to be another officer. *Vide* No. 142.

216. **Ṣānī Khān,** of Hirāt.

He was born at Hirāt, and belonged to the Arlāt (ارلات) clan. According to the *Akbarnāma* (I, 379), Mawlānā Ṣānī, "who is now called *Ṣānī*

Khān ", was in the service of Mīrzā Hindāl ; but after the Mīrzā's death (21st Zī Qaʿda, 958) he was taken on by Humāyūn. He served in the wars with Khān Zamān.

Badā,onī (III, 206) says that his real name was ʿAlī Akbar. He was a fair poet, but a heretic, and like Tashbīhī of Kāshān, wrote treatises on the Man of the Millennium, according to the Nuqṭawī doctrines (p. 502). Hence he must have been alive in 990.

217. **Sayyid Jamālᵘ 'd-Dīn**, son of Sayyid Aḥmad Bārha (No. 91).

Vide above, p. 447. He had also served in the final war with Khān Zamān.

218. **Jagmal**, the Pūwār.

He served in the second Gujrāt war after Akbar's forced march to Patan and Aḥmadābād (p. 458 note).

219. **Ḥusayn Beg**, brother of Ḥusayn Khān Buzurg.

220. **Ḥasan Khān Baṭanī.**[1]

The *Ṭabaqāt* classes him among the commanders of 1,000. He was at first in the service of the Bengal king Sulaymān, and was present with Sulaymān Manklī (p. 400) and Kālā Pahāṛ at the interview between Munʿim and Khān Zamān (No. 13) at Baksar (Buxar). *Akbarn.*, II, 325.

Ḥasan was killed with Bīr Baṛ in the Khaybar Pass ; *vide* p. 214. MSS. often call him wrongly *Ḥusayn* instead of *Ḥasan.*

221. **Sayyid Chhajhū,**[2] of Bārha.

The *Ṭabaqāt* says that S. Chhajhū was a brother of S. Maḥmūd (No. 75) and distinguished for his courage and bravery. From the family genealogies of the Bārha clan it appears that S. Ch. was a Kūndlīwāl. His tomb still exists at Majhera, and according to the inscription he died in 967.

222. **Munṣif Khān,** Sulṭān Muḥammad of Hirāt.

223. **Qāẓī Khān Bakhshī.**

Some MSS. have *Badakhshī* instead of *Bakhshī*. *Vide* No. 144.

224. **Ḥājī Yūsuf Khān.**

He was at first in Kāmrān's service. In the 12th year, he joined the corps of Qiyā Khān (No. 33), and rendered assistance to M. Yūsuf Khān, whom Khān Zamān (No. 13) besieged in Qanawj. In the 17th year, he operated under Khān ʿĀlam (No. 58) against M. Ibrāhīm Ḥusayn, and was present in the battle of Sarnāl. In the 19th year, he went with Munʿim to Bengal and Oṛīsā, and died after his return at Gaur (p. 407).

---

[1] *Baṭanī* is the name of an Afghān tribe, N.W. of Derā Ismāʿil Khān.
[2] The spelling " Chhajhū " is preferable to " Jhajhū ".

225. **Rāwul Bhīm**, of Jaisalmīr.

The *Tuzuk* says (p. 159):—"On the 9th Khurdād (middle of 1025), Kalyān of Jaisalmīr was introduced at Court by Rājā Kishn Dās, whom I had sent to him. Kalyān's elder brother was *Rāwul Bhīm*, a man of rank and influence. When he died, he left a son two months old, who did not live long. Bhīm's daughter had been married to me when I was prince, and I had given her the title of *Malika-yi Jahān*. This alliance was made, because her family had always been faithful to our house. I now called Bhīm's brother to Court, invested him with the *ṭīkā*, and made him Rāwul."[1]

For Kalyān, *vide* under No. 226. In the 12th year of Jahāngīr's reign he was made a commander of 2,000, one thousand horse (*Tuzuk*, p. 163).

226. **Hāshim Beg**, son of Qāsim Khān (No. 59).

After the death of his father (39th year) and the arrival of Qulij Khān (No. 42), the new governor of Kābul, Hāshim returned to Court. In the 41st year, he served under M. Rustam (No. 9) against Bāsū and other rebellious zamīndārs in the north-eastern part of the Panjāb, and distinguished himself in the conquest of Maụ. In the 44th year, he served under Farīd-i Bukhārī (No. 99) before Āsīr. Later, he went with Saʿādat Khān to Nāsik.[2] After the conquest of Tiranbak, he returned to Court (46th year), and was appointed, in the following year, to a command of 1,500.

In the first year of Jahāngīr's reign, he was made a commander of 2,000, fifteen hundred horse. In the 2nd year, his manṣab was increased to 3,000, two thousand horse, and he was made governor of Orīsā. In the 6th year, he was transferred to Kashmīr, his uncle Khwājāgī Muḥammad

[1] The list of Jahāngīr's wives on p. 323 may be increased by ten other princesses. (1) Malika-yi Jahān, daughter of Rāwul Bhīm of Jaisalmīr. (2) The beautiful daughter of Zayn Koka, mentioned on p. 369. There is a curious discrepancy between *Tuzuk*, p. 8, and *Akbarnāma*, III, 594: Jahāngīr says that Parwīz was his son by Zayn Koka's daughter, and Abū 'l-Faẓl says that Parwīz's mother was the daughter of Khwājah Ḥasan, Zayn Khān's uncle (*vide* also p. 367); but there is no doubt that Parwīz was born in the 34th year, on the 19th Ābān, 997, whilst Jahāngīr, only in the 41st year, fell in love with Zayn Khān's daughter (p. 369). It is therefore evident, assuming that Sayyid Aḥmad's text of *Tuzuk*, p. 8, be correct, that Jahāngīr had forgotten who among his many wives was mother to his second son. (3) Nūru 'n-Nisā Begum (married in Jumādha, II, 1000), sister of Mīrzā Muẓaffar Husayn, p. 464. (4) A daughter of the King of Khandesh. This princess died in the 41st year of Akbar's reign. (5) Ṣāliha Bānū, daughter of Qāʾim Khān, p. 401. (6) A daughter of Khwāja Jahān-i Kābulī (Dost Muḥammad). (7) A daughter of Saʿīd Khān Gakkhar. Her daughter, ʿIffat Bānū, is mentioned, *Akbarnāma*, III, 561. (8) The mother of Dawlat Nisā, *Akbarn.*, III, 597. The MSS. do not clearly give the name of the father of this princess. (9) A daughter of Mīrzā Sanjar, son of Khizr Khān Hazāra; *Akbarn.*, III, 607. (10) A daughter of Rām Chand Bundela (No. 248) married in 1018; *Tuzuk*, p. 77.

[2] This Saʿādat Khān had first been in the service of the Dākhin kings as commander of the Forts of Gālna and Tiranbak; but later he entered Akbar's service.

Ḥusayn (No. 241) officiating for him there till his arrival from Oṛīsā. His successor in Oṛīsā was Rāja Kalyān, brother of Bhīm (No. 225).

Hāshim's son is the renowned Muḥammad Qāsim K͟hān Mīr Ātish. He was, in the 18th year of Shāhjahān's, a commander of 1,000, five hundred and ninety horse. Dārog͟ha of the Topk͟hāna and Koṭwāl of the camp. He distinguished himself in Balk͟h, Andk͟hūd, received the title of Muʿtamid K͟hān,[1] and was made, in the 21st year, a commander of 2,000, one thousand horse, and Āk͟hta Begī. In the following year, he was promoted to a command of 3,000, and also got the title of Qāsim K͟hān. He then served under Awrangzīb in Qandahār, and was made, in the 28th year, a commander of 4,000, two thousand five hundred horse. In the next year, he destroyed Fort Sāntūr (سانتور), which the ruler of Srīnagar had repaired. Later, he was made by Dārā Shikoh a commander of 5,000, five thousand sihaspa-duaspa, received a present of a lac of rupees, and was appointed governor of Aḥmadābād (Gujrāt), whilst Jaswant Singh was made governor of Mālwa. Both were ordered to unite their contingents near Ujjain, and keep Prince Murād Bak͟hsh in check. When the Prince left Gujrāt, the two commanders marched against him *viâ* Bāswāra; but when approaching Khāchrod, Murād suddenly retreated 18 *kos*, and joined, 7 *kos* from Ujjain, the army of Awrangzīb. The two chiefs had received no information of Awrangzīb's march. They attacked him, however, but were totally defeated (near Ujjain, 22nd Rajab, 1068). In the first battle between Awṛangzīb and Dārā, at Samogar,[2] Qāsim commanded the left wing. Soon after, he made his submission, and received Sambhal and Murādādād as *tuyūl*, as Rustam K͟hān-i Dakhinī, the former jāgīrdār, had fallen at Samogar. Qāsim was then charged with the capture of Sulaymān Shikoh. In the 3rd year of Awrangzīb's reign he was appointed to Mathurā. On the way, he was murdered by a brother of his, who is said to have led a miserable life (1071). The murderer was executed at Awrangzīb's order.

227. **Mīrzā Farīdūn**, son of Muḥammad Qulī K͟hān Barlās (No. 31). He has been mentioned above, p. 364. His death took place at Udaipūr in 1023 (*Tuzuk*, p. 131).

228. **Yūsuf K͟hān** [Chak], king of Kashmīr.

Yūsuf's father was ʿAlī K͟hān Chak, king of Kashmīr. He died from a hurt he received during a game at *chaugān* (p. 309), having been violently thrown on the pommel of the saddle (*pesh-koha-yi zīn*). On his death, Yūsuf was raised to the throne (*Akbarnāma*, III, 237). He first surrounded

---

[[1] Succeeded by Kalyān, commander of 1,500, eight hundred.—B.]

[2] *Vide Journal Asiatic Society Bengal*, 1870, p. 275.

the palace of his uncle Abdāl, who aimed at the crown, and in the fight which ensued, Abdāl was shot. A hostile party thereupon raised one Sayyid Mubārak to the throne, and in a fight which took place on the *maydān* of Srīnagar, where the ʿĪd prayer is said, Yūsuf was defeated. Without taking further part in the struggle, he fled, and came, in the 24th year, to Akbar's Court, where he was well received. During his stay at Court, Sayyid Mubārak had been forced to retire, and Lohar Chak, son of Yūsuf's uncle, had been made king. In the 25th year (*Akbarn.*, III, 288) the Emperor ordered several Panjāb nobles to reinstate Yūsuf. When the Imperial army reached Pinjar, the Kashmīrīs sued for mercy, and Yūsuf, whom they had solicited to come alone, without informing Akbar's commanders, entered Kashmīr, seized Lohar Chak without fighting, and commenced to reign.

Some time after, Ṣāliḥ Dīwāna reported to the Emperor how firmly and independently Yūsuf had established himself, and Akbar sent Shaykh Yaʿqūb-i Kashmīrī, a trusted servant, with his son Ḥaydar to Kashmīr, to remind Yūsuf of the obligations under which he lay to the Emperor. In the 29th year, therefore, Yūsuf sent his son Yaʿqūb with presents to Akbar, but refused personally to pay his respects, although the Court, in the 30th year, had been transferred to the Panjāb; and Yaʿqūb, who had hitherto been with the Emperor, fled from anxiety for his safety. The Emperor then sent Ḥakīm ʿAlī (No. 192) and Bahāʾu 'd-Dīn Kambū to Yūsuf to persuade him to come, or, if he could not himself come, to send again his son. As the embassy was without result, Akbar ordered Shāhrukh Mīrzā (No. 7) to invade Kashmīr. The Imperial army marched over Pakhlī, and was not far from Bārah Mūlah, when Yūsuf submitted and surrendered himself (*Akbarn.*, III, 492).[1] Shāhrukh was on the point of returning, when he received the order to complete the conquest. Yūsuf being kept a prisoner, the Kashmīrīs raised Awlād Ḥusayn, and, soon after, Yaʿqūb, Yūsuf's son, to the throne; but he was everywhere defeated. Information of Yūsuf's submission and the defeat of the Kashmīrīs was sent to Court, and at Srīnagar the *khuṭba* was read, and coins were struck, in Akbar's name. The cultivation of *zaʿfarān* (p. 89)[2] and silk, and the right of hunting, were made Imperial monopolies (p. 452). On the approach of the cold season, the

---

[1] The *Akbarnāma* (III, 492) calls the pass near Bāra Mūlah, where Yūsuf surrendered, بولیاس. The *Maʾāṣir* has بولباس. It is evidently the same pass which the *Tuzuk* (p. 292) calls بهولباس کوتل, 2½ *kos* from Bārah Mūlah. The *Tuzuk* says that Bārah Mūlah means "place of the boar (*bārā*), which is one of the avatārs".

[2] Regarding the cultivation of *zaʿfarān* (saffron), *vide* also *Tuzuk*, p. 45.

army returned with Yūsuf Khān, and arrived, in the 31st year, at Court. Ṭoḍar Mal was made responsible for Yūsuf's person.

As Yaʿqūb Khān and a large party of Kashmīrīs continued the struggle, Qāsim (No. 59) was ordered to march into Kashmīr to put an end to the rebellion. Yaʿqūb was again on several occasions defeated.

In the 32nd year Yūsuf was set at liberty, received from Akbar a jāgīr in Bihār (*Akbarn.*, III, 547) and was made a commander of 500. He served in Bengal. In the 37th year, he accompanied Mān Singh to Oṛīsā, and commanded the detachment which marched over Jhāṛkand and Kokra [1] (Chutiyā Nāgpūr) to Mednīpūr (*Akbarn.*, III, 641).

Yaʿqūb Khān, soon after, submitted, and paid his respects to Akbar, when, in the 34th year, the Court had gone to Kashmīr (p. 412).

Yūsuf Khān is not to be confounded with No. 388.

229. **Nūr Qulij**, son of Āltūn Qulij.

Altūn or *āltūn* is Turkish, and means "gold".

Nūr Qulij was a relation of Qulij Khān (No. 42). He served under him in the expedition to Īdar, which Akbar had ordered to be made when moving, in the 21st year, from Ajmīr to Gogunda. In the fight with the zamāndār of Īdar, N. Q. was wounded. In the 26th year, he served under Sulṭān Murād against Mīrzā Muḥammad Ḥakīm. In the 30th year, he again served under Qulij Khān, who had been made governor of Gujrāt. He continued to serve there under Khānkhānān (No. 29), and returned with him, in the 32nd year, to Court.

230. **Mīr ʿAbdᵘ 'l-Ḥay**, Mīr ʿAdl.

The *Ṭabaqāt* calls him *Khwāja* ʿAbdᵘ 'l-Ḥay, and says that he was an Amīr. He had been mentioned above on pp. 468, 471.

231. **Shāh Qulī Khān Nāranjī.**

Abū 'l-Faẓl says that Shāh Qulī was a Kurd from near Baghdād. He

---

[1] *Kokra* was mentioned above on p. 438. It is the old name of Chutiya Nāgpūr, one of the parganas of which is still called Kokra or Khukra, as spelt on the survey maps. The Rāja, Col. Dalton informs me, once resided in Kokra, at a place in lat. 23° 20′ and long. 88° 87′, nearly, where there is still an old fort. *Vide* also Vth Report (Madras edition, vol. I, p. 503; old edition, p. 417).

The Rāja of Kokra, who, in the 30th year, succumbed to Shāhbāz Khān (p. 438) is called Mādhū. In the 37th year, Mādhū and Lakhmī Rāy of Kokra, served in Yūsuf Khān's detachment, to which the contingents also of Sangrām Singh Shāhā of Kharakpūr (p. 446 and Proceedings A.S. Bengal, for May, 1871), and Pūran Mal of Gidhor belonged (*Akbarnāma* III, 641).

Kokra is again mentioned in the *Tuzuk-i Jahāngīrī* (pp. 154, 155), where it is defined as a hilly district between south Bihār and the Dakhin. It was run over in the beginning of 1025, by Ibrāhīm Khān Fatḥ-jang, governor of Bihār, who was dissatisfied with the few diamonds and elephants which the Rājas sent him as tribute. The then Rāja is called Durjun Sāl. He was captured with several of his relations in a cave, and the district was annexed to Bihār.

The *Tuzuk* has (*l.c.*) a few interesting notes on the diamonds of Kokra.

was an old servant of Humāyūn. In the first year of Akbar's reign, he served under Khizr Khān (p. 394, note 1) in the Panjāb. He was much attached to Bayrām. In the 11th year, he was sent to Gadha, when Mahdī Qāsim Khān (No. 36) had left that province without permission for Makkah.

The *Tabaqāt* calls him a commander of 1,000.

His son, Pādishāh Qulī, was a poet, and wrote under the name of *Jazbī*. A few verses of his are given below in the list of poets.

232. **Farrukh Khān**, son of Khān-i Kalān (No. 16).

He was mentioned on pp. 338 and 384. According to the *Tabaqāt*, he served, in 1001, in Bengal.

233. **Shādmān**, son of Khān-i Aʿzam Koka (No. 21).

Vide above, p. 346.

234. **Hakīm ʿAynu 'l-Mulk**, of Shīrāz.

He is not to be confounded with Hakīmu 'l-Mulk ; *vide* below among the Physicians of the Court.

He was a learned man and a clever writer. He traced his origin, on his mother's side, to the renowned logician Muhaqqiq-i Dawwānī. The historian Badā,onī was a friend of his. Akbar also liked him very much. In the 9th year he was sent as ambassador to Chingiz Khān of Gujrāt. In the 17th year he brought Iʿtimād Khān (No. 67) and Mīr Abū Turāb to the Emperor. He also accompanied Akbar on his march to the eastern provinces of the empire. Afterwards, in 983, he was sent to ʿĀdil Khān of Bījāpūr, from where, in 985, he returned to Court (*Badā,onī* II, 250). He was then made Fawjdār of Sambhal. In the 26th year, when ʿArab Bahādur and other Bengal rebels created disturbances, he fortified Barelī, and refusing all offers, held out till the arrival of an Imperial corps, when he defeated the rebels. In the same year he was made Sadr of Bengal, and in the 31st year Bakhshī of the Sūba of Āgra. He was then attached to the Dakhin corps of ʿAzīz Koka (No. 21), and received Handi,a as jāgīr. When ʿĀzīz, for some reason, cancelled his jāgīr, he went without permission to Court (35th year), but was at first refused audience. On inquiry, however, Akbar reinstated him.

He died at Handia on the 27th Zī Hijja, 1003 (*Badā,onī* II, 403).

The Mīrzā'ī Masjid, also called Pādishāhī Masjid, in Old Barelī, Mīrzā'ī Mahalla, was built by him. The inscription on it bears the date 987 (24th year), when the Hakīm was Fawjjdār of Sambhal.

He was also a poet, and wrote under the *takhallus* of Dawā,ī.

235. **Jānish Bahādur**.

Jānish Bahādur was mentioned on p. 368. He was at first in the service of Mīrzā Muḥammad Ḥakīm king of Kābul. After the death, in the 30th year, of his master, he came with his sons to India. Soon after, he served under Zayn Koka (No. 34) against the Yūsufzāīs, and saved Zayn's life in the Khaybar catastrophe. In the 35th year, he served under the Khānkhānān in Thathah, and returned with him, in the 38th year, to Court. Later, he served in the Dakhin. He died in the 46th year (1009). He was an excellent soldier.

His son, *Shujāʿat Khān Shādī Beg.* He was made, in the 7th year of Shāhjahān's reign, a commander of 1,000, and received the title of Shād Khān. In the 12th year, he was sent as ambassador to Naẕr Muḥammad Khān of Balkh. On his return, in the 14th year, he was made a commander of 1,500, and was appointed governor of Bhakkar, *vide* Shāh Qulī Khān. Afterwards, on the death of Ghayrat Khān, he was made governor of Thathah and a commander of 2,000. In the 19th year he was with Prince Murād Bakhsh in Balkh and Badakhshān. In the 21st year he was appointed governor of Kābul, *vice* Sīwā Rām, and held, in the following year, an important command under Awrangzīb in the Qandahār expedition and the conquest of Bust. In the 23rd year, he was made a commander of 3,000, two thousand five hundred horse, and received the coveted distinction of a flag and a drum. Two years later, in the 25th year, he served again before Qandahār, and was made, on Shāhjahān's arrival in Kābul, a commander of 3,500, three thousand horse, with the title of *Shujāʿat Khān.* In the 26th year, he served under Dārā Shikoh before Qandahār, and with Rustam Khān Bahādur at Bust. He died soon after. He had a son of the name of Muḥammad Saʿīd.

236. **Mīr Ṭāhir-i** Mūsawī.

He is not to be confounded with Nos. 94, 111, and 201. According to the *Ṭabaqāt*, Mīr Ṭāhir is "the brother of Mīrzā Yūsuf Paẓawī (No. 37), and was distinguished for his bravery". It would thus appear that Abū 'l-Faẓl makes no difference between the terms *Raẓawī* and *Mūsāwī* (*vide* p. 414, under No. 61).

237. **Mīrzā ʿAlī Beg,** ʿAlamshāhī.

He is mentioned in the *Akbarnāma* among the grandees who accompanied Munʿim to Bengal and Orīsā, and took part in the battle of Takaro,ī (p. 406). After the outbreak of the Bengal Military revolt, he joined a conspiracy made by Mīr Ẕakī, ʿAbdī Kor, Shihāb-i Badakhshī, and Kūjak Yasāwul, to go over to the rebels. The plot, however, was discovered; they were all imprisoned, but Mīr Ẕakī alone was executed. *Akbarnāma,* III, 262.

His epithet *ʿAlamshāhī* is not clear to me.

He must not be confounded with the more illustrious [**Mīrzā ʿAlī Beg-i** Akbarshāhī].[1]

He was born in Badakhshān, and is said to have been a highly educated man. When he came to India he received the title of *Akbarshāhī*. In the 30th year, he commanded the Aḥadīs on Shāhrukh's expedition to Kashmīr (p. 535).

Later, he served under Prince Murād in the Dakhin. When the prince, after making peace, returned from Aḥmadnagar, Ṣādiq Khān (No. 43) occupied Mahkar. But new disturbances broke out under the Dakhin leaders, Azhdar Khān and ʿĀyn Khān, against whom Ṣādiq sent a corps under M. ʿAlī Beg He suddenly fell on them and routed them, carrying off much plunder and many dancing girls (*zanān-i akhāṛa*). In consequence of this defeat, Khudāwand Khān and other Amīrs of the Niẓāmshāh marched against the Imperialists with 10,000 horse, but Ṣādiq and M. A. B. defeated them. In the 43rd year, M. A. B. took Fort Rāhūtara (راهوتره) near Dawlatābād, after a siege of one month, occupied, in the same year, Paṭan on the Godāvarī, and took Fort Lohgaḍh. "Both forts," says the author of the *Maʾāṣir*, "have, from want of water, become uninhabitable (*mismār shuda*), and are so to this day." Later, M. A. B. served under Abū 'l-Faẓl, and distinguished himself in the conquest of Aḥmadnagar. In the 46th year, he received a drum and a flag, and continued to serve, under the Khānkhānān, in the Dakhin.

In the beginning of Jahāngīr's reign, he was made a commander of 4,000, jāgīrdār of Sambhal, and governor of Kashmīr. He served in the pursuit of Khusraw (*Tuzuk*, p. 30). Later, he received a *tuyūl* in Audh. When Jahāngīr went to Ajmīr, he went to Court. One day, he paid a visit to the tomb of Muʿīnu 'd-Dīn-i Chishtī. On seeing the tomb of Shāhbāz Khān (p. 439), he stooped down, and embracing it, exclaimed: "Oh! he was an old friend of mine." The same moment, he fell forward a corpse, and was buried at the same spot (22nd *Rabīʿ* I, 1025).

It is said that he kept few soldiers and servants, but paid them well. In his habits he was an epicurean. He was looked upon as a great patron of the learned. He died childless, at the age of seventy-five (*Tuzuk*, p. 163).

238. **Rām Dās,** the Kachwāha.

His father was a poor man of the name of Ordat (اوردت), and lived at Lūnī (or Baūlī, *vide* p. 435). Rām Dās was at first in the service of Rāy Sāl Darbārī (No. 106), and was recommended by him to the Emperor.

[1] The *Tuzuk* (p. 11) says he belonged to the *ulūs-i Dihlī*, a very doubtful term, as he belonged to Badakhshān. Perhaps we have to read *ulūs-i dulday* (p. 422).

His faithfulness was almost proverbial. In the 17th year, when Ṭoḍar Mal was ordered to assist Munʿim in Bihār, he was made his *nāʾib* in the Financial Department, and gained Akbar's favour by his regularity and diligence. He amassed a fortune, and though he had a palace at Āgra near Hatiyāpul, he lived in the guard house, " always watching with his 200 Rājpūts, spear in hand."

Immediately before Akbar's death he put his men over the treasures of the palace with a view to preserve them for the lawful heir. Jahāngīr, with whom he stood in high favour, sent him, in the 6th year, with ʿAbdᵘ 'llāh Khān to Gujrāt and the Dakhin, and gave him the title of Rāja and a flag, Rantanbhūr being assigned to him as jāgīr (*Tuzuk*, p. 98). It seems that he received the title of *Rāja Karan*. After the defeat of the Imperialists, Jahāngīr wished to make an example of the Amīrs who had brought disgrace on the Imperial arms. He ordered their pictures to be drawn, and taking the portraits one after the other into his hand, abused each Amīr right royally. Looking at Rām Dās's portrait, he said : " Now, when thou wert in Rāy Sāl's service, thou hadst a tanka *per diem* ; but my father took an interest in thee, and made thee an Amīr. Do not Rājpūts think flight a disgraceful thing ? Alas ! thy title, Rāja Karan, ought to have taught thee better. Mayest thou die without the comforts of thy faith." Rām Dās was immediately sent to Bangash, where, in the same year, he died (1022). When Jāhāngīr heard of his death, he said, " My curse has come true ; for the Hindūs believe that a man who dies beyond the Indus, will go straight to hell."

He was a liberal man, and gave rich presents to jesters and singers.

His eldest son, *Naman Dās*, in the 48th year of Akbar's reign, left the Court without permission, and went home. At the request of his father, Shāh Qulī Khān's men were to bring him back to Court by force. But Naman defied them ; a struggle ensued, and he was killed. Rām Dās was so grieved, that Akbar paid him a visit of condolence.

His second son, *Dalap Dās*, had the same character as his father ; but he died young.

In the *Tuzuk* (p. 312) a villa near a spring called Inch (اِنچ), between Bānpūr[1] and Kākāpūr in Kashmīr, is mentioned, which Akbar had given Rām Dās. *Vide* also *Tuzuk*, p. 39, l. 3.

239. **Muḥammad Khān Niyāzī.**

Abū 'l-Faẓl ranks him among the commanders of 500. Under Jahāngīr he rose to a command of 2,000. Like Mīrzā Rustam Ṣafawī and Abū

[[1] Panipūr ?—B.]

'l-Ḥasan Turbatī, he refused a title; for he said that his name was Muḥammad, than which no better name existed.

He served under Shāhbāz Khān (No. 80) in Bengal, and distinguished himself in the fights near the Brahmaputra. It is said that Shāhbāz was so anxious to retain his services, that he gave him a lac of rupees *per annum*. Later, he served under the Khānkhānān in the conquest of Thathah, and inflicted the final blow on Mīrzā Jānī Beg (No. 47) near Lakhī,[1] where he obtained a signal victory, though far outnumbered by the enemies. From that time, the Khānkhānān was his friend.

Under Jahāngīr, he took a leading part in the Dakhin wars, especially in the fights with Malik ʿAmbar near Kharkī, a famous battlefield (*vide* note to No. 255), and continued to serve there under Prince Shāhjahān.

He died in 1037. The *tārīkh* of his death is محمد خان اولیا بمرد, "Muḥammad Khān, the saint, is dead." He was a man of great piety. His day was carefully divided; religious exercises, the reading of commentaries on the Qurʾān, conversing with holy men, sleeping and eating, each had its fixed time. Nor did he ever depart from his routine except on the march. He never neglected the ablution (*wūẓū*) prescribed by the law. People told many miraculous stories (*khawāriq*) of him.

During his long stay in the Dakhin, he held Āshtī (in the Warda district) as jāgīr, and made it his home. He adorned the town with several mosques, houses, and gardens. "At present," says the author of the *Maʿāṣir*, "there is only one of his hundred houses left, the store house where his lamps were kept; the whole town and the neighbourhood are deserted, and do not yield a tenth part of the old revenue. Even among his descendants there is none left that may be called a man of worth (*kas-ī na-mānd ki rushd-ī dāshta bāshad*)."[2]

---

[1] *Vide* Dowson's edition of *Elliot's Historians*, Vol. I, p. 250.

[2] "The Emperor Jahāngīr gave the Āshtī, Amner, Paunār, and Tālīgāw (Barār) parganas in jāgīr to Muḥammad Khān Niyāzī. He restored Āshtī, and brought the country round under cultivation. A handsome mausoleum was built over his grave in Mughul style. Muḥammad Khān was succeeded by Aḥmad Khān, who died in 1061. A similar mausoleum was erected over his tomb, but smaller and of inferior workmanship. The two stand side by side within an enclosure, and are the sights of Āshtī. They are indeed striking monuments of art to find in such a remote spot as this. After the death of Aḥmad Khān, the power of the Niyāzīs gradually declined; in time Āshtī itself passed from their hands into the possession of the Marhatta officials, and now nothing remains to them save a few rent-free fields, sufficient merely for their subsistence. The tombs of their ancestors were already falling into disrepair, owing to the poverty of the family, when they were taken in hand by the district authorities as worthy objects of local interest, and restored from municipal funds. Lately, in consideration of the past history of the family, and the local respect which it commands, the Government conferred on Nawāb Wāḥid Khān, one of its representatives in Āshtī, the powers of an honorary magistrate."

"*Karanja.* A small octroi town in the Ārvī taḥṣil of the Warda district. It was founded some 260 years by Nawāb Muḥammad Khān Niyāzī of Āshtī." Extracts from C. Grant's *Gazetteer of the Central Provinces of India*, second edition, 1870, pp. 7 and 236.

He was buried in Āshtī. People often pray at his tomb.

The men of his contingent were mostly Niyāzī Afg̲h̲āns. If one of them died, he gave a month's pay to his family; or, if he had no children, half a month's pay to his heirs.

His son, Aḥmad K̲h̲ān Niyāzī, was in the 20th year of Shāhjahān's reign a commander of 2,500 (*Pādishāhnāma*, II, 386, 725).

240. **Abū 'l-Muẓaffar,** son of Ashraf K̲h̲ān (No. 74).

From the *Akbarnāma* (III, 248) we see that in the 24th year (987) he was stationed in Chanderī and Narwar, and was ordered to assist in suppressing the Bihār rebels (III, 273). In the 28th year he served in Gujrāt (III, 423), and *Badā,oni*, II (323). *Vide* also under No. 74.

241. **K̲h̲wājagī Muḥammad Ḥusayn,** Mīr Barr.

He is the younger brother of Qāsim K̲h̲ān (No. 59) and had the title of *Mīr Barr*, in contradistinction to that of his brother. He came in the 5th year with Munʿim (No. 11) from Kābul to India. When dissensions broke out between G̲h̲anī K̲h̲ān, Munʿim's son, and Ḥaydar Muḥammad K̲h̲ān Āk̲h̲tabegī (No. 66), whom Munʿim had left as his *nāʾibs* in Kābul, Ḥaydar was called to Court, and Abū 'l-Fatḥ,[1] son of Munʿim's brother, was sent there to assist G̲h̲anī. Muḥammad Ḥusayn accompanied Abū 'l-Fatḥ. He remained a long time in Kābul. After his return to India, he accompanied the Emperor on his march to Kashmīr. His honesty and punctuality made him a favourite with the Emperor, and he was appointed *Mīr Bakāwal* (master of the Imperial kitchen) and was also made a commander of 1,000.

In the 5th year of Jahāngīr, he officiated for Hāshim (No. 226) as governor of Kashmīr. On Hāshim's arrival he returned to Court, and died in the end of the 7th year (1021; *Tuzuk*, p. 114).

He had no children. The *Tuzuk* says that he was quite bald, and had neither moustache nor beard. His voice was shrill like that of a eunuch.

242. **ʿAbū 'l-Qāsim,** brother of Abdᵘ 'l-Qādir Āk̲h̲ūnd.

He is not to be confounded with Nos. 199 and 251. *Badā,oni* (II 323), calls him a native of Tabrīz, and says that his brother was Akbar's teacher (*āk̲h̲ūnd*). In 991, Abū 'l-Qāsim was made Dīwān of Gujrāt.

243. **Qamar K̲h̲ān,** son of Mīr ʿAbdᵘ 'l-Laṭīf of Qazwīn (No. 161).

He served under Munʿim (No. 11) in Bengal, and was present in the battle of Takaro,ī (p. 406). In the 22nd year he served under Shihāb

[1] Abū 'l-Fatḥ, who on p. 333, has erroneously been called ʿAbdᵘ 'l-Fatḥ, was the son of Faẓīl Beg, Munʿim's brother. *Badā,onī*, II, 56, has *Faẓāʾil* Beg, but the *Akbarnāma* and the *Maʾāṣir* have *Faẓīl*.

in Gujrāt (*Akbarn.*, III, 190) and in the 24th year under Ṭoḍar Mal in Bihār. In the 25th year he took part in the battle near Sulṭanpūr Bilharī[1] (p. 400, and *Akbarn.*, III, 305).

His son, Kawkab, fell into disgrace under Jahāngīr for some fault. He was flogged and imprisoned. Regarding his restoration to favour, *vide Tuzuk*, p. 219.

244. **Arjum Singh,**
245. **Sabal Singh,** } sons of Rāja Mān Singh (No. 30).
256. **Sakat Singh,**

Some MSS. have *Durjan*[2] instead of *Arjun*. The name of Sakat Singh, moreover, recurs again at No. 342. There is little doubt that at the latter place we should read *Himmat Singh*, though all MSS. have *Sakat*.

Nor is it clear why Abū 'l-Faẓl has not entered the name of Bhā,o Singh, who at Akbar's death was a commander of 1,000, and was gradually promoted during Jahāngīr's reign to a manṣab of 5,000. Like his elder brother Jagat Singh (No. 160), he died from excessive drinking (1030). His name often occurs in the *Tuzuk*.

Arjun Singh, Sabal Singh, and Sakat Singh, served in the 37th year in the conquest of Oṛīsā. Sakat Singh, in the 26th year (989), had served in Kābul. They died before their father.

Himmat Singh distinguished himself under his father in the wars with the Afghāns.

Col. J. C. Brooke in his *Political History of the State of Jeypore* (Selections from the Records, Government of India, Foreign Department, No. LXV, 1868) mentions six sons of Mān Singh, Jagat, Arjun, Himmat, Sakat, Bhīm, and Kalyān Singh. The last two are not mentioned by Muhammadan historians; nor are Bhā,o and Sabal mentioned by Brooke. *Vide*, " A Chapter from Muhammadan History," in the *Calcutta Review*, April, 1871.

246. **Musṭafa Ghilzī.**

A Sayyid Musṭafa is mentioned in the *Akbarnāma* (III, 416). He served in the 28th year in Gujrāt, and was present in the battle near Maisāna, 18 *kos* S.E. of Paṭan, in which Sher Khān Fūlādī was defeated.

247. **Naẓar Khān**, son of Saʿīd Khān, the Gakkhar.

A brother of his is mentioned below, No. 232. *Vide* Nos. 170, 171.

[[1] Or Bilahrī.—B.]

[2] The Lucknow edition of the *Akbarnāma* (III, 642) has also *Durjan*, and (by mistake) *Sīl* for *Sabal* Singh. The Subhān Singh mentioned in the same passage, would also appear to be a son of Mān Singh.

The *Ṭabaqāt* calls him Naẓar *Beg*, son of Saʿīd Khān, and says that in 1001 he was a Hazārī.

Mughul historians give the following tree of the Gakkhar chiefs :—

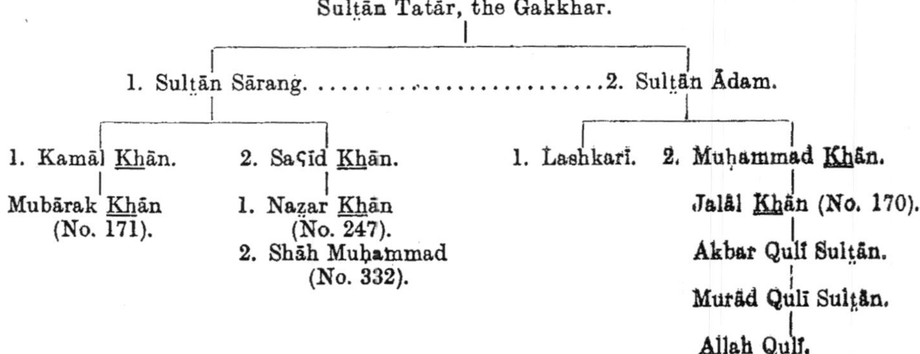

Jalāl Khān was killed in 1620 (15th year) in Bangash, and his son Akbar Qulī, who then served at Kāngṛa, was made a commander of 1,000, and sent to Bangash (*Tuzuk*, pp. 307, 308).

Jahāngīr, after the suppression of Khusraw's revolt, passed on his way to Kābul through the Gakkhar district (*Tuzuk*, pp. 47, 48). He left the Bahat (1st Muḥarram, 1016) and came to Fort Rohtās, the cost of which he states to have been 161,000,000 dāms, "which is equal to 4,025,000 rupees in Hindūstānī money, or 120,000 Persian tūmāns, or 1 *irb*, 2,175,000 silver Hālīs of Turānī money." After a march of 4¾ *kos*, he came to Ṭīla, *ṭīla* in the Gakkhar dialect meaning "a hill". He then came to Dih Bhakrāla, *bhakrā* meaning "forest". The way from Ṭīla to Bhakrā passes along the bed of the Kāhan river, the banks of which are full of *kanīr* [1] flowers. He then came to Hatyā, which was built by a Gakkhar of the name of Hāthī (mentioned in Mr. Delmerick's History of the Gakkhars, *Journal Asiatic Society Bengal*, 1871). The district from Mārgala to Hatyā is called Poṭhwār ; and from Rohtās to Hatyā dwell the Bhūgiyāls, a tribe related to the Gakkhars. From Hatyā, he marched 4¾ *kos* and reached *Pakka*, so called because it has a "*pucca*" sarā,ī. Four and a half *kos* further on, he came to Kuṛaṛ, which means in the Gakkhar dialect "rugged". He then went to Rāwalpinḍī, which is said to have been built by a Hindū of the name Rāwal, *pinḍī* meaning "a village", and gives a few curious particulars regarding the river and the pool of the place. From Rāwalpinḍī he went to Kharbūza, where a dome may be seen which has the shape of a melon (*kharbūza*). The Gakkhars used

[[1] *Kanīr*, probably *kaneṛ* m. "a species of oleander."—P.]

formerly to collect tolls there. He then came to the Kālāpānī, and to the Mārgala pass, *mār* meaning "killing" and *gala* "a carawan". "Here ends the country of the Gakkhars. They are a brutish race, always at feud with each other. I asked them to live in peace; but they will not." [1]

The *Pādishāhnāma* (II, 240, 264, 266, 722, 733, 740) mentions several Gakkhar chiefs :—

1. Akbar Qulī Sulṭān, a commander of 1,500, 1,500 horse, died in the 18th year of Shāhjahān's reign. His son Murād Qulī Sulṭān, was under Shāhjahān, a commander of 1,500, 1,000 horse (*Pādishāhn.*, II, 410, 485, 512, 523, 565, 595, 655, 730).

2. Jabbār Qulī (brother of Jalāl Khān),[2] 1,000, 800 horse.

3. Khizr Sulṭān (son of Hazar Khān),[2] 800, 500 horse, died in the 12th year Shāhj.'s reign.

The *Pādishāhnāma* (I, p. 432) mentions these Gakkhars' mules as famous.

The *Maᶜāṣir-i ᶜĀlamgīrī* (p. 155) also mentions Murād Qulī and his son Allah Qulī. Allah Qulī's daughter was married to Prince Muḥammad Akbar, fourth son of Awrangzīb, on the 3rd Rajab, 1087.

248. **Rām Chand,** son of Madhukar [Bundela].

He is also called *Rām Sāh,* and was mentioned on p. 356. He was introduced at court by Ṣādiq Khān (No. 43), when Akbar was in Kashmīr (1000). In the first year of Jahāngīr's reign we find him in rebellion, evidently because his right of succession was rendered doubtful by the predilection of the emperor for Bīr Singh De,o, Rām Chand's younger brother. In the end of the first year, he was attacked by ᶜAbd^u 'llāh Khān, who moved his jāgīr from Kālpī to Ūḍcha. On the 27th Ẕī Qaᶜda, 1015, Rām Chand was brought fettered to court; but Jahāngīr had his fetters taken off, gave him a dress of honour, and handed him over to Rāja Bāsū of Dhamerī. "He never thought that he would be treated so kindly" (*Tuzuk*, p. 42). But Ūḍcha was handed over to Bir Singh De,o as a reward for the murder of Abū 'l-Faẓl.

---

[1] For the geographical details of this passage, I am indebted to Mr. J. G. Delmerick. The *Tuzuk* has *Pīla* of *Tīla*; *Bhakrā* for *Bhakrāla,* and the Persian word *khāna* for *Kāhan* (کاهن), the name of the river near *Bhakrāla*—a most extraordinary mistake; *kor* for *Kuraṛ* or *Gūrā*, a village near Manikyāla; *Ponhūhār* for *Poṭhwār.* Mr. Delmerick also says that the river near Hatiyā or *Hāṭhiyā*, is called Kāsī, and that near Rāwalpinḍī is the Lahī, which forces a passage through low hills where there is a very deep pool, just before its junction with the Sohan Sarāᵉī Khārbūza is also called Sarāᵉī Mādhū.

On the same page of Sayyid Aḥmad's edition of the *Tuzuk*, we have to read *Khattar* and *Dila-zāk for Khar* and *Dila-zak.* The Khattars occupy the district called Khāṭar, and the Dila-zāks are found in the Chhach valley of the Indus. [*Vide* No. 373.—B.]

Poṭhwār is the country between the Jhelam and the Sohan; but Jahāngīr extends it to the Mārgala pass from Hatyā 30 miles from the Jhelam).

[2] So according to Mr. Delmerick.

In the 4th year of his reign (1018), Jahāngīr married Rām Chand's daughter at the request of her father (*vide Tuzuk*, p. 77 ; and also No. 225, note).

He appears to have died in 1021, and was succeeded by his son Bharat Singh. *Tuzuk*, p. 112.

Muhammadan historians give the following tree of the Ūḍcha Bundelas :—

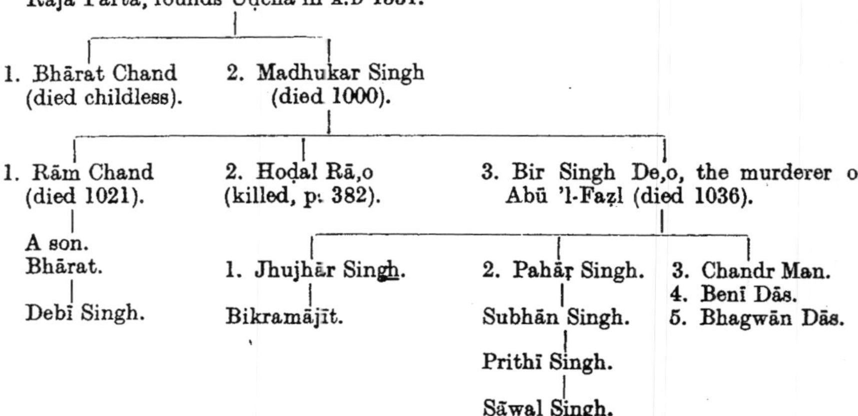

The *Maʾāṣir* contains biographical notes of nearly all of them. *Vide* also Thornton's *Gazetteer*, under *Oorcha.*

Benī Dās and Bhagwān Dās were killed by a Rājpūt in the 13th year of Shāhjahān's reign. They held commands of 500, 200 horse, and 1,000, 600 horse, respectively.

Chandr Man was in the 20th year of Sh. a commander of 1,500, 800 horse.

Vide Pādishāhnāma, I, 172 (where another Bundela of the name of Suhk Dev is mentioned), 205, 241, 368, 372, 425 ; II, 731, 734.

The *Maʾāṣir-i ʿĀlamgīrī* mentions several Bundelas, as Satr Sāl, Jāswant Singh, Indarman (*died* 1088) and the rebellious sons of Champat (*l.c.*, pp. 161, 163, 169, 273, 424). *Vide* also under No. 249.

Bīr Singh De,o, the murderer of Abū 'l-Faẓl is often called in bad MSS. *Nar* Singh Deo. Thus also in the printed editions of the *Tuzuk*, the 1st volume of *Pādishāhnāma*, the ʿĀlamgīrnāma, etc., and in Elphinstone's History. The temples which he built in Mathurā at a cost of 33 lacs of rupees, were destroyed by Awrangzīb in 1080. (*Maʾāṣir-i ʿĀlamgīrī*, p. 95.)[1]

[1] The Dutch traveller De Laët has an interesting passage regarding Abū 'l-Faẓl's death (*De Imperio Magni Mogulis*, Leyden, 1631, p. 209). He calls Bīr Singh *Radzia Bertzingh Bondela.*

249. **Rāja Mukatman**, the Bhadauriya.

Bhadāwar is the name of a district S.E. of Āgra; its chief town is Hatkānth (*vide* p. 341, note 4). The inhabitants are called Bhadauryas. They were known as daring robbers, and though so near the capital, they managed to maintain their independence till Akbar had their chief trampled to death by an elephant, when they submitted.

The next chief, Mukatman, entered the imperial service, and rose to a manṣab of 1,000. In 992 he served in Gujrāt (*Akbarnāma,* III, 423, 438).

Under Jahāngīr, we find a chief of the name of Rāja Bikramājīt, who served under ʿAbdu llāh against the Rānā, and later in the Dakhin. He died in the 11th year of Jahāngīr and was succeeded by his son Bhoj. Sayyid Aḥmad's edition of the *Tuzuk* (p. 108) mentions a Bhadaurya chief Mangat, who in the 7th year served in Bangash; but the name is doubtful.

Under Shāhjahān, the head of the Bhadauriya clan was Rāja Kishn Singh. He served in the first year under Mahābat Khān against Jhujhār Singh, and in the 3rd year against Khān Jahān Lodī and the Niẓāmu 'l-Mulk, who had afforded Khān Jahān protection. In the 6th year, he distinguished himself in the siege of Dawlatābād. Three years later, in the 9th year, he served under Khān Zamān against Sāhū Bhōnsla. He died in the 17th year (1053).

In the *Pādishāhnāma* (I, b., 309) he is mentioned as a commander of 1,000, 600 horse.

As Kishn Singh had only a son by a concubine, he was succeeded by Badan Singh,[1] grandson of Kishn's uncle. He was made a Rāja and a commander of 1,000. In the 21st year, at a darbār, a *mast* elephant ran up to him, took up one of his men with its tusks, when Badan Singh stuck his dagger into the animal, which, frightened as it was at the same time by a fire wheel, dropped the unfortunate man. Shāhjahān rewarded the bravery of the Rāja with a *khilʿat*, and remitted 50,000 Rs. out of the 2 lacs which was the assessment of the Bhadāwar district. In the 22nd year he was made a commander of 1,500. In the 25th year he served under Awrangzīb, and in the 26th under Dārā Shikoh, before Qandahār, where in the following year he died.

His son Mahā Singh was then made a Rāja and received a manṣab of 1,000, 800 horse. He served in the 28th year in Kābul. After Dārā's defeat he paid his respects to Awrangzib, in whose reign he served against

[1] So *Pādishāhnāma,* II, 732. The *Maʾāṣir* calls him Bad Singh or Bud Singh.

the Bundela rebels. In the 10th year he served under Kāmil Khān against the Yūsufzā'īs. He died in the 26th year.

He was succeeded by his son Odat Singh (*vide Ma'āṣir-i ʿĀlamgīrī*, p. 226 and p. 228, where the Bibl. Ind. edition has wrongly *Rūdar* Singh for *Odat* S.). He had before served under Jai Singh in the Dakhin, and was in the 24th year made commandant of Chītor (*l.c.*, p. 196).

250. **Rāja Rām Chandr**, zamīndār of Oṛīsā.

Regarding him, *vide* Stirling's report of Oṛīsā, *Asiatic Researches*, vol. xv. His name occurs often in the narrative of Mān Singh's conquest of Oṛīsā (37th year of Akbar's reign).

The province of Khurda (South Oṛīsā) was conquered and annexed to the Dihlī empire by Mukarram Khān (*vide* No. 260), in the 12th year of Jahāngīr's reign (*Tuzuk*, p. 215).

251. **Sayyid Abū 'l-Qāsim**, son of Sayyid Muḥammad Mīr ʿAdl (No. 140).

He served in the 25th year (998) in Bihār, and in the battle of Sulṭānpūr Bilharī; also, in the 33rd year, against the Yūsufzā'īs.

The Tārīkh Maʿṣūmī (Dowson, *Elliot's Historians*, I, p. 243) gives earlier but perhaps more correct dates regarding the appointment to Bhakkar and the death of the Mīr ʿAdl, *viz.* his arrival at Bhakkar, 11th Ramazān, 983, and his death there, 8th Shaʿbān, 984 (October, 1576). He was succeeded by his son Abū 'l-Faẓl, who is not mentioned in the Ā'īn. On the 9th Ẕī 'l-ḥijjah, 985 (Feb., 1578), Īʿtimād (No. 119) *arrived* at Bhakkar.

252. **Dalpat**, son of Rāy Rāy Singh.

He has been mentioned above, p. 386.

XVIII. Commanders of Four Hundred.

253. **Shaykh Fayẓī**, son of Shaykh Mubārak of Nāgor.

The name of this great poet and friend of Akbar was Abū 'l-Fayẓ. Fayẓī is his *takhalluṣ*. Towards the end of his life in imitation of the form of the *takhalluṣ* of his brother *ʿAllāmī*, he assumed the name of *Fayyāẓī*.

Fayẓī was the eldest son of Shaykh Mubārak of Nāgor. Shaykh Mubārak (*vide* pp. 178, 195, 207, 219) traced his origin to an Arabian dervish from Yaman, who in the 9th century of the Hijrah had settled in Sīwistān, where he married. In the 10th century, Mubārak's father went to Hindūstān and settled at Nāgor. Several of his children having died one after the other, he called his next child *Mubārak*. He was born in 911. When a young man, Mubārak went to Gujrāt and studied under

Khaṭīb Abū 'l-Faẓl of Kāzarūn and Mawlānā ʿImād of Lāristān. In 950, Mubārak settled at Āgra. It is said that he often changed his religious opinions. Under Islam Shāh, he was a Mahdawī, and had to suffer persecution in the beginning of Akbar's reign; he then became a Naqshbandī, then a Hamadānī, and lastly, when the court was full of Persians, he inclined to Shīʿism. But whatever his views may have been, the education which he gave his sons Fayẓī and Abū 'l-Faẓl, the greatest writers that India has produced, shows that he was a man of comprehensive genius. Shaykh Mubārak wrote a commentary to the Qurʾān, in four volumes, entitled *Mambaʿu 'l-ʿuyūn*,[1] and another work of the title of *Jawāmiʿu 'l-kalām*. Towards the end of his life, he suffered from partial blindness, and died at Lāhor, on the 17th Ẕī Qaʿda, 1001, at the age of 90 years. The *tārīkh* of his death will be found in the words *Shaykh-i kāmil*.

Shaykh Fayẓī was born at Āgra in 954. His acquirements in Arabic Literature, the art of poetry, and in medicine, were very extensive. He used to treat poor people gratis. One day he appeared with his father before Shaykh ʿAbdu 'n-Nabī, the Ṣadr (p. 282), and applied for a grant of 100 bīghas; but he was not only refused, but also turned out of the hall with every contumely on account of his tendencies to Shīʿism. But Fayẓī's literary fame reached Akbar's ears, and in the 12th year, when Akbar was on the expedition to Chītor, he was called to court. Fayẓī's bigoted enemies in Āgra interpreted the call as a summons before a judge and warned the governor of the town not to let Fayẓī escape. He therefore ordered some Mughuls to surround Mubārak's house; but accidentally Fayẓī was absent from home. Mubārak was ill-treated, and when Fayẓī at last came, he was carried off by force. But Akbar received him most favourably, and Fayẓī in a short time became the emperor's constant companion and friend. He was instrumental in bringing about the fall of Shaykh Abdu 'n-Nabī.

In the 30th year he planned a *khamsa*, or collection of five epics, in imitation of the Khamsa of Niẓāmī. The first, *Markizu 'l-adwār*, was to consist of 3,000 verses, and was to be a *jawāb* (imitation) of Niẓāmī's *Makhzanu 'l-asrār*; the *Sulaymān o Bilqīs* and the *Nal Daman* were to consist of 4,000 verses each, and were to be *jawābs* of the *Khusraw ᵒShīrīn* and *Laylą ᵒMajnūn* respectively; and the *Haft Kishwar* and the *Akbarnāma*, each of 5,000 verses, were to correspond to the *Haft Paykar* and the *Sikandarnāma*. In the 33rd year he was made *Maliku 'sh-Shuʿarā*,

[1] Badā,onī (III, 74) calls it *Mambaʿu nafāʾisi 'l-ʿuyūn*.

or Poet Laureate (*Akbarn.*, III, 559). Though he had composed portions of the Khamsa, the original plan was not carried out, and in the 39th year Akbar urged him to persevere, and recommended the completion of the Nal Daman. Fayẓī thereupon finished the poem and presented, in the same year, a copy of it to his imperial master.

Fayẓī suffered from asthma, and died on the 10th Ṣafar, 1004 (40th year). The *tārīkh* of his death is *Fayyāẓ-i ʿAjam.* It is said that he composed 101 books. The best known, besides his poetical works, are the *Sawāṭiʿu 'l-Ilhām*, and the *Mawārīdu 'l-Kalām*, regarding which *vide* below the poetical extracts. His fine library, consisting of 4,300 choice MSS., was embodied with the imperial library.

Fayẓī had been employed as teacher to the princes; sometimes he also acted as ambassador. Thus, in 1000, he was in the Dakhin, from where he wrote the letter to the historian Badā,onī, who had been in temporary disgrace at court.

Vide also pp. 112, 113, 192, 194, 207, 216, 218; and *Journal Asiatic Society Bengal* for 1869, pp. 137, 142.

254. **Ḥakīm Miṣrī.**

According to Badā,onī (III, 165) Ḥakīm Miṣrī was a very learned man and a clever doctor. He also composed poems. A satire of his is mentioned which he wrote against Khwāja Shamsu 'd-Dīn Khawāfī (No. 159). He died in Burhānpūr and was buried there.

Miṣrī is mentioned in the *Akbarnāma*, III, p. 629, and p. 843. In the latter passage, Abū 'l-Faẓl mentions his death (middle of 1009), and states that he saw his friend on the deathbed. It is impossible to reconcile Abū 'l-Faẓl's date with Badā,onī's statement; for Bādā,onī died in 1004 (*Journal Asiatic Society Bengal* for 1869, p. 143). But both Abū 'l-Faẓl and Badā,onī speak of the Ḥakīm as a man of a most amiable and unselfish character.

255. **Īrij**, son of Mīrzā Khānkhānān (No. 29).

He was mentioned on p. 339. During the reign of Jahāngīr he was made Ṣūbadār of Barār and Aḥmadnagar. He greatly distinguished himself during several fights with Malik ʿAmbar, especially as Kharkī,[1]

---

[1] کهرکی. Lachmī Narā,in Shafīq, the author of the *Ḥaqīqat-i Hindūstān*, says that it was called Kharkī from the Dakhin word کهرک, which means "stony", "a stony place". It lies 5 *kos* S.E. of Dawlatābād (the old Dhārāgaṛh and De,ogīr of ʿAlāʾu 'd-Dīn Khiljī). Kharkī under Jahāngīr was called Fatḥābad. In 1024 a canal was dug from Kharkī to Dawlatābād. Its name was *Chahārnahrī*, and the *tārīkh* of its completion is *khayr-i jārī* (pr. a running benefit). Later Awrangzīb changed the name of Kharkī to Awrangābād, under which name it is now known. Kharkī was the seat of Malik ʿAmbar.

for which victories he was made a commander of 5,000. In the 12th year he served under Prince Shāhjahān in the Dakhin.

It is said that he was a good soldier, but stingy, and careless in his dress. A daughter of his was married (2nd Ramaẓān, 1026) to Prince Shāhjahān. The offspring of this marriage, Prince Jahān-afroz, was born at Āgra on the 12th Rajab, 1028, and died at Burhānpūr, at the age of 1 year 9 months (*Padishāhnāma*).

According to Grant's *Gazetteer of the Central Provinces* (2nd edition, p. 128), Īrij's tomb is at Burhānpūr. "The tomb was built during his lifetime, and is really a handsome structure." The statement of the *Gazetteer* that Īrij, towards the end of his life, "lived as a recluse" at Burhānpūr, is not borne out by the histories; for according to the *Tuzuk* (p. 270) he died of excessive wine drinking.

At his death (1028) he was only thirty-three years of age. The manṣab of 400, which Ābū 'l-Faẓl assigns him, must therefore have been conferred upon him when he was a mere child.

256. **Sakat Singh,** son of Rāja Mān Singh (No. 30).

Vide above, under No. 244.

257. **ʿAbdᵘ 'llāh** [Sarfarāz Khān] son of Khān-i Aʿẓam Mīrzā Koka (No. 21).

Vide p. 316.

It was stated (p. 316) on the authority of the *Maʾāṣir* that he received the title of *Sardār Khān*, which had become vacant by the death of Takhta Beg (No. 195). But the *Tuzuk* (p. 71) gives him the title of *Sarfarāz Khān*. This is evidently a mistake of the author of the *Maʾāṣir*; for the title of *Sardār Khān* was in the 8th year (1022) conferred on Khwāja Yādgār, brother of ʿAbdᵘ 'llāh Khān Fīrūz-jang (*Tuzuk*, p. 116) when ʿAbdᵘ 'llāh Sarfarāz Khān was still alive.

The *Maʾāṣir* also says that ʿAbdᵘ 'llāh accompanied his father to Gwālyār (p. 317); but the *Tuzuk* (p. 141) states that he was imprisoned in Rantanbhur, from where, at the request of his father, he was called to court.

358. **ʿAlī Muḥammad Asp.**

Badā,onī says (II, p. 57) that "ʿAlī Muḥammad Asp, who is now in the service of the emperor, at the instigation of Jūjak[1] Begum, killed Abū 'l-Fatḥ Beg (p. 333)." In the 9th year he was in the service of Mīrzā Muḥammad Ḥakīm, king of Kābul. Afterwards, he came to India. In the 26th year (989) he served under Prince Murād against his former

[[1] *Chuckuk*, Turk.—B.]

master (*Akbarnāma*, III, 345); in the 30th year (993) he served in Kābul (III, 487, 490). In the 32nd year he distinguished himself under ʿAbdᵘ 'l-Maṭlab (No. 83) against the Tārīkīs (III, p. 541).

In the Lucknow edition of the *Akbarnāma* he is wrongly called ʿAlī Muḥammad *Alif.*

259. **Mīrzā Muḥammad.**

A. Mīrzā Muḥammad was mentioned on p. 399.

260. **Shaykh Bāyazīd** [Muʿaẓẓam Khān], grandson of Shaykh Salīm of Fatḥpūr Sīkrī.

Bāyazīd's mother nursed Prince Salīm (Jahāngīr) on the day he was born (*Tuzuk*, p. 13). In the 40th year of Akbar's reign B. was a commander of 400 and gradually rose to a command of 2,000. After Jahāngīr's accession he received a manṣab of 3,000 and the title of Muʿaẓẓam Khān. Soon after he was made Ṣūbahdār of Dihlī (*l.c.*, p. 37), and in the 3rd year a commander of 4,000, 2,000 horse. On his death he was buried at Fatḥpūr Sīkrī (*l.c.*, p. 262).

His son Mukarram Khān was son-in-law to Islām Khān Shaykh ʿAlāʾᵘ 'd-Dīn (another grandson of Shaykh Salīm), under whom he served in Bengal.[1] He distinguished himself in the expedition to Kūch Hājū, and brought the zamīndār Parīchhit before the governor.[2] At the death of his father-in-law, Muḥtashim Khān Shaykh Qāsim, brother of Islām Khān, was made governor of Bengal, and Mukarram Khān continued for one year in his office as governor of Kūch Hājū; but as he could not agree with Qāsim he went to court.

Later, he was made governor of Oṛīsā, and conquered the province of Khurdah (*l.c.*, pp. 214, 215), for which he was made a commander of 3,000, 2,000 horse. He seems to have remained in Oṛīsā till the 11th year (1029) when Ḥasan ʿAlī Turkmān was sent there as governor (*Tuzuk*, p. 308). In the 16th year M. Kh. came to court and was made Ṣūbadār of Dihlī and Fawjdār of Mewāt (*l.c.*, p. 352).

---

[1] Islām Khān was married to a sister of Abū 'l-Faẓl, by whom he had a son called Hoshang. Islām Khān died as governor of Bengal on the 5th Rajab, 1022 (*Tuzuk*, p. 126).

[2] The *Pādishāhnāma* (II, 64) where Mukarram Khān's expedition is related, distinguishes between Kūch Hājū and Kūch Bihār. The former was in the beginning of Jahāngīr's reign under Parīchhit, the latter under Lachmī Narā,in. Hājū is the name of a famous leader of the Kūch people, who in ethnological works is said to have expelled the Kachārīs and founded a dynasty which lasted two hundred years. His descendants still exercise *jura regalia* in Kūch Bihār Proper. Materials for a history of Kūch Bihār will be found in the *Akbarnāma* (Lucknow Edition, III, p. 208, annals of the 41st year); in the *Tuzuk-i Jahāngīrī* (pp. 147, 220, 221, 223); in the *Pādishāhnāma*, I, 496; II, 64 to 79, 87, 88, 94; and in the *Fatḥ-i Āshām*; *vide* also *Journal Asiatic Society Bengal*, vol. vii; Stewart's History of Bengal, p. 96; and above, pp. 315, 340, 343.

In the 21st year he was sent to Bengal as governor, *vice* Khānazād Khān. He travelled by boat. One day he ordered his ship to be moved to the bank, as he wished to say the afternoon prayer, when a sudden gale broke forth, during which he and his companions were drowned.

261. **Ghaznīn Khān**, of Jālor.

Ghaznīn Khān was in the 40th year of Akbar's reign a commander of 400. He is mentioned in the *Pādishāhnāma* (I, 167)[1] as having served during the reign of Jahāngīr against the Rānā.

Bird, in his *History of Gujrāt* (pp. 124, 405), calls him *Ghaznawī Khān* and *Ghaznī Khān*, and says he was the son of Malik Khanjī Jālorī. Ghaznīn Khān seems to have been inclined to join the insurrection of Sulṭān Muẓaffar. The Khānkhānān, on the 9th Muḥarram, 998, sent a detachment against Jālor; but perceiving that he was not in a fit condition to offer reṣistance, Ghaznīn went submissively to court. The emperor took compassion on him, and confirmed him in his hereditary possessions.

His son Pahāṛ was executed by Jahāngīr. "When I came to Dih Qāẓiyān, near Ujjain, I summoned Pahāṛ. This wretch had been put by me, after the death of his father, in possession of the Fort and the district of Jālor, his ancestral home. He is a young man, and was often checked by his mother for his bad behaviour. Annoyed at this, he entered with some of his companions her apartments, and killed her. I investigated the case, found him guilty, and had him executed." (Ṣafar, 1026; *Tuzuk*, p. 174).

Another son of Ghaznīn Khān is Niẓām who died in the 6th year of Shāhjahān's reign. He was a commander of 900, 550 horse (*Pādishāhn.*, I, b., 313).

Ghāznīn's brother Fīrūz was a commander of 600, 400 horse, and died in the 4th year (*Pādishāhn.*, I, b., 319).

The *Pādishāhnāma* (II, 739) mentions also Mujāhid of Jālor, who in the 20th year of Shāhjahān's reign was a commander of 800, 800 horse.

262. **Kījak Khwāja**, son of Khwāja ʿAbdu 'llāh.

The first volume of the *Akbarnāma* (p. 411) mentions a Kījak Khwāja among the grandees who accompanied Humāyūn to India. The third

[1] Wrongly called in the Bibl. Indica Edition of the *Pādishāhnāma* (I, 167), Ghazalī Khān.

Ghaznīn's *jāgīr*, before Akbar's conquest of Gujrāt, as detailed by Bird (p. 124) includes portions of Nāgor and Mīrtha, and fixes the revenue at nearly 10 lacs of rupees, with 7,000 horse. This can only have been nominal. Abū 'l-Faẓl, in his description of Ṣūba Ajmīr, IIIrd book, mentions 3½ lacs of rupees, with 2,000 horse, as the *jamaʿ* of Jālor and Sāṇchor (S.W. of Jālor).

volume of the same work (p. 470) mentions a Kījak Khwāja, who in 993 served against Qutlū Lohānī in Bengal. *Vide* No. 109.

263. **Sher Khān** Mughul.

264. **Fath[u] 'llāh,** son of Muḥammad Wafā.

He appears to be the Fatḥ[u] 'llāh mentioned in the *Akbarnāma* (III, 825) as the *sharbatdār* of the emperor. Akbar made him an Amīr. For some fault he was sent to the Dakhin ; but as he got ill, he was recalled. He recovered and went on sick leave to Māndū, where he died (1008).

265. **Rāy Manohar,** son of Rāja Lōkaran.

Rāja Lōkaran belonged to the Shaykhāwat branch of the Kachhwāhas. He served, in the 21st year, under Mān Singh, against the Rānā, and went in the same year with Rāja Bīr Baṛ to Dongarpūr,[1] the zamīndār of which wished to send his daughter to Akbar's harem. In the 24th year he served under Toḍar Mal in Bihār, and in the 24th year under the Khān Khānān in Gujrāt.

Manohar, in the 22nd year, reported to the emperor on his visit to Amber that in the neighbourhood an old town existed the site of which was marked by huge mounds of stone. Akbar encouraged him to rebuild it, and laid the foundation himself. The new settlement was called Mol Manoharnagar.[2] In the 45th year he was appointed with Rāy Durgā Lāl (No. 103) to pursue Muẓaffar Ḥusayn Mīrzā (p. 516), who was caught by Khwāja Waisī.

In the 1st year of Jahāngīr's reign he served under Prince Parwīz against the Rānā, and was made, in the 2nd year, a commander of 1,500, 600 horse (*Tuzuk*, p. 64). He served long in the Dakhin and died in the 11th year.

His son Prithī Chānd received after the death of his father the title of Rāy, and was made a commander of 500, 300 horse (*l.c.*, p. 160).

Manohar wrote Persian verses, and was called at court Mīrzā Manohar ; *vide* my article, " A Chapter from Muhammadan History," *Calcutta Review*, April, 1871.

266. **Khwāja ʿAbd[u] 'ṣ-Ṣamad,** Shīrīn-qalam (sweet-pen).

He is not to be confounded with No. 353.

Khwāja ʿAbd[u] 'ṣ-Ṣamad was a Shīrāzī. His father Khwāja Niẓām[u]

[1] The word *dongar*, which occurs in the names of places from Soraṭh to Mālwa and Central India, is a Gond word meaning *a forest*. There are many Dongarpūrs, Dongargāws, Dongartāls, Dongars, etc. Similarly, the word *bir* in Munḍārī signifies a jungle, whence Birbhūm (Western Bengal). Thus also Jhāṛkand, or jungle region, the general name of Chutya Nāgpūr. The above-mentioned Dongarpur lies on the N.W. frontier of Gujrāt (*Akbarn.*, III, 169, 170, 477).

[2] The maps give a Manoharpūr north of Amber, about Lat. 27° 20′.

'l-Mulk was Vazīr to Shāh Shujāʿ of Shīrāz. Before Humāyūn left Īrān he went to Tabrīz, where ʿAbdᵘ 'ṣ-Ṣamad paid his respects. He was even at that time known as a painter and calligraphist. Humāyūn invited him to come to him, and though then unable to accompany the emperor, he followed him in 956 to Kābul.

Under Akbar ʿA. was a commander of 400; but low as his *manṣab* was, he had great influence at court. In the 22nd year he was in charge of the mint at Fatḥpūr Sīkrī (*Akbarnāma*, III, 195); and in the 31st year, when the officers were redistributed over the several ṣūbas, he was appointed Dīwān of Multān.

As an instance of his skill it is mentioned that he wrote the *Sūratᵘ 'l-ikhlāṣ* (Qurʾān, Sur. CXII) on a poppy seed (*dānah-y khashkhāsh*). *Vide* p. 114.

For his son, *vide* No. 351.

267. **Silhadī,** son of Rāja Bihārī Mal (No. 23).

268. **Rām Chand** Kachhwāha.

Vide p. 422.

[**Rām Chand Chauhān.**] The *Maʾāṣīr* says that he was the son of Badal Singh, and a commander of 500. In the 17th year he served under M. ʿAzīz Koka (No. 21) in Gujrāt, and in the 26th year under Sulṭān Murād against M. Muḥammad Ḥakīm, king of Kābul. In the 28th year he was under M. Shāhrukh in the Dakhin. In the fight, in which Rāja ʿAlī of Khandesh fell, R. Ch. received twenty wounds and fell from his horse. Next day he was found still alive. He died a few days later (41st year, 1005).

269. **Bahādur Khān Qūrdār.**

He served in the beginning of the 18th year in Gujrāt (*Akbarnāma*, III, 25), in the 26th in Kābul (*l.c.*, 333) and in the siege of Āsīr (1008).

The *Pādishāhnāma* (I, b., pp. 311, 315) mentions Abābakr and ʿUsmān, sons of Bahādur Khān Qūrbegī, who seems to be the same officer. They died in the 8th and 9th years of Shāhjahān.

270. **Bānkā,** the Kachhwāha.

He served in the 26th year in Kābul (*Akbarn.*, III, 333). His son Haridī Rām was under Shāhjahān a commander of 1,500, 1,000 horse, and died in the 9th of his reign.

XIX. Commanders of Three Hundred and Fifty.

271. **Mīrzā Abū Saʿīd**
272. **Mīrzā Sanjar** } sons of Sulṭān Ḥusayn Mīrzā.

They were mentioned above on p. 328. Mīrzā Sanjar is not to be confounded with the Mīrzā Sankar mentioned on p. 533, note 1.

273. **ʿAlī Mardān Bahādur.**

The *Ṭabaqāt* mentions him as having been in 984 (21st year) at court, from where he was sent to Qulij Khān (No. 42) at Īdar, who was to go to Gujrāt to see the ships off which under Sulṭān Khwāja (No. 108) were on the point of leaving for Makkah. Later he served under the Khān Khānān in Sind,[1] and in the 41st year in the Dakhin. Subsequently, he commanded the Talingāna corps. In the 46th year, he marched to Pāthrī to assist Sher Khwāja (No. 176) when he heard that Bahādur Khān Gīlānī, whom he had left with a small detachment in Talingāna, had been defeated. He returned and attacked the enemies who were much stronger than he ; his men fled and he himself was captured. In the same year Abū 'l-Faẓl made peace, and ʿAlī Mardān was set at liberty. In the 47th year he served with distinction under Mīrzā Īrij (No. 255) against Malik ʿAmbar.

In the 7th year of Jahāngīr's reign he was attached to the corps commanded by ʿAbdᵘ 'llāh Khān Fīrūz-jang, who had been ordered to move with the Gujrāt army over Nāsik into the Dakhin, in order to co-operate with the second army corps under Khān Jahān Lodī. ʿAbdᵘ 'llāh entered the hostile territory without meeting the second army, and returned towards Gujrāt, now pursued by the enemies. In one of the fights which ensued, ʿA. M. was wounded and captured. He was taken before Malik ʿAmbar, and though the doctors did everything to save him, he died two days later of his wounds, in 1021 A.H. (*Tuzuk*, p. 108).

His son Karamᵘ 'llāh served under Jahāngīr (*Tuzuk*, p. 269) and was under Shāhjahān a commander of 1,000, 1,000 horse. He was for some time commandant of Fort Odgīr, and died in the 21st year of Shāhj.'s reign.

274. **Raẓā Qulī**, son of Khān Jahān (No. 24).

Vide above, p. 351.

275. **Shaykh Khūbū** [Quṭbᵘ 'd-Dīn Khān-i Chishti] of Fatḥpūr Sīkrī.

His father was a Shaykhzāda of Badā,on, and his mother a daughter of Shaykh Salīm. Khūbū was a foster-brother of Jahāngīr.[2] When the prince was at Ilāhābād in rebellion against Akbar, he conferred upon Khūbū the title of Quṭbᵘ 'd-Dīn Khān, and made him Ṣūbadār of Bihār.

---

[1] *Vide* Dowson, *Elliot's Historians*, I, p. 248.
[2] Jahāngīr says that Khūbū's mother was dearer to him than his own mother.

On his accession he made him Ṣūbadār of Bengal, *vice* Mān Singh (9th Jumāda I, 1015; *Tuzuk*, p. 37).

At that time, Sher Afkan ʿAlī Qulī Istajlū (*vide* No. 394) was tuyūldār of Bardwān, and as his wife Mihr^u 'n-Nisā [Nūr Jahān] was coveted by the emperor, Quṭb was ordered to send Sher Afkan to court, who however, refused to go. Quṭb, therefore, went to Bardwān, sending Ghiyāṣā, son of his sister, before him, to persuade Sher Afkan that no harm would be done to him. When Quṭb arrived, Sher Afkan went to meet him, accompanied by two men. On his approach, Q. lifted up his horse-whip as a sign for his companions to cut down Sher Afkan. "What is all this?" exclaimed Sher. Quṭb waved his hand to call back his men, and advancing towards Sher, upbraided him for his disobedience. His men mistaking Quṭb's signal to withdraw, closed round Sher, who rushed with his sword against Quṭb and gave him a deep wound in the abdomen. Quṭb was a stout man, and seizing the protruding bowels with his hands, called out to his men to cut down the scoundrel. Amba Khān, a Kashmīrī noble of royal blood, thereupon charged Sher Afkan, and gave him a sword cut over the head; but he fell at the same time, pierced through by Sher's sword (p. 529, note 1). The men now crowded round him and struck him to the ground. Quṭb^u 'd-Dīn was still on horseback, when he heard that Sher Afkan had been killed, and he sent off Ghiyāṣā to bring his effects and his family to Bardwān. He then was removed in a *pālkī*. He died whilst being carried away. His corpse was taken to Fatḥpūr Sīkrī and buried.

In 1013 he built the Jāmiʿ mosque of Badāʾon.

His son, Shaykh Ibrāhīm, was, in 1015, a commander of 1,000, 300 horse, and had the title of *Kishwar Khān*. He was for some time governor of Rohtās, and served in the beginning of 1021 against ʿUṣmān.

Ilahdiya, son of Kishwar Khān, is mentioned in the *Pādishāhnāma* (I, b., 100, 177, 307; II, 344, 379, 411, 484).

276. **Ẓiyāʾ^u 'l-Mulk,** of Kāshān.

The *Akbarnāma* (III, 590, 628) and the *Tuzuk* (p. 11) mention a *Ẓiyāʾ^u 'd-Dīn*.

The Hakīm Ẓiyāʾ^u 'd-Dīn of Kāshan, who under Shāhjahān held the title of Raḥmat Khān, can scarcely be the same.

277. **Hamza Beg Ghatrāghalī.**

He may be the brother of No. 203. The *Akbarnāma* (III, 255) mentions also a Ḥusayn Beg Ghatrāghalī.

278. **Mukhtar Beg,** son of Āghā Mullā.

Mukhtār Beg served under Aʿẓam Khān Koka (No. 21) in Bihār,

Gaḍha-Rā,isīn (*Akbarn.* III, 276, 473), and in the 36th year, under Sulṭān Murād in Mālwa.

Naṣru 'llāh, son of Mukhtār Beg, was under Shāhjahān a commander of 700, 150 horse, and died in the 10th year.

Fatḥu 'llāh, son of Naṣru 'llāh, was under Shāhjahān a commander of 500, 50 horse (*Pādishāhn.*, I, b., 318 ; II, 752).

Abū 'l-Fazl calls Mukhtār Beg the son of Āghā Mullā. This would seem to be the Āghā Mullā Dawātdār, mentioned on p. 398. If so, Mukhtār Beg would be the brother of Ghiyāṣu 'd-Dīn ʿAlī (No. 126), The Āghā Mullā mentioned below (No. 376), to judge from the *Tuzuk* (p. 27), is the brother of Āṣaf Khān III (No. 98), and had a son of the name of Badīʿu 'z-Zamān, who under Shāhjahān was a commander of 500, 100 horse (*Pād.*, I, b., 327 ; II, 751). In Muhammadan families the name of the grandfather is often given to the grandchild.

279. **Ḥaydar ʿAlī ʿArab.**

He served, in the 32nd year, in Afghānistān (*Akbarn.*, III, 540, 548).

280. **Peshraw Khān** [Mihtar Saʿādat].

Mihtar Saʿādat had been brought up in Tabrīz, and was in the service of Shāh Ṭahmasp, who gave him as a present to Humāyūn. After Humāyūn's death he was promoted and got the title of *Peshraw Khān.* In the 19th year Akbar sent him on a mission to Bihār, where he was caught on the Ganges by Gajpatī, the great zamīndār (p. 437, note 2). When Jagdespūr, the stronghold of the Rāja, was conquered, Gajpatī ordered several prisoners to be killed, among them Peshraw. The executioner, however, did not kill him, and told another man to do so. But the latter accidentally could not get his sword out of the scabbard ; and the Rāja, who was on the point of flying, having no time to lose, ordered him to take P. on his elephant. The elephant was wild and restive, and the man who was in charge of P. fell from the animal and got kicked, when the brute all at once commenced to roar in such a manner that the other elephants ran away frightened. Although P.'s hands were tied, he managed to get to the *kalāwa* (p. 135) of the driver and thus sat firm ; but the driver, unable to manage the brute, threw himself to the ground and ran away, leaving P. alone on the elephant. Next morning it got quiet, and P. threw himself down, when he was picked up by a trooper who had been searching for him.

In the 21st year he reported at court the defeat of Gajpatī[1] (*Akbarn.*, III, 163). In the 25th year he served in Bengal (*l.c.*, p. 289). Later he

[1] Gajpatī's brother, Bairī Sāl, had been killed (*Akbarn.*, III, 162).

was sent to Niẓāmu 'l-Mulk of the Dakhin, and afterwards to Bahādur Khān, son of Rāja ʿAlī Khān of Khāndesh. His mission to the latter was in vain, and Akbar marched to Āsīr. P. distinguished himself in the siege of Māligaḍh.

Jahāngīr made him a commander of 2,000, and continued him in his office as superintendent of the *Farrāsh-khāna* (Quartermaster).

P. died in the 3rd year, on the 1st Rajab, 1017. Jahāngīr says (*Tuzuk*, p. 71) "He was an excellent servant, and though ninety years old, he was smarter than many a young man. He had amassed a fortune of 15 lacs of rupees. His son *Ryāyat* is unfit for anything ; but for the sake of his father, I put him in charge of half the *Farrāsh-khāna*.

281. **Qāẓī Ḥasan** Qazwīnī.

In the 32nd year (995) he served in Gujrāt (*Akbarn.*, III, 537, 554, where the Lucknow edition has Qāẓī *Ḥusayn*), and later in the siege of Āsīr (*l.c.*, III, 825).

282. **Mīr Murād-i** Juwaynī.

He is not to be confounded with No. 380, but may be the same as mentioned on p. 380.

Juwayn is the Arabic form of the Persian Gūjān, the name of a small town,[1] in Khurāsān, on the road between Bisṭām and Nīshāpūr. It lies, according to the *Maʾāṣir* in the district of Bayhaq, of which Sabzwār is the capital, and is renowned as the birthplace of many learned men and poets.

Mīr Murād belongs to the Sayyids of Juwayn. As he had been long in the Dakhin, he was also called *Dakhinī*. He was an excellent shot, and Akbar appointed him rifle-instructor to Prince Khurram. He died, in the 46th year, as Bakhshī of Lāhor. He had two sons, Qāsim Khān and Hāshim Khān.

Qāsim Khān was an excellent poet, and rose to distinction under Islām Khān, governor of Bengal, who made him treasurer of the ṣūba. Later, he married Manīja Begum, sister of Nūr Jahān, and thus became a friend of Jahāngīr. An example of a happy repartee is given. Once Jahāngīr asked for a cup of water. The cup was so thin that it could not bear the weight of the water, and when handed to the emperor it broke. Looking at Qāsim, J. said (metre *Ramal*) :—

کاسه نازک بود آب آرام نتوانست کرد

The cup was lovely, so the water lost its rest—

---

[1] *Vide* Wüstenfeld's Yacut, II, 164

when Qāsim, completing the verse, replied :—

دید حالم را وچشمش ضبط اشک خود نکرد

It saw my love-grief, and could not suppress its tears.

In the end of J.'s reign, he was Ṣūbadār of Āgra, and was in charge of the treasures in the fort. When the emperor died, and Shāhjahān left the Dakhin, Qāsim paid his respects in the Bāgh-i Dahra (Āgra), which in honour of Jahāngīr had been called *Nūr Manzil*, and was soon after made a commander of 5,000, 500 horse, and appointed governor of Bengal, *vide* Fidā'ī Khān.

As Shāhjahān when prince, during his rebellion, had heard of the wicked practices of the Portuguese in Bengal, who converted natives by force to Christianity, he ordered Qāsim to destroy their settlement at Hūglī. In the 5th year, in Shaʿbān, 1041, or February, A.D. 1632 (*Pādishāhn.*, I, 435, 437), Q. sent a corps under his son ʿInāyat[u] 'llāh and Allah Yār Khān to Hūglī. The Portuguese held out for three months and a half, when the Muhammadans succeeded in laying dry the ditch in front of the Church, dug a mine, and blew up the church. The fort was taken. Ten thousand Portuguese are said to have perished during the siege, and 4,400 were taken prisoners. About 10,000 natives whom they had in their power were liberated. One thousand Musulmāns died as martyrs for their religion.[1]

Three days after the conquest of Hūglī, Qāsim died (*l.c.*, p. 444). The Jāmiʿ Masjid in the Atga Bāzār of Āgrah was built by him.

283. **Mīr Qāsin** Badakhshī.

He served in the Dakhin (*Akbarn.*, III, 830).

284. **Banda ʿAlī** Maydānī.

Maydānī is the name of an Afghān clan; *vide* No. 317. Banda ʿAlī served in the 9th year with Muḥammad Ḥakīm of Kābul, who was attacked by Mīrzā Sulaymān of Badakhshān (No. 5) and had applied to Akbar for help. In the 30th and 32nd years he served in Kābul (*Akbarn.*, II, 299; III, 477, 540).

The *Akbarnāma* (II, 209) also mentions a Banda ʿAlī Qurbegī.

285. **Khwājagī Fatḥ[u]** 'llāh, son of Ḥājī Ḥabīb[u] 'llāh of Kāshān.

He was mentioned above on pp. 386, 516. He served in the 30th year under Mīrzā ʿAzīz Koka (No. 21). *Akbarn.*, III, 473.

---

[1] The siege of Hūglī commenced on the 2nd Ẕī Ḥijjah, 1041, or 11th June, 1632, and the town was taken on the 14th Rabīʿ I, 1042, or 10th September, 1632. The village of Haldīpūr, mentioned in the *Pādishāhnāma* as having for some time been the head-quarters of the Mughul army, is called on our maps *Holodpūr*, and lies N.W. of Hūglī.

The Portuguese church of Bandel (a corruption of *bandar* ?) bears the year 1599 on its keystone.

286. **Zāhid**
287. **Dost** [Muḥammad]
288. **Yār** [Muḥammad]
} sons of Ṣādiq Khān (No. 43).

They have been mentioned above on p. 384. Zāhid, in the end of 1025, served against Dalpat (No. 252).

Regarding Zāhid, *vide* also a passage from the *Tārīkh-i Maᶜṣūmī*, translated Dowson's edition of *Elliot's Historians*, I, 246.

289. **ᶜIzzatᵘ** 'llāh Ghujdwānī.

Ghujduwān is a small town in Bukhārā.

The *Akbarnāma* (III, 548) mentions a Qāẓī ᶜIzzatᵘ 'llāh, who, in the 32nd year, served in Afghānistān.

XX. Commanders of Three Hundred.

290. **Āltūn Qulij.**

291. **Jān Qulij.**

Two MSS. have Āltūn Qulij, *son* of Khān Qulij, which latter name would be an unusual transposition for Qulij Khān. They are not the sons of Qulij Khān (No. 42) *vide* Nos. 292 and 293.

Āltūn Qulij is mentioned in the *Akbārnāma* (III, 554) as having served in Baglāna with Bharjī, the Rāja who was hard pressed in Fort Molher by his relations. Bharjī died about the same time (beginning of the 33rd year).

292. **Sayfᵘ 'llāh [Qulijᵘ 'llah]**
293. **Chīn Qulij**
} sons of Qulij Khān (No. 42).

Sayf is Arabic, and means the same as the Turkish *qulij*, a sword. Sayfᵘ 'llāh was mentioned under No. 203. In the beginning of the 33rd year he served under Ṣādiq Khān (No. 43) in Afghānistān.

Regarding Mīrzā Chīn Qulij, the *Maʾāṡir* says that he was an educated, liberal man, well versed in government matters. He had learned under Mullā Muṣṭafā of Jaunpūr, and was for a long time Fawjdār of Jaunpūr and Banāras.

At the death of his father, his younger brother Mīrzā Lāhaurī, the spoiled pet son of his father, joined Chīn Qulij in Jaunpūr. He had not been long there when he interfered in government matters and caused disturbances, during which Chīn Qulij lost his life. His immense property escheated to the state; it is said that it took the clerks a whole year to make the inventory.

In 1022, when Jahāngīr was in Ajmīr, he summoned Mullā Muṣṭafā, who had been the Mīrzā's teacher, with the intention of doing him harm.

While at court he got acquainted with Mullā Muḥammad of Thathah, a teacher in the employ of Āṣafjāh (or Āṣaf K͟hān IV ; *vide* p. 398), who had scientific discussions with him, and finding him a learned man, interceded on his behalf. Muṣṭafa was let off, went to Makkah and died.

Mīrzā Lāhaurī was caught and imprisoned. After some time, he was set at liberty, and received a daily allowance (*yaumiyya*). He had a house in Āgra, near the Jamna, at the end of the Darsan, and trained pigeons. He led a miserable life.

The *Maʾāṣir* mentions a few instances of his wicked behaviour. Once he buried one of his servants alive, as he wished to know something about Munkir and Nakīr, the two angels who, according to the belief of the Muhammadans, examine the dead in the grave, beating the corpse with sledge hammers if the dead man is found wanting in belief. When the man was dug out he was found dead. Another time, when with his father, in Lāhor, he disturbed a Hindū wedding-feast and carried off the bride ; and when the people complained to his father, he told them to be glad that they were now related to the Ṣūbadār of Lāhor.

The other sons of Qulij K͟hān, as Qulij[u] 'llāh, Chīn, Qulij, Bāljū Q., Bayrām Q., and Jān Q., held mostly respectable manṣabs.

The *Tuzuk-i Jahāngīrī* relates the story differently. Both M. Chīn Qulij and M. Lāhaurī are described as wicked men. Chīn Q., after the death of his father, came with his brothers and relations to court (Ṣafar, 1023 ; *Tuzuk*, p. 127) and received Jaunpūr as jāgīr. As the emperor heard of the wicked doings of M. Lāhaurī, from whom no man was safe, he sent an Aḥadī to Jaunpūr to bring him to court, when Chīn Qulij fled with him to several zamīndārs. The men of Janāngīr Qulī K͟hān, governor of Bihār, at last caught him ; but before he was taken to the governor, Chīn died, some say, in consequence of an attack of illness, others from wounds he had inflicted on himself. His corpse was taken to Jahāngīr Qulī K͟hān, who sent it with his family and property to Ilāhābād. The greater part of his property had been squandered or given away to zamīndārs (1024 ; *Tuzuk*, p. 148).

294. **Abū 'l-Fattāḥ Atāliq.**

295. **Sayyid Bāyazīd** of Bārha.

He served in the 33rd year (996) in Gujrāt (*Akbarn.*, III, 553). In the beginning of the 17th year of Jahāngīr's reign (1031) he received the title of Muṣṭafa K͟hān (*Tuzuk*, p. 344).

In the 1st year of Shāhjahān's reign he was made a commander of 2,000, 700 horse (*Pād.*, I, 183). His name is not given in the list of grandees of the *Pādishāhnāma.*

296. **Balbhadr**, the Rāṭhor.

297. **Abū 'l-Maˁalī**, son of Sayyid Muḥammad Mīr ˁAdl (No. 140).

298. **Bāqir** Anṣārī.

He was in Bengal at the outbreak of the military revolt. In the 37th year he served under Mān Singh in the expedition to Orīsā (*Akbarn.*, III, 267, 641).

299. **Bāyazīd Beg** Turkmān.

He was at first in Munˁim's service (*Akbarn.*, II, 238, 253). The *Pādishāhnāma* (I, b., 328) mentions Maḥmūd Beg, son of Bāyazīd Beg. *Vide* No. 335.

300. **Shaykh Dawlat** Bakhtyār.

301. **Ḥusayn**, the Pakhlīwāl.

The story of the origin of his family from the Qārlüqs under Tīmūr (*vide* p. 504) is given in the *Tuzuk* (p. 290). Jahāngīr adds, " but they do not know who was then their chief. At present they are common Panjābīs (*Lāhaurī-yi maraz*) and speak Panjābī. This is also the case with Dhantūr " (*vide* No. 392).

Sulṭān Ḥusayn, as he called himself, is the son of Sulṭān Maḥmūd. His rebellious attitude towards Akbar has been mentioned above on p. 504. When Jahāngīr in the 14th year (beginning of 1029) paid him a visit, Ḥusayn was about seventy years old, but still active. He was then a commander of 400, 300 horse, and Jahāngīr promoted him to a manṣab of 600, 350 horse

Ḥusayn died in the 18th year (end of 1032; *Tuzuk*, p. 367). His command and the district of Pakhlī were given to his son Shādmān.

Shādmān served under Dārā Shikoh in Qandahār (beginning of 1052) and was in the 20th year of Shāhjahān's reign a commander of 1,000, 900 horse. *Pādishāhnāna*, II, 293, 733.

The *Tuzuk* (p. 290) mentions a few places in the district of Pakhlī, and has a remark on the thick strong beer which the inhabitants made from bread and rice.

302. **Kesū Dās**, son of Jai Mal.

Vide No. 408. One MS. has *Jait Mal*, instead of *Jai Mal*. The *Pādishāhnāma* (I, b., 310) mentions a Rāja Girdhar, son of Kesū Dās, grandson of Jat Mal of Mirtha. The *Tuzuk* frequently mentions a Kesū Dās Mārū (*Tuzuk*, pp. 9, 37, 203).

303. **Mīrza Khān** of Nīshāpūr. One MS. has *Jān* for *Khān*.

304. **Muẓaffar**, brother of Khān ˁĀlam (No. 58).

My text edition has wrongly *Khān-i Aˁẓam* for *Khān ˁĀlam*.

305. **Tulsī Dās Jādon.**

He served in 992 against Sulṭān Muẓaffar of Gujrāt (*Akbarn.*, III, 422). The *Akbarnāma* (III, 157, 434, 598) mentions another Jādō Rāja Gopāl. He died in the end of the 34th year, and is mentioned in the *Ṭabaqāt* as a commander of 2,000.

306. **Raḥmat Khān**, son of Masnad-i ˤĀlī.

Masnad-i ˤĀlī is an Afghān title, as *Majlis*ᵘ *'l Majālis, Majlis-i Ikhtiyār*, etc. It was the title of Fattū Khān, or Fatḥ Khān, a courtier of Islam Shāh, who afterwards joined Akbar's service. He served under Ḥusayn Qulī Khān Jahān (No. 24) in 980 against Nagarkoṭ (*Badāˀonī*, II, 161). The *Ṭabaqāt* makes him a commander of 2,000). He seems to be the same Fatḥ Khān whom Sulaymān Kararānī had put in charge of Rohtās in Bihār (*Bad.*, II, 77).

He died in the 34th year in Audh (*Akbarn.*, III, 599).

A Raḥmat Khān served in the 45th year in the Dakhin. Raḥmat Khān's brother, Shāh Muḥammad, is mentioned below, No. 395.

307. **Aḥmad Qāsim Koka.**

He served in 993 against the Yūsufzāˀīs, and in 996 under Ṣādiq Khān, against the Tārīkīs (*Akbarn.*, III, 490, 552).

The *Tuzuk* (p. 159) mentions a Yār Beg, son of A. Q.'s brother.

308. **Bahādur** Gohlot.

309. **Dawlat Khān** Lodī.

He was a Lodī Afghān of the Shāhū-khayl clan, and was at first in the service of ˤAziz Koka (No. 21). When ˤAbdᵘ 'r-Raḥīm (No. 29) married the daughter of ˤAzīz, Dawlat Khān was transferred to ˤAbdᵘ 'r-Raḥīm's service, and ˤAzīz, in sending him to his son-in-law, said, "Take care of this man, and you may yet get the title of your father (Khān Khānān)." Dawlat distinguished himself in the wars in Gujrāt (p. 355, l. 24, where for *Dost Khān*, as given in the *Maˀāṣir*, we have to read *Dawlat Khān*), in Thatha and the Dakhin. His courage was proverbial. In his master's contingent he held a command of 1,000. Sulṭān Dānyāl won him over, and made him a commander of 2,000.

He died in the end of the 45th year (Shaˤbān, 1009) at Aḥmadnagar (*Akbarn.*, III, 846). It is said that Akbar stood in awe of him, and when he heard of his death, he is reported to have said, "To-day Sher Khān Sūr died."

Dawlat Khān's eldest son, whom the *Maˀāṣir* calls Maḥmūd, was half mad. In the 46th year, on a hunting tour, he left his companions, got into a quarrel with some Kolīs near Pāl, and perished.

Dawlat's second son is the renowned Pīr Khān, or Pīrū, better known in history under his title *Khān Jahān Lodī.* If Akbar's presentiments were deceived in the father, they were fulfilled in the son.

Pīr Khān, when young, fell out with his father, and fled with his elder brother, whom the *Maʿāṣir* here calls Muḥammad Khān, to Bengal, where they were assisted by Mān Singh. Muḥammad Khān died when young.

Like his father, P. Kh. was in the service of Sulṭān Dānyāl, who treated him like a friend, and called him " son ". On the death of the Prince, Pīr, then twenty years old, joined Jahāngīr's service, was made in the second year a commander of 3,000, and received the title of Ṣalābat Khān (*Tuzuk*, p. 42). He gradually rose to a manṣab of 5,000, and received the title of Khān Jahān, which was looked upon as second in dignity to that of Khān Khānān. Although Jahāngīr treated him like an intimate friend rather than a subject, Khān Jahān never got his position and formed no ambitious plans.

When Prince Parwīz, Rāja Mān Singh and Sharīf Khān (No. 351) were sent to the Dakhin to reinforce the Khān Khānān and matters took an unfavourable turn, Khān Jahān, in 1018, was sent with 12,000 troopers to their assistance. At the review, Jahāngīr came down from the state window, put his turban on Kh. J.'s head, seized his hand, and helped him in mounting. Without delaying in Burhānpūr, Kh. J. moved to Bālaghāt, where the imperial army was. At Mulkāpūr, a great fight took place with Malik ʿAmbar, and the imperialists unaccustomed to the warfare of the Dakhinīs, lost heavily. The Khān Khānān met him with every respect, and took him to Bālāghāt. According to the original plan, Kh. J. was to lead the Dakhin corps, and ʿAbdᵘ 'llāh Khān the Gujrāt army, upon Daulatābād (under No. 273). Malik ʿAmbar, afraid of being attacked from two sides, succeeded in gaining over the Khān Khānān, who managed to detain Kh. J. in Ẓafarnagar; and ʿAbdᵘ 'llāh, when marching forward, found no support, and had to retreat with heavy losses. Kh. J. got short of provisions; his horses died off, and the splendid army with which he had set out, returned in a most disorderly state to Burhānpūr.

Kh. J. accused the Khān Khānān of treason, and offered to conquer Bījāpūr in two years, if the emperor would give him 30,000 men and absolute power. This Jahāngīr agreed to, and the Khān-i Aʿẓam (No. 21) and Khān ʿĀlam (No. 328) were sent to his assistance. But though the Khān Khānān had been removed, the duplicity of the Amīrs remained what it had been before, and matters did not improve. The command was therefore given to the Khān-i Aʿẓam and Kh. J. received Thālner as jāgīr, and was ordered to remain at Īlichpūr. After a year, he returned to court, but was treated by the emperor in as friendly a manner as before.

In the 15th year, when the Persians threatened Qandahār, Kh. J. was made governor of Multān. Two years later, in the 17th year, Shāh ʿAbbās took Qandahār after a siege of forty days. Kh. J. was called to court for advice, having been forbidden to attack Shāh ʿAbbās, because kings should be opposed by kings. When he came to court, Prince Khurram was appointed to reconquer Qandahār, and Kh. J. was ordered back to Multān to make preparations for the expedition. It is said that the Afghān tribes from near Qandahār came to him in Multān, and declared themselves willing to be the vanguard of the army, if he would only promise every horseman five tankas, and each foot soldier two tankas *per diem* to keep them from starving; they were willing to go with him to Iṣfahān, and promised to be responsible for the supplies. But Kh. J. refused the proffered assistance, remarking that Jahāngīr would kill him if he heard of the attachment of the Afghāns to him.

In the meantime matters changed. Shāhjahān rebelled, and the expedition to Qandahār was not undertaken. The emperor several times ordered Kh. J. to return, and wrote at last himself, adding the curious remark that even Sher Khān Sūr, in spite of his enmity, would after so many requests have obeyed. The delay, it is said, was caused by severe illness. On his arrival at court, Kh. J. was made commandant of Fort Āgra, and was put in charge of the treasures.

In the 19th year, on the death of the Khān-i Aʿẓam, he was made governor of Gujrāt, and when Mahābat Khān was sent to Bengal, he was appointed *atālīq* to Prince Parwīz, whom he joined at Burhānpūr.

In 1035, the 21st year, Parwīz died, and the Dakhin was placed under Kh. J. He moved against Fatḥ Khān, son of Malik ʿAmbar, to Bālāghāt. His conduct was now more than suspicious: he accepted proposals made by Ḥamīd Khān Ḥabshī, the minister of the Niẓām Shāh, to cede the conquered districts for an annual payment of three lacs of hūns though the revenue was 55 krors of dāms (*Pādishāhn.*, I, 271), and ordered the imperial Fawjdārs and Thānahdārs to give up their places to the agents of the Niẓām Shāh and repair to Burhānpūr. Only Sipahdār Khān, who stood in Aḥmadnagar, refused to do so without express orders from the emperor.

Soon after, Mahābat Khān joined Shāhjahān at Junīr, and was honoured with the title of *Sipahsālār*. On the death of Jahāngīr, which took place immediately afterwards, Shāhjahān sent Jān Niṣār Khān to Kh. J., to find out what he intended to do, and confirm him at the same time in his office as Ṣūbadār of the Dakhin ; but as he in the meantime had formed other plans, he sent back Jān Niṣār without answer. He intended to rebel. It is said that he was misled by Daryā Khān Rohīla and Fāẓil Khān, the Dīwān of the Dakhin ; Dāwar Bakhsh, they insinuated, had been made emperor by the army, Shahryār had proclaimed himself in Lāhor, whilst Shāhj. had offended him by conferring the title of Sipahsālār on Mahābat Khān, who only lately had joined him ; he, too, should aim at the crown, as he was a man of great power, and would find numerous adherents.

Shāhj. sent Mahābat to Māndū, where Kh. J.'s family was. Kh. J. renewed friendly relations with the Niẓām Shāh, and leaving Sikandar Dutānī in Burhānpūr, he moved with several Amīrs to Māndū, and deposed the governor Muẓaffar Khān Maʿmūrī. But he soon saw how mistaken he was. The Amīrs who had come with him, left him and paid their respects to Shāhj. ; the proclamation of Dāwar Bakhsh proved to be a scheme made by Āṣaf Khān in favour of Shāhj., and Kh. J. sent a vakīl to court and presented, after Shāhj.'s accession, a most valuable present. The emperor was willing to overlook past faults, and left him in possession of the government of Mālwah.

In the second year, after punishing Jhujhār Singh, Kh. J. came to court and was treated by the emperor with cold politeness. Their mutual distrust soon showed itself. Shāhj. remarked on the strong contingent which he had brought to Āgra, and several parganas of his jāgīrs were transferred to others. One evening, at a darbār, Mīrzā Lashkarī, son of Mukhliṣ Khān, foolishly said to the sons of Kh. J., "He will some of these days imprison your father." Kh. J., on hearing this, shut himself up at home, and when the emperor sent Islām Khān to his house to inquire, he begged the messenger to obtain for him an *amān-nāma*, or letter of safety, as he was hourly expecting the displeasure of his master. Shāhj. was generous enough to send him the guarantee ; but though even Āṣaf Khān tried to console him, the old suspicions were never forgotten. In fact it would seem that he only feared the more for his safety, and on the night from the 26th to the 27th Ṣafar, 1039, after a stay at court of eight months, he fled from Āgra. When passing the Hatyāpul [1] Darwāza, he humbly threw the reigns of his horse over

[1] The two large stone elephants which stood upon the gate were taken down by Awrangzīb in Rajab, 1079, because the Muhammadan law forbids sculpture. *Maʾāṣir-i ʿĀlamgīrī*, p. 77.

his neck, bent his head forward on the saddle, and exclaimed, " O God, thou knowest that I fly for the preservation of my honour ; to rebel is not my intention." On the morning before his flight, Āṣaf had been informed of his plan, and reported the rumour to the emperor. But Shāhj. said that he could take no steps to prevent Kh. J. from rebelling ; he had given him the guarantee, and could use no force before the crime had actually been committed.

An outline of Kh. J.'s rebellion may be found in Elphinstone's history, where the main facts are given.

When he could no longer hold himself in the Dakhin, he resolved to cut his way to the Panjāb. He entered Mālwah, pursued by ʿAbdu 'llāh Khān and Muẓaffar Khān Bārha. After capturing at Sironj fifty imperial elephants, he entered the territory of the Bundela Rājah. But Jagrāj Bikramājīt, son of Jhujhār Singh, fell upon his rear (17th Jumāda, II, 1040), defeated it, and killed Daryā Khān (a commander of 4,000) and his son, Kh. J.'s best officers (*Padishāhn.*, I, 339 ; I, b., 296). On arriving in Bhānder,[1] Kh. J. met Sayyid Muẓaffar, and sending off his baggage engaged him with 1,000 men. During the fight Maḥmūd Khān, one of Kh. J.'s sons, was killed. On approaching Kālinjar, he was opposed by Sayyid Aḥmad, the commandant of the Fort, and in a fight another of his sons, Ḥasan Khān, was captured. Marching farther, he arrived at the tank of Sehōdā, where he resolved to die. He allowed his men to go away as his cause was hopeless. On the 1st Rajab, 1040, he was again attacked by ʿAbdu 'llāh Khān and S. Muẓaffar, and was mortally wounded by Mādhū Singh with a spear. Before Muẓaffar could come up, the soldiers had cut him and his son ʿAzīz to pieces (*Pādishāhn.*, I, 351). Their heads were sent to Shāhjahān at Burhānpūr, fixed for some time to the walls of the city, and then buried in the vault of Dawlat Khān, Kh. J.'s father.

Kh. J. had been a commander of 7,000 (*Pādishāhn.*, I, b., 293).

Several of Kh. J.'s sons, as Ḥusayn ʿAẓmat, Maḥmūd, and Ḥasan, had perished during the rebellion of their father. Another, Aṣālat Khān, a commander of 3,000, died during the rebellion at Dawlatābād, and Muẓaffar had left his father and gone to court. Farīd and Jān Jahān

---

[1] So the *Maʾāṣir*. The Bibl. Ind. Edition of the *Pādishāhnāma*, I, 348, has *Bāndhū*. So likewise for *Salwānī* (*Pād.*, I, 290), the *Maʾāṣir* has Lānjhī (Gondwānah), where Kh. J., after the fight near Dholpūr and his march through the Bundela State, for the first time rested.

Bhānder lies N.E. of Jhānsī. Sehōdā lies N. of Kālinjar, on the Ken.

were captured ; ʿĀlam and Aḥmad had fled, and went after some time to court. " But none of his sons ever prospered."

The historical work entitled *Makhzan-i Afghānī*, or some editions of it, contain a chapter in praise of Khān Jahān, after whom the book is sometimes called *Tārīkh-i Khān Jahān Lodī*.

310. **Shāh Muḥammad**, son of Quraysh Sulṭān (No. 178).

311. **Ḥasan Khān** Miyāna.

He was at first a servant of Ṣādiq Khān (No. 43), but later he received a *manṣab*. He died in the Dakhin wars.

Of his eight sons, the eldest died young (*Tuzuk*, p. 200). The second is *Buhlūl Khān*. He rose to a manṣab of 1,500 under Jāhangīr (*l.c.*, pp. 184, 200), and received the title of *Sarbuland Khān*. He was remarkable for his courage and his external appearance. He served in Gondwāna.

At the accession of Shāhjahān, B. was made a commander of 4,000, 3,000 horse, and jāgirdār of Bālāpūr. He joined Khān Jahān Lodī on his march from Gondwāna to Bālāghāt. When he saw that Khān Jahān did not succeed, he left him, and entered the service of the Niẓām Shāh.

A grandson of Buhlūl, Abū 'l-Muḥammad, came in the 12th year of Awrangzīb's reign to court, was made a commander of 5,000, 4,000, and got the title of *Ikhlāṣ Khān* (*Maʾāṣ. ʿĀlamgīrī*, p. 81).

For other Miyāna Afghāns, *vide Pādishāhn.*, I, 241 ; *Maʾāṣ. ʿĀlamgīrī*, p. 225.

312. **Ṭāhir Beg**, son of the Khān-i Kalān (No. 16).

313. **Kishn Dās** Tunwar.

He was under Akbar and Jahāngīr accountant (*mushrif*) of the elephant and horse stables. In the 7th year of J., he was made a commander of 1,000. A short time before he had received the title of Rāja (*Tuzuk*, p. 110).

314. **Mān Singh** Kachhwāha.

The *Akbarnāma* (III, 333, 335) mentions a Mān Singh Darbārī.

315. **Mīr Gadāʾī**, son of Mīr Abū Turāb.

Abū Turāb belonged to the Salāmī Sayyids of Shīrāz. His grandfather, Mīr Ghiyāṣ[u] 'd-Dīn, had come to Gujrāt during the reign of Quṭb[u] 'd-Dīn, grandson of Sulṭān Aḥmad (the founder of Aḥmadābād) ; but he soon after returned to Persia. The disturbances, however, during the reign of Shāh Ismāʿīl Ṣafawī obliged him to take again refuge in Gujrāt, where he arrived during the reign of Sulṭān Maḥmūd

Bīgaṛa.[1] He settled with his son Kamālᵘ 'd-Dīn (Abū Turāb's father) in Champānīr-Maḥmūdābād, and set up as a teacher and writer of school books (*darsiya kitāb*). Kamālᵘ 'd-Dīn also was a man renowned for his learning.

The family has for a long time been attached to the *Silsila-yi Maghribyya*, or Maghribī (Western) Sect, the " lamp " of which was the saintly Shaykh [2] Aḥmad-i Khaṭṭū. The name " Salāmī Sayyids " is explained as follows. One of the ancestors of the family had visited the tomb of the Prophet. When coming to the sacred spot, he said the customary *salām*, when a heavenly voice returned his greeting.

Abū Turāb was a highly respected man. He was the first that paid his respects to Akbar on his march to Gujrāt, and distinguished himself by his faithfulness to his new master. Thus he was instrumental in preventing Iʿtimād Khān (No. 67) from joining, after Akbar's departure for Kambhāyat, the rebel Ikhtīyārᵘ 'l-Mulk. Later, Akbār sent him to Makkah as Mīr Ḥajj, in which quality he commanded a large party of courtiers and begams. On his return he brought a large stone from Makkah, which bore the footprint of the prophet (*qadam-i sharīf*, or *qadam-i mubārak*) ; *vide* p. 207. The " tarīkh " of his return is *khayrᵘ 'l aqdām* (A.H. 987), or " the best of footprints ". The stone was said to be the same which Sayyid Jalāl-i Bukhārī at the time of Sulṭān Fīrūz had brought to Dihlī. Akbar looked upon the whole as a pious farce, and though the stone was received with great *éclat*, Abū Turāb was graciously allowed to keep it in his house.

When Iʿtimād was made governor of Gujrāt, Abū Turāb followed him as Amīn of the Ṣūba, accompanied by his sons Mīr Muḥibbᵘ 'llāh and Mīr Sharfᵘ 'd-Dīn.

Abū Turāb died in 1005, and was buried at Aḥmadābād.

His third son Mīr Gadāʾī, though he held a manṣab, adopted the saintly

---

[1] بیکره. This word is generally pronounced بیگره, and is said to mean having conquered two forts (*gaṛh*), because Maḥmūd's army conquered on one day the forts of Champānīr and Jūnāgaṛh. But Jahāngīr in his " Memoirs ", says that بیگره means *burūt-i bargashta*, " having a turned up, or twisted, moustache," which Sulṭān Maḥmūd is said to have had (*Tuzuk*, p. 212).

Champānīr, according to Bird, is also called Maḥmūdābād. The *Maʾāṣir* has Champānīr-*Muḥammadābād*.

[2] Born A.H. 738, died at the age of 111 (lunar) years, on the 10th Shawwāl, 849. Shaykh Aḥmad lies buried at Sarkhej near Aḥmadābād. The biographical works on Saints give many particulars regarding this personage, and the share which he had, as one of the four Gujrātī Aḥmads, in the foundation of Aḥmadābād (founded 7th Zī Qaʿda, 813). *Khazīnatᵘ 'l-Āṣfiyā* (Lāhor), p. 957.

Khaṭṭū, where Shaykh Aḥmad was educated by his adoptive father Shaykh Is-ḥāq-i Maghribī (died A.H. 776) lies east of Nāgor.

mode of life which his ancestors had followed. In the 46th year he served in the Dakhin.

316. **Qāsim Khwāja,** son of Khwāja ʿAbd[u] 'l-Bārī. *Vide* No. **320.**

317. **Nādi ʿAlī** Maydānī.

In MSS. he is often wrongly called *Yād* ʿAlī.

The word *nādi* is an Arabic Imperative, meaning " *call* ". It occurs in the following formula used all over the East for amulets.

Nādi ʿAliyan mazhara 'l-ʿajāʾib,
Tajid-hū ʿawnan fī kulli 'l-maṣāʾib.
Kullu hammin wa ghammin sa-yanjalī
Bi-mubuwati-ka yā Muhammad, bi-wilāyiti-ka yā ʿAlī.
Yā ʿAlī, yā ʿAlī, yā ʿAlī.

Call upon ʿAlī in whom all mysteries reveal themselves,
Thou wilt find it a help in all afflictions.
Every care and every sorrow will surely vanish
Through thy prophetship, O Muḥammad, through thy saintliness, O ʿAlī.
O ʿAlī, O ʿAlī, O ʿAlī!

The beginning of the amulet suggested the name.

In the 26th year Nādi ʿAlī served against M. Muḥammad Ḥakīm, in 993 (the 30th year) in Kābul, and two years later under **Zayn Koka** (No. 34) against the Tārīkīs.

In the 6th year of Jahāngīr's reign, he was made a commander of 1,500, chiefly for his services against the Kābul rebel Aḥdād. In the 10th year he served in Bangash, when he was a commander of 1,500, 1,000 horse. He died in the following year (1026); *vide Tuzuk*, p. 172. His sons were provided with manṣabs.

His son Bīzan (or Bīzhan) distinguished himself, in the 15th year, in Bangash, and was made a commander of 1,000, 500 horse (*l.c.*, pp. 307, 309).

The *Pādishāhnāma* (I, b., 322) mentions a Muḥammad Zamān, son of Nādi ʿAlī *Arlāt*, who in the 10th year of Shāhjahān was a commander of 500, 350 horse.

Nādi ʿAlī is not to be confounded with the Ḥāfiẓ Nādi ʿAlī, who served under Jahāngīr as Court Ḥāfiẓ (*Tuzuk*, p. 155, and its *Dībāja*, p. 19), nor with the Nādi ʿAlī who served under Shāhjahān (*Pādishāhn.*, II, 749) as a commander of 500, 200 horse.

318. **Nīl Kanṭh,** Zamīndār of Oṛīsā.

319. **Ghiyās Beg** of Ṭihrān [Iʿtimād[u] 'd-Dawla].

His real name is Mīrzā Ghiyāṣ^u 'd-Dīn Muḥammad. In old European histories his name is often spelled Ayās, a corruption of *Ghīyāṣ*, not of Ayāz (ایاز).

Ghiyāṣ Beg's father was Khwāja Muḥammad Sharīf, who as poet wrote under the assumed name of *Hijrī*. He was Vazīr to Tātār Sulṭān, son of Muḥammad Khān Sharaf^u 'd-Dīn Ughlū Taklū, who held the office of Beglar Begī of Khurāsān. After Tātār Sulṭān's death, the Khwāja was continued in office by his son Qazāq Khān, and on Qazāq's death, he was made by Shāh Ṭahmāsp Vazīr of Yazd.[1]

Khwāja Muḥammad Sharīf is said to have died in A.H. 984. He had two brothers, Khwāja Mīrzā Aḥmad, and Khwājagī Khwāja. The son of Kh. Mīrzā Aḥmad was the well-known Khwāja Amīn Rāzī (رازی, i.e., of the town of Ray of which he was *kalāntar*, or magistrate), who travelled a good deal and composed the excellent work entitled *Haft Iqlīm*, A.H.1002. Khwājagī Khwāja had a son of the name of Khwāja Shāpūr, who was likewise a literary man.

Ghiyāṣ Beg was married to the daughter of Mīrzā ʿAlāʾ^u 'd-Dawlah, *son of*[2] Āghā Mullā. After the death of his father, in consequence of adverse circumstances, Gh. B. fled with his two sons and one daughter from Persia. He was plundered on the way, and had only two mules left, upon which the members of the family alternately rode. On his arrival at Qandahār, his wife gave birth to another daughter, who received the name of Mihr^u 'n-Nisā (" the Sun of Women "), a name which her future title of Nūr Jahān has almost brought into oblivion.[3] In their misfortune, they found a patron in Malik Masʿūd, leader of the caravan, who is said to have been known to Akbar. We are left to infer that it was he who directed Ghiyāṣ Beg to India. After his introduction at Court in Fatḥpūr Sīkrī,[4] Gh. rose, up to the 40th year, to a command of 300. In the same year he was made Dīwān of Kābul, and was in course of time promoted to a manṣab of 1,000, and appointed *Dīwān-i Buyūtāt*.

---

[1] The *Dībāja* (preface) of the *Tuzuk* (p. 20) and the *Iqbālnāma* (p. 54) agree *verbatim* in Ghiyāṣ Beg's history. They do not mention Qāzāq Khān. For *Yazd* of the *Maʾāsir*, Sayyid Āḥmad's text of the *Tuzuk* has *Marw*; and the Bibl. Indica edition of the *Iqbālnāma* has خود " he made him his *own* Vazīr."

[2] The words *son of* are not in the *Maʾāṣir*, but in the *Tuzuk* and the *Iqbālnāma*. Two Āghā Mullās have been mentioned on p. 398, and under Nos. 278, 319, and 376.

[3] It is said that Nūr Jahān at her death in 1055 was in her seventy-second year. She would thus have been born in A.H. 984; hence Ghiyāṣ Beg's flight from Persia must have taken place immediately after the death of his father.

It is well to bear this in mind; for when Nūr Jahān was married by Jahāngīr (in 1020), she must have been as old as 34 (solar) years, an age at which women in the East are looked upon as old women.

[4] Where he had some distant relations, as Jaʿfar Beg (No. 98).

Regarding Mihr[u] 'n-Nisā's marriage with ʿAlī Qulī, *vide* No. 394.

In the beginning of Jahāngīr's reign, Ghiyās̤ Beg received the title of Iʿtimād[u] 'd-Dawla. In the second year, his eldest son, Muḥammad Sharīf,[1] joined a conspiracy to set Khusraw at liberty and murder the emperor ; but the plot being discovered, Sharīf was executed, and Iʿtimād himself was imprisoned. After some time he was let off on payment of a fine of two lacs of rupees. At the death of Sher Afkan (under 275) Mihr[u] 'n-Nisā was sent to court as a prisoner "for the murder of Quṭb[u] 'd-Dīn", and was handed over to Ruqayya Sulṭān Begum,[2] with whom she lived "unnoticed (*ba-nākāmī*) and rejected". In the 6th year (1020) she no longer slighted the emperor's proposals, and the marriage was celebrated with great pomp. She received the title of *Nūr Maḥall*, and a short time afterwards that of Nūr Jahān.[3]

Ghiyās̤, in consequence of the marriage, was made *Vakīl-i kul*, or prime-minister, and a commander of 6,000, 3,000 horse. He also received a flag and a drum, and was in the 10th year allowed to beat his drum at court, which was a rare privilege. In the 16th year, when J. was on his way to Kashmīr, Ghiyās̤ fell ill. The imperial couple were recalled from a visit to Kāngṛa Fort, and arrived in time to find him dying. Pointing to the emperor, Nūr Jahān asked her father whether he recognized him. He quoted as answer a verse from Anwarī :—

آنکه نابينای مادرزاد اگر حاضر بود   در جبين عالم آرا پس به بيند مهتری

"If one who is blind from birth stood here, he would recognize his majesty by his august forehead."

He died after a few hours. The *Tuzuk* (p. 339) mentions the 17th Bahman, 1031 (Rabīʿ I, 1031) as the day of his death, and says that he died broken-hearted three months and twenty days after his wife, who had died on the 29th Mihr, 1030, i.e., 13th Ẕī Qaʿda, 1030).

Ghiyās̤ Beg was a poet. He imitated the old classics, which ruling passion, as we saw, showed itself a few hours before he died. He was a clever correspondent, and is said to have written a beautiful *Shikasta* hand. Jahāngīr praises him for his social qualities, and confessed that his society was better than a thousand *mufarriḥ-i yāqūts*.[4] He was generally liked, had no enemies, and was never seen angry. "Chains,

[1] Who according to custom had the same name as his grandfather ; *vide* p. 497, No. 278.

[2] The *Tuzuk* and the *Iqbālnāma* have Ruqaiya Sulṭān Begum (p. 321). The *Maʾās̤ir* has *Salīma* Sulṭān Begum (p. 321). The *Iqbālnāma* (p. 56) has wrongly رقيه for رقيه.

[3] In accordance with the name of her husband *Nūr[u] 'd-Dīn Jahāngīr*.

[4] As the diamond when reduced to powder was looked upon in the East as a deadly poison, so was the cornelian (*yāqūt*) [garnet ?—P.] supposed to possess exhilarating properties. *Mufarriḥ* means an exhilarative.

the whip, and abuse, were not found in his house." He protected the wretched, especially such as had been sentenced to death. He never was idle, but wrote a great deal; his official accounts were always in the greatest order. But he liked bribes, and showed much boldness in demanding them.[1]

His mausoleum near Āgra has often been described.

Nūr Jahān's power over Jahāngīr is sufficiently known from the histories. The emperor said, "Before I married her, I never knew what marriage really meant," and, "I have conferred the duties of government on her; I shall be satisfied if I have a *ser* of wine and half a *ser* of meat per *diem*." With the exception of the *khuṭba* (prayer for the reigning monarch), she possessed all privileges of royalty. Thus her name was invariably mentioned on farmāns, and even on coins. The jāgīrs which she held would have conferred on her the title of a commander of 30,000. A great portion of her zamīndārīs lay near Rāmsir, S.E. of Ajmīr (*Tuzuk*, p. 169). She provided for all her relations; even her nurse, Dā,ī Dilārām, enjoyed much influence, and held the post of "Ṣadr of the Women" (*ṣadr-i anās*), and when she conferred lands as *suyūrghāls*, the grants were confirmed and sealed by the Ṣadr of the empire. Nūr Jahān is said to have particularly taken care of orphan girls, and the number whom she betrothed or gave outfits to is estimated at five hundred. She gave the tone to fashion, and is said to have invented the *ʿatr-i jahāngīrī* (a peculiar kind of rosewater). She possessed much taste in adorning apartments and arranging feasts. For many gold ornaments she laid down new patterns and elegant designs, and her *dudāmī* for *peshwāz* (gowns), her *pāchtoliya* for *oṛhnīs* (veils), her *bādla* (brocade), *kinārī* (lace), and *farsh-i chandanī*,[2] are often mentioned.

Her influence ceased with Jahāngīr's death and the capture of Shahryār, fifth son of the emperor, to whom she had given her daughter (by Sher Afkan) Lāḍlī Begum, in marriage. She had no children by Jahāngīr. Shāhjahān allowed her a pension of two lacs per annum.[3]

She died at Lāhor at the age of 72, on the 29th Shawwāl, 1055, and lies buried near her husband in a tomb which she herself had built (*Pādishāhn.*, II, 475).[4] She composed occasionally Persian poems, and

---

[1] So the Tuzuk and the Iqbālnāma.

[2] *Dudāmī*, weighing two dāms; *pāchtoliya*, weighing five tolas. The latter was mentioned on p. 101. *Farsh-i chandanī* carpets of sandalwood colour.

[3] Elphinstone has by mistake 2 lacs *per mensem*. The highest allowance of Begams on record is that of Mumtāz Mahall, *viz* 10 lacs *per annum*. *Vide Pādishāhn.*, I, 96.

[4] In the *Pādishāhnāma*, Nūr Jahān is again called *Nūr Mahall.*

like Salīma Sulṭān Begum and Zeb[u] 'n-Nisā Begum wrote under the assumed name of *Makhfī*.

Ghiyāṣ Beg's sons. The fate of his eldest son Muḥammad Sharīf has been alluded to. His second son, Mīrzā Abū 'l-Ḥasan Āṣaf Khān (IV), also called *Āṣaf-jāh* or *Āṣaf-jāhī*, is the father of Muntāz Maḥall (Tāj Bībī), the favourite wife of Shāhjahān whom European historians occasionally call Nūr Jahān II. He received from Shāhjahān the title of *Yamīn[u] 'd-Dawla* and *Khān Khānān Sipahsālār*, and was a commander of 9,000. He died on the 17th Shaʿbān, 1051, and was buried at Lāhor, north of Jahāngīr's tomb. As commander of 9,000 *du-aspa* and *sī-aspa* troopers, his salary was 16 krors, 20 lacs of *dāms*, or 4,050,000 rupees, and besides, he had jāgīrs yielding a revenue of five millions of rupees. His property at his death, which is said to have been more than double that of his father, was valued at 25 millions of rupees, and consisted of 30 lacs of jewels, 42 lacs of rupees in gold muhurs, 25 lacs of rupees in silver, 30 lacs of plate, etc., and 23 lacs of other property. His palace in Lāhor which he had built at a cost of 20 lacs, was given to Prince Dārā Shikoh, and 20 lacs of rupees, in cash and valuables, were distributed among his three sons and five daughters. The rest escheated to the State.

Āṣaf Khān was married to a daughter of Mīrzā Ghiyāṣ[u] 'd-Dīn ʿAlī Āṣaf Khān II (p. 398).

His eldest son is the renowned Mīrzā Abū Ṭālib Shāʾista Khān, who, as governor of Bengal, is often mentioned in the early history of the E.I. Company. Shāʾista was married to a daughter of Īrij Shāhnawāz Khān (No. 255), son of ʿAbd[u] 'r-Raḥīm Khān Khānān, by whom he had, however, no children. He died at Āgra in 1105, the 38th year of Awrangzīb's reign. His eldest son, Abū Ṭālib,[1] had died before him. His second son was Abū 'l-Fatḥ Khān. One of his daughters was married to Rūḥ[u] 'llāh (I), and another to Ẕū 'l-Faqār Khān Nuṣrat-jang.

Āṣaf Khān's second son, Bahmanyār, was in the 20th year of Shāhj. a commander of 2,000, 200 horse (*Pādishāhn.*, II, 728).

Ghiyāṣ Beg's third son is Ibrāhīm Khān Fatḥ-jang, who was the governor of Bihār (*vide* note to Kokra under No. 328) and Bengal. He was killed near his son's tomb during Shāhjahān's rebellion. His son had died young and was buried near Rājmaḥall, on the banks of the Ganges (*Tuzuk*, p. 383). Ibrāhīm Khān was married to Ḥājī Ḥūr Parwar Khānum, Nūr Jahān's maternal aunt (*khāla*). She lived up to the middle of Awrangzīb's reign, and held Kol Jalālī as *āltamghā*.

---

[1] Also called Muḥammad Ṭālib. *Vide Pādishāhn.*, II, 248.

An Aḥmad Beg Khān is mentioned in the histories as the son of Nūr Jahān's brother.[1] He was with Ibrāhīm Fatḥ-jang in Bengal, and retreated after his death to Dhākā, where he handed over to Shāhjahān 500 elephants, and 45 lacs of rupees (*Tuzuk*, p. 384). On Shāhj.'s accession he received a high manṣab, was made governor of Thathah and Sīwistān, and later of Multān. He then returned to court, and received as jāgīr the Parganas of Jāis and Ameṭhī, where he died. In the 20th year of Shāhj. he was a commander of 2,000, 1,500 horse (*Pādishāhn.*, II, 727).

.A sister of Nūr Jahān Manīja Begum was mentioned under No. 282.

A fourth sister, Khadīja Begum, was married to Ḥākim Beg, a nobleman of Jahāngīr's court.

The following tree will be found serviceable :—

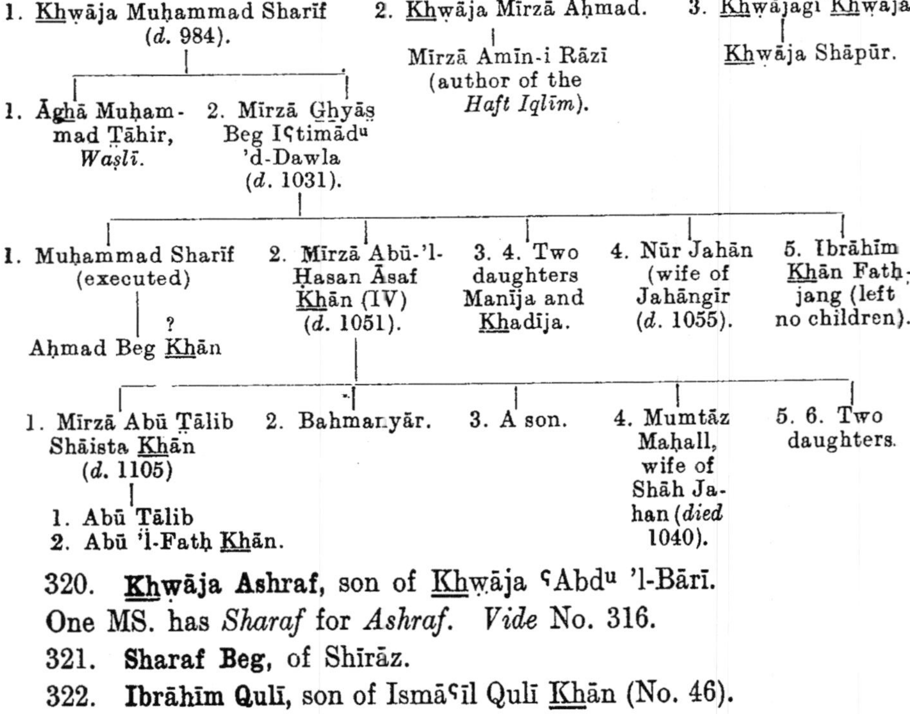

320. **Khwāja Ashraf,** son of Khwāja ʿAbdu 'l-Bārī.

One MS. has *Sharaf* for *Ashraf*. *Vide* No. 316.

321. **Sharaf Beg,** of Shīrāz.

322. **Ibrāhīm Qulī,** son of Ismāʿīl Qulī Khān (No. 46).

XXI. Commanders of Two Hundred and Fifty.

323. **Abū 'l-Fatḥ,** son of Muẓaffar, the Mughul.

324. **Beg Muḥammad** Toqbāʾī.

He served in the end of the 28th year in Gujrāt and was present in the fight near Maisāna, S.E. of Patan, in which Sher Khān Fūlādī was defeated, and also against Muẓaffar of Gujrāt (*Akbarn.*, III, 423).

---

[1] It seems therefore that he was the son of Muḥammad Sharīf.

Regarding *Toqbā'i*, *vide* No. 129.

325. **Imām Qulī** Shighālī.

The *Akbarnāma* (III, 628) mentions an Imām Qulī, who, in the 37th year served under Sulṭān Murād in Mālwa.

The meaning of *Shighālī* is unclear to me. A Muḥammad Qulī Shighālī played a part in Badakhshān history (*Akbarn.*, III, 132, 249).

326. **Ṣafdar Beg**, son of Ḥaydar Muḥammad Khān Ākhta Begī (No. 66).

A Ṣafdar Khān served, in the 21st year, against Daudā of Bundī (*vide* under No. 96).

327. **Khwāja Sulaymān** of Shīrāz.

He has been mentioned on p. 383 and under No. 172.

328. **Barkhurdār** [Mirzā Khān Āʕlam], son of ʕAbdu 'r-Raḥmān Dulday (No. 186).

Mīrzā Barkhurdār was in the 40th year of Akbar's reign a commander of 250. His father (No. 186) had been killed in a fight with the rebel Dalpat.[1] This Bihār Zamīndār was afterwards caught and kept in prison till the 44th year when, on the payment of a heavy *peshkash*, he was allowed to return to his home. But B. wished to avenge the death of his father, and lay in ambush for Dalpat, who, however, managed to escape. Akbar was so annoyed at this breach of peace that he gave orders to hand over B. to Dalpat; but at the intercession of several countries, B. was imprisoned.

As Jahāngīr was fond of him, he released him after his accession,[2] and made him *Qūshbegī*, or superintendent of the aviary.[3] In the fourth

---

[1] Dalpat is called in the *Akbarnāma* اجينيه, *Ujjainiya*, for which the MSS. have various readings, as اجنيه, اوجبتيه etc. Under Shāhjahān, Dalpat's successor was Rāja Pratāb, who in the 1st year received a manṣab of 1,500, 1,000 horse (*Pādishāhn.*, I, 221). From the same work we see that the residence of the Ujjainiya Rājas was Bhojpūr, west of Āra and north of Bhāsrām (Sasseram), a pargana in Sarkār, Rohtās, Bihār. Pratāb rebelled in the 10th year of Shāhjahān's reign, when ʕAbdu 'l-Allāh Khān Fīrūz-jang besieged and conquered Bhojpūr (8th Zī-Ḥajja, 1046). Pratāb surrendered, and was at Shāhj.'s order executed. His wife was forcibly converted, and married to Abdu 'l-Allāh's grandson. The particulars of this conquest will be found in the *Pādishāhnāma* (I, b., pp. 271 to 274).

The maps show a small place of the name of Pratāb near Bhojpūr.

It is said that the Bhojpūr Rājas call themselves *Ujjainiyas*, because they claim descent from the ancient Rājas of Ujjain in Mālwa.

In the 17th year of Shāhjahān, Dharnīdhar Ujjainiya is mentioned to have several in the second expedition against Palāmau; *Journal As. Soc. Bengal* for 1871, No. II, p. 123.

[2] If we can trust the Lucknow edition of the *Akbarnāma*, B. could not have been imprisoned for a long time; for in the end of the 44th year of Akbar's reign he served again at court (*Akbarn.*, III, 825).

[[3] Grand Falconer or superintendent of the *qūsh-khāna* or mews.—P.]

year (beginning of 1018), B. received the title of K͟hān ˁAlam (*Tuzuk*, p. 74). Two years later, in 1020, Shāh ˁAbbās of Persia sent Yādgār ˁAlī Sulṭān Ṭālish as ambassador to Āgra, and B. was selected to accompany him on his return to Persia. The suite consisted of about twelve hundred men, and was, according to the testimony of the *ˁĀlamārā-i Sikandarī*, the most splendid embassy that had ever appeared in Persia. In consequence of a long delay at Hirāt and Qum, caused by the absence of the Shāh in Āzarbājān on an expedition against the Turks, nearly one-half of the suite were sent back. In 1027 the Shāh returned to Qazwīn and received the numerous presents, chiefly elephants and other animals, which B. had brought from India. The embassy returned in 1029 (end of the 14th year), and B. met the emperor at Kalānūr on his way to Kashmīr. Jahāngīr was so pleased that he kept B. for two days in his sleeping apartment, and made him a commander of 5,000, 3,000 horse.

The author of the *Pādishāhnāma* (I, 427), however, remarks that B. did not possess the skill and tact of an ambassador, though he had not stated his reasons or the source of his information.

On Shāhjahān's accession, B. was made a commander of 6,000, 5,000 horse, received a flag and a drum, and was appointed governor of Bihār, *vide* M. Rustam Ṣafawī. But as he was given to *koknār* (opium and hemp), he neglected his duties, and was deposed before the first year had elapsed. In the fifth year (end of 1041), when Shāhj. returned from Burhānpūr to Āgra, B. was pensioned off, as he was old and given to opium and received an annual pension of one lac of rupees (*Pādishāhn.*, I, 426). He died a natural death at Āgra. He had no children.

B. is not to be confounded with K͟hwāja Bark͟hurdār, a brother of ˁAbdᵘ 'llah K͟hān Fīrūz-jang.

B.'s brother Mīrzā ˁAbdᵘ 's-Subḥān (No. 349) was Fawjdār of Ilāhābād. He was then sent to Kābul, where he was killed, in 1025, in a fight with the Āfrīdīs (*Tuzuk*, beginning of the 11th year, p. 158).

ˁAbdᵘ 's-Subḥān's son, Sherzād K͟hān Bahādur, was killed in the last fight with K͟hān Jahān Lodī at Sehōdah (*vide* under No. 309). *Pādishāhn.*, I, 349.

329. **Mīr Maˁṣūm** of Bhakkar.

Mīr Maˁṣūm belongs to a family of Tirmizī Sayyids, who two or three generations before him had left Tirmiz in Buk͟hārā, and settled at Qandahār, where his ancestors were *mutawallīs* (trustees) of the shrine of Bābā Sher Qalandar.

His father, Mīr Sayyid Ṣafāʾī, settled in Bhakkar, and received favours from Sulṭān Maḥmūd (*vide* under No. 47). He was related by marriage to the Sayyids of کهابروت in Sīwistān. Mīr Maʿṣūm and his two brothers were born at Bhakkar.

After the death of his father, M. M. studied under Mullā Muḥammad of Kingrī کنگری, S.W. of Bhakkar, and soon distinguished himself by his learning. But poverty compelled him to leave for Gujrāt, where Shaykh Is-ḥāq-i Fārūqī of Bhakkar introduced him to Khwāja Niẓāmᵘ 'd-Dīn Aḥmad, then Dīwān of Gujrāt. Niẓām was just engaged in writing his historical work, entitled *Ṭabaqāt-i Akbarī*, and soon became the friend of M. M., who was likewise well versed in history. He was also introduced to Shihāb Khān (No. 26), the governor of the province, and was at last recommended to Akbár for a manṣab. In the 40th year he was a commander of 250. Akbar became very fond of him and sent him in 1012 as ambassador to Īrān, where he was received with distinction by Shāh 'Abbās.

On his return from Īrān, in 1015, Jahāngīr sent him as Amīn to Bhakkar, where he died. It is said that he reached under Akbar a command of 1,000.

From the *Ākbarnāma* (III, 416, 423, 546) and Bird's *History of Gujrat* (p. 426) we see that M. M. served in 992 (end of the 28th year) in Gujrāt, was present in the fight of Maisāna, and in the final expedition against Muẓaffar in Kachh.

M. M. is well known as a poet and historian. He wrote under the poetical name of *Nāmī*. He composed a Dīwān, a Maṣnāwī entitled *Maʿdanᵘ 'l-afkār* in the metre of Niẓāmī's Makhzan, the Tārīkh-i Sindh, dedicated to his son, and a short medical work called *Mufridāt-i Maʿṣūmī*. The author of the *Riyāẓᵘ 'sh-Shuʿarā* says that he composed a *Khamsa*, and the Taẕkira by Taqī (*vide* under No. 352) says the same, viz., one maṣnawī corresponding to the Makhzan, the *Husn o Nāz* to the Yūsuf Zulaykhā, the *Parī Ṣūrat* to the Lailī Majnūn, and two others in imitation of the Haft Paikar and Sikandarnāma. Badā'onī (died 1004) only alludes to the *Husn o Nāz*, though he gives no title (III, 366).

M. M. was also skilled as a composer and tracer of inscriptions, and the Riyāẓᵘ 'sh-Shuʿarā says that on his travels he was always accompanied by sculptors. From India to Iṣfahān and Tabrīz, where he was presented to Shāh ʿAbbās, there are numerous mosques and public buildings which he adorned with metrical inscriptions. Thus the inscriptions over the gate of the Fort of Āgra, on the Jāmīʿ Mosque of Fatḥpūr Sīkrī, in Fort Māndū (*vide* under No. 52 and *Tuzuk*, p. 189) are all by him. Sayyid Aḥmad in his edition of the *Tuzuk* (Dībāja, p. 4, note) gives in full the inscription which he wrote on the side of the entrance to Salīm-i Chishtī's shrine at Fatḥpūr Sīkrī, the last words of which are:—"*Said and written by Muḥammad Maʿṣūm poetically styled Nāmī, son of Sayyid Ṣafāʾī of Tirmiz, born at Bhakkar, descended from Sayyid Sher Qalandar, son of Bābā Ḥasan Abdāl, who was born at Sabzwār and settled at Qandahār.*" Dowson, in his edition of *Elliot's Historians*, mentions Kirmān as the residence of Sayyid Ṣafāʾī, and gives (I, 239) a few particulars from the Tarīkh-i Sindh, regarding the saint Bābā Ḥasan Abdāl, who lived under Mīrzā Shāhrukh, son of Tīmūr. The town of Ḥasan Abdāl in the Panjāb, east of Aṭak, is called after him.

M. M. built also several public edifices, especially in Sakhar opposite to Bhakkar, and in the midst of the branch of the Indus which flows round Bhakkar he built a dome, to which he gave the name of Satyāsur (ستیاسر). "It is one of the wonders of the world, and its *Tārīkh* is contained in the words گنبد دریائی." water-dome, which gives A.H. 1007.

He was a pious man and exceedingly liberal; he often sent presents to all the people of Bhakkar, great and small. But when he retired, he discontinued his presents, and the people even felt for some cause oppressed (*mutaazzī*). It is especially mentioned of him that on his jāgīr lands he laid out forests for hunting.

His eldest son, for whose instruction he wrote the Tārīkh-i Sindh, was Mīr Buzurg. He was captured in full armour on the day Prince Khusraw's rebellion was suppressed, but he denied having had a share in it. Jahāngīr asked him why he had his armour on. "My father," replied he, "advised me to dress in full armour when on guard," and as the *Chaukīnawīs*, or guard writer, proved that he had been on guard that day, he was let off.

On the death of his father, Jahāngīr is said to have left Mīr Buzurg in possession of his father's property. He was for a long time Bakhshī of Qandahār, but he was haughty and could never agree with the Ṣūbahdārs. He spent the 30 or 40 lacs of rupees which he had inherited from his father. His contingent was numerous and well mounted. He subsequently served in the Dakhin; but as his jāgīr did not cover his expenses, he resigned and retired to Bkakkar, contenting himself with the landed property which he had inherited. He died in 1044. Some of his children settled in Multān.

330. **Khwaja Malik ʿAlī**, Mīr Shab.

His title of Mīr Shab implies that he was in charge of the illuminations and the games and animal fights held at night (p. 232).

331. **Rāy Rām Dās Dīwān.** *Vide* No. 238.

332. **Shāh Muḥammad**, son of Saʕīd Khān, the Gakkhar.

For his relations, *vide* under No. 247.

333. **Raḥīm Qulī**, son of Khān Jahān (No. 24).

334. **Sher Beg**, Yasāwulbāshī.

Karam Beg, son of Sher Beg, is mentioned in the *Akbarnāma* (III, 623).

XXII. Commanders of Two Hundred.

335. **Iftikhar Beg**, son of Bāyazīd Beg (No. 299).

He was alive in the end of A.H. 1007 (*Akbarn.*, III, 804).

336. **Pratāb Singh**, son of Rāja Bhagwān Dās (No. 27).

He was mentioned under No. 160.

337. **Ḥusayn Khān Qazwīnī**. *Vide* No. 281.

338. **Yādgār Ḥusayn**, son of Qabūl Khān (No. 137).

He was mentioned under No. 137. In the 31st year he served under Qāsim Khān in Kashmīr. The Yādgār Ḥusayn mentioned in the *Tuzuk* (p. 146) may be the same. He was promoted, in the 10th year of Jahāngīr's reign, to a command of 700, 500 horse, for his services in the Dakhin. *Vide* also *Pādishāhnāma*, I, b., p. 323, l. 2 from below.

He is not to be confounded with Khwāja Yādgār, a brother of ʕAbdu 'llāh Khān Fīrūz-jang.

339. **Kāmrān Beg** of Gīlān.

He served in the 33rd year (996) in Gujrāt and Kachh against Fatḥ Khān, the younger son of Amīn Khān Ghorī and Muẓaffar, and in the 36th year against Muẓaffar and the Jām. *Akbarn.*, III, 553, 621.

340. **Muḥammad Khān** Turkmān.

341. **Niẓāmu 'd-Dīn Aḥmad**, son of Shāh Muḥammad Khān (No. 95).

He is not to be confounded with the author of the *Ṭabaqāt*.

342. **Sakat Singh**, son of Rāja Mān Singh (No. 30).

Vide No. 256.

343. **ʕImādu 'l-Mulk.**

The *Akbarnāma* mentions a Qāzī ʕImādu 'l-Mulk, who in the end of 984 (21st year) accompanied a party of courtiers to Makkah.

344. **Sharīf-i Sarmadī.**

He was a poet. *Vide* below, among the poets of Akbar's reign.

345. **Qarā Bahr**, son of Qarātāq.

Qarātāq, whose name in the *Akbarnāma* is spelled *Qarāṭāq*, was killed by Gajpatī in the same fight in which Farhang Khān, son of Farḥat Khān (No. 145), was slain (No. 145).

346. **Tātar Beg,** son of ʿAlī Muḥammad Asp. (No. 258).

347. **Khwāja Muḥibb ʿAlī** of Khawāf.

Vide No. 159, note.

348. **Ḥakīm** [Jalālᵘ 'd-Dīn] **Muẓaffar** of Ardistān.

Ardistān is a Persian town which lies between Kāshān and Iṣfahān. He was at first a doctor at the court of Shāh Ṭahmāsp, and emigrated when young to India, where he was looked upon as a very experienced doctor, though his theoretical reading is said to have been limited. *Badāʾonī* (III, 169) and the *Tuzak* (p. 59) praise the purity of his character and walk of life.

He served in 988 (25th year) in Bengal, returned in the end of the 28th year with Mīrzā ʿAzīz (No. 21) to court, and served subsequently under him in Gujrāt and Kachh. *Akbarn.*, III, 283, 418, 620. Under Jahāngīr he was made a commander of 3,000, 1,000 horse (*Tuzuk*, p. 37). The emperor was fond of him, as he had been with him in Ilāhābād, when as prince he had rebelled against Akbar. The news of the Ḥakīm's death reached J. on the 22nd Jumāda I, 1016. For about twenty years before his death, he had suffered from *qarḥa*[1]*-yi shush*, or disease of the lungs, but his uniform mode of living (*yakṭawrī*) prolonged his life. His cheeks and eyes often got quite red, and when he got older, his complexion turned bluish. He was accidentally poisoned by his compounder.

349. **ʿAbdᵘ 's-Subḥān,** son of ʿAbdᵘ 'r-Raḥmān, Dulday (No. 186).

He was mentioned under No. 328.

350. **Qāsim Beg** of Tabrīz.

He served in the 36th year under Sulṭān Murād in Mālwa, and died on the 23rd Ābān (end of) 1007 ; *vide Akbarn.*, III, 628, 803. *Vide* below under the learned men of Akbar's reign.

351. **Sharīf** (Amīrᵘ 'l-Umarā), son of Khwāja ʿAbdᵘ 'ṣ-Ṣamad (No. 266).

Muḥammad Sharīf was the school companion of Prince Salīm, who was much attached to him. When the prince had occupied Ilāhābād in rebellion against Akbar, Sharīf was sent to him to advise him ; but he only widened the breach between the prince and his father, and gained such an ascendancy over Salīm, that he made the rash promise to give him half the kingdom should he obtain the throne. When a reconciliation had been effected between Salīm and Akbar, Sh. had to fly for his life, and concealed himself in the hills and jungles. He was reduced to starvation, when he heard of Akbar's death. He went at once to court,

---

[[1] *Qarḥa*, ulceration ?—P.]

and Jahāngīr, true to his promise, made him Amīr^{u} 'l-Umarā, Vakīl, entrusted him with the great seal (*ūzuk*) and allowed him to select his jāgīr lands. The emperor says in his Memoirs, "He is at once my brother, my friend, my son, my companion. When he came back, I felt as if I had received new life. I am now emperor, but consider no title sufficiently high to reward him for his excellent qualities, though I can do no more than make him Amīr^{u} 'l-Umāra and a commander of 5,000. My father never did more."

Sharīf seems to have advised the emperor to drive all Afghāns from India; but the Khān-i Aʿẓam (No. 21) warned Jahāngīr against so unwise a step. Though Sh.'s position at court was higher than that of Mīrzā ʿAzīz, the latter treated him contemptuously as a mean upstart, and Sh. recommended the emperor to kill ʿAzīz for the part he had played in Khusraw's rebellion. But ʿAzīz was pardoned, and advised to make it up with Sharīf, and invite him to his house. The Khān-i Aʿẓam did so, and invited him and the other Amīrs. At the feast, however, he said to him, in the blandest way, "I say, Nawāb, you do not seem to be my friend. Now your father Abd^{u} 'ṣ-Ṣamad, the *Mullā*, was much attached to me. He was the man that painted the very walls of the room we sit in." Khān Jahān (*vide* under 309) and Mahābat Khān could not stand this insolent remark, and left the hall; and when Jahāngīr heard of it, he said to Sh., "The Khān cannot bridle his tongue; but don't fall out with him."

In the second year, Sh. accompanied the emperor on his tour to Kābul, but fell so ill that he had to be left in Lāhor, Āṣaf Khān (No. 98) being appointed to officiate for him. On his recovery, he was sent to the Dakhin, but was soon afterwards called to court, as he could not agree with the Khān Khānān (No. 29). It is said that illness deprived him of the faculty of memory, and Jahāngīr was on the point of making him retire, when Khān Jahān interceded on his behalf. He was again sent to the Dakhīn, and died there a natural death.

Like his father, Sh. was a good painter. He also made himself known as a poet, and composed a Dīwān. His *takhalluṣ* is *Fārisī* (*Badāʿonī*, III, 310).

Sh.'s eldest son, Shāhbāz Khāb, died when young. A Sarāʿī near Lakhnau, about a *kos* from the town, bears his name.

His two younger sons, Mīrzā Gul and Mīrzā Jār^{u} 'llāh used to play with Jahāngīr at chess and *nard*; but this ceased at the death of their father. M. Jār^{u} 'llāh was married to Miṣrī Begam, a daughter of Āṣaf Khān (No. 98); but from a certain aversion, the marriage was never consummated. At Āṣaf's death, Jahāngīr made him divorce his wife, and married her to Mīrzā Lashkarī (No. 375), son of Mīrzā Yūsuf Khān (under No. 35).

Both brothers followed Mahābat Khān to Kābul, where they died.

352. **Taqiyā** of Shustar.

Taqiyā is the Īrānī from for *Taqī*. The *Ṭabaqāt* calls him Taqī Muḥammad. *Badāʿonī* (III, 206) has Taqiyᵘ 'd-Dīn and says that he was a good poet and a well-educated man. At Akbar's order he undertook a prose version of the *Shāhnāma*. He is represented as a " murīd " or disciple of Akbar's Divine Faith.

He was still alive in the 3rd year of Jahāngīr's reign (1017) when he received for his attainments the title of *Muʾarrikh Khān* (*Tuzuk*, p. 69, where in Sayyid Aḥmad's edition we have to read *Shushtarī* for the meaningless *Shamsherī*).

Taqiyā is not to be confounded with the more illustrious Taqiyā of Balbān (a village near Iṣfahān), who, according to the *Mirʾ-ātᵘ 'l-ʿAlam*, came in the beginning of Jahāngīr's reign to India. He is the author of the rare *Tazkira*, or Lives of Poets, entitled *ʿArafāt o ʿAraṣāt*, and of the Dictionary entitled *Surma-yi Sulaymānī*, which the lexicographer Muḥammad Ḥusayn used for his *Burhān-i Qāṭiʿ*.

353. **Khwāja ʿAbdᵘ 'ṣ-Ṣamad** of Kāshān.

354. **Ḥakīm Luṭfᵘ 'ullāh**, son of Mullā ʿAbdᵘ 'r-Razzāq of Gīlān.

He is the brother of Nos. 112 and 205, and arrived in India after his brothers. Badāʾonī (III, 169) calls him a very learned doctor.

355. **Sher Afkan** }
356. **Amānᵘ 'llāh** } sons of Sayf Khān Koka (No. 38).

Amānᵘ 'llāh died in the 45th year of Akbar's reign at Burhānpūr. " He was an excellent young man, but fell a victim to the vice of the age, and died from excessive wine-drinking." *Akbarnāma*, III, 835.

357. **Salīm Qulī** }
358. **Khalīl Qulī** } sons of Ismāʿīl Qulī Khān (No. 46).

359. **Walī Beg**, son of Pāyanda Khān (No. 68).

He served under Qāsim Khān (No. 59) in the conquest of Kashmīr.

360. **Beg Muḥammad** Uighūr.

361. **Mīr Khān** Yasāwul.

When Akbar during the first Gujrātī war (p. 480, note 2) had left Patan for Chotāna (Rajab, 980) it was reported that Muẓaffar of Gujrāt had fled from Sher Khān Fūlādī and was concealed in the neighbourhood; *vide* under No. 67. Akbar therefore sent Mīr Khān the Yasāwul and Farīd the Qarāwul, and afterwards Abū 'l-Qāsim Namakīn (No. 199) and Karam ʿAlī, in search of him. Mīr Khān had not gone far when he found the *chatr* and *sāyabān* (p. 52) which Muẓaffar had dropped, and soon after captured Muẓaffar himself in a field. Mīr Khān took him to Akbar.

362. **Sarmast Khān**, son of Dastam Khān (No. 79).

363. **Sayyid Abū 'l-Ḥasan**, son of Sayyid Muḥammad Mīr ʿAdl (No. 140).

364. **Sayyid ʿAbdu 'l-Wāḥid**, son of the Mīr ʿAdl's brother.

365. **Khwāja Beg Mīrzā**, son of Maʿṣūm Beg.

366. **Sakrā**, brother of Rānā Pratāb.

Sakrā is the son of Rānā Udai Singh, son of Rānā Sānkā (*died* A.H. 934). When his brother Pratāb, also called Rānā Kīkā, was attacked by Akbar, he paid his respects at court, and was made a commander of 200.

In the 1st year of Jahāngīr's reign he got a present of 12,000 rupees, and joined the expedition led by Prince Parwīz against Rānā Amrā, Pratāb's successor. In the end of the same year he served against Dalpat (*vide* under No. 44), and was in the 2nd year made a commander of 2,500, 1,000 horse. He received, in the 11th year, a manṣab of 3,000, 2,000 horse.

The *Akbarnāma* mentions another son of Udai Singh, of the name of *Sakat Singh*, who in the 12th year of Akbar's reign was at court. The emperor had just returned from the last war with Khān Zamān when he heard that Udai Singh had assisted the rebellious Mīrzās. He therefore resolved to punish the Rānā, and on a hunting tour in Pargana Bārī told Sakat Singh of his intentions, and expressed a hope that he would accompany him. Sakat, however, fled to his father, and told him of Akbar's intentions. This determined the emperor to carry out his plan without delay. Udaipūr was invaded, and Chitor surrendered.

367. **Shādī Be Uzbak** }
368. **Bāqī Be Uzbak** } sons of Nazar Be (No. 169).

They have been mentioned above. From the *Akbarnāma* (III, 628) we see that Nazar Be received a jāgīr in Handia, where he rebelled and perished (36th year).

369. **Yūnān Beg**, brother of Murād Khān (No. 54).

Some MSS. have *Mīrzā Khān* for *Murād Khān*.

370. **Shaykh Kabīr-r Chishtī** [Shujāʿat Khān, Rustam-i Zamān].[2]

---

[1] He is not to be confounded with another Shaykh Kabīr, who in the 25th year served in Bengal at the outbreak of the military revolt; in the 26th year, in Kābul; and in the 32nd year, against the Tārīkīs under Maṭlab Khān (No. 83). He died in the 36th year, in the war with the Jām and Muẓaffar of Gujrāt (*Akbarn.*, III, 283, 408, 541, 621, where the Lucknow edition calls him *the son* of *Mukammal Khān*).

[2] Khāfī Khān calls him wrongly (I, 273) *Shujāʿ Khān* and *Rustam Khān*.

The *Ma*ʿ*āṣir* calls him "an inhabitant of Mau". He was a relation of Islām Khān-i Chishtī, and received the title of Shujāʿat Khān from Prince Salīm, who on his accession made him a commander of 1,000 (*Tuzuk*, p. 12). He served under Khān Jahān (*vide* under No. 309) in the Dakhin as *harāwal*, an office which the Sayyids of Bārhā claimed as hereditary in their clan. Afterwards he went to Bengal, and commanded the imperialists in the last war with ʿUṣmān. During the fight he wounded ʿU.'s elephant, when the Afghān chief received a bullet, of which he died the night after the battle. The day being lost, Walī Khān, ʿUṣmān's brother, and Mamrez Khān, ʿUṣmān's son, retreated to a fort with the dead body of their relation, and being hotly pursued by Shaykh Kabīr, they submitted with their families and received his promise of protection. The 49 elephants which they surrendered were taken by Sh. K. to Islām Khān in Jahnāgīrangar (Dhākā), 6th Ṣafar, 1021 (*Tuzuk*, p. 104).

Jahāngīr gave him for his bravery the title of *Rustam-i Zamān*. The *Ma*ʿ*āṣir* says that Islām Khān did not approve of the promise of protection which Sh. K. had given the Afghāns, and sent them prisoners to court. On the road they were executed by ʿAbdᵘ 'llāh Khān at the emperor's orders. Sh. K., annoyed at this breach of faith, left Bengal. While on the way he received an appointment as governor of Bihār. At his entry in Patna he sat upon a female elephant, when another elephant suddenly came up against his. Sh. K. jumped down and broke his neck.

The *Tuzuk* tells the story differently, and says that Islām Khān appointed Sh. K. to Oṛīsā, and that on his way to that province the accident took place. Nothing is said about ʿUṣmān's relations.

Note on the death of ʿ*Uṣmān Lohānī.*

There are few events in Indian history so confused as the details attending the death of ʿUṣmān. Khwāja ʿUṣmān, according to the *Makhzan-i Afghānī*, was the second son of Miyān ʿIsā Khān Lohānī, who after the death of Qutlū Khān was the leader of the Afghāns in Oṛīsā and Southern Bengal. Qutlū left three sons—Naṣīb Shāh, Lodī Khān, Jamāl Khān. ʿIsā Khān left five sons, Khwāja, Sulaymān, ʿUṣmān, Walī, Ibrāhīm. Stewart makes ʿUṣmān a son of Qutlū (*History of Bengal*, p. 133). Sulaymān "reigned" for a short time. He killed in a fight with the imperialists, Himmat Singh, son of Rāja Mān Singh (*vide* No. 244) held lands near the Brāhmaputra, and subjected the Rājas of the adjacent countries. ʿUṣmān succeeded him, and received from Mān Singh lands in Oṛīsā and Sātgāw, and later in Eastern Bengal, with a revenue of 5 to 6 lacs *per annum*. His residence is described to have been the *Kohistān-i Dhākā*, or "hills of Dhākā" (Tipārah ?), the *vilāyat-i Dhākā*, or District of Dhākā, and Dhākā itself. The fight with ʿUs̱mān took place on Sunday, 9th Muḥarram, 1021, or 2nd March, 1612,[1] at a distance of 100 *kos* from Dhākā. My MS. of the Makhzan calls the place of the battle *Nek Ujyāl*.[2] Stewart (p. 134) places the battle "on the banks of the Subarnrīkhā river" in Oṛīsā, which is impossible, as Shujāʿat Khān arrived again in Dhākā on the 6th Ṣafar, or 26 days after the battle. According to the *Tuzuk*, Islām Khān was in Dhākā when the fight took place, and Walī Khān submitted to Shujāʿat, who had been strengthened by a corps under ʿAbdu 's-Salām, son of Muʿaẓẓam Khān (No. 260) ; but the Makhzan says that Islām besieged Walī in the Maḥalls where ʿUs̱mān used to live, between the battlefield and Dhākā, and afterwards in the Fort of Dhākā itself. Walī, on his submission, was sent to court with 7 lacs of rupees and 300 elephants taken from ʿUs̱mān, received a title of jāgīr, and was made a commander of 1,000, after which he lived comfortably. According to the *Mā*ʾ*as̱ir*, as said above, he was murdered before he came to court. The *Tuzuk* says nothing about him.

Stewart says (p. 136) that he was taken to court by Hoshang, Islām Khān's son ; but the *Tuzuk*, p. 115, though it has a long passage on the Mugs which he brought with him, does not mention the Afghān prisoners.

The Makhzan also says that ʿUs̱mān, after receiving his wound at the time when the battle was nearly decided in his favour, was carried off by Walī in a litter and buried on the road. When Shujāʿat came up to the place where he had been buried, he had ʿUs̱mān's corpse taken out, cut off the head, and sent it to court.

ʿUs̱mān is said to have been so stout that he was obliged to travel on an elephant. At his death he was forty-two years of age.

The Dutch traveller De Laët (p. 488, note) has the following interesting passage : *Rex* (Jahāngīr) *eodem tempore misit Tseziad ghanum Chiech zaden* (Shujāʿat Khān Shaykhzāda) *ad Tzalanghanum* (Islām Khān) *qui Bengalae praeerat, ut illum in praefecturam Odiae* (Oṛīsā) *mitteret. Sed Osmanchanus Patanensis, qui jam aliquot annis regionem quae Odiam et Daeck* (between Oṛīsā and Dhākā, i.e., the Sunderban) *interjacet, tenuerat et limites regni incursaverat, cum potentissimo exercitu advenit, Daeck oppugnaturus. Tzalanchanus autem praemisit adversus ipsum*

---

[1] According to Prinsep's Useful Tables, the 9th Muḥarram was a Monday, not a Sunday, *Tuzuk*, p. 102.

[2] There are several Ujyāls mentioned below among the Parganas of Sirkār Maḥmūdābād (Bosnah) and Sarkār Bāzūhā (Mymensing-Bogra).

(ʿUs̱mān) *Tzesiad chanum, una cum Mirza Ifftager et Ethaman chano* (Iftik͟hār K͟hān and Ihtimām K͟hān [1]) *et aliis multis Omerauvvis, cum reliquis copiis X aut XV cosarum intervallo subsequens, ut suis laborantibus subsideo esset. Orto dein certamine inter utrumque exercitum, Efftager et Mierick Zilaier* (Mīrak Jalāir—not in the *Tuzuk*) *tam acrem impressionem decerunt, ut hostes loco moverent; sed Osman inter haec ferocissimum elephantum in illos emisit, ita ut regii vicissim cedere cogerentur, et Efftager caederetur; Tzesiad gaunus autem et ipse elephanto insidens, ut impetum ferocientis belluae, declinaret, se e suo dejecit, et crus prefregit, ita ut aegre a suis e certamine subduceretur, et regii passim fugam capescerent; actumque fuisset de regiis, nisi inopinatus casus proelium restituisset; miles quidem saucius humi jacens, casu Osmano, qui elephanto vehebatur, oculum globo trajecit, e quo vulnere paulo post expiravit, cujus morte milites illius ita fuerunt consternati ut statim de fuga cogitarent. Regii vero ordinibus sensim restitutis, eventum proelii Tzalanchano perscripsere: qui biduo post ad locum venit ubi pugnatum fuerat, et Tzedsiatgano e vulnere defuncto, magnis itineribus fratrem* (Walī K͟hān) *et biduam atque liberos Osmanis assecutus, vivos cepit, eosque cum elephantis et omnibus thesauris defuncti, postquam Daeck Bengalae metropolim est reversus, misit ad regem Anno* . . . (the year is left out).

De Laët says that Shujāʿat K͟hān died from a fall from his elephant during the battle; but the accident took place some time later. The *Maʾās̤ir* says that he was on horseback when ʿUs̱mān's elephant, whom the Tuzuk calls *Gajpatī*, and Stewart *Buk͟hta* (?), knocked him over, but Sh. quickly disentangled himself and stuck his dagger into the animal's trunk.

The Mak͟hzan says that the plunder amounted to 7 lacs of rupees and 300 elephants.

371. **Mīrzā K͟hwāja,** son of Mīrzā Asad[u] 'llāh. *Vide* No. 116.

372. **Mīrzā Sharīf,** son of Mīrzā ʿAlāʾ[u] 'd-Dīn.

373. **Shukr[u] 'llāh** [Z̤afar Khān], son of Zayn Khān Koka (No. 34). He was mentioned above on p. 369. On the death of his father, he was made a commander of 700, and appears to have received, at the end of Akbar's reign, the title of Z̤afar K͟hān.

---

[1] The *Tuzuk* (p. 102) mentions Kishwar K͟hān (p. 497). Iftik͟hār K͟hān, Sayyid Ādam Bārhā, Shayk͟h Achhe, brother's son of Muqarrab K͟hān, Muʿtamid K͟hān, and Ihtimām K͟hān, as under Shujāʿat's command. Sayyid Ādam (the *Tuzuk*, p. 132, l. 4 from below, has wrongly Sayyid Aʿz̤am), Iftik͟hār, and Shayk͟h Achhe were killed. Later, ʿAbd[u] 's-Salām, son of Muʿaz̤z̤am K͟hān (No. 260) joined and pursued ʿUs̱mān.

As his sister was married to Jahāngīr (*vide* under No. 37, and note 2, to No. 225) Z. Kh. was rapidly promoted. When the emperor, in the second year of his reign, left Lāhor for Kābul, he halted at Mawẓaʿ Ahroʾī,[1] near Fort Aṭak, the inhabitants of which complained of the insecurity of the district arising from the predatory habits of the Khatar (p. 506, note 2) and Dilahzāk (note to No. 247). Ẓafar was appointed to Aṭak, *vice* Aḥmad Beg Khān (No. 191), and was ordered to remove the tribes to Lāhor, keep their chiefs imprisoned, and restore all plunder to the rightful owners. On Jahāngīr's return from Kābul, he joined the emperor, and was in the following year promoted to a manṣab of 2,000, 1,000 horse. In the 7th year he was made a commander of 3,000, 2,000 horse, and governor of Bihār. In the 10th year he was removed, went back to court, where he received an increase of 500 horse, and then served in Bangash. "Nothing else is known of him." *Maʾāṣir*.

From the *Tuzuk* (p. 343) we see that Ẓafar Khān died in the beginning of 1031, when Jahāngīr made his son Saʿādat a commander of 800, 400 horse.

Saʾādat Khān, his son. He served in Kābul, and was at the end of Jahāngīr's reign a commander of 1,500, 700 horse. In the 5th year after Shāhjahān's accession, he was made a commander of 1,500, 1,000 horse, and was promoted up to the 25th year to a full command of 3,000 horse. He again served in Kābul, and under Murād Bakhsh in Balkh and Badakhshān, was made commandant of Tirmiz and distinguished himself in repelling a formidable night attack made by Subḥān Qulī Khān, ruler of Bukhārā (19th year). Later he served in the Qandahār wars, was in the 29th year Fawjdār of Upper and Lower Bangash, and two years later commandant of Fort Kābul.

In 1069, the second near of Awrangzīb's reign, he was killed by his son Sherullāh. Mahābat Khān, Ṣūbahdār of Kābul, imprisoned the murderer.

374. **Mīr ʿAbdᵘ 'l-Mūmin**, son of Mīr Samarqandī.

Mīr Samarqandī was a learned man who came during Bayrām's regency of Āgra. *Badāʾonī*, III, 149.

375. **Lashkarī**, son of Mīrzā Yūsuf Khān (No. 35).

Vide above, p. 405, and for his wife under No. 351.

376. **Āgha Mullā** Qazwīnī. *Vide* No. 278.

377. **Muhammad ʿAlī** of Jām.

---

[1] The *Maʾāṣir* has اهروئی; the *Tuzuk*, p. 48, امروهی. I cannot find it on the maps. It is described as a green flat spot. The Khatars and Dilahzāks are estimated in the *Tuzuk* at 7 to 8,000 families.

Jām is a place in Khurāsān, famous for its *Bābā Shaykhī* melons. It has given name to the two poets Pūr Bahā and the renowned ʿAbdu r'-Rahmān Jāmī.

378. **Mathurā Dās,** the Khatrī.

379. **Sathurā Dās,** his son.

The latter served in the 26th year (989) under Sulṭān Murād in Kābul. *Akbarn.*, III, 333.

380. **Mīr Murād,** brother of Shāh Beg Kolabī (No. 148). *Vide* No. 282.

381. **Kallā,** the Kachhwāha.

He served in 989 under Prince Murād in Kābul.

382. **Sayyid Darwīsh,** son of Shams-i Bukhārī.

383. **Junayd Murul.**

A Shaykh Junayd served under Shihāb Khān (No. 26) in Gujrāt. He was killed in the Khaibar catastrophe (*Akbarn.*, III, 190, 498).

384. **Sayyid Abū Is-ḥāq,** son of Mīrzā Rafīʿu 'd-Dīn-i Ṣafawī.

He was mentioned under No. 149. In the 36th year he served against the Jām and Muẓaffar of Gujrāt.

His father Rafīʿu 'd-Dīn was a learned man of saintly habits, and died at Āgra in 954 or 957. One of his ancestors was Muʿinu 'd-Dīn, author of a commentary to the Qurʿan entitled *Tafsīr-i Maʿānī.*

385. **Fatḥ Khān,** superintendent of the leopards.

In 985, Akbar cured his sore eyes by blood letting, which Abū 'l-Faẓl describes, according to his custom, as a miracle. F. K. was in charge of the hunting leopards.

There is some confusion in the histories regarding the Fatḥ Khān of Akbar's reign. *First*, there is Fattū Khān Afghān. *Fattū* is the same as *Fatḥ.* His title is *Masnad-i ʿAlī*, and his son was mentioned above, No. 306. *Secondly*, Fatḥ Khān Fīlbān, who when young was Akbar's elephant driver (*fīlbān*). He was subsequently made Amīr, and according to my two MSS. of the *Ṭabaqāt*, died in 990. But Badāʾonī (II, 352) mentions Fatḥ Khān Fīlbān as alive in 994, when he accompanied Qāsim Khān (No. 59) on his march to Kashmīr; but the *Akbarnāma*, in the corresponding passage (III, 512) calls him *Fatḥ Khān Masnad-i ʿAlī.* Dowson's edition of *Elliot's Historians* (I, 244, 250) mentions a Fatḥ Khān Bahādur. A Fatḥ Khān Taghluq was mentioned under No. 187.

386. **Muqīm Khān,** son of Shujāʿat Khān (No. 51).

He served in the siege of Āsīr, and in the 46th year in the Dakhin. *Akbarn.*, III, 825, 865.

387. **Lāla,** son of Rāja Bīr Baṛ (No. 85).

The *Akbarnāma* (III, 835) calls him the *eldest* son of Rāja Bīr Baṛ. *Vide* under 85.

388. **Yūsuf-i Kashmīrī.** *Vide* No. 228.

389. **Ḥabī Yasāwul.**

Ḥabī is an abbreviation of *Ḥabīb*.

390. **Haydar Dost**, brother of Qāsim ʿAlī Khān (No. 187).

391. **Dost Muḥammad,** son of Bābā Dost.

392. **Shāhrukh** Dantūrī.

Dantūr, Dhantūr or Dhantāwar, is a district near the Kashmīr[1] frontier. The *Tuzuk* (pp. 287, 291) says that Dhantūr, during Akbar's reign, was ruled over by Shāhrukh, but now (in 1029, 14th year of Jahāngīr's) by his son Bahādur. Bahādur was a commander of 200, 100 horse, and served under Mahābat in Bangash.

393. **Sher Muḥammad.**

He served in 993 in the Dakhin. *Akbarn.*, III, 472.

A *Sher Muḥammad Dīwāna* was mentioned on p. 332. He had at first been in the service of Khwāja Muʿaẓẓam, brother of Akbar's mother. When Akbar, in the 10th year, was at Jaunpūr, engaged with the rebellion of Khān Zamān, Sher Muḥammad Dīwāna plundered several places in Pargana Samāna, the fawjdār of which was Mullā Nūr[u] 'd-Dīn Tarkhān. The Mullā had left his vakīl Mīr Dost Muḥammad in Samāna. Sh. M. D. invited him and treacherously murdered him at the feast. Plundering several places he went to Māler, when he was surprised by the Mullā at a place called Dhanūrī in Samāna. Sh. M. D. fled, but his horse ran against the trunk of a tree and threw him down. He was captured and executed, A.H. 973, *Akbarn*., II, 332.

394. **ʿAlī Qulī** [Beg, Istajlū, Sher Afkan Khān].

He was the *safarchī*,[2] or table-attendant of Ismāʿīl II, king of Persia. After his death he went over Qandahār to India, and met at Multān, the Khān Khānān (No. 29), who was on his march to Thatha. At his recommendation, he received a *manṣab*. During the war he rendered distinguished services. Soon after his arrival at court, Akbar married him to Mihr[u] 'n-Nisā (the future Nūr Jahān), daughter of Mīrzā Ghiyāṣ Ṭahrānī (No. 319). Ghiyāṣ's wife had accession to the imperial harem, and was on her visits often accompanied by her daughter. Prince Salīm saw her, and fell in love with her, and Akbar, to avoid scandal, married her quickly to ʿAlī Qulī.

---

[1] *Vide* Cunningham's *Geography of Ancient India*, p. 131. It lies on the Dor River, near Nawshahra.

[[2] *Sufra-chī*.—P.]

ʿAlī Qulī accompanied the prince on his expedition against the Rānā, and received from him the title of Sher Afkar Khān. On his accession, he received Bardwān as *tuyūl*. His hostile encounter with Shaykh Khūbū (No. 275) was related on p. 551. The *Maʾāṣir* says that when he went to meet the Ṣūbahdār, his mother put a helmet (*dubalgha*) on his head, and said, "My son make his mother cry, before he makes your mother weep," then kissed him, and let him go.

ʿAlī Q.'s daughter, who, like her mother, had the name of Mihr^u 'n-Nisā, was later married to Prince Shahryār, Jahāngīr's fifth son.

Jahāngīr, in the *Tuzuk*, expresses his joy at ʿA. Q.'s death, and hopes that "the blackfaced wretch will for ever remain in hell". Khāfī Khān (I, p. 267) mentions an extraordinary circumstance, said to have been related by Nūr Jahān's mother. According to her, Sher Afkan was not killed by Quṭb^u 'd-Dīn's men, but, wounded as he was, managed to get to the door of his house, with the intention of killing his wife, whom he did not wish to fall into the emperor's hands. But her mother would not let him enter, and told him to mind his wounds, especially as Mihr^u 'n-Nisā had committed suicide by throwing herself into a well. "Having heard the sad news, Sher Afkan went to the heavenly mansions."

His body was buried in the shrine of the poet Bahrām Saqqā (*vide* below among the poets); the place is pointed out to this day at Bardwān.

A verse is often mentioned by Muhammadans in allusion to four tigers which Nūr Jahān killed with a musket. The tigers had been caught (*Tuzuk*, p. 186) and Nūr Jahān requested Jahāngīr to let her shoot them. She killed two with one ball each, and the other two with two bullets, without missing, for which the emperor gave her a present of one thousand Ashrafīs. One of the courtiers said on the spur of the moment :—

نورجهان گرچه بصورت زن اشت   درصف مردان زن شیر افکن است

"Though Nūr Jahān is a woman she is in the array of men a *zan-i sher afkan*," i.e., either the wife of Sher Afkan, or a woman who throws down (*afkan*) tigers (*sher*).

395. **Shāh Muḥammad,** son of Masnad-i ʿAlī.

Vide Nos. 306 and 385.

396. **Sanwaldās Jādon.**

He accompanied Akbar on his forced march to Patan and Aḥmadābād (p. 458, note) and served in 989 under Prince Murād in Kābul. In 992 he was assaulted and dangerously wounded by some Bhāṭī. Akbar visited him, as he was given up by the doctors ; but he recovered after an illness of three years.

He was the son of Rāja Gopāl Jādon's brother (*vide* No. 305) and Abū 'l-Faẓl calls him a personal attendant of the emperor. *Akbarn.*, III, 24, 333, 435.

397. **Khwāja Ẓahīr[u] 'd-Dīn**, son of Shaykh Khalīl[u] 'llāh.

He served in the 31st year under Qāsim Khān (No. 59) in the conquest of Kashmīr, and in the 46th year in the Dakhin.

His father is also called *Shāh* Khalīl[u] 'llāh. He served in the 10th year against Khān Zamān, and under Munʿim Khān in Bengal and Oṛīsā, and died in 983 at Gaur of fever (p. 407).

Father and son are not to be confounded with the more illustrious Mīr Khalīl[u] 'llāh of Yazd and his son Mīr Ẓahīr[u] 'd-Dīn, who in the 2nd year of Jahāngīr came as fugitives from Persia to Lāhor. The history of this noble family is given in the *Maʾāṣir.*

398. **Mīr Abū 'l-Qāsim** of Nīshāpūr.

399. **Ḥājī Muḥammad** Ardistānī.

400. **Muḥammad Khān**, son of Tarson Khān's sister (No. 32).

401. **Khwāja Muqīm**, son of Khwāja Mīrakī.

He served under ʿAzīz Koka in Bengal, and returned with him to court in the 29th year. In 993 he served again in Bengal, and was besieged, together with Ṭāhir Sayf[u] 'l-Mulūk (No. 201) in Fort Ghorāghāt by several Bengal rebels. In the end of the 35th year (beginning of 999), he was made *Bakhshī*. *Akbarn.*, III, 418, 470, 610.

Vide Dowson's edition of *Elliot's Historians*, I, pp. 248, 251.

402. **Qādir Qulī**, foster-brother of Mīrzā Shāhrukh (No. 7).

He served in the 36th year in Gujrāt. *Akbarn.*, III, 621.

403. **Fīrūza**, a slave of the emperor Humāyūn.

Badāʾonī (III, 297) says that he was captured, when a child, by a soldier in one of the wars with India, and was taken to Humāyūn, who brought him up with Mīrzā Muḥammad Ḥakīm, Akbar's brother. He played several musical instruments and composed poems. He came to India with Ghāzī Khān-i Badakhshī (No. 144).

Badāʾonī also says that he was a Langā.

404 **Tāj Khān Khatriya.** *Vide* No. 172.

405. **Zayn[u] 'd-Dīn ʿAlī.**

He served in the 25th year (end of 988) under Mān Singh against M. Muḥammad Ḥakīm.

406. **Mīr Sharīf** of Kolāb.

407. **Pahāṛ Khān**, the Balūch.

He served in the 21st year against Daudā, son of Surjan Hāḍā (No. 96), and afterwards in Bengal. In 989, the 26th year, he was *tuyūldār* of G͟hāzīpūr, and hunted down Maʿṣūm K͟hān Farank͟hūdī, after the latter had plundered Muḥammadābād (*vide* under No. 175). In the 28th year he served in Gujrāt, and commanded the centre in the fight at Maisānā, S.E. of Patan, in which Sher K͟hān Fulādī was defeated. *Akbarn.*, III, 160, 355, 416.

Dr. Wilton Oldham, C.S., states in his "Memoir of the Ghazepoor District" (p. 80) that Fawjdār Pahāṛ K͟hān is still remembered in G͟hāzīpūr, and that his tank and tomb are still objects of local interest.

408. **Keshū Dās**, the Rāṭhor.

In the beginning of 993 (end of the 29th year) he served in Gujrāt. A daughter of his was married to Prince Salīm (*vide* under No. 4). From the *Akbarnāma*, III, 623, it appears that he is the son of Rāy Rāy Singh's brother (No. 44) and perished, in the 36th year, in a private quarrel.

409. **Sayyid Lād Bārha.**

In 993, Sayyid Lāḍ served with the preceding in Gujrāt, and in the 46th year, in the Dakhin.

410. **Naṣīr Maʿīn.**

Maʿīn (معين) or Munj, is the name of a subdivision of Ranghar Rājpūts, chiefly inhabiting Sarhind and the Bahat Duʿāb. "The only famous man which this tribe has produced is ʿIsā K͟hān Maʿīn. He served under Bahādur Shāh and Jahāndār Shāh." *Maʿāṣir.*

411 **Sānga**, the Pūwar.

412 **Qābil**, son of ʿAtīq.

413. **Adwand** } Zamīndārs of Oṛīsā.
414. **Sundar** }

415. **Nūram**, foster-brother of Mīrzā Ibrāhīm.

He served in the 31st year against the Afg͟hāns on Mount Terāh, and in 1000, under Mān Singh in the expedition to Oṛīsā. *Akbarn.*, III, 532, 642.

Mīrzā Ibrāhīm was Akbar's youngest brother, who died as an infant.

The above list of grandees includes the names of such Manṣabdārs above the rank of commanders of Five Hundred as were alive and dead in the 40th year of his Majesty's reign, in which this book was completed; but the list of the commanders from Five hundred to Two hundred, only contains such as were alive in that year. Of those who hold a lower rank and are now alive, I shall merely give the number. There are at present :—

of Commanders of 150	. . . .	53
Do.	120	1
Do.	100, or *Yūzbāshīs* . . .	250
Do.	80	91
Do.	60	204
Do.	50	16
Do.	40	260
Do.	30, or *Tarkashbands* . . .	39
Do.	20	250
Do.	10	224

[Total, 1,388 Manṣabdārs below the rank of a Commander of 200.]

Scarcely a day passes away on which qualified and zealous men are not appointed to manṣabs or promoted to higher dignities. Many Arabians and Persians also come from distant countries, and are honoured with commissions in the army, whereby they obtain the object of their desires. A large number again, both of old and young servants, receive their discharge, and are rewarded by his Majesty with daily allowances or grants of land, that render them independent.

As I have mentioned the Grandees of the state, both such as are still alive and such as have gone to their rest, I shall also give the names of those who have been employed in the administration of the government, and thus confer upon them everlasting renown.

The following have been *Vakīls*, or prime-ministers [1] :—

Bayrām Khān (No. 10); Munʿim Khān (No. 11); Atga Khān (No. 15); Bahādur Khān (No. 22); Khwāja Jahān (No. 110); Khān Khānān Mīrzā Khān (No. 29); Khān-i Aʿẓam Mīrzā ʿKoka (No. 21).

The following have been *Vazīrs* or ministers of finances :—

Mīr ʿAzīzᵘ 'llāh Turbatī; Khwāja Jalālᵘ 'd-Dīn Maḥmūd [2] of Khurāsān (No. 65); Khwāja Muʿīnᵘ 'd-Dīn Farankhūdī (No. 128); Khwāja ʿAbdᵘ 'l-Majīd Āṣaf Khān (No. 49); Vazīr Khān (No. 41); Muẓaffar Khān (No. 37); Rāja Toḍar Mal (No. 39); Khwāja Shāh Manṣūr of Shīrāz (No. 122); Qulij Khān (No. 42); Khwāja Shamsᵘ 'd-Dīn Khawāfī (No. 159).

The following have been *Bakhshīs* :—

Khwāja Jahān (No. 110); Khwāja Ṭāhir of Sijistān (No. 111); Mawlānā Ḥabī Bihzādī,[3] Mawlānā Darwīsh Muḥammad of Mashhad;

---

[1] Abū 'l-Faẓl's list is neither complete, nor chronologically arranged

[2] The MSS. and my text have wrong *Masʿūd* for Maḥmūd.

[3] Some MSS. have *Hai* instead of *Habī* (an abbreviation for *Habīb*).

Mawlānā ʿIshqī,[1] Muqīm of Khurāsān (No. 410); Sulṭān Maḥmūd of Badakhshān; Lashkar Khān (No. 90); Shāhbāz Khān (No. 80); Rāy Purukhotam; Shaykh Farīd-i Bukhārī (No. 99); Qāẓī ʿAlī of Baghdād; Jaʿfar Beg ʿĀṣaf Khān (No. 98); Khwāja Niẓāmu 'd-Dīn Aḥmad;[2] Khwājagī Fatḥu 'llāh (No. 258).

The following have been *Sadrs*[3]:—

Mīr Fatḥu 'llāh; Shaykh Gadāʾī, son of Shaykh Jamāl-i Kambū; Khwājagī Muḥammad Ṣāliḥ, descendant in the third generation from Khwāja ʿAbdu 'llāh Marwārīd; Mawlānā ʿAbdu 'l-Bāqī; Shaykh ʿAbdu 'n-Nabī; Sulṭān Khwāja (No. 108); Ṣadr Jahān (No. 194).

Concluding Note by the Translator of Akbar's Manṣabdārs.

The principal facts which Abū 'l-Faẓl's list of Grandees discloses are, *first*, that there were very few Hindūstānī Musulmāns in the higher ranks of the army and the civil service, most of the officers being foreigners, especially Persians and Afghāns; *secondly*, that there was a very fair sprinkling of Hindū Amīrs, as among the 415 Manṣabdārs there are 51 Hindūs.

The Mansabdārs who had fallen into disgrace, or had rebelled, have mostly been excluded. Thus we miss the names of Mīr Shāh Abū 'l-Maʿālī; Khwāja Maʿaẓẓam, brother of Akbar's mother; Bābā Khān Qāqshāl; Maʿṣūm-i Kābulī (p. 476, note); ʿArab Bahādur; Jabārī, etc. But there are also several left out, as Khizr Khwāja (p. 394, note 2), Sulṭān Ḥusayn Jalāʾir (*vide* under No. 64), Kamāl Khān the Gakkhar (*vide* p. 507), Mīr Gesū (p. 464), Nawrang Khān, son of Quṭbu 'd-Dīn Khān (No. 28), Mīrzā Qulī (p. 418), Rāja Āskaran (under No. 174), and others, for whose omission it is difficult to assign reasons.

Comparing Abū 'l-Faẓl's list with that in the *Ṭabaqāt*, or the careful lists of Shāhjahān's grandees in the *Pādishāhnāma*, we observe that Abū 'l-Faẓl has only given the *manṣab*, but not the actual commands, which would have shown the strength of the contingents (*tābīnān*). In other words, Abū 'l-Faẓl has merely given the *ẕātī* rank (p. 251). This will partly account for the discrepancies in rank between his list and that by Niẓāmu 'd-Dīn in the *Ṭabaqāt*, which may advantageously be given here. Niẓām gives only manṣabdārs of higher rank, viz.:—

---

[1] Regarding him *vide Akbarnāma*, III, 210. He was of Ghaznī.

[2] The Historian.

[3] *Vide* pp. 280 to 285. Regarding Maulānā ʿAbdu 'l-Bāqī, who was *Sadr* in the fifth year, *vide Akbarnāma*, II, 143.

In the *Ṭabaqāt*.	In *Abū 'l-Fazl's list*.
1. Khān Khānān Bayrām Khān .	No. 10. Manṣab, 5,000.[1]
2. Mīrzā Shāhrukh, 5,000 . .	„ 7 ; 5,000.
3. Tardī Beg Khān . . .	„ 12 ; do.
4. Munᶜim Khān . . .	„ 11 ; do.
5. Mīrzā Rustam, 5,000 . .	„ 9 ; do.
6. Mīrzā Khān Khānān . .	„ 29 ; do.
7. ᶜAlī Qulī Khān Zamān . .	„ 13 ; do.
8. Adham Khān . . .	„ 19 ; do.
9. Mīrzā Sharafu 'd-Dīn Ḥusayn .	„ 17 ; do.
10. Shamsu 'd-Dīn Muḥammad Atga Khān	„ 15 ; do.
11. Muḥammad ᶜAzīz Kokultāsh, 5,000	„ 21 ; do.
12. Khizr Khwāja . . .	not in the Āᵓīn ; *vide* p. 394.
13. Bahādur Khān, 5,000 . .	No. 22 ; 5,000
14. Mīr Muḥammad Khān Atga .	„ 16 ; do.
15. Muḥammad Qulī Khān Barlās*	„ 31 ; do.
16. Khān Jahān, 5,000 . .	„ 24 ; do.
17. Shihābu 'd-Dīn Aḥmad Khān, 5,000	„ 26 ; do.
18. Saᶜīd Khān, 5,000 . . .	„ 25 ; do.
19. Pīr Muḥammad Khān . .	„ 20 ; do.
20. Rāja Bihārā Mal [2] . .	„ 23 ; do.
21. Rāja Bhagwān Dās, 5,000 .	„ 27 ; do.
22. Mān Singh, 5,000 . . .	„ 30 ; do.
23. Khwāja ᶜAbdu 'l-Majīd Āṣaf Khān, maintained 20,000 horse	„ 49 ; 3,000.
24. Sikandar Khān Uzbak [2] .	„ 48 ; 3,000.
25. ᶜAbdu 'llāh Khān Uzbak .	„ 14 ; 5,000.
26. Qiyā Khān Gung [2] . .	„ 33 ; 5,000.
27. Yūsuf Muḥammad Khān Koka, 5,000	„ 18 ; 5,000.
28. Zayn Khān Koka, 5,000 .	„ 34 ; 4,500.
29. Shujāᶜat Khān, 5,000 . .	„ 51 ; 3,000.

[1] According to MS. No. 87, of the Library of the As. Soc., Bengal, and my own MS. The occasional differences in the names are mostly traceable to Akbar's hatred, which Abū 'l-Fazl shared, of the names " Muhammad ", " Aḥmad ".

[2] Mentioned in the *Ṭabaqāt* as belonging to the *Umarāᵓ-i kibār*, " the great Amirs," i.e., probably, the commanders of 5,000.

In the Ṭabaqāt.	*In Abū 'l-Faẓl's list.*
30. Shāh Budāgh Khān . .	No. 52 ; 3,000.
31. Ibrāhīm Khān Uzbak, 4,000 .	„ 64 ; 2,500.
32. Tarsō Muḥammad Khān, 5,000	„ 32 ; 5,000.
33. Vazīr Khān, 5,000 . . .	„ 41 ; 4,000.
34. Muḥammad Murād Khān [1] .	„ 54 ; 3,000.
35. Ashraf Khān [1]	„ 74 ; 2,000.
36. Mahdī Qāsim Khān [3] . .	„ 36 ; 4,000.
37. Muḥammad Qāsim Khān .	„ 40 ; 4,000.
38. Khwāja Sulṭān ʿAlī . .	„ 56 ; 3,000.
39. Rāja Toḍar Mal, 4,000 . .	„ 39 ; 4,000.
40. Mīrzā Yūsuf Khān Raẓawī, 4,000	„ 35 ; 4,500.
41. Mīrzā Qulī Khān [1] . .	not in the Āʾīn ; *vide* p. 418.
42. Muẓaffar Khān . . .	No. 37 ; 4,000.
43. Ḥaydar Muḥammad Khān, 2,000	„ 66 ; 2,500.
44. Shāham Khān Jalāʾir, 2,000 .	„ 97 ; 2,000.
45. Ismāʾīl Sulṭān Dulday . .	„ 72 ; 2,000.
46. Muḥammad Khān Jalāʾir [2] .	not in the Āʾīn.
47. Khān-i ʿĀlam, 3,000 . .	No. 58 ; 3,000.
48. Quṭbu 'd-Dīn Muḥammad Khān, maintained 5,000 horse .	„ 28 ; 5,000.
49. Muḥibb ʿAlī Khān, 4,000 .	„ 107 ; 1,000.
50. Qulij Khān, 4,000 . . .	„ 42 ; 4,000.
51. Muḥammad Ṣādiq Khān, 4,000	„ 43 ; 4,000.
52. Mīrzā Jānī Beg, 3,000 . .	„ 47 ; 3,000.
53. Ismāʿīl Qulī Khān, 3,000 [3] .	„ 46 ; 3,500.
54. Iʿtimād Khān Gujrātī, 4,000 .	„ 67 ; 2,500.
55. Rāja Rāy Singh, of Bīkānīr and Nagor, 4,000	„ 44 ; 4,000.
56. Sharīf Muḥammad Khān, 3,000	„ 63 ; 3,000.
57. Shāh Fakhru 'd-Dīn, Naqābāt Khān, 1,000	„ 88 ; 2,000.
58. Ḥabīb ʿAlī Khān . . .	„ 133 ; 1,000.
59. Shāh Qulī Maḥram, 1,000 .	„ 45 ; 3,500.

[1] Mentioned in the *Ṭabaqāt* as belonging to the *Umarāʾ-i kibār*, "the great Amīrs," i.e., probably the commanders of 5,000.

[2] He got insane. *Ṭabaqāt.*

[3] MS., 1,000.

In the Ṭabaqāt.	*In Abū 'l-Faẓl's list.*
60. Muḥibb ʿAlī Khān Rahtāsī, 4,000	not in the Āʾīn ; *vide* p. 466.
61. Muʿīnu ʿd-Dīn Aḥmad . .	No. 128 ; 1,000.
62. Iʿtimād Khān Khwājasarā .	„ 119 ; 1,000.
63. Dastam [1] Khān . . .	„ 79 ; 2,000.
64. Kamāl Khān, the Gakkhar, 5,000 5,000	not in the Āʾīn ; *vide* p. 507, and under No. 247.
65. Ṭāhir Khān Mīr Farāghat, 2,000	No. 94 ; 2,000.
66. Sayyid Ḥāmid of Bukhārā, 2,000	„ 78 ; 2,000.
67. Sayyid Maḥmūd Khān, Bārha, 4,000	„ 75 ; 2,000.
68. Sayyid Aḥmad Khān, Bārha, 3,000	„ 91 ; 2,000.
69. Qarā Bahādur Khān,[2] 4,000 (?)	„ 179 ; 700.
70. Bāqī Muḥammad Khān Koka, 4,000	„ 60 ; 3,000.
71. Sayyid Muḥammad Mīr ʿAdl .	„ 140 ; 1,000.
72. Maʿṣūm Khān Farankhūdī, 2,000	„ 157 ; 1,000.
73. Nawrang Khān, 4,000 . .	not in the Āʾīn ; *vide* p. 354.
74. Shāh Muḥammad Khān Atga, younger brother of Shamsu d'Dīn Atgah [3] . . .	not in the Āʾīn.
75. Maṭlab Khān, 2,000 . .	No. 83 ; 2,000.
76. Shaykh Ibrāhīm, 2,000 . .	„ 82 ; 2,000.
77. ʿAlī Qulī Khān, 2,000 . .	„ 124 ; 1,000.
78. Tolak Khān Qūchīn, 2,000 .	„ 158 ; 1,000.
79. Shāh Beg Khān Kābulī, 3,000	„ 57 ; 3,000.
80. Fattū Khān Afghān, 2,000 .	not in the Āʾīn ; *vide* No. 385.
81. Fatḥ Khān Fīlbān, 2,000 .	not in the Āʾīn ; *vide* under [No. 385.
82. Samānjī Khān Mughul, 2,000 .	No. 100 ; 1,500.
83. Bābū Manklī, 1,000 . .	„ 202 ; 700.
84. Darwīsh Muḥammad Uzbak, 2,000	„ 81 ; 2,000.
85. Shāhbāz Khān Kambū, 2,000 .	„ 80 ; 2,000.
86. Khwāja Jahān Khurāsānī .	„ 110 ; 1,000.

[1] The MSS. of the *Ṭabaqāt* also have wrongly *Rustam Khān*.
[2] MS. Bahādur Khān.
[3] This is probably a mistake of the author of the *Ṭabaqāt*.

In the *Ṭabaqāt*.	In *Abū 'l-Faẓl's list*.
87. Majnūn Khān Qāqshāl, kept 5,000 horse . . .	No. 50 ; 3,000.
88. Muḥammad Qāsim Khān,[1] 3,000	„ 40 ; 4,000.
89. Muẓaffar Ḥusayn Mīrzā, 1,000	„ 180 ; 700.
90. Rāja Jagannāth, 3,000 .	„ 69 ; 2,500.
91. Rāja Āskaran, 3,000 . .	not in the Āʿīn ; *vide* No. 174.
92. Rāy Lonkaran, 2,000 . .	not in the Āʿīn ; *vide* No. 265.
93. Mādhū Singh, "brother of R. Mān Singh," 2,000 . .	No. 104 ; 1,500.
94. Sayf Khān Koka . . .	„ 38 ; 4,000.
95. Ghiyāṣᵘ 'd-Dīn ʿAli Āṣaf Khān	„ 126 ; 1,000.
96. Pāyanda Khān Mughul, 2,000	„ 68 ; 2,500.
97. Mubārak Khān, the Gakkhar, 1,000	„ 171 ; 1,000.
98. Bāz Bahādur Afghān, 2,000 .	„ 120 ; 1,000.
99. Mīrak Khān Jinkjank (?) .	not in the Āʿīn.
100. Sayyid Qāsim Bārha, 2,000 .	No. 105 ; 1,500.
101. Rāja Kangār, 2,000 . .	not in the Āʿīn ; *vide* under No. 134.
102. Muḥammad Husayn Lashkar Khān, kept 2,000 horse .	No. 90 ; 2,000.
103. Ḥusayn Khān Tukriyah, 2,000	„ 53 ; 3,000.
104. Jalāl Khān, the Gakkhar, 1,500	„ 170 ; 1,000.
105. Saʿīd Khān, the Gakkhar, 1,500	not in the Āʿīn ; *vide* p. 508, and under No. 247.
106. Iʿtibār Khān, Eunuch, 2,000 .	No. 84 ; 2,000.
107. Khwājah Ṭāhir Muḥammad Tātār Khān . . .	„ 111 ; 1,000.
108. Moth Rāja, 1,500 . . .	„ 121 ; 1,000.
109. Mihtar Khān Khāṣa Khayl, 2,000	„ 102 ; 1,500.
110. Ṣafdar Khān, Khāṣa Khayl, 2,000[1]	not in the Āʿīn.
111. Bahār Khān, Khāṣa Khayl 2,000	No. 87 (?) ; 2,000.

[1] The same as No. 37 on p. 598 ?

In the Ṭabaqāt.	*In Abū 'l-Faẓl's list.*
112. Farḥat Khān Khāṣa Khayl, 2,000	No. 145 ; 1,000.
113. Rāy Sāl Darbārī, 2,000 . .	„ 106 ; 1,250.
114. Rāy Durgā, 1,500 [1] . .	„ 103 ; 1,500.
115. Mīrak Khān Bahādur,[2] 2,000 .	„ 208 ; 500.
116. Shāh Muḥammad Qalātī .	„ 95 ; 2,000.
117. Maqṣūd ʿAlī Kor . . .	„ 136 ; 1,000.
118. Ikhlāṣ Khān, the Eunuch, 1,000	„ 86 ; 2,000.
119. Mihr ʿAlī Sildoz, 1,500 . .	„ 130 ; 1,000.
120. Khudāwand Khān Dakhinī, 1,500	„ 151 ; 1,000.
121. Mīr Murtaẓā Dakhinī, 1,000 .	„ 162 ; 1,000.
122. Ḥasan Khān, a Batanī Afghān, 1,000	„ 220 ; 500.
123. Naẓar Beg, son of Saʿīd, the Ghakkhar, 1,000 . . .	„ 247 ; 500.
124. Rāja Gopāl, 2,000 . . .	not in the Āʾīn ; *vide* under No. 305.
125. Qiyā Khān, 1,000 . . .	No. 184 ; 700.
126. Sayyid Hāshim Bārha, 2,000 .	„ 143 ; 1,000.
127. Razawī Khān, 2,000 . .	„ 141 ; 1,000.
128. Rāja Bīr Bal, 2,000 . .	„ 85 ; 2,000.
129. Shaykh Farīd-i Bukhārī, 1,500	„ 99 ; 1,500.
130. Rāja Surjan, 2,000 . . .	„ 96 ; 2,000.
131. Jaʿfar Beg, Āṣaf Khān, 2,000	„ 98 ; 2,000.
132. Rāja Rūpsī Bairāgī, 1,500 .	„ 118 ; 1,000.
133. Fāẓil Khān, 1,500	„ 156 ; 1,000.
134. Shāh Qulī Khān Nāranjī, 1,000	„ 231 ; 500.
135. Shaykh Muḥammad Khān Bukhārī, 2,000	„ 77 ; 2,000.
136. Lāl Khān Badakhshī . .	„ 209 ; 500.
137. Khanjar Beg Chaghtā [3] . .	not in the Āʾīn.
138. Makhṣūṣ Khān, 2,500 . .	No. 70 ; 2,500.
139. Sānī Khān Arlāt	„ 216 ; 500.

[1] MS., 1,000.

[2] He died in the explosion of a mine before Chītor.

[3] " He belongs to the old Amīrs of the present dynasty. He was an accomplished man, excelled in music, and composed poems. There exists a well-known Maṣnawī by him, *dar bāb-i akhāṛā*, on the subject of dancing girls." *Ṭabaqāt. Vide Akbarnāma*, II, 82.

In the Ṭabaqāt.	*In Abū 'l-Faẓl's list.*
140. Mīrzā Ḥusayn Khān . .	No. 149 ; 1,000.
141. Jagat Singh, 1,500 . .	,, 160 ; 1,000.
142. Mīrzā Najāt Khān . .	,, 142 ; 1,000.
143. ʿAlī Dost Khān, 1,000 [1] . .	not in the Āʾīn.
144. Sulṭān Ḥusayn Khān . .	not in the Āʾīn.
145. Khwāja Shāh Manṣūr Shīrāzī .	No. 122 ; 1,000.
146. Salīm Khān, 1,000 . .	,, 132 ; 1,000.
147. Sayyid Chhajhū Bārha . .	,, 221 ; 500.
148. Darbār Khān, 1,000 . .	,, 185 ; 700.
149. Ḥājī Muḥammad Sīstānī, 1,000 (?)	,, 55 ; 3,000.
150. Muḥammad Zamān [2] . .	not in the Āʾīn.
151. Khurram Khān, 2,000 [3] . .	not in the Āʾīn.
152. Muḥammad Qulī Toqbāy, 1,000	No. 129 ; 1,000.
153. Mujāhid Khān, 1,000 [4] . .	not in the Āʾīn.
154. Sulṭān Ibrāhīm Awbahī [5] .	not in the Āʾīn.
155. Shāh Ghāzī Khān Turkmān .	not in the Āʾīn.
156. Sheroya, 1,000 . . .	No. 168 ; 1,000.
157. Kākar ʿAlī Khān, 1,000 .	,, 92 ; 2,000.
158. Naqīb Khān, 1,000 . .	,, 161 ; 1,000.
159. Beg Nūrīn Khān, 1,000 . .	,, 212 ; 500.
160. Qutlū Qadam Khān, 1,000 .	,, 123 ; 1,000.
161. Jalāl Khān Qurchī, 1,000 .	,, 213 ; 500.
162. Shimāl Khān Qurchī, 1,000 .	,, 154 ; 1,000.
163. Mīrzāda ʿAlī Khān . .	,, 152 ; 1,000.
164. Sayyid ʿAbdu 'llāh Khān .	,, 189 ; 700.
165. Mīr Sharīf-i Āmulī, 1,000 .	No. 166 ; 1,000.
166. Farrukh Khān . . .	,, 232 ; 500.
167. Dost Khān [6]	not in the Āʿīn.
168. Jaʿfar Khān Turkmān, 1,000 .	No. 114 ; 1,000.

[1] " He was a servant of Humāyūn. In Akbar's service he rose to a command of 1,000, and died at Lāhor." One MS. calls him ʿAlī Dost Khān *Nārangī*, the other has *Bārbegī*, an unusual title for the Mughul period.

[2] " Mūhammad Zamān is the brother of Mīrzā Yūsuf Khān (No. 35). He belonged to the commanders of 1,000, and was killed in Gaḍha." *Ṭabaqāt*.

[3] According to the *Ṭabaqāt*, he was dead in 1000. *Vide Akbarnāma*, II, 98, 108, 200, 284, 287.

He is not to be confounded with Mīrzā Khurram (No. 177).

[4] Mujāhid Khān was the son of Muṣāḥib Khān, one of Humāyūn's courtiers. He was killed at Konbhalmīr. *Akbarnāma*, III, 146, 168.

[5] He was the *khāl*, or maternal uncle, of the author of the *Ṭabaqāt*, and distinguished himself in leading a successful expedition into Kamāʾon.

[6] One MS. calls him بهاری, the other سهاري. " He belonged to the commanders of 1,000, and is now (A.H. 1001) dead."

	In the Ṭabaqāt.	*In Abū 'l-Faẓl's list.*
169.	Rāy Manohar . . .	No. 265 ; 400.
170.	Shaykh ʿAbd^{u} 'r-Raḥīm of Lakhnau	„ 197 ; 700.
171.	Mīrzā Abū 'l-Muẓaffar . .	„ 240 ; 500.
172.	Rāj Singh, son of Rāja Āskaran.	„ 174 ; 1,000.
173.	Rāy Patr Dās . . .	„ 196 ; 700.
174.	Jānish Bahādur . . .	„ 235 ; 500.
175.	Muḥammad Khān Niyāzī .	„ 239 ; 500.
176.	Rām Dās Kachhwāha . .	„ 238 ; 500.
177.	Mīr Abū 'l-Qāsim . .	„ 251 ; 500.
178.	Khwāja ʿAbd^{u} 'l-Ḥay, Mīr ʿAdl	„ 230 ; 500.
179.	Shams^{u} 'd-Dīn Ḥusayn, son of Aʿẓam Khān . . .	„ 163 ; 1,000.
180.	Khwāja Shams^{u} 'd-Dīn Khawāfī	„ 159 ; 1,000.
181.	Mīr Jamal^{u} 'd-Dīn Ḥusayn Injū, 1,000	„ 164 ; 1,000.
182.	Shaykh ʿAbd^{u} 'llāh Khān, son of Muḥammad Ghawṣ 1,000 .	„ 173 ; 1,000.
183.	Sayyid Rājū Bārha, 1,000 .	„ 165 ; 1,000.
184.	Mednī Rāy Chauhān, 1,000 .	„ 198 ; 700.
185.	Mīr Ṭāhir Raẓawī, brother of M. Yūsuf Khān . . .	„ 236 ; 500.
186.	Tāsh Beg Kābulī . . .	„ 172 ; 1,000.
187.	Aḥmad Beg Kābulī, keeps 700 horse	„ 191 ; 700.
188.	Sher Khwāja.	„ 176 ; 800.
189.	Muḥammad Qulī Turkmān .	„ 203 ; 600.
190.	Mīrzā ʿAlī Alamshāhī [1] . .	„ 237 ; 500.
191.	Wazīr Jamīl . . .	„ 200 ; 700.
192.	Rāy Bhoj, 1,000 . . .	„ 175 ; 1,000
193.	Bakhtyār Beg Turkmān . .	„ 204 ; 600.
194.	Mīr Ṣadr Jahān . . .	„ 194 ; 700.
195.	Ḥasan Beg Shaykh ʿUmarī .	„ 167 ; 1,000.
196.	Shādmān, son of ʿAzīz Koka .	„ 233 ; 500.
197.	Rāja Mukatmān Bhadaurya .	„ 249 ; 500.
198.	Bāqī Safarchī,[2] son of Ṭāhir Khān Farāghat . . .	not in the Āʾīn ; *vide* No. 94.

---

[1] "He is the brother of ʿAlamshāh, a courageous man, skilful in the use of arms." *Ṭabaqāt.* This remark is scarcely in harmony with the facts recorded under No. 237.

[[2] Or *Sufra-chī* ?—P.]

In the *Ṭabaqāt*.	In *Abū 'l-Faẓl's list*.
199. Farīdūn Barlās . . .	No. 227 ; 500.
200. Bahādur Khān Qurdār, a Tarīn Afghān	„ 269 ; 400.
201. Shaykh Bāyazīd-i Chishtī .	„ 260 ; 400.

In this above list, a few grandees are mentioned whom Abū 'l-Faẓl classes among the commanders of 400. Niẓām, however, adds the following note to his own list—" Let it be known that the title of *Amīr* is given to all such as hold Manṣabs from 500 upwards. *None of those whom I have enumerated holds a less rank.*"

The Historian Badā'onī has not given a list of Amīrs, but has compiled instead a very valuable list of the poets, doctors, learned men, and saints of Akbar's reign, together with biographical notices, which make up the third volume of the edition printed by the Asiatic Society of Bengal. With his usual animus he says (III, 1)—" I shall not give the names of the Amīrs, as Niẓām has given them in the end of his work, and *besides most of them have died without having obtained the pardon of God.*

I have seen none that is faithful in this generation ;
If thou knowest one, give him my blessing."

Of the Manṣabdārs whose names Abū 'l-Faẓl has not given, because the *Ā'īn* list refers to the period prior to the 40th year of Akbar's reign, the most famous are Mahābat Khān, Khān Jahān Lodī (*vide* under No. 309), and ʿAbdᵘ 'llāh Khān Fīrūz-jang.

We have no complete list of the grandees of Jahāngīr's reign ; but the Dutch traveller De Laët, in his work on India (p. 151) has a valuable note on the numerical strength of Jahāngīr's Manṣabdārs, which may be compared with the lists in the *Ā'īn* and the *Pādishāhnāma* (II, 717). Leaving out the princes, whose *manṣabs* were above 5,000, we have :—

Commanders of	*Under Akbar.* (Ā'īn)	*Under Jahāngīr.* (De Laët)	*Under Shāhjahān* (*Pādishāhnāma*)
5,000	30	8	20
4,500	2	9	0
4,000	9	25	20
3,500	2	30	0
3,000	17	36	44
2,500	8	42	11
2,000	27	45	51
1,500	7	51	52
1,250	1	0	0

Commanders of	Under Akbar. (Āʾīn)	Under Jahāngīr. (De Laët)	Under Shāhjahān (Pādishāhnāma)
1,000	31	55	97
900	38	0	23
800	2	0	40
700	25	58	61
600	4	0	30
500	46	80	114
Total	249	439	563
400	18	73	not specified.
350	19	58	
300	33	72	
250	12	85	
200	81	150	
Total	163	438	
150	53	242	not specified.
120	1	0	
100	250	300	
80	91	245	
60	204	397	
50	16	0	
40	260	298	
30	39	240	
20	250	232	
10	224	110	
Total	1,388	2,064	

The number of Aḥadīs under Jahāngīr, De Laët fixes as follows :—

Chahāraspas	741
Sihaspas	1,322
Duaspas	1,428
Yakaspas	950
	4,441 Aḥadīs.

Under Shāhjahān, 17 Grandees were promoted, up to the 20th year of his reign, to manṣabs above 5,000. There is no Hindū among them.

De Laët has not mentioned how many of the Amīrs were Hindūs. But we may compare the lists of the *Āʾīn* and the *Pādishāhnāma*.

We find under Akbar :—

among 252 manṣabdārs from 5,000 to 500 . .	32 Hindūs.
among 163 manṣabdārs from 400 to 200 . .	25 ,,

Under Shāhjahān (20th year of his reign), we have :—

among 12 manṣabdārs above 5,000 . . .	no Hindūs.
among 580 manṣabdārs from 5,000 to 500 . .	110 Hindūs

The names of commanders below 500 are not given in the *Pādishāhnāma*. Regarding other facts connected with the relative position of Hindūs and Muhammadans at the Mughul court, I would refer the reader to my "Chapter from Muhammadan History," *Calcutta Review*, April, 1871.

Āʾīn 30 (continued).

THE LEARNED MEN OF THE TIME.

I shall now speak of the sages of the period and classify them according to their knowledge, casting aside all differences of creed. His Majesty, who is himself the leader of the material and the ideal worlds, and the sovereign over the external and the internal, honours five classes of sages as worthy of attention. And yet all five, according to their light, are struck with his Majesty's perfection, the ornament of the world. The *first* class, in the lustre of their star, perceive the mysteries of the external and the internal, and in their understanding and the breadth of their views, fully comprehend both realms of thought, and acknowledge to have received their spiritual power from the throne of his Majesty. The *second* class pay less attention to the external world; but in the light of their hearts they acquire vast knowledge. The *third* class do not step beyond the arena of observation (*naẓar*) and possess a certain knowledge of what rests on testimony. The *fourth* class look upon testimony as something filled with the dust of suspicion, and handle nothing without proof. The *fifth* class are bigoted, and cannot pass beyond the narrow sphere of revealed testimony. Each class has many subdivisions.

I do not wish to set up as a judge and hold forth the faults of people. The mere classification was repugnant to my feelings; but truthfulness helps on the pen.

First Class.—Such as understand the mysteries of both worlds.

1. Shaykh Mubārak of Nāgor.[1]

Vide under No. 253. The *Ṭabaqāt* also mentions a Shaykh Mubārak of Alwar, and a Sayyid Mubārak of Gwālyār.

2. Shaykh Niẓām.

Abū 'l-Faẓl either means the renowned Niẓāmᵘ 'd-Dīn of Amethī, near Lakhnau, of the Chishtī sect, who died A.H. 979; or Niẓāmᵘ 'd-Dīn of Nārnaul, of the same sect, who died in 997.

3. Shaykh Adhan.

He also belonged to the Chishtīs, and died at Jaunpūr in 970.

4. Miyān Wajīhᵘ 'd-Dīn.

Died at Aḥmadābād in 998. The *Ṭabaqāt* mentions a contemporary, *Shaykh* Wajīhᵘ 'd-Dīn Gujrātī, who died in 995.

5. Shaykh Ruknᵘ 'd-Dīn.

He was the son of Shaykh ʿAbdᵘ 'l-Quddūs of Gango. Badāʾonī saw him at Dihlī at the time of Bayrām's fall.

6. Shaykh Abdᵘ 'l-Azīz (of Dihlī).

7. Shaykh Jalālᵘ 'd-Dīn.

He belongs to Thanesar, and was the pupil and spiritual successor (*khalīfa*) of ʿAbdᵘ 'l-Quddūs of Gango. Died 989.

8. Shaykh Ilāhdiya.

Ilāhdiya is Hindūstānī for the Persian *Ilāhdād*, "given (*diyā*) by God," "Theodore." He lived at Khayrābād and died in 993.

9. Mawlānā Ḥusāmᵘ 'd-Dīn.

"Mawlānā Ḥusāmᵘ 'd-Dīn Surkh of Lāhor. He differed from the learned of Lāhor, and studied theology and philosophy. He was very pious." *Ṭabaqāt*.

10. Shaykh ʿAbdᵘ 'l-Ghafūr.

He belongs to Aʿẓampūr in Sambhal, and was the pupil of ʿAbdᵘ 'l-Quddūs. Died in 995.

11. Shaykh Panjū.

He was wrongly called Bechū on p. 110, note 3. He died in 969. *Badāʾonī*, II, 53.

12. Mawlānā Ismāʿīl.

He was an Arabian, and the friend of Shaykh Ḥusayn, who taught in Humāyūn's Madrasa at Dihlī. He was a rich man, and was killed by some burglars that had broken into his house.

---

[1] The notes are taken from the *Ṭabaqāt*, the third volume of *Badāʾonī*, and the *Mirʾat 'l-ʿĀlam*.

13. Madhū Sarsutī.
14. Madhūsūdan.
15. Nārāyn Asram.
16. Harijī Sūr.
17. Damūdar Bhat.
18. Rāmtīrth.
19. Nar Sing.
20. Parmindar.
21. Ādit.

Second Class.—Such as understand the mysteries of the heart.

22. Shaykh Rukn^u 'd-Dīn Maḥmūd [1] Kamāngar (the bow maker).

23. Shaykh Amān^u 'llāh.

24. Khwāja ʿAbd^u 'sh-Shahīd.

He is the son of Khwājagān Khwāja, son of the renowned Khwāja Aḥrār. *Vide* No. 17 and No. 108. He died in 982, and was buried at Samarqand. He had been for twenty years in India, and held a jāgīr in Pargana جماري, in the Bārī Duāb, where he maintained two thousand poor.

25. Shaykh Mūsā.

He was a smith (*āhangar*), and performed many miracles. He died in the beginning of Akbar's reign, and was buried at Lāhor. The elder brother of Shaykh Salīm-i Chishtī also was called Shaykh Mūsā; *vide* under No. 82. *Vide* also below, No. 102.

26. Bābā Balās.

27. Shaykh ʿAlāʾ^u 'd-Dīn Majẕūb. *Vide Badāʾonī*, III, 61.

28. Shaykh Yūsuf Harkun.

The *Ṭabaqāt* calls him Shaykh Yūsuf Harkun Majẕūb of Lāhor.

29. Shaykh Burhān.

He lived as a recluse in Kālpī, and subsisted on milk and sweetmeats, denying himself water. He knew no Arabic, and yet explained the Qurān. He was a Mahdawī. He died in 970 at the age of one hundred years, and was buried in his cell.

30. Bābā Kipūr.

Shaykh Kipūr Majẕūb of Gwālyār, a Ḥusaynī Sayyid, was at first a soldier, then turned a *bihishtī*, and supplied widows and the poor with water. He died in 979 from a fall from his gate.

31. Shaykh Abū Is-ḥāq Firang. *Vide Badāʾonī*, III, 48.

32. Shaykh Dāʾūd.

He is called Jhannīwāl from Jhannī near Lāhor. His ancestors had come from Arabia and settled at Sītpūr in Multān, where Dāʾūd was born. *Badāʾonī* (III, p. 28) devotes eleven pages to his biography. He died in 982.

---

[1] *Badāʾonī* (III, p. 151) mentions a *Zayn^u 'd-Dīn Maḥmūd Kamāngar.*

33. Shaykh Salīm-i Chishtī.

He was a descendant of Shaykh Farīd-i Shakarganj, and lived in Fatḥpūr Sīkrī highly honoured by Akbar. Jahāngīr was called after him Salīm. He died in 979 Several of his relations have been mentioned above.

34. Shaykh Muḥammad Ghaws̤ of Gwālyār.

Vide No. 173.

35. Rām Bhadr. 36. Jadrūp.

Third Class.—Such as know philosophy and theology.[1]

37. Mīr Fatḥu 'llāh of Shīrāz.

Vide pp. 34, 110, 208, 234. His brother was a poet and wrote under the *takhalluṣ* of *Fārighī*; *vide Badā'onī*, III, 292. His two sons were Mīr Taqī and Mīr Sharīf.

38. Mīr Murtaẓā.

He is not to be confounded with Mīr Murtaẓā, No. 162. Mīr Murtaẓā Sharīf of Shīrāz died in 974 at Dihlī, and was buried at the side of the poet Khusraw, from where his body was taken to Mashhad. He had studied the Ḥadīs̤ under the renowned Ibn Ḥajar in Makkah, and then came over the Dakhin to Āgra. *Vide Akbarnāma*, II, 278, 337.

39. Mawlānā Saʕīd, of Turkistān.

He came in 968 from Māwara 'n-nahr to Āgra. *Bad.*, II, 49. He died in Kābul in 970; *l.c.*, III, 152.

40. Ḥāfiẓ of Tāshkand.

He is also called Ḥāfiẓ Kumakī. He came in 977 from Tāshkand to India, and was looked upon in Māwara 'n-nahr as a most learned man. He had something of a soldier in him, and used to travel about, like all Turks, with the quiver tied to his waist. He went over Gujrāt to Makkah; and from there to Constantinople, where he refused a vazīrship. Afterwards he returned to his country, where he died. *Vide Badā'onī*, II, 187.

41. Mawlānā Shāh Muḥammad.

Vide p. 112; *Bad.*, II, 295, *ll.*

42. Mawlānā Alāʕu 'd-Dīn.

He came from Lāristān, and is hence called *Lārī*. He was the son of Mawlānā Kamālu 'd-Dīn Ḥusayn and studied under Mawlānā Jalāl Dawwānī Shāfiʕī. He was for some time Akbar's teacher. Once at a darbār he placed himself before the Khān-i Aʕẓam, when the Mīr Tozak

---

[1] *Maʕqūl o manqūl*, pr. that which is based on reason (*ʕaql*) and traditional testimony (*naql*).

told him to go back. " Why should not a learned man stand in front of fools," said he, and left the hall, and never came again. He got 4,000 bīghas as sayūrghāl in Sambhal, where he died.

43. Ḥakīm Miṣrī. *Vide* No. 254.

44. Mawlānā Shaykh Ḥusayn (of Ajmīr).

He was said to be a descendant of the great Indian saint Muʿīn-i Chishtī of Ajmīr, was once banished to Makkah, and had to suffer, in common with other learned men whom Akbar despised, various persecutions. *Badāʾonī*, III, 87.

45. Mawlānā Mīr Kalān.

He died in 981, and was buried at Āgra. He was Jahāngīr's first teacher. *Bad.*, II, 170.

46. Ghāzī Khān. *Vide* No. 144.

47. Mawlānā Ṣadīq.

He was born in Samarqand, came to India, and then went to Kābul, where he was for some time the teacher of Mīrzā Muḥammad Ḥakīm, Akbar's brother. He then went back to his home, where he was alive in 1001. The *Ṭabaqāt* calls him Mullā Ṣādiq Ḥalwāʾī. *Badāʾonī* (III, 255, where the Ed. Bibl. India has wrongly *Halwānī*) puts him among the poets.

48. Mawlānā Shāh Muḥammad.

Vide No. 41. This seems to be a mere repetition. Other Histories only mention one Mawlānā of that name.

Fourth Class.—Such as know philosophy (ʿaqlī kalām).[1]

49. Mawlānā Pīr Muḥammad. *Vide* No. 20.

50. Mawlānā ʿAbdu 'l-Bāqī.

He was a Ṣadr ; *vide* pp. 282, 528 [and *Akbarnāma*, II, 143].

51. Mīrzā Muflis.

He was an Uzbak, came from Māwarā 'n-nahr to India, and taught for some time in the Jāmiʿ Masjid of Muʿīnu 'd-Dīn Farankhūdī (*vide* No. 128) at Āgra. He died in Makkah at the age of seventy. *Vide Bad.*, II, 187.

52. Mawlānāzāda Shukr.

53. Mawlānā Muḥammad.

He lived at Lāhor and was in 1004 nearly ninety years old. *Badāʾonī* (III, 154) calls him Mawlānā Muḥammad Muftī.

---

[1] This means chiefly religious testimony based on human reason, not on revelation. Abū 'l-Faẓl evidently takes it in a wider sense, as he includes the doctors in this class.

Abū 'l-Fazl, however, means perhaps Mawlānā Muḥammad of Yazd, a learned and bigoted Shīʿah, who was well received by Akbar and Abū 'l-Fazl, to whose innovations he at first agreed. But he got tired of them and asked for permission to go to Makkah. He was plundered on the road to Sūrat. *Mirʾāt*. But *Badāʾonī* tells quite a different story; *vide* p. 198.

Or it may refer to No. 140, p. 438.

54. Qāsim Beg.

Vide No. 350, p. 112. The *Ṭabaqāt* also says of him that he was distinguished for his acquirements in the *ʿaqlī ʿulūm*.

55. Mawlānā Nūr^u 'd-Dīn Tarkhān.

Vide under No. 393. He was a poet and a man of great erudition. Towards the end of his life "he repented" and gave up poetry. He was for a long time Mutawallī of Humāyūn's tomb in Dihlī, where he died.

The *Ṭabaqāt* says that he was a good mathematician and astronomer. According to the *Maʾāṣir*, he was born in Jām in Khurāsān, and was educated in Mashhad. He was introduced to Bābar, and was a private friend of Humāyūn's, who like him was fond of the astrolabe. He went with the emperor to ʿIrāq, and remained twenty years in his service. As poet, he wrote under the *takhalluṣ* of "Nūrī". He is also called "Nūrī of Safīdūn", because he held Safīdūn for some time as jāgīr. Akbar gave him the title of Khān, and later that of Tarkhān,[1] and appointed him to Samānah.

56. Nārāyn.
57. Madhūbhat.
58. Srībhat.
59. Bishn Nāth.
60. Rām Kishn.
61. Balbhadr Misr.
62. Bāsūdev Misr.
63. Bāmanbhat.
64. Bidyāniwās.
65. Gorīnāth.
66. Gopīnāth.
67. Kishn Paṇḍit.
68. Bhaṭṭāchārj.
69. Bhagīrat Bhaṭṭāchārj.
70. Kāshī Nāth Bhaṭṭāchārj.

Physicians.

71. Ḥakīm Miṣrī. *Vide* No. 254.

72. Ḥakīm^u 'l-Mulk.

His name is Shams^u 'd-Dīn and, like several other doctors of Akbar's court, he had come from Gīlān on the Caspian, to India. He was a very learned man. When the learned were driven from court and the innova-

---

[1] The title carried with it none of the privileges attached to it; *vide* p. 393. The *Maʾāṣir* has some verses made by Nūrī on his empty title.

tions commenced, he asked for permission to go to Makkah (988), where he died.

73. Mullā Mīr.

The *Ṭabaqāt* calls him Mullā Mīr Ṭabīb of Hairāt, grandson of Mullā ʿAbd[u] 'l-Ḥay Yazdī.

74. Ḥakīm Abū 'l-Fatḥ. *Vide* No. 112, p. 468.

75. Ḥakīm Zanbīl Beg. *Vide* No. 150, p. 490.

76. Ḥakīm ʿAlī of Gīlān. *Vide* No. 192, p. 519.

77. Ḥakīm Ḥasan.

He also came from Gīlān. His knowledge, says *Badāʾonī* (III, 167), was not extensive, but he was an excellent man.

78. Ḥakīm Aristū.

79. Ḥakīm Fatḥ[u] 'llāh.

He also came from Gīlān, knew a great deal of medical literature, and also of astronomy. He wrote a Persian Commentary to the Qānūn. In the first year of Jahāngīr's reign he was a Commander of 1,000, three hundred horse (*Tuzuk*, p. 34). The *Pādishāhnāma* (I, b., 350) says that he afterwards returned to his country, where he committed suicide. His grandson, Fatḥ[u] 'llāh, was a doctor at Shājahān's court.

80. Ḥakīm Masīḥ[u] 'l-Mulk.

He came from the Dakhin, where he had gone from Shīrāz. He was a simple, pious man, and was physician to Sulṭān Murād. He died in Mālwah.

81. Ḥakīm Jalāl[u] 'd-Dīn Muẓaffar. *Vide* No. 348, p. 582.

82. Ḥakīm Luṭf[u] 'llāh. *Vide* No. 354, p. 584.

83. Ḥakīm Sayf[u] 'l-Mulk Lang.

Badāʾonī and the *Ṭabaqāt* call him Sayf[u] 'l-Mulūk. Because he killed his patients, he got the nickname of *Sayf[u] 'l-Ḥukamā*, " the sword of the doctors." He came from Damāwand, and was in Āgra during Bayrām's regency. Later he went back to his country. He was also a poet and wrote under the *takhalluṣ* of " Shujāʾī ". He is not to be confounded with No. 201, p. 528.

84. Ḥakīm Ḥumām. *Vide* No. 205, p. 529.

85. Ḥakīm ʿAin[u] 'l-Mulk. *Vide* No. 234, p. 537.

86. Ḥakīm Shifāʾī.

The *Mirʾāt* mentions a Ḥakīm Shifāʾī, who in his poetical writings calls himself Muẓaffar ibn-i Muḥammad Al-ḥusaynī As-shifāʾī. He was born at Iṣfahān, and was a friend of Shāh ʿAbbās-i Ṣafawī. He died in 1037. There is a copy of his Masnawī in the Library of the Asiatic Society of Bengal (No. 795).

87. Ḥakīm Niʿmatu ʼllāh.

88. Ḥakīm Dawāʾī.

Dawāʾī was also the *takhalluṣ* of No. 85.

89. Ḥakīm Ṭalab ʿAlī.

90. Ḥakīm ʿAbdu ʼr-Raḥīm.

91. Ḥakīm Rūḥu ʼllāh.

92. Ḥakīm Fakhru ʼd-Dīn ʿAlī.

93. Ḥakīm Is-ḥāq.

94. Shaykh Ḥasan, and 95. Shaykh Bīnā.

Shaykh Ḥasan of Pānīpat, and his son Shaykh Bīnā were renowned surgeons. Instead of "Bīnā", the MSS. have various readings. The *Maʾāṣir* has *Phaniyā*, the *Ṭabaqāt Bhaniyā*.

Shaykh Bīnā's son is the well-known Shaykh Ḥasan, or Hassū, who under Jahāngīr's rose to great honours, and received the title of *Muqarrab Khān*. Father and son, in the 41st year, succeeded in curing a bad wound which Akbar had received from a buck at a deer-fight. Hassū was physician to Prince Salīm, who was much attached to him. After his accession, he was made a commander of 5,000 and governor of Gujrāt, in which capacity he came in contact with the English at Sūrat. He gave no satisfaction, and was recalled. In the 13th year (1027) he was made governor of Bihār, and in the 16th, governor of Āgra. In the beginning of Shāhjahān's reign, he was pensioned off, and received the Pargana of Kayrāna, his birthplace, as jāgīr. He constructed a mausoleum near the tomb of the renowned Saint Sharafu ʼd-Dīn of Pānīpat, and die dat the age of ninety. In Kayrāna, he built many edifices, and laid out a beautiful garden with an immense tank. He obtained excellent fruit-trees from all parts of India, and the Kayrāna mangoes, according to the *Maʾāṣir*, have since been famous in Dihlī.

Muqarrab's son, Rizqu ʼllah, was a doctor under Shāhjahān, and a commander of 800. Awrangzeb made him a Khān. He died in the 10th year of Awrangzeb.

Muqarrab's adopted son is Masīhā-i Kairānawī. His real name was Saʿadu ʼllah. He was a poet, and composed an epic on the story of Sītā. Rāmchandra's wife.

96. Mahādev.

97. Bhīm Nāth.

98. Nārāyin.

99. Sīwajī.[1]

[1] The *Ṭabaqāt* mentions a few other Hindū doctors of distinction who lived during Akbar's reign, *viz.* Bhīraū, Durgā Mal, Chandr Sen ("an excellent surgeon"), and Illī (one MS. has Abī).

Fifth Class.—Such as understand sciences resting on testimony (naql).[1]

100. Miyān Hātim.

He lived at Sambhal. The historian Badā*onī, when twelve years old, learned under him in 960. Hātim died in 969.

101. Miyān Jamāl Khān.

He was Muftī of Dihlī and died more than ninety years old in 984. He was a Kambū.

102. Mawlānā ʿAbdu 'l-Qādir.

He was the pupil of Shaykh Ḥāmid Qādirī (buried at Ḥāmidpūr, near Multān), and was at enmity with his own younger brother Shaykh Mūsā, regarding the right of succession. ʿAbdu 'l-Qādir used to say the *nafl*-prayers [2] in the audience-hall of Fatḥpūr Sīkrī, and when asked by Akbar to say them at home, he said, " My king, this is not your kingdom that you should pass orders." Akbar called him a fool, and cancelled his grant of land, whereupon ʿAbdu l-Qādir went back to Uchh. Shaykh Mūsā did better ; he joined the army, and became a commander of 500. *Vide* below, Nos. 109, 131.

The *Mir*-āt* mentions a Mawlānā ʿAbdu 'l-Qādir of Sirhind as one of the most learned of Akbar's age.

103. Shaykh Aḥmad.

The *Ṭabaqāt* mentions a Shaykh Ḥājī Aḥmad of Lāhor, and a Shaykh Aḥmad Ḥājī Pūlādī Majẕūb of Sind.

104. Makhdūmu 'l-Mulk. *Vide* p. 181.

This is the title of Mawlānā ʿAbdu 'llāh of Sulṭānpūr, author of the *ʿAṣmat-i Anbiyā*, and a commentary to the *Shamā*ilu 'n-Nabī*. Humāyūn gave him the titles of Makhdūmu 'l-Mulk and Shaykhu 'l-Islām. He was a bigoted Sunnī, and looked upon Abū 'l-Faẓl from the beginning as a dangerous man. He died in 990 in Gujrāt after his return from Makkah.

105. Mawlānā ʿAbdu 's-Salām.

The *Ṭabaqāt* says, he lived at Lāhor and was a learned man.

The *Mir*āt* mentions another Mawlānā ʿAbdu 's-Salām of Lāhor, who was a great lawyer (*faqīh*) and wrote a commentary to Baiẓāwī. He died more than ninety years old in the first year of Shāhjahān's reign.

106. Qāẓī Ṣadru 'd-Dīn.

Qāẓī Ṣadru 'd-Dīn Quraysbī ʿAbbāsī of Jālindhar was the pupil of Makhdūmu 'l-Mulk (No. 104). He was proverbial for his memory. He was attached to dervishes and held such broad views, that he was looked upon by common people as a heretic. When the learned were driven

---

[1] As religious law, Ḥadīṣ, history, etc.
[2] Voluntary prayers.

from court, he was sent as Qāẓī to Bharōch, where he died. His son, Shaykh Muḥammad, succeeded him. His family remained in Gujrāt.

107. Mawlānā Saʿadu 'llāh.

He lived at Bīyana, and was looked upon as the best grammarian of the age. He was simple in his mode of life, but liberal to others. Towards the end of his life he got silent, and shut himself out from all intercourse with men, even his own children. He died in 989.

108. Mawlānā Is-ḥāq.

He was the son of Shaykh Kākū, and lived at Lāhor. Shaykh Saʿadu 'llāh Shaykh Munawwar, and many others, were his pupils. He died more than a hundred years old in 996.

109. Mīr ʿAbdu 'l-Laṭīf. *Vide* No. 161, p. 496.

110. Mīr Nūru 'llāh.

He came from Shustar and was introduced to Akbar by Ḥakīm Abū 'l-Fatḥ. He was a Shīʿah, but practised *taqiya* among Sunnīs, and was even well acquainted with the law of Abū Ḥanīfa. When Shaykh Muʿīn Qāẓī of Lāhor retired, he was appointed his successor, and gave every satisfaction. After Jahāngīr's accession, he was recalled. Once he offended the emperor by a hasty word and was executed.

111. Mawlānā ʿAbdu 'l-Qādir.

He was Akbar's teacher (*ākhūnd*). *Vide* No. 242, p. 542.

112. Qāẓī Abdu 'l-Samī.

He was a Miyānkālī,[1] and according to *Badāʾonī* (II, 314) played chess for money and drank wine. Akbar made him in 990, Qāẓiyu 'l-Quẓāt, in place of Qāẓī Jalālu 'd-Dīn Multānī (No. 122). *Vide Akbarnāma*, III, 593.

113. Mawlānā Qāsim.

The *Ṭabaqāt* mentions a Mullā Qāsim of Qandahār.

114. Qāẓī Ḥasan. *Vide* No. 281, p. 559

115. Mullā Kamāl.

The *Ṭabaqāt* mentions a Shaykh Kamāl of Alwar, the successor and relative of Shaykh Salīm.

116. Shaykh Yaʿqūb (of Kashmīr). *Vide* below among the poets.

117. Mullā ʿĀlam. *Vide* p. 167, note.

He died in 991, and wrote a book entitled *Fawātiḥu 'l-Wilāyat*. *Bad.*, II, 337.

118. Shaykh ʿAbdu 'n-Nabī. *Vide* pp. 182, 186, 195, 197, 549, 616, note.

He was the son of Shaykh Aḥmad, son of Shaykh ʿAbdu 'l-Quddūs

---

[1] Miyānkāl is the name of the hilly tract between Samarqand and Bukhārā.

of Gango, and was several times in Makkah, where he studied the Ḥadīṣ. When he held the office of Ṣadr he is said to have been arbitrary, but liberal. The execution of a Brāhman, the details of which are related in *Badā'onī* (III, 80) led to the Shaykh's deposal.

Badā'onī (III, 83) places his death in 991, the *Mirʕāt* in 992. ʕAbdu 'n-Nabī's family traced their descent from Abū Ḥanīfa.

119. Shaykh Bhīk.

The *Ṭabaqāt* has also " Bhīk ", while *Badā'onī* (III, 24) has " Bhīkan ". Shaykh Bhīk lived in Kākor near Lakhnau. He was as learned as he was pious. He died in 981.

120. Shaykh Abū 'l-Fatḥ.

Shaykh Abū 'l-Fatḥ of Gujrāt was the son-in-law of Mīr Sayyid Muḥammad of Jaunpur, the great Mahdawī. He was in Āgra at the time of Bayrām Khān.

121. Shaykh Bahāʕu 'd-Dīn Muftī.

He lived at Āgra, and was a learned and pious man.

122. Qāẓī Jalālu 'd-Dīn Multānī. *Vide* pp. 183, 195.

He comes from near Bhakkar and was at first a merchant. He then took to law. In 990, he was banished and sent to the Dakhin, from where he went to Makkah. He died there.

123. Shaykh Ẓiyāʕu 'd-Dīn.

It looks as if Shaykh Ẓiyāʕu 'llāh were intended ; *vide* No. 173.

124. Shaykh ʕAbdu 'l-Wahhāb.

125. Shaykh ʕUmar.

126. Mīr Sayyid Muḥammad Mīr Adl. *Vide* No. 140, p. 485, and No. 251, p. 548.

127. Mawlānā Jamāl.

The *Ṭabaqāt* has a Mullā Jamāl, a learned man of Multān. *Badā'onī* (III, 108) mentions a Mawlānā Jamāl of تلنبہ, which is said to be a Maḥalla of Lāhor.

128. Shaykh Aḥmadī.

Shaykh Aḥmadī Fayyāẓ of Amethī, a learned man, contemporary of the saint Niẓāmu 'd-Dīn of Amethī (p. 607).

129. Shaykh Abdu 'l-Ghanī.[1]

He was born at Badā,on and lived afterwards in Dihlī a retired life. The Khān Khānān visited him in 1003.

130. Shaykh ʕAbdu 'l-Wāḥid.

---

[1] Sayyid Aḥmad's edition of the *Tuzuk* (p. 91, l. 11 from below) mentions that Jahāngīr when a child read the Ḥadīṣ under " *Shaykh ʕAbdu 'l-Ghanī*, whose fate is related in the *Akbarnāma*." This is a mistake for ʕAbdu 'n-Nabī (No. 118).

He was born in Bilgrām, and is the author of a commentary to the *Nuzhat*ᵘ *'l-Arwāḥ*, and several treatises on the technical terms (*iṣṭilāḥāt*) of the Ṣūfīs, one of which goes by the name of *Sanābil*.

131. Ṣadr-i Jahān. *Vide* No. 194, p. 522.

132. Mawlānā Ismāʿīl. *Vide* above, No. 12.

The *Ṭabaqāt* mentions a Mullā Ismāʿīl Muftī of Lāhor, and a Mullā Ismāʿīl of Awadh.

133. Mullā Abdᵘ 'l-Qādir.

This is the historian Badāʾonī. Abū 'l-Fazl also calls him *Mullā* in the *Akbarnāma*.

134. Mawlānā Ṣadr Jahān.

This seems a repetition of No. 131.

135. Shaykh Jawhar.

136. Shaykh Munawwar.

Vide p. 112. He was born at Lāhor, and was noted for his memory and learning. He is the author of commentaries to the *Mashāriq*ᵘ *'l-anwār* (Ḥadīs), the *Badīʿ*ᵘ *'l-bayān*, the *Irshād-i Qāẓī*, etc. When the learned were banished from court, he was imprisoned in Gwāliyār, where he died in 1011.

His son, Shaykh Kabīr, was also renowned for his learning. He died in 1026, in Aḥmadābād, and was buried in the mausoleum of the great Aḥmadābādī saint Shāh ʿĀlam. *Mirʿāt*.

137. Qāẓī Ibrāhīm.

Vide pp. 181, 183, 193. *Badāʾonī* and the *Ṭabaqāt* mention a Ḥājī Ibrāhīm of Āgra, a teacher of the Ḥadīs.

138. Mawlānā Jamāl. *Vide* above, No. 127.

139. Bijai Sen Sūr.

140. Bhān Chand.

Āʾīn 30 (continued).

THE POETS OF THE AGE.

I have now come to this distinguished class of men and think it right to say a few words about them. Poets strike out a road to the inaccessible realm of thought, and divine grace beams forth in their genius. But many of them do not recognize the high value of their talent, and barter it away from a wish to possess inferior store: they pass their time in praising the mean-minded, or soil their language with invectives against the wise. If it were not so, the joining of words were wonderful indeed; for by this means lofty ideas are understood.

He who joins words to words, gives away a drop from the blood of his heart.[1]

Every one who strings words to words, performs, if no miracle, yet a wonderful action.[2]

I do not mean a mere external union. Truth and falsehood, wisdom and foolishness, pearls and common shells, though far distant from each other, have a superficial similarity. I mean a spiritual union; and this is only possible in the harmonious, and to recognize it is difficult, and to weigh it still more so.

For this reason his Majesty does not care for poets; he attaches no weight to a handful of imagination. Fools think that he does not care for poetry, and that for this reason he turns his heart from the poets. Notwithstanding this circumstance, thousands of poets are continually at court, and many among them have completed a *dīwān*, or have written a *maṣnawī*. I shall now enumerate the best among them.

1. Shaykh Abū 'l-Fayẓ-i Fayẓī.

(*Vide* p. 548.)

He was a man of cheerful disposition, liberal, active, an early riser. He was a disciple of the emperor, and was thus at peace with the whole world. His Majesty understood the value of his genius, and conferred upon him the title of *Maliku 'sh-shuʕarā* or king of the poets.[3] He wrote for nearly forty years under the name of *Fayẓī*, which he afterwards, under divine inspiration, changed to *Fayyāẓī*, as he himself says in his "Nal Daman":—

Before this, whenever I issued anything,
The writing on my signet was "Fayẓī".
But as I am now chastened by spiritual love,
I am the "Fayyāẓī" of the Ocean of Superabundance (God's love).[4]

His excellent manners and habits cast a lustre on his genius. He was

---

[1] i.e., gives men something valuable.

[2] Saints perform wonderful actions (*karāmāt*), prophets perform miracles (*muʕjizāt*) Both in miracles, but the *karāmāt* are less in degree than the *mujʕizāt*. Whenever the emperor spoke, the courtiers used to lift up their hands, and cry "*karāmat, karāmat*", "a miracle, a miracle, he has spoken!" *De Laët.*

[3] Ghazālī of Mashhad (*vide* below, the fifth poet) was the first that obtained this title. After his death, Fayẓī got it. Under Jahāngīr Ṭālib of Āmul was *maliku 'sh-shuʕarā*, and under Shāhjahān, Muḥammad Jān Qudsī and, after him, Abū Ṭālib Kalīm. Awrangzīb hated poetry as much as he hated history and music.

[4] *Fayẓ* is an Arabic word meaning "abundance"; *Fayẓī* would be a man who has abundance or gives abundantly. *Fayyāẓ* is the intensive form of *Fayẓī*, giving superabundantly. *Fayyāẓī*, originally, is the abstract noun, "the act of giving superabundantly," and then becomes a title.

The form of *fayyāẓī* agrees with the form of *ʕAllāmī* Abū 'l-Faẓl's *takhalluṣ*, and some historians, as Badāʾonī, have maintained that the mere form suggested the change of *Fayẓī* to *Fayyāẓī*.

eminently distinguished in several branches. He composed many works in Persian and Arabic. Among others he wrote the *Sawāṭiʕᵘ 'l-ilhām* [1] (" rays of inspiration "), which is a commentary to the *Qurʕān* in Arabic, in which he only employed such letters as have no dots. The words of the *Sūratᵘ 'l-ikhlāṣ* [2] contain the date of its completion.

He looked upon wealth as the means of engendering poverty,[3] and adversity of fortune was in his eyes an ornament to cheerfulness. The door of his house was open to relations and strangers, friends, and foes; and the poor were comforted in his dwelling. As he was difficult to please, he gave no publicity to his works, and never put the hand of request to the forehead [4] of loftiness. He cast no admiring glance on himself. Genius as he was, he did not care much for poetry, and did not frequent the society of wits. He was profound in philosophy; what he had read with his eyes was nourishment for the heart. He studied medicine deeply, and gave poor people advice gratis.

The gems of thought in his poems will never be forgotten. Should leisure permit, and my heart turn to worldly occupations, I would collect some of the excellent writings of this unrivalled author of the age, and gather, with the eye of a jealous critic, yet with the hand of a friend, some of his verses.[5] But now it is brotherly love—a love which does

---

[1] I have not seen a copy of this work. It is often confounded with the *Mawāridᵘ 'l-kilam*, because the latter also is written *be nuqaṭ*, without the use of dotted letters. The *Mawārid* was printed at Calcutta in A.H. 1241, by the professors of the Madrasa and Maulawī Muḥammad ʕAlī of Rāmpūr. It contains sentences, often pithy, on the words *Islām, salām, ʕilmᵘ 'l-kalām, Ādam, Muḥammad, kalāmᵘ 'llah, ahlᵘ 'llah*, etc., and possesses little interest. Fayẓī displays in it his lexicographical abilities.

[2] This is the 112th chapter of the *Qurʔān*, which commences with the words *Qul huwᵃ 'allāhᵘ aḥad*. The letters added give 1002; Fayẓī, therefore, wrote the book two years before his death. This clever *tārīkh* was found out by *Mīr Haydar Muʕammāʔī* of Kāshān, poetically styled *Rafīʕī*. *Vide* below, the 31st poet.

[3] i.e., the more he had, the more he gave away, and thus he became poor, *or*, he considered that riches make a man poor in a spiritual sense.

[4] *Tārak*, properly the crown of the head. Putting the hand upon the crown of the head is an old form of the *salām*. Abū 'l-Faẓl wishes to say that Fayẓī was never mean enough to ask for favours or presents.

[5] Abū 'l-Faẓl kept his promise, and collected, two years after Fayẓī's death, the stray leaves of the *Markazᵘ 'l-adwār* (p. 549) regarding which the curious will find a notice by Abū 'l-Faẓl in the 3rd book of his *Maktūbāt*. The same book contains an elegy on Fayẓī's death.

MSS. of Fayẓī's Nal Daman are very numerous. His Dīwān, exclusive of the *Qaṣāʕid*, was lithographed at Dihlī, in A.H. 1261, but has been long out of print. It ends with a Rubāʕī (by Fayẓī), which shows that the words *Dīwān-i Fayẓī* contain the *tārīkh*, i.e., A.H. 971, much too early a date, as he was only born in 954. The *Mirʾātᵘ 'l- ʕĀlam* says that Fayẓī composed 101 books, Badāʔonī estimates his verses at 20,000, and Abū 'l-Faẓl at 50,000. The *Akbarnāma* (40th year) contains numerous extracts from Fayẓī's works. Dāghistānī says in his *Riyāẓᵘ 'sh-shuʕarā* that Fayẓī was a pupil of Khwāja Ḥusayn Sanāʔī of Mashhad, and it seems that Abū 'l-Faẓl has for this reason placed Sanāʔī immediately after Fayẓī. The same writer remarks that Fayẓī is in Persia often wrongly called *Fayẓī-yi Dakhinī*.

Many of the extracts given below are neither found in printed editions nor in MSS. of Fayẓī's works.

not travel along the road of critical nicety—that commands me to write down some of his verses.

Extracts from Fayẓī's Qaṣīdas (Odes).

1. O Thou, who existest from eternity and abidest for ever, sight cannot bear Thy light, praise cannot express Thy perfection.

2. Thy light melts the understanding, and Thy glory baffles wisdom; to think of Thee destroys reason, Thy essence confounds thought.

3. Thy holiness pronounces that the blood drops of human meditation are shed in vain in search of Thy knowledge: human understanding is but an atom of dust.

4. Thy jealousy, the guard of Thy door, stuns human thought by a blow in the face, and gives human ignorance a slap on the nape of the neck.

5. Science is like blinding desert sand on the road to Thy perfection; the town of literature is a mere hamlet compared with the world of Thy knowledge.

6. My foot has no power to travel on this path which misleads sages; I have no power to bear the odour of this wine, it confounds my knowledge.

7. The tablet of Thy holiness is too pure for the (black) tricklings of the human pen; the dross of human understanding is unfit to be used as the philosopher's stone.

8. Man's so-called foresight and guiding reason wander about bewildered in the streets of the city of Thy glory.

9. Human knowledge and thought combined can only spell the first letter of the alphabet of Thy love.

10. Whatever our tongue can say, and our pen can write, of Thy Being, is all empty sound and deceiving scribble.

11. Mere beginners and such as are far advanced in knowledge are both eager for union with Thee; but the beginners are tattlers, and those that are advanced are triflers.

12. Each brain is full of the thought of grasping Thee; the brow of Plato even burned with the fever heat of this hopeless thought.

13. How shall a thoughtless man like me succeed when Thy jealousy strikes down with a fatal blow the thoughts [1] of saints?

14. O that Thy grace would cleanse my brain; for if not, my restlessness (*quṭrub*) [2] will end in madness.

---

[1] *Literally,* strikes a dagger into the livers of thy saints.

[2] My text has *fitrat*; but several MSS. of Fayẓī's Qaṣīdas have *quṭrub*, which signifies incipient madness, restlessness of thought.

15. For him who travels barefooted on the path towards Thy glory, even the mouths of dragons would be as it were a protection for his feet (*lit.* greaves).[1]

16. Compared with Thy favour, the nine metals of earth are but as half a handful of dust; compared with the table of Thy mercies, the seven oceans are a bowl of broth.

17. To bow down the head upon the dust of Thy threshold and then to look up, is neither correct in faith, nor permitted by truth.

18. Alas, the stomach of my worldliness takes in impure food like a hungry dog, although Love, the doctor,[2] bade me abstain from it.

---

1. O man, thou coin bearing the double stamp of body and spirit, I do not know what thy nature is; for thou art higher than heaven and lower than earth.

2. Do not be cast down, because thou art a mixture of the four elements; do not be self-complacent, because thou art the mirror of the seven realms (the earth).

3. Thy frame contains the image of the heavenly and the lower regions, be either heavenly or earthly, thou art at liberty to choose.

4. Those that veil their faces in Heaven [the angels] love thee; thou, misguiding the wise, are the fond petted one of the solar system (lit. the seven planets).

5. Be attentive, weigh thy coin, for thou art a correct balance [i.e., thou hast the power of correctly knowing thyself], sift thy atoms well; for thou art the philosopher's stone (اکسیر اکبری).

6. Learn to understand thy value; for the heaven buys (*mushtarī*)[3] thy light, in order to bestow it upon the planets.

7. Do not act against thy reason, for it is a trustworthy counsellor; set not thy heart on illusions, for it (the heart) is a lying fool.

8. Why art thou an enemy to thyself, that from want of perfection thou shouldst weary thy better nature and cherish thy senses (or tongue)?

9. The heart of time sheds its blood on thy account [i.e., the world is dissatisfied with thee]; for in thy hypocrisy thou art in speech like balm, but in deeds like a lancet.

10. Be ashamed of thy appearance; for thou pridest thyself on the title of "sum total", and art yet but a marginal note.

---

[1] i.e., the terror of the mouths of dragons is even a protection compared with the difficulties on the road to the understanding of God's glory.

[2] *Literally,* Hippocrates.

[3] This is a pun. *Mushtarī* also means Jupiter, one of the planets.

11. If such be the charm of thy being, thou hadst better die ; for the eye of the world regards thee as an optical illusion (*mukarrar*).

12. O careless man, why art thou so inattentive to thy loss and thy gain ; thou sellest thy good luck and bargainest for misfortunes.

13. If on this hunting-ground thou wouldst but unfold the wing of resolution, thou wouldst be able to catch even the phœnix with sparrow feathers.[1]

14. Do not be proud (*farbih*) because thou art the centre of the body of the world. Dost thou not know that people praise a waist (*miyān*) when it is thin ? [2]

15. Thou oughtest to be ashamed of thyself, when thou seest the doings of such as from zeal wander barefooted on the field of love ; since thou ridest upon a swift camel [i.e., as thou hast not yet reached the higher degree of zeal, that is, of walking barefooted] thou shouldst not count thy steps [i.e., thou shouldst not be proud].

16. If thou wishest to understand the secret meaning of the phrase "to prefer the welfare of others to thy own", treat thyself with poison and others with sugar.

17. Accept misfortune with a joyful look, if thou art in the service of Him whom people serve.

18. Place thy face, with the humble mien of a beggar, upon the threshold of truth, looking with a smile of contempt upon worldly riches ;—

19. Not with the (self-complacent) smirk which thou assumest [3] in private, whilst thy worldliness flies to the east and the west.

20. Guard thine eye well ; for like a nimble-handed thief it takes by force the jewel out of the hand of the jeweller.

21. Those who hold in their hand the lamp of guidance often plunder caravans on the high road.

22. My dear son, consider how short the time is that the star of good fortune revolves according to thy wish ; fate shows no friendship.

23. [4] There is no one that understands me ; for were I understood,

---

[1] i.e., thou wouldst perform great deeds.

[2] *Proud*, in Persian *farbih*, pr. fat. In the East the idea of pride is suggested by stoutness and portliness. The Pun on *farbih* and *miyān* cannot be translated.

[3] As a hypocrite does.

[4] The next verses are *fakhriya* (boastful). All Persian poets write encomiums on themselves.

Wonderful stories are told about the mirror of Alexander the Great. He ordered his friend, the philosopher Balīnās, to erect in Alexandria a tower 360 yards high. A mirror was then placed on the top of it, 7 yards in diameter, and above 21 in circumference. The mirror reflected everything that happened in the world, even as far as Constantinople.

I would continually cleave my heart and draw from it the wonderful mirrors of Alexander.

24. My heart is the world, and its Hindūstān is initiated in the rites of idolatry and the rules of idol making [i.e., my heart contains wonderful things].

25. This [poem] is the masterpiece of the Greece of my mind; read it again and again; its strain is not easy.

26. Plunged into the wisdom of Greece, it [my mind] rose again from the deep in the land of Hind; be thou as if thou hadst fallen into this deep abyss [of my knowledge, i.e., learn from me].

---

1. The companion of my loneliness is my comprehensive genius; the scratching of my pen is harmony for my ear.

2. If people would withdraw the veil from the face of my knowledge, they would find that what those who are far advanced in knowledge call certainty, is with me (as it were) the faintest dawn of thought.

3. If people would take the screen from the eye of my knowledge, they would find that what is revelation (ecstatic knowledge) for the wise is but drunken madness for me.

4. If I were to bring forth what is in my mind, I wonder whether the spirit of the age could bear it.

5. On account of the regulated condition of my mind, I look upon myself as the system of the universe, and heaven and earth are the result of my motion and my rest.

6. My vessel does not require the wine of the friendship of time; my own blood is the basis of the wine of my enthusiasm [i.e., I require no one's assistance].

7. Why should I wish for the adulation of mean people? My pen bows down its head and performs the *sijda* in adoration of my knowledge.

Extracts from Fayẓī's Ghazals.

1. Rise and ask, in this auspicious moment, a favour at my throne; in noble aspirations I excel any army.

2. Expect in my arena the victory of both worlds; the banner of royalty weighs down the shoulder of my love.

3. When I cast a favourable glance upon those that sit in the dust, even the ant from my good fortune becomes possessed of the brain of Sulaymān.[1]

---

[1] The insignificance of the ant is often opposed to the greatness of Solomon. Once when all animals brought Solomon their presents, the ant offered him the leg of a locust as her only treasure.

4. The keepers of my door have their swords drawn; where is the desire that dares intrude on my seclusion?

5. Although I have buried my head in my hood, yet I can see both worlds; it may be that Love has woven my garment from the threads of my contemplation.

6. My eye is open and waits for the manifestation of truth; the spirit of the Universe flees before the insignia of my ecstatic bewilderment.

7. I am the simple Fayẓī; if you do not believe it, look into my heart through the glass of my external form.

---

1. The flame from my broken heart rises upwards; to-day a fiery surge rages in my breast.

2. In the beginning of things, each being received the slate of learning [i.e., it is the appointed duty of each to learn something]; but Love has learned something from looking at me, the duties of a handmaid.

3. May the eye of him who betrays a word regarding my broken heart be filled with the blood of his own heart!

4. O Fayẓī, thou dost not possess what people call gold; but yet the alchemist knows how to extract gold from thy pale cheek.

It were better if I melted my heart, and laid the foundation for a new one: I have too often patiently patched up my torn heart.

---

1. From the time that love stepped into my heart, nothing has oozed from my veins and my wounds but the beloved.[1]

2. The wings of angels have melted in the heat of my wine. Woe to the world, if a flash of lightning should some day leap from my jar [i.e., the world would come to an end, if the secret of my love were disclosed]!

---

[1] The beloved has taken entire possession of the poet. He has no blood left in him; for blood is the seat of life, and he only lives in the beloved who has taken the place of his blood. The close union of the lover and the beloved is well described in the following couplet by Khusraw:—

من تو شدم تو من شدي
من تن شدم تو جان شدی
تا کس نگوید بعد ازین
من دیگرم تو دیگري

I have become thou, and thou hast become I,
I am the body and thou art the soul.
Let no one henceforth say
That I am distinct from thee and thou from me.

1. Two difficulties have befallen me on the path of love ; I am accused of bloodshed, but it is the beloved who is the murderer.

2. O travellers on the right road, do not leave me behind ! I see far, and my eye espies the resting place.

I walk on a path [the path of love], where every footstep is concealed ; I speak in a place where every sigh is concealed.[1]

Although life far from thee is an approach to death, yet to stand at a distance is a sign of politeness.

---

1. In this world there are sweethearts who mix salt with wine, and yet they are intoxicated.

2. The nightingale vainly pretends to be a true lover ; the birds on the meadow melt away in love and are yet silent.[2]

---

1. My travelling companions say, " O friend, be watchful ; for caravans are attacked suddenly."

2. I answer, " I am not careless, but alas ! what help is there against robbers that attack a watchful heart ? "

3. A serene countenance and a vacant mind are required, when thou art stricken by fate with stripes from God's hand.[3]

---

1. The cupbearers have laid hold of the goblet of clear wine ; they made Khizr thirst for this fiery fountain.

2. What wine could it have been that the cupbearer poured into the goblet ? Even Masīḥ and Khizr are envious (of me) and struggle with each other to possess it.[4]

---

[1] A sigh indicates that a man is in love ; hence if the sigh is a stranger [*i.e.*, does not appear], the love will remain a secret. Eastern poets frequently say that love loses its purity and value, if it becomes known. The true lover bears the pangs of love, and is silent ; the weak lover alone betrays his secret. Hence the nightingale is often found fault with : it pours forth its plaintive songs to the rose, it babbles the whole night, instead of silently fixing its eye on the beauty of the rose, and dying without a murmur.

[2] Salt is an antidote against drunkenness. " Wine " stands for beauty, " salt " for " wit ". The nightingale is in love with the rose, but sings in order to lighten its heart ; the birds of the meadows, however, which are in love with the nightingale, show a deeper love, as they remain silent and hide their love-grief.

[3] Love is compared to robbers. The woe of love ought to be endured as a visitation of providence.

[4] Masīḥ (the " Messiah ") and Khizr (Elias) tasted the water of life (*āb i hayāt*). Wine also is a water of life, and the wine given to the poet by the pretty boy who acts as cupbearer is so reviving that even Messiah and Khizr would fight for it.

Ask not to know the components of the antidote against love: they put fragments of diamonds into a deadly poison.[1]

For me there is no difference between the ocean (of love) and the shore (of safety); the water of life (love) is for me the same as a dreadful poison.

I, Fayẓī, have not quite left the caravan of the pilgrims, who go to the Kaʿba; indeed, I am a step in advance of them.[2]

---

1. How can I complain that my travelling companions have left me behind, since they travel along with Love, the caravan chief?

2. O, that a thousand deserts were full of such unkind friends! They have cleared the howdah of my heart of its burden.[3]

---

1. I am the man in whose ear melodies attain their perfection, in whose mouth wine obtains its proper temper.

2. I show no inclination to be beside myself; but what shall I do, I feel annoyed to be myself.

---

1. Do not ask how lovers have reached the heavens; for they place the foot on the battlement of the heart and leap upwards.

2. Call together all in the universe that are anxious to see a sight: they have erected triumphal arches with my heart-blood in the town of Beauty.

---

1. Those who have not closed the door on existence and non-existence reap no advantage from the calm of this world and the world to come.

2. Break the spell which guards thy treasures; for men who really know what good luck is have never tried their good fortune with golden chains.[4]

---

[1] *Vide*, p. 573, note 4. Fragments of diamonds when swallowed tear the liver and thus cause death. Hence poison mixed with diamond dust is sure to kill. This is the case with every antidote against love: it does not heal, it kills.

[2] Fayẓī is ahead of his co-religionists.

[3] The beloved boy of the poet has been carried off. Fayẓī tries to console himself with the thought that his heart will now be free. But his jealousy is ill-concealed; for he calls the people unkind that have carried off his beloved.

[4] To the true Ṣūfī existence and non-existence are indifferent: he finds rest in Him. But none can find this rest unless he gives away his riches.

The bright sun knows the black drops of my pen, for I have carried my book (*bayāẓ*) to the white dawn of morn.[1]

O Fayẓī, is there anyone in this world that possesses more patience and strength than he who can twice walk down his street ? [2]

Desires are not to be found within my dwelling-place ; when thou comest, come with a content heart.

Renounce love ; for love is an affair which cannot be satisfactorily terminated. Neither fate nor the beloved will ever submit to thy wishes.

---

1. Come, let us turn towards a pulpit of light, let us lay the foundation of a new Kaʕba with stones from Mount Sinai !

2. The wall (*haṯīm*) of the Kaʕba is broken, and the basis of the *qibla* is gone, let us build a faultless fortress on a new foundation ! [3]

---

1. Where is Love, that we might melt the chain of the door of the Kaʕba, in order to make a few idols for the sake of worship.

2. We might throw down this Kaʕba which Hajjāj has erected, in order to raise a foundation for a (Christian) monastery.[4]

---

1. How long shall I fetter my heart with the coquettishness of beautiful boys ? I will burn this heart and make a new, another heart.

2. O Fayẓī, thy hand is empty, and the way of love lies before thee, then pawn the only thing that is left thee, thy poems, for the sake of obtaining the two worlds

---

How can I approve of the blame which certain people attach to

---

[1] Observe the pun in the text on *sawād*, *bayāẓ*, and *musawwada*.

[2] The street where the lovely boy lives. Can anyone walk in the street of love, without losing his patience ?

[3] If the *kaʕba* (the temple of Makkah) were pulled down, Islām would be pulled down ; for Muhammadans would have no *qibla* left, i.e., no place where to turn the face in prayer.

[4] When a man is in love, he loses his faith, and becomes a *kāfir*. Thus Khusraw says—*Kāfir-i ʕishqam, marā musalmānī darkār nīst*, etc., " I am in love and have become an infidel—what do I want with Islām ? " So Fayẓī is in love, and has turned such an infidel, that he would make holy furniture into idols, or build a cloister on the ground of the holy temple.

Zulaykhā? It would have been well if the backbiting tongues of her slanderers had been cut instead of their hands.[1]

I cannot show ungratefulness to Love. Has he not overwhelmed me with—sadness and sadness?

I cannot understand the juggler trick which love performed: it introduced Thy form through an aperture so small as the pupil of my eye into the large space of my heart, and yet my heart cannot contain it.

Flee, fate is the raiser of battle-fields; the behaviour of the companions is in the spirit of (the proverb) "hold it (the jug) oblique, but do not spill (the contents)." [2]

My intention is not to leave my comrades behind. What shall I do with those whose feet are wounded, whilst the caravan travels fast onwards?

This night thou tookest no notice of me, and didst pass by;
Thou receivedst no blessing from my eyes, and didst pass by.
The tears, which would have caused thy hyacinths to bloom,
Thou didst not accept from my moistened eye, but didst pass by.

---

1. On the field of desire, a man need not fear animals wild or tame: in this path thy misfortunes arise from thyself.

2. O Love, am I permitted to take the banner of thy grandeur from off the shoulder of heaven, and put it on my own?

---

1. O Fayẓī, I am so high-minded that fate finds the arm of my thought leaning against the thigh of the seventh heaven.

---

[1] When Zulaykhā, wife of Potiphar, had fallen in love with Yūsuf (Joseph), she became the talk of the whole town. To take revenge, she invited the women who had spoken ill of her to a feast, and laid a sharp knife at the side of each plate. While the women were eating, she summoned Yūsuf. They saw his beauty and exclaimed, "*Mā huwa basaran*," "He is no man (but an angel)!" and they suddenly grew so incontinent, that from lust they made cuts into their hands with the knives which Zulaykhā had placed before them.

[2] Fate leads you into danger (love); avoid it, you cannot expect help from your friends, they merely give you useless advice.

"You may hold (the jug) crooked, but do not spill (the contents)" is a proverb, and expressed that A allows B to do what he wishes to do, but adds a condition which B cannot fulfil. The friends tell Fayẓī that he may fall in love, but they will not let him have the boy.

2. If other poets [as the ancient Arabians] hung their poems on the door of the temple of Makkah, I will hang my love story on the vault of heaven.

---

1. O cupbearer Time, cease doing battle! Akbar's glorious reign rolls along, bring me a cup of wine:

2. Not such wine as drives away wisdom, and makes fools of those who command respect, as is done by fate;

3. Nor the harsh wine which fans in the conceited brain the fire of foolhardiness on the field of battle;

4. Nor that shameless wine which cruelly and haughtily delivers reason over to the Turk of passion;

5. Nor that fiery wine the heat of which, as love-drunken eyes well know, melts the bottles (the hearts of men):—

6. But that unmixed wine the hidden power of which makes Fate repent her juggling tricks (i.e., which makes man so strong, that he vanquishes fate);

7. That clear wine with which those who constantly worship in cloisters sanctify the garb of the heart;

8. That illuminating wine which shows lovers of the world the true path;

9. That pearling wine which cleanses the contemplative mind of fanciful thoughts.

In the assembly of the day of resurrection, when past things shall be forgiven, the sins of the Kaʿba will be forgiven for the sake of the dust of Christian churches.[1]

---

1. Behold the garb of Fayẓī's magnanimity! Angels have mended its hem with pieces of the heaven.

2. The most wonderful thing I have seen is Fayẓī's heart: it is at once the pearl, the ocean, and the diver.

The look of the beloved has done to Fayẓī what no mortal enemy would have done.

---

[1] The sins of Islām are as worthless as the dust of Christianity. On the day of resurrection, both Muhammadans and Christians will see the vanity of their religious doctrines. Men fight about religion on earth; in heaven they shall find out that there is only one true religion, the worship of God's Spirit.

1. The travellers who go in search of love are on reaching it no longer alive in their howdas ; unless they die, they never reach the shore of this ocean (love).

2. Walk on, Fayẕī, urge on through this desert the camel of zeal ; for those who yearn for their homes [earthly goods] never reach the sacred enclosure, the heart.

The dusty travellers on the road to poverty seem to have attained nothing ; is it perhaps because they have found there [in their poverty] a precious jewel ?

---

1. In the beginning of eternity some love-glances formed mirrors, which reduced my heart and my eye to a molten state [i.e., my heart and eye are pure like mirrors].

2. What attractions lie in the curls of idols, that the inhabitants of the two worlds [i.e., many people] have turned their face [from ideal] to terrestrial love ?

3. If a heart goes astray from the company of lovers, do not inquire after it ; for whatever is taken away from this caravan, has always been brought back [i.e., the heart for a time did without love, but sooner or later it will come back and love].

It is not patience that keeps back my hand from my collar ; but the collar is already so much torn, that you could not tear it more.[1]

---

1. If Laylī[2] had had no desire to be with Majnūn, why did she uselessly ride about on a camel ?

2. If anyone prevents me from worshipping idols, why does he circumambulate the gates and walls in the Ḥaram [the temple of Makkah] ?[2]

3. Love has robbed Fayẕī of his patience, his understanding, and his sense ; behold, what this highway robber has done to me, the caravan chief !

When Love reaches the emporium of madness, he builds in the desert triumphal arches with the shifting sands.

---

[1] A lover has no patience ; hence he tears the collar of his coat.

[2] Each man shows in his own peculiar way that he is in love. Laylī rode about in a restless way ; some people show their love in undergoing the fatigues of a pilgrimage to Makkah ; I worship idols.

1. Take the news to the old man of the tavern on the eve of the ʿĪd,[1] and tell him that I shall settle to-night the wrongs [2] of the last thirty days.

2. Take Fayẓī's Dīwān to bear witness to the wonderful speeches of a free-thinker who belongs to a thousand sects.

---

1. I have become dust, but from the odour of my grave, people shall know that man rises from such dust.

2. They may know Fayẓī's [3] end from his beginning : without an equal he goes from the world, and without an equal he rises.

O Love, do not destroy the Kaʿba ; for there the weary travellers of the road sometimes rest for a moment.

Extracts from the Rubāʿīs.

He [Akbar] is a king whom, on account of his wisdom, we call *ẕūfunūn* [possessor of the sciences], and our guide on the path of religion.

Although kings are the shadow of God on earth, he is the emanation of God's light. How then can we call him a shadow ? [4]

He is a king who opens at night the door of bliss, who shows the road at night to those who are in darkness.

Who even by day once beholds his face, sees at night the sun rising in his dream.

If you wish to see the path of guidance as I have done, you will never see it without having seen the king.

---

[1] The ʿīdu 'l-fiṭr, or feast, after the thirty days of fasting in the month Ramaẓān. Fayẓī, like a bad Muhammadan, has not fasted, and now intends to drink wine (which is forbidden), and thus make up for his neglect.

[2] Done by me by not having fasted.

[3] Fayẓī means the heart.

[4] A similar verse is ascribed by the author of the *Mir-ʾāt 'l-ʿĀlam* to the poet Yaḥyā of Kāshān, who, during the reign of Shāhjahān was occupied with a poetical paraphrase of the *Pādishāhnāma*.

گربی شریک خوانمت ای شاه دین رواست
زین گفته حاجتم بدلیل و بآیه نیست
تو سایهٔ خدائی و این همچو آفتاب
روشن بود که هیچ یکی را دو سایه نیست

If I call thee, o king of Islām " one without equal " it is but right.
I require neither proof nor verse for this statement.
Thou art the shadow of God, and like daylight ;
It is clear that no one has two shadows.

Thy old-fashioned prostration is of no advantage to thee—see Akbar, and you see God.[1]

O king, give me at night the lamp of hope, bestow upon my taper the everlasting ray!

Of the light which illuminates the eye of Thy heart,[2] give me an atom, by the light of the sun!

No friend has ever come from the unseen world; from the caravan of non-existence no voice has ever come.

The heaven is the bell from which the seven metals come, and yet no sound has ever come from it notwithstanding its hammers.[3]

In polite society they are silent; in secret conversation they are screened from the public view.

When you come to the thoroughfare of Love, do not raise dust, for there they are all surma-sellers.[4]

Those are full of the divine who speak joyfully and draw clear wine without goblet and jar.

Do not ask them for the ornaments of science and learning; for they are people who have thrown fire on the book.[5]

O Fayẓī, go a few steps beyond thyself, go from thyself to the door, and place thy furniture before the door.[6]

Shut upon thyself the folding door of the eye, and then put on it two hundred locks of eyelashes.

O Fayẓī, the time of old age has come, look where thou settest thy feet. If thou puttest thy foot away from thy eyelashes, put it carefully.

---

1 This is a strong apotheosis, and reminds one of similar expressions used by the poets of imperial Rome.

2 Kings receive a light immediately from God; *vide* p. III of Abū 'l-Faẓl's Preface.

3 *Muhrahā*, pl. of *muhrā*, according to the Bahār-i ʕAjam, the metal ball which was dropped, at the end of every hour, into a large metal cup made of *haft josh* (a mixture of seven metals), to indicate the time. The metal cups are said to have been in use at the courts of the ancient kings of Persia.

4 Lovers are silent in polite society. *Surma* is the well-known preparation of lead or antimony, which is applied to eyes to give them lustre.

5 The disciples of Akbār's divine faith have burnt the Qurʕān. They are different from the *ʕulamā fuẓalā*, the learned of the age.

6 Articles to be conveyed away are placed before the door immediately before the inmates travel away. Fayẓī wishes to leave the house of his old nature.

A pair of glass spectacles avails nothing, nothing. Cut off a piece from thy heart,[1] and put it on thine eye.

A sigh is a zephyr from the hyacinth bed of speech, and this zephyr has spread a throne for the lord of speech.

I sit upon this throne as the Sulaymān of speech; hear me speaking the language of birds.[2]

O Lover, whose desolate heart grief will not leave, the fever heat will not leave the body, as long as the heart remains!

A lover possesses the property of quicksilver, which does not lose its restlessness till it is *kushta*.[3]

O Fayẓī, open the ear of the heart and the eye of sense; remove thy eye and ear from worldly affairs.

Behold the wonderful change of time, and close thy lip; listen to the enchanter Time and shut thy eye.

What harm can befall me, even if the ranks of my enemies attack me? They only strike a blow on the ocean with a handful of dust.

I am like a naked sword in the hand of fate: he is killed that throws himself on me.

To-day I am at once both clear wine and dregs; I am hell, paradise, and purgatory.

Any thing more wonderful than myself does not exist; for I am at once the ocean, the jewel, and the merchant.

Before I and thou were thought of, our free will was taken from our hands.

Be without cares, for the maker of both worlds settled our affairs long before I and thou were made.

He held the office of a magistrate [4] and turned to poetry. He made himself widely known. His manners were simple and pure.

---

[1] For thy heart is pure and transparent.

[2] Solomon understood the language of the birds.

[3] *Kushta*, pr. killed, is prepared quicksilver, as used for looking-glasses. The lover must die before he can find rest.

[4] My text has *arbābī*. *Arbāb* is the plural of *rabb*, and is used in Persian as a singular in the sense of *kalāntar*, or *rīsh-safīd*, the head man of a place, *Germ.* Amtmann; hence *arbābī*, the office of a magistrate.

2. Khwāja Ḥusayn Sanā'ī of Mashhad.[1]

1. My speech is the morning of sincere men; my tongue is the sword of the morning of words.

2. It is clear from my words that the *Ruḥu 'l-quds* is the nurse of the Maryam of my hand [composition].[2]

3. It is sufficient that my pen has made my meanings fine, a single dot of my pen is my world.

4. In short, words exist in this world of brief duration, and my words are taken from them.

5. No one on the day of resurrection will get hold of my garment except passion, which numbers among those whom I have slain.

When thou goest out to mingle in society at evening, the last ray of the sun lingers on thy door and thy walls, in order to see thee.

---

1. In the manner of beauty and coquetry, many fine things are to be seen (as for example) cruel ogling and tyrannical flirting.

2. If I hold up a mirror to this strange idol, his own figure does not appear to his eye, as something known to him.[3]

3. If, for example, thou sittest behind a looking-glass, a person standing before it would see his own face with the head turned backwards.[4]

4. If, for example, an ear of corn was to receive its water according to an agreement made with thee [O miser], no more grain would ever be crushed in the hole of a mill.

---

1. A sorrow which reminds lovers of the conversation of the beloved, is for them the same as sweet medicine.

---

[1] The author of the *Ātashkada y: Āzar* says that Khwāja Ḥusayn was the son of ʿInāyat Mīrzā, and was in the service of Sulṭān Ibrāhīm Mīrzā Ṣafawī. But in his own Dīwān he is said to describe himself as the son of Ghiyāṣu 'd-Dīn Muḥammad of Mashhad, and the عنايت of the Ātashkada is a bad reading for غياث.

Regarding his poems the same author says, " either no one understands the meaning of his verses, or his verses have no meaning " —a critical remark which Abū 'l-Fazl's extracts confirm. Neither does Badā'onī (III, 208) think much of his verses, though he does not deny him poetical genius. The *Ṭabaqāt* again praises his poems. The *Mir'ātu 'l-ʿĀlam* says that " he was in the service of Ibrāhīm Mīrzā, son of Shāh Ṭahmāsp. On the accession of Shāh ʿIsmāʿīl II, Sanāʿī presented an ode, but Ismāʿīl was offended, as the poem did not mention his name, and accused the poet of having originally written it in honour of Ibrāhīm Mīrzā. Sanā'ī fled to Hindūstān, and was well received at court. He died at Lāhor in A.H. 1000. His Dīwān Sikandarnāma, and Sāqīnāma, are well known." Sprenger (Catalogue, pp. 120, 578) says that he died in 996. The *Ma'āṣir-i Raḥīmī* states that his bones were taken to Mashhad by his relation Mīrzā Bāqir, son of Mīr ʿArabshāh. It was mentioned on p. 619, note 5, that Fayẓī looked upon him as his teacher.

[2] *Ruḥu 'l-quds*, the spirit of holiness. *Maryam*, the Virgin Mary.

[3] So strange is the boy whom I love.

[4] This verse is unintelligible to me.

2. I exposed the prey of my heart to death, but the huntsman has given me quarter on account of my leanness and let me run away.[1]

3. If lovers slept with the beloved till the morning of resurrection, the morning breeze would cause them to feel the pain of an arrow.[2]

O sober friends, now is the time to tear the collar ; but who will raise *my* hand to my collar ? [3]

The messenger Desire comes again running, saying [4] . . .

It is incumbent upon lovers to hand over to their hearts those (cruel) words which the beloved (boy) took from his heart and put upon his tongue.

When my foot takes me to the Kaʿba, expect to fine me in an idol temple ; for my foot goes backwards, and my goal is an illusion.

---

1. The spheres of the nine heavens cannot contain an atom of the love grief which Sanāʾī's dust scatters to the winds.

2. Like the sun of the heaven thou livest for all ages ; every eye knows thee as well as it knows what sleep is.

3. Huznī of Ispahān.

He was an inquiring man of a philosophical turn of mind, and well acquainted with ancient poetry and chronology. He was free and easy and good hearted ; friendliness was stamped upon his forehead.[5]

---

1. I search my heart all round to look for a quiet place—and, gracious God ! if I do not find sorrow, I find desires.

2. Zulaykhā stood on the flowerbed, and yet she said in her grief that it reminded her of the prison in which a certain ornament of society [Yūsuf] dwelled.

3. I am in despair on thy account, and yet what shall I do with love ? for between me and it (love) stands (unfulfilled) desire.

---

[1] Or we may read *kurezam* instead of *girīzam*, when the meaning would be, "the huntsman has given me quarter on account of the leanness arising from my moulting." [This second reading is too far fetched and for practical reason may be dismissed.—P.]

[2] There are four verses after this in my text edition, which are unintelligible to me.

[3] The poet has no strength left in him to raise his hand to his collar. *Vide* p. 630, note 1.

[4] The remaining hemistich is not clear.

[5] The *Ṭabaqāt* calls him Mīr Ḥuznī, and says he left Persia with the intention of paying his respects at court, but died on his way to India. His verses are pretty The *Ātashkada* (p. 101 of the Calcutta edition) says he was born in Junābud, and was a merchant. The *Haft Iqlīm* says he was pupil of Qāsim-i Kāhī (the next poet).

Gabriel's wing would droop, if he had to fly along the road of love; this message (love) does not travel as if on a zephyr.

Whether a man be an Ayāz or a Maḥmūd, here (in love) he is a slave; for love ties with the same string the foot of the slave and the freeman.[1]

---

1. Last night my moist eye caught fire from the warmth of my heart; the lamp of my heart was burning until morning, to show you the way to me.

2. The power of thy beauty became perfectly known to me, when its fire fell on my heart and consumed me unknown to myself.

O Huznī, I sometimes smile at thy simplicity: thou hast become a lover, and yet expectest faithfulness from the beloved.

Don't cast loving eyes at me; for I am a withered feeble plant, which cannot bear the full radiance of the life-consuming sun [of thy beauty].

Alas! when I throw myself on the fire, the obstinate beloved has nothing else to say but "Ḥuznī, what is smoke like?"

I hear, Ḥuznī, that thou art anxious to be freed from love's fetters. Heartless wretch, be off; what dost thou know of the value of such a captivity!

To-day, like every other day, the simple-minded Ḥuznī was content with thy false promises, and had to go.

4. Qāsim-i Kāhī.[2]

He is known as Miyān Kālī. He knew something of the ordinary sciences and lived quiet and content. He rarely mixed with people in high position. On account of his generous disposition, a few low men had gathered round him, for which reason well-meaning people who did not know the circumstances, often upbraided him. Partly from his

---

[1] Ayāz was a slave of Maḥmūd of Ghāznī, and is proverbial in the East for faithfulness. There are several Maṣnawīs entitled Maḥmūd o Ayāz.

[2] *Kāhī*, "grassy," is his *takhalluṣ*. *Badāʿonī* (III, 172) says that his verses are crude and the ideas stolen from others; but yet his poems are not without merit. He was well read in the exegesis of the *Qurʿān*, in astronomy, mysticism, and the sciences which go by the name of *kalām*; he wrote on music, and was clever in *tārīkhs* and riddles. He had visited several Shaykhs of renown, among them the great poet Jāmī (died A.H. 899). But he was a free-thinker and was fond of the company of wandering faqīrs, prostitutes, and sodomites. "He also loved dogs, a habit which he may have contracted from Fayẓī."

own love of independence partly from the indulgence of his Majesty, he counted himself among the disciples and often foretold future events.

A low-minded man must be he who can lift up his hand for terrestrial goods in prayer to God's throne.

If lovers counted the hours spent in silent grief, their lives would appear to them longer than that of Khizr.[1]

Wherever thou goest, I follow thee like a shadow; perhaps, in course of time, thou wilt by degrees cast a kind glance at me.[2]

---

1. When I saw even elephants attached to my beloved, I spent the coin of my life on the road of the elephant.

Kāhī wrote a Masnawī, entitled *gul-afshān*, a reply or *jawāb*, to the Bostān, and completed a *dīwān*. An ode of his is mentioned in praise of Humāyūn and the Astrolabe.

He is said to have died at the advanced age of 120 years.

The *Ātashkada-yi Āzar* (Calcutta edition, p. 250) calls him "Mīrzā Abū 'l-Qāsim of Kābul", and says that he was born in Turkistān, and brought up in Kābul. One of his ancestors paid his respects to Tīmur, accompanied the army of that conqueror, and settled at last in Turkistān. Kāhī was well received by Humāyūn.

The same work calls him a *Gulistāna Sayyid*—a term not known to me. Hence, instead of "Mīrzā" we should read "Mīr".

The *Haft Iqlīm* has a lengthy note on Kāhī. Amīn of Ray (p. 512) says that Kāhī's name is Sayyid Najm^u 'd-Dīn Muḥammad, his *kunya* being Abū 'l-Qāsim. When fifteen years old, he visited Jāmī, and afterwards Hāshimī of Kirmān, who was called Shāh Jahāngīr. He went viâ Bhakkar to Hindūstān. Whatever he did, appeared awkward to others. Though well read, he was a pugilist, and would not mind fighting ten or even twenty at a time, and yet be victorious. No one excelled him in running. He followed no creed or doctrine, but did as the Khwājas do, whose formula is "*hosh dar dam, naẓar bar qudam, khalwat dar anjuman, safar dar waṭan,*" "Be careful in your speech; look where you set the foot; withdraw from society; travel when you are at home." He was liberal to a fault, and squandered what he got. For an ode in praise of Akbar, in every verse of which the word *fīl*, or elephant, was to occur (Abū 'l-Faẓl has given three verses of it), Akbar gave him one lac of tankahs, and gave orders that he should get a present of one thousand rupees as often as he should come to court. He did not like this, and never went to court again. He lived long at Banāras, as he was fond of Bahādur Khān (No. 22). Subsequently, he lived at Āgra, where he died. His grave was near the gate—my MS. calls it صارجاي با (?). He died on the 2nd Rabīʿ II, 988. Fayẓī's tārīkh (Rubāʿī metre):—

تاریخ وفات سال و ماهش جستم
گفتا دوم از ماه ربیع الثانی

gives 2nd Rabīʿ II, 978, unless we read دویم for دوم. Mawlānā Qāsim of Bukhārā, a pupil of Kāhī expressed the *tārīkh* by the words:—

رفت ملا قاسم کاهی

"Mulla Qāsim-i Kāhī died," which gives 988. *Vide* also *Iqbālnāma-yi Jahāngīrī*, p. 5; and above, p. 219.

Abū 'l-Faẓl calls him *Miyān Kālī*. Miyānkāl (*vide* p. 615) is the name of the hills between Samarqand and Bukhārā.

[1] *Khizr* is the "Wandering Jew" of the East.

[2] A verse often quoted to this day in India.

2. Wherever I go I, like the elephant, throw dust on my head, unless I see my guide above my head.

3. The elephant taming king is Jalāl^{u} 'd-Dīn Muḥammad Akbar, he who bestows golden elephants upon his poets.

---

1. O friend, whose tongue speaks of knowledge divine, and whose heart ever withdraws the veil from the light of truth,

2. Never cherish a thought of which thou oughtest to be ashamed, never utter a word for which thou wouldst have to ask God's pardon.

5. G͟hazālī of Mashhad.[1]

He was unrivalled in depth of understanding and sweetness of language, and was well acquainted with the noble thoughts of the Ṣūfīs.

I heard a noise and started from a deep sleep, and stared—the awful night had not yet passed away—I fell again asleep.[2]

Beauty leads to fame, and love to wretchedness. Why then do you speak of the cruelties of the sweetheart and the faults of the miserable lover ?

Since either acceptance or exclusion awaits all in the world to come, take care not to blame anyone ; for this is blameworthy.

---

[1] *Badāʿonī* (III, 170) says that G͟hazālī fled from Īrān to the Dakhin, because people wished to kill him for his heretical opinions. He was called by K͟hān Zamān (No. 13, p. 335) to Jaunpūr, where he lived for a long time. He afterwards went to court, and was much liked by Akbar, who conferred upon him the title of *Malik^{u} 'sh-Shuʿarā*. He accompanied the emperor in the Gujrāt war, and died suddenly on the 27th Rajab, 980. At Akbar's orders, he was buried at Sarkach, near Aḥmadābād. Fayẓī's clever tārīk͟h on his death is سنهٔ نهصد و هشتاد, " the year 980." At his death he left a fortune of 20 lacs of rupees.

The *Mirʿāt l'-ʿĀlam* mentions two books written by him, entitled *Asrār-i Maktūm* and *Rashahāt^{u} 'l-ḥayāt*, to which the *Haft Iqlīm* adds a third, the *Mirʿāt^{u} 'l-Kāynāt*. *Badāʿonī* and the *Mirʿāt* estimate his verses at 40 to 50,000 ; the *Haft Iqlīm* at 70,000 ; the *Ṭabaqāt Akbarī*, at 100,000. The *Ātashkada-yi Āzar* (p. 122) says that he wrote sixteen books containing 4,000 verses, and that he fled from Persia during the reign of Ṭahmāsp-i Ṣafawī. *Vide* Sprenger's Catalogue, pp. 61, 141, where particulars will be found regarding G͟hazālī's works. Sprenger calls him *G͟hazzālī*, an unusual form, even if the metre of some of his g͟hazals should prove the double *z*.

Badāʿonī relates a story that K͟hān Zamān sent him one thousand rupees to the Dakhin with a couplet, for which *vide Bad.* III, 170, where the *sar-i k͟hud* refers to the غ in *G͟hazālī's* name, because غ stands for 1,000.

The *Haft Iqlīm* mentions another G͟hazālī.

[2] This is to be understood in a mystic sense. *Badāʿonī* (III, 171) says that he had not found this verse in G͟hazālī's Dīwān.

1. O Ghazālī, I shun a friend who pronounces my actions to be good, though they are bad.

2 I like a simple friend, who holds my faults like a looking-glass before my face.

---

1. In love no rank, no reputation, no science, no wisdom, no genealogical tree is required.

2. For such a thing as love is, a man must possess something peculiar: the sweetheart is jealous—he must possess decorum.

---

1. The king says, "My cash is my treasure." The Ṣūfī says, "My tattered garment is my woollen stuff."

2. The lover says, "My grief is my old friend." I and my heart alone know what is within my breast.

---

1. If thy heart, whilst in the Kaʿba, wanders after something else, thy worship is wicked, and the Kaʿba is lowered to a cloister.

2. And if thy heart rests in God, whilst thou art in a tavern, thou mayest drink wine, and yet be blessed in the life to come.

6. ʿUrfī of Shīrāz.[1]

The forehead of his diction shines with decorum, and possesses a peculiar grace. Self-admiration led him to vanity, and made him speak lightly of the older classics. The bud of his merits withered away before it could develop itself.

---

[1] The *Maʾāṣir-i Raḥīmī* (MS. *As. Soc. Bengal*, p. 537) says that ʿUrfī's name was Khwāja Sayyidi (سیدی) Muḥammad. The *takhalluṣ* ʿUrfī has a reference to the occupation of his father, who as Dārogha to the Magistrate of Shīrāz had to look after *Sharʿī* and *ʿUrfī* matters. He went by sea to the Dakhin, where, according to the *Haft Iqlīm* his talent was not recognized; he therefore went to Fatḥpūr Sīkrī, where Ḥakīm ʿAbū 'l-Fatḥ of Gīlān (No. 112) took an interest in him. When the Ḥakīm died, ʿUrfī became an attendant on ʿAbdᵘ 'r-Raḥīm Khān Khānān, and was also introduced at court. He died at Lāhor, in Shawwāl, A.H. 999, according to the *Haft Iqlīm* and several MSS. of the *Ṭabaqāt*, of dysentery (*is-hāl*). He bequeathed his papers to his patron, in all about 14,000 verses, which at the Khān Khānān's order were arranged by Sirājā of Iṣfahān. He was at his death only thirty-six years old. The body was nearly thirty years later taken away by the poet Ṣābir of Iṣfahān and buried in holy ground at Najaf (*Sarkhush*). His early death, in accordance with an idea still current in the East, was ascribed to the abuse he had heaped on the ancients; hence also the *tārīkh* of his death—

عرفی جوانه مرگ شدي

"ʿUrfī, thou didst die young." The first edition of his poetical works contained 26 Qaṣīdas, 270 Ghazals, 700 Qiṭʿas and Rūbāʿīs; *vide* also Sprenger's Catalogue, p. 529.

The Tazkira by ʿAlī Qulī Khān-i Dāghistānī calls ʿUrfī Jamālᵘ ʿd-Dīn, and says that he was much liked by Prince Salīm towards whom ʿUrfī's attachment was of a criminal nature, and that he had been poisoned by people that envied him.

ʿUrfī was a man of high talent; but he was disliked for his vanity. *Badāʾonī* says (III, 285), "His poems sell in all bazaars, unlike those of Fayẓī, who spent the revenue of

Cling to the hem of a heart which saddens at the plaintive voice of the nightingale ; for that heart knows something.

If someone cast a doubt on the loftiness of the cypress, I melt away from envy ; for loftiness is so desirable that even a doubtful mention of it creates envy.

He who is intimate with the morning zephyr, knows that the scent of the Jasmin remains notwithstanding the appearance of chill autumn.

My wounded heart cannot endure a healing balm ; my turban's fold cannot endure the shadow of a blooming rose.

---

1. It is incumbent on me, when in society, to talk low ; for the sensible people in society are stupid, and I speak but Arabic.

2. Remain within the boundary of thy ignorance, unless you be a Plato ; an intermediate position is mirage and raving thirst.

Do not say that those who sing of love are silent ; their song is too fine, and the audience have cotton in their ears.

The more I exert myself, the more I come into trouble ; if I am calm, the ocean's centre is at the shore.

There is some hope that people will pardon the strange ways of ʕUrfī for the homeliness of his well-known poems.

---

his jāgīr in getting copies made of his verses ; but yet no one had a copy of them, unless it was a present made by Fayẓī." Ḥakīm Ḥāẕiq (*vide* under 205) preferred ʕUrfī's ghazals to his odes. His Masnawī, *Mājmaʕ*ᵘ *'l-Akbār*, is often wrongly called *Majmaʕ*ᵘ *'l-Afkār*.

One day ʕUrfī called on Fayẓī, whom he found surrounded by his dogs, and asked him to tell him the names of "the well-bred children of his family". Fayẓī replied, "Their names are *ʕurfī*" (i.e., well known). *Mubārak* (God bless us), rejoined ʕUrfī, to the intense disgust of Fayẓī, whose father's name was Mubārak.

Sprenger (Catalogue, p. 126) states on the authority of the Taẕkira Hamesha-Bahār that ʕUrfī's name was Khwāja Ṣaydī (صيدي), a mistake for *Sayyidī*. The *Ātashkada* also gives the name only half correctly, Sayyid Muḥammad. Taqī's note (loc. cit., p. 37) is wrong in the dates.

There exist several lithographs of ʕUrfī's Odes. The Calcutta printed edition of A.H. 1254 contains a Commentary by Aḥmad ibn-i ʕAbdᵘ 'r-Raḥīm (author of the Arabic Dictionary Muntahal Arab) of Ṣafīpūr.

No one has yet come into the world that can bear the grief of love; for every one has through love lost the colour of his face and turned pale.

O ʿUrfī, live with good and wicked men in such a manner, that Muhammadans may wash thee (after thy death) in Zamzam water, and Hindūs may burn thee.

If thou wishest to see thy faults clearly, lie for a moment in ambush for thyself, as if thou didst not know thyself.

ʿUrfī has done well to stand quietly before a closed door, which no one would open. He did not knock at another door.

To pine for the arrival of young spring shows narrowness of mind in me; for there are hundreds of pleasures on the heap of rubbish in the backyard, which are not met with in a rose garden.

My heart is sinking as the colour on Zalykhā's cheek when she saw herself alone; and my grief has become the talk of the market like the suspicion cast on Yūsuf.

---

1. On the day when all shall give an account of their deeds, and when the virtues of both Shaykh and Brāhman shall be scrutinized,
2. Not a grain shall be taken of that which thou hast reaped, but a harvest shall be demanded of that which thou hast not sown.

---

1. O thou who hast experienced happiness and trouble from good and bad events, and who art in consequence full of thanks and sometimes full of complaints,
2. Do not take high ground, so that thy efforts may not be in vain; be rather (yielding) like grass that stands in the way of the wind, or like a bundle of grass which others carry off on their shoulders.

---

1. O ʿUrfī, for what reason is thy heart so joyful? Is it for the few verses which thou hast left behind?
2. Alas! thou losest even that which thou leavest behind as something once belonging to thee. Thou oughtest to have taken it with thee; but hast thou taken it with thee?

7. Maylī of Hirāt.

His name was Mīrzā Qulī.[1] He was of Turkish extraction, and lived in the society of gay people.

Since I have become famous through my love, I shun all whom I see; for I am afraid lest my going to anyone might put thee into his thoughts.

I die and feel pity for such as remain alive; for thou art accustomed to commit such cruelties as thou hast done to me.

---

1. My heart derived so much pleasure from seeing thee, that fate—God forbid, that it should think of revenge.
2. Thou art neither a friend nor a stranger to me; what name is man to give to such a relation?

Thou knowest that love to thee does not pass away with the lives of thy lovers; for thou passest by the tombs of those whom thy love slew, and yet thou behavest coquettishly.

When thou biddest me go, cast one glance upon me; for from carefulness people tie a string to the foot of a bird, even if it be so tame as to eat from the hand.

My last breath is at hand! O enemy, let me have him (the lovely boy) but for a moment, so that with thousands of pangs I may restore him to thee.

---

1. I promised myself that I would be patient, and did not go to him (the boy); I had hopes to be content with loneliness.
2. But the woe of separation kills me, and whispers every moment to me, "This is the punishment of him who puts confidence in his patience."

---

[1] The Nafā'is mentions 979 and Taqī 983, as the year in which Maylī came to India (Sprenger, Catalogue, pp. 43, 54). The *Ātashkada* says, he was brought up in Mashhad. According to Dāghistānī, he belonged to the Jalāyr clan, lived under Ṭahmāsp, and was in the service of Sulṭān Ibrāhīm Mīrzā, after whose death he went to India. The *Tabaqāt-i Akbarī* says that he was in the service of Nawrang Khān (pp. 354, 596); and *Badā'onī* adds that his patron for some suspicion ordered him to be poisoned. He was in Mālwā when he was killed.

He is much praised for his poetry; the author of the *Ātashkada* says that he was one of his favourite poets.

1. Thy clients have no cause to ask thee for anything; for every one of them has from a beggar become a Crœsus in wealth.

2. But thou findest such a pleasure in granting the prayers of beggars, that they make requests to thee by way of flattery.

8. **Jaʿfar Beg** of Qazwīn.

He is a man of profound thought, has learnt a good deal, and describes very well the events of past ages. As an accountant he is unrivalled. From his knowledge of human nature he leans to mirth and is fond of jokes. He was so fortunate to obtain the title of Āṣaf Khān, and was admitted as a disciple of his Majesty.[1]

I am jealous of the zephyr, but I gladden my heart with the thought that this is a rose garden, and no one can close the door in the face of the wind.

When the town could not contain the sorrows of my heart, I thought that the open country was created for my heart.

I am prepared for another interview to-night; for I have patched up my torn, torn heart.

It is the fault of my love that he [the lovely boy] is an enemy. What is love worth, if it makes no impression?

I admire the insight of my heart for its familiarity with beauties whose ways are so strange.

He came and made me confused; but he did not remain long enough for me to introduce my heart to consolation.

As I am entirely at fault, do not threaten me with revenge; for the pleasure of taking revenge on thee makes me bid my fault defiance.

---

1. Dost thou show me thy face so boldly, Happiness? Wait a moment, that I may announce my love-grief.

---

[1] His biography was given above, No. 98. *Vide* also *Iqbālnāma-yi Jahāngīrī*, p. 5; *Dabistān*, p. 387. His *takhalluṣ* was Jaʿfar, as may be seen from Abū 'l-Faẓl's extracts.

The Masnawī by Jaʿfar mentioned by Sprenger (Catalogue, p. 444) may belong to Mīrzā Zaynu 'l-ʿĀbidīn, regarding whom *vide* above, p. 453, and Sprenger, loc. cit., p. 120, where for 1212 read A.H. 1021.

2. Jaʿfar came to-day so broken-hearted to thy house, that the hearts of the stones burnt on seeing his extraordinary condition.

---

1. Whoever has been in thy company for a night, is the companion of my sad fate.

2. Jaʿfar has found the road to the street of the sweetheart so difficult, that he can no more rise to his feet.

The morning zephyr, I think, wafts to me the scent of a certain sweetheart, because Jacob keeps his closed eye turned towards a caravan.[1]

A new rose must have opened out in the garden; for last night the nightingale did not go asleep till the morning.

9. Khwāja Ḥusayn of Marw.[2]

He possessed many excellent qualities, and sold his encomiums at a high price. He lived at the Court of Humāyūn, and was also during this reign highly favoured.

---

1. The realms of speech are in my possession, the banker of speech is the jeweller of my pearl strings.

2. Creation's preface is a sheet of my book, the secrets of both worlds are in the nib of my pen.

10. Hayātī of Gīlān.[3]

A stream from the ocean of thought passes by his house; correctness and equity are visible on his forehead. Serenity and truth are in him united; he is free from the bad qualities of poets.

---

[1] Jacob had become blind from weeping over the loss of Joseph. One day he smelled the scent of Joseph's coat, which a messenger was bringing to Egypt. When the coat was applied to his eyes, he recovered his sight.

[2] Khwāja Ḥusayn was a pupil of Mawlānā ʿIṣāmᵘ 'd-Dīn Ibrāhīm and the renowned Ibn Hajar of Makkah (*Haft Iqlīm*). Abū 'l-Faẓl's remark that he sold his encomiums at a high price seems to refer to Ḥusayn's Odes on the birth of Jahāngīr and Prince Murād, given in full by *Badāʾonī* (II, pp. 120, 132) for which the Khwāja got two lacs of tankas. The odes are peculiar, as each hemistich is a chronogram.

[3] The *Maʾāṣir-i Raḥīmī* says that Mullā Ḥayātī was born at Rasht in Gīlān and belonged to the *ādmīzādagān*, i.e., common people of the place. To better his circumstances, he went to India, was introduced by Ḥakīm Abū 'l-Fatḥ-i Gīlānī (No. 112) at Court, got a jāgīr, and was liked by Akbar. He joined the Khān Khānān in the Dahkin wars, and remained in his service, living chiefly at Burhānpūr where he built a villa and a mosque, which, according to the *Mirʾātᵘ 'l-ʿĀlam* was called *Masjid-i Mullā Hayātī.* He was still alive in 1024, when the *Maʾāṣir-i Raḥīmī* was composed.

The *Tabaqāt* and *Badāʾonī* praise his poems, and say that he belonged to the *ahl-i yārān-i dardmandān*, i.e., he was a man of feeling and sympathy. Sprenger (Catalogue, p. 58) translates this, "He was a friend of Dardmand."

1. Whenever you speak, watch yourself; repentance follows every word which gladdens no heart.

2. You do not require the swift wing of a bird; but since fortune is so, borrow the foot of the ant and flee.

A love-sick man is so entangled in his grief, that even the wish of getting rid of it does him harm.

Whatever you see is, in some way or other, a highway robber. I know no man that has not been waylaid.

---

1. This is the thoroughfare of love, it is no open market; keep your lips closed, no talk is required.

2. I, too, have been among the heathens, but have seen no waist worthy of the sacred thread.

3. Covetous people are, from covetousness, each other's enemies; in friendship alone there are no rivals.

---

1. Let every thorn which people sow in thy road, bloom in the lustre of thy smiles.

2. Say nothing, and heal the wound of the heart with poisoned arrows.

---

1. My love makes me delay over everything, even if it were a scent in the house, or a colour in the bazaar.

2. Thou knowest what people call me—"mad from shame, and dejected from baseness."

Since everything which I mended has broken again, my heart has gone altogether from trying to patch it.

---

1. I suffer thy cruelties and die; perhaps I thus complete my faithfulness.

2. Thou canst not deprive me of the means of union with thee, unless thou shuttest the zephyr in a box.[1]

This turf and this field have a tinge of madness; insanity and drunkenness have to-day a good omen.

---

[1] Because the zephyr wafts the breath of the beloved boy to the poet.

1. Love-grief is followed by an increase of sorrow, the desire to meet him is followed by bloody tears.

2. Neither the one nor the other, however, is the means of attaining love's perfection; be sound in mind, or else completely mad.

---

1. I am neither as high as the Pleiades, nor as low as the abyss; I neither cherish the old grief, nor do I possess a new thought.

2. If I am not the wailing nightingale, there is yet this excellence left, I am the moth and am pledged to the flame.[1]

---

1. I am the heart-grief of my dark nights, I am the misfortune of the day of my fate.

2. Perhaps I may go a step back to myself; it is a long time that I have been waiting for myself.

11. Shikebī of Iṣpahān.

He possesses taste and writes well. He is acquainted with chronology and the ordinary sciences; and the purity of his nature led him to philosophical independence.[2]

I have lived through nights of lonely sorrow, and am still alive; I had no idea of the tenaciousness of my life.

---

[1] The love of the moth for the candle seems to be a very ancient idea. Psalm xxxix, 11, Thou rebukest man and causest his delight to vanish as the moth vanishes in its delight, viz., the fire, where the word *Khamod* seems to have been purposely chosen to allude to the love of the moth. The passage in Saʿdī's preface to the Gulistān:—

عاشقان کشتگان معشوقند
برنیاید ز کشتگان آواز

"The lovers are killed by the beloved, no voice rises from the killed ones"—is also an allusion to the love of the moth.

[2] The *Maʿāṣir-i Raḥīmī* says that Mullā Shikebī was the son of Ẕahīru 'd-Dīn ʿAbdu 'llāh Imāmī of Iṣfahān. He studied under Amīr Taqiyu 'd-Dīn Muḥammad of Shīrāz, but left his native town for Hirāt when young, and became acquainted with the poets Sanāʾī, Maylī, and Walī Dasht Bayāẓī. When he was well known as a poet, he returned for a short time to Shīrāz, after which he went to India, and became the constant attendant of the Khān Khānān.

The *Mirʾātu 'l-ʿĀlam* says that later he fell out with his patron, and went from the Dakhin to Āgra, where Mahābat Khān introduced him at court. He asked for permission to return to Īrān; but Jahāngīr would not let him go, and appointed him Ṣadr of Dihlī. He died there at the age of sixty-seven, in 1023, the *tārīkh* of his death being صدر دهلی رفت. Another Chronogram, شکیبی رفت gives only 1022. For his Sāqīnāma, ʿAbdu 'r-Raḥīm gave him 18,000, or, according to the *Haft Iqlīm*, 10,000 rupees as a present. He wrote several other poems in praise of his patron. The *Maʿāṣiru 'l-Umarā* mentions a Maṣnawī on the conquest of Thatha (A.H. 999–1000), for which Jānī Beg and ʿAbdu 'r-Raḥīm gave him one thousand Ashrafīs. I do not know whether this Maṣnawī is the same as the Maṣnawī written by Shikebī in the Khusraw Shīrīn metre. [The As. Soc. of Bengal has a MS. of the *Kulliyāt-i Sanāʾī* in Shikebī's handwriting.—B.]

Grief, not mirth, is my ware. Why dost thou wish to know its price? I know that thou wilt not buy it, and that I shall not sell it.

On account of the jealousy of the watcher I had resolved to stay away from thy feast. I was deceived by my bad luck and called it jealousy, and stayed away.

O God, bestow upon my wares a market from the unseen world! I would sell my heart for a single interview; vouchsafe a buyer!

Thou art warm with my love; and in order to keep off bad omens, I sit over the fire, and burn myself as wild rue.[1]

I uprooted my heart from my being, but the burden of my heart did not leave my being. I severed my head from my body, but my shoulders did not leave my collar.

---

1. To-day, when the cup of union with thee is full to the brim I see Neglect sharpen the sword, in order to kill me.

2. Thou dost not dwell in my heart and hast girded thy loins with hatred towards me—ruin upon the house which raises enemies!

---

1. The plaintive song of my bird [heart] turns the cage to a rosebed; the sigh of the heart in which thou art, turns to a rosebed.

2. When thy beauty shines forth, covetousness also is love; straw, when going up in flames, turns to a rosebed.

---

1. Happy are we if we come to thee, through thee; like blind men we search for thee, through thee.

2. Increase thy cruelties till the tenaciousness of my life takes revenge on me, and thy cold heart on thee.

---

1. The world is a game, the winning of which is a loss; playing cleverly consists in being satisfied with a low throw.

2. This earthly life is like a couple of dice—you take them up, in order to throw them down again.

---

[1] *Sipand.* People even nowadays put the seeds of wild rue on heated iron plates. The smoke is said to drive away evil spirits. *Vide* p. 146, note 1.

12. Anīsī Shāmlū.[1]

His real name is Yol Qulī. He is a man of a happy heart and of pure manners; he is brave and sincere.

In seeking after thee, a condition is put upon us miserable lovers, viz., that our feet remain unacquainted with the hems of our garments.[2]

It is possible to travel along this road, even when one lightning only flashes. We blind lovers are looking for the ray of thy lamp.

If I remain restless even after my death, it is no wonder; for toil undergone during the day makes the sleep of the night restless.

---

1. How can the thought of thy love end with my death? for love is not like wine, which flows from the vessel when it is broken.

2. The lover would not snatch his life from the hand of death though he could. Why should the owner of the harvest take the grain from the ant?

---

1. The rosebed of time does not contain a songster like me, and yet it is from the corner of my cage that I have continually to sing.

2. In order satisfactorily to settle my fortune, I spent a life in hard work; but with all my mastership I have not been able to draw silk from reeds.

The nature of love resembles that of the magnet; for love first attracts the shaft, in order to wound the heart when it wishes to get rid of the point.

---

[1] The *Maʿāṣir-i Raḥīmī* says that Yol Qulī Beg belonged to the distinguished clan of the Shāmlū Turkmāns. He was a good soldier, and served as librarian to ʿAlī Qulī Khān Shāmlū, the Persian governor of Hirāt, where he made the acquaintance of Shikebī and Mahwī. He wrote at first under the *takhalluṣ* of Jāhī; but the Persian prince Sulṭān Ibrāhīm Mīrzā gave him the name of Anīsī, under which he is known in literature. When Hirāt was conquered by ʿAbdu 'llāh Khān, king of Turkistan and Māwarā 'n-nahr, Anīsī was captured by an Uzbak soldier and carried off to Māwarā 'n-nahr. He then went to India, and entered the service of Mīrzā ʿAbdu 'r-Raḥīm Khān Khānān, who made him his Mīr ʿArẓ, and later his Mīr Bakhshī. He distinguished himself by his intrepidity in the war with Suhayl-i Ḥabshī (p. 356). His military duties allowed him little leisure for poetry. He died at Burhānpūr in 1014. There exists a Maṣnawī by him in the Khusraw-Shīrīn metre, also a Dīwān, and several Qaṣīdas in praise of the Khān Khānān.

The Calcutta edition of the *Ātashkada-yi Āzar* (p. 19) calls him wrongly ʿAlī Qulī Beg, and his Hirāt patron ʿAlī Naqī Khān, after whose death he is said to have gone to India.

[2] i.e., our garments are always tucked up (Arab. *tashmīr*), as Orientals do when walking quickly. A lover finds no rest.

May God preserve all men from falling into my circumstances! for my sufferings keep the rose from smiling and the nightingale from singing.

Love has disposed of me, but I do not yet know who the buyer is, and what the price is.

Anīsī drinks the blood of his heart, and yet the vessel is never empty; it seems as if, at the banquet of love's grief, the red wine rises from the bottom of the goblet.

---

1. I am intoxicated with love, do not bring me wine; throw me into the fire, do not bring me water.
2. Whether I complain or utter reproaches, I address him alone, do not answer me!

---

1. I went away, in order to walk a few steps on the path of destruction, and to tear a few ties that bind me to existence.
2. I will spend a few days without companions, and will pass a few nights without a lamp till morning make its appearance.

---

1. O heart, beware! O heart, beware! Thus should it be; the hand of asking ought to be within the sleeve.[1]
2. O that I could but once catch a certain object! the hunter is for ever in the ambush.

13. Naẕīrī of Nīshāpūr.[2]

He possesses poetical talent, and the garden of thought has a door open for him. Outwardly he is a good man; but he also devises plans for the architecture of the heart.

Every place, whether nice or not, appears pleasant to me; I either rejoice in my sweetheart, or grieve for him.

---

[1] The heart should not ask, but patiently love.

[2] Muḥammad Ḥusayn Naẕīrī of Nīshāpūr left his home for Kāshan, where he engaged in poetical contests (*mushāʿara*) with several poets, as Fahmī, Ḥātim, etc. He then went to India, where he found a patron in Mīrzā ʿAbdu 'r-Raḥmīn Khān Khānān. In 1012, he went to Makkah on a pilgrimage, after which he is said to have become very pious. On his return to India, he lived at Aḥmadābād in Gujrāt, where he died in 1022. The *Tuzuk* (p. 91) says:—"I [Jahāngīr] had called Naẕīrī of Nīshāpūr to court. He is well known for his poems and poetical genius, and lives [end of 1019] in Gujrāt where he is a merchant. He now came and presented me with an encomium in imitation of a Qaṣīda by Anwarī. I gave him one thousand rupees, a horse, and a dress of honour." The

If thou destroyest the ware of my heart, the loss is for once; whilst to me it would be the loss of world and faith.

If thou wilt not put my cage below the rose-tree, put it in a place where the meadow hears my plaint.

It is from kindness that he [the beautiful boy] favours me, not from love; I can distinguish between friendship and politeness.

It is a generation that I have been girding my waist in thy service, and what am I worth? I must have become a Brahman, so often have I put on the badge (the thread).

Thy blood is worth nothing, Naẕīrī, be silent! Suffice it that he who slew thee, has no claim against thee.

I am costly and there are no buyers; I am a loss to myself, and am yet the ornament of the bazaar.

The impression which my sorrow makes upon him consists in depriving his heart of all sympathy; and the peculiar consequence of my reminding him of my love is that he forgets it.

Like a watch-dog I lie at his threshold; but I gnaw the whole night at my collar and think of chasing him, not of watching him.

MaʕāṣIr-i Raḥīmī says that Naẕīrī was a skilful goldsmith; and that he died, after having seen his patron in Āgra in 1022. at Aḥmadābād, where he lies buried in a mosque which he had built near his house. According to the *Mirʾatᵘ 'l-ʕĀlam*, he gave what he had to his friends and the poor. How esteemed he was as a poet may be seen from a couplet by the great Persian poet Ṣāyib, quoted by Dāghistānī:—

صایب چه خیالست شوي همچو نظیري
عرفي بنظیري نرسانید سخن را

O Ṣāyib, what dost thou think? Canst thou become like Naẕīrī?
ʕUrfī even does not approach Naẕīrī in genius.

The Tārīkh of Naẕīrī's death lies in the hemistich "*Az dunyā raft Hassanᵘ 'l-ʕAjam, āh!*" "The Ḥassān of Persia has gone from this world, alas!"—in allusion to the famous Arabian poet Ḥassān. This gives A.H. 1022; the other *tārīkh*, given by Dāghistānī, *markiz-i dāʾira-yi bazm kujā ast*, "where is the centre of the circle of conviviality," only gives 1021, unless we count the *hamzah* in دایرة as *one*, which is occasionally done in *tārīkhs*. Dāghistānī also mentions a poet Sawādī of Gujrāt, a pious man, who was in Naẕīrī's service. On the death of his master, he guarded his tomb, and died in A.H. 1031.

1. From carelessness of thought I transformed a heart, by the purity of which Kaʿba swore, into a Farangī Church.

2. The simoom of the field of love possesses so inebriating a power, that the lame wanderer thinks it sublime transport to travel on such a road.

3. The ship of love alone is a true resting-place; step out of it, and thou art surrounded by the stormy sea and its monsters.

4. Tell me which song makes the greatest impression on thy heart, so that I may utter my plaint in the same melody.

14 Darwīsh Bahrām.[1]

He is of Turkish extraction and belongs to the Bayāt tribe. The prophet Khizr appeared to him, and a divine light filled him. He renounced the world and became a water-carrier.

---

1. I have broken the foundation of austerity; to see what would come of it; I have been sitting in the bazaar of ignominy [love], to see what would come of it.

2. I have wickedly spent a lifetime in the street of the hermits; now I am a profligate, a wine-bibber, a drunkard, to see that will come of it.

3. People have sometimes counted me among the pious, sometimes among the licentious; whatever they call me I am, to see what will come of it.

15. Ṣayrafī [Ṣarfi] of Kashmīr.[2]

His name is Shaykh Yaʿqūb. He is well acquainted with all branches of poetry and with various sciences. He knows well the excellent writings of Ibn ʿArab, has travelled a good deal, and has thus become acquainted with many saints. He obtained higher knowledge under Shaykh Ḥusayn of Khwārazm, and received from him permission to guide others.

---

[1] Bahrām's *takhallus* is *Saqqa*, i.e., water-carrier. This occupation is often chosen by those who are favoured with a sight of the Prophet Khizr (Elias). Khizr generally appears as an old man dressed in green (in allusion to the meaning of the name in Arabic or to his functions as spring deity).

The Bayāt tribe is a Turkish tribe scattered over Āzarbāyjān, Erivan, Ṭihrān, Fārs, and Nīshāpūr.

Bahrām is worshipped as a saint. His mausoleum is in Bardwān near Calcutta. Regarding the poet himself and the legends connected with him, *vide* my "Arabic and Persian Inscriptions," *Journal Asiatic Society of Bengal*, 1871, pt. i, pp. 251 to 255.

[2] Shaykh Ḥusayn of Khwārazm, Yaʿqūb's teacher, was a pupil of Muḥammad Aʿẓam Ḥājī, and died in Syria in 956 or 958.

Shaykh Yaʿqūb also studied in Makkah for a long time under the renowned Ibn Ḥajar, the great teacher of the Ḥadīs, and then came to India, where he was held in high esteem

He stole from my heart all patience, and then took the whole mad heart itself; my thief stole the house with its whole furniture.

The weakness of the boy has brought the love-sick man into a strange position; from weakness he can no longer bear the weight of recovery.

16. Sabūḥi, the Chaghtāi.[1]

He was born in Kābul. Once he slept in the bedroom of Amīr Khusraw, when the shining figure of an old man with a staff in his hand awoke him and ordered him to compose a poem. As he had no power of doing so, he took the whole for a vision, and lay down in another place; but the same figure woke him up, and repeated the order. The first verse that he uttered is the following:—

When I am far from thee, my tears turn gradually into an ocean. Come and see, enter the ship of my eye, and make a trip on the ocean.[2]

My sweetheart saw the scroll of my faith, and burnt my sad heart, so that no one afterwards might read its contents.[3]

---

1. I have no need to explain him my condition; for my heart, if really burning, will leave a trace behind.

2. Weakness has overpowered me, and my heart has sunk under its sorrow. Who shall now inform him of my wretched state?

---

as a learned man and a poet. He was liked by Humāyūn and by Akbar, and was an intimate friend of the historian Badā'onī. His death took place on the 12th Zī Qaʿda, 1003, and Badā'onī found as *tārīkh* the words *Shaykh-i umam būd*, "he was the Shaykh of nations." A complete *Khāmsa*, a treatise on the *Muʿammā*, or riddle, and numerous Ṣūfistic Rubā'īs with a commentary, are said to have been written by him. A short time before his death, he had nearly finished a large commentary to the *Qur'ān*, and had just received permission from Akbar to return to Kashmīr, when he died. *Vide* above, p. 191, and under the poets.

His *takhallus* is variously given as *ṣayrafī* and *ṣarfī*. The latter seems the correct form, to judge from the metre of one of his verses preserved by Badā'onī (III, 148). Both words occur as *takhalluṣ*; thus there was a Qāẓī Ṣayrafī, encomiast of Fīrūz Shāh. *Vide* also poet No. 21.

[1] *Sabūḥī* means "a man that drinks wine in the morning". The real name of the poet is not given in the Taẕiras to which I have access. Badā'onī says that he lived an easy, unrestrained life; and the *Mirʾātu 'l-ʿĀlam* calls him a *rind* (profligate). He died at Āgra in 973, and Fayẓī found as *tārīkh* the words صبوحي، مي خوار, "Ṣabūḥī, the wine-bibber." Dāghistānī says, he was from Samarqand, and the *Ātashkada* calls him "Badakhshānī", but says that he is known as *Hurawī*, or from Hirāt.

[2] The verse, notwithstanding the vision, is stolen; *vide Badā'onī*, III, 180, under Ātashī.

[3] If this verse, too, was uttered at the time he had the vision, he stole thought and words from Āṣafī, Jāmī's pupil, who has a verse:—

دل که طومار وفا بود من محزون را
پاره کردند ندانسته بنان مضمون را

17. Mushfiqī of Bukhārā.[1]

I went to his street, and whilst I was there, a thorn entered deep into the foot of my heart. Thanks be to God that I have now a reason for staying in it!

---

1. Hindūstān is a field of sugar-cane, its parrots are sugar-sellers.
2. Its flies are like the darlings of the country, wearing the *chīra* and the *ṭakauchiya*.[2]

18. Ṣāliḥī.[3]

His name is Muḥammad Mīrak. He traces his descent from Niẓāmᵘ 'l-Mulk of Ṭūs.

Men without feeling tell me to use my hand and catch hold of his garment. If I had a hand [i.e., if I had the opportunity], I would tear my collar to pieces.

There are many reasons why I should be dead, and yet I am alive. O grief! thy forbearance has made me quite ashamed of myself.

---

[1] *Badāʿonī* (III, 328) says that he was originally from Marw, and came twice to India. For his *Qaṣīdas*, some called him "the Salmān of the age"; and Dāghistānī says that under ʿAbdᵘ 'llāh Khān he was *Malik 'sh-shuārā*. According to the *Haft Iqlīm*, he was born and died at Bukhārā. Sprenger (Catalogue, p. 508) says, he was born in 945, and his second Dīwān was collected in 983. From the *Akbarnāma* (Lucknow edition, III, p. 203) we see that Mushfiqī was presented to Akbar at Pāk Patan in the end of 985. He died in 994 (Vāmbēry's *Bokhara*, p. 301).

[2] This verse is a parody on the well-known Ghazal, which Ḥāfiẓ sent from Shīrāz to Sulṭān Ghiyāṣ of Bengal (Metre Muzāri).

شکر شکن شوند همه طوطیان هند
زین قند پارسي که به بنگاله میرود

The parrots of Ind will learn to enjoy sweets,
When this Persian sugar (the poem) *reaches Bengal.*

Abū 'l-Faẓl has meddled with Mushfiqī's verse; for the *Haft Iqlīm* gives instead of *nekūʿān-i diyār* the words *hindūʿān-i siyāh*; hence the verse is "India's flies are (black) like the black Indians, wearing like them a big turban (*chīra*) and a ṭakauchiya". This means, of course, that the Indians are like flies. The *ṭakauchiya* was described above on p. 94; the big head of a fly looks like a turban, and its straight wings like the straight Indian coat (*chapkan*). It may be that Abū 'l-Faẓl substituted the words *nekūʿān-i diyār*, the "dear ones of the country", with a satirical reference to the "learned", whom he always calls خالي درون عمیمه پوش "turban-wearing empty-headed", in which case we would have to translate "the simpletons of the country".

The verse is better given by *Badāʿonī* (III, 329).

[3] *Badāʿonī* calls him "Hirawī" (from Hirāt), and says that he was employed at court as a Munshī. He was a good penman. After his return to his country, he died. The Ātashkada says that he was a descendant of Khwāja ʿAbdᵘ 'llāh Marwārīd Kirmānī, and that his family had always been employed by kings.

Sprenger (Catalogue, p. 50) calls him wrongly *Muḥammad Mīr Beg*. The *Ātashkada* and the MSS. have Muḥammad Mīrak; and thus also his name occurs in the *Maʿāṣir-i Raḥīmī*.

I told him [the beautiful boy] my grief, he paid no heed. Oh, did you ever see such misery! I wept, he laughed—Oh, did you ever see such contempt!

My life is in his hand. It is quite clear, Ṣāliḥ, that even the falcon Death sits tame on his hand.

19. Maẓharī of Kashmīr.[1]

He made poems from his early youth, and lived long in ʿIrāq. From living together with good people, he acquired excellent habits.

---

1. I cannot understand the secret of Salmā's beauty; for the more you behold it, the greater becomes your desire.
2. What friendly look lay in Laylī's eyes, that Majnūn shut his eyes to friends and strangers?

I admire the looking-glass which reflects my sweetheart standing on a flower-bed,[2] although he is inside his house.

The good fortune of thy beauty has caused thy affairs to prosper; else thou wouldst not have known how to manage matters successfully.

---

1. Like a tail I follow my own selfish heart. Though the road is not bad, I make myself footsore.
2. Though I break through a hundred screens, I cannot step out of myself; I wander over a hundred stages, and am still at the old place.

I am a tulip of Sinai, and not like the stem-born flower. I cast flames over the slit of my collar instead of hemming it.[3]

He of whom my eye makes light, appears to heaven dull and heavy.

---

[1] Dāghistānī says that in ʿIrāq he was in company with Muḥtashim and Wahshī. After his return to India, Maẓharī was employed by Akbar as Mīr Baḥrī of Kashmīr, which employment he held in 1004 (*Badāʾonī*). He had turned Shīʿah, and as his father was a Sunnī, both used to abuse each other. His poems are said to contain several satires on his father. Maẓharī died in 1018. All Taẕkiras praise his poems.

[2] The eyes of the beautiful boy are crocus-like or almond-shaped; the chin is like an apple; the black locks, like *sumbuls*—in fact, his whole face resembles a garden.

[3] The hot tears of the poet fall like flames on his collar; hence he is surrounded by flames like a flower on Mount Sinai; for Mount Sinai is surrounded by God's glory.

20. Maḥwī of Hamadān.[1]

His name is Mug͟hīs. He tries to change the four mud walls of this worldly life into stone walls, and is intoxicated with the scent of freedom.

---

1. Once I did not know burning sorrow, I did not know the sighs of a sad heart.
2. Love has now left neither name nor trace of me—I never thought, Love, that thou art so.

---

1. You said that my condition was low from love-grief. A cup! bring me a cup! for my heart is stagnant.
2. Be ashamed of thyself, be ashamed! Which is the cup and which is the wine that has inebriated the nightingale?

---

1. O Maḥwī, beckon to a friend, and ring the bell of the caravan.
2. The stage is yet far and the night is near. O thou who hast fettered thy own foot, lift up thy foot and proceed!

---

1. A single lover requires hundreds of experiences, hundreds of wisdoms, and hundreds of understandings.
2. Thy luck is excellent, go away: love is a place where misery is required.

---

1. O Maḥwī, do not sing a song of the passion of thy heart, do not knock at the door of a single house in the street.
2. Thou hast seen this strange world, beware of speaking of a friend.

---

[1] **Mīr Mug͟hīṣ, according to the *Maʿāṣir-i Raḥīmī*, was born in Asadābād (Hamadān), and went, when twelve years old, to Ardabīl, where he studied for four years at the "Astāna-yi Ṣafawiya". From youth, he was remarkable for his contentment and piety. He spent twenty years at holy places, chiefly at Najaf, Mashhad, Karbalā, and Hirāt. Mawlānā Shikebī and Anīsī (pp. 646, 648) looked upon him as their teacher and guide. He held poetical contests (*mushāʿara*) with Mawlānā Sahābī (سحابى). He embarked at Bandar Jarūn for India, and was patronized by the K͟hān K͟hānān. After receiving from him much money, he went back to ʿIrāq, where the author of the *Maʿāṣir* saw him at Kāshān. He visited Najaf and Karbalā, and returned to Hamadān, where he died in 1016. He lies buried in the *Maqbara* of the Sayyids at Asadābād. The author of the *Maʿāṣir* edited Maḥwī's Rubāʿīs during his lifetime, and wrote a preface to the collection. Maḥwī is best known as a Rubāʿī writer: Abū 'l-Fazl's extracts also are all Rubāʿīs.**

The *Ātashkada* says that he is often called Nīshāpūrī because he was long in that town.

The *Mirʿāt* mentions a Maḥwī whose name was Mīr Maḥmūd, and says that he was for twenty-five years Akbar's Munshī.

21. Ṣarfī of Sāwah.[1]

He is poor and has few wants, and lives content with his indigence.

My dealer in roses wishes to take his roses to the bazaar, but he ought first to learn to bear the noisy crowd of the buyers.

I am shut out from the road that leads to the Kaʿba, else I would gladly wound the sole of my feet with the thorns of its acacias.[2]

I have no eye for the world, should it even lie before my feet ; he who takes care of the end, looks behind himself.

That which I desire [3] is too high to be obtained by stooping down. O that I could find myself lying before my own feet !

22. Qarārī of Gīlān.[4]

His name is Nūr^u 'd-Dīn. He is a man of keen understanding and of lofty thoughts. A curious monomania seized him : he looked upon his elder brother, the doctor Abū 'l-Fatḥ, as the personification of the world, and the doctor Humām as the man who represents the life to come, for which reason he kept aloof from them.

---

[1] The MSS. of the *Āʾīn* call him " Ṣayrafī ", but the metre of several verses given in the *Maʾāṣir-i Raḥīmī* shows that his takhalluṣ is " Ṣarfī ".

According to the Ātashkada, his name is Ṣalaḥ^u 'd-Dīn, and he was a relation of Salmān of Sāwaḥ. He was a pupil of Muḥtashim of Kāshān. The author of *Haft Iqlīm* says that he was a most amiable man, and marvellously quick in composing tārīkhs. He lived in the Dakhin, and went to Lāhor, to present Akbar with a Qaṣīda ; but finding no suitable opportunity, he returned to the Dakhin, and went to Makkah, where he died. The *Maʾāṣir-i Raḥīmī* states that he lived chiefly at Aḥmadābād, made Fayẓī's acquaintance in the Dakhin, and went with the Khān-i Aʿẓam (p. 543) to Makkah. According to *Badāʾonī*, he came with the Historian Niẓāms 'd-Dīn Aḥmad from Gujrāt to Lāhor, and accompanied Fayẓī to the Dakhin, where he died. Sprenger (Catalogue, p. 382) gives his name *Çalāhuddīn* : but the Ātashkada (the only work in which I have found his full name) has *Salāḥ^u 'd-Dīn*.

[2] The road of love (the ideal Kaʿba) is as difficult as the road to the Kaʿba in Makkah. Muhammadans do not lie down with their feet towards Makkah, which is against the law ; hence the poet says that he is prevented from stepping forward on the road of love.

[3] Self-knowledge.

[4] Nūr^u 'd-Dīn Muḥammad came in 983 with his brothers Abū 'l-Fatḥ (p. 468) and Humām (p. 529) to India. Akbar appointed him to a command in the army ; but Nūr^u 'd-Dīn was awkward, and had no idea how to handle a sword. Once, at a muster, he came without arms, and when some young fellows quizzed him about it, he said that military duties did not suit people of his class (literary men) ; it had been Timur's custom to place camels, cattle, and the baggage between the ranks, and the women behind the army, and when Timur had been asked where the learned were to go, he had said, " In the rear of the women." (This resembles the story of Napoleon I, who in Egypt had often to form squares against the hostile cavalry, and then invariably gave orders to place the

The longer the grief of separation lasts, the gladder I am; for like a stranger I can again and again make his acquaintance.

I doubt Death's power; but an arrow from thy eye has pierced me, and it is this arrow alone that will kill me, even if I were to live another hundred years.

He [the beautiful boy] must have been last night away from home; for I looked at his door and the walls of his house, but had no pleasure from looking.

If in that hour, when I tear the hood of my life, I should get hold of, what God forbid, Thy collar, I would tear it to pieces.

I envy the fate of those who, on the last day, enter hell; for they sit patiently within the fire.[1]

My madness and ecstasy do not rise from nightly wine; the burning of divine love is to be found in no house.

---

1. O heart! when I am in love, do not vex me with the jealousy of the watchman; thou hast made me lose my faith [Islām] do not speak ill of my Brahmanical thread.[2]

2. To be far from the bliss of non-existence seems death to him who has experienced the troubles of existence. O Lord! do not wake me up on the day of resurrection from the sleep of non-existence.

---

1. If the love of my heart should meet with a buyer, I would do something openly.

2. I have spread the carpet of abstinence in such a manner that every thread of the texture ends in a thousand Brahmanical threads.

---

donkeys and the savans in the middle.) Akbar, to punish him, sent him on active service to Bengal, where he perished in the disturbances, in which Muẓaffar Khān (p. 373) lost his life. *Badā,onī*, II, 211; III, 312.

Abū 'l-Faẓl is sarcastic in referring to Nūr[u] 'd-Dīn's monomania.. Nūr[u] 'd-Dīn wished to say that Abū 'l-Fatḥ was a man of intense worldliness (*ṭalib[u] 'd-dunyā*) and Humām longed for the pleasures of paradise as the reward of virtue (*ṭālib[u] 'lākhirat*), whilst he himself was a "true lover" (*ṭālib[u] l'mawlā*, one who feels after God).

The Ātashkadah adds that Nūr[u] 'd-Dīn had been in Gīlān in the service of Khān Aḥmad Khān, and that he went, after the overthrow of Gīlān, to Qazwīn.

[1] Whilst the fire of love deprives me of patience.

[2] Love has made the poet a heathen.

1. The drinking of my heart-blood has surfeited me ; like my sweetheart, I have become an enemy to myself.

2. I have killed myself, and, from excessive love to him, have cast the crime on my own shoulders.[1]

23. ʿItābī of Najaf.[2]

He possesses harmony of thought ; but his mind is unsettled, and he lives a disorderly life.

I am the nightingale of thy flower-bed. I swear by the pleasure of thy society that the rose has passed away, and I do not know where the garden is.

---

1. May all hearts rest peacefully in the black night of thy curls, when I, the miserable, wander restless from thy street !

2. I have knocked at the door of the seventy-two sects of Islām, and have come to the door of despair, hopeless of getting help from heathen and Musulmān.

3. I had come from the land of faithfulness : what wonder, if I vanish from the dear memory of the [faithless] fair ?

---

1. I have consumed my sober heart on the rubbish heap of passion ; I have burnt the Kaʿba candle at the idol temple's fate.

2. The flower-bed of a certain beloved has not wafted to me the fragrance of fulfilled desires, and hopelessly do I consume myself in my dismal corner.

3. No one has ever said the word " friend " to me, not even by mistake, though I consume myself before acquaintances and strangers.[3]

---

[1] Though in reality the beautiful boy murdered me.

[2] Sayyid Muḥammad of Najaf had lived for some time in the Dakhin, honoured as a poet, when he went to Hindūstān, and paid his respects to Akbar at Allahābād. He looked bold and slovenly (*bebāk u nāhamwār*). When asked whether he had in the Dakhin made satires on Shāh Fatḥu 'llāh, he said, " In the Dakhin, I would not have looked at a fellow like him." Akbar, who made much of Fatḥu 'llāh, was annoyed, imprisoned ʿItābī, and had his papers searched, to see whether he wrote satires on other people. A few compromising verses were found, and ʿItābī was sent for ten years (or according to the *Ṭabaqāt*, for two years) to Fort Gwālyār. At the request of Prince Salīm and several courtiers, he was at last released, and ordered to come to Lāhor. But he was as bad as before. The emperor gave him 1,000 rupees, and ordered Qulij Khān (p. 380) to send him from Sūrat to Hijāz ; but ʿItābī escaped, went to the Dakhin, and lived there as before. His Arabic and Persian poems are excellent ; he also was a clever *kātib* and letter-writer. *Badāʾonī*, III, 275.

The Ātashkada says that he came from Gulpāigān (or جرباذقان). Dāghistānī calls him " Mir ʿItābī ". *ʿItābī* means " worthy of reproach " ; compare *ruswāʾī*.

[3] The *Ṭabaqāt* ascribes this verse to a poet called Rukn 'd-Dīn, whose *takhalluṣ* is not given in my MS.

1. O heart, what portion of his wine-coloured lip dost thou keep in thy flagon, that thy inside is full of sighs and thy neck full of sobs.[1]

2. Love has thrown me into oceans of bloody tears; go, go away, that for once thou mayest reach the banks of the stream.

I have given thee permission to shed my blood without retaliation. I have said so, and give it thee black on white, and stamped with my seal.

Sometimes I am drowned in floods, sometimes burning in flames. Let no one build a house in my street!

In the name of God, let us go, if you belong to my travelling companions. This caravan [2] has no bell to sound the hour of starting.

In a realm where the word "faithfulness" produces tears, the messenger and the letter he brings [3] produce each separately tears.

---

1. Is the killing of a man like me worth a single sign of anger and hatred? Is shedding my blood worth the bending of thy arm (pr. thy sleeve)?

2. If thou art resolved to break my heart, is it worth while to ill-treat thy lovers?

24. **Mullā Muḥammad Ṣūfī** of Māzandarān.[4]

He is in affluent circumstances, but from virtuous motives he mixes little with the world. He seeks retirement by travelling about.

Look upon me, when standing below the revolving roof of the heavens, as a lamp concealed under a cover.

---

[1] In allusion to the gurgling noise in the neck of the bottle.

[2] The caravan of love.

[3] The messenger, because he comes from the beloved boy, and the letter, because it declines the request of a rendezvous.

[4] According to the Mirʾātu 'l-ʿĀlam, Mullā Muḥammad was called "Ṣūfī" from his gentle and mild character. Even at the present day, simple people are often addressed "Ṣūfī ṣāḥib", so much so that the word is often used as the equivalent of "a simpleton". Mullā Muḥammad early left his home, and lived chiefly at Aḥmadābād, where he was the friend and teacher of Sayyid Jalāl-i Bukhārī. The Mirʾāt and the *Haft Iqlīm*, praise his verses, and the former quotes from a *Sāqīnāma* of his.

The Ātashkada wrongly puts him under Iṣfahān, and mentions that some call him the maternal uncle of Mullā Jāmī—which is impossible.

1. O heart, thy road is not without thorns and caltrops, nor dost thou walk on the wheel of good fortune.

2. If it be possible pull the skin from the body, and see whether thy burden will be a little lighter.

---

1. You asked me, "How are you, Muḥammad, after falling in love with him ?—long may you live !" "I stand," said I, "below the heaven as a murderer under the gibbet."

25. Judāʾī.[1]

His name is Sayyid ʿAlī, and he is the son of Mīr Manṣūr. He was born and educated in Tabrīz, and attained, under the care of his Majesty, the greatest perfection in the art of painting.

The beauty of idols is the Kaʿba to which I travel; love is the desert, and the obstinacy of the worthless watchers[2] the acacia thorns.

I am a prey half-killed and stretched on the ground, far from the street of my beloved. I stagger along, tumbling down and rising up again, till I come near enough to catch a glimpse of him.

In the morning, the thorn boasts of having been together with the rose, and drives a nail through the broken heart of the nightingale.

26. Wuqūʿī of Nīshāpūr.[3]

His name is Sharīf.

Love and the lover have in reality the same object in view. Do not believe that I lose by giving thee my life.

---

[1] Judāʾī had been mentioned above on p. 107. He had the title of "Nādiru 'l-Mulk", and had already served under Humāyūn. He left a Dīwān ; but he has also been accused of having stolen Ashkī's Dīwān (*vide* below, the 37th poet).

[2] The Ātashkada and Taqī's Taẕkira mention another Judāʾī of Sāwah.

[3] Muḥammad Sharīf Wuqūʿī belonged, according to the *Maʾāṣir-i Raḥīmī*, to a distinguished family of Sayyids in Nīshāpūr. His mother was the sister of Amīr Shāhmīr, who had been for a long time assay master under Shāh Ṭahmāsp. He died in 1002.

Badāʾonī (III, p. 378) says that Sharīf was a relation of Shihāb Khān (p. 352). "His name was Muḥammad Sharīf. Alas, that so impure a man should have so excellent a name ! His heretical opinions are worse than the heresies of those who, in this age, bear the same name [Sharīf-i Āmulī, pp. 185, 502 ; and the poet Sharīf-i Sarmadī, mentioned below, No. 53—two archheretics in the eyes of Badāʾonī]. Though he belongs neither exclusively to the Basakhwānīs (p. 502, note 2) nor to the Ṣabāhīs, he holds an intermediate place between these accursed and damned sects ; for he strenuously fights the doctrine of the transmigration of souls (*tanāsukh*). One day, he came to me at Bhimbar on the Kashmīr frontier, asking me whether he could accompany me to Kashmīr. Seeing large blocks of

1. I do not care for health.[1] O Lord, let sorrow be my lot, a sorrow which deprives my heart of every hope of recovery !

2. I am smitten by the eye which looks so coquettishly at me, that it raises, openly and secretly, a hundred wishes in my heart.

27. Khusrawī of Qā'in.[2]

He is a relation of [the poet] Mīrzā Qāsim of Gūnābād [or Junābād, or Junābīd, in Khurāsān]. He writes *Shikasta* well, and is a good hand at shooting with the bow and the matchlock.

If the dust of my body were mixed with that of others, you would recognize my ashes by their odour of love.

Thy coming has shed a lustre on the ground, and its dust atoms serve as *surma* for my eyes.

The lions of the Ḥaram should not stain their paws with my blood. O friend, give the dogs of the Christian monastery this food as a treat.

What do I care for comfort ! I think myself happy in my misery ; for the word "rest" is not used in the language of this realm [love].

28. Shaykh Rahā'ī.[3]

He traces his descent from Zain^u 'd-Dīn Khāfī. He pretended to be a Ṣūfī.

---

rocks of several thousand *mans* lying about near my house, he exclaimed with a sigh, "All these helpless things are only waiting to assume human form." Notwithstanding his wicked belief, he composed poems in praise of the Imāms ; but he may have done so, when he was young. He was an excellent *kātib* and letter-writer, and was well acquainted with history. He died in A.H. 1002.

[1] Health is the equivalent of "indifference to love".

[2] Qā'in lies between Yazd and Hirāt. Dāghistānī calls him Sayyid Amīr Khusrawī, and says that he excelled in music. According to *Badā'onī*, his mother was Mīrzā Qāsim's sister, and he came to India after having visited Makkah. He was in the service of Prince Salīm (Jahāngīr).

[3] His name is Mawlānā Sa'd^u 'd-Dīn, of Khāf, or Khawāf (p. 493). The Ātashkada quotes the same verse as Abū 'l-Faẓl. *Badā'onī* says, he left a well-known dīwān. In Dāghistānī, two Rahā'īs are mentioned, one Mawlānā Rahā'ī, "known in literary circles"; and another Rahā'ī from Ardistān. Sprenger (Catalogue, p. 58) calls him *Rihā'ī* ; and says that, according to the Nafā'is, he died in 980.

Zayn^u 'd-Dīn Khāfī, from whom Rahā'ī traced his descent, is a famous saint, who died in the beginning of Shawwāl, A.H. 838. He was first buried at Mālīn (or Bālīn), then at Darwīshābād, then at Hirāt. His biography is given in Jāmī's *Nafḥāt^u 'l-Uns*, and he is not to be confounded with the saint Zayn^u 'd-Dīn Tā'ibādī, mentioned above.

No one has, in thy love, been more brought up to sorrow than I; and that thou knowest not my sorrow is a new sorrow.

I took to travelling in order to allay my grief, not knowing that my road would pass over hundred mountains of grief.

29. Wafāʿī of Iṣfahān.[1]

He possesses sparks of taste. He had been for some time wandering in the desert of retirement, but has now put the mantle of worldliness on his shoulders.[2]

I do not call him a buyer who only wishes to buy a Yūsuf. Let a man buy what he does not require ! [3]

Knock at night at the door of the heart; for when it dawns, the doors are opened, and the door of the heart is closed.

I am secure from the dangers of life: no one deprives the street-beggar of his bareness.

---

1. The dart of fate comes from the other side of the armour; [4] why should I uselessly put on an armour ?
2. Flash of death, strike first at me! I am no grain that brings an ear to the harvest.

Joy and youth are like the fragrance of the rose that chooses the zephyr as a companion.

30. Shaykh Sāqī.[5]

He belongs to the Arabians of the Jazāʿir. He has acquired some knowledge.

---

[1] *Badāʿonī* says (III, p. 385) that Wafāʿī was for some time in Kashmīr, went to Lāhor, and entered the service of Zayn Khān (p. 367). According to the Ātashkada, he belonged to the ʿImādiya Kurds, and was brought up at Iṣfahān; his Rubāʿīs are good. Dāghistānī calls him a Turk, and states that Wafāʿī at first was an *uttūkash* (a man who irons clothes). From a fault in his eye, he was called *Wafāʿī-yi kor*, " The blind Wafāʿī."

[2] " His impudent flattery was proverbial." *Dāghistānī.*

[3] As, for example, love, grief.

[4] i.e., a place where man is not protected, because he does not expect an arrow from that side.

[5] *Badāʿonī* also calls him *Jazāʿirī*, i.e. from the islands. His father, Shaykh Ibrāhīm, was a distinguished lawyer and was looked upon by the Shīʿahs as a Mujtahid. He lived in Mashhad, where Sāqī was born. Sāqī received some education, and is an agreeable poet. He came from the Dakhin to Hindūstān, and is at present [in 1004] in Bengal.

1. I became a cloak to ruin, Sāqī, and like the Kaʿba, a place of belief and heresy.

2. I have found no trace of love, much as I have travelled among the hearts of the infidels and the faithful.

My heart is still ardent with love, and thou art still indifferent. sweetheart, speak, before I openly express myself.

31. Rafīʿī of Kāshān.[1]

His name is Ḥaydar. He is well acquainted with the *ars poetica* and is distinguished as a writer of riddles and *tārīkhs*.

My heart is sensitive, you cruel one; what remedy is there for me? Although a lover, I have the temper of the beloved—what can I do?

---

1. A recluse does not sin [love] and calls thee a tyrant; I am plunged into crime [love] and think that thou art forgiving.

2. He calls thee a tyrant, I call thee forgiving; choose whatever name pleases thee most.

32. Ghayratī of Shīrāz.[2]

His diction is good, and he knows the history of the past.

I am smitten by the eyelash of my murderer, who has shed my blood without letting a drop fall to the ground.[3]

---

[1] His full name, according to Taqī-yī Awḥadī, is Amīr Rafīʿᵘ 'd-Dīn Ḥaydar. He was a Ṭabāṭibā Sayyid of Kāshān. The *Maʾāṣir-i Raḥīmī* states that he left Persia in 999, on account of some wrong which he had suffered at the hand of the king of Persia, went from Gujrāt in company with Khwāja Habībᵘ 'llāh to Lāhor, and was well received by Akbar. For the *tārīkh*, mentioned above on p. 619, note 2, Fayẓī gave him 10,000 rupees. After a stay of a few years in India, he returned to his country, but suffered shipwreck near the Mukrān coast, in which he not only lost property to the amount of two lākhs of rupees, but also (as *Badāʾonī* spitefully remarks) the copies of Fayẓī's poetical works which he was to have distributed in Persia. Sprenger (Catalogue, p. 58) says that Ḥaydar was drowned; but the fact is, that he was saved and returned to India. His losses created much sympathy, and he received, at Akbar's wish, valuable presents from the Amīrs. From the Khān Khānān alone, he got, at various times, about a lākh. After some time, he again returned, his two sojourns in India having lasted about eight lunar years. He went to Makka and Madīna, where he stayed four years. In 1013, he returned to Kāshān, found favour with Shāh ʿAbbās, and received some rent-free lands in his native town. According to the Ātashkada he died in A.H. 1032, the *tārīkh* of his death being the Arabic words, "*wa kānᵃ zalikᵃ fī sanah.*" His son, Mīr Hāshim-i Sanjar, is mentioned on the next page; and Ṭāhir-i Naṣrābādī mentions in his Taẕkira another son of the name of Mīr Maʿṣūm, a friend of Mullā Awjī. MSS. often give his name wrongly رفيقي, *Rafīqī*.

[2] The Ātashkada says that Ghayratī travelled about in ʿIrāq, went to Hindūstān, and lived after his return in Kāshān, where he fell in love with a boy of a respectable family. From fear of the boy's relations, he went to Shīrāz, where he died.

[3] Because the heart only was broken.

The present age asks God for a mischief-maker like thee, who makes the days of the wretched bitterer.[1]

I am free from worldliness; for my aspirations do no longer lean against the wall of confidence.

I am smitten by the fearless glance of a Christian youth, for whose sake God will pardon, on the day of resurrection, the slaughter of a hundred Musalmāns.

Even death mourns for those who are killed by the grief of separation from thee.

The street of the sweet boy is a beautiful land; for there even heaven's envy is changed to love.

I saw the heart of another full of grief, and I became jealous; for there is but one cruel tyrant in these regions.[2]

33. Hālatī of Tūrān.[3]

His name is Yādgār. He is a selfish man.

Leave me to my grief! I find rest in my grief for him. I die, if the thought of the possibility of a cure enters my heart.

When my eye caught a glimpse of him, my lips quivered and closed. Oh that life remained but a moment within me!

To whatever side I turn in the night of separation, my heart feels pierced by the thought of the arrow of his eyelash.

---

[1] That is, my beloved boy causes the greatest mischief among the hearts of men.

[2] No boy is lovelier than the beloved of the poet. If the poet, therefore, sees another man love-sick, he gets jealous; his beloved boy must have bestowed favours on the other man.

[3] *Badā*ᶜ*onī* says that his father was a poet, and wrote under the name of *Wālihī*. Yādgār traced his descent from Sulṭān Sanjar; but the *Ṭabaqāt* calls him a Chaghtāᶜī. He served in Akbar's army.

"His son Jalāl Khān had the *takhalluṣ* of Baqāᶜī, though from his unprofitableness he styled himself *Ruswā*ᶜ*ī*, 'the blackguard.' He gave his father poison from his mother on account of a fault," and Akbar ordered him from Kashmīr to Lāhor, where he was executed by the Kotwāl.

The *Akbarnāma* (Lucknow Edition, III, p. 486) says that Yādgār served in 993 in Kābul. He is not to be confounded with Mīr Ḥālatī of Gīlān.

34. Sanjar of Kāshān.[1]

He is the son of Mīr Ḥaydar, the riddle-writer. He has a taste for poetry, and lives in good circumstances.

I came from the monastery of the Guebres, and wear, from shame on account of improprieties, a sacred thread twisted round my waist, and a wailing gong under my arm.[2]

I am jealous and I shall die from the aggressions of fickle lovers. I am a fresh plant, but shall die from the heap of rubbish about me.

I, too, have at last perished in the century of thy love. Alas! none is now left of Majnūn's tribe.[3]

Sorrows rush from every side on my heart without first knocking at the door. I cannot help it; my house lies on the highway.

35. Jazbī.[4]

His name is Pādishāh Qulī, and he is the son of Shāh Qulī Khān Nāranjī of Kurdistān, near Baghdād.

See how extremely jealous I am. My bewilderment leaves me, if any one alludes to him [the beautiful boy] whose memory causes me bewilderment.

---

[1] Sanjar came in A.H. 1000 from Persia to India, and met his father (p. 662 (?)). For some crime, "to mention which is not proper," Akbar imprisoned him. When again set free, he went to Aḥmadābād; but not thinking it wise to remain there, he went to Ibrāhīm ʿĀdil Shāh of Bījāpūr. Some time after, he received, through the influence of his father, a call from Shāh ʿAbbās of Persia to return. But before he could leave, he died at Bījāpūr, in A.H. 1021. Regarding the value of his poems people hold opposite opinions. *Maʾāṣir-i Raḥīmī.*

The *Khizānā-yi ʿĀmire* and Mr. T. W. Beale of Agrā, the learned author of the *Miftaḥu 'l-Tawārīkh*, give the following verse as *tārīkh* of Sanjar's death (metre *Muẓāriʿ*):—

انگند بادشاه سخن چتر سنجری

The king of literature has thrown away the royal umbrella,

of which the words *pādishāh-i sukhun* give 1023; but as the pādishāh throws away the umbrella, we have to subtract a ب, or 2; for the figure of the Arabic ب if inverted, looks like an umbrella.

[2] i.e. love has made the poet forget his faith, and he has become a heathen or a Christian. The Christians in many eastern countries used gongs because they were not allowed bells.

[3] The poet only is a true lover. He alone resembled Majnūn.

[4] The Tazkiras give no details regarding *Jazbī*. His father has been mentioned above on p. 537; and from the *Akbarnāma* (III, p. 512) we know that Pādishāh Qulī served in Kashmīr under Qāsim Khān (p. 412). "Jazbī" means "attractive"; a similar takhalluṣ is "Majzūb", "one who is attracted by God's love."

Badāʾonī (III, 213) ascribes the last verses given by Abū 'l-Faẓl to Pādishāh Qulī's father.

1. Sometimes I break my vow of repentance and sometimes the wine-bottle ; once, twice, incessantly, I break my plaintive flute [my heart].

2. O Lord, deliver my heart from these bad practices ! How often shall I repent and again break my vow of repentance !

36. Tashbīhī of Kāshān.[1]

His mind, from his youth, was unsettled. He belongs to the sect of the Maḥmūdīs ; but I know nothing of his origin, nor of his present condition. The Masnawī entitled " Ẕarrah o Khurshīd ", " the Atom and the Sun ", is written by him.

Dust of the graveyard, rise for once to joy ? Thou enclosest a corpse like mine, slain by his hand and his dagger.

Dress in whatever colour thou wilt ; I recognize thee when thy figure shines forth.

---

[1] The Ātashkada calls him " Mīr ʕAlī Akbar Tashbīhī. Though a decent man, he was singular in his manners, and was not widely known. Whilst in Hindūstān he tried to improve the morals of the people, dressed as a Faqīr, and did not visit kings ". Dāghistānī says that he was a heretic, and lived for forty years in Hindūstān a retired life. He generally lived in graveyards. *Badāʕonī* (III, 204) has the following notice of him, " He came twice or three times to Hindūstān, and returned home. Just now (A.H. 1004) he has come back again, and calls the people to heresies, advising them to follow the fate of the Basākhwānīs (*vide* above, p. 502). He told Shaykh Abū 'l-Faẓl that he was a Mujtahid, or infallible authority on religious matters, and asked him to introduce him to the emperor, to whose praise he had composed an ode, the end point of which was the question why the emperor did not direct his policy to the overthrow of the so-called orthodox, in order that truth might assume its central position, and pure monotheism might remain. He also wrote a pamphlet in honour of Abū 'l-Faẓl according to the manner of the Nuqtaqī sect and their manner of writing the letters [singly, not joined, as it appears from the following], all which is hypocrisy, dissimulation (*tazrīq*) and agreement of the numerical value of the letters. Ḥakīm ʕAynᵘ 'l-Mulk (*vide* above, p. 537) discovered that " Tashbīhī " has the same numerical value (727) as " Tazrīqī ", " the hypocrite." Tashbīhī has composed a Dīwān. When I wrote my history, he once gave me, in Abū 'l-Faẓl's presence, a pamphlet on Maḥmūd of Basākhwān, and I looked at it. The preface was as follows :—" O God ! who art praiseworthy (*Maḥmūd*) in all Thy doings, I call upon Thee. There is no other God but Allah. Praise be to God, whose mercies are visible in all his works, who has shown the existence of all his works . . . [the text is unintelligible]. He knows Himself ; but we do not know ourselves, nor Him. He is an existence not existing except through Himself, and a place of existence independent of others ; and He is the most merciful. *Question* : What is meant by " nature " ? *Answer* : what people call creation or nature, is God, etc. Dirt upon his mouth, for daring to write such stuff ! The grand point of all this lying is, of course, " the four *nuqṭas*." At the end of the pamphlet, I saw the following :— " This has several times been written on the part of the Persian Mujtahid M, i, r, ʕA, l, ī, A, k, b, a, r, T, a, sh, b, ī, h, ī, the Amīnī, the last, the representative." And the rest was like this—may God preserve us from such unbelief ! "

" The Atom and the Sun " is a mystical subject. The atoms of dust dance in the sun's rays and love it, and are emblematical of man's love to God. But as Akbar worshipped the sun, the poem, no doubt, referred to the peculiar views of the emperor.

Pass some day by the bazaar of the victims of thy love, and behold the retribution that awaits thee; for there they buy up every one of thy crimes at the price of a hundred meritorious actions.[1]

O thou that takest the loaf of the sun from this warm oven, thou hast not given Tashbīhī a breakfast, and he asks thee for an evening meal.[2]

---

1. I am that Tashbīhī who, from foresight, chooses to dwell in a graveyard.

2. I like to dwell in a graveyard, because dwelling in a graveyard lies before our sight.

The hands of this world and of the world to come are empty. With me is the ring !—all other hands are empty.[3]

57. **Ashkī** of Qum.[4]

He is a Ṭabāṭibā Sayyid, and is a poet of some talent.

Those who are slain by thee lie everywhere inebriated on the ground : perhaps the water of thy steel was wine.

---

[1] This verse is an example of a well-known rhetorical figure. The word " retribution " leads the reader to expect the opposite of what Tashbīhī says. The lovely boy has, of course, broken many hearts and shed the blood of believers ; nevertheless, all are ready to transfer the rewards of their meritorious actions to him, and thus buy up his crimes.

[2] The sun looks round like a loaf.; the warm oven is the heat of the day.

[3] In allusion to a game, in which the players secretly pass a ring from one to another, and another party has to find where the ring is. " The ring is with Tashbīhī," i.e., he has chosen truth, he is the elect.

[4] We know from the *Haft Iqlīm* that Mīr Ashkī was the son of Mīr Sayyid ʿAlī Muḥtasib (public censor) of Qum in Persia. Ashkī's elder brother Mīr Ḥuẓūrī also is known as a poet. Ghazālī's fame and success (*vide* p. 634) attracted Ashkī to India, but he did not meet Ghazālī. The number of his verses exceeded ten thousand ; but when on his deathbed, he gave his several Dīwāns to Mīr Judāʾī (*vide* p. 660) to arrange. Mīr Judāʾī, however, published whatever he thought good in his own name, and threw the remainder into water. Ṭarīqī of Sāwah alludes to this in the following epigram :—

اشکیٔ نامراد را کشتی
عقل حیران خون خفیهٔ اوست
بتو واماند چهار دیوانش
شعر واماندهٔ تو گفتهٔ اوست

Thou hast killed poor Ashkī,
And I wonder at thy crime being hidden.
With thee four Dīwāns of his remained,
And what remains of thy poems, is his.

Dāghistānī says that Ashkī died in Mīr Judāʾī's house, and he ascribes the epigram to Ghazālī ; but as he only quotes a hemistich, the statement of the contemporary *Haft Iqlīm* is preferable.

Badāʾonī says that Ashkī's poems are full of thought, and that he imitated (*tatabbuʿ*) the poet, Āṣafī. He died at Āgra.

My body melts in the fire of my madness, when he [the lovely boy] is away; and if you should hang an iron chain to my neck, it would flow (molten) to my feet.

Whenever I have to bear the pang of separation from my beloved, no one bears with me but death.

Ashkī, I think my tears have turned watchers; for whenever I think of him, they rush into my face.[1]

38. **Asīrī** of Ray.[2]

His name is Amīr Qāẓī. He is a man of education.

The messenger was a watcher in disguise, and I did not see his cunning. The cruel wretch succeeded in putting his contrivance between us.

I have pardoned my murderer, because he did not take his hand away from me; for as long as life was left within me, his murderous hands were properly employed.

His love has so completely filled my breast, that you can hear him breathe in my breath.

39. **Fahmī** of Ray [Ṭihrān].[3]

Give him no wine who feels no higher pleasure in the juice of grapes; do not even give him water when he lies as dust before the door of the tavern.

---

[1] So do the watchers of the beloved boy rush up against Ashkī, when he declares his love.

[2] Asīrī was, according to *Badā'onī*, an educated man, and the best pupil of Ḥakīmᵘ 'l-Mulk (p. 611). But the climate of India did not agree with him, and he did not find much favour with the emperor. He therefore returned to Ray, his home, where he died (i.e., before A.H. 1004).

[3] *Badā'onī* gives three poets of the name of Fahmī:—1, Fahmī of Ṭihrān, who travelled much, and was for some time in India; 2, Fahmī of Samarqand, son of Nādirī, an able riddle-writer, who was also for some time in India; 3, Fahmī of Astrābād, who died at Dihlī. The *Ma'āṣir-i Raḥīmī* mentions a Fahmī of Hurmuz (Ormuz) well known in Lār and Hurmuz, who came to India, presented an ode to the Khān Khānān, got a present, and returned. Dāghistānī mentions a fifth Fahmī from Kāshān, and a sixth, of whom he gives no particulars.

As the *Ṭabaqāt* and *Dāghistānī* ascribe the same verse to Fahmī-yi Ṭihrānī, which Abū 'l-Faẓl gives to Fahmī of Ray, the identity of both is apparent. In fact, it looks as if Abū 'l-Faẓl had made a mistake in calling him "of Ray", because no *Taẕkira* follows him.

I have no patience when in love, and have lost in reputation. Tell reputation to go, I cannot be patient.

40. Qaydī of Shīrāz.[1]

He spent some time in the acquisition of such sciences as are usually studied; but he thinks much of himself.

As thou hast never gone from my heart, I wonder how thou couldst have found a place in the hearts of all others.

---

1. Thou drovest me away, and I came back, not from jealousy, but because I wish to confess that I feel ashamed of my love having had jealousy as a companion.

2. My tears derive a lustre from the laughter of cruel wretches; else a wound inflicted by thee could never produce such bloody tears.

A lover may have many reasons to complain; but it is better not to unburden the heart before the day of judgment.

If I desire to accuse thee of shedding, in every look, a hundred torrents of lover's blood, my lot, though hostile enough, would be ready to be my witness.

I am gone, my reason is gone! I want a flash of madness to strike my soul, so as to keep it burning [with love] till the day of judgment.

---

1. Last night union [with the sweet boy] raised her lovely form before me, and the gloomy desert of my heart shone forth in raptures.

2. But the bat had no power to gaze at the sun; else the sun would have revealed what is now behind the screen.

---

[1] Qaydī came from Makkah to India, and was well received by Akbar. Once, at a court assembly, he spoke of the injustice of the *Dāgh o Maḥallī*-Law, on which Akbar had set his heart (*vide* p. 252) and fell into disgrace. He wandered about for some time as Faqīr in the Byāna District, and returned to Fatḥpūr Sīkrī, suffering from piles. A quack, whom he consulted, cut open the veins of the anus, and Qaydī died. He was an excellent poet. *Badāʿonī.*

Dāghistānī says that he was a friend of ʿUrfī, and died in A.H. 992.

41. Payrawī of Sāwah.[1]

His name is Amīr Beg. He was a good painter.

Where is the wine of love given to wretches without feeling? Loving idols, is a drunkenness; let men be careful to whom to give it!

O God! I cannot reach the world of the ideal; forgive me if I worship form.[2]

42. Kāmī, of Sabzwār.[3]

His mind is somewhat unsettled.

If I knew that tears could make an impression, I would altogether turn to blood and trickle from the eye.

Whether I see him [the beautiful boy] or not, my heart is in raptures. Have you ever seen such a sight?

I wished I could like a breeze pass away from this base world. This is not the street of the sweetheart, from which one cannot pass away.

My blood dances from mirth in my vein like a flame; the look he gave me commences to work, and my heart is effectually wounded.

43. Payāmī.[4]

His name is ʿAndu 's-Salām. He is of Arabian extraction, and has acquired some knowledge; but he is not clear to himself.

---

[1] Payrawī imitated the poet Āṣafī. He wrote a poem on "Form and Ideal", of which Abū 'l-Faẓl has given the first verse, and completed a Dīwān of Ghazals.

[2] This verse, the beginning of Payrawī's "Form and Ideal", contains the rhetorical figure, *istihlāl*, because it gives the title of the poem.

[3] Kāmī's father, Khwāja Yaḥyā, was a grocer (*baqqāl*) and lived in the Maydān Maḥallah of Sabzwār, in Khurāsān. Occasionally he wrote poems. When the Uzbaks took Sabzwār, Mīr Yaḥyā went to India, and left Kāmī, then twelve years old, with one of his relations in Sabzwār. At the request of his father, Kāmī came to India, and was frequently with the Khān Khānān. He went afterwards back to Khurāsān and the author of the *Maʾāṣir-i Raḥīmī* saw him, in 1014, in Hirāt. In travelling from Hirāt to his house, he was killed by robbers, who carried off the property which he had acquired in the Khān Khānān's service.

The *Haft Iqlīm* says that his poems are good, but that he was irascible and narrow-minded.

Badāʾonī also mentions him; but he wrongly calls *Qumī* "from the town of Qum". He says, Kāmī is a young man and has just come to India (1004); his thoughts are bold.

[4] Payāmī, according to Dāghistānī, was a pupil of the renowned ʿAllāmī Dawwānī. He was for a long time Vazīr to Shāh ʿAlaʾu 'l-Mulk ibn-i Nūru 'd-Dahr of Lār. His services were afterwards dispensed with, and a Jew of the name of Yaʿqūb was appointed instead. But this change was not wise; for soon after, Shāh ʿAbbās sent an army under Ilāh Virdī Khān to Lār, who conquered the country.

Fortune cheats in play, loses, and takes back what she paid. One cannot play with a companion that is up to such tricks.

---

1. How long do you file down your words and polish them; how long do you shoot random arrows at the target?
2. If you would take one lesson in the science of silence, you would laugh loud at your silly conversation.

---

1. I keep a thousand thunderbolts concealed below my lip. Go away, go away, take care not to put your finger on my lip.
2. I have come to the public square of the world, but I think it were better if my Yūsuf were yet in the pit than in the bazaar.[1]

Patience, in order to console me, has again put me off with new subterfuges, and has stitched up the book of my happiness the wrong way.

---

1. My heart has overcome the grief of separation, and has gone from this land; it has tucked the hem up to the waist and has gone.
2. My heart saw among the companions no trace of faithfulness; hence it smiled hundred times by way of friendship and went away.

44. Sayyid Muḥammad [Fikrī].[2]

He is a cloth-weaver from Hirāt. He generally composes Rubāʿīs.

---

1. On the day when the lover kindled the fire of love, he learnt from his beloved what burning grief is.
2. This burning and melting has its origin in the beloved; for the moth does not burn till it reaches the candle.

---

1. On the day of judgment, when nothing remains of the world but the tale, the first sign of Eternity's spring will appear:

---

[1] Yūsuf means here "life"; pit, "non-existence"; bazaar, "existence."

[2] Sayyid Muḥammad's poetical name is *Fikrī*, the "pensive". He came, according to the *Haft Iqlīm*, in 969 to India; and his excellent rubāʿīs induced people to call him the "Khayyām of the age", or "Mīr Rubāʿī". He died on his way to Jaunpūr, in 973, the *tārīkh* of his death being *Mīr Rubāʿī safar namūd*.

2. The beloved will raise like plants their heads from the dust, and I, too, shall raise my head in courtship.[1]

45. Qudsī of Karabalā, Mīr Ḥusayn.[2]

I am utterly ashamed of the dogs of thy street; for they have made friendship with a man like me.

I am in misery; and you would know the sadness of my lot, if you were instead of me to suffer for one night by being separated from him [the beautiful boy].

Who am I that thou shouldst be my enemy, and shouldst care for my being or not being?

46. Ḥaydarī of Tabrīz.[3]

He is a merchant and a poet; he works hard and spends his gains liberally.

Show no one my black book of sorrows; let no one know my crimes [love].

---

[1] This verse reminds me of a verse by Kalīm, I think (metre *Rajaz*):—

روز قیامت هر کسے بدست گیرد نامهٔ
من نیز حاضر مي شوم تصویر جانا در بمغل

Each man on the day of resurrection, will seize a book (the book of deeds), I, too, shall be present, with my sweetheart's picture under my arm.

[2] Dāghistānī says that Mīr Ḥusayn's father left Karbalā for Sabzwār. Qūdsī was a great friend of Muḥammad Khān, governor of Hirāt. *Badāʿonī* (III, 376) says that Mīr Muḥammad Sharīf Nawāʿī, Qudsī's brother, also came to India, and "died a short time ago", i.e., before A.H. 1004.

[3] Ḥaydarī was three times in India. The first time he came he was young, and found a patron in Muḥammad Qāsim Khān of Nīshāpūr (*vide* above, p. 376). His company, says the *Haft Iqlīm*, was more agreeable than his poems. The Maṣnawī which he wrote in imitation of Saʿdī's Bostān, is insipid, and remained unknown. Though he made money in India, he said:—

در کشور هند شادي و غم معلوم.
انجا دل شاد و جان خرم معلوم
جائے که بیک روپیه دو آدم بخرند
آدم معلوم و قدر آدم معلوم

On his second return to India he found a patron in the Khān-i Aʿẓam (p. 343), who gave him one thousand rupees for an ode. Muḥammad Khān Atga (p. 337) introduced him at court. For an ode on the elephant, Akbar presented him with two thousand rupees and a horse. The third time he came to India, he attached himself to the Khān Khānān, whom he accompanied on his expedition to Gujrāt (p. 254), and received liberal presents for an ode on the victory of Sarkich. He returned to Kāshān, the governor of which town, Āghā Khizr Nahāwandī (brother of the author of the *Maʾāṣir-i Raḥīmī*) befriended him. As Tabrīz had just been destroyed by the Turks of Rūm, he settled in ʿIrāq, at a place called in the MSS. بثر; which for its excellent climate and fruits had

O Ḥaydarī, try, like the virtuous, to attain some perfection in this world of sorrow; for to leave this world deficient in anything, is like leaving the bath in a dirty state.

47. Sāmri.

He is the son of the preceding. His versification is good.

My disgrace has made me famous, and my shame [love] has rendered me well known; perplexed I ask myself why I remain concealed.

The farmers have committed their seeds to the field, and now hope to receive aid from the flood of my tears.

48 Farebī of Ray (?).[1]

His name is Shāpūr. He is a good man, but is in bad circumstances. If he is diligent, he may become a good poet.

---

1. I go and heat my brain with the love of a certain sweetheart; I sit in the midst of the flame, and breathe a hot sigh.

---

no equal in ʿIrāq or Khurāsān. About that time Shāh ʿĀbbās came to the place to hunt pheasants (*kabg*). [*Kabk* is the *Chukor* partridge of India.—P.] It happened that the king's own falcon flew away, and sat down on the house of a darwīsh, who, notwithstanding that the king had gone personally to his house, refused to open the door. "The foaming ocean of the king's wrath rose in high waves," and he ordered a general massacre of the people of the place, which was happily prevented through Ḥaydarī's influence. The same falcon was killed on the same day by an eagle on a steep hill, about a farsang from ؟ ; and the king, out of love for the animal, had a large house built on the top of the hill, which has now become a place of resort for the surrounding country. But as the hill is inaccessible for beasts of burden, the building must have cost a great deal of money and labour. Ḥaydarī died there, beloved by all, in A.H. 1002.

He had also written a book entitled *Lisānᵘ 'l-ghayb*, in praise of his teacher, the poet Lisānī, who had been attacked in a pamphlet entitled *Sahwᵘ 'l-Lisān*, "the Slip of the Tongue," which was written by his base pupil Mīr Sharīf-i Tabrīzī. The *Maʾāsir-i Raḥīmī* gives a few passages from the book.

Dāghistānī says that the poet Darwīsh Ḥaydar of Yazd, mentioned in *Tazkiras*, is very likely the same as Mawlānā Ḥaydarī of Tabrīz, who is sometimes called "Yazdī" from his friendship with Waḥshī of Yazd.

Sāmrī, Ḥaydarī's son, came to India after his father's death, and was made by the Khān Khānān *Mīr Sāmān* of his household. He was also a good officer, and was killed during the Dakhin wars, when with Shahnawāz Khān, the son of his patron.

[1] The second verse shows that the *takhalluṣ* of the poet is Shāpūr. Farebī is scarcely known. With the exception of Dāghistānī's work, which merely mentions that Farebī lived during the reign of Akbar, I have not found his name in the Tazkiras. Sprenger (Catalogue, p. 52) mentions a Farebī of Bukhārā; but as he is said to have died in A.H. 944, he must be another poet. The name of his birthplace is doubtful; the MSS. of the *Āʾīn* have Ray, Rahī, and Dīhī, or leave out the word, as Dāghistānī has done. Rāzī is the usual form of the adjective derived from "Ray" the well-known town in Khurāsān.

2. It is not my intention to be in ardours for myself, Shāpūr; my object is to bring a certain sweetheart before the world.

I am the thorny shrub without leaves in the desert; no bird takes shelter with me from fear of accidents.

---

1. If the martyr of thy love-grief is to have a tomb, let it be the gullets of crows and kites, or the stomachs of wild beasts.

2. Until I pass along the torrent of restlessness [love], I cannot plunge into the shoreless ocean.

49. Fusūnī of Shīrāz.[1]

His name is Maḥmūd Beg. He is an excellent accountant, and knows also astronomy well.

When the eye has once learned to see [to love] it loses its peaceful sleep; when the heart has once learned to throb, it loses its rest.

The passion which I feel for other lovely ones, has made my heart like a bud which has been forced open by blowing upon it.

When I wish to kiss his foot, I first wipe it with my wet eye; for the eye feels, more than lip, the sweet sorrow of kissing his foot.

Woe me, if my blood is not shed for the crime of my love! To pardon my faults were worse than to take revenge on me.

Sole friend of my chamber! I feel jealous of those who stand outside disappointed. Sweet companion of my feast! I feel jealous of the spectators.

---

1. If I flee from thy cruelties tell me what dust I am to scatter on my head when far from thee.

2. If I sit in the dust of the earth on which I wander, whose victim shall I be when I arise?[2]

---

[1] Abū 'l-Faẓl says that Fusūnī was from Shīraz; *Badā*ᵉ*onī* and Taqī call him Yazdī; and Dāghistānī and the Ātashkada says that he came from Tabrīz. *Badā*ᵉ*onī* says that Fusūnī came over Tattah and entered the service of the emperor, and Dāghistānī adds that he also served under Jahāngīr and Shāhjahān as Mustawfī. The Mirᵉātᵘ 'l-ʿĀlam mentions a Fusūnī, who was an Amīr under Jahāngīr and had the title of Afẓal Khān.

[2] The original contains a pun on *khāk gird* and *gard*, which I cannot imitate.

50. Nādirī of Turshīzī.[1]

I am as if blind and wander about seeking for something. I pant after this mirage [love], though I hold a cooling drink in my hand.

Nādirī, I complain of no one; I have myself set fire to this heap of thorns.

51. Nawʿī of Mashhad.[2]

He is a poet of talent; if sharply spoken to, he writes very well.

I am dead, and yet the blisters of my wandering foot do not dry up; neither death nor the life to come can bring the journey towards this stage [love] to a close.

No eye is fit to behold my glory; my figure in the looking-glass even appears veiled.

If that be Manṣūr's love, do not grieve, O heart. Not every weak-minded man is fit to love.[3]

---

[1] The author of the *Haft Iqlīm* says that Nādirī went two years before the completion of the *Haft Iqlīm*, i.e., in 1000, to India; but he does not know what became of him.

Dāghistānī mentions three poets of the name of Nādirī: (1) Nādirī of Samarqand, who came to Humāyūn in India, (2) a Nādirī from Shustar; and (3) a Nādirī from Syālkoṭ.

Turshīz, or Turshīsh, lies near Nīshāpūr.

[2] Mullā Muḥammad Riẓā comes from Khabūshān near Mashhad. On his arrival in India, says the *Maʿāṣir-i Raḥīmī*, he found a patron in Mīrzā Yūsuf Khān of Mashhad (p. 369); but soon after, he entered the service of the Khān Khānān (p. 334) and stayed with him and Prince Dānyal at Burhānpūr. For his *Sāqīnāma*, the Khān Khānān gave him an elephant and a present of 10,000 rupees. He also composed several odes in praise of the prince. Some people say that his poems are like the *shutur o gurba*, i.e., you find chaff and grains together; but most people praise his poems. The Khizāna-yi ʿĀmira says that his Maṣnawī entitled *Soz o Gudāz* is quite sufficient to establish his fame as a great poet. This poem, of which the Asiatic Society of Bengal has a copy, contains the story of a Suttee. Nawʿī had not yet arranged his Qaṣidas and Ghazals in form of a dīwān, when he died in 1019, at Burhānpūr.

Badāʾonī says that he claims descent from Hazrat Shaykh Ḥājī Muḥammad of Khabūshān; but his doings belie his claim. He is very bold, and is now (in 1004) with the youngest prince.

[3] Manṣur attained a high degree of pantheistic love; he saw God in everything, and at last proclaimed, Anā al-ḥaqq "I am God"—for which he was killed. The poet here accuses Manṣūr of weakness, because he proclaimed his love; he should have kept it to himself, as is proper for true lovers (*vide* p. 625, note 1).

Intrinsic beauty cannot be seen ; and he who looks into the looking-glass sees, indeed, his figure, but forms no part of the glass itself.[1]

Make thyself a heart as large as the orb of heavens, and then ask for an atom. Do not be satisfied, Nawʿī, with a ray of the sun ; cherish the lofty aspirations of the little mote.[2]

52. Bābā Ṭālib of Iṣfahān.[3]

He is a thoughtful poet, and is experienced in political matters.

I would not exchange my lonely corner for a whole world, and I am glad that my intercourse with the people of the world has left me this impression.

It is no wonder that my little heart expands into a wide plain, when it is filled with thy love.

I cannot raise, from weakness, my hands to my collar, and I am sorry that the rent in my collar reaches so late the hem of my garment.[4]

1. In being separated from me thou givest me poison to taste and yet askest " what does it matter ? " Thou sheddest my blood, thou drivest me away, and yet askest " What does it matter ? "

2. Thou dost not care for the havoc which the sword of separation has made ; sift the dust of my grave and thou wilt know what it matters.[5]

---

[1] The poet means by the looking-glass the beautiful face of the beloved boy. He sees in it his woeful figure ; but does not become one with him.

[2] Properly, half a mote. The dust atoms that play in the sun rays are in love with the sun.

[3] According to the *Haft Iqlīm*, Bābā Ṭālib had been for nearly thirty years in Kashmīr, patronized by the rulers of that country. When Akbar annexed the province, he came to Hindūstān, where he was much liked. The *Maʿāṣir-i Raḥīmī* says that he was often in the company of Ḥakīm Abū 'l-Fatḥ (p. 468), Zayn Khān Kokah (367), Abū 'l-Fazl, and Shaykh Fayẓī ; at present, i.e. in 1025, he is Ṣadr of Gujrāt. *Badāʿonī* says that he was nearly eight (twenty ?) years in Kashmīr, was at first a dervish, but took afterwards an employment, and entered Akbar's service. The emperor once sent him as ambassador to ʿAlī Rāy, ruler of Little Tibbat. On his return he gave Abū 'l-Fazl a treatise on the wonders of that land, which was inserted into the *Akbarnāma*. His poems are good, and breathe fine feeling. The *Iqbālnāma* (*Bibl. Indica* Edition, p. 133) confirms these remarks, and adds that Bābā Ṭālib died in the end of Jahāngīr's reign, more than a hundred years old.

[4] *Vide* p. 560, note 1.

[5] This Rubāʿī pleased Jahāngīr so much, that he entered it with his own hand in the Court album. *Iqbālnāma*, loc. cit.

53. Sarmadī of Iṣfahān.[1]

His name is Sharīf. He possesses some knowledge, is upright, and zealous in the performance of his duties. His rhyme is excellent. He understands arithmetic.

Fortune has been faithful in my time; I am the memorial tablet of Fate's faithfulness.

I was at home, and thou camest to me with drunken eyes and with roses under the arm; the very dust of this house of grief budded forth to see the sight of thy arrival.

---

1. What have I not done to myself in the heat of transgression! What crimes have I not committed whilst trusting to Providence!

2. I and my heart have soared up to a rose bed, and we are jealous of the zephyr's going and coming.

3. A lover has hundreds of wishes besides union with him [the beautiful boy]; I still want thee, Fortune, for many things.

I have in contempt set my foot upon both worlds; neither joy nor sorrow have overpowered my heart.

---

1. I cherish a love which will be talked of on the day of resurrection; I cherish a grief which no tale can relate.

2. A grief which can coquet with the grief of others, which no thought can comprehend and no pen can describe.

54. Dakhlī of Iṣfahān.[2]

He is a man without selfishness, and of reserved character. Though he says but little, he is a man of worth.

---

[1] Muḥammad Sharīf was mentioned above on p. 581, No. 344, as a commander of Two Hundred. *Badāʿonī* says that he was at first Chaukī-nawīs, and is at present (i.e., 1004) with Sharīf-i Āmulī (p. 502) in Bengal. He used at first to write under the *takhalluṣ* of "Fayẓī"; but in order to avoid opposition to Fayẓī, Abū 'l-Faẓl's brother, he chose that of Sarmadī. *Badāʿonī* looked upon him as a heretic, and often abuses him (*Bad.* II, 335). From the *Akbarnāma*, we see that Sharīf served in the 31st year in Kashmir, and in the end of the 32nd in Gujrāt. In 1000 he was sent to Bengal with Sharīf-i Āmulī, and in the beginning of 1001 we find him fighting in Oṛīsā against Rām Chandr, Rāja of Khurda. Dāghistānī says he died in the Dakhin.

[2] The *Maʿāṣir-i Raḥīmī* is the only work in which I have found a notice of this poet. His name is Malik Aḥmad, and he was the son of Maliku 'l-Mulūk Maqṣūd ʿAlī, proprietor of Werkopāʿī, twelve farsakhs from Iṣfahān. (The MS. belonging to the Society had originally Dorkopāi; but the author appears to have corrected the *d* to a *w*). His mother's father was the great Shaykh Abū 'l-Qāsim, who had

1. I have burnt the furniture of my strong and wise heart; I have set fire to the house of my aspirations and burnt it.

2. I have given up heresy and faith, and, half-way between the Kaʿba and the idol temple, I have burnt the sacred thread and the rosary.

---

1. I know of no plaint that has made impression; I know of no evening that was followed by a cheerful morn.

2. They say that grief is followed by joy, but this is an error; I know but of sorrows being followed by sorrows.

55. Qāsim Arslān of Mashhad.[1]

He possesses some talent. He works hard in order to collect wealth, and spends it in a genial way.

I am intoxicated with the pleasures of the society of wits: for there the subtleties of expression vanish at a hint.

Word and thought weep over my circumstances, when without thee I look into the book (of my poems).

My life is half gone—what am I worth now when a single look from thee is valued a hundred lives?

Thou hast the brilliancy of the rose and the colour of wine. How wonderful, what a freshness!

---

such influence with Ṭahmāsp that several legacies (*awqāf*) in Persia belonging to Makkah were transferred to him, and of other foundations he was appointed Mutawallī. His circumstances thus became affluent, and so many dervishes, pupils, learned men, travellers, poets, etc., collected around him, that people persuaded Ṭahmāsp that Abū 'l-Qāsim was bent on rebellion or heresy. He was, therefore, blinded, and lived a retired life in the village. Some time after he presented a poem to Ṭahmāsp, which procured him a pension. In this poem, which the *Maʾāṣir* has partly preserved, the village is called Kuhpāya. In his retirement he used to write under the *nom de plume* of Amrī, and employed Dakhlī to arrange his poems. This occupation gave Dakhlī a taste for poetry, and he received from Abū 'l-Qāsim the takhalluṣ of "Dakhlī". After having attended on his maternal uncle for some time, Malik Aḥmad went to Iṣfahān, where he gained a reputation as a poet.

In 997, he came to India, and was for five years in Akbar's service. In 1003 he went to the Dakhin, and found a patron in the Khān Khānān, in whose service he was in 1025, when the *Maʾāṣir-i Raḥīmī* was written. He also was a good soldier.

[1] Arslān is Qāsim's *nom de plume*. He chose this name, because his father claimed descent from Arslān Jāẕib, an Amīr of Maḥmūd of Ghaznī. The family came from Ṭūs, and Qāsim was brought up in Transoxania. He was a good poet, and excelled in *tārīkhs*. *Badāʾonī* quotes an ode written by Arslān on the Mountain of Ajmīr. He died in 995, probably in Lāhor. Dāghistānī says he died at Aḥmadābād. *Vide* p. 109.

56. Ghayūrī of Ḥiṣār.[1]

Manliness shines on his forehead, and simplicity is the ornament of his life.

When longing directs its way to that door [love] it overthrows all possibility of returning.

---

1. The door of Shāh Akbar, the victorious, is a paradise of rest;
2. And if I shave my beard, I do so not to beautify myself,
3. But because beards, like crimes, are of a deep black dye, and can therefore have no place in a paradise.[2]

57. Qāsimī of Māzandarān.[3]

He lives as a Faqīr, and wanders bare-footed and bare-headed through the world.

I do not compare thee in beauty with Yūsuf; Yūsuf was not so, I do not flatter.

---

1. My sickness has increased to-night in consequence of the pain of separation, and my wretched condition arises from the hundred excesses of yesterday.
2. The wine of desire flows every night freer. What shall I to-night do with my unsteady heart?

58. Sherī.[4]

He belongs to a Panjābī family of Shaykhs. Under the patronage of his Majesty he has become a good poet.

The beloved [boy] came, and blotted out my name; nay, he made me quite beside myself.

---

[1] Ghayūrī is called in the *Akbarnāma* Mullā Ghayūrī, and Dāghistānī calls him Ghayūrī of Kābul. This shows that he came from Ḥiṣar in Kābul and not from Ḥiṣār Fīrūza. The *Haft Iqlīm* tells us that Ghayūrī was at first in the service of Mīrzā Muḥammad Ḥakīm, Akbar's brother and king of Kābul. On the death of his patron, he entered Akbar's service, and was a Yūzbāshī, or Commander of One Hundred. He was killed, in 994, with Bīr Baṛ, in the Khaybar Pass catastrophe (under 34, p. 367).

[2] Akbar, in 1000, forced his courtiers to shave off their beards; *vide* p. 217.

[3] Dāghistānī mentions a Qāsim of Māzandārān. Qāsimī seems to be an unknown poet.

[4] Mullā Sherī has been mentioned above, pp. 112, 207, 212, 214. He was born in Kokūwāl in the Panjāb (Bārī Duāb). His father's name was Mawlānā Yaḥyā. He belonged to a tribe called in *Badā'onī* "Mājī".
Sherī was killed with Bīr Baṛ, in 994, in the Khaybar Pass.

The beloved has so closely surrounded himself with an array of coquetry, that even Desire found access impossible in this dense crowd.

O Zephyr, the beloved has entirely filled the mould of my desire. I am thy devoted servant, but thou art rather too devoted to his street.

---

1. My heart has polluted itself with revealing its condition. Though I am silent, the language of my looks has betrayed me.

2. A little thing [love] offers thousands of difficulties; an object apparently within reach offers hundreds of impossibilities.

59. **Rahī** of Nīshāpūr.

His name is Khwāja Jān. He is a good man.

---

1. O Rahī, no longer cunningly twist this thread [thy religious belief]; give up ideas of future life, beginning, and the purgatory.

2. Put the thread into the fire of love, so that the offensive smell of the water of the corpse may not go to hell (?).

* * * * * * *

The above (59) poets were presented at Court. There are, however, many others who were not presented, but who sent from distant places to his Majesty encomiums composed by them, as for example, Qāsim of Gūnābād; Ẓamīr of Iṣfahān; Waḥshī of Bāfa; Muḥtashim of Kāshān; Malik of Qum; Ẓuhūrī of Shīrāz; Walī Dasht Bayāẓī; Nekī; Ṣabrī; Figārī; Ḥuẓūrī; Qāẓī Nūrī of Iṣfahān; Ṣāfī of Bam; Ṭawfī of Tabrīz; and Rashkī of Hamadān.

Āʾīn 30 (*concluded*).

THE IMPERIAL MUSICIANS.[1]

I cannot sufficiently describe the wonderful power of this talisman of knowledge [music]. It sometimes causes the beautiful creatures of the

---

[1] We have to distinguish *goyanda*, singers, from *khwānandas*, chanters, and *sāzandas*, players. The principal singers and musicians come from Gwālyār, Mashhad, Tabrīz, and Kashmīr. A few come from Transoxania. The schools in Kashmīr had been founded by Īrānī and Tūrānī musicians patronized by Zaynᵘ 'l-ʿĀbidīn, king of Kashmīr. The fame of Gwālyār for its schools of music dates from the time of Rāja Mān Tunwar. During his reign lived the famous Nāʾik Bakhshū, whose melodies are only second to those of Tānsen. Bakhshū also lived at the court of Rāja Bikramājīt, Mān's son; but when his patron lost his throne, he went to Rāja Kīrat of Kālinjar. Not long afterwards he accepted a call to Gujrāt, where he remained at the court of Sulṭān Bahādur (A.D. 1526 to 1536). Islem Shāh also was a patron of music. His two great singers were Rām Dās and Mahāpāter. Both entered subsequently Akbar's service. Mahāpāter was once sent as ambassador to Mukund Deo of Orīsā.

harem of the heart to shine forth on the tongue, and sometimes appears in solemn strains by means of the hand and the chord. The melodies then enter through the window of the ear and return to their former seat, the heart, bringing with them thousands of presents. The hearers, according to their insight, are moved to sorrow or to joy. Music is thus of use to those who have renounced the world and to such as still cling to it.

His Majesty pays much attention to music, and is the patron of all who practise this enchanting art. There are numerous musicians at court, Hindūs, Īrānīs, Tūrānīs, Kashmīrīs, both men and women. The court musicians are arranged in seven divisions, one for each day in the week. When his Majesty gives the order, they let the wine of harmony flow, and thus increase intoxication, in some, and sobriety in others.

A detailed description of this class of people would be too difficult; but I shall mention the principal musicians.

1. Miyān Tānsen,[1] of Gwālyār. A singer like him has not been in India for the last thousand years.
2. Bābā Rāmdās,[2] of Gwālyār, a singer.
3. Subḥān Khān, of Gwālyār, a singer.
4. Srigyān Khān, of Gwālyār, a singer.
5. Miyān Chand, of Gwālyār, a singer.
6. Bichitr Khān, brother of Subḥān Khān, a singer.
7. Muḥammad Khān, Ḍhāṛī,[3] sings.
8. Bīr Mandal Khān, of Gwālyār, plays on the *sarmandal*.
9. Bāz Bahādur, ruler of Mālwa, a singer without rival (p. 473).
10. Shihāb Khān, of Gwālyār, performs on the *bīn*.
11. Da'ūd Ḍhāṛī,[3] sings.
12. Sarod Khān, of Gwālyār, sings.
13. Miyān Lāl,[4] of Gwālyār, sings.
14. Tāntarang Khān, son of Miyān Tānsen, sings.
15. Mullā Is-ḥāq Ḍhāṛī,[3] sings.
16. Ustā Dost, of Mashhad, plays on the flute (*nay*).

---

[1] Regarding Tānsen, or Tānsain, or Tānsīn, *vide* p. 445. Rām Chand is said to have once given him one kror of tankas as at present. Ibrāhīm Sūr in vain persuaded Tānsen to come to Āgra. Abū 'l-Faẓl mentions below his son Tāntarang Khān; and the *Pādishāh-nāma* (II, 5—an interesting passage) mentions another son of the name of Bilās.

[2] *Badā'onī* (II, 42) says, Rām Dās came from Lakhnau. He appears to have been with Bayrām Khān during his rebellion, and he received once from him one lakh of tānkas, empty as Bayram's treasure chest was. He was first at the court of Islam Shāh, and he is looked upon as second only to Tānsen. His son Sūr Dās is mentioned below.

[3] Dhāṛī means "a singer", "a musician".

[4] Jahāngīr says in the *Tuzuk* that Lāl Kalāwant (or *Kalānwat*, i.e., the singer) died in the 3rd year of his reign, "sixty or rather seventy years old. He had been from his youth in my father's service. One of his concubines, on his death, poisoned herself with opium. I have rarely seen such an attachment among Muhammadan women."

17. Nānak Jarjū, of Gwālyār, a singer.
18. Purbīn Khān, his son, plays on the *bīn*.
19. Sūr Dās, son of Bābū Rām Dās, a singer.
20. Chānd Khān, of Gwālyār, sings.
21. Rangsen, of Āgra, sings.
22. Shaykh Dāwan Ḍhāṛī,[1] performs on the *karnā*.
23. Raḥmatu 'llāh, brother of Mullā Is-ḥāq (No. 15), a singer.
24. Mīr Sayyid ʿAlī, of Mashhad, plays on the *ghichak*.
25. Ustā Yūsuf, of Hirāt, plays on the *ṭambūra*.
26. Qāsim, surnamed Koh-bar.[2] He has invented an instrument intermediate between the *qūbūz* and the *rubāb*.
27. Tāsh Beg, of Qipchāq, plays on the *qūbūz*.
28. Sulṭān Hāfiz Husayn, of Mashhad, chants.
29. Bahrām Qulī, of Hirāt, plays on the *ghichak*.
30. Sulṭān Hāshim, of Mashhad, plays on the *ṭambūra*.
31. Ustā Shāh Muḥammad, plays on the *surnā*.
32. Ustā Muḥammad Amīn plays on the *ṭambūra*.
33. Hāfiẓ Khwāja ʿAlī, of Mashhad, chants.
34. Mīr ʿAbdu 'llāh, brother of Mīr ʿAbdu 'l-Ḥay, plays the *Qānūn*.
35. Pīrzāda,[3] nephew of Mīr Dawām, of Khurāsān, sings and chants.
36. Ustā Muḥammad Ḥusayn, plays the *ṭambūra*.[4]

---

[1] Dhāṛī means "a singer", "a musician".

[2] Koh-bar, as we know from the *Pādishāhnāma* (I, b., p. 335) is the name of a Chaghtāʾī tribe. The *Nafāʾisu 'l-Maʾāṣir* mentions a poet of the name of Muḥammad Qāsim Kohbar, whose *nom-de-plume* was Ṣabrī. *Vide* Sprenger's Catalogue, p. 50 (where we have to read *Koh-bar* for *Gūh-paz*).

[3] Pīrzāda, according to *Badāʾonī* (III, 318) was from Sabzwār. He wrote poems under the *takhalluṣ* of Liwāʾī. He was killed in 995 at Lāhor, by a wall falling on him.

[4] The *Maʾāṣir-i Raḥīmī* mentions the following musicians in the service of the Khān Khānān—Āghā Muḥammad Nāʾī, son of Ḥājī Ismāʾīl, of Tabrīz; Mawlānā Aṣwātī, of Tabrīz; Ustād Mīrzā ʿAlī Fāthagī Mawlānā Sharaf of Nīshāpūr, a brother of the poet Naẓīrī (p. 649), Muḥammad Mūmin, *alias* Ḥāfiẓak, a ṭambūra-player; and Ḥāfiẓ Naẓr, from Transoxania, a good singer.

The *Tuzuk* and the *Iqbālnāma* mention the following singers of Jahāngīr's reign—Jahāngīrdād; Chatr Khān; Parwīzdād; Khurramdād; Mākhū; Hamza.

During Shāhjahān's reign we find Jagnāth, who received from Shāhjahān the title of *Kabrāʾī*; Dirang Khān; and Lāl Khān, who got the title of *Gunsamundar* (ocean of excellence). Lāl Khān was son-in-law to Bilās, son of Tānsen. Jagnāth and Dirang Khān were both weighed in silver, and received each 4,500 rupees.

Awrangzīb abolished the singers and musicians, just as he abolished the court-historians. Music is against the Muḥammadan law. Khāfī Khān (II, 213) tells a curious incident which took place after the order had been given. The court-musicians brought a bier in front of the Jharokha (the window where the emperors used to show themselves daily to the people), and wailed so loud as to attract Awrangzīb's attention. He came to the window, and asked whom they had on the bier. They said, "Melody is dead, and we are going to the graveyard." "Very well," said the emperor, "make the grave deep, so that neither voice nor echo may issue from it." A short time after, the Jharokha also was abolished.

END OF VOLUME I.

ADDITIONAL NOTES.

Page 31, note 1.

Ṭoḍar Mal. For correcter and fuller biographical notes, *vide* p. 376.

Page 35, note 2.

Qulīj Khān. The correct year of his death is given on p. 381.

Page 36, line 20.

Bābāghūrī. This word is not in the Dictionaries; but there is no doubt that it means "White Agate". The word is also mentioned in the 4th Book (my Text Edition, II, 60), where it is said that all the weights used at court for weighing jewels were made of "transparent Bābāghūrī". Ṭāhir Naṣrābādī, in his *Tazkirah*, under Jalāl, has the following. "When the case came on," he said to Mīrzā Taqī, "I have often counted with the point of my penknife the Bābāghūrī threads (the veins) of your eye—there are seventeen."

در روز دیوان با میرزا تقي میگفت که مکرر بنول قلمتراش زنار باباغوريْ چشم شما را شمرده ام هفده زنار دارد اا

Page 46, middle.

Salaries of the Begams. Under Shāhjahān and Awrangzīb, the queens and princesses drew much higher salaries. Thus Mumtāz Maḥall had 10 lākhs per annum, and her eldest daughters 6 lākhs, half in cash and half in lands. Awrangzīb gave the "Begam Ṣāḥib" 12 lākhs *per annum.*

Regarding Nūr Jahān's pension, *vide* p. 574, note 3.

Page 49, note 7.

Gulbadan Begam. From Badāonī, II, 14, we see that she was Akbar's paternal aunt, i.e. she was Humāyūn's sister. She was married to Khizr Khwāja; *vide* pp. 207, 394.

Page 58, line 4, from top.

Sorūn. Sorō is the correct name of a town and Pargana is Sirkār Kol. It lies east of the town of Kol (ʿAlīgaṛh), near the Ganges.

Page 58, line 14, from below.

Panhān. This I believe to be a mistake for "Paṭhān" or "Paṭhānkoṭ". The MSS. have پنهان or سنهان, but as the initial *sīn* in MSS. is often written with three dots below it, it is often interchanged with پ, and reversely. The spelling پیتهان, *Paithān*, for *Paṭhān*, is common in Muhammadan historians. My conjecture is confirmed by the distance mentioned in the text.

Page 69, note 2.

KĪLĀS. Mr. F. S. Growse, C.S., informs me that *gīlās* is to the present day the Kashmīrī term for *cherries*.

Page 75, line 7.

MAHUWĀ. This partly confirms Elliot's note under *Gulū* (Beames' Edition, *Races of the N.W. Provinces*, II, p. 335) and corrects Shakespeare's Dictionary.

Page 77, line 7, from below.

PĀN LEAVES. In the 3rd Book of the Āʿīn (Text, p. 416, l. 20) Abū 'l-Faẓl mentions another kind of *pān*, called *Makhī* or *Mukhī*, grown in Bihār.

Page 84, line 7.

QAYṢŪRĪ. Col. Yule tells me that the correct name is FANṢŪRĪ. According to Marco Polo, Fanṣūr was a state in Sumātra, probably the modern Barūs.

Page 87, note.

ZĪRBĀD. This should be ZERBĀD, for *zer-i bād*, i.e. "under the wind", leeward, the Persian translation, as Col. Yule informs me, of the Malay *Bāwaḥ angīn*, "below the wind," by which the Malays designate the countries and islands to the east of Sumātra.

Khāfī Khān (I, p. 11) couples Zerbād with Khatā, over both of which Tūlū Khān, son of Chingiz Khān, ruled.

Page 93, note 6.

کرکراق. I have since seen the spelling کرکیراق which brings us a step nearer to etymology. *Yarāq* means "supellex"; and *kürk* means "fur".

Page 93, line 2, from below.

AḤMADĀBĀD. The comma after Aḥmadābād may be wrong. Aḥmadābād is often called Aḥmadābād-i Gujrāt.

Page 94, line 17.

GHIYĀṢ-I NAQSHBAND. We know from the *Tazkira* of Ṭāhir Naṣrābādī that Ghiyāṣ was born in Yazd. "The world has not since seen a weaver like him. Besides, he was a good poet. Once he brought a piece of *mushajjar* brocade, on which there was among other figures that of a bear between some trees, to Shāh ʿAbbās (1585–1629), when a courtier after praising the stuff admired the bear. Ghiyāṣ said on the spur of the moment.

خواجه در خرس بیش میبند   هرکسے نقش خویش میبیند

"*The gentleman looks chiefly at the bear. Each looks at his own likeness.*"

Bears in the East are looked upon as stupid animals. A proverb says,

خرس در کوه ابوسینا

"*A bear on the hill is an Avicenna,*" i.e. a fool among bigger fools is a philosopher. Naṣrābādī quotes some of Ghiyāṣ's verses.

Page 100, middle.

Cotton Cloths. Of the various cotton cloths mentioned by Abū 'l-Faẓl.

Chautār was woven in Ḥawelī Sahāranpūr.
Sīrī Ṣāf and Bhīraū, in Dharangā,on, Khāndesh.
Gangājal, in Sirkār Ghorāghāt, Bengal.
Mihrkul, in Allāhābād,
and Pāchtoliya was mentioned on p. 574, in connexion with Nūr Jahān.

Page 105, note 2.

Ādam-i Haft-hazārī. I find that this expression is much older than Abū 'l-Faẓl's time. Thus Ziāʾu 'd-Dīn Baranī in his preface to the *Tārīkh-i Fīrūzshāhī* (p. 5, l. 6), states that the Khalīfa ʿUmar lived seven thousand years after Ādam.

Page 107, note 8.

Ashraf Khān. A correcter and fuller biography of this grandee was given on p. 423. He died in 983, not 973.

Page 108, note 3.

Khandān. The collection of Dehli MSS. belonging to the Government of India has a copy of the *Tazkiratu 'l-Awliyā* written by Khandān in 920 A.H., and yet the *Mirʾatu 'l-ʿĀlam* gives 915 as the year of his death.

Page 110, note 3, line 4.

Bechū. Though Bechū is a common Hindūstānī name, there is little doubt that the correct name of the saint is Panchū, or Panjū, *vide* p. 607. Badāonī (II, 54) gives as *tārīkh* of his death the words شیخ پنجو and tells the reader to subtract the middle letter (پ), i.e. 971 − 2 = 969. *Vide* also my Essay on "Badāonī and his Works", *Journal Asiatic Society of Bengal*, 1869, p. 118.

Page 123, line 18.

Sangrām. Akbar's favourite gun. We know from the Tuzuk (p. 20) that Akbar killed with it Jatmall, the champion of Chītor.

Page 129, lines 27 to p. 130, line 2.

The reader is requested to substitute the following :—

Elephants are found in the following places. In the Ṣūbah of Āgrah, in the jungles of Bayāwān and Narwar, as far as Barār; in the Ṣūbah of Ilāhābād, in the confines of Pannah, (Bhath) Ghorā, Ratanpūr, Nandanpūr, Sirguja, and Bastar; in the Ṣūbah of Mālwah, in Handiah, Uchhod, Chanderī, Santwās, Bījāgaṛh, Rāisīn, Hoshangābād, Gaṛha, and Hariāgaṛh; in the Ṣūbah of Bihār, about Rohtās and in Jhārkhand; and in the Ṣūbah of Bengal, in Oṛīsā and in Sātgāṇ. The elephants from Pannah are the best.

Page 179, note 3.

Sulaymān Kararānī reigned in Bengal from 971 to 980.

Page 192, note 1.

Prince Murād was born on the 3rd Muḥarram, 978. *Badāonī*, II, 132. *Vide* below.

Page 203, middle, and note.

In the *Proceedings of the Asiatic Society of Bengal*, for May, 1870 (p. 146), I have shown that the unclear words in Badāonī's text are :—

کنابلان که خوشگاه ایشان است

"the cunabula which is their time of mirth."

By "cunabula" the Jesuits meant the representations of the birth of Christ, in wax, etc., which they used to exhibit in Āgrah and Lāhor.

Page 281, line 8.

The Ṣadr read the *khuṭbah* in the name of the new king, and thus the *julūs* became a fact. *K͟hāfī K͟hān*, I, p. 52, l. 2, from below.

Page 282, middle.

MAWLĀNĀ ʿABDᵘ 'L-BĀQĪ. *Vide* p. 596, note 3.

Page 321.

AKBAR'S WIVES. For *Raqiyah* the diminutive form *Ruqayyah* is to be substituted. Regarding Jodh Bāī *vide* next note.

Sulṭān Salīma Begum. She *is* the daughter of Gulruk͟h Begum, a daughter of Bābar. Mīrzᵘ Nurᵘ 'd-Dīn Muḥammad, Gulruk͟h's husband, was a Naqshbandī K͟hwāja.

Gulruk͟h Begum must not be confounded with another Gulruk͟h Begum, who was the daughter of Mīrzā Kāmrān and wife of Ibrāhīm Husain Mīrzā (*vide* p. 516).

Of other women in Akbar's harem, I may mention (1) the daughter of Qāẓī ʿĪṣā (p. 498); (2) an Armenian woman, *Tuzuk*, p. 324. *Vide* also Keane's *Agra Guide*, p. 38. (3) Qismiyah Bānū, married by Akbar in the 19th year (*Akbarn.*, III, 94); (4) a daughter of S͟hamsᵘ 'd-Dīn Chak (*Akbarn.*, III, 659).

SULṬĀN MURĀD. He was married to a daughter of Mīrzā ʿAzīz Koka (p. 343). Their child, Sulṭān Rustam, did not live long (*Akbarn.*, III, 539, 552).

SULṬĀN DĀNYĀL. The correct date of his birth seems to be the 2nd Jumāda I, 979, not the 10th; but the MSS. continually confounded دوم and دهم. His first wife was a daughter of Sulṭān K͟hwāja (p. 466), by whom he had a daughter of the name of Saʿādat Bānū Begum, who was born in 1000 (*Akbarn.*, III, 643).

Page 323.

JAHĀNGĪR'S WIVES. An additional list was given on p. 533, note 1. Besides them, I may mention, (1) a daughter of Mubārak Chak of Kashmīr; (2) a daughter of Husain Chak of Kashmīr (*Akbarn.*, III, 659); (3) another Kashmīrī lady, mentioned in *Akbarn.*, III, 639.

Page 329, middle.

DEATH OF MĪRZĀ RUSTAM. Thus the date is given in the *Ma'āṣirᵘ 'l-Umarā*; but from the *Pādishāhnāma* (II, 302) we see that Mīrzā Rustam died on, or a few days before, the 1st Rabīʿ I, 1052. The author adds a remark that "the manners (*awẓāʿ*) of the Mīrzā did not correspond to his noble birth, which was perhaps due to the absence of nobility in his mother".

Page 329, line 4, from below.

QARĀ QŪILŪ TURKS. The correct name is Qarāqoinlū. The Calcutta Chag͟htᵃāi Dictionary gives Qarāqūnīlū. Vambéry (*History of Bok͟hārā*, p. 265, note) mentions the Ustajlū, Shāmlū, Nikallū, Bahārlū, Zū 'l-Qadr, Kājār, and Afshār, as the principal Turkish tribes that were living in Transcaucasia, on the southern shore of the Caspian and in the west of Khurāsān. Qarāqoinlū means " the black sheep tribe ".

Page 332, note 1.

The correct name of the place where Bayrām was defeated is Gūnāchūr, گوناچور, which lies S.E. of Jālindhar. The word کنور پهلور, which the Bibl. Indica Edition of Badā,onī gives, contains " Phillaur ", which lies S.W. of Gūnāchūr.

Page 342, note.

I do not think that Pīr Muḥammad came from the Sharwān mentioned in this note. It is more likely that he was a Shirwānī Afghān.

Page 343, note.

This note has been corrected on p. 445, line 14, and p. 458, note.

Page 348, line 6, from below.

Zū'l-Qadr is the name of a Turkmān tribe; *vide* above.

Page 361, last line.

Goganda. Regarding the correct date of the battle, *vide* p. 460, note 2.

Page 376.

Ṭoḍar Mal. The *Ma'āṣir*ᵘ *'l-Umarā* says that Ṭoḍar Mal was born at Lāhor. But it is now certain that Ṭoḍar Mal was born at Lāharpūr, in Audh; *vide Proceedings Asiatic Society Bengal*, September, 1871, p. 178.

Page 402, note 2.

Miyān Kāl. The note is to be cancelled. Miyān Kāl has been explained on p. 615, note

Page 404, line 4.

Yūsuf Khān. Regarding his death, *vide Tuzuk*, p. 328. His son ʿIzzat Khān is wrongly called in the Bibl. Indica Edition of the *Pādishāhnāma* (I, *b*, p. 302) غيرت خان His name was ʿAzīzᵘ 'llah; hence his title *ʿIzzat*.

Page 412, line 1.

Qāsim Khān. I dare say the phrase " Chamanārāī Khurāsān " merely means that he was Governor of Kābul.

Page 413, line 24.

Bāqī Khān. He is often called " Khān Bāqī Khān ".

Page 423, line 15.

Mīr Bābūs. The spelling " Uigur " is now common; but in India the word is pronounced " Īghur ". The query may be cancelled; *vide* p. 488, note 1.

Page 435, line 9.

Dastam Khān. Vambéry spells " Dostum ".

Page 454, middle.

SHAYKH FARĪD-I BUKHĀRĪ. That the name of Farīd's father was Sayyid Aḥmad-i Bukhārī, may be seen from the short inscription on the "Bukhārī Mosque" in the town of Bihār, which was built by Shaykh Lāḍ, at the cost of Farīd-i Bukhārī, and bears the date 16th Rajab, 1017.

Mr. J. G. Delmerick has sent me the following inscription from Farīd's Jāmiʿ Masjid in Farīdābād :—

بعهد شاه نور الدین جهانگیر شهنشاهے بدین و داد واحسان
اساس این بنای خیر بنهاد فرید عصر و ملت مرتضی خان
بعز وشوکت و جودو سخاوت خلف ابن الخلف تا شاه مردان
رقم خیر البقاع از خامه سرزد پئی تاریخ این جاوید بنیان

1. *In the reign of Shāh Nur*[u] *'d-Dīn, a king who is pious, just, and liberal,*

2. *Murtaẓā Khān, the unique one* (farīd) *of the age and faith, erected this religious building.*

3. *He is honoured, powerful, generous, and liberal, a worthy descendant of the king of men* [ʿAlī].

4. *As Tārīkh of this lasting structure, the words* Khayru'l-Biqāʿ *issued from the pen.*

This gives 1014 A.H.

Page 468, middle.

KHWĀJA ṬĀHIR MUḤAMMAD. He is mentioned as a Sijistānī on p. 528, among the Bakhshīs.

Page 476, note 1.

MAʿṢŪM KHĀN-I KĀBULĪ. This rebel, who gave Akbar no end of trouble, had the audacity to assume royal prerogatives in Bengal. The following inscription I received, through Bābū Rājendralal Mitra, from Rāja Pramatha Nāth, Rāja of Dīghaputi, Rājshāhī. It was found in a ruined mosque at a village called Chatmohor, not very far from Dīghaputi.

این مسجد رفیع در زمان سلطان الاعظم عمدة السادات ابو الفتح محمد معصوم خان خلد الله
ملکه ابدا یا رب و یا باقي بناکرد خان رفیع مکان عالیشان خان محمد بن توي محمد خان قاقشال
في سنه تسع و ثمانین و تسعمایة اا

This lofty mosque was built during the time of the great Sulṭān, the chief of Sayyids, Abu 'l-Fātḥ Muḥammad Khān—May God perpetuate his kingdom for ever, O Lord, O Thou who remainest! by the high and exalted Khān, Khān Muḥammad, son of Tūī Muḥammad Khān Qāqshāl, in the year 989.

This was, therefore, nearly two years after the outbreak of the Bengal Military Revolt (9th Ẕī Hajjah, 987); *vide* p. 486.

Page 485, line 7.

SAYYID MUḤAMMAD. Regarding the correct date of his death, *vide* p. 548.

Page 499, line 27.

SŪRAT. There is every probability that Sorath, and not Sūrat, is intended.

Page 506.

THE GAKKHARS. *Vide* pp. 544, 545.

The places Pharwāla and Dāngalī (دانگلی, not Dangālī) mentioned in the note as the principal places in the Gakkhar District, are noticed in E. Terry's *Voyage to East India* (London, 1655, p. 88). "*Kakares*, the principal Cities are called *Dekalee* and *Pūrhola*; it is a large Province, but exceeding mountainous; divided it is from Tartaria by the Mountain Caucasus; it is the extremest part North under the *Mogol's* subjection."

De Laët also gives the same passage.

Page 512, line 1.

YARĀQ KHĀN. The correct name is, I believe, Borāq Khān. *Vide* Vambéry's *Bokhara*, p. 153.

Page 552, middle.

KŪCH HĀJŪ. Regarding Kūch Hājū and Kūch Bihār and Mukarram Khān, *vide* my article on these countries in *Journal Asiatic Society Bengal* for 1872, p. 54.

Page 553, line 5.

GHAZNĪN KHĀN, of Jālor.

"The Pahlunpūr family is of Afghān origin, belonging to the Lohānī tribe, and, it is said, occupied Bihār in the reign of Humāyūn. They subsequently took service with the king of Dihlī; and from Akbar Shāh, in A.D. 1597, Ghaznīn Khān, the chief, obtained the title of Dīwān, for having successfully repulsed an invasion of Afghān tribes; for his services on this occasion, he was also rewarded with the government of Lāhor. In A.D. 1682, Fatḥ Khān Dīwān received the provinces of Jālor, Sānchor, Pahlunpūr, and Dīsah from Awrangzīb. Fatḥ Khān died in 1688, leaving an only son, Pīr Khān, who was supplanted in his rights by his uncle Kamāl Khān, who, subsequently, being unable to withstand the increasing power of the Rathors of Māṛwāṛ, was compelled, in A.D. 1698, to quit the country [Jālor], and retire with his family and dependents to Pahlunpūr, where the family has remained ever since.—*Selections, Bombay Government Records*, No. XXV.—*New Series*, p. 15.

Page 591, line 27.

ʿALĪ QULĪ BEG ISTAJLŪ. Vambéry spells Ustajlü, which is the name of a Turkish tribe; *vide* p. 687.

INDEX TO THE FIRST VOLUME

OF THE

Āʾīn-i Akbarī

[The numbers refer to the pages; *n.* means "footnote". When names occur twice or several times on a page, they have been entered only once in the Index.
The geographical names form a separate Index.]

INDEX

OF

GEOGRAPHICAL NAMES

IN THE FIRST VOLUME

OF THE

Āʿīn-i Akbarī